ENCYCLOPEDIA OF
POLITICS AND RELIGION

ENCYCLOPEDIA OF POLITICS AND RELIGION

Second Edition

Robert Wuthnow, *Editor in Chief*

VOLUME I

A Division of Congressional Quarterly Inc.
Washington, D.C.

CQ Press
1255 22nd Street, NW, Suite 400
Washington, DC 20037

Phone: 202-729-1900; toll-free, 1-866-4CQ-PRESS (1-866-427-7737)
Web: www.cqpress.com

Cover design: Matthew Simmons

Printed and bound in the United States of America

10   09   08   07   06   1   2   3   4   5

LIBRARY OF CONGRESS CATALOGING-IN-PUBLICATION DATA
Encyclopedia of politics and religion / Robert Wuthnow, editor in chief. — 2nd ed.
        p.   cm.
    Includes bibliographical references and index.
    ISBN-13: 978-0-87289-323-8 (set : alk paper)
    ISBN-10: 0-87289-323-5 (set : alk paper)
    ISBN-13: 978-0-87289-321-4 (v. 1 : alk paper)
    ISBN-10: 0-87289-321-9 (v. 1 : alk paper)
    [etc.]
    1. Religion and politics--Encyclopedias.   I. Wuthnow, Robert.   II. Title

    BL65.P7E53   2006
    322'.103--dc22   2006034642

About the Editors

CHARLES KURZMAN is associate professor of sociology at the University of North Carolina at Chapel Hill, where he helped found the Carolina Center for the Study of the Middle East and Muslim Civilizations. He is the author of *The Unthinkable Revolution in Iran* (2004) and editor of the anthologies *Modernist Islam, 1840–1940* (2002) and *Liberal Islam* (1998).

DAVID MAXWELL is senior lecturer in African and imperial history at Keele University. He was editor of the *Journal of Religon in Africa* from 1998 to 2005. He is the author of *African Gifts of the Spirit: Pentecostalism and the Rise of a Zimbabwean Transnational Religious Movement* (2007) and *Christians and Chiefs in Zimbabwe: A Social History of the Hwesa People* (1999). He is currently researching a project on the missionary and African roots of colonial science in the Belgian Congo.

Contents

Preface

The *Encyclopedia of Politics and Religion* was initially created to fill a void for those seeking to examine the interconnections of politics and religion and understand how these two elemental institutions of society have combined to shape public discourse, affect social attitudes, spark and sustain collective action, and influence policy, especially during the past two centuries.

Since the publication of the first edition of the encyclopedia in 1998, the al-Qaida attacks of September 11, 2001, and the subsequent launch of the U.S. government's "global war on terror" have thrust religio-political issues to the forefront of public consciousness. Today, this thoroughly revised second edition of the encyclopedia is more relevant than ever in a world seeking reliable, authoritative information.

The principle of the separation of church and state, and the related idea that politics and religion are and ought to be distinct, has been one of the most crucial factors in the rise of national secular states. Although it is the bedrock of modern political institutions and international relations, this principle has been challenged in recent years to the point of becoming a fault line in societies and religious movements around the world. Clearly, religion increasingly plays a major role in much of the political conflict of our era. Any effective analysis of or long-lasting solution to such turmoil requires attention to religion in its political context. The encyclopedia's aim is to present the historical roots of the relations between politics and religion in the modern world and to explain their global interconnections. This updated, second edition of an award-winning work continues to serve as a sorely needed guide to understanding, scholarship, and communication.

In preparing this work, the editors and contributors sought to represent the vast diversity of ways in which religions and political systems are influencing each other throughout the contemporary world. Expanded to 281 articles by prominent scholars from many nations, the encyclopedia examines broad themes, such as millennialism and pluralism, as well as articles on specific religions, individuals, geographical regions, institutions, and events. More than half of the existing articles have been updated or partially revised to complement the more than twenty-five new or completely revised entries, including Creationism and Evolution, Palestine, and Radical Islam.

The articles, ranging from a few hundred to eight thousand words, are written to be accessible to students and interested adults as well as to scholars. Most articles include references to related entries and brief bibliographies to assist in further reading. Each volume of the work contains a detailed index.

In addition to the articles, the encyclopedia includes an introduction by Robert Wuthnow of Princeton University, who once again served as editor in chief. The appendix contains excerpts and complete texts from source documents related to articles in the volume. The appendix also includes excerpts from world constitutions with provisions on religion, a glossary of terms, and a compilation of Internet sites that may be of use to readers.

Acknowledgments

The second edition of the *Encyclopedia of Politics and Religon* reflects the work of numerous authors, editors, and researchers. The editorial process has been under the general direction of Professor Wuthnow, who was assisted throughout the project by an editorial board of five scholars, each expert in his or her own field. Members of the editorial board, all of whom offered advice throughout the preparation of the work, are Grace Davie, University of Exeter (England); John C. Green, University of Akron; Charles F. Keyes, University of Washington; Charles Kurzman, University of North Carolina at Chapel Hill; and David Maxwell, Keele University (England). In the end, the volume is the product of the editors and authors who gave generously of their time to share their knowledge.

It should be noted that the originator of the idea for the *Encyclopedia of Politics and Religion* was Ann Davies, now director of editorial operations at CQ Press. Editorial development of this edition of the encyclopedia at CQ Press fell under the direction of Andrea Pedolsky, chief, editorial acquisitions; acquisitions editor Mary Carpenter; and development editor David Arthur. Tim Arnquist, Iman Ali, Liza Baron, Sarah Myers, and Joshua Stager also made valuable contributions.

Project editor Nancy Matuszak and production editor Joan Gossett oversaw manuscript editing and the production process. Steve Pazdan, Paul Pressau, and Margot Ziperman contributed resources and support to the project. Freelance editors Joanne Ainsworth, Colleen McGuiness, and Sabra Ledent assisted with editing the manuscript. Joe Fortier, Inge Lockwood, and Kate Stern proofread the typeset pages, and Sally Ryman prepared the index. Matthew Simmons designed the book, and MacPS composed it.

A Note on Transliteration

The editors have used diacritics sparingly in transliterating names of people and places from languages such as Chinese and Arabic, not written in Latin characters. In general, transliterated words appear in a form that should be familiar to English-speaking readers.

Kathryn Suárez
Director
Library Reference Publishing

Alphabetical List of Articles and Contributors

A

'Abduh, Muhammad
DONALD MALCOLM REID
Georgia State University

Abolitionism
JOHN M. GIGGIE
University of Texas at San Antonio

Abortion
CLYDE WILCOX
Georgetown University

al-Afghani, Jamal al-Din
NIKKI R. KEDDIE
University of California at Los Angeles

Afghanistan
LUDWIG W. ADAMEC
University of Arizona

Africa, West: The Mande World
JAN JANSEN
Leiden University

African American Experience
TIMOTHY P. HARRISON

Ahmad Khan, Sir Sayyid
HAFEEZ MALIK
Villanova University

Algeria
ALLAN CHRISTELOW
Idaho State University

Anabaptists
FRED KNISS
Loyola University-Chicago

Anglicanism
JOHN WOLFFE
The Open University

Angola
DIDIER PÉCLARD

Anticlericalism
JEAN BAUBÉROT
*École Pratique des Hautes Études
(Vème section)–Sorbonne*

Anti-Semitism
BENJAMIN GINSBERG
Johns Hopkins University

Atatürk, Kemal
ŞERIF MARDIN
Sabancï University

Atheism
PAUL G. CROWLEY
Santa Clara University

B

Bahai
SAID AMIR ARJOMAND
Stony Brook University

Balkan States
NIKOS KOKOSALAKIS
Panteion University

Banna, Hasan al-
DONALD MALCOLM REID
Georgia State University

Baptists
ORAN P. SMITH
Palmetto Family Council

Barth, Karl
RICHARD H. ROBERTS
Lancaster University

Base Communities
DANIEL H. LEVINE
University of Michigan

Bonhoeffer, Dietrich
DANIEL HARDY
University of Cambridge

Botswana
BARRY MORTON

Bourguiba, Habib
KENNETH J. PERKINS
University of South Carolina

Brazil
ANDREW CHESTNUT
University of Houston

Buddha
CHARLES F. KEYES
University of Washington

Buddhism, Theravada
CHARLES F. KEYES
University of Washington

Buddhism, Tibetan
PETER K. MORAN
University of Washington

Burke, Edmund
DOUGLAS STURM
Bucknell University

C

Calvinism
GARY SCOTT SMITH
Grove City College

Canada
MARK A. NOLL
Wheaton College

Capitalism
RICHARD H. ROBERTS
Lancaster University

Catholicism, Roman
R. SCOTT APPLEBY
University of Notre Dame

CELAM
EDWARD L. CLEARY
Providence College

Censorship
BHIKHU PAREKH
University of Hull

Contributors to the First Edition

The authors listed below wrote the original versions of the following articles.

Angola
LAWRENCE W. HENDERSON

Brazil
ROWAN IRELAND
La Trobe University, Australia

Egypt
DONALD MALCOLM REID
Georgia State University

Evangelicalism
JAMES L. GUTH, LYMAN A. KELLSTEDT, AND CORWIN E. SMIDT
Furman University,
Wheaton College,
Calvin College

France
DANIÈLE HERVIEU-LEGER
L'École des Hautes Études en Sciences Sociales

Freedom of Religion
PAUL J. WEBER
University of Louisville

Germany
UWE BERNDT
Arnold Bergstraesser Institut

Ghana
PATRICK J. RYAN
Fordham University

Hungary
MIKLÓS TOMKA
Peter Pazmany Catholic University

India
T. N. MADAN
Institute of Economic Growth, Delhi University

Ireland
JOHN FULTON
St. Mary's University College

Islam's Encounters with the West
KENNETH CRAGG

Israel
KEVIN AVRUCH
George Mason University

Jehovah's Witnesses
KAREN E. FIELDS

Jesuits
PETER MCDONOUGH
Arizona State University

Judaism
DANIEL J. ELAZAR
Jerusalem Center for Public Affairs

Korea
LAUREL KENDALL
American Museum of Natural History

Nongovernmental Organizations
BRIAN H. SMITH
Ripon College

Pakistan
VALI NASR
Naval Postgraduate School

Poland
LEONARD T. VOLENSKI

Russia
MICHAEL BOURDEAUX

Saints
AVIAD M. KLEINBERG
Tel Aviv University

Sexuality
GARY DAVID COMSTOCK
Wesleyan University

Syria
JOSHUA M. LANDIS
University of Oklahoma

Turkey
ŞERIF MARDIN
American University

War
LESTER KURTZ
University of Texas

Zimbabwe
TITUS LEONARD PRESLER
Episcopal Theological Seminary of the Southwest

Zionism
KEVIN AVRUCH
George Mason University

List of Appendix Materials

Documents on Politics and Religion

Reference Materials

Introduction

During the past decade interest in the relationships between religion and politics has burgeoned both in the academic literature and on the world stage. Evidence of the growing importance of religion in world affairs can hardly be missed, whether one is a government official, religious leader, scholar, or rank-and-file consumer of the mass media. Religion's role in international diplomacy, as a source of armed violence or as a facilitator of humanitarian efforts, is increasingly apparent. Staying abreast of these fast-changing developments, not to mention their historic and cultural roots, is a major challenge.

One indication of the increasing importance of relationships between religion and politics is the growing number of books, scholarly essays, and news articles about these topics. Between 1996 and 2005, the Library of Congress recorded nearly 1,200 new books about religion and politics, almost double the number published during the previous decade. In the same period, newly published scholarly articles about religion and politics listed in the Social Science Citation Index grew from 450 to 660. Popular articles indexed by the Dow-Jones Factiva service climbed even more steeply, reaching a total of more than 121,000 published between 1996 and 2005, compared with fewer than 37,000 from 1986 to 1995. No longer was religion relegated to the community events section of local newspapers. During a single six-month period in 2005, *Le Monde* carried more than 300 articles about religion, the *London Times* included more than 600, and the *Washington Post* published more than 850.

The event that contributed most to the awakening of popular interest in religion and politics was, of course, the September 11, 2001, terrorist attacks on New York City and Washington, DC. Although it was disputed whether the attackers were as motivated by Muslim convictions as by other grievances, the ensuing debate brought religion and its potential for violence squarely into the public arena. Across campuses and among heads of state, controversy flared about the teachings and practices of Islam and about the appropriate manner for people of other faiths to respond. Discussions of terror, evil, morality, and respect all took on new meaning. Just as the Iranian revolution had done a generation earlier, the events of that Tuesday reminded leaders everywhere of how salient a political force religion can be.

Other events in recent years have prompted growing awareness of the importance of religion in political life as well. In 2001, within the first few days of his administration, U.S. president George W. Bush announced the formation of a White House Office of Faith-Based and Community Initiatives. This program was designed to expand significantly the possibilities for religious congregations and service organizations to receive government funding for their activities. Unlike the Charitable Choice legislation that had been passed in 1996 for a similar purpose, the Bush initiative favored a more proactive role for government in promoting faith-based social programs. Supporters argued that religion made caregivers more effective and thus deserving of public funds, while critics suggested that the constitutional wall separating church and state was being breached. The debate added fuel to an already smoldering fire of discussion about the free exercise of religion and whether religious groups were being fairly or unfairly excluded from participation in American public life. Local referenda and court cases focused on such topics as whether and how evolution and creationism should be taught in public schools, what rights or restrictions should be associated with gay marriage, and what to think about prayers and religious texts being performed or displayed in public places.

During 2002 the United States' military invasion of Afghanistan moved to the center of world attention and again raised questions about religion's relationships to public policy. Afghanistan's Taliban leadership represented a unique blend of Islamist and ethnic nationalist interpretation. The Taliban's role in harboring al-Qaida leader Usama bin Ladin, the alleged planner of the attacks on New York and Washington, prompted U.S. leaders to call for its overthrow. As the war unfolded, broader questions about the United States' relationship to the Muslim world emerged. Religion and politics were joined not only in these discussions but also in debates about "just war" theory in Christianity. Even broader questions about the applicability or inapplicability of Western understandings about religion's place in democratic government became part of the public debate.

In 2003 the main theater of U.S. military action moved to the Middle East as policymakers perceived an opportunity to depose Iraqi president Saddam Hussein and turn the country into a model of Western-style democracy. The end of Hussein's regime opened opportunities for longstanding ethnic, religious, and regional differences to reappear. The role of religion thus became an important consideration during the process of formulating and ratifying a new Iraqi constitution. The war reinforced broader discussions about relationships between the Muslim world and the West. Within the United States, discussions also emerged about the religious foundations of human rights and sanctions against torture.

The attention to Islam that was stimulated by these events became an increasing aspect of European politics for different reasons. By 2002, an estimated 14 million Muslims were living in western Europe, of whom approximately 5 million lived in France, 3 million lived in Germany, and more than 1 million lived in the United Kingdom. These numbers represented dramatic increases that were largely a result of guest worker programs and migration from former colonies. Policies sometimes excluded immigrants from becoming citizens and in other cases resulted in continuing economic hardships. Sporadic violence was a recurring feature of relationships between immigrants and the majority population. Religion thus became a matter of dispute among the various political parties and their leaders.

Discussions of religion's role in European affairs grew in intensity in 2004 in conjunction with debates about ratification of a constitution for the European Union (EU). Although a majority or significant minority of the EU countries' populations identified with a Christian denomination, few of the countries' constitutions included references to religion and most provided for separation of church and state. Proposals emerged nevertheless for the EU constitution to include some reference to God, to Christian values, or to Europe's Christian heritage. These proposals were hotly contested, revealing the pronounced differences between more secular countries, such as France, and more religious ones, such as Poland. The debate also raised questions about relationships between the EU and Muslim countries and the possible inclusion of countries with predominant Muslim populations, such as Turkey, in the European Union.

In eastern Europe the collapse of the Soviet Union continued to reverberate in the form of conflicts among religious and ethnic groups. The Orthodox Church gained adherents and political influence in Russia, but these gains generated concerns about the harassment of minority religious groups, such as Jehovah's Witnesses, Seventh-day Adventists, and Mormons. In Croatia, where 85 percent of the population is Catholic, Serbian Orthodox leaders reported continuing instances of harassment and violence. Bosnia and Herzegovina maintained a delicate balance among Muslim Bosniaks, Catholic Bosnian Croats, and Orthodox Bosnian Serbs, with religious discrimination being more common than uncommon and nationalistic sentiments often associated with religious appeals. Tensions between Christians and Muslims also continued in eastern Europe. One of the most visible instances of religious violence took place in 2004 when Muslim Chechen militants killed hundreds of women and children at a school in the southern Russian town of Beslan.

In Central Asia religion has been of continuing concern in constitutional interpretation and governmental policy. For instance, Kyrgyzstan's constitution mandates religious freedom, which the government seeks to enforce by requiring religious groups to be officially registered and by prohibiting religion from being taught in the nation's schools. Kazakhstan's policies toward religion also promote religious freedom, although a law passed in 2005 permits the government to punish members of religious groups deemed to be encouraging political extremism. Uzbekistan, in contrast, aggressively prosecutes Islamic groups that have not been approved by the government and prohibits Christian groups from proselytizing.

Elsewhere, the role of religion in national and regional affairs has become increasingly important as a result of armed conflicts between religious groups as they struggle for political and economic advantage. For instance, the United Progressive Alliance in India has championed secular government and religious tolerance, while the opposing Bharatiya Janata Party has argued that Hindu religious and cultural norms should be given a more prominent role in school textbooks and in interpretations of local laws. Riots between Hindus and Muslims and between Christians and Hindus have necessitated armed intervention in several parts of India. In Pakistan more than 125 deaths occurred in 2004 as a result of conflict among religious groups. In Indonesia conflicts between Christians and Muslims have been a persistent problem in Central Sulawesi and the Moluccas.

In Latin America and Africa the most notable religious development has been the rapid growth of Christianity, especially in variants of Protestant Pentecostalism. This growth is widely assumed to be the result of indigenous preaching and religious practices that appeal to the lower socioeconomic strata. Globalization, however, is also a significant factor, both as an influence on local economic and political conditions and as a means of communicating religious teachings via international travel and television. Although Pentecostalism is generally described as an apolitical religion, it has gained notable influence in some countries and been promoted by government officials in others. For instance, an amendment to the Zambian constitution has declared the country a Christian nation; similarly, Ghanaian policies of free trade and democratization have significantly facilitated the growth of Christian churches in that country.

The impact of globalization can be seen in a wide variety of religious developments. Discussions of globalization generally emphasize growth of international travel and communication and increasing integration of economic markets. Because of this emphasis on technology and trade, religion is sometimes viewed separately as a manifestation only of local, traditional, and even tribal loyalties. Globalization sometimes threatens these loyalties, however, causing them to be held with greater conviction than before, and in other instances provides new resources that alter traditional practices. A sacred tribal ceremony in a remote village in Papua New Guinea being performed to disco music is one example. The popularity of holy hip-hop music of Ghanaian origin in Atlanta, Georgia, is another.

China's ascendancy in global markets has been striking not only in economic terms, but also in its implications for the changing relationships between religion and politics. In rural China the continuing paucity of health care and other government services has encouraged the popularity of faith healers and other religious self-help movements, such as Falun Gong. On the one hand, township officials sometimes tolerate these practices as long as they are deemed to be politically neutral; on the other hand, improved communication and transportation have made it easier for the police to suppress these groups. In the more prosperous coastal cities, underground churches coexist with growing officially registered churches, sometimes financed by "boss Christians" who run successful companies, as well as large "passport churches" attended by Koreans, Americans, and other expatriate workers. The political implications of this apparent upsurge of religious activity remain to be understood and, in the short term, depend considerably on balances within the ruling regime and relations with other countries.

The scholarly response to these numerous developments in religion and politics has varied from discipline to discipline. The relevant disciples are of course the social scientists. Yet social scientists interested in religion have had to confront three significant hurdles in tackling the relationships between politics and religion. One is that the social sciences have long held that religion would become increasingly passé in the modern world. In this view, religion was something that benighted people of yesteryear believed, but that those with knowledge of science, with training in higher education, and with the comforts of modern existence would no longer take seriously. Thus it might be of interest to study religion historically, as a scholar of Late Antiquity or the Middle Ages might do, but not to credit it with much significance in contemporary affairs. A second and related hurdle is the assumption that religion, even if it does persist as a private passion in personal life, is not an important consideration in political or economic life. In this view, what may appear to the untutored as a religious impulse is to more thoughtful minds a reflection of rational choices, self-interest, social class, and power. Efforts to understand public policy, therefore, should focus on the nuts and bolts of what can be planned and predicted, not on the whims of the religiously inclined. The third hurdle is the fact that hardly any social scientists themselves, at least not in the United States or western Europe, are themselves religious believers or practitioners. Thus, to the extent that personal experience informs one's outlook on the world, it has been easier for social scientists to ignore religion than attempt to understand it.

These intellectual barriers have finally been challenged in recent years and, in the view of scholars who know the most about religion, are in the process of being thoroughly discredited. Science and economic development have altered the ways in which people practice their faith but have shown few signs of discouraging it from being practiced at all. Even in western Europe, where secularism has been most evident, religion continues to be an influence in public affairs, and that role appears to be increasing as a result of immigration and political integration. Empirical studies there, in the United States, and elsewhere show that religious participation shapes not only what people do in their private lives, but also how they vote, which political party they favor, and what they think about a wide range of social issues. Although it is true that social scientists themselves are generally uninvolved in religion, no educated person can fail to see that religion is an important part of the contemporary world and needs to be better understood.

The discipline in which the greatest strides have been made toward taking religion seriously in relation to politics is political science. It is perhaps not surprising that this should be so, given the abundance of evidence that religion and politics commingle. The extent of this interest, however, is surprising from one perspective. In the development of political theory, at least in the West, religion did not feature as an important topic of concern. It was certainly in the background, especially in the Lockean tradition for which overcoming religious conflict through tolerance and constitutional liberalism was key. Political theory nevertheless progressed largely as a discussion of rational and procedural norms, grounded in such universal values as justice and fairness, rather than through continuing consideration of religious communities or traditions. In recent years, the renewal of interest in religion has thus been accompanied by criticisms of this strand of political theory. These criticisms have emphasized the reality of religious communities as crucibles for the formation and expression of values and the validity of bringing religious values into the public sphere. Among empirically oriented political scientists, inquiries into the political attitudes and electoral behavior of religious constituencies have become common, especially in the United States, where political candidates routinely invoke connections with these various constituencies. Qualitative research has focused increasingly on religious conflict, on constitutional debates about religion, and on the political implications of fundamentalist and extremist groups.

Leaving aside economics, in which interest in religion has been limited to controversial studies purporting to show that rational choice theories were as applicable to the soul as to markets, the discipline that has shown a striking lack of interest in religion and politics is sociology. This lack of interest is notable for two reasons. One is that discussions of religion were central to the figures that sociologists generally count as their "founding fathers" (Karl Marx, Max Weber, and Emile Durkheim). The other is that many sociologists do in fact study various aspects of religion. Few of these studies, however, focus on the interplay between religion and politics. They usefully illuminate the religious beliefs and practices of individuals, and they sometimes provide rich de-

scriptions of religious movements, communities, or congregations. The results sometimes include a discussion of how individuals feel about "hot button" issues (such as abortion or homosexuality). To the extent that they deal with "power," though, the focus is more likely to be on power in interpersonal relations or over one's emotions than within the political arena. Of course there are significant exceptions to this pattern, including treatments of the public role of religion and of the political factors that reshape religious identities. The larger problem within sociology is nevertheless that religion tends to be excluded rather than incorporated into the dominant considerations of the discipline. Few of the top-ranked graduate research departments include faculty who specialize in religion, and relative to other topics, religion is seldom the focus of articles in the discipline's primary journals. Although religion is sometimes included in empirical studies as a single variable (such as church attendance), its connections with other aspects of social life are largely ignored. For example, social class is studied without considering the extent to which religion contributes to class disparities. Race and gender are prominent preoccupations among sociologists, whereas religious diversity and its connections with race and gender are not.

Compared with sociology, anthropology has been a significantly richer source of inquiries about religion and politics. This interest is partly a reflection of the fact that anthropology has emphasized culture to a greater extent than sociology has and, in so doing, has recognized that religious symbolism and ritual is an important part of culture. To a much greater extent than sociologists, anthropologists have also covered the world, as it were, studying locations in Africa, Indonesia, the Middle East, and other countries where religion is not only prominent, as it is in the United States, but is also the source of ongoing change and political tension. In focusing less on statistical manipulations and model building, anthropological work has considered the character of whole communities as well, and for this reason has had to take the political factors influencing those communities into account.

The work of scholars in religious studies, history, international relations, and public policy has also focused increasingly on religion and politics. Religious studies and history continue to hold accountable the work of scholars with interest in politics by producing studies that illuminate the past and that emphasize knowledge of religious texts and traditions. Increasingly, discussions in religious studies also challenge assumptions about what constitutes religion and how religion as a cultural category is influenced by social and political developments (such as colonialism and post-colonialism). New emphasis on "lived religion"—the practices of real people outside as well as inside religious organizations—converges with anthropological perspectives. This emphasis is especially valuable in giving policy discussions a "bottom up" or grassroots dimension. International relations and other policy studies, for their part, have focused increasingly on religion for practical reasons. The bread and butter of these studies is to offer recommendations deemed relevant to governmental decisions. Thus, the range of topics of current interest in policy circles runs the gamut from faith-based services to war and from constitutional questions to the role of religious organizations in promoting economic development.

The Encyclopedia's Approach

The entries in this *Encyclopedia* are meant to serve both beginning students and more seasoned scholars whose work increasingly leads them into unfamiliar territory. Apart from disinterest, the biggest deterrent to scholars paying greater attention to religion is probably the fact that religion is such an enormously complicated subject. A scholar who stumbles in naming the three persons of the Trinity or confusing Eid and Divali risks sufficient embarrassment to avoid these topics at all. Treating religion as a variable (such as frequency of church attendance) betokens no more understanding of the subject than does treating race in the same way. The entries included here are meant to overcome some of the reluctance that unfamiliarity with the basics of religion may induce. These entries, though, are specifically tailored to emphasize the relationships between religion and politics. Many of the essays focus on individual countries. They summarize the essential ways in which religion and politics have influenced each other in the past and at present in these countries. We have not sought to include separate entries for each of the approximately 225 countries in the world. Rather, we have emphasized large countries and countries in which the dynamics of religion and politics have been especially important in recent years. We have also included essays that combine discussions of several countries under a single regional rubric.

In addition to the essays about countries, we have included three other kinds of entries. One set provides historical and cultural background information. For instance, the essays about crusades, Confucianism, and the English revolution are largely of this nature. A second category includes essays about specific individuals who have played a prominent role in the relationships between religion and politics. The essays about Dorothy Day, Mohandas Karamchand Gandhi, and Theodor Herzl are examples. The remaining essays deal with important issues, developments, or concepts and are thus organized by topic. Some of these focus on issues that will be of primary interest to scholars based in the United States and concerned about the nation's religion and politics. Evangelicalism is an example. Others deal more broadly with issues that span countries and regions, such as environmentalism and globalization.

This second edition of the *Encyclopedia* differs from the first in two important respects. First, we have updated more than half of the original entries. These updates emphasize developments that have taken place during the past decade. They also draw on the latest scholarship and include references to this scholarship in the respective bibliographies. In some instances, recent developments have also necessitated refocusing the discussion of preceding events or recasting the essay from scratch. Second, we have added twenty-five new entries. These have been added to reflect recent scholarly interest or because of events in the world itself. Entries for Demographic Shifts in Global Christianity, Islam in the United States, and Media and Religion are examples.

No single scholar nor any single essay can provide an authoritative guide to current thinking about religion and politics in the social sciences. Specific research topics nevertheless require framing in terms of larger debates and assumptions. In the remainder of this introduction, I discuss five such debates, each of which rests on broad assumptions about the nature of religion and how it might be related to politics. Readers should think of these topics as orienting frameworks. How one thinks about specific relationships between religion and politics is likely to be shaped by one's understanding of these larger issues.

The Global Context

The fact that goods, people, and information flow over longer distances in greater volume and faster than ever before is well documented. Despite rising fuel prices, shipping costs have declined. So have long-distance telephone rates. The volume of both goods shipped and calls made has climbed dramatically. Email further facilitates long distance communication. Satellite television transmission and the

Internet make global information more accessible. Meanwhile, neoliberal economic policies and democratization have reduced trade barriers and opened new markets. The global economic dependence that has resulted consists not only of more importing and exporting, but also of cheaper consumer goods, greater specialization and thus interdependence, increasing international financial flows, and an enlarged pool of available investment capital. Although many of these developments have been good for rich countries, the effects for poor countries have been mixed, benefiting some but making it harder for others to compete.

Scholarly opinions differ about the consequences of this new global economy, as it is sometimes called, for religion. In one view, religion is rooted primarily in local communities. It sacralizes attachments to home, to places of origin, to kin networks, and to tribal, ethnic, or familial identities. The main implication of global integration, in this view, is to threaten the local communities in which religion is rooted. Religious adherents can respond to these threats in one of two ways. They can accept them or resist them. Acceptance means passively acknowledging that religion is no longer as meaningful as it once was. Being a believer and a practitioner is now less important than being an Internet surfer, a Wal-Mart shopper, or a producer for the world market. Resistance means fighting back. The tension between one's distinctive heritage and the wider world now becomes more acute. Religious participation takes on added meaning. Being a believer is a way to preserve the past, defend one's home, and protect an entire way of life. That is one view. The other view is that religion itself adapts more easily to the changing global context. A person does not surf the Internet only for news; he or she also uses the new technology to learn more about fellow believers in other parts of the world. Shopping at Wal-Mart does not negate one's religious identity; one can now purchase Bibles and inspirational books more cheaply at Wal-Mart because they have been produced with low-cost labor in China.

Whether religion is local or global naturally depends on which religion and which population is at issue. What is evident in any situation is that the global context needs to be taken into account. Religious uprisings that take on political significance may well be inspired by the sense that one's way of life is threatened. They may also result from the fact that global markets benefit some groups more than others. The feeling of being left behind can be a powerful motive for resisting regimes, policies, and other nations deemed responsible for changing circumstances. At the same time, global expansion brings new opportunities and new resources that religious leaders may use to enhance their political role. Links to foreign countries, broadcasting technology, and the legitimation provided by prestigious visitors from outside one's community all help to strengthen the place of well-positioned religious leaders.

The changing global context of religion is not only a source of resources and motives that result in struggles for power. It is also a source of shifting perspectives and priorities. For instance, it is notable that religious organizations in the United States and Europe have paid increasing attention in recent years to world hunger. This attention cannot be explained in terms of an increasing share of the world suffering from hunger or increasing disparities between rich and poor. It stems in large measure from the fact that images of starvation are more readily communicated. Concerns about environmental policy provide another example. Religious organizations express greater interest in the health of the planet because economic interdependence raises awareness of mutual responsibilities.

The growing integration of the world's economies appears likely to continue, barring scarcities or negative consequences that encourage governments to restrict trade and communication. The process of integration has thus far been bumpy, however, meaning that the future will likely proceed in fits and spurts as well. These uncertainties will also affect the relations between religion and politics. For example, a regime that seeks to reduce international trade or restrict immigration may well gain popular support from nativistic religious groups that find a wider platform for their arguments.

Although the widening global context of religion and politics creates ample opportunities for new research to be conducted on these topics, one line of inquiry that has attracted attention does not, in my view, appear as promising as it did initially. This is the so-called neo-institutionalist approach to social organizations. This approach is so broad as to have hardly any distinct meaning, other than to suggest that organizations are influenced by the form of other organizations, and that what they display about themselves may be different from what they actually do. In recognition of the growing integration of the world economy, scholars working in this tradition have posed the bold argument that organizations will increasingly all resemble one another. Restaurants around the world will all look like McDonald's, retail stores will all look like Wal-Mart, government agencies will all look like the U.S. State Department, and so on. The implication is that a world culture of commonly accepted norms is coming into existence. Buddhist temples in India and Christian churches in the United States will increasingly adopt these common norms. They will also relate to their governments in the same ways.

The reason this argument does not appear promising is that it flies in the face not only of an increasing amount of empirical evidence but also of logic itself. Organizations do not take shape simply by imitating one another. They also adapt to their local environments. Even McDonald's restaurants incorporate different themes and provide different menus in Beijing and Bangalore than they do in inner-city Los Angeles or suburban Dallas. Religious organizations have all the more reason to distinguish themselves and to develop distinctive styles in different contexts. It would be convenient, of course, if they all looked the same, for studying one would constitute understanding them all. That, however, is not the current reality.

The more likely consequence of global integration is that religious diversity will increase. An organization in one country may adopt music from another. Not far away, a different religious organization caters to immigrants from a variety of home nations. The unique mix of beliefs and practices is different from those in any of these home countries. Local practices are altered by people and ideas from other places. The political implications thus become harder to predict.

State Expansion and Contraction

Thus far I have described how changes in the global context may affect religious communities. Governments' roles in relation to these wider considerations are also changing. The primary scholarly debate at present is whether the ruling regimes and their governing functions in national societies are more likely to expand, contract, or possibly fluctuate between expansion and contraction. The argument for expansion appears to be supported by considerable evidence. Authoritarian and democratic regimes alike have been able to extract resources in large amounts from their respective economies. They do this by monopolizing the power to provide national security. They also provide a growing number of social services, ranging from transportation and old-age insurance to education and meat inspection. Government expansion means variously that a larger share of the population may be employed by government, that the best or most stable jobs may be in government, that tax rates are higher,

that a larger proportion of the public pays taxes, or that people are increasingly defined as citizens, shaped by public schooling, and linked to government through identification cards or membership in organizations regulated by government. That government functions *should* expand in the context of increasing global competition is also arguable on grounds that strong states become more necessary to negotiate such competition. Thus, the strong centralized government in China does a good job of steering its economy in the direction of strong growth. Weaker states in Africa or Latin America compete less effectively.

The possibility that national state power is contracting as a result of changing global conditions has also been of interest. Because this possibility is more about future than past developments, it is grounded less in empirical evidence than in arguments. The main argument is that states' ability to control and thus extract revenue from their economies is shrinking. For instance, a business subject to high taxes or strict environmental regulations in one society can simply move to a different one. Or, even more easily, it can transfer more of its revenue to a branch office in another country. Another reason that national states may play a less important role in the future is that supranational organizations gain strength as they are called on increasingly to negotiate in global markets. The European Union's growing power in relation to that of its individual nation states might be an example.

Fluctuations involving periodic expansion and contraction of state power are also a reasonable possibility. During times of global economic growth, the role of states could contract, whereas economic downturn could encourage protectionist policies enforced by strong governments or more strategic political intervention in economic affairs. Differences among countries are also likely possibilities. For example, China, the United States, and the European Union could well pursue policies that strengthen their respective governments, while African governments might experience greater difficulty either in promoting economic growth or in maintaining their own stability.

Governmental expansion, contraction, and fluctuation obviously have implications for the role of religion under these various conditions. Strong centralized regimes have made it possible for religious communities to be almost completely suppressed, as in the case of the Soviet Union or China. In other cases, appeals to religious authorities have been used to strengthen regimes and thereby reinforce the power of a monopoly religion. Weak or contracting states are likely to have a different relationship with religious communities. In instances where central government is incapable of enforcing basic law, extremist religious groups may be able to operate with impunity. In other situations where governmental power is moderately reduced or divided, political factions are more likely to seek alliances with religious groups to strengthen their position against other factions. Certainly in the policy sphere, religious groups can be found arguing both in favor of and against proposals that would strengthen or reduce the power of national governments.

Non-State Actors

An important set of issues that necessarily frames current thinking about religion and politics derives from the observation that the role of non-state actors has probably increased dramatically since the end of the cold war. In international relations, for instance, the prevailing orientation during and after World War II was that the heads of national states were the main players in world affairs, and for this reason negotiations involving treaties, alliances, and summit meetings needed to take place at this level. After the cold war, it was less clear that this view was still operative. Although centralized regimes still held power, it was increasingly evident that local associations, nongovernmental organizations, businesses, social movements, and in some cases mafiosa and tribal warlords were reasserting their place in civic affairs. Following 9/11, it seemed further evident that non-state actors were a more significant political force. Dealing with al-Qaida was different from meeting with official representatives of nations at the United Nations or in The Hague or Beijing.

Non-state actors range from terrorist groups to nongovernmental organizations such as Amnesty International or Habitat for Humanity. They are not duly elected and they do not represent the legitimate authority within a territorially defined nation. They nevertheless command resources, exercise political power, carry out administrative and social service functions either with or without government support, and sometimes use violence or the threat of violence. Non-state actors typically represent a distinct constituency and function in the interests of that constituency, although they may also claim to speak for the common good or some universal principle (such as human rights or environmental justice). Religion is often a source of non-state organizations. These groups variously claim to speak for God, mobilize

people through religious networks, and differentiate themselves from other religions or from such enemies of religion as secularism and materialism. Radical or extremist religious groups are often labeled as such because of the distinctive values they hold and their willingness to engage in nonlegal means of furthering those values. The majority of non-state actors, however, work within prevailing laws. They provide international emergency relief, lobby for environmental protection or human rights, promote marriage and childrearing, sponsor missionaries, or monitor abuses of prisoners.

Non-state actors are essentially voluntary associations in that members join freely and do not in most instances rely on force to achieve their ends. In this respect, they are features of the nineteenth century as much as of the twentieth or twenty-first centuries. They bear a strong relationship with democracy, providing checks and balances against strong centralized state bureaucracies and serving as the means through which citizens express political claims. In more recent parlance, they generate social capital in the form of networks and norms of trust and cooperation, and this capital can be used to further peaceful aims but can also be deployed to sell drugs, rob banks, or bomb buildings.

Discussions of non-state actors generally locate them within larger treatments of civil society. Civil society refers to the fact that citizens organize themselves in ways that both influence governmental structures and circumvent those structures. For instance, the voluntary associations of which civil society is composed include nonprofit food pantries and homeless shelters that, on the one hand, encourage government to be more responsive to the needs of the poor and, on the other hand, help the poor even without the assistance of government. Religion is sometimes considered an important source and continuing aspect of civil society because it encourages people to band together and engage in altruistic behavior of this kind.

Several reasons can be advanced for thinking that non-state actors have become increasingly important in recent years. One is that global communication makes it possible for people to organize more easily and for scattered activities to be coordinated in ways other than the bureaucratic hierarchies involved in national governments. Another is that governments themselves rely increasingly on non-state actors to assist in administering ever more complicated social services. For instance, rich countries that seek to promote economic development or improved health facilities in poor countries do not simply hire bureaucrats to go abroad or send money to officials in those countries; instead, they work with nongovernmental associations, foundations, and churches to administer these efforts. A more specific reason is that non-state actors are increasingly used by democratic governments to promote democracy from the ground up, so to speak, in formerly authoritarian societies. For example, nongovernmental organizations have been a popular means of attempting to build civil society in eastern Europe and other areas previously controlled by the Soviet Union.

Whether or not non-state actors are becoming more important, they are a significant consideration in discussions of the relationships between religion and politics. For one thing, these organizations mediate between individual citizens and central governing bodies, meaning that individuals often mobilize and voice their political views through religious or quasi-religious groups. The political behavior of religious people cannot be understood, therefore, simply in terms of what they believe or how they vote; it must also take account of how they are organized. For this reason, scholars pay increasing attention to religious congregations as places where political opinions are shaped or where people are recruited to join social movements. In addition, non-state actors increasingly work hand in hand with public officials and receive funding from government agencies. In this way, as well as through requirements for reporting or accountability to the public, religious groups are shaped by the political context in which they function. Clearly, it is quite different for a religious group to hire professional grant writers and secure large sums through government contracts than for it to recruit volunteers to spend a few free evenings helping the poor.

A related consideration concerns the ability of religious groups, community organizations, and other non-state actors to encourage political participation. Two opposing trends underlie the interest in this consideration. On the one hand, voluntary associations have responded to changes in communication patterns and the enlarged scope of government functions by altering their basic structure. More of these associations are national membership organizations that raise money through direct mail but do little else to promote social interaction. Others are nonprofit service organizations with specialized functions and professional staff. On the other hand, grassroots organizations that create lasting bonds among people and draw them into larger networks appear to have declined. As a result, some kinds of civic participation also seem to be diminishing. Thus, the ebb and flow of participation in religious groups is of interest not only to religious leaders but also to social observers who view these dynamics as part of a larger story. To the extent that religious participation encourages political involvement and volunteering, a decline in levels of religious participation may also signal an erosion of civic life more generally.

Porous Institutions

In the social sciences religion and politics are often described as social institutions. This means that they presumably perform distinct societal functions and operate according to different norms. For instance, religion relates people in some way to the sacred, supernatural, or transcendent and is organized by clergy who carry out these functions, whereas the political sphere sets the society's goals and pursues these goals through coercive means administered by people trained in policymaking and law. Institutions are said to be relatively autonomous from one another insofar as they can generate their own resources and set their own standards. Thus, religion raises its money through voluntary contributions and decides to devote these funds to paying clergy salaries and maintaining houses of worship; government generates revenue through taxes and spends it for national security, administration, and public services. The standards by which clergy are evaluated are thus different from those used to judge the performance of government officials.

Social theory has long held that institutions such as religion and politics are more clearly differentiated from one another in modern societies than they probably were in earlier societies. For instance, a holy man may have doubled as tribal leader in earlier times, but it would be less common today for a member of the clergy to be an elected official. Historic efforts to draw a clear line of demarcation between church and state are often mentioned as watersheds in the increasing differentiation of religion and politics. Once a king is no longer head of the church, for instance, religion has greater freedom to set its own course and government does not need to be as concerned about how its actions may or may not conform to religious teachings. In the same way that religion and politics have become more distinct, other institutions have also gained greater autonomy. Professional medicine is much more distinct from religion now than it was at a time when the shaman also provided cures for illnesses. Other examples include a greater separation of art from religion, higher education from religion, and therapy from religion.

What the idea of separate and distinct institutional spheres neglects is the fact that these spheres continue to interact. Just because the king does not double as the pope does not mean that the two no longer influence one another. Indeed, a related argument in social theory is that the more something becomes specialized and distinct, the more it has to interact with other specialized groups or organizations. A farmer who raises cattle but no longer bakes his own bread has to interact with another farmer who grows wheat or a baker who specializes in baking. In this view, political functionaries might not be so good at presiding over military funerals and thus would need to call on clergy for this task, or clergy would need to enlist the help of a public official to work out a complex zoning question when constructing a place of worship. It is worth noting, though, that these continuing and perhaps increasing interactions have often been neglected in the social sciences. The reason is that religion's roles have not been considered as essential as those of public officials, doctors, or business leaders. In this view, religion simply existed because people could not deal with their problems in better ways. Once these ways were found, religion would disappear or at least shrink to insignificance.

Yet religion has continued to be much more important in modern societies than social scientists predicted. To be sure, popular participation in religious worship services is much more common in some societies than in others. Yet there are few societies in which religion fails to be a public presence. If it is not a presence through large numbers of people participating in congregations, it is evident in state ceremonies, magnificent historic cathedrals, or activist minority political movements. Despite being well-differentiated from the formal functions of government, religion continues to interact with government. Political candidates appeal for votes by proclaiming themselves to be in favor of or in opposition to policies that affect religious groups. Clergy have sufficient followings to seize political power or serve as powerbrokers in the drafting of constitutions. Ordinary citizens assemble at places of worship and talk about public policy as well as about the sacred.

That social institutions with distinct norms and functions interact with one another is important to consider in framing discussions about religion and politics. Whether the distinction is formalized as constitutional separation of the two or not, the differences in functions must be taken into account. For instance, when congregations become locations for political oratory or for administering government service programs, questions arise about the consequences for definitions of the sacred. Not without reason, religious leaders have often insisted that the mundane be kept separate from the sacred. Similarly, when public officials proclaim that their policies should be accepted because they resulted from prayer or studying sacred texts, questions must be asked about whether these policies can be defended through rational deliberation and are to be enacted by competent people. The fact that religion spills into politics and vice versa is equally important. In the same way that the environmental impact of public policy is taken into account, the religious impact also warrants consideration. For example, a policy that provides large sums of government funding to relocate low-income families from urban neighborhoods to small towns or suburbs will clearly have a detrimental influence on the religious organizations that serve those neighborhoods. Similarly, a zoning law that prevents any new religious organization from being established will have greater consequences for a mosque or temple initiated by recent immigrants than for a congregation long in existence. Because policies with implications like these are so common, litigation and other means of expressing religious concerns are a continuing aspect of contemporary politics.

These interactions between religion and politics are likely to increase because of the growing porousness of institutions. Porousness refers to the fact that people, goods, and information flow more often and more easily across institutional boundaries, just as they do across geographic terrain. The change can be imagined in the following way: When travel and communication are difficult, coordination can be organized on any sizable scale only through a rather well-defined hierarchical structure. In this form of organization, people supervise those below them and report to those above them; information flows through channels. In contrast, instant communication via email or even telephone alters the possibilities. Electronic computation especially means that financial information does not have to be coordinated in one place. Accounts can be decentralized. People do not have to be employees of an organization; they can be brought in as subcontractors or temporary workers and yet their performance can be monitored more easily. This means that a business can reduce its overhead costs without significantly increasing its risks by dealing with independent suppliers and keeping inventories low. By the same token, it means that communication and coordination can also occur more easily across institutional sectors. A government agency can contract with a nonprofit organization, which in turn hires a for-profit publicity firm, raises additional revenue from a private foundation, and works through a network of religious organizations to provide tutoring for children from low-income families.

Porousness is increasingly evident in the religious sphere. Although it might be supposed that religious leaders would guard their special relationship with the sacred, they have instead made strategic use of opportunities to build alliances with leaders in other sectors and to import ideas or export them to those sectors. This kind of porousness can be illustrated by the relationships between religion and the communications industry. Especially in the United States, religious organizations have made increasing use of radio and television technology. Although this practice is sometimes regarded as nothing more than borrowing technology, religious television programming has also spilled directly into the entertainment business, resulting in profitable cable television endeavors. In addition, religious productions in congregations sometimes air on network television, places of worship become venues for art exhibits and concerts, and specialists trained in communications or the arts gain experience in religious settings and then move into secular organizations.

The interaction between religion and the communications industry is relevant to considerations about religion and politics because the latter is more likely to be considered a public domain and subject to government regulation. Once religion enters that sphere, its interests in public policies affecting communications shift. In addition, experience gained in mass communication and entertainment can also transfer to political marketing or lobbying. Not surprisingly, religious leaders who are deeply involved in mass communication have not only gained influence within the religious sphere itself but have also become a voice in political affairs. Other cross-institutional activities have had similar consequences. For instance, one of the largest organizations in the United States that specializes in family issues draws large sums from religious individuals and congregations and in turn uses some of this money to seek influence in national politics. Less visibly, religiously sponsored counseling centers draw religion increasingly into the public sphere through the regulations regarding insurance and privacy that are mandated by government.

Porousness means that both religion and politics must be understood as taking increasingly complex and innovative organizational forms. Although research on religion correctly recognizes that congregations are usually the primarily way in which faith is organized, attention also needs to be paid to other forms. So-called parachurch or quasi-religious organizations are one example. A service organization that is motivated by religious convictions and partly funded by religious organizations is nevertheless different from a congregation and plays a different role in the community and in relation to government. Complex alliances that involve government agencies, businesses, nonprofit organizations, and religious organizations are another example. How public policies or laws pertain to these alliances are open questions. Informal networks among public officials, corporate executives, and clergy are especially interesting because of their potential for shaping major political decisions. Finally, the Internet's role in mobilizing people across different religious traditions in support of political causes is a topic of growing importance.

Cultural Pluralism

Another lens through which the relationships between religion and politics must be viewed is the essentially pluralistic character of modern culture. Pluralism refers not only to the fact that norms and values are diverse but also to the idea that this diversity is a good thing. It contrasts sharply with situations in which consensus or homogeneity is required. Pluralism is always political. It arises from groups with different traditions needing to form an alliance to protect themselves or being joined by trade or intermarriage. It often emerges because of regimes being imposed on more than one local or ethnic subculture. Increasingly, pluralism is also the result of migration and travel. The idea that pluralism is desirable is reinforced by governments (in the name of tolerance), by businesses (as an impetus for expanded markets), and by universities (as the mark of an educated person).

When diverse religious groups intermingle, the stakes are typically higher than they are for those involving any other kind of difference. This is because religion cannot be understood in terms of phenotypical characteristics, accident of birth, or comforting traditions. The major religions present themselves as manifestations of divine truth. Although there may be similarities among religious claims, each religion embodies a distinct understanding of truth and is organized around that understanding. Islam, Judaism, and Christianity, for example, are quite different from one another, even though they share some of the same figures and stories. When adherents of different religions live within the same political space, therefore, cultural work is required to adjust their views of themselves and of one another.

The most obvious difficulties posed by religious diversity include violent struggles, hate crimes, discrimination, and intolerance. Several political solutions have been devised to address these difficulties. One is repression. A strong authoritarian regime can simply repress all religions or those minority religions that happen to be in disfavor with the majority. Repression may not be sufficient to eradicate private religious convictions, but forcing them to be practiced in secret or held only as matters of conscience may severely dampen their longevity. Keeping minority religions in their place takes a variety of forms, ranging from withholding the right to meet or to worship, to forced emigration, to genocide. All of these techniques have been practiced in recent decades as well as throughout history.

In democratic societies the more common means of managing the potential for conflict among religious groups is by guaranteeing freedom of religious expression but circumscribing the forms such expression may take. Minority and majority religions alike are typically free to meet as long as they do so peacefully. Individual adherents and religious leaders can exercise their right to speak publicly about their convictions as long as they do not instigate violence in the process. Religious groups can seek to influence elections and lawmaking, but cannot enlist the coercive powers of government to do so. They cannot, for instance, call on the police to harass members of other religions or use money raised through the government's powers of taxation to support themselves. There are, of course, wide variations among constitutional democracies in how these principles are applied. What must be underscored is simply the great extent to which considerations about religious diversity are part of the heritage that has shaped modern constitutional thought and jurisprudence.

The direct role of political processes in governing religious diversity does not, however, exhaust the significant implications of this diversity for the political sphere and for the practice of religion itself. A case in point is the tension between believing privately that one's religious convictions are the unique revelation of divine truth and treating "unbelievers" as equals in civic life. This tension has been the source of deep philosophical debates, such as those about the possibilities of common moral principles underlying all religions. In civic life, universal suffrage has in practice been rooted in assumptions about common morality or a natural law that is not restricted to one or another interpretation of divine truth. Understandings of religious truth itself, though, are affected by these civic concerns. For example, some research suggests that exposure to religious diversity is associated with a weakening of commitment to the practices of one's own religion or to placing greater emphasis on the mysterious nature of the divine and the inscrutability of divine will. The important point is that civic norms and religious convictions do not operate in separate spheres. Although institutional arrangements encourage people to speak and talk differently in different contexts (e.g., in school or at one's congregation), their religious convictions influence how they think about other groups and about questions of respect and tolerance.

Some of the most vociferous disagreements about the relationships between religion and politics stem from different views of how best to accommodate religious pluralism. These disagreements surface in questions about how much or how little religious convictions should be taken into consideration by judges in decisions about important constitutional questions, in questions about the desirability of granting full rights of citizenship to immigrants and other minority groups, and in debates about issues that appear to be grounded in religious convictions, such as abortion, homosexuality, and the propriety or impropriety of presenting school children with alternatives to instruction about evolution. Although the term "culture war" is often misused to overstate the popular extent of these disagreements, there is no question that conflicting views about deeply held religious beliefs have been part of the civic culture of many societies in recent decades. One of the underlying tensions in these debates is whether a particular interpretation of divine truth is being unfairly boxed in by considerations about pluralism or whether pluralism itself is of sufficient value to warrant such restrictions.

Pluralism is thus about much more than simply creating a civic climate in which people of different religions can live together without killing one another. It is also a deeper question that can only temporarily be resolved by citizens retreating into themselves and saying, in effect, leave me alone. As long as people continue to take their religious faith seriously (a prospect that by all indications is likely), the question of how much those convictions should influence the collective life of societies will remain important. Deep differences and even acrimony will be part of how this question is debated. The purpose of democratic government, however, is not to quash differences or to eradicate acrimony. Debate about fundamental values is essential to any thriving democracy. There is positive value to the fact that people of different religions are willing to engage one another in public debate. The danger is that powerful political interest groups can also manipulate these discussions and their various constituencies simply for self-interested political gain.

The Challenges Ahead

Scholarly inquiries are generally driven by one or another of two goals. The quest for intrinsic knowledge is one. In the case of religion and politics, curiosity alone is a powerful reason to know more. A scholar might say, here is a new way to use the Internet to conduct an experiment about religious belief; I wonder what I can learn. Or, let's see what happens if we apply a new statistical technique to the information we have from surveys. A scholar could become passionate about the quest for new knowledge in these ways. The other motive for scholarly investigation is the quest for practical knowledge. The idea of practical knowledge is often misunderstood to be any knowledge that can be used. Thus, information that can be used to blow up buildings or annihilate populations is as practical as research to cure an illness. This interpretation leads to the cynical view that scholarly inquiry should not be very concerned with its practical uses because any of these could be harmful instead of beneficial. A better understanding of practical knowledge implies a strong normative commitment to engage in scholarship oriented toward improving the human condition and the circumstances bearing on this condition and for which humans can assume responsibility. Any consideration of religion and politics is surely a reason to engage in the pursuit of practical knowledge. Both the enormous problems associated with religion and its vast potential for good cry out for investigation.

Yet, the conclusion that knowledge about religion and politics is of value for its practical consequences cannot be so readily assumed in the contemporary academy. To the extent that scarce resources are invested, many would argue that religion is simply a realm of idle speculation, a topic for pointless chatter on a Sunday morning or at parties, not a subject for serious investigation in the modern university.

The long reach of the Enlightenment remains strong in the twenty-first century. Was not the Enlightenment the triumph over years of superstition and religion-inspired bloodshed? Did it not lead to the glorious age of modern science? The priority for universities should thus be science, not the study of religion. Improvements to life are better accomplished through cancer research and studies of the brain. Let people fight about religion if they will, but scholars should move on, take the high road, and learn a better way.

In short, academics should ignore the real world. Ignore the fact that religion matters so deeply that people are willing to die for it, even if cancer research would ensure them a long life. Ignore the fact that the United States remains one of the most religious countries in the world, despite its high levels of education and scientific achievements. Ignore the fact that the normal way to understand something better is not to ignore it but to learn more about it. This is the kind of ignorance that reflects badly on scientists and university administrators alike. It results in policymakers pursuing adventures that backfire because they overemphasize technology and take religion too little into account.

The challenge involved in gaining a clearer understanding of the relationships between religion and politics is in the first instance a matter of learning the extent to which religion is or is not a significant part of the lived experiences of individuals and communities. This is a fundamental question to which there are as yet surprisingly few answers. It cannot be assumed that religion is simply important in all circumstances and to all aspects of life, any more than it can be assumed to be irrelevant. How individuals and groups make choices and defend those choices remains poorly understood. Interdisciplinary research that includes, but extends beyond, questions about religion is required. A promising start is to recognize that people may or may not make rational choices but generally do want their decisions to seem reasonable. What counts as reasonable, though, varies considerably from context to context. The accounts that people give of their behavior, whether religious, scientific, self-interested, or something else, are ways of legitimating their decisions in relation to the norms and values they consider important. Studies of decision-making processes that pay close attention to the discourses of legitimation are thus a promising avenue for enhancing knowledge about religion and politics.

A related challenge is to maintain the delicate balance between studies of abstract or disaggregated constructs and

real-life situations. For instance, the study of decision making and its legitimating rationale may usefully be conducted
in the laboratory or through computerized simulations. At
the same time, ethnographic research provides a reality check
on these assumptions built into experiments and simulations.
The global context in which religion and politics intersect
means that greater attention must be devoted to regional and
cultural differences. Language skills and familiarity with local customs and religious traditions are essential. Fortunately,
increases in global communication also greatly facilitate the
sharing of such knowledge.

An additional challenge is to balance scholarship that reflects a rich understanding of religion itself with studies that
relate religion to other aspects of social life, such as social
class, gender, health policy, the mass media, or the pursuit of
democracy. On the one hand, specialists in the study of particular religious traditions provide valuable information
about the origins and history of sacred texts, schools of interpretation, and associated ritual practices. On the other
hand, a specialist in health policy or national security brings
a wealth of knowledge to the table that helps in understanding how religion may be relevant to these issues. Increasingly, collaborative scholarship is required, whether it is conducted in universities or in policy institutes. Such collaboration is of course best facilitated by centers, seminars, and
other interdisciplinary programs.

A final challenge is simply a cautionary note. The events
of 9/11 are a reminder of how quickly interests in religion
and politics can be altered by world affairs. Because religion
interacts constantly with its social environment, its flanks are
also exposed to changes in that environment. Wars, natural
disasters, waning or waxing economic fortunes, and acts of
violence can all have profound effects on religion. The task
of scholarship is not only to respond with new information
but also to provide a foundation of knowledge from which
to launch the search for that information. The entries in this
Encyclopedia aim to serve this purpose.

BIBLIOGRAPHY

Almond, Gabriel A., R. Scott Appleby, and Emmanuel Sivan. *Strong Religion: The Rise of Fundamentalisms around the World.* Chicago: University of Chicago Press, 2003.

Barrett, David B., George T. Kurian, and Todd M. Johnson. *World Christian Encyclopedia: A Comparative Survey of Churches and Religions in the Modern World.* 2d ed. New York: Oxford University Press, 2001.

Casanova, José. *Public Religions in the Modern World.* Chicago: University of Chicago Press, 1994.

Esposito, John L., and Michael Watson. *Religion and Global Order.* Cardiff: University of Wales Press, 2000.

Fetzer, Joel S., and J. Christopher Soper. *Muslims and the State in Britain, France, and Germany.* New York: Cambridge University Press, 2005.

Hanson, Eric O. *Religion and Politics in the International System Today.* New York: Cambridge University Press, 2006.

Heclo, Hugh, and Wilfred M. McClay. *Religion Returns to the Public Square: Faith and Policy in America.* Washington, D.C.: Johns Hopkins University Press, 2003.

Jenkins, Philip. *The Next Christendom: The Coming of Global Christianity.* New York: Oxford University Press, 2007.

Juergensmeyer, Mark. *Terror in the Mind of God: The Global Rise of Religious Violence.* 3d ed. Berkeley: University of California Press, 2003.

Norris, Pippa, and Ronald Inglehart. *Sacred and Secular: Religion and Politics Worldwide.* New York: Cambridge University Press, 2004.

Orsi, Robert A. *Between Heaven and Earth: The Religious Worlds People Make and the Scholars Who Study Them.* Princeton, N.J.: Princeton University Press, 2005.

Philpott, Daniel. *Revolutions in Sovereignty: How Ideas Shaped Modern International Relations.* Princeton, N.J.: Princeton University Press, 2001.

Putnam, Robert D., ed. *Democracies in Flux: The Evolution of Social Capital in Contemporary Society.* New York: Oxford University Press, 2002.

Stern, Jessica. *Terror in the Name of God: Why Religious Militants Kill.* New York: Ecco, 2003.

Stout, Jeffrey. *Democracy and Tradition.* Princeton, N.J.: Princeton University Press, 2004.

Wuthnow, Robert. *America and the Challenges of Religious Diversity.* Princeton, N.J.: Princeton University Press, 2005.

———. *Saving America? Faith-Based Services and the Future of Civil Society.* Princeton, N.J.: Princeton University Press, 2004.

ENCYCLOPEDIA OF POLITICS AND RELIGION

'Abduh, Muhammad

Muhammad 'Abduh was an Egyptian reformer and a pioneer of Islamic modernism and nationalism. Of peasant stock from Lower Egypt, 'Abduh (1849–1905) studied at the village Qur'an school, the Ahmadi mosque in Tanta, and the great mosque-university of al-Azhar in Cairo. Sufism (Islamic mysticism) and his apprenticeship with the Iranian pan-Islamist Jamal al-Din al-Afghani (1839–1897) strongly influenced his outlook. When Afghani was expelled from Egypt in 1879, his disciple 'Abduh was dismissed from teaching duties at al-Azhar and returned to his village.

'Abduh came back to Cairo in 1880 as editor of the government's *Official Journal.* Because he supported a revolt against Egypt's domination by Europeans and the Turkish-speaking elite in the army and palace, the British (after occupying Egypt in 1882) exiled 'Abduh to Beirut in what is now Lebanon.

In 1884 'Abduh joined Afghani in Paris to publish a short-lived journal, *The Indissoluble Bond,* which preached Muslim unity against Western imperialism. In 1888 he returned to Egypt and became a judge on the National Courts; eleven years later he became grand mufti, Egypt's highest official interpreter of the *shari'a* (Islamic law). From his seat on al-Azhar's administrative council, he tried unsuccessfully to reform the institution. Conservatives blocked his efforts, and shortly before his death in 1905 he resigned in frustration.

'Abduh and Afghani believed that Muslims everywhere must cooperate to reverse internal decline and counter European imperialism. They called for a return to the spirit of early Islam and a reinterpretation of the Qur'an and the *sunna* (precedent) of the prophet Muhammad in light of modern times. They believed that limited borrowing from Western ideas was permissible and that properly used reason could not conflict with religious revelation.

Although the shock of defeat and exile, and Afghani's spell, had briefly drawn him back into political activism in Paris, 'Abduh came to believe that political protest was futile without reform from within. This belief led him to limited cooperation in social reform with Lord Cromer, the British consul general and real ruler of Egypt from 1883 to 1907. It also alienated him from the local ruler, khedive Abbas Hilmi II, and Mustafa Kamil's circle of nationalists, all of whom pushed for immediate independence from the British.

After 'Abduh's death his closest disciple, the Syrian reformer Muhammad Rashid Rida (1865–1935), continued to carry his message throughout the Islamic world. Rida's magazine, *al-Manar,* spoke for the Salafiyya movement, which sought inspiration in the example of virtuous early Muslims (the *salaf,* or ancestors). Rida grew more anti-Western and intransigent after World War I, deeply influencing Hasan al-Banna and the Muslim Brethren, the leading revivalist Islamic movement in the Arab world in the mid-twentieth century. Islamist radicals today prefer Afghani, the relentless activist, to 'Abduh, the patient reformer.

'Abduh's legacy also lived on among his secular nationalist and liberal followers. These men—mostly lawyers and teachers rather than *ulama,* or scholars of Islam—set the tone of Egypt's dominant liberal nationalism until a military coup in 1952 overthrew the government. Thereafter liberal Egyptian nationalism was on the defensive, first against Gamal Abdel Nasser's Arab nationalism and socialism and then against the Islamist resurgence that began in the late 1960s.

See also *Afghani, Jamal al-Din al-; Banna, Hasan al-; Egypt; Islam; Islam's Encounters with the West.*

Donald Malcolm Reid

BIBLIOGRAPHY

Adams, Charles C. *Islam and Modernism in Egypt.* New York: Russell and Russell, 1968.

Ahmed, Jamal Mohammed. *The Intellectual Origins of Egyptian Nationalism.* Oxford and New York: Oxford University Press, 1960.

Enayat, Hamid. *Modern Islamic Political Thought.* Austin: University of Texas Press, 1982.

Hourani, Albert. *Arabic Thought in the Liberal Age, 1798–1939.* London: Oxford University Press, 1970.

Kerr, Malcolm H. *Islamic Reform: The Political and Legal Theories of Muhammad Abduh and Rashid Rida.* Berkeley: University of California Press, 1966.

Abolitionism

Abolitionism is the political and religious conviction that the practice of human bondage is morally wrong. It is impossible to study the political and social history of the Americas without studying the history of slavery. The modern development of the countries of the Americas proceeded hand in hand with the practice of slavery. Questions of slavery's economic value, political viability, and morality greatly influenced the character of these countries from the moment of initial contact between the indigenous peoples and European settlers until abolitionism took firm root and led eventually to the end of the practice of human bondage.

The United States legalized slavery from its birth as a nation until the end of the Civil War in 1865. As long as slavery existed, groups of men and women condemned it as a moral and political evil. Slaves themselves protested against and resisted human bondage, seeking to increase their liberty and control over their lives through sabotage and work slow-downs, flight, and occasionally revolt. The political fires of abolitionism burned brightest from 1830 to 1860, the thirty-year period preceding the Civil War. Before that time, only a few Anglo-Americans viewed slavery as a moral or ethical evil, though there were notable exceptions. Some of the most prominent of the founders, including George Washington and Thomas Jefferson, questioned the morality and political wisdom of holding slaves and wondered, at least in private, if a nation conceived in liberty could survive with slavery as a common practice.

Religious groups have historically censured slavery. In 1758 the Quakers condemned it at their annual conference and remained resolute in their conviction. The Baptists and Methodists also condemned the practice at the turn of the nineteenth century, arguing that no man could serve as master over his brother because all were equal in the eyes of the Lord. These two groups, however, ultimately softened their opposition. By the early 1800s they had traded their antislavery stances for a measure of social respectability after becoming convinced that few politicians or slaveholders would sanction emancipation under any circumstance.

Early Abolitionists and U.S. Politics

The American Colonization Society—established in 1816 by a coterie of affluent northerners dedicated to the gradual and voluntary emancipation of enslaved Americans—was the most famous organized and sustained resistance to slavery before 1831. Officials of the organization proposed that masters be financially compensated for freeing their slaves and that freed people be repatriated to Africa. The society actually transported several thousand blacks to Africa in the early 1800s, particularly to Liberia. Its activities, however, ignited a firestorm of protest from pro-slavery groups and particularly northern free blacks, who countered that no one should be forced to emigrate against his or her will. Richard Allen, founder of the country's first all-black denomination, the African Methodist Episcopal Church (in Philadelphia in 1816), along with David Walker, Frederick Douglass, and other prominent spokespersons for the free black community stood steadfastly against slavery. Unlike most white politicians, these abolitionists unflaggingly portrayed human bondage as a wicked act against God and called for immediate emancipation. Notwithstanding these acts and words of protest, until the early 1800s most white Americans generally viewed black slaves as naturally inferior and consigned by God to bondage.

Abolitionism emerged as a dominant debate within national politics in the 1830s because of major transformations in the country. First, innovations in technology made it easier to build large, national political movements. Canals and railroads expanded at an unprecedented rate. Improvements in printing dramatically lowered the cost and increased the speed of producing newspapers and pamphlets. These developments allowed people from distant corners of the country to share ideas and organize support for issues like abolitionism. At the same time, a powerful series of religious revivals swept through the West and the East, popularizing new ideas about sin and salvation and nurturing a reform-minded culture in which abolitionism flourished. Beginning in the late 1700s, revivals burst forth in Kentucky and Tennessee and gradually spread eastward, touching residents of the hinterlands and the cities alike. Charles Finney, a one-time Presbyterian and the best known of the new evangelists, conducted revivals in western New York State in the late 1820s and in New York City in the early 1830s. Finney taught that man was not predestined for heaven or hell but instead could affect his eternal future through his behavior. Man could strive to address his sins and those of his society, instructed Finney, and thus prepare the way for the imminent return of Jesus and the subsequent start of the millennium. In this world of evangelical Protestantism, there was no compromise with the devil, no backing down from sin. In this world, few sins were more heinous than slavery.

Evangelical Protestantism and Free Labor

Opposition to slavery seemed to some people a natural extension of evangelical Protestantism. Evangelists taught that modern society was a battleground between humans' moral free agency and duty to follow God and their unregulated passions. No one should tolerate individuals or institutions that corrupted humans' ability to act on their own; all must labor to liberate their spirits from social influences that imprisoned them, be it alcohol, prostitution, or work on Sundays and especially slavery. Slavery was the worst of these sins because, for hundreds of years, it had disfigured not only the slave's capacity to act freely but also the master's, binding both to an economy in which humans were trafficked, beaten, abused, and sold. Indeed, for many evangelical Protestants, slavery was part of a world that they hoped to change forever.

Perhaps no one embodies the intersection of evangelical Protestantism and abolitionism better than William Lloyd Garrison, who founded the *Liberator* as an antislavery newspaper on the first day of 1831. He spoke to the hearts of many evangelists when he called for an utter and instant end to slavery. Unlike many earlier opponents of human bondage, in particular members of the American Colonization Society, Garrison condemned slavery as a national sin that divided Americans from God and required expiation in the form of immediate emancipation. He founded the American Anti-Slavery Society in Philadelphia in 1833 and articulated the antislavery leanings of many northerners,

especially residents of New England, western New York, and southern Ohio—places where Protestantism and changes in technology had been the greatest.

Abolitionism as a single-issue political movement never attracted widespread support. Its most radical spokespersons, like Garrison, drew relatively few disciples. Rather, many evangelists, including Finney, argued that emancipation, though a lofty goal, must be accomplished slowly and proceed only as slave owners experienced conversion. Talk of immediate action, they feared (prophetically) risked alienating slaveholders and driving the nation to the brink of civil war. Still, the issue of abolitionism stoked the flames of a new political consciousness in the antebellum era, forcing people into two categories—those who opposed slavery and those who did not—and providing a critical plank in the platform of the Republicans, a new and rising electoral political party in the 1850s.

Republican politicians, most notably Abraham Lincoln of Illinois, rose to prominence by fusing the issue of antislavery to new economic and political philosophies and creating the ideology of free labor. As the term suggests, *free labor* posits that the health of a civilization depends directly on the ability of its laborers to work freely. All men desire to improve themselves and thus would naturally practice those habits that promise the greatest chances of success, namely thrift, discipline, diligence, and temperance. A man, regardless of the station in life into which he is born, could work his way up the ladder of success. Work done by hand and for hire is honorable because it is temporary, only a starting point from which free men of drive and ambition could advance to become their own bosses. The presence of social mobility in a free-labor ideology, however, rests on the absence of slavery. Slavery denies its workers a chance to lift themselves out of their status, and thus a system of bonded workers, without hope for social advancement, works inefficiently. Slavery also degrades the dignity of manual labor by equating it with fixed servitude.

Preserving the Union

In addition to opposing slavery for economic reasons, most Republicans shared with evangelical Protestants a belief in the immorality of human bondage. African Americans, they claimed, were by nature inferior to whites, but they still deserved an opportunity to earn bread by the sweat of their own brows and receive a modicum of civil liberties. Yet Republicans in the 1850s stopped far short of demanding immediate emancipation. Instead, they called for the containment of slavery within its borders while arguing the inevitability of emancipation because slavery was unprofitable and doomed to fail. The Republican cry for containing slavery was self-serving. Free-labor ideology relied on free soil or the fresh acquisition of lands free of slavery. Indeed, to advance, people must have access to free soil. The issue of such land had became critical in the first half of the 1800s with the rapid transformation of the North's largely agrarian economy to an industrial economy in which men worked factory jobs that promised little opportunity for advancement. The chance to move up and out, to start a farm or a business in a place of limited competition and cheap land represented the basic solution to dead-end manufacturing jobs. Thus, as Kansas, Nebraska, and other territories petitioned for statehood in the 1850s, free-labor ideologues insisted that they enter the Union as states free of slavery, while pro-slavery spokespersons asserted the opposite. Tensions flared in Congress, and bloody skirmishes erupted in the midwestern territories, prefacing the battles over slavery fought in the Civil War.

When the North and the South took up arms in 1861, the issue of abolitionism in the United States received its final hearing. When President Lincoln issued the Emancipation Proclamation on January 1, 1863, he officially freed all slaves in the Confederate states and explicitly made the war into a struggle about the fate of slavery. In his second inaugural address, on March 4, 1865, Lincoln directly linked the cause and ultimate meaning of the war to slavery, arguing that the widespread loss of life occasioned by the fighting was a type of national atonement for the sin of human bondage.

Slavery's demise in North America came at the point of a bayonet, but any charting of the political career of abolitionism cannot fully capture the steady trajectory of resistance by slaves themselves to their earthly fate. Slaves challenged their condition from the start. Whether at the original point of enslavement on the western coast of Africa, during the middle passage across the Atlantic, on the sugar or cotton plantation, or in the domestic household, they worked the system of human bondage to its minimum disadvantage through flight, rebellion, malingering, sabotage, theft, and deception. Changes in the North's economy, the spread of evangelical Protestantism, and the rise of the Republican Party made it possible for abolitionism to occupy center stage in national and sectional politics, but antislavery had always been at the center of politics for African Americans, free or enslaved.

Abolitionism throughout the Americas

The Union victory in the U.S. Civil War invigorated the cause of abolition throughout the Americas. Slaves in other countries and colonies historically had challenged their fate through various sorts of resistance. As early as 1522, for example, slaves in southeastern Hispaniola had staged the first significant slave revolt, on a sugar plantation owned by a son of Christopher Columbus. The modern age of emancipation in the Caribbean and Central and South America perhaps began in 1791, when slaves in the French colony of Saint-Domingue rebelled against their oppressors and fought for independence. Thirteen years later, when the smoke finally cleared and victory was declared, the insurgents renamed the country Haiti. The rebellion reflected diverse influences, including the fiery ideology of the French Revolution, a history of slave resistance, a widely shared popular religion called Vodun, a common language of Creole, and the superb generalship of Toussaint L'Ouverture.

The Haitian revolution—as a rebellion that led directly and speedily to emancipation—was distinctive, but it served as a symbol and source of energy for the cause of antislavery throughout the region, making the issue of emancipation critical to changing ideas of citizenship and economy. In 1792 Denmark became the first European colonial power to abolish the slave trade, reflecting a growing popular sentiment across Europe to end slavery as the philosophy and demands of international commerce changed. In 1834 the British Parliament, bowing to public support for abolitionism that grew also from the popularization of evangelical Christianity at the turn of the nineteenth century, abolished slavery throughout its Caribbean colonies. By 1848 France and Holland had followed suit.

In the Americas, the Haitian revolution led to official acts of abolition in several newly independent states: Chile in 1823, the countries of Central America in 1824, and Mexico in 1829. Other countries, often those with large concentrations of slaves, were slower to initiate emancipation. In these cases, slaveholding elites fought to retain the privileges of power, limit the rights and freedoms of former slaves, and ease the transition from slave-based economies to ones based on wages for hire. Uruguay abolished slavery in 1846, Colombia in 1850, the Argentine Republic in 1853, Venezuela and Peru in 1854, and finally Paraguay in 1870.

In Cuba and Brazil, elites successfully circumvented the end of the slave trade for a while longer. Whether for sugar plantations in the Spanish colony of Cuba or coffee plantations in imperial Brazil, rulers continued to bring new slaves directly from Africa, develop new lands in their own countries, and nurture new overseas markets. Yet these strategies ultimately failed to sustain plantation slavery as a profitable enterprise. Along with the insatiable need to buy more slaves, the problem of domestic insurgency grew. Cuban rebels forced Spain to enact cautious laws of gradual emancipation in 1870. Within sixteen years, a persistent rebellion in eastern Cuba and widespread resistance by slaves forced Spain to declare an end to bondage, in 1886. In Brazil, laws of gradual emancipation went into effect in the early 1870s, as many urban professionals believed that the future of the economy lay not in slavery, but in immigrant labor. Slave resistance, particularly in the form of flight and theft, accelerated the process and forced reluctant plantation owners to move quickly toward emancipation. In 1888 abolition became the rule of the land in Brazil and, finally, throughout all the Americas.

See also *Evangelicalism; Human Rights.*

John M. Giggie

BIBLIOGRAPHY

Klein, Herbert S. *African Slavery in Latin America and the Caribbean.* New York: Oxford University Press, 1986.

Sewell, Richard H. *Ballots for Freedom: Antislavery Politics in the United States, 1837–1860.* New York: Oxford University Press, 1976.

Stewart, James B. *Holy Warriors: The Abolitionists and American Slavery.* New York: Hill and Wang, 1976.

Tomich, Dale W. "The 'Second Slavery': Bonded Labor and the Transformation of the Nineteenth Century World Economy." In *Rethinking the Nineteenth Century: Movements and Contradictions,* edited by Francisco O. Ramirez. New York: Greenwood Press, 1988.

Wade, Peter. *Blackness and Race Mixture: The Dynamics of Racial Identity in Colombia.* Baltimore: Johns Hopkins University Press, 1993.

Walters, Ronald G. *American Reformers, 1815–1860.* New York: Hill and Wang, 1978.

Abortion

Governments worldwide are struggling with the issue of whether and in what conditions women should be allowed to terminate pregnancies, a procedure known as abortion. At stake are conflicting values and worldviews, often embodied in a clash between religious conservatives, on the one hand, and religious progressives and secular citizens, on the other.

Many religious conservatives argue that life begins at conception and that the termination of a pregnancy amounts to the killing of an unborn child. Most feminists and civil libertarians argue that there is no consensus on when or if a fetus is an unborn child, a potential child, or merely tissue growing in a woman's body and that a pregnant woman should be allowed to make the complex moral decision to terminate a pregnancy without interference from the state. Many liberal religious groups have adopted positions that are generally supportive of women's right to choose an abortion.

Although abortion has been used to control reproduction for most of recorded human history, it has been a source of moral and religious controversy. Greek philosophers in the fifth century B.C. disagreed on the moral justification for abortion; and abortion and infanticide were widespread in ancient Rome, where they were a subject of at least some debate. During this period, however, infanticide was more common than abortion because most abortion procedures posed grave risks to the life and health of the mother. In the nineteenth and twentieth centuries, as medical procedures for both abortion and childbirth became safer, religious groups began to confront the moral issue. Today most religious bodies have officially considered a position on abortion, although many lack an explicit policy.

In the United States the abortion debate rose to a new level of controversy after the U.S. Supreme Court ruled, in 1973, in *Roe v. Wade* that women's rights to privacy entailed a right to an abortion during the first two trimesters (the first six months) of pregnancy. The Court's ruling overturned state laws regulating or banning abortion in most states and invalidated many national laws as well. After the Court ruling, anti-abortion forces organized a "right to life," or "pro-life," movement to seek to reverse the decision, while supporters of abortion rights reorganized existing abortion-reform organizations into "pro-choice" groups.

In the 1990s the debate over abortion turned violent in the United States, as radicals on the fringe of the pro-life movement shot abortion providers and bombed abortion clinics. The pro-life movement generally condemned this violence, although some ideological leaders publicly sympathized with the frustration of those who resorted to violence, perhaps thereby signaling acceptance.

In the 2000s pro-life groups in the United States were hopeful that new appointees to the Court would overturn *Roe v. Wade* and return the issue of abortion to the states. In anticipation, South Dakota banned all abortions except those that were needed to save the life of the mother. The

Demonstrators on both sides of the abortion debate gather in front of the U.S. Supreme Court to await the Court's decision in Planned Parenthood of Southeastern Pennsylvania v. Casey *(1992). In that case the Court upheld the right to an abortion while permitting some state restrictions.*

law was considerably more conservative than opinion in the state and suggested that if abortion were returned to state governments, pro-life forces would push to ban all abortions even if public opinion did not support it.

The Roman Catholic Position

The Roman Catholic Church is the largest organized religious opponent of legal abortion. The Catholic Church holds that abortion is murder because the fetus is a child from the moment of conception. The church opposes abortion in all circumstances, including cases in which the mother's life would be put in danger by completion of the pregnancy. Catholic opposition to abortion is grounded in the teachings of religious leaders, especially popes, who based their arguments on natural law.

Although Catholic theologians have grappled with abortion for centuries, the position of opposition to all abortions was solidified during the nineteenth and twentieth centuries. Many but not all early Catholic thinkers distinguished between abortions performed before the fetus was active in the mother's womb, a time when the soul was thought to enter the fetus, and those performed afterward. By the end of the nineteenth century, however, the church officially opposed abortions in almost all circumstances. In the twentieth century Pope Pius XII declared that the right to life from God was immediate, and Pope Paul VI in his 1968 encyclical *Humanae Vitae* opposed abortion and contraception as interfering with the procreative nature of sexual union and thereby perverting the purpose of the divine gift of human sexuality.

Although the Catholic position on abortion has been clearly enunciated, *Humanae Vitae* is a teaching document, not an *ex cathedra* papal pronouncement that is considered infallible. Nonetheless, the Catholic bishops in the United States have focused more on abortion than on any other political issue, and at times Catholic leaders have threatened to excommunicate Catholic lawmakers who support abortion rights. Many Catholic bishops have subsumed the abortion issue into a larger doctrine of the "seamless garment of life," which includes a series of "life-affirming" stances on issues such as opposition to abortion, the death penalty, and nuclear weapons and support for programs that provide nutrition assistance for poor pregnant women.

The Catholic Church has lent its considerable organizational resources to the pro-life movement. Most Catholic priests deliver at least one homily on abortion each year, and many dioceses have organized pro-life groups that are supported in large part by the church. The Catholic bishops organized the National Committee for a Human Life Amendment in 1973, to attempt to push a constitutional amendment to ban abortions, and the group received considerable grassroots support from Catholic parishes. The church also commissioned polling to help influence the debate on abortion.

Considerable dissent exists among the Catholic laity and some Catholic religious elites in the United States and in other countries to the official church position on abortion. Despite the clear teaching of a hierarchical religious institution, there is also little evidence that Catholics have fewer abortions than other Americans. In the United States and other countries, Catholics are generally more conservative on abortion than are other citizens, but only a small minority support a ban on all abortions, even among those who attend Mass regularly.

Evangelical Opposition

A second religious source of opposition to legal abortion in the United States comes from the evangelical Protestant community. Evangelical Protestant churches in the United States are generally critical of abortion, and most denominations' official position allows abortions only in limited circumstances, such as to save the life and health of the mother. A number of evangelical denominations, especially fundamentalist Baptists and pentecostal Assemblies of God, have served as the organizational backbone of the pro-life movement in the South and Midwest and have lent their considerable resources to opposing legal abortion. Moreover, evangelical organizations of the Christian right, such as the Christian Coalition and Concerned Women for America, have lobbied for restrictive policies on abortion in national and state legislatures.

Evangelical churches base their opposition to abortion on biblical scripture, especially Exodus 21:22–23: "If men strive, and hurt a woman with child, so that her fruit depart from her, and yet no mischief follow: he shall be surely punished, according as the woman's husband will lay on him; and he shall pay as the judges determine. And if any mischief follow, then thou shalt give life for life." Pro-life evangelicals argue that this verse prescribes penalties for abortion providers; a few even suggest that this verse dictates the death penalty. Evangelical pastors also point to verses that suggest activity by John the Baptist and Jesus in their mothers' wombs and

to the commandment against killing. Pro-choice evangelicals offer alternative readings and argue that the verse from Exodus seems to describe a miscarriage brought on by violence, not an abortion.

The congregants in evangelical churches are generally slightly more conservative than American Catholics in their views on abortion, and members of the Assemblies of God exhibit the highest level of opposition to legal abortion of any U.S. denomination. Yet even among evangelicals, there are more pro-choice than pro-life congregants, even among those who attend church regularly.

Other Views

Mainline Protestant churches in the United States and much of Europe, while generally criticizing "frivolous" abortions, have usually supported a woman's legal right to choose. Their reasoning is that the fetus is not a fully developed human with a soul. For example, the American Episcopal Church in its 1968 general convention held that the church "emphatically oppose[d] abortion as a means of birth control, family planning, sex selection or any reason of mere convenience." Members considering abortion were encouraged to seek counsel from the Christian community and to pray. Most mainline Protestant churches have similar official positions. Many mainline Protestant denominations are members of the Religious Coalition for Reproductive Choice, which seeks to ensure that abortion remains legal in the United States.

In Europe, mainline Protestants and Catholics have occasionally disagreed visibly on abortion politics, especially in countries such as Germany with large numbers of adherents to both faiths. Members of mainline Protestant churches in the United States and Europe are more liberal than other citizens on abortion, but those who attend church regularly are more conservative than those who attend infrequently.

Orthodox Jews hold that abortion is mandatory if necessary to save the life of the mother but that it should generally be avoided; the decision is usually left to the family. Many Orthodox rabbis support pro-life politics. Reform, Conservative, and Reconstructionist Jews take a pro-choice position by viewing threats to the mother's health in the broadest possible way. American Jews are overwhelmingly pro-choice. Muslims generally have supported abortion as a medical procedure when the health of the mother is in question but otherwise have discouraged it. Islamic doctrine concerning the role of women in society and within their families, and the Islamic condemnation of extramarital sex, all combine to make many Muslim theologians take conservative positions. Yet by no means is this a unanimous view.

The denominational differences in attitudes toward abortion are echoed to a lesser extent in the attitudes of elites. Studies have shown that votes on abortion in the U.S. Congress and in state legislatures are at least somewhat predictable by taking into consideration the religious affiliation of individual members. A significant number of Catholic legislators, however, support pro-choice policies.

Conservatives and Secularists

Religion has been a source of the political debate on abortion in the United States and in other countries in several ways. First, religious denominations have provided support in the form of money, infrastructure, and official doctrine for both sides of the conflict. Second, religious activists have been visible on both sides of the debate. Third, religious rhetoric and values have been used in framing the debate. Pro-life forces, however, have received significantly greater support from organized religion than has the pro-choice side. Churches have provided the resources to form pro-life groups and lent their facilities for meetings, endorsed the cause from the pulpit, and instructed their lobbyists to work to restrict access to abortion.

The activist struggle over abortion is often portrayed as a struggle between religious conservatives and secularists. Kristin Luker's classic study of abortion activists in California, for example, found that pro-life activists were intensely religious and disproportionately Catholic converts, while many pro-choice activists lacked formal ties to organized religion. The intense religiosity of the pro-life activists led them to view unplanned pregnancies as a gift from God and never an obstacle to career or family goals.

Among nonactivist citizens, this split between secular and religious citizens is smaller, but within every religious tradition (including those that take an official pro-choice position), frequent attenders at religious services are more likely to oppose abortion than are those who attend less often. Thus, for all groups, strong commitment to religious values appears to be associated with greater opposition to abortion. Some researchers suggest that this connection between strong commitment and opposition to abortion is because frequent attenders are likely to encounter pro-life activists in church services. Others argue, however, that those who frequently attend church are likely to be traditional in their views of sexual morality and to believe that events (such as unexpected pregnancies) are God's will.

Within every religious group there is at least some debate about the official doctrine on abortion. As new technologies continue to transform the possibilities of childbirth and abortion, it seems likely that the religious debate on abortion will continue. In the 2000s, the debate about abortion spilled over into the funding of scientific research that used embryonic stem cells to find cures for neurological diseases such as Parkinson's and Alzheimer's. Embryonic stem cell research involves the destruction of an embryo and the extraction of cells that are then cloned. The issue divided the pro-life camp. Some argued that the embryos would be destroyed regardless of whether they are used in research, for they were discarded by couples who created them as part of fertility treatment. Others argue that the research is complicit in the destruction of human life.

See also *Feminism; Lobbying, Religious; Medicine; Morality; Natural Law; Sexuality.*

Clyde Wilcox

BIBLIOGRAPHY

Bowen, Donna Lee. "Abortion, Islam, and the 1994 Cairo Population Conference." *International Journal of Middle East Studies* 29 (1997): 161–184.

Connery, John. *Abortion: The Development of the Roman Catholic Perspective.* Chicago: Loyola University Press, 1977.

Cook, Elizabeth Adell, Ted G. Jelen, and Clyde Wilcox. *Between Two Absolutes: Public Opinion and the Politics of Abortion.* Boulder, Colo.: Westview Press, 1992.

Ellington, Mark. *The Cutting Edge: How Churches Speak on Social Issues.* Grand Rapids, Mich.: Eerdmans, 1993.

Luker, Kristin. *Abortion and the Politics of Motherhood.* Berkeley: University of California Press, 1984.

Noonan, John T., Jr. "An Almost Absolute Value in History." In *The Morality of Abortion: Legal and Historical Perspectives,* edited by John T. Noonan Jr. Cambridge: Harvard University Press, 1970.

Adventism

See *Seventh-day Adventism.*

al-Afghani, Jamal al-Din

Muslim reformer and anticolonialist. Jamal al-Din al-Afghani (1838 or 1839–1897) was one of the first to restate the Muslim tradition in response to Western encroachments. He reinterpreted Islam, stressing such modern values as activism, human reason, and the need for political and military strength and unity. In seeking these values in Islamic traditions, he could influence believers more than could those who simply appropriated Western ideas. He is a parent of later trends that reject both pure tradition and pure Westernism. Best known as a pan-Islamist, Afghani is also identified with Islamic modernism, Islamic revivalism, and even pan-Arabism and other nationalisms. Although his influence is often exaggerated, he remains one of the world's best-remembered Islamic activists and thinkers, and his style of interpreting the Islamic past in modern or nationalist terms has grown in popularity throughout the Muslim world.

Although Afghani claimed to have been born and brought up in Afghanistan, overwhelming evidence points to his being born and raised in Iran and receiving a Shi'i, rather than a Sunni, education. His followers, mostly Sunnis, often discount the evidence of his Iranian origin and Shi'i education. Iranians call him Asadabadi, after the town of his birth.

From his first appearance in the political record in Afghanistan, in 1864, Afghani expressed strongly anti-British views. He encouraged the Afghan emir to join Russia in fighting against the British. This anti-British sentiment was probably aroused during his first trip to India during the time of the Indian mutiny of 1857. Anti-British agitation continued to be a leitmotif during most of Afghani's life, and he used language later identified with anti-imperialism, though he was rarely severe in his criticisms of French or Russian imperialism.

Afghani became a public figure in 1869–1870 in Istanbul, where he was appointed to the Council on Education. In a public lecture, he displayed his debt to the great Islamic philosophers—including the controversial theologian and physician Abu Ali Husayn Ibn Sina (980–1037), known to the West as Avicenna—who were still taught in religious schools in Iran but were considered heretical by Sunni clerics. Afghani's talk was taken as an excuse to expel him. He went to Egypt, where he helped to educate a generation of Egyptian reformist and nationalist intellectuals, including Muhammad 'Abduh, a prominent religious reformer.

After being expelled from Egypt by the new khedive, Taufiq, in 1879, Afghani went to Hyderabad, India, where he wrote several important articles and his only treatise, *The Refutation of the Materialists.* In 1883 he traveled to London and then Paris, where he entered into debate with Ernest Renan on Islam and science. Writing for a Western audience, Afghani abandoned the religious tone he used in the Muslim world and criticized religion as limiting and intolerant, although he regarded it as needed by the nonintellectual masses. In 1884 he made his first major appearance as a pan-Islamist in an Arabic newspaper co-edited with Muhammad 'Abduh. The newspaper, *al-'Urwa al Wuthqa* ("The Strongest Link"), was distributed throughout the Muslim world.

After becoming involved in London with the schemes of a pro-Arab Englishman, Wilfrid Blunt, to settle with the Sudanese Mahdi, Afghani spent two years in Russia trying to get its leaders to start a war with Britain. In late 1889 he returned to Iran, where he helped to inspire agitation against a series of economic concessions to the British. Blaming a fiery anticoncession leaflet on Afghani, the shah expelled him to Iraq in early 1891. There he contacted the leader of the Shi'i *ulama* (Muslim scholars) who became a central figure in a successful uprising against a British tobacco concession in 1891–1892.

Afghani accepted an invitation from Ottoman sultan Abdulhamid to come to Istanbul, where he spent the last five years of his life. Although Abdulhamid forbade Afghani to write or speak publicly, the sultan did encourage him to try to persuade Shi'i clergy through Iranians in Istanbul to support the sultan as the head of all Islam. Resentful toward the shah for expelling him, Afghani encouraged a disciple to assassinate Naser al-Din Shah in Iran, in 1896. He himself died of cancer in 1897.

Although many of Afghani's ideas were borrowed, and his activism fluctuated between appeals to the powerful and appeals to the masses against the powerful, his example, his writings, and his myth have inspired a wide variety of figures and movements in the Muslim world.

See also *'Abduh, Muhammad; Islam; Islam's Encounters with the West.*

Nikki R. Keddie

BIBLIOGRAPHY

Keddie, Nikki R. *An Islamic Response to Imperialism: Political and Religious Writings of Sayyid Jamal ad-Din "al-Afghani."* Berkeley: University of California Press, 1968.

———. *Sayyid Jamal ad-Din "al-Afghani": A Political Biography.* Berkeley: University of California Press, 1972.

Kedourie, Elie. *Afghani and Abduh: An Essay on Religious Unbelief and Political Activism in Modern Islam.* Portland, Ore.: Frank Cass, 1997.

Afghanistan

Located in Central Asia at the crossroads between Europe, East Asia, and the Indian subcontinent, Afghanistan has been a gateway of invasions from the days of Alexander the Great in the fourth century B.C.E. to the Soviet intervention in the 1980s, and the American intervention in 2001. The population is heterogeneous with the Pashtu, Persian (Farsi), and Turki speakers the major communities, largely of the Sunni school of Islamic jurisprudence with a Shi'i minority of about 15 percent. The country owes its existence to the martial character of its people, to the inhospitable terrain, and, since the eighteenth century, to the fact that it formed a buffer between Russia and the British Empire in India. The country was ruled both by the sword and by Islamic law.

Since Ahmad Shah founded the state of Afghanistan in 1747, religion has limited the powers of tribal rulers, kings, and presidents. Islamic law (*shari'a*), administered by religious functionaries (*ulama*), governs the state, and even the rulers of a short-lived Marxist regime (1978–1992) gave it respect. There always, however, existed a dichotomy between customary law (the "king's law") and the *shari'a* ("God's law"), with the latter increasingly relegated to the sphere of family law.

Ahmad Shah (r. 1747–1773) had absolute power. The courts were in the hands of the *ulama,* but the death penalty had to be approved by the king or a governor. Ahmad Shah forbade the mutilation of limbs, a traditional form of punishment, and made the first attempt at drafting a legal code. Little was changed until the time of Amir Abd al-Rahman (1888–1901), who centralized all power in his hands. The "Iron Amir" claimed temporal and spiritual powers, and the only restraint on his arbitrary rule was the obligation to conform to the rules of Islamic law, as interpreted by his council of *ulama.*

The central government did not extend its jurisdiction into every community of the country. Tribal councils (*jirga* or *majlis*) adjudicated disputes within a tribe according to local traditions. Disputes between tribes were settled by negotiation in which members of the *ulama* who did not belong to the tribes served as mediators. The same was true for village communities where local dignitaries tried to solve problems without referring them to central authorities. In the major towns, governors or district chiefs controlled police powers. They were assisted by the *muhtasib,* a market inspector and overseer of public morals, to "command the good and forbid the evil" (*al-amr bi al-ma'ruf wa al-nahy'an al-munkar*). He was to discourage sinful behavior, encourage attendance at prayers, check measures and weights in the bazaars, and ascertain that foodstuffs were not adulterated. The *muhtasib* was appointed by a judge (*qadi*), paid from the public treasury, and empowered to administer whippings for minor offenses.

A process of secularization began with King Amanullah (1919–1929), who proclaimed a constitution in 1924 that enumerated the prerogatives of the ruler and the rights of the ruled. Police courts began to replace the institution of the *muhtasib,* but in the rural areas the traditional system continued. The new constitution formed the basis for further democratization under Zahir Shah (1933–1973), whose reforms culminated in the promulgation of the 1964 constitution. Members of the royal family could no longer hold ministerial positions. The system of education was greatly expanded: Kabul University, founded in 1932, was upgraded to international standards. Coeducation was introduced in the 1960s, and by 1970 secondary schools existed in every province except Zabul. Zahir Shah's efforts, however, were limited by a lack of resources. There were not enough trained teachers to man the new provincial schools, and most of the development was confined to the major towns. Universal education, envisioned by the constitution, was an aim rather than a reality. The introduction of secular schools, in addition to the traditional mosque system, produced two essentially competing elites, of which at first the modernists gained political power until they were challenged by traditional elements.

Muhammad Daud, a cousin of the king, staged a coup in 1973 and proclaimed a republic; Daud set up a one-party government, a "democracy based on social justice." His constitution, promulgated on February 14, 1977, was intended to give power to the majority—farmers, workers, and youth. Land reforms were to be carried out and cooperatives were to be encouraged. Women were to enjoy equal rights and obligations, and every Afghan citizen eighteen years or older was to have the right to vote. The constitution centralized the legal establishment, and the vestiges of separation of power were abolished as the ministry of justice took over the functions of chief justice. When some of his Marxist followers overthrew Daud in 1978, a national council replaced parliament and the revolutionary council became the highest authority in the state. Revolutionary and extraordinary courts were set up for political offenses, but religious courts were not abolished.

Resistance to the Marxist regime turned into a war of liberation after Soviet forces entered Afghanistan in December 1978. Refugee camps in Pakistan became a source of manpower, supplemented by a veritable foreign legion of young Muslim fighters, and international material and diplomatic support provided the means for a ten-year struggle in which the *mujahadin* prevailed. Islam was the rallying cry, and it was the Hanbali interpretation of Islamic jurisprudence that gained considerable influence in this process. An Islamist International under the leadership of such individuals as Usama bin Ladin has since continued the war against Eastern and Western governments.

After the fall of the communist regime in 1992, a period of civil war ensued until the Taliban regime was able to take over a large part of the country and establish its theocratic rule. Taking advantage of Pashtun nationalism, the people's yearning for stability, and considerable assistance from the Pakistan side of the border, the Taliban were able to consolidate their control of the Pashtun areas as a basis for the conquest of the north. Mulla Muhammad Omar adopted the title "Commander of the Faithful," and members of the *ulama* held most ministerial and administrative positions. The Islamic Emirate of Afghanistan began to implement its version of the "Islamic state" in which the *shariʿa* comprised the constitution and all manifestations of Westernization were abolished. Women, who had been active in the professions, were no longer permitted to carry out their duties; they were forced to wear a veil covering the entire body. Schools for girls were closed; radio and television were permitted only to broadcast religious programs. Music, photography, and various games were forbidden, and men were enjoined to grow full beards and wear traditional dress. Attendance at prayers became obligatory. Islamic punishments, long discontinued, were reinstated: adultery was punished with stoning, and the penalty exacted for theft was mutilation. Attempts to eliminate the worship of "idols" led to the irreparable loss of pre-Islamic artifacts at the Kabul Museum and the destruction of the famed Buddha statues in Bamian.

Although the Hanifite school of Sunni Islam is dominant in Afghanistan, some of the Taliban leadership were graduates or followers of the restrictive Deobandi school, which tended to adopt the stricter interpretation of the Hanbali school. Traditionally, acts in Islamic law are divided into five categories: 1.) obligatory (*fardh* or *wajib*), duties whose performance is rewarded and whose omission is punished; 2.) meritorious (*mandub, sunnah*), actions whose performance is rewarded but whose omission is not punished; 3.) indifferent (*mubah* or *jaʿiz*), actions whose performance or omission is neither punished nor rewarded; 4.) reprehensible, actions that should be avoided but will not be punished; and 5.) forbidden (*haram*), actions that are forbidden and punishable. The Taliban did not recognize these distinctions and punished reprehensible actions and enforced meritorious actions, as for example the growing of beards. They called Shiʿite Hazara "unbelievers" and were continuously engaged in campaigns against them. They attempted to impose Islamic restrictions even on non-Muslim members of the foreign aid organizations. The Taliban, however, were selective in their persecutions. They benefited from the lucrative production of drugs, making Afghanistan one of the world's biggest opium suppliers. It was "only for export," they maintained. Only as a result of international pressure did the Taliban eventually forbid poppy cultivation.

The theocratic regime was finally destroyed as a result of the American intervention of October 2001, and elections resulted in the establishment of a government, headed by Hamid Karzai. A new constitution was drafted, patterned in part after the constitution of 1964. The former king, Zahir Shah, returned to Afghanistan to hold the ceremonial position of "Father of the Nation," and Afghanistan was proclaimed an Islamic republic. The new constitution provided for the equality of all Afghans, regardless of sex or sectarian affiliation, but all laws or actions of the new government were required to conform to Islam. This provision grants the judiciary branch considerable power, and it remains to be seen if the religious establishment will follow a modernist interpretation of the law.

Afghanistan is nominally independent, but as of the mid-2000s, American forces continued to be engaged in hunting remnants of al-Qaida and the Taliban regime, and NATO forces remained employed in peacekeeping efforts. It appears that the United States expects to eventually withdraw its forces and transfer the task of pacification to NATO and the Afghan national army. Islamist groups increased their activities in 2005–2006 and imported techniques of warfare from Iraq. Socio-economic conditions likely must be improved significantly to convince the Afghan people that the country's new ideology, called democracy, is a desirable innovation.

Ludwig W. Adamec

BIBLIOGRAPHY

Abou El Fadl, Khaled M., et al. *Democracy and Islam in the New Constitution of Afghanistan.* Santa Monica, Calif.: RAND, 2003.

Adamec, Ludwig W. *Historical Dictionary of Afghan Wars, Revolutions and Insurgencies.* 2nd ed. Lanham, Md.: Scarecrow Press, 2005.

Crile, George. *Charlie Wilson's War: The Extraordinary Story of the Largest Covert Operation in History.* New York: Atlantic Monthly Press, 2003.

Nawid, Senzil. *Religious Response to Social Change in Afghanistan, 1919–1929: King Aman-Allah and the Afghan Ulama.* Costa Mesa, Calif.: Mazda, 1999.

Rashid, Ahmed. *The Taliban, Islam, Oil, and the New Great Game in Central Asia.* London: I. B. Taurus, 2002.

———. *Taliban: Militant Islam, Oil and Fundamentalism in Central Asia.* New Haven, Conn.: Yale University Press, 2000.

Roy, Olivier. *Afghanistan: From Holy War to Civil War.* Princeton, N.J.: Darwin Press, 1995.

Rubin, Barnett R. *The Fragmentation of Afghanistan: State Formation and Collapse in the International System.* 2d ed. New Haven, Conn.: Yale University Press, 2002.

Africa, West: The Mande World

The Mande world is an area in sub-Saharan West Africa that covers large parts of Mali, Guinea, Guinea-Bissau, The Gambia, Senegal, Côte d'Ivoire, and Sierra Leone. It is inhabited by linguistically, socially, and culturally related ethnic groups that share the memory of a common heritage and political unity. The Mande world, however, is not equal to the area where Mande languages are spoken.

The ethnic groups living in the Mande world—among them the Bamana (Bambara), Maninka (Malinke), Mandingo, Mandenka, Soninke, and Jula (Dioula)—trace their descent to ancient or medieval empires such as Ghana, Wagadu, and Mali (or Mande), which are celebrated in epic oral traditions. Scholars generally associate the founding of the medieval Mali empire with some of the Mande peoples and note its central place in the political history of West Africa, based on reports from medieval Muslim writers. Probably through expansion and trade, state policies, and internal dynamics, Mande cultural and social traits have spread over large parts of West Africa and provide the basis for national and ethnic identities.

Cosmology and Social Organization

Alleged indigenous traditional religion in the Mande world has known Islam as a constituent factor for centuries already. To suppose that it is pre-Islamic would be a severe error. Yet, the Mande world has shown a great variety in ritual practices that clearly do not have an Islamic source of inspiration or origin. Trees, wells, bushes, and stones could be sacred sites devoted to sacrifices. These communal rituals expressed concern for the fertility of the land and the veneration of ancestors. Nowadays, many of such religious expressions have become marginal and have even disappeared in large parts of the Mande world. Socioreligious rituals are practiced more extensively in communities in the southern part of the Mande world.

Ceremonies involving carved masks and vibrant dances, for example, were commonly performed to celebrate the harvest, rites of passage, or merely social well-being. Komo societies, in which blacksmiths perform a central role, also observe a well-known set of ceremonies related to initiation into esoteric knowledge. Ceremonies in the Mande world however, face opposition because of the growing influence of Islam and changes in wider society. Most notable are changing labor relations within extended families and other transformations associated with the shift from self-sufficiency to a cash-crop economy. Nonetheless, hunters' societies, another widespread socioreligious form of organization, flourish and attract people from both urban and rural areas even though game has almost disappeared in large parts of the Mande world because of environmental deterioration and growing population.

The Mande world is characterized by an ideology based on social division in three status categories—noble freemen, slaves, and artisans (*nyamakalaw*). To this last group belong male blacksmiths, female blacksmiths (who do pottery), bards, and leather workers. Membership in a social category is ascriptive. Since the formal abolition of slavery under colonial rule, the tripartite division has gradually transformed itself into an opposition between freemen-agriculturists and nyamakalaw, although national charters that stress the equality of all people deny this distinction.

A central concept in Mande culture is *nyama,* which might best be translated as "transformative power" (some

would even suggest "occult power"). Nyama is released by certain actions, such as offerings of food, the killing of animals, and nyamakalaw activities. Only specialists, the Mande people believe, can cope with nyama. The concept of nyama is explicitly incorporated into the social identity of the nyamakalaw. Nyamakalaw groups clearly identified with these powers are blacksmiths, potters, and leather workers, who transform raw material (iron ore, clay, skins) into usable products, and bards, who achieve a similar end by attributing historically rooted identities to individuals, thus structuring society. Hunters also release nyama in their activities but are not considered nyamakalaw in large measure because the killing of game occurs in the bush, far outside the borders of

villages. Despite their invaluable contributions to society, nyamakalaw have an ambivalent status in the Mande world because they release nyama within the borders of the village or close to the village.

Political Organization and National Identities

Although the Mande people may be historically connected to great empires, their political organization in the nineteenth century did not resemble that of a centralized state. Society was segmented, petty kings and war leaders were numerous, and rule was not direct over a territory but indirect and over people. Elaborate royal rituals, such as existed in the Benin and Ashante kingdoms of the West African coast, were not practiced. At every level of society, people forged alliances relying on kinship relations as the basis for collaboration. Bards had a crucial role in this process, both as diplomats and history-brokers.

Descent from Sunjata, founder of the Mali empire, was used most often in creating political alliances. In the republic of Mali, where Mande groups have dominated politically, they expressed this solidarity by renaming their independent nation Mali in 1960 (it was formerly the French colony of Sudan). Other nation-states where Mande ethnic groups form a large part of the population also trace their nations' history to Sunjata. Mande cultural concepts and images have become dominant in national politics in Guinea and The Gambia, as well as in Mali, as a means of building feelings of national unity. Radio programs, records, films, dance performances, and theater plays were used to link the people to the heritage of Sunjata and the Mali empire.

Mande solidarities also operate below the level of national politics. The most obvious means of appeal to a shared history is the patronymic. There are relatively few patronymics in West Africa—within the limits of one region, large parts of the population may bear patronymics such as Keita, Traore, Camara, Diawara, or Toure or patronymics related to these according to oral tradition. Each of them traces its origin from Sunjata himself or from a legendary male hero who helped him. In this way, the past lives in the present.

Such stories about the ancestors are sometimes wrongly portrayed as a part of traditional religion. Families used to have cults celebrating famous male ancestors within their own patrilineage, but such expressions of traditional religion must not be confused with the status and glory expressed by and represented by the patronymic. The great deeds remembered and evoked by the patronymic are prerequisites for establishing and maintaining social relationships with non-kin in all levels of society, and whatever religious opinion.

Mande patronymics offer the postcolonial governments vehicles for constructing historical national identities that appeal to every single person as a member of a specific social group. In this way nation-states seek the legitimacy that would befall the successor regimes to the great medieval empires, the Mali empire in particular. Governments in these countries of West Africa employ bards to instill feelings of national unity. In this respect it is noteworthy that in 2003 the United Nations Educational, Science, and Cultural Organization (UNESCO) recognized Guinea's demand to put the cultural space of the Sosbala (the Sosobala is an instrument that features in the Sunjata epic and that, in a restored version, is guarded in a village in northern Guinea) on the World Heritage List as a Monument of Intangible Heritage. This is remarkable, because the cultural space of the Sosobala would at least encompass parts of Mali.

The Kamabolon ceremony in Kangaba in southern Mali is another example of this complex relationship between heritage and politics. In the traditional septennial restoration of the Kamabolon sanctuary, the authorized version of the Sunjata epic is performed in the Kamabolon. Outsiders are not allowed in this performance, and the ultimate truth thus remains a secret. The Kamabolon ceremony was once a regional event in which the deceased kings were celebrated and a new age group was inaugurated, but nowadays the Malian government financially supports the ceremony. Thus the sanctuary has acquired the status of a national emblem, expressing, among other things, Sunjata's role as the founder of the nation.

Islam

Postindependence regimes, dictatorial or not, have apparently not been eager to promote traditional religion. Islam increasingly is becoming a feature of society, although governments stick to the idea of secularism (a heritage from the French era). West African ruling classes had already practiced Islam at least since the eighteenth and nineteenth century *jihads,* or holy wars, which, originating from different areas and reflecting the charisma of their leaders, successively spread over West Africa. After El Haji Oumar Tall's mid-nineteenth century jihad, Samori Toure—a Malinke of humble origin—organized a jihad that greatly influenced the Mande world. In the second half of the nineteenth century he conquered large parts of today's Guinea, Mali, and Côte d'Ivoire before he was captured by the French colonial forces in 1898. Samori's war made the Mande people more open to conversion to Islam, although traditional religious rituals were abandoned on a grand scale only after the 1950s, when Islam became the hegemonic religion in the Mande world.

Islam is not the official state religion in any of the Mande nation-states, but Islam's symbolism is present in every level of civil society, in particular thanks to the quickly developing and innovating mass media. Fundamentalism is a growing political factor in some urban areas. Islamic organizations and practices have affected society politically in different ways. For instance, in Senegal Islamic brotherhoods such as the Mourides help mold national politics, and in Mali some Muslim spiritual leaders are considered to be a powerful force in national politics. These *marabouts* are religious specialists trained in knowledge of the Qur'an, as well as in traditional medicine, the making of amulets, and occult science. They embody the complex relationship among state, Islam, and traditional religion in West Africa. Sometimes maraboutic knowledge gives way even to a kind of counterculture. This is, for instance, the case with the Guinean Suleyman Kante, who invented a writing system for his own Maninka language, called Nko, and set up a literacy program that is gaining ground far beyond Guinea. This literacy program produces texts on religion, history, and medicine, thus clearly representing the complexities of the present-day Mande world.

See also *Islam; Jihad; Senegal; Traditional Religions, African.*

Jan Jansen

BIBLIOGRAPHY

Austen, R. A., ed. *In Search of Sunjata: The Mande Epic as History, Literature, and Performance.* Bloomington: Indiana University Press, 1998.

Hanson, J. H. *Migration, Jihad, and Muslim Authority in West Africa.* Bloomington: Indiana University Press, 1996.

Launay, R. *Beyond the Stream: Islam and Society in a West African Town.* Berkeley: University of California Press, 1992.

Levtzion, N. *Ancient Ghana and Mali.* London: Methuen, 1973.

Oyler, D. W. *The History of the N'ko Alphabet and Its Role in Mande Transnational Identity: Words as Weapons.* Cherry Hill, N.J.: Africana Homestead Legacy Publishers, 2005.

Soares, B. F. *Islam and the Prayer Economy: History and Authority in a Malian Town.* Edinburgh: Edinburgh University Press, 2005.

African American Experience

The civil rights movement—the social and political movement in the United States to desegregate public institutions and transportation and to provide civil protections to African Americans in voting and employment—was one of the most significant events of the African American experience. From labor organizations to women's clubs to citizens' groups, many bearers took part in the social and political activism of the twentieth century. One of the most significant elements has been the awakened political religiosity of African American communities of faith. As a source of indigenous strength for the civil rights movements of the 1950s and 1960s, this political religiosity stood at the center of effective civil resistance. At difficult yet pivotal moments in U.S. social and political history, it also provided a platform for cultivating new leaders, essential for radical new movements, in racial liberation, interracial cooperation, and feminism.

Indigenous Strength: Black Women and the Church

Among the key organizational strengths of the civil rights movement, three indigenous collectives were critical to the origins of its social activism: southern branches of the National Association for the Advancement of Colored People (NAACP), especially its Legal Defense and Education Fund; southern black colleges and their many determined and hopeful students; and southern black Baptist churches and the thousands of women who comprised the majority of the parishioners. Front and center of what is commonly known as the origins of the civil rights movement and the heart and soul of the political activism of the 1950s and 1960s is this meeting of the black church and black women. In launching an effective political mobilization, each of these three collectives occupied an important niche. The NAACP chapters and its legal unit focused on desegregating public schools; the black colleges worked on integrating lunch counters. The black church fought simultaneously for the desegregation of public institutions and public transportation.

As the center of most black communities, the church was a likely place for fomenting political activism. It had financial resources, well-respected community leaders, a stable physical structure for meetings, and, most important, thousands of members who could be spurred into action. It offered an ideal location for educating the community, opening lines of communication, and building networks. The church provided a common space where similar people with similar grievances and like experiences could come together and push for needed societal and political reforms. The black church's importance within black communities made it an essential and critical factor in the civil rights movement.

The presence of the thousands of black women in churches across the South provided the civil rights movement with the necessary numbers for effective boycotts and marches. Many of these women, like their male counterparts, were frustrated and angry with the treatment they received in public spaces. They found energy by sharing their griev-

Future U.S. Supreme Court justice Thurgood Marshall, fourth from right, and other NAACP Legal Defense and Education Fund attorneys for the plaintiffs in the landmark school desegregation decision Brown v. Board of Education *(1954) congratulate each other on their monumental victory.*

ances and becoming politically active, which engendered the demonstrations during the early days of the movement. The lives of southern black women in the 1950s were filled with hard work, low pay, long days, and little respect. The racial indignities they endured for years could no longer be tolerated. The church, although often a haven and escape for blacks, had not always or even typically been a source of political activism, but the decades of shunning political engagement gradually gave way to a new age of political involvement.

The well-documented and well-known bus ride of Rosa Parks in 1955 provided the necessary spark that transformed ordinary church women into activists. One day that year in Montgomery, Alabama, Parks, a black woman who had trained in nonviolent resistance, refused to vacate her seat on a Montgomery city bus, as was law and custom if a white

patron needed one. Parks was arrested. In response, the black church and its women members organized a boycott of the transportation system that eventually led not only to the integration of Montgomery city buses, but also spawned movements in other cities. The church of the Reverend Ralph Abernathy, a Baptist minister, emerged as the center of the boycott movement. It is there that parishioners became educated on the issues and organized. It was also there that a young Reverend Martin Luther King Jr. began his ascent to the leadership of the civil rights movement.

Political Action

The use of civil disobedience in the Birmingham, Alabama, campaign in 1963 and in the march from Selma, Alabama, to Montgomery in 1965 highlights one of the most effective tactics employed by the civil rights movement. It required that demonstrators place themselves in cities where they risked immediate and often brutal reactions from hostile whites. The tactic enabled parishioners to actualize Jesus' teaching to "turn the other cheek," thus building a political religiosity out of religious religiosity. The sit-ins, marches, and demonstrations provoked the most vicious of responses. The likes of Bull Conner, the Birmingham police chief, and Jim Clark, his counterpart in Selma, ruthlessly attempted to retain the status quo of segregation. Increasingly receptive media, however, etched assaults on marchers into the public memory. Vivid images showed authorities turning powerful fire hoses against peaceful demonstrators and police dogs attacking them, including children. The spectacle of these events pressured President Lyndon B. Johnson and Congress to pass the Civil Rights Act of 1964 and the Voting Rights Act of 1965, high points of the civil rights movement.

As with the Montgomery bus boycott, the black religious community sponsored and led the march from Selma to Montgomery and the Birmingham campaign for justice and the end to racial segregation. With the Southern Christian Leadership Conference and its members spearheading demonstrations and church women and men sacrificing their safety in the nonviolent campaigns, the civil rights movement took an important turn in the early 1960s. Church leaders held invitational periods at mass meetings to ask for volunteers for the campaigns. Thousands of "soldiers" joined the movement, a parallel to the classic Baptist "invitation" to give oneself over to Christ. The devout viewed the mass meetings for political action as part and parcel of their religious duty and obligation. Those who attended church infrequently were also drawn into the church to listen and volunteer. The campaigns echoed the African American spirituals of freedom, love, redemption, and nonviolence. Met with hate and brutal violence in the South, the campaigns exposed the immorality, inhumanity, and contradictions among the opposition, most of whom claimed Christianity as their faith.

Cultivating Leadership

Although self-admittedly not born civil rights leaders, Martin Luther King Jr. and Ralph Abernathy among others were groomed by their church, proponents of nonviolent struggle, and the exigencies of their time to assume leadership roles that might otherwise have gone unfilled. As point men and women of the movement present for the worst of the opposition's response, these leaders were forced to grapple with the contradictions of their faith. Through their activities they became easy targets for criticism, assault, and assassination. The cultivation of leadership also spread beyond the ordained. The often unsung leaders of the civil rights movement include devoted lay persons called to action. Ella Baker and Fannie Lou Hamer were both grounded in the black church. As executive director of the Southern Christian Leadership Conference (SCLC), Ella Baker helped spearhead the development of the Student Nonviolent Coordinating Committee (SNCC), one of her many contributions. The political activist Fannie Lou Hamer led the Mississippi Freedom Democratic Party in the fight for black inclusion during the 1964 Democratic Party Convention. The efforts of both women in the pursuit of change were anchored by a commitment to justice and equality and facilitated by a religious zeal that sustained them when the opposition turned brutal or when change proved slow in coming. Both ordained and lay leaders were essential to the mix of forces in the civil rights movement.

Radical Religiosity

At the core of the civil rights movement, the activism of thousands of participants was at once religious—rooted in the theistic traditions of Christianity and Judaism—and secular—concerned with the dignity and deliverance from bondage of all persons. This existential Christianity rested upon a strong belief in the individual's worth, plight, possession of free will, and struggle with right and wrong. That philosophy led to principles of rights, equality, democracy, and self-worth. This amalgamation of the religious and the secular perhaps radicalized the social activism of the 1950s and 1960s and made it universally appealing to supporters of the civil rights movement worldwide.

The liberating elements of the civil rights movement, however, came from factions within American Christianity, Judaism, and the Democratic Party that were left of center. None of the factions should be confused, however, with extreme left ideologies or factions of religion and politics. Although transformative and consequential, the underlying ethos of the civil rights movement was not revolutionary; the leaders, activists, and ideas that predominantly shaped the civil rights movement did not seek to overthrow the U.S. government or undo the basic governing fabric, laws, and traditions of the United States. Rather, the movement revolved around reformist social activism.

The reform movement driving the civil rights activism of the 1950s and 1960s sought inclusion into the mainstream for the excluded black population. Other movements, including the women's movement and the gay and lesbian movement, among others, agitated for new antidiscrimination laws with enforcement power and prodded Americans to live up to the principles embedded in their democratic tradition, namely, liberty, equality, and justice. Taking guidance and moral legitimation from religion, activists pushed for social and political reforms that ultimately challenged and tested the limits of a democratic society. In refashioning what it meant to be Christian, the thousands of activists not only exposed centuries of religious contradictions, but more specifically challenged the tacit acceptance by Christians of racial oppression. Moreover, they demonstrated that their faith must be employed to fight the injustices inflicted on others and on themselves.

The paradoxes of Christianity were evident in the 1950s and 1960s. On the one hand, black and white Christians created new forms of interracial cooperation and a burgeoning radical feminism. On the other, those same Christians were heirs to a tradition that promoted separation between the races and shaped sexist, even misogynist, conceptions of women and their "rightful" place in society. The thousands of black women, from college coeds to grandmothers, who joined black men in boycotting, marching, and leading demonstrations were joined by white women and men.

Traditional gender norms had a rebirth after World War II, and black communities did not escape it. At critical moments, therefore, women like Rosa Parks, Ella Baker, and Fannie Lou Hamer forthrightly challenged not only sexualized norms and expectations but also those ministers and churches that were reluctant to take an active role in the movement. As leaders willing to speak out on injustice and lead resistance actions, they confronted community leaders who were accustomed to being the "race leaders" but unaccustomed to women's assuming prominent roles. As usual, they found the means to undo the status quo.

Participation in the movement by many southern white women similarly began in their churches. In challenging the contradictions of their faith, which housed racist and sexist norms, many of them found inspiration and guidance from the black women involved in the struggle for justice and equality. In crossing borders of race, sex, and class, especially in working with and developing political, social, and sexual relationships with black men, these women fought not only for the liberation of blacks but for their own. The activism among these women was critical to providing some of the building blocks for and fomenting the modern women's movement of the 1960s and 1970s. Many of the early participants of the women's movement had been active in the civil rights movement and had begun to question, rethink, and reshape putative gender norms and to reawaken a dormant political feminism. As in the case of black women, the church and societal custom that had long resisted the notion of any significant presence of women in the public sphere was ultimately used to fight for racial and gender justice. The antiegalitarian and antipolitical strains of Christianity and of Judaism that particularly worked to keep white women out of the public and political sphere were transformed into an idealism and passionate concern for social justice.

The involvement of white women and many white men of the Christian and Jewish faiths also speaks to the use of religion to sponsor interracial cooperation and coalitions. From white campus ministries and groups like the Methodist Student Movement, Young Women's Christian Association, and United Student Christian Council to interracial organizations such as the NAACP and SNCC in its early days, the civil rights movement showcased an experiment with interracial cooperation in the struggle for justice that had not been seen except perhaps during the abolitionist movement. Despite religious norms that harbored racist and sexist ideas and practices, black and white activists culled elements of their faiths with which to build new movements for racial liberation, feminism, and interracial cooperation. The civil rights movement highlights the vibrancy of political religiosity during the 1950s and 1960s and stands as one of the most significant movements of the twentieth century.

See also *Civil Disobedience; Civil Rights Movement; Human Rights; King, Martin Luther, Jr.*

Timothy P. Harrison

BIBLIOGRAPHY

Evans, Sara. *Personal Politics: The Roots of Women's Liberation in the Civil Rights Movement and the New Left.* New York: Vintage Books, 1979.

Giddings, Paula. *When and Where I Enter: The Impact of Black Women on Race and Sex in America.* New York: William Morrow, 1984.

King, Martin Luther, Jr. *Stride toward Freedom.* New York: Harper and Row, 1958.

Lincoln, C. Eric, and Lawrence H. Mamiya. *The Black Church in the African American Experience.* Durham, N.C.: Duke University Press, 1990.

McAdam, Doug. *Political Process and the Development of Black Insurgency, 1930–1970.* Chicago: University of Chicago Press, 1982.

Marable, Manning. *Race, Reform, and Rebellion: The Second Reconstruction in Black America, 1945–1990.* Jackson: University Press of Mississippi, 1991.

Payne, Charles M. *I've Got the Light of Freedom: The Organizing Tradition and the Mississippi Freedom Struggle.* Berkeley: University of California Press, 1995.

Piven, Francis Fox, and Richard A. Cloward. *Poor People's Movements: Why They Succeed, How They Fail.* New York: Vintage Books, 1977.

West, Cornel. *Prophesy Deliverance! An Afro-American Revolutionary Christianity.* Philadelphia: Westminster Press, 1982.

African Traditional Religions

See *Traditional Religions, African.*

Ahmad Khan, Sir Sayyid

Indian modernist writer, educational and religious reformer, and political leader. Khan (1817–1898) claimed descent from the prophet Muhammad. Khan's ancestors migrated to Mughal India from Afghanistan in the seventeenth century, and his family, despite having lived in India for nearly two hundred years, remained conscious of their foreign origin. Khan's formal education was strictly traditional, and he ceased formal schooling at eighteen. Conservative critics considered him unqualified to undertake the reforms he proposed for the modernization of Islam, yet through personal study and independent investigation he laid the groundwork for a modern interpretation of the religion.

While working in the court system of the British Raj, Khan lived through the Indian Mutiny of 1857–1859. He emerged from this ordeal as both a loyal functionary of the British government and a staunch Muslim nationalist. Khan worked to create understanding between Muslims and Christians, to establish scientific organizations to help Muslims understand the secret of the West's success, and to analyze objectively the causes for the revolt. He was the only Muslim scholar to venture a commentary on the Old and New Testaments, which he presented in *Mahomedan Commentary on the Holy Bible* (1862).

In light of the British belief that the mutiny had been led by Muslims, Khan wrote *An Account of the Loyal Mahomdans of India* (1860–1861) to show that the majority of influential Muslims remained loyal to the British government and that they were by no means enemies of the British. This attempt enabled him to elicit British support for a fair Muslim share in the Indian political system.

In May 1869 Khan arrived in London and remained in Britain for fifteen months to study British culture, including modern scientific education and the capitalist economy characterized by social and political laissez-faire. In London he published *A Series of Essays on the Life of Mohammad* (1870). To study British educational institutions he visited the universities of Cambridge and Oxford as well as private preparatory schools. These educational models enabled him to develop the blueprint for the Mohammedan Anglo-Oriental College, which he established in 1875 at Aligarh. In 1920 the college became Aligarh Muslim University.

Equipped with modern ideas and orientations, Khan returned to India in October 1870 and initiated a movement of religious and cultural modernism among Muslims. He resigned his position in the judicial service in 1876, and until his death devoted himself to modernizing the life of Muslims in the Indian subcontinent. Most of his efforts went toward promoting modern education among Muslims, especially through the All-India Mohammedan Educational Conference, which was active from 1886 to 1937. From 1886 to 1898 the conference competed with the All-India National Congress, which espoused secular Indian nationalism. Khan endorsed a form of Muslim nationalism that accentuated separatist Muslim politics in India and gave rise to the All-India Muslim League, which in the 1930s and 1940s spearheaded the movement for the creation of Pakistan.

Khan promoted an Islamic modernism that drew inspiration from the writings of Indian rationalist Islamic reformer Shah Waliy Allah (1703–1762) and emphasized a rational approach to Islam and social reforms in Muslim culture. What made Khan controversial was his emphasis on religious modernism, which rejected the traditional practices and orientations of the orthodox, and his advocacy of modern education, which lured young Muslims from orthodox religious seminaries into Western-style schools and colleges. The British government knighted him in 1888 in recognition of his accomplishments.

See also *India; Islam; Pakistan.*

Hafeez Malik

BIBLIOGRAPHY

Malik, Hafeez. *Sir Sayyid Ahmad Khan and Muslim Modernization in India and Pakistan.* New York: Columbia University Press, 1980.

———, ed. *Political Profile of Sir Sayyid Ahmad Khan: A Documentary Record.* Islamabad: National Institute of Historical and Cultural Research, 1982.

———, ed. *Sir Sayyid Ahmad Khan's Educational Philosophy: A Documentary Record.* Islamabad: National Institute of Historical and Cultural Research, 1989.

Troll, Christian W. *Sayyid Ahmad Khan: A Reinterpretation of Muslim Theology.* New Delhi: Vikas, 1978.

Algeria

Algeria, a North African country with a population that is almost entirely Muslim, borders the Mediterranean Sea in the north and reaches far into the Sahara to the south. The majority of the population is Arabic speaking, with minorities speaking Berber dialects. Previously made up of a number of smaller political formations, Algeria took shape in the early sixteenth century, when inhabitants of the region appealed to the Ottoman Empire for help in defense against Spanish incursions. Turkish-speaking Ottoman soldiers ruled the country until 1830, when the French began their conquest of Algeria, but the Ottomans remained a small minority of the population.

Traditionally, Islamic religious leadership in Algeria involved a combination of knowledge of the written sources of Islam with prestige inherited from a forebear renowned for piety. Families of religious leaders had an identity clearly distinct from military and political leaders. In both city and countryside, Sufi mystical orders played a major role in religious life; their rituals supplemented the core practices of Islam, creating bonds of community among initiates. In times of crisis, Sufi initiates lent their influence to political mobilization. Women also participated in Sufi activities with their own distinct organizations.

The Colonial Period

For four decades after 1830 the French occupiers faced widespread resistance in which Islamic leaders and Sufi orders were the moving forces. Amir 'Abd al-Qadir, the most prominent of these, fought the French from 1832 until his surrender in 1847. He was allowed to go into exile in Damascus where he lived until 1882. During his exile he became an important exponent of the pursuit of a vision combining modern values and Islamic spirituality.

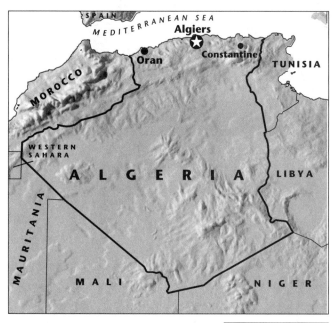

Algeria was declared French territory in 1848. The French feared the potential of Islamic leaders to inspire rebellion but saw their ability to promote peace. Thus French policy vacillated between repression and conciliation. The French restricted Islamic law to family matters and subordinated Muslim courts to the French Court of Appeal. Although the European settlers never exceeded 15 percent of Algeria's total population, they were a majority in major cities.

By the early 1900s a combination of socioeconomic change and the extension to Algeria of the French law of 1905 separating church and state stimulated the rise of a new form of voluntary organization that emphasized modern Islamic education. By 1931 local groups had coalesced into a nationwide organization, the Algerian Association of Ulama (Muslim scholars), led by 'Abd al-Hamid Ben Badis. As well as maintaining an educational role, this group, usually termed Islamic reformists, opposed what it viewed as the heterodox practices of Sufism.

After the death of Ben Badis in 1940, Bashir al-Ibrahimi assumed leadership of the Association of Ulama. The years immediately after World War II were marked by a rapid growth of the association and by the emergence of a strong nationalist movement. Ibrahimi campaigned for the return of Islamic endowment properties confiscated by the French in the previous century, hoping that these would ensure the autonomy of religious leaders and insulate them from the pressures of politics. Opposed by the French administration and by the Sufi orders, Ibrahimi's campaign failed. Frustrated, he went into exile in Cairo, Egypt, where he formed ties with the Muslim Brethren, a radical religious organization that sought the establishment of an Islamic state.

Another important Islamic voice to emerge in the colonial period was that of Malek Bennabi. His emphasis was on the need for Muslims to develop "efficacity" through the study of science and technology. He also railed against the demagoguery of popular political leaders such as Messali Hajj and stressed the importance of individual responsibility and initiative.

In November 1954 a revolution against colonial rule broke out in Algeria. It was led by the National Liberation Front (FLN), an outgrowth of secular nationalist political parties. The Association of Ulama supported the revolution, and many of its younger members joined the ranks of the FLN. Through nearly eight years of war (1954–1962), the FLN stressed the connection between Islam and the Algerian national identity. They used *fatwas,* or Islamic judicial rulings, to further the ends of the nationalist cause. A widely followed injunction against tobacco consumption, which cut into the revenues of the French tobacco monopoly, demonstrated the public support given the FLN.

During the war some members of the Roman Catholic clergy in Algeria, including the archbishop of Algiers, Léon-Étienne Duval, worked to support the cause of independence and denounced the human rights abuses carried out by the French military and the police. At the end of the war Duval took the initiative to return the cathedral of Algiers, which had been a mosque seized by the French in 1832, to the Algerian government for reconsecration as a mosque. Nearly all the French settlers left Algeria at independence in 1962.

After Independence

The first independent Algerian regime, led by Ahmad Ben Bella from 1962 to 1965, had a mainly secular and socialist orientation. During the war the Association of Ulama had been dismantled, its assets confiscated by the French. Thus it was not in a position to act as an independent force in the early postrevolution period. Nonetheless, Ibrahimi spoke out against Ben Bella's secularism, and Ibrahimi's funeral in 1965 was an occasion for public protest against the regime.

Houari Boumedienne, a soldier who replaced Ben Bella as president in a 1965 coup, was the product of a religious education. He enlisted reformist religious leaders in the service of his regime, while opposing the Sufi orders that he saw as tied to conservative rural interests. The most prominent Algerian Islamic thinker of the day, Malek Bennabi, worked briefly as the minister of higher education, but for the most part he remained on the political sidelines, publishing provocative essays and holding seminars in his apartment.

The main thrust of the Boumedienne regime was a program of rapid industrialization, along with the promotion of Arabic in place of French as the medium of instruction. He and his successor, Chadeli Benjedid, who came to power in 1979, promoted Islam as the "religion of the state." Their regimes constructed mosques, trained and employed religious personnel, and catered to conservative Islamic views in matters of family law. But the Islamic resurgence they helped to advance soon was beyond their control.

A new grassroots Islamic movement first expressed itself in the 1970s as urban neighborhood groups began building mosques without first requesting government authorization. As President Benjedid began his own version of Soviet leader Mikhail Sergeyevich Gorbachev's policy of *glasnost,* or dismantling authoritarian control, Islamic groups established a political organization, the Islamic Salvation Front (FIS). Its leaders included 'Abbasi Madani, who in the 1970s pursued a doctorate in education at the University of London. There he came into contact with Islamic intellectuals from many countries and joined in their quest to create an Islamic political ideology viable in the modern world. Madani was widely seen as the leader of the FIS's moderate wing. The radical element found its expression in 'Ali Ben Hajj, the youthful *imam,* or leader, of a mosque in a poor neighborhood near the center of Algiers, who was known for his fiery oratory.

The FIS drew its support from a variety of sources, including older, traditionally conservative Muslims; well-educated members of a younger generation, for whom Islam served as a symbol of personal identity and pride; and angry young people with few prospects, living on the margins of urban society, for whom the Islamic resurgence held out the hope of a better life.

The Islamic resurgence also took root in Algerian and other immigrant Muslim communities in France, where, by the 1970s, many immigrant workers had begun to see themselves as permanent residents. They voiced demands for prayer rooms and mosques in their factories and places of residence. Many French institutions, including corporations, labor unions, housing authorities, and the Catholic Church worked to accommodate these new demands. At the same time, right-wing French groups, such as Jean-Marie Le Pen's National Front, expressed increasing hostility to Muslim immigrants.

In the mid-1980s, with the decline of prices for oil and gas (Algeria's primary exports) and a rapidly growing population of youth, the Algerian government faced a severe challenge. Following violent riots by frustrated urban youth in October 1988, President Benjedid committed himself to a process of democratic opening. Some analysts argue that he sought to turn the Islamic movement to the advantage of his own reformist, free-market followers within the FLN. But the old guard within the governing elite, still tied to state-controlled economic policies, opposed his strategy.

In local elections in June 1990 the FIS scored major victories, especially in urban areas, while other opposition parties had only localized support. Many FIS activists were young, idealistic, and well educated. In running municipal governments they gained a reputation for honesty and competence. In some cases, such as in enforcing strict dress codes for women, they also proved dogmatic. Legislative elections were scheduled for January 1992, but the military moved to block them, ousted Benjedid, and outlawed the FIS, arresting its principal leaders. Some Islamic activists then took to guerrilla warfare, forming the Armed Islamic Group (GIA).

The result was a spiral of violence that continued over the next five years. Initially the government seemed in a precarious situation, challenged both by the disaffection of large segments of the population at home and by the success of FIS acitivists abroad at winning credibility with Western governments and human rights activists. The most hopeful moment was the 1995 Rome conference of Algerian opposition parties, organized by the Community of Sant' Egidio, a lay Catholic group that, just three years earlier, had a role in brokering the successful peace agreement between the government and rebels in Mozambique.

But this peace effort failed to gain traction. The more radical GIA intensified violence against civilians and became embroiled in internal factional quarrels. Many of its militants gained their first military experience in Afghanistan fighting the Russians. GIA established links with other Islamic groups that helped with the publication of a newspaper, *al-Ansar,* based in London. One by-product of this was that the FIS leaders abroad lost their stature as moderates who could contain radical elements. Anwar Haddam, the FIS representative in the United States, was arrested in 1996 and held in detention until 2000 on the basis of secret evidence.

The Algerian government seized the opportunity to open a transition from military rule to controlled democracy, with elections open to moderate Islamists, such as Mahfudh Nahnah's Hamas Party. Islamists became more polarized between pragmatists willing to negotiate their way back into the system and radicals bent on pursuing armed struggle. Internal quarrels within the GIA led in 1996 to the emergence of the Salafist (Fundamentalist) Group for Predication and Combat (GSPC), which had at least loose connections to al-Qaida. The GSPC is thought to be the group behind the effort to set off an explosion at Los Angeles Airport, a scheme that was thwarted when the bomber, Ahmed Ressam, was arrested with a carful of explosives in Port Angeles, Washington, in December 1999 as he departed a ferry from Canada.

Stability began to take hold in 1999 with the election of President Abdelaziz Bouteflika, a figure closely associated with the optimism of the 1970s under Boumedienne, whom he had served as foreign minister. His policy was to come to terms with all those willing to renounce violence, granting amnesty to rebels who laid down their arms, and persuading exiled intellectual and political leaders to return to Algeria, including, by late 2005, Anwar Haddam. Armed attacks, usually attributed to the GSPC, still occurred episodically, but not on a scale to challenge the government. With the return of stability there has been a revival of interest in modern pragmatic visions of Islam, such as that of Malek Bennabi

See also *Colonialism; France; Islam; Islam's Encounters with the West; Sufism; Violence.*

Allan Christelow

BIBLIOGRAPHY

Boukrouh, Nour Eddine. *Islam sans islamisme: vie et pensée de Malek Bennabi.* Algiers: Editions Samar, 2006.

Burgat, François, and William McDowell. *The Islamic Movement in North Africa.* Austin: University of Texas Press, 1993.

Christelow, Allan. *Muslim Law Courts and the French Colonial State in Algeria.* Princeton: Princeton University Press, 1985.

Clancy Smith, Julia. *Rebel and Saint: Muslim Notables, Populist Protest, Colonial Encounters (Algeria and Tunisia, 1800–1904).* Berkeley: University of California Press, 1994.

Entelis, John. *Algeria: The Revolution Institutionalized.* Boulder, Colo.: Westview Press, 1986.

Impagliazzo, Marco. *Duval d'Algeria: une chiesa tra Europa e mondo arabo (1946–1988).* Rome: Edizioni Studium, 1994.

Kepel, Gilles. *Les banlieues de l'Islam: Naissance d'une religion en France.* 2nd ed. Paris: Editions du Seuil, 1991.

Martinez, Luis. *La guerre civile en Algérie.* Paris: Karthala, 1998.

Roberts, Hugh. *The Battlefield Algeria, 1881–2002: Studies in a Broken Polity.* London: Verso, 2003.

Rouadjia, Ahmed. *Les frères et la mosquée: Enquête sur le mouvement islamique en Algérie.* Paris: Karthala, 1990.

Ruedy, John, ed. *Islamism and Secularism in North Africa.* New York: St. Martin's, 1994.

Amish

See *Anabaptists.*

Anabaptists

Anabaptists emerged in mid-sixteenth-century Europe as a radical wing of the Protestant Reformation. The term *Anabaptist,* from the Greek for "rebaptizer," denotes their practice of rebaptizing adult converts. Anabaptism itself had multiple origins and took a variety of forms. The earliest groups developed in Austria, Germany, Moravia, the Netherlands, and Switzerland. There is ongoing scholarly debate about the breadth of Anabaptist origins and whether it is even correct to speak of Anabaptists as Protestants. Because they opposed infant baptism and religious establishment, they frequently experienced repression by Catholic as well as Protestant religious and political authorities. In the face of opposition, most Anabaptist groups abstained from violent resistance. Thus frequent migrations in pursuit of religious freedom or tolerance mark their history. Most of the migrations from the seventeenth century onward were either westward, to North America, or eastward, to Prussia and Russia.

Two core religious ideas profoundly shaped Anabaptist involvement in politics. First, they held to a "two-kingdom" theory that posited a sharp antinomy between the "kingdom of God" and the "kingdom of the world." Second, most Anabaptist groups adhered to the principle of "nonresistance," which called for the renunciation of warfare and other coercive means in pursuit of personal or social interests. These core ideas interacted with varying social and political contexts to produce a range of political responses by Anabaptists. Some early Anabaptists combining the two-kingdom notion with powerful apocalyptic impulses attempted to establish the kingdom of God using political and military force. For example, Anabaptist followers of Melchior Hoffman in northern Germany took control of Münster, the major city of Westphalia, for sixteen months during 1534 and 1535. They established a sociopolitical regime marked by community of goods and polygamy. The two-kingdom idea and the principle of nonresistance more commonly combined to produce a more passive sectarian withdrawal from the political world. By the late sixteenth century, sectarian nonresistance had become an Anabaptist norm. Thereafter, Anabaptists usually responded to political opposition by accommodating or migrating to more hospitable regions. The tension between the activist and sectarian impulses, however, continued to shape Anabaptist politics into the modern period.

Anabaptists in North America

Mennonites and Amish are the largest North American religious groups descended from the European Anabaptist movement. (The Brethren in Christ denomination and the Hutterite communes in the western United States and Canada also have roots in the European Anabaptist movement.) Mennonites derive their name from Menno Simons, an early Dutch Anabaptist leader. Records indicate that some Dutch Mennonites lived in New York as early as 1644, but the first successful U.S. settlement was established in Germantown, Pennsylvania, near Philadelphia, in 1683 by immigrants from the Lower Rhine in Germany. Later waves of migration arrived from Alsace-Lorraine, southern Germany, and Switzerland until the mid-1800s. These groups settled first in eastern Pennsylvania but later went directly to Ohio and Indiana. Within the United States, their migrations continued westward from Pennsylvania, north into Canada, and south into Virginia in pursuit of farmland and in flight from war. Still later, successive waves of Mennonite immigrants arrived from Russia in flight from political upheaval and military conscription. These Russians settled primarily in the plains regions of Canada and the United States.

Because of their commercial and tourist appeal, the Old Order Amish are probably the most well known American group of Anabaptist descent. Amish groups originated in a schism among Swiss Anabaptists in 1693 led by Anabaptist bishop Jakob Ammann (c. 1644–c. 1730). Ammann promoted stricter cultural restrictions, more frequent observance of

The Amish are among the largest of the North American groups to grow out of the European Anabaptist movement. They were involved in the efforts to recognize conscientious objectors during the world wars and remain involved in politics in those areas that affect their way of life. In most political matters, however, the Amish practice passive nonresistance towards the state.

communion, and enforcement of shunning, the practice of social ostracism of members who transgress church discipline. Amish immigrants began coming to the United States in the 1730s, and the first American Amish congregation was established in 1749.

Parallel communities of Mennonites and Amish emerged in most states and provinces where Mennonites settled. The key distinction between the two was the Amish community's greater emphasis on congregational polity. That is, among the Amish groups, primary religious authority lay at the congregational level rather than in regional or denominational hierarchies. About 1865, the American Amish experienced a schism in which traditionalists withdrew to form what came to be known as the Old Order Amish. Most of the more progressive and culturally accommodative Amish groups merged with their Mennonite counterparts in the late 1800s and early 1900s.

North American Mennonite and Amish groups exhibit a broad range of religious forms and political stances. By 1996, in the United States alone, the broader Mennonite "family" of religious groups consisted of thirty-two organizationally independent multicongregational bodies. ("Denominations" is a problematic term for some of these groups.) At least twelve other distinct groups exist only in Canada. This variety results from a complicated history of immigration from various parts of Europe during various periods and numer-

ous schisms within U.S. and Canadian groups. The two largest groups in the United States (excluding the Old Order Amish, who have about 65,000 members) are the Mennonite Church General Assembly (90,139 members in 970 congregations) and the General Conference Mennonite Church (34,040 members in 226 congregations). The distinction between these two groups has its earliest roots in a schism in eastern Pennsylvania in 1847. In 1995 the two denominations voted to approve a process leading to merger, which took effect in 2002.

With such organizational variety, it is not surprising that Anabaptist groups can be found across the entire political spectrum. Some groups have acclimated themselves to North American culture, while others have remained sectarian. Even within groups, the emphasis on religious voluntarism—in other words, membership by choice rather than by birth, and relatively easy congregational switching—and congregational polity have produced a wide variety of political stances. Some congregations embrace conservative politics and values, while others are more leftist and activist in their politics, taking an oppositional approach to the state and mainstream political institutions and policies. Support for political positions on both the right and the left can be found in Anabaptist tradition. The Anabaptist emphasis on biblical and communal moral authority has affinities with many conservative positions in the North American context.

On the other hand, Anabaptists' pacifism and their goals of building an alternative social order in the here and now have affinities with the left. Amid this variety, there exist two general and interrelated trends that deserve more detailed discussion: the ongoing negotiation of the relation between church and state, especially with respect to military conscription, and the the move from sectarian nonresistance to active pacifism as the dominant political stance, especially among North American Mennonites.

Church-State Relations: From Sectarian Nonresistance to Active Pacifism

For Anabaptist groups, relations between church and state are complicated by a two-kingdom theory that views the church as the embodiment of the kingdom of God and sees the state as representing the kingdom of the world (to which the kingdom of God is essentially opposed). The constitutional separation of church and state in North America (and the small size of Anabaptist groups) permitted such an oppositional stance and made repression by external authorities less likely. Tension between Anabaptists and the state emerged most explicitly when the state made demands that would require Anabaptists to violate principles that they believed essential to their citizenship in the kingdom of God. Such tension was sharpest during times of war and military conscription. Over the past two centuries in North America, the relations between Anabaptist groups and the state have been hammered out in the crucible of war time.

During the American Revolution, Mennonites and Amish tried to maintain a neutral stance. Most of them refused to join militias, take oaths of allegiance, or provide direct material support to the revolutionary cause. State and local responses included special taxation of conscientious objectors, fines or forfeitures, withholding of political rights (such as voting privileges), and occasionally imprisonment. Mennonites and Amish disagreed among themselves over whether it was legitimate for individuals to pay substitutes to join the military in their stead. They also differed over whether to refuse payment of taxes that were explicitly in lieu of military service. The war served to heighten distinctions between Anabaptist groups and their neighbors. As their sectarian identity became stronger, their involvement in routine political activity, such as voting, decreased.

By the time of the U.S. Civil War (1861–1865), Mennonite and Amish enclaves had become relatively prosperous agricultural communities on both sides of the North–South divide. Under the draft laws of President Abraham Lincoln's administration, conscientious objectors to war could hire substitutes or pay a $300 exemption fee. Most Anabaptist groups willingly accepted these options, though a few Mennonites enlisted in the Union army. In Virginia, Mennonites were not likely to be sympathetic to the Confederate cause. They were not slaveholders, and they had ties of kinship and loyalty to Mennonite communities in the North. No Mennonites willingly joined the Confederate army, and when forced into service, they refused to shoot. To avoid forced conscription, some Mennonites hired substitutes, others hid, and a few suffered imprisonment. After 1862 Virginia passed a law allowing conscientious objectors to avoid military service by paying a $500 fee and a 2 percent tax on property, a provision most Mennonites accepted willingly. Because Mennonites largely sympathized with the Northern cause, the consequences of the Civil War were an increased tolerance by Anabaptists for the state and a willingness to accept its provisions for conscientious objection without opposing state militarism.

World War I brought renewed tensions with the state and caught Mennonites and Amish unprepared. Almost fifty years had passed since the Civil War, and the new generation of Mennonite and Amish leaders were unschooled and naive in dealing with the government. Further, the Anabaptists' Germanic culture did not facilitate an easy accommodation between their church and the state's war effort. As a consequence, they failed to obtain meaningful concessions for conscientious objectors. Young men who were drafted were required to report to military camps. There, if they demonstrated the sincerity of their convictions by conscientiously refusing to follow orders, they were considered for agricultural furloughs. This led to a rather chaotic situation in the camps, where military officers varied in the extent to which they understood or followed this policy. Many conscientious objectors were subjected to ill treatment, and some were imprisoned following courts martial.

The Mennonite and Amish not conscripted faced other issues in their home communities. One divisive question concerned the purchase of Liberty Bonds to support the war effort. Official denominational policy opposed their purchase, but the policy's application was varied and at times confusing. Some communities worked out creative compromises with bankers so that Mennonites technically would not purchase war bonds, but would deposit money in local banks, thus freeing other bank funds for investment in Liberty Bonds. During this period, Mennonites and Amish learned much about dealing with the state. They benefited as well from occasional cooperation with the more politically savvy Quakers. They became active participants in postwar relief efforts and began to develop ideas and institutions to support alternative service during times of war. During World War II, they would further develop alternative service for conscientious objectors.

World War II did not catch Mennonites so unaware as did World War I. Their leaders had gained experience in dealing with government officials, and they institutionalized their official position as conscientious objectors through various church programs, and outsiders recognized it. Throughout 1940 representatives of the historic peace churches and officials of the legislative and executive branches of the U.S. government held long series of complicated negotiations. The upshot was President Franklin D. Roosevelt's Executive Order 8675 in 1941 establishing the Civilian Public Service (CPS). Initially the CPS plan assigned drafted objectors to conservation camps, where they would work in soil conservation and forestry projects. Later in the war, as the number of conscientious objectors grew, groups of young men were assigned to a variety of other projects as well, including work in mental hospitals, hookworm eradication projects in the South, forest-fire skydiving units in the West, and service as "guinea pigs" for various experiments at the National Institutes of Health. World War II resulted in Anabaptist groups strengthening their identity as pacifists and developing attitudes, skills, and institutions supporting greater social and political activism outside their sectarian communities.

By the time of the Vietnam War, the U.S. government had recognized conscientious objection as legitimate and had institutionalized alternative service provisions. This position freed Anabaptist groups to take a more aggressive oppositional stance to government military policies, and they were more likely to do so because of their increasingly active social involvement during and following World War II. Throughout the 1960s, various official denominational statements challenged the U.S. government's militarism, especially its involvement in Vietnam. By the late 1960s and early 1970s, many Mennonites had become active in the antiwar movement through institutionalized means, such as lobbying Congress and writing the president, and through noninstitutionalized means, such as protest marches and draft resistance. Both of the largest Mennonite denominations issued official statements declaring legal alternative service pro-

grams and illegal draft resistance as valid expressions of nonresistance.

Since the end of the Vietnam War, official Mennonite statements and program policies have moved beyond the pursuit of peace to a larger concern for "justice." Mennonite positions have trended toward the left on a variety of social and economic issues, such as opposition to capital punishment, support for the rights of women and minorities, and solidarity with environmental concerns. The exception to this trend is the issue of abortion, on which Mennonites have tried to articulate a "consistent pro-life" position that envelops opposition to militarism, capital punishment, and abortion.

Qualifying the General Trend

There are several important qualifications regarding the general trend from passive nonresistance to active pacifism. The first is that Amish communities have not been part of the shift toward political activism. Although they cooperated with Mennonites and other peace churches in the attempts to gain concessions for conscientious objectors during both world wars, they did not accompany Mennonites on their path to activism in the 1960s. Their stance toward political involvement continues to be one of passive nonresistance. Their interactions with the state, via the National Amish Steering Committee, have been primarily defensive attempts to gain concessions from regulations that would require them to violate their religious convictions. Court cases regarding education have been the most publicized, but the Amish have also clashed with the state in cases concerning traffic and occupational safety issues, health concerns, and land use issues. These cases have helped to define the boundaries of federal and state protection of the free exercise of religion. The most important court decision was *Wisconsin v. Yoder* (1972), in which the Supreme Court established a four-part test regarding religious liberty that significantly increased the state's burden of proof in such cases.

A second important caveat is that the experience of Anabaptist groups in Canada differs in significant respects from that of U.S. groups. Canadian Mennonites and Amish have found the Canadian government quite hospitable to their particular religious and cultural interests. In addition, Anabaptist groups in Canada have not faced issues of war and militarism as intensely as their U.S. counterparts. For this reason there has been less of an adversarial relationship between Anabaptists and the state, along with higher rates of participation in political institutions. Canadian Mennonites are significantly more likely to vote and hold public office than are Mennonites in the United States.

It is important to stress that the left-leaning political activism that has characterized official Mennonite institutions and policies during the past few decades is not unambiguously reflected in the Mennonite populace. As noted above, local congregations, even within the same denomination or regional conference, exhibit a broad range of political views and activities. The same holds for Mennonite individuals. Good survey data are available from 1972 and 1989 only, but they indicate that in the United States a significant (and increasing) plurality of Mennonite individuals identify themselves as conservative Republicans. The number of Mennonites identifying themselves as liberal Democrats also increased from 1972 to 1989, but was less than 10 percent. A similar pattern exists in Canada, with the largest number of Canadian Mennonites (47 percent) identifying themselves as Progressive Conservatives in 1989.

See also *Freedom of Religion; Pacifism; Separation of Church and State; Traditionalism; Violence; War.*

Fred Kniss

BIBLIOGRAPHY

Driedger, Leo, and Donald B. Kraybill. *Mennonite Peacemaking: From Quietism to Activism.* Scottdale, Pa.: Herald Press, 1994.

Epp, Frank H. *Mennonites in Canada, 1886–1920: The History of a Separate People.* Toronto: Macmillan, 1974.

———. *Mennonites in Canada, 1920–1940: A People's Struggle for Survival.* Toronto: Macmillan, 1982.

Graber Miller, Keith. *Wise as Serpents, Innocent as Doves: American Mennonites Engage Washington.* Knoxville: University of Tennessee Press, 1996.

Kauffman, J. Howard, and Leo Driedger. *The Mennonite Mosaic: Identity and Modernization.* Scottdale, Pa.: Herald Press, 1991.

Keim, Albert N., and Grant M. Stoltzfus. *The Politics of Conscience: The Historic Peace Churches and America at War, 1917–1955.* Scottdale, Pa.: Herald Press, 1988.

Kniss, Fred. *Disquiet in the Land: Cultural Conflict in American Mennonite Communities.* New Brunswick, N.J.: Rutgers University Press, 1997.

Kraybill, Donald B., ed. *The Amish and the State.* Baltimore: Johns Hopkins University Press, 1993.

Redekop, Calvin. *Mennonite Society.* Baltimore: Johns Hopkins University Press, 1989.

Schlabach, Theron, ed. *The Mennonite Experience in America.* 4 vols. Scottdale, Pa.: Herald Press, 1985–1996.

Anglicanism

The tradition of Christian belief and practice associated with the Church of England is known as Anglicanism, or the Anglican Communion. The Church of England became the established church in England after King Henry VIII renounced the authority of the pope in 1533. Since the late eighteenth century Anglicanism has spread to many other countries. A balanced appreciation of the political significance of contemporary Anglicanism requires both an understanding of the nature of the tradition's origins and historical development in early modern England and an awareness of the diversifications that have occurred during the past two centuries.

Origins

The initial chain of events leading to the formation of the Church of England was only indirectly connected to the wider pattern of religious reform and revolt in mid-sixteenth-century Europe. Henry VIII's motivation for setting himself up as "supreme head" of the Church of England and repudiating the authority of the pope in Rome was essentially political rather than religious. In particular, he desperately wanted a male heir and therefore sought legitimacy, which the pope had denied him, for his decision to divorce Catherine of Aragon and remarry. More generally, his government sought to repudiate what it saw as papal interference in English internal affairs. Henry, however, had no desire otherwise to change the Catholic character of the Church of England. During the short reign of the boy-king Edward VI (1547–1553), however, the Reformers gained the ascendancy, although under Mary I (1553–1558), an uncompromising supporter of Roman Catholicism and the pope, strenuous efforts were made to reassert the authority of Rome.

A lasting settlement was achieved only in 1559, at the beginning of the reign of Elizabeth I. The Act of Supremacy established the position of the queen and her successors as "supreme governor" (rather than head) of the church. The Act of Uniformity required the use of the Book of Common Prayer and made absence from church punishable by a fine, a measure directed against Roman Catholics and Protestant separatists (who rejected the Church of England as insufficiently reformed). Elizabeth's intention was that the Church of England should be as comprehensive as possible, thereby enabling it to serve as a focus for national unity and as a key support of the Crown. The Church of England retained the extensive property holdings of the medieval church and its episcopal organizational structure. Its authority extended over Wales as well as England, and a parallel Church of Ireland was established. In Scotland, however, the Reformation followed a very different course: a Presbyterian state church developed, while episcopalians in the region were a small and often persecuted minority. Scottish episcopalianism developed as a tradition organizationally distinct from the Church of England.

Only after the Elizabethan settlement did the Church of England begin to define its theological and doctrinal position. The first step came with the issuing of the Thirty-nine Articles, a statement of the church's doctrine, in 1563. Richard Hooker was the church's leading apologist. In his *Laws of Ecclesiastical Polity* (1594–1597) he deferred to natural law (rather than biblical scripture) as the ultimate source of authority, argued that the church still possessed valid continuity with the medieval English church, and defended the maintenance of the church's governance by bishops. The word *Anglican,* which was not used at all in the Elizabethan era, gained only a limited currency in the seventeenth century. Gradually, however, it came into use, denoting a middle way between Roman Catholicism and Calvinism. In summary, Anglicanism was characterized by a rejection of papal supremacy but the retention of bishops; a limited belief in the rites of the sacraments but advocacy of justification by faith; and acknowledgment of the authority of reason and tradition alongside that of scripture.

Meanwhile, the church was closely bound up with the turbulent politics of the seventeenth century. In the 1630s attempts by the archbishop of Canterbury, William Laud, to restore aspects of pre-Reformation liturgical practice outraged the Puritans, who wanted to move the church closer to Calvinist reforms, and contributed to the tensions that erupted in the Civil War. After the victory of Parliament and the execution of Charles I in 1649, episcopacy was temporarily abolished and an attempt was made to extend a Scottish-style Presbyterian system of church governance to England. In 1655 Oliver Cromwell, the Lord Protector, prohibited the use of the prayer book. In 1660, however, the restored monarchy brought back the bishops, and the Act of Uniformity of 1662 reimposed a modified version of the Book of Common Prayer, which remains the official liturgy of the Church of England. Clergy who were unwilling to conform left the church, thereby beginning the history of other Protestant denominations in England, known as Dissenters and later as Nonconformists.

In subsequent decades both Parliament and the Church of England became divided between those who asserted that royal and ecclesiastical authority was divinely sanctioned (Tories and High Churchmen) and those who held to a more limited view of monarchy and episcopacy and a more fluid interpretation of doctrine (Whigs and latitudinarians). These struggles reached their climax in the Glorious Revolution of 1688, in which James II, who was believed to want to restore Catholicism to England, was removed from the throne and the crown was offered to William of Orange and his wife Mary (James's daughter). The Glorious Revolution gave political ascendancy to the Whigs and to Parliament and ensured the Protestant succession, while Tory and High Church attitudes continued to enjoy considerable ecclesiastical support. The Act of Settlement of 1701 required that future monarchs and their consorts be Protestants and "join in Communion" with the Church of England. It has remained in force.

Following the accession of George I, in 1714, tensions subsided and the eighteenth century saw the Church of England in relatively stable and close alliance with the secular fabric of politics and society. The choice of bishops was likely to be made in the political interests of the government; the parish clergy often came to enjoy considerable local political power as magistrates and landlords. Meanwhile, the conflicts of earlier ages had left their mark in considerable internal doctrinal diversity.

Reform and Expansion

From the late eighteenth century onward England became increasingly industrialized and urbanized. These changes were associated with substantial increases in the strength of religious dissent—in part because of disruption of the Anglican-dominated social fabric of pre-industrial society, and in part because of the development of new industrial settlements remote from existing Anglican churches. From Dissenters came irresistible pressure to reform the relationship between the Church of England and the state to reflect the more diverse nature of society. Nonconformists, Roman Catholics, and, eventually, Jews and atheists became eligible to take seats in Parliament, thus ending the illusion that the practice of politics was exclusively Anglican. An Ecclesiastical Commission, the ancestor of the modern Church Commissioners, was set up in 1835 to administer the church's wealth on behalf of Parliament. New dioceses and parishes were created in response to the enormous growth in population. Tithes and church rates (a local levy on property), which had obliged landowners and taxpayers to contribute to the support of the church, were gradually reformed and removed. The Church of Ireland was disestablished in 1871, and there was considerable pressure for a complete severance of ties between church and state in England. This radical step was successfully resisted, although the Church in Wales was to be disestablished in 1920. All these changes were a source of considerable political controversy and parliamentary debate.

Meanwhile, the religious identity of Anglicanism was intensely contested in struggles between Evangelicals, Anglo-Catholics, and Broad Churchmen. At stake was the question of whether Anglicanism was essentially Protestant (but not sectarian), essentially Catholic (but not Roman), or comprehensive in ethos and liberal—or at least nonprescriptive—in theology. By the end of the nineteenth century an uneasy stalemate had resulted, in which all parties had secured their position within the church but none had gained an incontestable ascendancy. The inclusiveness of the Church of England in the late nineteenth and twentieth centuries was both cause and consequence of its continued ties with the state insofar as its all-encompassing nature rendered the church a credible representation of the religious life of the nation as a whole.

During this period Anglicanism began to be exported outside England, Wales, and Ireland. There had been a substantial Anglican presence in North America in colonial times, but no local bishops were appointed. After American independence Samuel Seabury sought consecration as the first bishop of what was to become the Protestant Episcopal Church in the United States. It was impossible for him to be consecrated in England because the order of service there required an oath of allegiance to the king. No such difficulty existed in Scotland (because the Episcopal Church was not established), and accordingly Seabury was consecrated in Aberdeen, in 1784. A process of gradual convergence between the Church of England and the Scottish Episcopal Church can be dated from this period. Subsequently British colonization and missionary endeavour was associated with the expansion of Anglican organization into other parts of the world, symbolized by the appointment of the first bishops for British North America (1786), India (1814), the West Indies (1824), Australia (1836), New Zealand (1841) and

South Africa (1847). A bishopric of Jerusalem was also set up in 1841 to represent an Anglican presence in the Holy Land. These Anglican churches (including the Scottish Episcopal Church and the Church in Wales after its disestablishment) were in an ambivalent relationship to the state. Their formation often arose from government initiatives, but they lacked the formal constitutional status of the Church of England itself. Ecclesiastical lines of authority were also uncertain: they came to operate as largely autonomous ecclesiastical provinces under the umbrella of the Anglican Communion in which the archbishop of Canterbury has a primacy of prestige, but not of authority. In 1867 the first Lambeth Conference of all Anglican bishops from around the world was held in London, and these gatherings have continued at ten-yearly intervals, except when delayed by the two world wars. The Conference of 1888 affirmed the so-called Lambeth Quadrilateral of scripture, creeds, the sacraments of baptism and communion, and the historic episcopate "locally adapted" as the essence of Anglicanism.

The Modern Era

The twentieth century saw the further substantial geographical expansion of Anglicanism, not only in regions initially under British colonial control, notably in Africa and Asia, but also in continental Europe and South America. Estimates of global membership in the mid-2000s are around eighty million.

During the twentieth century the internal diversity of Anglicanism increased still further. The Evangelical and Anglo-Catholic wings adopted strongly contrasting liturgical practices as well as theologies, while some liberals moved toward radical rejection of traditional Christian dogma. Further sources of dissension since the 1960s have been the influence of the charismatic movement, which sought to exercise the gifts of the Holy Spirit in the worship and ministry of the contemporary church, and the debate over the ministry of women. In the Protestant Episcopal Church in the United States women were first ordained in 1974 and the first woman bishop appointed in 1988. In 1992 the General Synod of the Church of England allowed the ordination of women to the priesthood and in 2006 began the process that will enable them to become bishops. A significant body of Anglican opinion remains, however, opposed on principle to women assuming priestly, let alone episcopal orders. The Church of England has become something of a microcosm of the wider divergencies within the Anglican Communion.

As leader of the worldwide Anglican Communion, the archbishop of Canterbury represents the commun- ion in international affairs. In a one-year anniversary service in remembrance of British victims of the September 11, 2001, terrorist attacks in the United States, Archbishop of Canterbury George Carey is led to the alter at St. Thomas Church in New York City.

Ties between the Church of England and the state also underwent significant change in the twentieth century. In 1919 the Enabling Act created the Church Assembly, to which Parliament delegated the discussion of legislation concerning the church, while itself retaining a right of veto. In 1970 this body was combined with the Convocations (historic assemblies of the clergy) to constitute the General Synod. Nevertheless, substantial links between church and state remain. The sovereign continues as supreme governor of the church and therefore must be an Anglican. Diocesan bishops and some other senior clergy are formally appointed by the Crown on the recommendation of the prime minis- ter, although procedures introduced in the 1970s ensure that in practice the church exercises considerable influence on the process. The archbishops and the twenty-four most sen- ior bishops have seats in the House of Lords. Although no public money is given to support its religious functions, the church continues to benefit from the substantial endow- ments managed by the Church Commissioners; these funds, however, have been somewhat depleted in the late twentieth and early twenty-first centuries, leading to a much greater dependence on the voluntary offerings of congregations. The Church of England, through its tenure of the cathedrals and numerous historic churches and other buildings, is the custodian of a major portion of the British national heritage.

It continues to be the religious point of reference for a sub- stantial proportion of the population—though in 1989 only slightly more than 3 percent of the English population regu- larly attended Anglican Sunday worship. (A survey in 1974 had suggested that 41.6 percent of the population retained a nominal identification with Anglicanism.)

In a predominantly secular age the Church of England has moved toward the periphery of political life in Britain, but it retains the capacity to sometimes capture the lime- light. Notable occasions were in 1927–1928, when a revised prayer book proposed by the Church Assembly was rejected by Parliament, and in the later phases of World War II, when George Bell, bishop of Chichester, strenuously opposed the saturation bombing of German cities. In the 1960s Arch- bishop Michael Ramsey took a strong stand against racism, while in the 1980s bishops were among the strongest critics of the economic and social policies of Margaret Thatcher's governments. Such occurrences show that the continuing state connection does not necessarily render the church sub- servient to the government of the day, although it does tend to contribute to an avoidance of political positions that could be construed as narrowly partisan. The possibility of disestablishment continues to periodically resurface in Eng- land, but there seems to be no inherent reason why the state connection is more vulnerable now than it has been in the recent past. What is clear, however, is that, in view of the historic role of Anglicanism in the whole fabric of English national and constitutional identity, serious future debate over disestablishment would raise far-reaching questions.

Outside England, the political contexts in which Anglicans operate vary widely. In general their situation is a minority one, whether in the predominant secularity of countries such as Australia or Canada, as a relatively small group within the Christian plurality of the United States, or in the context of the majority Roman Catholicism of South America, or of the ascendancy of Islam in the Middle East and other parts of Asia. Thus potential for effective political influence is limited. On the other hand, in Africa, the continent where committed Anglicans were most numerous in the early twenty-first century, they have on occasion assumed a prominent political profile. In 1977 Archbishop Janani Luwum was murdered because of his defiance of the Idi Amin regime in Uganda; in South Africa in the 1980s and 1990s Archbishop Desmond Tutu played an important role in ending racial apartheid and in promoting subsequent reconciliation; David Gitari, archbishop of Kenya from 1997, has been a weighty critic of the Moi regime in that country.

At the beginning of the twenty-first century the Anglican Communion has come under acute strain because of issues relating to human sexuality, especially the wish of some parishes and dioceses to bless same–sex unions, and above all the consecration in 2003 of a practicing gay man, Gene Robinson, as bishop of New Hampshire. Anglicans in Africa, and elsewhere in the global south, as well as the conservative minority within the American Church itself were appalled by what they perceived as rejection of the clear moral teaching of the Bible. Archbishop of Canterbury since 2002, Rowan Williams struggled to maintain unity. Eventual outcomes remain uncertain, but attempts at compromise look fragile, and it is probable that there will be a schism or at least a significant reorganization of the Anglican Communion with authority operating through interdiocesan and international networks as well as traditional territorial dioceses and provinces. Tensions in the early to mid-2000s should be understood in the context of the historic internal diversity of Anglicanism, which was originally shaped for political purposes, with a view to achieving as great a degree of comprehensiveness as possible, and subsequently expanded to become a global church that, in Archbishop Williams's words, "is neither tightly centralized nor just a loose federation of essentially independent bodies."

See also *Burke, Edmund; Catholicism, Roman; English Revolution; Great Britain; Ireland; Protestantism; Reformation; Religious Organization; State Churches.*

John Wolffe

BIBLIOGRAPHY

Chadwick, Owen. *The Victorian Church.* New York: Oxford University Press, 1966–1970.

Collinson, Patrick. *The Religion of Protestants: The Church in English Society, 1559–1642.* Oxford: Clarendon Press, 1982.

Habgood, John Stapylton. *Church and Nation in a Secular Age.* London: Darton, Longman, and Todd, 1983.

Hastings, Adrian. *A History of English Christianity, 1920–1990.* 3d ed. London: SCM Press, 1991.

Jacob, W. M. *The Making of the Anglican Church Worldwide.* London: SPCK, 1997.

Parsons, Gerald, ed. *The Growth of Religious Diversity: Britain from 1945.* New York: Routledge, 1993–1994.

Parsons, Gerald (with James Moore and John Wolffe), ed. *Religion in Victorian Britain.* 5 vols. Manchester: Manchester University Press, 1997.

Spurr, John. *The Restoration Church of England, 1646–1689.* New Haven and London: Yale University Press, 1991.

Sykes, Norman. *Church and State in England in the Eighteenth Century.* Cambridge: Cambridge University Press, 1934.

Walsh, John (with Colin Haydon and Stephen Taylor), ed. *The Church of England, c. 1689–c. 1837.* Cambridge: Cambridge University Press, 1993.

Williams, Rowan (Archbishop of Canterbury). *The Challenge and Hope of Being An Anglican Today.* London: Lambeth Palace, 2006.

Wingate, Andrew, Kevin Ward, Carrie Pemberton and Wilson Sitshebo, eds. *Anglicanism: A Global Communion.* London: Mowbray, 1998.

Angola

Angola, on Africa's Atlantic coast between Namibia to the South and the Democratic Republic of the Congo (DRC) to the North, is a former Portuguese colony that became independent in 1975. Although potentially one of the richest African countries because of its vast mineral resources (primarily oil and diamonds), the country has been devastated by nearly three decades of civil war, and its population is among the poorest on the continent. Religion and politics in Angola have been closely intertwined for many centuries. Christian churches in particular, present in the country since the late fifteenth century, have had a rich and complex relationship with pre-colonial, colonial, and post-colonial authorities, and a strong influence on the shaping of social identities.

Early Colonial Period (Sixteenth to Nineteenth Centuries)

In 1491, eight years after the Portuguese explorer Diogo Cão had disembarked at the mouth of the river Congo, the first Catholic missionaries set foot in what was to become Angola. Within a few weeks, the party had reached Mbanza Kongo, the capital of the Kongo kingdom in the north of present-day Angola. They were welcomed by the Mani Kongo (king), Nzinga Kuvu, who was converted to Catholicism and baptized on Easter of the same year as João I. This baptism marked the symbolic beginning of the evangelization of Central Africa.

After this rapid start, the development of a Christian presence in the area took a different turn. For the next two-and-a-half centuries the missionary presence remained very thin, with a historic low of five priests in 1853. One of the remarkable features of this early encounter between Christian missionaries and African societies, however, was the rapid development of an indigenous church. Far from dying out with the diminishing missionary presence, the new faith was appropriated by Kongolese as a new dimension of their own bakongo religion, and it thus developed into diverse forms of popular Christianity.

From this very early date there was a close and complex relationship between the Catholic Church and the Portuguese crown. Indeed, in the middle of the fifteenth century the Vatican granted special rights to the two countries that extended their control over most of the known world. This regime of *Padroado* (Patronage) conferred Portugal (and Spain) special powers in the nomination of bishops, as well as in the definition of ecclesiastical frontiers (dioceses). Additionally, the Vatican could not send missionaries to Portuguese territories without the king's approval. In counterpart, Portugal committed itself to financially sustaining Catholic missions. As the colonial exploration of the country continued, these links intensified and diversified, especially towards the end of the nineteenth century.

Colonial Conquest and the "Second Evangelization" of Angola

Up until the last quarter of the nineteenth century Portugal's military and political hold over Angola was far from complete or even extensive. In fact, its control was still largely limited to the coastal towns of Luanda, Benguela, and Moçâmedes, as well as to two corridors reaching westward from Luanda to the interior city of Malanje, and from

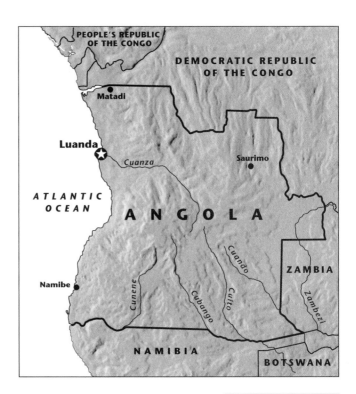

Benguela towards the central highlands, even though a number of explorers, travellers, commercial agents, and petty traders were present in many places in the interior of the colony. Beginning the late 1880s, this changed quite dramatically over a period of approximately four decades.

After the Berlin conference of 1885, Portugal was pressed to establish actual military control over the territories that had been recognized under its jurisdiction. Pressured from without by Germany and Britain, its colonial neighbors, and from within by a rising colonial lobby, the Portuguese government seized the initiative and mounted numerous military expeditions throughout the colony, especially between 1902 and 1920. During these two decades the Portuguese army spent most of its time marching and raiding the Angolan interior. Despite several episodes of strong armed resistance on the part of Angolans, the military conquest of most of the country was achieved by the mid-1920s.

It is against this historical backdrop that Christianity developed at an unprecedented pace in Angola. The Catholic Church, which had left the survival and development of the church founded in the sixteenth-century Kongo kingdom mainly in the hands of local priests, decided to again take the initiative. From five in 1853, the number of priests grew to more than one hundred in 1910, with as many religious brothers and sisters. This new impulse was mainly the result of one particular Catholic missionary order, the French Congregation of the Holy Ghost Fathers.

The development of the Catholic missions in Angola followed two paths. In Cabinda, a Portuguese enclave on the northern bank of the river Congo, the Holy Ghost Fathers took up the evangelization work initiated by Italian Capuchins and opened a mission station in Lândana in 1873, from where the Catholic Church expanded in the northern part of Angola. A few years later, the Holy Ghost Fathers developed their work from the south of the country.

The evangelization of the country had a further boost with the coming of Protestant missionaries. During the last quarter of the nineteenth century, three Protestant mission societies started their work in Angola. In 1878 British Baptist missionaries settled in the capital of the former Kongo kingdom, by then called São Salvador. Two years later, North-American Congregationalist missionaries arrived at Benguela, the country's second city on the Atlantic coast, a few hundred miles south of Luanda. They quickly made their way into the interior and opened their first mission station at Bailundo that same year, in an area not yet under Portuguese control. In 1885 the American Methodist bishop William Taylor disembarked in Luanda. Within a few years the Methodist missionaries had reached the interior city of Malange. Additionally, various non-mainstream Protestant (and related) missionary societies also began work in Angola at a later stage: Plymouth Brethren, Seventh-day Adventists, the Swiss-based Philafrican Mission, and others.

By the 1920s a vast network of Christian mission stations spread all over Angola. As in most African colonies, these stations were not just centers for the diffusion of Christianity. They all had schools, hospitals, and programs of rural development that contributed largely to their success among local populations—even more so perhaps in Portuguese colonies than elsewhere. Indeed, Portugal's investments in the social infrastructure of its colonies remained extremely low up until the late 1960s. Therefore, access to primary or secondary education, to vocational and technical training, or to health services for the vast majority of the Angolan population was only possible through mission stations, while the colonial state seemed more concerned with providing the colonial plantation economy with the unskilled labour force it requested.

In other words, Christian missions had a prominent role in the modernization of Angolan societies, albeit in a paradoxical way. Indeed, much of the missionaries' modernising discourse and practices were based on the re-invention, or reconfiguration, of African cultural values in a Christian mold, rather than on their mere destruction and substitution by Western values. Thus, it became possible within missionary circles to be "modern" in a "traditional" manner. Since missions were also very firmly rooted in very local constituencies and peoples, they contributed to reinforcing preexisting divisions between different social groups within Angolan society. This was to have a lasting impact on pre- and post-independence Angolan politics.

The Salazar Years

In 1926 a military coup d'état put an end to Portugal's First Republic, the regime that had overthrown the monarchy in 1910. The 1926 "revolution" paved the way to the accession to power by António Oliveira Salazar four years later. Once in power, Salazar established a dictatorial regime that lasted until 1975. A staunch Catholic himself and a close friend of the patriarch (religious leader) in Lisbon, Salazar was to have a strong impact on the relationships between religion and politics in Portugal as well as in its colonies.

One of the hallmarks of the First Republic had been its anticlericalism. Led in part by Freemasons, it launched a severe campaign against the Catholic Church, banning missionary orders, closing seminaries, and even trying, albeit without success, to replace Catholic missions in the colonies with lay missions. Contrary to the First Republic's policies, Salazar's strategy was to use the power and legitimacy of the Catholic institution in order to reinforce his own grip on power.

The high point of this strategy came in 1940, when a concordat was signed between the Vatican and Lisbon, accompanied by a Missionary Accord that set new rules for the evangelization of Portuguese territories. With the Accord the Catholic Church was granted special rights, such as control over the whole primary education system and special subsidies; additionally, missionaries were granted rights and privileges similar to those of state employees. Protestant missions, on the contrary, were not granted any legal recognition. This was very much in line with official Portuguese policy that, since Protestant mission societies first settled in Angola, treated them as potentially dangerous representatives of foreign powers keen on undermining Portuguese rule.

With the concordat and the missionary accord, the "sacred alliance" between Portugal and its colonies seemed stronger than ever. The situation, however, was more complex.

Both the concordat and the missionary accord were the result of a protracted battle between the state and the Catholic Church around the symbolic control over Portuguese society. As much as Salazar tried to control the church, the church was pursuing its own objectives in an attempt to prevent the state from intervening in its own "private domain." Additionally, Portugal never had sufficient means to sustain its political objectives: the subsidies that were granted to the church did not allow it to fulfill all of the tasks that it had been assigned, especially in the area of teaching. This contributed, on the one hand, to the extremely low level of education in Angola, as well as, on the other, to the continued importance of Protestant missions in this respect. The role of the Catholic Church in the "portugalisation" of the "natives" was further undermined by the lack of Portuguese missionaries and the necessity for the church to draw on foreign missionary orders to fulfil its charge. Finally, the situation of Protestant missions was more contrasted than could have been expected. Their role in the provision of services such as schooling, health, and rural development was such that it could simply not be done away with, especially as their contribution to the development of Angola was often highly esteemed at the local level even by Portuguese officials.

Nationalism, War, and Independence

After the end of World War II, social, political, and racial tensions started to soar in Angola. Despite unprecedented economic growth mainly resulting from a sharp increase in coffee production and exports, social upward mobility for the small minority of Angolan educated elites was becoming increasingly difficult. As waves of poor immigrants from rural Portugal literally swamped their "jewel" colony in the hope of reaping some fruits of the coffee boom (white population in Angola more that tripled from 1940 to 1960), educated Africans were pushed to the far margins of the colonial world on the basis of their skin color and their racial origins, despite their education and qualifications, which were often much higher than those of most of the new settlers. For the rest of the Angolan population, this centrifugal force was even stronger, both in the cities and in rural areas, as social and economic pressure mounted with white immigration.

Portugal's official discourse and colonial policy was in complete contradiction with this reality. In 1953 its colonies were legally turned into "overseas provinces" and thereby nominally integrated into a single Portuguese nation stretching over three continents. Clearly, in Salazar's Portugal, decolonization was not the order of the day, and any sign of political dissent was closely watched by the International Police for the Defense of the State (PIDE), the regime's political police, which set up a vast network of informants throughout Angola at the end of the 1950s.

Against this strongly authoritarian backdrop, however, a complex network of clandestine political associations and movements began to emerge, especially in Luanda and among the bakongo population in the north of the country. By the early 1960s these organizations had coalesced into two nationalist movements, the Popular Movement for the Liberation of Angola (MPLA), and the National Front for the Liberation of Angola (FNLA). In February and March 1961 two unrelated uprisings in Luanda and in the coffee growing area in the north marked the beginning of a fourteen-year decolonization war, which ended with Angola's independence on November 11, 1975. In the course of the war, in 1966, a third nationalist movement appeared, the National Union for the Total Independence of Angola (UNITA). Divisions between the three branches of Angolan nationalism were such that, throughout the war, the three movements fought each other in addition to fighting the Portuguese army.

All three movements had ties with Christian missions. Their leaders were educated in Protestant schools, as were many of their members. In the eyes of Portuguese officials, this meant that Protestant missions were responsible for the rise of Angolan nationalism, and repression against them in the aftermath of the 1961 uprisings was particularly harsh: mission stations were closed, some foreign missionaries expelled, and countless Angolan Protestants were harassed, arrested, deported to detention camps, or even killed. The war was considered by colonial authorities as the "proof" that Protestant missions had indeed always been a hotbed for anti-colonial and anti-Portuguese feelings and activities.

The influence of Christian missions over the historical dynamics of nationalism in Angola, however, was less straightforward and more complex. The question to be asked here is not so much whether they were in favor or against Portuguese rule, but how they impacted on the social fabric of identities or how they contributed to shaping the social groups that led the struggle for independence. With their prominent role in education and vocational training, Christian missions were crucial in the making of Angolan elites in the twentieth century. Consequently, they were also, and most important perhaps, spaces where competing visions of the Angolan nation were forged and discussed before they were eventually turned into political projects and movements. Christian missions in general, and Protestant missions in particular, however, did not officially offer arenas where these different nationalist conceptions could be brought together. On the contrary, missions reinforced social, ethnic, and cultural differences between emerging elites by locating their work in clearly demarcated historical and geographical spaces.

Thus, more than just offering the breeding ground for Angolan nationalism, Christian missions in Angola were producers and reproducers of deep social divisions. These not only paved the way for competing nationalist movements, but also nourished the moral economy of the civil war that followed independence.

Churches in the Midst of War

Angola became independent on November 11, 1975, some eighteen months after the Salazar regime was overthrown in Lisbon by a military coup led by left-wing officers. Independence was achieved in the midst of heavy fighting between the MPLA, the FNLA, and UNITA, all of which tried to take control of the capital city of Luanda. It was eventually to the Luanda-based MPLA that Portuguese authorities handed over power. Quickly, the fighting between nationalist movements turned into an internationalized civil war fuelled by cold war strategy. The MPLA received military and financial support from Cuba and the Soviet Union, while UNITA rapidly became the champion of the United States and South Africa, especially after the FNLA lost the confidence of its American backers.

In May 1991, after long negotiations, a peace agreement was signed between the warring parties, and in 1992 Angola's first and only democratic elections (as of 2006) took place. The electoral process, however, was set up hastily in a context where neither the MPLA nor UNITA were ready to lose in the ballot box what they had been trying to achieve on the battlefield, and war broke out again immediately after the declaration of the first election results. Despite a new agreement signed in 1994 and the formation of a government of national unity in 1997, fighting continued until 2002, when the death of UNITA leader Jonas Savimbi finally paved the way for a stable peace.

In the course of these twenty-seven years of war, more than five hundred thousand people died; one third of Angola's approximately twelve million inhabitants were forced into internal exile, causing the overpopulation of Luanda and other major cities; and an estimated 450,000 refugees were forced to flee the country. The economic and social infrastructures also suffered greatly, and the millions of anti-personnel mines that were spread throughout Angola during the war continue to be a great obstacle to the recovery of agricultural production. In the mid-2000s, even as most of the internal refugees have returned home, and as international investors rushed to gain a share of Angola's vast mineral riches, the majority of Angolans lived in great poverty, and very few have seen the "dividends of peace" promised since the end of the war.

As the fighting dragged on, Angolan churches played an increasing role in an attempt to alleviate the suffering of the population through social and humanitarian aid. However, they never managed to impact the course of war or make their repeated calls for dialogue, negotiated settlement, and national reconciliation heard by the warring parties. Several elements can account for this.

One of the main obstacles that prevented Christian churches from playing an active role in promoting peace were the divisions inherited from the colonial period. Indeed, the identification between the main Protestant churches and nationalist movements grew stronger with independence and civil war. The Luanda-based Methodist Church remained a close ally of the ruling elite of the MPLA, despite the latter's official Marxist–Leninist policy, and the Congregationalist Church of the central highlands partly allied with UNITA. Additionally, Protestant and Catholic churches in post-colonial Angola were opposed by their colonial past, the Catholic Church struggling to rid itself of its image as "the church of the colonizers" in the face of "nationalist" Protestant churches. This made ecumenical dialogue and common initiatives for the promotion of peace very difficult, especially as the government's strategy was to play the churches against each other.

By the late 1990s, however, Angolan Christian churches overcame their divisions and joined their efforts in the creation of an "Inter-church committee for Peace" (COIEPA). Despite many difficulties, COIEPA quickly managed to get momentum and to represent an important actor within civil society. Its repeated calls for a negotiated settlement between the MPLA and UNITA, as well as its efforts towards national reconciliation, also gained international support. These efforts, however, were annihilated by the government's military strategy, and peace in Angola was eventually attained not through negotiations but through the military defeat of UNITA. While peace was welcomed by a population exhausted by twenty-seven years of civil war, national reconciliation in the divided country remains shaky into the mid-2000s. Additionally, since its military victory over its arch enemy, the MPLA's grip over power is greater than it ever was, and the room for civil society organizations such as churches to maneuver or have a say in Angolan politics remains extremely limited.

Didier Péclard

BIBLIOGRAPHY

Birmingham, David. "Angola." In *A History of Postcolonial Lusophone Africa,* by Patrick Chabal et al. London: C. Hurst, 2002, pp. 137–184.

Edwards, Adrian C. *The Ovimbundu under Two Sovereignties, A Study of Social Control and Social Change among a People of Angola.* London: Oxford University Press, 1962.

Henderson, Lawrence W. *The Church in Angola. A River of Many Currents.* Cleveland, Ohio: Pilgrim Press, 1992.

Heywood, Linda. *Contested Power in Angola, 1840s to the Present.* Rochester, N.Y.: University of Rochester Press, 2000.

Marcum, John. *The Angolan Revolution.* Vol. 1. Cambridge, Mass.: M.I.T. Press, 1969.

Messiant Christine. "Angola: The Challenge of Statehood." In *History of Central Africa. The Contemporary Years since 1960,* edited by David Birmingham and Phyllis Martin. London: Longman, 1998, pp. 131–165.

Messiant, Christine, et al., eds. "Des protestantismes en 'lusophonie catholique.'" *Lusotopie* (1998). [English abstracts and full-text articles available online at: http://www.lusotopie.sciencespobordeaux.fr/somma98.html.

Messiant, Christine. *L'Angola Colonial, Histoire et Société. Les Prémisses du Mouvement Nationaliste.* Basel, Switzerland: P. Schlettwein Publishing, 2006.

Péclard Didier. "Religion and Politics in Angola : The Church, the Colonial State and the Emergence of Angolan Nationalism, 1940–1961." *Journal of Religion in Africa* 28, no. 2 (1998): 160–186.

Anticlericalism

Anticlericalism is a social movement found in some societies that challenges the cultural and political domination of Roman Catholicism. Although criticism of the clergy can be found in many countries and during many times, the term *anticlericalism* usually refers to the hostility toward and struggle against the Catholic Church's position of power and influence on cultural and social policy in Europe, particularly in France.

Anticlericalism is linked to the ideas of the eighteenth-century Enlightenment, the French Revolution, and nineteenth-century liberalism. The revolution in France took away the privileges of the clergy (the clerics) that dated from the Middle Ages and confiscated the church's large property holdings. Anticlerics—who accused the clergy of claiming special privileges and attempting to dominate the minds and morals of the people and the government—worked to emancipate civil and political society from the influence of the church, particularly in social matters relating to marriage, divorce, and education.

Anticlerical movements have also arisen in other countries where Catholicism predominates; among them are Belgium, Italy, Mexico, Portugal, and Spain. The *Kulturkampf* ("culture struggle") in Germany in the 1870s was closely akin to anticlericalism. Under Chancellor Otto von Bismarck the government of the newly united German state clashed with the Vatican over control of social institutions.

Three basic ideas are behind the Catholic Church's claim to precedence, and each of these must be present before an anticlerical movement arises. First, the church makes a distinction between the clergy and the laity—a difference in essence, not just in function—with the clergy taking on the nature of the sacred. Second, the church claims doctrinal authority based on biblical revelation, ecclesiastical tradition, and natural ethics and makes universal judgments in these domains. And, third, the church proclaims itself to be a universal institution.

The church becomes a target of anticlericalist sentiment when these three elements are not conditioned by moderating forces (for example, the pressure for religious freedom that led to the reforms instituted by the Second Vatican Council in the 1960s) and when the doctrines of the church conflict with civil society. With the elimination of widespread illiteracy, it becomes much more difficult for the church to justify its position that clerics are naturally superior to the laity. When culture and religion become independent, and when Catholicism is one doctrine among others, the church cannot maintain its claim to supremacy. And when the structure of nation-states is based on citizenship and nationality, political interference from a supranational church is regarded as abusive.

A conflict does not necessarily exist between clericalism and anticlericalism in predominantly Catholic countries. Catholicism can represent national feeling (for example, in Ireland under British rule and in Poland under communism). Furthermore, a decline in anticlericalist feeling is evident when the church agrees to a separation between civil law and religious law. Examples are Spain (1976–1980), where reform laws were instituted after the death of Francisco Franco, the dictator who had been supported by the church, and Italy after Vatican II.

Confrontation between clericalist and anticlericalist elements continued in France until 1905, when a law was passed separating church and state. The conflict in France involved two political and cultural forces, both convinced that they represented universal values: Catholic France (regarded as defender of the monarchy) and secular France (the promoter of human rights). But this conflict was transformed into the normal tension that occurs in any democratic society. Disagreements continue, however, especially concerning public funds for private Catholic schools and over questions of birth control.

Generally, the process of secularization prevents clericalism (and therefore anticlericalism). New forms of conflict that might be characterized as anticlericalism have, however, arisen between conservative religious groups and secularized societies. Examples are evident in Islamic countries (for example, Turkey and Iran), in Israel (ultra-Orthodox Jews), in the United States (fundamentalist Christians), and even in Europe with the growing presence of Islam. This tendency was increasing, not decreasing, in the early years of the twenty-first century.

See also *Catholicism, Roman; Christian Democracy; France; Pluralism; Secularization; Vatican Council, Second.*

Jean Baubérot

BIBLIOGRAPHY

Baubérot, Jean. *Morale laïque ou ordre moral.* Paris: Le Seuil, 1997.
Bertocci, Pietro. *Republican Anticlericalism and Cultural Politics in France, 1848–1890.* Princeton, N.J.: Princeton University Press, 1978.
Martin, David. *A General Theory of Secularization.* Oxford: Blackwell, 1978.
Remond, René. *L'Anticléricalisme en France depuis 1815 à nos jours.* Paris: Fayard, 1976; Brussels: Complexe, 1985.
Sanchez, J. M. *Anticlericalism: A Brief History.* Notre Dame, Ind.: University of Notre Dame Press, 1972.
Schapiro, J. S. *Anticlericalism: Conflict between Church and State in France, Italy, and Spain.* Princeton, N.J.: Princeton University Press, 1967.

Anti-Semitism

Anti-Semitism, or the hostility toward Jews that occasionally manifests itself in discriminatory legislation, hostile political movements, and even violence, has been a recurrent feature of political life in the modern world. Most theories endeavoring to explain anti-Semitism seek to identify its roots in ethnic hatred. Some theorists locate the source of such hatred in economic relations. Others emphasize the role of religious institutions. Still others look to cultural differences and misunderstandings.

No doubt, all of these explanations have some validity. However, it is not clear that there is any mystery to be explained. Whatever its psychological, social, economic, or even evolutionary basis, suspicion of strangers is the norm in all societies, while acceptance of outsiders is unusual and generally ephemeral. When times are good and foreigners play a recognized and useful role in the community, they may be tolerated. When times are hard and outsiders seem to compete with their hosts, any latent popular xenophobia is more likely to manifest itself and foreigners may become useful targets for rabble-rousing politicians. Attacks on immigrants in Western Europe in the 1990s are unambiguous examples of this phenomenon.

Certainly, everywhere that Jews have lived, their social or economic marginality—their position "outside society," as social theorist Hannah Arendt put it—sooner or later exposed them to suspicion, hostility, and discrimination. In the United States, Jews currently appear to be accepted by the larger community. Nevertheless, at least in part by their own choosing, American Jews continue to maintain a significant and visible measure of communal identity and distinctiveness in religious, cultural, and political matters. At the same time, many Gentiles continue to perceive Jews to be a distinctive group. Although Jews have learned to look, talk, and dress like other Americans, they are not fully assimilated either in their own minds or in the eyes of their neighbors. Even in America the Jews' marginality makes them at least potentially vulnerable to attack. This potential has been realized during several periods in American history, most recently during the New Deal era of the 1930s, when anti-Semitic movements flourished.

Moreover, in the United States as elsewhere Jews are outsiders who often are more successful than their hosts. Because of their historic and, in part, religiously grounded emphasis on education and literacy, when given an opportunity Jews have tended to prosper. Furthermore, Jews often secretly or not so secretly conceive of themselves as morally and intellectually superior to their neighbors. Jews by no means have a monopoly on group or national snobbery. In contemporary America, every group is encouraged to take pride in its special heritage and achievements.

The roots of anti-Jewish sentiment are not as difficult to understand as the conditions under which such sentiment is likely to be politically mobilized. Where an anti-Semitic politics becomes important, usually more is involved than simple malice toward the Jews. In politics, principles—even as unprincipled a principle as anti-Semitism—are seldom completely divorced from some set of political interests. Major organized campaigns against the Jews not only reflect ethnic hatred, but they also represent efforts by the political opponents of regimes or movements with which Jews are allied to destroy or supplant them. Anti-Semitism has an instrumental as well as an emotive character. Thus, to understand the cycle of Jewish success and anti-Semitic attack, it is necessary to consider the place of Jews in politics, particularly, as Arendt noted, their relationship to the state.

Jews and the State

For nearly two thousand years, from the time of their exile from Palestine in 586 B.C.E., Jews lived as scattered minorities while preserving a considerable measure of communal identity and cultural distinctiveness from the societies that surrounded them. This distinctiveness was maintained by Jews' religious and communal institutions and was often reinforced by the hostility of their neighbors and the antipathy of Muslim and Christian religious institutions. Because Jewish religious practice required male participants to read prayers and other texts, Jewish men received a measure of education that made them considerably more literate and numerate than the people among whom they lived. Their geographic dispersion and literacy combined to help Jews become important traders in the medieval and early modern worlds. Jewish merchants, linked by ties of religion, culture,

and often family, played an important role in international commerce.

At the same time, however, their literacy, commercial acumen, and even their social marginality often made Jews useful to kings, princes, and sultans. Into the eighteenth century rulers regularly relied upon Jews as a source of literate administrators and advisers. European monarchs, moreover, depended upon Jewish financiers to manage their fiscal affairs and relied heavily upon Jewish merchants and bankers for loans. In addition, because Jews remained outsiders to the societies in which they lived, sovereigns found them useful instruments for carrying out unpopular tasks, notably collecting taxes.

For their part, Jews, like Sikhs of northern India and other ethnic minorities provided with the state's protection in exchange for services, have usually considered it to be to their advantage to undertake these tasks. Jews often saw this acquiescence as their only viable alternative. Social marginality made Jews the objects of popular hostility that at times shaded into violence, and kings could offer a Jewish community protection in exchange for its services. At the same time, the Crown could provide Jews with financial opportunities and allow them to enter commercial fields that otherwise would have been closed to them. This exchange of protection and opportunity for service was the foundation for a centuries-long relationship between Jews and the state. Such alliances were responsible for the construction of some of the most powerful states of the Mediterranean and European worlds, including the Habsburg, Hohenzollern, and Ottoman Empires of Central Europe and modern-day Turkey.

These patterns persisted into the nineteenth and twentieth centuries. Jews have maintained a sense of distinctiveness from surrounding societies and have, as a result, continued to experience a measure of suspicion, hostility, and discrimination. Concern about their neighbors' attitudes toward them has continued to lead Jews to seek the protection of the state. At the same time, modern Jewish secular culture, like its religious antecedents, has emphasized education. This focus has enabled Jews to acquire professional and technical skills that can make them as valuable to presidents and prime ministers as they had been to monarchs.

Where Jews have been unable to obtain protection from existing states, they have often played active roles in movements seeking to reform or supplant these regimes with new ones more favorably disposed toward them. Thus, in the nineteenth century, middle-class Jews were active in liberal movements that advocated the removal of religious restrictions. At the same time, working-class Jews were prominent in socialist and communist movements that sought the overthrow of existing regimes in the name of full social equality. In some cases, including Germany and Austria-Hungary, regimes provided access to a small number of very wealthy Jews while subjecting the remainder to various forms of exclusion. In those cases, Jews could be found both at the pinnacles of power and among the leaders of the opposition.

Over the past several centuries, then, Jews have played a major role both in strengthening existing states and in working to supplant established regimes with new ones. Their relationship to the state has often made it possible for Jews to attain great wealth and power. At the same time, however, relationships between Jews and states have been the chief catalysts for organized anti-Semitism.

Even when they are closely linked to the state, Jews usually continue to be a separate and distinctive group in society and so to arouse the suspicions of their neighbors. In the service of the state, Jews have often become visible and powerful outsiders and thus awakened more suspicion and jealousy than ever before. As a result, the relationship between Jews and the state is always problematic. An identification with Jews can weaken the state by exposing it to attack as the servant of foreigners. Correlatively, Jews' identification with the state invites political forces that are seeking to take over or destroy the established order to make use of anti-Semitism as a political weapon.

In contemporary America, for example, radical populist fringe groups such as The Order and the White Aryan Resistance refer to the administration of the United States as the ZOG, or Zionist Occupation Government—a corrupt tool of the Jews who are prominent in the American political elite. Not so differently, columnist and 1996 presidential candidate Patrick Buchanan has referred to the U.S. Congress as "Israeli occupied territory," thus defining a political institution controlled by his liberal Democratic foes as nothing more than a Jewish front. It is in these struggles between regimes and their enemies that popular suspicion of Jews is often mobilized by contending political forces and transformed into organized anti-Semitism.

The Politics of Anti-Semitism

Historically, alliances between Jews and states or state-building movements have been the chief catalysts for organized anti-Semitism. Anti-Semitic campaigns proceed from a mixture of motives. Pure hatred of Jews obviously is one important animus for the participants in anti-Semitic groups and movements. However, in societies in which an anti-Semitic politics becomes important, usually more is involved than simple dislike of Jews. Anti-Semitism can have an important instrumental aspect.

Anti-Semitism is likely to become an important political force under three circumstances. First, political forces that oppose a state in which Jews are prominent may seek to undermine the regime and its supporters by attacking its Jewish backers and depicting the government as the puppet of an alien group. Typically, in this circumstance, anti-Semitic appeals are used to create what might be termed coalitions of the top and bottom. In the modern world these are associated with Nazism, but in early modern Europe they were sometimes associated with efforts by the church or aristocracy to rally popular support against the crown. They are used by forces that attempt to mobilize the masses while avoiding threats to the interests and property of the elite. Thus anti-Semitic ideologies are typically espoused either by radical populists who court elite support or by a segment of the upper class seeking to arouse and mobilize a mass base for an assault on the established order.

Elites normally are fearful of popular mobilization, especially when it develops to the level of excitement and, perhaps, violence associated with the overthrow of a regime. They are, moreover, fearful of the rabble-rousers with whom they may have to ally themselves in coalitions of the top and bottom. As a result, such coalitions are likely to emerge only when elites face the most severe economic crises or political threats. Anti-Semitism in the French Third Republic (1871–1940) and the many anti-Semitic movements that manifested themselves in Weimar Germany (1919–1933) are major cases in point. American anti-Semitic movements during the Great Depression of the 1930s also follow this pattern.

The destruction of a regime associated with Jews by a coalition of the top and bottom is sometimes followed by the continued use of anti-Semitic appeals to attack and discredit institutions and social classes affiliated with the old political regime. Attacks on the Jews can help the new regime clear away the vestiges of the old order and prepare the way for the construction of a new one. Early modern Spain (in the fifteenth century) and Nazi Germany (1930s and 1940s) are the most important cases. In both Spain and Germany, regimes were able to institutionalize the

Following their rise to power, the Nazis sought to shore up the new political regime by directing anti-Semitic attacks against the old. Scenes like this one, in which a Nazi soldier stands guard outside a Jewish-owned department store, were not uncommon in Germany in the 1930s. The sign reads, "Germans! Defend yourselves! Don't buy from Jews!"

anti-Semitic fervor they had mobilized. In Spain this was accomplished through the Inquisition, an organ of the Roman Catholic Church that sought out Jews, and in Nazi Germany through the SS, the secret police, and the incorporation of anti-Semitic principles throughout the civil administration. Both these regimes were able simultaneously to discourage sporadic anti-Semitic agitation—a source of turmoil and instability—and to use anti-Semitism as a source of state power.

Second, anti-Semitic campaigns often emerge from the internal politics of a regime linked to Jews. Campaigns against the Jews may develop when Jews' erstwhile allies feel that they can consolidate and enhance their own power by casting off their former Jewish associates. Russia under Joseph Stalin from 1929 to 1953 is a case in point. Often, rival factions within a governing coalition endeavor to displace their nominal Jewish colleagues and so to aggrandize their own power. This strategy was typical of court politics in the medieval Middle East. Similarly, in contemporary America, the use of anti-Semitic rhetoric by some black politicians is designed to serve the purpose of expanding African American influence within the liberal Democratic coalition at the expense of the Jews who, since the New Deal, have been an important force within that alliance. Jesse Jackson is one prominent African American politician who has used this tactic.

In a related sense, when a regime linked to Jews comes under external attack, Jews' allies may feel compelled (or see an opportunity) to throw the Jews to the wolves to save themselves. For example, in twelfth-century England Jewish financiers provided the funds that supported the British Crown's efforts to expand its authority in relation to the aristocracy. As a result, when the barons moved to restrict the powers of the Crown during the thirteenth century, the Jews were among their chief targets. In the Magna Carta of 1215 the barons compelled King John to accept limits on the capacity of the Jews to recover debts from the landed gentry. The king was also forced to agree to accept limits on his own ability to acquire and recover debts that members of the gentry originally owed to the Jews. The acquisition of such debts had been a significant—and hated—mechanism through which the Crown extracted resources and enhanced its power over the nobility. Subsequently, the Crown distanced itself from the Jews, first imposing severe restrictions on them and later expelling them from England—though not before expropriating as much of their capital as could be found.

Hungary is a more recent example. In pre–World War I Hungary, the Magyar governing class was closely allied with the Jews, who dominated business and the professions and extended Magyar influence in the provinces. As a result of this alliance, Hungarian Jews enjoyed complete political freedom and social acceptance. Jews were sometimes given access to noble status. Between the two world wars, however, the Magyar elite's relationship with the Jews came under attack from radical populists within Hungary as well as from Hungary's German allies. To save itself, the aristocracy agreed to restrict the political, economic, and civil rights of its former partners. Ultimately, large numbers of Hungarian Jews perished at the hands of the Germans.

Similarly, Jews in seventeenth-century Ukraine were aligned with the Polish nobility, whom they served as estate managers, tax collectors, administrators, and operators of such enterprises as mills and breweries. In 1648, however, the Ukrainian peasantry led by Bogdan Chmielnicki revolted against the Poles and their Jewish subordinates. The Poles sought to save themselves by handing the Jews over to the Ukrainians in exchange for their own lives. Thousands of Jews were killed when denied access to or evicted from the fortified Polish towns where they had sought refuge. In the United States, nineteenth-century business elites who had been closely allied with Jewish financiers and bankers rid themselves of their Jewish colleagues when this alliance came under attack from the Populists and from groups that wanted to restrict immigration.

Finally, when Jews play a major role in efforts to supplant an existing regime, the state or social forces under attack may respond with an anti-Semitic campaign designed to protect the established order and discredit its antagonists. Generally, such a campaign involves inciting popular forces by claiming that the government's opponents are unpatriotic and linked to Jews and other foreign elements. Because most governments view rabble-rousing of this sort as destabilizing and potentially dangerous, they generally endeavor to keep the popular forces they mobilize on a short leash and to rein them in as soon as possible. Tsarist Russia is an important example.

Thus, over the past several centuries, Jews have played important roles in the construction of states as well as in movements seeking to reform or supplant regimes to which they were unable to obtain access. Jews have traditionally offered their services to the state in exchange for the regime's guarantee of security and opportunity. Ironically, however, precisely this relationship between Jews and the state has often sparked organized anti-Semitic attacks. To be sure, where Jews forge a close relationship with the state, they may well obtain protection and a considerable measure of power. In ancient Babylonia all citizens were required to bow before the leader of the Jewish community. During the eighteenth-century heyday of the European court Jew, Shakespeare's *Merchant of Venice* could be performed in Berlin only if preceded by an apology to Jewish members of the audience. In twentieth-century Russia, Jews helped to build and lead powerful instruments of terror and repression.

The power and protection offered Jews by the state, however, has tended to be evanescent. It lasts only as long as Jews' allies in governing coalitions continue to find them useful and "their" state continues to have the capacity to defend them from attack. In the meantime, by employing the state to hold off their enemies, the Jews add its foes to their own.

See also *Genocide; Holocaust; Inquisition; Judaism.*

Benjamin Ginsberg

BIBLIOGRAPHY

Arendt, Hannah. *The Origins of Totalitarianism.* Rev. ed. New York: Harcourt, 1967.

Birnbaum, Pierre, and Ira Katznelson, eds. *Paths of Emancipation: Jews, States, and Citizenship.* Princeton: Princeton University Press, 1995.

Dinnerstein, Leonard. *Anti-Semitism in America.* New York: Oxford University Press, 1994.

Ginsberg, Benjamin. *The Fatal Embrace.* Chicago: University of Chicago Press, 1993.

Hilberg, Raul. *The Destruction of the European Jews.* New York: Holmes and Meier, 1985.

Johnson, Paul. *A History of the Jews.* New York: Harper, 1987.

Langmuir, Gavin. *Toward a Definition of Anti-Semitism.* Berkeley: University of California Press, 1990.

Mearsheimer, John, and Stephen M. Walt. "The Israel Lobby and U.S. Foreign Policy." Working paper. John F. Kennedy School of Government, March 2006.

Pulzer, Peter. *The Rise of Political Anti-Semitism in Germany and Austria.* Cambridge: Harvard University Press, 1988.

Rapoport, Louis. *Stalin's War against the Jews.* New York: Free Press, 1990.

Apocalyptic Literature

See *Millennialism.*

Assemblies of God

See *Pentecostalism.*

Assimilation, Opposition to

See *Nativism.*

Atatürk, Kemal

Turkish soldier, nationalist, and statesman. Mustafa Kemal Atatürk (1881–1938) was the founder of modern republican Turkey and its first president. The National Assembly bestowed the name Atatürk (Father Turk) on him in 1934 for his service to his country.

On November 30, 1918, the Ottoman government signed the armistice of Mudros, which recognized the defeat of the Ottoman Empire by the Allied forces in World War I. Atatürk had been serving in the Ottoman military in Syria as commander of the Special Ottoman Army Corps. After the Greeks occupied Izmir in May 1919, with the encouragment of British prime minister David Lloyd George, Atatürk joined the broad-based resistance to the occupation of Anatolia, the rump of the Ottoman Empire. Sent to the city of Samsum to disband the remnants of the Ottoman army, he instead organized a gathering of officials, the military, and notables in a congress at Erzurum, with himself as commander of the Turkish army in order to create a new Turkish government to replace the dissolved Istanbul government. Atatürk set up a provisional government at Ankara in April 1920. In 1921 Atatürk's nationalist supporters elected him president of a new government, the Grand National Assembly. In the fall of 1922 this new government defeated the Greeks, who then evacuated Anatolia.

On October 29, 1923, the Turkish Republic was proclaimed, and Atatürk was elected president by the new nation's Grand National Assembly. A constitution was accepted on April 20, 1924. Determined to make Turkey a secular state, Atatürk declared the truest brotherhood to be that of "civilization," by which he meant the Western social, political, economic, and cultural systems that were the source for his drive toward secularization. Under Atatürk's guidance, Turkey adopted a civil code based on that of the Swiss and a criminal code based on that of the Italians. Other measures followed: Turkish replaced Arabic as the language of the call to prayer; the nation adopted the Latin alphabet and the Western calendar , with "A.D." denoting dates in the common era; the government eliminated Arabic and Persian from the schools; and Islam lost its constitutional standing as the state religion. In 1934 women gained the right to vote in national elections and to seek election to the parliament. A 1937 amendment of the constitution declared the Turkish state republican, nationalist, populist, secular, and reformist.

Atatürk distrusted the *ulama,* Muslim clerics, whose influence he feared. He instead promoted Turkish nationalism and the secular foundation of the republic. Secularism proved to be successful to the extent that it blended with Turkish nationalism. It was most effective while the single party that Atatürk had created held power. Later, with the transition to a multiparty system in 1946, the antisecular sentiments of a large number of Turkish citizens outside the secular vanguard began to be reflected in the parliament. National elections in 1995 and 2003 were won by Islamic movements that proclaimed the end of "Kemalist" secularism but adopted much of Atatürk's pro-Western ideology.

See also *Turkey.*

Şerif Mardin

BILIOGRAPHY

Kinross, Lord [John Patrick Balfour]. *Atatürk, the Rebirth of a Nation.* 2d ed. London: Weidenfeld and Nicolson, 1964.

Mango, Andrew. *Atatürk.* London: John Murray, 1999.

Pettifer, James. *The Turkish Labyrinth: Atatürk and the New Islam.* London: Penguin Books, 1998.

Atheism

Atheism is the rejection of belief in and the existence of God. The word derives from the Greek *a* (without; not) and *theos* (god). The term *atheism* has a range of inconsistent and seemingly contradictory meanings and a long history marked by controversy. Its meaning in any specific instance depends on how it is defined and on the persons to whom it refers. For example, when Roman state authorities accused early Christians of being atheists because they refused to participate in the state-sponsored cults, the word was a term of opprobrium. What the Christians denied was a particular *theism* enshrined in the state religion; they were called atheists by others who rejected the theistic beliefs of the Christians. By contrast, the followers of Madalyn Murray O'Hair, who founded American Atheists in 1965, actively took upon themselves the label *atheist.* They have flaunted the term as a quasi-theological position and have taken it to imply a strict separation of church and state and of religion from culture. Atheism is to be distinguished from *agnosticism,* a term coined by Thomas H. Huxley, an English biologist, in the nineteenth century. Agnosticism is the refusal to enter into judgment, either affirmative or negative, about the existence of God.

In general, references to atheism place it in the category of serious philosophical positions, such as some forms of idealism and of materialism, that reject traditional theological arguments for the existence of God and by implication reject the notion of belief in God. These positions emerged from the period of the eighteenth-century Enlightenment, with its stress on emancipation from traditional religious authorities, including the authoritative interpretation of the Bible. Philosophical and even theological questions gradually focused on natural philosophy and the possibility of a universal mechanics that would make nature intelligible on its own terms. Arguments for the existence and attributes of God rested largely on the design, pattern, and order of nature. These arguments were gradually superseded by later extrapolations from Isaac Newton's physics to a self-sustaining and self-explanatory universe without a god, but the Enlightenment itself was in some ways the final flowering of an earlier Renaissance humanism. This humanism gave the world a new idea of science freed from theology, an interest in the agency of the human person in the political sphere, tremendous religious and theological change, and the rediscovery of academic skepticism. The Catholic theologian Henri de Lubac argued that these philosophic forms of atheism must be taken seriously on their own terms if one is to understand how profound their implications are for the social and political order and a recovery of authentic humanism.

These philosophic forms of atheism cannot be adequately understood apart from that which they reject, which is not only a belief in a god per se but often also the theologies and religious and cultural structures that have traditionally supported the transmission of belief in a god. As the Catholic theologian Michael Buckley has argued, atheism is "parasitic" in that it feeds on that which it rejects. The earliest forms of modern atheism depended in part on the repudiation of theologies that had unsuccessfully argued for the existence and attributes of a god, often on the basis of physical or natural principles rather than strictly theological ones. In this sense, Buckley argues, religion generated its own antithesis.

For some, ecclesiastical infighting and power intrigues and the scandals of religious wars created a context within which the rejection of religious belief in God was made easier. Such was the case for many of the disaffected intelligentsia in postrevolutionary France. In the twentieth century, the systematic atheism of Soviet communism represented not only the ideological expression of Marxist atheism, but a rejection of the religious and political culture that had helped sustain the Orthodox faith in Russia prior to the revolution of 1917.

In considering the relationship between atheism and politics, one must distinguish among the atheism of the Enlightenment and post-Enlightenment periods, the structured acceptance or adoption of atheism in political systems, and the newer forms of atheism that have emerged from "postmodern" cultures. Here one must also consider the newest forms of atheism that do not bear the name of atheism but which can be seen in the irrelevancy of God as a question, in the political and economic struggles of developing nations, and in the various forms of nihilism, both nonreligious and religious, that emerge from a lack of transcendence.

Enlightenment and Post-Enlightenment Atheism

The origins of modern atheism are often traced to the emergence of the rational ego in the philosophy of René Descartes, the seventeenth-century French mathematician and philosopher. For Descartes, ideas held by the rational ego displaced as the ultimate foundation of knowledge the philosophy of being (ontology) and the traditional foundations of metaphysics that had been handed down from Plato and Aristotle through Thomas Aquinas. This autonomy of the rational ego allowed for the elaboration of a universal mathematics that would explain the world and would be the source of any real affirmation of God. Around the same time, the British mathematician Isaac Newton developed a universal mechanics in which the physical universe was understood as a vast and comprehensible system that had been set in motion and was kept in motion by God, the provident governor and designer of the universe. Newton's achievement was enthusiastically received by some theologies, such as that of Samuel Clarke, which had argued for the existence and attributes of a god on the basis of physical or natural principles. This helped give rise to a permutation of the traditional Christian theology of God, *deism,* in which God was perceived as the distant creator of a well-designed universe that otherwise ran according to its own internal laws of motion, with very rare instances of a provident divine intervention.

It was a short step from deism to conscious attempts to explain the universe on purely materialistic grounds without the benefit of God whatsoever. The first phase of this development of atheism is found in the eighteenth century in the writings of the French Enlightenment's *philosophes,* especially Voltaire and Denis Diderot. These intellectuals railed vehemently at least as much against religion and its institutions as against belief in God per se, but their writings opened the door for more concerted philosophical efforts to deny the existence of God altogether. Atheism received its clearest philosophical expression in Paul-Henri Dietrich d'Holbach's *System of Nature* (1770). In it, D'Holbach argues for a completely materialistic universe and deliberately sets forth a scheme for a thoroughgoing philosophical denial of the existence of God as a transcendent being. Deism and the theology that supported it had become the natural ancestor of an atheism that held that the universe could be explained without any further need of the hypothesis of God.

The second phase in the development of modern atheism occurred during the post-Enlightenment period of early German idealism and, later, romanticism. In the work of the German philosopher G. W. F. Hegel (1770–1831), the rational ego of Descartes is transformed into a pure consciousness. Within that consciousness, according to Hegel, the knowledge of all of reality is collapsed in a dialectical relation between the world as object of knowledge and the knower's self-consciousness as subject. Immanuel Kant (1724–1804) shifted the entire field of philosophical inquiry from traditional metaphysics to epistemology, the study of the basis of knowledge. In Kant's philosophy, practical judgment and morality, rather than metaphysics or even traditional epistemology, were where one could establish the existence of God. In making moral judgments, the human person requires an ultimate confirmation of the direction and rightness of those judgments. That ultimate confirmation is God, and to the German theologian Friedrich Schleiermacher (1768–1834), this God is known through an experience he called "feeling." The absence of metaphysics and such a strong turn to experience placed the metaphysical grounds for the affirmation of the existence of God in jeopardy.

Another German philosopher, Ludwig Feuerbach, was among the first to see this slippage in metaphysical foundations for belief in God. In *The Essence of Christianity* (1841), Feuerbach asserts that belief in God is merely the projection onto the "sky" of the deepest aspirations and inner necessities of the self-conscious human subject, who is a member of a larger species sharing the same aspirations and needs. "Species consciousness" thus marks the human from other species. The gods themselves are a projection of this species consciousness. The existence of a god is therefore finally dependent on the transcendental subjectivity of human persons, that is, the capacity to transcend oneself in knowledge. In fact, no god exists apart from human subjectivity. The deepest reality about religion is that it is a veiled atheism. In its focus on gods and powers to whom humans must be sub-servient, religion results in an alienation of human persons from themselves and from others. Emancipation from this alienation comes from a critical understanding of the funda-mental atheism underlying religion.

Sigmund Freud (1856–1939) built on Feuerbach's philo-sophical foundations in his psychoanalytic theory and saw the nature of belief as the struggle of the id in relation to the ego and the superego. The model for this struggle for free-dom is the individuation of the son from the mother and the ensuing rejection of the father. Religion thus comes to be understood as a playing out of primitive psychological forces. Final emancipation arrives in the form of atheism. In an early work, *The Future of an Illusion,* Freud developed yet another thesis: God is a human response to the fear of death and the terrors of nature. Religion itself can be explained as the social framework within which this fear is ritualized and tamed. Human beings, Freud believed, must free themselves from the tyranny of religion.

Friedrich Nietzsche stood in this tradition by arguing in *The Gay Science* (1882) that God is dead. His point is that God no longer serves even as a projection of consciousness; the marketplace and its bourgeois social and political values replaced God with a nihilism in which traditional meta-physics no longer function and the eternal truths are no longer certain. The issue is not whether God exists as a pro-jection of consciousness, but of acknowledging that the con-ditions for the possibility of such a projection no longer exist because the consciousness that had given rise to God is dead. In Nietzsche's book, the "Madman" in the marketplace shouts that God has been murdered. Human beings are left with a will to power and the ultimate achievement of a new form of humanity (the *Übermensch,* or "superman").

Karl Marx stood in Feuerbach's lineage in his understand-ing of belief in God as an expression of the alienation of the subject (worker) from himself as well as from other human beings. This alienation is a remote expression of the funda-mental alienation from self that religion brings about. It can be overcome only through actual historical events in the playing out of dialectical materialism. Marx argues in *The Economic and Philosophic Manuscripts of 1844* that until that final emancipation, religion will serve as the sigh of the oppressed creature, an opiate for the masses. Atheism is thus intrinsic to Marxist theory as a quasi-theological foundation and as an anticipated result of the dialectical forces of eco-nomic history.

In addition to these developments in Germany, a flower-ing of atheism occurred during the nineteenth century in England and in the United States. This can be attributed in part to the rising faith in economic progress, the emergence of Darwinism as an alternative to what was considered benighted religion, the appeal of social Darwinism to the educated classes, and a positivist view of science. In the United States, the influence of the philosopher John Dewey (1859–1952) cannot be underestimated as a source of secu-larist and even atheistic ethics. Dewey's thought, which heavily influenced American thinkers such as Reinhold Niebuhr, was to go far toward building what would later be called "civil religion."

Political Implications of Modern Atheism

The beliefs that gained currency during the Enlighten-ment and after it had significant political implications. As measured by the religion and piety of the American founders, the deist god—not the god of the much earlier Puritans or of a later evangelical Christianity—undergirded the United States as a great political project of the Enlight-enment. Although certainly not intended as a form of athe-ism, deism did allow for the possibility of toleration of a range of theological convictions and insisted on the freedom to pursue them. Deism was fed by the streams of Unitarian-ism (an offshoot of Anglicanism that denied the traditional Christian theology of God) and Freemasonry (a quasi-reli-gious movement that tolerated and even encouraged athe-ism). Out of these streams emerged two principles dear to the American political project: freedom of religion and the separation of church and state, both enshrined in the First Amendment to the U.S. Constitution. The Enlightenment rejection of religious authority and monarchy fueled these principles as much as did memories of past religious perse-cution. The First Amendment helped shelter within U.S. political culture the development and toleration of various expressions of atheism. Nevertheless, the United States became a nation of extraordinary religious vitality, and athe-ism has never been embraced by the masses.

France was another country that devised new political structures strongly shaped by Enlightenment thought. The development of atheism was inextricably intertwined with anticlericalism and the cultural skirmishes between the Catholic Church and the new French state. It also bore the marks of a rejection of religion, not only by intellectual elites but also by significant portions of the working classes.

Perhaps the most important development in the American project was civil religion, that is, the notion of a society in which belief in God stands alongside political culture and in some ways supports it but does not officially buttress or undergird it except in formulaic ways (for example, "In God We Trust," the slogan on American currency). The emergence of this civil religion in the United States allowed for the development of a markedly secular society within which some religious values could nevertheless thrive. As the sociologist Robert Bellah has demonstrated, civil religion encourages individualist religious philosophies and spiritual quests. It has contributed to the development of a society in which belief in God is largely held as a matter of private pursuit and where questions about God as a public or common intellectual matter have never taken root, even in academic circles. There has thus emerged a society within which believers—Christians, Jews, Muslims, and others—coexist alongside atheists and agnostics, although differences have often played out in the political and legal domains. This contrasts sharply with theocracies (Iran's, for instance) where atheism, unimaginable except as a sin within a religious context, is also treated as a civil crime.

The second phase of the development of modern atheism, the post-Enlightenment thought following upon Feuerbach, led in subtle ways to the development of two of the major political phenomena of the twentieth century: Nazi fascism and Soviet communism. Political fascism, at least in its National Socialist (Nazi) form, depended on some religious (church) cooperation and actually made use of religious and quasi-religious imagery. As an ideology, however, it fundamentally rejected a society based on faith, substituting for belief in God submission to the Führer and the ideology of racial purity as a transcendent ideal and concrete political goal. In this sense it was profoundly a-theistic. Although Nietzsche's Madman announces the "death of God," and although the Übermensch represents a will to power without the benefit of God, Nietzsche is too easily invoked as the philosophical forebear of the "atheism" of Nazi socialism. In fact, it could be argued that Nietzsche was calling for the discovery of a new sense of the transcendent, outside traditional theologies, despite his dark and pessimistic social outlook. This recovery of transcendence has been the aim of some "postmodern" thought.

As an explicitly and aggressively atheistic system, Soviet communism attempted to institutionalize what Marx had limned in theory. The Soviet system, however, was based on a fundamental misreading of Marxist atheism that can be attributed to the totalitarian nature of the system itself. Whereas Marx believed that religion would eventually be overcome through the dialectic of economic forces, the Soviet system began with the brutal suppression of religion and the imposition of official state atheism. Atheism was an intrinsic philosophical foundation of Marxist theory, but in Soviet communism it became an intrinsic part of the political process, as it did also in China under Mao Zedong. The demise of the Soviet system in 1989–1991 demonstrated that the roots of belief in God remained just below the surface of official atheism. It has also been amply demonstrated, however, that a totalitarian regime can, over a few short generations, succeed in seriously crippling that belief by retarding its development and by violently hacking at its roots.

Nazi fascism, Soviet communism, and even Maoism emerged in an age when it was possible to imagine the total rejection of the theistic (or more broadly, religious) underpinnings of Western societies by political organizations. This could only have happened after atheism had become established as an alternative to faith in God. The atheism of fascism and of communism has been echoed in various forms of totalitarianism that depend on strict control of religion and, implicitly, on denial of God as transcendent reality.

Postmodern Forms of Atheism

Unbelief, idolatry, and the lack of a sense of transcendence (a position expounded by former Czech president Václav Havel) represent forms of atheism that do not correspond to the older, "traditional" forms that emerged earlier in the Western world and depend on a well-conceived philosophical position.

Unbelief is to be distinguished from older "modern" atheism in that in many respects God as a possible reality is not explicitly in question in the first place. According to the Catholic theologian Karl Rahner (1904–1984), this stance is based not so much on rejection of the idea of God as on the tacit assumption that the question of the existence of God is irrelevant, at least as a matter of common intellectual concern. In its most severe forms, unbelief folds into nihilism, a loss of the values and common points of reference that have enabled cultures to cohere in the past. The roots of unbelief are complex. Secularism, the forces of the market economy, the assurances of technology, and the dominance of a positivist view of science have all contributed to its pervasive influence. Secularism, the belief that a culture best functions in the absence of religious influence, is an axiom of Western political societies. As an ideology, it is to be distinguished from the principle of separation of church from state, from which it partly derives. The principle of separation of church and state allows for religious influence upon culture, as in civil religion, but secularism seeks to cleanse culture of religion.

Secularism has paved the way for a market ideology within which the market economy assumes the absolute value that religion once held. This development, in which economies of variant cultures are radically dependent on one another, and in which these economies function according to wholly secular principles, has resulted in a pan-culture in which "unbelief" is a tacit assumption, even in non-Western societies. Various libertarian political and economic programs, originally propounded by such thinkers as Ayn Rand (1905–1982), have also promoted a radical secularism. Libertarianism stresses the absolute authority of reason, rugged individualism, government minimalism, and the "objective" power of market forces over any transcendent values, political or religious.

Linked with these developments is the universal influence of technology, which has given human beings the illusion of the ultimate comprehensibility of the universe and, on a more mundane level, a certain hubristic confidence in the manageability of problems without any reference to transcendence. Certain philosophically naive views of science, involving a nearly unquestioning confidence in the truth claims of science, have also contributed to the phenomenon of unbelief. In this arena, as in the universe of market ideology, unbelief characterizes certain sectors of the educated elites not only in the Western world but beyond it. In this sense, one could speak, for example, of a culture of unbelief in some of the countries of Asia, including Japan.

Idolatry is a category of analysis employed by some followers of liberation theology. The theology of liberation was the outgrowth of the work of the Catholic theologian Gustavo Gutiérrez in the 1970s. It addresses the problems of poverty in developing countries and the socioeconomic and political structures that helped give rise to and sustain it. In most liberation theologies, atheism per se is not at issue. Atheism in the modern sense exists in these countries but primarily among the educated elites and in those sectors, such as labor unions, that have traditionally been influenced by anticlericalism in these cultures. Modern atheism is not generally found among the vast masses of the poor and mid-

dle classes. Theologies of liberation, therefore, invoke the tradition of the biblical prophets and inveigh against various forms of "idolatry" that characterize a "godless" society.

The Salvadoran theologian Jon Sobrino cites the idolatries of wealth, materialism, and political power wielded by the rich over the poor. The theological question thus becomes not whether one believes in God, but in which god one believes. The "idols" of wealth, materialism, and power demand that the human person offer himself or herself up to the mechanisms of an unjust political order. Later writings in the theology of liberation, especially those since the advent of neoliberalism in the 1990s, stress not so much the divide between rich and poor as they do a "communitarian" approach to the solving of social problems, balancing a social justice agenda with a prudent use of market economics.

The lack of a sense of transcendence has been noted especially in Western Europe, where the structures and traditions of the Christian faith and Judaism (because of the Holocaust) suffered massive implosions in the last half of the twentieth century. As political leaders such as Havel have noted, this pervasive lack of the transcendent does not necessarily obviate the quest for transcendence on a personal or cultural level through politics. Indeed, the "postmodern" alienation from religion is ironically often tied to a quest for the spiritual or the transcendent but outside the traditional theologies of God. Havel's political and philosophical writings stress the importance of this postmodern search for transcendence in the face of the absence of God, not only as a personal quest but as a dimension of life that societies badly need to recover if they are to survive. Havel's writings generally stress as well that the transcendence for which people are searching will not necessarily be found in traditional religions or theologies.

Theological Reactions to Atheism

Although it has been established that religion contributed to the rise of atheism, there have been notable theological reactions to atheism that have had some political implications. These can be included generally under the headings of political theology and explicit ecclesiastical responses to atheism.

Political theology emerged in Europe, primarily in Belgium, France, and Germany, after World War II. The aim of political theology was to pursue the implications of faith at a time when it was clear that the Christendom of Old Europe, including belief in God, no longer held sway. The question became what faith and politics together might look like in a post-Christian age. Theologians like the Catholic Johannes B. Metz reinterpreted the imagery of the Book of Revelation and searched its apocalyptic imagery for keys to recovering a sense of God in building a new society, while the Protestant Jürgen Moltmann produced a theology of hope that took into account the full force of the cross as a symbol of divine involvement in social and political suffering. In American Protestantism this political interest took the form of a "secular" theology, in which some theologians argued for finding God within the political and cultural world. These thinkers were following an older and well-established path of political theology in Protestantism going back to John Calvin, the sixteenth-century Protestant reformer. In the mid-twentieth century it was forcefully expressed as an American political theology by Reinhold Niebuhr and, in the categories of Christ and culture, elaborated by his brother H. Richard Niebuhr. In Europe, the theologians Karl Barth and Dietrich Bonhoeffer had elaborated these themes in the context of the experience of the Protestant churches during the Third Reich.

The ecclesiastical response of the Western churches to atheism has been most forcefully expressed by the Roman Catholic Church. In its "Pastoral Constitution on the Church in the Modern World" *(Gaudium et Spes),* the Second Vatican Council (1962–1965) moved beyond its traditional position of repudiating atheism as a sinful rejection of God to an expressed desire for dialogue with atheists. The theological reasons for this shift are complex and depend on developments in theological anthropology and in an understanding of God's self-communication (grace) as a divine offer made to all human beings, not only to Christians or believers. The reasons are also conciliatory. The dialogue with atheists, therefore, is for the "political" goal of the common good.

Catholic theologians such as Karl Rahner engaged in active dialogue with Marxists and atheists in the years following World War II. A Vatican Secretariat for Non-Believers was established in 1965. In that same year, Pope Paul VI commissioned the Society of Jesus (Jesuits) to undertake dialogue with atheists as a primary mission and to devote their intellectual attention to the problem of atheism in the modern world. These missions of the church toward engagement with atheism were intended not only to combat atheism, which the church continued to view as incompatible with Christian faith, but to engage it positively with the goal of finding common horizons in the interest of the good of humanity.

As some indication of how the thinking of the Roman Catholic Church has changed in regard to the phenomenon of atheism, the name of the Secretariat for Non-Believers was changed in 1991 to the Pontifical Council for Dialogue with Non-Believers and in 1993 to the Pontifical Council on Culture. This reflects a tacit admission that the phenomenon of atheism is no longer an intellectual position alone, the "modern" rejection of the existence of and belief in God, but is a reality embedded in the secular culture that increasingly involves all social and political systems around the globe.

See also *Barth, Karl; Bonhoeffer, Dietrich; Civil Religion; Communism; Communitarianism; Enlightenment; Fascism; Freedom of Religion; Havel, Václav; Liberation Theology; Marxism; Niebuhr, Reinhold; Nietzsche, Friedrich; Secular Humanism; Separation of Church and State.*

Paul G. Crowley

BIBLIOGRAPHY

Bellah, Robert. *Habits of the Heart: Individualism and Commitment in American Life.* New York: Harper and Row, 1986.

Buckley, Michael J. *At the Origins of Modern Atheism.* New Haven: Yale University Press, 1987.

De Lubac, Henri. *The Drama of Atheistic Humanism.* New York: New American Library, 1963.

Gallagher, Michael John. *What Are They Saying about Unbelief?* Mahwah, N.J.: Paulist Press, 1995.

Jacoby, Sudan. *Freethinkers: A History of American Secularism.* New York: Henry Holt, 2004.

Murray, John Courtney. *The Problem of God.* New Haven: Yale University Press, 1964.

Sobrino, Jon. *Jesus the Liberator: A Historical-Theological View.* Translated by Paul Burns and Francis McDonagh. Maryknoll, N.Y.: Orbis Books, 1993.

Ayatollah

See *Islam.*

B

Bahai

The Bahai faith traces its origin to the Babi movement, a millenarian movement of the Shi'ite Muslims of mid-nineteenth-century Iran. Its founder, Sayyid Ali Muhammad of Shiraz (d. 1850), first proclaimed himself the Gate (*bab*) to the Hidden Twelfth Imam, whom the Shi'ites believed to be the mahdi, the rightly guided leader of the end of time. At the close of 1844, the twenty-five-year-old Bab, as he became generally known, declared himself to be the Hidden Imam, returning after a thousand years of concealment.

His movement spread rapidly in his native land and culminated in a series of millenarian uprisings between 1848 and 1850 in which his followers abrogated Islamic law to mark the beginning of the new era. The Bab was imprisoned and condemned as a heretic by the Shi'ite clergy in 1848 and was executed in 1850. The movement was ferociously suppressed after a group of Babis unsuccessfully attempted to assassinate the monarch in 1852. Mirza Husayn Ali Nuri (1817–1892), a government official who had joined the Babi movement in 1844, was imprisoned. Cleared of the charge of complicity in the plot, he nevertheless suffered exile to Ottoman Baghdad in 1853. Ten years later, in a garden in Baghdad, he proclaimed himself to be "he whom God shall manifest," of whom the Bab had spoken. He assumed the title of Baha'ullah (the Glory of God), and his followers considered him the last prophet and manifestation of God.

The Bahai religion, which may be considered the youngest of the world religions and has about five million followers throughout the world, was thus founded in April 1863. The great majority of Babis accepted Baha'ullah's messianic claims and became Bahais. A small minority led by his brother, known as the Subh-i Azal (Dawn of Eternity), refused to do so, however, and remained Babis.

The Ottoman government exiled Baha'ullah to Palestine in 1868. From there, he sent epistles, tablets, and missionaries to Iran and the rest of the world until his death in 1892. In 1873 the Bahai community in Iran asked for a book of law to supersede the Bab's as well as Islamic law, and he sent them the Most Holy Book (*Kitab i-Aqdas*). During Baha'ullah's lifetime, the Bahai community in Iran grew to an estimated one hundred thousand, and the Bahai faith expanded mainly in the East, in the Caucasus, Egypt, India, Iraq, Syria, Turkey, Turkistan. From 1892 to 1921, under the leadership of his son and designated successor, Abbas, known as Abdul-Baha' (the Servant of the Glory), the Bahai religion expanded globally, spreading into East Asia, Europe, North America, South Africa, and South America. The first Bahai mission in the United States was established in Chicago by Ibrahim George Kheialla in 1894. When Abdul-Baha' visited the United States in 1912, there were already several thousand American Bahais. These Americans had a considerable effect on the evolution of the Bahai religion.

The expansion of the Bahai faith continued under the vigorous leadership of Shoghi Effendi (1899–1957), the grandson of Abdul-Baha', from 1921 to 1957. Shoghi Effendi died childless, and because he had excommunicated his eligible relatives, Bahai leadership devolved upon a Universal House of Justice that Baha'ullah had envisioned. Its trustees are elected every five years. The first Universal House of Justice trustees were elected by the International Bahai Council in 1963. Five of its nine trustees were American, two

The Shrine of the Bab in Haifa, Israel, is the second most holy place in the Bahai world.

British, and two Iranian. Since 1957 mass conversions to Bahaism have been recorded in Bolivia, India, and Uganda. The historically important mother community in Iran now constitutes only 10 percent of the world's Bahais.

The development of the Bahai religion from Babi millenarianism illustrates the transition from revolutionary militancy to political pacifism and from a theocratic fusion of religion and politics to their strict separation within the framework of participatory government. Two historical factors were decisive for this transition: the early exposure of Baha'ullah and Abdul-Baha' to the Ottoman reform movement and constitutionalism in the 1860s and 1870s and the expansion of the Bahai religion in the United States.

From the beginning, Baha'ullah distanced his "realized messianism" from the militant millenarianism of the Babis

by declaring that his religion had abrogated holy warfare, "the rule of the sword." At the same time, he declared the separation of religion and politics in marked divergence from their fusion in Babism. These declarations paved the way for constitutionalist ideas concerning government, on the one hand, and the advocacy of universal peace, on the other. The influence of the Ottoman reforms and constitutionalist ideas are evident in Baha'ullah's writings in the late 1860s and 1870s. Baha'ullah advocated the rule of law and constitutional monarchy, hailing the advent of constitutionalism and parliamentary government as the final manifestation of reason among mankind. Baha'ullah adopted the idea of universal peace, which was popular among the Ottoman and Egyptian intellectuals of the period, as an extension of his abolition of holy war and made it a cornerstone of the universalism of his religion.

The Ottoman administrative reforms, especially those of 1856 concerning the self-regulation of the religious minorities, also influenced Baha'ullah's institution of consultative forms of self-regulation for the Bahai communities. His Most Holy Book called for local councils, "houses of justice," consisting of at least nine members, to act as governing bodies of Bahai communities. These local councils became the basic units of Bahai administration. These elected councils administer the religious and civic affairs of Bahai communities, and their growth prevented the emergence of any Bahai clergy out of the nucleus of original missionaries.

During the constitutional decade (1870s), Baha'ullah had told his son not to leave the writing on political affairs to nonbelieving intellectuals, but to write a book on the science of politics. In a book (1875) he wrote on the subject and in a prologue to his anonymous history of the Babi movement (1888), Abdul-Baha' presented equality, liberty, and universal human rights as the signs of the latest stage of civilization. During the Iranian constitutional revolution (1906–1911), however, Abdul-Baha'—now the leader of the Bahai religion in his own right—refused to support the Iranian constitutionalists, primarily because of the prominent role of his more radical sectarian rivals, the Azali Babis. Abdul-Baha' did, however, stress the separation of religion and politics. This separation was reaffirmed by his grandson and successor, Shoghi Effendi, who also confirmed that the machinery of the internal administration of the Bahai communities should not supersede the governments of their respective countries.

The increasing influence of the American Bahai community largely accounts for the ending of the separation of men and women during the leadership of Abdul-Baha', who was also prevailed upon to allow women to serve in the local house of justice. The American Bahais have since been influential in reinforcing the machinery of self-regulation in Bahai communities and in the development of national and international conventions. The Bahais of Iran attracted international attention again after the Islamic revolution of 1979. Although they consistently confirmed the separation of religion and politics and reaffirmed the apolitical nature of their faith in the 1970s, they have been severely persecuted by the Islamic theocratic regime in Iran, which from a religious perspective considers them defectors from Shi'ism and, from a political perspective, agents of imperialism and Zionism. The government has confiscated Bahai properties and dissolved all their local councils. Hundred of Bahais have been killed and imprisoned and thousands purged from the army and civil service or forced to recant.

See also *Iran; Iraq; Islam; Mahdi.*

Said Amir Arjomand

BIBLIOGRAPHY

"Bahai Faith or Bahaism." *Encyclopaedia Iranica.* Vol. 3. London: Routledge and Kegan Paul, 1989.

Cole, J. R. I. *Modernity and the Millennium.* New York: Columbia University Press, 1998.

Smith, Peter. *The Babi and Baha'i Religions: From Messianic Shi'is to a World Religion.* New York: Cambridge University Press, 1987.

Balkan States

The Balkan states, which include the former Yugoslavia, Bulgaria, Romania, Albania, and Greece, are predominantly Eastern Orthodox, but they also have significant Muslim and Roman Catholic populations. Politics and religion have interacted in the Balkans at least since the ninth century, when Byzantine missionaries led by Cyril and Methodius christianized the Slavs and the Bulgarians. From about the same time, three major religious cultures—Eastern Orthodoxy, Roman Catholicism, and Islam—have been involved in a complex religious-ideological and political struggle in the region. Over the second millennium, religion and politics in the Balkans have been shaped by empires and their legacies, especially the Orthodox Byzantine, which ended in

the fifteenth century with the conquest of Constantinople (today Istanbul in Turkey) by Mehmet II (1453), and the Muslim Ottoman, which lasted from the fifteenth to the twentieth century. In the early twentieth century the largely Catholic Austro-Hungarian Empire (1867–1918) wielded considerable influence in the region, and from 1945 to 1990, religion endured communist rule.

The collapse of empires resulted in long-lasting social, political, and cultural consequences, with nation building as overarching objective. Religion and ethnicity have been central in the pursuit of this objective. Over the past two hundred years, social change and the interaction of religion and politics in the Balkans have been deeply affected by the collapse of the Ottoman and the Austro-Hungarian Empires and the socialist bloc. Since the collapse of the socialist block in 1990 the region entered a period of tension and radical transformation with religion exercising a new active role in politics. Basic to this transformation and its prospects is the European Union (EU) orientation of all the Balkan states.

Independence and Modernization

In Western societies modernity, modernization, capitalism, industrialization, democratization, and secularization developed in unison. Not so in the Balkans, where modernity had little chance to take firm root within the ailing Ottoman Empire of the eighteenth and nineteenth centuries. Influenced in some measure by the ideas of the Enlightenment and above all by the spirit of nationalism then sweeping Europe, one after the other the people of the Balkans rose to claim their independence from the Turkish yoke during the nineteenth century. Orthodoxy, a central element of the ethnic identity of these people, played a crucial, legitimizing, ideological role in the independence of Greece (1830), Serbia (1830), Romania (1862), Bulgaria (1878), and Albania (1920). But "independent," in this case, must be carefully qualified. These new nation-states were not just economically dependent on loans from the Great Powers (Britain, France, Prussia, Russia), but in large measure they also were under their political tutelage.

With the exception of Serbia, the first monarchs of the new Balkan states were Catholics called to rule over predominantly Orthodox populations. Political institutions in the region were largely superimposed from outside. Throughout this period national borders kept shifting as the Ottoman and the Austro-Hungarian Empires gradually disintegrated and wars became endemic in the region. The Crimean War (1854–1856), the Russo-Turkish War (1875–1878), the Greek-Turkish War (1897), the Balkan Wars (1912–1913), and the First World War (1914–1917) all involved extensive outside intervention and interest. Ethnoreligious factors were central to these conflicts and crucial to the consolidation of the nation-state. The ethno-religio-political puzzle in the region, which still remains unresolved and unpredictable, must be understood as it relates to globalization.

Industrialization and capitalism, for example, came late in the Balkans because most of the region consisted of peasant societies up to the 1960s. (In the 1950s, 78 percent of the working population in Yugoslavia was in agriculture; 75.5 percent and 70 percent, respectively, in Bulgaria and Romania.) But although the communist regimes that took over after 1945 emphasized fast industrialization, a real industrial infrastructure has never developed in these countries. Class structure, social organization, and division of labor never followed Western patterns either, so industrial working and middle classes similar to those of Western Europe never developed in the Balkans. Politics in the region developed along clientilistic and ethnic-nationalistic lines. Votes were exchanged for personal or family favors arranged by local patrons representing politicians. So, given the mosaic of ethnoreligious groups and the historical divisions among the major religions in the region, socioeconomic and political issues have tended to express themselves as ethnoreligious conflicts.

In the aftermath of such ethno-religio-political strife in the former Yugoslavia after the collapse of the socialist regime in 1990, American political scientist Samuel P. Huntington has implied that Orthodoxy and Islam are religious cultures that, if not incompatible, certainly are not conducive to democracy and pluralism. That thesis must be rejected for Orthodoxy. Orthodox theology poses the person and personal freedom as the central social ideal of Christianity. Unlike Roman Catholicism, Orthodoxy does not accept the authority and infallibility of the pope. In principle Orthodoxy is not a hindrance to democracy, and, as a political culture, it is deeply democratic. This being the case, the reason democracies have not fared well in the Balkans cannot be sought in the culture of Orthodoxy, which is the major religion in the region. In the Balkans secularization is less advanced than in the West, but apart from the historical explanation for this, the fact that Orthodoxy is resistant to secularization but Protestantism seems compatible with it does not mean that Orthodoxy is undemocratic or antipluralist.

A better explanation for the historical ethnoreligious conflict in the Balkans comes from the interaction of political and socioeconomic developments and the role of religion in galvanizing the nationalist claims of various Orthodox, Catholic, and Muslim communities. Moreover, these developments should be understood within the context of global socioeconomic and political change. In their aspirations to become independent states, ethnoreligious communities in the region were caught in the political void of the collapsed socialist Yugoslavia and the necessity to survive and get a place in a modern globalized economy. The revival of old intercommunal hatreds made the conflict bloodier than ever. Since the turn of the century, violent conflict, which involved the North Atlantic Treaty Organization (NATO) itself, has eased down as the prospects of the Balkan states to join the EU have opened up.

Church and State Relations

Theologically, church and state relations in the Orthodox tradition are based on the biblical principle "Give unto Caesar...." In Byzantium, which was the seat of Eastern Christendom between 320 and 1453, religion and politics were diffused in a Christian, theocentric commonwealth, but there was no confusion in the exercise of sacred and political authority. Sacred authority belonged to the church in the person of the ecumenical patriarch of Constantinople, who had honorary primacy *(primus interpares*—first among equals) among other Orthodox patriarchs, and political authority belonged to the emperor, who was also holy. This schema has been called *Caesaropapism,* meaning political subjugation of church to state. Some modern scholars reject this interpretation, however, because emperors sometimes lost not just their thrones but also their heads because of their religious policies.

During Ottoman rule (1453–1923) the Orthodox Church, led by the patriarch of Constantinople, became the social and civil administrator of the Orthodox people under the sultan. This strengthened the bonds of the Balkan peoples to Orthodoxy and gave the church a new political status. But this standing changed radically with the emergence of the nation-states in the nineteenth century. As they acquired their independence, one after the other also demanded a church independent *(autocephalous,* or with its own head bishop) from the ecumenical patriarchate, which in each case the patriarchate had to concede reluctantly as a fait accompli. From then on most national churches in the Balkans have been under the almost total control of the state and have been made to serve ethnic and even party and sectional political ends. At the same time large Muslim minorities within these states were presenting a serious problem.

With the coming of communist rule after 1945, church-state relations in the Balkans entered their worst phase in history. In socialist society the presence of the church was an anomaly in the eyes of the state. But because it could not be abolished altogether, despite the persecution, it had to be used and tolerated for propaganda purposes insofar as it was cooperating with the regime. If they wanted to survive, the churches had to play that game. With the collapse of communist rule, church-state relations have been caught within the new tensions of fanatic, nationalist ethnoreligious conflicts on the one hand and the demands of modernization on the other.

Former Yugoslavia

The kingdom of Yugoslavia was established after the First World War, in 1920. With a population in 1990 of about 24 million, 50 percent of the people were classified as Orthodox, 30 percent as Roman Catholic, 19 percent as Muslim, and 1 percent as other (Jews, evangelicals, and so on). The Orthodox live mainly in Serbia and Montenegro, the Catholics in Croatia and Slovenia, and the Muslims in Bosnia and Kosovo. But there have long been significant Serbian Orthodox minorities within Bosnia and Croatia,

Muslim women pray in remembrance of family members who perished in July 1995 when Bosnian Serb forces captured Srebrenica, a suburb of Sarajevo, during the war in Bosnia.

where brutal war broke out (1991–1994) after these provinces declared their independence from Yugoslavia. Sarajevo, the center of the conflicts, was also the city that sparked the First World War after the 1914 assassination there of Archduke Franz Ferdinand, heir to the Habsburg throne, by a Serb nationalist.

The Serbian church was established in 1219 by Savas Nemania, its first archbishop, who gave it an ethnic character prevalent to the present day. In 1879 it acquired autocephalous status from the ecumenical patriarchate. Since 1920 its coexistence with the Catholic Church of Croatia and Slovenia within a single state has been a source of conflict and tension, as the Vatican often intervened to protect or promote the interests of the Catholics. During the Second World War, Serbs and Croats found themselves in opposing camps as Croatia, then under the pro-Fascist, Croat nationalist party, attempted to exterminate its Serbian minority. With Nazis in power, the Serbs as a whole paid a heavy toll, with about one million slaughtered, including six Orthodox bishops, four hundred priests, and many monks. Because of this, traditional mistrust and tension between the two communities turned into deep hatred.

The communist regime (1945–1990) of Josip Broz Tito's Yugoslavia could not eradicate such hatred. At first the regime opposed all religions. Then came a period of mutual toleration between church and state, followed by a period of mutual compromise. The Serbian church, however, was used as a tool of foreign policy to show the world that religious freedoms were not suppressed. This stance increased Croat fears of Serbianization and the loss of their ethnic identity. In 1990 Croats welcomed the collapse of the communist bloc, and they, along with their fellow Catholic Slovenians, were first to declare Croatia and Slovenia sovereign states (1991). But cutting the umbilical cord with Yugoslavia was not easy. Significant Serbian Orthodox minorities lived in Croatia and Slovenia, and with recent hatreds now revived, their extrication led to bloodshed and atrocities on both sides and hundreds of thousands of refugees. Slovenia, however, by joining the EU in 2003, seems now to have extricated itself from traditional Balkan ethnoreligious conflicts. The prospects of Croatia also seem good as she has signed a Stabilisation and Association Process (SAP) agreement with the EU, which means that she can join the union as soon as she meets the necessary socioeconomic criteria.

The situation in Bosnia proved even worse. According to the 1981 census the republic consisted of Muslims (39.5 percent), Serbs (32 percent), and Croats (18.4 percent) mixed and scattered throughout Bosnia. The actual number of Muslims is estimated at 2.5 million. In 1990 a Muslim-led coalition elected Alija Izetbegović its leader and was in favor of a loose confederation of sovereign states within former Yugoslavia. This angered the Serbs of Bosnia, who declared that they would create their own autonomous regions. It also angered the Croats and the government of Slobodan Milošević in Belgrade. A savage war broke out in the province in 1992 that lasted more than three years, cost hundreds of thousands of lives, and caused incalculable human suffering. In 1995 the Dayton-Paris peace agreement put an end to war by establishing the Federation of BiH and the Republika Srpska—a makeshift political structure—involving the participation of the Muslim, Serbian Orthodox, and Croat Catholic communities under United Nations (UN) supervision.

The situation in Serbia involved the military intervention of NATO in 1999 with the United States heading the operation. The objective was to punish the Serbian government for its military polices in the region and prevent ethnoreligious bloodshed and refugee fleeing from Kosovo, something that the bombardment of Serbia by NATO did not achieve. Since 2000, with Milošević gone, Serbia is struggling to reconstruct itself with international aid and negotiations to enter a SAP with the EU.

After the war, Kosovo is under NATO supervision with the peacekeeping force, KFOR. The Serbian Orthodox minority dwindled to about ninety thousand with the Albanian Muslim majority demanding an independent state. Montenegro also, with Orthodox majority, is pursuing independence and is likely to achieve it by the end of 2006.

In 1992 Macedonia declared its independence and was accepted by the UN as the Former Yugoslavian Republic of Macedonia (FYROM). It has a population of 2.2 million (Orthodox, 60 percent; Muslim, 40 percent). Ethnically, the Muslims are mostly of Albanian origin, and the Orthodox are mostly of Bulgarian origin. Greece refuses to recognize Macedonia under that name for historical and cultural reasons and because a major northern province of Greece is also called Macedonia. FYROM now has signed a SAP with the EU, but joining the union will depend on many factors.

The International Commission for the Balkans (ICB) has been actively working to resolve problems and the tensions within the new states of the former Yugoslavia. The reports of the commission recommend that the moving of the

Balkan states toward EU membership is the only way to prevent them from turning into the black hole of Europe.

Bulgaria

In 1878 the Treaty of Berlin established the Bulgarian state, but the Bulgarian Orthodox Church had already declared its independence from the ecumenical patriarchate in 1870 as a prelude to its nationalist aspirations. The patriarchate did not endorse this act and declared the church schismatic. Like the Serbian and the Greek churches, the Bulgarian church acquired an intensely ethnic character that has been used to promote nationalist interests in the various conflicts in the region. As in Greece, the Bulgarian monarchy was initially Catholic but later became Orthodox; unlike Greece, the church has not been closely tied to the state. The ecumenical patriarchate granted the church autocephalous status in 1945, just as it fell under a hostile communist regime. At first the party attempted to disrupt the church from within but later started using it as a tool for its nationalist policy and as a banner of the ethnic culture. Since the collapse of socialism in the country, the church has attempted to reorganize itself, and, without being involved in politics, it takes active part in the post-communist reconstruction. Political and economic developments, however, tend to create tensions in the church.

Apart from the Orthodox, who make up the great majority in Bulgaria, there exists a significant Muslim minority, who consider themselves Turks. In 1989, at the height of the conflict of the Muslim community with the (still Communist) government, 350,000 Muslims left for Turkey, most of them to return later, still uncertain about their economic prospects in Bulgaria. Bulgaria now has made considerable socioeconomic progress and will join the EU in 2007.

Romania

In the nineteenth century Romania was perhaps the richest and most cultured area in the Balkans, thanks to its Greek Phanariot (so called from the Greek quarter of Constantinople, from which many came) princes. But when the independent Romanian kingdom was established in 1862, King Charles Hohenzollern, a Catholic, expropriated most church property, closed down ecclesiastical presses, and declared the Romanian Orthodox Church independent. The ruling classes were secularized and kept the church low in status and despised. Formal recognition of its independence by the ecumenical patriarchate came in 1885. After the First World War the church was strengthened when Transylvania, with its substantial Orthodox population, was incorporated into the Romanian kingdom, making it the largest Orthodox Church after the Russian.

After the Second World War state policy toward the church, especially during Nicolae Ceausescu's regime, was contradictory. Religion was repudiated and the church was persecuted through expropriation of its lands and imprisonment of its clergy. Yet religion and the church (which has its clergy paid by the state) were used to support the special brand of Romanian nationalism the regime promoted. Since 1990 the Orthodox Church has become again one of the major cultural institutions in Romania, and much of Romania's friendship and cooperation with Serbia grows out of the common religious tradition of the two countries. There is, however, tension with the Catholic Hungarian minority (about 17 percent). Romania, although still struggling with socioeconomic problems, will join the EU in 2007.

Albania

The last of the Balkan states to be liberated from the Turks (1920), Albania has a population of 3.2 million, of which the majority (about 65 percent) are Muslims and the rest are Orthodox (22 percent) and Catholic (13 percent). Even before independence the nationalists promoted establishment of an independent Orthodox Church, which the patriarchate recognized in 1937. The communist regime of Enver Hoxha (1945–1985) proved the most antireligious of all Marxist-Leninist states. After 1951 there was total suppression of religious freedom. A decree (4337 13.11.1967) formally declared Albania the first Marxist-atheist state. All ecclesiastical schools were closed, along with 2,169 religious establishments. Violation of religious and human rights continued in the 1980s, bringing severe protests from Greece and from many European states. After Hoxha's death the penal code was modified, and in 1991 the new democratic government in its constitution (Articles 7 and 45) restored religious and political freedoms.

The Orthodox Church was reestablished (1991) with Anastasios Gianoulatos, a professor from the Theological Faculty of Athens, appointed as archbishop by the ecumenical patriarchate. The majority of the Orthodox are ethnically Greek and live in Southern Albania (Northern Epirus), which was Greek territory for a while before 1921. The Orthodox Church has contributed significantly to the general social reconstruction of the country and has promoted intercultural and interfaith life in an exemplary manner. Catholics also have reconstituted their religious organization with a papal nuncio and four bishops, and Muslims have been opening mosques increasingly.

Greece

Greece differs from the rest of the Balkan states not only in its language, history, and culture but also in its relatively advanced economy and membership in the European Union. The great majority (95 percent) of the country's population (about 11 million) are Orthodox. The rest are Catholics, Muslims, Jews, Jehovah's Witnesses, and members of various Protestant denominations and sects.

After its war of independence in the 1820s, Greece was a small state. It was first a republic under President Ioánnis Kapodistrias (1827–1831) and then a monarchy from 1833 to 1862 under the young Bavarian prince Otto of Wittelsbach, who became King Otto I, a Catholic. The head of his Bavarian regency council—Otto was only seventeen years old at his accession—was a Protestant. The Bavarian administration attempted to modernize society without considering Orthodox religious culture. It declared the Greek church independent from the ecumenical patriarchate, made it subservient to the state, and closed more than four hundred monasteries, expropriating their lands. In 1852 the patriarchate recognized the church as autocephalous. By then Greek nationalism and Orthodoxy had combined to form the "great idea," a romantic vision of reestablishing modern Greece within its pre-Ottoman occupation boundaries. That dream ended on September 9, 1922, in what has come to be known in Greece as "the Asia Minor catastrophe." On that date—perhaps the most significant in twentieth-century Greece—the Turkish troops of Mustafa Kemal (later known as Atatürk) routed Greek forces at Smyrna. More than one million Greeks fled to Greece from Asia Minor before the January 1923 refugee convention allowed the exchange of Christian and Muslim populations between Greece and Turkey.

Orthodoxy continued to be the dominant religion, and the Orthodox Church, always tied to the state, continued to exercise an indirect cultural hegemony over Greek society. Church and religion followed the patterns of the turbulent political history of the country. Throughout the twentieth century, not a single archbishop was elected according to normal canonical procedures, and several times the synod of the hierarchy—the highest governing body of the Church of Greece, which is presided over by the archbishop of Athens and all Greece and includes all diocesan bishops— was abolished and reinstated by the state.

After the Second World War and the civil war that followed in Greece, the church was involved even more in political developments. During a military dictatorship that lasted from 1967 to 1974, the ruling junta used the church and religion to support and legitimize its own special brand of Greek-Christian civilization. Since the return to civilian rule in 1975, there has been periodic tension between church and state. Although the constitutional subjugation of church to state has not changed, there has been a gradual disengagement of religion from politics. However, Greek nationalism and Orthodoxy are still significantly linked.

Since the mid-1990s the government has been pursuing modernization policies that often clashed with the church. One such policy has been the removal of religious affiliation from civilian identity cards. Also as Greek society becomes more pluralistic, with about one million immigrants entering the country since the early 1990s, church and state relations are due for revision.

See also *Globalization; Orthodoxy, Greek; Religious Organization; State Churches; Yugoslavia.*

Nikos Kokosalakis

BIBLIOGRAPHY

Critic, Christopher. *Remaking the Balkans.* London: Royal Institute of International Affairs, Pincer Publishers, 1991.

Huntington, Samuel P. "The Clash of Civilizations?" *Foreign Affairs* (September–October 1993).

Kavalski, Emilian. "The Western Balkans and the EU: The Probable Dream of Membership." *South East European Review* 1–2 (2003).

Jelavich, Charles. *The Establishment of the Balkan National States, 1804–1920.* Seattle and London: University of Washington Press, 1977.

Poulton, Hugh. *The Balkans: Minorities and States in Conflict.* London: Minorities Rights Group, 1991.

Ramet, Pedro, ed. *Eastern Christianity and Politics in the Twentieth Century.* Durham, N.C.: Duke University Press, 1988.

Wolf, Robert Lee. *The Balkans in Our Time.* Cambridge: Harvard University Press, 1956.

Bangladesh

See *Pakistan.*

Banna, Hasan al-

Egyptian teacher, Islamic reformer, and founder of the Muslim Brethren. Hasan al-Banna (1906–1949) was the son of a teacher and *imam* (leader in prayer) at a mosque near Alexandria. Banna attended Qurʾanic school briefly and joined a mystical Sufi order, but he took his formal schooling in government primary and teacher-training schools and at Dar al-Ulum, a college in Cairo. The mix of religious and modern subjects at Dar al-Ulum, from which he graduated in 1927, prepared him for teaching. A post as a primary teacher in Ismailiyya marked the beginning of a nineteen-year career with the Ministry of Education.

In 1928 Banna founded the Society of Muslim Brethren *(al-Ikhwan al-Muslimin),* to oppose secularization and promote a return to the ideals of early Islam as found in the Qurʾan. Inspired by the teachings of Jamal al-Din al-Afghani, Muhammad Abduh, and Muhammad Rashid Rida, Banna emphasized piety, education, and religious charity, while denouncing Christian missionaries, the West as morally bankruptcy, Egyptians who aped Western ways, and Egypt's British occupiers. (Britain occupied Egypt in 1882 and continued to substantially control Egyptian affairs, even after declaring the country nominally independent in 1922.) Ismailiyya's location in the Suez Canal Zone, where resentment of the foreign-owned Suez Canal Company and British occupation troops was strong, facilitated recruiting for the Brethren.

When Banna obtained a teaching post in Cairo in 1932, he moved the Brethren's headquarters there. He set up branches throughout Egypt and later also established them in neighboring countries. He insisted that the Muslim Brethren was not a political party, but the economic hardships of the Great Depression of the 1930s, the Zionist challenge of Jewish settlers in Palestine, and Britain's repression of Egyptian nationalists during World War II inexorably drew him into politics. By 1949 Banna had created a mass organization that challenged the status quo from outside the parliamentary and constitutional system. Despairing of peaceful, legal change, the Brethren's underground "secret apparatus" planned some of the assassinations and bombings that struck Egypt in the late 1940s. Banna approved of *jihad,* or struggle, against the British, but his writings did not preach terrorist violence. The degree of his responsibility for terrorist attacks remains elusive.

When the Egyptian government armed volunteers to fight against the new Jewish state in Palestine in 1948, the Muslim Brethren secretly stockpiled arms for use at home. Egypt's defeat by Israel called the regime's legitimacy into question. When Cairo's chief of police was killed in a student riot in December 1948, Prime Minister Mahmud Fahmi Nuqrashi banned the Brethren on charges of conspiring against the government. He arrested most of its leaders and was then assassinated by a student member of the Brethren. Banna denounced Nuqrashi's killing and denied any conspiracy, but his sloganeering continued to challenge the regime: "The Qurʾan is our constitution" and "No other constitution but the Qurʾan and Muhammad is our model." Realizing that the government's failure to arrest him meant that his life was in danger, Banna tried desperately to rein in the secret apparatus. On February 12, 1949, the political police shot him dead. His killers were convicted in 1954, but the nearly certain culpability of higher officials went unproved.

After experiencing torture and the death of comrades in jail under President Gamal Abdel Nasser, surviving leaders of the Brethren renounced violence in pursuit of their cause. Alternately tolerated and repressed, and still not formally legal, the Muslim Brethren today remain a mass movement that carries on Banna's work in Egypt and in other Arab countries. Extremist offshoots have embraced terrorist tactics and denounced the mainstream movement for selling out its principles.

See also *ʿAbduh, Muhammad; al-Afghani, Jamal al-Din; Fundamentalism; Islam; Islam's Encounters with the West; Jihad; Nasser, Gamal Abdel; Qutb, Sayyid.*

Donald Malcolm Reid

BIBLIOGRAPHY

Abu-Rabiʾ, Ibrahim M. *Intellectual Origins of Islamic Resurgence in the Modern Arab World.* Albany: State University of New York Press, 1996.

Carré, Olivier. "Banna, Hasan al-." In *The Oxford Encyclopedia of the Modern Islamic World.* Oxford: Oxford University Press, 1995, 1:195–199.

Carré, Olivier, and Gérard Michaud. *Les Frères Musulmans, Egypt et Syrie, 1928–1982.* Paris: Gallimard, 1983.

Mitchell, Richard P. *The Society of the Muslim Brothers.* London: Oxford University Press, 1969.

Baptists

Baptists are evangelical Christians who trace their roots to England but enjoy their strongest current following in the American South. Born in the seventeenth century out of differences with mainline Protestants on several theological issues, Baptists have since gained converts around the world through their aggressive missionary work. Traditionally, Baptists have believed in a strict separation of church and state and emphasize an independent, personal approach to faith based on biblical scripture. Local Baptist congregations are democratic in polity, operate autonomously, and are not governed by hierarchies, synods, or bishops. Individual Baptist denominations cover the spectrum of theological and political Protestantism from left to middle to right, from mainline to evangelical to fundamentalist, though most adherents are evangelical and conservative.

Baptists got their name from their belief that baptism should be by immersion and for professing believers only. Only adults and children mature enough to make a public profession of faith in Christ are baptized. The usual method of Baptist baptism is a minister's plunging of a believer completely under water ("buried with Christ") and then returning that person to the standing position ("risen with Christ to walk in a newness of life"). These immersion-style baptisms are usually performed in indoor facilities built into Baptist churches for this purpose, but Baptists have been known to baptize in lakes, rivers, and even portable baptisteries on a battlefield.

Even given their separationist views, from the beginning of American history Baptists have influenced politics and government. In the seventeenth century, with their fierce opposition to church entanglement with matters of state, Baptists helped to change the way religion and government would interact, and a "wall of separation" appeared. But for a time in the 1990s, the Baptist political roll call of American government included all four top-ranking national officers: President Bill Clinton, Vice President Al Gore, House Speaker Newt Gingrich, and Senate president pro tempore Strom Thurmond. African American Baptist political figures have been influential as well. These include the Rev. Dr. Martin Luther King Jr., Rep. Adam Clayton Powell Jr. (D-N.Y., 1945–1967, 1969–1971), Rep. John Conyers Jr. (D-Mich., 1965–), Rep. John Lewis (D-Ga., 1987–), Rep. William H. Gray III (D-Pa., 1979–1991), Del. Walter E. Fauntroy (D-D.C., 1971–1991), Rep. Barbara Jordan (D-Texas, 1973–1979), Rep. J. C. Watts (R-Okla., 1995–2003), and Rep. Kweisi Mfume (D-Md., 1987–1996, and president, National Association for the Advancement of Colored People [NAACP], 1996–2004).

European Heritage, American Growth

The Baptist faith traces its history to 1609, when an English Nonconformist minister, John Smyth (not Captain John Smith, who was associated with Pocahontas), rejected infant baptism most dramatically by rebaptizing himself and several adult followers. Preaching in Amsterdam at the time, Smyth had fled England when Anglican (Church of England) authorities found his ideas heretical and led a crackdown. By the time Thomas Helwys succeeded Smyth in 1611, the group felt safe to return to England, but Helwys was in prison there within a year. Soon, however, the Act of Toleration of 1689 opened up new religious choices to the English people, and Baptists thrived. By the middle of the seventeenth century, Baptists enjoyed such strength that in true Baptist fashion rival Baptist denominations formed, each with its unique brand of faith.

Baptists had their roots in the Old World, but it is in America that they have flourished. When Roger Williams, a Cambridge-educated Nonconformist clergyman, immigrated to the Massachusetts Bay colony from England in 1631, he refused an invitation to pastor a Boston church because it had not broken its link to the Church of England. To Anglicans, Williams was a "dissenter." He believed in the concept of separation of church and state and resisted a state church, like the Anglican Church, funded by government tax collections. Williams was so controversial in Anglican-Puritan Massachusetts that he was banished from that colony in 1635. Fleeing to what later became Rhode Island, he had baptized several believers within a year and established, in Providence, what is considered the first Baptist church in America. Williams later left the church he established but remained in public life, becoming president of the Rhode Island Colony in 1654.

The Baptists in what Anglicans called "Rogues Island" were evangelical, however, and spread their faith throughout Britain's American colonies. More stable Baptist congregations were soon established in Newport, Rhode Island, and in Philadelphia, Pennsylvania. In 1707 the Philadelphia Association of Baptist Churches was organized, linking Baptists throughout the colonies. A southern association was founded in 1751 in Charleston, South Carolina, to establish a fellowship for the growing number of Baptists in the South. (The First Baptist Church of Charleston had been established in 1696.) In 1814 a national organization, the General Missionary Convention of the Baptist Denomination in the United States of America for Foreign Missions, was established. Because it met every three years, it was soon known unofficially by the shorter name Triennial Convention.

Some scholars of religion still call the Baptist faith "the American religion," a faith that is to religion what Coca-Cola is to beverages: a phenomenon created by and for Americans and exported to the world.

Missionary Work

Baptists in America began ambitious world missionary efforts even before they were well established at home. An Englishman, William Carey, went to India in 1792 as the first Baptist missionary, but he was soon followed in 1812 in Burma by three Americans: Ann Hasseltine Judson, Adoniram Judson, and Luther Rice. In 1846 American missions expanded to Africa with the appointment of black Baptists John Day and A. L. Jones, who began service in Sierra Leone and Liberia. Two years later Thomas J. Bowen, a white Baptist from Georgia, went to Nigeria with African Americans Robert F. Hill and Harvey Goodale. Already active in Baptist work, African Americans, by the end of the century, would have their own denomination and two mission boards, the National Baptist Convention and the Lott Carey Baptist Foreign Mission Convention. (The latter was named in honor of an African American Baptist from Richmond, Virginia, who founded the first African Baptist missions society in 1815.)

With the creation of the Baptist World Alliance, in 1905, Baptist missions became more coordinated. For example, Northern Baptists directed Baptist work in northern and central Europe, while Southern Baptists looked to southern and later to eastern Europe. Conferences in London, England, in 1920 and 1948 assisted with this coordination. After World War II, European Baptists affiliated with the alliance began to send missionaries as well as receive them; more than six hundred were serving at the end of the twentieth century.

North and South

When delegates south of the Mason-Dixon Line (a line drawn between Pennsylvania and Maryland separating North and South) broke from the Triennial Convention in 1845 over the issue of slavery and other disputes, there were almost ten thousand Baptist churches nationwide, up from ten in 1700. Southerners called themselves the Southern Baptist Convention, and Northerners became the American Baptist Missionary Union. In 1907 the northern group became the Northern Baptist Convention before reverting to the American Baptist Convention in 1950 and finally, in 1972, the American Baptist Churches U.S.A.

For decades, the two denominations grew in their respective regions, with the northern group taking a looser, voluntary approach and the southerners becoming more and more denominational in their organization. After the Civil War (1861–1865), Southern Baptists struggled with the war's legacy of poverty, leaning on the border states and Texas to fund their work. (Southerners and Southern Baptists would not fully recover economically from the Civil War until after World War II ended in 1945.) But just as the founding of the new democratic nation afforded the evangelical democratic Baptists fertile ground for planting churches (it was the largest denomination in the country by 1800), the growth of the Sunbelt states in the twentieth century made the Southern Baptist Convention (SBC) the country's largest Protestant denomination (at fourteen million members by the 1990s). This phenomenal size led Martin Marty, a scholar of religion, to jest that "in the South, there are more Baptists than people."

The "American Religion"

For Baptists, rapid growth in America is no mere coincidence, however. Certain elements had to be in place for this faith to take root. The founding of the United States in the eighteenth century came from several notions about how government should be run. These included the belief that all men are created equal (Declaration of Independence, 1776), that there is a social contract in government that protects the liberty of the people (Declaration), that the church and the state must be kept separate (First Amendment to the Constitution, 1791), that the preponderance of power should be at the local level (Tenth Amendment to the Constitution, 1791), and that the economic system should be based on the idea of capitalist free enterprise.

These are Baptist ideas as well. The keystones to the Baptist faith as it touches politics are "the priesthood of all believers," which makes forgiveness of sin a personal matter; "soul liberty," which makes scriptural interpretation a matter between the individual soul and the Holy Spirit; and a localistic view, which makes Baptist congregations the most independent of any organized denomination. Local Baptist churches buy land, build buildings, call ministers, adopt budgets, and accept or reject members, all with little supervision from the national organization. That is why it is improper in most cases to refer to the national organization as "the Baptist Church" as one might the Roman Catholic Church or the Episcopal Church. A person may be a Baptist but not a member of "the Baptist Church," unless the reference is to a single, local congregation. As for capitalism, Baptists have few rivals in fund raising among their members and in attracting new "customers" through an aggressive entrepreneurial approach. Many congregations borrow marketing techniques from free enterprise to build "seeker-friendly megachurches" the size of shopping malls.

The Baptists also grew because of their evangelical nature. Baptists have few rivals in their eagerness to spread the Gospel message and gain converts. In the individualistic, entrepreneurial American culture, Baptists found fertile ground in the marketplace of ideas. Free enterprise promoted an up-front, no-holds-barred willingness to "sell" like nowhere else on the globe. The Baptists seized on this with vigor, using the openness to new ideas to build the largest communion in the country. Like siblings in a family, the Baptist denomination grew along with the United States. Evangelicalism is so closely identified with Baptists that, unlike among the Lutherans or Methodists or Presbyterians, there is no Evangelical Baptist Church denomination of any significance. Such a name would be redundant.

An old joke among Baptists is that "we multiply by division," and it is difficult to name the many different "flavors" of Baptists in America. There are at least a couple of ways to group Baptists, however. The easier is by denomination. But there are certain characteristics that cut across denominations. In general, Baptists are either "regular" (or "Charleston tradition" after the South Carolina city where this tradition was best known) or "pietistic" (or "Sandy Creek tradition" after Sandy Creek, North Carolina, where it was popular). In general, the regular Baptists were of a city-oriented, Calvinistic, High Church tradition, and the pietistic Baptists were more rural, evangelistic, and Low Church in their worship. In their long history, Baptists have also been labeled General Baptist and Particular Baptist, following a demarcation similar to regular and pietistic. As for denominations, there are Progressive Baptists, National Baptists, Southern Baptists, independent Baptists, Free Will Baptists, Primitive Baptists, American Baptists, Reformed Baptists, Conservative Baptists, North American Baptists, and even Pedo-Baptists.

Baptist Politics

The type of Baptist faith one chooses has political implications. Former Democratic presidential candidate Rev. Jesse Jackson, Christian Coalition founder Pat Robertson, Moral Majority co-founder Jerry Falwell, and presidential spiritual adviser Billy Graham have all identified themselves as Baptists at one time. Jackson helped infuse the Democratic Party with a host of African American civil rights activists. Robertson and Falwell brought conservative Christians into the Republican Party. Graham has served as informal spiritual counselor to a half-dozen U.S. presidents of both parties.

African American Baptists have been associated with the Democratic Party since the 1932 election, when Franklin D. Roosevelt was first elected president. But before that, the party of Abraham Lincoln, the Republican Party, enjoyed almost universal support from the black Baptist community. In all cases, however, the local Baptist church has been a central meeting ground for black political activism. Candidates in local or national Democratic primaries often attend black churches to promote their campaigns, and civil rights leaders in need of support for their legal and political work tap into church fund-raising networks.

Civil rights organizational leadership (NAACP, Urban League, Southern Christian Leadership Conference) and black Baptist leadership have overlapped at times also. A number of African American political leaders have been Baptist leaders. Martin Luther King Jr. first attracted the attention of the nation as pastor of the Dexter Avenue Baptist Church in Montgomery, Alabama, in 1954. He later became co-pastor of his father's Atlanta church in 1960. King Jr. and King Sr. were Baptist leaders, as was Adam Clayton Powell Jr., a prominent black clergyman and politician. The National Baptist Convention USA (NBCUSA), the largest African American Baptist group, was formed with the merger of three smaller denominations in 1895. It has roughly 8.5 million members and thirty-three thousand churches. Other African American Baptist groups include the National Missionary Baptist Convention of America (NMBCA, 1880), the National Baptist Convention of America (NBCA, 1915), and the Progressive National Baptist Convention (PNBC, 1961). The PNBC is particularly aggressive in promoting social justice through political activity. The four groups held a historic joint meeting in Nashville in 2005 to work for common goals and share fellowship.

Independent Baptists are as Republican as African American Baptists are Democratic. Independent Baptists are fundamentalist Baptists who either seceded from major national Baptist groups or have chosen not to align themselves with major denominations whose practices and belief they consider too liberal. Most associate themselves informally with other independents as part of a fellowship, however. During the last decade of the twentieth century, the most well-known independent Baptist was Jerry Falwell. Falwell's Thomas Road Baptist Church in Lynchburg, Virginia, was for decades a part of a loose association of independent Baptists called the Baptist Bible Fellowship International (BBFI). This group was founded in 1950 and by the beginning of the twenty-first century had more than 1.4 million members. Falwell mobilized the independent Baptists and other conservative Christians in the early 1980s as a part of the Moral Majority, the first real attempt to organize conservative Christians politically. The Christian Right in its infancy focused on the issues that kindled its founding: banning abortion, restoring school prayer, and electing Ronald Reagan president. (Falwell has since moved his congregation into the Southern Baptist Convention citing his new level of comfort with the SBC in the wake of its conservative resurgence.)

The even more fundamentalist Bob Jones University (BJU), though Methodist in origin, is mostly Independent Baptist as well. Many of the churches in the fifty-state network that supply Bob Jones with students belong to the Fundamental Baptist Fellowship or similar groups, and most of the university's ministerial graduates become Independent Baptist preachers and evangelists. Bob Jones University graduates, faculty, and staff are very politically minded. The school all but controls local Republican politics in its hometown (Greenville, South Carolina) and regularly hosts leading national conservative politicians in chapel. (Then-candidate George W. Bush was chastised by his political opponents for his appearance at BJU when material opposing Roman Catholic doctrine was discovered on the university website.) Many fundamentalists associated with Bob Jones have been active Republicans since Barry Goldwater's presidential campaign in 1964; others were energized by Reagan's social agenda in 1976 and 1980. Bob Jones University has a great deal of national political influence through its many graduates, but unlike the Moral Majority in its heyday, BJU is not a political mobilizer or part of any movement per se.

Southern Baptists, at just under sixteen million members, hold several numerical distinctions: the largest Protestant denomination in North America, the North American denomination with the most churches, and the largest Baptist organization in the world.

When the SBC shifted from moderate to conservative control in 1979, grassroots political organizing and secular political issues played a key role, and politics has influenced Convention life ever since. Part of this campaign atmosphere is built in, given that the SBC elects a president at a convention. The Convention meeting and the Convention organization (which carry the same name) seem by their nature to play to political type issues and political intrigue. In the first decade of conservative control (1979–1990), powerless moderates unwilling to admit defeat complained from the convention floor of the uniform hard line the Convention began to take on the inerrancy of the Bible, women in ministry, and doctrinal control of Convention colleges and seminaries. Centrists cited political concerns as well, opposing the new leadership's call for returning prayer to public schools as a violation of the historic Baptist demand for separation of church and state.

The second decade of conservative leadership led to the founding of rival organizations. The Cooperative Baptist Fellowship (CBF) and to some extent the Alliance of Baptists have since served as way stations on the road to a new denomination for moderate Baptists of varying levels of disgruntlement. Former president Jimmy Carter officially cut his ties to the SBC in 2000 and aligned himself with the CBF. This has trickled down to the state level as well. Texas and Virginia now have rival Convention organizations.

With wide popular support in a third decade of leadership, fundamentalists in the SBC enjoy a free hand to work for theological purity in Convention agencies and doctrinal statements, aggressive evangelistic programs, and a socially conservative political agenda. Theological issues finding their way onto the national radar screen have included the addition of a paragraph in *The Baptist Faith & Message* (BFM) that called on women to "submit graciously" to the leadership of their husbands, a reassertion of the belief in the pastorate as an institution for males only, a call for missionaries to adhere to BFM, and withdrawal of support for the Baptist World Alliance (a global organization of 211 Baptist groups). Evangelistic efforts gaining wide political attention have included efforts to convert Mormons, homosexuals, Jews, and Muslims.

Much of the political muscle of the SBC is exerted through the Ethics and Religious Liberty Commission in Washington, D.C., headed by Dr. Richard Land. The Oxford-educated, larger-than-life Texan has made the Convention a huge player in national politics, maintaining a close relationship with other evangelical leaders and leaders of the Republican Party at the highest levels. Under the leadership of Land and others, the SBC forged alliances with theologically conservative African Americans and politically conservative Catholics in the late 1990s. No strangers to the culture war, Southern Baptists initiated a boycott of the Walt Disney Company in 1997 over its gay-friendly theme parks and personnel policies and its less-than-family-friendly Miramax film unit. But with the departure of Michael Eisner as chief executive officer, the divestiture of Miramax, and the release of films such as *The Chronicles of Narnia,* the SBC called off the boycott. Financially, with the exception of some retrenchment at the North American Mission Board, the Convention has remained on solid footing. Its Lifeway Christian Bookstore chain and Broadman and Holman publishers unit seized the opportunity represented by the multi-million-dollar Christian media market, with bestsellers that include Beth Moore Bible studies for women and Southern Baptist Pastor Rick Warren's *The Purpose Driven Life.* A 2005 proposal to change the name from Southern Baptist to North American Baptist Convention was rejected.

Other white Baptist groups include Conservative Baptists, the General Association of Regular Baptist Churches (GARBC), Primitive Baptists, Free Will Baptists, Seventh Day Baptists, and various Reformed Baptist entities. These groups differ in some respects from one another and from Southern and Independent Baptists, but as a whole represent a large portion of "the Republican Party at prayer."

American Baptists (American Baptist Churches USA), the old Northern Baptist Convention, which numbers 1.5 million people (fifty-eight hundred congregations), tend to be less political than Southern Baptists. From the beginning, the denomination was much less willing to create a denominational structure than were its brothers and sisters to the south. Many members of the Cooperative Baptist Fellowship and the Alliance of Baptists, both of which came out of the moderate wing of the Southern Baptists, have sought to forge ties with the American Baptist Churches. American Baptists claim Dr. Martin Luther King Jr. as well.

Counting Baptists can be difficult. But to sort out the relative strength of Baptist groups, a good rule of thumb is to remember that about half of the nation's Baptists are Southern Baptist (sixteen million) and half of African American Christians are members of Baptist churches (thirteen million).

Harvesting New Fields

Worldwide, there are approximately thirty-five million Baptists. Much of this strength is accounted for in the relatively recent expansion of Baptists into Europe. One Baptist historian reported that at the time of the Battle of Waterloo (1815) there was no Baptist church on the Continent, but by the end of World War I (1918) there were between one million and two million European and Asian Baptists. Areas cited as particularly fruitful for the Baptist harvest during that period were Russia (which had "the largest Baptist community in Europe" at the time of the 1918 revolution) along with Germany, Sweden, Romania, Latvia, Estonia, Poland, and Hungary.

Eastern-bloc Baptists struggled under communism, the most notable Baptist dissident being Georgi Vins, general secretary of the Council of Evangelical Christian-Baptist Churches in the Soviet Union. Vins was a political prisoner in Siberia from 1974 until 1979, when U.S. president Jimmy Carter, himself a Baptist, negotiated Vins's release and with great drama attended a Baptist church with him in Washington several days later.

Communist regimes were unpredictable in their attitudes toward Baptists and acted inconsistently from country to country. Because Baptists were thought to undermine the hold of the Russian Orthodox Church, the Soviet Union was somewhat friendly to Baptists at the country's beginning, in 1918, but the regimes of Joseph Stalin and Nikita Khrushchev restricted religious exercise severely. With the collapse of the Soviet Union in 1991, Baptists expanded in eastern Europe and Asia but struggled in the new millennium with resistance from Orthodox Church authorities and a revival of interest in the mother church with more religious freedom of choice.

In its new frontiers, as in seventeenth-century England and America, Baptists are expanding their version of "simple democratic Christianity." With a worldwide missionary force supported by more than fifty Baptist mission agencies in the United States alone, Baptists have begun the twenty-first century with renewed hope, faith, and resources.

See also *African American Experience; Calvinism; Civil Rights Movement; Evangelicalism; Fundamentalism; Graham, Billy; King, Martin Luther, Jr.; Russia.*

Oran P. Smith

BIBLIOGRAPHY

Ammerman, Nancy Tatom. *Baptist Battles: Social Change and Religious Conflict in the Southern Baptist Convention.* New Brunswick, N.J.: Rutgers University Press, 1990.

Baker, Robert A. *The Southern Baptist Convention and Its People, 1607–1972.* Nashville, Tenn.: Broadman Press, 1974.

Estep, William R. *Whole Gospel, Whole World: The Southern Baptist Foreign Mission Board, 1845–1995.* Nashville, Tenn.: Broadman and Holman, 1994.

Hankins, Barry. *Religion and American Culture.* Tuscaloosa and London: University of Alabama Press, 2002.

Hill, Samuel S., ed. *The Encyclopedia of Southern Culture.* Chapel Hill: University of North Carolina Press, 2006.

Lincoln, C. E., and L. Mayima. *The Black Church in the African-American Experience.* Durham, N.C.: Duke University Press, 1990.

Martin, Sandy D. *Black Baptists and African Missions: The Origin of a Movement, 1880–1915.* Macon, Ga.: Mercer University Press, 1989.

McBeth, H. Leon. *A Sourcebook for Baptist Heritage.* Nashville, Tenn.: Broadman, 1990.

Montgomery, William E. *Under Their Own Vine and Fig Tree: The African-American Church in the South.* Baton Rouge: Louisiana State University Press, 1994.

Shurden, Walter B. *The Baptist Identity: Four Fragile Freedoms.* Macon, Ga.: Smyth and Helwys, 1993.

Smith, Oran P. *The Rise of Baptist Republicanism.* New York and London: New York University Press, 1997.

Smith, R. Drew, ed. *Long March Ahead: African American Churches and Public Policy in Post–Civil Rights America.* Durham, N.C.: Duke University Press, 2005.

Barth, Karl

Swiss-German theologian in the Reformed Church tradition and one of the most significant Protestant thinkers of the twentieth century. Barth (1886–1968) studied at universities in Switzerland and Germany. After a period of ministry in neutral Switzerland during World War I, he became a professor of theology at Göttingen and Bonn, in Germany, where he was an early opponent of the Nazi regime. After Barth refused to take an oath of allegiance to the führer, Germany expelled him in 1935. He spent most of the remainder of his career at Basel, in Switzerland. Barth's political thought was theologically driven and contextually related to the time. It was also frequently controversial.

Karl Barth.

Early Work

In his student days in Marburg, Barth had followed the path of nineteenth-century liberal rationalism. This phase came to an abrupt end in 1914, with the outbreak of World War I, when ninety-three German intellectuals issued a manifesto endorsing the war policy of the German kaiser, Wilhelm II. For Barth, the presence of the names of his most respected theological teachers on this list represented a catastrophic ethical failure. Their action ignited his theological creativity, and throughout the war he engaged in a quest for the basic meaning of Christianity and became a radical critic of liberal theology's accommodation to modern society. Becoming a Christian socialist, Barth regarded the European conflict as an imperialist struggle between the elites of rival capitalist nations that was contrary to the interests of the working classes. As a preacher and well-known local political activist, he rediscovered the theology of St. Paul, the early Christian interpreter of Jesus' life and work, exploring Paul's writings through preaching and testing his ideas in daily correspondence with his life-long friend Eduard Thurneysen.

In 1919 Barth published the *Römerbrief,* a renowned theological commentary on Paul's Epistle to the Romans. Later that year at the Tambach conference of Christian socialists, he presented the lecture "The Christian in Society," arguing that the Gospel and Jesus' teachings should take precedence in society. In 1922 he rewrote the *Römerbrief* in more radical terms. The second *Römerbrief* is one of the most important theological texts of the twentieth century. The political consequences of his theology, known as dialectical theology, amounted to a paradox: insofar as it succeeded in focusing the rhetorical power and charismatic energy sufficient to launch a new theological movement within Protestant Christianity, to that extent it distanced Christian theory and practice from the mediation and compromise that attend politics understood as the "art of the possible." Barth later moved away from dialectical theology.

The major crisis of Barth's life occurred after the German general election of March 1933, when Adolf Hitler's National Socialists extended their control to the church and to the teaching of theology. As a professor at Göttingen and Bonn, Barth resisted this process, claiming the absolute autonomy of the God and Gospel of the Bible. In stiffening theological resistance to Nazism in the church, and above all through his role in formulating the Barmen Declaration of May 1934, Barth saw himself as acting politically. The Barmen Declaration was the foundation of the "Confessing Church," which declared itself to be the evangelical church in Germany in contrast to the established German church that accommodated the Nazi regime. Simply to undertake the task of theology under such conditions "as though nothing had happened" (as he maintained in June 1933) was simultaneously to enact a political act and to follow a theological vocation. Barth's contribution to the resistance of the Confessing Church to Hitler may nonetheless be regarded as the political high point of his life.

Later Work and Influence

With the end of World War II in 1945, Barth again applied his political theology, this time under the more ambiguous circumstances of the communist revolutions across Eastern Europe. Jan Hromadka, a Czech Reformed theologian, attempted with Barth's support to equate Christian and socialist commitments. For Hromadka, this advocacy was to have tragic personal consequences, for Marxism was to show as little mercy for free thinking as had Nazism. Barth's apparent ambivalence toward Marxist socialism, as contrasted with his outright opposition to National Socialism, attracted much criticism.

The interpretation of Barth's work has always been controversial. Ernst Bloch, a German Marxist philosopher, for example, maintained in 1923 that Barth propounded a bourgeois theology that had negative implications for emancipatory politics, whereas Friedrich-Wilhelm Marquardt has argued that Barth's theology explores and enacts a revolutionary revealed God. By contrast, R. W. Ward, an English historian of religious socialism, represented Barth as a man solely concerned with abstract theological issues and out of touch with real politics. He regarded Barth as a poseur whose interventions were little more than an inflated pseudo-political discourse that masked a relentless theological drive toward self-maximization and dominance.

Barth's politics were always subordinated to theological concerns. The relative success or failure of the former was more the product of contingent interaction with changing historical contexts than the conscious result of the discrimination and adjustments that might be characteristic of the genuinely politically minded.

See also *Communism; Fascism; Germany; Marxism.*

Richard H. Roberts

BIBLIOGRAPHY

Barth, Karl. *The Epistle to the Romans.* (English translation of *Der Römerbrief.*) Translated by Edwyn C. Hoskyns. Oxford: Oxford University Press, 1933.
———. *The Word of God and the Word of Man.* Translated by Douglas Horton. Boston: Pilgrim Press, 1928.
Busch, Eberhard. *Karl Barth: His Life from Letters and Autobiographical Texts.* Translated by John Bowden. London: SCM Press, 1976.
Hunsinger, George A. *Karl Barth and Radical Politics.* Philadelphia: Westminster, 1976.
Marquardt, Friedrich-Wilhelm. *Theologie und Sozialismus: Das Beispiel Karl Barths.* Munich: Kaiser Verlag, 1972.
Roberts, Richard H. *A Theology on Its Way? Essays on Karl Barth.* Edinburgh: T. and T. Clark, 1991.

Base Communities

Base communities, a form of association that began emerging in Roman Catholicism in Latin America in the late 1960s, originally rose in response to clergy shortages. The goal had been to provide small-scale, familiar, and accessible environments in which people could meet for reflection and common action without the presence of clergy. The creation of base communities is best understood in relation to the emergence and overall effect of liberation theology in Latin America during this period. The two are linked historically, related as theory is to practice. Base communities formed in a pattern of simultaneous creation—there was no "first" base community—as activists inspired by liberation theology began to "go to the people," identifying with their struggles for freedom and economic justice and creating new organizations, base communities among them.

The full name of this phenomenon is "base ecclesial community" (in Spanish, *comunidad eclesial de base*). A common working definition takes off from the meaning of these three words: striving for *community* (small and homogeneous); stressing the *ecclesial* (links to the church); and constituting a *base* (either the faithful at the base of the church's hierarchy or the poor at the base of a class-and-power pyramid). Whatever else they may be, most base communities are small groups of ten to thirty people homogeneous in social composition, most commonly poor and female. Whatever else they may do, they gather regularly (once every week or two) to read and comment on the Bible, to discuss common concerns, and occasionally to act together toward some concrete end. Reading and commenting on the Bible in a community setting soon became the common foundation of group activities. Stress on participation and equal access to sacred knowledge, through the Bible, reinforces ideas of egalitarianism and action in common as the outgrowth of a transformed religious faith.

A New Autonomy

The newness of base communities is found above all in the model of governance created and the degree of autonomy claimed within the church. Governance was conceived in an egalitarian and participatory way. Breaking with traditional Catholic trickle-down models—in which the bishop knows more than the priest, the priest knows more than the sisters, the sisters know more than the laity, and so on down to the bottom—base communities and similar groups with different names underscored equal access to knowledge (through the Bible) and equal participation in managing group affairs. Relative autonomy left groups free, at least in principle, to seek alliances with others, rather than checking everything with clerical advisers.

The working model of community put into practice gave place of preference to ideals of active and informed participation, with religious practice structured around small, self-governing groups able to operate without clerical supervision. Learning from experience in familiar settings where all participate as equals lays the groundwork for new models of governance in everyday practice. The value placed on participation in the day-to-day routine of base communities spills over to a general insistence that participation is good in itself. Strategies and tactics that enhance and extend participation to the utmost are an ideal to be pursued.

There is much dispute over precisely what counts as a base community. Widely varying organizations are often lumped together and presented under this heading. What passes for a base community in El Salvador or Brazil often bears little relation to groups of the same name encountered in Colombia or Argentina. A group that meets all of the normal definitions may conversely not call itself a base community. There is also intense competition within countries between alternative models, as progressives and conservatives each try to advance their goals through groups referred to as base communities. Such groups are rarely spontaneous creations, springing unbidden and full blown "from the people." Rather, they are born linked to the churches, specifically to initiatives by bishops, religious orders, priests, nuns, or lay agents commissioned by the church. These ties are maintained through a regular routine of courses, visits by clergy and especially sisters, and through the distribution of mimeographed circulars, instructional material, and cassettes. Base communities may be popular in social composition, but they are not autonomous or isolated from the institutional church. To the contrary, all base communities begin with pastoral agents reaching out to communities, and they are constantly influenced by the church and subject to its monitoring and control. Initial contact is most often made by nuns in conjunction with seminarians. Popular receptivity has not been a given; in many cases, clerics tried but failed to create base communities. Failure has been more likely when pastoral agents attempt to encourage the formation of highly politicized groups from the outset.

Religion, Community, and Action

The success of base communities has been more common when religion and community were initial and continuing goals. The ordinary practice of most base communities is religious in quite conventional ways. Members pray a lot, individually and as a group. They also value and practice a number of traditional prayers and rites (rosaries, nocturnal vigils, adorations, and celebrations like processions and pilgrimages) often spurned by Catholic radicals anxious to move on to the "real work" of social and political transformation. The clash of popular desires for liturgy with activist stress on "useful" collective action is a permanent feature of much base community life.

Most base community meetings follow a standard pattern. The group gathers weekly or biweekly in a church facility or community center or on a rotating basis in the homes of members. The session opens with reading from the Bible, followed by commentary and discussion aimed at connecting the scriptural passage to personal and community issues. Although the Bible is central to group life, base communities should not be confused with fundamentalists. They do not view the Bible as an inerrant text, a source of formulas to be applied in some mechanical fashion, but rather as a set of values, ideals, and role model. Discussion is active and open, with members jumping in to point out how what is spoken of in the Bible is happening here and now, to people like them.

The links between base communities and explicitly political action have varied, but all such action begins with a community decision to address some pressing local need. Health committees, cooperatives, schools, and local efforts to supplement subsistence (for example, by organizing community kitchens) are common. These short-term connections are amplified by the way participation in base communities legitimizes activism and autonomous organization. By diffusing skills of organization and providing spaces for the practical expression of democracy and self-governance, base communities contribute to a general democratization of culture. Efforts to translate these cultural and religious predispositions into direct political activism have rarely been successful.

Part of the difficulty in building political movements out of base communities arises from a palpable gap between the hopes and expectations of activists and intellectuals and the goals and dispositions of members. Contrary to what early commentators believed, members of base communities rarely come from the very poorest of the poor. Members are more likely to be recruited from the stable poor: peasants with some land, city dwellers with steady jobs. Members are also overwhelmingly female. Because church organizations are culturally sanctioned vehicles for women, they draw hitherto silent voices into public spaces, but many women remain wary of specifically political activism and are constrained by family obligations, including pressure from male relatives, to stay out of politics, which is regarded as men's work.

Together these issues shape the kind of activism that most members are disposed to support. Commitment is more limited, local, and less confrontational than many activists have wanted to recognize. Goals are distinctly modest, nonpolitical, and nonrevolutionary. Members look for fellowship, moral support, and specific improvements, like access to water, education, credit, or health services. No matter what the social or political agenda may be, from child care to sewing circles, from cooperatives to strikes or land invasions, in all instances there is great stress on prayer, Bible study, and liturgy. In any event, most of the social and political agenda at issue is quite conventional. Typical activities include sewing, visiting the sick, or social action, which usually means collecting money, clothing, or food for those in extreme need. There are also attempts to found cooperatives, which for the most part remain limited to very small scale savings-and-loan operations or at most to collective-marketing or common-purchase arrangements.

Repression and Grassroots Activism

Although the initial impetus behind the formation and spread of base communities was religious, not political, in practice communities have had subtle and far-reaching effects on politics. From the beginning, base communities developed in ways that responded to the needs of popular sectors for participatory experiences that could provide meaning, structure, and support as they faced a difficult and changing world. All this was appealing and would have had some impact in any event, but in those countries where the communities later became particularly visible in politics (for example, in Brazil, Chile, El Salvador, and Nicaragua), repression and authoritarian rule decisively magnified and extended their impact. By restricting political spaces and closing organizations such as unions and political parties, fearful governments drove activists into the churches. There was often nowhere else to go.

It is precisely those regimes that ironically complain most bitterly about the "political" impact of liberation theology and base communities, and about excessive "politicization" of the churches generally, that have been prime creators of what they deplore and condemn so strongly. Their own intense repression created a clientele and made the logic of resistance and activism all the more meaningful. In Latin America, authoritarianism was a prime growth medium for popular religious movements. Instead of frightening activists into apathy, official threats and violence reinforced the dedication of many bishops and pastoral agents, who intensified efforts to create and defend base communities.

At issue here is a complex process of exchange and mutual influence among new commitments to the poor articulated through liberation theology, social changes, and repression. When the churches began to promote ideas about justice, rooting them in participatory, reinforcing group structures, they found a ready audience. The moral sanction of the churches, reinforced by solidarity and mutual support in the groups, helped sustain membership and uphold its commitments as possible and correct, even in the face of great danger. As the needs of members were echoed and reinforced by guiding ideas derived from liberation theology, originally limited religious agendas broadened. Together these changes undergirded a range of new commitments and activities.

Legacy

Beginning in the mid-1980s, the resolution of Central America's civil wars and the return of civilian rule and democratic politics elsewhere in Latin America reduced the pressures that helped turn base communities to politics. More open conditions also have led to a proliferation of organizational alternatives. Base communities now encounter vigorous competition from a wide range of groups, including political parties and trade unions, as well as evangelical and Pentecostal Protestants and Catholic charismatics, who stress gifts of the Holy Spirit such as healing or speaking in tongues. At the same time, many of the movements that had spun off from base communities in earlier years divided or simply failed. They fell victim to a combination of repressive violence (which took a particularly heavy toll in Central America) and, in some sense, the impact of democracy itself. As the common enemy of military and authoritarian rule disappeared, members split among available alternatives, and in many instances movements were left in the lurch as allies on the left splintered or pursued their own agendas.

The legacy of base communities is a heightened awareness of the possibilities for participation and democratic self-governance, not only within the church but also in society and politics as a whole. The appeal of Bible study is evidence of the powerful attraction of literacy in newly mobile communities. Among the people of Latin America, as among the Puritans of sixteenth-century England, equality of access to sacred knowledge laid the foundation for a claim to equality in general. Participation as equals in religious life provided a groundwork for a practical theory of rights manifest in the creation of an active citizenry that can play a continuing role in democratizing society and politics over the long haul.

See also *Brazil; Liberation Theology.*

Daniel H. Levine

BIBLIOGRAPHY

Azevedo, Marcello. *Basic Ecclesial Communities in Brazil: The Challenge of a New Way of Being Church.* Translated by John Drury. Washington, D.C.: Georgetown University Press, 1987.

Berryman, Phillip. *Religious Roots of Rebellion: Christians in the Central American Revolutions.* Maryknoll, N.Y.: Orbis, 1984.

Bruneau, Thomas C. *The Church in Brazil: The Politics of Religion.* Austin: University of Texas Press, 1982.

Burdick, John. *Looking for God in Brazil: The Progressive Catholic Church in Urban Brazil's Religious Arena.* Berkeley: University of California Press, 1993.

Hewitt, W. E. *Base Christian Communities and Social Change in Brazil.* Lincoln: University of Nebraska Press, 1991.

Levine, Daniel H. *Popular Voices in Latin American Catholicism.* Princeton: Princeton University Press, 1992.

Belgium

See *Low Countries.*

Bhutto, Zulfiqar Ali

See *Pakistan.*

Bible

See *Christianity.*

Bonhoeffer, Dietrich

German Lutheran theologian, pastor, and leader of church resistance to the Third Reich who was executed for conspiring against Adolf Hitler. Bonhoeffer (1906–1945) was the sixth son of a professor of neurology at the University of Berlin. His family's tradition of responsibility in scientific and public life took an unexpected form as he chose to study theology and later to be ordained. His research into the church as the worldly reality in whose formation and witness God is active in the world, unusual for its time, qualified him as a university teacher. It gave him a distinctive Christian voice and also sensitized him to the perversion of society by Hitler. He came to a fresh understanding of how the state is circumscribed by its Creator and of the prophetic responsibility of the church. Its task is to care for social order, declaring the limitations of the state, especially where it steps beyond its legitimate sphere, as it had in dealing with the Jews.

Correcting the Church, Resisting the State

Bonhoeffer was among the relatively few to recognize the complicity of the conventional religion of his time with Hitler's strategy of using religion as an instrument of his policies. Bonhoeffer's approach to the task of correcting the church and resisting the encroachments of the state was more clear headed and down to earth than most. No less theological because practical, he sought to allow God to enable the church to act responsibly in the contingencies of political struggle. Engaging with major theological influences, he concluded that God had in Christ bound himself to human social life in history with definite consequences for responsible social life (the scriptural "mandates" of labor, marriage, government, and church). For Bonhoeffer, these were not abstract theological considerations but decisive for the "Confessing Church"—a church that confesses itself to be for its Lord and against its enemies—as it formed itself in resistance against the "German" church that succumbed to Hitler's strategy. His own thought emerged in fragmentary form as he responded to the urgencies of the struggle.

What was particularly remarkable about Bonhoeffer's thought was the depth of his critique of religious rationalizations of church and state ("cheap grace") and his recognition of the involvement of God in the sufferings of people in the world where they found freedom in living responsibly for each other ("costly grace"). In this, and in his attempts to work out the ethical and political consequences,

he was convinced that in Christ God was always nearby and active in the human social struggle for justice.

It is clear that Bonhoeffer's capacity to live "outside" himself in his duties to Christ, church, and social order gave his life an extraordinary Christian integrity. This capacity can be seen in his activities as university teacher, spokesman for the Confessing Church (and for those endeavoring to stop Hitler and his regime) abroad, director of the community in which Confessing Church pastors were educated, pastor in England and underground in Germany, and—in conscious opposition to Lutheran tradition—participant in the conspiracy on Hitler's life. It was also evident during his year-long imprisonment before his execution only three weeks before Hitler's suicide. This integrity, which shines through Bonhoeffer's writings and biography, accounts for his wide influence since then.

During his year in prison, freed of direct responsibilities and made accountable to secular authorities, Bonhoeffer began to see how drastically modern life undercut "religion" in its usual forms (teaching, piety, and "exploiting human weakness or human boundaries"). This realization led him to ask what Christianity and the lordship of Christ might then mean. There is yet hope that God will then be "not on the boundaries but at the center," "not in death and guilt but in human life and goodness," revealing true human freedom in discipline, action, suffering, and death.

These remarkable views gave rise to far-reaching discussions about God, Christ, church, world, and human responsibility. Bonhoeffer was in effect re-situating God in the historical situation of the world and taking modern atheism as an opportunity to investigate the Christian concept of God anew—not, as some claimed, advocating the death of God.

Concentration of Influence

Bonhoeffer's influence has been concentrated in two main arenas: among those concerned with the position and intelligibility of the Christian faith and church in modern thought and life and among those confronted by oppressive regimes. In the first, his insights about God, Christ, community, and sociopolitical responsibility in a post-Enlightenment world have figured importantly in the work of those reconsidering God and identifying God's activity in the achievement of just social life in history, but his ideas are not easily reconstructed or transferred.

In the second arena, Bonhoeffer's influence is seen where the churches must reconsider their role in society, as in Eastern Europe, Latin America, and South Africa. His conception of the church was particularly influential in the German Democratic Republic. His claim that there is no disjunction between the reality of the world and the reality of God, and that the brokenness of this world is reconciled with God through Jesus Christ, enabled the church to move from opposition to critical dialogue in its relations with the state. Bonhoeffer's view of the church as "for others," that it is not so much concerned for itself as for society as a whole, allowed the church to participate in the political process in such a way as to make the kingdom of God visible without legitimating an unjust socialism.

See also *Fascism; Genocide and "Ethnic Cleansing"; Germany; Holocaust; Lutheranism.*

Daniel W. Hardy

BIBLIOGRAPHY

Bethge, Eberhard. *Dietrich Bonhoeffer: A Biography.* New York: Harper and Row, 1970.

De Gruchy, John, ed. *Bonhoeffer for a New Day: Theology in a Time of Transition.* Grand Rapids, Mich.: Eerdmans, 1997.

Floyd, Wayne Whitson, Jr., ed. *Dietrich Bonhoeffer Works.* Vols. 1–16. Minneapolis: Augsburg Fortress, 1996.

Kelly, Geffrey B., and F. Burton Nelson. *A Testament to Freedom: The Essential Writings of Dietrich Bonhoeffer.* San Francisco: HarperSan Francisco, 1990.

Botswana

A landlocked democracy of 1.4 million people, Botswana lies to the north of South Africa. Until it gained independence from Great Britain in 1966, it was known as the Bechuanaland protectorate. Since gaining independence, it has become one of Africa's wealthiest nations. Although a multiethnic society, with more than a dozen language groups, the country has long been dominated by Tswana-speaking people.

Botswana today is predominantly Christian. There are no organized religious movements that seek to influence policy in the country's two main centers of power—the legislature and the government bureaucracy. Indeed, since independence, the government and all major political parties have rarely consulted or worked with religious organizations in any formal way.

This emphasis on secular politics is not a long-standing practice. During the previous hundred years, mission churches played a central role in buttressing the powers of

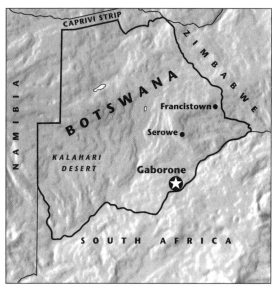

the Tswana chiefs, each of whom patronized a single church and refused to allow competitors in his territory. As a result, Christianity was linked closely to the chiefs, and because the chiefs lost practically all their power after independence, the churches have since lacked a formal role in Botswana's government. Religious freedom, which came with independence, encouraged the introduction of large numbers of small churches, thus further diminishing the role of religious institutions. Formal religious influence on politics has therefore been restricted to lobbying, although in recent years many small denominations have begun to forge relationships with opposition politicians in a bid to win greater recognition for their congregations.

Traditional Religion and Colonization

The various people of Botswana were traditionally animists, with a worldview similar to that of many other Africans. They believed in witchcraft and sorcery and generally thought that the spirits of their ancestors, who were thought to punish those who failed to live by custom, influenced many events. Traditional leaders, the chiefs of the various Tswana groups, played an important role in sacred practices, such as rainmaking, and held a preeminent spiritual role in society.

When Christian missionaries began to evangelize the Tswana peoples in the mid-1800s, they found a receptive audience among the elite—particularly the chiefs, their relatives, and the traditional doctors. After being adopted by the elite, Christianity spread downward to the commoners and slaves. This process occurred among the five major Tswana chieftaincies: the Bangwato, Bakwena, Bangwaketse, Batawana, and Bakgatla. Once the chiefs and the elite became Christians, they began to replace animist practices. For instance, formal prayer sessions just before the plowing season replaced rainmaking. "Heathen" practices involving marriage, rites of passage, inheritance, and the like were gradually outlawed and replaced by Christian ones.

The nondenominational London Missionary Society was by far the most important of the Christian groups working among the Tswana, sending missionaries into Botswana as early as 1824. The society established a religious monopoly among four of the major Tswana chieftaincies, and because of its links to the leading chiefs, it became dominant across the country. This situation was strengthened by the arrival of colonialism in 1885, when the British system of "indirect rule" required the British colonizers to govern through the traditional chiefs. As a result, British authorities supported the chiefs' attempts to retain a single church within each of their territories. Colonialism thus cemented the ties between the chiefs and their "state" churches.

For a long period, the London Missionary Society used its position to promote social change. It successfully persuaded chiefs to banish traditional practices and to institute Christian practices and ritual in their place. For the dominant Tswana especially, Christianity became part of their daily lives.

Close ties between the London Missionary Society and the chiefs meant that independent, African-run "Ethiopian" and "Zionist" churches were slow to spread in Botswana. Chiefs like Khama III of the Bangwato (1875–1923) routinely expelled preachers and converts of these churches, because they viewed them as potentially hostile political factions. Only during the mid-1930s did British authorities intervene to end the London Missionary Society's monopoly by allowing Seventh-day Adventists into several regions where the Adventists offered to build the country's first hospitals.

During the 1950s and 1960s independent churches, particularly Zionist ones, emerged, though they continued to be banned by all the major chiefs until 1966. These new churches proved to be particularly popular among ethnic minorities, many of whom resented their subjugation under Tswana rule. The Kalanga, especially those living on government land outside the control of the Tswana chiefs, estab-

lished the first vibrant independent churches. Such groups as the Spiritual Healing Church and St. John's Apostolic Faith Healing Church had become well established by 1960, after which they surreptitiously moved into Tswana regions. The Zion Christian Church, another important group, attracted many adherents who had to live on government-owned land to avoid persecution by the chiefs.

Modern Botswana

After 1966, the newly elected independent government drastically altered the status quo, first by gutting chiefly power and second by allowing complete religious freedom for the first time. Power moved away from British officials and chiefs and ended up in the hands of the ruling Botswana Democratic Party, which created a large new bureaucracy. Although elections were held regularly beginning in 1966, the Botswana Democratic Party did not face serious opposition until the 1990s.

The weakness of the opposition was mirrored by a weakness in civil society generally, as power came to be centered within the government bureaucracy. Popularly elected politicians in the legislature held little influence, and the few private organizations could not counteract government dominance. Until the mid-1980s, for instance, no independent press or media existed.

Whereas the London Missionary Society—which became the Botswana synod of the United Congregational Church of South Africa, or UCCSA—and other sanctioned churches had had direct access to chiefs and government officials, they now lacked formal avenues to the government. Moreover, the rapid growth of dozens of small independent churches after 1966 allowed groups like the Zion Christian Church and Spiritual Healing Church to outstrip the UCCSA in membership. Christians in the country thus divided into a large number of denominations, none of which had the clout formerly held by the London Missionary Society. Although a national body called the Botswana Christian Council, which incorporates all of Botswana's churches, has the potential to wield political influence, it has nonetheless avoided any open political role since its inception in the 1960s.

The UCCSA continues to have some influence in the ruling party because of its historical role in education and health. One of its missionaries, Dr. A. M. Merriweather, for instance, was the country's first parliamentary Speaker. Botswana's second president, Sir Ketumile Masire (who took office in 1980), is also a life-long UCCSA member; both he and his predecessor, Sir Seretse Khama, were educated in its schools.

Although churches since independence have eschewed any formal role in elections and in formal government, there can be no doubt that they have influenced the government to practice a range of socially conservative policies and have prevented the introduction of liberal ones. This situation is most clear in the case of pornography: the government prohibits the distribution of sexually explicit material. Abortion is another area in which groups like the Zionists and the UCCSA have taken a strong stand. In 1994, when government officials tried to legalize abortion, they met with strong opposition from church leaders. This represents one of the few instances in Botswana's history where public protests led to the government's withdrawing proposed legislation.

In the 1990s, although mainline religious groups like the UCCSA have tended to be implicit supporters of the government, smaller churches have come to identify with the opposition. The left-leaning Botswana National Front, which dominates the urban vote, has to some extent courted ministers of independent and Zionist churches capable of delivering votes. In particular, the registration of smaller churches has been an important factor for the Botswana National Front because the government will recognize only registered churches. To register, a church must formulate a constitution and go through a cumbersome administrative process. Tedious registration formalities have often led aspiring churches to feel that they are being victimized by the government and thus have led them to identify with the opposition. In a large number of cases, independent ministers have continued to work with the opposition, even after completing registration.

It is likely that in the future two religious-political blocs will coalesce: a mainline church allied with the Botswana Democratic Party, on the one hand, and an independent church and Botswana National Front partnership on the other. At present, though, Botswana's large Christian population is disorganized and split. As the rest of the country's civil society becomes more sophisticated, it is probable that the country's churches will assume a greater role in national politics.

See also *Christianity in Africa; Traditional Religion, African.*

Barry Morton

BIBLIOGRAPHY

Amanze, James. *African Christianity in Botswana.* Gweru, Zimbabwe: Mambo, 1998.

———. *Botswana Handbook of Churches: A Handbook of Churches, Ecumenical Organizations, Theological Institutions, and Other World Religions in Botswana.* Gaborone: Pula Press, 1994.

Boschman, Don. *The Conflict between New Religious Movements and the State in the Bechuanaland Protectorate prior to 1949.* Studies on the Church in Southern Africa. Vol. 3. Gaborone: Department of Theology and Religious Studies, University of Botswana, 1994.

Landau, Paul. "The Spirit of Pigs and Demons: The 'Samuelites' of Southern Africa." *Journal of Religion in Africa* 29, no. 3 (1999).

———. *The Realm of the Word: Language, Gender, and Christianity in a Southern African Kingdom.* Portsmouth, N.H.: Heinemann; London: J. Curry, 1995.

Schapera, Isaac. *Tribal Innovators: Tswana Chiefs and Social Change, 1795–1940.* London: Athlone, 1970.

Setiloane, Gabriel M. *The Image of God among the Sotho-Tswana.* Rotterdam: Balkema, 1976.

Bourguiba, Habib

Habib Bourguiba (1903–2000) led the Tunisian nationalist movement and served as the first president of Tunisia after it received its independence from France, in 1956. After attending secondary schools in Tunis, Bourguiba earned a law degree from the University of Paris. Returning to Tunisia, he renewed an earlier association with the nationalist Dustur (Constitution) Party but became an outspoken critic of party leaders' unwillingness to challenge French rule. Expelled from the Dustur in 1934, Bourguiba helped form the Neo-Dustur Party, which, under his direction, supplanted the older party as the vehicle of nationalist sentiment and, in 1957, assured its popular leader a victory in the first postindependence presidential elections. After he won reelection in 1964 and 1969, the National Assembly appointed him president for life in 1974.

Bourguiba initiated a sweeping program of social change designed to foster the emergence of a secular, Westernized state. Many of his reforms targeted Muslim customs that he viewed as impediments to progress and development. He spearheaded campaigns to restore to individual ownership properties held as religious trusts and to bring all education under state instead of religious control. He oversaw the introduction of a legal system that minimized the influence of Islamic law, most dramatically exemplified by the enactment of a code radically altering traditional practices (such

Habib Bourguiba.

as outlawing polygamy and legitimizing marriages between persons of different faiths). The government, accusing religious leaders of trying to preserve their power at the expense of the national good, forcefully curbed protest demonstrations.

Despite Bourguiba's enormous popularity and the considerable powers vested in the president by the constitution, some aspects of Islam remained impervious to change. In 1960, for example, Bourguiba failed to persuade his countrymen to ignore the religious obligation to fast during the month of Ramadan, despite his ingenious assertion that all Tunisians were waging a *jihad* (struggle) against underdevelopment and that Islam exempted persons engaged in *jihad* from observing the fast.

An uneasy truce developed as the religious establishment was brought to heel, but memories of Bourguiba's assault on Islam, combined with the conviction that his policies had created serious social and economic ills, gave rise in the 1970s and 1980s to a potent religiously based opposition epitomized by the Islamic Tendency Movement. Although the constraints of a single-party state and Tunisia's faltering economy also engendered secular opposition movements,

Bourguiba responded to his religious adversaries with particular vehemence. In 1987 a number of Islamist militants were tried on charges of plotting to overthrow the government, and several received capital sentences. Bourguiba acceded to his advisers' pleas to commute the death sentences to deprive the movement of martyrs, but his abhorrence of the Islamists soon led him to disavow this pragmatic decision and demand that the executions be carried out.

Prime Minister Zine el-Abidine Ben Ali attributed Bourguiba's erratic behavior in this, as in other matters, to his failing health. In accordance with a provision of the constitution, Ben Ali convoked a team of physicians who declared the president unable to fulfill his duties. Bourguiba retired to his home town of Monastir. For the thirteen years of his life that remained, the man known to Tunisians as "The Supreme Combattant" played no role in public life.

Kenneth J. Perkins

BIBLIOGRAPHY

Brown, L. Carl. "Bourguiba and Bourguibism Revisited: Reflections and Interpretation." *Middle East Journal* 55, no. 1 (Winter 2001): 43–57.

Hopwood, Derek. *Habib Bourguiba of Tunisia: The Tragedy of Longevity.* New York: St. Martin's Press, 1992.

Perkins, Kenneth. *A History of Modern Tunisia.* Cambridge: Cambridge University Press, 2004.

Brazil

The largest and most populous country of South America, the Federative Republic of Brazil, is home to three major religious families: Roman Catholicism, Protestantism (especially its Pentecostal forms), and spiritism. Each of these religious families—which have wide variations in belief and practice within them, not least between popular and educated forms—has a claim to dominance in Brazil's social and cultural life. Catholicism was brought by the Portuguese who colonized the area in the sixteenth century. Protestantism is more recent, arriving with missionaries over the past century and a half but developing strong local roots in the latter half of the twentieth century. The popular forms of spiritism, often designated Afro-Brazilian spiritism, have developed from the religions of the African slaves.

Catholicism looms large as the foundation religion of colonial Brazil. The calendar is organized around its feast

days, and despite separation of church and state since the constitution of 1891, dignitaries of the Catholic Church still preside over public occasions as though Catholicism were the established religion. In a population approaching 180 million, more than 70 percent describe themselves as Catholic. Nominally Brazil is the largest Catholic country in the world, but numerical preponderance and public presence are not accompanied by any kind of hegemony exercised by the church, and even on the numbers the other religions mount an increasing challenge. The Pentecostal churches are growing at an extraordinary rate, and the number of Protestants attending church regularly now exceeds the number of Catholics, though a best estimate of their proportion in the population is 16 percent. In any of the poorer suburbs and shantytowns of Brazil's big cities it may be difficult to locate the local Catholic church, but there will be a dozen or more Pentecostal temples—the Assemblies of God, Brazil for Christ, the Four Square Gospel Church (among others), and now, the fastest growing of them all, the Universal Church of the Kingdom of God.

In coastal cities the hymns and sermons of the Protestants, broadcast on loudspeakers for all to hear, may be drowned out by the sound of drums and chanting from the Afro-Brazilian religions, Candomblé (more traditionally African) and Umbanda (more of a blend). These religions are part of a larger family of spiritist religions, distinguished by belief in a world of spirits to which the living, through mediums, may have recourse to obtain strength, healing, and protection. The spiritist family includes forms of spiritism imported from France in the nineteenth century. But the African elements of Candomblé, in particular, reflect the fact that Afro-Brazilian spiritist religions were brought from Africa by African slaves and kept alive by them and their descendants since the abolition of slavery in 1888. Because many devotees of spiritism consider themselves to be Catholics as well, and so report themselves in the census, it is difficult to guess their proportion in the population. But if practitioners of these religions are included with the millions of Brazilians who periodically consult a spirit medium, then spiritism has a claim to approximately the same percentage of Brazilians as Protestantism.

The Role of the Catholic Church

The three religious traditions are woven deeply, and intricately, into the fabric of political life in Brazil. The most obvious and direct involvement occurs when religious leaders enter into the political arena or mobilize the faithful for political ends. The Catholic Church's political involvement was especially intense during the years of the country's military dictatorship from 1964 to 1985. The Brazilian Conference of Bishops endorsed the coup of April 1964, judging it necessary to restore order and defeat communism. But from the early 1970s the church gradually became the major institutional source of opposition to military authoritarian rule and the social injustices believed to be worsened by its policies.

This political radicalization occurred for a number of reasons. One was reaction to the imprisonment and torture of clerical and lay Catholic radicals who sought democracy and social justice. Another was the diffusion of critical social analysis and pastoral initiatives, including the fostering of grassroots base communities, which were inspired by the liberation theology movement. According to liberation theology, the vocation of the church is to struggle for justice on the side of the poor and oppressed and to prefigure the biblical Kingdom of God in its own practices and structures. The base communities, consisting of groups in poor neighborhoods brought together by clergy, were an attempt, meeting varying degrees of success, to realize that vocation. By the early 1980s, in the years of gradual restoration of democracy in Brazil, Catholic clergy as well as laity were frequently involved in mobilizing support for parties of the opposition. The Catholic contingent in the coalition of radical groups that came together to form the new socialist Workers' Party was substantial.

It should not be concluded, however, that the Catholic Church has been uniform or entirely effective in mobilizing support for the political left. Although there have been instances of individual radical clergy urging a vote for left-leaning candidates and parties, the closest the church has come to direct support for the left has been in a few dioceses such as São Paulo where voter education programs have been organized. These programs reach only a small proportion of Catholics. Since the return of democracy to Brazil, Catholics of the left often have been disappointed to discover that those Catholic citizens who could be mobilized to support political initiatives expressing the church's "preferential option for the poor" in the early 1980s now distribute their votes across the political spectrum. This outcome appears to be how the majority of the bishops at the beginning of the twenty-first century would want it: they are persuaded that with the military returned to the barracks, the clergy should return to the sacristy and the church should refrain from direct involvement in politics. Among politicians, the designation "Catholic" conveys nothing about an individual's policies or allegiances. There is no Catholic party even of the unofficial kind such as the Christian Democrats in Chile.

New Directions

For a while in the mid-1980s, following the restoration of democracy, it seemed that Protestants, and the Pentecostal churches in particular, would enter the political arena as a coherent and influential bloc, just as the Catholic Church, in effect, was leaving. Pentecostal pastors became active in national politics for the first time. Previously, although pastors might intervene in local politics, most were apolitical, engaged with their congregations in the defining practices of Pentecostals: celebrating and cultivating the gifts of the Holy Spirit, mutually supporting a strict Christian morality, proselytizing, and providing social services to members of the congregation. In 1985, however, leading pastors of the Assemblies of God organized to have members of their church elected to the federal legislature. In the Constituent Assembly (the Senate and House of Deputies combined) that produced the 1988 constitution for postmilitary Brazil, a Protestant caucus of mainly Pentecostal politicians (eighteen of the thirty-three Protestant deputies) was extremely influential for a time. The caucus did not survive, however. It received bad press, in part because of the political inexperience of the Pentecostals but mainly because it could all too easily be depicted as selling its votes for various benefits to the churches. Toward the end of the 1980s and into the 1990s, leaders of the Pentecostals were able to mobilize votes against the Workers' Party candidate for the presidency and at local levels to win support for Pentecostals or candidates prepared to extend patronage to their churches. However, in a surprising about-face, the Universal Church of the Kingdom of God (the second largest Pentecostal church in Brazil) mobilized in support of Lula da Silva, the Workers' Party candidate, in the presidential election of 2002. At the grassroots there are reports of Pentecostals who actively support the Workers' Party and take political positions for social justice not so different from those espoused by Catholics of the base communities.

The direct involvement of Afro-Brazilian spiritism in the political arena has been largely at the local level. The leaders of spiritist centers frequently enter into the exchanges of urban patronage politics. But like the other two major religious families of Brazil, spiritism connects to politics in less direct ways. In some Afro-Brazilian groups religious engagement has led to involvement in something like a black civil rights movement. But in others belief and practice dispose members to accept the political and economic status quo.

Similar divergent tendencies can be seen in the other two religious families. Affinities between popular Catholicism and rural patronage politics, and the connection between Pentecostal belief and an attitude of aversion to all political engagement, have long been observed. However, certain forms of Catholicism and Pentecostalism dispose the faithful toward what might be called social movement politics. From the Catholic base communities various residential movements of the urban poor have emerged. The most important movement of the late 1990s and beginning of the twenty-first century, the Landless People Movement, developed from the church's pastoral work with the rural poor and its sustained advocacy of land reform over three decades. In dioceses in which communities have been fostered by church authorities, these primarily religious associations have motivated members and provided them with the means to participate in struggles for land tenure and basic services in such areas as health, education, and transport. In the course of these struggles, new forms of local exchange and cooperation have developed. In this way, forms of participation in the religious sphere have generated transformations in civil society, which arguably enrich and strengthen Brazilian democracy.

Several case studies of Pentecostalism have shown that out of many a local temple come new citizens critical of the gender, racial, and class inequities of contemporary Brazil and disposed to challenge them, at least at the local level. Certain forms of Pentecostalism encourage and empower followers of the new faith to seek improvement for their families and neighborhoods and to invent new forms of local cooperation for achieving it. Further, Pentecostalism as a way of life, involving the reining in of machismo, scrupulous self-discipline, and consequent transformations of family life, may be transforming civil society more effectively than the struggling base communities.

There is much debate among students of the religions of Brazil about these more indirect links between religion and politics, and that debate is fed by uncertainty regarding developments within each of the religious families. What will be the effect of the decline in the bishops' support for the Catholic base communities and their growing support for the Charismatic Renewal, a vibrant Pentecostal-style lay movement? In the Protestant family, what are the implications, religious and political, of the spectacular rise of the Universal Church of the Kingdom of God? Which of several streams of Afro-Brazilian spiritism, if any, will appeal to a generation of Brazilians who move to the beat of the global African diaspora? Among all the uncertainties and through the debates surrounding them, one thing is clear: Brazil remains a society in which neither politics nor religion can be understood except in their intertwining.

See also *Base Communities; Catholicism, Roman; Latin America; Liberation Theology; Pentecostalism.*

R. Andrew Chestnut

BIBLIOGRAPHY

Burdick, John. *Looking for God in Brazil: The Progressive Catholic Church in Urban Brazil's Religious Arena.* Berkeley: University of California Press, 1993.

Chesnut, R. Andrew. *Born Again in Brazil: The Pentecostal Boom and the Pathogens of Poverty.* New Brunswick, N.J.: Rutgers University Press, 1997.

———. *Competitive Spirits: Latin America's New Religious Economy.* New York: Oxford University Press, 2003.

Cleary, Edward L. "The Brazilian Catholic Church and Church-State Relations: Nation Building." *Journal of Church and State* 39 (Spring 1997): 253–272.

Freston, Paul, ed. *Evangelical Christianity and Democracy in Latin America.* New York: Oxford University Press, 2006.

Ireland, Rowan. *Kingdoms Come: Religion and Politics in Brazil.* Pittsburgh: University of Pittsburgh Press, 1991.

Mainwaring, Scott. *The Catholic Church and Politics in Brazil, 1916–1985.* Stanford: Stanford University Press, 1986.

Buddha

According to legendary history the person known to most of the world as the Buddha—the "enlightened one"—was before his enlightenment a prince living in northern India. This prince is remembered as having had the name Siddhartha Gautama, as belonging to a tribe or clan known as the Sakyas, and as having been born and raised in the northern Indian city of Kapilavastu. Most followers of Buddhism believe Prince Siddhartha was born in 624 B.C.E., but the consensus of Buddhist scholars today is that he was born and died in the fourth century B.C.E. The Buddha is believed to have lived a long life, dying at the age of eighty. The Buddhist calendar begins with the date of his death, traditionally calculated as 543/544 B.C.E.

Little in the popular stories of the life of the Buddha can be historically verified, but scholars agree that behind the legends there existed a historical person who as an adult renounced secular life, assumed the life of an ascetic, and left behind a set of teachings that have profoundly shaped the lives of millions of people in what are today South Asia, Southeast Asia, and East Asia.

Legends surrounding the Buddha depict him as having had the potential to be a *chakravartin,* a world conqueror, that is, one who would have wielded exceptional power. He is believed to have been reared in a royal palace, to have married as a young man, and to have become a father. When he

Bronze Buddha, from Kashmir. Despite Kashmir's Muslim majority, Buddhism has been practiced in the region since around 245 B.C.E.

was twenty-nine he witnessed the "four sights"—a man suffering from illness, an elderly man, a corpse, and a religious ascetic. This experience shattered his sheltered life within the confines of the court. From reflection on these sights he realized that there could be no escape from suffering (*dukkha*), even as a powerful ruler, and vowed to follow the path of a homeless seeker of a way to transcend suffering. He left his wife and son and the luxury of the palace and for three years pursued the life of a wandering ascetic.

The Dharma

After having rejected the extreme practices of others, he discovered the "middle way." At the end of a period of intense meditation, he gained deep insight into the fundamental nature of human existence. Having been enlightened, he set forth at the age of thirty-three to teach the *dharma,* the truths he had learned, to others.

The dharma is predicated on the "Four Noble Truths": that suffering is fundamental to human experience, that the cause of suffering is desire (or craving), that the cessation of desire will release one from suffering, and that the way to achieve such cessation is the "Noble Eightfold Path." By cultivating wisdom (*prajña*), or right understanding and right thought, morality (*sila*), or right speech, right action, and right livelihood, and mental discipline (*samadhi*), or right effort, right mindfulness, and right concentration, one can ultimately escape from the wheel of suffering to which one is bound by *karma,* or "the consequence of one's actions," and achieve Nirvana.

The Sangha

The Buddha acquired a following of men, and subsequently a few women, who subjected themselves to the "discipline" that he established. Those who followed this discipline came to be known collectively as the *sangha.* Members of the sangha, distinguished still today by their distinctive robes and shaven heads signifying nonattachment to possessions or to bodily adornment, did not, however, separate themselves from society. Instead, they remained in close relationship to society to teach the dharma to others and to exemplify the dharma in their own actions. The Buddha, the dharma, and the sangha (those who maintain and teach the dharma) constitute the "Three Gems" upon which all Buddhist congregations are based.

The Buddha made the sangha, through the discipline he instituted, dependent for their food, clothing, shelter, and medicines on the generosity of the laity. Such generosity would be forthcoming only if lay people recognized the sangha as being a source of religious merit. Herein lies an apparent paradox: while the Buddha's message entails renunciation of the world, the survival of his message depends on the support of those who remain in the world, especially those with wealth and power.

Religious and Secular Authority

So long as the Buddha was alive, he held the authority to determine whether a member of the sangha was a "field of merit" for the laity. When he died, however, the question became who could ensure that the sangha would adhere to the discipline and would embody his dharma. By the time the Mauryan ruler Aśoka, who reigned from 270 to 230 B.C.E., became emperor of much of India, sectarian divisions had developed within the sangha. Aśoka used his secular authority to call a council of Buddhist monks to resolve conflicting interpretations of the Buddha's teachings. He also assumed responsibility for keeping the memory of the Buddha present in the world through the construction of "reminders" of his presence in the form of stupas, tumulus structures housing relics of the cremated Buddha, and by spreading the message of the Buddha abroad through a program of missionization.

The moral authority—also called dharma—of the righteous monarch thus was joined with religious truths of the Buddha to create a distinctive symbiosis between religious and secular authority. Buddhists in South Asia and Southeast Asia would follow the model of the "two wheels of the dharma" until modern times. The model was first adopted in East Asia but was subsequently undermined as Chinese and Japanese rulers looked to religious sources other than Buddhism for legitimating their power. In the Himalayan areas, another model would emerge, one that united the two types of dharma, that is, both religious and secular authority, under one theocratic system. Nowhere has the dharma of the Buddha prospered without the patronage of those holding secular power.

See also *Buddhism, Theravada; Buddhism, Tibetan.*

Charles F. Keyes

BIBLIOGRAPHY

Carrithers, Michael. *The Buddha.* New York: Oxford University Press, 1983.

Lamotte, Etienne. "The Buddha: His Teachings and His Sangha." In *The World of Buddhism: Buddhist Monks and Nuns in Society and Culture,* edited by Heinz Bechert and Richard Gombrich. London: Thames and Hudson, 1984.

Reynolds, Frank E., and Charles Hallisey. "Buddha." In *The Encyclopedia of Religion,* edited by Mircea Eliade. Vol. 2. New York: Collier Macmillan, 1987.

Thomas, Edward J. *The Life of Buddha as Legend and History.* Rev. ed. London: Routledge and Kegan Paul, 1975.

Buddhism, Theravada

Theravada Buddhism is the tradition of Buddhism dominant today in Sri Lanka (formerly Ceylon), Burma (Myanmar), Thailand (formerly Siam), Laos, Cambodia, and some other small communities. Theravada Buddhism as an institutionalized religion has had since its beginnings a marked interdependence with the political structures in the societies in which it has become the dominant religion. The relationship between Buddhism and politics has, however, undergone radical changes in all the societies in which Theravada Buddhism is dominant since the emergence of modern political systems.

Basic Characteristics

Theravada Buddhism is one of the major divisions of Buddhism, the others being Mahayana and Tibetan Buddhism. *Theravada* means the "way of the elders," a term that points to the centrality of monks (*bhikkhu*) who collectively make up the *sangha,* or clergy in this religious tradition. The sacred language of Theravada Buddhism is Pali, not Sanskrit. Pali, like Sanskrit, is an ancient Indian language believed to have been used at the time of the Buddha. Buddhist terms, such as *dhamma* instead of *dharma* and *kamma* instead of *karma,* used in this article follow the Pali, not Sanskrit, forms.

Theravada Buddhists commit themselves to "take refuge" in the "Three Gems," the Buddha, the *dhamma,* and the sangha. The Buddha was one Siddhattha Gotama believed to have died in the sixth century B.C.E. after having discovered the way to transcend the condition of suffering that all who are born as human experience and having taught this way to others for nearly half a century. The Buddha is remembered through images and the tumulus as well as monumental structures known as stupas, which even if they contain no actual relic represent the mound in which his remains were enshrined after his death.

Members of the sangha are looked to both as the exemplars of the way taught by the Buddha by virtue of their adherence to the "discipline" (*vinaya*) that he laid down during his lifetime and as the propagators of the way through their communication of the Buddha's teachings in rituals and sermons. Most monks (*bhikkhu*) and novices (*samanera*) in Theravada Buddhist societies, easily recognizable by their distinctive robes (which are usually yellow, but sometimes are brown or even red), will not remain within the sangha for life. Monks not only must abide by the basic moral precepts incumbent on all Buddhists, but they also must follow a cloistered life characterized by chastity, poverty, and asceticism. Although there has been no order of *bhikkhuni*, female members of the sangha, in any Theravadin society since about the eleventh century, some women still take religious roles. Such "nuns," who often wear distinctive plain robes, leave the life of a householder and, like monks and novices, forgo any sexual relations, reject ornamentation for the body, eat only what is necessary for sustenance in meals consumed before noon, and live a life without gold or silver or entertainments. Nuns became noticeable in the twentieth century as a consequence of changing ideas about religion and gender.

The foundation of the dhamma is the doctrine of *dukkha,* by which it is understood that all who are born will experience "suffering" directly as pain or indirectly as the cessation of that which is pleasurable, with death—often a combination of both—being the culmination of dukkha. The Buddha taught that transcendence of dukkha can be attained through following the "way" or "path" that includes the practice of "morality" (*sila*), mental concentration (*samadhi*), and cultivation of wisdom (*pañña*).

For lay Buddhists, *sila* is understood primarily as entailing the offering of "alms" (*dana*) to the sangha in the form of food, clothing, shelter, and medicines and following the "five precepts." In return for alms, lay persons accumulate "merit" or "positive kamma" (*puñña*). By adhering to the moral precepts to refrain from taking life, stealing, lying, and improper sexual relations, one avoids accumulating "demerit" or "negative kamma" (*pappa*). The balance of one's kamma will condition the relative degree of dukkha one will experience in both this life and in future existences. The kamma one inherited at birth is understood to have generated some of the physical and social conditions of one's present life.

The fifth precept—a commitment to refrain from ingesting substances (notably, alcohol and drugs) that conduce toward heedlessness—represents a step toward the cultivation of "mindfulness." Through such cultivation as well as the practice of "mental concentration" (meditation) one seeks to acquire the ability to detach oneself from those desires that lead to increased dukkha. If one is successful in practicing mental concentration, one will gain that insight into the self that is a basic form of wisdom.

Buddhist Monarchies

Theravada Buddhism exists as a major religion not only because of the "truths" (*dhamma*) discovered by the Buddha and propagated by him and his "sons," the members of the sangha, but also because of the patronage of rulers. Theravada Buddhists trace the origin of such patronage to Aśoka, the great emperor who extended his authority over much of India in the third century B.C.E. From this period up to the nineteenth century, Theravada Buddhism depended on what is referred to the "two wheels of the dhamma," one being the sangha and the other the Buddhist monarch.

Buddhist rulers were expected to be the chief patrons of the sangha and to assume responsibility for ensuring that members of the sangha adhered to the "discipline" (*vinaya*) that was made the basis for religious life by the Buddha. Although the sangha in turn was the source of symbolic legitimacy for Buddhist rulers, it lacked the ability to impose any real sanctions on a king who was an unbeliever or who acted against the tenets of Buddhist morality. While Buddhism failed to receive the patronage in India that would have ensured its success in competition with other religions in the subcontinent, Theravada Buddhist kingdoms were established in Sri Lanka and subsequently in Southeast Asia.

In Sri Lanka in the first century of the Christian era, monarchs provided patronage for monks who were the first to write down the teachings of the Buddha, previously transmitted only through oral traditions, that came to constitute the canon for all Theravada Buddhists. The canonical collection of the discourses of the Buddha, the record of the origin of disciplinary rules for the sangha, and compilation of metaphysical summaries of the teachings of the Buddha, collectively known as the *Tripitaka* or "three baskets" (of the dhamma), were written in the Pali language.

Although Buddhist (as well as Hindu) religious thought and practices spread to Southeast Asia from at least the beginning of the Christian era, Theravada Buddhism had a limited following until the eleventh century. In the eleventh through fifteenth centuries, kings in what is today Burma, Thailand, Laos, and Cambodia became patrons of missionizing monks and of monks writing in vernacular languages who made Theravada Buddhism the popular religion throughout much of mainland Southeast Asia. The religion also spread to neighboring areas in northeastern India and Bangladesh, southern China, northern Malaya, and southern Vietnam, although it always remained the religion of a small minority in these countries primarily because in these areas royal patronage was notably absent. By the fifteenth century, several distinctive forms of Theravada Buddhism had become established in mainland Southeast Asia, each associated with a different written language and a different set of polities.

The Challenge of Colonialism and Christianity

Beginning in the sixteenth century, but especially in the nineteenth, Buddhism in Sri Lanka and Southeast Asia underwent radical change in the wake of challenges posed by Christian missionaries and colonial rulers. Sri Lanka was the first of the Theravadin countries to be strongly influenced by the West. The Portuguese established a colonial foothold on the island in the sixteenth century, and Catholic missionaries gained a small following in areas under Portuguese rule. Then in the seventeenth century the Dutch replaced the Portuguese and introduced Dutch Reformed Christianity in the expanded area under their control, although an independent kingdom controlled most of the island from the capital of Kandy in the highlands. The political turmoil of the period, however, almost led to the disappearance of the sangha in Sri Lanka. In the late eighteenth century, Kandyan kings had reestablished the sangha with aid from monks from Siam (as Thailand was known before 1939) and Burma. But in 1815 the British conquered Kandy, abolished the monarchy, and ended forever the patronage of the religion once provided by the monarchy in Sri Lanka.

In 1824, soon after this conquest, the British began a series of wars with the Burmese. By 1885 the whole of Burma was under British rule and, as in Sri Lanka, the British abolished the monarchy. They also, again as in Sri Lanka, disestablished the Buddhist religion.

The political upheavals in these countries and the efforts of Christian missionaries to convert local people posed significant challenges to Buddhism. In both countries, religious leaders emerged who in the late nineteenth and early twentieth centuries instituted significant reforms of the religion. In Sri Lanka, reformed Buddhism has been termed "Protestant Buddhism" because it emerged in direct response to the efforts of Protestant missionaries and because, as in Protestant Christianity, reformed Buddhism also rejected many pre-modern rituals as hindering the practice of the true faith. In Burma, where Christian missionaries were far less successful, reformed Buddhism continued to coexist side by side with ritual-centered traditions.

In both countries, nationalist leaders succeeded in promoting the premise that colonial rule was a threat to Buddhism. Although Buddhist nationalism was more militant in Burma prior to independence, militant Buddhism would in Sri Lanka come after independence to be a defining influence on politics of that country.

Thailand (or Siam as it was known before 1939) was never colonized, and the encounter with Christianity was never seen as a serious threat. Nonetheless, Christian missionaries played a significant role in stimulating the reforms undertaken in Siamese Buddhism through their encounters with the princely monk who spearheaded these reforms in the middle of the nineteenth century. This monk would later become King Mongkut (1851–1868). The reformed Buddhism that he began became the basis for an established religion that from 1902 on placed all monks under the authority of a state-sponsored hierarchy.

Cambodia and Laos were both incorporated into French Indochina in the period from 1863 to 1907, and while monarchies in both countries were left in place, they were allowed no real power throughout the colonial period, which lasted until 1954. While in neither country did an autonomous reform Buddhist movement emerge, a French-sponsored Buddhist Institute in Cambodia would provide the breeding ground for a radical nationalism that was eventually taken over by communists.

Buddhist Politics in Postcolonial Societies

The radical changes imposed on Buddhist polities during the colonial period laid the groundwork for the distinctive Buddhist politics that have developed in the postcolonial period.

Sri Lanka. In Sri Lanka, even though approximately one-third of the population is not Buddhist, those who have held power since the mid-1950s have succeeded in promoting a constricted Buddhist nationalism that relegates those who are not Buddhists or speakers of Sinhalese, the dominant language in the country, to a marginalized place within the national community. This narrowly defined and often militant Buddhist nationalism, supported by some leading monks and opposed by others, has been a major cause of the ongoing and often violent conflict between Sinhalese and Tamils.

S. W. R. D. Bandaranaike, who was elected prime minister in 1956, set forth a nationalist program that would shape Sri Lankan politics for the next four decades. Bandaranaike was a convert to a reformed Buddhism linked to a nationalist agenda. As prime minister he succeeded in having Sinhalese made the national language to the exclusion of English and Tamil, made the myths concerning Sri Lanka being the chosen land of Buddhism central to the nationalist ideology, and emulated former Buddhist kings providing patronage for the religion in his role in the celebration of the twenty-five hundredth anniversary of the Buddhist era.

During Bandaranaike's premiership, monks became actively involved in politics for the first time in the postcolonial period, one tragic consequence being the assassination of Bandaranaike himself by a monk. This act did not lead to a change in nationalist policy, and Bandaranaike's successors, including his wife, Sirimavo Bandaranaike, continued to promote policies favoring the Buddhist Sinhalese majority. Even when the main opposition party succeeded in wresting power away from Sirimavo Bandaranaike in 1977, the government of Junius R. Jayawardene instituted changes in economic, not nationalist, policies. Supported by certain leading monks, the Jayawardene government took a hard line toward the Tamil minority.

The increasing rift between Tamils and Sinhalese erupted into violence in 1983 when the Liberation Tigers of Tamil Eelam (LTTE) began a war to gain independence for a Tamil state in northern Sri Lanka. In response, and with the tacit backing of the government, a reign of terror was let loose on Tamils living in Sinhalese-dominant areas.

The intensity of violence in Sri Lanka since 1983, which had claimed the lives of at least 60,000–100,000 by the end of 2005, including that of President Ranasinghe Premadasa in 1992, has seemed to many to make a mockery of Buddhist ideals of nonviolence. Although a significant number of Buddhist monks have denounced the violence, others have offered moral justification for the killing of non-Buddhists to ensure that the religion will remain dominant in the country. Since taking power in 1994, the government of President Chandrika Bandaranaike Kumaratunga, the daughter of the two previous Bandaranaike prime ministers, has undertaken negotiations with the Tamil nationalists on several occasions, but the legacy of violence has proven too great for these negotiations to succeed. The negotiations collapsed, in part because of controversy over the distribution of aid in Tamil areas following the tsunami in late 2004 and then the assassination of the country's foreign minister, Lakshman Kadirgamar, by a sniper in August 2005. President Kumaratunga has been pressed by the National Buddhist Front, an organization of many monks, to continue the war and even ban non-Buddhist nongovernmental organizations (NGOs) from working in the country. Buddhist nationalism has been a major factor for the tragedy of Sri Lanka, a tragedy that as yet does not seem to have an end.

Burma. In Burma (or Myanmar as is today the official name), efforts by the first independent government to make Buddhism a state religion exacerbated ethnic conflicts that had erupted even before independence. Although a nominally secularist government was installed after the military, under General Ne Win, staged a coup in 1962, Ne Win and his associates still drew heavily on Buddhism in promoting the "Burmese Way to Socialism." Ne Win's government also provided conspicuous support for many of the major shrines throughout the country, and members of the ruling elite were also evident among the followers of leading meditation monks.

In 1988, after Ne Win nominally retired and socialist policies were abandoned, significant public opposition developed to the continued rule by a military oligarchy. Daw Aung San Suu Kyi, who has provided the charismatic leadership of this opposition, draws her moral authority not only from being the daughter of the revered leader of the independence movement but also from her strong links to reformed Buddhism. Monks have also played a significant role in the opposition. In reaction, the ruling military junta placed Daw Aung San Suu Kyi under house arrest for many years, used coercive force against opposition monks (as well as against others opposed to their regime), and has sought legitimacy through the patronage for compliant monks, support for revered shrines, and sponsorship of significant rituals.

The military has continued to control Burma since Ne Win's retirement despite clear evidence that emerged in a 1990 election that the vast majority of the population preferred the creation of a new political order under Aung San Suu Kyi's guidance. In the continuing tensions and sometimes open conflict, between followers of Aung San Suu Kyi and the military junta, both sides have looked to Buddhism to provide legitimacy for their political visions. The military junta has sought to replicate the practices of Buddhist monarchs in the past by sponsoring the building of stupas, the display of a famous relic, and conspicuous support for favored members of the Buddhist sangha. Aung San Suu Kyi has gained respect for her devotion to Buddhist meditation. The junta, however, has used its monopoly on coercive power instead of Buddhist politics to maintain itself in power.

Cambodia. The radical communist revolutionaries referred to as the Khmer Rouge who succeeded in taking power in Cambodia in 1975 attempted to eliminate the Buddhist sangha and eradicate Buddhism from Khmer culture and society altogether. This extreme cultural revolution (strongly influenced by the Chinese prototype) was undertaken even though Prince Sihanouk, the successor to the pre-modern Buddhist monarchs, had allied himself with the Khmer Rouge after being ousted from power in a coup in 1970. But Sihanouk was allowed no role in the new order, although he, unlike at least two million of his compatriots, survived the Khmer Rouge period. The Khmer Rouge sought to build wholly new order without links to the Buddhist monarchies of the past.

In late 1979 Vietnamese forces pushed the Khmer Rouge out of most of Cambodia and installed a new government made up of more moderate Communists. This new government allowed Buddhism to be reestablished but strongly restricted its role for many years.

Throughout the 1980s the Vietnamese-backed government led by Hun Sen was treated as a pariah by all but Soviet-bloc countries. Despite the atrocities committed by the Khmer Rouge, it gained some international support by entering into an alliance with royalist and republican groups. In the early 1990s negotiations carried out under the United Nations (UN) compelled the government in Phnom Penh to agree to the holding of elections in which all factions would compete. In anticipation of a new electoral-based politics, Hun Sen and other erstwhile members of the Cambodian Communist Party assumed a major public patronage role toward monks and shrines, culminating in making Buddhism the state religion.

In 1991, after the UN-sponsored accord was reached, Sihanouk returned to Phnom Penh as king, and political leaders who had been in exile for many years organized new political parties. All factions have sought to associate themselves publicly with leading monks and with patronage of the religion. Maha Ghosananda, a senior monk who was outside Cambodia when the Khmer Rouge took over, has emerged as a charismatic leader of a movement without affiliation with any political faction that seeks to make Buddhist ideals the basis for transcending the violence of Cambodia. This movement has, however, been eclipsed by Hun Sen's domination of the Khmer polity.

Laos. A government led by a communist party also took control of state power in Laos in 1975. While this government initially sought to ban some of the most popular traditional Buddhist rituals and to restrict significantly any new recruitment to the sangha, the Lao Communist Party did not attempt as did its counterpart in Cambodia to eradicate Buddhism. By the late 1970s most Buddhist rituals were once again permitted, and in the 1980s the sangha was allowed to recruit new members. By the mid-1980s, the government had undertaken a volte-face, began actively to promote some Buddhist activities, and even started to use monks in carrying out the educational role of the state. But the sangha in Laos remains very much under the control of the state, and the only politics involving the religion are those allowed by the government.

Thailand. Because Thailand remained independent politically throughout the colonial period, appeals to Buddhism as the foundation for Thai nationalist identity have been promoted by the state instead of in opposition to the state. In the early decades of the twentieth century, some opposition to the imposition of the authority of Bangkok in areas that had previously enjoyed relative autonomy coalesced around certain local Buddhist leaders. This opposition was eliminated, however, by a combination of coercive force and cultural policies. The latter, carried out primarily through both monastic and secular education, eventually succeeded in inculcating in the populace an identification with a nation based on a shared Buddhism and the monarchy. In contrast to all other Theravadin countries, in Thailand Buddhism became the de facto state religion, and the religious establishment was co-opted in state-sponsored efforts to integrate the nation and modernize the society.

The very success of these efforts created the conditions for a new politics in which Buddhism has been a significant factor. Through a coup carried out in 1932, members of a small nonroyal elite succeeded in transforming the polity into a constitutional monarchy. The "promoters" (as they were known) of the 1932 coup were educated in secular schools and shared a modern perspective on the world. But the ideal of "democracy" in the name of which the coup was staged held little meaning for the vast majority of the populace who still lived in rural communities where life was organized around the agricultural and Buddhist ritual cycles. By the late 1930s, the old monarchical absolutism had been replaced by a new authoritarianism that was legitimated, in part, by state-sponsored Buddhist ritualism.

After World War II, the economy of Thailand began to grow significantly, and from the 1960s until the late 1990s it was one of the fastest growing in the world. This growth led to the emergence of an expanding middle class. By the late 1960s, many, especially students, from this middle class had begun to question the right of a military oligarchy to exercise unchecked power. In the early and mid-1970s the challenge to military rule was predicated primarily on secular, including communist, ideologies. This challenge initially succeeded on October 14, 1973, when a student-led movement forced the military junta to resign and, with the backing of the king, a new constitution was written. But this constitution was soon eclipsed as right-wing forces mobilized to support the re-institution of an authoritarian regime. These forces acquired backing from both the Buddhist establishment, which allowed a former dictator to be ordained temporarily, and from a charismatic monk who offered moral justification for the killing of "communists."

A bloody coup on October 6, 1976, that resulted in the killing or imprisonment of many in the student movement and led many others to flee to the jungle to join a communist-led insurrection seemed to mark the triumph of a militant Buddhism. This proved, however, not to be the case. Some military leaders for whom Buddhist values of tolerance were more compelling succeeded in taking power away from the most radical right-wing elements and instituted an amnesty for communist insurrectionaries. This coupled with the Communist Party of Thailand's loss of external backers led to the ultimate collapse of the communist challenge.

In the 1980s, as the economy continued to boom, the political system evolved into what has been termed a "demi-democracy," in which groups representing diverse interests among the now even larger middle class were able to exert increasing influence on policy making through the parliament, through the media, and through a growing number of nongovernmental organizations. Some of these NGOs based their mission explicitly on Buddhist critiques of materialism and social inequalities. One politician who became mayor of Bangkok and the leader of the opposition to yet another effort to re-institute military rule in 1991–1992 was closely associated with a new movement whose leader was expelled for heterodoxy from the established sangha. Efforts on the part of a junta that held power for a year in 1991–1992 to make legitimate its role through links with establishment Buddhism clearly failed.

In the 1990s the Thai people faced the worst HIV/AIDS epidemic in Asia, environmental degradation and pollution (especially in Bangkok), and, in the late 1990s, an unprecedented economic crisis that began with the collapse of the value of the currency. In confronting these modern forms of dukkha, people in Thailand often turned to monks offering a significant diversity of interpretations of the Buddhist way. Among the most conspicuous are the "commercial monks" who seem to offer shortcuts to attaining reduction of suffering for those who make large gifts in support of the religion. Other monks have rejected such religious materialism and have called for moral regeneration through the cultivation of spirituality centered on meditation. Yet others advocate a "socially engaged Buddhism" that emphasizes joining together with others, sometimes in opposition to governments, to address problems of social injustice, poverty, illness, and destruction of the environment. In such a pluralistic environment, it is no longer possible for any government to claim for itself as did governments prior to the 1970s the sole mantle of Buddhist legitimacy.

Following an election in early 2001 Thai politics entered a new period. The Thai Rak Thai Party led by Thaksin Shinawatra, who promoted a populist nationalism, gained control of parliament. The Muslim peoples of southern Thailand, who had previously been courted by the opposition Democrat Party, became increasingly alienated. This alienation was exacerbated by the Thaksin government's support of the American war in Iraq. It contributed to the emergence of a Muslim insurgency in southern Thailand beginning in early 2004. The Thaksin government responded with force in a series of deadly incidents that further alienated Thai Muslims. The rhetoric of the Thaksin government echoed the constricted Buddhist nationalism of Sri Lanka.

Although the Thaksin government was returned to power in 2005 with an even greater majority in parliament, the media, university faculty, and NGOs steadily increased their criticisms of both government actions in Muslim areas and of misuse of power for personal gain by the prime minister, a media magnate, and his family. By early 2006 an intense crisis of legitimacy developed as Thaksin lost the support of the king and many highly respected Buddhist monks and senior Buddhist lay leaders. In September 2006 Thaksin was overthrown in a military coup.

Violence versus Pacifism

Although the taking of human life is a cardinal sin according to Theravada Buddhism, violent conflict has often taken place in societies in which Theravada Buddhism is dominant. In modern times, militant Buddhist nationalism has been promoted by governments in Sri Lanka, Buddhist nationalism has been evoked to justify suppression of Muslim insurgents in Thailand, a highly repressive regime in Burma has sought to clothe itself with Buddhist legitimacy, and Buddhist monks have been the targets of violence in Cambodia. In all Theravada Buddhist countries, governments have sought to impose strict controls on the sangha, the community of Buddhists monks. Nonetheless, the fundamental pacifism of Buddhism continues to be used by monks and lay people to criticize the misuse of power. In Sri Lanka, Burma, Thailand, Cambodia, and Laos politics are deeply intertwined with Buddhist cultures.

See also *Buddha.*

Charles F. Keyes

BIBLIOGRAPHY

Evans, Grant. "Buddhism and Economic Action in Socialist Laos." In *Socialism: Ideals, Ideologies, and Local Practice,* edited by C. M. Hann. London and New York: Routledge, 1993.

Gombrich, Richard. *Theravada Buddhism: A Social History from Ancient Benares to Modern Colombo.* London: Routledge and Kegan Paul, 1988.

Gombrich, Richard, and Gananath Obeyesekere. *Buddhism Transformed: Religious Change in Sri Lanka.* Princeton: Princeton University Press, 1989.

Jackson, Peter A. *Buddhism, Legitimation, and Conflict: The Political Functions of Urban Thai Buddhism.* Singapore: Institute of Southeast Asian Studies, 1989.

Keyes, Charles F. "Buddhist Politics and Their Revolutionary Origins in Thailand." In *Structure and History,* edited by S. N. Eisenstadt. Special issue of the *International Political Science Review* 10, no. 2 (1989): 121–142.

———. "Buddhist Economics and Buddhist Fundamentalism in Burma and Thailand." In *Remaking the World: Fundamentalist Impact,* edited by Martin Marty and Scott Appleby. Chicago: University of Chicago Press, 1993, pp. 367–409.

———. "Communist Revolution and the Buddhist Past in Cambodia." In *Asian Visions of Authority: Religion and the Modern States of East and Southeast Asia,* edited by Charles F. Keyes, Laurel Kendall, and Helen Hardacre. Honolulu: University of Hawaii Press, 1994, pp. 43–73.

Sarkisyanz, E. *Buddhist Backgrounds of the Burmese Revolution.* The Hague: Martinus Nijhoff, 1965.

Schober, Juliane. "Buddhist Just Rule and Burmese National Culture: State Patronage of the Chinese Tooth Relic in Myanmar." *History of Religions* 36, no. 3 (1997): 218–243.

Smith, Bardwell L., ed. *Religion and the Legitimation of Power in Sri Lanka.* Chambersburg, Pa: Anima, 1978.

———. *Religion and Legitimation of Power in Thailand, Laos, and Burma.* Chambersburg, Pa.: Anima Books, 1978.

Stuart-Fox, Martin, and Rod Bucknell. "Politicization of the Buddhist Sangha in Laos." *Journal of Southeast Asian Studies* 12, no. 1 (1982): 60–80.

Swearer, Donald K. "Fundamentalist Movements in Theravada Buddhism." In *Fundamentalisms Observed.* Vol. I: *The Fundamentalism Project,* pp. 628–690, edited by Martin E. Marty and R. Scott Appleby. Chicago: University of Chicago Press, 1991.

Tambiah, Stanley Jeyaraja. *World Conqueror and World Renouncer: A Study of Buddhism and Polity in Thailand against a Historical Background.* Cambridge, U.K.: Cambridge University Press, 1976.

———. *Buddhism Betrayed? Religion, Politics, and Violence in Sri Lanka.* Chicago: University of Chicago Press, 1992.

Buddhism, Tibetan

Tibetan Buddhism is the predominant religion of Tibet, of bordering areas in the Himalayan plateau, and, in the twentieth and twenty-first centuries, of Tibetan refugees living in India and elsewhere. From about the seventh century C.E. until the early 1950s, when the People's Republic of China incorporated Tibet as a province (Xizang), Tibetan Buddhism was the primary organizing principle in the development of Tibet's unique political system.

The Tibetan Buddhist Tradition

Beginning in the seventh century, with the spread of Mahayana Buddhism and esoteric forms of Buddhism from India, several kings of central Tibet became patrons of the faith. Following the suppression of Buddhism by one king in the ninth century, and his subsequent assassination, there followed a period of decentralized authority that lasted until the thirteenth century. Although political authority was in the hands of local rulers, scattered Tibetan monks and pious lay people continued to invite Buddhist scholars and teachers from India and Nepal. From these teachers the important Mahayana doctrines and practices of the period were received, and major portions of Buddhist scripture were translated from Sanskrit into Tibetan.

The four main sectarian traditions of Tibetan Buddhism in the modern world trace their origins to the teaching lineages of different Indian Buddhists. With the power vacuum in central Tibet created by the demise of the kings, petty Tibetan rulers sought to increase their political influence by forming relationships first with Indian and then with Tibetan religious authorities (called lamas). At the same time, some lamas sought the protection and support of political leaders against their rivals from other Tibetan Buddhist sects. This trend continued, with far-reaching results, for most of Tibetan history. Beginning with the patron-priest relationship between the lama Sakya Pandita and the Mongol king Godan in the thirteenth century, Tibetan lamas from various sects received patronage from foreign powers. These included the lords of different Mongol tribes as well as the Mongol, Han, and Manchu emperors of China.

In Tibet, the ideal of the bodhisattva, a spiritual adept who deliberately seeks to be reborn in the world in order to aid suffering beings, led to the religious and political institution of reincarnate lamas, beginning in the thirteenth century. Such a person is usually recognized from a young age as the rebirth of a previous spiritual master. There were hundreds of recognized reincarnate lamas in Tibet, only some of whom also held considerable political power as the spiritual heads of large monasteries or sectarian traditions. The dalai lamas eventually became the most powerful of these, though other reincarnation lineages, such as the panchen lama, also held considerable religious and political authority.

In the seventeenth century, during the reign of the powerful fifth dalai lama, Lozang Gyatso (1617–1682), central Tibet became unified as a state explicitly governed by the principle of religion and politics combined. Yet even after the time of the "Great Fifth" Dalai Lama and his centralization of power in Lhasa, large, semi-independent monasteries owned vast estates, collected taxes on them from peasant landholders, and even raised their own military forces. Thus lamas from these important monasteries had considerable political as well as religious influence on what was often a weak central government. In short, the lay nobility and the monastic rulers were the twin poles of power in Tibetan

politics. From the seventeenth century onward, both lay and monastic officials were appointed as government ministers. This system was institutionalized in the late nineteenth century, and the long-standing political clout of certain clergy was incorporated into the central Tibetan government.

In the centuries following the fifth dalai lama's reign, patron-priest relationships between the dalai lamas in Lhasa (as well as other high-ranking lamas) and foreign monarchs were vital in the political climate of the Tibetan state. These relationships were described in both political and religious terms, with the dalai lamas as spiritual preceptors to the political rulers. When Mongol and later Manchu emperors were strong, the Chinese empire's political influence on Tibet was equally strong. Contemporary Chinese historians interpret this as evidence of Tibet's subservience and dependence on the Chinese state. Many Tibetan and Western historians, however, point to Tibet's independence from Chinese political influence at other points in history, stressing that the patron-priest relationship did not militate against the temporal power that the dalai lamas held in their own domains.

Chinese Rule and Resistance

After the communist revolution in China in 1949, the People's Liberation Army entered eastern Tibet, claiming it had come to "liberate" Tibet from feudal serfdom. Many Tibetans regarded the Chinese army as a foreign invader; this perception was reinforced by the profound differences between the atheistic communism of Mao Zedong, the Chinese leader, and their own Buddhist faith. After the flight of the fourteenth dalai lama, Tenzin Gyatso (1935–), to India in 1959, Tibet's religious-political system was dismantled and replaced by institutions under the direction of the Chinese government in Beijing. Since 1959 approximately 130,000 Tibetans have followed their leader into exile. Most settled in India, where the Dalai Lama's government was reconstituted as a government in exile. One of the principal aims of this exile government was to see that the religious culture of Tibet would be preserved among the refugees. Refugees continued to leave Tibet into the twenty-first century, and more Tibetans have gone on to settle in Europe and North America. Despite this geographical dispersal, faith in the Dalai Lama and in Tibetan Buddhism have linked Tibetan exiles worldwide. For many Tibetans, Buddhism is one of the most important markers of their ethnic and national identity.

A Tibetan monk holds the flag of his country while listening to protest speeches at a November 1997 rally in Vancouver, British Columbia, demanding independence for Tibet. Buddhist monks and nuns have been at the forefront of the movement to end the Chinese occupation of Tibet.

In the decades following the Chinese invasion of Tibet, the institutions and even the practice of Buddhism were suppressed. This political repression reached its height during the Cultural Revolution (1966–1976), in which Mao's directive to eradicate old and outmoded systems of thought led to the destruction of thousands of Tibetan (as well as Chinese) Buddhist shrines and monasteries, which were believed to be strongholds of superstition and feudal society. When Chinese policy changed in the early 1980s, allowing for the return of Tibetan customs and religious practice, it was obvious that years of political reeducation and social reorganization introduced from Beijing had not weakened the beliefs of many Tibetans. The harsh slogans brought against the exiled Dalai Lama and religion produced an opposite effect. Both the Dalai Lama and Buddhism itself became symbols of Tibet's cultural and political independence from China.

Despite linguistic, historical, and cultural differences between Chinese and Tibetans, religion has proved to be the primary means through which Tibet's cultural uniqueness, and indeed its political sovereignty, is articulated.

In the autumn of 1987 the first popular Tibetan protests against Chinese rule were witnessed by Western tourists in Lhasa. Since then protests have continued in Lhasa and in other areas of Tibet, despite China's massive military presence and the Chinese government's willingness to crush all opposition. After Tibetan independence protests in the spring of 1989, martial law was imposed in Lhasa; it was not lifted until more than a year later.

During this time the figurehead of the struggle for an independent Tibet, the fourteenth dalai lama, was awarded the Nobel Peace Prize for his efforts to bring a solution to Tibet's ongoing crisis. Tibetans both within Tibet and those in exile reacted with jubilation. In 1995, in accordance with Tibetan Buddhist protocol, the Dalai Lama recognized a boy found in Tibet as the rebirth of the Panchen Lama, who had died in 1989. The government in Beijing rejected the Dalai Lama's candidate and replaced him with its own choice, thus indicating Chinese attempts to control Tibetan politics by way of its religion. Despite his worldwide acclaim, no world government has ever recognized the Dalai Lama as the legitimate political leader of an independent Tibetan nation. Because of Chinese pressure, he is treated at best as a religious dignitary, never as Tibet's head of state.

Many of the pro-independence demonstrations, which have aimed at bringing China's repression in Tibet to the attention of the world, have been led by Buddhist monks and nuns. Monasteries and nunneries represent an autonomous sphere of Tibetan culture, despite Chinese attempts to reconfigure them as merely religious places in service to a unified China. Instead, monastics have exemplified the cultural, religious, and political autonomy of Tibet in relation to the People's Republic. Drawing on their pre–Chinese invasion role as upholders of tradition, monks and nuns have come to symbolize, once again, the unity of religion with politics that is part of Tibet's history and culture. Tibetan Buddhist symbols, practices, institutions, and clergy have become the most potent way of asserting Tibet's cultural and political independence in the face of Chinese rule.

One of the most significant effects of the post-1959 Tibetan diaspora has been the burgeoning international attention that Tibetan Buddhism has received. The most important lamas of each of Tibetan Buddhism's four main traditions are now all international travelers; they have established Buddhist centers widely in Western Europe, North America, and Australia, in addition to Malaysia, Taiwan, Russia, Brazil, and Mexico. Ironically, even as Buddhism is one of the primary forces unifying Tibetans in exile and in Tibet, Tibetan Buddhism has also attracted tens of thousands of non-Tibetan converts in ever increasing numbers. This in turn reinforces the visibility of Tibetans internationally, perhaps making religion the most important political tool that pro-independence activists possess.

See also *Communism; Dalai Lama.*

Peter K. Moran

BIBLIOGRAPHY

Goldstein, Melvyn. *A History of Modern Tibet, 1913–1951: The Demise of the Lamaist State.* Berkeley: University of California Press, 1989.

Schwartz, Ronald D. *Circle of Protest: Political Ritual in the Tibetan Uprising.* New York: Columbia University Press, 1994.

Shakabpa, Tsepon W. D. *Tibet: A Political History.* New Haven: Yale University Press, 1967.

Stein, R. A. *Tibetan Civilization.* Translated by J. E. Stapleton Driver. Stanford: Stanford University Press, 1972.

Burke, Edmund

British politician and political theorist. In opposition to the royal absolutists, for whom the king's will represented the ultimate principle of government, Burke (1729–1797) joined with the moderate Whig Party, for whom the settled customs of the people constituted the fundamental law of the land. His political perspective, contrasting sharply with dominant intellectual trends of the time, has been variously classified over subsequent centuries, perhaps most significantly as the archetype of classical conservatism.

Burke became well acquainted with diverse religious communities throughout Great Britain in his early years. He was born in Dublin into a religiously divided family—his father and brothers being Protestant and his mother and sister being Roman Catholic. Burke attended a Quaker school and graduated from Trinity College. Contrary to unverified rumors of a secret liaison with the Jesuits, Burke was a devout communicant of the established Anglican Church throughout his life. In 1756 he married Jane Nugent, daughter of a Roman Catholic father and a Presbyterian mother. In Burke's judgment, religious sensibilities, while assuming various forms, constitute an indispensable means of comprehending the fundamental meaning of life and of sustaining social stability and growth throughout history.

Burke rose to become a prominent member of the House of Commons for nearly three decades (1765–1794), addressing the critical issues of his time in speeches, pamphlets, and letters through which his political understanding was developed. He opposed the rationalism of the French *philosophes* (Voltaire, Denis Diderot, and others), whose principles of natural rights—rights derived by reason from human nature rather than dictated by social custom or legislative decision—were influential in the French Revolution. Instead, Burke invoked the ancient wisdom of humankind transmitted through long-standing cultural and social institutions. In matters of fundamental political judgment, the prejudices and prescriptions of our common history—most profoundly present in established religions and conveyed through an aristocracy of the wise and virtuous—are, according to Burke, more to be trusted than the speculative reasoning of the solitary individual.

Divine Providence, in Burke's assessment, works its way through the processes of history, but not uncritically, given the concern of Providence for the true happiness of all humankind. On the strength of that conviction, Burke vigorously opposed the oppressive practices of the East India Trading Company in South Asia as inconsistent with the traditions of that ancient civilization. He strongly supported moves to relieve Roman Catholics in Ireland and England of arbitrary restrictions on their religious practices and political participation, and he promoted the cause of the American colonies in their struggle against King George III, despite his lack of sympathy with the natural rights appeals of the revolutionaries. Social change, Burke avowed, if it follows the insights of an informed prudence, does not run contrary to the principle of prescription.

Burke, however, expressed some limits. In his most famous tract, *Reflections on the Revolution in France* (1790), he denounces the arch-individualism and atheism of the French revolutionaries—the intellectuals as well as the monied interests—as destructive of the foundations of European civilization and productive of social anarchy. Whereas the Glorious Revolution of 1688 in England—in which the Roman Catholic king was ousted and replaced by Protestant successors at the invitation of parliamentary leaders—resulted in a restoration of the prescriptive rights of the English, the French Revolution threatened the dissolution of ancient bonds of the European commonwealth. Burke's support of military action against revolutionary France as a religious war led to his rupture with the prevailing powers in the Whig Party. Their support for the new French regime manifested, from Burke's perspective, profound ignorance of the dynamics of human history.

See also *Conservatism*.

Douglas Sturm

Edmund Burke.

BIBLIOGRAPHY

Burke, Edmund. *Reflections on the Revolution in France,* edited with introduction by J. G. A. Pocock. Indianapolis: Hackett, 1987.

Cobban, Alfred. *Edmund Burke and the Revolt against the Eighteenth Century.* London: Allen and Unwin, 1929.

Macpherson, C. B. *Burke.* New York: Hill and Wang, 1980.

Stanlis, Peter J. *Edmund Burke: The Enlightenment and Revolution.* New Brunswick, N.J.: Transaction Publishers, 1991.

C

John Calvin.

Caliphate

See *Islam*.

Calvinism

Calvinism, a widely adopted theological system largely based on the teachings of John Calvin (1509–1564), has significantly influenced political developments in the modern Western world. In the sixteenth century, John Calvin, inspired by the new Protestant Reformation set in motion by Martin Luther, sought to reform Roman Catholicism. He developed a theological system based on belief in biblical authority, divine sovereignty, predestination, and the responsibility of Christians to serve God in all areas of life. Born in France and educated in theology and law, Calvin was forced to flee Paris in 1533 because of his radical views. He went to Switzerland, first to Basel and then to Geneva, where, after a period of exile, he helped Protestant leaders establish control over the civil government. By pastoring the Protestant congregation in Geneva, training numerous Protestant leaders, publishing numerous theological works, and maintaining an extensive correspondence with church and governmental officials, Calvin had a substantial impact on political events during his lifetime.

In the next three centuries, his followers helped shape political theory and practice in several Western nations, especially in England, Scotland, Holland, and the United States. Some scholars argue that because Calvin espoused an authoritarian concept of government, opposed the right of individuals to worship as they chose, persecuted "heretics," and endorsed theocracy (a system of government in which God rules), Calvin provided little foundation for modern notions of democracy. They claim that individual liberty and democracy were neither a logical implication nor an explicit teaching of Calvinism but instead developed accidentally from the competition and conflict between Catholics and Protestants during the sixteenth and seventeenth centuries. Other scholars counter that because liberal democracy first arose precisely in the places where Calvinism was most deeply rooted and had the greatest influence on national life, a connection must exist between the two. They contend that Calvinist convictions helped prepare the way for, or convinced people to accept, modern democratic principles and practices.

Calvin's Theology

Although Calvin did not publish treatises on politics, his theological teachings and writings had powerful political implications, and he was deeply involved in contemporary political events. He campaigned for governmental policies favorable to Protestants and frequently offered advice to kings. He played a major role in political affairs in Geneva, a city that sought to create a Christian commonwealth in the years after 1541. Although Calvin held a political office in the city, he codified its civil and constitutional laws and had a tremendous influence on its development as a republic admired by his contemporaries for its administration of justice, hospitality, and civic righteousness. The congregations Calvin helped establish were based on representative and democratic principles and provided a model for republican governments. At the same time, however, Geneva was a paternalistic community that enforced the observance of the Christian faith through extensive regulations and rigorous surveillance of private life.

Unlike Lutheranism and Anabaptism, the other major movements associated with the Protestant Reformation and both of which placed little emphasis on temporal affairs, Calvinism insisted that Christians must participate in political life as part of their calling to glorify God in all areas of life. Calvin rejected views that Christians should shun political involvement because the state existed solely to restrain humanity's sinful nature. He and his followers considered the state to be an instrument of God, a positive good, not a necessary evil, and sought whenever possible to create a holy commonwealth. Calvin argued that God ordained civil government to serve his purposes and that magistrates, whether they acknowledged it or not, were under God's authority.

While arguing that the Bible did not mandate any particular form of government, Calvin was critical of monarchy, the prevailing political system of his day. He contended that a mixture of aristocracy and democracy (a form of representative government) like that which governed Geneva represented the best form of government. He feared that a completely democratic government would degenerate into mob rule and anarchy. Rule by an aristocracy, by the most talented and politically astute citizens, not a hereditary class, would ensure the most just society.

In the midst of the political upheaval produced by the Reformation's break with the Catholic Church, Calvin strove to assure magistrates that Protestants were loyal citizens, not political revolutionaries. He urged all Christians to obey their rulers and advised Protestants living under unjust governments to pray for their rulers and even suffer persecution rather than engage in civil disobedience or revolt as private citizens. He argued, however, that Christians could criticize their civil leaders and that they had a right, even a moral duty, to depose a wicked ruler, if led by the lesser magistrates who stood between them and kings. In the 1550s and 1560s, when the Catholic Counter Reformation threatened to exterminate Protestants, Calvin asserted that magistrates who exceeded their power violated their office and were reduced to the status of private citizens. Individual Christians could, therefore, disobey them. These teachings prepared the way for rebellions, led by the people's representatives, of largely Calvinist populations in Holland, Scotland, England, and the United States.

Deeply influenced by the medieval views of the relationship of church and state, Calvin did not believe in religious toleration, ideological pluralism, or the separation of church and state as it has developed in many Western nations since the late eighteenth century. Although he insisted that church and state have different leaders, he argued that their work must complement one another and that civil government must protect "the outward worship of God," defend "sound doctrine" and the position of the church, and help promote civil righteousness. To accomplish these ends, magistrates must compel citizens to adhere to all of the Ten Commandments and ensure the practice of true religion in their jurisdictions. Both Calvin and Luther believed that church and state should work together and argued that the state should promote true religion. Luther, unlike Calvin, however, asserted that God ruled only indirectly over the secular world, prohibited revolt against tyrannical government, and did not seek to create a distinctively Christian state.

Calvinist Expansion and Influence

Calvin's teachings and his political policies in Geneva inspired and served as a model for his followers in France, Scotland, England, Holland, and the United States. New political situations led Calvinists in these nations to alter and apply Calvin's political views to fit their contexts. In the 1570s and 1580s, for example, the Huguenots, a Calvinist minority in France, devised a theory of religious and political freedom that went beyond Calvin's more restrained position and had a substantial impact on other nations. In a series of revolutionary tracts, the Huguenots asserted that liberty was based on both a divinely ordained covenant and a concept of popular sovereignty that gave people the right to select and depose their rulers.

Calvinist thought was embodied most fully on a national level in Scotland. In numerous political pamphlets, John Knox (1513–1572), a Scottish Protestant reformer, insisted that Christians had the right to rebel against ungodly tyrants even without the leadership of lower elected officials. By stressing religious concerns, especially eternal salvation, Knox galvanized the Scots to political action that made the nation a Calvinist stronghold, and Calvinism became the basis of the Scottish Presbyterian Church. Three important concepts that developed in Scotland in the late 1500s went on to become widely accepted in Great Britain by the early 1700s: the church has an equal legal right and standing with the civil state, citizens have the right to hold political officials responsible for performing their duties as prescribed by transcendent law, and democratic structures based on Presbyterian polity provides for the participation of ordinary people in government.

In the 1640s, a civil war in England deposed the king, Charles I, and established a Commonwealth (1649–1660) under the leadership of the Puritan leader Oliver Cromwell. The Puritans were English Calvinists who wished to "purify" the church of Catholic doctrine and liturgy. The war stemmed in large part from the Puritans' opposition to Charles's belief in the divine right of kings and their resistance to the harsh persecution they suffered. In 1643 the Scots and English approved a Solemn League and Covenant that sought to balance individual and national liberty with the necessity of state authority and guaranteed the right of Presbyterians to worship freely in Scotland, England, and Ireland. The Westminster Confession, adopted by English and Scottish Calvinists in 1646, urged magistrates to maintain piety, justice, and peace and protect the church without giving preference to any denomination; it counseled citizens to pray for rulers, honor them, and obey their lawful commands.

The Glorious Revolution of 1688 was based in part on the principles of the Scottish Covenanters. It replaced the Catholic king of England, James II, with his Protestant daughter, Mary, and her husband, William III of Holland. The justification for this action rested largely on the teachings of Knox and fellow Scots Andrew Melville and Samuel Rutherford who argued that kings who violated their covenant with God and their people could justly be deposed.

Across the Atlantic, Calvinism helped shape the U.S. political system and inform its values. Although three major streams of thought—the ideas of the Commonwealth men of seventeenth-century England, the several varieties of the European Enlightenment, and the Judeo-Christian tradition—converged to direct the development of the U.S. Constitution and government, the Calvinist contribution to U.S. independence and democracy was substantial. It is evident in the ideological similarities between Calvinist theology and U.S. political theory, the historical leadership and models provided by Calvinist leaders and groups, and the role that Calvinists played in the American Revolution.

The Puritans who had settled New England in the seventeenth century wanted to create a biblical commonwealth that glorified God and adhered to divinely revealed norms. Their society acknowledged its dependence on God, recognized that God ordained government to promote the common good, and affirmed the rule of law. The state established a church, required church attendance, prevented other religious groups from worshipping, banished dissenters, and limited the vote to church members. More rigorously than almost all other religious groups, the Puritans applied the law of God to all aspects of society, including the state. The law was God's means for ordering a sinful world and helping to restrain the unregenerate and redeem the elect.

Scholars have stressed the role that seventeenth-century natural law theories and the eighteenth-century Enlightenment had on shaping the American understanding of civil authority and responsibility in the colonial period.

Nevertheless, it is clear that the Puritans had a direct and powerful effect on the spirit of American democracy. Puritanism taught that government is under divine law and that people are capable of self-government. These concepts, combined with the Calvinist emphasis on self-discipline, individual calling, and education, helped inspire citizens to participate actively in politics, care deeply about civic righteousness and the structure and practice of government, and live responsibly under the law.

Calvinists contributed to the American Revolution that began in 1776 in a number of ways. During the 1730s and 1740s, the First Great Awakening, a colony-wide revival based largely on Calvinist theology, helped unify colonists and prepare them for their break with England. In sermons and pamphlets, numerous Calvinists argued that God's law was higher than the decrees of kings or the acts of Parliament. Because people were created in the image of God, Calvinists declared, they possessed certain inalienable rights. Calvinists joined other patriots in asserting that the success of a republic depended on the virtue of its citizens. Because of human depravity, written constitutions defining, limiting, and balancing power were necessary. Congregationalists and Presbyterians, the most influential denominations in colonial America in 1776, supplied much of the ideological support, political leadership, and soldiers for the revolution.

To a significant extent, the political foundation for the American Revolution and the U.S. Constitution, ratified in 1789, rests upon the thought of John Locke (1632–1704). Locke, however, was substantially influenced by his Puritan forbears. His ideas were acceptable in America largely because they restated familiar principles forged by Calvinists during the English Civil War. Samuel Rutherford, in *Lex Rex* (1644), had used almost every argument later employed by Locke, including the claims that the people were ultimately sovereign, government originated in a contract between the governor and the governed, and citizens had a right to revolt when this contract was broken. Even Locke's influential views on religious toleration restated Puritan convictions that human beings were fallible, church and state had different objectives, and government depended on the consent of the governed.

Calvinists in all nations emphasized the sovereignty of God and insisted that the state existed to promote the common good, not that of any individual or group. Because God had designed different institutions to direct other areas of life—the family, school, business, church—the powers of government, Calvinists argued, were limited to preserving the peace, ensuring justice, and advancing the corporate welfare. These convictions, coupled with Calvinism's emphasis on human sinfulness, contributed to the U.S. Constitution's principles of limitation and balance of power.

Modern Calvinism

Since 1790 Calvinism has influenced political life in a variety of ways. It produced the outstanding Dutch statesman and leader Abraham Kuyper (1837–1920). Kuyper published dozens of analyses of political issues, edited a daily newspaper, founded and led a Christian political party, and served several terms in the Dutch parliament. As prime minister from 1901 to 1905, he fought to expand voting rights to all social classes, improve education, and ensure that all religious groups were treated equally. In South Africa, Calvinism helped to provide a theological foundation for Boer nationalism and apartheid (racial segregation and inequality) by teaching that the Dutch who settled the area in the nineteenth century were God's chosen people, superior to indigent Africans. In the twentieth century, the Reformed Church in South Africa did little to protest the nation's rigid racial segregation.

The stance of American Calvinists toward political activism during the nineteenth century varied greatly. Northern Presbyterians and Congregationalists provided extensive support for the benevolent societies spawned by the Second Great Awakening (1800–1840) that strove to abolish slavery, reduce drunkenness, improve education, and help the indigent. Reformed Presbyterians, a group rooted in dissenting Scottish Covenanters that formally organized in the United States in 1833, refrained from political participation because the United States refused to amend its Constitution to recognize Christ's lordship over the nation. After 1860 most Southern Presbyterians adopted the position that the church in its organized capacity should not attempt to influence government. By contrast, President Woodrow Wilson, son of a Presbyterian minister, practiced a "missionary diplomacy" designed to help developing nations become stable democracies. During his presidency (1913–1921) he attempted to base international relations on ethical principles, most notably by devising his Fourteen Points as a foundation for a treaty to end World War I and helping create the League of Nations.

Contemporary Calvinists, who reside primarily in the Netherlands, Scotland, the United States, and South Africa, hold varying positions about government and political life. Some espouse Christian reconstructionism, the belief that Old Testament law, moral and civil, except as it is specifically canceled by the New Testament, should be rigorously applied to present-day nations. Others, adhering to the national confession position, contend that all nations should officially declare allegiance to Jesus Christ in their constitutions and devise governmental structures and policies based on general biblical tenets. A third group of Calvinists, strongly influenced by Kuyper and Herman Dooyeweerd, a Dutch philosopher, advocate principled pluralism. They argue that God has established several basic independent structures—state, society, school, workplace, church, marriage, and family—that must work together to accomplish his designs in the world (structural pluralism). They also contend that governments should accept the presence of differing faith communities within their borders and ensure that all citizens, regardless of their religious convictions, receive equal rights (confessional pluralism).

Despite these fundamental differences, contemporary Calvinists agree that God's word is authoritative for all areas of life, including government and politics, and that the Bible provides transcendent norms for governing political life. They also affirm that political authority ultimately stems from God, not the consent of the governed, and that all earthly rulers are therefore subject to him. They believe that governments exist to enhance and enrich the lives of their citizens, especially by preserving order and ensuring justice.

See also *Anabaptists; Enlightenment; Lutheranism; Natural Law; Presbyterianism; Reformation; Theocracy; Weber, Max.*

Gary Scott Smith

BIBLIOGRAPHY
Davies, A. Mervyn. *Foundation of American Freedom.* New York: Abingdon, 1955.
Gamble, Richard C., ed. *Articles on Calvin and Calvinism.* Vol. 3: *Calvin's Work in Geneva.* New York: Garland, 1992.
Hunt, George L., ed. *Calvinism and the Political Order.* Philadelphia: Westminster Press, 1965.
Kelly, Douglas F. *The Emergence of Liberty in the Modern World: The Influence of Calvin on Five Governments from the Sixteenth through the Eighteenth Centuries.* Phillipsburg, N.J.: Presbyterian and Reformed, 1992.
Kingdon, Robert, and Robert Linder, eds. *Calvin and Calvinism: Sources of Democracy?* Lexington, Mass.: D.C. Heath, 1970.
McNeill, John T. *The History and Character of Calvinism.* New York: Oxford University Press, 1954.
Reid, W. Stanford, ed. *John Calvin: His Influence on the Modern World.* Grand Rapids, Mich.: Zondervan, 1982.
Smith, Gary Scott, ed. *God and Politics: Four Views on the Reformation of Civil Government.* Phillipsburg, N.J.: Presbyterian and Reformed, 1989.
Stone, Ronald H. *Reformed Faith and Politics.* Washington, D.C.: University Press of America, 1983.
Wallace, Ronald F. *Calvin, Geneva, and the Reformation.* Grand Rapids, Mich.: Baker Book House, 1990.

Canada

Canada, like its much more populous neighbor to the south, the United States, has since its earliest days experienced close connections between religion and politics, although not in the same way or for the same reasons. The modern history of Canada began in the early seventeenth century with French settlements in what is now the province of Quebec. Unlike in the United States, Catholicism was important politically from the first. Even today, the corporate conception of civic life that characterizes Roman Catholic societies continues to exert an especially strong influence in Quebec, although levels of religious practice in the province have fallen dramatically.

The Catholic factor loomed large in almost all major Canadian political developments until recent times. After the Treaty of Paris (1763), which granted Britain control of Quebec, British success at accommodating the province's Catholic establishment prepared the way for Catholic loyalty to the Crown during the American Revolution. When patriots invaded Canada in 1775, Bishop Briand of Quebec labeled support for the Americans "heresy," and most of his fellow religionists took the message to heart.

The tragic career of Louis Riel, who twice attempted to set up quasi-independent governments in Manitoba for the *métis* (mixed bloods of French Canadian and Indian parentage), also involved religion in several ways. Riel's execution in 1885, after his second rebellion failed, fueled bitter conflicts between Protestants eager to extend British religious hegemony and French-speaking Catholics who felt Riel had been wronged. Ill will generated by the Riel episode came to an end only when Wilfrid Laurier, the Liberal Party leader in the 1896 national election and a Roman Catholic, successfully assuaged the wounded sensibilities of both sides.

Even with the easing of Catholic-Protestant antagonism over the past half-century, Catholicism still makes a difference in Canadian electoral politics. In the mid-1980s

Richard Johnston found that Catholic-Protestant differences explained electoral variance more than any other social structural trait and, moreover, that these differences were not just a reflection of Anglophone-Francophone differences. In the 1995 Quebec referendum, as documented by the Canadian pollsters Andrew Grenville and Angus Reid, active Francophone Catholics were much less likely to vote in favor of sovereignty for Quebec than were nominally Catholic or secular Quebecois.

Rejecting Revolution

Religion has played an important role in the persistent Canadian rejections of revolution as a means of altering the political system and of American liberalism as the sole norm for political life. Catholic gratitude for the Quebec Act of 1774, which secured civil rights for Canadian Catholics that their co-religionists in Britain did not gain until 1829, helps explain Quebec's rejection of American pleas to join the War of Independence. In the Maritimes, a much smaller, more Protestant population also refused to join the patriot cause. In that case, at least part of the reason was the apolitical pietism fostered by Henry Alline and other leaders of the revivalist "New Light Stir" that began about the same time as the war.

The greatest stimulus to the creation of an anti-American Canadian nationalism, however, was the War of 1812. When undermanned militia and British regulars repelled the attacks of American troops in the Niagara peninsula and on the Great Lakes in 1813 and 1814, Canadian ministers hailed God's providential rescue of His people from tyranny with the same assurance that Americans had employed after their struggle against Britain a generation before. Loyalty to the king and trust in God constituted the Canadian "Shield of Achilles" that frustrated the perceived despotic plans of the American democratic mob.

The rejection of revolution, commemorated by the descendants of the fifty thousand loyalists who eventually settled in the Maritimes and Ontario and sealed decisively by the War of 1812, encouraged a spirit that several scholars, most famously Seymour Martin Lipset, have described as the critical element in Canadian politics. It is not as though the individualism, free market advocacy, and democratic principles that have meant so much in the United States are absent in Canada. Instead, in Canada liberalism always has been balanced by the corporate visions of the left and the right, and often with significant religious support. For example, the fundamentalist preacher William "Bible Bill" Aberhart embodied populist and communitarian principles in Alberta's Social Credit Party, which he led to power in the 1930s. A Baptist minister and contemporary of Aberhart, Tommy Douglas, exploited principles from the Social Gospel in organizing the Cooperative Commonwealth Federation in the prairies during the same Great Depression years. That movement eventually was transformed into the New Democratic Party, Canada's socialist alternative to the Liberals and Conservatives. The party has held power in several provinces at various times since the 1960s. The redoubtable Christian philosopher George Parkin Grant was only the most forceful of several prominent spokespersons in the 1950s and 1960s for a kind of statist conservatism that excoriated Canada's drift into American economic, political, and intellectual orbits.

Contrasting Approaches

Catholic corporatism as well as several varieties of Protestant loyalism have together encouraged in Canada an approach to questions of church and state that differs from the strict separation characterizing the U.S. system. The Catholic establishment in Quebec relinquished control of the school systems, hospitals, and labor organizations of the province only in the decades after the end of the Second World War. In the Maritimes and Ontario, the Anglican and Presbyterian Churches never received the same levels of governmental support that their established counterparts enjoyed in England and Scotland, but direct forms of aid to the churches did not end until the Clergy Reserves (land set aside for the use of the churches) were secularized in 1854.

Even after that contentious event, indirect government support continued for many religious agencies. Denominational colleges, for example, were folded into several of the major provincial universities so that to this day a few such colleges exist as components of the universities. In addition, varying kinds of aid are still provided to at least some church-organized primary and secondary schools in every Canadian province. In Newfoundland, the publicly funded educational system was conducted by the various denominations until the late 1990s, at which time general public schools not connected to the churches appeared for the first time.

Canadian distinctiveness is suggested by other differences with the United States—for example, stricter enforcement of Sunday closing laws and much stricter restrictions on independent religious broadcasters. By contrast, the religious views of major political leaders have usually been subject to much less public scrutiny than has become customary in the United States. Thus national political campaigns have been little affected by the fact that Canadian prime ministers Alexander Mackenzie (1873–1878) and John G. Diefenbaker (1957–1963) were practicing Baptists; John Turner (1984) was a serious Catholic; William Lyon Mackenzie King (1921–1926, 1926–1930, 1935–1948) was a Presbyterian spiritualist who enjoyed talking to his long-dead dog and mother; Pierre Elliott Trudeau (1968–1979, 1980–1984) and Brian Mulroney (1984–1993) were more ambiguously Catholic; and John A. Macdonald (1867–1873, 1878–1891) was a casual Presbyterian who (late in life) established a close connection with the evangelists H. T. Crossley and John E. Hunter.

To be sure, significant exceptions have emerged to the general pattern of not scrutinizing the personal faith of political leaders. Canadian political conservatism has recently been rejuvenated through the efforts of effective leaders from the Canadian West, including Preston Manning (head of the Reform Party, 1987–2000), Stockwell Day (head of the Canadian Alliance, 2000–2002, which succeeded the Reform Party), and Stephen Harper (head of a reconstituted Conservative Party, 2002–   , which pulled together the Alliance and remnants of the old Progressive Conservative Party). In each case, these leaders' evangelical Protestant convictions and their views on issues such as abortion and gay marriage featured large in federal elections, including the January 2005 vote that brought Harper to power as Canada's prime minister. Also significant was that the October 3, 2000, funeral of former Liberal premier Pierre Elliott

Trudeau was conducted as a formal Catholic service in Montreal's Notre Dame Basilica. It was probably the most widely noticed religious event in all Canadian history, and Trudeau's life-long (but private) Catholic practice has been the subject of significant recent reevaluation. Nonetheless, even with these developments, Canadian religious-political intersection remains much less prominent than witnessed in the United States during the civil rights era or during the rise of the Christian Right.

One of the most important reasons for structural differences in religion and politics between the two nations arises from the varied proportions of religious adherence. A major cross-border survey conducted by the Angus Reid group in October 1996 revealed that although about the same proportions of the two national populations were adherents to mainline churches (15 percent in the United States, 16 percent in Canada), in the United States a much higher proportion of citizens belonged to conservative Protestant churches (26 percent to 10 percent) and to African American Protestant churches (9 percent to less than 1 percent). In addition, a higher proportion of Canadians were adherents to the Roman Catholic Church (26 percent to 20 percent), and a much higher proportion were secular or only nominal in religious attachments (40 percent to 20 percent). The fact that each of these large blocs is constituted differently in the two countries—with, for example, the Mennonites and Dutch Reformed relatively more important among Canadian conservative Protestants and Baptists much more important in the United States—helps further to explain different religious tendencies.

At the same time, however, contrasts between Canada and the United States on questions of religion and politics are intriguing precisely because they coexist with so many similarities between the two nations. Those similarities include an active evangelical voluntarism that in the nineteenth century (outside of Quebec) came close to establishing an informal Protestant establishment. Part of the dominant nineteenth-century Protestant culture was a propensity to use biblical imagery for the aspirations of Canadian nationalism that also mirrored practices south of the border. For example, when the Dominion of Canada was formed in 1867, it seemed only natural for the Methodist Leonard Tilley of New Brunswick to apply the words of Psalm 72:8 to his country ("He shall have dominion also from sea to sea"). Also like the United States, Canada had a dismal record of Protestant-Catholic violence in the nineteenth century,

fueled sometimes by Catholic resentment of Protestant missionaries and sometimes by demonstrations of the Irish Protestant Orange Order.

In the immediate past, social scientific research has provided another way of comparing Canada and the United States. In both countries a "God's party" vote appears to be associated with politically conservative movements, but that association is considerably stronger in the United States than in Canada. Whereas 72 percent of self-identified fundamentalists and evangelicals who regularly attend church voted for the Republican presidential candidate in 1992, only 41 percent of church-attending adherents to conservative Protestant denominations voted for the Reform Party in Canada's 1993 parliamentary election.

The Angus Reid poll of October 1996 showed that on some issues Canadians and Americans are virtually the same—for example, in percentages who take a religiously motivated stance on abortion or who report that their clergy speak out on social issues. But Americans are considerably more likely (by at least 10 percentage points) to say that Christian values should influence politics, to express confidence in organized religion, to belong to a church or a religious group, to say that Christians should get involved in politics to protect their values, and to affirm that religion is important for political thinking. By contrast, Canadians are more likely (again, by at least 10 percentage points) to say that churches and religious organizations should be required to pay taxes, to express confidence in the news media, and to vote for a self-described atheist running for high political office. Such polling results suggest that processes of secularization have moved more rapidly in Canada than in the United States. They also suggest that, though Canadians and Americans share many social attitudes and experiences, historical differences in approaching questions of religion and politics continue to make at least something of a difference.

See also *Nationalism; Revolutions; Secularization; Social Gospel.*

Mark A. Noll

BIBLIOGRAPHY

Adamson, Christopher. "God's Continent Divided: Politics and Religion in Upper Canada and the Northern and Western United States, 1775 to 1841." *Comparative Studies in Society and History* 36 (July 1994): 417–446.

English, John, Richard Gwyn, and P. Whitney Lackenbauer. *The Hidden Pierre Elliott Trudeau: The Faith behind the Politics.* Ottawa: Novalis, 2004.

Ferrin, Scott Ellis, et al. "From Sectarian to Secular Control of Education: The Case of Newfoundland." *Journal of Research on Christian Education* 10 (Fall 2001): 411–430.

Gauvreau, Michael. *The Catholic Origins of Quebec's Quiet Revolution, 1931–1970.* Montreal and Kingston: McGill-Queen's University Press, 2005.

Grant, George Parkin. *Lament for a Nation: The Defeat of Canadian Nationalism.* Princeton, N.J.: Van Nostrand, 1965.

Grenville, Andrew, and Angus Reid. "Catholics and Voting No." *Christian Week,* January 30, 1996, p. 7.

Hamelin, Jean. *Histoire du catholicisme québécois: Le XXe siècle.* Vol. 2: *De 1940 à nos jours.* Montreal: Boréal, 1984.

Johnston, Richard. "The Reproduction of the Religious Cleavage in Canadian Elections." *Canadian Journal of Political Science/Revue Canadienne de Science Politique* 18 (March 1985): 99–114.

Lipset, Seymour Martin. *Continental Divide: The Values and Institutions of the United States and Canada.* New York: Routledge, 1990.

Miedema, Gary R. *For Canada's Sake: Public Religion, Centennial Celebrations, and the Re-making of Canada in the 1960s.* Montreal: McGill-Queen's University Press, 2005.

Noll, Mark A. "What Happened to Christian Canada?" *Church History* 75 (June 2006): 1–29.

Rawlyk, George A. "Politics, Religion, and the Canadian Experience: A Preliminary Probe." In *Religion and American Politics from the Colonial Period to the 1980s,* edited by M. A. Noll. New York: Oxford University Press, 1990.

Reimer, Sam. *Evangelicals and the Continental Divide: The Conservative Protestant Subculture in Canada and the United States.* Montreal and Kingston: McGill-Queen's University Press, 2003.

Van Die, Marguerite, ed. *Religion and Public Life in Canada: Historical and Comparative Perspectives.* Toronto: University of Toronto Press, 2001.

Capitalism

The word *capitalism* is contentious and impossible to define without offending the many vested interests that have disputed for, against, or about this system of economic activity, in the dominant reality of our time. For present purposes, capitalism may be defined as an economic system that sanctions the private and corporate accumulation, exchange, and deployment of wealth as a means of organizing the work of others from whose labor it is possible to extract a surplus—a profit that may in turn be reinvested in the original or another enterprise or that may be otherwise directed.

Development

Classical capitalism appeared in the course of the eighteenth century and was first fully theorized by Adam Smith, a Scottish economist, in the *Wealth of Nations* (1776). Max Weber, a German sociologist, later argued that capitalism understood simply as great individual financial undertakings is as old as history, whereas capitalism as an economic system is a modern phenomenon. Since the publication of Weber's *Protestant Ethic and the Spirit of Capitalism* (1920) the capitalist system has developed enormously and diversified. There are many new markets in the globalized economy and innovative ways of manipulating capital for profit; and there are, besides, many cultural adaptations of capitalism.

According to Weber, the mentality associated with the capitalist mode of production had historical connections and affinities with Protestant asceticism, which developed as a result of the sixteenth-century Reformation. It is therefore a customary (but not undisputed) idea to link the nascent "spirit of capitalism" with the much disputed "Protestant ethic," and, above all, with the Reformed Christian tradition. Weber explored the affinities between the single-minded and ascetic pursuit of God and an equally focused desire for profit. Work by Donald Hay, Douglas Meeks, and others in the late 1980s and early 1990s has provided Christian theologies of "God the Economist" and discussions of the ethics of distribution. In North America, "prosperity theology," with its relatively uncritical endorsement of capitalism, has remained a popular theological genre.

Theologically informed and critical evaluations of capitalism were rare in the period between the First and Second World Wars. It was only after the Second World War, and with a gradual thaw in the ensuing cold war, that this situation changed. In Germany "political theology," which linked Protestant theology with various strands of revisionist Marxism, developed in the 1960s and 1970s. Insights from political theology were transplanted to Central and Latin America, where, after the Second Vatican Council (1962–1965) and the Second General Conference of Roman Catholic bishops at Medellín, Colombia, in 1968, the liberation theology movement arose. This theology drew perspectives from the Marxist analysis of capitalist society, in particular, the class struggle and the need to liberate the poor, but sidestepped the atheistic aspects of Marxism. It attained its most radical critique of capitalism by representing the imbalanced distribution of wealth in the global economy between rich and poor nations as a religious issue.

Since the late nineteenth century Roman Catholic social teaching has provided a sustained, if limited, critique of capitalism and its chief antagonist, Marxist socialism. In 1891, after lengthy discussions, the pope produced the encyclical *Rerum Novarum,* the first modern papal document on social issues. The church's position with regard to the historic struggle between capital and labor was defined in terms of a conflict between the competing rights and obligations of owners and workers, over which the church was to exercise a moderating role. Both parties were to recognize their mutual rights and obligations while acknowledging the Beatific Vision (the state of the blessed in heaven who enjoy direct knowledge of God) as the sole and legitimate goal of humankind. During the pontificate of John Paul II a deeper level of cultural analysis became apparent in the encyclical *Centesimus Annus* (1991). In this encyclical the integrity of the human agent is defended against the depredations of both unrestrained capitalism and Marxist socialism, each of which is represented as an aspect of a destructive, secular modernity in need of comprehensive reevangelization.

New Directions

During the 1980s, when Margaret Thatcher was prime minister of England and Ronald Reagan was president of the United States, resurgent capitalism was driven by a new right version of political economy. The collapse of Marxist socialist regimes in Eastern Europe in 1989–1990 removed what was regarded by some as the final barriers to the triumph of capitalism. This encouraged Francis Fukuyama to proclaim the "end of history" (in *The End of History and the Last Man,* 1992), in which the unfettered enactment of victorious capitalism is attended by the managerial regularization of the whole world. An exceptional few, the enterprise heroes and "last men," must lead a mass humanity happily domesticated by capitalism. Fukuyama's vision of historic closure leaves unasked the many questions that first arose in Karl Marx's much-maligned critique of capitalism. As a rebellious, atheistic Jew, Marx had attacked both the alienated theology of the West and its displaced surrogates, the state and the accumulated power of money in dynamic, world-transforming capital. By the end of the twentieth century there seemed to be few, if any, constraints upon such power.

In the late twentieth and early twenty-first centuries the market expanded and commodification correspondingly extended in ways scarcely foreseeable. Information technology increased the speed with which capital can circulate to the point that time is to all effect abolished. Globalization displaced the class struggle within nations with a world system that pits developed countries against developing nations. This is the era of what the Roman Catholic writer Michael Novak has called "magic capitalism." In his comprehensive

inversion of Marxist socialism, Novak has argued that humankind has to abandon the naïve and infantile "dream" (that is, the false consciousness) of Marxist socialism and recognize the universality of necessary alienation. Experience of the latter is a universal rite of passage in which each must encounter the "empty shrine" of "democratic capitalism." So, matured through alienation, humankind may then draw upon spirituality, theology, and religious values (supremely those of Christianity and Judaism) for strength to compete and survive in the face of the inner emptiness of capitalism.

There are, however, further dimensions of contemporary capitalism. In a globalized world system in which the consciousness of humanity (and its virtual enhancement) is refracted through the World Wide Web and the Internet, the parameters of the human and the natural are displaced in ways only remotely foreshadowed by Marx and others.

There is no one single "new" spirit of capitalism; but it is safe to assert that there are many and increasingly intimate synergetic interactions between religions, innovative spiritualities, and the cultures of capitalism. Moreover, any vestiges of ascetic denial have largely disappeared and have been replaced by a celebration of the consuming self in an expanding global market of human—and inhuman—opportunities.

See also *Globalization; Liberation Theology; Marxism; Protestantism; Reformation; Weber, Max.*

Richard H. Roberts

BIBLIOGRAPHY

Duchrow, Ulrich. *Global Economy: A Confessional Issue for the Churches?* Translated by David Lewis. Geneva: WCC Publications, 1987.

Fukuyama, Francis. *The End of History and the Last Man.* New York: Free Press, 2006.

Hay, Donald A. *Economics Today: A Christian Critique.* Grand Rapids, Mich.: Eerdmans, 1991.

Meeks, M. Douglas. *God the Economist: The Doctrine of God and Political Economy.* Minneapolis, Minn.: Fortress Press, 1989.

Novak, Michael. *The Spirit of Democratic Capitalism.* Lanham, Md.: Madison Books, 1991.

Ray, Larry "The Protestant Ethic Today." In *Classic Disputes in Sociology,* edited by R. J. Anderson, J. A. Hughes, and W. W. Sharrock. London and Boston: Allen and Unwin, 1987.

Roberts, Richard H, ed. *Religion and the Transformation of Capitalism: Comparative Approaches.* London and New York: Routledge, 1995.

Schumpeter, Joseph A. *History of Economic Analysis.* Edited from manuscript by Elizabeth Boody Schumpeter. New York: Oxford University Press, 1954.

Thrift, Nigel. "The Rise of Soft Capitalism." *Cultural Values* 1 (1997): 29–57.

Weber, Max. *The Protestant Ethic and the Spirit of Capitalism.* 3d. Roxbury ed. Translated by Stephen Kalberg. Los Angeles, Calif.: Roxbury Pub., 2002.

Carter, Jimmy

See *Presidents, American.*

Catholicism, Roman

Led by the pope, the bishop of Rome, Roman Catholicism is the faith of nine hundred million people, making it by far the largest church body within Christianity and putting it on a scale similar to that of Islam and Hinduism among the world's major religions. Whatever Catholics may affirm about the church's immunity to substantive historical change, there is such a thing as modern Roman Catholicism. The construction of Catholicism's modern identity began in the immediate aftermath of the French Revolution. It gained momentum with the papal condemnations of liberalism and republicanism in the first half of the nineteenth century and reached initial culmination in the pontificate of Pope Pius IX (1846–1878).

A hostile, defensive attitude toward secular, post-Enlightenment philosophies and political developments defined this first phase of modern Catholicism. Known as "fortress Catholicism," the attitude was exemplified in Pius IX's "Syllabus of Errors" (1864), a list of purportedly misguided notions compiled from erstwhile papal condemnations of modern science and evolutionism, liberalism, democracy, and the secular idea and ideal of "progress." In this mode the church viewed itself as a persecuted and suffering but ultimately triumphant "eternal society," the spotless bride of Christ. It alone possessed the truth that could save the world from its own sinful excesses.

The fortress mentality served to alienate the church from an increasingly secular and atheistic world and to parochialize a faith that had previously projected itself as universal and open to all that was good in the realms of politics, art, science, and religion. While the Roman curia and conservative bishops waged a war against modernity, however, some Catholic intellectuals set about to develop an alternative to

Pope John XXIII.

Catholic antimodernism, thereby launching a second phase of modern Roman Catholicism.

These progressive or liberal Catholics, whose number eventually included bishops and cardinals as well as priests, women religious (nuns), and laity, believed that the church had much to learn from and to teach the modern world. They sought to effect a type of rapprochement or even a synthesis between the ancient faith and modern thought. An attitude of hopeful openness toward modern science (including evolution), democratic polities, religious liberty, and other liberal ideals informed their research, writing, preaching, and teaching. Known as "liberal Catholicism," this attitude was personified by Pope John XXIII (served 1958–1963), who convened the Second Vatican Council in 1962 as a dramatic and decisive way to pursue *aggiornamento* ("updating" the church) through *ressourcement* (selective retrieval of neglected but newly relevant Catholic theological and spiritual traditions). In this mode the church portrayed itself as an imperfect pilgrim on the path to salvation instead of a heavenly kingdom aloof from and untouched by the errors and sins of the world.

It would be inaccurate to portray these overlapping phases of modern Roman Catholicism as strictly sequential. From the early nineteenth century, the two Catholic "parties" developed through interaction with one another as well as with the outside world. The progressive mentality was apparent as early as the 1820s in the writings of Félicité Robert de Lamennais (1782–1854), the French Catholic champion of liberalism. It informed at least some aspects of the social teaching of Pope Leo XIII (served 1878–1903), but it did not gain full ascendancy in the church until the pontificate of John XXIII.

In the decades following the Second Vatican Council, furthermore, liberal Catholicism was itself transformed according to the mind and example of Pope John Paul II (served 1978–2005), the Polish actor, theologian, and mystic who reigned longer than any pope of the twentieth century, wielded papal power with extraordinary skill, and exercised enormous influence over the internal life and geopolitical aspects of the postconciliar church.

This overview focuses on four themes—religious, cultural, socioeconomic, and political—that together describe the two-hundred-year transition from fortress Catholicism in its Europeanized mode to the global, multicultural Catholicism of the late twentieth century. In each case the examples are necessarily illustrative, not comprehensive.

From Transcendence to Immanence: The Religious Turn

Prior to the Second Vatican Council the Roman Catholic Church considered itself an institution set apart from the world for the purpose of saving the world from damnation through its sacred teachings, offices, and rituals. The official Catholic theology of priesthood provides a window into this worldview. No human office is more important than the priesthood, wrote the Rev. John A. O'Brien in a popular 1943 textbook. He reminded seminarians that St. Thomas Aquinas (1225–1274) had declared the consecration of the eucharist to be the greatest act of which man is capable. In presiding over the transformation of the sacramental bread and wine into the body and blood of Christ during the Mass, O'Brien explained, the priest speaks with the authority of Christ himself. The Catholic priest was, in the theological terminology of the day, *alter Christus,* "another Christ."

The intellectual framework within which this conception of priesthood made sense was known as "neoscholasticism." Derived originally from the summas of the scholastics (or "schoolmen") of the thirteenth century, especially Thomas Aquinas, neoscholasticism was a formalized and routinized version of the medieval synthesis of philosophy and theology. It was, that is, an attempt to apply medieval thought to modern problems. The neoscholastic application, however, was often formulaic and driven by institutional needs (for example, the production of standardized manuals of moral theology for confessors) instead of by intellectual curiosity and creativity. By the nineteenth century it had taken on numerous accretions and was less historically minded than Thomas's own theology (Thomism).

Neoscholasticism was nonetheless presented in Catholic seminaries as an absolute, unified, and self-contained system of thought identical with Catholic orthodoxy. Its most ideologically driven proponents were sometimes called "integralists," for they affirmed the literal truth of each Christian doctrine (in its neoscholastic formulation) as necessary to the integrity of the whole, and they saw scholasticism's emphasis on divine revelation, grace, and the centrality of the church as the perfect antidote to agnosticism, Marxism, and a host of related irreligious modern philosophies.

By the dawn of the twentieth century the integralists feared that such philosophies were gaining sympathizers within the church itself. To challenge the doctrine of the virgin birth of Christ or the Mosaic authorship of the Pentateuch on the basis of the latest findings of the higher criticism of the Bible—as a handful of European Catholic biblical scholars and theologians seemed to be doing—was, in their minds, to threaten to unravel the web of Catholic doctrine, each strand emanating as it did from divine revelation as communicated in scripture and apostolic tradition. In 1907 Pope Pius X (served 1903–1914) condemned as "modernists" the Catholic priests who were experimenting with nonscholastic methods and ideas.

The official Catholic theology of the time posited an unchanging spiritual essence as the principle of identity: a person is a human being by virtue of a soul, a priest is a priest by virtue of an indelible mark on the soul. The modern enemies of the church, by contrast, identified human history with the history of matter or consciousness, denying it a transcendence or spiritual significance compatible with Christian theism. In formulating an authoritative response to this theory, the Vatican's theologians rejected the notion that ordinary human experience is an arena for God's self-revelation—an ironic decision in that it undermined Catholicism's ancient commitment to salvation in and through this world.

Enshrined in Vatican I's document on revelation, this dictum was known as "extrinsicism." Its proponents denied that the human subject is inherently a "hearer of the word." Instead, divine self-revelation is an event entrusted to the church and utterly foreign to the everyday experience of the individual. The philosophy of extrinsicism was the integralists' attempt to protect the "objective, external fact" of revelation and to preserve the unique and irreplaceable role of the church in the saga of human redemption. It was, in other words, a defense against the modern turn to the human subject (what the integralists called "Kantian subjectivism"), which led inevitably, the Vatican warned, to "vital immanence," the belief that the Spirit is indwelling, intimately present to each individual prior to and apart from any concrete apprehension of a specific revelation.

The notion of vital immanence, by shifting the locus of divine redemptive activity to the individual, called into question the institutional church's claim to be the exclusive or even a privileged mediator of saving grace. The acceptance of immanence as a defining theological model therefore carried significant ecclesial and political consequences. It spelled doom for hierarchical, monarchical, and any other systems of governance of church or state that failed to take into account the inherent dignity and "godliness" of every individual, baptized Catholic or otherwise. And it promised to shift the church's gaze, and orientation, from Heaven to Earth as the arena of redemptive action.

Resisting the turn to the subject and thus to history as the vehicle of religious "progress," the neoscholastic theologians promoted a kind of church-world dualism that shaped European and American Catholic sensibilities during the early decades of the twentieth century. In this view, history, which had produced Protestants, materialists, and atheistic communists, was merely the chronicle of a fallen, secular world. Born to such a world, the faithful were predisposed to sin, unworthy to approach the altar of the living God. Their one recourse was to the church, a perfect society untainted by the sin of its members and possessed of an objective moral law and sacraments of saving grace legitimated in and of themselves (*ex opere operato*) instead of by the personal, subjective qualities of the priest. The church enjoyed this objective authenticity, the reasoning went, by virtue of the com-

mission, promise, and perfect holiness of its founder, Jesus Christ.

While the Catholic hierarchy emphasized God's remote majesty and the necessity of the church's mediating role, the laity continued to experience the sacred more immediately in their daily lives—and daily devotions. If the mystifying transcendence of God stood behind the elaborate formalism of the Latin liturgy, a palpable sense of divine immanence inspired a "devotional revolution" in late nineteenth- and early twentieth-century Europe and America. Lay Catholics rejoiced in the delights or recoiled from the terrors of the supernatural world by means of constant access to familiar patron saints and the Virgin Mary, whose association with humanity was uninhibited by the burdens of full divinity.

This balancing act was accomplished within the system of transcendence developed by the integralists. Catholic social outreach, for example, was conducted within the parameters of the neoscholastic worldview. The emphasis was on saving souls, not transforming the world. Charitable organizations such as the St. Vincent de Paul Society helped the poor and underprivileged recover from, or cope with, the debilitating consequences of life in an unjust society and sinful world. They did not, however, bring the resources of faith to bear upon the intractable situation or complex economic structures that had left the neighbor homeless or penniless in the first place.

As the twentieth century unfolded, however, the concept of immanence—and the religious worldview it implied—gradually made a remarkable comeback. A moderate version even reentered the official theology in Vatican II's document on divine revelation. The recovery of the Catholic belief in a strikingly catholic (universal and inclusive) Holy Spirit, a God who is always already present to laity as well as priests, and even to non-Catholics as well as Catholics, was revolutionary in its implications. It stood behind Vatican II's embrace of religious liberty, ecumenism, and a new ecclesiology that saw the church as the "People of God."

Immanence made its comeback, ironically, with the help of neoscholasticism. It began when Pope Leo XIII called for a renewal of scholasticism by a return to its original sources in the thought of St. Thomas. Only on the "safe" grounds of Thomism could a Catholic intellectual revival serve as an antidote to modernism. By encouraging the serious study of history, however, neo-Thomism opened the possibility that the entire history of the church (not just the High Middle Ages) would become the subject of inquiry. German

Benedictine monks began to study the earliest Catholic liturgies, for example, and theologians influenced by their work argued that the modern church should look not to the medieval model of Christendom but to the apostolic church, which thrived at a time when much of the surrounding society was pagan (or "pre-Christian," in ways roughly analogous to the "post-Christian" beliefs and practices of the twentieth century).

Two encyclicals of Pope Pius XII (served 1939–1958), who died five years before Vatican II, also fostered the kind of theological creativity that led to a new appreciation for historical development and the dynamism of the Holy Spirit in the life of the church. *Divino Afflante Spiritu* (1943) gave conditional approval to Catholic study of the Bible using critical methods. Among other advances, this encyclical allowed Catholic scholars to examine the New Testament Christian community in its historical context. *Mystici Corporis* (1943) drew upon St. Paul's letters to describe the church as the "Mystical Body of Christ," a scriptural image rich in implications for a new understanding of the church defined by a shared faith and spirituality, not by visible boundaries. This noninstitutional view of the church opened the way to reconceptualizing the relationship of Roman Catholicism to other Christian denominations and eventually to other religions and even to nonbelievers.

In 1950 Pius attempted to forestall further innovation by promulgating the encyclical *Humani Generis,* which seemed to condemn the "new theology" emerging in postwar Europe in the writings of priests such as M. D. Chenu and Henri de Lubac. But those theologies would triumph at the Second Vatican Council.

Vatican II reflected and refined these developments by describing the church as the "People of God," a biblical instead of an institutional description (in its dogmatic constitution, *Lumen Gentium),* by declaring the church's openness to and respect for human cultures (in its pastoral constitution, *Gaudium et Spes)* and by affirming the right of every person, regardless of religious affiliation, to worship God (or not) according to his or her conscience and without coercion from church or state (in the decree on religious freedom, *Dignitatis Humane).* Thus Roman Catholicism embraced religious pluralism as a good in itself. In official teaching Roman Catholic Christianity remains the true and most complete human expression of the love and will of the Creator, but it acknowledges the holiness of many other religions as well.

From Mission to Dialogue: The Cultural Turn

The Second Vatican Council had enormous impact on the way the church conceptualized and lived its dual identity as a universal communion with its center of authority in Rome and a network (or "mystical body") of thousands of local churches, each rooted in its own "cultural horizon of self-understanding," as the theologian Karl Rahner (1904–1984) put it. In the years following the council, *inculturation* became the code word for the church's new understanding of its evangelical mission to the world.

Informed by a sophisticated awareness of the diverse social forms Christianity has taken over the two millennia of its history, the concept of inculturation describes the process by which the Gospel is adapted to a particular culture. With Rome's recognition that a monolithic European model was ill-suited to a culturally diverse church thriving on five continents, Catholics began to rethink their methods and purposes in preaching the Gospel to people inside and outside the church's visible institutional borders. After Pope John XXIII's revolution, Catholic missionaries no longer presumed to introduce the living God to pre-Christian or non-Christian peoples. Instead, believing itself to be blessed with the clearest and fullest revelation of God's redemptive activity in the world, the church strove merely to lift up, embrace, purify, and clarify all that is good and productive of holiness in the diverse cultures of its peoples. (This formula is found in *Lumen Gentium,* Vatican II's "Dogmatic Constitution on the Church in the Modern World.")

Popes, bishops, theologians, and missionaries gradually worked out the pastoral and ecclesiological implications of inculturation after the concept was discussed in *Gaudium et Spes,* Vatican II's pastoral constitution. In his 1975 apostolic exhortation, *Evangelii Nuntiandi* ("On Evangelization in the Modern World"), Pope Paul VI (served 1963–1978) described evangelization as comprehensive of the entire mission of the church and provided a blueprint for pastoral initiatives carried on from within the cultures of humankind. Evangelization is about liberation from every form of sin and oppression, the pope wrote. It occurs when Christians give "witness to an authentically Christian life" through lives of poverty and detachment from the world, through the liturgy and popular piety, and through the pursuit of justice.

The emergence of a movement known as liberation theology also shaped the new Catholic understanding of evangelization. Gustavo Gutiérrez, Jon Sobrino, and other Latin

American theologians fostered the movement by wedding social scientific (and, in some cases, "Christian Marxist") analyses of political and social structures to a retelling of the New Testament message that portrayed Jesus as a radical revolutionary ("Christ as Liberator"). In 1968 the Latin American bishops meeting at Medellín, Colombia, lamented the massive poverty of the continent and focused attention on the social and political factors responsible for the oppression of the poor. Citing Vatican II's embrace of a "new humanism" in which human beings were defined primarily by their joint responsibility for history, the bishops denounced what they saw as the "institutionalized violence" of Latin American society and demanded "urgent and profoundly renovating transformations" in the social structures of their countries. The bishops urged each episcopal conference to present the church as "a catalyst in the temporal realm in an authentic attitude of service" and to support grassroots organizations for the "redress and consolidation of their [the poor's] rights and the search for justice." Finally, the bishops called for Catholics worldwide, in exercising their political and religious responsibilities, to adopt a "preferential option for the poor."

These events transformed Roman Catholicism's presence in the postcolonial developing nations in two ways, one following upon and more profound than the other. First, the traditional goal of converting souls to Catholicism in the European mode gave way to inculturation, by which indigenous customs and rituals that did not contradict or undermine the doctrine of the faith were incorporated into the Roman liturgies and other religious practices. In Africa, for example, there was notable success in blending African tribal rituals and dances into the celebration of the Roman Catholic Mass. The conciliar respect for the integrity of cultures thereby resulted in the promise of a new, truly globalized Catholicism. It did not result, however, in a repudiation of the church's claim to be the "privileged instrument" instituted and raised up by Christ to work within the world and within history to help prepare humankind to become the Kingdom of God.

The second and deeper transformation entailed a change of attitude toward missionizing itself, a radical calling into question of its purposes and methods.

Ad Gentes Divinitus, Vatican II's "Decree on the Church's Missionary Activity," categorically stated that the "pilgrim church is missionary by her very nature." This declaration raised a pivotal question, however: what attitude best suits a "pilgrim missionary"?

Religious orders such as the Maryknoll missioners were deeply influenced not only by theologies of inculturation but also by the liberation theologians' scathing indictments of the church's historical alliances with colonial governments and imperialist projects. These alliances, it was charged, had served to keep native peoples in economic and social subjugation. In response to such critiques, missionaries began to emphasize the demands of justice at least as much as the necessity for doctrinal orthodoxy.

Coupled with this emphasis on the need for social solidarity with the poor and oppressed was a new respect for non-Catholic Christians and for non-Christian religions. In part this attitude was an effect of the church's formal participation in the ecumenical movement after Vatican II; in part it stemmed from the immanentist and experience-based theologies achieving prominence within the church itself, such as various forms of feminism and liberation theologies. In any case, the postconciliar generation of Catholic missionaries and catechists pioneered a radical rethinking of the nature and purpose of their vocations.

In the Philippines, for example, Roman Catholic missionaries encountered both Filipino Catholics in Manila and other parts of Luzon and a Muslim majority throughout the nation's numerous southern islands. If inculturation was the appropriate response to the former, conversion was no longer seen as an appropriate goal in dealings with the latter. In the 1980s and 1990s proselytization was replaced by dialogue, a difficult and delicate process of mutual self-disclosure, sharing, and self-criticism designed not to create new Catholics but to build peace and trust between peoples of different faiths, classes, and races.

According to promoters of dialogue-as-mission in the Philippines, the church's task was not mainly to convert postcolonial peoples but to promote their total human liberation. For this purpose, the Episcopal Commission for Tribal Filipinos and other social justice organizations were established. In addition, Catholic women religious, lay women, and priests working among the poor in the southern Philippines founded dialogue groups such as Silsilah ("chain") dedicated to living among the people in a spirit of service, humility, and shared prayer across religious and cultural boundaries. In such groups, an interest grew in understanding the dynamics of folk religiosity in the hope of harnessing its potential for popular political mobilization in the cause of liberation.

Evangelization continues to exist alongside dialogue, but

the traffic between the metropolitan churches of the old world and the younger churches of the colonies is no longer in one direction. In the postconciliar era every local church must be a sending church, a conviction that emboldened the Catholic Church in the Philippines to establish the Philippine Missionary Society.

The postconciliar experiences of Catholic missionaries in the southern Philippines and in similar contexts elsewhere in Asia and Africa raised the question: what happens to Catholic theology when it is conducted in an interfaith context? Aloysius Pieris, a Sri Lankan Jesuit, has been one of the most prominent advocates of genuine dialogue with other religious traditions as a resource for Christian theological reflection. Father Pieris's writings also emphasize the importance and applicability of liberation theology outside the Latin American context. They demonstrate that "liberation" and "inculturation" are two names for the same process in the Asian context, thereby posing a challenge to the Catholic Church in Asia to become a fully inculturated Church of Asia and no longer the outpost of a European colonial mission.

The Catholic turn from proselytization and "soul winning" to inculturation, dialogue, and political activism rests on the conviction that the extent and depth of structural injustice in the world requires Christians to speak and act in full solidarity with those who are suffering. Most Catholic missions after Vatican II have continued to provide "traditional" relief work to alleviate suffering, and many have strived to support economic development and political change as well. Thus the building up of the local Catholic Church has taken on a new and different meaning: success in the mission field is to be judged not by the number of converts or new Catholic churches planted but by progress toward genuine evangelization, which encompasses a dialogue with the other local religious communities and solidarity with the masses of the poor and oppressed in the region. In this conceptualization evangelization is integral, historical, and social, involving the whole person (not only the soul). The Catholic evangelist asks how the church can become present to the people in question, with their particular history and culture and in their present specific economic, political, and cultural situation.

From Charity to Social Justice: The Economic Turn

The cultural turn coincided with and informed the church's changing relationship to modern states and their economic systems. Throughout the early modern period Catholic religious orders and laity dedicated to serving the poor focused on the works of mercy—feeding the hungry, caring for the sick, educating the ignorant, visiting the prisoner. They established hospitals, schools, orphanages, and other such institutions to counter the debilitating effects of the industrial age. Analysis of the social, political, and economic structures and "causes" of poverty, racism, and economic exploitation—what a later age would call "social injustices"—was rare.

A new awareness and approach emerged in 1891, with the appearance of the first official statement of modern Roman Catholic social doctrine, Pope Leo XIII's encyclical letter Rerum Novarum ("The Condition of Labor"). By systematically addressing the pressing social and economic questions of the day, such as the strengths and weaknesses of capitalist and socialist economic visions, the desirability of labor unions, and the plight of the industrial worker, Rerum Novarum set Catholics on a pathbreaking, century-long intellectual journey that prepared them to articulate and espouse not only the rights of workers but the liberation of all peoples from every form of oppression and discrimination based on race, religion, or class.

The era of Vatican II saw enormous strides in Catholic social teaching. Pope John XXIII's social encyclical, Mater et Magistra (1961), revisited Catholic social teaching on property, the rights of workers, and the obligations of government in light of the new interdependence of peoples bound together by a global network of technology, mass communications, and big business that threatened to accelerate the division of the postcolonial world into prosperous nations on one side and their developing clients on the other. Vatican II's pastoral constitution, Gaudium et Spes, aligned the church with the social, political, and economic aspirations of all people seeking equality and opportunity for self-improvement. In 1971 a synod of Catholic bishops meeting in Rome to reflect on the legacy of Vatican II developed a memorable formula, in Justice in the World, expressing Catholicism's commitment to political and social change. Action on behalf of justice, they proclaimed, is a constitutive dimension of the Gospel and of the church's mission for the redemption of the human race and its liberation from every form of oppression.

The church's prescriptions for economic development were distinctive, rooted as they were in the Catholic understanding of the moral obligations imposed by the laws of nature, which were seen as being continuous with revealed truth and the divine will. In 1968, for example, Pope Paul VI reaffirmed the prohibition by the magisterium (the church's teaching authority) of artificial birth control. Instead of advocating population reduction as a primary means for addressing the perceived shortage of resources in the developing world, as many liberal foundations and relief agencies chose to do, the church pointed to the gross inequalities in wealth within and among nations and criticized the exploitation of workers by the new and powerful multinational corporations.

Speaking before the United Nations General Assembly on October 4, 1965, Pope Paul VI argued that the church, as "an expert in humanity" by virtue of its divine mandate and its long historical experience, has a special, and unique, role to play in the formulation of social policy. He identified the church with the voice of the poor, the dispossessed, the suffering, and all those who seek freedom and justice commensurate with the dignity of human life.

The social magisterium of Pope John Paul II has further deepened the church's commitment to global leadership. In 1991, on the centennial of *Rerum Novarum,* he issued *Centesimus Annus* ("The Hundredth Year"). A celebration of Leo's (and the church's) decision to engage the moral aspects of political economy, the encyclical both summarized and advanced the modern tradition of Catholic social teaching by addressing the realities of the post–cold war world and the apparent triumph of the free-market economy over Soviet-style state socialism. Its central affirmation, however, was the priority of the moral and cultural dimensions of human existence over specific political and economic systems. The correct view of the human person, the pope wrote, is the guiding principle of the church's social teaching.

In *Centesimus Annus*'s closely reasoned argument about the proper relationship among the political, economic, and cultural spheres of the social order—which has been described as a blueprint for "the economics of human freedom"—one encounters a fresh and dynamic application of Catholic social doctrines. This occurs in the creative conjoining of disparate principles in such a way as to reveal their overall coherence. Thus, for example, the right to own private property (established, against the socialists, in *Rerum Novarum)* is considered in light of the church's equally profound commitment to a preferential option for the poor (also known as the principle of solidarity). The interaction and synthesis of such principles yield corollary truths.

Hence, the possession of goods is not an absolute right, the pope argued, and work should be directed not to the accumulation of personal wealth but to the service of others.

Debate continues over whether *Centesimus Annus* signals an unqualified endorsement of democratic capitalism, or what the pope referred to as "the free economy." Prior to its promulgation, some people read Catholic social doctrine as sympathetic to a Christian socialism, while others have construed Catholic social teaching as promoting a "third way" between socialism and capitalism. Catholic neoconservatives in the United States argued, however, that with the 1991 encyclical the pope and the church definitively acknowledged the superiority of a laissez-faire capitalist economy. They pointed to the pope's criticisms of the excesses of the "welfare state" as a clear violation of the principle of subsidiarity (established by Pope Pius XI in the 1931 encyclical *Quadragesimo Anno)*. The principle of subsidiarity holds, against the encroachments of the modern state, that a community of a higher order should not interfere in the internal life of a community of a lower order, depriving the latter of its appropriate functions. Also protected by this principle is the Catholic affirmation of the family as the primary educator of children.

Yet the thought of John Paul II was subtle and not easily categorized. Addressing the cultural community at the University of Latvia, once a Marxist academic center, he noted that church social teaching is neither a third way between capitalism and socialism nor a "surrogate for capitalism." *Centesimus Annus* is replete with qualifications of its support for democratic capitalism as practiced in the contemporary world. While the free market appears to be the most efficient instrument for utilizing resources and effectively responding to needs, the pope acknowledged, many human needs are not addressed by it. It is therefore necessary to go beyond the market, he continued, to help needy people acquire expertise and develop their skills. Clearly, the encyclical continues, the state has a right and obligation to intervene when and where lower forms of government and community organization are unwilling or unable to meet these needs.

In the same vein, wrote the pope, the church acknowledges "the legitimate role of profit" but cautions that profitability is secondary to the human dignity of the people employed by the firm, which is, in the final analysis, "*a community of persons.*" Capitalism should be promoted as the model for countries of the developing world, he maintained, only if economic freedom is circumscribed within a strong juridical framework that places it at the service of human dignity.

Even democratic capitalism can fail to serve legitimate human aspirations, the pope taught, if it is allowed to develop outside and apart from the encompassing vision of humanity proclaimed by the church. Catholicism has proven itself to be the bane of economic and political regimes that ignore or reject this vision. Without claiming that it was the sole actor in the fall of oppressive regimes in some Latin American, African, and Asian countries in the 1980s, or in the liberation of Eastern Europe from the grip of Soviet totalitarianism in 1989, Pope John Paul II praised the church's commitment to defend and promote human rights as the "decisive contribution" to such developments.

Whatever history's final apportioning of credit for the wave of democratization that swept over parts of the world in the 1980s and 1990s, the Catholic Church was a tireless promoter of human rights, especially religious freedom, in these decades. During his pontificate the charismatic John Paul himself carried this message to five continents, dozens of nations (including Cuba, France, Korea, Poland, Russia, the United States, and Zaire), and millions of Catholic and non-Catholic admirers. And *Centesimus Annus* rightly acknowledges the heroic witness to the inviolability of human dignity and rights borne by pastors, Christian communities, and other people of good will.

From State Church to Pillar of Civil Society: The Political Turn

The credibility of the church's social doctrines, including its teachings on economic justice, received a powerful boost when Catholicism formally renounced any claim to temporal sovereignty or political authority over states (beyond the tiny Vatican city-state). By virtue of this historic shift from a state-oriented "foreign policy" to a global, transnational approach based not on concordats with regimes but on the goal of strengthening the church's role in civil society, the church became a "disinterested" or nonpartisan player in local—and global—politics.

"Civil society" refers to the nongovernmental mediating institutions situated between the state and the individual citizen. Democracies tend to thrive when and where a strong civil society exists. A stable configuration of schools, labor unions, political parties, a free press, and other voluntary associations contributes significantly to the process of moderating the competing claims of ethnic, religious, and socio-

economic groups within pluralist societies. In the spirit of Vatican II and subsequent synods, the Catholic Church in recent decades has played a vigorous leadership role in civil society in nations as different as Poland, Spain, and the United States.

In Poland, workers, inspired by the Polish pontiff, John Paul II, joined together under the banner of the outlawed labor union Solidarity to agitate for economic justice, civil liberties, and human rights. Polish cardinals, bishops, and priests gave moral and tactical support to the "nonviolent revolution" and served as effective mediators between the people and the Soviet-backed government in the dramatic events leading to the fall of the communist government and the transition to democracy.

In Spain Catholicism reversed itself after years of supporting the fascist regime of General Francisco Franco. Imbued by the spirit of Vatican II, priests and religious helped found the voluntary associations and political organizations that contributed mightily to the renaissance of civil society and strengthened the traditions of democratic action.

For more than a century Catholics in the United States have sponsored and staffed the kind of institutions associated with civil society. In the 1990s the work continued in nongovernmental organizations as Catholic Charities' extensive network of fourteen hundred charitable agencies served eighteen million people; Catholic Health Association's six hundred hospitals and three hundred long-term care facilities served twenty million people; and Campaign for Human Development's two hundred local antipoverty groups empowered the poor by improving policies, practices, and laws affecting low-income individuals.

In 1968 the National Conference of Catholic Bishops created a prominent social action and public policy office to influence the nation's debate about the common good and to lobby for political change in Washington, D.C. On the one hand, this decision merely continued the public witness the bishops had begun in 1917 with the establishment of the National Catholic War Council. On the other hand, the bishops brought to this new initiative a keener sense of the necessity of acting in a fully collaborative and consultative manner within the church (which Vatican II described as "collegiality") and a new appreciation for the art of persuasion in the pluralistic American political arena. In the 1980s the bishops put these virtues on display during the writing of two controversial pastoral letters, one assessing (and criticizing) U.S. policy on the arms race and nuclear deterrence and the other strongly implying that the economic policies of President Ronald Reagan's administration amounted to a preferential option for the rich.

While bishops' conferences and other official organs of the Roman Catholic Church have been active in shaping civil society in their respective countries, social movements of lay Catholics (often with some element of clerical leadership) have arisen as a dynamic response to Pope John Paul II's call for a more vigorous engagement with the political cultures in which Catholics find themselves.

A New Vision of "Evangelical Catholic Power": Comunione e Liberazione

Within Italy this development unfolded in a typically culture-specific pattern. Secular movements seeking democratic reform and political unity in the eighteenth and nineteenth centuries eroded much of the church's cultural and political influence, especially among the urban working classes. From ancient times Catholicism had been an urban reality in Italy; by the dawn of the twentieth century it was in full retreat, reduced to a minority culture. This dismal period culminated in the Catholic hierarchy's ineffectiveness in the face of the fascist regime. In the generation following the Second World War a succession of Catholic movements attempted to revitalize the church and return Italian society to some measure of religious-moral commitment. They did so amidst the general disarray in postwar Italian politics that saw a series of failed political experiments and governments, the cumulative effect of which was to weaken Italian culture, customs, and traditional ways of life.

In this context Luigi Giussani, a Catholic priest and theologian, founded Comunione e Liberazione (CL) in Milan in 1956. By the 1990s the movement had spread to thirty countries, including the United States, with particularly vibrant chapters in Brazil, Germany, Spain, Switzerland, and Uganda. CL is a Christian revivalist movement whose intrinsic moral authority comes from its members' experience of "saving grace" and their belief in the actual presence of Jesus Christ in their lives. Members learn to recognize the event of grace by imitating a person who already lives the values of the movement.

As Catholics they naturally seek social, corporate, and political expression of this experience, which they see as the central source of inspiration for the renewal of culture, economy, politics, and all of life. Thus CL developed a network of diverse economic, cultural, and political organizations, at the center of which are the *Scuole di Comunita* centers ("schools of community"), the local branches of the movement in which members are educated and formed in Giussani's version of Catholicism.

With considerable support from the hierarchy, CL opposes the cultural form of secularization that has led to the marginalization of the church in Italian society. According to the movement's ideology, the church itself provides the principle of authority in society, the principle by which the moral quality of freedom is to be judged. By embodying the presence of Christ, CL claims, the church wields authority that is binding on society at large.

Dario Zadra, a sociologist who has studied the movement extensively, has documented Comunione e Liberazione's diverse and flexible forms of membership. Approximately one hundred thousand middle-class high school and university students and young adults take part in the Scuole di Comunita. In these groups priests or older laymembers of CL lead discussions of social and cultural problems and identify Christian solutions. Other CL members join related international organizations, the Fraternita and the Memores Domini. The Fraternita is a lay secular association recognized in 1983 by the Catholic Church as a canonically constituted entity within the jurisdiction of the church. In 1991, according to Zadra, the Fraternita had twenty thousand members, mostly between twenty-eight and thirty-five years of age. Members of the Memores Domini take vows of perpetual poverty, celibacy, and obedience.

Each CL member contributes a portion of his or her income to the international missions and the national organizations of the movement, attends several annual meetings and retreats, and participates in the weekly activities of the Scuole di Comunita, in the Sunday liturgy in their parishes, and in the social enterprises of the group. Members of CL often refer to each other as *militanti* ("activists").

Le Opere ("the Works")—the social and cultural activities and institutions of the movement—include the religious schools, workshops, and businesses that CL members see as the building blocks of a new Christian society. They bolster the finances of the movement and enhance its political influence. These initiatives are formally independent of the diocese, parish, or other levels of church organization. Instead, they are coordinated by two main institutions of CL, namely, Compagnia delle Opere and, the political arm, Movimento Popolare. Compagnia delle Opere, a nonprofit organization founded in 1986, promotes cooperation among companies and cooperatives to reduce unemployment and share resources. The main Milan office, Zadra writes, is organized like a service center, with departments for sales, finance, marketing and communication, foreign development, employment and training, and the startup and development of companies. The Compagnia has thirty-two branch offices in Italy and others in Brussels and Warsaw. Although each local CL group is financially independent, ideology and organizational policy are centralized around a council established by Giussani in Milan, also home of the related international organizations—the Fraternita and the Memores Domini.

CL's diverse panoply of charitable, economic, cultural, financial, and educational endeavors numbers approximately four thousand member companies and institutions having an impact at both the local and national levels. Its national networks include a center that assists the homeless and drug addicts, centers for health care and for the study of health care legislation, an organization that provides humanities teaching materials to primary schools and teachers, a parliamentary lobby for legislation affecting the family, and a cooperative that provides student housing, cafeterias, and student centers in the major universities (and receives government funding). The movement also owns and staffs professional centers that offer consultations on technical, architectural, and environmental aspects of private and public development projects. Finally, the *associazioni professionali* bring together professionals such as engineers, doctors, lawyers, and scientists for religious study and philanthropic work.

In the realm of culture CL established the Italian Association of Cultural Centers in 1983 to contribute to the cultural, social, and artistic development of Italian society. Since 1988 a CL research center for social change has organized the International Academy of Science and Culture, which promotes ties with foreign universities and institutes. The movement also runs Jaca Books, a large and respected academic publishing house based in Milan; *Il Sabato,* a popular weekly political and cultural magazine; the monthly periodical *30 Giorni,* which is published in six languages; and literary works and treatises dedicated to the defense of human rights in the former Soviet Union. Among the most visible of CL's national activities is the Meeting of Peace (at Rimini), a major cultural event in Italy that is televised nationally. It features major European political and cultural figures and attracts approximately 150,000 people.

Comunione e Liberazione is emblematic of late modern Catholic social movements in that it takes full advantage of Roman Catholicism's redefined role in contemporary society. In the Catholic world of postwar Italy, several such movements have arisen among the 85 percent of the adult Italian population who identify themselves as Catholic, 10 percent of whom—approximately four million people—claim to belong to a religious group, association, or movement. These religious associations, groups, and movements are diverse in organizational structures as well as in purpose. Some are dedicated solely to spiritual renewal, while others give their energies to voluntary charitable works or to missionary activity. Some, such as the prolife movement, are specialized or single-issue movements. Others have a more comprehensive religious goal, which is pursued in collaboration with the Italian Bishops' Conference (for example, Italian Catholic Action) or with the Vatican itself (for instance, international movements such as Opus Dei and Focolari). Comunione e Liberazione, by contrast, has an autonomous international status recognized by the pope, but it also enjoys a direct connection with each diocesan bishop and local parish organization.

CL sees culture as its primary arena of influence: by means of the education and formation provided in the Scuole and the economic and social initiatives of the Opere, the movement hopes to reshape society for the long term. It does not form theologians, scholars, or religious specialists. Instead, it prepares lay people for cultural leadership and social action.

CL's entry into the Italian political arena came in 1974 with its participation in the national referendum on divorce. Yet CL did not attempt to establish a Catholic political party. It pursued specific political goals through Il Movimento Popolare (MP), a support organization for individuals and groups that promote the Catholic tradition in local and national political institutions and cultural organizations. MP also functions as an independent power broker and shaper of public opinion. It nominates and campaigns for candidates who favor the Compagnia delle Opere and its initiatives. Although MP has allied itself with the Christian Democrats, CL has criticized the party harshly for supposedly capitulating to the unacceptable cultural and political principles of the modern state. The party failed to transform its political hegemony into cultural hegemony. Il Movimento Popolare is CL's response. It has proved effective at every level of the electoral process and has become an influential insurgent within the Christian Democrat Party by electing its representatives in every major local and national election.

Tension and Diversity in the Modern Church

Comunione e Liberazione is a fascinating mixture of both types of modern Catholicism. Ideologically, its antimodern and countercultural spirit has more in common with the preconciliar Catholic attitude toward the modern world and the secular political realm. By denying the fact of the Christ event, CL maintains, modernity is atheistic and divested of any viable spiritual value. Movement ideology holds that the modern state has attempted to usurp the power that rightly belongs to the religious and moral foundations of a just political order, namely, the church. Communism was one inevitable result of this error, in Giussani's view, but even democracy can become an illusory morality, he warned, if it marginalizes religion.

In its organizational structure and social location, however, CL is clearly a product of the Second Vatican Council. It is primarily a lay society dedicated to bringing about change "from below" through cultural renewal complemented by direct political action on social issues facing the Italian electorate. The political program of Il Movimento Popolare is encapsulated in the slogan "less state, more society"—an ironic twist on the old secular motto. CL promotes religious authority as the guide for both the individual conscience and the state, especially on matters pertaining to morality, faith, education, and family legislation.

Yet CL clearly resists certain aspects of Vatican II's program of liberalization. In the view of many CL leaders, the Second Vatican Council's endorsement of church-state separation and religious pluralism undermined the church's constitutional position in areas of family life, morals, and education. Instead of demanding greater pluralism and popular participation, CL seeks what its critics call a new type of Catholic hegemony. While stopping short of calling for a Catholic state (a move that would violate the letter as well as the spirit of Vatican II), CL makes no secret of its conviction that the church should wield political influence and exercise public power. Only the church, it believes, can legitimately establish normative structures that govern human existence.

This is not to be confused with the political model of church-state union associated with the old regime. Giussani assumes that cultural pluralism will continue to exist, but he and his movement wish to restore decisive cultural power to the church. This is not primarily a matter of the official position and role of religion vis-à-vis the state, Dario explains. It is a new social ethos based on Catholic solidarity and sustained from within by hierarchical authority. Presumably, political change will follow. Giussani has denied that he holds a confessional state to be the political ideal, but he does envision a state guided by religiously observant leaders.

Many Italian Catholics, fearing any form of hegemonic religion, reject CL's political and cultural agenda. They prefer to see Catholicism thrive as an apolitical moral and spiritual force in a genuinely pluralist society. Such open and sometimes vehement disagreements among Catholics living in the same society reflect a striking diversity of Catholic political and cultural orientations. This is one of the most important legacies of the Second Vatican Council.

In relocating its public presence instead of abandoning its commitments to the commonweal and the public good, Roman Catholicism is perhaps the preeminent example of a powerful world religion that refuses to become "privatized" in the late modern era. More than a few commentators have noted an irony in the fact of the Catholic Church, with its decidedly nondemocratic patterns of internal governance, standing as a powerful champion of pluralist, democratic societies in the modern world. Yet this is one striking result of the creative tension, built up over two centuries, caused by the two radically different attitudes and approaches to the modern world coexisting and competing for dominance within the church itself.

Similarly, the Roman Catholic teaching on the relationship between social justice and charity, brought into stark relief by the Second Vatican Council and the notion of a "preferential option for the poor," continues to evolve. A papal encyclical, promulgated on Christmas Day in 2005, suggests a renewed emphasis on charity, perhaps at the expense of social justice.

Upon Pope John Paul II's death in 2005, Joseph Ratzinger, a German cardinal and longtime prefect (director) of the Vatican's Congregation for the Doctrine of the Faith, was elected by his fellow cardinals as the 264th successor to St. Peter. The new pope took the name Benedict XVI and embarked on a pontificate dedicated to opposing what he called "a dictatorship of relativism" infecting modern society and to reconciling the Roman Catholic, Orthodox, and Protestant Christian churches with one another. Pope Benedict XVI's first encyclical, entitled "Deus Caritas Est" ("God is Love"), was a meditation on the relationship between divine love and various types of human love. The opening section of the encyclical, devoted entirely to this theme, received widespread praise from non-Catholics and Catholics alike. The second part of the encyclical was controversial, however, in that it seemed, to many progressive Catholics, to identify the Church with the hierarchy and clergy, and to restrict or even reject the Church's previously proclaimed commitment to working for the transformation of unjust social structures. "The Church cannot and must not take upon herself the political battle to bring about the most just society possible," the encyclical warned. Elsewhere in the text, Benedict XVI does acknowledge the role of "the lay faithful" in fulfilling "the direct duty to work for a just ordering of society."

During the twenty-six years of John Paul II's pontificate, Ratzinger earned a reputation as a strict and uncompromising enforcer of traditional interpretations of Catholic doctrine. By silencing controversial theologians or taking away their right to teach as Catholic theologians, Ratzinger attempted to eliminate dissent against received Catholic teaching on birth control, homosexuality, and the exclusion of women from the priesthood. Notably, Ratzinger attempted to squelch a number of innovative movements within the church, among them the theology of liberation that emerged in Latin America in the 1980s. Like John Paul II, then-cardinal Ratzinger despised Marxism and feared what he saw as a strong Marxist tendency in liberation theology. As Pope Benedict XVI, Ratzinger remained consistent, by echoing previous condemnations of Marxism and insisting that "Christian charitable activity must be independent of parties and ideologies." As of September 2006, "Deus Caritas Est" was the only encyclical issued thus far by the new pope, and the jury was still out on the question of its implications for the modern Church's commitment to the work of social justice as well as charity.

See also *CELAM; Christian Democracy; Civil Society; Liberation Theology; Maryknoll; Papacy; Vatican; Vatican Council, Second.*

R. Scott Appleby

BIBLIOGRAPHY

Alberigo, Giuseppe, and Joseph Komonchak, eds. *Announcing and Preparing Vatican Council II: Toward a New Era in Catholicism.* Vol. 2: *History of Vatican II.* Maryknoll, N.Y.: Orbis Books/Peeters, 1995.

Benedict XVI. "Deus Caritas Est." *Libreria Editrice Vaticana,* 2005.

Burns, Gene. *The Frontiers of Catholicism: The Politics of Ideology in a Liberal World.* Berkeley: University of California Press, 1992.

Casanova, Jose. *Public Religion in the Modern World.* Chicago: University of Chicago Press, 1995.

Gremillion, Joseph, ed. *The Church and Culture since Vatican II: The Experience of North and Latin America.* Notre Dame: University of Notre Dame Press, 1985.

———. *The Gospel of Peace and Justice: Catholic Social Teaching since Pope John.* Maryknoll, N.Y.: Orbis Books, 1976.

Gutierrez, Gustavo. *Theology of Liberation.* Maryknoll, N.Y.: Orbis Books, 1976.

Hastings, Adrian, ed. *Modern Catholicism: Vatican II and After.* Oxford: Oxford University Press, 1991.

Himes, Michael J., and Kenneth R. Himes. *Fullness of Faith: The Public Significance of Theology.* Mahwah, N.J.: Paulist Press, 1993.

John Paul II. *Centesimus Annus.* Reprinted in *First Things* (August/September 1991).

McBrien, Richard P. *Lives of the Popes: The Pontiffs from Saint Peter to John Paul II.* San Francisco, Calif.: HarperCollins, 1997.

McBrien, Richard P., ed. *The HarperCollins Encyclopedia of Catholicism.* San Francisco, Calif.: HarperCollins, 1995.

Novak, Michael. *The Catholic Ethic and the Spirit of Capitalism.* New York: Free Press, 1993.

Zadra, Dario. "Comunione e Liberazione: A Fundamentalist Idea of Power." In *Accounting for Fundamentalisms: The Dynamic Nature of Movements,* edited by Martin E. Marty and R. Scott Appleby. Chicago: University of Chicago Press, 1994.

CELAM

The Consejo Episcopal Latinoamericano (or CELAM), known in English as the Latin American Bishops Conference, is the regional organization of Roman Catholic bishops from twenty-two Latin American and Caribbean conferences. CELAM studies common issues, proposes practical approaches, and coordinates transnational activities among the Latin American nations. Its four general conferences have established the Catholic Church's policy for the region.

Latin American bishops met for the First General Conference in Rio de Janeiro, Brazil, July 25–August 4, 1955. The Vatican, especially through Italian archbishop Antonio Samoré, then the pope's chief of staff, had encouraged the bishops to form a permanent organization for the Latin American church. In September 1955 the new body set up a general secretariat in Bogotá, Colombia. During the 1950s CELAM served as the example for many national churches organizing similar permanent secretariats. CELAM influenced Latin American and developing world churches through a shift from emphasizing traditional piety and individual charity to concern for political and social issues affecting the lower classes. The Latin American conference also emphasized much broader participation of lay Catholics within the church and in politics.

Early assemblies took place in Rome during the years of the Second Vatican Council (1962–1965), which Pope John XXIII convoked to revitalize the Roman Catholic Church and which became the symbol of the church's openness to the modern world. Vatican II's renewed visions of the church—emphasizing a new ecumenical openness toward other Christian churches, the collective responsibility of the bishops in the church's mission, more acute concern for political and social issues, reform of priestly education, and partial diversity in theology and local practices—strongly influenced the Latin American bishops. Vatican II's final document, *The Church in the Modern World,* provided a this-worldly method that CELAM has followed for many years: a description of reality, biblical and theological reflection, and proposals for action.

Before the council concluded, Pope Paul VI (who became pope in 1963) accepted CELAM's proposal that it apply the teachings of Vatican II to Latin America. Liberation theologians and progressive advisers strongly influenced an important set of documents, which were modified and approved by the bishops at the Second General Conference at Medellín, Colombia (1968). Several Protestant observers attended, helping other churches understand the Catholic renewal movement.

The Medellín conference was a landmark meeting for church renewal. Theological and pastoral innovations such as liberation theology, base Christian communities, and preferential option for the poor were emphasized, especially in the documents on justice and peace. These issues and the bishops' analysis of economic and social inequalities brought moderate and progressive church leaders into conflict with military governments and conservative Catholics and Protestants over repressive political governance and human rights abuses.

The Third General Conference at Puebla, Mexico (1979), by and large, ratified positions taken at Medellín. But the election of Archbishop Alfonso López Trujillo as president of CELAM the year before signaled a conservative shift within the organization that lasted for more than a decade. Under the imprint of John Paul II (who was elected pope in 1978) conservative leadership was evident at CELAM's Fourth General Conference at Santo Domingo, Dominican Republic (1992). CELAM celebrated its sixtieth anniversary in 2005 while looking forward to its Fifth General Conference at Aparecida, Brazil, in 2007, with Pope Benedict XVI in attendance.

See also *Base Communities; Central America; Human Rights; Liberation Theology.*

Edward L. Cleary

BIBLIOGRAPHY

Cleary, Edward L. *Crisis and Change: The Church in Latin America Today.* Maryknoll, N.Y.: Orbis Books, 1985.

Hennelly, Alfred T., ed. *Santo Domingo and Beyond.* Maryknoll, N.Y.: Orbis Books, 1993.

Second General Conference of Latin American Bishops. *Position Papers and Conclusions: The Church in the Present-Day Transformation of Latin America in the Light of the Council.* 2 vols. Bogotá: General Secretariat of Consejo Episcopal Latinoamericano, 1970.

Censorship

Censorship, the prohibition of public expressions of ideas and opinions, has three components. First, it is concerned with ideas and opinions, not with conduct. Banning communist parties or unconventional sexual practices, for example, is not censorship, but banning the advocacy of either activity is. Second, censorship is not concerned with ideas or opinions that individuals might express in the privacy of their homes but with the public expression of them. The term "public expression" refers to what is in principle accessible to others and includes ordinary utterances; philosophical, literary, scientific, and other works; and artistic performances. Third, censorship implies prohibition—that is, an official ban accompanied by a threat of sanctions.

There are two kinds of prohibition: preventive, in which certain ideas are denied public expression, and punitive, in which ideas are allowed to be published but authors of them are subject to prosecution and punishment. Mere disapproval, however strong, of a body of ideas or vague threats of undesirable consequences to those who articulate them do not amount to censorship. The disapproval must be explicitly expressed by the governing authority, and the threats must be clearly specified and enforceable.

Censorship can be imposed by anyone in a position of authority. In the early twenty-first century, in its most obvious form, censorship is imposed by the state, but it can also be imposed by educational and religious institutions. Publishing houses, libraries, theaters, cinemas, television companies, and museums can exercise censorship by refusing to publish or circulate books or to display certain kinds of material. Powerful social, economic, and religious groups exercise censorship when they threaten to boycott certain products or programs as a way of imposing their views on others. Individuals too can engage in self-censorship by voluntarily refraining from publicly expressing their ideas for fear of unpleasant consequences.

Because all societies seek to reproduce themselves, and see certain sets of ideas as threats to their survival and identity, censorship in one form or another has existed in every society. In the West it was introduced by the Greek city-state Sparta, which banned not only unconventional ideas but also some forms of poetry, dancing, and music that were thought likely to encourage licentiousness and effeminacy. Classical Rome was far more tolerant, but it too instituted censorship; indeed, the term itself is Roman in origin. Censors, the guardians of Roman virtues, wielded considerable power. Although their primary duty was to ensure manliness and probity in public life, and thus to regulate personal and public conduct, they also banned ideas likely to undermine faith in Roman values and way of life.

Unlike Sparta and Rome, which were primarily concerned with regulating conduct and took only a limited interest in censoring ideas, the Roman Catholic Church emphasized the latter. The Church, which began to consolidate itself in the third century after Christ, was deeply concerned with developing and imposing a theological orthodoxy, and it banned heretical writings. Its censorship was largely punitive and consisted in punishing transgressors in various ways. (The medieval practice of inquisition is the best known.) It also issued a list of forbidden books, the *Index Librorum Prohibitorum*, first published in 1559. Catholics were forbidden to read these books on the grounds that they spiritually and morally corrupted their readers and undermined their allegiance to the only "true faith." Later, with the emergence of Protestantism, advances in the natural sciences, and the popular fascination with black magic, the *Index* was expanded to include Protestant writings; some scientific, medical, and philosophical works; books on magic and astrology; some Jewish writings; manuals on exorcism; and some pacifist books.

Challenges to State Censorship

With the disintegration of the medieval Church's power and the rise of the nation-state in Europe, governments began to assume the function of censorship. Initially, state censorship was preventive. No work was allowed to be pub-

"The Bookworm" cartoon, circa 1925. Censorship of books deemed "obscene" by the government and by civil watchdog groups such as the New England Watch and Ward Society was widespread through Prohibition and led to the coining of the phrase "Banned in Boston."

lished without the prior approval of government officers, and no one was allowed to set up a printing press without obtaining a strictly controlled government license. Over time, the practice was relaxed and censorship became punitive. Anyone could set up a printing press and authors could publish books, but both alike were subject to prosecution and punishment.

State censorship covered a wide range of books and artistic expressions, though it concentrated on three kinds of writings—the subversive, the blasphemous, and the obscene. The authoritarian—and insecure—early states banned works critical of the institution of government, the ruling dynasty, and the dominant political ideology. Such works, it was believed, weakened the authority of the government, threatened civil disorder, and encouraged disloyalty and disobedience. Because these states were religiously based, attacks on Christianity were banned in the interest of that faith, the state, and social and personal morality. Obscene works were banned on the grounds that they corrupted public morality, violated and weakened the established norms of decency and good taste, offended public sentiments, and encouraged licentiousness and prurience.

Almost from its beginning, and especially from the eighteenth century onward, state censorship came under considerable criticism. Although the criticism was mounted by different groups on different grounds, most critics drew their inspiration from liberalism, a body of ideas that had begun to emerge in the seventeenth century and acquired philosophical coherence in the eighteenth. Liberalism, which stressed individual autonomy, rationalism, progress, and the omnipotence of truth, articulated a vision of society in which self-determining individuals, pooling together their rational resources in public debate, could discover moral truths on which to base their personal and collective lives. Freedom of expression, which encompassed artistic and other forms of self-exploration as well as freedom of speech, was crucial to human progress and well-being.

Basing their objections on these and related ideas, liberal writers challenged all forms of censorship. Censorship was unacceptable to them for several reasons. Truth and progress resulted from a clash of ideas; so to suppress the latter was to foreclose the possibility of either. Because it was impossible to know what ideas were false except by openly confronting and criticizing them, censorship perpetuated ignorance and falsehood. Because new ideas could not be suppressed forever, all censorship ultimately was futile. Indeed, suppressed ideas acquired glamour and the halo of martyrdom and were widely embraced even when wrong, thereby rendering censorship counterproductive. Finally, censorship treated people as children unable to think for themselves, thus at the same time insulting them and arresting their intellectual growth.

Having questioned the basic presuppositions of censorship, liberals went on to challenge its three dominant forms. Political censorship was bad because it concealed the misdeeds of government, led to abuse of power, prevented the emergence of enlightened public opinion, and hindered the growth of responsible citizenship and democratic culture. Freedom could be misused, but the remedy lay not in restricting but expanding it.

Religious censorship was considered bad for similar reasons. God was too great to be blasphemed, and in any case he did not need the protection of human law to maintain his honor. Furthermore, theological truths could be interpreted in several different ways, and each individual had to decide which one was rationally most acceptable. Because religion was a matter for individual conscience, the state had no right to interfere with it. Although people could be swayed by wrong ideas, the best way to counter those ideas was not to suppress them but to refute them in public debate.

Censorship of obscenity was the last to be attacked. Although critical of the prevailing economic, political, and religious ideas, liberals—who were generally drawn from the ranks of the middle classes—were often conservative and even puritanical in sexual matters. Only in the last few decades of the twentieth century did they begin to mount a radical critique of the censorship of obscenity. Obscenity, they argued, is a matter of individual opinion and cannot be objectively defined, and there is no evidence that pornography corrupts public morals. Indeed, it is likely to act as a safety valve, to offer vicarious gratification to unconventional sexual desires and fantasies, and thus to lead to moral health. The human mind is complex, and reading the right kind of wrong book has advantages the narrow, puritanical imagination does not appreciate. What is more, it is up to self-determining adults to decide what sexual material to read; the state has no right to act as their guardian.

Political censorship in the early twenty-first century is almost nonexistent in liberal states, the major exception to it being the widely accepted need to protect vital state secrets. Religious censorship has declined considerably. Some states, such as Great Britain, still have antiblasphemy laws, but these are largely defunct and there is considerable pressure to abolish them. Some forms of censorship on pornography and obscenity remain, but they are increasingly being relaxed.

Many non-Western countries believe they have a right to uphold moral and religious values that are necessary to their survival as a particular kind of society. Those values represent a collective inheritance, a sacred trust, which society has a duty to transmit to succeeding generations. Censorship is therefore considered wholly legitimate. It is a form of collective self-discipline and as essential to building national character as moral discipline is to cultivating individual character. For these societies, which include many Muslim and some East Asian countries, the West has taken its liberal antipathy to censorship too far and is paying the price in the form of moral confusion and social disintegration.

Unresolved Questions

Moral and political questions are never completely resolved. Feminists in the late twentieth and early twenty-first centuries have reopened the question of censorship of obscenity, and several religious leaders, especially Muslim migrants to the West, have reopened that of religious censorship. Some feminist writers have demanded a ban on pornography, especially material that depicts female bodies in exploitative and demeaning ways. Pornography, they argue, degrades women, undermines their self-respect, violates their dignity, and represents them as mere sex objects. Furthermore, it encourages men to believe that they may take sexual liberty with women and that women welcome this behavior. Many feminist writers argue that unless pornographic material has redeeming features, which it rarely has, it should be banned. Pornography may rightly be curtailed when the liberal doctrine of self-expression comes into conflict with the liberal respect for persons.

The question of religious censorship was dramatically placed on the public agenda with the publication in 1988 of a novel by Salman Rushdie, a well-known Indian writer of Muslim descent who then lived in Britain. Although Rushdie defended *The Satanic Verses* as an allegorical work, Muslims in England and abroad declared it to be "a form of religious pornography" that had taken unacceptable liberties with their religious heritage. It presented the prophet Muhammad as an unscrupulous businessman doing shady deals with the archangel and God and as a debauchee who married women out of lust. It treated the Islamic holy book, the Qur'an, as a collection of politically convenient verses, not an authentic divine revelation.

For Muslims, *The Satanic Verses* insulted, trivialized, and told lies about their faith; demeaned them in their own and in others' eyes; crossed all limits of decency; and gratuitously insulted the Prophet, his wives, and followers. They demanded that the book be banned or at least purged of the offending passages. They argued that while free speech is vital to the pursuit of truth, Rushdie's book was abusive and insulting and did not provide a rational critique of Islam. Free speech promotes progress, they agreed, but it is difficult to see how a book of this kind promotes either intellectual or moral progress. Free speech is necessary to expose crude exploitation of religious beliefs; however, Rushdie had instead pandered to crude prejudices against Islam. The right to self-expression is important, but so are the rights of every individual to self-respect and of every religious community to the integrity of its beliefs and heritage. Muslims believed it was wrong, even irrational, to privilege self-expression and to allow it always to trump other rights. They appealed to the principle of equality and demanded that Britain's antiblasphemy law cover not only Christianity but also Islam and other religions.

Although some of these arguments are unconvincing, others have force. The liberal response that *The Satanic Verses* was a work of fiction, that Muslims were oversensitive about their religion, and that free speech was a more or less absolute value does not address some of the important questions that were raised. The issues remain unresolved. In 1989 the Iranian leader, Ayatollah Ruhollah Khomeini, issued a death sentence on Rushdie, and Rushdie was forced to go into hiding for most of the 1990s. In 2005 a Danish newspaper's publication of a cartoon depicting Muhammad with a bomb in his turban led to sometimes violent protests and renewed debate over religious censorship.

In recent years hate speech has become a subject of debate. It is argued that racially and ethnically denigratory utterances violate the liberal principle of respect for persons, demean the target group in its own and others' eyes, and create a hostile climate against it. Since hate speech serves no worthwhile goals and in fact harms individuals, some advocate restricting it.

Because of these and other challenges, the liberal doctrine of minimum restriction on freedom of expression has come under scrutiny. The consensus built up over the past two centuries has weakened. Since state censorship is not the answer, there is a search for other ways of dealing with gross misuse of the freedom of expression.

See also *Conservatism; Fundamentalism; Inquisition, Khomeini, Ruhollah Musavi; Liberalism.*

Bhikhu Parekh

BIBLIOGRAPHY

Ernst, Morris L., and Alan U. Schwartz. *Censorship: The Search for the Obscene.* New York: Macmillan, 1964.

Haiman, Franklyn S. *Freedom of Speech.* Skokie, Ill.: National Textbook Co., 1976.

MacKinnon, Catharine A. *Feminism Unmodified: Discourses on Life and Law.* Cambridge: Harvard University Press, 1987.

Mill, John Stuart. *On Liberty and Other Writings.* Edited by Stefan Collini. Cambridge, England; New York: Cambridge University Press, 1989.

Parekh, Bhikhu. *Rethinking Multiculturalism: Cultural Diversity and Political Theory.* Cambridge: Harvard University Press, 2000.

Webster, Richard. *A Brief History of Blasphemy.* London: Orwell Press, 1990.

Central America

Forming an isthmus that bridges North America and South America, Central America is predominantly Roman Catholic and is made up of the countries of Belize, Costa Rica, El Salvador, Guatemala, Honduras, Nicaragua, and Panama.

In the mid- to late 1970s, revolutionary movements emerged and gained ground in Nicaragua, El Salvador, and Guatemala in response to long-standing poverty and decades of repressive rule. When the leftist Sandinista National Liberation Front (FSLN) took power in Nicaragua in mid-1979, successful revolution seemed possible in the region. Throughout the 1980s revolutionary and counterrevolutionary forces—with heavy outside intervention, especially by the U.S. government—made Central America a battleground. Unlike what had happened at the time of the Cuban revolution (1959), church people were significantly involved in these revolutionary struggles.

Nicaragua, El Salvador, and Guatemala were alike in many ways. They were small agro-export countries under repressive rule (the Somoza family's dictatorship in Nicaragua since the 1930s and de facto military control in El Salvador and Guatemala for decades). Over time, large agricultural producers expanded their operations, taking large tracts of the best land. The rural poor had less and less land, often of poorer quality, to pass on to their children. In each country several leftist guerrilla groups had been operating with little success for a number of years. In the 1970s mass political organizations of peasants, labor, the urban poor, and students emerged. They were Marxist-inspired and, as it eventually became clear, had ties to the guerrilla organizations that began to show new strength by the middle of the decade.

In the period of renewal of the Roman Catholic Church following the Second Vatican Council (1962–1965) and the meeting of the Council of Latin American Bishops in Medellín, Colombia (1968), Catholic clergy and lay workers began new pastoral experiences with the poor (for example, setting up base communities or small religious study groups). In all three countries there were connections between such pastoral work and the emergence of the militant mass organizations, some of which were founded by church activists.

Nicaragua

The Catholic Church, which had largely accepted the Somoza dictatorship since its inception in the 1930s, began to move toward a more critical stance. For example, in 1970 Archbishop Miguel Obando y Bravo refused President Anastasio Somoza's gift of a Mercedes-Benz. When Somoza and his circle shamelessly profiteered from international aid arriving after the 1972 earthquake, opposition began to spread even among the elites. Archbishop Obando was called on to mediate after a daring Sandinista hostage operation in 1974 (and again in 1978). Catholic Church representatives documented and publicized the killing and disappearance of hundreds of peasants by Somoza's National Guard. In 1977 the Sandinistas took the offensive, and mass opposition developed, with significant church participation. After a year and a half of a struggle that cost an estimated thirty thousand lives, the dictator departed, and the first successful Latin American revolutionary movement in twenty years took power.

Some believers were convinced that the Nicaraguan revolution represented a unique new opportunity for the church, a chance to embody the option for the poor in an effort to make structural change and to create a new kind of society. In this view, it was not only legitimate for Christians to be involved, but such involvement also followed from their commitment to the Gospel. Others were concerned that the Sandinista revolution was Marxist and hence inevitably antireligious, whatever the Sandinistas might claim. As a rule, Protestants felt less impelled to take public stands, in part because they were regarded as a minority in a society considered Catholic.

Despite some initial misgivings, the Catholic bishops seemed to accept the revolutionary government during an early honeymoon phase, as illustrated by a November 1979 pastoral letter in which they accepted socialism. Three hundred members of religious orders were active in the 1980 Sandinista-sponsored literacy campaign. But the honeymoon lasted less than a year. Over a number of years, the bishops expressed their fear that the Sandinistas would set up a Marxist regime that would put constraints on the church. They said that Catholics, and especially priests, who openly supported the revolution were causing division in the church. Shortly after the two members representing the business elite resigned from the government junta, the bishops went into opposition, ordering four priests in ministerial positions to resign.

In the early 1980s much of the public debate between Sandinista partisans and adversaries was presented in theological terms. In October 1980 the Sandinistas published

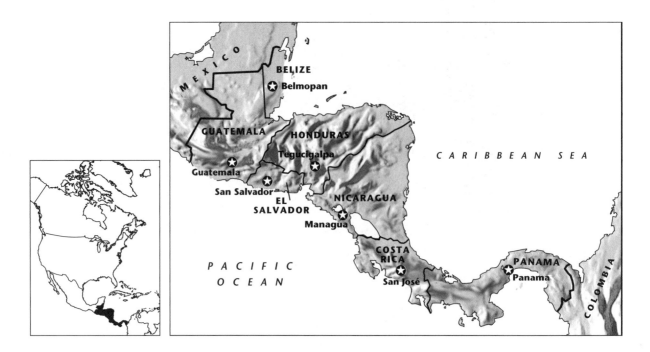

their "Statement on Religion," which consciously broke away from a century of Marxist opposition to religion, noting that Christians had been active in the fight to overthrow the dictatorship and that this fact opened new possibilities "in the phase of building a new society."

By 1982 the U.S.-supported *contra*—for *contra revolutionario* or counter revolutionary—army (made up initially of former Somoza troops) was staging major attacks in Nicaragua, killing and terrorizing civilians. The Catholic bishops refrained from condemning these actions while opposing the Sandinistas repeatedly.

In a 1982 letter Pope John Paul II had admonished Nicaraguan Catholics to follow their bishops, seemingly endorsing their anti-Sandinista stance. On his arrival at the airport for his 1983 visit and in front of the world's television cameras, he wagged a finger at Father Ernesto Cardenal, the poet and minister of culture, and told him to leave the government and resume a normal priestly life. At an afternoon Mass attended by several hundred thousand people, Sandinista supporters who had hoped in vain for some word of comfort over the recent killing of seventeen young people began to chant for peace. The pope shouted back "Silence!" three times. Whether the chanting was spontaneous, as Sandinista supporters claimed, or an orchestrated insult to the pope, the images transmitted around the world fueled the notion that the Sandinista regime was hostile to

the church. In making Archbishop Obando a cardinal in 1985, the Vatican further polarized the situation.

Lacking the same historic role in Nicaraguan society, Protestant churches were less likely to be thrust into similar public disputes. Nevertheless, one network of anti-Sandinista Protestant pastors was formed with U.S. embassy support as an alternative to an ecumenical organization deemed cooperative with the government.

Through the rest of the decade lines remained firmly drawn as the conflict played itself out. The Sandinista government, forced to combat the contras and maintain a military capable of withstanding a potential U.S. invasion, diverted resources to defense and put its ambitious development programs on hold. The bishops, far from condemning the contra war, seemed to endorse it, especially when Cardinal Obando appeared in Washington in 1986 in support of $100 million in U.S. aid to the contras. In mid-1986 the Sandinistas expelled one prominent bishop for supporting the contras.

The Central America peace plan of 1987 prepared by the presidents of the region finally established guidelines for reversing the ever-deepening conflict. Cardinal Obando and Baptist leader Gustavo Parajon were appointed to the peace commission. Hundreds of priests, sisters, and Protestant pastors served on local reconciliation commissions around the country.

Starting in the mid-1980s living standards began to drop, and inflation turned to hyperinflation. A disenchanted electorate voted the Sandinistas out of office in 1990, surprising most pollsters. The winning coalition under President Violeta Chamorro was split between moderates, who strove for an accommodation with the Sandinistas, and more hard-line members of her coalition, who urged harsher policies, particularly to eliminate as much of the Sandinista policies as possible. For example, Humberto Belli, a member of the conservative Catholic organization Opus Dei and a fierce anti-Sandinista critic, oversaw the redesign of school curricula and textbooks. Cardinal Obando and the bishops inclined to side with the hard-liners. By the late 1990s Obando was tarnished by association with the government of President Arnoldo Aleman, who was subsequently jailed for corruption. In the post-Sandinista years the political role of the Catholic Church declined.

El Salvador

El Salvador had been under harsh military and oligarchical control since 1932, when the army had killed ten thousand to thirty thousand peasants in suppressing an uprising. High population density made rural landlessness even more acute. As early as 1970, repression was being used against priests working with the rural poor. Mass organizations formed in the mid-1970s became militant. When the Universidad Centroamericana José Simeón Cañas, also known as the University of Central America, supported a mild government-proposed land reform in 1976, bombs were set off in the institution as warnings. Conflict became extreme in the first several months of 1977. Several priests were expelled, others beaten; Fathers Rutilio Grande and Alfonso Navarro were killed. Outside the cathedral opposition figures protesting the electoral fraud were beaten, and several dozen were killed. Security forces swept the area around the town of Aguilares, abducting dozens of people and taking over the town church and holding its Jesuit staff captive. This was the setting of the first few months of Oscar A. Romero's tenure as archbishop of San Salvador. By 1980 approximately a dozen priests had been murdered by official forces or right-wing death squads.

As tensions rose, Archbishop Romero came to be seen as the "voice of the voiceless." In 1979, observing what had happened in Nicaragua, a group of officers overthrew President Carlos Humberto Romero and installed a junta, which immediately announced its intention of carrying out reforms. In practice, however, the level of violence increased until a thousand people a month were being killed or "disappeared" in early 1980. Archbishop Romero insistently called for dialogue to head off the civil war that seemed imminent. He himself was murdered by a right-wing assassin in March. The country slid toward civil war. In December, shortly after the brutal murder of six opposition figures, four North American women—three nuns and a lay worker—were abducted by National Guard troops, raped, and murdered. Only after intense American pressure and substantial delay were some lower-ranking soldiers sentenced to jail terms for this crime.

In January 1981 the leftist FMLN (Farabundo Marti National Liberation Front) formally launched an insurrection, but it failed to ignite great popular support among an already terrorized population. The guerrillas then withdrew to rural areas in the hills along the northern border with Honduras. Some priests, sisters, and lay people carried out pastoral work in guerrilla-controlled areas.

Romero's replacement, Archbishop Arturo Rivera y Damas, repeatedly urged that the war be resolved through dialogue or negotiations. Pope John Paul II angered the right and the military by also using the word "dialogue" in his 1983 visit, thereby giving it respectability. Although Rivera's approach was more evenhanded than Romero's had been (Rivera insisted, for example, that the church human rights office document violations by guerrillas as well as official and right-wing forces), he and his associates earned the ire of the army by denouncing the frequent human rights abuses. The other bishops did not support Rivera and, at least by default, supported the government.

The United States played a major role in funding the Salvadoran government and military and in pressuring the military toward at least formal democracy. In 1984 José Napoleón Duarte, who had been defrauded of the 1972 election, was elected, but his role was largely that of executing an overall plan designed by the Americans, in which the primary objective was to prevent a guerrilla victory and to isolate the FMLN.

Throughout the 1980s the University of Central America, under its rector, Ignacio Ellacuría, a Jesuit theologian, philosopher, and advocate of a negotiated end to the war, was a major center of independent research and analysis. In public forums it became a place where representatives of all political sectors—from right to left—could present their views. Although the government did little to carry out the

Central America peace plan, repression abated somewhat, and the leftist opposition could have at least a minor political presence.

In November 1989 the FMLN launched an offensive in the capital, San Salvador. In response, army troops went to Catholic University and murdered six Jesuits, including Ellacuría, as well as a housekeeper and her daughter who had taken refuge there. The offensive again failed to spark a general uprising, and both sides were forced to face the fact that the war was at an impasse and could not be resolved militarily. The killing of the Jesuits by the U.S.-trained elite Atlacatl Battalion hastened the end of U.S. patience for the war, especially after an ensuing attempt at a cover-up. In October 1991 several lower-ranking officers were put on trial, but only two were found guilty. Shortly afterward, a formal peace accord was signed.

Guatemala

After a 1954 Central Intelligence Agency–organized overthrow of its democratically elected government, Guatemala was under military rule. A complex guerrilla movement arose in the 1960s and was put down at the cost of six thousand to eight thousand civilian lives. Church workers came under suspicion when an attempt by two Maryknoll priests and a sister, along with a number of students, to join a guerrilla group was foiled in late 1967. In the early 1970s hundreds of labor union members and other activists were murdered each year. In the mid- to late 1970s guerrilla groups began to operate again, and there arose new mass popular movements, particularly of labor and peasants. A number of pastoral workers were involved in these. At least three priests joined the guerrillas, and one was killed in combat.

Although the Guatemalan bishops' conference made several eloquent statements condemning injustice and violence, they were generally offset by conservative Cardinal Mario Casariego of Guatemala City. After Casariego's death in 1983, his replacement, Archbishop Prospero Penados, became more forthright in opposition to state-sponsored violence.

As in El Salvador, approximately a dozen priests were murdered during 1978–1982 by the army or right-wing death squads. Repression was so acute in the Quiché diocese that in June 1980 all Catholic Church personnel decided to leave the diocese, and the bishop went into exile outside the country (although in fact a few priests managed to maintain a low-key presence). In 1981–1983 the army launched a "dirty war" in areas of guerrilla influence, carrying out well-

documented massacres of sometimes more than two hundred or three hundred people in a single village. Those viewed as leaders, including Catholic catechists and Protestant pastors, were singled out for abduction, torture, and murder. In 1982 the bishops said that more than a million Guatemalans (out of a total population of seven million at that time) had been forced to leave their homes.

Such brutal tactics were effective, and by the mid-1980s the guerrillas had lost civilian support and were reduced to a minor presence. Very slowly, new organizations for human rights, labor, and indigenous rights began to form. Of particular interest was Rigoberta Menchú, a young Quiché Maya woman who as a teenager had gone from being a catechist to a peasant organizer before having to flee the country (her father, mother, and two brothers were all murdered by the army). Menchú carried on her work on behalf of Guatemalan human rights from her refuge in Mexico, and in 1987 she began to make occasional visits to Guatemala, in the wake of the Central America peace plan. In 1992, the five hundredth anniversary of the European discovery of the Americas (also proclaimed the Year of the Indigenous), she was awarded the Nobel Peace Prize, to the chagrin of the Guatemalan military.

Protestants also came to play a public role. By the 1980s they were estimated to be 15 percent of the population and, in terms of actual church attendance, were on a par with Catholics. General Efraín Rios Montt, who took over the government in the wake of a military coup in 1982, was a member of the neopentecostal Church of the Word (based in Eureka, California). He was often blamed for the massacres in the highlands. His public moralizing and authoritarian attitude and actions (for example, setting up special courts for quick verdicts and even executions with no legal safeguards) made him increasingly a liability, and he was deposed in 1983. In the 1990 election Jorge Serrano Elias's Protestant identity helped him win the election (and become the first Protestant elected head of state in Latin America). He was forced out of office in 1993 after he attempted to close the congress and shut down the judicial system.

In 1995 the Catholic Church began an extensive project called REHMI (Recovery of Historic Memory) to bring to light the violence in Guatemala. Testimonies were collected through approximately seven thousand interviews with ordinary people, especially the indigenous. The testimonies were then summarized and analyzed in a four-volume report presented in April 1998 by Bishop Juan Gerardi. Two days later he was bludgeoned to death in his garage as he returned home, in obvious retaliation for the report. Three lower-level perpetrators were eventually put on trial and imprisoned, but the real authors (retired or active military) of the crime were not pursued.

When, on a 1985 visit to Nicaragua, Brazilian theologian Leonardo Boff said that the revolution there embodied "all our utopias," he was expressing a shared hope that the struggles in Central America were a sign of Latin America's future, that is, that a different kind of society could be created. In hindsight, however, those struggles marked not the beginning of a utopia but the end of the 1960–1990 period in which revolution seemed possible. Many people, including Christians who had wagered their lives on revolution, were left perplexed by the world of the 1990s, which seemed to offer no alternative to a globalized economy that aggravated extremes of wealth and poverty. Both the FMLN and FSLN coalitions split, and many of their supporters, including prominent Christians, were left disillusioned.

The witness of Archbishop Romero, the murdered church women, the Jesuits, and many thousands of other martyrs remains alive in the groups that continue to defend human rights and to seek forms of development that include the poor.

See also *Base Communities; CELAM; Genocide and "Ethnic Cleansing"; Human Rights; Latin America; Liberation Theology; Maryknoll; Romero, Oscar A.; Sanctuary.*

Phillip Berryman

BIBLIOGRAPHY

Berryman, Phillip. *The Religious Roots of Rebellion: Christians in Central American Revolutions.* Maryknoll, N.Y.: Orbis Books, 1984.

———. *Stubborn Hope: Religion, Politics, and Revolution in Central America.* Maryknoll, N.Y.: Orbis Books, 1984.

Dunkerley, James. *Power in the Isthmus: A Political History of Modern Central America.* New York: Verso, 1988.

Hennelly, Alfred T., ed. *Liberation Theology: A Documentary History.* Maryknoll, N.Y.: Orbis Books, 1990.

Human Rights Office of the Archdiocese of Guatemala. *Guatemala: Never Again! Recovery of Historical Memory Project (REMHI): The Official Report of the Human Rights Office, Archdiocese of Guatemala.* Maryknoll, N.Y.: Orbis Books, 1999.

Kirk, John M. *Politics and the Catholic Church in Nicaragua.* Gainesville: University of Florida Press, 1990.

Whitfield, Teresa. *Paying the Price: Ignacio Ellacuría and the Murdered Jesuits of El Salvador.* Philadelphia: Temple University Press, 1995.

Central Asia

The five countries that make up what is commonly referred to as Central Asia are Kazakhstan, Kyrgyzstan, Tajikistan, Turkmenistan, and Uzbekistan, each of which attained independence from the former Soviet Union in 1991. Sunni Islam, the more conservative sect of the Islamic religion and the one that comprises some 83 percent of the Muslim world, is the dominant religion, introduced by the Arabs in the seventh century. The Fergana Valley, which spreads across parts of what are now Uzbekistan, Tajikistan, and Kyrgyzstan, was the heart of Islamic influence in the eighth century as a populous region of the Tian Shan mountain ranges, situated on the Silk Road, the major trade route between China and the Mediterranean Sea.

The vast area of Central Asia, variously defined and demarcated over thousands of years, was ruled or dominated by many, including the Samaritans, Chinese, Turks, Mongols, Persians, Huns, Arabs, Uzbeks, and Russians. Because of their location on and near the Silk Road, the territories were subject to many influences (nomadic horsemen to the north, China to the east, India to the southeast, and Middle Eastern populations to the southwest). Clans and tribal loyalties rather than religious affiliations influenced political activity over millennia, evolving from the traditional relationships rooted in the nomadic Turkic and Mongol tribes. The populations of Uzbekistan and Tajikistan—the latter mainly of Persian descent—were the most influenced by Islam, followed by the tribal societies of Kazakhstan, Kyrgyzstan, and Turkmenistan, which had less exposure to the religion. In the nomadic populations, Islam was less of a cultural factor. (The dominance of the nomadic tribes ended in the sixteenth century with the introduction of firearms and explosives to the settled populations.) In the more settled populations, the emir or khan relied on *shari'a,* or Islamic law, to enhance his rule and as the basis for economic and political policies. The elite classes (land owners, the clergy, and the merchants) in turn used aspects of *shari'a* to their advantage. The Muslim clergy operated the schools that trained the government bureaucrats. The khan rewarded the clergy with *waqf,* a religious endowment of land. The landowners provided the khan money from sharecropping arrangements, and the merchants loaned money to the khan. The elite classes also gave one-tenth of their income to religious and educational efforts, in accordance with Islamic law. The beneficiaries were primarily the well-to-do, leaving the urban and rural poor more vulnerable to forces of change and conquest.

As early as the tenth century, when Russian princes expressed their desire to learn about Islam, Central Asian Muslims had the opportunity to spread their religion, but few conversions took place because the Russians rejected many of the main Islamic customs and restrictions. Historians point out that there were no crusades to convert populations, even as the Russians adopted Christianity and Mongols ruled the territory in the thirteenth century. By the sixteenth century, religion became an issue mainly in regard to pilgrimages (as the route to the holy city of Mecca crossed Russia but was blocked in places by opposing Shi'i Muslims) and marriage (as tsars prohibited Russian women who married Central Asian merchants from returning to Central Asia with their husbands). In 1716 Peter I became the first Russian leader to send a military expedition into Central Asia and the first to lead a major effort to convert Muslims. Under Catherine II in the late 1700s, during the age of Enlightenment, however, Russian policy toward Muslims changed significantly, in keeping with the age's move toward religious tolerance.

In the mid- to late 1800s, Russia began its domination of the territories by conquering the lands that now make up the five republics after most of the latter had mounted unsuccessful revolts against the Bolsheviks. Ultimately, through the 1920s, the territories were incorporated into the Russian Soviet Federative Socialist Republic. Boundaries were drawn arbitrarily, based on ethnic and nationalistic divisions, defined more by region than by religion. Secularism was enforced, though other aspects of the socialist society were closer to Islamic tradition, such as emphasis on the collective group rather than on the individual, social justice, and a paternalistic, albeit authoritarian, ruler. The five states were divided into culturally similar population groups that were encouraged to retain their identity through language and customs yet still become a part of a greater Soviet socialist system. Religion, except as it influenced cultural practices, was proscribed, and mosques, religious schools, waqfs, and clergy were eliminated.

In 1943 the Soviets established the Muslim Board of Central Asia, controlled by the Kremlin, which required the loyalty of the clergy. From the 1960s into the 1980s anti-religion efforts were revived, including strictures against Islam, with mosques converted for secular use, among other measures. Following one Muslim board leader's attempts at polit-ical reform and enhanced recognition of Islam in Tajikistan, the board member was forced to flee the country after the civil war and subsequently was charged with treason.

Modern Era Revival

With the introduction of *perestroika* or restructuring under Soviet leader Mikhail Gorbachev in the late 1980s, the strictures against religion were relaxed, and some holidays and other traditions were allowed to be celebrated openly. Also, beginning in the early 1990s, some 15,000 mosques were opened in the five Central Asian republics, as well as numerous Islamic schools. By the early twenty-first century, courses for women were offered at traditionally male schools. The influence of the Muslim Board of Central Asia disintegrated. Despite the emergence of Islamic instruction and practices, however, Islam in Central Asia is less formalized and more "folk" oriented than in other regions of the world, in part due to nomadic and tribal traditions, in part because of the influence of mystical Sufism, whose influence predates the Soviet takeover, and in part because of the lingering influence of decades of atheistic, secular Russian rule.

It was not until the modern post-independence era, however, that a greater Islamic revival occurred, partly in reaction to repressive measures under Soviet rule, particularly in Uzbekistan and Tajikistan. Some analysts have pointed out that the banning of Islamic movements and political groups may have inevitably strengthened them, even while forcing their leaders underground. Since religion was not fostered under the secular states concept of Russian authority, there was no building on Islamic traditions until independence. The leaders of the former Soviet republics continued to favor a secular state, although the constitutions developed by some of the republics mandate religious freedom. The Islamic political movement, while a major force influencing social and cultural aspects, was typically banned from organized politics within the republics in the mid-2000s.

Radical Islam

A move toward more radical Islam has occurred in the modern era, though a majority of the Muslims throughout Central Asia are generally described as mainstream. The governments of the five republics, however, have been increasingly concerned with a growing extremist movement, which some analysts have said is related to a cultural link to past traditions that were all but extinguished under communist atheism. As Soviet education and secularism replaced Islam, only the daily rituals regarding birth, marriage, and death were permitted in the decades of Soviet rule. More radical Islamist elements began appearing in Central Asia in the 1970s, influenced to a great extent by the Muslim Brotherhood, a worldwide organization whose branches are perhaps more in the forefront throughout the Middle East. It is thought that Islamic extremists moved into Central Asia through the Fergana Valley, which is home to Uzbeks, Kyrgyz, and Tajiks, and operated underground during Soviet rule. Their stated goal has been to overthrow the secular governments and establish Islamic states or caliphates. The governments of the republics have been wary of a resurgence of fundamentalism in the early to mid-2000s and have tried to rein in politically active religious groups or movements. The most repressive response has been from the government of Uzbekistan.

The Islamic Rebirth Party (IRP), the first Islamic party to be established in the former Soviet Union, counted the majority of its members in the Central Asian republics in the early 1990s, with the exceptions of Turkmenistan and Kyrgyzstan. In the latter two, the Islamic fundamentalism so central to the IRP did not make inroads on the political scene. Generally, the Central Asian republics tended to be more nationalistic than religion-based societies; Islamic cultural and traditional practices were respected and incorporated, but were not prevalent in political activity. With the formation of the Islamic Movement of Central Asia in the early 2000s, an umbrella organization was established for many of the more radical organizations. Terrorist attacks in Uzbekistan in 2004 and antigovernment uprisings in Kyrgyzstan and in Andizhan, Uzbekistan, in 2005 are evidence of increasing focus on the more radical elements of Islam in Central Asia. The most popular radical Islamist group in Central Asia has been thought to be *Hizb ut-Tahrir,* the Muslim Brotherhood founded by a Palestinian cleric in the 1920s and soon established in Egypt.

Kazakhstan

The fourth largest of the former Soviet republics in population and the second largest in land area (four times the size of Texas), Kazakhstan is bordered by Siberia to the north, China to the east, and Kyrgyzstan, Uzbekistan, and Turkmenistan to the south. Slightly more than half the 15 million people are Kazakhs, with Russians making up most of the rest of the country's inhabitants. Kazakh replaced Russian in 1989 as the official language. Following independence, many ethnic Russians, Germans, and Ukrainians emigrated. The Russians in particular viewed new citizenship and language laws as discriminatory.

The territory now known as Kazakhstan became part of the Russian Soviet Federative Socialist Republic on August 26, 1920, and a constituent republic of the Union of Soviet Socialist Republics on December 5, 1936. Kazakhs retained their strong clan and kinship traditions despite the Soviet Union's attempts to disrupt them.

President Nursultan Abishevich Nazarbayev was first elected by the Supreme Soviet as its chair in 1990; he assumed the newly created post of president after independence in December 1991. A new constitution was approved in 1995. Under the Law of Political Parties adopted in 2002, political parties based on religion, ethnicity, or gender were outlawed. The National Freedom Party, or *Alash,* a nationalist, Islamist group, repeatedly has not been allowed to register as a legal political party.

Some 57 percent of the people are Sunni Muslims, while about 40 percent are Christians, mostly Russian Orthodox. However, many other religions are represented. Although most of the citizens are affiliated with a religion, most of them are not "deeply religious" due, in great part, to their nomadic and Soviet history.

In 2006 the president, in what was viewed with great regional interest, called for establishing an international center of cultures and religions in Kazakhstan.

Kyrgyzstan

This republic of about five million people is bordered by Kazakhstan on the northwest, China on the east, Tajikistan on the south, and Uzbekistan on the southwest. Its official languages are Kyrgyz and Russian; some 65 percent of the population are Kyrgyz. Russians (14 percent) and Uzbeks (13 percent) make up most of the rest of the inhabitants. The majority are Sunni Muslims; the Russians are either atheist or Russian Orthodox.

The territory now known as Kyrgyzstan staged an unsuccessful revolt against the Bolsheviks before becoming part of the Russian Soviet Federative Socialist Republic on February 1, 1926. Kyrgyzstan became a constituent republic of the Union of Soviet Socialist Republics on December 5, 1936, and became an independent nation in 1991. Prior to independence, the region's worst ethnic violence was centered in Kyrgyzstan as deadly clashes erupted between the Kyrgyz and the Uzbeks.

The republic's constitution, promulgated in 1993, prohibits religious influence in matters of state, and it provides for equal treatment for all ethnic groups. A provision based on following Islamic moral values was dropped at the behest of the president. President Kurmanbeck Bakiyev led the country in 2006, overseeing a government in which religion-based groups were not among the most politically active parties. The republic, like most others in Central Asia, has been concerned about a fundamentalist Islamic revolution and thus has tried to keep religion and state separate. In an effort to provide balance, Kyrgyzstan recognizes a number of different religious holidays as national holidays (Orthodox Christmas and the Muslim New Year, for example). The population in the north of Kyrgyzstan, which has stronger ties to their nomadic past, mix shamanistic practices with Islamic traditions. In the south, the people have stronger ties to Islam, dating to the seventeenth century.

Tajikistan

The Republic of Tajikistan, most of whose seven million inhabitants are of Iranian descent, is bordered by Kyrgyzstan on the north, China on the east, Afghanistan on the south, and Uzbekistan on the west. Russia conquered most of the lands in the late 1800s; uprisings against the Bolsheviks continued into the 1920s. In 1924 Tajikistan became part of the Uzbek Soviet Socialist Republic, and on October 16, 1929, became a constituent republic of the Union of Soviet Socialist Republics. It declared independence in 1991, and its constitution was promulgated in 1994.

The Islamic Rebirth Party was at the forefront of Islamic political activity in Tajikistan in the 1990s. For thirteen years the party was under the leadership of Said Abdullo Nuri (who died in August 2006). The party began organizing demonstrations against the government following a failed assassination attempt against Soviet leader Mikhail Gorbachev in 1991, and the subsequent withdrawal of the Communist Party of Tajikistan from the Communist Party of the Soviet Union. The Islamic Rebirth Party formed a prodemocracy alliance with the Democratic Party of Tajik and ultimately obtained posts in the new republic's cabinet. Subsequently, fighting between pro-communist forces and the Islamic opposition resulted in hundreds of deaths, and after several government changes, the Islamists were removed from the cabinet. Civil war continued for five years, with the opposition boycotting the constitutional referendum and legislative elections. Many of the opposition leaders went into exile in Afghanistan. A cease-fire agreement in 1997 officially ended the civil war, though fighting continued for another year. With the seating of a new assembly in 2000, stability returned for the most part. The constitution adopted in 1994 outlines laws for a secular, democratic republic, and later amendments provide for secular political parties.

The Islamic Rebirth Party, though rejecting the description of itself as fundamentalist, has sought to turn Tajikistan into an Islamic republic. Islam is seen as influencing even the most nationalistic parties and groups, with the emphasis being on cultural and ethnic traditions rather than on religious aspects.

Turkmenistan

Turkmenistan is the southernmost of the former Soviet republics, bordered by Kazakhstan on the northwest, Uzbekistan on the north and northeast, Afghanistan on the southeast, Iran on the south, and the Caspian Sea on the west. About 80 percent of the land area is part of the Kara Kum Desert. Of the nearly 5 million people, ethnic Turkmens make up 77 percent of the population, with Uzbeks about 9 percent, Russians, 7 percent, and Kazakhs, 2 percent. The Turkmens are mainly Sunni Muslims.

In 1924 historic Turkestan, then a republic within the Russian Soviet Federative Socialist Republic, was split into two parts: Turkmenistan in the west and Uzbekistan in the east. Both became part of the Union of Soviet Socialist Republics in 1925. Turkmenistan declared independence on October 27, 1991, and a constitution was adopted in 1992. Freedom of religion is guaranteed under the constitution, though the country has been repeatedly cited by international human rights groups for its repressive policies. The abolition in 2004 of criminal penalties for unregistered religious activities reportedly did not have much real impact.

Turkmens, who have been cut off from broader Islamic influences, maintain many nomadic traditions and generally do not follow religious practices of Islam. They do not attend mosque services, and they support a revival of Islam only as part of their national cultural heritage. Principles of Islam are taught in public schools; religion classes are held in religious schools and mosques. Under the secular government, political parties based on religion are proscribed, and religious groups are not allowed to proselytize or to distribute religious literature. Some Muslim leaders, however, have continued to try to spread the influence of Islam throughout society.

Uzbekistan

Home to some 26 million people, Uzbekistan is documented as one of the world's oldest civilizations. The country shares a short southern border with Afghanistan and is otherwise bordered by Kazakhstan on the north and west, Kyrgyzstan on the northeast, Tajikistan on the southeast, and Turkmenistan on the south. Uzbeks, the majority of whom are Sunni Muslims, make up 69 percent of the population, Russians account for 11 percent, and Tatars, Kazakhs, and Tajiks, 4 percent each.

In the nineteenth century, Russians conquered much of the territory, and in 1920 it became part of the Turkestan Soviet Socialist Republic within the Russian Soviet Federative Socialist Republic. On May 12, 1925, Uzbekistan became a constituent republic of the Union of Soviet Socialist Republics. It declared independence in 1991, and its constitution was adopted in 1992.

Although the constitution upholds freedom of religion, a law passed in 1998 severely restricts religious freedom, with the strictest controls on Muslims. Religious groups are banned from missionary work, and religious education and publication of religious materials are strictly limited. Since religious education is controlled by the state, Islamic clergy are also under the control of the government. Islamic Web sites are blocked and religious groups are banned from holding meetings unless the groups have registered in accordance with the law. The registration restrictions, however, prevent many Muslim and Christian groups from becoming legal. Violations are punished by fines or detention. The outlawed Islamic Movement of Uzbekistan has long been a target of the government as well.

According to international human rights groups, the government in 1997 significantly intensified its seven-year campaign against independent Muslims, blaming radical Islamists for the brutal deaths of several policemen in Namangan. The government reportedly detained and allegedly beat up some one hundred people. Subsequently, the government closed mosques, allegedly harassed religious leaders, and expelled students who wore Islamic garb from state-run universities. By the early to mid-2000s government repression and persecution had become more widespread, targeting groups other than Muslims, including but not limited to Jehovah's Witnesses and Protestants. After a mass antigovernment uprising in Andizhan in 2005, government forces killed hundreds of civilians, claiming they were Islamic extremists and terrorists.

See also: *Fundamentalism; Islam; Orthodoxy, Russian.*

Judy Isacoff

BIBLIOGRAPHY

Allworth, Edward, ed. *Central Asia: 130 Years of Russian Dominance, A Historical Overview.* 3d ed. Durham, N.C.: Duke University Press, 1994.

Banks, Arthur S., Thomas C. Muller, and William R. Overstreet, eds. *Political Handbook of the World.* Washington, D.C.: CQ Press, 2006.

Baran, Zeyno, S. Frederick Starr, and Svante E. Cornell. "Islamic Radicalism in Central Asia and the Caucasus: Implications for the EU." Washington D.C.: Central Asia-Caucasus Institute, Silk Road Studies Program, July 2006. Available online at http://www.silkroad-studies.org/new/inside/publications/silk_road.htm.

Burghart, Dan, and Theresa Sabonis-Helf, eds. *In the Tracks of Tamerlane: Central Asia's Path to the 21st Century.* Washington, D.C.: National Defense University, Center for Technology and Security Policy, 2004.

Geiss, Paul Georg. *Pre-Tsarist and Tsarist Central Asia: Communal Commitment and Political Order in Change.* London: RoutledgeCurzon, 2003.

Gross, Jo-Ann, ed. *Muslims in Central Asia: Expressions of Identity and Change.* Durham, N.C.: Duke University Press, 1992.

Haghayeghi, Mehrdad. *Islam and Politics in Central Asia.* New York: St. Martin's Press, 1996.

Hunter, Shireen T. *Central Asia since Independence.* Westport, Conn.: Praeger, 1996.

Hunter, Shireen T., and Human Malik, eds. *Modernization, Democracy, and Islam.* Westport, Conn.: Praeger, 2005.

Jones Luong, Pauline. *Institutional Change and Political Continuity in Post-Soviet Central Asia: Power, Perceptions, and Pacts.* Cambridge, England: Cambridge University Press, 2002.

Keller, Shoshana. *To Moscow, Not Mecca: The Soviet Campaign Against Islam in Central Asia, 1917–1941.* Westport, Conn.: Praeger, 2001.

Khan, Aisha. *A Historical Atlas of Uzbekistan.* New York: Rosen Publishing Group, 2003.

Mandelbaum, Michael, ed. *Central Asia and the World: Kazakhstan, Uzbekistan, Tajikistan, Kyrgyzstan, and Turkmenistan.* New York: Council on Foreign Relations Press, 1994.

Naumkin, Vitaly V., ed. *Central Asia and Transcaucasia: Ethnicity and Conflict.* Westport, Conn.: Greenwood Press, 1994.

Rumer, Boris, ed. *Central Asia: A Gathering Storm?* Armonk, N.Y.: M. E. Sharpe, 2002.

Schatz, Edward. *Modern Clan Politics: The Power of "Blood" in Kazakhstan and Beyond.* Seattle: University of Washington Press, 2004.

Charity

See *Philanthropy.*

China

The cultural and geographic center of East Asia, China has a population of approximately 1.3 billion, characterized by considerable religious and ethnic diversity. This article traces the relationship of politics and religion in this vast nation from the late imperial period to the present day.

The Late Imperial Period

The relationship of politics and religion in late imperial China (1368–1911) differed from the European experience in that secular and spiritual power were never split between the state and an autonomous church. Instead, the state monopolized both functions, legitimizing its rule by reference to a state religion strongly shaped by Confucianism. It advocated a tripartite cosmology in which the emperor mediated the cosmic relationship of humanity with Heaven and Earth by means of a complex system of rituals and sacrifices. Imperial rule was legitimized by the conferral of "the mandate of Heaven" upon the emperor, who was regarded as "the son of Heaven." A concept of sacral kingship thus endowed the state with cosmic significance and gave the social and political order upheld by it a sacred and inviolable quality.

This state religion ideally was to structure all of society, defining the social, moral, and religious obligations of every class, from the emperor downward to the commoners. In reality, the traditional state was neither strong enough to enforce its orthodoxy throughout the empire, nor was this orthodoxy, geared as it was toward the state and the collective good of society, ever able to satisfy the religious needs of the individual. Thus the state always had to deal with the presence of religious alternatives within Chinese society. These alternatives can be grouped into two basic categories: institutional religions with their own sacred literature and professional clergy, such as Buddhism, Daoism, Islam, and Christianity; and a popular religion whose beliefs and practices were diffused through the institutional structure of local society.

The state's approach toward both types of religion was a combination of control and co-optation. The institutional religions were denied any autonomous status and were subjected to strict control. For example, the state regularly decreed caps on the number of Buddhist and Daoist clergy permitted in any area of the empire and enforced these regulations through specialized government agencies under the Ministry of Rites, the department responsible for the state cult and court ceremonial affairs. Within this framework of administrative control, the institutional religions were allowed to practice their respective faiths without much government interference—as long as they did not question the state orthodoxy. Unwillingness to integrate into the officially sanctioned ethical and political order never failed to trigger a heavy-handed reaction from the state. The power of the state was felt, for example, by the Jesuit mission in the early eighteenth century, when the pope's refusal to allow Chinese Catholics to venerate their ancestors, a vital expression of the Confucian cardinal virtue of "filial piety," led to the prohibition of all missionary work in China.

Suppression was the routine response of the state toward any radical religious challenge of its orthodoxy. In the history of late imperial China, such a challenge was put forth principally by popular sects, whose millenarian preoccupations often led them to compare the perfections of the kingdom to come unfavorably with the shortcomings of contemporary society. The state frequently moved to suppress these sects even if they did not pose any immediate political threat, but were content to await the millennium in an attitude of quietistic pietism. Sometimes, however, sects did take violent political action, attempting to hasten the advent of the millennium by overthrowing the temporal order. The history of China's last dynasty, that of the Qing (1644–1911), records numerous bloody campaigns against so-called religious bandits. The greatest of these sectarian rebellions, that of the Taiping, lasted from 1850 to 1864. In the course of the rebellion huge areas were devastated and millions of lives lost. The state's tolerance of religious diversity ended whenever its orthodoxy was questioned in a radical manner and the offender refused to join its fold.

The state's relationship with popular religion was predicated on the same assumption of official orthodoxy, and the state could move against any popular cult that it classified as "licentious" or "excessive." A basic problem faced by the state in this domain, however, was that most of the deities and religious practices of popular religion were, strictly speaking, noncanonical and thus theoretically heterodox. They grew out of and answered the religious needs of commoners, for whom little provision was made in the official rosters of permissible and prescribed sacrifices. Furthermore, the deities at the center of village and township temples were focal points of local identity, and the determination of their status in relation to the official orthodoxy thus always

involved a balance between local and national interests. As markers of local identities and interests, the status of local deities often became a matter of negotiation between state authorities and local elites. The latter championed the local cults, which defined their power base, while trying at the same time to interpret their meaning in a manner compatible with the state orthodoxy from which these elites, too, drew their legitimation. The state, on the other hand, was interested in assimilating local society into its ritual hierarchy by giving its gods the stamp of official approval and weakening their status as carriers of local identity.

Revolution, Communism, and the Two Chinas

Imperial rule ended in China with the revolution of 1911. The emperor was replaced by a series of regional warlords and eventually by a unified republican government. The new government adopted Western concepts of the separation of church and state, though it interpreted them in the light of Chinese political experience. This principle was taken to mean a separation of politics and religion: religion was to be banished from the public realm of a thoroughly secularized state and not allowed to "meddle" in politics.

Although the state thus effectively barred religion from legitimate participation in the political realm, the principle of separation did not work the other way around to shield religion from state interference. The traditional subordination of religion to the state was maintained and even strengthened by the increasing effectiveness of state control in a modernizing society. The traditional state orthodoxy was replaced by a modern one, a radical secularism that could take a decidedly antireligious turn. In the years following the revolution, Buddhist monasteries were taken over, Christian institutions secularized, and village temples turned into army barracks or primary schools.

Such antireligious zealotry was discouraged after the consolidation of the republican regime under Gen. Chiang Kai-shek, leader of the Nationalist Party. From about the early 1930s, the nation began a more careful approach to enlist religious support for purposes of nation building. The national emergency created by the war with Japan (1937–1945) left little time for the further development of this approach, though it became dominant again at the end of the Chinese civil war that broke out after the defeat of Japan.

The civil war erupted when the uneasy coalition of Nationalists and Communists, who had made huge gains in numbers during the 1930s and 1940s, broke apart. It ended with a Communist victory and the declaration of the People's Republic of China (PRC), in 1949. The defeated Nationalists under Chiang Kai-shek withdrew to the island of Taiwan, off the southeastern coast of China, and established the provisional capital of their Republic of China (ROC) in Taipei. These "two Chinas" henceforth followed separate trajectories of development, creating a national division that persists to the present day. Both regimes—as far apart as they were ideologically—adopted similar policies toward religion. A clear line was drawn between the institutional religions and popular religion, with official recognition being extended only to the former. In the People's Republic the recognized religions were Buddhism, Daoism, Islam, Roman Catholicism, and Protestantism; the Republic of China recognized these "big five" plus a number of smaller indigenous religions.

Both regimes, the Communists in mainland China and the Nationalists in Taiwan, tried to co-opt these institutional religions into a united front to work alongside other social forces in the great task of national reconstruction. The agenda to be followed was to be set by the party-state, and the religions were to propagate this agenda among their adherents. To facilitate communication of policy directives, national associations of the officially recognized institutional religions were formed. Following the corporatist model, these associations had a monopoly on the representation of their respective constituencies. The purpose of these associations was not to lobby the government but to serve as channels for the transmission of government policies toward their members. To deal with the day-to-day business of maintaining tight administrative control over the religions, both

regimes established bureaus of religious affairs. This approach restricted religious liberty by subjecting religious organizations to tight state control, but it also created a legitimate space for religion in the new society and shielded it from the zealotry of the radical secularists in both regimes.

The size of that space differed between the two regimes, with Taiwan generally allowing a much greater degree of religious freedom. An important difference in policy application was, for example, the PRC's insistence on the "Three-Self Movement": Religious bodies had to be self-funded, self-guided, and self-propagating. This policy excluded any support from foreign sources and led to the expulsion of all foreign missionaries. In the case of Catholics, for example, it resulted in the establishment of a national Catholic Church without any ties to the Vatican. As a result, Chinese Catholics were split between an officially recognized Catholic Patriotic Association and an underground church loyal to the pope, who denied the sacramental authority of the "patriotic" priests and bishops. The ROC, by contrast, did not require its religious associations to cut international relationships but, to the contrary, used these links to counteract its increasing diplomatic isolation. Thus the Catholic Church on Taiwan has always maintained close contact with the Vatican, which, to this day, maintains diplomatic relations with the ROC.

The united front collapsed in the PRC with the onset of the Cultural Revolution in 1966. The Cultural Revolution was Communist Party chairman Mao Zedong's campaign to create a new society overnight by eradicating all vestiges of the old. Along with intellectuals and government officials, innumerable clerics and lay believers of all religious traditions suffered, with untold thousands killed, thrown into prison, or forcibly secularized by the Red Guards. The Cultural Revolution ended officially in 1976 with the overthrow of the radical Maoists known as the Gang of Four and the assumption of power by the reformist wing of the Communist Party.

New Approach to Religion

The following period brought with it a significant relaxation of the suppression of religion and a return to the united front approach of the 1950s and early 1960s. It was now believed that religion still had a useful function to fulfill within Chinese society and that religious organizations should therefore be allowed to contribute to the construction of China. The new approach was sanctioned in the so-called Document 19, issued by the Party's Central Committee in 1982. It was enshrined as well in Article 36 of the PRC's 1982 constitution, which stated that citizens had freedom of religious belief. Since 1982 this more liberal approach has dominated PRC policy, granting the officially recognized religions again a legitimate, though restricted, sphere of activity. Many temples, monasteries, mosques, and churches have been returned to their communities, and sometimes public funds have been allocated for their restoration, especially if the edifices represent cultural treasures and have the potential to draw tourists. The legal framework for religious life was systematized with a new set of "Regulations for Religious Affairs" that took effect on March 1, 2005.

With this new relative freedom, a "religion fever" began in the 1990s that was widely interpreted as a sign that the decay of communist values and of the Party's ideological credibility had produced a spiritual vacuum that could be filled with religious content. Official sources claim that in 2005 there were more than 100 million religious believers in the PRC. Specific figures given for the five officially recognized religions, however, are much lower. There are said to exist 20 million Muslims, 16 million Protestants, and 5 million Catholics. For Buddhism and Daoism only the number of full-time clergy is given: 200,000 for Buddhists and 25,000 for Daoists. These official statistics are to be treated with caution. Unofficial estimates mention 100 million Buddhists, more than 30 million Protestants, and eight to ten million Catholics. The higher number of Buddhists includes lay adherents, while the difference in the numbers of Christians is due to the existence of many Protestant and Catholic communities that are not affiliated with the official religious associations. Underground Catholics loyal to the pope, as well as Protestant house churches remain frequent targets of police raids and arrests.

In the ROC, some restriction on religious activities continued until the lifting in 1987 of the rule of martial law, which had first been imposed in 1949, shortly before the arrival of Chiang Kai-shek's government on Taiwan. Since 1987 Taiwan has been undergoing a process of rapid democratization that has done away with many aspects of the authoritarian one-party regime, including the corporatist handling of religion. With the gradual development of democratic pluralism, state ideological control of religions became weaker, and religious groups came to have much greater leeway to play a role in all aspects of social life,

including politics. The strict secularist separation of politics and religions is being watered down, and the two realms of discourse are beginning to merge. For example, some political leaders have sought endorsements from prominent Buddhist clerics, while others have demonstrated their sensitivity to grassroots concerns by actively participating in popular religious festivals and pilgrimages. Buddhist participation in the political process has been especially notable.

In the 1990s efforts began to design a new comprehensive "Law on Religious Organizations" that would replace the old administrative regulations, some of which date back to the 1920s. As of early 2006 the law had not yet passed and was still the subject of debate among religious leaders.

According to government statistics, among a total population of just under 23 million, Taiwan in 2005 counted roughly 7.6 million Daoists; 5.5 million Buddhists; 791,000 Yiguan Dao adherents; 605,000 Protestants; 300,000 Catholics; and more than one million followers of other faiths. Again, these statistics are to be treated with caution as there exists no well-defined membership criteria for Daoism and Buddhism.

Popular and Minority Religions

Many studies of religion and politics in the PRC tend to neglect the importance of popular religion. This is due in large part to the fact that popular religion is not recognized as religion at all but is relegated to a hazy category of "feudal superstitions." This means that popular religion is not protected by the constitutional guarantee of religious freedom, which applies only to the five institutional religions recognized by the state. In spite of its legally insecure status, popular religion has made a strong comeback in many areas of China, in particular in the south and southeast of the country, where active village temples and earth god shrines are again a common sight. Popular practices such as ancestor worship have been reevaluated by the authorities: ancestor worship, previously regarded as "feudal superstition," is now seen as an expression of positive moral values and thus in principle permissible. On the other hand, popular religious practices such as shamanism, fortune telling, and geomancy continue to meet with censure and are subject to intermittent suppression. Although popular religion operates in a legal gray zone and is vulnerable to shifts in government policies, it is reestablishing itself in some areas of China as a forum for local and national identities, much as it functioned in late imperial China.

A reemerging field of religious contestation has appeared in the form of new popular sects. Mindful of imperial China's experience with millenarian religious movements, soon after the revolution of 1949 the new communist government had initiated a major campaign against religious sects all over China and had effectively stamped them out. With the loosening of state controls some of the traditional sects reestablished themselves, often in rural areas. More significant or—in the government's perception—threatening was the emergence in the 1990s of large numbers of new sects. Many of these had only local or regional influence, but a few gained a nationwide profile. The best-known among them is the Falun Gong movement (literally, "Practice of the Dharma Wheel"). Its founder, Li Hongzhi (c. 1951–) claims that Falun Gong is not an organized religion, but rather a system of advanced spiritual practice based on Li's adaptation of traditional qigong gymnastics. A perusal of Li's writings, however, shows a considerable development of this core into an elaborate belief system that draws on Buddhist, Daoist, and scientific notions, and even on UFO beliefs. The movement proved hugely successful in attracting and mobilizing large numbers of followers (up to 70 million, according to some estimates). This success fully came to the government's attention when, on April 25, 1999, thousands of Falungong followers staged a peaceful protest outside the Zhongnanhai area of Beijing, where many high government officials and party cadres reside. Reading this action as an unprecedented challenge to its authority, the government swiftly cracked down on Falun Gong. From the summer of 1999 to the early twenty-first century, a concerted effort has been under way to suppress all Falun Gong related activities and news, as well as to arrest and "reeducate" members. The brutal persecution of Falun Gong as (in the government's terms) an "evil cult" has led to the deaths of numerous adherents in detention. This and similar crackdowns on popular sects show that the government remains highly sensitive to the political potential of religious movements that operate outside the state-approved and state-controlled organizations.

In Taiwan, where tensions between the Taiwanese majority and the small ruling elite of Nationalist mainlanders who fled to the island in 1949 has constituted a persistent political undercurrent, the political dimension of popular religion was often noted by scholars. While remaining disdainful of the "irrationalism" of Taiwanese folk religion, the government never suppressed it violently; instead, it followed an only moderately successful approach of administrative con-

trol and interpretative co-optation. In the absence of genuinely democratic political channels of expression during the period of martial law, Taiwanese popular religion played an important role as a realm of symbolic protest. The Taiwanese, for example, could express their identity by holding lavish traditional temple festivals in the face of government efforts to curb the attending "superstition" and "waste of resources." In addition, popular religious cults continued to figure prominently in village and township politics, even though secularism dominated at the national level. Government policy towards popular sects was uneven, with some being banned while others received official recognition. After the lifting of martial law in 1987, such restrictions on religious groups ended. This new freedom has resulted in the growth of the number of officially recognized religions (26 as of the mid-2000s), including previously banned "heterodox sects" such as the Way of Unity (Yiguan Dao), a modern successor to an ancient Chinese tradition of popular sectarianism focusing on the worship of a primordial mother deity. It is now the third largest religious community in Taiwan.

A final area of great importance to Chinese policymakers is the role of religion in the state's relationship with ethnic minorities. This is a significant issue primarily in the PRC, where many minority groups live in sensitive border areas and have historically been treated with a mixture of strict control and careful accommodation. Religion is usually a significant element in these minorities' ethnic self-identity and thus must be given special consideration. On the other hand, the state does not hesitate to come down heavily on any attempt to use religion to further political aims of minorities that are incompatible with the state's interests.

The limits of religious freedom are made very clear every time the authorities quell Muslim demonstrations in the predominantly Muslim autonomous region of Xinjiang in western China or conduct mass arrests of Tibetan Buddhist monks supporting the exiled Dalai Lama. After the terrorist attacks on the World Trade Center in New York City and the Pentagon on September 11, 2001, the Chinese government intensified its efforts to suppress or root out Islamic fundamentalism and ethnic separatism in Xinjiang province. As these two aspects of resistance are often intertwined, in practice these policies have severely limited the religious freedoms of Xinjiang Muslims. Thus, in spite of the more relaxed climate since the late 1970s, religion in the PRC remains vulnerable to periodic shifts in the state's policy agendas. The PRC thus continues a long-standing Chinese political tradition by resolutely insisting on the subordination of religion and religious freedom to the overriding interests of the state.

See also *Buddhism, Tibetan; Communism; Confucianism; Dalai Lama; Millennialism; Separation of Church and State.*

Philip Clart

BIBLIOGRAPHY

Clart, Philip, and Charles B. Jones, eds. *Religion in Modern Taiwan: Tradition and Innovation in a Changing Society.* Honolulu: University of Hawaii Press, 2003.

Dean, Kenneth. *Taoist Ritual and Popular Cults of Southeast China.* Princeton, N.J.: Princeton University Press, 1993.

DuBois, Thomas David. *The Sacred Village: Social Change and Religious Life in Rural North China.* Honolulu: University of Hawaii Press, 2005.

Gladney, Dru C. *Muslim Chinese: Ethnic Nationalism in the People's Republic.* Cambridge, Mass.: Council on East Asian Studies, Harvard University, 1991.

Katz, Paul R., and Murray A. Rubinstein, eds. *Religion and the Formation of Taiwanese Identities.* New York: Palgrave Macmillan, 2003.

Laliberté, André. *The Politics of Buddhist Organizations in Taiwan, 1989–2003: Safeguard the Faith, Build a Pure Land, Help the Poor.* New York: RoutledgeCurzon, 2004.

Luo Zhufeng, ed. *Religion under Socialism in China.* Translated by Donald E. MacInnis and Zheng Xian. Armonk, N.Y.: M. E. Sharpe, 1991.

MacInnis, Donald E. *Religion in China Today: Policy and Practice.* Maryknoll, N.Y.: Orbis Books, 1989.

Munro, Robin, ed. and trans. "Syncretic Sects and Secret Societies: Revival in the 1980s." Thematic issue of *Chinese Sociology and Anthropology* 21 (1989), no. 4.

Palmer, David A. *La fièvre du Qigong: Guérison, Religion et Politique en Chine, 1949–1999.* Paris: Éditions de l'École des Hautes Études en Sciences Sociales, 2005.

Overmyer, Daniel L., ed. *Religion in China Today.* The China Quarterly Special Issues, New Series, no. 3. New York: Cambridge University Press, 2003.

Wickeri, Philip L. *Seeking the Common Ground: Protestant Christianity, the Three-Self Movement, and China's United Front.* Maryknoll, N.Y.: Orbis Books, 1988.

Yang, C. K. *Religion in Chinese Society: A Study of Contemporary Social Functions of Religion and Some of Their Historical Factors.* Berkeley: University of California Press, 1961.

Yu, Anthony C. *State and Religion in China: Historical and Textual Perspectives.* Chicago: Open Court, 2005.

Christian Coalition

See *Conservatism.*

Christian Democracy

Christian Democracy is a largely lay Catholic response to the challenges of modern, industrial society. Rooted in the social teachings of the Catholic Church and in the works of modern Catholic social thinkers such as Luigi Sturzo (1871–1959), Jacques Maritain (1882–1950), and Emmanuel Mounier (1905–1950), it developed a Catholic approach to politics that managed to reconcile Catholic beliefs with such modern aspirations as freedom, democracy, and lay autonomy from ecclesiastical authority in social and political matters. During much of the twentieth century, it was an important political force in both Europe and Latin America, occupying a reformist middle ground between secular left and traditional conservative forces. The varied and occasionally divergent ideological perspectives of its adherents have led them to differ in interpreting and applying their shared Christian values. For these reasons, the orientations and cohesiveness of Christian Democratic parties have tended to reflect their particular political contexts and the forces with which they have had to compete, more than their doctrinal heritage as such. Toward the end of the twentieth century, in increasingly secular settings and in evolving political contexts, their appeal diminished notably. Once strong parties experienced crisis and decline, and those that retained their following found themselves being pulled rightward along the party and political spectra.

Origins

The notion of a Christian democracy was first embraced by Pope Leo XIII (reigned 1878–1903), who hoped to rescue elements of democracy and reform from the skeptical and individualistic foundations with which they were often associated in the nineteenth century. In his encyclical *Rerum Novarum* (on capital and labor) in 1891, Leo called for social justice, improvements in the lot of workers and the poor, and lay Catholic participation in politics, especially where liberal and socialist currents were threatening Catholic values and interests. Tensions quickly arose, however, as lay activists ran afoul of both conservative bishops and political authorities. In a second encyclical, *Graves de Communi Re,* issued ten years later, Leo decried the movement's excessively political character, urged Catholics not to challenge existing social structures or distinctions or to favor a particular form of government over any other, and reaffirmed the need for ecclesiastical oversight.

The church thus continued to be dependent on socio-economically conservative Catholic parties. These parties were almost always political instruments of elites that were being challenged on various levels—religious, socioeconomic, and political. As industrialization proceeded, and as reform-minded working- and popular-class elements emerged politically in the late nineteenth and early twentieth centuries, conservative parties grew progressively weaker, and Church leaders began to look for new strategies.

Gradually and unevenly, they began to distance themselves from their elite allies and patrons. They abandoned the notion of obligatory political unity for Catholics and accepted, reluctantly at first, "liberal" demands for religious freedom, separation of church and state, lay autonomy in political affairs, and greater social and political democratization. In addition, with an eye to reclaiming the fallen-away Catholic masses, Church authorities gave renewed emphasis to Catholic social teaching. In 1931, on the fortieth anniversary of *Rerum Novarum,* Pope Pius XI issued the encyclical *Quadragesimo Anno* (on reconstructing the social order). The Church began to train and assign lay men and women to apostolic activities through the Catholic Action movement and Young Christian Workers and Young Christian Students groups. Church authorities thus came to rely on the leavening impact of lay people in their parish communities and work places. The experience of many middle-class and some working-class Catholics in these organizations helped them to reconcile their faith with their increasingly progressive social inclinations. It also led some to join with other, largely secular, forces in opposing Nazi parties in the 1930s and in resisting German occupation during the Second World War.

These developments formed a breeding ground in which "liberal" Catholic sentiments could arise and exert appeal. They also provided a context in which reform-minded Catholic parties were the logical next step. And so it was, in the late 1940s and 1950s, that Christian Democratic parties emerged in both Europe and Latin America. Blessed with extraordinary lay leadership, and with a ready constituency among former Catholic Action and anti-Nazi activists, Christian Democratic parties quickly became major players in the politics of the postwar period. Helping to establish Christian Democratic parties in these years were strong leaders such as Robert Schuman in France, Alcide De Gasperi in Italy, Konrad Adenauer in Germany, and Eduardo Frei in Chile.

The Postwar Period

In Europe, Christian Democratic parties attracted Catholic voters in Germany, Italy, Belgium, and the Netherlands, where traditional right-wing groups were weak and more progressive responses to Marxist and anti-clerical forces were possible. In France, the initially promising Popular Republican Movement was eclipsed by Gen. Charles de Gaulle's triumphal return to the political arena in the late 1950s, and it later merged with other groups in various centrist and independent fronts. Spain's Christian Democrats were less liberal Catholics who sided with Franco in the civil war but then grew increasingly unhappy with him in ensuing decades. By the 1960s and early 1970s, most had gone over to the opposition and were on fairly good terms with the country's various leftist parties and unions. Fearing the continuation of clerical–anti-clerical polarization in the post-Franco period, church leaders decided not to encourage the formation of a catchall Christian Democratic Party. Spanish Christian Democrats ended up forming a faction of the center-right Unión de Centro Democrático (Democratic Center Union or UCD) or were drawn leftward into the Socialist Workers Party or rightward into the Popular Party.

European Christian Democrats have generally appealed to wide-ranging social forces by generating growth and helping to sustain a prosperous, if less than ideal, socioeconomic status quo. The German party is a union of the larger Christian Democratic Union and the staunchly Catholic Christian Social Union of Bavaria. It dominated the country's politics, usually in coalition with the centrist Free Democrats, from 1949 to 1969, and again, after fourteen years of intervening Social Democratic governments, from 1983 to 1998. It is widely credited with having produced the postwar "German miracle" of solid growth and generous social benefits. In Italy, the Christian Democrats were a similarly dominant force during these years, heading up virtually all of that country's coalition governments and presiding over a similarly prosperous, if more tumultuous and scandal-ridden, postwar recovery. Christian Democratic parties were frequent partners in ruling coalitions in both Belgium and the Netherlands as well.

Most European Christian Democratic parties have clear ties to the Catholic Church and traditions of their countries, using them to substantial political advantage. But they also have made a point of operating independently of Catholic authorities. They remain open to Catholic and non-Catholic members alike and while acknowledging their inspiration in Catholic social teaching claim a rightful autonomy in deciding upon its practical application. For the most part, local Catholic authorities have been willing to accommodate them, albeit more readily on socioeconomic and political issues than on moral and cultural concerns.

In Latin America, widespread poverty and the intransigence of socioeconomic and political elites pushed some socially conscious Catholics in a more decidedly reformist direction, at least initially. Christian Democrats came to power in Chile (1964–1970), Venezuela (1969–1974), El Salvador (1984–1988), Ecuador (1981–1984 and 1984–1988), the Dominican Republic (1986–1996), and Costa Rica (1990–1994), in opposition to secular left and populist forces and, where it had been strong, against the right as well. Their economic and political performances compared favorably with those of many preceding and ensuing governments. In many cases, however, tensions arose between rival moderate and progressive factions. The latter favored deeper transformations and often urged alliance with left-wing groups but were generally overruled by others who were suspicious of the left and determined not to alienate local elites or potential foreign investors. In the process, several of these parties, and the smaller Peruvian party as well, lost some of their younger members to mainline leftist parties, Christian-Marxist splinter movements, and other supporters to more conservative Social Christian offshoots (for example, the Popular Christian Party of Peru).

Decline

In the changing cultural and political contexts of the late twentieth and early twenty-first centuries, Christian Democracy has struggled to maintain its identity and appeal. In an era of ongoing secularization, its Christian values are less appealing or reassuring, and they mean increasingly different things to different people. On issues such as artistic expression, divorce, abortion, euthanasia, homosexuality, AIDS prevention, and sex education, for example, liberal and conservative Christian Democrats are as likely to disagree with one another and to be closer to people in parties to their left and their right. In most instances, party leaders have sided with those backing restrictive policies, although less, perhaps, from conviction than because they hope not to alienate Catholic authorities and thus risk losing their formal or informal blessings. In addition, in a post–cold war world in which socialism is no longer an option, free markets are everywhere triumphant, and competitive advantage

has become a categorical imperative, Christian Democracy's idea of a "third economic way" between traditional lefts and rights has less appeal than it did in the 1960s and 1970s. And, finally, in both Europe and Latin America, tripartite political and party systems have given way to bipolar contexts in which Christian Democrats must compete (with secular Social Democrats) for both control and survival in the crowded political center, or must move rightward, or remain on the right, to anchor or represent more conservative interests.

Where Christian Democracy remains a major political force in Europe, it generally has espoused and defended right-wing or conservative political and economic interests. Measured in the percentage of seats held in the lower house of national legislature, Christian Democrats are still a major force, and the country's leading right-wing or conservative political party, in Spain (49 percent), whose conservative Popular Party now considers itself a Christian Democratic party, and headed the government between 1996 and 2004; Austria (43 percent), where Christian Democrats, also operate as the Popular or People's Party; Luxembourg (40 percent); and Germany (37 percent). Christian Democrats are also a substantial political force in the Netherlands (29 percent); Ireland, where they are represented by Fine Gael (19 percent); Switzerland (14 percent); Norway (13 percent); and Belgium (12.7 percent). The once-dominant Italian Christian Democrats capsized in a sea of scandal and corruption in the early 1990s, with some party members moving leftward and others resurfacing as a secondary element (under 6 percent) in Silvio Berlusconi's rightist coalitions. In Portugal, the center-right (and largely Christian Democratic) Popular Party has won roughly 5 percent of the seats in that country's lower house in recent elections, but Christian Democrats are no longer a significant political force in Finland, France (3 percent), or Denmark.

Christian Democracy's evolution and decline have been even more dramatic in Latin America. At present, it is strongest in Mexico, where the traditionally conservative Partido Acción Nacional (National Action Party or PAN, with 31 percent of the seats in the Chamber of Deputies) has recently affiliated with the Christian Democrat and Democratic Center International. It is also a significant force, but seemingly in decline, in Chile, where it has been a leading element in the several center-left coalition governments that have governed the country since 1990. It currently holds 20 percent of the seats in the lower house and faces a strong challenge from the right by the conservative, and staunchly Catholic, Unión Demócrata Independiente (Independent Democratic Union or UDI). Christian Democracy is also a substantial political force in Ecuador (24 percent) and the Dominican Republic (21 percent), where it defends center-right positions and interests, and a less significant force in Costa Rica (9 percent) and El Salvador (6 percent). It once had a substantial political following, but no longer does, in Nicaragua, Panama, Peru, Uruguay, or Venezuela.

The decline of the Partido Social Cristiano de Venezuela (Social Christian Party of Venezuela or COPEI) has been particularly dramatic. For thirty years, it alternated in power with its social democratic partner–rival Acción Democrática (AD), pursuing broadly similar policies, splitting the votes cast in most elections, and channeling patronage to their respective elite supporters and to their organized labor, peasant, and middle-class clients. This "party-archical" system worked well through the 1980s but collapsed in the 1990s when popular forces excluded from resources and benefits rallied in support of Hugo Chavez' abortive coup in 1993 and his successful presidential campaigns of 1998 and 1999. As Chavez' star rose, those of the AD and COPEI fell, and by 2000, the latter had disintegrated, and its leaders and militants retired from politics, or began opposing Chavez from bastions within civil society, or from left-wing groups such as Movimiento al Socialismo (MAS).

Christian Democracy is still a significant political force in both Europe and Latin America, but is not as cohesive or relatively progressive as it was, or aspired to be, in the 1960s or 1970s. Economic, political, and cultural changes in the last thirty years have weakened both its cohesiveness and its appeal. The Catholics making up the bulk of its electoral base are increasingly divided on important economic (for example, globalization) and moral (for example, divorce and abortion) issues. More and more, it seems, they are finding common ground more readily with nominal and non-Catholics to their right and their left than with their fellow Catholics.

See also *Anticlericalism; Catholicism, Roman; Conservatism; Liberalism; Vatican.*

Michael H. Fleet

BIBLIOGRAPHY

Baum, Gregory, and John Coleman, eds. *The Church and Christian Democracy.* Edinburgh: Clark, 1987.

Cary, Noel D. *The Path to Christian Democracy: German Catholicism and the Party System from Windthorst to Adenauer.* Cambridge: Harvard University Press, 1996.

Einaudi, Mario, and François Goguel. *Christian Democracy in Italy and France.* Notre Dame: University of Notre Dame Press, 1952.

Fleet, Michael H. *The Rise and Fall of Chilean Christian Democracy.* Princeton: Princeton University Press, 1985.

Fogarty, Michael P. *Christian Democracy in Western Europe, 1820–1953.* Notre Dame: University of Notre Dame Press, 1957.

Hanley, David, ed. *Christian Democracy in Europe: A Comparative Perspective.* London: Pinter; New York: St. Martin's, 1994.

Kalyvas, Stathis. *The Rise of Christian Democracy in Europe.* Ithaca, N.Y.: Cornell University Press, 1996.

Maritain, Jacques. *Integral Humanism.* New York: Scribner's, 1968.

———. *Man and the State.* Chicago: University of Chicago Press, 1951.

Mounier, Emmanuel. *Personalism.* Notre Dame: University of Notre Dame Press, 1970.

Sturzo, Luigi. *Church and State.* New York: Longmans, Green, 1939.

Warner, Carolyn M. *Confessions of an Interest Group: The Catholic Church and Political Parties in Europe.* Princeton: Princeton University Press, 2000.

Christian Right

The Christian Right is an American social movement among conservative Christians dedicated to restoring "traditional values" in public policy. The movement emerged in the late 1970s and became a central part of the American right and a fixture of American politics. Its main organizations included initially the Moral Majority and the Religious Roundtable and more recently the Christian Coalition, Concerned Women for America, the Family Research Council, and Focus on the Family. The Christian Right has supported the broader political agenda of American conservatism, including cuts in government social spending and economic regulation, militant anticommunism (until the end of the cold war), and the war on terrorism (after September 11, 2001). However, its focus has been on restoring traditional morality. The Christian Right represents a unique connection between conservative religion and conservative politics in Western democracies.

The Christian Right and Conservatism

Since the mid-twentieth century conservatism has been a political position that seeks to reduce the role of government in the economy and to reestablish moral order in the face of a culture deemed too secular and too permissive. These two goals have been called, respectively, "economic libertarianism" and "moral traditionalism." A nationalist and aggressive foreign policy has often been part of conservatism, first anti-communism and more recently opposition to militant Islam.

Whether characterized as capitalist, industrial or postindustrial, modern or postmodern, Western societies inevitably generate problems of moral order, community, and meaning, to which conservative religious politics are one response. The moral traditionalism of conservative ideology takes a distinctive approach to these problems. It rarely focuses on only discrete issues such as abortion or gay rights. It is more concerned with the general moral trends that these issues reflect and promote. It decries the growing secularization of society, especially the declining belief in God and absolute standards of right and wrong. It also usually attributes these broader problems not primarily to impersonal social forces but to a secular culture actively created and sustained by liberal or radical elites in government, the media, universities, and other cultural institutions.

Political conservatism in this sense has a clear affinity for the theological conservatism of various religious groups, especially those that emphasize literal readings of scripture and a personal commitment to God. The most active and growing relationship between conservatism and religion is found in the United States. Consequently, what is known as the "Christian Right" is an independent conservative political movement in the United States rooted primarily in theologically conservative white Protestant religious groups.

Although other Western societies may face social problems and political issues similar to those in the United States, these are not framed in the same religious terms. Contemporary observers frequently comment on the greater role religion plays in American society and politics. Americans are more likely to attend church, and churches play bigger roles in everyday life than in the countries of Western Europe. Societies such as those in France, Germany, and Great Britain have strong rights of various kinds, but independent, religion-based political movements play a relatively small role in them. Even where the right is most active in Western Europe, the connection with religion is fairly weak. Perhaps this is why scholars looking for cross-national analogies compare the Christian Right with "fundamentalist" political movements primarily in the non-Western, less industrialized, less modern world. However, Islamic fundamentalism in Iran and Hindu fundamentalism in India are clearly different: their critique of secularism is tied to the rejection of Western influences and occurs in a far different political context. It thus has different implications.

Constituencies of the Christian Right

The constituencies on which the Christian Right draws most heavily have been variously called evangelical, fundamentalist, charismatic, and Pentecostal. The term *evangelical* refers to these groups generally, meaning all those who combine a relatively literal reading of the Bible, regarded as the final authority in all moral matters, with an emphasis on individual salvation through a personal relationship with God and a born-again experience. Others have called this group "conservative Christians." Some groups in this category may place more emphasis on biblical authority; others on religious experience. Some may belong to relatively large, mainstream denominations; others may belong to independent churches. The Christian Right also draws strength from a strong set of evangelical religious networks, from the broader religious polarization of Americans, and from other forces on the right.

Not all white evangelicals support the Christian Right, and not all supporters are evangelicals. Evangelicals have a wide range of political beliefs and often view the world in ways that are not captured in any simple ideology. Although the Christian Right emerged in the white evangelical world, by the end of the twentieth century, it had built major alliances with conservative Catholics as well.

Central to the politics of the Christian Right are the basic themes of moral traditionalism: most of America's many problems stem from the dominance of a secular humanist culture, purveyed by elites in government as well as in the media, universities, and other cultural institutions. This culture fundamentally denies God or any transcendent source of morality and thus removes religion and any moral moorings from public life. As a result, this culture leads to a general moral crisis and is tied to a host of specific problems as well: the decline of the conventional family, feminism, homosexuality, pornography, and even the growth of government. In addition to attacking this secular culture and calling for the reassertion of religious values in politics, the New Christian Right has supported, among other things, a variety of specific measures to outlaw abortion; prevent the spread of gay rights; permit religious activities in schools and other public places; ensure that public school curricula praise capitalism, the conventional family, and the virtues of America; and reinforce the conventional heterosexual family.

For example, writing in 2003 as federal and state courts were striking down antisodomy laws and legalizing same-sex marriage, James Dobson, head of Focus on the Family, presented a classic conservative analysis. (Dobson 2003) At issue, he wrote, was not simply the constitutionality of state anti-sodomy laws, the rights of gays to marry, or even the legitimacy of homosexuality. At issue was the institution of marriage itself. God designed heterosexual marriage, Dobson reminded his readers, and it "has been the cornerstone of every civilization from the beginning of humanity." However, in the last few decades, he continued, marriage had come under attack by enemies identified variously as the "homosexual activist movement," "radical feminists," the liberal establishment, and activist judges. The consequences are dire: "The institution of marriage is on the ropes and western civilization itself appears to hang in the balance."

Significance of the Christian Right

Religion is no newcomer to conservative politics in democratic capitalist societies. Generally, devout members of established or high-status churches have tended to support conservative political parties, whereas members of lower-status churches and those with no religious affiliation have voted for more liberal or leftist parties. Historically, struggles over the relationship between church and state sometimes have coincided with class conflict between right and left. As a result, the religious bases of voting often have both cross-cut and overlapped with the class bases of voting.

The Christian Right, however, represents a different and currently more significant kind of religious involvement in conservative politics. Although closely allied with the broader American right, it is an independent movement with its own leaders, organizations, and agenda. It is rooted not in the highest-status churches, but in ones that, historically at least, have been lower status. It speaks not with the quiet voice of privilege, but with a loud, moralistic voice, condemning sin wherever it sees sin.

The Christian Right is unique to the United States among democratic capitalist nations. Politics has moved to the right in nearly all these countries since the 1970s. As global economic competition heated up and as welfare state expenses outran the ability of governments to pay for them, conservative governments such as those of U.S. president Ronald Reagan (1981–1989) and British prime minister Margaret Thatcher (1979–1990) came to power seeking to cut government spending and regulation, weaken unions, and generally promote free enterprise. (In the meantime, social democratic parties have often moved to the center, forsaking any ambitious programs for building democratic

socialism.) Conservative regimes also have often emphasized a return to traditional values centered on individual responsibility, self-control, and hard work. And, until the end of the cold war, they often featured a militant anticommunism. Only in the United States, however, has an independent, religion-based political movement played a significant role in promoting this agenda.

The distinctive role of religion in the American right becomes clearer when it is compared with the rights of two otherwise similar societies, those of Great Britain and Canada. In each country the right has sought to cut back big government, enliven free markets, and restore the entrepreneurial spirit and traditional values. And in each case the issues have been cultural as well as economic. Only in the United States, however, has "cultural" become tied so closely to "religious." In Great Britain under Prime Minister Thatcher, the cultural battles focused in complicated ways on social class. The right wing of the Conservative Party fought against an upper-class Tory paternalism as well as working-class union militancy. In Canada the Reform Party became prominent in the 1990s by focusing on the linguistic and regional issues that have pitted French-speaking Quebec against the rest of English-speaking Canada, especially the western provinces, where the Reform Party built its base. The British and Canadian rights certainly have invoked traditional or Judeo-Christian values, but they have not generated an independent religious movement.

The Christian Right may seem akin to fundamentalist political movements that have proliferated in recent years, particularly in the Islamic and Hindu worlds, in former communist countries, and to some extent in Latin America. The Christian Right shares with these movements a rejection of a fully secular society and an effort to reorganize political discourse at least in part around a belief in a transcendent moral authority. To this end all such movements selectively retrieve and redefine beliefs and practices from a putative sacred past. To place the Christian Right in this context, however, is to reemphasize how unique it is. These other political movements have developed chiefly in non-Western societies. Their antisecularism often is characterized by an anti-imperialism, an opposition to the legacies of Western or communist domination. And these movements occur in societies in which the secular state they attack is weak or relatively new, or in which religious issues are tied closely to ethnic conflicts over political boundaries and rights. The only other Western countries that can be said to have independent fundamentalist political movements—Northern Ireland and Israel—are precisely the ones still rent by ethnic conflict over political identity.

Many observers have sought to explain the rise of the Christian Right by referring to the broad social changes common to all democratic capitalist societies. Some have argued that the Christian Right is a reaction to modern society; that is, a society that as it industrializes becomes not only increasingly secular but also increasingly specialized (with different societal activities carried on in different institutional settings) and rationalized (with more and more of life organized by formal rules). Others have argued that it is part of a new set of political conflicts that emerge in a postindustrial society: as older class-based economic conflicts have become muted, conflicts over values and lifestyle become more important. Still other observers have argued, in a somewhat different vein, that the Christian Right is a response to what neo-Marxist philosopher Jürgen Habermas calls the "colonization of the lifeworld," that is, the growing intrusion of market forces and government rules into everyday life. Whatever one makes of these explanations, they cannot be the whole story because Christian right movements have not sprouted up everywhere these forces are at work. At best these theories describe endemic discontent with the impersonal, meaningless, and materialistic nature of life in the West. They do not explain how under some circumstances some people channel their discontent with the moral quality of life into a particular kind of religious movement. To understand why the Christian Right emerged in the United States when it did, one must look at what makes U.S. society different from those of other countries as well as what it shares with them.

The Salience of America's Religious Past

Some of the roots of the contemporary Christian Right lie deep in America's religious past, especially in the strength of religious institutions in civil life and the distinct kind of moralism propagated by certain religious groups. The United States always has had a relatively high degree of separation of church and state. This separation has not meant that religious issues have not been important politically, or that religious institutions have not been involved in political life, or that government has not acted at times to favor one religion or another. It does mean that there has not been an established church, one that enjoys consistent official recognition and substantial public subsidies.

The lack of public recognition and support, ironically perhaps, has encouraged, not discouraged, the proliferation of religious institutions and activities, because churches have had to compete to get and hold members. Since the early nineteenth century, foreign observers of life in the United States such as French writer and politician Alexis de Tocqueville have noted the large percentage of Americans attending churches and the strength of these institutions in everyday life. Compared with the citizens of other countries, Americans have allocated a relatively large share of the fruits of economic growth to religious institutions, with several results. First, churches are easily available to would-be members and are more likely to become the focus of a civic life that in other countries might be dominated by political parties and unions. Second, a vast array of seminaries and theologians are available to articulate religious ideas. Third, Americans have, with relative ease, developed the habit of attending church and orienting themselves to religion. In short, religious institutions in America occupy a central place in everyday life. This does not mean that U.S. churches necessarily provide a basis for political mobilization but that they are well placed to do so.

A significant part of this religious activity always has been oriented toward a distinctive kind of Protestant moralism. This moralism has emphasized several themes that remain important among evangelical Protestants today: the importance of individual salvation gained through a born-again experience and a personal relationship with God; an emphasis on "Christianizing" and otherwise reforming a sinful world; a belief in the Bible as the sole source of moral authority; and the idea of America as a "new Israel" destined to play a special role in the divine plan for humanity. Together these beliefs do not necessarily encourage political activism. (They may encourage radical withdrawal from a society deemed irretrievably corrupt.) They do, however, provide a powerful basis for a thorough critique of the secular tendencies of modern societies.

The religious groups that became known as fundamentalist (beginning in the early 1900s) and evangelical (around mid-century) are some of the most important products of this religious heritage. They were sporadically involved in American politics in the first six decades of the twentieth century, from battles over the teaching of evolution in the 1920s to anticommunist crusades in the 1950s to conflicts about sex education and school curriculum in the 1960s and early 1970s.

The most important precursors to the rise of the Christian Right in the 1970s, however, were cultural, not political. Beginning in the late 1940s, evangelicals and fundamentalists built a dense network of religious institutions. Bible institutes, colleges, seminaries, journals, and publishing houses flourished. Evangelical radio and television programs, youth organizations, and mass revival meetings (notably those of Billy Graham) enjoyed considerable success. Above all, evangelical and fundamentalist Protestant churches continued to grow, even in the 1970s when theologically moderate and liberal churches were losing members. Some enterprising ministers began building mega-churches with thousands of members and an increasingly wide range of activities. Others took to the airwaves to develop electronic ministries on cable television. In a pattern that has continued and grown, these institutions became the cultural and organizational basis for political mobilization.

Mobilization of the Christian Right

By the early 1970s, then, an organizational base for a Christian Right existed, but this in itself did not lead to political mobilization. From the 1950s through the early 1970s, evangelicals, if anything, were relatively depoliticized. They participated less in politics than other Americans and were less likely to condone the participation of their churches. In the 1960s and 1970s religion in politics took the form of the active involvement of the liberal churches in the civil rights and anti–Vietnam War movements.

This picture changed dramatically in the mid-1970s. From then on, according to most surveys, evangelicals became more politically active than other Christians. They registered to vote and voted in increasing numbers; they lobbied their elected representatives and worked on political campaigns. They also increasingly approved of their clergy becoming politically involved, and their religious leaders were eager to oblige. Above all, a network of leaders and political organizations dedicated to mobilizing this constituency rapidly developed.

Why this happened can be understood in terms of the emergence of both new issues and new political opportunities. Although evangelical and fundamentalist Christians for a long time had condemned the secularism of American culture and identified it as a cause of many important social problems, from the 1960s on a host of new issues emerged in American society that made that critique especially salient. Commentators called these "social" and later "cultural"

issues. Conflict over these issues came to be known as "culture wars." They were not economic—that is, they were not primarily about how the costs and benefits of economic growth were distributed and what role government played in this. Instead, they concerned matters of social order and morality such as crime and drug use, sexuality, family and gender roles, affirmative action, and the values taught by America's cultural institutions (schools, mass media, and family).

These cultural issues emerged in part because of broad changes in American society and in part because of liberal social movements. For example, the rise of women's rights issues such as equal rights and abortion partly reflected long-term changes in the family and gender roles: the increasing percentage of women (especially those with young children) working outside the home, rising rates of divorce and single parenthood, and more permissive sexual mores. But the emergence of these issues also stemmed from the rapid growth after the mid-1960s of the women's movement, which placed these issues on the political agenda.

New political opportunities also encouraged the mobilization of the Christian Right, of which three stand out in particular. First, the involvement of largely nonevangelical religious leaders and organizations in the liberal social movements of the 1960s, especially the civil rights and antiwar movements, legitimated the mixing of religion with politics. The 1976 presidential campaign of Democrat Jimmy Carter, himself an evangelical Christian, stressed the need to return morality to government and appealed in particular to evangelicals, albeit from a centrist position. This development, too, gave evangelicals a heightened sense of political legitimacy and entitlement.

Second, a series of changes in the religious world made it easier for evangelical Christians to find sympathetic allies and form cross-denominational alliances. Beginning in the 1950s, boundary lines between the various traditional religious denominations in the United States, especially within Protestantism, blurred as the old regional and ethnic differences that once distinguished them declined in importance. At the same time, the religious world became somewhat polarized along secular and religious lines as the ranks of both the religiously unaffiliated and the more theologically conservative churches grew, while those of moderate and liberal churches declined. Moreover, within many religious denominations a growing cleavage developed between the more orthodox and more progressive elements. This general realignment in the religious world provided the basis for the culture wars and thus created political opportunities for the Christian Right.

Third, the Christian Right benefited from the rise of conservatism in American politics generally in the late 1970s and early 1980s. After the debacle of Watergate in 1974, the Republican Party rebuilt itself into a potent political force. The party used direct-mail fund-raising techniques to develop a mass base of contributors. Their donations allowed the party to develop strong national organizations, which systematically cultivated new generations of political candidates and provided them with sophisticated political technology and other resources.

At about the same time, large corporations began mobilizing to push American politics to the right. Concerned about increasing government economic regulation, in particular, and a political system they believed too hostile to capitalism, in general, business leaders and large corporations formed new organizations (such as the Business Roundtable) for high-level lobbying, directed an increasing percentage of corporate campaign donations to conservative Republican congressional candidates, and poured money into conservative think tanks.

Most important, a secular conservative political movement came of age at the same time. Born with the founding of the journal *National Review* by William F. Buckley Jr. in 1955, this movement had by the mid-1970s developed into a vast network of political activists and organizations. The emerging leaders of the movement, including Howard Phillips and Paul Weyrich, cultivated the first leaders and helped them create the first organizations of the Christian Right in the late 1970s. Having identified white evangelical Christians as a largely untapped constituency for the right, they approached several television preachers and helped one of them, Jerry Falwell, establish Moral Majority. They also helped to create Christian Voice and the Religious Roundtable, the other two organizations with broad political agendas, and to bring other TV evangelists, notably Pat Robertson, into politics.

Growth of Political Activism

The political activism of the Christian Right that began in the mid-1970s focused on specific issues of concern to evangelical Christians: the proposed Equal Rights Amendment, gay rights initiatives, the tax status and rights of private Christian schools, and the content of public school text-

The Rev. Jerry Falwell. A figurehead of right-wing Christianity, Falwell's political activism has made him both an influential figure and a subject of controversy for his outspoken statements of social conservatism.

books. These initially disparate efforts fed at the end of the decade into the formation of Moral Majority, Christian Voice, and the Religious Roundtable.

These organizations were led typically by TV preachers and the ministers of mega-churches. They drew on preexisting religious networks and leaders. Each was associated with a major TV preacher—Moral Majority with Jerry Falwell, Christian Voice with Pat Robertson, and Religious Roundtable with James Robison. Moral Majority also featured ministers from some of America's largest mega-churches on its board of directors, and it recruited most of its state leaders from the ranks of the Baptist Bible Fellowship, an organization of independent fundamentalist churches. It drew on the computerized mailing list of Falwell's television show, *Old-Time Gospel Hour,* to raise money.

More generally, the Christian Right relied especially on evangelical church congregations and the networks of ties these produced to mobilize its rank-and-file membership. Only those evangelicals heavily involved in their churches—not evangelicals generally—were politicized and moved to the right. Frequent church attendance among white evangelicals correlated as well with conservative positions on issues such as abortion and the Equal Rights Amendment. Evangelical congregations provided both a religious ethos and a network of social ties conducive to conservative political mobilization.

When Ronald Reagan assumed the presidency and Republicans took control of the Senate as a result of the 1980 elections, the Christian Right gained considerable notoriety, and many commentators came to regard it as a decisive force in American politics. Others, however, questioned how much substance there was to the image. They pointed out that few Americans had heard of Moral Majority in 1980 (and most of those who had were opposed to it), that evangelical Christians were not a monolithically conservative force, and that there was little evidence that the Christian Right had had an independent effect on the 1980 elections.

By 1984, however, the impact of the Christian Right had become clearer. That year, 80 percent of white evangelical Christians voted for Ronald Reagan, and subsequent Republican presidential candidates enjoyed similar majorities even as their overall shares of the popular vote rose or fell. Polling data showed that white evangelical Christians in all regions of the country, especially those who attended church frequently, were shifting their political allegiance significantly to the Republican Party. In addition, they were becoming the most important source of new conservative grass-roots political activism. Clearly, then, white evangelical Christians were a new political force for right-wing politics.

Solid political accomplishments were harder to come by, however. The Christian Right won few victories during the Reagan years. The Family Protection Act, an omnibus bill addressing many of the movement's concerns, failed to pass. Legislation favoring school prayer and limiting abortion also went nowhere.

Since the mid-1980s, the fortunes of the Christian Right have risen and fallen largely with the fortunes of the Republican Party and of the right generally. At each turn commentators have been quick to pronounce it either all-powerful or moribund.

In the late 1980s, Christian Right organizations and leaders that represented them seemed to fall on hard times. All three major Christian Right organizations were inactive by 1986. Many of the television evangelists from whose ranks Christian Right leaders had come found their electronic ministries beset by financial problems and had to retrench; a few faced moral scandals as well. Most significant, the well-financed campaign of Pat Robertson for the 1988 Republican presidential nomination fell flat, failing even to gain strong support among all evangelicals, let alone expand beyond those ranks.

This malaise, however, turned out to be only a brief downturn in the fortunes of the Christian Right. By the early 1990s, a new generation of organizations (most notably, the Christian Coalition, the Family Research Council, and Focus on the Family) and new leaders (Ralph Reed, Gary Bauer, and James Dobson) emerged to push the religious right's agenda. These new organizations sought to develop a broader base of support and to present their position less in sectarian religious rhetoric and more in pluralist secular language. Thus organized prayer in school was justified as a matter of student rights and religious liberty, as was putting religious values back into education. Battles over the content of school textbooks were presented as a matter of securing parental rights to control curriculum as well as countering a secular humanist culture.

The Christian Right has managed to sustain itself through good times and bad. It has been able to work at both the national level, lobbying for major pieces of legislation, and the local level around issues of school curricula, antigay ordinances, and the like. It has maintained deep roots in the white evangelical religious world. It has also been able to connect the political and the personal for its supporters. Focus on the Family, for example, in its radio broadcasts, publications, and Web site addresses a myriad of everyday issues such as rearing children, making marriages work, and dealing with drug addiction. People who have learned to trust it on personal matters are more open to its political messages.

Finally, the Christian Right has been able to find big issues around which to mobilize supporters. In the late 1990s and early 2000s, the Christian Right has focused on preventing the extension of marriage rights to same-sex couples and opposing local gay rights ordinances. It has also sought to chip away at abortion rights through measures such as the Partial Birth Abortion Ban and the Unborn Victims of Violence Act. During George W. Bush's presidency, it has pushed consistently for putting more conservative judges on the federal courts. At the local level, it has supported abstinence-only sex education and the teaching of intelligent design along with the theory of evolution in public schools.

In recent years, a clear pattern of conservative politics and religion has emerged. The Republican Party has become increasingly conservative. Its center of gravity has moved to the South and Southwest. The generations of conservatives who came of age in the 1980s have assumed positions of leadership. Americans have become increasingly polarized by degree of religious involvement. Presidential elections from 1996 on have shown record gaps among white voters between frequent church attenders, who vote overwhelmingly Republican, and nonattenders, who vote heavily Democratic. White evangelicals, especially church-going ones, have become the most reliable Republican constituency and are generally viewed as the party's base. Christian Right leaders such as Dobson of Focus on the Family and Tony Perkins of the Family Research Council have become major voices in the Republican Party. In the 2004 elections, the Republican drive to get out the vote trumped a strong Democratic effort, by working through evangelical churches and with Christian Right organizations.

A similar pattern can be seen on the issue of same-sex marriage. In the fall of 2003, as gay rights and same-sex marriage became especially visible, contentious issues, surveys showed that white evangelicals were more likely to oppose same-sex marriage than either Catholics or Mainline Protestants. Frequent church attenders in all three groups were more likely to oppose it, but level of church attendance made the biggest difference among white evangelicals. Overall, white evangelicals were more likely to hear about the issue in church and more likely to get negative messages from their pastors. (Pew Center for the People and the Press, "Religious Beliefs Underpin Opposition to Homosexuality," November 18, 2003)

Still, some caveats are in order. Although the Christian Right and its opponents are engaged in a broad culture war, most Americans have not enlisted. Public opinion on most issues, even among religious people, hugs the political center. Although political parties are increasingly polarized, the American public is not. Although the Christian Right is powerful and likely to remain so, the ranks of the "unchurched" (those reporting no affiliation) is increasing and the number of Protestants in particular is declining.

Overall, the important point is this: the most vibrant connection between conservative politics and religion is the Christian Right in the United States. In other Western democracies, connections between religion and the right reflect the inertia of past commitments instead of continually renewed engagement.

See also: *Conservatism; Lobbying, Religious.*

Jerome L. Himmelstein

BIBLIOGRAPHY

Diamond, Sara. *Not by Politics Alone: The Enduring Influence of the Christian Right.* New York: Guilford Press, 1998.

Dobson, James. "Marriage on the Ropes." *Dr. Dobson's Newsletter,* September 2003.

Fiorina, Morris P., Samuel J. Adams, and Jeremy C. Pope. *Culture War? The Myth of a Polarized America.* New York: Pearson Longman, 2005.

Himmelstein, Jerome L. *To the Right: The Transformation of American Conservatism.* Berkeley: University of California Press, 1990.

Green, John C., Mark J. Rozell, and Clyde Wilcox, eds. *The Christian Right in American Politics: Marching to the Millennium.* Washington, D.C.: Georgetown University Press, 2003.

———. *The Values Campaign? The Christian Right and the 2004 Election.* Washington, D.C.: Georgetown University Press, 2006.

Irvine, Janice M. *Talk about Sex: The Battles over Sex Education in the United States.* Berkeley: University of California Press, 2002.

Martin, William C. *With God on Our Side: The Rise of the Religious Right in America.* New York: Broadway Books, 1996.

Micklethwait, John, and Adrian Wooldridge. *The Right Nation: Conservative Power in America.* New York: Penguin, 2004.

Pew Center for the People and the Press. "Religious Beliefs Underpin Opposition to Homosexuality." The Pew Forum on Religion and Public Life, November 18, 2003. Available online at http://pewforum.org/docs/index.php?DocID=37.

Wilcox, Clyde. *Onward Christian Soldiers? The Religious Right in American Politics.* 3d ed. Boulder, Colo.: Westview Press, 2006.

Christian Science

Christian Science is the name applied to the teachings of the Church of Christ, Scientist, a sometimes politically controversial religious organization established in 1879 in Boston, Massachusetts. It is based on the writings of its founder, Mary Baker Eddy (1821–1910). Her book *Science and Health with Key to the Scriptures* summarizes major elements of the religion. Since its publication in 1875, her book has served as the key writing that distinguishes the church from other Christian-based churches.

Theology and Practice

Christian Science theology places a strong emphasis on the spiritual in contrast to the material. The primary teaching of Christian Science is that God is at once omnipotent, omnipresent, and omniscient Divine Principle, Mind, Soul, Spirit, Truth, and Love. Creation, it is taught, is the spiritual expression of God, and man and woman are made in "God's image and likeness." The thrust of this theology is unitarian, the healings of Jesus being defined as examples of applying the scientific truth that Eddy discovered and began to practice following her own apparently spontaneous healing after a serious accident.

Perhaps the best known and most controversial concept from Christian Science theology concerns *spiritual healing.* The term refers to the treatment of physical ailments, depression, grief, stress, business problems, and marital crises through prayer alone. Christian Science teaches that healing will result if one will but depend completely on God and accept the basic truths of Christian Science theology.

In any healing situation the Christian Scientist focuses on establishing a proper relationship between the individual patient and God. A person seeking spiritual healing through Christian Science will often turn for help to specially trained *practitioners* or *teachers,* who have an established record of healing and are fully dependent on their healing ministry for their livelihood. Christian Science practitioners are reimbursed under some private insurance plans, although they have never received payments under any state or federal government programs.

In recent years controversy has ensued over spiritual healing in the United States, especially as it is used in cases involving seriously ill children, some of whom have died. People have become relatively accustomed to spiritual healing, a factor contributing to the fact that many states have granted formal exemptions for such healing to laws concerning child endangerment and neglect. Children's deaths in the last two decades, however, have led to criminal charges being filed against parents in a few cases. Some of the cases have led to convictions, although most convictions have been overturned on appeal. The cases have brought about much negative publicity for the church, which has had a difficult time getting the media and the public to accept its explanations. These cases have led to some reexamination of Christian Science theology and practice concerning spiritual healing.

Mary Baker Eddy.

Sociology and Organization

The Mother Church in Boston has established more than twenty-two hundred branches in more than sixty countries. Most of the branches are in the United States. The estimated number of church participants worldwide is 350,000 to 450,000. This estimate reflects a decline in church membership in the United States and some European countries in recent decades but a growth in some developing countries. A high proportion of members are middle-aged and elderly women from middle- and upper-class origins. Females make up nearly 85 percent of the more than two thousand practitioners and about half of the higher-status teachers.

Members have active social and political lives and are not encouraged to be reclusive or ascetic. Little emphasis is put on communal life or collective living. They do not use tobacco or alcohol, believing that such substances impair moral judgment and spiritual development. Members also eschew gambling, which they believe indicates a dependence on chance instead of God's law and will. Marriage is sanctioned, and celibacy is neither promoted nor scorned.

The church has no ordained clergy and few overt rituals. It does not, for instance, practice baptism or celebrate Easter or Christmas through special services. Because of the lack of official clergy, marriage ceremonies are not performed in the church. In regular church services, lay readers present material from the Bible and *Science and Health* selected by the church authorities in Boston. The same material is used in all branch churches for the week. Services, held in austere surroundings, tend to be unemotional and include silent and audible prayer, readings, and some hymn singing. Midweek testimonial meetings are also held. Most of the churches have a Sunday School for younger participants, and each one operates a "reading room," which is open to the public and contains all church publications and works by biblical commentators acceptable to the church.

The church and its branches are still governed by principles laid down by Eddy in the *Manual of the Mother Church,* published first in 1895 and revised by her several times. A five-person self-perpetuating board of directors governs the Mother Church and develops broad policy consistent with the *Manual.* Local branches operate on democratic principles. Members who desire to do so can participate in governance of the local church by being elected to a local church office.

A church Committee on Publication in each state monitors the media and state legislatures to make sure the church is not dealt with unfairly. The church also has a legal arm in Washington, D.C., that monitors federal cases and legislation to some extent.

The church has several major regular publications, the best known of which is the *Christian Science Monitor,* a daily newspaper of high standing among journalists and the general public. The newspaper is known for its lack of sensationalism and its thorough coverage of international issues. Eddy began the paper in 1908, two years before her death, as a way of making a statement about the practical implications of her spiritual philosophy. The other major regular publications of the church are the monthly *Christian Science Journal,* the weekly *Christian Science Sentinel,* and the weekly *Herald of Christian Science,* which is published in many different languages. These publications include articles on various aspects of Christian Science faith and practice; reports on the work of the church; reports on spiritual healings; and lists of Christian Science churches, reading rooms, organizations on college campuses, and practitioners and teachers around the world. More than fifty thousand reports of spiritual healings have appeared in these publications during the past hundred years.

See also *Medicine.*

James T. Richardson

BIBLIOGRAPHY

Christian Science Publishing Society. *Christian Science: A Sourcebook of Contemporary Materials.* Boston, Mass.: Christian Science Publishing Society, 1990.

Eddy, Mary Baker. *Science and Health with Key to the Scriptures.* Boston, Mass.: Christian Science Publishing Society, 1934.

Gottschalk, Stephen. *The Emergence of Christian Science in American Religious Life.* Berkeley and Los Angeles: University of California Press, 1973.

Peel, Robert. *Spiritual Healing in a Scientific Age.* San Francisco, Calif.: Harper and Row, 1987.

Richardson, James T., and John DeWitt. "Christian Science Spiritual Healing, the Law, and Public Opinion." *Journal of Church and State* 34 (summer 1992): 549–562.

Christianity

Christianity, the religious movement that grew out of the ministry and crucifixion of Jesus of Nazareth two thousand years ago, has spread in a variety of forms and churches across the globe. Jesus was a Jew; his followers never abandoned the Jewish scriptures, although little by little they added to the Jewish "Old Testament" a further collection of writings that became the "New Testament" of their Bible. Christian beliefs and practices in every area have to be understood as a mix of elements and influences, in part derived from their Hebrew ancestry, in part the product of the teachings of Jesus or the situation in which Christianity subsequently developed.

Judaism was the religion of a single people, claiming to be uniquely chosen by God and to have been given a particular territory as its own. Its sense of political identity was reinforced by the way in which so many of its sacred books were historical in character, relating to the rise and fall of a kingdom of Israel centered upon Jerusalem. Inevitably, this sort of political focus was entirely lost in a religious movement that contrasted itself with Israel precisely in terms of not being a "people" in a national sense but being instead a "new people of God" chosen from all peoples of the world. Whether or not this universalism was implicit in the teaching of Jesus himself, it was a decisive characteristic of the

Christian Church within a generation of his death and was at the heart of the teaching of his most influential follower, Saint Paul.

The politicism inherent in the Judaism from which Christianity came could have no possible place in a community stressing in theory and achieving in practice a rapidly growing "catholicity," that is to say openness on equal terms to people of every race and language. Although Jesus must undoubtedly have spoken in Aramaic or Hebrew and never, so far as we know, left Palestine, the books about him and early Christian literature as a whole were written in Greek—the most widely spread language of the time. Christianity's very adoption of Greek expressed its claim to a nonethnic, non-national, nonpolitical identity, especially as Greek was not made into the one privileged language of the community. Once it had spread into western Europe among non-Greek speakers, its scriptures and liturgy were translated into Latin. In Syria they were translated into Syriac, in the interior of Egypt into Coptic, in Armenia into Armenian. The claim to universality extended well beyond the borders of the Roman Empire, and Christianity grew as naturally in Armenia or Persia as in the former.

Jesus was someone who had exercised no political power, who was quoted as distinguishing fairly clearly between the claims of religion and politics—give to Caesar the things that are Caesar's and to God the things that are God's—and who had died as a condemned criminal. Here was no glorification of political power but rather an assertion that "the Kingdom of God," which Jesus proclaimed, could be attained in a totally apolitical way, by turning the power system of the world on its head. After Jesus' crucifixion, the cross, a particularly cruel instrument of execution, a symbol of oppression and ignominy, became instead a symbol of liberation and glory. This was possible only because of the intense other-worldliness of the early Christian movement: the victory being sought was one not of this world but of the next. Enthusiastic early Christians had to be discouraged by the church from actually seeking martyrdom.

Nevertheless, some aspects of Old Testament political religion, the prophetic aspects especially, passed at once into Christianity—its highly ethical disposition and its concern for justice, the poor, and the oppressed. In a sense, taking for granted this prophetic concern, Jesus positioned himself and his movement as identified with the oppressed. Because the oppressed were politically powerless, this attitude could seem a withdrawal from the political, but in the long term it

proved not to be. Instead, it established as first priority an inescapable foundation for the reshaping of the political with the needs of the poor. It did so by proclaiming an authority in some way vested in the church, something in no way identical with normal political authority—Caesar—but nonetheless sanctioned to speak out about the world of political power and its misuse. The Christian tradition is thus intrinsically dualist: it recognizes the secular authority of Caesar, derived from God and the natural order, but it also asserts that there is within the church an independent, more directly God-given authority that can and must carry on the prophetic concern for justice, and Jesus' own identification with the most innocent and the most oppressed, by challenging the state in a vast range of matters that the state considers political and not religious.

The Constantinian Revolution

Until the beginning of the fourth century, the apolitical character of Christianity must have seemed overwhelmingly obvious. It had spread with striking rapidity yet without any political or military support whatsoever. On the contrary, it had undergone numerous persecutions because Christians refused to take part in emperor worship and had never responded by any sort of organized resistance. Most of its members were pacifists and few belonged to a governing class. Nevertheless, in various parts of the eastern Mediterranean world Christians had become so numerous that it was increasingly difficult for government to function effectively without their cooperation. The last great persecution, which began under the emperor Diocletian and lasted from 303 to 311, was a huge failure. Christians, by and large, refused to return to traditional worship, the numerous executions of harmless people discredited the state, and society was disrupted. In 313 the young emperor of the Western empire, Constantine, identified himself and his cause with Christianity. He proved stunningly successful, defeated all rivals, and established a new Christian capital for the empire at Byzantium on the Bosporus, renamed and rebuilt as Constantinople. He died in 337, having transformed the entire relationship between Christianity and politics.

Why did Constantine become a Christian? It remains hard to know. The pragmatic answer makes little sense. At the time, Constantine was struggling for control of the Latin West, where Christians still formed a small proportion of the population. His religious background had been one of solar monotheism. Somehow, by vision, inspiration, or contact with Christians this religious inclination was transmuted into a Christian faith that included the conviction that his own victorious career depended on it. Constantine's conversion led to the principles of the Edict of Milan (313), agreed to with his eastern rival, Licinius, whereby all religions were to be tolerated. Only at the end of the fourth century, under the emperor Theodosius, did Christianity become formally the one official religion of the empire. But already Constantine was giving the church privileges in all sorts of ways and, particularly after his conquest of the Eastern Empire in 324, incorporating it within the machinery of government.

It is understandable enough that Christians for the most part went along enthusiastically with this revolutionary change of status. It was not only that wealth and power had their attractions, or even that it was hard to question the propriety of a development that encouraged an enormous increase in the number of church members; it was also that in the eyes of men like Eusebius, bishop of Caesarea, the outstanding church historian of his age, and the Latin theologian Lactantius what had happened seemed to reflect the designs of divine Providence: church and empire were meant for each other. Luke's Gospel had already stressed how Jesus was born at a moment when the whole world was united as never before under the authority of the emperor Augustus. Where hitherto persecution had held the two apart, intensifying an apolitical otherworldliness in Christianity and negating any claim that the empire could truly be part of God's benign providence, Constantine had joined the two together. No wonder Constantine was acclaimed as the thirteenth apostle, providing the church with an overt political dimension it would ever after have the greatest difficulty in escaping. Some of the early Christian ideals, like the tradition of pacifism, simply faded away in consequence, whereas the high social status accorded the bishops, incorporating them into the class of the powerful, set them apart from other Christians and deeply affected the church-state relationship, by partially encapsulating it inside a single ruling class.

There were other consequences as well. Christians outside the Roman Empire were put at once in an invidious position. If Rome was officially Christian, and if Christianity was indeed now in some sense Roman, then Persian Christians might be seen as agents of Rome. With the development of Constantinople as a completely Christian capital, an explicitly Greek form of Christianity became preeminent within what we can begin to call a Byzantine Empire.

Constantine I.

Christians at odds with the Eastern emperor and his Greek-centered world, whether within or without the borders of empire, became inclined to opt for a form of Christianity different from that patronized in Constantinople.

It was Constantine who had endeavored to resolve the Arian controversy in 325 by calling the bishops together in a council at Nicaea. Arius, a priest in the church at Alexandria, Egypt, and his followers held a view on the nature of Christ that deviated from that of the majority. At Nicaea, Constantine had paid the bishops' expenses, he addressed them in person, and he expected them to agree to a line of doctrine that would not be politically divisive. Disagreement was to be punished by exile. Although neither Constantine nor most of his successors claimed to make doctrine, they expected the bishops to do so in the way they directed. What grew up in consequence was a monist system of control of the church by the state that was appropriate to the Roman tradition but profoundly alien to the Christian.

If this imperial control never fully took root, it was because the authority of the bishops was already too well advanced. Although in practice bishops might often be chosen by an emperor, in principle their consecration and source of authority came from elsewhere—the apostolic succession. This doctrine maintained that the bishops derived their authority through the apostles as direct descendants of Jesus. Already in the time of Constantine and his immediate successors, Athanasius, bishop of Alexandria, had incurred exile after exile for not conforming to imperial policy. By his obstinacy and clarity of mind, Athanasius did much to maintain a sense of surviving dualism, which was in danger of disappearing within the privileged servility of an imperial church.

Dualism, however, survived even more emphatically in the West for two reasons. The first was the existence of the See of Rome, which claimed apostolicity in the fullest sense because its founders were the apostles Peter and Paul. The emperors were inclined to regard the undoubted superiority of the Roman church as due to its being the church of the first imperial capital and to claim that, for the same reason, the church of Constantinople should be next in importance. For the church in Rome, however, its imperial connection had no significance at all. Its authority came from the apostles. In consequence, the papacy (the bishopric of Rome) remained a bulwark against a creeping monism. Pope Gelasius, in particular, formulated the theory of the two swords given by God: the earthly to the emperor, the spiritual to pope and church. Basically, this idea represents simply a reformulation of Christianity's traditional position: to recognize the validity of secular authority but to deny that such authority could be exercised over the church and to assert the claim of the church to challenge the misdeeds of the secular, as the prophets of Israel had once done.

The second reason that the leanings toward a unified church and empire of Constantine, Theodosius, and Justinian—the greatest Eastern emperor of the sixth century—failed to take root in the Latin world was that the empire itself collapsed in the West under invasion from Germanic tribes moving west across the Rhine. In consequence, the mirage of a single universal community of church and empire faded fast. In the early fifth century Augustine of Hippo, facing the collapse in morale occasioned by the sack of Rome by the Goths in 410, wrote his *City of God,* in which he took the Roman Empire to pieces as a work of man, no more privileged than any previous empire and wholly to be distinguished from the church as the City of God, which would continue across whatever change of political regime might occur.

Although the ideal of a unified Christian empire continued to haunt the West, stimulating the revival and survival of a "Holy Roman Empire" effectively limited to Germany and parts of Italy, the reality was moving toward a multitude of separate states. In each of these the church had to find a home and a measure of freedom.

The Papacy, Nationalism, and Protestantism

The attempt of the papacy in its most venturesome period, from the eleventh to the thirteenth century, to provide political leadership for a Christian community still imagined as single provided a watershed in Christian political history. To the pope, it was now claimed, both swords—the temporal and the spiritual—had been confided. The political role of a king was essentially inferior to that of the pope.

This attempt to achieve a Western kind of monism, unified not in a royal but clerical form, could not conceivably succeed. In reality, the power of the popes, bureaucratically far more efficient than anyone else, was simply too limited. Even at the level of a universalist ideology, the popes were continually challenged in the thirteenth and fourteenth centuries by people like the Florentine poet Dante and Marsilius of Padua, who continued to believe in the dominating role of a universal emperor. But far more decisively were they defeated by the rising power of national monarchies, which were actually fortified by the underlying sentiment of Christian dualism, something that had been dangerously impaired by the papal claim to a sort of universal monarchy. The latter's supreme military embodiment, the Crusades, had also proved disastrous in religious terms and a long-term failure in political ones. The popes had drawn a religion that began as largely committed to pacifism and that had then been driven by political circumstances to allow a "just war" to fling itself into something very different, "holy war." Holy war is an expression of monism. Both the Crusades and the papacy of the High Middle Ages reflected a disastrous abandonment of the inherent dualistic balance between the religious and the political, and they were to lead in reaction to the large-scale lay and national takeover of the church in the following period.

As this happened, however, a new side of Christianity's political impact was revealed: its nation-building propensity. If on one side a united church, glorying in a single "communion" open to every people and language, naturally linked itself with a universal empire, which at its best cherished similar aspirations, on the other side the church retained in its Bible the Hebrew scriptures, which evoked a quite different political model, one that can be not absurdly described as that of a national state, keen to defend its identity against invading powers. Western Christians, as they forged a series of national identities—English, Scottish, French, German, and the rest—were greatly assisted both by the political model of Israel they found in their Bibles and by the encouragement that the church gave to the development of literature in the vernacular languages. Christianity from the start had been a religion of translation, and this activity continued, despite the high value accorded to the role of Latin by the political and clerical elites.

The early emergence of vernacular literature in Welsh and Irish, English and French, German and Dutch was not accidental. It was inherent in Christianity's relationship to language—a relationship stressed still further at the Protestant Reformation in the sixteenth century. The extensive writing of a given vernacular solidified the community that possessed it, particularly when this literature included the Bible. The national state was the result, and it came to claim somewhat inevitably the sort of control over its own church that Constantine had exercised over the universal church. It is striking that when Henry VIII declared himself to be supreme ruler over the church in England in 1534, he did so by asserting England to be an "empire," and he appealed explicitly to the example of Constantine and Justinian.

All Protestants did not, however, sit down quietly to the consequence of such a claim—a multitude of monist church-states, in each of which the ruler claimed to control the church by divine authority and the subjects followed the religion of their ruler (a doctrine known as *cuius regio, eius religio*). If this formula was effectively endorsed in Germany and England by the Lutheran and Anglican traditions, as it had been for centuries by the Eastern Orthodox, so that in all three a state church became the norm, it was not at all the case in regard to Calvinism or to any other of the more radical wings of the Reformation. Here, on the contrary, the essential freedom of the church from the state was asserted,

although, since this could lead (as in John Calvin's Geneva) to the effective subordination of the state to the church, the bonding of the two might look much the same to the outside observer. With time, however, the Calvinist position led in practice as well as in theory to the reemergence of a "Free Church," that is to say, a church uncontrolled by the state. This pattern was evolving very notably in seventeenth-century England and in its overflow to New England in North America. Although the English Puritans, for the most part, had wanted to impose their own model of church upon everyone, and to a large extent did so during the years of the Commonwealth after the civil war and abolition of the monarchy, the very dividedness of their own views rendered this prospect impossible. If the authority of the state to impose uniformity upon the church was denied, no other entity could do so, and the unity of church and state was bound to come to an end.

Historically, the Christian tradition thus presents a whole range of models for the relationship of religion and politics, models deriving from different periods and circumstances. This diversity was possible and remains possible largely because of the lack of any overt political dimension in early Christianity. In consequence, it has remained highly malleable to cultural circumstances and pressure from the state. That pressure, characteristic of almost all Christian history subsequent to Constantine, was systematized within the Eastern Orthodox tradition first in the Byzantine Empire and then in the Russian Empire and elsewhere. It was later systematized in the West as the modern state system developed, claiming sovereignty even in the field of religion.

Nevertheless, the basic dualism always implicit within Christianity was not suppressed. This is most obvious in the cases of Roman Catholicism and Calvinism. It is true that in practice the state governments within Catholic Europe, such as Spain and France, exercised almost as great a control over the running of the church as happened in Lutheran and Anglican countries. But the existence of the papacy maintained in principle a distinct religious source of authority. Moreover, even in Orthodoxy, Lutheranism, and Anglicanism the claims of monism remained to some extent restricted by the recognition that fundamental doctrine could not be altered by the state. When in England a Roman Catholic, James II, ascended the throne in 1685, an inherently contradictory situation resulted. The bishops could neither obey him nor disobey him. To obey him could lead to the overthrow of the established Protestant church; to disobey him meant reneging on their religious obligation to accept royal authority. The result was revolution, which the bishops could not sanction but could also hardly deplore. A subsequent law confined the crown to Protestants.

The Modern Period

If the Constantinian model of a single church controlled and protected by a single emperor ceased to be practical once the empire broke apart in the centuries following Constantine's death, the resurrection of that model in national terms characteristic of the Reformation, in which the state holds authority over religion, has also been discredited. The modern church is back very largely with a clear dualism—the separation of church and state, whether the church itself is conceived of in unitary, more or less Roman, terms, or whether it is seen as a more fragmentary network of diverse groups. On the one side, such a fragmentary network may not be wholly unfaithful to the sort of decentralized communion of churches existing in the pre-Constantinian era; on the other, the World Council of Churches, in full existence since 1948, has endeavored to make the network less fragmentary and more comparable with what in the Catholic communion is achieved by the Vatican in Rome.

When in modern times we consider the relationship of Christianity to politics, we must look at four levels: denominations, leaders, laity, and intellectuals. The first is the denominational level. Although in most parts of the world—the major exception being eastern Europe—the specific approach of the various denominational traditions has greatly weakened, these still provide an underlying point of departure, alike for church leaders, the laity, and intellectuals. Anglicans continue to look at the political dimension of religion with preconceptions a little different from those of Lutherans or Catholics, although these differentiations that were still strong at the start of the twentieth century were enormously weakened by the beginning of the twenty-first.

Second, when a political problem arises with religious or moral implications people often say, "The church should speak out," meaning almost always the bishops or other church leaders. An analysis of the relations between Christianity and politics must distinguish carefully between church leadership, the laity, and intellectuals. All three are important. In a traditional but little educated society, the political leadership of bishops may remain all important in an emergency. Yet what is striking is the caution of bishops even in circumstances where one might expect them to give a strong lead. It may well be, nevertheless, that more political guidance has been offered in the late twentieth century by the Catholic episcopate, in particular in the form of pastoral letters, than ever before.

Third, the central relationship between Christianity and politics remains a lay one. Even during the time of the Reformation it was claimed that kings, in excluding the power of the papacy and altering the doctrine and practice of the church, were acting by virtue of a basic lay responsibility for the church and its relationship to society. The state's control of the church was justified in terms of the church membership of those exercising control. It could be seen as a necessary piece of anticlericalism, the only way to curb the huge power bishops and popes had exercised hitherto. Thus a certain kind of lay role shaped the way in which the relationship between religion and politics was conceived. When it was challenged, it was mostly by other lay people. In the early twentieth century in places where the Catholic Church was often discriminated against on account of the dominance of either Protestantism or anticlericalist feelings, Catholics developed new forms of lay activity, particularly Catholic Action, a network of lay groups active in the social arena, together with lay-organized but religiously based political parties, chief among them the Christian Democratic parties that were powerful in Europe and Latin America after World War II. But lay Christian involvement in politics in the modern world, especially in democratic societies, is often and increasingly on a purely individual basis. Although it may be important that a Christian witness be brought to bear in regard to political issues, this generally happens in almost anonymous ways so that it becomes difficult to analyze the interaction of Christianity and politics. Where Christians continue to be mobilized within a pluralist society on a specifically political platform, it is usually on a basis of single-issue politics and may well be symbolic of a feeling of weakness.

Fourth, there is the level of intellectual or charismatic leadership. One may think of Reinhold Niebuhr, Jacques Maritain, Barbara Ward, Paulo Freire, Martin Luther King Jr., and Gustavo Gutiérrez. Perhaps even more poignantly one can recall the roles of Karl Barth and Dietrich Bonhoeffer in challenging Nazism. None of these people could in a formal way speak in the name of the church, and what they said was repudiated at the time by many Christians. Nevertheless, it is the teaching of such individuals that has very largely shaped the subsequent attitudes of Christians toward politics. These are the people who can most aptly be called the heirs to the prophets of Israel. Free to speak less cautiously than ecclesiastical authority, capable of analyzing both Christian faith and contemporary circumstances, they provide the sharp edge of the encounter between religion and politics. It could be claimed that the church as a politically conscious community is guided largely by the inspiration of such action-oriented thinkers, so long as they keep sufficiently in touch with the grass roots and with a popularly recognizable expression of faith.

Finally, beyond the four basic levels, there is the role of the subgroup to consider. Quite often it is in this form that Christianity is most effective in relating to the political order. Consider, for example, the Jesuits, especially as they were before the dissolution of their order in 1773 and as they are again today, or the Clapham Sect, a group of upper-class Anglican evangelicals who did much to bring about the British abolition of the slave trade in the early nineteenth century. Consider the way a century later the Anglican Church Missionary Society lobbied successfully for the establishment of a British protectorate over Uganda, or the influence of the Quakers on legitimizing pacifism and conscientious objection. Maryknoll, the London Catholic Institute for International Relations, and Opus Dei are other contemporary examples of relatively small, well-organized groups with a consistent outlook or lobbying policy operating at the interface of religion and politics with an effectiveness generally unobtainable either by charismatic individuals, able as they may be, or ecclesiastical authorities bound to represent and be restrained by the apathy and mixed viewpoint characteristic of any larger group of Christians.

Five Contrasting Tendencies

Post-Reformation Christianity has made an impact on the shaping of politics, principally in five different, yet overlapping, directions. These five directions may be described as tendencies toward autocracy, nationalism, imperialism, democracy, and, socialism.

Autocracy. Kingship was sacralized and idealized in the Middle Ages, but it was held in check by various other things no less important—the church and the papacy, natural law, even parliaments of various sorts. Ultimate authority in medieval eyes, at least nonpapalist eyes, was usually conceived in terms of the supremacy of law. The Renaissance downplayed everything except the king. Catholicism, Lutheranism, and Anglicanism all went in this direction, although the absolutist tendencies in Anglicanism were rendered ineffectual by the seventeenth-century victory of Parliament over king. Nevertheless, in general, at the beginning of the modern period Christianity's political doctrine appeared to be one supremely justificatory of authority, especially royal authority. Romans 13 was its prime text: "The authorities that exist have been established by God. Consequently he who rebels against the authority is rebelling against what God has instituted." In a democratic age such a text could, of course, apply to democracy, but in a Europe still overwhelmingly autocratic it appeared to justify absolute monarchy and to condemn anyone who sought to change it. The fearfully antireligious consequences of the French Revolution greatly strengthened this conviction in most Catholic minds but, perhaps, hardly less in Lutheran or Orthodox ones. Throughout most of the nineteenth century, in consequence, the central political sympathy of Christianity appeared to be toward autocracy. Even in England most ecclesiastics supported the Tory Party in opposing moves toward a liberalization of the state.

In the nineteenth century some Catholics, like the French priest and philosopher Félicité Robert de Lamennais, saw already how dangerous a policy of crown and altar could be, and, despite the extreme antiliberalism of Pope Pius IX, they were encouraged to some extent by his successor, Leo XIII. The Catholics who formed the Center Party may well have been the best democrats in Germany from the 1870s to the 1930s, and they were followed by the Catholics led by Luigi Sturzo, a priest and political leader who formed the Italian Popular Party in 1919, but both were sacrificed by the Vatican in a vain bid to placate Adolf Hitler and Benito Mussolini. From the age of France's Louis XIV to that of Hitler, the majority Christian view favored autocracy as a political system. It was protective of the no less autocratic character of the pope's rule in the Papal States, which survived until 1870, when they were incorporated into the newly unified Italy, and within the church itself. If the French Revolution had pressed church leadership into the autocratic embrace, so did the coming of communism. It is striking how willing even leading English Catholics were in the 1930s to sympathize with Mussolini and Hitler, seen as comparable with Portugal's António de Oliveira Salazar and Spain's Francisco Franco, because they were all enemies of communism. Only with World War II did the preference for autocracy effectively disappear.

Nationalism. Next comes a fostering of nationalism. Here too the roots are ancient. The English nation-state, proto-model of Europe's political nations, was being fostered by the great monk historian Bede no later than the eighth century. When Joan of Arc encouraged Frenchmen to repel the English invaders of France in the fifteenth century, she had no hesitation in declaring "all those who fight against the holy kingdom of France fight against the Lord Jesus." When John Milton appealed to the English Parliament in 1640, he did not hesitate to ask "Why else was this Nation chosen before any other?" In each case a linked reading of the Bible and national history had fostered the conviction that God had chosen those in France, England, Spain, Russia, or America as his "elect people," to whom he had confided a unique destiny and whose cause, in consequence, had a special sanctity. The Reformation immensely enhanced England's consciousness of being an elect nation, a consciousness carried in the seventeenth century across the Atlantic. Nationalism backed by religion from then to the present has proved a formidably ruthless tool for eliminating enemies and the unwanted.

In many cases, a religious nationalism that started defensively later turned into an offensive force and, in doing so, stimulated counter-nationalisms among its neighbors. Thus Russian and German nationalism stimulated Polish nationalism, and English nationalism triggered Irish nationalism. It is when conflicts of this sort are exacerbated by a religious frontier that the religious undergirding of nationalism is most acute. The English invasion of Ireland from the reign of Elizabeth I onward was very much a Protestant invasion intended to ensure that Ireland remained in Protestant hands. As the Irish insisted for the most part on remaining Catholics, their nationalism took on a predominantly Catholic character. Church and nation went together in self-defense against the linked domination of the English and Protestantism. Although English Protestant nationalism eventually faded at home, in Ireland it remained very much alive. The Ulster unionism born in the twentieth century is essentially the last continuation of an English Protestant identity forged in the years after the Spanish Armada, when England was threatened by invasion from Catholic Spain and Ireland was seen as in danger of falling to Spanish power. The Catholic character of Polish nationalism was forged in much the same way as a reaction to Orthodox Russia and Protestant Prussia's partitioning Catholic Poland.

Nationalist fervor is almost universally heightened by a somewhat mythical reading of history. Nowhere has this been clearer than in Serbia. Here, national identity was for centuries maintained by the institutions of the Serbian Orthodox Church, although the nation itself was divided between the Muslim Ottoman Empire and the Catholic Habsburg Empire. The foundation myth was that surrounding the Battle of Kosovo in 1389, when the Serb prince Lazar died in battle with an invading Ottoman army. The figure of Lazar eating his last meal before the battle and prophesying that one of his lords would betray him was transformed into the image of Christ, a mystical identity stressed in literature and art, particularly in the nineteenth century, when the modern Serb state was coming into existence. No nationalism has had a more intense religious undergirding able to stimulate the most powerful hostility toward Muslims and Catholics.

Imperialism. An aggressive nationalism turns naturally into imperialism, and here close connections with Christianity must be noted. Imperialism expresses the dominance of the Christian West over the rest of the world from the sixteenth to the twentieth century. Europe's sudden, highly successful expansion was seen by Catholics and Protestants alike as best explicable in providential terms. It was perhaps forgotten how many defeats had been suffered in previous centuries, how many previously Christian lands had passed to Islam. If they were remembered, it seemed merely to highlight what was then happening.

It was the Spaniards, as the vast extent of the new world of America dawned on them, together with their own rather easy conquest of huge tracts of it, who first developed a belief that all this must be intended by God. They were, it seemed, uniquely favored. The division of all newly discovered lands between Spain and Portugal by Pope Alexander VI, in 1494, simply confirmed the religious significance of their empire, proclaimed again and again as a tool for evangelization. However badly the native inhabitants of America were treated, however bitterly Bartolomé de Las Casas, a sixteenth-century Dominican, denounced the behavior of the conquistadores, there never was a closer link between government and church than in Spanish America. The king of Spain entirely controlled the church in his overseas dominions even more than he controlled it at home. Nor in this was the Portuguese empire any different. Christianization was conceived as Portugalization even into the second half of the twentieth century. The religious undergirding of Portuguese imperialism, reconfirmed by, for instance, the concordat and missionary agreement with the Vatican of 1940, was a matter at once of ideology, of the political organization of Portuguese overseas territories, and even of the methodology of missionary activity.

As economic and political power in Europe shifted away from the Iberian peninsula to Britain, France, and, later, Germany, something similar happened, although Christianity was seldom tied quite so closely to their forms of imperialism. Nevertheless, the British Victorian sense of being a chosen people, providentially destined to carry the Gospel and its benefits throughout the world precisely through imperial and economic power, was clear. As Edward Benson, archbishop of Canterbury, declared in 1894, "The Church of England is now charged with the world's Christianity."

The scale of the British Empire and the diversity of churches within nineteenth-century Britain made it impossible, however, to establish the sort of relationship between the British Empire and the Church of England that Spain had established between its empire and Catholicism. Britain, on the contrary, early learned the benefits of religious tolerance. It knew that it could rule Catholic Quebec and Hindu and Muslim India only if it did not push Protestantism down the throats of its imperial subjects. Moreover, its willingness to admit Christian missionaries of all nationalities as well as many churches into its dominions ensured a further watering down within the imperial-Christian alliance. Nevertheless, it was also true that the churches were offered in many ways a privileged position in India and elsewhere—the Church of England above all. In a subtle if undefinable way Christianity validated imperialism in moral terms and imperialism offered Christianity what looked like an open door to most of the world and encouraged Asians and Africans to respect Christianity as the religion of both civilization and power. If the effect in Asia was relatively limited, in Africa it proved overwhelming.

The second half of the twentieth century saw this relationship fade away in regard to Europe, only because the empires of Europe faded away while that of the United States—less formal but still more world-embracing—replaced them. Here too a relationship between imperialism and Christianity has been unmistakable. Whereas European missions have declined, American missionaries have greatly increased in number since the 1950s, above all from the most emphatically Protestant denominations, evangelical and fundamentalist. Although it is not the case that all American missionaries are in some way agents of American imperialism, some have been so, even in organizational terms. But far

more important than the latter is the ethos they spread, an ethos that sees America as God's chosen people so that the fortunes of Christianity everywhere are in some way tied to American success, just as in earlier ages they were tied to Spanish or British success. The face offered by Christianity in many parts of Latin America, Asia, and Africa remains a distinctly imperialistic one. What has changed is that the imperialism in question is now American.

Democracy. If Christianity was in many ways a foundation stone for autocracy, it has been no less a nurse for democracy. Both have roots in the Middle Ages. If the church's episcopal government had assumed a highly autocratic form by then—although bishops remained controlled by a canon law of exceptional complexity—Christian life had long had its more democratic side, which took the form in the late Middle Ages of lay confraternities and guilds. It may be in these urban associations that we can find the most lively roots of Western democracy, but they were naturally linked with the medieval development of parliamentary institutions. Although many withered during the Renaissance, the English Parliament weathered royal autocracy and retained its sense of a tradition that dated back at least to the Magna Carta (1215). When civil war broke out in England in 1642, both sides claimed religious sanctioning. King Charles I based his claim on the divine right of kingship; Parliament, and some of its radical supporters, developed a theory of government based on the Bible as seen through Calvinist eyes and on English medieval and parliamentary tradition. What followed the Restoration of Charles II was a mixed constitution upholding both the theory of kingship and the effective primacy in power of Parliament, representing for the most part the landed and the urban middle class. Although this was certainly not a recognition of democracy, the claims of democracy rising to the surface in Oliver Cromwell's army during the civil war years were carried implicitly across to New England and came to prevail in America before being recognized in England.

If modern Western democracy owes most to the American experience and example, that experience would hardly have been possible without its matrix in New England Calvinist Protestantism. It is noticeable that in Europe the countries where democracy, even if still somewhat limited in scope (especially in regard to women), first flourished are almost all ones with a religious culture, either Calvinist or closely comparable—for example, Switzerland, Holland, Scotland. A Presbyterian or Congregationalist form of church government prepared the way for a democratic form of state government. The more divided Protestantism became, as in the United States, the more democracy flourished. This was not merely a matter of forms of government but rather of a whole program of what can be described as the liberal reform of society. It is noticeable how closely the Free Churches in England became linked to the Liberal Party and then to the early Labour Party, which, it has been claimed again and again, owed more to Methodism than to Marxism.

By the late nineteenth century it was probably taken for granted by many that Protestant Christianity made for a liberal and parliamentary government, Catholic Christianity for an illiberal autocracy. Yet, even for that time, this would be a simplification. Catholics in Britain, America, or Germany could be as much at home with parliamentary government as Protestants. Indeed, in Germany the Protestant identity of the kaiser and the political doctrine of Lutheranism kept Lutherans far happier with a rather autocratic state than it did Catholics. Only after World War II, however, did the Vatican and European Catholics as a whole become reconciled to a democratic system. This change occurred under the impact not only of the war and the discrediting of right-wing Catholic politics represented by Marshal Henri-Philippe Pétain and the Vichy regime in France but also of influential Catholic theorists like Jacques Maritain and Christopher Dawson. From this point, any large contrast between Catholic and Protestant forms of Christianity in relation to democracy and autocracy disappears, even though it would continue to exist for a few more years in what were at the time culturally backward areas such as Spain, Portugal, and much of Latin America. Yet it may still seem ironic, in light of past history, that Christians in the late twentieth century have so often taken it for granted that Christianity and democracy go hand in hand.

Socialism. Beyond liberalism, one may say, lies socialism. The Christian encouragement of socialism across the past hundred years is as important as anything in shaping the modern political face of Christianity. William Temple, archbishop of Canterbury (1942–1944) and one of the great Anglican leaders of the twentieth century, once remarked while still a young man that there was only one choice to be made: between socialism and heresy. Socialism can be defined and practiced in many different ways, but the most interesting political question as regards modern Christianity is whether Christianity can avoid being socialist without losing its own soul. Temple's close friend, R. H. Tawney, became the leading theorist of the Labour Party and wrote several of its manifestos and an immensely influential book, *Equality* (1931). He was also a devout Anglo-Catholic. The symbolic model behind Christian socialism is the account in the first chapters of Acts where the first believers "held everything in common. Selling their possessions and goods, they gave to anyone as he had need" (Acts 2: 44–45). It was an ideal that many Christians have sought to implement across the ages, mostly in monasteries or in other forms of "alternative community" removed from the inequalities of the ordinary world. Instead of opting out, however, should one not struggle to realize a greater measure of equality in the whole of society?

If such was the thrust behind various socialistic movements in the nineteenth and early twentieth centuries in Europe, and still more recently in the liberation theology of Latin America, one may come to recognize in retrospect that the great social tragedy of the twentieth century was the hijacking of socialism by Marxism and its consequent wide discrediting. Nevertheless, the concern for social justice apparent in a series of papal encyclicals beginning in 1891 with Leo XIII's *Rerum Novarum* (on capital and labor), in the Second Vatican Council's *Pastoral Constitution on the Church in the Modern World* (1965), and in numerous documents of the World Council of Churches makes sense only within what one can best call a socialist approach. Despite the denunciation of socialism in the 1980s, the age of Ronald Reagan and Margaret Thatcher (both of whom could appeal to Christianity when it suited them), it seems unlikely that the churches will entirely abandon this approach, which appears in the context of the twenty-first century the most plausible reembodiment of the message of the Old Testament prophets Amos and Isaiah. It is countered by those who claim that the true social message of Christianity is one that encourages individuals to be successful and then to be charitable in their success, rather than one focused on the public protection of the poor and the unsuccessful.

These two views may provide the terrain on which the future relationship of Christianity to political society will be fought. The one side is grounded on a tradition that condemned usury in the Middle Ages, that stimulated the trade guilds with their meticulous control of commercial processes, and that has insisted upon concepts like the just wage and the just price—the belief that the determination of wages and prices should depend not only on market forces but on the responsibility of society to ensure that work is rewarded according to the reasonable needs of workers. The other side looks back on the way in which Protestantism provided the ground for the rise of capitalism through its release of the values of individualism and the pursuit of prosperity. It is significant that Tawney, whose *Equality* has been for many the bible of a non-Marxist socialism, was also a historian who wrote the hardly less well-known work *Religion and the Rise of Capitalism* (1926). It may be that Max Weber's attempt (in *Protestant Ethic and the Spirit of Capitalism,* 1920) to link Protestantism and capitalism is too simplified at the theoretical level, but it is not open to question that the modern capitalist economy largely began in Protestant England and expanded first to other predominantly Protestant countries.

The deep theological contrast between Catholic and Protestant approaches to the church, to salvation, and moral life can hardly not be reflected in approaches to public justice and the right ordering of society. It could well be that continental Europe remains primarily shaped by Catholic approaches, modern America by Protestant ones. If so, the one will seek what in a large sense can be called socialist solutions, and the other will remain wedded to capitalist ones. But a socialist Christianity as represented most recently by liberation theology goes deeper than that because it challenges the covert collusion between church leadership and the class of the rich that has dominated Christian history, both Catholic and Protestant, ever since the Constantinian revolution.

Christianity and the Political Order

The impression left by a review of the relations between Christianity and political reality is their flexibility and the near impossibility of considering any one relationship normative. Although Islam began its history in a highly public and military way, which has always provided a normative model for the ideal Muslim political order, no such thing exists in Christianity. In many ways this absence of a model is characteristic of every side of Christianity. Just because Jesus wrote nothing, and what was written about him was written by many different hands in a language other than his own, there is a lack of precision from the start that has enabled Christianity to reshape itself time and again. This is particularly true of its relationship with the political order. Although the intense politicization of the Constantinian era has never quite been thrown off, it cannot obliterate the fact

that for centuries before Constantine Christian life could be characterized by its strongly apolitical and otherworldly values. Christianity's incarnational tendency has made it enter into the culture and sociopolitical construction of remarkably different peoples and periods, and the resulting diversities in the political face of the church can seem overwhelming.

What is there in common? Four elements seem fairly constant. First comes the dualism that separates religious from secular authority. Although, as we have seen, this element has frequently been under threat, it has quickly reemerged again and again, and where it has been denied, the authenticity of Christianity itself can be seen as imperiled. Second, and linked with the recognition that Caesar has rights in an order derived from God but independent of the Christian dispensation, goes a wider recognition of natural law. Although some Christians, especially within the Protestant tradition, have dismissed the claims of natural law, nevertheless their recognition has been one of the most central and characteristic marks of Christian political thought, and it explains why much of the latter is universalist by its nature. Such thought is about the world—God's world—as a whole and not just about Christian societies. Third, there is in the Gospels a hard-to-interpret balance between present and future, between what may be called this-worldliness and other-worldliness. This balance—or, perhaps, jerky pursuit of a balance—leads to quietism on the one hand, to social activism on the other. The central Christian tradition has perennially laid claim to both. Finally, there is the voice of the prophets. Christianity inherited Amos, and Amos refuses to be silenced. In vastly different ages and circumstances the simple duty to speak out in favor of the poor and the oppressed has regularly demonstrated the vitality of the tradition. An absence of such prophetic activity may provide the litmus test as to whether in this or that place the subtle ability of the state and secularity to emasculate Christianity or replace it with a counterfeit model, more congenial to the powers of this world, has indeed succeeded.

See also *Anticlericalism; Calvinism; Capitalism; Catholicism, Roman; Christian Democracy; Christianity in Africa; Christianity in Asia; English Revolution; Enlightenment; Europe, Eastern; Europe, Western; Jesus; Natural Law; Protestantism; Reformation; Social Gospel; State Churches; Vatican; Vatican Council, Second; Weber, Max; World Council of Churches.* See also specific countries and denominations.

Adrian Hastings

BIBLIOGRAPHY

Barnes, T. D. *Constantine and Eusebius.* Cambridge: Harvard University Press, 1981.

Baum, Gregory. *Theology and Society.* New York: Paulist Press, 1987.

Brayshaw, David. *The First America.* Cambridge: Cambridge University Press, 1991.

Brouwer, Steve, Paul Gifford, and Susan D. Rose, eds. *Exporting the American Gospel.* New York: Routledge, 1996.

Burns, J. H., ed. *The Cambridge History of Medieval Political Thought, c. 350–c. 1450.* Cambridge: Cambridge University Press, 1988.

Cullmann, Oscar. *The State in the New Testament.* London: SCM, 1955.

D'Entrèves, A. P. *Natural Law.* London: Hutchinson, 1951.

Frend, W. H. C. *The Rise of Christianity.* London: Darton, Longman, and Todd, 1984.

Hastings, Adrian. *Church and State: The English Experience.* Exeter: University of Exeter Press, 1991.

———. *The Construction of Nationhood: Ethnicity, Religion, and Nationalism.* Cambridge: Cambridge University Press, 1997.

Kee, Alistair. *Constantine versus Christ.* London: SCM, 1982.

Morris, Colin. *The Papal Monarchy.* Oxford: Clarendon Press, 1989.

Norman, Edward. *Christianity in the Southern Hemisphere: The Churches in Latin America and South Africa.* Oxford: Oxford University Press, 1981.

Temple, William. *Christianity and Social Order.* London: SCM, 1942.

Troeltsch, Ernst. *The Social Teaching of the Christian Churches.* London: Allen and Unwin, 1931.

Christianity in Africa

Christian Africa has a continuous history from the second century C.E., antedating the expansion brought by Roman Catholic missionaries since the fifteenth century and Protestant missionaries since the eighteenth century. Christianity in Africa has since its early manifestations in Ethiopia tended to develop distinctively African features. The missionary period (which was coming to an end in the late twentieth century) provided the basis for much of Africa's educational and health services. The dissemination of Christian ideas has had a profound effect on the political systems of the African states, just as the states have influenced the development of the Christian churches.

Within the Roman Empire

In the parts of Africa that lay within the Roman Empire (the Mediterranean coastlands and their hinterlands up to the Atlas Mountains and the desert, and Lower Egypt and Upper Egypt), Christianity spread rapidly as a popular movement, challenging the official cult. After the Roman Empire granted favored status to Christianity early in the fourth century, Africa produced expressions of the faith reflecting local political and social priorities, often at variance with the official forms. The form of Christianity called "Donatist" became the majority religion in Roman Africa (modern Tunisia) and in the less Romanized areas westward. It eventually declined through its failure to take hold outside Africa. From the fifth century, Egypt largely defied imperial pressure for confessional unity in favor of its own confession, often called "monophysite." This confession, influenced by Egyptian thought and religious practice, described the union of the human and divine natures in Christ in a way that to Western Christians appeared to undermine his humanity.

Outside the Roman Empire

Several African states outside the Roman Empire also adopted Christianity. Most important was Aksum in the Horn of Africa, whose king converted in the fourth century. The Upper Nile states of Alwah, Makkurah, and Nobatia united in a single Nubian Christian state in 710. Here, too, the conversion of the monarchs led to the official adoption of Christianity. All these states maintained ecclesiastical relationships (usually monophysite) with Christians in the Roman Empire.

The North African Christian communities dwindled away over several chaotic centuries, the Muslim Arabs being the last of many invaders. In Egypt, where alienation from the Roman Empire led monophysite Christians at first to see Arab rule as liberation, Christians gradually passed from majority to hereditary minority with *dhimmi* status. Dhimmis were Jewish, Christian, or other religious communities under Islamic sovereignty. Although accorded political security, dhimmis were subject to restrictions on religious practice and sometimes to civil disabilities. Nubia, flowering in the tenth century, retained its Christian status until around 1450. Aksum became the kernel of an inland Ethiopian state.

Ethiopian Christianity

Ethiopian Christianity, developed in the highlands, was a unique blend of Judeo-Semitic and African elements and a vital constituent of Ethiopian identity. Ethiopian territorial expansion took with it Ethiopian Christianity, Amharic language and culture, and a distinctive Ethiopic tradition of literature and learning. Despite frequent isolation, Ethiopia maintained a link with Christians elsewhere by bringing its *abuna* (bishop) from the (monophysite) church of Alexandria, in Egypt. Down to the last emperor, Haile Selassie II (reigned 1928–1974), the monarchy (claiming descent from the biblical Solomon) was a periodic source of reform of the church. Equally, the church was a periodic brake on the power of the monarchy, which it has outlived. In the nineteenth and twentieth centuries Ethiopia, as representing an Africa primordially Christian, became a powerful symbol elsewhere in Africa and in the Caribbean. Many African religious movements, especially those asserting a Christianity independent of Western domination, have adopted the name Ethiopian.

Afro-Portuguese Christianity

The Portuguese arrival in Africa in the late fifteenth century initiated an ongoing relationship with Europe and, through the Atlantic slave trade, with the Americas. In a pan-Christian alliance Portuguese troops helped Ethiopia to survive a fierce Muslim *jihad* in the 1540s. Ethiopia shook off a subsequent attempt to bring its church into Latin Christianity. In Angola and Mozambique Christian communities arose from Portuguese settlement, occupation, and intermarriage. In other areas the Portuguese tried to negotiate agreements with African rulers that included the adoption of Christianity. There was at least one notable success: the elective monarchy of Mbanza Kongo at the Congo mouth, whose king accepted baptism in 1491, developed as an African Christian state, uncomfortable with its relations with Portugal and seeking direct links with Rome.

The slave trade, adopted into the economies of African coastal states, produced a vast permanent transatlantic African population. In Brazil an Afro-Catholic leadership emerged with some influence in the Portuguese capital of Lisbon. The diplomacy of one such leader, Lourenço da Silva de Mendonça, "procurator-general of the congregation of Blacks and Mulattos of Our Lady," reached beyond the Portuguese court to the Vatican and secured an explicit, if ultimately ineffectual, papal condemnation of African slavery in 1686.

Early Protestant Christianity

As Portugal's power faded, North European powers succeeded to much of her commercial interest in Africa. In the seventeenth century the Dutch established a colony at the Cape of Good Hope; by the eighteenth, Britain had become the chief carrier for the Atlantic slave trade. These Protestant nations showed little official enthusiasm for the Portuguese policy of extending Christendom. Thus the early Protestant missions to the Khoi, the aboriginal people of the Cape, were by 1742 effectively squeezed out by European settlers.

The Protestant missionary movement combined evangelicalism and humanitarianism in strong opposition to slavery. The establishment of the colony of Sierra Leone (founded 1787; refounded 1792; crown colony of Great Britain, 1808) was intended both to demonstrate the viability of an African economy without slavery and to provide a base for missions in the interior. Its first stable population consisted of Christian Afro-Americans, former slaves. It was later strengthened, after British abolition of its slave trade in 1807, with recaptives from the slave ships, brought to Christianity by missionary effort. Sierra Leone helped to inspire a parallel settlement of Christian Africans from America in Liberia.

The settlements in Sierra Leone and Liberia strengthened the concept of an African Christian civilization—free of slavery, African-led, but in all essentials resembling the Protestant West. The most influential statement of this vision was Thomas Fowell Buxton's *African Slave Trade and Its Remedy* (1840), which argued for British policy in Africa to stimulate agriculture, stifle the slave trade, and develop an independent economy. Suffering Africa could be redeemed by drawing out her own resources, economic and human, and could share in the interrelated blessings of Christianity, commerce, and civilization. The Niger Expedition of 1841, which was intended to give this policy expression, led to the loss of so many lives that the government quickly abandoned the project, but Buxton's ideals continued to influence missions and, even more, the Christian populations in West Africa and the Caribbean, producing the seed of a Christian pan-Africanism. In the Cape similar humanitarian ideals brought the chief spokesman of missions, John Philip (1777–1851), into sharp conflict with the settlers, both Dutch and English speaking, who saw those ideals as a threat to their interests.

Outside the small European colonies, early nineteenth century missions entered into relationships with traditional African states. Frequently they worked with multiple agendas, providing a service desired by the state, such as Western education, while seeking to gather a Christian community within it and to influence social customs in such matters as slave trading, war, or ritual killing. African states, which often found missionaries useful intermediaries with whites, reacted variously. Calabar accepted a gradual modification of religious and social institutions. Abeokuta opened the way to a Buxtonian economic policy and other aspects of modernization. King Moshoeshoe (c. 1786–1870), while slow to identify personally with Christianity, built the Sotho nation by mission-guided religious and social reform. Chief Khama III enthusiastically embraced Christianity as a powerful integrative force in his Tswana state. In Buganda the party identifying with Protestantism emerged victorious in a power struggle with Catholic and Muslim rivals.

Other African states resisted all attempts by Christian missionaries to implement change. Traditional rulers often found the Christian community, living in open breach of many established African customs, threatening to their authority.

Colonial Influences

The rapid European occupation of Africa after 1880 was generally welcomed by the missions as providing conditions in which Christianity could spread freely. Missionary endeavor expanded under colonial rule. Protestant missions flourished most in British territory, Catholic missions in French territory, and both in the Belgian Congo. Colonial conditions created higher demand for Western education, a regular feature of mission activity. The colonial state, always on restrictive budgets, found it economical to use missions to provide the infrastructure for education and health services. With the articulation in the 1920s of a British government policy of subsidizing (and inspecting) mission schools, missions increasingly saw education as a means of influencing Africans in a time of social change, a view reflected in the Le Zoute conference of the International Missionary Council (1926), which urged missions to greater investment in education.

Elsewhere, missionary and colonial interests often collided. Administrative considerations restricted mission entry in areas under Muslim rulers. A substantial Islamic advance followed in Nigeria and Sudan, and missions tended to complain that colonial governments favored Islam. Nevertheless, in spite of these obstacles to missionary work, the International Missionary Council helped to mitigate the conditions of forced labor in East Africa and to secure from Britain a declaration of the importance of African interests in Kenya, which also had white and Indian populations.

Colonial rulers tended to marginalize the educated African leadership that had emerged in the earlier "emancipation phase" of missions and had little sympathy with their pan-African ideals. Moreover, missions in the colonial period were less ready than their predecessors to put Africans in full charge. Some Africans, frustrated, established independent

African-led institutions. Nevertheless, church structures gave Africans leadership opportunities not open to them in most other spheres, and social and political networks wider than the locality or ethnic group. Mission education exposed people to ideas—some of biblical origin, some of secular—that strengthened desires for self-determination. During and after the First World War, a series of movements led by African prophets aroused hostility in colonial governments and ambivalence in missions. In inspiration and intent, these movements represented African appropriations of Christian doctrine and principles and their application to contemporary life.

Emergence of African Nation-States

The dissemination of Christian ideas, mission education, and experience of church life contributed to the movement for decolonization and the emergence of the new African states, which came into being after World War II. However, few mission churches (as distinct from their individual members) were active in the independence movement. The new states followed colonial, not traditional or ethnic, boundaries. Most were religiously plural and, outside the Islamic north, adopted secular institutions. (Botswana, an exception, had an established church.) Early national leaders, frequently from mission schools, articulated themes from Christian teaching. The churches acknowledged responsibilities in nation building through education, health and social services, and moral and spiritual influence. Western Christian missions, rapidly declining in significance locally, were prominent in the movement for Western economic and humanitarian aid to Africa.

The mission situation under colonial rule did not encourage a steady church critique of government, and this critique developed slowly. It emerged first in Ghana, the first new state, originally on specifically religious issues (for example, President Kwame Nkrumah's use of libation to the ancestors at state ceremonies). It intensified when governments tried to take over education and broadened as issues of injustice, corruption, and abuse of power multiplied. The vehicles of criticism included the national Councils of Churches (representing the older Protestant churches) and the Catholic Bishops' Conferences. In Uganda even churchmen who were identified with the traditionally otherworldly revival movement became politically conscious under the regime of Idi Amin in the 1970s. Social and political concern was equally reflected at the regional and national levels in the conferences and publications of the All Africa Conference of Churches and its Association of Member Episcopal Conferences of East Africa. Autocratic rulers responded with favors to African independent, evangelized, and pentecostal churches outside the Protestant mainstream represented by the councils.

The late 1980s and early 1990s saw movements for democratization overthrowing many dictatorial or oppressive regimes. In Madagascar and Malawi the churches were direct agents in effecting political change. In Ghana, Kenya, and even in Muslim Mali they highlighted governmental abuses. In Benin, Congo-Brazzaville, Gabon, Togo, Zaire (now the Democratic Republic of the Congo), and Zambia, church leaders provided the machinery for the transition to democracy. In many countries the churches were the main, or even only, form of civil society still functioning vigorously.

South Africa offers a special case of the democratization process. Here a highly localized thread of Calvinistic theory within the Dutch Reformed Church, one centered on race and the hierarchy of power, was used by a white government to legitimize permanent white rule of the other races. Reformed churches outside South Africa denounced this theory as heretical, as did most black Reformed Christians. Many members of English-speaking churches in South Africa, while not espousing the theory, contentedly accepted the practice. A Christian alternative to the apartheid doctrine was pressed by dissident Reformed ministers, notably Beyers Naude, and affirmed by the South African Council of Churches. For several years the churches, despite many of their white members, formed the most effective legal opposition to the white South African government. Among black Christians several streams of "Black Theology" developed. Some of these simply stood apartheid theology on its head; others affirmed continuity with the established Reformed tradition. All stressed the God-given value and dignity of black identity. In Rhodesia (later Zimbabwe), which entrenched white rule without the ideological underpinning of apartheid, some, but not all, of the leaders of the black nationalist movements identified with the Christian churches.

Two African nations reflect particularly complex relations of religion and identity. Nigeria has perhaps a quarter of the continent's population and roughly equal numbers of Muslims and Christians. Christianity was part of the self-identity of the southeastern territory of Biafra in its secession and the subsequent civil war (1966–1970). Heavy Islamic dominance in the north has encouraged several attempts to make Nigeria an Islamic state. The contiguity of Muslim and Christian populations in the middle belt makes that area a frequent center of religious tension and political struggle. In Sudan power has always lain with the Arabized north, which sees itself as part of the Islamic world. The different identities of many of the African peoples in the south of the country have been sharpened by the widespread adoption of Christianity. The area has known decades of bitter warfare.

The rapid spread of Christianity in sub-Saharan Africa, which has taken place since the mid-nineteenth century under precolonial, colonial, and postcolonial conditions alike, and Christianity's increasing adaptation to African society are likely to remain significant factors in political developments in the continent.

See also *Africa, West: The Mande World; Colonialism; Egypt; Ghana; Independent Churches, African; Kenya; Missionaries; Nigeria; Sudan; Tunisia; Zimbabwe.*

Andrew Walls

BIBLIOGRAPHY

Bayart, Jean-Francois. *The State in Africa: The Politics of the Belly.* London and New York: Longman, 1993.

Elphick, Richard, and Rodney Davenport, eds. *Christianity in South Africa: A Political, Social, and Cultural History.* Berkeley and Los Angeles: University of California Press, 1997.

Fyfe, Christopher, and Andrew Walls, eds. *Christianity in Africa in the 1990s.* Edinburgh: Centre of Asian Studies, 1996.

Gifford, Paul, ed. *The Christian Churches and the Democratisation of Africa.* Leiden: Brill, 1995.

Gray, Richard. *Black Christians and White Missionaries.* New Haven: Yale University Press, 1990.

Hastings, Adrian. *The Church in Africa: 1450–1950.* Oxford: Clarendon Press; New York: Oxford University Press, 1994.

———. *A History of African Christianity, 1950–1975.* Cambridge and New York: Cambridge University Press, 1979.

Sanneh, Lamin. *Piety and Power: Muslims and Christians in West Africa.* Maryknoll, N.Y.: Orbis Books, 1996.

Taddesse Tamrat. *Church and State in Ethiopia.* Oxford: Clarendon Press, 1972).

Christianity in Asia

From the first century the Christian faith entered portions of Asia, which is defined as East Asia (China, North and South Korea, Japan, Taiwan, Macao, and Mongolia), South Central Asia (Afghanistan, Bangladesh, Bhutan, India,

Kazakhstan, Kyrgyzstan, Maldives, Nepal, Pakistan, Sri Lanka, Tajikistan, Turkmenistan, and Uzbekistan), and Southeastern Asia (Brunei, Cambodia, East Timor, Indonesia, Laos, Malaysia, Myanmar, Philippines, Singapore, Thailand, and North and South Vietnam).

According to tradition, Christianity first entered Asia in India with the arrival there in 52 C.E. of the Apostle Thomas. Nestorian Christianity, which derived its name from Nestorius, fifth-century patriarch of Constantinople, came to China in 635. In the next several centuries its missionaries also went to India and Central Asia. Roman Catholic missionaries reached China for a short period in the thirteenth century. Their greatest impact, however, came from the fifteenth to nineteenth centuries as they introduced Christianity into India, Indonesia, Cambodia, Vietnam, the Philippines, China, and Korea.

The Protestant form of Christianity was brought to Taiwan by the Dutch in the early seventeenth century. In the nineteenth and twentieth centuries Protestant missionary representatives from several Western colonial powers went to many Asian countries where Roman Catholics had preceded them. Orthodox Christianity came to Russia in 988, but its message did not reach Central Asia, which throughout most of the twentieth century belonged to the Soviet Union (and in the early 1990s, with the fall of communism there, became several independent nations). Indigenous Christianity, often an offshoot of earlier Catholic and Protestant efforts, has spread widely in many countries since World War II. Early missionization had been closely associated with the expansion of the colonial empires of Western countries. As a consequence, Christians in Asia were frequently considered as representatives of colonial powers.

The response to the Christian message in Asia has varied. Before World War II the most receptive audience were people who previously had adhered to folk religions not intimately associated with one of the major historic religious faiths. This was because, in part, there was no text-based religion with a formal hierarchy among these peoples. Often marginalized culturally, economically, religiously, and politically as ethnic minorities in modern states, they sometimes found Christianity to offer them a path to self-identity and self-esteem.

South Central Asia

Since the time when Christianity first entered India in the first century, both Roman Catholic and Protestant mission groups have been active. Best known of the Catholic missionaries were Francis Xavier (1542–1545), the first foreign missionary to India, and Robert de Nobili (1605–1645), an Italian Jesuit, who concentrated on winning the higher castes to the Christian faith. William Carey and Alexander Duff are considered among the most significant of the Protestant representatives. Active missionary work was prohibited by the East India Company in its territories (1706–1823), but much more freedom came for evangelization when India came under British control in 1858. With independence from Great Britain in 1947, India declared itself a "secular" state, guaranteeing equal protection for all religions and noninterference by the state in matters purely religious. Although there is freedom for local Christians, the government has made it difficult for expatriate missionaries to enter the country.

Despite many instances of local persecution, Christianity has been able to spread freely, particularly by movements of mass conversion in Andhra Pradesh in the southeast, very early in the Portuguese colony of Goa, and among tribal groups in the north among the Khasi, Garo, Mizo, and Naga peoples. Catholics, Protestants, and Orthodox Christians constitute only about 4 percent of the total population of India, but in the small northern states of Mizoram, Meghalaya, and Nagaland the percentage is a dominant 85 percent. Despite the relatively small number of Christians, nearly two hundred indigenous Indian mission societies have sprung up with a total of eleven thousand missionaries.

The Apostle Thomas may also have introduced Christianity to Sri Lanka. Subsequent Christian influence came through colonial efforts by the Portuguese in 1505, the Dutch in 1655, and the British in the nineteenth century. During the past 275 years the Christian population decreased from 21 percent to 8 percent, largely because of the influence of nominalism, a weak form of Christianity, and the anti-Christian attitude of Buddhism, which was declared Sri Lanka's state religion in 1972.

Although the Christian message came early to Pakistan through the Nestorians in the eighth century and through the Jesuits in 1594, no lasting results were achieved. Modern Catholic Christianity began in 1842, after the conquest of Sindh by the British. The early twenty-first century the work of the Catholic Church, whose members constitute less than 1 percent of the population, was maintained by three indigenous congregations of sisters and ten foreign orders and congregations of priests, brothers, and sisters.

Protestant Christianity was introduced to Pakistan in 1833. A large revival that occurred in 1904 ultimately resulted in six of the thirty "scheduled" Hindu castes becoming Christian by 1930. Despite the fact that Pakistan declared itself an Islamic republic in 1956, nine years after independence, many new Protestant agencies entered the country. In the early 2000s Protestant Christianity numbered no more than 2 percent of the population. This, however, totals about 900,000 believers, making it one of the largest Christian communities in the Muslim world. The social impact of the Christian faith, both Protestant and Roman Catholic, includes a large number of local schools, five seminaries, four Bible schools, and over thirty hospitals providing fifteen percent of Pakistan's medical care. Adherents of all Christian persuasions face the pressure of increasing Islamization.

Bangladesh, formerly East Pakistan, became independent from Pakistan in 1971 and after a period when it was a secular state (1971–1988) became an Islamic republic. Both Catholics and Protestants came into this area in the nineteenth century, but growth of Christianity was minimal except for mass movements among the tribes of the Chittagong Hills. The total Christian population of the country is less than 1 percent. Most of the Christians are from a Hindu background, creating a natural barrier between them and the 85 percent Muslim majority in the country. Despite this religious and political barrier, more Bangladeshis are adopting the Christian faith than at any previous time.

Whatever Christian influence existed early in Afghanistan's history was wiped out by Timur, a Mongol conqueror, in the fourteenth century. In the early twenty-first century the Christian community comprised slightly less than 0.1 percent of the population. It was composed largely of foreign technicians, diplomats, and visitors. Very few of the local populace have converted to Christianity in the face of fierce opposition by radical Islamic factions fighting for control of the country. Although the military occupation by the United States and its allies that began in 2001 has brought some social and political freedom to Afghanistan, there has been no significant increase of the Christian population.

The Himalayan region along the northern boundary of India has a population of about twenty-two million and is composed of Nepal, a Hindu kingdom; Bhutan, with Buddhism as the state religion; and Sikkim, formerly a Buddhist hereditary monarchy and now an Indian state. All of these states have traditionally been resistant to the Christian faith, but revival movements have occurred, so that nearly 15 percent of Sikkim's population and 10 percent of Nepal's people have committed themselves as Christians. Proselytization is forbidden by the government in both Nepal and Bhutan. Christians face increasing difficulties because of the ongoing conflict between "Maoist" rebels and government forces in these two countries.

The five states—Kazakstan, Kyrgyzstan, Tajikistan, Turkmenistan, and Uzbekistan—that were formerly part of the Soviet Union are now independent and seek to overthrow, often with internal conflict, the yoke of communism. Although declaring themselves to be secular or undetermined, their populations are largely Islamic, in many cases a folk variety influenced heavily by animism. Christians, largely Orthodox of immigrant minorities, number as low as 4–5 percent in Tajikistan, Turkmenistan, and Uzbekistan and as high as 11 percent and 27 percent in Kyrgyzstan and Kazakstan, respectively. Protestants, particularly in Uzbekistan, face persecution from the government even though Christianity is legal.

Southeastern Asia

Although Buddhism was declared the state religion of Myanmar (Burma) in 1961, this government edict was withdrawn in 1965, and there is now freedom of religion, albeit under a totalitarian government. For nationalistic reasons, the government expelled all foreign missionaries in 1966. It has not interfered directly with the work of the churches.

Nestorians reached Burma in the tenth century, Catholics by 1544, and Protestants by 1813. In the early twenty-first century Baptists, whose founder in Burma was Adoniram Judson, and Catholics are the two largest Christian groups. Most of the Baptist Christians are not found among the Burmese peoples but among the Karen, Chin, and Kachin ethnic groups in the northern section of the country. Protestants number 5 percent of the population and Catholics 1 percent.

Christianity first reached Indonesia when Portuguese traders and missionaries came to the Moluccan isles (Maluku) in 1512. Several Catholic missionary orders came later in the sixteenth century and gained many converts, often promising them Portuguese protection against enemy neighboring kingdoms. Dutch traders expelled the Portuguese, including missionaries, in 1605, thus inaugurating the eras of the Dutch East Indies Trading Company

(1605–1800) and Dutch colonial control (1816–1945). Dutch ascendancy in the area resulted in the arrival of many European and, sometime later, American mission agencies. Some of the established churches, largely Dutch Reformed, were under state control. The Dutch colonial administration occasionally prohibited missionary work in socially and politically sensitive areas.

The growth of Christianity in Southeastern Asia has been uneven, with large people movements to Christ in areas dominated by traditional folk religion. Beginning in the mid-1960s, some of the greatest growth of both Protestant and Catholic Christianity in the world has occurred in Indonesia. A revival, sparked largely by lay people, occurred on the island of Timor in the eastern part of the archipelago in the early 1960s. Other movements to Christ resulted from the violent anticommunist repression following the abortive attempt by communist rebel forces to take over the Indonesian government in 1965. The Indonesian constitution, formulated in 1945 after the country's independence, granted freedom of religion despite the country's overwhelming Muslim majority. This freedom, however, was not extended to those following localized animistic religions. Religion was defined under the "five principles" (*pancasila*), adopted in 1965, to be those that had written texts. In effect, this meant that Indonesians have the freedom to embrace a belief in Islam, Protestantism, Catholicism, or Hindu-Buddhism. The easiest, least politically complicated option for many was to choose the Christian faith.

Areas of Indonesia that have experienced the greatest growth in Christianity are east and central Java, Karoland in north Sumatra, and east and west Kalimantan. For all of Indonesia Protestants average 9 percent of the total population of two hundred million, and Catholics represent 3 percent. Christians number 30–85 percent in many of the island provinces such as East Timor (annexed in 1975, independent since 2002), Irian Jaya (annexed in 1963), Maluku, and the E. Lesser Sunda Islands.

The Philippines is one of only two predominantly Christian countries in Asia. Catholic priests reached these islands under the protection of Spanish armor in 1565. After five decades of evangelization directed toward the Malayo-Indonesian inhabitants, the entire country nominally embraced Christianity. Many Protestant mission agencies, with the door opened by American annexation of the Philippines in 1898, sent their representatives in the early 1900s. As a group they were outnumbered by the predominantly Catholic population. Nevertheless, they established comity agreements—plans for dividing the territory and work in such a way as not to compete directly with one another.

About 1 percent of the population, largely mountain dwellers dispersed through the nation, continue to believe in traditional folk religion. Muslim believers, tracing their origin to 1380, number about 8 percent and live largely in the southwest, Mindanao, the Sulu islands, and Palawan. Roman Catholicism, including the Philippine Independent Church, remains the dominant faith of nearly 80 percent of the population. Adherents of Protestant Christianity number 8–9 percent but have grown dramatically in the last decade. Filipino Christians, following a tradition that goes back about 500 years, are sending missionaries to the Pacific Islands and Asia. Since the time of American rule, church and state in the Philippines have been separated.

After the Philippines and East Timor, Vietnam is the most Catholic country in Asia. In the first sixty years of missionary work, beginning from 1580, there were eighty thousand Catholics in the north and fifty thousand in the south. Growth continued at a slower pace until the late 1800s, but always with much persecution, until 1884, when France imposed a protectorate as French Indochina (including what is now Vietnam, Laos, and Cambodia). Catholic Christianity continued to grow in both North and South Vietnam, although with the victory of communism in the north, as many as six hundred thousand Catholic believers took refuge in the south, where they formed an influential anticommunist bloc supporting the government. With the fall of the regime in the south in 1975, and reunification of South and North Vietnam under the communists, the church, 9 percent Catholic and less than 1 percent Protestant, has continued to exist but with the repression characteristic of a Marxist regime.

The evangelical church of Vietnam in the south was formally recognized in 1971 by the government. Minority peoples are still harassed for their faith, but many have house fellowships. A new Ordinance of Religion in mid-November 2004 calls for a tightening of state control over religion.

Growth of Christianity in both communist Laos and Buddhist Kampuchea (Cambodia) has been very slow, with Christians numbering 2 percent and less than 1 percent of the population, respectively. Both the Catholic and Protestant churches suffered under the Pol Pot regime in the 1970s, but have grown much better into the twenty-first century. In Thailand the Christian faith, with no more than 1 percent of the population classified as adherents, has not been able to penetrate the Buddhist majority. Most of its converts have come from the Vietnamese, the Chinese, the Montagnards, and other ethnic minorities in the north of the country.

Catholic Christianity arrived in Malaysia with the Portuguese in the sixteenth century, and Protestantism was brought later by the Dutch and the British. The most responsive group has been the Chinese, followed by the Indians and aboriginal minorities. Very few Christians are found among the Malays, who are almost entirely Muslim. Protestants number about 5 percent and Catholics 4 percent. With similar ethnic and linguistic composition, the Republic of Singapore is 8 percent Protestant and 6 percent Catholic, with adherents largely from the Chinese and Indian populace. Because of Singapore's multiethnic and multifaith composition, the government has imposed restrictive legislation limiting overt evangelism.

East Asia

Christianity first entered East Asia during the Tang Dynasty in 635, with the arrival of Nestorian missionaries in China. A Franciscan Catholic missionary reached Beijing in 1294, but Catholicism did not establish itself until the Jesuits, led by Matteo Ricci (1552–1610), came at the end of the sixteenth century. Protestant Christianity commenced in 1807 with the arrival of Robert Morrison (1782–1834) of the London Missionary Society.

Both the Protestant and Catholic missionary movements were hindered greatly by being associated with the "unequal treaties" arising out of British efforts to import opium into China. (These treaties were imposed on China by Great Britain, which defeated it in 1840, and by other nations. When missionaries followed foreign diplomats and business people entering China under the terms of the treaties, the missionary movement came to be linked with imperialism and militarism.) Subsequently, Christianity was known as the foreign religion. With the coming of the communist People's Republic of China in 1949, Christian missionaries were forced to leave China, and Chinese Christians, with both Catholics and Protestants numbering about two million, faced a difficult period of persecution, forced unity, loss of denominational identity, and destruction of meeting places and Bibles. This persecution was particularly intense during the Cultural Revolution (1966–1976). Churches began to reopen in the late 1970s, and since that time the number of Christians has increased greatly, with estimates placed anywhere from fifteen to sixty million. Catholic believers are divided between the government-approved Catholic Patriotic Association and those many congregations that retain their loyalty to the pope in Rome. Protestant Christians are found in the China Christian Council, related to the Three-Self Patriotic Movement, in thousands of autonomous house churches, and in student Christian fellowships on many college and university campuses. Technically, the constitution guarantees freedom of religion, but this has been interpreted diversely in many parts of the country. In some areas, freedom does indeed exist; in other sections, persecution and harassment continue. In the southwestern areas of China—Yunnan, Guangxi, and Guizhou—Christians from among the minority nationalities outnumber Han Chinese (culturally Chinese) Christians.

In the 1990s and into the 2000s a great migration has occurred in China, bringing tens of millions to the cities in order to find jobs and a better life. Both Protestant and Catholic churches have developed new departments for social work, often in cooperation with the government and NGOs, in and outside of China, to give help in job-searching, education for children, and medical needs. China's embrace of the World Trade Association (WTO) and her successful bid for the 2008 Summer Olympics have given it a new relationship to the world community, one with both social and economic benefits.

Christianity in both its Protestant and Catholic forms first came to Taiwan in the early 1600s. At this time about six thousand of the tribal people converted to Christianity under the Dutch, but this movement ceased with the Dutch expulsion by the Chinese in 1662. Protestant and Catholic missionaries returned to the island in the mid-1860s, and, apart from the World War II period, have been engaged in evangelism and nurturing of churches. Despite a great influx of missionaries coming after the fall of China's mainland to the communist People's Republic of China in 1949, Christian growth for both Catholics and Protestants has not exceeded 5 percent of the population. Among the mountain tribal people, now labeled original inhabitants, Christianity is espoused by at least 50 percent of the population of three hundred thousand.

Christianity came to Hong Kong in 1842 after the territory was ceded to Great Britain. Christians are estimated to make up about 15 percent of the population. With the return of Hong Kong to China in 1997, its churches were promised continued freedom of religion within their own territory as long as they did not interfere with churches on the mainland. A vigorous Hong Kong Evangelism 2000 program was promoted by Protestant churches.

Catholic missionaries reached Macao, a tiny peninsula about forty miles west of Hong Kong, in 1557 and used it as a base to send missionaries into China. Protestants arrived in 1807. About 10 percent of Macao's people are Christian. Much effective evangelism has been done in recent years among workers who have come from mainland China. With Macao's reversion to China in 1999, its churches were expected to be under the same guidelines as those in Hong Kong.

Catholicism entered Korea in the last decade of the eighteenth century, largely through Koreans who had learned of the faith in China. Korean scripture portions—translations of various books of the Bible—were distributed in Korea from China in 1831, and one year later the first Protestant missionary entered the country. These various Catholic and Protestant contacts led to many efforts of indigenous evangelization among the populace, whose major religious faith was shamanism, a religion centering on spirits and spirit mediums. When religious freedom was gained in 1882, as a result of a treaty with the United States, many Koreans openly asked for baptism. Protestant Christians in Korea actively resisted the former Japanese colonial regime in 1919 and participated in moves to strengthen the country's national identity.

By the early twenty-first century the Christian population of South Korea, with nearly twelve million Catholics (6 percent) and Protestants (28 percent), exceeded that of all other nations in Asia except the Philippines. Church growth continued at a rapid pace of nearly 6 percent annually in the south, bolstered by vigorous evangelistic efforts and also by the favor of the government, which viewed Christianity as an ideological means of resisting the encroachment of communism. In North Korea, a strong center of Christianity before its separation from the south following Word War II, all religions have been harshly suppressed, and the number of Christians is unknown.

The Catholic presence in Japan commenced in 1549 with the visit of Francis Xavier. By 1593 Catholic Christians numbered three hundred thousand, but with government prohibition in 1611, a severe persecution occurred. The church went through two hundred years of silence, emerging only when Catholic missionaries returned in 1859. Prot-estant missionaries arrived in Japan the same year and engaged in medical and educational activities. When the government removed all anti-Christian activities in 1878, both Catholics and Protestants were able to engage actively in evangelism. The Japanese constitution of 1889 made Shinto, the ancestral religion of Japan, the state religion. In December 1945, as a result of Japan's defeat in World War II, Shinto was separated from the state, and freedom of religion was guaranteed to all. More Protestant and Catholic missionaries, proportionally to the population, have been working in Japan than in any other country. Despite this, Christians number only seven hundred thousand, about 3 percent of Japan's total population.

See also *China; Colonialism; Korea; Missionaries.*

Ralph R. Covell

BIBLIOGRAPHY

Athyal, Saphir, ed. *The Church in Asia Today: Challenges and Opportunities.* Singapore: The Asia Lausanne Committee for World Evangelization, 1996.

Barrett, David B., George T. Kurian, and Todd M. Johnson. *World Christian Encyclopedia: A Comparative Survey of Churches and Religions in the Modern World.* Oxford; New York: Oxford Univeristy Press, 2001.

Covell, Ralph R. *The Liberating Gospel in China: The Christian Faith among China's Minority Peoples.* Grand Rapids, Mich.: Baker, 1995.

Hoke, Daniel E., ed. *The Church in Asia.* Chicago: Moody, 1975.

Hunter, Alan, and Kim-Kwong Chan. *Protestantism in Contemporary China.* New York: Cambridge University Press, 1993.

Johnstone, Patrick. *Operation World: A Day-by-Day Guide to Praying for the World.* Grand Rapids, Mich.: Zondervan, 1993.

Sunquist, Scott W., ed. *A Dictionary of Asian Christianity.* Grand Rapids, Mich.: Eerdmans, 2001.

Christianity, Baptist

See *Baptists.*

Christianity, Lutheran

See *Lutheranism.*

Christianity, Orthodox

See *Orthodoxy, Greek; Orthodoxy, Russian.*

Christianity, Pentecostal

See *Pentecostalism*.

Christianity, Protestant

See *Protestantism*.

Christianity, Roman Catholic

See *Catholicism, Roman*.

Church Property

See *Taxation*.

Citizenship

Citizenship refers to the liberties, rights, and obligations that define an individual's membership in the nation-state. The terms of membership and participation in the nation-state evolved in Europe and North America in the nineteenth and twentieth centuries. The conditions for membership in society are on the whole framed in terms of the rights and obligations of individual citizens in their relations with one another and with the state authority. Together with struggles over the place of the church (or different religions) in national public life and the issues of distributive justice, the terms of citizenship—that is, the admission of the lower strata into full civic, political, and economic national membership—have been and remain the defining issue of the modern era.

Definitions of Citizenship

With the emergence of the modern nation-state, the medieval traditions of corporatism and privileged classes gave way to the principle of the direct relation of each and every citizen to the authority of the state. The legal and institutional codification of this relation took the form of equality before the law for even previously excluded groups such as those defined as dependent persons (wage laborers) and certain religious "out groups" such as Jews, who in most western European countries gained full legal citizenship only after the French Revolution (1789–1799). From John Locke's *Letter on Toleration* in 1689 through the end of the nineteenth century, the issue of equal rights for religious minorities (whether Catholics and dissenters in seventeenth-century England or Jews in nineteenth-century Germany) was at the center of the raging debate over the meaning of citizenship in western Europe.

As the nineteenth century progressed the legal equality of citizens came to be perceived as the right of the franchise. In Europe the struggles over the right to vote were the single most important aspect of political integration in the nineteenth century. By the turn of the twentieth century and in the years following the First World War when universal male suffrage was granted in most western European nations, the terms of citizenship were being increasingly perceived as containing a certain modicum of economic welfare and maintenance. These changing and expanding definitions of citizenship became political issues, often subject to struggle. In western Europe these issues were at the center of often violent conflict throughout the nineteenth and early twentieth centuries.

In lectures delivered in 1949 in Cambridge, England, the British political scientist T. H. Marshall framed the historical evolution of the nature of citizenship in terms that since have become classic. Marshall distinguished among the civil, political, and social aspects of citizenship. The civil element of citizenship was made up of those rights necessary for individual freedom: liberty of person; freedom of speech, belief, and faith; and the right to private property and so to contract and due process. The political aspect of citizenship was the right to participate in the decision-making process of society and so the right to exercise political power as an elector. The social aspect of citizenship was defined as the right to share in the material standards of society and to live a life that would partake of that society's full material and social heritage. The historical benchmarks used by Marshall to identify the founding moments of the first and second aspects of citizenship in England were the Reform Act of 1832 and the Electoral Act of 1918. In many countries people continue to struggle over the social aspects of citizenship such as welfare and other entitlements. For Marshall, however, the trajectory of social citizenship in England ran from expansion of the Workmen's Compensation Act in 1906 to the Old Age Pension Act of 1908 to the National Insurance Act of 1911 and the Unemployment Insurance Act of 1920 to the National Health Service Act of 1946.

The attributes of citizenship are nowhere fully institutionalized, and the concrete implications of these criteria have never been fully agreed upon. In the United States struggles over, among other things, welfare entitlements, labor relation laws, minimum wage agreements, women's rights, and the place of homosexuality in American culture—that is, struggles over the place of diversity and public recognition of diverse cultural and ethnic groups and traditions as well as the legal representation of that recognition—are all, to no small degree, struggles over the definition of citizenship. Significantly, in many parts of the world struggles over citizenship continue to revolve around issues of religion. These struggles may take the form of tensions between religious law and secular constitutionalism (in Israel and in the Islamic world from Turkey and Iran to Pakistan and Indonesia) or efforts to gain toleration and equal rights for religious minorities, especially when the minorities also share a unique ethnic designation (for example, the aboriginal cultures in the United States, Canada, and Australia—countries that have dealt with the claims of these groups in very different ways).

Current debates in western Europe and the North Atlantic contexts over the meaning and extent of social entitlements as well as over the very principles of national integration (as in the province of Quebec's relationship to Canada or Scotland's relationship to Great Britain) highlight the degrees to which the different definitions and criteria of citizenship are contested in different parts of the world. For example, throughout eastern Europe and east central Europe the emerging civic polities are all struggling to define new principles of social organization and solidarity along a fault line of so-called principles of demos, which establish absolute individual equality among the citizenry, or principles of ethnos, which privilege one or another ethnic group as more representative of the nation, its values, and social heritage than other groups. The exclusive and exclusionary aspects of the ethnos model have been especially attractive to the political elites in many of the Balkan states and the states of the former Soviet Union.

Similarly, many of the exclusionary definitions of citizenship and of membership and participation in the nation-state are predicated along religious lines, which in fact often overlap with ethnic divisions with tragic results such as the 1992–1995 war in the former Yugoslavia. Unfortunately, precedent can be found for such exclusionary practices, ultimately belying any possible integration. One need only look at the 1947 breakup of India and Pakistan following the end of colonial rule and at the formal division of Ireland in 1920 into a self-governing, predominantly Catholic south and a British-governed, predominantly Protestant north.

No given polity can be defined solely by its acceptance of one or the other of these models. Instead, a polity, especially ethnically and religiously heterogeneous societies, should be defined by a mix of both—that is, by differential definitions of the terms of mutuality, solidarity, and obligations and rights of citizenship of different ethnic groups within society.

Citizenship and Historical Development

The very existence of multiple definitions of citizenship in different parts of the world and even in different parts of Europe lends credence to the claim that the definitions of citizenship reigning in the West are not universally relevant and are, moreover, rooted in the particular path of historical development that characterized western European societies. Thus citizens and scholars increasingly have realized that the trajectory of the West was unique and not repeatable, and that, to understand the particular developmental paths of different societies, it is more and more important to understand the models of citizenship evolving in those societies.

In contemporary Europe the historical trajectory of nation building and state formation is of major importance to understanding the terms of citizenship. The long, drawn-out process of state making and nation building in western Europe was characterized by the only gradual integration of different ethnic and religious groups into one national identity (characterized by its own territory; economy; legal, educational, and cultural systems; and historical memories). Central to this process were the different features of linguistic assimilation, social mobilization, and, at a much later date, mass education and the effects of mass media. In this process, and as the American sociologist Daniel Lerner noted more than thirty years ago, the formation of "psychologically mobile personalities" enabled the establishment of "empathy" between individuals of different ethnic and religious traditions. This empathy rested on the replacement of traditional, often religiously defined, criteria of solidarity and collective membership and participation with the "modern" values of individual rights and universal citizenship.

Providing the background for these developments was a unique set of historical features. These included large autonomous cities that provided independent locales for the organization of different social interests; an autonomous legal system (rooted in the legacy of Roman law) with traditions of legal reciprocity; and a recognition of representative institutions (the medieval *Stände*). These factors, together with the critical separation and independence of the church from the empire and the relatively little overlap among ethnic, religious, class, and political groups, all provided a degree of pluralism and recognition of social interests independent of the state and its rulers that tended to be unique in world history. As a result, to different extents the countries of western Europe saw, first, the crystallization of a national identity out of different ethnic groups. In England, France, and Spain this development occurred around an ethnic core group and in Greece or Switzerland without such core groups. The formalization and universalization of the criteria for membership and participation in this national entity followed, based on the principles of citizenship and mass participation in the social and political life of the nation.

In other parts of the world this process was very different. In eastern Europe, for example, the nation-state—or more precisely the administrative-bureaucratic structures of state rule—emerged (after the First World War) before the nation itself. Contributing to this process were the political elites who in the nineteenth century, while leading the nationalist movements in east central Europe, did not identify national independence with more than their own corporate interests. Moreover, the democratic component of national movements was submerged in these corporate interests; social reforms were minimal. The very ethnic fragmentation of these societies led to the view that the state itself produces national sentiment and not the other way around. By the mid-nineteenth century all the ruling elites had agreed that the nation stemmed from the state and were focusing solely on the state's role as a cultural, administrative, or coercive producer of nationalism. Thus the type of mass mobilization around social reforms that characterized Western nationalism and united diverse communities into one national identity did not come to pass.

The pattern of development in eastern Europe had clear implications for the problem of citizenship in contemporary east central Europe. The necessary preconditions for modern forms of citizenship—based on the legal autonomy of the individual agent (freed from communal, religious, or ethnic identities) and existing in legal and political equality with other citizens—did not develop. Instead, the historical development of this region has seen the continued existence of strong ethnic and group solidarities that have continually thwarted the emergence of those legal, economic, and moral individual identities on which modern democratic forms of political identity are founded.

Thus in the most general of terms the existence of the individual social actor—freed from ascriptive identities—who was the foundation of Western, democratic models of social citizenship stemmed from the twofold historical moment of national integration and then the universalization of citizenship within the nation-state. In east central Europe, the first process took place in only a partial and mediated manner. The second process of universal citizenship was never realized.

Eastern Europe is not, however, a unique case, and latecomers to the process of modern state building and the formation of a democratic citizenry face daunting tasks in institutionalizing the principles of citizenship that are identified with western European regimes. High dependence on an external (extraterritorial) center of power, low levels of elite and social unification, and equally low levels of institutional readiness for the demands of mass participation in the political process, together with high demands for a politics of economic redistribution, all combine to make the implementation of citizenship on a Western model highly problematic.

Contemporary Debates over Citizenship

Even more important than the structural and historical differences of various societies in understanding current debates over citizenship is the very ideological rejection of some of the tenets of Western citizenship that began to emerge in the final decades of the twentieth century across the globe. Principles of individual autonomy and liberty, which have been strongly identified with the citizenship process, are being increasingly questioned from the perspective of different national or even civilizational heritages. From areas as diverse as Southeast Asia and the Islamic Middle East new political elites are offering very different ideas of what the principles of citizenship may mean. Certainly the Islamic militancy movement that has spread to different parts of the world is questioning the universality of the Western model. With its rejection of secularization as part of the "package" of modern citizenship and its reaffirmation of the relevancy of sometimes ethnic, sometimes religious criteria to the terms of citizenship, the Islamic world (including Muslims in western European societies) is challenging Western conceptions of citizenship in new ways with as-yet-untold results.

This is true not only in those parts of the world that one typically thinks of as Muslim—the Middle East, for example—but also in many of the countries of the former Soviet Union. From the reemergence of shamanism among the Yakuts in northeastern Siberia to the importance of Orthodox Christianity to postcommunist Russian nationalism, religious identities continue to serve as the center of people's individual and collective senses of self, providing them with the core terms of membership and participation in the political and social orders. Moreover, these modes of membership contrast and often conflict with more civic ideas of a liberal political order founded on the equality of the citizenry before the law. Thus, while the 1980s saw the Soviet leadership alarmed at the growth of Islamic ritual and belief within its central Asian republics, the 1990s witnessed growing ethnic competition and conflict in the region, intensified by the various religious commitments of the parties involved.

To some extent the contention over the terms of citizenship and participation in the nation-state taking place in such parts of the world is echoed within western European societies as well. For example, the overriding value of secularization, once identified with liberal ideas of citizenship, seems increasingly problematic. The important role played by the Catholic Church in the transition to democratic rule in Spain as well as the continual resistance waged by the Catholic Church to the Communist Party in Poland point to very different types of political action than those associated with the more conservative role of the Catholic Church before the Second Vatican Council in the 1960s. Likewise, the role played by the clergy in the overthrow of the apartheid regime in South Africa and in the processes of democratization in other African countries (such as Kenya) have led scholars to reassess the role of religion in the modern world.

The growth of religious, especially Christian pentecostal, affiliations in Latin America, Asia, and the United States also have increased social conflict over fundamental issues of citizenship such as individual rights, autonomy, and what is known in the United States as individual choice. Debates over abortion, school prayer, homosexuality, and most especially the role of religion in public life, all refer in one way or another to the fundamental terms of individual citizenship and the role of the state in organizing and directing the life of its citizenry.

Some observers have described these debates as ones over liberal versus republican visions of citizenship—that is, a vision of the state as a morally neutral realm where its citizens are free to pursue their own vision of the good versus a vision of a "moral community" of citizens dedicated to a particular vision of good, a vision that takes precedence over that of any particular member (citizen) of the community. As this debate is influenced by and draws on the changing nature of religious affiliations in the United States and the world at large, it becomes clear that the idea of citizenship was as conflict-ridden and problematic at the close of the twentieth century as it was at its onset.

See also *Civil Society.*

Adam B. Seligman

BIBLIOGRAPHY

Arjomand, Said, ed. *The Political Dimensions of Religion.* Albany, N.Y.: SUNY Press, 1993.

Bendix, Rienhart. *Nation-Building and Citizenship.* Berkeley and Los Angeles: University of California Press, 1977.

Dahl, Robert. *Polyarchy: Participation and Opposition.* New Haven: Yale University Press, 1971.

Eisenstadt, S. N. *Modernization, Protest, and Change.* Englewood Cliffs, N.J.: Prentice Hall, 1966.

Hall, John, ed. *States in History.* Oxford: Blackwood, 1986.

Lindsay, A. D. *The Modern Democratic State.* New York: Oxford University Press, 1962.

Maier, Charles, ed. *Changing Boundaries of the Political.* Cambridge: Cambridge University Press, 1987.

Marshall, T. H. *Class, Citizenship, and Social Development.* Westport, Conn.: Greenwood Press, 1973.

Civil Disobedience

Civil disobedience is the act of nonviolently disobeying a state-imposed law or command on grounds of conscience. Nonviolence distinguishes civil disobedience from armed rebellion or revolution. Conscience distinguishes it from mere law breaking. Other traits are sometimes added to the definition: that the disobedience must be public and the legal penalty accepted, that only unjust laws may be broken, or that the goal must be reform and not overthrow of the state.

These additional traits do not always apply. Civil disobedience cannot always be public and the penalty accepted; for example, consider those conveying slaves to freedom and those who hid Jews in Nazi-occupied Europe. The act cannot always be violation of an unjust law; those protesting nuclear arms testing could not violate the authorizing laws directly, so they violated admittedly just trespass laws in order to bring the issue to the public. The goal has not always been reform; Mohandas Gandhi's campaigns in India from 1920 until Indian independence in 1947 aimed not at reforming British rule but at getting rid of British rule. Even nonviolence has not been invariable; consider war protestors' destruction of draft records and other property to oppose U.S. involvement in the Vietnam War in the 1960s and 1970s.

There are, then, different types and strategies of civil disobedience depending on the goals sought and practical considerations of effectiveness. Rescuers in oppressive states must act secretly. Reformers utilize public, nonviolent, opinion-mobilizing techniques. Those aiming at the fall of a regime may engage in large-scale acts of noncooperation against state commands.

Moral Foundations

Civil disobedience is grounded in the understanding that there are obligations superior to the obligation to obey the commands of a state. Typically these are obligations to God, to natural law or natural right, or to a community. In this vein, Jewish midwives, during captivity in Egypt, fearing God more than Pharaoh, disobeyed Pharaoh's command to kill all newborn males (Exod. 1:15–17). Shadrach, Meshach, and Abednego braved death by fire rather than obey idolatrous commands by Nebuchadnezzar (Deut. 3). Christians, commanded to "render . . . to Caesar the things that are Caesar's" (Matt. 22:21), and informed that the powers that be are of God and should be obeyed (Rom. 13:1–7), nevertheless held that, in case of conflict, God must be obeyed rather than Caesar (Acts 5:29). The early Christians followed this understanding even to martyrdom.

In other traditions, Gandhi, drawing on certain aspects of his Hinduism and traditions East and West, led a movement of noncooperation against India's British colonial rulers. In classical Greece this understanding was embodied in literature in Sophocles' heroine Antigone, who defied the Theban king when he forbade her to bury her brother, and in

philosophy in the distinction between what is right by nature and what is merely conventional. In classical Rome it was embodied in the natural law tradition. Marcus Tullius Cicero (106–43 B.C.E.), statesman and philosopher, gave this tradition its classic expression, holding that there is a true law, right reason, which accords with nature, applies to all, is unchangeable and eternal, and cannot be invalidated by human law. God is the author of this law. This tradition paralleled that in the Christian tradition of the Apostle Paul (c. 10–62) and cohered with that of St. Augustine (354–430) and St. Thomas Aquinas (1225–1274). It was continued by the Dutch jurist Hugo Grotius (1583–1645), modified by the English political theorist John Locke (1632–1704) into a theory of natural rights, and in this form given expression in the American Declaration of Independence (1776), the French Declaration of the Rights of Man and of the Citizen (1789), and the United Nations Universal Declaration of Human Rights (1948).

Notable examples of civil disobedience include religious resistance to idolatry or persecution from ancient times to the present, religious and secular conscientious objection and resistance to military service, and opposition to war taxes, to war itself, or to particular wars, and to arms races and types of arms, such as nuclear weapons. Slavery evoked civil disobedience. In the United States, slaves were spirited out of the South by sympathizers who assisted them on the Underground Railway, and there was resistance in the North to the fugitive slave laws, which would have forced them back. In the era of Nazi conquest in Europe in the 1930s and 1940s, Jews were similarly sometimes hidden or aided in their escape and in a few instances defended by mass noncooperation. Civil disobedience was a major part of Gandhi's efforts for civil rights in South Africa in the early years of the twentieth century, as it later was to free India from British rule. Civil disobedience was employed as well in other nationalist movements, and it has been a mainstay of labor and environmental movements around the globe.

In the United States, civil disobedience was a galvanizing force in the civil rights movement of the 1950s and 1960s. At the beginning of World War I, it played a significant role at a crucial time in the women's suffrage movement, and it has been used, to a greater or lesser degree, in virtually all civil rights movements since then, including those for homosexuals, and in the struggle over abortion. Civil disobedience has become a standard part of protest against injustice and has been used even in totalitarian and authoritarian societies.

An estimated 200,000 to 500,000 demonstrators marched on Washington, D.C., for civil rights and jobs on August 28, 1963. The march is now considered one of the culminating moments of the civil rights movement.

Indeed, the use of massive noncooperation against state commands played a major role in the collapse of the communist governments in Eastern Europe in 1989, but it failed spectacularly in China that same year, when the government violently crushed democracy movement protests in Tiananmen Square.

Theory and Practice

Objection to slavery provided the impetus for Henry David Thoreau's essay "Civil Disobedience" (1849), the best-known defense of civil disobedience in the nineteenth century. In the twentieth century, Gandhi and Dr. Martin Luther King Jr. provided the principal theoretical expositions on civil disobedience and led the most admired and emulated movements. Each of these men captured the imagination of the world as they helped bring about dramatic change. Gandhi, drawing on his interpretations of Hinduism and combining these with like elements he found in Christianity and Buddhism (as well as Thoreau), developed the concept of *satyagraha,* which he defined as "truth-force." *Satyagraha,* which employed civil disobedience, aimed to achieve justice and reconciliation without violence or hatred. King, an ordained Baptist minister, drew on Gandhi, as well as his own interpretation of the proper social applications of Christian love and Jesus' Sermon on the Mount,

the tradition of natural law, and the principles of the Declaration of Independence, to provide moral direction to the civil rights movement of the 1950s and 1960s.

King, whose public life, from 1955 until his assassination in 1968, spanned a period of tense years of race relations in the United States, believed that unjust privilege is rarely given up without a struggle. He was more ready than Gandhi to acknowledge that a degree of coercion must be used in the struggle for civil rights, but the goal remained justice and reconciliation, so the means must be nonviolent and persuasive. King would typically pick a symbolic site for protest that would capture the public imagination or present a clear conflict between justice and injustice. After trying for negotiation—rarely effective without coercion—he would prepare for a campaign of nonviolent protest, usually involving civil disobedience. Protesters were to accept voluntarily the penalty for disobedience of the law to show that there was no disrespect for law as an institution. Nonviolence was necessary on principle (good ends require pure means) and as a tactic (nonviolence helps to defuse the issue of "law and order," while any harsh or violent reaction to the protesters, a common occurrence, poses the moral issues in the clearest possible terms). King's use of nonviolence resulted in a kind of morality play, highlighting the confrontation between justice and injustice, reasonable protest and unreasonable resistance. Such a campaign holds the potential to be both coercive and persuasive. It created a crisis that required a decision or response. In addition, by presenting the confrontation as a contest between good and evil, it was often effective in bringing about political action against the injustice and in delegitimizing the injustice.

The anti–Vietnam War movement of the late 1960s and early 1970s increasingly practiced civil disobedience. Among the more prominent members of that movement were the Berrigan brothers, Daniel and Philip, Roman Catholic priests (though Philip left the priesthood). Perhaps their most memorable tactic was destroying draft files, which they did in two well-publicized protests. The first occurred on October 27, 1967, at the Baltimore Customs House, where Philip led a group of four in pouring blood on draft records. The second protest took place on May 17, 1968, at Catonsville, a Baltimore suburb, where the brothers led a group of nine in burning draft files with homemade napalm. Using dramatic tactics, fleeing from authorities, and appearing in famous trials (as the Baltimore Four and the Catonsville Nine), the brothers helped merge the secular and Roman Catholic antiwar movements and contributed to a rethinking, by many Roman Catholics and others, of their support for the Vietnam War and "just war" theory.

Civil disobedience soon became a tactic in other protest movements, including the antiabortion and sanctuary movements. In 1973 the U.S. Supreme Court decided, in *Roe v. Wade,* that the U.S. Constitution protects abortion. The decision provoked protest that continues a quarter of a century later, conducted mainly by Roman Catholics and evangelical Protestants. The best-known antiabortion organization employing civil disobedience in this protest movement was Operation Rescue. Following the biblical injunction to "rescue those who are being taken away to death; hold back those who are stumbling to slaughter" (Prov. 24:11), the group attempted to peacefully block entry to abortion clinics. By the early 1990s, federal legislation—including legislation designed to curb racketeering—and strong penalties had largely curbed these "rescues."

In the early 1980s, the sanctuary movement employed civil disobedience in its attempt to shelter political refugees in the United States illegally from deportation to their conflict-ridden homelands, particularly El Salvador or Guatemala, where they faced possible retribution. Individual congregations, loosely linked nationally, would formally declare their churches sanctuaries for the refugees, many of whom were attempting to get to Canada. This movement drew on an ancient tradition of churches offering sanctuary or shelter to those fleeing civil punishment.

Critics note that civil disobedience may fail and that rebellion, revolution, and war are sometimes justified or required. Others argue that civil disobedience may produce disrespect for law and that it may even lead to general lawlessness and to eruptions of violence and anarchy. Still, it has become an often effective part of the arsenal of protest in democratic and nondemocratic nations.

See also *Civil Rights Movement; Colonialism; Gandhi, Mohandas Karamchand; Human Rights; King, Martin Luther, Jr.; Natural Law; Pacifism; Sanctuary; Social Justice; Violence; War.*

William R. Marty

BIBLIOGRAPHY

Childress, James F. *Civil Disobedience and Political Obligation: A Study in Christian Social Ethics.* New Haven, Conn.: Yale University Press, 1971.

Cohen, Carl. *Civil Disobedience: Conscience, Tactics, and the Law.* New York: Columbia University Press, 1971.

Gandhi, M. K. *Non-Violent Resistance (Satyagraha).* New York: Schocken Books, 1961.

King, Martin Luther, Jr. *Why We Can't Wait.* New York: Signet, 1964.

Moskos, Charles C., and John Whiteclay Chambers II, eds. *The New Conscientious Objection: From Sacred to Secular Resistance.* New York: Oxford University Press, 1993.

Pateman, Carole. *The Problem of Political Obligation: A Critical Analysis of Liberal Theory.* New York: Wiley, 1979.

Thomas, Owen, ed. *Henry David Thoreau, Walden, and Civil Disobedience: Authoritative Texts, Background, Reviews, and Essays in Criticism.* New York: Norton, 1966.

Walzer, Michael. *Obligations: Essays on Disobedience, War, and Citizenship.* Cambridge, Mass.: Harvard University Press, 1970.

Civil Religion

Civil religion is a set of cultural symbols that draw connections between a nation and some conception of the sacred. These symbols usually consist of beliefs and practices that make explicit reference to a divine being (for example, prayers for the well-being of the nation or acknowledgment of God on the currency). Some treatments also include symbols that legitimate the nation with reference to the transcendent or with some other idea of ultimate reality (such as fundamental human rights, the laws of nature, or a Marxist notion of universal class struggle).

The idea of civil religion was first advanced by the French philosopher Jean-Jacques Rousseau (1712–1778) in his effort to understand the social principles underlying democratic societies. Rousseau argued that it was in the self-interest of individual citizens to form cooperative relationships with one another but that the resulting restrictions on individual freedoms required certain beliefs that would render the new relationships legitimate. In traditional societies a common religion had often provided such beliefs, but in modern nations a unifying set of beliefs needed to be found that would not exclude citizens who ascribed to minority religions or who were nonreligious. The religious wars between Protestants and Roman Catholics that devastated seventeenth-century Europe persuaded Rousseau that organized religion was likely to be divisive and therefore should be replaced, or at least augmented, by beliefs that pertained to the entire nation but that also inspired devotion in the way that organized religion had done in the past. Rousseau suggested that nations would (and should) develop a civil religion that would embrace all citizens, giving them reasons to practice civic virtue and to be patriotic.

The ingredients of civil religion, according to Rousseau, were to be relatively simple so that citizens could agree upon them and remember them. They should include belief in the existence of a divine being or order characterized by its power, wisdom, and goodness. They should also include some conception of the future, of justice, and of punishment, and they should emphasize the sanctity of the social bonds that link people together and the laws to which they are subject. Rousseau emphasized that civil religion should promote tolerance. The divine being in Rousseau's conception is thus a symbol that crystallizes the qualities people should admire in their nation and willingly commit themselves to upholding. Insofar as the divine being is both benevolent and just, and insofar as the life to come (whether on this earth or in heaven) is regarded positively, citizens will presumably be motivated to think well of their society.

Together, these ingredients provide a concept of reality in relation to which the specific activities of leaders can be assessed, for example, by providing cause for ending a particular regime but giving continuity to the nation's higher values and traditions. This concept of reality nevertheless legitimates the basic institutions of the nation by encouraging citizens to realize their dependence on a sovereign power,

Jean-Jacques Rousseau.

the ways in which their dependence on one another is conducive to achieving their highest values, and their need to be tolerant of one another.

Contemporary Views

Interest in the idea of civil religion was rekindled in the 1960s, in particular by the work of sociologist Robert N. Bellah. Focusing primarily on the United States, Bellah stressed that civil religion exists to some extent among all people as the way in which each nation interprets its historical experience in the light of transcendent reality. The most important aspect of civil religion is thus a "myth of origin" that explains how a people came into being, who their heroic leaders were, and what the principles were on which their nation was founded. A myth of origin unifies citizens by pointing to common ancestors and a shared heritage. It also emphasizes times of crisis during which citizens worked together or perhaps engaged in conflict to resolve some fundamental ambiguity in their vision of who they should be. For the United States, stories about the early colonists, about the War of Independence and the Civil War, and about such figures as George Washington, Benjamin Franklin, and Abraham Lincoln provide a myth of origin in which current events can be interpreted in light of a time when sacred principles were perhaps especially clear. Following Mircea Eliade, a historian of comparative religion, Bellah suggested that ordinary time is often distinguished from mythic time, the latter being a period set apart in which humans communicated directly with the gods or took on characteristics that made them larger than life. In civil religion, mythic time is the period of founding or prehistory of a people.

Besides a myth of origin, civil religion includes beliefs that legitimate who is or who is not regarded as eligible for the full rights and privileges of citizenship. By drawing distinctions between citizens and noncitizens, civil religion reinforces loyalties among the former and encourages them to exercise their civic responsibilities. It also provides reasons for excluding certain groups from participating in civic activities. As definitions of citizenship are redefined (for example, to include people who do not own property or to permit women or eighteen-year-olds to vote), the civil religion is generally reinterpreted to legitimate these changing definitions. More negatively, the civil religion stigmatizes certain groups deemed to be threatening to the sanctity of the nation (for example, conspirators, witches, communists, aliens, subversives).

Civil religion also includes ideas about the goals, purposes, or destiny of a nation. These ideas help to mobilize the energies of citizens, especially when they are called on to sacrifice for their country. The goals specified by civil religion range from those that are specific (such as waging war against an ungodly foe) to more general or abstract values (such as upholding freedom or promoting world peace). The civil religion undergirds the nation's purposes by showing that its goals are not arbitrary or mean-spirited but are consistent with sacred ideals and moral absolutes. Because political leaders are charged with the task of setting national goals and mobilizing commitment to those goals, civil religion is often articulated in the speeches of the leaders.

In contemporary discussions of civil religion, commentators have paid considerable attention to the rituals that maintain it. National holidays, state funerals, elections, and speeches by major leaders provide special occasions for reinforcing the civil religion. In the inaugural addresses of U.S. presidents, for example, some explicit reference to God is not uncommon; inaugurations typically include prayers and swearing of oaths on the Bible. Some rituals also provide citizens with an opportunity to reenact parts of the myth of origin, thus reminding them of its importance and altering it in light of present circumstances. Enactments of major battles are one example. Rituals are important because they bring people together physically or through mass communication, encouraging them to recognize that they are a people with a collective identity and stirring their emotions so that abstract symbols and historic narratives become personally meaningful.

Research on civil religion suggests that it is not as consensual or unified as earlier writers assumed. The effective functioning of civil religion depends on its capacity to incorporate themes and traditions that are meaningful to different segments of the population or that have been prominent at different periods in history. Western countries typically incorporate themes from Judaism and Christianity into their civil religions, but they also draw on ideas about republicanism or democracy that stem from Greek and Roman traditions or the Enlightenment. A study of Italy suggests that its civil religion is composed of several historic layers, including popular Christianity, Roman Catholicism, democratic liberalism, socialism, and activism. Japan's civil religion combines elements of Shinto and Buddhism. Muslim countries generally combine elements both of Islam and of modern secular political theory in their civil religions. The new nations that have emerged from the former Soviet Union have had to draw together democratic and Eastern Orthodox ideas with other themes to forge legitimating myths of origin. Because of the different traditions from which civil religions are generally composed, it is often helpful to distinguish the unifying (and often implicit) values on which they are based from "public theology," which articulates a particular tradition or vision of what the nation should be.

The Connection with Organized Religion

The relationships between organized religion and civil religion appear to vary considerably. On the one hand, many instances can be found in which the strength of one reinforces that of the other. For example, societies with large numbers of clergy are more likely to include specific references to God in their public commemorations than are societies with relatively few clergy. On the other hand, religious leaders who push for a specific interpretation of the civil religion sometimes find themselves with few resources when these interpretations fall into disfavor with particular regimes. In either case, it is important to acknowledge the differences between civil religion and organized religion. The former is more likely to represent a "least common denominator" faith, whereas the latter can emphasize the traditions of particular groups. The former may not be compelling because it focuses on the entire nation, whereas the latter (especially when it is organized around congregations) can reinforce local understandings and loyalties.

In general, the process of political modernization has resulted in greater differentiation between organized religion and political institutions, but it has not led uniformly to a weakening of civil religion. Because civil religion is largely cultural, not institutional, strong symbolic links can be maintained between the nation and various conceptions of the sacred, even when formal separation of religion and politics is present. In such conditions, the civil religion provides a way to legitimate the separate activities of religious and political functionaries, encouraging them to fulfill their particular roles and thus permitting organized religion to be a voice in the public arena without presuming it to be the only voice. Recognizing the continuing presence of civil religion is important in scholarship on modern societies because it shows that religion is not entirely "privatized" or relegated to the personal lives of individuals.

Current Approaches to Scholarship

The study of civil religion has mostly taken the form of qualitative research focusing on a single country over a period of time. Studies of this kind are valuable for sorting out the complex threads of a particular civil religion and for showing how it changes in response to new economic or political realities. For example, research on civil religion in South Africa shows how it has been shaped by British and Dutch colonialism, by indigenous religions, and by the country's experiment with the racial segregation of apartheid. A few studies have examined civil religion comparatively, and some have done so by developing quantitative measures. For example, it is possible to examine constitutions, national anthems, and presidential speeches to determine the presence or absence of religious content.

Current scholarship appears to be shifting away from an emphasis on civil religion toward concepts such as national identity; public religion, ritual, and theology; and civil society and civic engagement. One reason for this shift is that civil religion may have fairly limited value as a concept for understanding the complex relationships between religion and politics, especially when it is defined narrowly to mean the use of religious language in reference to the nation. Conversely, civil religion becomes too broad a concept to be useful when it is defined as any transcendent event used in relation to the nation. In addition, scholars have sometimes objected to the idea of civil religion because it appeared to be used as a prescription for a certain kind of cultural renewal instead of as an analytic concept.

Normative Concerns

Concerns have been raised about civil religion from a normative perspective. These concerns indicate that the study of civil religion often focuses on established or elite views, instead of on the folk religion or popular beliefs and practices of ordinary people. Some writers point to the importance of sectarian civil religion—that is, beliefs about the relationship between sacred teachings and civil authorities that are espoused by religious groups outside the social mainstream. The civil religions evident in teachings of American Quakers, Mennonites, or Jews are examples. Other writers emphasize the need for a more diverse conception of civil religion, especially one that moves beyond tolerance toward a more positive evaluation of diversity itself. In these treatments, civil religion is said to benefit from internal conflict and disagreement that encourages it to change or to engage in self-criticism.

Recent discussions about the decline of civic engagement in a large number of advanced industrial societies nevertheless point to the continuing importance of examining some of the core ingredients of civil religion. Civil society is strengthened not only by specific networks of social interaction, or by instrumental norms that tell people how to work together, but also by unifying symbols that define them as having a common history and sharing a common destiny. Engaging in cooperative pursuits and working for the public good is often difficult to justify in terms of self-interest alone. Rousseau's insight that people need to know that it is legitimate to sacrifice some of their own freedoms to work together remains valid.

Although recent scholarship often does not refer explicitly to civil religion, the debate to which the idea of civil religion remains most relevant is that between writers who argue in favor of procedural agreements as the basis for democratic society and those who argue for substantive agreements. The former suggest that deep symbols, values, and traditions of the kind embodied in civil religion are likely to be disruptive and should thus be replaced by greater emphasis on laws, governmental procedures, and rational modes of public discourse. The latter argue that commitment to the common good cannot be sustained by procedures alone but must be reinforced by citizens' identification with the community, collective memory, and shared values.

Recent scholarship also emphasizes that popular understandings of civil religion raise normative questions about the future of democracy among societies experiencing changes in religious composition as a result of immigration. In the United States a large majority of the population continues to believe that America is a "Christian nation" founded on Christian principles and morally strong because of its commitment to biblical principles. Yet the reality is one of increasing religious diversity, including large numbers of Muslim, Hindu, and Buddhist immigrants. Among the population convinced of the importance of historic understandings of U.S. civil religion, resistance to non-Christian immigrants is acute. In western Europe, a more secularized civil religion that applauds tolerance and purely privatized spirituality has come into similar conflict with immigrant groups who believe that religion should be practiced more collectively and publicly.

Considerations of civil religion raise the important normative concern of whether deeply taken-for-granted shared narratives serve primarily to preserve the status quo or whether they can be usefully examined and deployed in the interest of progressive social change. Historic narratives that define a nation's collective purposes are often reduced to short phrases about "freedom," "prosperity," "God's blessings," "rags to riches," or "our way of life." When this happens, audiences tacitly accept that something appropriate has been said, but they are less likely to question the rhetorical uses of these phrases. A strong democracy requires more than tacit agreement; it also necessitates taking time to reflect on the meanings of widely shared symbols and myths. In the past, civil religion has helped to legitimate campaigns against slavery and has encouraged compassion and social justice in the form of private charity and ameliorative welfare legislation. These efforts typically required cultural inertia to be overcome through the work of advocacy groups that questioned shared assumptions and raised consciousness about the gap between ideals and reality.

See also *Citizenship; Civil Society; Communitarianism; Holidays; Individualism; Nationalism; Nativism; Presidents, American; Tocqueville, Alexis de; Traditionalism; Theology, Public; Voluntarism.*

Robert Wuthnow

BIBLIOGRAPHY

Angrosino, Michael. "Civil Religion Redux." *Anthropological Quarterly* 75 (2002): 239–267.

Bellah, Robert N. *Beyond Belief: Essays on Religion in a Post-Traditional World.* New York: Harper and Row, 1970, chap. 9.

———. *The Broken Covenant: American Civil Religion in Time of Trial.* New York: Seabury, 1975.

Davie, Grace. "Global Civil Religion: A European Perspective." *Sociology of Religion* 62 (2001): 455–473.

Goldberg, Chad Alan. "Social Citizenship and a Reconstructed Tocqueville." *American Sociological Review* 66 (2001): 289–315.

McClay, Wilfred M. "The Soul of a Nation." *Public Interest* (Spring 2004): 4–19.

Noll, Mark A. *America's God: From Jonathan Edwards to Abraham Lincoln.* New York: Oxford University Press, 2003.

Rousseau, Jean-Jacques. *The Social Contract and Discourse on the Origin of Inequality,* edited by Lester G. Crocker. New York: Washington Square Press, 1967.

Stout, Jeffrey. *Democracy and Tradition.* Princeton: Princeton University Press, 2003.

Wuthnow, Robert. *America and the Challenges of Religious Diversity.* Princeton, N.J.: Princeton University Press, 2005.

———. *American Mythos: Why Our Best Efforts to Be a Better Nation Fall Short.* Princeton, N.J.: Princeton University Press, 2006.

Civil Rights Movement

The modern civil rights movement in the United States arose in the mid-1950s around the initial aim of dismantling the system of Jim Crow segregation, which had developed in the South in the decades following the abandonment of post–Civil War Reconstruction in 1877. Although resistance to white domination has been a constant of the African American experience in the United States, the modern civil rights movement can be said to have begun in December 1955, with the onset of the bus boycott in Montgomery, Alabama. The civil rights phase of the struggle gradually gave way in the mid-1960s to what has been called the "black power" movement and was then dealt a critical blow with the assassination of Martin Luther King Jr. in April 1968.

The role of religion in social movements constitutes one of the notable "silences" in the study of collective action. What causes this silence is not clear. What is clear, however, is that the neglect of the topic seriously understates the often close connection between religion and collective protest activity. Religious institutions have long been among the most common social settings within which protest is likely to develop. Throughout history, religious groups have been the key source of animating ideologies, leaders, rank and file activists, and other organizational resources for countless social movements.

This connection between churches and protest movements has been especially true in the United States, where rates of church attendance and professed religiosity have remained high in the face of the trend toward secularization in virtually all other Western democracies. From the nineteenth-century abolition movement to the present-day Nation of Islam, from pro-life activism to the enduring tradition of religious pacifism, a long and varied list of American social movements has been nurtured and shaped by an equally long and varied list of American religious traditions. But perhaps no social movement better illustrates the close connection between religion and collective action in the United States than the modern civil rights movement. This essay highlights the role of the black church in the movement and, by extension, its influence in setting in motion other instances of religiously inspired activism around the globe. The example of Archbishop Desmond Tutu in the South African anti-apartheid struggle is only one prominent instance. Tutu was awarded the Nobel Peace Prize in 1984.

The Black Church as the Organizational Center

It would be hard to overstate the black church's central role in the civil rights movement. As the opening act in the civil rights struggle, the Montgomery bus boycott illustrates, even as it helped to cement, the close relationship between the movement and the southern black church. On December 1, 1955, Rosa Parks, a black woman, was arrested for quietly defying Montgomery's policy of segregated seating on city buses. E. D. Nixon, the head of the state chapter of the National Association for the Advancement of Colored People (NAACP), the country's oldest and most influential civil rights organization, posted bail for Parks. The next morning he called Martin Luther King Jr. and Ralph Abernathy of Montgomery's First Baptist Church to apprise them of the events of the previous evening. The three men agreed to organize a meeting of church and other civic leaders that evening at the Dexter Avenue Baptist Church. The purpose of the meeting was to call for a one-day symbolic boycott of Montgomery's buses. The boycott was to take place the following Monday, December 5.

The proposal was enthusiastically endorsed by Montgomery's black leadership, and the ministerial elite who formed the core of the leadership agreed to use their pulpits on Sunday to call for support for the boycott. The call worked. On Monday, between 90 and 95 percent of Montgomery's black bus patrons stayed off the buses. Buoyed by

Rosa Parks is fingerprinted after being arrested for refusing to sit at the back of a segregated bus in Montgomery, Alabama, in December 1955. This act by Parks was the spark that helped launch the civil rights movement in the United States.

the unprecedented show of solidarity by Montgomery's black community, the leaders laid plans that evening at yet another meeting at Dexter Avenue to continue the boycott until the group's demands were met. The civil rights struggle had been joined.

The events in Montgomery illustrate the four organizational contributions made by the black church to the movement. These contributions were the provision of "free space" in which to mobilize, a group of established leaders, a communications network, and members of the congregation to serve as the movement's "foot soldiers."

Free space. Scholars of social movements and organizers alike have long stressed the importance of free space to the embryonic beginnings of collective action. Free spaces are the social settings controlled by prospective insurgents and within which they can safely engage in the activities necessary to launch a protest movement. Within the oppressive confines of the Jim Crow South, the black churches—and, in particular, the largest and best-heeled urban black churches—were the most significant institutional free spaces available to the burgeoning movement. In Montgomery, even though an NAACP official initiated action, his first move was to mobilize the black clergy and secure the sponsorship of the church. From that moment on control and direction of the movement and of the organization it spawned (the Montgomery Improvement Association) passed to a network of black ministers and the churches they headed. As the sociologist Aldon Morris has noted (in *The Origins of the Civil Rights Movement,* 1984), what was true in Montgomery was true for the movement as a whole. Organized protest activity was centered in local networks rooted in the black church. The reason was simple: the black church was the central organization and the only truly independent institution in the southern black community.

Leaders. The church also provided the movement with a large share of its formal leadership. Martin Luther King Jr., who first achieved national prominence in Montgomery, is only the most obvious example. But without denying King's unquestioned centrality to the movement, it is important to note that his leadership was a reflection of the more general pattern. King was only the most prominent of a host of black ministers who spearheaded the struggle. In fact, he was not even the first to do so. In 1953 the Reverend Theodore Jemison of Baton Rouge, Louisiana, had organized a bus boycott on which the Montgomery campaign was modeled. Considering that the movement was so closely tied to the church, the dominance of black clergy in formal leadership roles is hardly surprising. Established ministerial leadership was only one of the organizational resources the movement appropriated by tying itself closely to the church.

Communications. Although we tend to think of social movements as large-scale national events, in fact most movements are collections of local campaigns, knit together by a dense communications network to create a semblance of national breadth and coordination. Such was the case with the civil rights movement. The black church served as the basis for the communications network that transformed Montgomery into a regional coalition of local movements that eventually garnered national support and attention. The nature of this communications network is suggested by the previous reference to the Baton Rouge bus boycott. When King, Abernathy, and the other leaders in Montgomery were laying plans for the boycott, they knew they had to talk with Jemison. They knew this because they were linked to Jemison through a series of formal and informal ministerial networks that connected black clergy throughout the South.

Similarly, King's ties to other locally prominent black ministers facilitated the spread of the boycott tactic well beyond Montgomery. The Reverend Charles Steele visited King in the winter of 1956 and returned home to Tallahassee, Florida, to organize a boycott there. In short order, other campaigns, patterned along the lines of the Montgomery movement, were organized in Atlanta, New Orleans, Birmingham, Chattanooga, and Rock Hill, South Carolina. As in Montgomery, all were church-based operations headed by a minister. From this collection of local campaigns the Southern Christian Leadership Conference (SCLC) was forged at a gathering held in Atlanta in January 1957. With King at the helm, SCLC was to spearhead the national movement through the 1960s.

Church members. Perhaps the single most remarkable feature of the Montgomery campaign was the extraordinary rate of compliance of black bus riders with the demands of the boycott. The key to the 90–95 percent compliance rate lies in the church's imprimatur, which legitimized the boycott. More generally, throughout its heyday the movement was able to mobilize large segments of the black community because of the fundamental embedding of the struggle in the black church. By centering the movement in the church, civil rights leaders were able to recruit congregations virtually en masse, thereby sparing themselves the much more difficult task of developing a membership from scratch.

In his 1963 book *Why We Can't Wait,* King likened the recruitment of movement volunteers at church-based mass meetings to the "invitational periods that occur every Sunday morning, when the pastor projects the call." Indeed, it may be more accurate to say that participants in church-based campaigns were not so much recruited from the ranks of active churchgoers as it was a case of church membership itself being redefined to include civil rights activity as a primary requisite of the role.

The Black Church as Cultural "Tool Kit"

Ann Swidler (in "Culture in Action: Symbols and Strategies") has described culture as a kind of "tool kit" that facilitates action. This analogy points to another set of functions performed by the black church in the civil rights movement. These functions relate to the church's role as a repository of cultural materials, ideas, and symbols that motivated and legitimated protest activity. We can distinguish three cultural resources that the church afforded the movement: an ideology that legitimated the movement, the mass meeting that became the movement's basic building block, and a rhetorical style that arose from the imagery and language of black preachers. We will look at each of these in turn.

Ideology. The civil rights movement drew ideological inspiration from a number of sources. No one embodied the unique combination of these sources better than did Martin Luther King Jr. In his blending of familiar Judeo-Christian themes, conventional democratic theory, and the philosophy of nonviolence, King brought to the struggle a compelling, yet accessible, mix of ideas. At the core of this rich ideological stew was Christian theology. In employing traditional Christian themes, King not only rooted the movement in one of the ideological bedrocks of American culture but diverged sharply from the more conservative theological stance that had tended to mark the southern black church in the early decades of the twentieth century. In part, this conservatism can be seen as little more than the temporary ascendance of one perspective in black theology over another—a stress on "other-worldly reward" over an emphasis on the everyday demands of the social gospel. This orientation, however, must also be seen as a rational adaptation to a repressive system of caste restrictions. That is, whites' efforts at social control during this period encouraged an "acceptable" content in the overt teachings of the black church.

The fact that King and other young black ministers saw fit to break with the dominant "accommodationist" tradi-

tion was due both to their youth and the theological perspectives to which they had been exposed and to the relative freedom from white control they enjoyed by virtue of the large, urban congregations they headed. Regardless of the factors that allowed them to make the break, however, their reappropriation of the traditions of the Social Gospel served the movement well in a number of ways.

First, it resonated with the experience and values of the southern African American community, steeped as it was in the church and its teachings. Any account of the movement's ability to mobilize the black masses must begin with its foundation in the language and imagery of traditional Christian theology. Second, the themes of Christian forgiveness and redemptive healing that were central to King's philosophy were instrumental in gaining the broad support the movement received in white America. These themes were deeply reassuring to a white America burdened (as it still is) by guilt and fear of black anger and violence. King's emphasis on Christian charity and nonviolence promised a redemptive and peaceful healing of America's long-standing racial divide. He thus invited a level of white support for the struggle that had until then been unimaginable. This support included the active backing of a host of religious institutions (for example, the National Council of Churches) and prominent figures outside the world of black Protestantism (among them Reinhold Niebuhr and Abraham Heschel). Finally, when coupled with the movement's appropriation of Christian themes, the practice of nonviolence effectively tied the hands of southern segregationists. That is, by embodying the image of peaceful, Christian petitioners, the movement drastically reduced the options of social control that had been open to its opponents. The free hand that southern authorities had once enjoyed in repressing civil rights forces was gone.

Mass meetings. From Montgomery onward, the mass meeting was the movement's basic organizational building block. Almost always held in a church, the mass meeting became the principal vehicle by which people were mobilized for action. In its basic form, it was but a transparent variant on the Sunday church service. Each meeting opened with announcements and the singing of "freedom songs," often included the kind of invitational period described by King, and generally closed with singing and one or more rousing "sermons" by movement leaders.

Although the form was initially adapted by King and other activist ministers for use in the movement, it became a staple of civil rights organizing more generally. Organizers in such nominally secular groups as the Student Nonviolent Coordinating Committee (SNCC) and the Congress of Racial Equality (CORE) readily adopted the mass meeting as well. In this way, the cultural familiarity and resonance of the congregational-style meeting was appropriated by the movement.

Rhetoric. During its heyday, the dominant rhetorical style associated with the movement was that of the black preacher. The dominance of this style is hardly surprising. Indeed, rooted as the movement was in the language and images of the black church, the surprise would have been if the rhetoric had been something other than ministerial. Then, too, the disproportionate role played by ministers in formal leadership positions in the movement made the adoption of this style logical and culturally comprehensible. Finally, once the mass meeting form had been firmly established within the movement, yet another pressure for adoption of this rhetorical style emerged. The strong cultural affinity between the mass meeting and the ministerial style of address prompted even secular organizers to adopt the style and mannerisms of the black preacher.

The southern black church, then, was both the organizational base and cultural template for much of the civil rights struggle. Indeed, so functional was the marriage of church and movement that a case could be made that the increasing secularization of the struggle during its black power phase contributed to the decline of the movement during the late 1960s and early 1970s. The turn toward black power, with its emphases on black pride, "self-defense," and the mobilization of the political and economic resources of the black community, and the geographic shift northward (where the church was not the central institution it was in the South) deprived the movement of its strong foundation in the church. The movement was left with neither the central organizational vehicle nor the resonant cultural "tool kit" it had enjoyed in the South.

See also *African American Experience; Civil Disobedience; Heschel, Abraham Joshua; Human Rights; King, Martin Luther, Jr.; Niebuhr, Reinhold; Prejudice; Social Gospel.*

Doug McAdam

BIBLIOGRAPHY

Findlay, James F. *Church People in the Struggle: The National Council of Churches and the Black Freedom Movement, 1950–1970.* New York: Oxford University Press, 1993.

Garrow, David. *Bearing the Cross.* New York: Morrow, 1986.

King, Martin Luther, Jr. *Stride toward Freedom: The Montgomery Story.* New York: Harper and Brothers, 1958.

———. *Why We Can't Wait.* New York: Harper and Row, 1963.

McAdam, Doug. *Political Process and the Development of Black Insurgency, 1930–1970.* Chicago: University of Chicago Press, 1982.

Morris, Aldon. *The Origins of the Civil Rights Movement.* New York: Free Press, 1984.

Payne, Charles M. *I've Got the Light of Freedom.* Berkeley: University of California Press, 1995.

Swidler, Ann. "Culture in Action: Symbols and Strategies." *American Sociological Review* 51 (1986): 273–286.

Watters, Pat. *Down to Now: Reflections on the Southern Civil Rights Movement.* Athens: University of Georgia Press, 1993.

Civil Society

Civil society is the realm of social voluntarism, the organization of interests outside of the state, and the existence of intermediary associations, mediating between the individual citizen and the state. The idea of civil society as a political concept expressing liberal and democratic norms gained currency in the eighteenth century, only to be revived in the 1980s in East Central Europe and later in many other parts of the world.

In response to the disruption of old certainties of territorial, kinship, and religious-based obligations and expectations, the notion of civil society emerged in the eighteenth century as thinkers sought to find a new basis for collective life, for social solidarity, and for trust among members of society. Eventually, the idea of civil society provided one of the earliest formulas for the modern, democratic form of political life that would, by the twentieth century, be identified with citizenship within the democratically organized nation-state.

The Modern Idea of Civil Society

While the idea of civil society has a long history in the traditions of Western political thought—its roots go back to Christian natural law—its modern emergence dates to the writings of the Scottish moralists. For the eighteenth-century thinkers of the Scottish Enlightenment, civil society was primarily a vision of society held together by the force of "moral sentiments" and "natural affections." In the writings of Francis Hutcheson, Hugh Blair, Adam Ferguson, and Adam Smith, the establishment of civil society came to be identified with the realization of the moral sense within humankind. As a form of sociability this sense would provide the foundation for the moral community. Consequently, this moral sense would assure mutuality, compassion, and empathy among individuals, all of which would take them beyond calculation of purely economic interests in their dealings with one another.

Thus for these writers and publicists of mid-eighteenth-century Scotland, the idea of civil society was primarily a new principle for the organization of society and the expression of men and women's fundamental ties with one another. In that sense, it replaced the medieval idea of the Catholic Church as a *universitas fidelium* (university of the faithful) with a new, more inclusive definition of membership in society based on the moral sense within humankind. No longer able to conceive of society in the hierarchic terms of medieval orders and estates but instead as a grouping of discrete and autonomous individuals, the thinkers of the day had to find a new bond among these individuals.

For Scottish thinkers such as Adam Ferguson and Adam Smith this bond was based on the assumed need of people for recognition and consideration by others. At the epistemological level the notion of civil society is thus an attempt to ground the very idea of society in an intimately human propensity to mutuality, to something that in fact closely approximates the idea of friendship. Building on the social nature of human existence, the writers of the Scottish Enlightenment saw the essence of civil society in the continuing need of people to be validated and recognized by their fellow citizens. Eschewing the explanation that society and social interaction were organized solely by the pursuit of material goods and interest (that is, by market exchanges), these eighteenth-century thinkers recognized that mutual approbation was no less critical in explaining the transactions of the marketplace and counting house.

What stood at the core of all attempts to articulate a notion of civil society in the eighteenth century were the increasingly problematic relations between the private and the public, the individual and society, public ethics and private morals, individual passions and public concerns. More to the point, the question of civil society was, and still is, how could individual interests be pursued in the social arena and, similarly, how could the social good be pursued in the individual or private sphere? Scottish thinkers looked to the idea of natural sympathy and innate mutuality to resolve these contradictory tensions by positing the natural propensity to sociability within the breast of civilized man.

This "solution" to the problem of society, this "formula" for a civil society with its particular reading of civility as something beyond polite manners, was not, and could not be, a lasting one. Very quickly in fact the idea of an innate propensity to goodness and sociability was countered—most especially in the writings of Scottish philosopher and historian David Hume—with an argument for society organized solely by the mutual pursuit of individual interests. Bernard Mandeville's *Fable of the Bees* (1714), in which the British philosopher and satirist maintained that private vices produced public goods, gained acceptance, and David Hume's famous argument that the exchange of services was based not on any kindness but rather solely on self-interest (in the mutual exchange of such services) became the reigning theory by which the organization of society was explained.

By the time German philosopher G. W. F. Hegel wrote his *Philosophy of Right* in 1821, the idea of civil society had lost its moorings in any idea of natural sympathy or mutual benevolence, and for Hegel, as for the social philosopher Karl Marx after him, civil society was identified solely with that realm of social action in which the interests of different social groups compete with one another. Thus by the turn of the nineteenth century, civil society was, for Hegel, Marx, and others, made up of a heterogeneity of classes, social groups, professional associations, and the like, each with its own interests and agendas, each competing with the others in pursuit of its own particular good. In many ways civil society became almost totally identified with that society of free competitors that one immediately correlates with the logic of the marketplace. For both Hegel and Marx this contradictory and tension-filled existence of society had to be resolved. Their solutions, however, were very different. For Hegel the conflict of particular wills that made up civil society would be resolved in the ethical entity of the universal state; for Marx the resolution of civil society's tensions could be accomplished only by the establishment of a classless society.

By the mid-nineteenth century civil society had taken on a whole new set of meanings. As it became increasingly identified with what was privately owned and market regulated, so it was also contrasted to the state. In fact, thinkers began to conceive of civil society and the state as dichotomous social realities, and among certain thinkers such as American political philosopher Thomas Paine and, later, French writer and politician Alexis de Tocqueville a healthy civil society was seen as necessary protection against the development of a despotic state.

Civil Society and Citizenship

This evolving understanding of civil society as a phenomenon existing apart from and often in opposition to the state had much to do with the retreat of the concept from scholarly use and public debate in the second half of the nineteenth century and first half of the twentieth. For it was in this period that the problems originally viewed as remedied by civil society—that is, the problems of providing a new basis for the organization of societal interests and the establishment of new criteria for membership and participation in society—became, on the whole, subsumed under the developing idea of citizenship. The great struggles at the end of the nineteenth century and early in the twentieth century over workers' rights, unionization, and, most essentially, the right to vote and establishment of universal suffrage became the arena in which the institutionalization of any idea of civil society was played out. Civil freedom, economic autonomy, and the moral agency of the individual man and woman became, to a great extent, identified with the rights and obligations of citizenship as defining the terms of membership in the social and political orders.

In this period, therefore, the idea of citizenship became more or less conterminous with that of civil society. The extension or universalization of the rights of citizenship and the legal and institutional spheres of its workings (from equality before the law, to the right to vote, to different forms of social entitlement) became the concrete and practical forms taken by the idea of civil society in the nineteenth century. The social problems that, in the eighteenth century, had been discussed in terms of civil society were in no small measure transformed into problems that people in the nineteenth and twentieth centuries would discuss (and struggle over) in terms taken from the lexicon of citizenship.

This was the case until sometime in the 1980s, when the idea of civil society enjoyed a renewal and resurgence that have continued unabated. This more contemporary revival of the idea of civil society began in Eastern Europe, especially in Poland in the 1970s during the struggle between the Polish workers' movement and the coercive apparatus of the state. There, civil society reentered the lexicon of political and social usage—this time, however, more as a political slogan and as a cudgel to batter the totalitarian state than anything else. Its strong civic associations and resonance of social voluntarism and activities and spheres of action free of state regulation and intervention made it an especially favorable political slogan within the context of the Soviet-style totalitarian regimes of Eastern Europe and Central Eastern Europe. Use of the term spread from Poland to the revolutionary movements under way in all the countries of the area.

With so much of social life regulated by the state and with private life rendered virtually meaningless in so many Eastern European countries, the banner of civil society presented a potent rallying point for those wishing to reclaim from the state a social (and a private) space free from the state and its regulative agencies. Freely organized voluntary organizations of a civic, religious, and political nature became focal points for new demands to implement a civil society around what became the new political parties and employer and employee associations—and often religious organizations—of the post-1989 revolutions in Eastern Europe. Here, too, civil society gave itself over, when circumstances finally permitted, to the dynamics of citizenship and of interest representation within a democratically organized political order.

Although the concept of civil society proved useful as a political slogan and rallying call under totalitarian and repressive regimes, many in Eastern Europe found in the post-1989 period that its usefulness in constructing an institutional order was limited. The drafting of new constitutions and rules of public order, the growth of free political parties, and the development of new market economies—each with its own dynamics, tensions, challenges, and sets of problems—have tended to reorient debate around more familiar concepts such as liberalism and democracy.

The Ambiguities of the Idea of Civil Society

A look at the changing role of the Catholic Church in Poland illustrates the ambiguity at the heart of the notion of civil society. In the period of communist rule (1945–1989) the Polish church was the center of protest to the regime, preserving in its very existence the meanings, identities, and commitments that had been suppressed by the communist state. In its role as a symbol of resistance to the regime and as an association that was to a great degree successful at preserving its independence and autonomy from the state, the Polish church became a model to many of the phenomenon of civil society.

Yet today the Polish church is not what it was before the triumph of the workers' union Solidarity and the overthrow of communism in 1989. The major battle lines in contemporary Poland are in fact between Catholicism and liberal democracy, and the church may be poised to reassert its lost privileges in the realm of state making and policy promulgation. Certainly the role of the church in the development of Polish policy on religious education and abortion in the 1990s would lead one to question its continuing role as supporter of universal human rights, individual autonomy, and, in fact, civil society. It is one thing to assign the church a role as political actor within a pluralist civil society—a role akin to that of any other interest group—but it is quite another to identify the church with the very essence of that national entity that supposedly finds expression in the workings of civil society as often is the case in contemporary Poland. There, where the idea of civil society has a markedly national cast, where it resonates strongly with the Polish people, with national independence and with national institutions, the role of the church is very different from its role in the West. The political strength of the church and its public and deprivatized position in society as a political actor in its own right raise serious questions about the role of such an institution within civil society. Similar questions can be raised about the organization of xenophobic political movements and parties within the multiethnic and nationally heterogeneous societies of eastern Europe, and in western Europe as well.

All these phenomena lead to the question: just how civil, or how representative of civil society, are organizations whose political programs are by nature antidemocratic, socially exclusive, or even racist? If civil society is the realm of social voluntarism, in which associations representing interests apart from the state mediate between the individual citizen and the state, then organizations such as the Montana militias and the Ku Klux Klan in the United States, the Muslim Brotherhood in Egypt, and fundamentalist terrorist groups such as Hamas on the West Bank also would qualify as examples of civil society. One could therefore conclude that civil society is not always an unmitigated good thing. While people may like to believe that voluntary associations and civic groups are all based on liberal individualist assumptions and honor universal human rights, that often is not the case. Civil society, then, must refer to something more than just a generous number of different forms of association. A vibrant civil society also must include associations dedicated to and organized around certain principles of tolerance and recognition of civility that may not be far at all from the original ideas of the Scottish moralists in the mid-eighteenth century.

To be sure, this understanding has not yet been accepted by all users of the term *civil society*. The idea of civil society continues to be used by political groups and thinkers on both the right and the left, although in Europe it most often is the province of the left, and in the United States it has been appropriated by both groups to advance their political agendas. Thus for right-of-center thinkers as well as for libertarian followers of the Austrian economist and philosopher Friedrich von Hayek, the quest for civil society is a mandate to deconstruct many of the powers of the state and replace them with intermediary institutions based on social voluntarism.

Many of these thinkers and followers, however, refuse to recognize that voluntary organizations can be of a particularly nasty nature and based on primordial or ascriptive principles of membership and participation that put to shame the very foundations of any idea of civil society. For many liberals civil society is identified with social movements, also existing beyond the state. But they are blind to the fact that the Achilles heel of any social movement is its institutionalization, which, one way or the other, must be through the state and its legal (and coercive) apparatus. In the meantime, both communitarians and liberals continue to assimilate the idea of civil society into their own terms, invest it with their own meanings, and make of it what they will as the term is identified with everything from multiparty systems and the rights of citizenship to individual voluntarism and the spirit of community.

The present confusion in the use of the term notwithstanding, the idea of civil society continues to be usefully invoked as a political slogan in the quest for more democratically organized societies that give greater scope to individual freedom and self-determination. Muslim societies in the Middle East and beyond (Indonesia, for example) have adopted this concept not only as a slogan in protest of existing institutional arrangements but also as the basis of a more theoretical and critical attitude toward the Islamic tradition itself, which has its own sources and unique potentialities for the formation of modern associations out of Islamic religious traditions and even kinship structures. Within Muslim societies there are many indigenous forms of association, from tribal forums, to the traditionally male *diwaniyyah* where people gather in the homes of leading citizens to discuss social issues, to the religiously endowed organizations of the *Awqaf*, all of which can and have played a role in the exponential growth of civic associations in

Muslim countries. In the Middle East, with its authoritarian, autocratic, and patrimonial regimes, demands for a civil society of freely organized citizens seem to have as much resonance now as they did earlier in the communist countries of Eastern Europe.

See also *Citizenship; Europe, Eastern.*

Adam B. Seligman

BIBLIOGRAPHY

Bell, Daniel. "American Exceptionalism Revisited: The Role of Civil Society." *Public Interest* 95 (1989): 38–56.

Bobbio, Norberto. *Democracy and Dictatorship.* Minneapolis: University of Minnesota Press, 1989.

Casanova, Jose. *Public Religions in the Modern World.* Chicago: University of Chicago Press, 1994.

Hall, John A., ed. *Civil Society: Theory, History, Comparisons.* Oxford: Polity Press, 1995.

Keane, John. *Civil Society and the State.* London: Verso Press, 1988.

Norton, Augustus R., ed. *Civil Society in the Middle East.* Leiden: E. J. Brill, 1995.

Seligman, Adam B. *The Idea of Civil Society.* New York: Free Press, 1992.

Taylor, Charles. "Modes of Civil Society." *Public Culture* 3 (1990): 95–118.

"Clash of Civilizations"

"Clash of civilizations" is a popular phrase used to describe relations between the Islamic world and the West.

In the waning days of the cold war, specialists on international relations speculated on the types of challenges and opportunities the United States and Europe might face in a world relieved of Soviet machinations. Among those whose views commanded attention at the time was Samuel P. Huntington, a professor in the Department of Government at Harvard University, whose article "The Clash of Civilizations" appeared in the summer 1993 issue of the journal *Foreign Affairs.* Huntington predicted that future world conflicts would be confrontations between different civilizations. In particular, Islamic civilization, possibly in alliance with what he called Confucian civilization, would challenge the West with its vision of a universal Muslim social and political order.

Within the political science and foreign policy communities, extensive debate developed over the specifics of Huntington's theory. At the same time, many people who knew little or nothing about the theory adopted the phrase as a shorthand way of expressing their fear that Islam and the West were either becoming, or always had been and always would be, incompatible, and that past historical episodes of hostile engagement were destined to recur indefinitely into the future, largely in the form of terrorism.

Political Science

The dominant schools of thought in international relations at the time that Huntington wrote stressed either ideological or economic factors: "conflicts of power" or "conflicts of interest." Culture, which lay at the foundation of Huntington's concept of a civilization, had faded from the theoretical picture to the degree that expert scholarship on non-Western parts of the world was dismissed as mere "local knowledge" of little relevance to the real structure of world politics. After all, the cold war had demonstrated that communism and liberalism might find themselves in conflict in a wide variety of cultural settings, and international competition for energy supplies, growing tides of labor migration, and the globalization of private corporations and capital markets were all taking place with minimal regard for cultural differences. "Bringing culture back in," to use the political science designation for the new direction of thought being advanced by Huntington and others, therefore questioned the very bases of scholarly thinking about the world political system.

Academic critiques within the political science profession ranged widely. Some felt that Huntington's conflict scenarios could be accommodated within the framework of cold war balances of power or conventional calculations of national interest. Others criticized Huntington for failing to define *civilization* in sufficient detail for the concept to be of analytical use and for ignoring differences and conflicting interests within civilizations. They offered examples of conflict situations that failed to fit his theory, such as the membership of Muslim Arab states in the largely Western coalition that forced Iraqi leader Saddam Hussein's army out of Kuwait in 1992, the widespread Muslim acceptance of the need to fight against al-Qaida terrorists who advertised themselves as Muslim holy warriors fighting the West, and the extensive military cooperation between Israel, considered a part of the West, and Turkey, a predominantly Muslim country. Still others argued that Huntington based his thinking on deeply biased "orientalist" stereotypes that presented Islam as utterly different from, and inferior to, the West. In this view, Huntington's true objective was sometimes seen, especially after the terrorist attacks of September 11, 2001, on the United States, as providing support for an anti-Muslim U.S. foreign policy.

However, most of these critiques appeared in academic journals that gained far less notice among the general public than did Huntington's article and the follow-up book he published in 1996, *The Clash of Civilizations and the Remaking of World Order*. Thus his title phrase frequently became divorced in public discourse from both the theory it was intended to encapsulate and the academic critiques of that theory. As a consequence, the other meanings imputed to the phrase, and the arguments surrounding them, are as important to understanding its significance to debates on Islam and the West as Huntington's original formulation.

Foreign Policy

Issues related to Islam first became central concerns for American foreign policy at the time of the Iranian Revolution of 1979. Most Americans, including those in policy positions and with specialized backgrounds in studies of revolutions, found the overthrow of Shah Muhammad Reza Pahlavi utterly baffling. In a cold war world that conventionally associated revolution with leftist or nationalist militancy, a parallel degree of militancy based on Islam, which was conventionally seen as a conservative social force, made little sense, and the scanty literature available on contemporary Islam provided little elucidation. Thus in the early 1980s some analysts suggested that the particular doctrines of Shi'i Islam made it susceptible to militant distortion—some people used the word *fanatic*—but that Sunni Islam was entirely different. Yet world events quickly showed this theory to be erroneous. Other analysts glossed over the Sunni-Shi'i division and speculated that a worldwide network of Islamic fanaticism based in Tehran might supplant worldwide communism as the enemy of the West. Subsequent world events, particularly the success of al-Qaida in claiming Sunni revolutionary leadership for Usama bin Ladin, again undermined a theory based more on speculation than deep knowledge.

Without a coherent vision of the function of religion in Muslim societies, or of the ideological uses to which Islam was being put in the contemporary world, American foreign policy proceeded along mutually contradictory paths. On the one hand, the revolutionary regime that took over in Iran, and that held American diplomatic personnel hostage in 1980–1981, was vigorously opposed because of its religious extremism and its apparent desire to export its revolution. On the other hand, equally (or more) extreme religious movements in Afghanistan, mostly Sunni, received massive American military and financial support in the Afghans' fight against Soviet military occupation. In another contradiction, on the one hand, Saudi Arabia, an absolute monarchy known for punitive enforcement of Islamic moral strictures of the sort that most Americans deplored, continued to be a close friend of the United States. On the other hand, Iraq, whose one-party Ba'athist government was similarly absolutist, but also avowedly secular and strongly in favor of women's rights, was condemned for being totalitarian.

These contradictory attitudes toward Muslim regimes and movements confused the American public and encouraged knowledgeable scholars to write books and articles offering clarification. In 1990 Bernard Lewis, a well-known Princeton professor of Middle Eastern history, wrote an article in the *Atlantic Monthly* entitled "The Roots of Muslim Rage." Lewis's use in this article of the phrase "clash of civilizations" was later picked up by Huntington. In 1998 John L. Esposito, a professor of religion at Georgetown University, presented an opposing view in *The Islamic Threat: Myth or Reality?* In this and subsequent works, including *Unholy War: Terror in the Name of Islam,* he and other scholars discounted the idea that Islam and the West were on a collision course. They also stressed the many varieties of contemporary Islamic thought and observance and the scarcity of Muslims drawn to participate in terrorist organizations.

With both the general public and the government uncertain about how to think about Islam and Muslims in the world arena, and with specialist scholars presenting strongly opposing views, the stage was set for Huntington's launch of his catchphrase. Leaving aside the debate generated by the "clash of civilizations" theory in political science circles, the phrase itself proceeded to achieve wide dissemination and popularity, because it seemed to encapsulate the evolving state of world affairs in an easy slogan. Its popularity increased still further after the terrorist attacks of September 11.

Outside the scholarly world, however, there was no agreement on what the phrase meant, because Huntington's actual words were seldom read by those who mouthed it. Questions abounded; answers conflicted. What was a civilization? What was Islamic civilization? Did Muslims living in America or France or Bosnia belong to Islamic civilization or to Western civilization? Could someone be part of more than one civilization? Was the clash between Islam and the West a continuation of the Arab conquests of the seventh century, the Crusades that began in the eleventh century, and the Ottoman takeover of eastern Europe in the fourteenth through seventeenth centuries? Or was it a recent phenomenon rooted in a Muslim loathing of the modern world created by the West? Would the clash someday come to an end, or was enmity between Islam and the West inevitable and permanent? The appeal of the "clash of civilizations" catchphrase was its broad but undefined scope, its avoidance of explicit religious bigotry, and the illusion that it offered meaningful guidance in a dangerous twenty-first-century world.

The post–September 11 war on terror and the invasion of Iraq placed Muslims squarely in the gun sights of American soldiers and on the watch lists of American intelligence agencies. Yet the American government also stated that the United States had no quarrel with Islam, which President George W. Bush recognized as a religion of peace. The words "clash of civilizations" disappeared from policy pronouncements as specific challenges of great complexity prompted responses tailored to local situations. In Iraq, the United States placed hopes for democratic progress firmly on the leadership of strongly Shi'i political parties, while in Somalia it supported secular warlords against a Muslim religious leadership that was increasingly effective in gaining popular support. Huntington himself departed from his own theo-

retical formulation when asked by *Newsweek* magazine in December 2001 for his opinion on what policies the United States should adopt in light of the attacks of September 11.

Religion

Samuel Huntington made no claims to being an expert on Islam, and his theory of post–cold war conflict did not hinge on religion per se. His "Confucian civilization," for example, took its name from an age-old Chinese ethical and political outlook, not from a religion. Nevertheless, his choice of the word *Islamic* inevitably thrust his "clash of civilizations" formulation into the midst of religious debate. Thus religious uses and critiques paralleled, but seldom overlapped, the critiques by political scientists.

One line of thought fully endorsed the most Islamophobic interpretation of Huntington's phrase: Islam is now and always has been an evil religion, hostile to Christianity and Judaism, discriminatory toward the adherents of those faiths, abusive of human rights and women, and cruel in its legal code. This attitude was expressed more on the Internet and on talk radio than in more formal venues, but it undoubtedly reflected the mindset of millions of believing Christians and Jews, as well as that of many secular individuals. To some extent, the specifics of this indictment derived from anti-Islamic polemics of great antiquity. But because popular awareness of Islam as a religion was rare prior to September 11, much of the detail used to particularize the indictment

An imam *speaks to supporters before the Swiss house of parliament in protest of the cartoon depictions of the prophet Muhammad published in a Danish newspaper. The cartoons sparked riotous, often violent, protests throughout the Islamic world, resulting in more than 120 deaths. The riots served as an illustration of the conflicting views and growing chasm between the Islamic and Western worlds.*

came from current headlines about martyrdom operations, honor killings, resistance to cultural assimilation among diaspora Muslim communities, curtailment of women's freedoms by Muslim governments, and so forth. Deeper reflections, counterexamples, and discussions of the shortcomings of Western culture counted for little in this discourse, and it was taken for granted that "clash of civilizations" aptly summarized the relations between Islam and the West.

On a more sophisticated level, many Muslim, Christian, and Jewish leaders, some holding religious positions, saw danger in the "clash of civilizations" phraseology and worked explicitly to discourage its use or promote a substitute formulation. Dozens of ecumenical conferences and meetings have been held—most of them since September 11—at which the "clash of civilizations" idea has been widely (but not universally) denounced. Organizations created specifically to sponsor such meetings and promote ecumenical harmony include the Royal Institute for Inter-Faith Studies in Amman, Jordan; the International Centre for Dialogue among Civilizations in Tehran, Iran; and Dialogues: Islamic World-U.S.-The West in New York City.

The prominence of the word *dialogue* as an alternative to *clash* stems from the successful proposal of Iranian president Muhammad Khatami to have the United Nations designate 2001 as the year of civilizational dialogue. President Khatami's statements on this subject explicitly mention his preference for the phrase "dialogue of civilizations" over "clash of civilizations." In 2005 the United Nations took a further step by endorsing an initiative chaired by the prime ministers of Spain and Turkey to create an "alliance of civilizations."

History

Tacitly underlying the phrase "clash of civilizations" is the assumption that it is reasonable to divide the world into civilizations. This idea emerged during the course of the nineteenth century as remains of ancient cultures were discovered by archaeologists, but it gained its most explicit formulations in the twentieth century, particularly in the writings of Arnold Toynbee (d. 1975), whose massive work *A Study of History* (12 vols., 1934–1961) presented accounts of many civilizations in a repeating pattern of rise and fall. In 1923, after serving as a British delegate to the Paris Peace Conference following World War I, Toynbee published *The Western Question in Greece and Turkey: A Study in the Contact of Civilizations*. The implication of this title that the neighboring countries of Greece and Turkey belonged to different civilizations was picked up three years later by Basil J. Mathews, the literature secretary of the World's Alliance of YMCAs, in his book *Young Islam on Trek: A Study in the Clash of Civilizations*. Though there is no direct link between Mathews's little-known work and Huntington's 1993 article, Mathews's anti-Muslim tone and missionary exhortations indicate that Christians in the West have long been ready to accept the idea that the Islamic world belongs to a different and objectionable civilization.

The counteridea that historical research could be productively based on the opposite assumption—namely, that the West and Islam belong to a single civilization based on a shared heritage of Hellenistic culture; close relations between Jewish, Christian, and Muslim scriptures; and a history with many close parallels and as many periods of fruitful exchange as of hostility—has been proposed by Richard W. Bulliet, a historian at Columbia University, in his book *The Case for Islamo-Christian Civilization* published in 2004. In his view, not only is there no need to conceive of a "clash of civilizations," but there is much to learn about both Islam and the West by treating them as parts of the same civilization and studying their histories in tandem.

See also *Islam's Encounters with the West.*

Richard W. Bulliet

BIBLIOGRAPHY

Berman, Paul. *Terror and Liberalism.* New York: Norton, 2003.
Bulliet, Richard W. *The Case for Islamo-Christian Civilization.* New York: Columbia University Press, 2004.
Esposito, John L. *Unholy War: Terror in the Name of Islam.* New York: Oxford University Press, 2002.
Hunter, Shireen T. *The Future of Islam and the West: Clash of Civilizations or Peaceful Coexistence.* Westport, Conn.: Praeger and CSIS, 1998.
Huntington, Samuel P. "The Age of Muslim Wars." *Newsweek,* December 17, 2001, 42–47.
———. "The Clash of Civilizations?" *Foreign Affairs* 72 (summer 1993): 22–28.
———. *The Clash of Civilizations and the Remaking of World Order.* New York: Simon and Schuster, 1996.
"Religion and International Relations." Special issue, *Millennium: Journal of International Studies* 29, no. 3 (2000).
Said, Edward W. "The Clash of Ignorance." *Nation,* October 22, 2001.
Schmiegelow, Henrik, ed. *Preventing the Clash of Civilizations: A Peace Strategy for the Twenty-First Century.* New York: St. Martin's Press, 1999.

Colonialism

Colonialism involves extension of political and economic control by a usually technologically or organizationally superior people or state over a foreign area—populated or unpopulated. It has existed since antiquity and can be driven by motives as diverse as the desire to expand and control trade, the search for land and resources, the quest for freedom from religious persecution, and the zeal to convert indigenous peoples to the colonial power's faith.

Modern European colonialism virtually emerged from the Crusades, the military expeditions western European Christians undertook between 1095 and 1270 to recover from Muslim control Jerusalem and the other Palestinian places of pilgrimage known to Christians as the Holy Land. The first forms of modern colonialism were perpetrated by Portugal and Spain in South America beginning in the sixteenth century. The central purpose was to extract gold and silver, bringing great wealth to the Iberian kingdoms and money for the foremost maritime power in Europe. Spanish America's own supremacy over the Low Countries did not go unchallenged by the Dutch and British, however. A series of raids by English navigator and explorer Sir Francis Drake (1540?–1596) and other adventurers siphoned off much of the Spanish and Portuguese bullion. The Dutch had a much larger fleet than did the English and so built it up to take control of port cities in Southeast Asia. The British tried to challenge the Dutch but were repulsed. In the early seventeenth century, the British relocated in ports in India. France was also active in several parts of India, and both countries were reduced to a state of intermittent war. Because India was so vast, these conquered areas were quite restricted and most of the subcontinent remained under Indian control.

At the end of the Napoleonic Wars (1799–1815) in which the Netherlands had been a French auxiliary, British claims were asserted in the Cape Colony in Africa and Dutch sugar colonies in the Caribbean. Most of the Dutch possessions in Indonesia were returned to them, although Britain retained Singapore and Penang. These changes left most of the developing world still under its own rulers. The other European powers entered the colonial race after 1870. Britain and France secured their colonial possessions by sea. Other powers absorbed territory by landward expansion—thus Russia absorbed the Islamic states of Central Asia, and Japan took over Korea and much of China. It can be argued that the area the United States occupied in Mexico in 1846 was a similar landward acquisition of empire. The colonizing powers followed different patterns of government. Britain left indigenous rulers in charge of vast tracts, where they remained powerful. The French largely ruled directly, introducing their own officials as the colonial rulers. Both kinds of colonization left the new rulers in supreme control.

For the most part, colonial powers worked out their rivalries without direct antagonisms. The boundaries between the colonial regimes bore only a casual resemblance to their previous territorial divisions, and peoples with different languages were often put together. Because of these agreements between the colonial powers, major wars seldom broke out between them; at most there were minor frontier conflicts. The main period of rivalry extended from about 1890 to 1914.

When World War I erupted in 1914, African and Asian troops were employed not only in their own areas but also in western Europe. The French deployed African soldiers on the western front, and the British brought in Indian troops. Although these encounters produced no immediate political consequences, it has been argued that colonial peoples' serious political awareness took root in this wartime experience. The 1920s and 1930s saw a much greater demand for autonomy, particularly in India. Latin America had attained formal independence from Spain and Portugal, although political power was the monopoly of a small minority of whites, such as Simón Bolívar. The United States retained ultimate political power in the region, however, and whenever conditions there were deemed dangerous for American interests, the marines were dispatched to restore order. British policy in Asia looked forward to eventual self-government for Asians but on a time scale so distant as to be quite unrealistic.

Africa, however, did not seem to be a seedbed of nationalist feelings. Africans were believed to be limited by concepts of tribalism that inhibited all but local and regional groupings, and no thought was given to changing the existing social forces. The only major change was that the former dominance of hunters gave way to the landed classes. Groups without land were at the very bottom of the social scale and were not able to rise. In general, land ownership was along traditional lines, although in a few, very limited areas traditional agriculture gave way to modern forms of cultivation. Thus in West Africa there was a move into the production of cocoa and in East Africa into tea and coffee. These changes shifted greater wealth to some within the landed groups who moved into commerce, law, and other commercial activities. In a way, they had become the allies or customers of the colonial overlords, which constituted the main change in the social deployment. Meanwhile, a few attempts were made to directly challenge the Western overlords, the most notable being the Zulu rebellion in which a British force was defeated. Generally, though, because of the superior weapons technology of Westerners, the Africans stood no real chance.

Perhaps it seemed that the colonial relationship would continue indefinitely, but colonialism came to an end more because of world forces than because of the local pattern. With the rise of the ideas of national sovereignty and self-determination in the twentieth century, quite suddenly the deployment of colonial military power symbolized not an advanced role in international relations but, to the contrary, international backwardness. Different Western countries came to this view at rather different times. The United States and Britain were the first to understand that in the postwar world after 1945 there was no longer a place for colonialism. The French and Dutch were slower to change their attitudes. The first to take up colonialism, the Portuguese were also the last to discard it. There was also the phenomenon of colonized states that, in turn, had become colonizers. They were mainly in the south of Africa—notably Rhodesia (Zimbabwe) and South Africa. Here colonialism had been strictly along racial lines, but in a few short years it also disappeared.

Spanish and Portuguese conquests in South America witnessed a massive interaction of church and state. Every colonial city was dominated by a striking church of great size and splendor. The head of the church community, the archbishop, was also sometimes the head of secular affairs. In fact, the ordinary people remained largely unaffected by the new religion, but formally the tone of society was Catholic.

In British colonies, the religious spirit was much less in evidence. Indeed, before 1800 Christian missionaries were excluded from India and some other areas of British control. Thereafter, as the spirit of religion became even stronger in Britain, there was a greater degree of Christian activity in India and other colonies. During the first half of the nineteenth century, many Christian values were introduced in India and elsewhere. Higher education was much influenced by Christian thinking, and the colleges in Calcutta, Madras, and other cities were explicitly Christian in tone. All this was modified by the end of the century. There was a good deal of conversion to Christianity, but it was mostly among the poorer elements in society.

Only in the Philippines was the whole population converted to Christianity during three centuries of Spanish Catholic rule. Although the Spaniards were replaced by an American form of government, the existing system of society and politics was sufficiently well established to maintain the status quo.

French colonial possessions were second only to those of the British in size and importance. Even though France is a Catholic country, the spirit of the French Revolution (1789–1799) was sufficiently pervasive to maintain the secular system to a large extent. The institutions of government and administration in French colonies were therefore not greatly influenced by Catholicism, but, as in the British colonies, lawyers and landlords dominated the new politics. Although the increased democratization of forms of government brought new elements into the administrative structure, these did not fundamentally affect the nature of the system of control. Thus the interaction of politics and religion remained limited in Asia and Africa.

What difference, then, did colonialism make to the developing world? Even though there were terrible injustices in colonialism, it did stimulate an overall quiet advancement that nevertheless brought Asia and Africa into the modern world. And yet the stains, such as the slave trade, are striking; the gains are not. What seems clear is that colonialism did not contribute to the division of the world into advanced and backward sectors, but in general led to the evolution of one world, which, however stark its differences, contributed to wholeness.

See also *Conversion; Missionaries; Nationalism.*

Hugh Tinker

BIBLIOGRAPHY

Brunschwig, Henri. *French Colonialism, 1871–1914: Myths and Realities.* London: Praeger, 1966.

Emerson, Rupert. *From Empire to Nation: The Rise of Self-Assertion of Asian and African Peoples.* Cambridge, Mass.: Harvard University Press, 1960.

Fieldhouse, D. K. *The Colonial Empires: A Comparative Survey.* London: Weidenfeld and Nicolson, 1966.

Furnivall, J. S. *Colonial Policy and Practice.* Cambridge: Cambridge University Press, 1948.

Lapping, Brian. *End of Empire.* New York: St. Martin's Press, 1985.

Smith, Tony, ed. *The End of European Empire: Decolonisation after World War Two.* Lexington, Mass.: Heath, 1975.

Tinker, Hugh. *Men Who Overturned Empires: Fighters, Dreamers and Schemers.* Basingstoke, U.K.: Macmillan, 1987.

Communication

Communication, broadly defined as the exchange of information between individuals or groups, plays an important role in American religion and American politics. Communication encompasses sources that are both formal or structured, as in a daily newspaper, and informal and unstructured, such as exchanges between friends at church about who to vote for in an upcoming election. In addition, communication sources are both secular and religious in content.

The importance of both formal and informal sources of religious communication is growing in the United States in the first part of the twenty-first century. This development is tied to the flourishing of religious institutions in American society. Attendance at places of religious worship remains high, charitable giving is growing, and voluntary activity in worship and in religion-related institutions is elevated as well. Despite some evidence of secularization in American society, the "religious factor," as scholar Gerhard Lenski called it a generation ago, remains strong.

In addition, the role of religious communication in determining the public's political beliefs may be stronger than ever, relative to other, more traditional sources of influence. Political party organizations at the local level no longer have the clout that they once did; local precinct workers knocking on doors to ask support for their candidates is far less common than in the past. Into that vacuum come a variety of forces, lobbying for the voter's attention, including political candidates themselves, the national media, or local networks of the voter's friends, neighbors, and fellow congregants. Indeed, the latter act as sources of personal influence and have great potential for making an impact on the political attitudes and behaviors of the mass public. Given the strength of religious identifications and local bodies of worship, such as the church, the potential for religious influence is great, relative to other sources. In addition, places of worship serve as mobilizing environments, as places where people gather, with vote-seeking politicians never far behind.

Despite strong indications that religious communication has political consequences, the relationships between religion, communication, and political behavior remain problematic because a systematic body of literature is just beginning to develop in this area. Scholars of religion have tended to ignore these relationships, except when they have been important to an understanding of the television evangelists

and the role of the media in the careers of American evangelists like Aimee Semple McPherson (1890–1944) and Billy Sunday (1862–1935). Similarly, experts in the field of political communications have tended to overlook the role of religion.

We begin by examining the sources of communication, both secular and religious, including the mass media and other forms of communication. Next the receipt of communication, especially among religious people, is examined. Finally, the impact of communication on the political behavior of the public is explored. Throughout, special attention is given to evangelical Protestantism, the religious tradition that is both the source of and the object of many religious communications. In fact, it is reasonable to suggest that religious radio and television have made a major contribution to the development of evangelicalism in the United States as a self-conscious religious movement.

Sources of Communication

What are the sources of communication that affect political behavior? There are the familiar secular sources like newspapers, radio, television, and magazines. But there are also numerous sources of religious communication such as those through periodicals, radio, and television. These religious sources of communication have grown significantly since the 1920s. Religious publishing houses flourish in the United States, representing a variety of denominations. Religious periodicals abound, from narrowly focused denominational publications to interdenominational magazines like *Christianity Today,* the unofficial voice of American evangelicalism. *Christian Century* serves mainline Protestantism, while *Commonweal* is but one of many publications directed mainly toward a Roman Catholic audience. "Christian orthodoxy" is represented by *First Things,* a journal with a strong intellectual and conservative voice. Finally, a variety of Jewish media are available, from the more general publications like *Moment* to the more intellectual *Commentary* and *Tikkun.*

Almost from the beginning of the radio boom in the 1920s, American religious broadcasters made their mark, from the hyper-energetic Aimee Semple McPherson to the demagogic Father Charles Coughlin (1891–1979). The latter began on a single station in Detroit in 1926, but by 1930 had a national program on CBS Radio. From the start, religious broadcasting was viewed as a service in the public interest. As a result, both networks and local stations offered religious groups access to the airwaves. But Father Coughlin's strong attacks on President Franklin D. Roosevelt (1882–1945) led to a reassessment of this policy by his network. CBS set up an in-house advisory board for religious broadcasting and sought the outside guidance of the Federal Council of Churches (now the National Council of Churches) to advise the network on religious programming. For a ten-year period ending with the conclusion of World War II, only the Mutual Broadcasting System offered commercial time without restriction to religious broadcasters. Evangelicals were effectively shut out from the airwaves during this period, leading to the founding in 1944 of the National Religious Broadcasters, which lobbied the Federal Communications Commission (FCC) for airtime for religious programming that was fair to all groups. Differences between religious groups were never settled, but a 1960 FCC ruling opened the door for paid religious broadcasting on both radio and television stations at the local level. Prior to the ruling, 47 percent of all religious broadcasting was free, whereas by the late 1970s that figure had dropped to 8 percent.

Although network-wide religious broadcasting in the United States was sparse in the early 2000s, local radio and television stations offered a wide variety of religious programs. A religious cable channel, BeliefNet, was also established. In this environment of paid religious programming, individuals and churches representing the evangelical religious tradition and its associated movements—fundamentalism and the charismatic or pentecostal movement—have been at the forefront. In terms of religious radio, an evangelical presence was a fixture in almost every community in the nation. Some local stations acquired an exclusive or predominantly evangelical focus. The Moody Radio Network, for example, blanketed the nation with programs. Such personalities as the radio psychologist James Dobson became household names in Christian circles. Partly as a result of his radio show, *Focus on the Family,* Dobson became a leader in "Christian Right" politics. Christian radio, then, has been a pervasive presence in American society. Although spreading the Gospel of Jesus Christ has been its first priority, promoting traditional conservative values has been a close second. It has been estimated that three-quarters of religious broadcasting (radio and television) comes from the evangelical religious community.

The story of religious media would be incomplete without a careful examination of religious television. The precursors of modern televangelism were the nineteenth-century American revivalists Charles Grandison Finney (1792–1875) and Dwight Lyman Moody (1837–1899) and their twentieth-century American counterpart Billy Sunday. These leaders established evangelistically focused organizations that were separate from traditional denominations, developed successful techniques for mass evangelism, and brought sound business principles to their ventures, along with rhetorical gifts of persuasion. They serve as exemplars for religious television and its practitioners in the early twenty-first century.

Religious television began to make its mark in the United States in the 1950s with the network program of Roman Catholic bishop Fulton Sheen (1895–1979) and the televising of the Billy Graham (1918–) crusades. Since Sheen went off the air in the late 1950s over a dispute with New York's cardinal Francis Spellman, and in the aftermath of the 1960 FCC ruling noted above, the field has been left increasingly to evangelicals who have successfully raised the money to put and keep programs on the air. Mainline Protestantism has only a limited presence on religious television, compared with that of its evangelical brethren.

As a result, almost all of the best-known televangelists have been evangelicals, from Graham, Rex Humbard, and Oral Roberts to Robert Schuller, Jerry Falwell, Pat Robertson, Jimmy Swaggart, and Jim and Tammy Bakker. Despite scandals associated with Swaggart and Bakker, programs like Falwell's *Old-Time Gospel Hour* and Robertson's *700 Club* continued to play to sizable audiences into the early twenty-first century, dispensing the now familiar mixture of old-time evangelism and conservative politics. Both Falwell and Robertson were leaders of national political movements that had their beginnings in their religious television programs, with the media exposure helping to secure them a national following. In good measure, then, Falwell's Moral Majority and Robertson's Christian Coalition were the products of religious television. The organizations of the Christian Right, as important as they are, however, may not be the most important contribution of the religious media. As noted earlier, religious media contributed a sense of identity to an interdenominational movement, American evangelicalism, with implications not only for politics but for different aspects of life as well.

Other sources of religious communication exist apart from the mass media. The growth of religious interest groups like the Moral Majority, the Christian Coalition, Concerned Women for America, the Coalition for Traditional Values, and the Family Research Council (the public policy arm of Focus on the Family) have made these organizations influential participants in the political process. All of these groups are conservative in their political outlook. They have spawned opposition groups of religious people on the left of the spectrum, like the Inter-Faith Alliance and the Call to Renewal. Groups such as these and the Washington offices of the major American denominations have altered the face of national politics. Many of these groups have networks that extend to the local level with participants meeting regularly, and they are often actively involved in politics.

Local places of worship are also locations for frequent political communication. The Roman Catholic Church in America has never been hesitant to send political messages to its member congregations; the pastoral letters from Catholic bishops are only the most recent form of this activity. The African American church has always been a place for local political activity, and it became the organizational focus for the civil rights movement. White Protestant clergy, particularly the mainline variety, were also active in the civil rights and peace movements, although neither movement had broad grassroots support within mainline denominations. White evangelical pastors have joined the fray in recent decades (partly as a result of the increasing number of religious right organizations in the early 2000s), pushing a moral reform agenda with a particular focus on abortion and gay rights. Both pastors and religious activists are in strategic positions to influence the politics of active laity within their congregations. This influence can take the form of pastoral communications from the pulpit, or it may find expression in one of the many informal means that pastors and other leaders use to communicate their views to the flock. For example, many evangelical clergy may feel uncomfortable about endorsing candidates from the pulpit, given potential legal penalties for such activity, but might be comfortable with voter guides being handed out after the service or discussing issues from a conservative perspective.

Methods of Receiving Political Communication

The sources of political communication are many, but how important are they to the mass public? Recent research has attempted to answer this question. In 1996 a national sample of approximately twenty-four hundred Americans was asked to assess the importance of various sources of voting information. Sixty-six percent of the respondents mentioned newspapers as a key source; 64 percent cited televi-

sion news; 57 percent noted "this year's political campaign"; 46 percent mentioned radio; and 30 percent noted coworkers or friends. All of these, of course, are secular sources. Smaller percentages referred to religious sources: 14 percent mentioned their church or place of worship; 12 percent cited religious publications; another 10 percent noted religious television, with 8 percent mentioning religious radio; and, finally, 9 percent cited mail from religious groups. These figures increase significantly, however, when only the target group for most of these religious sources, white evangelical Protestants, is examined. The percentages increase even more when the examination is limited to "traditionalist" evangelicals—in other words, those with strongly orthodox Christian beliefs and very high levels of religious practice.

Traditionalists, who made up almost 10 percent of the population in 1996, are much more likely than the public at large to regard religious radio as an important source of voting information (29 percent). Other important sources for traditionalists include religious publications (27 percent), religious television (24 percent), information obtained at their place of worship (21 percent), and mail received from religious interest groups (21 percent). In other words, in 1996 a significant portion of the population both received religious communications and regarded them as important to their political behavior. A follow-up survey in 2004 showed almost identical patterns, with secular sources more widely used by the general public but with religious sources regarded as much more important by traditionalist evangelicals, a group that had increased to almost 12 percent of the population over the eight-year time span. In 2004 both secular and religious sources increased in importance compared to 1996 with the religious sources showing the greatest increase. For example, among traditionalist evangelicals, the importance attached to information obtained at church doubled from 1996 to 2004.

Impact of Communication on Political Behavior

Although secular sources of communication outnumber the religious, the latter are more important for evangelical Christians than for most other Americans and are particularly influential with the most orthodox and observant among them. Do these religious communications matter in terms of voting decisions, and do they matter more than the secular communications? In terms of the secular sources of communication, respondents that regarded newspapers and television news as important factors in their voting decisions were more likely to have voted for Bill Clinton than for Bob Dole in 1996 and for John Kerry as opposed to George W. Bush in the 2004 election.. In contrast, individuals that relied on radio and interest-group mail in making their voting decisions were somewhat more likely to have voted Republican in both years.

Communications from the political campaign itself and from friends and coworkers made little difference in voting choices in 1996 and 2004. The secular sources, then, exhibited no consistent pattern in relationships with the vote.

Communications from religious sources, however, consistently benefited the Republican Party. Religious radio made the most difference in both 1996 and 2004. Percentages for the other religious sources were not as striking but still in the same direction. This Republican bias among those who regarded religious sources of communication as important held up for traditionalist evangelicals as well. As documented in the scholarly literature, many forces are pushing evangelicals in the direction of the Republican Party, and religious sources of communication are certainly part of the explanation. They support efforts by the Republican Party and its candidates to mobilize evangelicals, who have become the base of the GOP voting coalition.

Is there evidence about the content of pastoral political communication? The classic studies of Protestant clergy emphasized the liberal bias of pastors in communicating with their congregations. But there is evidence of change. In recent research on the Protestant clergy, mainline and evangelical pastors were asked what political subjects they talked about in church. Their theological positions predicted their responses, with the theologically orthodox emphasizing a moral reform agenda focusing on abortion, gay rights, sexual promiscuity, and moral decline; the theologically liberal, on the other hand, emphasized a social justice agenda focusing on race, poverty, equal rights, and the environment. Clerical conservatives, the research showed, were as politically active as their liberal counterparts. In a 1996 survey, the mass public was asked what political issues their clergy had spoken about in the past year. Seventy-four percent said their pastors had talked about hunger and poverty, 55 percent mentioned abortion and sexual behavior, while just 19 percent noted "candidates and elections," and only 9 percent said their clergy had spoken about foreign policy or defense-related issues. For traditionalist evangelicals the percentages increased significantly on the abortion, sexual behavior, and "candidates and elections" items while declining on the

other two issues. A 2004 survey asked a similar, but not identical, set of items. Pastoral speech against abortion declined somewhat in 2004 (although it was still high in traditionalist evangelical circles), but a new measure found that "same-sex marriage," a hot topic in the campaign, was discussed by 26 percent of pastors, and fully half of the clergy for traditionalist evangelicals. The Iraq War (2003–) and the issue of terrorism was talked about by 31 percent of pastors (39 percent of traditionalist evangelical clergy spoke out on this topic). In 2004 hunger and poverty were discussed by almost one-third of pastors (less among evangelicals), while education and the environment received even less attention.

Do these communications make an electoral difference? Both 1996 and 2004 surveys showed that when respondents claimed that their clergy discussed abortion or sexual behavior, these same respondents sided with the Republicans. The same was the case with same-sex marriage in 2004. When poverty and hunger or foreign policy and defense issues were discussed, including the war in Iraq and terrorism in 2004, respondents leaned toward the Democrats. So there is evidence that the content of pastoral communications is related to the vote choices of those who receive the messages. It appears that pastors can sway their congregations simply by talking about issues, even if they shy away from candidate endorsements. If Republican clergy focus on abortion, the issues of gay rights, and personal morality, while Democratic pastors choose poverty and hunger and other "social justice" issues, both sides should move the laity in their preferred direction.

Finally, in the same surveys, a series of questions were asked about secular and religious contacts made during the campaign itself. Here the disparity between secular and religious contacts was much less pronounced than that between secular and religious media communications. In 1996, in terms of campaign contacts, 29 percent of Americans claimed to have been contacted by a candidate for office, while 32 percent mentioned a contact by a political party. In 2004 contacts increased to 35 percent from candidates and 43 percent from parties. Among traditionalist evangelicals, in 2004 the percentages were even higher, 45 percent from candidates and fully 52 percent from parties showing that the GOP and its candidates were targeting their base.

Examining religious contacts, 35 percent of the 1996 respondents received at least one religious contact from a variety of sources (a religious interest group, information available in their church, clergy or friends in church urging them to vote). This figure increased to 48 percent in 2004. Among traditionalist evangelicals these figures were 48 and fully 82 percent, respectively. This dramatic increase reflects the highly charged religious atmosphere in the 2004 campaign and the organized effort by the Republican Party to use religious sources to its advantage.

The evidence supports the conclusion that secular contacts have had modest effects on recent election outcomes. Religious contacts, however, have had a much greater impact, especially among evangelicals. These findings are far from conclusive but suggest that targeted contacting efforts can pay off in election campaigns. Traditionalist evangelicals are a natural target because their political attitudes are relatively homogeneous and they are easy to reach in the church setting.

Audiences for Communication

The secular and religious media clearly communicate to different audiences. Secular communications are received by large segments of the population, including the highly religious, while religious communications are rarely, if ever, received outside religious circles. Increasingly, many religious communications are received by the evangelical community only. In that community their impact is greatest among traditionalist evangelicals and is closely related to their voting decisions.

See also *Conservatism; Evangelicalism; Fundamentalism; Graham, Billy; Pentecostalism.*

Paul M. Kellstedt and Lyman A. Kellstedt

BIBLIOGRAPHY

Green, John C., et al. *Religion and the Culture Wars: Dispatches from the Front.* Lanham, Md.: Rowman and Littlefield, 1996.

Guth, James L., et al. *The Bully Pulpit: The Politics of Protestant Clergy.* Lawrence: University Press of Kansas, 1997.

Hadden, Jeffrey K. *The Gathering Storm in the Churches.* Garden City, N.Y.: Doubleday, 1969.

Hadden, Jeffrey K., and Anson D. Shupe. *Televangelism, Power, and Politics on God's Frontier.* New York: Henry Holt, 1988.

Hertzke, Allen D. *Representing God in Washington: The Role of Religious Lobbies in the American Polity.* Knoxville: University of Tennessee Press, 1988.

Horsfield, Peter G. *Religious Television: The American Experience.* New York: Longman, 1984.

Quinley, Harold E. *The Prophetic Clergy: Social Activism among Protestant Ministers.* New York: Wiley, 1974.

Schultze, Quentin. "Evangelical Radio and the Rise of the Electronic Church, 1921–1948." *Journal of Broadcasting and Electronic Media* 32 (1988): 289–306.

Sweet, Leonard I., ed. *Communication and Change in American Religious History.* Grand Rapids, Mich.: Eerdmans, 1993.

Wald, Kenneth D. *Religion and Politics in the United States.* 3d ed. Washington, D.C.: CQ Press, 1997.

Communism

Communism set out—in theory—to bring about a society in which all would be equal: everyone would contribute to it according to ability and everyone would draw upon its resources according to need, a prelude to the withering away both of the state and of religion. However, in practice every communist or Marxist regime promoted hostility to, often persecution of, religion as one of its defining features. Karl Marx, the founding father of communism in the nineteenth century, did not write extensively about religion, but he defined it as "the opium of the people"—an unhealthy palliative necessary during the painful transformation of society to its "socialist" phase. Religion, Marx believed, would die a natural death when economic conditions improved to the point that all humanity shared the world's economic bounty. Not until October 1917, with the accession to power of Vladimir Ilyich Ulyanov, the Russian revolutionary known to history as Lenin, did communism execute a program of active persecution of religion.

Lenin and Stalin

Lenin's intentions were soon made clear. The Russian Orthodox Church was forced not only to dissociate itself from its tsarist past, when it had been a subservient state religion, but also to be extirpated from society forthwith. Since the time of Peter the Great, tsar from 1682 until 1725, the state had nominated its own lay representative as head of the church, but the collapse of the tsarist regime in March 1917 provided an opportunity for the assertion of independence. The church elected a supreme head, Tikhon, the first patriarch since Peter the Great's abolition of the office two hundred years earlier.

Lenin's first legislative act was to abolish private ownership of land, including land that belonged to monasteries and churches. The Law on Separation of Church and State and of School from Church followed in January 1918. Although Lenin's constitution proclaimed the right of individuals to religious liberty, believers nevertheless were bereft of their religious heritage, and violent persecution followed. Church leaders (including Tikhon as well as the minority Roman Catholics and later the Baptists), along with uncounted millions of ordinary believers, were harassed, imprisoned, often murdered, or starved to death.

When Stalin (Joseph Vissarionovich Djugashvili) succeeded Lenin in 1925, the lot of believers deteriorated further. The assertion of unconditional loyalty to the state by the intimidated acting head of the church, Metropolitan Sergi, in 1927, was unavailing, even though this vow of loyalty became the theoretical standard for church-state relations until 1985, when Mikhail Sergeyevich Gorbachev became Soviet leader. Stalin's constitution replaced Lenin's right to "freedom of religion" by the much more restrictive phrase "freedom of religious worship." But even that right was severely limited by compulsory state registration of places of worship, which in practice the authorities usually refused. The continued proclamation of separation of church and state was no more than a legal fiction.

The suffering of believers in Stalin's purges of the 1930s was the most comprehensive and organized persecution in Christian history, not excluding that of the early Christians under the Roman Empire. The church, both as an institution and as a worshiping community, virtually ceased to exist by 1941. The results of that devastation are still visible—the ruined relics of countless churches and monasteries—in nearly every town and village in Russia, Belarus, and Ukraine.

World War II and Its Consequences

The Great Patriotic War, as the Russians call the Second World War, had a positive effect on the life of the Russian Orthodox Church. However, the effect on all the territories that fell under Soviet domination at its conclusion was negative. The beneficial effect worked in two ways. Western areas of the Soviet Union (Belorus and huge tracts of Ukraine and of Russia itself) were temporarily liberated from Soviet domination by the incursion of the Nazi German army in June 1941. Almost everywhere behind the German lines there was an immediate revival of religion. Churches reopened and, as from nowhere, clergy and laity emerged, ready to maintain them. These actions would soon become a contributory factor to increased persecution, for when the Soviets reconquered these territories they were looking for scapegoats who could be accused of collaboration with the enemy.

In the Russian heartland and even in the non-Russian

republics of the Soviet Union, Stalin used the call to patriotism to revive the morale of a nation that had been duped into a feeling of security by the Ribbentrop-Molotov pact. (This pact supposedly guaranteed nonaggression between the communist and fascist regimes.) After having abused religious believers for a decade and a half, Stalin called on their church to promote patriotism. Priests and pastors were released from prison on condition that they take an oath of loyalty to the Soviet state.

Stalin even received the surviving rump of the church leaders in 1943 and rewarded them for their loyalty with the promise of concessions as soon as practicable. Until recently, the substance of this meeting was unknown. But with the fall of communism and the opening of Soviet records, researchers have been able to dig through the archives and locate the protocol. It is evident that Stalin exhibited a benign face, making far-reaching promises about the reopening of churches, monasteries, and theological seminaries; the publication of a journal; and the election of a patriarch for the first time since the death of Tikhon, in 1925. Stalin generally kept to the promises he made, though his price was continuing political loyalty on the lines of Metropolitan (later Patriarch) Sergi's assertion of 1927, particularly offering moral support for the subjugation of the new parts of the Soviet empire acquired by conquest at the end of the First World War.

This unofficial concordat between church and state lasted until the accession to power of Nikita Sergeyevich Khrushchev in 1958. Khrushchev instituted a new period of active persecution, with the reclosure of many churches, from 1959 until his ousting in 1964.

Soviet Expansion and Cold War Policy

The Soviet Union expanded westward at the end of the war in 1945, to encompass the Baltic states (Estonia, Latvia, and Lithuania), which had been independent in the 1920s and 1930s. A huge swathe of territory, stretching from the Arctic to Moldavia in the south, was incorporated, in every part of which the church was flourishing. Protestant areas (predominantly Lutheran Estonia and Latvia) came under Soviet domination for the first time. Millions of indigenous Roman Catholics were in Lithuania, parts of Belorus, and Ukraine. In Moldavia the Orthodox Church had a vigorous parish and monastic life. Every one of these areas had to be sovietized in its own way, but without exception subjugation of the church was a key issue, and the brutality with which this was done contrasted with the improved situation in the Russian heartland.

A special case was Western Ukraine, where the Eastern Rite Catholics flourished—a church with developed education, a strong hierarchy, and an identification with Ukrainian nationalism. Its origins went back 250 years, and its development as a Catholic Church loyal to Rome but using the Slavonic liturgy and Orthodox Church order (allowing priests to marry, for example) had always been somewhat contentious. In 1946 Stalin's commissars forcibly incorporated it into the Russian Orthodox Church. Even this latter name was anathema to those upholding such a strong tradition of Ukrainian nationalism, but any who protested—many clergy, all the bishops, and the redoubtable Metropolitan Slipyj—immediately lost their liberty and some even their lives. The Ukrainian Catholic Church regained its legitimacy only at the time of Gorbachev's visit to the pope in December 1989.

From the end of World War II, Soviet influence spread further, as the parameters of the cold war were established. The new Communist bloc of Eastern Europe and Central Europe presented a massively diversified religious picture. While each regime had limited autonomy to deal with the religious question in its own way, nowhere did the new rulers relinquish the basic communist tenet of state atheism.

Of all these countries Poland experienced the least direct persecution. After an unsuccessful attempt to gag Cardinal Stefan Wyszynski, an outspoken opponent of the government's repression of religious freedom, by imprisoning him from 1953 to 1956, the regime had burned its fingers in the fire of popular dissent. From then on a variety of even less successful antireligious tactics, all negated by the election of Cardinal Karol Wojtyla as pope in October 1978, were to occur. The new pope, John Paul II, was to become an instrumental figure in Poland's move toward liberation. Never before had the College of Cardinals elected a pope from Eastern Europe. The immediate effect, from the moment of his first visit back to his homeland in 1979, was to destabilize the country in a political sense, leading directly to the founding of the Christian trade union Solidarity.

Other Catholic leaders faced longer imprisonment than Cardinal Wyszynski, the best known of whom were Cardinals József Mindszenty in Hungary, Josef Beran in Czechoslovakia, and (in a country never fully incorporated into the Soviet bloc) Aloysius Stepinac in Yugoslavia. However, despite the temporary rise of various "peace priest" movements, which sought to reconcile communism and Christianity and promote pro-regime sentiments among the populace, nowhere did the Catholic Church capitulate to the political demands of the ruling faction.

One cannot make such a generalization of the Protestant or Orthodox churches. In the Soviet Union the Baptists, who had been present in Russia and Ukraine in small numbers since the 1860s, at first appeared to do the political bidding as required, but from the early 1960s, in response to the renewed persecution under Khrushchev that affected all denominations, a resistance movement evolved uniting many congregations. The leaders of the *Initsiativniki* (initiators of a movement to set up a free congress), as they were called, or Reform Baptists, put up decades of resistance to brutal treatment, but they succeeded in a way no other religious group in the Communist bloc ever did in attracting worldwide publicity and international support. The leadership of the registered Baptist congregations meanwhile made strenuous efforts to undermine the credibility of these reformers, both inside the Soviet Union and worldwide.

In Hungary a compromised but strong leadership of the Reformed Church, smaller than the majority Catholic Church, predominated over the anticommunist opposition in 1948 and again after the uprising of 1956. The resulting "diaconia theology," which was in effect a New Testament phrase for accommodation with the powers that be, exercised a telling influence on international bodies such as the World Council of Churches and the World Alliance of Reformed Churches, which, in their turn, were diverted from any front they might have established against Communist atheism. The Orthodox Churches of Eastern Europe played an even more prominent part in defining such a policy.

In the German Democratic Republic the majority Lutheran Church evolved a much more critical stance, never abandoning its determination to criticize the regime if it intruded too crassly into the administration of church affairs. Nevertheless, Christians found themselves to be second-class citizens, suffering discrimination in education and career opportunities.

The situation was very different in neighboring Czechoslovakia, where the minority Church of the Czech Brethren evolved its policies under the leadership of Josef Hromadka. As well as accepting the Soviet worldview, promoted by the Christian Peace Conference, which Hromadka established in 1958, the Czech Brethren put a unique emphasis on dialogue with the Communists. This effort drew together theologians from East and West in a series of meetings in the 1960s. The meetings ended abruptly when the Soviet invasion of August 1968 annihilated the so-called Prague Spring, the attempt under Alexander Dubček to introduce "communism with a human face." Those who had promoted the dialogue found themselves persecuted, but they, as well as the more traditional opposition to communism, undoubtedly contributed to the evolution of a civic consciousness.

The Orthodox Church outside the Soviet Union unquestionably played a role in pacifying the people and, directly or indirectly, persuading them to accept their lot under the new regime. In Bulgaria, communism in its early years instigated brutal persecution of all believers, especially the small Protestant and Catholic Churches, but Patriarch Kiril sacrificed independence of speech to preserve the structural unity of the Orthodox Church. From 1971 his successor, Patriarch Maxim, built relations that might almost be described as cordial.

In Romania the situation was not that different, though on the world stage the Orthodox Church, as the second largest after the Russian, played a more prominent role. Patriarch Justinian exercised his office for almost the first thirty years of the communist state, evolving his own, less compromised version of diaconia theology. The massive popular support for Orthodoxy was never confronted by the closure of churches such as happened in the Soviet Union. The Romanian Orthodox Church was the strongest visible Christian presence in a Communist country, even though the price, as a small number of dissenters and many Protestants discovered to their cost, was political conformity.

A total contrast to these countries was Albania, a predominantly Muslim country, though there was a significant Catholic and Orthodox presence as well. Following the precept of Chinese leader Mao Zedong, who never finalized the plan of closing every place of worship in China, Enver Hoxha, the Albanian premier, alone totally outlawed religion (1967), closing more than two thousand mosques and churches and imprisoning all religious leaders.

Many Albanian Muslims who lived on the Yugoslavian side of the frontier, in Kosovo, were at that time better off (though they were to suffer more after the breakup of Yugoslavia in 1989). Muslims in Bosnia (then part of Yugoslavia) were also treated tolerantly, which could not be said of Muslims in Azerbaijan and the five Soviet republics of Central Asia (or of other Muslim enclaves in Russia).

Although Islam was never outlawed, Soviet Muslim institutions collapsed in the early days of communism and there was a massive closure of mosques.

Other Communist Countries

After the consolidation of Soviet power in Eastern Europe and Central Europe, other countries in a wide diversity of geographical locations went over to the Communist sphere of influence. Although their relations with Moscow varied considerably, every one of them adopted state atheism in some form or other.

The most significant of these was China, which signaled its adoption of communism under Mao by the immediate expulsion of all foreign missionaries. The local churches had to become indigenous almost overnight, and political loyalty was demanded after the Soviet model. This situation led to a split in the Catholic Church between those who remained loyal to a "foreign regime" (Rome) and were forced to go underground and a new Chinese Catholic Church. Among Protestants of various denominations, who were forced to unite, there was a similar development. During the Cultural Revolution of the late 1960s and early 1970s, Christians, especially those belonging to the unofficial "house churches," suffered appalling deprivation, along with many other sectors of the population. The traditional Chinese religions such as Confucianism were less structured and survived with a low profile, though Islam, strong in the less populated western region of Xinjiang, suffered repression.

A special case was Tibet, which lost its independence as a result of the Chinese invasion of 1959. From that year on, following the escape of the Dalai Lama, Tibet's spiritual leader, to India, the Buddhist faith, which embraced the whole nation, was locked in a life-or-death struggle to survive. Buddhist monasteries and cultural institutions were under daily attack. The spirit of the people and their loyalty to the exiled Dalai Lama never succumbed, however.

Even Cuba, far distant from the hub of communist power, became a loyal satellite of Moscow. In 1959 Fidel Castro demonstrated his intentions, after seizing power, by expelling all foreign, particularly American, missionaries. The majority Catholic Church was subjected to pressure and discrimination, if not open persecution. In more recent years Castro has shown himself to be more positive to issues such as Bible distribution, and the visit of Pope John Paul II to Cuba in 1998 seems finally to have reversed Cuban antireligious policies. North Korea, slavishly following Chinese

Cuban president Fidel Castro signs a book of condolence for Pope John Paul II in April 2005. Pope John Paul II was the only pope to ever visit the communist nation.

policies, has come close to eradicating public religious life, though doubtless there is much below the surface which will one day be revealed. The African states of Angola, Ethiopia, and Mozambique all operated antireligious policies of one kind or another in the 1970s and 1980s, but none was systematic enough to have much beyond a short-term effect on religious life.

The Collapse of the Berlin Wall

The churches contributed to the rapid and relatively bloodless collapse of communism in Eastern Europe at the end of 1989 and two years later in the Soviet Union. The election of the Polish pope led directly to the open resentment expressed by the tens of millions of Catholic Poles at the domination of their country by an alien ideology. Pope John Paul II visited his country in the summer of 1979 for the first time since his election and encouraged his people to take the initiative in the struggle for full religious liberty and their independence from false ideologies. Following the

pope's visit, Lech Walesa (who would later be the first president of an independent Poland) gained massive support when he established Solidarity as a Christian trade union. Bishops, priests, and working laity were united. Fr. Jerzy Popieluszko became a Christian spokesman for political reform and attracted the attention of the nation before his murder by the police in 1985. The imposition of martial law could only fail to suppress freedom of thought, unless backed by a Soviet invasion, something that became unthinkable after the accession of Gorbachev.

In the German Democratic Republic the Protestant Church began to provide a remarkable safe haven for political protesters in 1989. The churches in Czechoslovakia and Hungary were involved in the popular protests that led to increasing demands for the freedom to travel. The removal of the first brick from the Berlin Wall, which had stood as a symbol of a divided Europe since 1961, released a flood tide that no political edict could stem. Gorbachev and his right-hand man, Eduard Shevardnadze, the foreign minister, chose a policy that saved Europe from a bloodbath: the Soviet army would not intervene, as it had done in Hungary in 1956 and in Czechoslovakia in 1968. In Romania, which by then had an especially tough regime under Nicolae Ceausescu, a leader of the Reformed Church, Laszlo Tokes, led the first popular protests in Timisoara. These protests eventually resulted in the deposition and execution of the dictator.

In the Soviet Union the role of the churches in the period of glasnost and perestroika, Gorbachev's watchwords for examining the past and restructuring society, had been less dramatic but not insignificant, as they moved into the public domain for the first time since 1917. From 1988, when the state permitted—even encouraged—the Russian Orthodox Church to celebrate the millennium of its founding in Kiev, believers established social work in prisons, hospitals, and orphanages. In 1990, a year before the collapse of the Soviet Union, new laws were passed that guaranteed complete religious liberty and brought to fruition the efforts of thousands of all denominations who, in the 1970s and 1980s, had risked their freedom and even their lives to achieve religious liberty and transform the face of a repressive regime.

See also *Atheism; Balkan States; Buddhism, Tibetan; China; Cuba; Europe, Eastern; Hungary; Marxism; Orthodoxy, Russian; Poland; Russia; Yugoslavia.*

Michael Bourdeaux

BIBLIOGRAPHY

Beeson, Trevor. *Discretion and Valour.* 2d ed. London: Collins, 1982; Philadelphia: Fortress Press, 1982.

Bourdeaux, Michael. *Gorbachev, Glasnost, and the Gospel.* London: Modder and Stoughton, 1990; published in the United States as *The Gospel's Triumph over Communism.* Minneapolis: Bethany House, 1991.

Ellis, Jane. *The Russian Orthodox Church: A Contemporary History.* London and New York: Routledge, 1988.

Pospielovsky, Dimitry. *The Russian Church under the Soviet Regime, 1917–1982.* 2 vols. Crestwood, N.Y.: St. Vladimir's Seminary Press, 1984.

Walters, Philip, ed. *World Christianity: Eastern Europe.* Monrovia, Calif., and Eastbourne, Sussex: MARC, 1988.

Weigel, George. *The Final Revolution: The Resistance Church and the Collapse of Communism.* New York: Oxford University Press, 1992.

Communitarianism

Communitarianism, a contemporary social movement and political philosophy, developed in reaction to the individualist tendencies of Western culture. Its proponents seek to find remedies to the crisis of social disintegration, evidenced by the breakdown of family life, poverty, violence, and political fragmentation, through the development of communities. They advocate a renewed sense of responsibility for persons as parents, workers, employers, neighbors, and citizens.

Philosophically, communitarianism defines itself against liberalism, the dominant Western view that highlights individual liberty in personal, economic, and political life. Communitarianism holds that exaggerated individualism is the root cause of society's moral and social problems. It is distinct from communism in that it does not seek to subsume the dignity of the individual under the collective whole. Communitarianism aims to create a balance between persons and community, individual freedom and the social good. It is most developed in the United States and Great Britain.

Philosophical Characteristics

The fundamental argument of communitarianism is that liberal individualism presents a distorted description of what it means to be a person. Communitarians describe persons as social beings. They hold that persons are formed within relationships and have no identity apart from relationships. Personal autonomy, the ability to choose freely, is dependent in many ways on human relationships. People, born within traditions, develop their own identity—who they are, what they think and feel—in relation to other people. Communitarians thus use such phrases as "the socially embedded self" or "the dialogical self" or "persons-in-community" to describe the essential social nature of persons.

Liberals defend a stance of neutrality on the notion of social good: it is up to individuals or businesses to define their own good. It is thus inappropriate for society to define social good in a way that would limit individual or corporate liberty. Communitarians hold that society can and must seek a shared meaning of the good. They believe the well-being of society is the element that should determine morality and social policy. Communitarians defend a strong notion of participatory democracy. The public good, to be truly a public good, must be discussed publicly.

In contrast to liberals, communitarians are suspicious of "rights" language, which in contemporary culture dominates moral discourse. Rights, by definition, are moral claims that individuals make against society. Communitarians argue that rights are proclaimed independently of particular social contexts and without concern for related responsibilities. Communitarians, although split on the significance of rights, as we shall see, are united in their concern for the priority of responsibility and the social nature of persons.

Types of Communitarians

There are two forms of communitarians, moderate and radical. Moderate communitarians are postliberal in that they build on the strengths of liberalism, especially its concern for social equality, while challenging its lack of social integration. They defend basic human rights but argue that the liberal understanding of rights is impoverished. Moderate communitarians call for a balance between rights and responsibilities. Their political positions do not fit neatly into categories. For example, they advocate strengthening the structure of the family by such politically diverse means as making divorce less accessible than it is now and by ensuring that employers provide maximum support for working parents. They support teaching values of tolerance, conflict resolution, personal responsibility, and democracy in schools. They believe a healthy society is built on healthy institutions and thus promote participation in local institutions, schools, places of worship, and neighborhood groups. Radical communitarians reject the notion of human rights because they reject any attempt to develop an ethic that is applied universally to all communities and cultures. They hold that moral standards arise within particular communities as expressions of their history and tradition.

Both forms of communitarianism tend toward a relativistic morality. They typically reject transcommunal, or objective, moral claims in favor of a morality developed by consensus within a particular community. However, moral relativism within a community, they argue, is ultimately destructive to the community. Moderate communitarianism looks outward and focuses on civic responsibility. Radical communitarianism looks inward and focuses on preserving the identity of a particular community.

Role of Religion

Communitarianism has allies in Christianity and Judaism. Roman Catholic social thought, with its strong sense of people as social beings, its moral tradition of promoting the common good, its hierarchical structure that directs local communities to focus on larger communities, and its natural law tradition (moral truth is open to all persons of good will), has strong affinities with moderate communitarianism. The biblical notion of covenant, as found in some Protestant and Jewish theology, corresponds with the communitarian notion of persons being bound in community, united by a common morality, and directed toward a good beyond the self.

The communitarian public virtues of rational dialogue, diversity, toleration, and a commitment to the social well-being resonates with fundamental concerns of contemporary Jewish and Christian life. Some forms of Protestantism that stress the place of the individual against larger social structures would be critical of the communitarian emphasis on the secular community. There is a strong affinity between radical communitarianism and some forms of Protestant and Jewish thought. Just as radical communitarians seek to promote particular communities, some Jewish and Christian groups advocate forming alternative communities distinct from the world.

Criticisms

A tension between communitarianism and organized religion lies in the question of moral authority. Although contemporary Christianity and Judaism support democracy in political organization, there is concern about defining all moral value through a democratic method of a particular society—that is, moral relativism. Other critics note that community ought not to be an end in itself and that many communities have oppressive histories. It has been suggested that communitarianism is a nostalgic philosophy, recalling a simpler time, and that the radical pluralism of modern societies makes it impossible to speak of a substantive social good.

See also *Communism; Covenant; Human Rights; Individualism; Liberalism; Natural Law; Pluralism.*

Bernard V. Brady

BIBLIOGRAPHY

Bellah, Robert, Richard Madsen, William Sullivan, Ann Swidler, and Steven Tipton. *Habits of the Heart: Individualism and Commitment in American Life.* Berkeley: University of California Press, 1985.

Daly, Markate, ed. *Communitarianism: A New Public Ethics.* Belmont, Calif.: Wadsworth, 1994.

Dyck, Arthur. *Rethinking Rights and Responsibilities: The Moral Bonds of Community.* Cleveland: Pilgrim Press, 1994.

Etzioni, Amitai. *The Spirit of Community: Rights, Responsibilities, and the Communitarian Agenda.* New York: Crown, 1993.

———, ed. *New Communitarian Thinking: Persons, Virtues, Institutions, and Communities.* Charlottesville: University of Virginia Press, 1995.

Glendon, Mary Ann. *Rights Talk: The Impoverishment of Political Discourse.* New York: Free Press, 1991.

MacIntyre, Alasdair. *After Virtue: A Study in Moral Theory.* Notre Dame, Ind.: University of Notre Dame Press, 1984.

Sandel, Michael. *Liberalism and the Limits of Justice.* Cambridge: Cambridge University Press, 1982.

Community Organizing

Community organizing encompasses a wide variety of efforts to empower residents in a local area to participate in civic life or policy making. In the United States, most community organizing operates in low- or middle-income areas and has adopted at least some of the tactics and techniques pioneered by Saul Alinsky (1909–1972), a controversial community activist and reformer. Such efforts focus on building the political power of an organization composed of local residents, and using that power to influence issues and decisions affecting those residents.

Community organizing has taken many forms, often differentiated according to whether they are "neighborhood-based," "issue-focused," "race-based or multiracial," or "congregation-based" (also called "broad-based" or "faith-based"). From the 1940s to the 1960s Alinsky and his allies drew on labor organizing experiences to pioneer neighborhood-based confrontational tactics—initially in Chicago but later throughout the United States and in Tanzania, the Philippines, South Korea, and elsewhere. The U.S. federal government funded some community organizing in the 1970s, and several local governments sponsored community organizations in the 1990s. By the mid-2000s most community organizing was sponsored by nongovernmental organizations funded by charitable organizations, foundations, and individuals. Primary funding came from several major foundations and religious organizations such as the Catholic Campaign for Human Development, various Protestant denominations, and the Jewish Fund for Justice.

For scholars of religion and politics, congregation-based community organizing has been of greatest interest. It draws on the social ties within religious congregations to recruit participants, then draws on religious commitment and participants' economic interests to motivate vigorous engagement in civic life. Through "actions"—large public gatherings at which officials are asked to commit to a specific course of action—these organizations push for public policies that serve the interests of low-income residents. Sponsored by a single religious congregation, a citywide federation of congregations, or a statewide network, these actions may draw from a hundred to several thousand participants. They typically incorporate music from the congregations, prayer led by local clergy, and religious language invoked by lay leaders to define a specific issue as important and suggest an appropriate role for religious believers in the public realm. The action serves to highlight a specific issue and pressure political or corporate leaders to respond to the organization's concern. By negotiating with officials, an organization may also seek to shape long-term public policy.

In the United States four large networks link most of congregation-based community organizations: the Industrial Areas Foundation (based in Chicago), the PICO National Network (based in California), the Gamaliel Foundation (Chicago), and Direct Action, Research, and Training (Florida). Federations affiliated with these networks have addressed issues of economic development, housing policy, educational reform, public safety, city services, government block grant programs, bank lending practices, and minimum wage levels. Many have gained significant influence on local policy regarding these issues and, in some cases, on state-level policy (most prominently the Texas Industrial Areas Foundation in the 1990s, the PICO California Project in the 1990s and 2000s, and Louisiana Interfaith Together in the 2000s);

none have yet played decisive roles in shaping national policy. Such national-level efforts, however, were launched in the early 2000s, most prominently the "PICO New Voices" initiative. Gamaliel's work on economic development in broad metropolitan regions has also been prominent.

Internationally, community organizing efforts directly affiliated with the U.S. networks exist in Great Britain, Central America, Mexico, and South Africa. More broadly, quite distinct forms of community organizing developed in association with liberation theology in Latin America, the theology of struggle in the Philippines, *minjung* theology in South Korea, the Solidarity movement in Poland, and the Islamist movement in the Middle East.

Congregation-based community organizing has drawn the attention of scholars of religion and politics for two reasons. Those interested in democratic theory and social movements have studied its successes and limitations in changing public policy, reforming authoritarian regimes, and empowering low-income urban residents. Those interested in the importance of religion in the public realm have studied congregation-based organizing as one example of how religious motivations and organizations foster participation in the secular political world.

See also *Base Communities; Civil Society; Economic Development; Liberation Theology; Lobbying, Religious; Maryknoll; Nongovernmental Organizations; Philanthropy.*

Richard L. Wood

BIBLIOGRAPHY

Alinsky, Saul D. *Rules for Radicals: A Practical Primer for Realistic Radicals.* New York: Random House, 1971.

Boyte, Harry. *Commonwealth: A Return to Citizen Politics.* New York: Free Press, 1989.

Cortes, Ernesto, Jr. "Reweaving the Fabric: The Iron Rule and the IAF Strategy for Power and Politics." In *Interwoven Destinies: Cities and the Nation,* edited by Henry G. Cisneros. New York: Norton, 1993.

Greider, William. *Who Will Tell the People: The Betrayal of American Democracy.* New York: Simon and Schuster, 1992.

Horwitt, Sanford D. *Let Them Call Me Rebel: Saul Alinsky—His Life and Legacy.* New York: Vintage Books, 1992.

Swarts, H. "Setting the State's Agenda: Church-Based Community Organizations in American Urban Politics." In *States, Parties, and Social Movements: Protest and the Dynamics of Institutional Change,* edited by Jack A. Goldstone. New York: Cambridge University Press, 2003.

Warren, Mark R. *Dry Bones Rattling: Community Rebuilding to Revitalize American Democracy.* Princeton, N.J.: Princeton University Press, 2001.

Wood, Richard L. *Faith in Action: Religion, Race, and Democratic Organizing in America.* Chicago: University of Chicago Press, 2002.

Conference of Latin American Bishops

See *CELAM.*

Confucianism

Based on the teachings of the Chinese political and ethical philosopher Confucius (551–479 B.C.E.), Confucianism is a set of institutional practices grounded in the centrality of familial relations. By the second century B.C.E. this guide to statecraft and moral teaching had become the official creed of China.

Confucianism has undergone any number of alterations since its inception. Throughout these transformations, however, it has remained remarkably consonant with the original teaching of Confucius. As a philosophic or religious vision, Confucianism has been expressed through a line of scholars who have continued to elaborate on the canonical texts (*Analects*) passed on after Confucius's death, thereby extending the way of living that the "Master" had begun.

Although the influence of Confucius was felt soon after his death, thanks to a number of dedicated disciples, it was not until the Han dynasty (206 B.C.E.– 220 C.E.) and the establishment of Confucianism as the state ideology that his school of thought became unchallenged orthodoxy. From this period on, the fundamental insights of Confucius's thought—the importance of family, friendship, education, and community—were central to the Chinese cultural and political experience.

The Terms of Confucianism

Use of oneself as a measure for gauging others describes *shu,* the standard by which both self-realization and social harmony may be attained. As Confucius characterizes *shu:* "Do not impose on others what you yourself do not desire" (*Analects,* 15:24). *Shu* is an act of comparison in which one takes oneself as starting point and attempts to discover the desires of others.

If one is able to act in accordance with *shu,* it is essential that the standard from which one begins—one's self as socially constituted—be expressive of appropriate moral character. In other words, it is essential that one be truly human. The notion expressive of such humanity is *ren,* often translated as benevolence or human-heartedness. This term also alludes to the process of becoming human. Human-heartedness involves both the sense of being fully human and the sense of acting humanely toward others.

Ritual activity (*li*) provides the more or less formal structure that permits the embodiment of *ren* and *shu. Li* comprises the various roles and relationships making up the family and the sociopolitical order beyond. The most important relationships for Confucius are those of father and son and elder brother and younger brother. These hierarchical relationships help to establish the grounds for respect within both the biological and the broader political families. Much of the ritual activity associated with the Confucian vision is modeled on familial relationships. Thus *li* constitutes a code of formal behaviors for stabilizing and disciplining life situations.

Charting a harmonious path within and among the world of others is a principal task for those who want to achieve real humanity. Such an effort leads to a search for the proper way, or *dao,* a crucial term in Confucianism. Confucius characterizes *dao* in terms of cultural inheritance. In this sense *dao* is a cultural resource specifiable in terms of particular individuals or ritual forms. The *dao* of a particular person, or a particular social situation, is a specification of this general inheritance. Thus there is a *dao* of music and of archery, a *dao* of the bureaucrat, as well as a *tian dao*—a way of heaven. All these ways have their source in the rituals, actions, institutions, and writings that have survived in the cultural memory. *Dao,* then, is not some specific norm in accordance with which a person acts; rather, *dao* is realized in the performance of appropriate conduct. The person of *ren* acting with *shu*—within the context provided by *li*—is therefore able to discern the proper way of conducting himself or herself.

Confucianism in a Broader Context

One characteristic of Confucianism that flies in the face of most Western understandings of its vision is its porousness and adaptability. Confucius called himself a transmitter, not a creator, of cultural traditions—that is, he simply adapted the wisdom of the past to his own historical present. Confucius's principal resource was the institutions of the Duke of Zhou who lived some five hundred years earlier. It was from the Duke of Zhou that he inherited the insight of employing the family as the model of all sociopolitical relations.

Just as Confucius reinvented the culture of the Zhou and earlier dynasties for that of his own era, the disciples of Confucianism sought to accommodate many of the ideas of its competing schools (among others, Mohism, Daoism, Legalism, and emerging Buddhism), and in doing so to interweave elements of these sensibilities into their own. This same process of accommodation was to take place after the decline of the Han dynasty. From the third to the tenth centuries Daoist and Buddhist elements began to exert renewed intellectual influence, often strongly competing with Confucianism. Thus since its inception in the eleventh century, a neoclassical form of Confucianism has expressed an interweaving of Confucian, Daoist, and Buddhist ideas.

In either its traditional or neoclassical form, Confucianism dominated Chinese thought after the Han synthesis and largely remained the unchallenged orthodoxy of the Chinese empire until the fall of the Qing dynasty in 1911. Indeed, perhaps this continues to be true today, for a strong argument can be made that just as a composite of Daoism, Buddhism, and Confucianism produced neo-Confucianism, the combination of Marxism and Confucianism in the twentieth century created but another kind of neoclassical Confucianism. Evidence of this development has been China's renewed interest in Confucianism beginning in 1976 just after the death of Communist Party chairman Mao Zedong. Ideological Marxism is fading under the impact of foreign capitalism, but that same impact has led to a reemphasis on the classic Confucian values of discipline, thrift, and task orientation, which harmonize well with the capitalist sensibility. Such an appeal to traditional values could make the transition to a capitalist society much less traumatic.

Meanwhile, the values of Confucianism have had a far-ranging impact on the educational and political institutions of numerous Asian countries—notably Korea, Japan, and Vietnam. Elsewhere in Asia, Singapore has made a conscious attempt to reform its political and educational institutions along traditionally Confucian lines. South Korean schools require formal exposure to Confucian values. Everywhere in Asia where the impact of Western individualism has been felt, there has been a return to Confucianism as a means of reasserting the communitarian model of society.

See also *China; Confucius; Korea.*

David L. Hall

BIBLIOGRAPHY

Chan, W. T. *A Source Book in Chinese Philosophy.* Princeton, N.J.: Princeton University Press, 1963.

Confucius. *The Analects.* Translated by D. C. Lau. Hong Kong: Chinese University Press, 1992.

———. *Mencius.* Translated by D. C. Lau. Hong Kong: Chinese University Press, 1984.

De Bary, W. T., et al. *Sources of the Chinese Tradition.* New York: Columbia University Press, 1960.

Graham, Angus. *Disputers of the Tao.* La Salle, Ill.: Open Court Press, 1989.

Hall, D. L., and R. T. Ames. *Anticipating China—Thinking through the Narratives of Chinese and Western Culture.* Albany: State University of New York Press, 1995.

Confucius

No philosophic or religious visionary, whether Plato or Aristotle, Jesus, Buddha, or Muhammad, is more significant than Confucius (551–479 B.C.E.), who founded in China an entire culture. Even today, in a China nominally influenced by Marxism, Confucianism remains the foundation of the society and culture.

Confucius (K'ung Fu-tzu) was born in the state of Lu (Shandong province in contemporary China) during the decline of the Zhou dynasty (1027–267 B.C.E.). For much of his life he was an itinerant scholar who traveled among competing Chinese states, offering advice on the art of rulership. But Confucius never achieved real practical influence, either in his home state of Lu, where he was for a short period police commissioner, or in any of the other states in which he briefly resided. Somewhat frustrated, Confucius returned to Lu late in life, serving as a councilor of the lower rank, while he continued teaching a small number of disciples who later would begin to disseminate his ideas more broadly.

Among his other accomplishments, Confucius established a school in the state of Lu for the education of future "statesmen"—Plato's academy would not appear until more than a century later. The curriculum of Confucius's school was based on a collection of poetry, music, historical documents, and annals that chronicled the events at the Lu court, along with an extensive commentary on the *Book of Changes,* a divination book containing all the permutations of a six-line figure made up of straight (yang) and broken (yin) lines and consulted to understand the best action in a particular situation. These works, which provided a shared cultural vocabulary for his students, would become the classics of Chinese culture and the standard curriculum for the Chinese literati in the centuries to come.

The principal source of Confucius's own thinking is the *Lunyu*—traditionally translated as the *Analects,* or sayings—which records his life and teachings. The earlier-written portions of the work contain disciples' remembrances of Confucius the man, recording his personal habits and interests. Later portions, particularly the last five of the twenty chapters, were likely recorded by disciples well on their way to becoming mature interpreters of Confucian thought. In these chapters, although Confucius remains the focus, the disciples often speak in their own voices.

Confucius's vision of the means to social and political harmony was grounded in the rites and institutions originated by the Duke of Zhou some five hundred years before Confucius. The Zhou feudal system made family relations the basis of political loyalties. Thus Zhou feudal lords were both vassals and blood relatives of the king.

Building on the vision of the Duke of Zhou, Confucius articulated and elaborated on the importance of the family as a sociopolitical model. The family provides the context within which an individual becomes who he or she is. Moreover, the state itself is patterned on the model of the family. One does not, as Aristotle asserted, move out from the privacy of the family to become a public person, a "citizen"; rather, one is always a member of a family—both of the biological unit into which one is born and of the political "family," which urges a broader set of allegiances. The importance of the family as a model for all sociopolitical relations was the grounding principle from which Chinese civilization was to emerge.

See also *Confucianism.*

David L. Hall

BIBLIOGRAPHY

Confucius. *The Analects.* Translated by D. C. Lau. Hong Kong: Chinese University Press, 1992.

———. *Mencius.* Translated by D. C. Lau. Hong Kong: Chinese University Press, 1984.

Graham, Angus. *Disputers of the Tao.* La Salle, Ill.: Open Court Press, 1989.

Hall, David L., and Roger T. Ames. *Thinking through Confucius.* Albany: State University of New York Press, 1987.

A woman walks by a statue of Confucius, where devotees have left prayers.

Congo, Democratic Republic of the

The Democratic Republic of Congo, known previously as the Congo Free State (1885–1908), the Belgian Congo (1908–1960), the Democratic Republic of Congo (1960–1971), and Zaire (1971–1997), is one of Africa's largest and most populous countries, located around the Congo River Basin in Central Africa. Although sometimes cooperating with the government, religious groups in the Democratic Republic of Congo have often provided an independent social voice. Prior to colonialism, the nearly three hundred distinct societies in what is today Congo presented an extraordinary diversity of political arrangements and religious practices. Political systems ranged from the decentralized stateless societies of the rainforest to the large centralized kingdoms such as the Luba, Lunda, and Kongo in the coastal and savannah regions. Religious beliefs varied widely, including animism, ancestral veneration, spirit worship, and belief in a high god. In most societies, little distinction was made between a secular and sacred realm, and political leaders held religious authority and ritual responsibilities.

In the late 1400s, Catholic missionaries arrived in the coastal Kongo Kingdom, whose territory is today divided between Angola, the Democratic Republic of Congo, and the Republic of Congo. King Nzinga a Nkuwu converted to Christianity in 1491, and his son, who became King Alfonso, declared Kongo a Christian kingdom. Christianity remained strong in Congo for over two centuries, until the slave trade devastated the kingdom. Christian symbols and rites were then subsumed into other religious practices, though traces of a vernacular Christianity persisted in core areas of Catholic activity.

Colonial Congo

Christian missionaries returned to Congo even before Henry Morton Stanley began to claim land in the name of King Leopold II of Belgium in 1879. Sharp competition between Catholic and Protestant missionary groups characterized colonial missionary activity. Although King Leopold, who held Congo as a personal possession until 1908, at first favored Protestant missions, a close alliance between the Catholic Church and the Belgian colonial government soon developed, as most Belgian colonial administrators were themselves Catholic and the Vatican shrewdly gave precedence to Belgian missionary groups, including Trappists, Redemptorists, the Sisters of Notre Dame de Namur, and Belgian branches of the Jesuits and White Fathers. The Catholics benefited from their privileged position in recruiting members, and by independence over half of Congo's population was Catholic. Despite their generally good ties with the state, Catholic missionaries occasionally clashed with the regime, as in a major struggle over control of education in the 1950s. The Catholic Church was one of the first voices calling for Congolese self-rule in the mid-1950s.

To compete more effectively with the Catholics and avoid competition among themselves, American, British, and Scandinavian Protestant missionary societies divided up the colony under a comity agreement, creating a regional base for Protestant churches that persists to the present. The Protestants periodically clashed with the colonial regime, which mistrusted their foreign origins. In the first decade of the 1900s, English and American Protestants organized an international campaign against the brutal forced labor practices, used in the collection of red rubber, that were devastat-

ing the population of the Congo Free State. The Congo reform movement forced the Belgian parliament in 1908 to remove the monarchy's control and assume direct authority over the territory, changing its name to the Belgian Congo. Despite the disadvantaged position of Protestant missionaries, nearly a quarter of the population was Protestant by the time of independence.

During the colonial period, several indigenous Christian churches also emerged. The most important of these was founded by Simon Kimbangu, a former Baptist evangelist from the Kongo group who began a healing ministry in 1921 in the Bas Congo region. Colonial authorities soon arrested him, and he remained in prison until his death in 1951. Nevertheless, the movement he founded flourished. The Church of Jesus Christ on Earth through the Prophet Simon Kimbangu (known as the Kimbanguism) with its message of healing and deliverance from evil spirits attracted many people seeking an alternative to the Western-controlled missionary churches.

Church and State under Mobutu

After independence on June 30, 1960, Congo swiftly disintegrated, as the prime minister and president challenged one another for power and the regions of Katanga and Kasai declared independence. The churches regarded Prime Minister Patrice Lumumba with suspicion, because of his radical politics and intentions of establishing a secular state, and they did not object to his removal from office in 1960 and assassination in 1961. Although United Nations troops intervened and brought Kasai and Katanga back into Congo and defeated a rebellion in eastern Congo by Lumumba's supporters, the country remained unstable until the leader of the army, Joseph Mobutu, seized power in 1965.

The churches initially welcomed Mobutu's presidency, because he promised to bring order to the country. Clashes between church and state soon emerged, however, as President Mobutu viewed the churches as obstacles to increasing his political and social control over society. Catholic and Protestant leaders first objected to Mobutu's presentation of himself in messianic terms and his use of symbols associated with indigenous magic, such as his staff, which rumor claimed he could transform into a snake. In 1971 the government nationalized the premier Catholic educational institution, Lovanium University. Mobutu further angered church leaders by requiring church schools to allow his political party to establish branches in their institutions. The

Zairian president Mobutu Sese Seko disembarks from his plane in 1977. Mobutu's nearly thirty years of rule left the country, now called the Democratic Republic of the Congo, in a shambles. The years since his overthrow have been marked by civil war and unrest in the region, resulting in more than three million deaths.

Catholic Church publicly opposed his authenticity campaign, which sought to promote traditional African culture, because it required citizens to give up the Christian names taken at baptism and adopt traditional African names. Tensions with the government led the Vatican briefly to withdraw Cardinal Joseph Albert Malula to Rome in 1972. Although Malula was allowed to return to the country (whose name Mobutu had changed from the Democratic Republic of Congo to Zaire in 1971) later in the year, Mobutu continued his assault on church power, but the expulsion of Malula made the churches less open to speaking out. In 1973 Mobutu banned church youth groups and outlawed several dozen church publications. In an attempt to centralize his control over them, Mobutu forced all fifty-three Protestant groups in the country to come together in a single institution, the Church of Christ in Zaire. Some groups that resisted state control, such as the Kitawilsts, an outgrowth of the Watchtower Movement that rejected all earthly authority, were brutally suppressed. In 1975 Mobutu nationalized church schools, which constituted over half of the country's educational establishments, but church leaders offered only mild objections.

Few church–state conflicts emerged over the next decade. Mobutu's power gradually waned, as the population grew weary of his corrupt and authoritarian style, and his mismanagement of the economy led to an economic downturn and decline in the standard of living. As government services declined, churches moved in to fill the gap, expanding health and development services. The government, unable to provide financial support for all the country's schools, returned much of the education system to church control. By the end of the 1980s, the churches had gained considerable popular good will, even as Mobutu's popularity had diminished severely.

With over 90 percent of Congo's population affiliated with a Catholic, Protestant, or Kimbanguist community, the churches became an important base for challenging the Mobutu regime. The Catholic Church in particular provided important support for the democracy movement that emerged in the early 1990s. The council of bishops issued an important pastoral letter in April 1990 that condemned corruption and called for political reform. The bishops' frank declarations inspired many others in the society to voice their criticisms of the regime. Both Protestant and Catholic churches sponsored new independent newspapers and human rights groups in the early 1990s. Under strong pressures from the churches and others, in 1991 Mobutu begrudgingly allowed a Sovereign National Conference to convene, bringing together Zairian politicians, civil society activists, business leaders, and religious leaders, to chart the country's future. Catholic archbishop Laurent Monsengwo of Kisangani was elected president of the National

Conference, because of the belief that he could act as a neutral mediator.

Despite the emergence of open opposition, Mobutu's deft political skills allowed him to hang onto political power. Mobutu succeeded in dividing and undercutting the National Conference, at first accepting their choice for prime minister, then replacing him with someone of his choosing. While the Catholic hierarchy remained critical of Mobutu, he maintained good relations with the leadership of the Kimbanguists and with the head of the united Protestant group, the Church of Christ in Zaire, Bishop Bokeleale, who came from his home region Equateur. As Mobutu felt his power increasingly challenged, he turned to the exploitation of ethnic differences as a means of dividing the population, and this strategy also fostered ethnic tensions in the churches.

Church and State Since Mobutu

Ultimately, outside intervention removed Mobutu from power. The 1994 genocide in Rwanda resulted in a refugee crisis, when more than one million mostly Hutu refugees poured across the border into eastern Zaire. Fearing the destabilizing effects of the refugee camps across their frontier, the new Rwandan government sponsored a movement of Zairian rebels, the Alliance of Democratic Forces for the Liberation of Congo-Zaire (ADFL), in 1996. With backing from Burundian, Rwandan, and Ugandan troops, the ADFL advanced quickly across Zaire, gaining support from many dissident Zairians and local militias. In May 1997, Mobutu fled as the troops approached the capital, and the leader of the ADFL, Laurent Kabila, became president, changing the name of the country back to the Democratic Republic of Congo. When President Kabila proved less pliable than they had hoped, Rwanda and Uganda organized another uprising in eastern Congo in 1998 and again sent in their troops, but this time other African countries, including Namibia and Zimbabwe, sent troops to back the regime, creating a military stalemate that lasted for several years.

Christian churches served as a major voice condemning human rights abuses committed during the two wars and promoting efforts to seek peace. The Second Congo War came to a formal end with a peace accord in July 2003, though violence continued in parts of the country. The war was highly disruptive and is estimated to have contributed to the deaths of more than three million people, mostly through disease and starvation. Churches played a

major role in providing assistance to those in need because of the war.

Several local militia groups involved in the two wars turned to indigenous religious practices to back their cause. The best known of these groups is called Mai-Mai, derived from the Swahili word for water, because of the reputed ability of ritually pure fighters to turn bullets into water droplets. Mai-Mai militia members undergo elaborate rituals and observe taboos to gain ritual purity that is said to guarantee their military success.

See also *Catholicism, Roman; Christianity in Africa; Missionaries.*

Timothy Longman

BIBLIOGRAPHY

Adelman, Kenneth Lee. "The Church-State Conflict in Zaire." *African Studies Review* 18, no. 1 (April 1975): 102–116.

Boyle, Patrick M. "Beyond Self-Protection to Prophesy: The Catholic Church and Political Change in Zaire." *Africa Today* 39, no. 3 (1992): 49–66.

Kabongo-Mbaya, Phillippe. *L'Eglise du Christ au Zaire.* Paris: Editions Hurtubise, 1992.

MacGaffey, Wyatt. *Modern Kongo Prophets: Religion in a Plural Society.* Bloomington: Indiana University Press, 1983.

Schatzberg, Michael. *The Dialectics of Oppression in Zaire.* Bloomington: Indiana University Press, 1988.

Consejo Episcopal Latinoamericano

See *CELAM.*

Conservatism

Conservatism, once on the wings of the American political stage, played a leading role on center stage by the early to mid-2000s. Despite conservatism's emergence as a powerful political force, however, misunderstandings abound about its meaning and nature—economically, philosophically, politically, religiously, and socially.

In 1860 Abraham Lincoln succinctly summed up conservatism in New York City's Cooper Union: "What is conservatism? Is it not adherence to the old and tried, against the new and untried?" This simple effort to define conservatism, however, masks important differences within its ranks. Indeed, complexity, not simplicity, best describes conservatism. For several reasons it is something more than the other side of the ideological coin, something more than liberalism's opposite. Although commonly considered an ideology, many of conservatism's foremost intellectuals dispute this notion. And while it is often simply presented as a counter-balance to liberalism, conservatism defies a generally accepted definition. Additionally, although thought to embody a standard set of principles, conservatism's principles frequently conflict. Many leading intellectuals, liberal and conservative, believe that conservatism lacks a significant tradition in the United States, but it has contributed more to American public life than the credit lines indicate. Finally, although usually thought to feature homogeneity among its adherents, in truth conservatism features heterogeneity not only among its adherents but also in its ideas.

A Definition of Conservatism

Even though conservatives may differ in how they define conservatism, the following definition captures the mainstream of conservative thought: Conservatism is the defense of the political, economic, religious, and social status quo from the forces of abrupt change, based upon the belief that to maintain continuity and stability in society, established customs, laws, and traditions should guide change.

To amplify this definition by contrasting it with liberalism, conservatives generally (1) place more emphasis on orthodox and traditional religious values; (2) express less faith in the goodness, reason, and perfectibility of mankind; (3) voice greater opposition to the power of centralized government; (4) connect more with state and local governments in the federal system; (5) identify with nationalism more than with internationalism, such as voicing less support for the United Nations and other international organizations; (6) express a more fervent nationalistic and patriotic spirit; (7) put greater emphasis upon the responsibilities and duties of individuals and less upon their rights; (8) trust capitalism and free markets more than government regulation in determining economic policy; and (9) believe that gradual changes within existing institutions offer more hope and greater opportunity to maintain the economic, political, religious, and social stability of society.

Ten Canons of Conservative Ideas

The ten canons presented here represent a synthesis of the tenets of conservatism found in important books espousing conservative ideas, discussed below.

1. *Continuity* stands out as the most widely accepted canon of conservative thought, primarily because conservatives value order in society. Preferring organic change, meaning a slower rate of change within existing institutions, conservatives oppose large-scale and abrupt changes that would disrupt and threaten a stable society. Their respect for the past reflects a desire to incorporate change within existing community institutions, standards, and traditions, making continuity from generation to generation the most essential canon of conservative thought.

2. *Authority* manifests itself as a natural corollary of continuity in the social order. Conservatives believe that the government must protect society from foreign challenges and domestic disturbances that would disrupt the continuity of community.

3. *Community* emerges high on lists of conservative tenets because conservatives believe communities provide the structure for organic change and serve as a countervailing force against the abuses of power concentrated in the government. Conservatives place a premium on private and voluntary organizations, including professional associations, churches, and service organizations, along with universities, trade unions, newspapers, private business, and local government.

4. *Deity* holds a place on most lists of conservative tenets, if for no other reason than this: Conservatives usually believe in traditional moral values and manifest a distrust of human nature. Put another way, they believe that natural or divine law transcends human law, which makes man and government ultimately accountable to God.

5. *Duty* or personal responsibility ranks higher in conservative thinking than personal rights. When personal rights transcend individual responsibilities, conservatives contend that citizens think more about what government can do for them rather than what they can do for themselves, which leads to an ever larger government.

6. *Democracy* in the conservative mind exists within the context of constitutional constraints. Because the U.S. Constitution limits the power of government, conservatives advocate its "strict interpretation," contending that the courts should interpret the law rather than make law

and should observe the "original intentions" of the founders in interpreting the constitution.

7. *Property* and its ownership enable individuals to have a stake in society, according to conservatives, who maintain that when people have a stake in their community, they are more likely to function as responsible citizens who desire to preserve the social order. A sound social order not only creates opportunities for people to own property, thereby strengthening their ties to the community, but it also helps them rise in economic and social status. The opportunity to own property, therefore, is a key to an open society.

8. *Liberty* rises higher than equality in its importance to the social fabric, but conservatives deem the relationship like that of a "big brother." Liberty cannot exist without equality, lest it create anarchy. Nor can equality exist without liberty, lest it create totalitarianism. So on balance, society must balance the two, but give preference to liberty. According to conservatives, when equality supersedes liberty, it leads to the creation of an enlarged government to determine the appropriate levels of equality among individual citizens and groups and to the loss of incentive for citizens to excel as a direct consequence of their dependence on government.

9. *Meritocracy* reflects the conservative belief in merit and ability in the selection of leaders. Conservatives believe that orders and classes of people naturally exist in society and that the leadership class helps to provide order by guiding and governing society. Because the American founders rejected the idea of an aristocratic leadership class of titled nobles found in Edmund Burke's England, conservatives in the United States believe in a "natural aristocracy," open to those whose merit and ability qualify them.

10. *Antipathy* to communism and an enlarged government created by the New Deal and the Fair Deal stoked the fires of contemporary conservatism. All of the conservative books in the 1940s and 1950s attacked one or both of these conservative adversaries.

These ten canons represent ten principles to guide conservatives in their personal lives and in their communities and to restrain the role of government in society. Social harmony and stability stand out as their ultimate goal.

The Emergence of Contemporary Conservative Ideas

In 1950 Lionel Trilling declared in *The Liberal Imagination* that "liberalism is not only the dominant but even the sole intellectual tradition. For it is the plain fact that nowadays there are no conservative… ideas in general circulation." But even as Trilling chiseled an epitaph on the conservative tombstone, contemporary conservatism had already risen from the dead as a reaction to communism's rise internationally and to the emergence of a powerful central government in Washington, D.C., via the New Deal and Fair Deal. These rapid changes internationally and domestically struck at core conservative beliefs: a slow rate of political and social change; decentralization of economic and political power; fiscal responsibility; decreased government spending; a reduction in governmental regulation of society; personal freedom; and traditional religious faith.

Intellectually and philosophically many books undergirded the rise of contemporary conservatism. In 1944 Friedrich von Hayek's *The Road to Serfdom* challenged the rise of a state-managed economy, whether in the form of communism or of liberalism's ascendance through the New Deal. In 1948 Richard Weaver's *Ideas Have Consequences* argued that the dominant ideas of the times would produce disastrous consequences for personal freedom and the social order. One year later, Ludwig von Mises' *Human Action* presented a powerful case for free-market economics. Also in 1949, Peter Viereck's *Conservatism Revisited* drew praise from the *Times* of London for laying out a set of traditional conservative principles based on the ideas of British parliamentarian and intellectual Edmund Burke. These books represent but a few of the thoughtful presentations of conservatism that appeared before Lionel Trilling's premature burial of conservatism in the graveyard of history.

In rapid-fire order between 1950 and 1953 many influential conservative books appeared on the scene, including but certainly not limited to William F. Buckley's *God and Man at Yale* (1951), Eric Vogelin's *The New Science of Politics* (1952), Russell Kirk's *The Conservative Mind* (1953), Leo Strauss's *Natural Right and History* (1953), and Robert Nisbet's *The Quest for Community* (1953). All of these books, whether written before or after 1950, continue to enjoy significant influence more than five decades later.

Appearing like a *double fortissimo* on a musical score expressing the crescendo of influential conservative books, Clinton Rossiter's *Conservatism in America: The Thankless Persuasion* received the Charles A. Beard Memorial Prize in

1955. Rossiter's book not only won a major literary award, but it sparked a heated debate about the meaning of conservatism. For example, some viewed Rossiter's book as a defense of the mainstream or moderate center of American politics rather than as a counterweight on the right to liberalism's ascendance on the left. Regardless of the positions taken in this debate, conservatism had come of age.

Not only have these writers had continuing influence for more than fifty years, but also others have followed in their footsteps, including Pulitzer and Nobel Prize winners. Among the leading authors and their books are Milton Friedman, *Capitalism and Freedom* (1962); James Buchanan and Gordon Tullock; *The Calculus of Consent* (1962); Forrest McDonald, *E Pluribus Unum* (1965); Edward Banfield, *The Unheavenly City* (1970); Harvey Mansfield, *The Spirit of Liberalism* (1978); George Gilder, *Wealth and Poverty* (1981); Herbert Storing, *The Antifederalists* (1981); Richard Neuhaus, *The Naked Public Square* (1984); Charles Murray, *Losing Ground* (1984); Allan Bloom, *The Closing of the American Mind* (1987); E. D. Hirsch, *Cultural Literacy* (1987); and Shelby Steele, *The Content of Our Character* (1991).

The titles alone illustrate the breadth and division of conservative interests, which makes a simple defining of conservatism all the more challenging.

Common Manifestations of Conservative Ideas

Seven manifestations of conservatism and liberalism—authoritarian, economic, international, political, populist, religious, and social—reveal much about conservatism's complexity and its differences with liberalism. In each instance, however, their manifestations of differences represent diverse tendencies or directions in their thinking, not absolute disagreements.

1. First, Alexander Hamilton's authoritarian conservatism emphasized elitism as contrasted with Thomas Paine's radical egalitarianism. Elitist and egalitarian thought continue to influence American society, but not as much as either Hamilton or Paine would have liked. Hamilton liked the idea of rule by aristocrats, and Paine very much wanted to wipe out class distinctions. Just as conservative thought today exhibits a greater affinity for elitism, liberalism reveals a greater kinship with egalitarianism. On the whole, however, neither totally rejects the other's inclination.

2. Economic conservatism as manifested in the writings of Milton Friedman emphasizes free markets, while economic liberalism as presented by John Kenneth Galbraith underscores the role of government in managing the economy. Relatively speaking, economic conservatism places more emphasis on capitalism, while economic liberalism places greater emphasis on socialism. That is not to say that economic liberals are socialists, but rather that their thinking leans more in that direction. In the same way not all conservatives oppose all government initiatives that embody socialist tendencies, such as Social Security, Medicare, and Medicaid. All things considered, conservatives and liberals lean in different directions economically.

3. Realism stands out as the byword of international conservatism, while idealism manifests itself as the byword of international liberalism. Again as a matter of relative importance, liberals rely more on international organizations, while conservatives put more faith in power politics and pragmatism. President Ronald Reagan's build-up of the American military to challenge communism and President Jimmy Carter's idealism and emphasis upon human rights illustrate this point of contrast.

4. Conservatism stresses liberty, while liberalism emphasizes equality, but neither to the total neglect of the other. President Reagan peppered his speeches with references to liberty and freedom, while his opponents used the word *equality* much more. Both liberty and equality possess a long history in American politics, going at least as far back as the opening line of the Declaration of Independence.

5. Moral impulse motivates conservatives and liberals with populist agendas. Conservative populists view such issues as school prayer and abortion through a moral lens, whereas liberal populists look at such issues as the excesses of corporate greed through a moral lens. Conservatives want to implement into public policy their personal morality, while liberals want the government to create economic equity.

6. Religious conservatives hand out the calling card of orthodoxy in their promotion of absolute standards of right and wrong. On the other hand, relativism stands out as the mark of religious liberals. For example, regarding the Ten Commandments, religious conservatives customarily interpret them strictly, while religious liberals interpret them more loosely, contending that individual situations should determine the degree of adherence to them. To no one's surprise, religious con-

servatives stand in the front lines of Americans fighting for public displays of the Ten Commandments and for school prayer, even as religious liberals fervently oppose them.

7. In the matter of change in society, conservatives advocate gradual change, and liberals, faster change. Conservatives believe that a faster rate of change may endanger the social order and the stable implementation of justice, equality, liberty, and prosperity in society. By contrast, liberals argue that faster change will enable more people to benefit from these goals in a timelier manner, which would enhance stability by more quickly spreading the benefits of democracy to a broader cross-section of people. In short, how much change and at what speed can society absorb it without creating the liabilities of social disorder? During debates about President Lyndon Johnson's Great Society proposals, conservatives contended that they represented too much change too soon. Subsequent studies of these policies generally conclude that conservatives were right. The performance of Great Society programs never measured up to their promise, and most of them no longer exist.

Besides these seven manifestations of differences with liberalism, four other comparisons merit mention: neo-conservatism, libertarianism, Midwestern conservatism, and attitude versus action conservatism.

Neo-conservatives began to come under the conservative tent during the late 1960s and early 1970s. Disaffected by liberalism's increasing preference for a weaker military and for enlarged social programs, neo-conservatives found themselves attracted to the conservative ideals of nationalism and a slower rate of social change. Geographically located primarily in the Northeast, New York City in particular, however, they do not share the same passion for religious conservatism as that found in the South and in the Sunbelt states.

Libertarians appear like conservatives some of the time, and like liberals at other times. Critics call them chameleons. On one hand, they ardently advocate autonomy of the individual, a minimal role for government, and a vibrant free market economy. But on the other, they steadfastly oppose governmental action to limit or ban abortion, to allow school prayer, and other initiatives supported by traditional conservatives, who argue that libertarians, by placing undue emphasis on liberty, constitute a form of unbridled individualism that fails to respect community customs and traditions.

Midwestern conservatives differ from other conservatives, particularly those in the South and the Sunbelt. Laying claim to the pragmatic mantle of Abraham Lincoln, they are less ideological and more prone to compromise, as illustrated by the pragmatic leadership of these former conservative leaders: Senators Robert A. Taft (R-Ohio), Everett McKinley Dirksen (R-Ill.), Robert Dole (R-Kan.), and President Gerald Ford (R-Mich.). Ideology guides, but does not govern, Midwestern conservatives, unlike the emergent conservative leaders from the South and Sunbelt, such as Newt Gingrich (R-Ga.) and Tom Delay (R-Tex.). For pragmatic and humanitarian reasons, Midwestern conservatives may promote policies that would enlarge the size of the national government. To illustrate, Senator Taft advocated public housing during the late 1940s, and Senator Dirksen provided the absolutely essential support needed to pass the Civil Rights Act of 1964 and the Voting Rights Act of 1965. Gingrich and Delay not only pursued a staunchly conservative platform, but they also did it with a very sharp cutting edge in their manner. Under conservative Midwestern leadership in Congress, Republicans and Democrats got along quite well, but under Gingrich and Delay, ideological and political animosities increased.

Is conservatism an attitude or an activist ideology? A state of mind marks attitude conservatives, who believe in conservative ideals and principles, such as the importance of the local community, tradition, and a slow rate of change. Action conservatives typically hold to the same ideals and principles, but they offer a seriously prepared plan for ideological and political action, and in the matter of social change, action conservatives frequently favor a faster rate of change to achieve their ideological objectives. When Newt Gingrich replaced Robert Michel (R-Ill.) as the leader of Republicans in the U.S. House of Representatives, he used the lever of the "Contract with America" to strengthen activist conservatism and to usher in a faster rate of public policy change from a conservative perspective.

Given the complexity of conservatism, does it offer a generally accepted set of principles? Do certain ideas almost always mark conservatism, regardless of its myriad manifestations? In a nutshell, can conservatism be boiled down to several readily identifiable canons? By synthesizing conservative tenets from a variety of conservative thinkers, the answer is "yes."

See also *Christian Right*.

Charles W. Dunn

BIBLIOGRAPHY

George H. Nash. *The Conservative Intellectual Movement in America Since 1945.* Wilmington, Del.: Intercollegiate Studies Institute, 1998.

Charles W. Dunn and J. David Woodard. *The Conservative Tradition in America.* Lanham, Md.: Rowman and Littlefield, 2003.

Constitution, U.S.

The U.S. Constitution, the world's oldest surviving written constitution, is the fundamental law of the country, simultaneously specifying a structure of government and limiting the power of that government. In contrast to patterns of government in European nations in 1787, when the Constitution was adopted, and even in variance with the Declaration of Independence of 1776, the Constitution is strictly secular; that is, it does not claim an explicit theological or religious base. This omission was primarily because its framers limited the federal government to a few areas of defined powers, mostly regarding interstate and international commerce and defense. The individual states remained responsible for determining any government relation to religion. Thus the Constitution addressed religion in only the briefest terms.

Article VI, clause 3, of the Constitution prohibits religious tests for individuals holding federal office. This clause was adopted because the framers thought religious affiliation should not be a bar to service to one's country. Several state constitutions did have bars to public office, excluding nonbelievers, Catholics, and Jews. Maryland and Massachusetts, for example, at first stipulated that only a Christian could become governor.

The most significant reference to religion in the Constitution was added after its adoption, in the First Amendment of the Bill of Rights, which was ratified in 1791: "Congress shall make no law respecting an establishment of religion or prohibiting the free exercise thereof." These religion clauses affirmed that Congress has no power to establish religion or to interfere with the exercise of religious faith. This position was extraordinary for its time, contravening the pattern that had prevailed in Europe for one and a half millennia, since the fourth century, when the Roman emperor Constantine adopted Christianity (313) and his successor, Theodosius, made it the official religion of the state (380). James Madison and other founders at the Constitutional Convention had carefully read the history of religion and state patronage, finding that the fusion debilitated both. Thus, for the first time in Western history, they decided to establish a government that neither was legitimated by religion nor was the patron of religion. The two spheres would be separated from the onset.

In 1970 the Supreme Court, in *Walz v. Tax Commission,* noted that the relationship between religion and government must be one of "benevolent neutrality." This means that American government, though secular in purpose, is not hostile to religion but is generally sympathetic to religious faith. Determination of the precise parameters of religion-state relations has not been easy; therefore, this task has usually been left to the courts.

The Nineteenth Century

Before the twentieth century, jurisdiction over most religion cases rested in the states rather than the federal government. Thus the highest court, the Supreme Court, heard only a few cases. In two cases that dealt with disputes in U.S. territories, *Reynolds v. United States* (1879) and *Davis v. Beason* (1890), the Supreme Court said that freedom of religion did not reach to the Mormon practice of polygamy. *Watson v. Jones* (1872) declared that the federal government had no power to intervene in disputes between competing Christian sects or congregations. Justice Samuel Miller, writing for the Court, stated emphatically, "The law knows no heresy, and is committed to the support of no dogma, the establishment of no sect."

In *Bradfield v. Roberts* (1899) the Supreme Court, for the first time, addressed establishment of religion. *Bradfield* held that congressional funding to a religiously affiliated organization (in this case a hospital in Washington, D.C.) that accomplished a secular purpose of providing medical care for the indigent did not constitute a case of establishment of religion in violation of the First Amendment.

The Twentieth Century

During the twentieth century the Supreme Court began incorporating provisions of the Bill of Rights into the Fourteenth Amendment as a restraint on state actions. *Cantwell v. Connecticut* (1940) witnessed the incorporation of the free exercise clause. The Court ruled that Connecticut could not prohibit Jehovah's Witnesses from distributing literature in support of their faith. On the matter of incorporation, the Court stated, "The fundamental concept of liberty embodied in the [Fourteenth] Amendment embraces the liberties guaranteed by the First Amendment . . . . The Fourteenth Amendment has rendered the legislatures of the states as incompetent as Congress to enact laws" prohibiting the free exercise of religion. The Court incorporated the establishment clause seven years later, in *Everson v. Board of Education of Ewing Township.* In this decision the Court upheld a city's subsidizing the transportation of students to and from both public schools and private religious schools, reasoning that the aid went to students and their parents and not to the support of religious instruction. *Everson* also included a broad definition of the unlawful establishment of religion, setting a significant precedent for establishment clause jurisprudence.

Incorporation of the religion clauses ushered in a new era of federal jurisdiction in religion cases. The Supreme Court has since then heard more than one hundred religion cases. Faced with the challenge of balancing the demands of ensuring freedom from the imposition of religion by law (no establishment) and freedom for religion (free exercise), the Court has found religion cases to be among the most difficult to decide with consistency.

Free Exercise Clause Jurisprudence

The Supreme Court, in *Sherbert v. Verner* (1963), held that South Carolina's denial of unemployment benefits to Adell Sherbert, who had lost her job because of her refusal to work on Saturday, her day of worship, was an unconstitutional restriction on Sherbert's free exercise of religious rights. This case is notable for broadening free exercise claims and establishing the precedents that a state must show a compelling state interest to justify infringing religious rights and that its method of enforcement of that interest must be the least restrictive means available.

A major shift in jurisprudence came in *Employment Division v. Smith,* decided in 1990. In this case the Court abandoned the compelling-interest test for a rule of neutral applicability, upholding a law prohibiting unemployment benefits to employees fired for drug use, even when associated with religious worship. In 1993 Congress responded specifically to the *Smith* decision by passing the Religious Freedom Restoration Act. The act, in holding that the government could "substantially burden" free exercise of religion only when a law furthered a compelling state interest and was the least restrictive means for doing so, reinstated the test principles enunciated in *Sherbert* thirty years previously.

In *Boerne v. Flores* (1997) the Court found the act unconstitutional, at least when applied to the states, not because of its insistence on the compelling interest–least restrictive test, per se, but because the act was found to violate the constitutional separation of powers.

Free exercise questions have often arisen in relationship to education. *West Virginia State Board of Education v. Barnette* (1943) upheld the right of Jehovah's Witnesses to abstain from pledging allegiance to the American flag, warning against making use of governmental means to coerce religious and ideological unanimity. *Wisconsin v. Yoder,* decided in 1972, upheld the right of Amish parents to withdraw their child from school after the eighth grade, to avoid worldly influences. In *Widmar v. Vincent* (1981) the Court ruled that a public university could not bar religious groups from meeting in buildings in which the school allowed nonreligious groups to meet. *Rosenberger v. Rector and Visitors of the University of Virginia* (1995) determined that a public university could not withhold funding from a Christian-oriented student newspaper when the school also funded other publications. In a 5–4 decision, the majority of the Court applied the general notion of neutral treatment of all speech, whether religious or nonreligious, instead of deciding the case strictly as an establishment issue. In *Locke v. Davey* (2004) the Court allowed the State of Washington to deny scholarship funds to theology students. Petitioner Davey alleged that neutrality required the state to fund all students, including theology students, but the Court held that an exclusion for those pursuing degrees in devotional theology did not violate the free exercise clause.

Tax policy has, on occasion, clashed with religious liberty claims. In *Murdock v. Pennsylvania,* decided in 1943, the Court held that states could not condition the distribution of religious literature on the payment of a licensing fee. In *Murdock* the Court considered an ordinance of Jeannette, Pennsylvania, which conditioned door-to-door solicitations for merchandise of any kind on payment of a licensing fee. The Pennsylvania borough held that Jehovah's Witnesses, who were distributing literature and soliciting people to purchase their books, were subject to the ordinance. The Court determined that application of the ordinance to the Witnesses was unconstitutional, finding that it would amount to a tax on free exercise of religion. In *Christian Echoes National Ministry v. United States* (1973) the Court upheld rules from the Internal Revenue Service (IRS) that did not allow any religious organization involved in political activities to declare a tax

Walter Gobitas and his children, William and Lillian. The Gobitases, Jehovah's Witnesses, challenged the children's expulsion from school after refusing to salute the flag as an infringement on their religious beliefs in Minersville School District v. Gobitis *[sic] (1940). The U.S. Supreme Court's ruling upholding the requirement was overturned in* West Virginia State Board of Education v. Barnette *(1943).*

exemption. In *Bob Jones University v. United States* (1983) the Court upheld the IRS policy disallowing tax exemption to any religious organization that practiced racial discrimination. *Swaggart Ministries v. California Board of Equalization* (1990) held that requiring religious organizations to collect sales tax on the sale of religious literature did not violate free exercise. The Court's reasoning was that the tax was applied generally and was only an incidental burden on religion.

Establishment Clause Jurisprudence

In 1968 the Court considered how to apply the *Everson* precedent on funding of religious education, in *Board of Education v. Allen,* ruling that the loan of secular texts to private religious schools did not establish religion. More direct aid to private religious schools was first rejected in 1971, in *Lemon v. Kurtzman. Lemon* determined that state funding of secular instruction in private religious schools was an unconstitutional establishment of religion. *Lemon* was also notable in that it was the first establishment case to combine the secular purpose, primary effect, and entanglement tests developed in *Abington and Walz*. These three components have since been referred to as the *Lemon* test.

In 1973, in *Committee for Public Education and Religious Liberty v. Nyquist,* the Supreme Court struck down, as unconstitutionally advancing religion, a New York program that provided grants to religious schools that served low-income families, gave tuition reimbursement to low-income parents with children in nonpublic schools, and allowed tax deductions for middle-income parents with children in nonpublic schools. In *Mueller v. Allen* (1983) the Court upheld Minnesota's policy of providing a tax deduction to parents with children attending any school, private or public. *Tilton v. Richardson* (1971) allowed funding under Title I of the Higher Education and Facilities Act of 1963 for financing buildings on the campuses of church-related colleges and universities, but only if the buildings were used for nonreligious purposes.

In *Agostini v. Felton* (1997) the Court altered the *Lemon* test. The Court retained the first two prongs (purpose and effect) but then provided three criteria to be used to determine effect: (1) Does the program result in indoctrination of participants? (2) Does the program choose recipients on religious grounds? (3) Does the program result in an excessive entanglement between religion and government? The Court later used these criteria to uphold a state program to provide nondiscriminatory aid (to religious and nonreligious schools) made up of computers, videos, library materials, and so on (*Mitchell v. Helms,* 2000) and to uphold a nondiscriminatory voucher plan (*Zelman v. Simmons-Harris,* 2002).

Several disputes over religious exercises in public education have ended up in federal courts. *McCollum v. Board of Education* (1948) ruled that public schools could not allow religious instruction during the school day, even though participation was voluntary and the instruction was given by local religious leaders who were not paid from tax moneys. The ruling in *Zorach v. Clauson* (1952) clarified the limits of *McCollum,* however, holding that public schools could release students early to attend religious instruction off campus.

A controversial ruling in 1962, *Engel v. Vitale,* held that student recitation of a government-written prayer was unconstitutional, noting that a showing of compulsion to participate in a practice was not required to reach an establishment prohibition. *Abington Township School District v. Schempp* (1963) prohibited both the daily recitation of the Lord's Prayer and the reading of ten Bible verses, allowing, however, the study of religious documents in an academic, nondevotional manner, as literature or comparative religious history. *Abington* reasoned that a policy must have a secular purpose and that its primary effect must neither advance nor inhibit religion. In *Wallace v. Jaffree* (1985) the Court extended that rationale to the "minute of silence" proviso some state legislatures and school boards had adopted as an alternative to school-sponsored prayer. An Alabama statute (1978) had provided for a time of silence, which could be used "for meditation." When it was amended in 1981 to add "voluntary prayer," the Court held it unconstitutional, reasoning that this would characterize prayer as a favored practice, a violation of the secular purpose test in *Lemon. Lee v. Weisman* (1991) dealt with prayer at school graduation. The principal of a Rhode Island middle school had invited a rabbi to give opening and closing prayers and to do so with guidelines set by the school board. The majority opinion set aside the argument that graduation prayer was simply a long-held tradition favored by most people, finding instead an unconstitutional "psychological coercion" of those at the ceremony who disagreed with the practice.

Under the Equal Access Act of 1984, schools that provided a limited open forum in which student organizations could meet must also allow student-initiated and student-led religious organizations to meet. The Supreme Court upheld the Equal Access Act in *Board of Education of the Westside Community Schools v. Mergens* (1990).

Does granting of tax exemptions to churches constitute an unconstitutional establishment of religion? In *Walz v. Tax Commission* (1970) the Court upheld New York's policy of allowing property tax exemptions to churches, finding that the policy was not an unlawful establishment of religion

because it applied broadly to charitable institutions. Also the Court noted an important rule that has become a major factor in establishment clause jurisprudence—the entanglement test. This test prohibits government interference with religious activities when interference would create an excessive entanglement with religion.

Government-supported religious traditions have given rise to numerous legal challenges. *Marsh v. Chambers* (1983) reviewed state funding of legislative chaplains. Instead of applying the *Lemon* test, the Court opted to uphold the practice as a long-established tradition. In *Lynch v. Donnelly* (1984) the Court, applying a new "endorsement" test proposed by Justice Sandra Day O'Connor, allowed a city's sponsorship of a nativity scene, accompanied by secular symbols of Christmas. The endorsement test was later used to strike down a Christmas display on public property that was oriented around strictly Christian themes (*Allegheny v. Pittsburgh ACLU,* 1989), reject a Kentucky courthouse display of the Ten Commandments that was erected to promote religion (*McCreary Co. v. Kentucky,* 2005), and approve a Ten Commandments monument on the Texas State Capitol grounds that was erected without proselytization designs but rather to acknowledge passively the historical importance of the Ten Commandments (*Van Orden v. Perry,* 2005).

Challenges to religious exemptions from labor laws have resulted in several cases that defined the relationship between labor laws and religion. In *National Labor Relations Board v. Catholic Bishop of Chicago* (1979) the Court ruled that a religious school was not subject to the National Labor Relations Act. In 1972 Congress amended Section 702 of the Civil Rights Act of 1964, to allow religious organizations to discriminate in employment on the basis of religion. Subsequent decisions in *Southwestern Baptist Theological Seminary v. Equal Employment Opportunity Commission* (1980) and *Alamo Foundation v. Secretary of Labor* (1985) determined that religious exemptions from labor laws do not apply to nonministerial employees or employees engaged in commercial employment. In *Church of Latter-day Saints v. Amos* (1987) the Court upheld the dismissal of an employee working in a Mormon-owned gym, a nonprofit service related to a religious mission of the Mormon church.

A lively debate over the proper relationship of religion to government has continued for more than two hundred years. Although the fine points of this relationship will never be entirely resolved, the U.S. Constitution will continue to offer a framework for peaceful discussion of church-state issues.

See also *Education; Freedom of Religion; Separation of Church and State; Taxation; United States of America.*

Derek Davis

BIBLIOGRAPHY

Ariens, Michael S., and Robert A. Destro. *Religious Liberty in a Pluralistic Society.* Durham, N.C.: Carolina Academic Press, 1996.

Cord, Robert L. *Separation of Church and State: Historical Fact and Current Fiction.* New York: Lambeth Press, 1982.

Curry, Thomas. *The First Freedoms: Church and State in America to the Passage of the First Amendment.* Oxford: Oxford University Press, 1986.

Davis, Derek. *Religion and the Continental Congress, 1774–1789: Contributions to Original Intent.* Oxford: Oxford University Press, 2000.

Miller, Robert T., and Ronald B. Flowers. *Toward Benevolent Neutrality: Church, State, and the Supreme Court.* 5th ed. Waco, Texas: Baylor University Press, 1996.

Pfeffer, Leo. *Church, State, and Freedom.* 2d ed. Boston: Beacon Press, 1967.

Stokes, Anson Phelps. *Church and State in the United States.* 3 vols. New York: Harper, 1950.

Conversion

Religious conversion is the process by which the identity, relationships, and personal values of an individual or group are reformulated as new religious ideals. Although today many people think of it as a uniquely individual event, throughout history broad changes in politics and society have prompted religious conversion. In ancient times the incorporation of tribal and nonstate peoples into multiethnic empires was often accompanied by their conversion to more socially expansive and doctrinally formalized religions, including those known today as the world religions. In modern times religious conversion has assumed new forms, in a manner deeply influenced by world politics, global communications, and the accelerated pace of social change.

Christians and Muslims in the Modern Macrocosm

More than most other religions, Christianity and Islam have demonstrated a remarkable ability to adapt to the modern era and communicate their message to growing numbers of believers. Restricted to Europe and portions of the Middle East during the Middle Ages, Christianity in the early modern era benefited from the colonial ascent of western Europe, extending its reach to all corners of the globe. Some scholars have argued that the often close collaboration of mission and colonial authorities during this time amounted to a "colonization of consciousness." Although they often did facilitate mission establishment and compel conversion, the attitudes of colonial authorities toward missionaries varied widely. In Mexico, East Africa, and Sumatra, authorities promoted the establishment of missions in recently colonized territories but later restricted missionary privileges when church leaders sought to defend native populations from exploitative labor programs. Elsewhere, as in Muslim portions of Africa and the Dutch East Indies, colonial officials barred missions outright, on the grounds that proselytization among Muslims might provoke unrest and jeopardize European economic concerns.

Christian missionaries in colonial times, therefore, were not everywhere agents of European domination. What is clear is that Western expansion presented a forceful challenge to localized and politically vulnerable religions. On some islands in the South Pacific, nineteenth-century natives discarded their cults shortly after European contact, hoping that adoption of the new arrivals' religion would allow them to tap into European military and economic power. Elsewhere, as in portions of Southeast Asia and sub-Saharan Africa, missionaries required converts to adopt European dress, worship, and etiquette. As a result, many natives rejected Christianity as "the religion of Europeans." Not coincidentally, the ranks of native Christians in Asia and Africa swelled dramatically after World War II, when church leadership devolved from European to native clerics, and the identification of Christianity with European colonialism weakened.

Since the end of that war, Christian conversion has continued in large portions of the developing world in a manner that again reflects changing political realities. In contemporary Africa, Christian conversion has been accompanied by the growth of "African" and independent churches. Some of these new religious movements maintain orthodox belief and ritual, but many draw on indigenous styles of leadership and worship. More dramatic yet has been the recent expansion of evangelical Christianity in Africa, eastern Europe, Latin America, and Southeast Asia. In Latin America, upward of 15 percent of the population has converted to the new faith since 1960. Although North American missions pioneered the movement in many countries, today evangelicalism's grass roots are locally sustained. As with Methodism in nineteenth-century England, many poor and marginalized urbanites view evangelical Christianity as an avenue to direct religious participation and social dignity. Women converts look to the faith to provide checks on abusive macho males. In societies plagued by political violence, evangelicalism also provides believers a means to express alternative ethical values without encoding that alternative in a political form and thereby inviting repression by local authorities.

In parts of the Old World, the European expansion also accelerated the process of Islamic conversion. When, in the sixteenth century, the Portuguese seized "spice island" entrepôts in Southeast Asia (in what is today the island nation of Indonesia), Muslim rulers responded by attacking and converting their Hindu neighbors, whom the Muslims saw as potential allies of the Europeans. As nineteenth-century colonialism improved roads and economic infrastructures in Asia and Africa, Muslim preachers often followed in their wake. Like their Christian counterparts, Muslim preachers were identified by native peoples as the carriers of a powerful and cosmopolitan religion. Islam appealed to many converts because colonial penetration undermined local authorities and ideals, unleashing a desire for a religion capable of responding to the challenge of an expanded social universe. In numerous instances, too, Islam was drawn into the struggle against European colonialism.

At several points in modern history Islamic conversion came about through political conquest. Islam's contemporary growth, however, has more to do with the Muslim community's voluntarism, proselytizing zeal, and grassroots organization, qualities that it shares with evangelical Christianity. Still, the usual process of conversion differs between the two religions. Unlike mission Christianity (especially its Protestant variant), Islam rarely requires converts to demonstrate early in the process a comprehensive knowledge of theology; conversion is effected through a simple profession of the faith. As a community of believers grows, however, Muslim practices of almsgiving, collective worship (required of all males on Fridays), pilgrimage, and religious education create strong pressures for a deepening orthodoxy. Islam has no centralized church structure or even a formal clergy; religious leadership is instead assumed by jurists or religious scholars known collectively as *ulama*. Unlike nineteenth-century Christianity, mainline Islam has allowed converts in new Muslim lands to rise quickly to leadership positions. In newly converted regions of Africa, South Asia, and Southeast Asia, the permeability of Islamic leadership to local recruits has allowed converts quickly to identify their new faith as indigenous, discouraging the development of nativist sects like those that have proliferated in African Christianity.

Internal Conversion

Islam and Christianity have been the two most powerful agents of religious conversion in modern times. However, an equally significant reformulation of religious identity has occurred among other believers, not through the adoption of a new faith, but through the reconfiguration or "rationalization" of the religion with which individuals have long been affiliated. Scholars refer to this reformulation of identity within an already-professed religion as "internal conversion."

In the modern era internal conversion has often been prompted by Muslim or Christian challenges to other faiths. In early twentieth-century India, for example, Christian and Muslim success in converting untouchables led Hindu leaders to develop their own programs of religious proselytization. In so doing, the Hindu leadership standardized and simplified their religion's organization and doctrine in a manner that showed strong Protestant influences. Elsewhere, as in Muslim Southeast Asia, the recent Islamic revival has prompted the adherents of minority religions to defend their faith by adopting educational and organizational reforms similar to those promoted by reformist Muslims. In the majority Buddhist nations of Burma, Sri Lanka, and Thailand, finally, government officials have supported efforts by reform-minded Buddhists to convert minority populations within their borders.

Not all cultures are equally susceptible to conversion appeals. In the eighteenth and nineteenth centuries, as they reshaped their diverse populations into a more homogeneous citizenry, many western European countries developed ethnonationalist traditions that diminished religion's role in political life and dampened popular interest in formulating expressly religious public identities. In premodern China and Japan, too, ruling elites discouraged the development of exclusive religions in favor of a civilizational tradition in which confessional religion played a secondary and nonexclusive role. In the twentieth century, the bitter experience of Japanese colonialism, civil war, and cultural disorientation led many Koreans to depart from this East Asian pattern and convert to Christianity in large numbers. More recently, Japan, Taiwan, Hong Kong, and even mainland China have witnessed the development of proselytizing religions promoting conversion and exclusive affiliation. Evangelical Christianity has figured in some of these new religious movements, but confessional sects of Buddhism and Daoism, as well as assorted "new religions," have emerged as well. Despite these developments, East Asia remains a region in which conversion and the idea of exclusive religious affiliation are less prevalent than in many other parts of the world.

Modern politics, economics, and communications have drawn growing numbers of people into a fast-changing and multicultural macrocosm. In many communities this development has also increased social differentiation, accelerated the collapse of locally organized traditions, and unleashed aspirations for voluntarism and popular participation in religious affairs. Having originated in the empires of the ancient world and been reformulated through their encounter with modernity, Christianity and Islam developed values and organizations well suited to the challenges of the modern era. Other religions have followed suit, promoting widespread movements of religious renewal and conversion. Inasmuch as world events continue to challenge popular morals and identity, conversion will likely remain a central feature of contemporary politics, contradicting forecasts of modern religion's demise.

See also *Colonialism; Evangelicalism; Islam in Southeast Asia; Missionaries.*

Robert W. Hefner

BIBLIOGRAPHY

Geertz, Clifford. " 'Internal Conversion' in Contemporary Bali." In *The Interpretation of Cultures,* edited by Clifford Geertz. New York: Basic Books, 1973.

Hefner, Robert W., ed. *Conversion to Christianity: Historical and Anthropological Perspectives on a Great Transformation.* Berkeley: University of California Press, 1993.

Keyes, Charles F., Laurel Kendall, and Helen Hardacre, eds. *Asian Visions of Authority: Religion and the Modern States of East and Southeast Asia.* Honolulu: University of Hawaii Press, 1994.

Kipp, Rita Smith. *The Early Years of a Dutch Colonial Mission.* Ann Arbor: University of Michigan Press, 1993.

Lewis, I. M. *Islam in Tropical Africa.* 2d ed. Bloomington: Indiana University Press, 1980.

Martin, David. *Tongues of Fire: The Explosion of Protestantism in Latin America.* Oxford: Blackwell, 1990.

Sanneh, Lamin. *West African Christianity: The Religious Impact.* London: C. Hurst, 1983.

Van der Veer, Peter. *Religious Nationalism: Hindus and Muslims in India.* Berkeley: University of California Press, 1994.

Covenant

Covenant, a political idea whose sources are deep in Western religion and rooted in biblical monotheism, defines political justice, shapes political behavior, and directs humans toward a civic synthesis of the two within a context of what theologians know as federal liberty. Covenant is one of the seminal political ideas of humanity. It is particularly significant for its political and religious origins and its theo-political character. It may also be the oldest political idea providing for human liberty, with law antedating the idea of natural law by centuries.

The term *federal* is from the Latin *foedus,* which means covenant. Hence federal liberty is the liberty to do that which is right and proper by the terms of a particular covenant, thereby providing a basis for resolving the problem of balancing liberty and authority with which every society must grapple. As such, covenant is an idea whose importance is akin to natural law in defining justice and to natural right in delineating the origins and proper constitution of political society. This is especially true in periods of crisis or transition, such as transition from the late medieval period to the modern epoch, which took place from the Reformation early in the sixteenth century to the great revolutions of the eighteenth century. Although somewhat eclipsed since the shift to organic and then positivistic theories of politics, which began in the mid-nineteenth century, covenant persists as a factor shaping political behavior in those civil societies whose foundations are grounded in the effort to translate covenant ideas into political reality and in others attempting to build a democratic order on federalist rather than centralist principles.

Since its beginnings, political science has identified three basic ways in which polities come into existence: conquest, organic development, and covenant. In *Federalist* No. 1 (1787), one of the defining documents of American constitutionalism, these were referred to as force, accident, and reflection and choice. These questions of origins are not abstract; the mode of founding of a polity does much to determine its subsequent political life. The covenant worldview is one of the two or three "mother" views shared by humanity. It may even be rooted in the very psyches of people, in the sense that every personality, as formed by nature and culture, has a tendency toward hierarchical, organic, or covenantal perceptions of human relationships.

The uses of covenant demonstrate how political conceptualization and expression go hand in hand. In ancient Israel the Jews—and during the sixteenth and seventeenth centuries the Scots, Dutch, and English Puritans—not only conceived of their worlds in covenantal terms but wrote national covenants to which loyal members of the body politic subscribed. Similar covenants were used in the founding of many of the original colonies in British North America. Covenantal thinking was the common mode of political conceptualization and expression during the American Revolution, where it was reflected in any number of constitutional documents. More recently, the call for a social contract in England to create a new set of relationships between labor and management and the covenant inaugurated in Boston, Massachusetts, by the city's major religious groups in 1979 in an attempt to bring racial peace to that city are but two of many examples of the continuing use of covenant and its derivations as forms of political conceptualization and modes of political expression.

As a source of political ideology, covenant shapes the worldviews or perspectives of whole societies, defining their civil characters and political relationships and serving as a touchstone for testing the legitimacy and often even the efficiency of their political institutions and those who keep them going. Perhaps most important is the role of covenant as an element in shaping political culture and behavior. This element is the most difficult to measure, and yet it is operationally the most significant dimension of covenant.

The Idea of Covenant

A covenant is a morally informed agreement or pact between people or parties having an independent and sufficiently equal status; it is based on voluntary consent and established by mutual oaths or promises witnessed by the relevant transcendent authority. A covenant provides for joint obligation and action to achieve defined ends (limited or comprehensive) under conditions of mutual respect that protect the individual integrities of all the parties to it. Every covenant involves consent. Most are meant to be of unlimited duration, if not perpetual. Covenants can bind any number of partners for a variety of purposes, but in essence they are political in that their bonds are used principally to create relationships best understood in political terms.

In its original biblical form, covenant embodies the idea that relationships between God and humanity are based on morally sustained compacts of mutual promise and obliga-tion. God's covenant with Noah (Genesis 9), which came after Noah had harkened fully to God's commands in what was, to say the least, an extremely difficult situation, is the first of many examples. In its political form, covenant expresses the idea that people can freely create communities and polities, peoples and publics, and civil society itself through morally grounded and sustained compacts (whether religious or otherwise in impetus), establishing thereby enduring partnerships.

In all its forms the principal focus of covenant is on relationships. A covenant is the constitutionalization of a set of relationships of a particular kind. As such, it provides the basis for the institutionalization of those relationships; but it would be wrong to confuse the order of precedence.

It is possible that covenant ideas emerged spontaneously in various parts of the world. If covenant thinking is rooted in human nature as well as nurture, it is to be expected that some people everywhere would be oriented toward the idea. For an idea to take root and spread, however, it is not sufficient for random individuals to be disposed to it. Somehow a culture or civilization must emerge that embodies and reflects that idea.

All the evidence points to the existence of certain covenantal peoples whose political cultures are informed by covenantal and related concepts, which in turn influence their political behavior. Those people emerged from two nuclear concentrations. The first was at the western edge of southwestern Asia three thousand to four thousand years ago in what was once known as the Fertile Crescent, especially in Israel. Its principal manifestations were the Bible and the Jewish people, who were to foster the covenant idea and its practice through the introduction of monotheism.

The second concentration was in northwestern Europe, especially in Switzerland and the region stretching northward up the Rhine River valley through what is today western Germany, Alsace, Belgium, and the Netherlands, extending across the North Sea to Scotland, and continuing along the western coast of Scandinavia. These peoples, who drew their covenantal ideas from the Hebrew Bible, subsequently settled and shaped various "new worlds" from Iceland and North America to South Africa and Australia.

From these covenantal peoples emerged Judaism and Christianity with their biblical covenantal base, Reformed Protestantism with its federal theology, federalism as a political principle and arrangement, modern constitutionalism, civil societies based on interlocking voluntary associations, and almost every other element that reflects social organization based on what has loosely been called "contract" rather than "status." Moreover, these covenantal peoples seem to have internationalized a covenantal or federalistic approach to life to a greater or lesser extent.

The first such civilization or culture area was that of ancient Israel whose people transformed and perfected a device originally developed among the Amorite and Hittite peoples who inhabited the area. The first known uses of the term *covenant* (*biritum* in Akkadian) were the treaties through which the empire builders of southwest Asia secured the fealty of conquered peoples and their domains through pacts secured by oath before their respective deities. These pacts laid out the form that covenants have taken ever since. They included four elements: a prologue indicating the parties and purposes involved, a preamble stating the general purposes of the covenant and the principles behind it, a body of conditions and operative clauses, and an oath to make the covenant morally binding. The oath stipulated the agreed-upon sanctions to be applied if the covenant was violated. These first covenants simultaneously established the political purposes and moral bases for covenanting.

The domestic political and religious usages of covenant emerged either parallel to or derived from these ancient vassal covenants. The two were connected in the Bible to transform the idea of covenant into the classic covenant tradition. God's covenant with Israel established the Jewish people and founded it as a body politic, while at the same time creating the religious framework that gave that polity its purpose, its norms, and its constitution, as well as the guidelines for developing a political order based on proper, that is, covenantal, relationships.

Biblical adaptation of the forms of the vassal covenants involved a transformation of purpose and content so great as to mean a difference in kind, not merely degree. A covenant was used to found a people, making their moral commitment to one another far stronger and enduring than that of a vassal to an imperial overlord. The Bible draws a distinction between "children of the covenant," *bnei brit* in Hebrew, and "masters of the covenant," or *ba'alei brit*. On the one hand, children of the covenant is used where the covenant has established a new entity whose partners are bound together as children within a family. The covenant that unites and forms the Jewish people in the biblical account and in all subsequent Jewish history makes all Jews *bnei brit*. On the other hand, where the term used is *ba'alei brit,* it is essentially

an international treaty. It does not create a new entity but establishes a relationship of peace and mutual ties between separate entities that remain for all purposes separated despite the limited-purpose pact.

This new form of covenant brought God in as a partner, thus informing it with religious value and implication for the Israelites, who saw no distinction between its religious and political dimensions. The covenant remained a theo-political document with as heavy an emphasis on the political as could be. The strong political dimension reflected God's purpose in choosing one people to be the builders of a holy commonwealth that would be a model for all others.

It was only later with the rise of Christianity and the beginning of the long exile of the Jews from their land that covenant took on a more strictly religious character for some. The political dimension was downplayed, if not ignored, by Christian theologians and diminished by Jewish legists. Christianity embraced the covenant idea as one of its foundations, but Christians reinterpreted the old biblical covenant establishing a people and a polity to be a covenant of grace unilaterally granted for individual humans and mediated through Jesus. Jewish legists simply took the basic covenantal framework of Judaism for granted and concentrated on the fine points of the law as applies to daily living or the expected messianic redemption.

Within the Jewish world, the political dimension of covenanting received new impetus in the eleventh through the fourteenth centuries to provide a basis for constituting autonomous local Jewish communities throughout Europe. That effort ran parallel to the establishment of municipal corporations throughout the Continent that were legitimized by royal charter, usually negotiated between the municipality and the throne. Although these efforts found some expression in political thought, it was really not until the Reformation that covenant reemerged as a primary political category, first in political theology and then in political philosophy.

The Reformation and Federal Theology

It was then that the covenant idea emerged as a powerful force in the second major cultural area, that of western and, most particularly, northwestern Europe. What cultural predispositions lay behind the receptivity of the peoples of that area to covenant as a concept remain to be uncovered, if they can be. It cannot be an accident that the federal theology emerged simultaneously in the sixteenth century in four separate places in Switzerland (Zurich, Basel, Berne, and Geneva), where confederal political arrangements had been dominant since the late thirteenth century. The other major covenantal polity was the United Netherlands, formed as a confederation by its revolt against Spain inspired by Reformed Protestantism.

The Reformed churches turned to the covenant concept with relish, finding in it the most appropriate expression of their theological ideas and expectations for church polity and the new search for religious and political liberty. The first great use of the concept in an overtly political manner in this period was the *Vindiciae contra Tyrannos* (claim against kings, 1579), thought to be written by Philippe Du Plessis-Mornay, a Huguenot leader, and based on scriptural discussions of the legitimate right of resistance to tyrannical kings. The very term *Huguenot,* which was applied to French Calvinists, is from the German *eidgenossen,* meaning "covenant."

Drawing heavily on biblical sources, the foundations of religious and political freedom were established through the federal theology developed by theologians and political thinkers such as Johannes Althusius, a German political theorist, who, as the intellectual father of modern federalism in the late sixteenth century, stimulated the systematic political application of the covenant idea. In the next century, covenant was given secular form by Thomas Hobbes, John Locke, and Benedict de Spinoza. By the late seventeenth century the concept had taken on an independent life of its own in the ideas of political compact, civil society, and modern constitutionalism.

From northwestern Europe, covenantally grounded civilization spread to the new worlds opened by northwestern European colonization. Those covenantal societies ranged from Iceland, settled by Danes and coastal Norwegians in the tenth century, to the United States, settled in the early seventeenth century by Scots and Puritans from the British Isles and Netherlanders and Huguenots. Where settlers from those traditions were dominant, new peoples were established by covenant, and they in turn wrote constitutions that realized the covenantal dimension through a network of political institutions. At the end of the eighteenth century the American Revolution translated the concept into a powerful instrument of political reform, but only after merging it with the secularized covenantal idea of compact. American constitutionalism is a product of that merger.

Covenant, Compact, and Contract

Covenant is tied in an ambiguous relationship to two related terms, *compact* and *contract*. On the one hand, both compacts and contracts are in a sense derived from covenant, and sometimes the terms are even used interchangeably. On the other hand, there are very real differences that need clarification.

Both covenants and compacts differ from contracts in that the first two are constitutional or public and the last is private in character. As such, covenantal or compactual obligation is broadly reciprocal. Those bound by one or the other are obligated to respond to one another beyond the letter of the law rather than to limit their obligations to the narrowest contractual requirements. Covenants and compacts, then, are inherently designed to be flexible in certain respects as well as firm in others. As expressions of private law, contracts tend to be interpreted by each party as narrowly as possible as to what is explicitly mandated by the contract itself.

A covenant differs from a compact in that its morally binding dimension takes precedence over its legal dimension. In its heart of hearts, a covenant is an agreement in which a higher moral force, traditionally God, is either a direct party to or a guarantor of a particular relationship. When the term *compact* is used, moral force is involved only indirectly. A compact, based as it is on mutual pledges rather than on guarantees by or before a higher authority, rests more heavily on a legal—although still ethical—grounding for its politics. In other words, compact is a secular phenomenon.

This statement is historically verifiable by examining the shift in terminology that took place in the seventeenth and eighteenth centuries. Although those who saw the hand of God in political affairs in the United States as a rule continued to use the term *covenant,* those who sought a secular grounding for politics turned to the term *compact*. Although the distinction was not always used with strict clarity, it does appear consistently. The issue was further complicated by the eighteenth-century French theorist Jean-Jacques Rousseau and his followers, who talk about the "social contract," a highly secularized concept that, even when applied for public purposes, never develops the same level of moral obligation as either covenant or compact.

Covenantal Relationships

Over the centuries the ideas of covenant, natural law, and constitutionalism became intertwined. In 1776, for example, when the Americans formally declared themselves an independent people in the Declaration of Independence—itself a covenant establishing a new relationship based on precepts of natural rights—they saw constitution making as a way of further covenanting or compacting together to form civil instruments designed to carry out the premises of the Declaration. The resulting state and federal constitutions were seen as compacts embodying the principles of natural law, especially in their Declarations of Rights. The propriety of subsequent legislation was, therefore, to be judged in light of its "constitutionality," or, in other words, its conformity to both the natural law and the covenant, one step removed.

Normally, a covenant precedes a constitution to establish a people or civil society, which then proceeds to adopt a constitution of government for itself. Thus a constitution involves the implementation of a prior covenant into an actual structure of government. The constitution may include a restatement or reaffirmation of the original covenant, as does the Massachusetts Constitution of 1780 in its preamble: "The body-politics is formed by a voluntary association of individuals: It is a social compact, by which the whole people covenants with each citizen, that all shall be governed by certain laws for the common good."

Covenant relationships have often been compared to marriages in their permanency, promise of trust, mutuality of responsibility, and respect for the integrity of each of the partners within the community created by wedding (an ancient Anglo-Saxon term for sealing a contract). The analogy also highlights the way in which covenant links consent and kinship. In the biblical-covenantal view of marriage, two independent and otherwise unrelated persons consent to become "one flesh" and establish a family.

In politics, covenant connotes the voluntary establishment of a people and body politic. The Declaration of Independence is an excellent example of this kind of covenant. Through it, the diverse inhabitants of the thirteen colonies reaffirmed that they consented to become a people. It was not without reason, therefore, that President Abraham Lincoln fondly described the union created by that act as "a regular marriage." The partners do not unquestionably live happily ever after, but they are bound by covenant to struggle toward such an end, a commitment well understood and made explicit by Lincoln during the Civil War years in the 1860s.

To the extent that covenant is both a theological and political concept, it is also informed by a moral or ethical perspective that treats political relationships in the classical manner. That is, it links power and justice—the two faces of politics—and preserves the classic and ancient linkages between ethics and politics. Again, the emphasis is on relationships rather than structures as the key to political justice. Structures are always important, but ultimately, no matter how finely tuned the structures, they come alive (or fail to) only through the human relationships that inform and shape them.

Parallel to the theological and philosophic dimensions is the sociopolitical aspect of the covenantal founding of new societies. A principal, although not necessarily universal, characteristic of new settlements is that they tend to promote equality. People come together in a new place, away from the established civil order and must organize their own political life. The natural inclination is for them to do so on the basis of equality because of the equal risks involved. Moreover, they can do so only through some contractual means whereby each agrees to accept the jurisdiction of the whole. They are likely to do so only if each preserves those liberties deemed essential and acquires some share in the common decision-making processes. The further removed a new settlement is from older political orders, whether physically or in other ways, the more likely it is that this will be the model for its founding. Where previously existing political authority can effectively be extended over new territories, and older constitutional arrangements enforced, there is less room for the application of this model than otherwise, although even in such cases the very fact of new settlement tends to bring some of its elements into play. Where the old order cannot be effectively extended, or where it actively encourages a contractual founding in the new territory, the model is more likely to be implemented in its fullness.

The case of Switzerland illustrates this point. The territories of what is today Switzerland were for many generations wild lands at the peripheries of the various royal, imperial, and feudal domains of Europe. People seeking to be free of autocratic rule fled to those lands, where they organized themselves into communities of equals with a minimum of outside interference. When the Habsburg emperors sought to impose their rule on those communities, the Swiss fought back, organizing to do so by applying the same federal principles to the confederation of communities that they had to earlier unions of individuals and families.

The covenant idea has been important for the growth of democratic government and society, whatever the starting point. It presupposes the independence and worth of each individual and the truth that each person possesses certain inalienable rights because only free people with rights can enter into agreements with one another. It also presupposes the necessity for government and the need to organize political society on principles that ensure the maintenance of those rights and the exercise of power in a cooperative or partnerlike way.

Still, covenantal or federal liberty is not simply the right to do as one pleases. Federal liberty is the liberty to pursue the moral purposes for which the covenant was made. This latter kind of liberty requires that moral distinctions be drawn and that human actions be judged according to the terms of the covenant. This does not preclude changes in social norms, but the principles of judgment remain constant. Consequently, covenantal societies, founded as they are on covenantal choice, tend to emphasize constitutional design and choice as a continuing process, whether in the form of state constitutional referendums in the United States or the recurring referendums in Switzerland or whatever.

The Dynamics of Covenant

The dynamic dimension of covenant emphasizes relationships and their proper shaping, which finds expression in the language of covenantal peoples. All covenantal peoples have appropriate covenantal language. The Hebrew examples discussed here present only a few samples, drawn from a rich covenantal terminology.

To take one example, a central Hebrew term for defining human relationships is *haver,* which means friend, partner, or comrade. This term is developed extensively in the Talmudic literature of Jewish civil and religious law and in medieval Jewish thought in ways that have clear covenantal connotations. The modern Zionist pioneers transformed the term into the Hebrew equivalent for *comrade,* deepening its built-in connotation of partnership. Most covenantal societies have a similar term. It is significant that the form of address of the archetypical American folk figure, the cowboy, is *pardner,* and *partnership* is the term of choice for describing American federalism. In Australia, the term is *mate,* and *mateship* is a basic concept in Australian society.

The essence of covenantal dynamics lies in three biblical terms expressed in Hebrew as *brit* (covenant), *hesed,* and *shalom* (peace). *Biritu,* the original Semitic term for covenant itself suggests a dynamic process and relationship. It reflects two actions, cutting and binding—that is, the separating of something into parts and its reunification in such a way that

the parts remain separate in their identities. Indeed, the biblical term for making a covenant is *lichrot brit,* to "cut a covenant." In the ancient Near East, the original covenant ritual involved the division of a sacrificial animal, the parties passing between it, and the animal being reunited through a rebinding. This imagery can be found in other covenantal rituals and ceremonies among Jews and other peoples. Thus both the language and the ritual reflect the dynamics of the covenantal way.

Hesed, which is sometimes translated as "grace" and sometimes as "lovingkindness," is not really translatable into English. It is best understood as the loving fulfillment of the obligations flowing from a covenant bond. Here we shall use the term *covenant obligation* as the equivalent of *hesed.* The Bible recognized the problem of all contractual relationships; namely, the tendency of the parties to a contract to interpret it as narrowly as possible in their own interests. *Hesed* is a dynamic concept designed to reinforce mutuality. Every *brit* creates a *hesed* relationship, whereby the obligation of the parties to it is not narrowly contractual but broadly covenantal. Thus they are required to go beyond the letter of the law in dealing with covenantal matters. The Bible is a record of God's *hesed* toward Israel, his constantly going beyond the letter of the law in dealing with his people who, despite their basic loyalty to the covenant, persistently violate its strict standards in one way or another. At the same time, it is a record of the equivalent response of the people or at least some important segment of the people to God and to each other. A person who acts in the way of *hesed* is called a *hasid,* that is to say, one who builds one's life around the rendering of *hesed* to the covenant partners. The whole concept of Hasidism in Jewish life, both in the biblical period and subsequently, is an outgrowth of this dynamic approach to covenantal relationships.

The Supreme Constitutional Court of the German Federal Republic has developed the concept of *bundestreue* or *bundesfreundlichkeit* as a civil equivalent of the biblical idea of *hesed* and has applied it to adjudicate intergovernmental issues. It calls for a kind of federal friendship and loyalty among the federal government and the constituent states of the German federation, requiring them to go beyond the letter of the law in certain issues, so as to promote more effective intergovernmental cooperation. There are situations in which the federal government or the states may be able to claim that the federal constitution does not require them to respond to their partners. But since such a stance reflects a lack of cooperative spirit, which could paralyze governance, the court has developed this concept as a constitutional norm that it will apply to ensure that the parties go beyond the letter of the law in order to fulfill its spirit.

In the United States the term *partnership* is the American quasi-constitutional equivalent of *hesed*. Although it has not gained similar legal status, it has tremendous normative power. Even its misuse is revealing; every effort of linkage is labeled partnership even when hegemony of one "partner" is the goal.

Shalom, the third term, means peace. Etymologically, it suggests completeness, wholeness, coming together; that is, it is covenantal in its echoes and implications. Thus peace itself, in biblical terminology, is dynamic; it involves the completing of something, bringing things together to create a new whole. Peace is obtained through a *brit shalom,* a covenant of peace, which can be maintained only through the *hesed* of the parties to it.

See also *Civil Society; Communitarianism; Judaism; Natural Law; Reformation.*

Daniel J. Elazar

BIBLIOGRAPHY

Elazar, Daniel J. *The Covenant Tradition in Politics.* 4 vols. New Brunswick, N.J.: Transaction, 1995.

———, ed. *Kinship and Consent: The Jewish Political Tradition and Its Contemporary Uses.* 2d ed. New Brunswick, N.J.: Transaction, 1997.

Elazar, Daniel J., and John Kincaid, eds. *The Covenant Connection: Federal Theology and Politics.* New York: Lexington Books, 2000.

Hillers, Delbert R. *Covenant: The History of a Biblical Idea.* Baltimore, Md.: Johns Hopkins University Press, 1969.

Miller, Perry. *The New England Mind.* Boston: Beacon Press, 1961.

Niebuhr, H. Richard. "The Idea of Covenant and American Democracy." *Church History* 23 (1954).

Snaith, Norman H. *The Distinctive Ideas of the Old Testament.* New York: Schocken Books, 1966.

Thundyil, Zacharas P. *Covenant in Anglo-Saxon Thought.* Madras, India: Macmillan, 1972.

Walzer, Michael. *The Revolution of the Saints.* Cambridge, Mass.: Harvard University Press, 1965.

Creationism and Evolution

Almost one hundred fifty years after British scientist Charles Darwin published his groundbreaking theory on the origins of life, Americans are still fighting over evolution. Evolution, according to most scientists, is the process by which life developed on Earth: from a common descendent, billions of years ago, to the wide-ranging diversity of species that exist today. If anything, the controversy over evolution is growing in both size and intensity. From 2002 through 2004 alone, challenges to the teaching of evolution in one form or another were mounted in school boards, town councils, and legislatures in more than half the states, including Wisconsin, Ohio, Kansas, Pennsylvania, and Washington.

More broadly, through much of the twentieth century evolution opponents either tried to strike the teaching of Darwin's theory from school science curricula or urged schools to teach as well the creation story found in the Old Testament book of Genesis. Creationism or creation science, as it is variously called, attempts to reconcile the biblical account of creation in the Old Testament book of Genesis with the fossil record as well as other evidence of life's origins and development. Beginning in the 1960s, however, the Supreme Court issued some important decisions that imposed severe restrictions on evolution opponents. As a result, school boards, legislatures, and government bodies are now barred from banning the teaching of evolution, or teaching creationism, either along with evolutionary theory or in place of it.

In the early twenty-first century, partly in response to these court decisions opposition to evolution itself evolved, with opponents changing their goals and tactics. Some local and state school boards in Kansas, Pennsylvania, and elsewhere considered teaching what they contend are scientific alternatives to evolution. The most comprehensive of these approaches is the concept of "intelligent design," which posits that life is too complex to have developed without the purposeful direction intervention of an outside force. Other education officials have tried to require students to hear or read disclaimers encouraging them to think of evolution as "a theory, not a fact."

Polls indicate that challenges to Darwinian evolution have substantial support among the American people. According to an August 2005 survey sponsored by the Pew Forum on Religion and Public Life and the Pew Research Center for the People and the Press, 60 percent believe that humans and other animals have either always existed in their present form or have evolved over time under the guidance of a supreme being. In addition, the same poll found that 64 percent of Americans support teaching creationism alongside evolution in the classroom.

This view is not shared by the nation's scientists, almost all of whom contend that evolution is an established scientific theory, not a mere "hunch" or "guess." They dismiss creationism as religion, not science, and usually describe intelligent design as little more than creationism dressed up in scientific jargon.

So if, as many scientists claim, evolution is a well-established part of science, why are people still arguing about it? The answer lies in part in the possible theological implications of evolutionary thinking. For example, the Darwinian view of life—as a panorama of brutal struggle and constant change—conflicts with the Judeo-Christian concept of an active and loving creator. This perceived incompatibility, coupled with the deep and abiding religious faith of many Americans, has ensured the teaching of evolution a prominent place in the country's wider culture war.

A Dangerous Idea

Scientists had been debating whether animals evolved for decades before Charles Darwin first publicized his theory in the late 1850s. Darwin's achievement was to offer a compelling explanation for how species evolve and to use this explanation to trace the history of life's origins and development. All existing creatures, he argued, share a common ancestor, a single progenitor species from which every living thing has evolved. This evolution, Darwin wrote, stems from two factors. First, each individual animal is subtly different from its parents because of what today would be deemed genetic mutation, although Darwin called these differences "variations" owing to the fact that in his day genetics had not yet become a field of scientific endeavor and would not become one until the early twentieth century. Second, although these "variations" are random, some of them inevitably convey distinct advantages—such as superior camouflage, a heartier constitution, and greater speed—that help a creature to better survive in its environment. Greater chance of survival also means a greater chance to breed and to pass on this advantage to a greater number of offspring. Over time, the advantage would spread throughout the species, because the creatures with the advantage would be more likely to endure ("the survival of the fittest") and reproduce. Over the course of many generations, many of these subtle changes would then accumulate in a species, eventually producing big changes and even new species.

The publication *On the Origin of Species* in 1859 quickly brought Darwin's ideas to the wider world. But while many scientists in Britain and elsewhere quickly embraced the theory, it was vigorously rejected by British and American churches as being contradictory to many of the core teachings of the Christian faith. Darwin's notion that existing species, including man, had developed over time was in clear opposition to the idea that all creatures had been created "according to their kind" by God, as described in the first chapter of the book of Genesis. Darwinian thinking also contradicted the notion, central to Christianity and most other major faiths, that man had a special, God-given place in the natural order. In response, proponents of evolution pointed to signs in human anatomy—remnants of a tailbone, for example—showing common ancestry with other mammals. And finally, the idea of a benevolent God who loved his creation was challenged by Darwin's depiction of the natural world as a savage and cruel place.

Darwin's ideas provoked a harsh and immediate response from religious leaders in Britain. Samuel Wilberforce, the Anglican archbishop of Oxford and one of the most highly respected religious figures in England, gave talks condemning natural selection, including a now famous speech on its scientific deficiencies at an 1860 meeting of the British Association for the Advancement of Science. At one point, Wilberforce jokingly asked biologist Thomas Henry Huxley, who was present at the meeting, if he was related to an ape on his grandmother's side or his grandfather's side. Huxley, whose vigorous defense of evolutionary theory earned him the nickname "Darwin's bulldog," evidently replied that he would rather be the ancestor of a monkey than an advanced and intelligent human being who employs his "knowledge and eloquence in misrepresenting those who are wearing out their lives in the search for truth."

Huxley's jibe at Wilberforce was judged to be a stunning rebuke of religious resistance to Darwinian thinking. And although it did not end the public disagreement over evolution between ecclesiastical and scientific authorities, it made religious thinkers much more wary of directly challenging evolution on scientific grounds. Instead, many churches in the late nineteenth and early twentieth centuries directed much of their energy toward resisting a particular part of evolutionary theory: the idea that man had evolved from lower animal orders and thus had no special place in creation or, for that matter, a soul.

American Reactions

Darwinism came to America at roughly the same time it burst onto the scientific and cultural scene in Britain. But while debates raged in England, the religious establishment in the United States initially ignored the issue; it was preoccupied with other, more pressing concerns such as the Civil War, slavery, and Reconstruction. Still, by the 1870s some American religious leaders and thinkers began considering the theological implications of Darwin's theory. Not surprisingly, many attacked evolutionary thinking. For example, Presbyterian theologian Charles Hodge, in his book *What Is Darwinism?* (1874), argued that natural selection was unacceptable because it directly contradicted belief in a benevolent and all-powerful God. Others, though, such as famed Congregationalist minister Henry Ward Beecher, tried to create a rapprochement between evolutionary thinking and Christianity, arguing that evolution was simply God's method of creation.

But these early debates over faith and evolution, while important, were largely confined to intellectual circles. The issue did not filter down to the wider American public until the end of the nineteenth century, when a large number of popular Christian authors and speakers, such as the evangelist Dwight L. Moody, began to inveigh against Darwinism as a threat to biblical truth and public morality.

The wide exposure of Darwinian thinking to the American public consciousness coincided with the advent of dramatic shifts in the country's religious landscape. From the 1890s to the 1930s, the major American Protestant denominations—which, in spite of doctrinal differences, had maintained a unity on basic issues of faith—gradually split into two camps: modernists (or liberals) and fundamentalists (or conservatives). This fundamentalist–modernist schism was caused by some important developments, including new questions about the historical accuracy of biblical accounts and provocative and controversial new ideas by thinkers such as Sigmund Freud and Karl Marx as well as the spread of new scientific thinking. Modernists sought to integrate these new theories and ideas into their religious doctrine, whereas fundamentalists resisted these developments in the name of traditional doctrine.

By the early 1920s evolution had become one of the most, if not *the* most, important controversies in this Protestant divide, in part because Darwin's ideas were spreading to public school curricula. Not surprisingly, the issue became a mainstay for evangelists, including Billy Sunday, the most popular preacher of this era. "I don't believe the old bastard theory of evolution," he said during a 1925 revival meeting in Memphis. "I believe I am just as God Almighty made me." But it was William Jennings Bryan, a man of politics, not the cloth, who ultimately became the leader of a full-fledged national crusade against evolution.

Bryan, a great populist orator and devout Christian who three times had run unsuccessfully for president, believed that the presence of Darwinism in the nation's classrooms would result in the moral destruction of American youth. He argued that an education in evolution would ensure that whole generations would grow up believing that the Bible was no more than "a collection of myths," undermining the nation's Christian faith and replacing a religion of love and peace with the doctrine of "survival of the fittest."

Bryan's fear of social Darwinism was not entirely unfounded. Evolutionary thinking had helped to give birth to the eugenics movement, which maintained that one could breed a better person in the same way that farmers bred better sheep and cattle. Eugenics led to now discredited theories of race and class superiority that helped to drive the debate in the United States over immigration and led some American states to enact sterilization laws to stop "mental deficients" from having children.

Most who favored the teaching of evolution in public schools were not supporters of eugenics, but simply wanted students to be exposed to the most up-to-date scientific thinking. For others, such as supporters of the newly formed American Civil Liberties Union (ACLU), it was an issue of freedom of speech as well as the maintenance of the separation of church and state. Still others, such as well-known lawyer Clarence Darrow, saw the battle over evolution as a proxy for a wider cultural conflict between progress and modernity, on one side, and, on the other, what they viewed as backwardness and religious superstition. Darrow, for one, believed that religion, particularly Christianity, was an enemy of social progress.

Scopes and Its Aftermath

As with so many controversies in the United States, the battle over teaching evolution eventually became an issue of law. At the urging of Bryan and other fundamentalist leaders, efforts were made in the early 1920s to ban the teaching of Darwin's theory in some states, including Kentucky and Florida. Although these efforts failed, opponents won a victory in 1925 when the Tennessee legislature overwhelmingly approved legislation making it a crime to teach "any theory that denies the story of the Divine Creation of man as taught in the Bible, and to teach instead that man has descended from a lower order of animal."

Soon after the Tennessee law was enacted, the ACLU offered to defend any science teacher in the state who was willing to break it. John Scopes, a teacher in the small rural town of Dayton, agreed to take up the ACLU's offer.

Meanwhile, Bryan and then Darrow agreed to assist the prosecution and defense, respectively, thereby turning an already highly publicized event into a media circus. Indeed, the Scopes trial was one of the first true "media events" of the modern era and certainly the first modern media trial. It was covered in hundreds of newspapers and broadcast live on radio.

From the start, both sides understood that the case was being tried more in the court of public opinion than in a court of law. With that in mind, Darrow and the ACLU legal team focused their attacks on the Tennessee statute (as a violation of church-state separation) and on the notion that biblical revelation could be an adequate substitute for science in the classroom. But state prosecutors effectively blocked this effort, arguing that the issue before the court was not the Bible or even the statute, but whether Scopes had violated the law.

As the trial progressed, it seemed increasingly clear that the defense team's hope to make the case into a public debate on the merits of evolution were being stymied by state prosecutors. Just when it seemed that the Scopes case might end with a whimper, Darrow made the highly unorthodox request of calling a member of the prosecutorial team—Bryan—to the witness stand. Although the politician was under no obligation to testify, he acceded to Darrow's invitation.

With Bryan on the stand, Darrow proceeded to ask a series of detailed questions about biblical events that could be viewed as inconsistent, unreal, or both. For example, the lawyer asked how there could be morning and evening during the first three days of creation when the sun was not formed until the fourth? And was Jonah really swallowed by a whale? Bryan responded to these and similar questions in different ways. Often, he defended the biblical account in question as the literal truth, the work of a God of miracles. On other occasions, though, he admitted that something in scripture might need to be interpreted in order to be fully accepted.

Although the largely local crowd observing the two-hour exchange was clearly on Bryan's side, most journalists and other observers believe that Darrow's cross-examination made his opponent seem inconsistent, flustered, and, at times, even buffoonish. The next day, many big city papers hailed Darrow and savaged Bryan, who unexpectedly died less than a week later.

The trial, particularly Darrow's questioning of Bryan, created a tremendous amount of positive publicity for the pro-evolution camp, especially in northern urban areas, where the media and cultural elites were sympathetic. But this post-Scopes momentum did not destroy the anti-evolution movement. Indeed, in the years immediately following the Scopes trial, two state legislatures—in Mississippi and Arkansas—enacted bills similar to the Tennessee act. Other states, particularly in the South and Midwest, passed resolutions condemning the inclusion of material on evolution in biology textbooks. These actions, along with a patchwork of restrictions from local school boards, prompted most publishers to remove references to Darwin from their science textbooks.

Efforts to make evolution the standard in all biology classes would have to wait decades before bearing any fruit, in large part because the First Amendment's prohibition on religious establishment applied only to federal actions and not state ones until the Supreme Court's 1947 decision in *Everson v. Board of Education.* Efforts to mandate the teaching of evolution in public schools also received a boost ten years after *Everson,* in 1957, when the surprise Soviet launch of the first satellite, *Sputnik,* prompted the United States to make science education a national priority.

Epperson and Edwards: The Supreme Court Intervenes

In 1968, more than twenty years after *Everson* applied the establishment clause to the states, the Supreme Court finally turned its attention to anti-evolution laws. *Epperson v. Arkansas* concerned a challenge to the 1928 post-Scopes Arkansas law that made it a crime to teach evolution in a public school or state university. In a 9-0 decision, the Court ruled that the law violated the First Amendment's establishment clause because it ultimately had a religious purpose, in this case preventing students from learning a particular viewpoint antithetical to fundamentalist Christians. "There can be no doubt that Arkansas has sought to prevent its teachers from discussing the theory of evolution because it is contrary to the belief of some that the Book of Genesis must be the exclusive source of doctrine as to the origin of man," Justice Abe Fortas wrote for the majority.

Epperson put an end to prohibitions on teaching evolution. But even before the case had been decided, a new anti-evolution movement, dubbed creation science or scientific creationism, was taking shape and beginning to influence the wider debate. Proponents of creation science contend that the weight of scientific evidence supports the creation story as described in Genesis—with the formation of the earth and the development of life occurring in six twenty-four-hour days. The presence of fossils and evidence of significant geologic change are attributed to the great catastrophic flood described in the eighth chapter of Genesis, in which all life on the earth's surface was destroyed, save that of Noah, his family, and the animals they had taken with them in the ark.

Throughout the late nineteenth and early twentieth centuries, many fundamentalist Christians had come to believe that the earth was much older than the six thousand or so years biblical scholars had long estimated it to be. A turn back toward stricter biblical literalism can be traced to 1961, when engineer Henry M. Morris and theologian John C. Whitcomb published *The Genesis Flood*. The book, which became and remains a bestseller, is the bible of the creation science movement, purporting to present scientific explanations for the creation, destruction, and repopulation of the earth as described in the book of Genesis.

In the wake of *Epperson*, creation science provided an alternative to the now unconstitutional efforts to ban the teaching of evolution. In the early 1980s, two states, Arkansas and Louisiana, embraced creation science, passing "balanced treatment" laws, which forbade the teaching of evolution in public schools unless accompanied by instruction in the theory of creation science. But both statutes were ultimately the subject of legal challenges. In 1982 the Arkansas law was struck down by a federal district court in *McClean v. Arkansas Board of Education*. The Supreme Court entered the creation science debate five years later in *Edwards v. Aguillard* (1987), which concerned a challenge to the Louisiana statute.

In its analysis of the law, the Court relied on its 1971 decision in *Lemon v. Kurtzman*, which set out a three-prong test to determine whether a government action violates the establishment clause. Under the *Lemon* test, an action must (1) have a bona fide secular purpose; (2) not advance or inhibit religion; and (3) not excessively entangle the government with religion. If the challenged action fails any one of the three parts of the test, it is deemed to have violated the establishment clause. In a 7-2 decision, the Supreme Court then ruled that the Louisiana statute violated the establishment clause because it did not meet the first, or "secular pur-

pose," prong of the *Lemon* test. The Court did not bother to consider parts two and three of the test, because failure to satisfy any of the three is sufficient to nullify a government action.

Writing for the majority, Justice William J. Brennan Jr. stated that "the preeminent purpose of the Louisiana legislature was clearly to advance the religious viewpoint that a supernatural being created humankind." He dismissed the state's defense: that the aim of the act was to protect academic freedom and make the teaching of science more comprehensive. Actually, Brennan argued, the Louisiana law severely limited both aims by prohibiting the teaching of evolution unless certain other conditions were met. Indeed, the justice added, teaching scientifically based critiques of evolution is entirely appropriate, so long as it is done with a secular intent.

New Challenges: Disclaimers and Intelligent Design

Edwards essentially ended state efforts to bring creationism into public school science classes. But efforts to challenge evolution in the classroom continued, with opponents turning their attention to other strategies, such as disclaimers and, most recently, intelligent design.

Attempts to require either oral or written evolution disclaimers have not met with success in federal courts. In a 1999 decision, *Freiler v. Tangipahoa Parish Board of Education,* the Fifth Circuit Court of Appeals invalidated a disclaimer that teachers were reading biology classes in Tangipahoa, Louisiana, urging students learning about evolution "to exercise critical thinking." It also stated that teaching evolution was "not intended to influence or dissuade the biblical version of Creation or any other concept."

In another, more recent case, *Selman v. Cobb County School District* (2005), a federal district court struck down an effort by the school board in Cobb County, Georgia, to affix stickers to textbooks simply stating that evolution was "a theory, not a fact" and urging students to approach the subject "with an open mind." In both *Freiler* and *Selman,* the courts determined that the disclaimer had violated the second or "effect" prong of the *Lemon* test, prohibiting actions that in this case had the effect of advancing religion.

Another 2005 court challenge was in response to an effort by the school board in the rural community of Dover, Pennsylvania, to insert intelligent design into the high school biology curriculum. As already noted, advocates of intelligent design argue that living systems are so complex that

An election sign in Dover, Pennsylvania, depicts the teaching of "intelligent design" as the basis for a school board platform. The debate over the teaching of evolution in schools continued in 2005, as eight families contested their schools' refusal to offer intelligent design as an alternative to evolution in their curriculum.

they could not have evolved purely by evolution through natural selection and instead must have been purposely directed by an outside force, most likely—but not necessarily—God. In particular, supporters of intelligent design point to what they say are "irreducibly complex" systems, such as the eye and the process by which blood clots, as proof that Darwinian evolution is not adequate to the task of explaining the development of life.

The great majority of scientists reject intelligent design, arguing that it is little more than creationism dressed up in scientific jargon. In fact, many scientists do not even want to debate intelligent design proponents, maintaining that doing so would give the movement a legitimacy it does not deserve. For example, pro-evolution scientists refused to testify in May 2005, when the Kansas Board of Education held hearings on a proposal to insert criticism of Darwinian evolution into the state's science education standards.

Still, a small but highly visible cadre of researchers and thinkers contend that intelligent design will soon become a full-fledged, legitimate scientific theory. The movement is not even two decades old, they point out, having its origins in the writings of Phillip E. Johnson, a law professor at the University of California at Berkeley, who published his first book on the subject, *Darwin on Trial,* in 1991. Indeed, the

nation's premiere intelligent design think tank, the Discovery Institute in Seattle, opposed the Dover school board's efforts to insert even a mention of intelligent design into the high school biology curriculum, arguing that, at this stage, the theory is not developed enough to be taught in high schools.

In October 2004, however, the Dover school board passed a resolution requiring biology teachers to read a lengthy disclaimer stating that evolution is a "theory" and that the theory of "intelligent design" offers an alternative viewpoint. Som earea families with children in the public school system then sued the board in federal district court, claiming that the new policy was unconstitutional.

In the ensuing case, *Kitzmiller v. Dover Area School District,* the court struck down the new requirement, arguing that because the school board singled out evolution for a disclaimer and introduced a religion-friendly alternative, "an objective student would view the disclaimer as a strong official endorsement of religion." The judge also rejected all scientific arguments for intelligent design, saying that it was "nothing less than the progeny of creationism."

Unlike *Selman,* the *Kitzmiller* decision was not appealed. In November 2005, a month before the decision, all but one of the school board members who endorsed the curriculum change were voted from office in local elections. Their replacements did not support teaching intelligent design, and so had no interest in continuing to fight for a policy they fundamentally opposed.

And yet the *Kitzmiller* decision is unlikely to be the final word on the constitutionality of intelligent design or the last high-profile case involving evolution. Practically every week, someone in a state legislature or on a municipal board of education raises a challenge to the teaching of evolution in the classroom. The issue has even come up in Congress, where in 2001 Sen. Rick Santorum (R-Pa.) succeeded in adding language to the conference report of the "No Child Left Behind" education law encouraging the teaching of all sides of scientific controversies "such as biological evolution."

More than eighty years ago, many secular and liberal Christian commentators saw the Scopes trial as a turning point in the battle between evolution and "superstition," as Darrow termed fundamentalist Christian belief. By the 1960s, even *Time,* in its famous April 1966 cover story, pondered whether God was dead—a question that ultimately proved to be premature.

Throughout the twentieth century, religious traditionalism in the United States showed itself to be very resilient. And in the last thirty years, conservative Christians have returned from their post-Scopes political exile to become a significant force in the American political landscape, exercising great influence in many of the nation's social, moral, and even foreign policy debates. This influence has helped to place the controversy over teaching evolution squarely on the national agenda, where it is likely to remain for some years to come.

David Masci

BIBLIOGRAPHY

Darwin, Charles. *The Origin of Species.* New York: Random House, 1993.

Desmond, Adrian, and James Moore. *Darwin: The Life of a Tormented Evolutionist.* New York: Warner Books, 1991.

Johnson, Phillip E. *Darwin on Trial.* Downers Grove, Ill.: InterVarsity Press, 1991.

Larson, Edward J. *Evolution: The Remarkable History of a Scientific Theory.* New York: Random House, 2004.

———. *Trial and Error: The American Controversy over Creation and Evolution.* Oxford: Oxford University Press, 2003.

Crime and Criminal Justice

A crime is any act deemed an offense against the state that is punishable according to law. Criminologists consider religion a deterrent to conventional crime and a factor in shaping criminal justice policy.

The interdisciplinary field of criminology studies the making of laws, the breaking of laws, and the formulation of responses to the breaking of laws. Religion plays a role in all three processes. For example, in the United States religious motives and organizations have been active in writing laws concerning alcohol, pornography, drugs, abortion, homosexuality, and race relations. Furthermore, religious beliefs can both increase the volume of crime by motivating adherents to break the law on behalf of their convictions (as in the case of civil disobedience) and decrease the volume of crime by serving as a deterrent and as a reinforcer of secular laws. Finally, religion often is a central ingredient in the formation of public opinion and eventually public policy concerning the goals of punishment and the methods used to treat offenders.

Two issues have received considerable attention in criminological research: the importance of religion as a deterrent to conventional crime and delinquency and the relationship between religious beliefs and views about the appropriate response to criminal offenders.

Religion as a Deterrent

Perhaps surprisingly, religion was not recognized as an important variable in most theories of social control developed in the 1950s and 1960s. These theories were aimed at identifying forces that deter people from violating the law. Though one of the early statistical studies in criminology in the United States reported in 1950 that only 40 percent of a sample of juveniles with court records attended church regularly, compared with 67 percent of a matched sample of nondelinquents, religion still was not considered a prominent variable in control theories developed over the next two decades.

The most influential control theory, presented by Travis Hirschi and supported by research conducted in the late 1960s on a large sample of California junior and senior high school males, found no evidence that religious beliefs and religious participation were factors in deterring people from engaging in illegal behavior. Although acceptance of conventional moral values and respect for the law (measured with reports from research subjects and juvenile court records) did inhibit delinquency, frequency of church attendance was not related to acceptance of conventional values or to respect for the law. Furthermore, while church attendance fostered a belief in supernatural sanctions for violating the law, the belief in sanctions had no effect on involvement in delinquency.

Hirschi's findings seemed to defy common sense and sparked a flurry of research that continues today. After all, sacred proscriptions and prescriptions typically overlap with secular laws so that commitment to sacred teachings should reinforce one's commitment to the legal order. But perhaps because of Hirschi's influence in the field of criminology, theory and research on the effects of religious beliefs and behavior on crime, delinquency, and other forms of deviance remain somewhat isolated from the dominant theoretical perspectives in criminology.

Charles Tittle and Michael Welch in 1983 identified sixty-five studies containing information on the relationship between religiosity (measured by either frequency of church attendance or the strength of persons' religious beliefs in their daily lives) and rule breaking. Of these, fifty-five found a significant positive association between religiosity and compliance, at least under some conditions: those who were more religious were more compliant with rules. Although most of these studies concerned juveniles, six examined adult crime and deviance, and all of the adult studies found that religiosity deterred people from violating conventional laws and norms. The importance of the findings concerning adults, apparent also in more recent research such as Christopher G. Ellison and his colleagues' study of domestic violence, should be stressed. Among juveniles, measures of religiosity such as frequency of participation in religious activities might reflect parental coercion instead of the juvenile's true level of religiosity. Research on adults potentially provides more conclusive evidence concerning the deterrent effect of religion.

The question of whether religious beliefs and behavior inhibit criminal and other deviant behavior continues to be a topic of research and has been addressed in the National Study of Youth and Religion, under the direction of Christian Smith. Smith's 2005 book *Soul Searching: The Religious and Spiritual Lives of American Teenagers* provides some of the most recent evidence that religious adolescents are more compliant with conventional norms. Systematic reviews of this recent literature by Colin J. Baier and Bradley R. E.

Wright and by Darren E. Sherkat and Christopher G. Ellison confirm the earlier conclusion of Tittle and Welch. Nevertheless, religious variables remain on the outside of the core theoretical paradigms in criminology—social learning, strain, and social control—that are presented in standard criminology textbooks such as Freda Adler, Gerhard O. W. Meuller, and William S. Laufer's fifth edition of *Criminology* (2004). Religion, as Byron R. Johnson and his colleagues note in their review, remains "the forgotten factor" in mainstream theories of the determinants of crime and delinquency.

By the end of the 1980s criminologists generally agreed that at least in some conditions religion was a deterrent to crime. Though still outside the mainstream of criminology, theories and tests of them became more sophisticated. During the two decades after Hirschi's conclusion, scholars sought to identify the conditions in which religiosity had its greatest deterrent effect on illegal behavior. Three themes emerged in the literature.

One line of research focused on the nature of the community. Researchers partially replicated Hirschi's study in Atlanta, Georgia, where they found a significant inverse effect of church attendance on self-reported delinquency among high school students. In other words, in a southern city where religion presumably was a more central part of people's lives, and contrary to Hirschi's findings from California (presumably a more secular region of the country), as church attendance increased, delinquency decreased. A theory that emerged from this and other studies was that religiosity had a stronger inhibiting effect on conventional illegal behavior in communities where religion was a more prominent force in day-to-day life ("sacred communities") than in communities where religious convictions generally were weak ("secular communities").

Not all research, however, supported this conclusion, and in fact the inconsistent research findings prompted Tittle and Welch to develop a different theory. They noted that religion is but one of many social institutions and sources of values that promote compliance with the law. According to their theory of secular social disorganization, religion has its strongest deterrent effect when secular moral guidelines are weak or have lost their authority. In these kinds of communities, where the institutions of family, education, and politics are in disarray and fail to provide clear moral guidelines, the institution of religion serves as a last resort to instill compliance with the law.

A second attempt to understand the relationship between religiosity and illegal behavior addressed the nature of particular laws and came to be called the anti-asceticism hypothesis, which is similar to the secular social disorganization theory. Scholars noted that some acts are more consistently condemned throughout all societal institutions than are others. According to the anti-asceticism hypothesis, behaviors that are consistently condemned, such as murder or robbery, are not strongly influenced by religious beliefs. The messages from secular institutions are sufficient to deter people from these kinds of behavior, whether or not they have religious convictions. But there are other behaviors, labeled anti-ascetic forms of deviance, for which secular condemnation is weaker or ambiguous—underage drinking, drug use, tax fraud, employee theft, traffic law violation, and so on. According to the anti-asceticism hypothesis, religiosity should have its greatest deterrent effect on these kinds of behavior for which secular proscriptions are not as compelling. Much like Tittle and Welch's secular disorganization theory, the anti-asceticism hypothesis proposed that religiosity serves as a deterrent to crime and deviance primarily when other forces have failed to elicit conformity.

A third approach to specifying conditions in which religiosity affects deterrence emphasized religious denomination; it has been called the norm qualities hypothesis. The argument focuses primarily on the distinctions between more and less conservative denominations. Conservative denominations expect total commitment and uniform interpretation of sacred teachings, leaving little room for individual discretion in decisions concerning compliance or noncompliance with rules. Consequently, it might follow that religiosity, viewed either as personal religious commitment or frequency of participation, would be a stronger deterrent to crime and deviance among people affiliated with conservative denominations than among those affiliated with less conservative denominations. The extent to which religiosity deters crime depends on the content of the religious norms to which one adheres. With some exceptions, however, research has failed to support this theory, finding instead that religiosity is a significant deterrent regardless of religious affiliation.

By the end of the 1980s the search for conditions in which religiosity has an impact on deterrence seemed to have run its course. Scholars almost unanimously reached the conclusion that religiosity had at least some, though not an extremely strong, deterrent effect on conventional crime and delinquency in nearly all conditions. Prominent scholars such as John Cochran and Ronald Akers called for an end to this line of inquiry. Attention then shifted to the processes through which religiosity had its deterrent effect on crime.

Harold G. Grasmick and his collaborators resurrected Hirschi's earlier concern with religion as a possible sanctioning system and attempted to link religion to the rational choice theory of crime that was gaining respect in criminology and other areas. According to the theory, criminal behavior is like any other behavior: it occurs when the rewards for it outweigh the costs.

Religion potentially contributes to the cost side of the equation in two ways. First, to the extent that sacred norms overlap with secular law, those people for whom religion plays a prominent role in everyday decision making would be more likely than others to feel ashamed if they violate the law. Shame is a self-imposed sanction, enhanced by the importance of religion in one's life and occurring even when others are unaware of one's transgression. Second, to the extent that participation in religious organizations brings one into contact with others who endorse legal norms, individuals actively involved in religious organizations risk greater embarrassment if they choose to violate the law. Embarrassment is a socially imposed sanction, experienced as a loss of respect from others who become aware of one's transgression. Rational choice theory, therefore, has shifted attention away from attempts to specify conditions in which religion is a deterrent to concern with how religion functions as a deterrent. From this theory's perspective, the multiple dimensions of religiosity, religious commitment, and organizational participation, which were not clearly distinguished in earlier research, receive special attention.

The consensus seems to be that religion serves at least as a modest deterrent to conventional crime and delinquency in most conditions. The process through which this effect occurs stems from both the personal and the social dimensions of religiosity.

Religion and Responses to Criminal Offenders

Public opinion concerning preferred societal reactions to criminal offenders is an important topic because policy makers take public opinion into account when formulating criminal justice policies. Since about the mid-1970s Americans have become increasingly punitive in their reaction to crime. For example, in the 1960s the majority of Americans opposed the death penalty, but by the late 1990s an overwhelming majority (over 80 percent by nearly all estimates), when asked whether they generally favored or opposed the death penalty, said that they favored it.

At the same time there has been a growing disillusionment with rehabilitation and even deterrence as a goal of criminal justice policy and increasing public support for retribution (often called "just deserts") as the objective of the criminal justice system. The goal of punishment, according to the retributivist doctrine, is to punish offenders simply because they deserve it, whether the punishment rehabilitates them or deters others.

Earlier research examined the effect of standard socioeconomic and demographic factors (race, age, sex, education, and others) on attitudes toward punishment and justice, finding only weak relationships at best. Other scholars considered the possibility that America's increasing punitiveness was linked to an increasing crime rate, but studies failed to find evidence that victimization or fear of crime affected people's opinions about appropriate punishments.

Sparked in part by David Garland's work on the history of punishment, research in the 1990s explored the previously neglected link between religion and people's views about the goals of punishment and the appropriate punishment for offenders in American society. In contrast to the previously cited research on religion and involvement in crime, in which strength of religious commitment was shown to be more important in determining compliance with laws than religious affiliation or adherence to particular religious doctrines, research on attitudes toward punishment focused on religious affiliation and the nature or content of one's religious beliefs.

Evidence suggests that individuals affiliated with more conservative Protestant denominations are the strongest proponents of retribution as the goal of punishment. This effect of conservative Protestant affiliation is stronger than the effects of socioeconomic and demographic variables, and it appears that this support is linked to conservative Protestants' more literal interpretation of the Bible. Kenneth Wald has noted that conservative churches are especially well equipped to influence public policy. And it has been speculated that the movement toward retribution in the American criminal justice system, as well as in the juvenile justice system, is connected to the revival and growth of such denominations in contemporary American society.

Not only are conservative Protestants more inclined to favor retribution as the objective of criminal justice policy, but they also appear to be more punitive in their response to crime. Compared with others, conservative Protestants are more supportive of the death penalty for adults and for juveniles; they are more likely to believe the courts should be harsher in their punishment; and they are more likely to favor stiffer laws. Again, the effect of conservative Protestantism is greater than the effects of socioeconomic and demographic variables and political party affiliation. Some evidence, however, suggests that the effect is restricted to whites, with blacks affiliated with conservative denominations being less punitive toward offenders than are other blacks.

Grasmick and his colleagues have attempted to explain why conservative Protestants are stronger supporters of retribution and more punitive in their response to crime, noting, as have others, that conservative Protestants are more punitive toward the transgressions of their own children. In the field of social psychology, attribution theory addresses variations in what people consider to be the causes of behavior. Some people are more inclined to think that behavior results from the "will" or character of the actors. These people are said to have a dispositional attribution style. Others who believe that the behavior is the product of forces in the actors' environment are said to have a situational attribution style. Dispositional, not situational, attributions of criminal behavior render the actor more blameworthy and thus, from the perspective of the one making the attribution, more deserving of punishment. Evidence is convincing that those who make dispositional attributions of criminal behavior are more punitive in their response to offenders.

Drawing on the work of Phillip Greven and Robert Wuthnow, Grasmick and his colleagues proposed that conservative Protestantism promotes a dispositional attribution style. A main ingredient in this religious perspective is an emphasis on the "character" of a person. Behavior consistent with religious prescriptions and proscriptions reflects good character; behavior inconsistent with such teachings reflects weak character. From this frame of mind, situational influences have little impact on what a person does.

Grasmick and his colleagues further argued that conservative Protestants, compared with more moderate Protestants, Catholics, and those with no affiliation, are more punitive in their response to crime because they are more likely to attribute criminal behavior to dispositional factors. They tested the argument by studying preferred responses to punishments for juvenile offenders. Their research yielded four conclusions. First, people who adhere to a literal interpretation of the Bible are more punitive in their preferred response to juvenile delinquents. Second, adherence to a literal interpretation of the Bible is closely linked with making a dispositional attribution—that is, with attributing the causes of delinquency to the character of delinquents instead of to environmental influences. Third, this dispositional attribution style strongly increases the punitiveness of people toward juvenile offenders. And, finally, the dispositional attribution style associated with interpreting the Bible accounts for more than half of the greater punitiveness among those who are biblical literalists.

At the same time, this emphasis on the disposition of offenders underlies the motives of faith-based voluntary organizations to rehabilitate offenders, the largest of which is Prison Fellowship, which includes more than fifty thousand trained volunteers who provide Bible studies and seminars to prison inmates. Prison Fellowship and similar organizations assume that offenders are in need of spiritual transformation and that such a transformation while incarcerated can reduce inmates' likelihood of recidivism upon release. A handful of studies, with mixed conclusions, have addressed the effectiveness of such prison programs. In the most recent and most methodologically sound of these, Byron R. Johnson reports short-term effects for about two years, but then the effect begins to diminish so that after eight years beyond release from prison those who participated and those who did not were equally likely to have been rearrested and reincarcerated.

Harold G. Grasmick and Miyuki Fukushima

BIBLIOGRAPHY

Adler, Freda, Gerhard O. W. Mueller, and William S. Laufer. *Criminology.* 5th ed. New York: McGraw-Hill, 2004.

Baier, Colin J., and Bradley R. E. Wright. "If You Love Me, Keep My Commandments: A Meta-Analysis of the Effect of Religion on Crime." *Journal of Research in Crime and Delinquency* 38 (February 2001): 3–21.

Cochran, John, and Ronald Akers. "Beyond Hellfire: An Exploration of the Variable Effects of Religiosity on Adolescent Marijuana and Alcohol Use." *Journal of Research in Crime and Delinquency* 26 (May 1989): 198–225.

Ellison, Christopher G., John P. Bartkowski, and Kristin L. Andersen. "Are There Religious Variations in Domestic Violence?" *Journal of Family Issues* 20 (January 1999): 87–113.

Garland, David. *Punishment and Modern Society: A Study in Social Theory.* Chicago: University of Chicago Press, 1993.

Grasmick, Harold G., and Anne L. McGill. "Religion, Attribution Style, and Punitiveness toward Juvenile Offenders." *Criminology* 32 (February 1994): 23–46.

Grasmick, Harold G., Elizabeth Davenport, Mitchell B. Chamlin, and Robert J. Bursik Jr. "Protestant Fundamentalism and the Retributive Doctrine of Punishment." *Criminology* 30 (February 1992): 21–45.

Grasmick, Harold G., John Cochran, Robert J. Bursik Jr., and M'Lou Kimpel. "Religion, Punitive Justice, and Support for the Death Penalty." *Justice Quarterly* 10 (June 1993): 289–314.

Grasmick, Harold G., Robert J. Bursik Jr., and John Cochran. "Render unto Caesar What Is Caesar's: Religiosity and Taxpayers' Inclinations to Cheat." *Sociological Quarterly* 32 (Summer 1991): 251–266.

Greven, Phillip. *Spare the Child: The Religious Roots of Punishment and Psychological Impact of Physical Abuse.* New York: Random House, 1991.

Hirschi, Travis. *Causes of Delinquency.* Berkeley: University of California Press, 1969.

Johnson, Byron R. "Religious Programs and Recidivism among Former Inmates in Prison Fellowship Programs: A Long-term Follow-up Study." *Justice Quarterly* 21 (June 2004): 329–354.

Johnson, Byron R., Spencer De Li, David B. Larson, and Michael McCullough. "A Systematic Review of the Religiosity and Delinquency Literature." *Journal of Contemporary Criminal Justice* 16 (February 2000): 32–52.

Sherkat, Darren E., and Christopher G. Ellison. "Recent Developments and Current Controversies in the Sociology of Religion." *Annual Review of Sociology* 25 (1999): 363–394.

Smith, Christian. *Soul Searching: The Religious and Spiritual Lives of American Teenagers.* New York: Oxford University Press, 2005.

Tittle, Charles, and Michael Welch. "Religiosity and Deviance: Toward a Contingency Theory of Constraining Effects." *Social Forces* 61 (March 1983): 653–682.

Wald, Kenneth. *Religion and Politics in the United States.* 3d ed. Washington, D.C.: CQ Press, 1996.

Wuthnow, Robert. *The Consciousness Reformation.* Berkeley: University of California Press, 1976.

Crusades

The Crusades were military expeditions launched by various popes during the Middle Ages and beyond to achieve what was seen in the Christian West as a righteous end: most commonly but never exclusively to capture or establish control over Jerusalem. The city of Jerusalem, which was holy to Jews, Christians, and Muslims, had been under Muslim control since 638. In 1095 Pope Urban II launched the First Crusade, which captured Jerusalem in 1099.

This notion of holy war had no clear sanction in the Bible, which defines no particular attitude toward violence. Rather, it arose from contemporary religious and political developments that led the church to interpret the Christian religion in new ways. Medieval churchmen knew that it was impossible to stop the violence of medieval society; instead, they tried to harness it to Christian ends.

In the latter part of the eleventh century, in what is known as the investiture contest, the popes threw off domination of Rome by the German emperors and established the principle that the church should be governed by the clergy. As a result, the Western church was centralized under the control of a papal monarchy that saw its role as reordering society to increase people's chances of salvation. A natural outcome was the use of war as an instrument of policy against opponents. The papacy was conceived of as universal, although the Eastern Orthodox Church—the dominant religious force within the Byzantine Empire centered in Constantinople—had always been reluctant to recognize papal supremacy. By 1071 this empire had lost Asia Minor to an Islam resurgent under the Turks. Two popes, Gregory VII (ruled 1073–1085) and Urban II, tried to reassert supremacy over the Orthodox Church by offering military aid against Islam.

Rise of the Crusading Movement

Urban II was able to mount a successful expedition, the First Crusade, for two reasons: he had cultivated good relations with the Byzantine emperor, Alexius I Comnenus (ruled 1081–1118), and he cast his appeal to European knights in the form of a pilgrimage to Jerusalem, offering to all who participated the hope of eternal life. The First and all subsequent Crusades were penitential wars in which every step forward and every blow were acts of penance that would free a man's soul from hell. It was this brilliantly original notion that created the special character of the crusading movement. The crusader was a soldier, but—rather like a monk—he was also under a spiritual discipline that would earn him forgiveness of his sins. From this idea sprang the Knights Templars and the Knights Hospitalers, military orders of monks sworn to a lifetime in the Holy Land in search of salvation by fighting those they considered Muslim infidels. Ironically, the crusading eruption revived the Qur'anic injunction to *jihad,* the religious duty of Muslims to wage war for the spread of Islam. This imperative formed the rallying cry for the Muslim resistance to crusader conquest that ultimately would drive Westerners from the Holy Land.

The crusaders' establishment of principalities in the East created an obligation for Western Christians to support them, and after 1099 a stream of expeditions great and small went to the Holy Land. For the European upper class, the idea of crusading became an integral part of the chivalric code, which supported knights in their role as the arms-bearers of the church. Crusading to the Holy Land reached a climax after the capture of Jerusalem by Saladin, the sultan of Egypt, in 1187, and in the thirteenth century the papacy gave the movement a new definition and organization. But Jerusalem was not the only goal of crusades.

Only the pope could launch a crusade, and although the idea was intimately associated with the Holy Land, the pope was free, as an assertion of his leadership in Christian society, to define other objectives. In the early twelfth century, crusades were launched to Spain, much of which was under Moorish control. The Second Crusade was launched to rescue Edessa (in modern-day Turkey), which fell to Islam in 1044. Many German crusaders, however, were allowed the crusading reward for fighting the pagans of eastern Europe; others received the same benefit for wars in Spain and Portugal. In 1199 Innocent III promulgated a crusade against his enemy, Markward of Anweiler, in Sicily, and in 1208 against the Cathar heretics of southern France. His successors used crusades against the German Hohenstaufen emperors who were gaining strength in Italy.

Redirection

Scholars today tend to perceive these crusades as political, rather than religious, and so did their victims at the time. But most people in western Europe did accept papal authority—especially because the liberation of Jerusalem was widely desired. By the mid-thirteenth century, however, failure to retake Jerusalem caused Western thinkers to question whether God wanted them to succeed.

By the late thirteenth century, greater forces were at work. The church developed means other than crusading to allow its followers to escape the burden of sin. The European world of 1095 had been dominated by relatively small principalities and kings with limited power, and among these the authority of the papacy had towered. But by the mid-thirteenth century, France and England had developed efficient monarchies that demanded allegiance from their subjects and had the means to enforce it. Monarchs disputed the right of the pope to take men and money for wars in the East and even tried to limit the power of the papacy to tax their subjects and regulate their lives in the name of the church. In a series of conflicts between the French monarchy and the papacy at the turn of the thirteenth into the fourteenth century, the role of the church was much more tightly circumscribed than ever before. Crusading continued to be an ideal of late medieval society, but the institutional decline of the papal monarchy deprived it of vitality. It became increasingly an idea dependent upon the initiative of individuals, particularly of secular kings.

The rulers of Spain and Portugal, influenced by the crusading ideal, encouraged voyages of discovery in the hope of finding new ways of attacking Islam, but other factors, such as hopes of commercial success, tended to become dominant. The Protestant Reformation, in full swing in the sixteenth century, delivered a fatal blow to crusading, because it was as the leader of a united Christendom that the pope had launched the Crusades. Once that fundamental political condition of a united church had been shattered, the movement, which had been dogged by failure and eclipsed by new social and political developments, increasingly became an abstract ideal. However, the notion of crusade as a war inspired by moral righteousness lives on in the consciousness of the modern Christian world. Preaching missions are called crusades, and the cold war was often portrayed in the West as a crusade against communism. Conversely, there is an echo of the worst features of crusading in the use of the word as a synonym for fanatical, unreasoning belief, reinforced by Nazi invocations of the crusading spirit against their enemies.

See also *Islam's Encounters with the West; Jerusalem; Jihad; Orthodoxy, Greek; Papacy; Reformation; Sacred Places.*

John France

BIBLIOGRAPHY

Brundage, James A. *The Crusades, a Documentary Survey.* Milwaukee, Wis.: Marquette University Press, 1962.

Edgington, S. B. *The First Crusade.* New Appreciations in History, no. 37. London: Historical Association, 1996.

France, John. *Victory in the East: A Military History of the First Crusade.* Cambridge: Cambridge University Press, 1994.

Maalouf, Amin. *The Crusades through Arab Eyes.* Translated by Jon Rothschild. New York: Schocken, 1985.

Riley-Smith, Jonathan. *The Crusades: A Short History.* New Haven, Conn.: Yale University Press, 1987.

Cuba

Religious beliefs have historically permeated the Caribbean island of Cuba, whereas the influence of churches has waxed and waned. With the Spanish conquest of the island in the early sixteenth century, the indigenous population was decimated and pre-Columbian religions largely disappeared. Spanish colonial control established Roman Catholicism as the official religion, while the importation of Africans as slaves, primarily in the eighteenth and nineteenth centuries, spread Yoruban and Bantu beliefs, among others. Beginning in the 1880s Protestant churches targeted the island, intensifying their efforts after the United States intervened in Cuba's war of independence (1895–1898). The U.S. protectorate imposed in 1901 facilitated the penetration of North American churches, which regarded themselves as promoters of democracy and modernization.

By the 1940s both Catholics and Protestants were reassessing their growth strategies particularly in the face of increasing competition from secular groups, including Marxist political parties and labor unions. European imports such as the Federation of Young Catholics and Catholic Action promoted socioeconomic justice as a means of combating socialism, secularism, and Protestantism. A 1957 Catholic Action survey found that only 52 percent of four thousand rural families identified themselves as Catholics, with 53.5 percent stating they had never laid eyes on a priest. Nevertheless, more than 96 percent expressed a belief in God. African spiritist beliefs, popularly known as Santería, were, however, prevalent both in urban and rural areas.

By the 1950s the Catholic Church in Cuba was widely regarded as the weakest in Latin America: only about 70 percent of the population identified with it, reflecting its failure to penetrate the rural areas and limited pastoral emphasis. Protestants were estimated at 3–8 percent, and Jews constituted less than 1 percent.

The Cuban Revolution

In 1952 Fulgencio Batista, the Cuban dictator from 1934 until 1944, seized control of the government. Fidel Castro, a lawyer and political activist, led a populist movement to overthrow Batista. Most church people supported the insurrection. They expected a multiparty reformist government to replace the dictator and were taken somewhat aback when Castro consolidated his power in 1959 and proposed extensive agrarian reform and increased state control of private school curricula. Such initiatives, together with a fear of communism, generated a backlash. In November 1959 an estimated one million Cubans gathered in Havana for a National Catholic Congress, where shouts of "Cuba, sí, comunismo, no!" rang out. As criticism of the government increased, both domestically and in the United States, Castro sought allies, including the Popular Socialist Party, the fore-runner of Cuba's Communist Party, and the Soviet Union. In 1961 he declared himself a Marxist-Leninist in the immediate aftermath of the Bay of Pigs invasion, thereby cementing his identification with communism both nationally and internationally.

Tensions between church people and government supporters contributed to a growing exodus of Catholics, Protestants, and Jews from the island. Of approximately seven hundred priests in Cuba in 1960, 70 percent had left by 1963, including 8 percent who were expelled by the government for alleged counterrevolutionary activities. The Methodists, Presbyterians, and Episcopalians lost virtually all of their ministers and 40–70 percent of their congregations. By 1965 the Jewish community had declined from more than twelve thousand to approximately twelve hundred. Such losses help explain why so many churches shut down and many denominations became refuges for the disaffected. The nationalization of private schools in the aftermath of the Bay of Pigs, together with the induction of some clerics and seminarians into Military Units to Aid Production in the mid-1960s, confirmed the fears of many church people. Armed resistance to the revolution by small groups of fundamentalist Christians in the interior of the country in the mid-1960s fueled the government's suspicions of all religions.

In the late 1960s tensions began to lessen as Catholic and mainline Protestant denominations, as well as the government, sought rapprochement. In 1969 the Catholic Church issued two pastoral letters criticizing the U.S. embargo of Cuba, imposed after Cuba nationalized some U.S.-owned properties, and urging the faithful to support government programs that contributed to the common good. Several mainline Protestant denominations initiated dialogues with the government, with the Presbyterians and Methodists, in particular, praising state health and educational programs. Castro responded in the early 1970s by stating that he saw no contradiction between religion and Marxism and praising the emergence of progressive Christian groups throughout Latin America.

In 1976 a new constitution guaranteed freedom of conscience and the right to profess or practice any religion, although it was illegal to oppose one's faith or beliefs to the revolution. It also asserted that the state was obligated to educate all Cubans in scientific materialism, a commitment abandoned in 1992. Constitutional guarantees did not, however, end discrimination against believers, especially in schools and workplaces. The government continued to condemn such groups as the Assembly of God and Jehovah's Witnesses, in part because of their opposition to universal military service and to work and school on Saturdays.

Easing of Church-State Tensions

By the mid-1980s church-state relations had been regularized through a special office of the Communist Party's Central Committee. Among other matters, it provided for the importation of materials necessary for religious activities and travel of church people to and from Cuba. Relations were also improved after Castro granted a book-length interview on religion to a Brazilian friar that was published in 1985.

In 1986 the Catholic Church held a National Encounter in an effort to revitalize itself. It recommended greater lay participation, more intensive evangelization, and dialogue among all Cubans. The church hastened to affirm that it was not in competition with the government because it was promoting a religion, not an ideology, and that it was not against socialism.

The end of the cold war and the breakup of the Soviet Union in 1991 ended foreign aid from that country and helped precipitate economic crisis in Cuba. Food subsidies and government welfare programs were cut back, causing the churches to seek international humanitarian assistance. Difficult economic conditions contributed to a new exodus of Cubans. As a result, the Catholic Church in 1993 called for a reassessment of public policies as well as the initiation of a dialogue aimed at reconciling all Cubans on the island and abroad. This declaration prompted a series of sharp responses from the government, which regarded it as overstepping the bounds of legitimate church activities. Church-state tensions intensified but were held in check somewhat by a desire not to exacerbate internal divisions as well as by a pragmatic interest in retaining assistance from religious aid organizations.

Ten years after the Catholic Church's first National Encounter, the faithful again gathered to assess the state of the church and the nation. Dialogue and reconciliation were seen as even more necessary than in 1986. The church criticized the government's repression of human rights activists and called for greater respect for the rights of all citizens. It reasserted its strong criticism of the U.S. embargo of Cuba and specifically condemned the 1996 Helms-Burton law, which tightened it. The government responded positively to this condemnation, while essentially ignoring the calls for dialogue and reconciliation. The Catholic Church received a boost when Pope John Paul II visited the island in 1998. Among his concerns were moral regeneration, greater freedom for evangelization, revitalization of the family, and power to influence the course of Cuba's future. The government was interested in having the pope condemn the U.S. embargo and lend legitimacy to a fading regime, which he did.

Since the late 1980s virtually all religions in Cuba have been growing, in part because of the pressures resulting from economic and political crises. A 1994 survey by the *Miami Herald* estimated that 20 percent of the population had attended services in the previous month, significantly higher than in 1958. In addition, a 1989 study by the Cuban Center for Psychological and Sociological Research found that 84 percent of the population professed some form of religious belief. These data suggest a remarkable survival of religious belief after many years of Marxist government and promotion of materialist atheism. At the outset of the twenty-first century speculation increased about a possible role for religion in an increasingly active civil society. To date neither Cuban religions nor civil society have succeeded in generating a consensual agenda with broad-based popular support that might influence the transition that is beginning in Cuba.

See also *Marxism; Revolutions.*

Margaret E. Crahan

BIBLIOGRAPHY

Castro Ruz, Fidel. *Fidel and Religion.* New York: Simon and Schuster, 1987.

Gómez Treto, Rafael. *The Church and Socialism in Cuba.* Maryknoll, N.Y.: Orbis Books, 1988.

Kirk, John M. *Between God and the Party: Religion and Politics in Revolutionary Cuba.* Tampa: University of South Florida Press, 1989.

Pérez-Stable, Marifeli. *The Cuban Revolution: Origins, Course, and Legacy.* New York: Oxford University Press, 1993.

Cults

Cults, as they are generally understood today, are new and unconventional religious groups, many of which grew rapidly in the 1960s and gave rise to controversies about their teachings and practices. The term "cult" is problematic partly because its range of meanings is wide and partly because it has become pejorative. Its range extends from the practice of special veneration for holy figures or relics (as in the Christian cult of the Virgin Mary) to allegedly authoritarian religious movements (as in Sun Myung Moon's Unification Church, or "Moonies," founded in Korea in 1954). In addition, popular usage of "cult" refers to celebrities or cultural products that attract the unusually intense devotion of admirers (as in cult movies or the cult of Elvis Presley) as well as to political leaders such as Mao Zedong, Kim Jong Il, and Fidel Castro who inspire or impose mass adulation. All meanings of the word emphasize intense devotion and commitment, but popular usage nowadays implies that intensity can degenerate into fanaticism and irrationality, as in the case of Christian Patriot, survivalist, or neo-Nazi cults.

The Controversial Nature of Cults

The meaning of the term "cult" has changed significantly since about 1960. It used to mean a small group of enthusiasts for esoteric or spiritual beliefs whose activities were secretive or marginal to mainstream social life. Cult members were usually considered to have little interest in politics because they were preoccupied with their personal beliefs and practices. Few cultic groups had enough resources to make an impact on public affairs. This particular conception of cults began to change in the 1960s, however, when a large number of new religious movements began to attract followers and public attention, initially in the United States and subsequently in other advanced industrial democracies. Many of these new movements such as the International Society for Krishna Consciousness, the Church of Scientology, the Unification Church, and the Neo-Sannyas movement were based on beliefs and values deriving from non-Western and non-Christian philosophies.

In addition to being charged with perverting or rejecting the main Christian traditions, religious groups regarded as cults were accused of having harmful effects on the fabric of society and on the mental health of their followers. Accusations that cults brainwashed their recruits, exploited them, and ruined their education or careers became commonplace in the 1970s. The relatives and friends of some recruits fought hard to get them out of cults either by persuasion or by forcible deprogramming.

By the mid-1990s about six hundred groups were probably identifiable as cults in the United States, with the number of their members being estimated at roughly 200,000. Although controversies have concerned only a dozen or so cults, the public image of all cults has been heavily influenced by the controversial ones. Because "cult" has become value-laden, most social scientists who study emergent, alternative, or unorthodox religious groups prefer the term "new religious movement."

Most marginal religious movements are not controversial, but a series of tragedies affecting a small number of so-called cults has kept them in the public eye. These events include the suicide or murder of more than nine hundred followers of Jim Jones at the People's Temple compound in Jonestown, Guyana, in 1978; the death of eighty-eight members of the Branch Davidian group led by David Koresh in Waco, Texas, in 1993; the murder or suicide of sixty-seven members of the Order of the Solar Temple at various sites in Canada, France, and Switzerland in 1994 and 1995; the death of eleven victims of the sarin gas attacks carried out on the Tokyo subway by followers of Aum Shinri-kyo in 1995; and the suicide in 1997 of thirty-seven members of the Heaven's Gate unidentified flying object cult in California.

The fact that the People's Temple and the Branch Davidians were Christian churches exploited by unscrupulous leaders, not new movements with esoteric teachings, did not prevent their critics and opponents from labeling them as cults. These collective tragedies, along with other, less well publicized, incidents involving death or damage to individual members of new religious movements, have helped to fuel the suspicion that any unorthodox religious movement outside the Christian mainstream might have cultic tendencies. At a time when levels of active participation in mainstream religious organizations are declining in most advanced industrial societies, unease about movements lumped together as cults shows no sign of abating.

Religious cults are politically significant for two main reasons. First, some cults have tried to exercise political influence directly. Second, cult controversies have raised political questions about public responses to challenging or unorthodox religious movements. The strength of public concern about cults fluctuates over time—though journalists keep cults in the public eye even when there is a shortage of newsworthy stories about them. But there have also been major scandals, disasters, and tragedies that have not only thrust cults into the headlines temporarily but also provoked official investigations into the "cult phenomenon" in general.

Cults in Politics

Although most religious cults are rarely involved in organized politics, a few have been politically active in various countries. Virtually the only thing these political activities have in common is that they have been controversial. By comparison, the political activities of major Christian, Jewish, and other well established religious organizations have attracted relatively little public interest and criticism.

The Unification Church, under its high-profile founder and leader Sun Myung Moon, stands out as one of the few cults that are known to have tried to exercise influence over politics in the United States, the Republic of Korea, and elsewhere. The Unification Church's teachings do not support the idea of a sharp distinction between the affairs of the everyday world and those of a transcendent, heavenly realm. Consequently, Unificationist theologians argue that it is a religious responsibility to work toward the perfection of human societies on Earth. The Unification Church's ambitious and varied programs of social change and cultural improvement are therefore inseparable from political activity—especially campaigns against communism and in favor of free-market economics in a unified world. Numerous lobbyists for Unificationist ideals worked in Washington, D.C., in the 1970s and 1980s in support of various conservative issues, not only in the United States but also in the cult's place of origin and in Latin America. Moon's launch of a new daily newspaper, the *Washington Times,* in 1982, was further evidence of his intention to shape American politics. Two major controversies developed in response to this direct political activity.

First, the Unification Church was accused of lobbying U.S. political leaders on behalf of Korean companies that stood to suffer large financial losses if the U.S. administration withdrew American troops from South Korea in an attempt to reduce its budget deficit and to foster better relations with communist regimes in China and North Korea. Second, the Unification Church's links with right-wing regimes and political interests in Central America and South America were furthered by one of its political front organizations, CAUSA (the Confederation of Associations for the Unity of Societies of the Americas), throughout the 1980s.

Similar accusations of political and economic influence peddling have been made against some of the massive new religions that mushroomed in Japan after World War II. The largest of them, Soka Gakkai, has been at the center of numerous controversies associated with the activities of the

Komeito, a political party to which it was formally connected between 1964 and 1970. Soka Gakkai, a lay Buddhist movement of about sixteen million members, officially separated itself from Komeito (Clean Government Party) to reduce the risk of offending Japanese sensibilities about the mixing of religion and politics. The movement's leaders, however, did not refrain from trying to keep certain political issues in the forefront of members' minds, especially in relation to global peace, disarmament, environmental protection, and racial discrimination. Komeito's continuing ideological sympathy with Soka Gakkai's values and ideals also ensures that the movement remains in a position to influence Japanese politics indirectly.

Few cults have matched the aspirations of the Unification Church and Soka Gakkai to exercise direct political influence on a national or international level, but some of them have occasionally been active in broadly political campaigns that cut across the boundaries of political parties. The Church of Scientology, founded by L. Ron Hubbard in 1953, for example, has campaigned for many years against what it considers to be the abuses of institutional psychiatry. The Scientologists' strategies have included direct lobbying of politicians and government officials, publication of campaign literature, and attempts to gain control over voluntary associations in the field of mental health. Similarly, Scientology has sought to tackle drug abuse and crime by mounting programs to change public attitudes and conduct.

Regional and local administrations have necessarily interacted with cults that occupied premises in their areas. Questions about zoning applications, the education of the children of cult members, and public health concerns loom large in places where religious movements have residences or businesses. Local journalists often play an important role in alerting public authorities to alleged problems. This is notably the case in Japan where, ten years after Aum Shinri-kyo's lethal attack on the Tokyo subway system, local opposition to the continuing operation of the cult's successor organization, Aleph, remained intense.

In the 1980s local and state officials in Oregon clashed with the followers of the Bhagwan Shree Rajneesh, who founded the Rajneesh Foundation International in India and expanded it to the United States. Controversy arose over the way in which the Rajneeshpuram commune constructed and ran its vast settlement in remote surroundings. There were allegations that the cult breached immigration regula-

tions, tried illicitly to control local politics, brutally repressed critics, and plotted to kill at least one of its opponents. In Japan the official investigation into Aum Shinri-kyo's criminal activities also raised the possibility that there had been complicity or negligence on the part of local officials or politicians in covering up the cult's potential threat to its own members and the public. In several countries similar allegations have been made about the complicity of politicians and police in the possibly illegal activities of the Order of the Solar Temple, including connections with well-placed neo-Nazi supporters in France. Luc Jouret, who founded this apocalyptic cult in 1977, led many of his followers to commit suicide and possibly murder in 1994 and 1995 in Canada, France, and Switzerland.

All these cases illustrate the general point that public attitudes toward the minority of religious cults that are directly involved in politics tend to be distinctly suspicious, if not hostile. The belief is widespread that new or controversial religious movements exploit their members and their fiscal privileges unfairly or deceptively for the sake of gaining power and wealth. Meanwhile, fears also have arisen that strong criticism of cults has served as a stalking-horse to conceal broader attacks on the privileges enjoyed by most religious organizations.

The Politics of Cults

The central issue in the politics of cults is the extent to which democratic and pluralist societies can afford to tolerate religious beliefs and actions that may appear to be intolerant in themselves. As a classic dilemma of liberalism, the issue of the limits of tolerance in a tolerant society arises particularly in countries that recognize the freedom of citizens to practice the religions of their choice.

This dilemma has arisen in an especially poignant and ironic form in countries of central Europe and eastern Europe, which were under Soviet domination until the early 1990s. The opportunity for autonomy and democracy might have been expected to lead to an explosion of unorthodox and nontraditional activities in all spheres of social life. Instead, a concern to protect individual citizens and the social fabric from the dangers of exploitation has given rise to campaigns and new laws to prevent Christian churches and religious movements that did not have large followings or that had not been active in these countries for generations from operating legally. It is as if the advent of democratic political systems has convinced many people that complete freedom of religion would be an unacceptable risk to take in their newly democratic countries.

The fact that movements labeled "cults" in advanced industrial societies tend to originate in the United States or Asia and to involve ideas foreign to the former Soviet spheres of influence makes them especially vulnerable to political campaigns for the control of nonindigenous forms of religion. The vested interests of the Orthodox and Catholic Churches in these countries create still more obstacles to the implantation of cults. Yet the ideological vacuum left by state socialism offers a golden opportunity for new religious movements to achieve a rapid expansion of their sphere of operations.

The growth of extreme nationalistic sentiments has also created a political atmosphere of hostility toward religious organizations that have no association with the history of the nations concerned. For example, a new law enacted in Russia in 1997 was designed to halt the missionary activities of most mainstream and cultic religious groups originating outside the country. Since then, the frequency of legal actions against cults and minority religious groups such as Jehovah's Witnesses has increased, and misgivings are widespread about political interference in some trials as well as about the lack of due process in others. Attempts to introduce new laws to control the activities of cults have also occurred in other countries, including Croatia, the Czech Republic, Hungary, and Poland.

Cults face the same legal disabilities as those faced by other foreign religious organizations in countries that restrict or prohibit any religious activity except that permitted by the state. The People's Republic of China is particularly noteworthy for its legal and administrative measures to suppress the activities of movements such as Falun Gong and Zhong Gong, which are officially designated as "evil cults." Chinese authorities and anticult groups are especially vigilant about the uses that illegal religious groups make of the Internet and satellite broadcasts to communicate with their followers and supporters in China and other countries. But even countries that formally or informally guarantee freedom of religion—as in the regions of western Europe, North America, and Australasia—the "problem of cults" is framed in such a way that new religious movements encounter obstacles ranging from the denial of fiscal privileges to the prohibition of some of their normal activities. The range of official and quasi-official investigations into cults extends from ad hoc inquiries to full-scale parliamen-

tary reports such as those commissioned in the 1990s by the French National Assembly, the German Parliament, the Japanese Religious Corporation Council, and the Belgian Chamber of Representatives. The French report aimed to take stock of the dangers allegedly presented by cults to individuals and society and to identify appropriate countermeasures. The German inquiry was concerned primarily with collecting information about new religious movements and analyzing the social background to their emergence and spread. The Japanese report was more narrowly focused on whether the official procedures for registering religious movements needed to be tightened in the wake of the Aum Shinri-kyo incident.

The Belgian parliamentary report of 1997, which listed 189 harmful cults, led indirectly to a new law in 1998 and to the creation of an Information and Advisory Centre to monitor cultic activity. But the political response to cults is more forceful and better coordinated in France than in any other European country. The parliamentary report of 1996, which identified 173 dangerous cults, was followed by the creation of three interministerial agencies in succession that were responsible for the official "fight against cults." In addition, the About-Picard Law of 2001 not only made it illegal to exploit the physical or psychological dependency of other people but also empowered officially recognized anticult organizations to pursue legal action against any group suspected of breaking this law.

Alongside these high-level initiatives are numerous voluntary anticult or cult-watching associations running campaigns to monitor or suppress the activities of new religious movements. In turn, groups concerned with protecting civil liberties and the separation of church and state are opposed to many of these cult-monitoring activities on the ground that they threaten religious freedoms. Moreover, the U.S. State Department's annual reports on religious freedom have often noted concerns about the French response to cults and other minority religious groups. The Parliamentary Assembly of the Council of Europe invited the French government in 2002 to reconsider the About-Picard Law.

It is important to keep the topic of cults in perspective. The number of cults involved directly in politics has never been large, and their effect has been negligible. Only a handful of highly controversial cults have attracted attention, but public opinion and journalistic practice tend to lump all cults together and to portray them as uniformly destructive and threatening. It is therefore important to emphasize that most cults display little interest in politics and prefer to turn their back on the world. The major political controversies concern a small number of religious groups that are not representative of other new religious movements but that have become embroiled in public controversies and political disputes. Controversial cults are politically significant mainly because they test the outer limits of religious toleration and the freedom of religion. The advent of the Internet and of global flows of people, resources, and ideas has raised the stakes both for cults and for their opponents.

See also *Denominationalism; Millennialism; Religious Organization; Survivalism; Unification Church; Voluntarism.*

James A. Beckford

BIBLIOGRAPHY

Arweck, Elisabeth. *Researching New Religious Movements: Constructions and Controversies.* London: Routledge, 2005.

Beckford, James A. *Cult Controversies: The Societal Response to New Religious Movements.* London: Tavistock, 1985.

Dawson, Lorne L., ed. *Cults and New Religious Movements: A Reader.* Oxford, U.K.: Blackwell, 2003.

Richardson, James T., ed. *Regulating Religion.* New York: Kluwer, 2004.

Robbins, Thomas. *Cults, Converts, and Charisma.* Beverly Hills and London: Sage, 1988.

D

Dalai Lama

The highest ranking religious and political figure of Tibetan Buddhism. Tenzin Gyatso (1935–), the fourteenth dalai lama, was born in northeastern Tibet and, in the early twenty-first century, lived in exile in northern India. As a small boy he was recognized as the rebirth of the thirteenth dalai lama and was enthroned as the secular and spiritual ruler of Tibet. Like all dalai lamas (a title first bestowed by the Mongolian ruler Altan Khan in 1578), he is also believed to be an emanation of Tibet's patron deity, Chenresig or Avalokiteshvara, the Bodhisattva of Compassion. In 1950, when the fourteenth dalai lama was fifteen, Chinese troops entered Tibet and soon incorporated it as a province into the newly formed People's Republic of China. In 1959 the Dalai Lama escaped to India, where he reestablished his government in exile.

Since the 1980s the Dalai Lama has traveled extensively in his capacity as a spiritual and political leader. In 1987 he presented his Five Point Peace Plan for Tibet before the U.S. Congress, calling for an end to the increasing Chinese immigration to Tibet; the establishment of Tibet as a neutral "zone of peace"; respect for Tibetan human rights; implementation of safeguards to protect Tibet's natural environment; and initiation of earnest negotiations leading to a resolution on Tibet's future. Such proposals have been denounced by the Chinese government as attempts to split Tibet from China, but in other statements the Dalai Lama has indicated that he is willing to forgo full independence for Tibet if he can be assured of real autonomy within the Chinese nation. Envoys from the Tibetan government in exile have traveled repeat-

Tenzin Gyatso, the fourteenth dalai lama, attends a conference on women in California on September 26, 2006.

edly to China for private negotiations, but there has been no public change in the Chinese government's stance that Tibet is an inalienable part of the Chinese nation and that the Dalai Lama is a political rebel in monk's robes.

241

The Dalai Lama was awarded the Nobel Peace Prize in 1989 in recognition of his attempts to work out a political solution for Tibet through peaceful measures. As a Buddhist monk, he is guided in his political work by principles of nonviolence; he has also cited Mahatma Gandhi and the Reverend Martin Luther King Jr. as exemplars of his political philosophy. A prolific author and lecturer as well as a strong proponent of interreligious dialogue, the Dalai Lama has become internationally known not only as a religious leader but also as a champion of human rights. He has participated in a number of conferences with neuroscientists and medical doctors since the mid-1980s, as part of his deep interest in the study of the mind from both empirical scientific and Buddhist perspectives. Traveling widely as a Buddhist master, he has also taught and performed rituals in places as diverse as Los Angeles, Sydney, Moscow, and Ulan Bataar, Mongolia. In early 2006, for the thirtieth time in his long rule, the Dalai Lama performed an important Tibetan Buddhist ritual cycle known as the Kalachakra, or "Wheel of Time," before a crowd of more than 100,000 Tibetan, East Asian, and Euro-American Buddhists in southern India.

See also *Buddhism, Tibetan; Human Rights.*

Peter K. Moran

BIBLIOGRAPHY

Dalai Lama. *Freedom in Exile: The Autobiography of the Dalai Lama.* New York: HarperCollins, 1990.

———. *The World of Tibetan Buddhism: An Overview of Its Philosophy and Practice.* Translated and edited by Geshe Thupten Jinpa. Boston, Mass.: Wisdom Publications, 1995.

———. *My Land and My People: The Original Autobiography of His Holiness the Dalai Lama of Tibet.* New York: Warner Books, 1997.

Day, Dorothy

American reformer and journalist. Day (1897–1980) cofounded the radical Catholic Worker Movement in 1933 and published a monthly newspaper, the *Catholic Worker.* Her unique blend of pacifism, anarchism, and fidelity to Christian principles of charity and justice led her and the movement she founded to oppose many social policies. Whether criticizing child labor, the exploitation of blacks, and anti-Semitism during the 1930s or protesting the treatment of migrant workers, the Vietnam War, and the nuclear arms race in the 1960s and 1970s, the *Catholic Worker* consistently chal-

Dorothy Day.

lenged Americans to think through the implications of public policy.

Born in Brooklyn, Day grew up in Chicago, where she learned of the struggles of the labor movement in the decades preceding World War I. As a student at the University of Illinois, she rejected religion because of its lack of social vision and joined the campus socialist group. Arriving in New York in 1915 to pursue a career in journalism, she wrote for left-wing journals and newspapers and, during the war, participated in draft protests and marches for women's suffrage.

In the early 1920s Day lived with her common-law husband, had a child, and mingled freely with the political and cultural left wing of Greenwich Village. She became interested in Roman Catholicism, which satisfied her hunger for prayer and transcendence. It was her association with the French peasant-philosopher Peter Maurin, however, that enabled her to synthesize her radical political commitments and religious beliefs. Together they founded the Catholic

Worker Movement with the intention of reconstructing the social order in accordance with the norms of the Christian Gospels.

The *Catholic Worker* was as critical of capitalist economics as it was skeptical of Marxist revolutionary claims. Day's movement was also distinguished by its commitment to pacifism during the Spanish Civil War of the 1930s, World War II, and the cold war that followed. In the early 1940s Day and her colleagues sponsored the Association of Catholic Conscientious Objectors, which promoted alternative service rather than military combat. In the 1950s she was arrested for refusing to participate in compulsory air-raid drills. In the 1960s and 1970s the Catholic Worker supported critics of the Vietnam War and advocates of disarmament. Day's was an authentic religious pacifism, an opposition to violence and war that was rooted in the Gospels and tradition.

A second contribution of the Catholic Worker Movement was the establishment of simple "houses of hospitality" to feed the hungry, clothe the naked, shelter the homeless, and promote interracial justice. Under Day's influence, some forty houses grew up across the country. Day herself lived a life of voluntary poverty among the destitute and the homeless on New York's Lower East Side. The task at Catholic Worker Movement houses was to live out the Christian ideal of personal charity, respect for human dignity, and practical assistance to the needy. Day's movement thus combined political activism against injustice with direct assistance to the poor. As both a political radical and a Catholic, Day embodied a remarkable integration of religion and politics in twentieth-century American culture.

See also *Humanitarianism; Pacifism; Social Justice; Vietnam.*

Mary C. Segers

BIBLIOGRAPHY

Day, Dorothy. *The Long Loneliness.* New York: Harper, 1952.

Ellsberg, Robert, ed. *By Little and by Little: The Selected Writings of Dorothy Day.* New York: Knopf, 1983.

Klejment, Anne. *Dorothy Day and the Catholic Worker: A Bibliography and Index.* New York: Garland, 1986.

Miller, William D. *Dorothy Day: A Biography.* San Francisco, Calif.: Harper and Row, 1982.

Piehl, Mel. *Breaking Bread: The Catholic Worker and the Origins of Catholic Radicalism in America.* Philadelphia, Pa.: Temple University Press, 1982.

Segers, Mary C. "Equality and Christian Anarchism: The Political and Social Ideas of the Catholic Worker Movement." *Review of Politics* 40 (April 1978): 196–230.

Demographic Shifts in Global Christianity

In the centuries after a religion is founded, one would expect most of its adherents to live near its place of origin. But for religions such as Christianity, Islam, and Buddhism, trade routes and missionary activity facilitated the rapid spread of the faith—followers were thriving in areas thousands of miles from where their founders once walked. It is in this transregional sense that these religions came to be "global" and that the demographic weight of each religion shifted far from its original center.

One way to track the demographic shift of a religion is to utilize the concept of a statistical center of gravity—that is, where an equal number of followers are found to the north, south, east, and west of a specific geographic location at a specific time in history. In the first century, the statistical center of Christianity was Jerusalem. By the end of the second century, Christians could be found as far north as Britain and as far east as Afghanistan. Nevertheless, its statistical center remained in Western Asia for its first millennium. For these thousand years, Christians were equally divided between Europe and Africa or Asia. After 1000, however, Christianity declined in Asia, so that by the time of the Protestant Reformation, 92 percent of all Christians were European and the statistical center of Christianity had moved north to Hungary. By 1900, because of the European settlement of the Americas, the statistical center of global Christianity was near Madrid in Spain. Yet by the beginning of the twenty-first century, the statistical center had moved again; it was near Timbuktu in Mali—over 60 percent of all Christians were in Africa, Asia, Latin America, and Oceania. If present trends continue, by 2010 the center will be in northern Nigeria, and over 75 percent of all Christians will be found outside of Europe and North America. The trajectory created by joining all of these points in a line traces the serial expansion of Christianity from Asia and Africa to Europe and back again.

Table 1 shows the demographic shift of global Christianity in terms of North and South in 1900 and 2005. At first glance, there appears to have been little change in global Christianity—Christians represented about one-third of the world's population throughout the twentieth century. Nevertheless, one can readily see internal changes within Christianity; 82 percent of all Christians lived in the North in 1900 but only 39 percent by 2005. Correspondingly, in the

Table 1

Christians by Six UN Regions, Global South and Global North, 1900 and 2005

	1900			2005		
	Christians	% Christian	% of all Christians	Christians	% Christian	% of all Christians
Africa	9,939,000	9.2	1.8	410,973,000	46.3	19.3
Asia	21,898,000	2.3	3.9	350,628,000	9.0	16.4
Latin America	62,003,000	95.2	11.1	517,103,000	92.6	24.2
Oceania	4,838,000	77.5	0.9	26,460,000	80.2	1.2
Global South	**98,678,000**	**8.7**	**17.7**	**1,305,164,000**	**24.2**	**61.2**
Europe	380,642,000	94.5	68.2	553,301,000	76.4	25.9
Northern America	78,812,000	96.6	14.1	275,364,000	82.9	12.9
Global North	**459,454,000**	**94.9**	**82.3**	**828,665,000**	**78.4**	**38.8**
Global Christians	**558,132,000**	**34.5**	**100.0**	**2,133,829,000**	**33.1**	**100.0**

Source: Center for the Study of Global Christianity, Gordon-Conwell Theological Seminary.

South Christians grew from 18 percent of all Christians in 1900 to over 60 percent by 2005.

The decline of Christianity in the North can be attributed mainly to the unexpected massive defections of Christians in 1900 because of the secularism in Western Europe, communism in Eastern Europe, and materialism in North America. At the same time, large numbers of conversions to Christianity took place in Africa. Christians there numbered fewer than 10 million in 1900, rising dramatically to over 410 million by 2005. Most of these converts came from tribal backgrounds and not from other world religions. In addition, the conversions came after the colonial powers left. Other factors in this phenomenal growth are the delayed effects of Bible translation (into Africa's mother tongues) and the rise of African pastors and evangelists. Today, conversion is no longer the main driver of Christian growth in Africa. Of the 41,000 new Christians per day, only 1,500 are converts; the rest are children born to Christian parents. Globally, however, the number of Christians grows each year by 22.2 million, a number produced by four separate dynamics: 42.1 million Christian births plus 19.7 million converts to Christianity minus 21.9 million Christian deaths minus 17.7 million defections from Christianity. The future of Christianity is thus directed by demography (birth and death) and religious change (conversion and defection).

Christianity now has over two billion followers in the world. Every year, these followers are increasingly from the Global South. This shift is largely the result of the indigenization of Christianity in Africa, Asia, and Latin America. In the middle of the twentieth century, as southern countries increasingly declared their independence, foreign missionaries became less visible while national workers took over leadership of the churches.

Table 1 also shows that in Asia Christians, one of the fastest-growing categories, represent less than 10 percent of the population of that region. Although Christians are in the minority in Asia, in Africa they are increasingly in the majority. At the same time, the percentage of Christians is decreasing in nearly every country in Europe and North America.

Table 2 shows the basic shift in the number of Christians over the past century in terms of cultural tradition. European hegemony has declined, falling from 78.6 percent in 1900 to only 34 percent by 2005. During the same period, African, Asian, and Latin American Christians (understood ethnically and culturally) increased from 21.4 percent in 1900 to 66 percent of all Christians over the same period. In fact, Christians now use more languages (4,000 out of 6,700) for worship, theology, and witness than any other religionists. Christian missionaries and later local church leaders forged strategic alliances with local conceptions of religion—in particular, using local names for God. This interaction was so profound that one historian writes of the "indigenous discovery of Christianity" rather than the "Christian discovery of indigenous societies." This diversity

Table 2

Global Population and Christians, by Major Cultural Tradition, 1900 and 2005

Cultural tradition	1900				2005			
	Population	% of World Pop.	Christians	% of all Christians	Population	% of World Pop.	Christians	% of all Christians
African (Bantu, Nilotic, Sudanic)	68,220,000	4.2	2,297,000	0.4	590,972,800	9.2	337,732,000	15.8
African American (U.S. black, Creole)	23,326,000	1.4	22,597,000	4.0	148,325,000	2.3	135,330,000	6.3
Asian (Chinese, Indo-Malay, Korean)	682,718,000	42.2	34,530,000	6.2	2,437,332,000	37.8	389,618,000	18.3
European (Caucasian, Germanic, Slav)	440,971,000	27.2	438,553,000	78.6	937,644,200	14.5	724,053,000	33.9
Indo-Iranian (Dravidian, Iranian, North Indian)	302,351,000	18.7	6,670,000	1.2	1,527,652,000	23.7	83,140,000	3.9
Latin American (Mestizo, Amerindian)	47,778,000	2.9	42,910,000	7.7	389,981,000	6.0	382,260,000	17.9
Middle Eastern (Arab, Berber, Ethiopic)	51,708,000	3.2	9,310,000	1.7	404,299,000	6.3	66,690,000	3.1
Oceanic (Fijian, Melanesian, Papuan)	2,556,000	0.2	1,265,000	0.2	17,423,000	0.3	15,006,000	0.7
Global Population	1,619,628,000	100.0	558,132,000	100.0	6,453,629,000	100.0	2,133,829,000	100.0

Source: Center for the Study of Global Christianity, Gordon-Conwell Theological Seminary.

of cultures and languages is transforming Christianity worldwide by presenting new concepts and worldviews with which Christians must grapple in new mother tongues. It is also clear that global Christianity is moving in the direction of more equally representing the world's population.

Table 3 lists the top ten countries in global Christianity in 1900 and 2005, along with the form of government found in each at that time. The table reveals that northern countries, mostly monarchies, are no longer normative for Christians, who today live mainly under various kinds of republics. Yale University historian Lamin Sanneh sees the rise of Christianity in the global south as a stream moving in the opposite direction of that of the secularizing North or West. From this viewpoint, he speaks of a post–western Christianity in contrast with a post–Christian West. The bulk of Christians are already found in the less secular South. In the postcolonial era, the countries that found their freedom by becoming independent from colonial masters have not followed the European pattern of secularization. Instead, people in newly

independent countries tend to be more religious and their governments seem less interested in promoting secularism. At the same time, with the decline of communism in Europe and its continued presence in Asia, the statistical center of atheism dramatically moved from Europe in 1900 to Asia in 2005. The prototypical atheist today is Chinese, not Swedish or French.

Table 3 also demonstrates that Christians are less concentrated today than they were a hundred years ago. In 1900 the top ten countries (eight in Europe) contained over 67 percent of all Christians. Today, the top ten represent slightly less than half of the world's Christians. In fact, in two-thirds of the world's 238 countries, Christians now form a majority of the population.

Political Implications

Christianity in the global south tends to be more conservative in theology and moral teaching than northern Christianity. The churches growing in the South, whether Angli-

Table 3
Top Ten Christian Countries, 1900 and 2005

1900			2005		
Country	Christians	Type of government	Country	Christians	Type of government
United States (N)	73,270,000	Federal republic	United States (N)	250,642,000	Federal republic
Russia (N)	61,545,000	Absolute hereditary monarchy	Brazil (S)	166,847,000	Multiparty republic
Germany (N)	41,533,000	Hereditary monarchy	China (S)	110,956,000	Single-party people's republic
France (N)	40,731,000	Republic	Mexico (S)	102,012,000	Federal republic
Britain (N)	37,125,000	Constitutional monarchy	Russia (N)	84,495,000	Federal multiparty republic
Italy (N)	32,903,000	Constitutional monarchy	Philippines (S)	73,991,000	Unitary republic
Ukraine (N)	28,501,000	Absolute hereditary monarchy	India (S)	68,190,000	Multiparty republic
Poland (N)	21,990,000	Hereditary monarchy	Germany (N)	61,702,000	Multiparty republic
Spain (N)	18,797,000	Constitutional monarchy	Nigeria (S)	61,438,000	Federal republic
Brazil (S)	17,319,000	Republic	DR Congo (S)	53,371,000	Republic
Total	373,714,000	67% of all Christians	Total	1,033,644,000	48% of all Christians

Note: N = North, S = South.

Source: Center for the Study of Global Christianity, Gordon-Conwell Theological Seminary.

can, Roman Catholic, or Pentecostal, have a strong supernatural orientation emphasizing healing, prophecy, and, in some cases, prosperity. Conservative bishops and church leaders in the global south have had an interesting impact on the world's Christian communions, opposing same-sex marriage and emphasizing scriptural authority. Some observers equate this theological conservatism among southern Christians with western political conservatism. But whereas northern Christians have tended to emphasize moral conservatism, southern churches have been equally interested in social and economic justice. Northern Christians are encouraged to practice their faith in private, while southern Christians feel an obligation to family, community, and the public square. In addition, northern politics is heavily conditioned by strict separation of church and state as well as by strong secular ideology. Southern Christians do not generally operate under this worldview, but show greater loyalty to religious institutions than political ones.

One example of southern Christian activism is the rise of Pentecostals in Latin America. Initially thought to be politically "quiet," they have become increasingly drawn into politics. Their involvement normally starts locally in social concerns, but it has gradually manifested itself in voting blocs. This bottom-up view of the church transforming society is prevalent in Africa, Asia, and Latin America. An interesting outcome might be that Christians in the global south, given their unique position, could finally solve the problem of the

artificial bifurcation between the gospel and social action so prevalent in western Christianity.

At the same time, the role of women continues to grow in significance, because global Christianity is in many ways a woman's movement. Some 70 percent of Christian church members in Africa and Asia are women. Women carry out the bulk of evangelism, teaching, and discipling, and yet often they are kept out of key leadership positions. This imbalance could have far-reaching political implications, especially if movements similar to women's suffrage emerge.

Because Christians in the South are more likely to face persecution and martyrdom, religious liberty is likely to have a significant role to play in the future of global Christianity. Over the entire history of Christianity, 70 million Christians have been killed for their faith. Over half of these deaths were in the twentieth century alone, when the perpetrators were communists, fascists, and atheists. The twenty-first century could look quite different as the age of empires gives way to more localized persecution. One example is China, where Christians in one district are given government funds to build a church while in another they are persecuted or killed.

The future of relations between Christian and non-Christian is also shifting to the South. Demographically, the fastest-growing Christian populations are found in predominantly non-Christian countries. Christians as a minority are sometimes well treated, but often they are persecuted or oppressed. One can look to Indonesia and Sudan for examples of Muslim-Christian conflict, to India and Nepal for Hindu-Christian conflict, or to Myanmar and Sri Lanka for Buddhist-Christian conflict. At the same time, some observers have noted a "marbling effect" where people from different religions learn to live in close contact with each other. This effect seems to be a trend in northern countries such as the United States and France as well as in southern countries such as Singapore and India. Proximity seems to give equal opportunity to conflict and harmony.

Finally, the economics of the southern shift of Christianity will be important as well. Currently, one out of every seven Christians lives in absolute poverty, and over 100 million Christians live in the world's twenty-six poorest countries. Over the past forty years, some northern Christians tried to uplift the Christian poor by encouraging liberation theology and other revolutionary strategies. Southern Christians, however, continue to want to solve their economic problems on their own terms. Meanwhile, the gap between the rich and poor continues to widen—an obvious challenge of the central message of equality in global Christianity. A potential source of hope lies with the future economic superpowers of the South: Nigeria, China, and India. Each of these countries has burgeoning Christian movements, and perhaps they will rise up in behalf of social and economic justice.

Conclusion

The massive twentieth-century shift of Christianity from North to South has many global ramifications for Christians and for the world. These range from theological and ecclesiastical issues within global Christianity to political and social impacts on the world's population. By understanding this shift and similar changes within the world's religious and nonreligious communities policy makers and other leaders will be better able to solve some of the world's most intractable problems.

See also *Christianity.*

Todd M. Johnson

BIBLIOGRAPHY

Barrett, David B., and Todd M. Johnson. *World Christian Trends, AD 30–AD 2200.* Pasadena, Calif.: William Carey Library, 2001.

Barrett, David B., George T. Kurian, and Todd M. Johnson. *World Christian Encyclopedia.* 2d ed. New York: Oxford University Press, 2001.

Jenkins, Philip. *The Next Christendom: The Coming of Global Christianity.* New York: Oxford University Press, 2002.

Johnson, Todd M., and Sun Young Chung. "Tracking Global Christianity's Statistical Centre of Gravity, AD 33–AD 2100." *International Review of Mission* 93, no. 369 (April 2004): 166–181.

Juergensmeyer, Mark, ed. *Global Religions: An Introduction.* New York: Oxford University Press, 2003.

Sanneh, Lamin. *Whose Religion Is Christianity? The Gospel Beyond the West.* Grand Rapids, Mich.: William B. Eerdmans, 2003.

Walls, Andrew F. *The Cross-Cultural Process in Christian History.* Maryknoll, N.Y.: Orbis Books, 2002.

Denominationalism

Denominationalism, a system of institutionalized division among many competing religious organizations, is made possible by a constitution that separates the affairs of government from those of the church, a culture of religious voluntarism, and societal differentiation. A denomination is a type of religious organization defined not so much by its internal characteristics as by the social milieu in which it is found. A denomination emerges in a society that has no established church but permits and encourages the practice of religion by the various organized religious communities. Unlike a church, it emphasizes voluntary allegiance. Unlike a sect, it makes no exclusive claim to religious truth. Although denominations tend to develop complex administrative structures (for example, to take care of mission work, education, fund raising, lobbying), this outcome is not inevitable and is not unique to this religious form.

Denominationalism sometimes refers to a constellation of religious organizations, whose forms have come to resemble each other (more than their own ancestors) and who coexist in a relationship of institutionalized division. At other times the term is used to refer to a normative system—a set of values and rules—undergirding a voluntary religious order. Denominationalism, in this sense, presupposes religious pluralism, accepts the claims to legitimacy of competing groups, and expects religious organizations to be "this worldly" and publicly engaged—although sectlike in the idea that individuals should obey their own conscience and should adhere voluntarily. Denominationalism provides space for individuals to exist outside or alongside any religious establishment, making it possible for them to join or not join. Each believer is responsible for his or her own faith, within the framework of the church, which he or she has helped to build.

Historical Relation between Denominationalism and Disestablishment

Denominations have flourished in the United States, but they are not unique to the United States and did not originate there. The theological idea that the church has no necessary earthly form can be traced to the Independents of seventeenth-century England. Ironically, many of the religious groups that settled the United States (especially Anglicans) did not share this view and considered themselves transplanted representatives of the true church in their homeland. They were soon to find that the idea of a state church was impracticable in the New World, where a wide variety of social groups existed and space abounded for the religiously discontented to move away and found a religion of their own. In eighteenth-century America, congregations were important focuses of community solidarity—the key to neighborhood stability, ordered family life, and the education of children. Denominations grew out of efforts by these scattered congregations to propagate the Christian faith independent of civil power. They became an important link between the local community and the emerging national society. All this happened before the colonies declared independence from Britain in 1776.

Revivalism also helped created conditions conducive to denominationalism. The Great Awakening, which occurred some thirty years before the War of Independence, was made possible by the liberties enjoyed in the more sparsely settled regions. It added a new pietistic element to the American religious life, giving birth to denominations such as the Disciples of Christ, attracted many new adherents to recent imports from England (for example, Methodism), and gave fresh energy to some of the more established denominations (for example, Presbyterianism).

In short, the attempts to replicate European church-state relations in the New World had largely failed by the outbreak of the Revolutionary War. The separation of church and state was a result, as much as the cause, of denominationalism. Once in place it fostered and protected it. Independence, and the Constitution (1787) and Bill of Rights (1791) that followed, made it possible to distinguish between being a member of society and a member of a church—a distinction crucial to denominationalism.

Effect of Disestablishment

The granting of religious freedom and toleration was a political necessity that actually went against the principles and beliefs of many of the early settlers. It was the result of a tacit bargain between evangelicals, who wanted to keep politics out of religion, and rationalists, who wanted to keep religion out of politics. By denying the establishment of any religion and granting the free exercise of religion to all (in the First Amendment to the Constitution), the state could no longer support regulation that denied privileges to or imposed sanctions on specific religious organizations—or their members. Unshackled from government control, American congregations were free to choose whichever form of association they believed conformed most closely to the scriptural ideal.

It is important to note that disestablishment in the United States means freedom of religion, not mere toleration. This is different from the European model, which assumes that there is a favored church but allows others to exist—on sufferance. Tolerance in the United States—a society preoccupied with questions of national identity—has always been conditional: Jews, Catholics, Mormons, and many sects have at various times been excluded from the list. But there has been enough tolerance to allow social mobility of religious denominations, as their members' fortunes change or as they compete for new adherents in the religious marketplace, to a degree unknown in most other countries.

Not to be ignored in this account of the effect of disestablishment on denominationalism is the acknowledged legitimacy of secular claims for freedom of expression. This secular spirit not only prevents the state from playing favorites with particular religions but also discourages the state from overtly favoring religion in general. This ideal sits in uneasy tension with an equally powerful set of ideals that attach the founding of the United States to larger religious purposes. Ironically, the absence of an established church has made it easier for there to emerge an inchoate but nevertheless meaningful "civil religion" to which all or most of the established denominations contribute but which is reducible to none of them in particular.

Influence of Other Social Factors

The separation of church and state is a necessary, but not sufficient, condition for denominationalism. Church and state are separate in other countries (the Netherlands, for instance) without the same proliferation of denominations and frequency of mergers and schisms. First, the social and ethnic diversity of the early settlers in the United States and subsequent immigrants encouraged great diversity of religious expression. Denominations came to express differences in ethnicity, community, and the social status of their clientele. Freedom of choice was thus somewhat limited—by ties such as race and ethnicity and by social class. Second, vast, unsettled spaces made it possible for people to find room for their own religious expression or no religion at all. Third, the economic needs of an expanding frontier and growing industrial sector—especially the need for cheap, mobile labor—provided a disincentive to religious discrimination and intolerance. Fourth, and perhaps most important of all, denominationalism resonates with American values, most notably those encouraging activism, pragmatism, reformism, individualism, freedom of choice, pluralism, and toleration. The denomination offers a way for Americans to be involved in a faith that is neither authoritarian nor privatistic.

Protestant, Catholic, Jew

The denominational form is associated most closely with Protestantism. However, it is a feature of denominationalism that the organization, beliefs, and practices of all religions become absorbed within it, and a process known as "structural isomorphism" occurs whereby religious organizations of many different persuasions come to resemble each other. With respect to Roman Catholicism, the immigration experience of Irish and Italians at the turn of the century, in the context of disestablishment, led many to "discover" their Catholicism and use it as a means of self-identification. Catholicism had become a source of group affiliation rather than a taken-for-granted ethnic or national identity. Subsequent generations of Catholics have enjoyed considerable social mobility, and the church has lost its "sectarian" position as a result. Although theological differences might remain, cooperation in dealing with civic problems at the grassroots level is now common.

The denominationalization of the Catholic Church was accelerated by a political event, the election of John F. Kennedy as president, in 1960. No longer were Catholics outside the mainstream. The reforms of the Second Vatican Council enacted in the 1960s made it easier for the U.S. Catholic Church to involve lay people in the running of the church and to cooperate with non-Catholic organizations in religious and secular activities. As a result, the Catholic Church became less distinctive, less mysterious, to outsiders. Today, the individualism, congregationalism, and pragmatism of denominational America has begun to replace the communal, hierarchical, and sacramental understandings of the original church. More and more Catholics see the church as just another voluntary association. This tendency goes along with the greater freedom enjoyed by Catholic bishops to enter "civil society" and speak as a group on social issues, such as poverty, social injustice, and abortion.

Judaism has also had to adapt to American realities. For Jews, the choice of denominational preference expresses what it means to be a Jew in the United States. A tripartite structure of national religious organizations has emerged resembling Protestant denominationalism in its representation of various shades of belief and practice and in the social differentiation of adherents into different religious communities. Reform Judaism (39 percent) embraces sacred-secular dichotomies and narrowly defines the arena of the sacred. Orthodoxy (6 percent) speaks for a Judaism with a strong continuity and sense of exclusivity. Conservatism (42 percent) occupies a midway point. Some argue that, given the strength of voluntarism and congregationalism in the Jewish community, the "denominations" are more akin to movements, little more than paper organizations, forced to tolerate a wide range of behaviors and attitudes between local synagogues. This is especially true of Orthodoxy. As in the Catholic and Protestant faiths, tolerance is a matter of degree in the Jewish community. To Orthodox Jews, Conservative and Reform Judaism are not legitimate expressions of the faith.

Denominations as Group Political Affiliations

The choice of denomination in the United States is based less on detailed knowledge of specific positions than on an awareness of where the denomination falls on a broad continuum, from conservative to liberal. Members of denominations develop particular political outlooks—even if their affiliation is nominal. Denominational preferences are systematically associated with political partisanship, issue positions, and voting patterns. Although denominational affiliations overlap with race, ethnic, and social class identities, they are also independent forms of group identification because they represent cultural traditions and personal attachments.

There are hundreds of religious denominations in the United States today. No single denomination constitutes more than 40 percent of the American population, and nearly half the U.S. population resides in counties in which no single denomination has majority status. It is common practice to group denominations into "families" or "traditions." Protestants are typically grouped into evangelical Protestant (for example, Baptist, Adventist, Holiness, Pentecostal, some Lutheran, some Presbyterian); mainline Protestant (for example, United Church of Christ, Methodist, Disciples of Christ, Episcopal, some Lutheran, some Presbyterian); black Protestant (for example, National Baptist Convention, African Methodist Episcopal Church); conservative nontraditional (for example, Jehovah's Witnesses, Mormons); and liberal nontraditional (for example, Unitarians, New Age). The other two religious "families" are Catholics and Jews. White mainline Protestants, evangelical Protestants, and Catholic affiliates constitute about one-quarter each of the American population. The rest are black Protestants (10 percent), Jews (2 percent), and the unaffiliated (13 percent).

Denominational affiliation is stable over the life-course of individuals: 69 percent of evangelicals, 76 percent of mainline Protestants, and 81 percent of Catholics surveyed in 1989 still belonged to the tradition in which they were raised. Switching from one denomination to another is more common—somewhere between one-third and one-half of all Americans will do this at least once during their lifetime. Many people switch to bring their politics and the politics of their denomination (on civil rights, abortion, and so forth) into line. Given the overlap between race and religious identification, it is no surprise that little switching occurs between white and black denominations, even within the same tradition.

There is a clear pattern of association between denominational family and political attitudes and behavior (differences between denominations within families are less predictable). In the 1994 congressional elections, 75 percent of white evangelicals voted Republican (an interesting pattern, considering that most evangelicals are drawn from lower social classes, which traditionally do not support Republican candidates). In comparison, 56 percent of the white mainline Protestants, 53 percent of Catholics, 39 percent among other religions, and 44 percent among those with no affiliation voted Republican. Hispanic Catholics largely support the Democratic Party, but they are less likely to vote than are other groups. Very little is known about the politics of the minor religious traditions. The Orthodox churches (Russian, Greek) tend to behave like traditional Roman Catholics; Mormons and Jehovah's Witnesses resemble highly sectarian evangelicals; and Christian Scientists and Unitarians are close to the liberal mainline. Within Judaism, Reform Jews are the most liberal, followed by Conservatives, with Orthodox Jews being the most conservative.

Changing Alignments

During most of the twentieth century, white mainline Protestants constituted the core of the Republican Party. They shared a common north European ancestry, an impulse for moral and social reform, and support for the principles of the free market. Catholics were predominantly Democratic, as were the (mainly Baptist and Methodist) white Protestants in the South. Since the 1960s the core groups of the New Deal coalition—namely, white evangelicals and white Catholics—have begun to desert the Democratic Party. However, members of the mainline Protestants have left the Republican Party in large numbers. Evangelicals have moved into the Republican Party coalition, and mainline Protestants have become less solidly Republican than they were. The partisan attachment of evangelicals is magnified by their large and growing numbers, bolstered by high religious commitment, and fostered by the conviction that their religion is relevant to politics. During the same period, black Protestants have joined the Democratic coalition, Jews have remained loyal to it, and Catholics have become less Democratic than formerly as their social heterogeneity increases.

Do Denominations Matter Any More?

Some scholars believe that the day of the denomination is past. The denominational form is thought to be weakened by the membership losses of the mainstream denominations, the alienation of members and congregation from the national leadership (especially during the civil rights era), the resulting diversion of resources away from denominational coffers and into local projects, and growing divisions between liberals and evangelicals within denominations. Large, pluralistic denominations, such as the Methodists and Episcopalians, have lost adherents to the opposing forces of secularism and evangelicalism. Their replacements tend to be less committed than are those born into the faith. Internal dissension and organizational decline have further weakened them. Their ties to the state have atrophied, and more vigorous pandenominational organizations, such as the Christian Coalition, seem to command more political attention. The political stage is now occupied by a host of paradenominational groups (such as pro-life, environmental, and health reform groups), each pursuing its own issue-specific agenda. The fastest membership growth today is in the nondenominational sector of churches. These churches, which are generally evangelical, do not affiliate with larger bodies and prefer to call themselves "community churches."

Recent years have also healed many previously bitter social divisions upon which denominations were formed—the exception being race. This is the result of increased educational opportunities, social and geographical mobility, the civil rights movement, the culture of experimentation fostered during the 1960s, and the controversy over the Vietnam War. These trends not only blur the boundary around denominations but add to their internal heterogeneity. Partially as a result, religious belief and practice have become more personal, and the ties to the denomination have weakened. Individual congregations now actively seek a "niche" within their local religious community as they compete for survival in a culture where individual choice is prized as never before. This, in turn, creates much variation within denominations and makes them less viable.

It would be wrong to conclude from the erosion of strength and distinct identity of the mainline Protestant denominations that the denominational form is extinct. The past generation has witnessed a counterbalance to this decline: the emergence onto the political scene of a revitalized evangelical family of denominations, which have shaken off their southern and lower-class origins to identify with the Republican Party, especially on social issues. Evangelicals have grown richer, they have become more involved in their community as the result of becoming property owners, and their higher levels of education have imparted political self-confidence and sophisticated political skills. Although they skillfully use a variety of organizational forms to mobilize political action, they do not show any signs of abandoning the denominational form as a primary organizational tool. There is every promise, in conclusion, that denominationalism will continue to undergird religious freedom in the United States and sustain its contribution to cultural pluralism and political toleration.

See also *Civil Religion; Constitution, U.S.; Freedom of Religion; Pluralism; Separation of Church and State; Voluntarism.*

John Wilson

BIBLIOGRAPHY

Carroll, Jackson W., and Wade Clark Roof, eds. *Beyond Establishment: Protestant Identity in a Post-Protestant Age.* Louisville, Ky.: Westminster Press, 1993.

Finke, Roger. "Religious Deregulation: Origins and Consequences." *Journal of Church and State* 32 (Summer 1990): 609–626.

Lazerwitz, Bernard, J. Alan Winter, Arnold Dashefsky, and Ephraim Tabory. *Jewish Choices: American Jewish Denominationalism.* Albany: State University of New York Press, 1998.

Leege, David C., and Lyman A. Kellstedt, eds. *Rediscovering the Religious Factor in American Politics.* Armonk, N.Y.: M. E. Sharpe, 1993.

Mullin, Robert Bruce, and Russell Richey, eds. *Reimagining Denominationalism.* New York: Oxford University Press, 1994.

Richey, Russell. *American Denominational Organization.* Pasadena, Calif.: William Carey Library, 1980.

Wald, Kenneth. *Religion and Politics in the United States.* 3d ed. Washington, D.C.: CQ Press, 1997.

Wilson, Bryan. "Religious Organization." In *International Encyclopedia of the Social Sciences.* Vol. 13. New York: Macmillan, 1968.

Diaspora

See *Judaism.*

Discrimination

See *Prejudice.*

Douglass, Frederick

American abolitionist, writer, and orator. Douglass (1817–1895), born a slave in Tuckahoe, Maryland, became an ardent social reformer and a profound moral and political voice for most of the nineteenth century. His father was a slave owner, and his mother was a slave. Douglass himself stood between two different worlds bound together by a brutal institution.

Douglass's career can be divided into two interrelated phases: the pre–Civil War and wartime period (early 1840s–1865) and the period during and after Reconstruction until his death. The first phase marks Douglass as an impassioned abolitionist and early advocate of women's rights. Although often drawing on moral suasion to convince the United States of the evil of slavery, he parted company with those abolitionists who rejected out of hand the resort to force.

The latter phase consists of his activity within the Republican Party and the eventual waning of his sphere of political

Frederick Douglass's powerful oratory established his reputation as the spokesperson for African Americans in the nineteenth century. His writings remain classics to this day.

and moral influence. Douglass's journey from slavery to become one of the leading moral and political voices of the nineteenth century has been chronicled in his three autobiographies: *Narrative of the Life of Frederick Douglass* (1845), *My Bondage and My Freedom* (1855), and *Life and Times of Frederick Douglass* (1881, amended 1892). From the moment the *Narrative* appeared, Douglass took his place in the United States' literary imagination.

Douglass is often characterized as black America's first "Jeremiah." His activism, like that of the biblical Jeremiah, called attention to the failure of his community to live up to its stated ideals. Indeed, Douglass expressed deep dissatisfaction with the nation and urgently challenged the United States to rid itself of the evils that threatened it, particularly the evils of slavery and racism. Douglass worked within the American tradition of public exhortation: the political sermon called the American Jeremiad, which joins social criticism with calls for moral renewal.

From his first encounter with the abolitionist William Lloyd Garrison in 1841, to the creation of his own newspaper, the *North Star,* to his death in 1895, Douglass consistently reminded the nation of its stated commitments to the ideals of democracy, freedom, and equality. He drew on the cultural repertoires and styles of black America, particularly the oratorical style of the black preacher, to exhort black Americans to act for themselves and to convince white Americans that slavery and racism threatened the nation and compromised Christian principles.

Douglass judged the South for its support of the institution of slavery, but he saved his harshest criticism for those in the North who professed themselves Christian but continued to allow the evil of slavery and racism to exist in the United States. For Douglass, it was more than a contradiction that a Christian nation would allow these two evils to exist: such practices were an abomination. Nevertheless, Douglass held an abiding faith in the United States. He even served the nation in his later years as the U.S. ambassador to Haiti. But, forever the Jeremiah, he continued to remind the nation—even when most would not listen—of the United States' promise and its failure to live up to it.

Eddie S. Glaude Jr.

BIBLIOGRAPHY

Douglass, Frederick. *Frederick Douglass: New Literary and Historical Essays.* Edited by Eric J. Sundquist. New York: Cambridge University Press, 1990.

———. *The Frederick Douglass Papers.* Edited by John W. Blassingame. New Haven: Yale University Press, 1979.

Howard-Pitney, David. *The Afro-American Jeremiad: Appeals for Justice in America.* Philadelphia: Temple University Press, 1990.

Quarles, Benjamin. *Frederick Douglass.* Washington, D.C.: Associated Publishers, 1948.

Waldo, Martin. *The Mind of Frederick Douglass.* Chapel Hill: University of North Carolina Press, 1984.

Druze

The Druze are a tightly-knit religious community of about 1.2 million people concentrated mainly in Lebanon and to a lesser extent in Syria and Israel. Druze immigrants and their descendants live in other parts of the world as well. The Druze faith was born within the Ismaili Shi'i sect of Islam in Egypt during the reign of al-Hakim bi Amr Allah (985?–1021), the sixth caliph of the Egypt-based Fatimid dynasty. Although religion was and remains the primary cause of the cohesiveness of the Druze community, the group's status as a minority has also been a factor.

Al-Hakim and the New Faith

Although the Fatimids were Ismaili Shi'is, al-Hakim formulated a new faith that dissented from the Ismaili doctrine, which he announced in 1017. Under this new faith, al-Hakim was viewed as a manifestation of God. The adherents of the new faith became known as Druze. The name came from Muhammad al-Darazi, an Ismaili missionary from Bukhara, who, with Hamza ibn Ali, an Iranian Ismaili theologian, and Hamza's disciple Baha al-Din al-Samuki, had the main responsibility for propagating the new religion. The new doctrine was first spread by missionaries in Lebanon and other parts of the Middle East.

Doctrinal divisions soon surfaced between Hamza and al-Darazi. Al-Darazi believed that *tawil* (the inner interpreted truth) is superior to the *tanzil* (the revealed outer truth) and attributed supernatural powers to al-Hakim. Al-Darazi advocated conversion by force, while Hamza believed in using persuasion to promote the faith. In 1019 al-Darazi was assassinated, and his name became anathema to the Druze, who refer to themselves as Muwahidun (Unitarians) because of their emphasis on the oneness of God. Hamza, who now led the missionary movement, went beyond al-Hakim's concepts and proclaimed that al-Hakim was the incarnation of the divinity.

The spread of the Druze doctrine continued unabated until al-Hakim mysteriously disappeared in 1021. His successor, al-Zahir li I'zaz Din Allah, rejected the new faith and persecuted its followers, leading many to recant and others to go underground. For safety, some of the new converts joined others residing in the Chouf in Mount Lebanon and in the ante-Lebanon mountain range. Despite the persecution, Hamza and Baha al-Din continued to spread the message. Between 1027 and 1043 Baha al-Din collected into six books, known as al-Hikmah al-Sharifa (the Noble Wisdom), the epistles of the faith (believed to be written by al-Hakim and his close disciples) and the proclamation made by al-Hakim. The last epistle was added in 1042, after which no new adherents were accepted into the faith. The closing of conversion has allowed the Druze to maintain a high level of solidarity and to successfully defend their community. The overwhelming majority of the Druze community in the early twenty-first century are the descendants of the original

Druze. Among the largest converts to the Druze faith were members of the Arab Tannukh tribe, who had settled in the Levant area and had several confrontations with the Crusaders.

The Belief System

The Druze faith was for a long time surrounded by mystery. Some parts of it remain so today. Its tenets were kept secret even from most Druze, except for a small number of initiates know as 'Uqqal, or enlightened ones. The remaining group, known as Juhhal, are the uninitiated ones. The religion requires that all follow a simple code regarding moral and ethical behavior and loyalty toward one another. The Druze religion is believed to have been influenced by a variety of sources, including Greek philosophy, Hinduism, Christianity, and Islam.

Over the centuries the secrecy of the religion has been misunderstood by some Muslim religious scholars, who have generally considered the Druze to be heretics, even infidels, and sometimes people without religion. They have also been wrongfully accused of engaging in peculiar practices. In response, the Druze practiced dissimulation (*taqiyya*) and were outwardly allowed to deny their faith and to pose as adherents of the dominant religion to survive. In later periods, the Druze denied the principles of the faith to those whom they considered unfit to receive the wisdom.

There are several main articles of faith that must be accepted by all Druze. In addition to a strict Unitarian concept of God, the Druze revere al-Hakim as the tenth, last, and most perfect manifestation of God. It is believed that al-Hakim has only temporarily gone from view and will reappear, along with Hamza, to establish universal justice, at which time the truly pious will lead the world.

The Druze believe in five divine messengers. These messengers represent specific theological concepts and are equated with major figures in the religious history of the Druze and with three lesser figures. In addition to Hamza, there were four other *hudud,* or luminaries, who played a major role in propagating the Druze faith. These *hudud* represent the universal mind of God and stand as the spiritual fathers of the faith. The four others are Ismail al-Tamimi, who is seen as the al-Nafs, or the universal soul that unites believers; Muhammad ibn Wahb, who represents al-Kalima, or the Logos through which the faithful were called to the faith; Salama al-Samiri, or al-Sabiq, the cause which motivates the call for the faithful; and Ali ibn Ahmed and Baha al-Din, both of whom represent al-Tali, or the effect, which represents the glory of achieving unity with God. The Druze faith emphasizes that there are prophets who preceded the luminaries and who represent the expression of the divine intelligence as forerunners to the beginning of the call to the faith. These prophets include Adam, Noah, Abraham, Jesus, and Muhammad. In addition to these prophets, there are minor prophets, called *Natiq* or spokespersons, and *asas* or the foundation, who have under them twelve disciples. The minor prophets are simply propagating the message of their chief prophet. Among the lesser prophets are people from biblical, Greek, and Islamic history, including Aaron, Simon, Ali, Enoch, Daniel, Plato, and Socrates. God, according to the Druze faith, created the universal mind, and through careful, rational thought, members of the community can join with God.

There are also several precepts to which all Druze must adhere: truthfulness, the giving of mutual aid to all Druze, rejection of all other religions, maintenance of the secrets of the religion, detestation of evils, and submission to and acceptance of God's will. Additionally, the Druze believe in reincarnation, or the transmigration of souls, which is foreign to some religions such as Islam and Christianity. They believe in reincarnation for all members of the community. After death the soul is reborn into another human body. The last judgment is the last transmigration and the last divine manifestation. The revelations of al-Hakim are viewed as the ultimate truth.

The Druze Emirate and Later

The twelfth century witnessed the emergence of a Druze emirate, or principality, in Lebanon, but the Druze did not play a prominent role until the sixteenth century, when Fakhr al-Din al-Ma'ni allied himself with the victorious Ottoman Turks against the Egyptian Mamluks. Fakhr al-Din II greatly expanded the emirate and opened his country to Western influences. He was harassed, however, and ultimately defeated by the Ottoman overlords. The influence of the Druze declined under their Ma'nid successor, the Shihab dynasty, in the eighteenth century, as rivalries emerged between different factions, one of which fled to the Hawran region of Syria, later known as the Druze Mountain. Ottoman and European meddling in the nineteenth century, as well as changing demographic and political patterns, led to confrontations between the Druze and their Christian neighbors and to massacres of Christians in 1860 in Lebanon and Damascus. These events resulted in European, mainly French, involvement and to a new autonomous system of government in Lebanon under a governor who was required to be a Christian Ottoman. The political influence of the Druze leaders greatly declined in Lebanon in the nineteenth century as a result of a decline in their number relative to the rise in the numbers of other communities.

Present-day Druze

Kamal Junblat, of the influential Druze Junblat family, played a significant role in Lebanese politics from the 1950s and allied himself with the Palestine Liberation Organization. He was assassinated in 1977, and his son Walid replaced him. The Arslan family continued to be traditional rivals to the Junblats. Leading Druze families in Syria and Israel have been the Atrash family, which led the 1925 nationalist revolt against the French in Syria, and the Tarif family, respectively. The Druze in Israel, unlike most other Arabs, serve in the Israeli military.

Since the assassination of Lebanon's pro-western prime minister, Rafiq al-Hariri, Druze leader Walid Junblat has emerged as a key leader in the anti-Syrian coalition, better known as the March Fourteenth Movement. This included Hariri's son Sa'd, a parliamentarian and leader of the al-Mustaqbal (Future) Party, and Samir Ja'ja, the Maronite Christian leader of the Lebanese Forces party. Junblat's role in Lebanon and his authority there far exceed his Druze constituents', although he has a challenger and rival in Talal Arslan, the leader of another Druze faction. Junblat has emerged as one of the most influential figures in the anti-Syrian coalition, and has accused the Syrian government of being responsible for the assassination of his late father, Kamal Junblat. He has also been active in an attempt to weaken and remove Lebanese president Emile Lahhoud, who is seen as having close ties to Syria and to the Si'i Hizb Allah Party in Lebanon. He has publicly called for the disarmament of Hizb Allah. Wahid Junblat has also sought to cooperate with Syrian anti-regime opponents, and was issued a summons by a Syrian military court in the mid-2000s, along with two other figures who held similar views, for allegedly "inciting the U.S. administration to occupy Syria."

See also *Israel; Syria.*

Edmund Ghareeb

BIBLIOGRAPHY

Abu Izzeddin, Najla M. *The Druzes: A New Study of Their History, Faith, and Society.* 2d ed. Leiden, the Netherlands: Brill, 1993.

Betts, Robert. *The Druze.* New Haven, Conn.: Yale University Press, 1988.

Chassaud, George Washington. *The Druze of Lebanon: Their Manners, Customs, and History.* London, 1855.

Hitti, Philip Khuri. *The Origins of the Druze People and Religion.* New York: Columbia University Press, 1928.

Makarin, Sami Nasib. *The Druze Faith.* Delmar, N.Y.: Caravan Books, 1974.

Najjar, Abdullah. *The Druze: Millennium Scrolls Revealed.* Translated by Fred I. Massey. Atlanta, Ga.: American Druze Society, 1973.

Durkheim, Emile

French sociologist regarded as one of the founders and giants of modern sociology. Durkheim (1858–1917) was born at Epinal, in the eastern province of Loraine, France. The son of a rabbi, and descended from a long line of rabbis on both sides of his family, he studied Hebrew, the Hebrew Bible, and the Talmud (the writings that constitute Jewish civil and religious law), while at the same time attending secular schools in his native city. At the age of thirteen Durkeim had a brief mystical experience under the influence of a Roman Catholic teacher, but soon afterwards he turned forever from all religious involvement. Yet religious phenomena and the religious roots of societal forces remained at the center of his theoretical concerns throughout his life.

Durkheim studied philosophy at the Ecole Normale Supérieure, the traditional training ground of the French intellectual elite, and soon was regarded by fellow students and teachers as a man of great promise, though somewhat aloof. Graduating in 1882, he taught in a number of provincial academic schools from 1882 to 1887, when he moved to the University of Bordeaux. It was there that he first had the occasion to teach sociology, hitherto a taboo subject in the eyes of both pro- and anticlericalists. In 1902, by then a widely recognized student of society, Durkheim was called to the Sorbonne, the traditional first citadel of French academic life. Partly because of his position at the Sorbonne and partly because of the growing prestige of the *Année Sociologique,* a journal that he founded in 1898, Durkheim became the leading spirit of French sociology and attracted a gifted group of young French scholars and disciples. He

remained until his death an eminent, though controversial, figure in French intellectual life and social thought.

Basic Teachings

In part in reaction to the turmoil and conflict-ridden early years of the French Third Republic (1870–1940), to which he was passionately devoted, Durkheim centered his teaching on a diagnosis of the ways in which common bonds could bind individuals together for the common good. Such bonds, he concluded, had in the past been provided by religious institutions but had largely eroded. What, then, he asked, could provide functional equivalents to the largely decayed religious commitments of individuals?

Among Durkheim's early contributions to the science of social thought was his distinction between mechanical and organic solidarity. In societies based on mechanical solidarity, which had predominated for most of human history, the social edifice is founded on the fundamental likeness of individual components and the minimization of individual differences. Organic solidarity, on the other hand, develops from differences rather than from likenesses. In the former, most people are engaged in a similar course of life and activities. In the latter, people's lives and activities vary, and they must cooperate with others engaged in different pursuits. With increasing differentiation of functions in modern society come increasing differences among its members.

A central concept in Durkheim's sociology is *anomie* (lawlessness or rootlessness), a term that denotes a state of affairs in which the social bonds that support the social body have so corroded that they can no longer control and guide individual action. Although human drives and propensities tend to be unlimited, social forces can counteract and control them. When social regulations erode, the controlling influence of society on individuals breaks down and leaves individuals to their own, insufficient, devices. Social scientists can use their knowledge to point to ways of overcoming societal crisis and breakdown.

The Role of Religion

Durkheim's early major works, such as *The Division of Labor in Society* (1893) and *Suicide* (1897), did not focus on religious phenomena and the role of religious institutions. In his later work, *Elementary Forms of Religious Life* (1912), Durkheim did concentrate on the religious bonds that he believed were necessary for social cohesion. In this volume, he analyzed the functions of religion in primitive societies, in particular, among Australian aborigines. He maintained that these functions are still central to the analysis of modern societies based on developed forms of labor and organic solidarity. Whereas previously Durkheim had focused on external factors of control, such as legal institutions, he now emphasized internal forces rooted in individual consciousness. Religion was the major force that created within individuals a sense of moral obligation to adhere to society's demands. What, then, if it was true that religious observance had decayed in the modern world? Was not Ivan Karamazov, in Fyodor Mikhailovich Dostoyevsky's novel *The Brothers Karamazov* (1912), right when he asked in despair, "Once God is dead, does not everything become permissible?"

Many nineteenth-century thinkers had urged a return to religion as the remedy to Karamazov's despair. But Durkheim—an agnostic—searched for functional substitutes for religion. He argued that the deities that people worship are projections of the power of society. Religions are not just social creations but are society divinized. Durkheim did not follow his intellectual ancestors Saint-Simon and Auguste Comte, both French social reformers, in their attempts to institute new humanitarian cults. Instead, he searched for ways that would allow individuals to transform their egos in a new civic morality rooted in collective social phenomena. Religion brings about cohesion; its ceremonies bring people together in a shared experience. It is a vitalizing force in society. When Australian aborigines gather together for a ceremony, they celebrate the victory of collective existence over the dispersion of mundane social life; they revitalize the social world of which they are a part.

This same revitalization occurs in many other social phenomena that are not obviously religious in character. Every effervescence in society, whether the revolutionary manifestations of the overthrow of the monarchy in the French Revolution (1789–1794) or the ceremonial observance of Bastille Day on July 14, revitalizes the sense of collective bonds and moral cohesion by bringing into the collective consciousness the glory and the power of the bonds of social living. Every incidence of collective effervescence documents the force of social cohesion and rekindles the flames of solidarity in the face of anomic doubt and existential despair. The decline of formal religion then need not herald the dissolution of society. Durkheim urged collective engagement and communitarian revival as the cure to the sickness of modern society.

See also *Civil Religion; Communitarianism.*

Lewis A. Coser

BIBLIOGRAPHY

Coser, Lewis A. "Emile Durkheim." In *Masters of Sociological Thought: Ideas in Historical and Social Context.* 2d ed. New York: Harcourt Brace Jovanovich, 1977.

Durkheim, Emile. *The Division of Labor in Society.* Translated by W. D. Halls. Introduction by Lewis A. Coser. New York: Free Press, 1984.

———. *The Elementary Forms of Religious Life.* Translation and introduction by Karen E. Fields. New York: Free Press, 1995.

———. *Suicide: A Study in Sociology.* Translated by John A. Spaulding and George Simpson. Edited and with an introduction by George Simpson. Glencoe, Ill.: Free Press, 1951.

Lukes, Steven. *Emile Durkheim: His Life and Work: A Historical and Critical Study.* Stanford: Stanford University Press, 1985.

E

Economic Development

Economic development is the process of generating a sustained rise in per capita incomes that leads to the elimination of mass poverty—the fate of humankind till the era of modern economic growth. This modern era of *intensive* growth, when per capita incomes have risen, can be contrasted with the much longer period of *extensive* growth, when per capita incomes stagnated—with output growing at a rate equal to the growth in population.

Limits on Economic Growth

Before the Industrial Revolution, output growth was limited by the fixed factor of production—land. The produce from such land supplied food, clothing, housing, fuel (charcoal), and the raw materials required for all economic uses in agriculture, industry, and transport. Also the mechanical energy needed in these "organic" economies depended on human or animal muscle, which again required nutrients provided by land. Once the land frontier was reached, returns diminished. The principle of population growth put forward by the English economist Thomas Robert Malthus in 1798 (that is, that population tends to increase faster than the means of subsistence) meant that, in the long run, the masses would languish at a near-subsistence standard of living.

Even in these organic economies there was some possibility of intensive growth through the greater division of labor made possible by international trade, as the eighteenth-century Scottish economist Adam Smith argued in *The Wealth of Nations*. But if the resulting growth in opulence led to population increase, the per capita standard of living would revert to subsistence. "Smithian" intensive growth accounted for the prosperity of the Mauryan Empire in India, the Roman Empire, the Abbasid Empire of the Muslims, and the empire of the Chinese Sung dynasty. In each case a larger geographical area was economically integrated by imperial arms, creating a wider market. But the rise in per capita income could not be sustained, given the fixed amount of land, and these areas reverted to extensive growth.

The Industrial Revolution

It was not, however, till the Industrial Revolution in Europe, which led to the substitution of a mineral-based energy economy for the traditional "organic" economy, that "Promethean" intensive growth based on science and technology became possible worldwide. Coal and the steam engine allowed virtually unlimited supplies of mechanical energy, and the land constraint on the raw materials required to raise aggregate output was removed. The alleviation of mass poverty became possible, because, contrary to Malthus, the rising prosperity led to a fall in the birth rate as richer parents began to trade quality for quantity in their desired families. This "demographic transition" has occurred not only in the West but also in many developing countries—particularly in East and now South Asia—that have been able to eliminate poverty by transforming their organic into mineral-based energy economies.

Religion and Politics

Given these contemporary possibilities, the relevance of religion and politics to economic development is twofold.

257

First, there is the historical question of why the Industrial Revolution occurred in Europe and not in China, which under the Sung had developed all the necessary technology and science well before the West. The German sociologist and economist Max Weber saw the materialist and individualist ethic promoted by Protestantism as being the spur for the creation of the new economy in Europe. His thesis is unpersuasive because all the economic institutions responsible for the rise of the West predate the emergence of Protestantism. More recent research, reported by Deepak Lal in *Unintended Consequences,* indicates that it was the revolutions of Pope Gregory I in the sixth century A.D., which concerned the family and promoted individualism, and then of Pope Gregory VII in the eleventh century, which created all the institutions of a market economy, that are in large part responsible for the rise of the West.

Equally important was the decentralized nature of European polities after the fall of the Roman Empire, which forced rulers to grant various forms of property rights to feudal lords in return for revenue. By contrast, China for millennia maintained a system of bureaucratic authoritarianism that despised merchants and commerce—the life-blood of a market economy.

More recently, the role of religion and politics in economic development has been raised in relation to the prospects of current developing countries. Confucianism is thought by many to be responsible for the spectacular development of East Asia. Others believe that without democracy economic development will be retarded. The available evidence does not support either position.

Deepak Lal and Hla Myint have found that the immediate causes of the differential postwar growth performance of twenty-one developing countries were the rate and efficiency of investment. Moreover, the latter depended on the policy environment. Countries that adopted central planning and state controls and whose economies were insulated from the world economy had lower growth rates than those with open, market-friendly economies. But these differences in policy were not associated with a particular type of government (for example, democracy) but rather with the countries' initial endowment of resources, in particular, the availability or lack of natural resources. Countries poor in resources—such as the East Asian ones—irrespective of the nature of their government, were forced to develop their only resource: their citizens. The performance of such countries was much better than that of countries rich in natural resources, such as Brazil and Mexico. This was because of the inevitable politicization of the income that natural resources yield, which damages economic performance as people scramble for this unearned income, instead of undertaking productive economic activities. Countries such as China and India, with endowments of resources that fall between these extremes, swerved between following the policies of their resource-abundant and resource-poor cousins, with a resulting indifferent economic performance.

Economic performance could be affected in regions and countries where religion and politics have been combined—as by the Hindu fundamentalists in India and Islamic fundamentalists in the Middle East—to try to stop the process of modern economic growth to maintain the social systems associated with their old agrarian economies. With the rise and global expansion of the West these ancient Eurasian civilizations faced a dilemma. With their ancient equilibrium disturbed, most often by force of superior arms, how could their wounded civilizations come to terms with the West without losing their souls? The first was to modernize by imitating the West: by adopting its material beliefs, including the artifacts that provide military and economic strength, but without adopting Western cosmological beliefs. The scond was to adopt the attitude of the clam, for fear of a modernization that would undermine ancient traditions. The third was to find a middle way between tradition and modernity. Japan during the Meiji revolution took the first route. The second was advocated by various cultural nationalists such as Gandhi in India and until recently by his followers in the Hindu nationalist party, the Bhartiyqa Janata Party. The third route was taken by all those countries that found a middle way in various forms of socialism to reconcile the modernity offered by its Enlightenment strand and tradition as offered by its romantic strand associated with the British socialists William Morris and Tawney. Nehru's India and Maoist China epitomized this route. The countries of Islam have tried all three routes, from Atatürk's Turkey to Nasser's Egypt taking the first and third routes, to the current Islamists who want to follow the second route. With the two emerging Asian giants—China and India—now following the first route, recognizing, as Japan has done, that it is possible to modernize without westernizing, the lands of Islam (apart from Turkey) still need to accept that they can achieve prosperity while keeping their souls.

See also *Confucianism; Individualism; Protestantism; Science and Technology; Weber, Max.*

Deepak Lal

BIBLIOGRAPHY

Becker, Gary. *A Treatise on the Family.* Enl. ed. Cambridge: Harvard University Press, 1991.

Lal, Deepak. *The Poverty of Development Economics.* 2d ed. London: Institute of Economic Affairs, 1997.

———. *Unintended Consequences: The Role of Factor Endowments, Culture, and Politics on Long-Run Economic Performance.* Cambridge: MIT Press, 1998.

———. *Reviving the Invisible Hand: The Case for Classical Liberalism in the Twenty-first Century.* Princeton: Princeton University Press, 2006.

Lal, Deepak, and Hla Myint. *The Political Economy of Poverty, Equity, and Growth: A Comparative Study.* Oxford: Clarendon Press, 1996.

Little, Ian. *Economic Development.* New York: Basic Books, 1982.

Marty, Martin E., and R. Scott Appleby, eds. *Fundamentalisms and the State.* Chicago: University of Chicago Press, 1993.

North, Douglass, and R. P. Thomas. *The Rise of the Western World.* Cambridge: Cambridge University Press, 1973.

Wrigley, E. A. *Continuity, Chance, and Change: The Character of the Industrial Revolution in England.* Cambridge: Cambridge University Press, 1988.

Education

Education, used here to refer to the provision of organized socialization and training conducted by formally qualified instructors, has been prominent at the intersection of politics and religion throughout the modern era. The learned personnel produced by the church's educational institutions figured prominently in the rise of the modern state in Europe, and the church served as the primary model for state bureaucracies and the incorporation of entire populations in centrally administered, society-wide structures and activities. Education in the early modern era was highly restricted, however, focusing mainly on the production of clergymen, lay professionals, and a small range of bourgeois occupations. For the vast majority of children and youth, especially peasants, learning was simply living.

This article mainly discusses primary education, particularly mass schooling, while higher education is treated briefly. Secondary education is omitted because the religion issue in secondary schools has received relatively little attention and less systematic information about secondary school curricula and practice is available.

Religion and Primary Education in Citizen Formation

The role of religion in primary education is best understood in the context of the genesis and institutionalization of mass schooling in Europe. Two large-scale developments were of primary importance. The first was directly religious: the Reformation of the sixteenth and seventeenth centuries shifted the focus of religiosity from rituals conducted by clerical elites to confessions of faith experienced in the heart of individual parishioners. As this "interiorized" view of religion took hold, both Protestants and Counter-Reformation Catholics, especially the Jesuits, turned to schooling as a means of winning and keeping souls. Compulsory schooling laws formalized this notion as early as 1619 in Lutheran Weimar and 1642 in Puritan Massachusetts, although these laws had more symbolic than practical consequences.

The second development of crucial importance for mass schooling was the consolidation of the European state system in the seventeenth and eighteenth centuries, which led to rapidly expanding state administrative capacities and deliberate nation-building efforts, particularly from the eighteenth century onward. State expansion and nation building entailed the gradual displacement of the church by the state as the primary central institution in society, settling the long church-state struggle in the state's favor. Open conflict about this displacement with regard to education occurred mainly at the university level. Primary education remained decentralized and sporadic until the nineteenth century, by which time the state's supremacy over the church was far advanced even in strongly Catholic countries.

Religious groups played a major role in the expansion of schooling in some countries, most notably the United States and England, but for the most part the mass schooling systems that emerged after 1800 were state creations. By this period, the driving motivation for schooling was no longer the struggle for souls. Instead, it was a new, progress-oriented ideology that emerged as European countries began to rationalize agriculture, industrialize production, professionalize occupations, and formalize state-citizen relations. What would later be called "modernization" had taken firm root, and societal modernization entailed extensive and increasingly state-directed restructuring.

Mass schooling became one of the central mechanisms for this restructuring. In line with emerging theories of childhood socialization, individual malleability, and the utility of formalized systems for the pursuit of explicit goals, a vision of societal progress as dependent on the formation of carefully socialized citizens came to dominate the European arena and its colonial extensions. Schooling would endow children with new skills and capacities, imbue them with loyalty and commitment to the nation, and foster proper moral character. Schooling, so the emerging doctrine held, must accomplish these goals for all children, because every individual, regardless of sex, social status, or future occupation, was a potential contributor to national development. In short, schooling was to fashion productive and committed national citizens of the entire population, and national success was contingent on educational success. While schooling's potential to encourage rebellion among the lower classes was a concern among aristocratic and bourgeois elites, by the end of the century the imperative of schooling had become a self-evident and virtually unchallenged tenet.

The mass schooling systems that spread rapidly in the nineteenth century were heavily secularized, emphasizing basic literacy skills, arithmetic, and rudimentary geography and history. Nevertheless, religion was deemed an indispensable element of schooling in most places. National political and economic citizenship had become the central focus, but religious citizenship—active and sincere participation in the religious polity—was a necessary complement. Religious piety and moral virtues would impel children, particularly those of the lower classes, to become conscientious, God-fearing adults, respecting authority and working diligently as agriculturalists, factory workers, and parents. Hence, though religious education as such typically occupied only a small portion of the school day, religious materials (above all, Martin Luther's *Little Catechism* and various abbreviated Catholic catechisms) were a mainstay of reading instruction in many European countries. In the latter half of the century, as labor unions formed and voting rights were extended to ever larger segments of the population, elite concern for the potential unruliness of modestly educated but self-assertive lower classes made the rhetorical importance of religion in the schools even more prominent.

Making religion a distinct subject in the primary curriculum, and emphasizing the subjective character-building potential of religion, paralleled the transformation of religion in broader terms. Religion was being compartmentalized as a distinct social sector, subordinate to the state and the market; religion was narrowing its focus primarily to the level of individual inner faith and moral propriety. Secularization did not mean the end of religion but its circumscription as one among many institutions, and so it was in the schools of most countries.

With few exceptions, above all the United States, sectarianism in mass primary education systems was not a problem. While most European and New World countries had made formal commitments to religious tolerance by the end of the nineteenth century, in the schools the predominant religion of the country was usually the sole doctrine propagated—whether it be Lutheran Protestantism in the highly homogeneous Scandinavian countries or Catholicism in the Mediterranean and Latin American countries. Hence the principle of separation of church and state that became an axis of recurrent conflict in the United States had little meaning for schooling elsewhere. The principle was largely ignored even in the United States until the latter part of the nineteenth century, when established Protestant denominations felt threatened by the rising waves of Catholic immigrants from Europe. Catholics objected to the entrenched Protestantism that prevailed in the schools; Protestants abhorred the papal threat and the obdurate Catholic capacity to build separate schools not subject to state control. Yet the imperative of enrolling Catholics in standardized public schools was great, for no other mechanism seemed able to ensure the Americanization of these polyglot immigrants. The pragmatic resolution eventually reached was the doctrine of absolute nonsectarianism in the public schools, so that Protestants and Catholics could attend side by side without the religiously based eruptions that explicit religious instruction would likely trigger.

Twentieth-Century Developments

In the twentieth century much of the institutional apparatus that had developed in Europe and the European-dominated independent countries of the New World became standard equipment for new states formed out of the collapsing colonial empires. Virtually without exception, the social imperative of schooling as essential to progress and modernization was accepted as self-evident truth: only modernized children could produce strong, progressive, wealthy societies. The striking breadth of this imperative appears in both national constitutions and legislation (which embody not only political philosophy but also social theory about how to build the good society) and in data on school enrollments that show how philosophy and theory yield durable organizational practices. The right to education appeared in about two-fifths of the 39 constitutions in existence in 1870; in 1970 the proportion was about two-thirds of 141 constitutions; and in 2000 it was about three-fourths of the more than 180 constitutions in force. Notably, newer countries are more likely than older countries to make education a constitutional right, and constitutions usually make of education not only a right but also a duty (57 percent of constitutions in 1970 and more than 60 percent in 2000 obligated all children to attend schools). Where the right and duty to education are not constitutionally specified, they are legislatively enacted. Almost all countries now make primary education free and compulsory, and 80 percent of the world's countries make at least a portion of secondary education obligatory.

School enrollment data demonstrate that this formalized commitment to mass schooling is hardly mere rhetoric. In the past hundred years, the expansion of schooling has been nothing less than astonishing. On average, in 1870 about a third of school-age children were enrolled in primary schools in the 40 countries and colonies for which data are available. By 1940, this mean enrollment ratio had risen to about 41 percent, while the number of countries and colonies reporting data rose to 120. By the latter date, practically all school-age children were enrolled in most developed countries. After World War II schooling exploded in every region of the world as new states everywhere devoted substantial resources to educational development. By 2000 the median enrollment ratio was above 90 percent for more than 170 countries reporting enrollment data; only 14 percent enrolled less than 70 percent of eligible children. As this state-controlled educational explosion has proceeded, traditional educational practices, often based on religious instruction (for example, in Buddhism, Confucianism, or Hinduism) or rooted in the spiritualistic practices of African and pre-Columbian American peoples, have largely disappeared or become marginal activities almost everywhere.

International organizations have provided a major impetus to the expansion of schooling in the postwar era of rapid globalization. Of central importance is the United Nations Educational, Science, and Cultural Organization (UNESCO), which promotes models of educational systems, provides organizational and technical advice, and gathers worldwide data on education. Numerous other intergovernmental organizations (IGOs) within and outside the United Nations family, and hundreds of international nongovernmental organizations (INGOs), help to promote schooling worldwide, aid new states in building comprehensive and effective school systems, improve the working conditions and pay of teachers, and so on. Notable examples include Education International, which represents more than twenty-nine million unionized or associated educators in 166 countries; the International Association for Educational Assessment, which focuses on improving and measuring educational quality; the International Schools Associa-

tion, which represents international schools around the world and was the first NGO to gain consultative status with UNESCO; and the International Council for Adult Education, concerned with adult learners and educators. Cooperation between IGOs and INGOs is extensive and increasingly formalized. For example, in 1988 the UNESCO/NGO Collective Consultation on Higher Education was established to regularize cooperation between UNESCO and some sixty international higher education organizations.

Though states have dominated in the worldwide expansion of primary education, religion has remained a standard curricular concern throughout the twentieth century, both in the older developed countries and in newer countries. Nowhere, however, is religion the primary curricular concern; modern schooling is decidedly secular. Available data on primary school curricula throughout the world show that, on average, religious education accounted for less than 5 percent of total curricular time in the 1970s and 1980s (82 countries). Early in the century, during the 1920s and 1930s, the average share of school time devoted to religion was only slightly above 5 percent (49 countries), and it was even lower in the middle of the century (under 4 percent in the 1950s and 1960s, for 125 countries). In contrast, language, mathematics, and the natural and social sciences consume upward of two-thirds of curricular time in the world's schools, and their predominance goes back to the nineteenth century.

Yet religious instruction has endured as a widespread element of the curriculum. Religion is taught in the public schools of over half of all countries (55–60 percent throughout most of the twentieth century, dropping to about 51 percent by 2001). Wherever religion has entered the primary curriculum, it has remained on the books almost without challenge, and recent research indicates that where religion is part of the primary curriculum, its share of total instructional time has risen slightly (to about 8 percent in 2001). Regional variations are large, however. Religion is most prominent in the school systems of Islamic countries, especially in the Middle East and North Africa, where it accounted for nearly 12 percent of curricular time in the 1970s and 1980s. Religion is also relatively prominent in the developed Western countries of Europe and Anglo-America, with almost 5 percent of curricular time in recent decades. Meanwhile, religion was entirely absent from the curriculum of the countries of Eastern Europe until the collapse of communism (Catholic Poland and Lithuania added religion to the curriculum, with Poland devoting 9 percent of curricular time in 2001), and it receives only scant attention in Latin American and Caribbean countries (about 2 percent of curricular time).

These figures reflect the varied institutional role of religion in different societies. States in countries dominated by the Islamic faith not infrequently define themselves as formally Islamic and build their commitment to Islam into state-directed institutions. The most extreme cases are Saudi Arabia and Yemen, where over 25 percent of the primary school curriculum is devoted to religion. However, despite the expansion of Islamic fundamentalism in recent decades, religion in Islamic schools is on the decline overall, falling to about 10.5 percent of curricular time for all Muslim countries that incorporate religion in primary school instruction. Northern and western European countries with an established state church regard religion in the schools as a matter of course—in England, religion has always been a compulsory subject—but not as a central curricular element, hence the relatively high but still small proportion of curricular time given to religion in developed Western countries. In Catholic countries where the French Revolutionary example has been followed (the state subordinating the church and building barriers to church influence in nonreligious matters), religion is rare in the curriculum. This mode of state-church relations applies most regularly in Latin America, whence the low proportion of school time reserved for religion despite the almost universal Catholicism of Latin American populations.

An additional dimension of importance with respect to primary education is the parallel system of religious schools that prevails in a number of countries. In Western countries where religious groups played important roles in the general expansion of mass schooling, parallel systems are still prominent. For example, in Ireland most schools, while formally public, are directed by local boards with strong church representation, and in the Netherlands a majority of schools have either Protestant or Catholic affiliation. In Australia, Belgium, Britain, and France, religious schools are less numerous but equally durable, and in many Latin American countries the Catholic schools consistently enroll 10–20 percent of primary students. An unusual model is that of the United States, where a great variety of denominational schools operate in a highly decentralized governance structure. Enrolling in toto some 10 or 11 percent of all primary students (having declined in recent decades), these schools are increasingly the province of children from affluent families.

Outside the Western sphere, most school systems are thoroughly state creations. Parallel systems are limited to former or contemporary missionary schools that enroll a few percent of primary pupils at best. The exception here is religiously infused states, such as Israel (where religious schools, most of which are formally within the state school system, enroll nearly a third of all pupils) and some Muslim countries. In the latter, traditional forms of schooling involving a scholar imam and his associated pupils, often focused on the Qu'ran, may be common. In Indonesia such schools enroll more than 10 percent of primary students, and in parts of northern Nigeria they enroll more children than state schools.

In most instances, the curricula even of religious schools have become increasingly secular, and state regulation and funding of these parallel systems have expanded considerably. Often states provide the vast bulk of funds. With the exception of some Muslim countries, religious primary schools are usually similar to public schools, even where they enroll large numbers of children. Religious schools include more direct religious instruction, but religion is still only a small part of the normal school day, except in a few places.

Though religion remains a fixture in school curricula and religiously affiliated schools have a substantial presence in many countries, usually the relationship between state and religion is unproblematic. Where state commitment to secular education is especially strong, however, conflict has become common. In France, Germany, and the Netherlands, for example, tensions related to immigrant groups have led to the suspension or expulsion of Muslim students wearing headscarves and Sikh students wearing turbans on the grounds that such symbols constitute religious proselytizing. At issue are the conflicting principles of respect for religion and non-denominationalism in the schools, and court rulings and state policies have been inconsistent. France recently banned all conspicuous religious symbols (including, for example, the Christian cross and the Jewish yarmulke), while other countries such as Canada have explicitly embraced a policy of accommodation and called on France to reverse its ban.

Another political issue played out in the schools—in this case, mostly at the secondary level—reflects the moral agenda of fundamentalist and evangelical Christian groups. Recurring disputes over evolution versus creationism, sex education, homosexuality, and so on have flared up as elements of the "culture wars" of recent decades. Such disputes are concentrated in the United States but are also found in some other predominantly Christian countries.

While politicized religion is thus evident in the schools, in recent decades the content of religious instruction has shifted toward increasingly ecumenical approaches, especially in the liberal Western democracies. Cultural relativism and globalization have made "religious tolerance" and "diversity" important watchwords in many school systems, with the result that teachers typically teach about many religions, not a particular faith. The ideologies of individual rights and freedom of conscience lead states to avoid imposing religious beliefs on children, so religious advocacy is out of bounds. Religion courses are likely to include surveys of the major world religions and sometimes include brief forays into "primitive" religions such as totemism and shamanism. This sort of desacralization of religious instruction is not common in many Islamic countries, however.

Higher Education

If religion in primary education has been largely a subsidiary complement to the dominant secular focus, the same can hardly be said of higher (tertiary) education. In Europe from the fourteenth century, the struggle between church and state was as evident in higher education as it was in the Vatican and royal courts. Early universities or their cathedral-school predecessors were church institutions whose establishment was prompted by the intellectualization of the church and the commitment of strong bishops to improving the training and piety of the clergy. As the Renaissance unfolded, humanistic subjects began to make inroads in the universities, but a convenient ideology of complementarity between Augustine's "City of God" and "City of Man" was maintained as long as the church remained a major landowner and social institution.

During the seventeenth and eighteenth centuries, however, when the church had been Protestantized or largely dispossessed in many places, this contingent complementarity began to erode as states undertook the expansion and secularization of higher education in earnest. Nation building was in process; rationalized knowledge (science) was coming to be seen as crucial for national success; a common national language was deemed necessary for internal cohesion, while the classic languages of Greece and Rome were considered all but dead. Thus states pushed to make secular subjects, especially science, medicine, and mathematics, elements of the core curriculum. Latin and Greek

became optional languages of instruction and written expression, and the production of personnel useful to the state took precedence over the production of clergy. This process was hastened by a proliferation of universities founded by states and operated largely outside church control; it was opposed bitterly by many church officials but proved to be unstoppable.

As with primary education, religion was gradually compartmentalized at the higher level. Seminaries and other religious institutes did not necessarily decline. With the ongoing expansion of societal resources, they often expanded in absolute terms. But religion became the focus of distinct schools or faculties of theology in universities, and university faculty became increasingly lay and secular in orientation, even in Jesuit and other schools with strong religious affiliations. By the time of the great expansion of higher education after World War II, states were clearly the primary actors, both in the developed West and in the newly independent countries, most of which eagerly established state universities. Hence public universities of fully secular character accounted for the great majority of this worldwide expansion. Considerable variation persists in the degree to which tertiary institutions are formally linked to religion. In Catholic countries, in particular, church-related universities have a sizable share of university enrollments and are often noted for their general excellence. But, in practice, religion is almost always a small and optional part of the average student's curriculum, and little tension remains between states and religious bodies regarding the mainly secular orientations and purposes of higher education.

The major exceptions to this pattern of largely harmonious relations between secular states and religious bodies regarding higher education are various Muslim countries. In places such as Afghanistan, Algeria, Egypt, Iran, Pakistan, and officially secular Turkey, Islamization advocates question such standard features of higher educational systems as equal access for women and coeducational instruction, and they urge the institutionalization of Islamic principles in all aspects of higher education. Secularists and religious minorities oppose such efforts; the resulting conflicts are often bitter. Even where Islamization has occurred, however, it generally appears to be more symbolic than substantive in that most students continue devoting nearly all of their studies to secular subjects oriented to secular occupations, and women's participation in higher education has not suffered significantly. On average women account for larger proportions of higher education enrollments in officially Islamic states than in other countries with Muslim-majority populations, and women's share of enrollments in such professions as law and medicine has been rising as quickly in Muslim countries as elsewhere.

See also *Citizenship; Globalization; Individualism; Jesuits; Reformation; Secularization; Secularization, Non-Western; State Churches.*

John Boli

BIBLIOGRAPHY

Bereday, George Z. F., and Joseph A. Lauwerys, eds. *The World Yearbook of Education: Church and State in Education.* New York: Harcourt, Brace, and World, 1966.

Boyd, William, and Edmund J. King. *The History of Western Education.* 11th ed. London: Adam and Charles Black, 1975.

Cameron, John, Robert Cowan, Brian Holmes, Paul Hirst, and Martin McLean, eds. *International Handbook of Education Systems.* 3 vols. Chichester, England: John Wiley, 1983.

Cummings, William K., and Noel F. McGinn, eds. *International Handbook of Education and Development: Preparing Schools, Students, and Nations for the Twenty-first Century.* Oxford: Pergamon, 1997.

Meyer, John W., David Kamens, Aaron Benavot, Yun-Kyung Cha, and Suk-Ying Wong. *School Knowledge for the Masses.* London: Falmer Press, 1992.

Meyer, John W., Francisco O. Ramirez, and Yasemin Soysal. "World Expansion of Mass Education, 1870–1980." *Sociology of Education* 6, no. 2 (1992): 128–149.

Mor, Menachem, ed. *International Perspectives on Church and State.* Omaha, Neb.: Creighton University Press, 1993.

Postlethwaite, T. Neville, ed. *The Encyclopedia of Comparative Education and National Systems of Education.* Oxford: Pergamon, 1988.

Reagan, Timothy. *Non-Western Educational Traditions: Alternative Approaches to Educational Thought and Practice.* Mahwah, N.J.: Lawrence Erlbaum Associates, 1996.

Rivard, Jean-François, and Massimo Amadio. "Teaching Time Allocated to Religious Education in Official Timetables." *Prospects* 33, no. 2 (June 2003): 211–217.

"Special Issue: The State of the Art: Twenty Years of Comparative Education." *Comparative Education Review.* 21, no. 2–3 (1977): 151–416.

Tomaševski, Katarina. *Free and Compulsory Education for All Children: The Gap between Promise and Performance.* Lund, Sweden: Raoul Wallenberg Institute of Human Rights and Humanitarian Law, 2001.

United Nations Educational, Science, and Cultural Organization, Institute for Statistics. *Global Education Digest 2004: Comparing Education Statistics across the World.* Montreal: UNESCO Institute for Statistics, 2004.

United Nations Educational, Science, and Cultural Organization, International Bureau of Education. "Education and Religion." *Prospects* 33, no. 2 (2003).

Egypt

The Arab Republic of Egypt, located in northeast Africa and bordered by Libya, Sudan, Israel, and the Gaza strip has a predominantly Sunni Muslim majority and a significant Coptic Christian minority. Small Shi'i Muslim and Bahai populations are also present. Of Egypt's seventy-eight million people 90–93 percent are Sunnis, and 6–10 percent are followers of the indigenous Coptic Church, which separated from both Constantinople and Rome in the early days of Christianity. Other Christian groups total about 1 percent of the population. With Islam as the religion of state, and the vast majority of the population Muslim, Copts have been unable to achieve full equality with Muslims. Before 1956 Egypt's population included significant numbers of Greeks, Italians, Armenians, Levantines, Jews, and others. Following the 1948 war and the creation of the new state of Israel, most Jews were forced to emigrate. Most of the other foreign populations emigrated after the 1956 war and the subsequent waves of nationalization.

Historical Background

Egyptian politics and religion have been bound together throughout history, since the ancient pharaohs, who were considered semidivine by their subjects. In the early days of the Christian church, Egyptian Christians died for refusing to worship the Roman emperor. In Byzantine times, Egyptians expressed their distinct identity through the Coptic Church's resistance to dogma endorsed by the Greek-speaking Orthodox emperors of Constantinople.

The Arab Muslims who conquered Egypt in 640 made no theoretical distinction between religion and state. The caliph, or successor to the prophet Muhammad, was duty-bound to apply Islamic law (*shari'a*) and defend the Muslim state and community. Christians and Jews who did not follow the majority of Egyptians in converting to Islam obtained tolerated but inferior status under their own religious leaders. From the twelfth century through the Ottoman period that ended in 1882, Turkish-speaking military elites ruled. They depended on Islamic scholars (*ulama*) for legitimacy and ties to their Arabic-speaking subjects. As prayer leaders, preachers, teachers, *shari'a* court judges, and legal experts (*muftis*), the *ulama* were well placed to voice popular grievances. The Islam of the *ulama* was centered in the great mosque-university of al-Azhar, which drew students to Cairo from throughout the Islamic world.

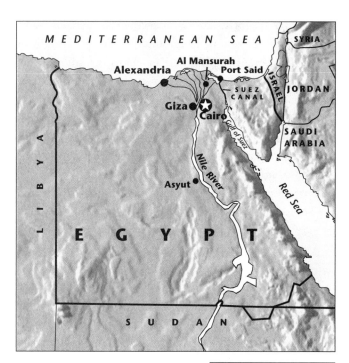

pressured Britain into granting limited independence, in 1922, though British interference and military bases lasted into the 1950s.

The Western-inspired constitution of 1923 articulated a new political framework. Egypt became a constitutional monarchy with elections and a parliament. Islam remained the religion of state. Turkey's abolition of the caliphate in 1924 led Egypt's King Fu'ad (ruled 1917–1936) and his successor Faruq (ruled 1936–1952) to bid unsuccessfully to revive the office. In 1925 Ali Abd al-Raziq, a *shari'a* judge, attacked the caliphate as a post-Qur'anic innovation lacking religious sanction and demanded separation of religion and state. Al-Azhar anathematized him as an atheist and drove him from his judgeship.

By the 1940s British interference, royal authoritarianism, and the inability of the Wafd Party—the main Egyptian nationalist party—to achieve either independence or socio-economic reform had tarnished liberalism, capitalism, and constitutionalism in Egyptian eyes. Hasan al-Banna's Muslim Brotherhood, established in 1928 in Ismailiyya, a provincial town in the Suez Canal zone, surged forward with an Islamist challenge. Banna denounced colonialism and the foreign exploitation of Egypt, corrupt government, Zionism, and the new state of Israel. Government agents assassinated Banna in 1949, but the organization quickly turned into a mass movement with the ultimate goal being the establishment of a truly Islamic state and society.

Military Coup and Islamist Revival

After overthrowing King Faruq in 1952, Col. Gamal Abdel Nasser and a military group known as the Free Officers broke with the Muslim Brotherhood, one of whose members allegedly tried to kill Nasser in 1954. Mass arrests, torture, and executions shattered the Brotherhood during the 1950s and 1960s. The secular-minded Nasser, who became president in 1956 after serving as prime minister, developed Arab nationalism and socialism as the ideologies of his authoritarian rule. He presided over the union of Egypt and Syria as the United Arab Republic from 1958 to 1961, when Syrian secession ended the union. In 1961 he struck at the *ulama,* forcing al-Azhar to admit women and to add medicine, engineering, science, and agriculture to its religious curriculum. Egypt's defeat by Israel, and the Israeli occupation of the Sinai peninsula in 1967, dealt a blow to Arab nationalism, paving the way for an Islamist revival throughout the Arab world and beyond.

Al-Azhar, one of the oldest universities in the world, remained an influential seat of Islamic learning into the twenty-first century.

Sufism (Islamic mysticism) offered an alternative to al-Azhar's formal, legalistic Islam. Permeating many levels of society, Sufism encompassed ecstatic rituals, celebrations of saints' birthdays and pilgrimages to their tombs, and charms against disease and infertility. By the eighteenth century even many Azhari scholars had joined Sufi orders.

To Muhammad Ali, who became governor of Egypt in 1805 and ruled until 1848, building a modern centralized state included seizing control of religious endowments and turning the *ulama* into salaried bureaucrats. Rulers and reformist *ulama* like Jamal al-Din al-Afghani and Muhammad 'Abduh, however, had little success in modernizing al-Azhar. Sometimes al-Azhar was easier to bypass than to reform: the result was separate state and religious education systems, with Mixed Courts deciding cases involving foreigners and National Courts sitting alongside the old *shari'a* courts.

Nineteenth-century Egypt became an economic dependency of industrial Europe, with cotton as the cash crop for export. Political control followed when the British occupied the country in 1882. A national uprising in 1919

Anwar al-Sadat, elected president in 1970 after Nasser's death, freed jailed members of the Brotherhood, dubbed himself "the Believer President," enshrined the *shariʿa* in the 1971 constitution as the main source of legislation, and fostered Islamist student groups to counter leftist groups opposed to his rule. Even some leftists began going over to Islamism. Saudi oil money, both governmental and private, helped underwrite the Islamist surge. Additionally, many Egyptians working in Saudi Arabia and other parts of the Gulf returned to Egypt with money, as well as conservative customs, habits, and ideas about Islam and politics.

Like other parts of the Arab and Muslim world, Egypt experienced increasing religiosity among both Copts and Muslims during this period. This manifested itself, for example, in greater numbers of women wearing the *hijab*, or veil, the emergence of popular Islamist preachers, growing conservatism in society and popular culture, and increased sectarian tension. Islamists also gained support by delivering social welfare services such as health care and education that the government failed to provide.

Islamists increased their appeal to students by offering them practical assistance at the overcrowded universities. By the late 1970s disciplined Islamists controlled many student organizations. Islamists broke with Sadat when he made peace with Israel, and one of them, Khalid al-Islambuli, assassinated him in 1981.

Sadat was succeeded by Husni Mubarak, who set out to separate nonviolent from violent Islamists. The line, however, proved difficult to draw. At first, in 1984 and 1987, Mubarak let Muslim Brothers win parliamentary seats under the banners of other parties. In the 1990s he squeezed most Islamists out of parliament, but they returned in leadership positions in student councils and professional syndicates. He curtailed these organizations' activities and limited press freedoms, only to have Islamists win several important cases in civil court. Mubarak enlisted the official *ulama* of al-Azhar to refute the radicals, but even the Azharis were not always reliable. Secularists and Copts complained that the government had already conceded too much to the Islamists.

In the 1990s Islamist extremists intermittently targeted and killed policemen, outspoken secularists, Copts, and foreign tourists. They also made attempts on the lives of Nobel Prize–winning novelist Naguib Mahfouz and President Mubarak himself. Mass arrests, torture, summary military trials, and executions ran the risk of radicalizing the uncommitted. Islamist militants often quoted Sayyid Qutb, a Muslim Brethren theorist who was executed in 1966. The radicals were mostly young, lower-middle-class provincials or recent immigrants to the urban slums. Outside Cairo, extremist Islamism was strong in underdeveloped Upper Egypt in Asyut and Minya provinces, where there were also many Copts. A number of Islamist extremist leaders had studied science or technology but were only narrowly self-taught in religion. A few Azhar-educated *ulama* joined the extremists; among them was Shaykh Umar Abd al-Rahman, who was convicted on terrorism charges in connection with the bombing of the World Trade Center in New York City in 1993.

A number of Egyptians were also involved in al-Qaida, the group that executed the September 11, 2001, attacks on the United States. Ayman al-Zawahiri, an Egyptian medical doctor and formerly one of the leaders of Egypt's Islamic Jihad, served as the number two man in al-Qaida, while Mohamed Atta was one of the nineteen men who executed the attacks on the Pentagon and the World Trade Center. Between 2004 and 2006, religious extremists also struck Egypt's tourist sector with several attacks in the Sinai peninsula that left more than 100 people dead.

Moderate Islamists made increasing political gains in the Egyptian parliament during this period. The Muslim Brotherhood won 17 seats in the 2000 elections and 88 seats in the 2005 elections, despite state interference in the electoral process, to become the largest opposition bloc in parliament and the most important opposition force in Egyptian politics.

Long-standing authoritarian rule, high rates of unemployment, corruption, and the inability of the Egyptian government to provide basic social services partially account for the popularity of Islamist groups such as the Muslim Brotherhood. Although the Brotherhood presents itself as striving for greater political freedom, less corruption, and better governance, many question the group's commitment to democracy, believing that minority and women's rights would be threatened if the organization came to power.

Egypt's strong tradition of religious tolerance is being tested, and it is likely that religion and politics will remain closely intertwined, regardless of future political developments.

See also *ʿAbduh, Muhammad; al-Afghani, Jamal al-Din; Banna, Hasan al-; Fundamentalism; Islam; Jihad; Islam's Encounters with the West; Nasser, Gamal Abdel; Qutb, Sayyid.*

Samer Shehata

BIBLIOGRAPHY

Baker, Raymond William. *Islam Without Fear: Egypt and the New Islamists.* Cambridge: Harvard University Press, 2003.

———. *Sadat and After: Struggles for Egypt's Political Soul.* Cambridge: Harvard University Press, 1990.

Binder, Leonard. *Islamic Liberalism: A Critique of Development Ideologies.* Chicago: University of Chicago Press, 1988.

Delanoue, Gilbert. *Moralistes et politiques: Musulmans dans l'Egypte du XIXe siècle (1798–1882).* 2 vols. Cairo: Institut Français d'Archéologie Orientale, 1982.

Eccel, Chris. *Egypt, Islam, and Social Change: al-Azhar in Conflict and Accommodation.* Berlin: Klaus Schwarz, 1984.

Ibrahim, Saad Eddin. *Egypt, Islam and Democracy: Critical Essays, With a New Postscript.* Cairo; New York: American University in Cairo Press, 2002.

Kepel, Gilles. *Muslim Extremism in Egypt: The Prophet and the Pharaoh.* Berkeley: University of California Press, 1985.

Mitchell, Richard P. *The Society of the Muslim Brothers.* London: Oxford University Press, 1969.

Mawsilili, Ahmad S. *Radical Islamic Fundamentalism: The Ideological and Political Discourse of Sayyid Qutb.* Beirut: American University of Beirut, 1992.

Sagiv, David. *Fundamentalism and Intellectuals in Egypt, 1973–1993.* London: Frank Cass, 1995.

Wickham, Carrie Rosefsky. *Mobilizing Islam: Religion, Activism and Political Change in Egypt.* New York: Columbia University Press, 2002.

English Revolution

The English revolution of the mid-seventeenth century refers to a diverse set of events that brought England through two civil wars, the execution of a king, a brief period of republican rule, and the Restoration of the monarchy. The near fusion of religion and politics during this period can be attributed to institutional and cultural contexts. Institutionally, disagreements over the future of the state church—the Church of England—defined political issues that divided rival political parties. Culturally, this was an age whose inhabitants saw the hand of Providence in all dimensions of existence, natural and social. Hence conflict over esoteric doctrines or minute organizational matters quickly became entangled with different views on a broad range of secular issues, including foreign policy, economic justice, and models of government.

The Civil War Years

The interweaving of religion and politics is evident in the events that led to the outbreak of civil war. After eleven years of ruling without the aid of Parliament, Charles I convened Parliament in 1640. His ability to rule alone ended when he tried to impose his religious policy on Scotland. The Scots refused to conform to the liturgy of the Church of England or give obedience to its bishops. Northern England was occupied by a Scottish army pledged to defend its Presbyterian model of John Calvin's church in Geneva, Switzerland. Confronted by an alliance between his rebellious Scottish subjects and domestic opponents of his rule, Charles summoned what was to be known as the Long Parliament, so called because it was not dissolved until 1660.

The issue that eventually drove members of Parliament into rival camps was Charles's unyielding opposition to the Puritans' demands for religious reforms. The Puritans were Calvinists who had left the Church of England and wanted to "purify" the church of its Roman Catholic traditions and practices. Among their demands were imposition of religious discipline (detection and punishment of "ungodly" behavior), repression of Catholics, and limits on the powers of bishops. Street demonstrations led to Charles's flight from London in 1642.

Religious issues remained central to subsequent developments. A broad consensus in the Long Parliament on the need for moderate religious and constitutional reforms led to intractable conflict between Royalist and Parliamentarian parties that culminated in civil war. The first civil war lasted until 1646. Royalists not only supported a prominent place for royal prerogative in political decision making but also regarded bishops and the established ecclesiastical order of the Church of England as an essential pillar of the monarchy. Perhaps the strongest source of popular support for the Royalist cause was widespread attachment to the established liturgy and suspicion of its critics. Chief among supporters of Parliament was the main body of Puritans, religiously committed Protestants who rejected the bishops and liturgy of the Church of England but supported the ideal of a national church. An abortive coup against Parliament in 1647 was followed by a second civil war in 1648. The civil war ended with the execution of Charles and the abolition of the House of Lords in 1649.

Sectarian Divisions

During the first civil war Puritan support for Parliament disintegrated into rival factions, principally Presbyterian and Independent factions. The terms have distinct political and religious referents. Not all political Presbyterians, who advocated conservative social and military policies, were religious

Presbyterians; not all religious Independents, who preferred a Congregationalist model to the coercive model of church discipline in Presbyterianism, sided with the policies of political Independents in Parliament.

Independent opposition to Presbyterian efforts to reconstruct a state church facilitated the appearance of many radical sectarian groups with a variety of political and religious commitments. Although it took many forms, radical religion upheld the possibility of spiritual perfection and the priority of inner spirit over rituals and organization. This view devalued precisely those aspects of religion that traditionalists thought made society orderly. For example, unyielding hostility to mandatory tithes to the established church and fierce anticlericalism among Quakers and other sectarian groups led traditionalists to equate sectarianism with sedition.

An ethos of egalitarian individualism in religious life pervaded radical sectarianism. Some versions, like the Levellers, Diggers, and Fifth Monarchy Men, combined this egalitarian spirit with an explicit, radical political agenda; others, like the Baptists, Ranters, and Seekers, generally did not. Moreover, radical politics exhibited great variation. Levellers such as John Lilburne advocated a greatly expanded franchise, religious toleration, and freedom of the press. Diggers, led by Gerrard Winstanley, advanced primitive communism as a means to a moral utopia. Fifth Monarchists, who expected the imminent return of Christ, were led by these millennial beliefs to participate in violent, abortive uprisings.

Quakers came from the middle reaches of society, especially its mobile, literate segments, such as artisans, yeomen farmers, and shopkeepers. In the 1650s they recruited members from mainstream Puritan denominations, its sectarian offshoots (Baptists, for example), and heretical groups that until then had led a furtive existence apart from Puritanism. Quakerism arose in the northern areas of England as George Fox and other itinerant preachers, in 1652, first mobilized followers who were united by economic as well as religious grievances. They opposed high rents as well as mandatory tithes. The New Model Army, like other radical political groups, was a fertile source of recruits to Quakerism. (Indeed, in the 1650s Quakers sometimes served in the Parliamentary party's New Model Army and the county militia; they did not adhere to pacifism as a principal tenet until after the Restoration.)

Like other radical sectarians, Quakers were not consistent in their political alliances and views, though they generally supported abolition of the monarchy and the House of

Oliver Cromwell, a devout Puritan, was the first commoner to rule England. Cromwell served as Lord Protector under England's only written constitution, the Instrument of Government, from 1653 until his death on September 3, 1658.

Lords. Individual Quakers held government and military positions during Oliver Cromwell's Protectorate, which replaced an experiment in republican government that lasted until the end of 1653, despite Cromwell's suppression of agitation to remodel England as a holy commonwealth. At the same time, Quakers supported republican proposals to institutionalize parliamentary democracy when this seemed the best option for preventing the return of the Stuart monarchy, the bishops, and a state church.

When the monarchy was restored, in 1660, under Charles II, in part because of widespread fear of Quakers and other sectarian groups, Quakers responded to defeat by retreating from politics and embracing pacifism as a doctrinal tenet. Under Charles, the Church of England and the House of Lords were restored. Modest legal and constitutional changes formally abolished lingering remnants of feudalism, limited the Crown's powers to raise revenue, required Parliaments to be called every three years, and took the first steps toward toleration of religious dissent.

See also *Anglicanism; Friends, Society of (Quakers); Protestantism; Reformation; State Churches.*

David Zaret

BIBLIOGRAPHY

Finlayson, Michael George. *Historians, Puritanism, and the English Revolution: The Religious Factor in English Politics before and after the Interregnum.* Toronto and Buffalo: University of Toronto Press, 1983.

Hill, Christopher. *The English Bible and the Seventeenth-century Revolution.* London: Allen Lane; New York: Penguin, 1993.

———. *The World Turned Upside Down: Radical Ideas during the English Revolution.* London: Temple Smith; New York, Viking, 1972.

Lindley, Keith. *Popular Politics and Religion in Civil War London.* Aldershot, U.K.: Scolar Press, 1997.

Morrill, John S. *The Nature of the English Revolution.* London and New York: Longman, 1993.

Reay, Barry. *The Quakers and the English Revolution.* London: Temple Smith; New York: St. Martin's, 1985.

Seaver, Paul S. *Wallington's World: A Puritan Artisan in Seventeenth-century London.* Stanford, Calif.: Stanford University Press, 1985.

Underdown, David. *Pride's Purge: Politics in the Puritan Revolution.* London and Boston: Allen and Unwin, 1985.

———. *Revel, Riot, and Rebellion: Popular Politics and Culture in England, 1603–1660.* Oxford: Clarendon Press; New York: Oxford University Press, 1985.

Enlightenment

The Enlightenment, a historical period and a European intellectual movement, radically redefined the relationship between religion and politics. The *Enlightenment* is an ambiguous term, and scholars debate its historical duration, geographical location, leading figures, and dominant characteristics.

In narrowest terms the Enlightenment, often identified simply as the French Enlightenment or the Age of Reason, was an intellectual movement in eighteenth-century France. It ended with the French Revolution of 1789 and the revolution's failure to achieve most of its Enlightenment-defined goals (many of which were achieved in the nineteenth century and continue to shape contemporary life).

In broadest terms the characteristics of the Enlightenment define the leading characteristics of modernity. Intellectual forerunners of the Enlightenment date to classical Greece and especially to the Renaissance and the Reformation. Viewed broadly, the Enlightenment began in seventeenth-century England, particularly with John Locke's approaches to knowledge, politics, and religion. English and Scottish Enlightenment thinkers included Joseph Priestley, Francis Hutcheson, Adam Smith, Edward Gibbon, David Hume, and Jeremy Bentham. The French Enlightenment was dominated by Voltaire, baron de Montesquieu, Denis Diderot, Jean le Rond d'Alembert, and Jean-Jacques Rousseau, while the leading figures of the German Enlightenment were Christian Wolff, Moses Mendelssohn, G. E. Lessing, and Immanuel Kant. The North American Enlightenment was led by Thomas Paine, Benjamin Franklin, and Thomas Jefferson and found expression in the American Declaration of Independence of 1776. In each of these places, the Enlightenment takes somewhat different forms, not least with respect to religion.

Characteristics of the Enlightenment

The dominant, medieval, European, pre-Enlightenment approach to politics and religion emphasized the hierarchical supremacy of supernatural religious authority. It upheld divine revelation, religious scripture and tradition, the church, and clerical authority. The monarchy and political institutions were derivative, receiving their legitimacy by appeals to supernatural and religious authority.

Proponents of the Enlightenment rejected this approach to politics and religion and upheld reason and nature, not the supernatural realm, as the primary sources of and authorities over objective knowledge and human progress. They emphasized critical reasoning, laws of nature, objectivity, and universality; a scientific outlook; progress; natural rights, liberty, and equality; utility; toleration; and freedom from superstition, irrationality, and dependence on religious and other forms of external authority.

According to Kant's famous definition of 1784, Enlightenment is characterized by the emergence of human beings from a self-imposed immature condition in which they lack the determination and courage to use their own capacity for understanding and instead depend on the external authority and guidance of another. Individuals must have the courage and will to think for themselves about politics and religion instead of depending for their views on political and religious authorities.

Moreover, human beings must be true to their nature and exercise their central capacity for reason as the sole means for gaining objective knowledge and understanding of politics and religion. Critical reasoning exposed irrational dogma and externally imposed, religious, and political structures of domination. Reason freed human beings from religious dogma and superstition, from irrational and oppressive legal systems, and from political and moral injustice and suffering. By developing their rational capacity, humans made progress and moved toward greater perfection.

Although many Enlightenment thinkers had confidence in the human rational capacity and in its potential for progress, others were more skeptical about human nature and focused on the conditions and limits of objective knowledge. These thinkers believed, along with their less skeptical counterparts, that rationality was a universal human capacity, and they called for a new sense of egalitarianism in which individual human beings were free to exercise their own critical reason and to enjoy individual liberty, equality before the law, and equal tolerance. There was and continues to be a huge gap between such Enlightenment ideals and their limited applications and actual practices in modern political and religious life.

According to these ideals, in studying politics and religion human beings must rationally investigate nature, including human nature. Nature has a rational structure exhibited through universal natural laws. Natural phenomena, religious and political institutions, and human behavior were to be investigated using the same fundamental conceptions and a common methodology. Nature, including human, scientific, religious, and political phenomena, was to be understood by breaking complex phenomena into simple component parts and by uncovering relations of cause and effect. For example, political authority could be analyzed in terms of rational individuals voluntarily coming together to form a social contract and then transferring power to a sovereign ruler. Enlightenment thinkers disagreed on the nature and content of the social contract, the extent to which power should be transferred to the sovereign, and the political relationship between the ruler and the ruled.

Politics and Religion of the Enlightenment

Unlike many counter-Enlightenment thinkers, proponents of the Enlightenment asserted that the methods of investigating and verifying the truth in politics and religion were the same. Uncritical dogma, superstition, and irrationality were to be uprooted, whether in religion or politics. At the same time and in contrast, natural law, natural rights, critical reasoning, and objective knowledge were to be upheld, whether in religion or politics.

The Enlightenment world view affirmed both religious and political tolerance. Toleration was necessary for human beings to develop their natural capacity to reason and to decide what to believe. Both political and religious intolerance restricted human beings' ability to develop their universal, natural, rational capacity for arriving at objective knowledge. It also prevented them from establishing political and other relationships that maximized their potential for human development and for the realization of liberty and happiness.

Compared with pre-Enlightenment figures, Enlightenment thinkers were critical of past interactions and intersections of politics and religion. Although they approached religious and political phenomena using the same fundamental conceptions and the same methodology, they tended to discourage the intersection of religion and politics and to affirm their separation. This tendency was clear in the formulations of atheists of the Enlightenment who saw no value in religion and were determined to free politics from religious authority, dogma, ignorance, and superstition. Other Enlightenment thinkers affirmed a natural and rational deism, a rational theology, and a natural religion over a religion of supernatural revelation. However, even these religious figures of the Enlightenment opposed religion's using supernatural revelation, dogma, scripture, and institutional and clerical authority to interact with and restrict political life.

Furthermore, any legitimate view of religion and politics was based on humans' critical understanding arising from their nature as rational beings. Religion, based on reason and nature, must respect the rational, natural foundation of politics and the universal, equal, and political rights and liberties of others, including those of nonbelievers and believers alike. Politics, also based on reason and nature, must ensure human beings' freedom from religious and other forms of domination. At the same time it should protect their liberties, including religious liberty, so that they could freely and critically pursue the truth of religious, political, and all other matters. Pushed to the extreme, there is a sharp tension between these two ideas.

See also *Natural Law; Secular Humanism.*

Douglas Allen

BIBLIOGRAPHY

Cassirer, Ernst. *The Philosophy of the Enlightenment.* Princeton, N.J.: Princeton University Press, 1951.

Gay, Peter. *The Enlightenment: An Interpretation.* 2 vols. New York: Knopf, 1966, 1969.

Hazard, Paul. *European Thought in the Eighteenth Century.* New Haven, Conn.: Yale University Press, 1954.

Horkheimer, Max, and Theodor W. Adorno. *Dialectic of Enlightenment.* New York: Herder and Herder, 1972.

Himmelfarb, Gertrude *The Roads to Modernity: The British, French, and American Enlightenments.* New York: Vintage Books, 2005.

Im Hof, Ulrich. *The Enlightenment.* Cambridge, Mass.: Blackwell Publishers, 1994.

Manuel, Frank E. *The Eighteenth Century Confronts the Gods.* Cambridge, Mass.: Harvard University Press, 1959.

Yolton, John H., ed. *The Blackwell Companion to the Enlightenment.* Cambridge, Mass.: Blackwell Publishers, 1992.

Environmentalism

The rise of environmentalism has been occasioned by the growing perception of a crisis in the relationship between modern societies and the natural environment, a crisis manifest in humanly induced climate change. This is evident in raised land temperatures, the melting of frozen tundra, the recession of all land glaciers, and the shrinking of polar ice caps; in the extinction of many species caused by deforestation and industrial farming and fishing methods; in the spread of deserts and the erosion of soils in many of the earth's regions; in atmospheric and water pollution; and in dangers from toxic and industrial waste. Those most affected by environmental problems, including climate change, desertification, over-fishing, and deforestation, are poor rural and indigenous peoples in developing countries whose lands, rivers and coastlands are often pillaged by industrial corporations and governments without regard to their needs or wishes.

The crisis therefore has a significant political dimension because it relates to local, national, and global decision making about wealth distribution, land use, resource allocation, and economic development. There is also a religiocultural dimension to the environmental crisis. Some environmentalists argue that certain religious beliefs, rituals, and behaviors are implicated in the growth of ecologically destructive attitudes and practices. Other environmentalists, and many religious adherents, propose that the ritual systems, mythological beliefs, and moral and spiritual values of religious communities provide significant resources for resisting the ecologically destructive impacts of industrial capitalism and the practices and values of mass consumerism.

Environmentalism and Political Thought

Environmentalists point to a fundamental conflict between the dominant values and practices of modern civilization—economic growth, technological progress, consumerism—and the fragile and finite character of the biosphere of the earth. Many environmentalists believe that the exploitative tendencies of modern life in relation to the earth originated in religiocultural attitudes toward nature fostered by the Christian religion, including the biblical idea of human dominion over creation. Ecofeminists such as Rosemary Ruether point to the influence of dualistic accounts of the relationship between mind and matter, and body and soul in the Christian doctrine of salvation, and to the influence of patriarchy in scriptural texts and Christian traditions as crucial elements in the construction of modern exploitative attitudes towards the earth. Ruether also suggests that the scriptures and traditions of Christians and Jews contain within them significant resources for challenging the exploitation of women and the environment.

Representing a significant adapation of modern political thought and practice, environmentalism in this sense is also a regional and global program of political, economic, and even civilizational reform. For example, the 1987 United Nations Commission on Environment and Development report *Our Common Future* promoted the concept of sustainable development. Furthermore, world leaders who met to discuss global environmental problems at the Rio Earth Summit in June 1992 adopted *Agenda 21*, which identified the deterioration of ecosystems and the worsening of poverty, hunger, and ill health as a defining moment in human history requiring remedial action by local communities and national governments, and by international cooperation and treaty. Many city and state authorities have made efforts since 1992 to incorporate elements of sustainable development into their planning and regulatory systems. The principle "the polluter pays" has also achieved growing recognition, and pollution taxes and trade in pollution permits are the two principal ways in which this principle has been integrated into the market economy.

Environmentalism has been less successful internationally than regionally or locally. The Montreal Protocol, signed by all developed and most developing countries in 1987, agreed to dramatic reductions in the production of ozone-depleting chlorofluorocarbons (CFCs) and initiated an international quest for less-damaging refrigerants. Similar efforts at the Rio Earth Summit, and at the Johannesburg Earth Summit in 2002, to set globally agreed limits to tropical deforestation and industrial fishing, however, were less successful. Similarly, although more than ninety countries ratified the Kyoto Protocol on Climate Change in a combined effort to significantly reduce global emissions of global warming gases—

particularly of carbon dioxide—by the mid-2000s few countries had made progress in actually reducing their greenhouse gas emissions, and the United States and Australia, the heaviest users of greenhouse gases per head of population, refused to ratify the Kyoto Protocol.

Environmentalism may also be seen as a countercultural or postmodern social movement whose proponents see the environmental crisis as representing the defining-limit problem of modern civilization. They seek to rebalance the utilitarian quest for maximum human welfare with the welfare of other species, and even of the planet, or *gaia*. James Lovelock, who originated the now widely accepted gaia hypothesis, proposes that the earth is a total living system in which organic life forms modulate the atmospheric, climatological, geological, and marine environments necessary for life. As the full dimensions of the threat to the planet represented by global warming are exposed by climate scientists, however, the gaian perspective on planetary systems has moved into the mainstream of environmental science. This perspective challenges the reductionism and narrow specialism of the scientific enterprise, but the implications of this challenge remain widely resisted.

Ecocentric philosophers point to the Cartesian metaphor of the cosmos as machine as a major cause of the disharmony between modern, technologically driven societies and the fragile and complex organic balances of ecological systems. Ecocentric environmentalism is manifest in a range of alternative political, economic, and lifestyle projects involving direct action, alternative communities, and a rejection of the core values of the dominant society. Countercultural environmentalists argue that, like the social and ritual systems of indigenous peoples, production and exchange systems should be fashioned not with the primary aim of reordering the natural world after human purposes, but rather of promoting human and nonhuman welfare by mirroring the balances and recycling patterns of ecological systems.

Ecocentric environmentalism has its origins in the nineteenth-century Romantic movement, which, in reaction to Enlightenment rationalism and early modern industrialization, sought to relocate ethical goods and spiritual values in the intrinsic beauty and order of the natural world. Ecocentric environmentalists argue that exalting wealth accumulation and luxury over ecological goods is a sign of the moral impoverishment of an urban industrial culture out of touch with the sustaining spiritual energies of the planet and that puts material acquisition before relationships of care and responsibility between people, and between people and their environment.

Environmentalism and Religion

The spiritual and religious dimensions of environmentalism are of growing significance to environmentalism as global political policy and as a new social movement. The environmental crisis is seen by many, particularly ecocentric, environmentalists and by many religious adherents as a spiritual crisis of modern civilization. There is also a pragmatic motive that recognizes the continuing cultural power of religions as a resource for moral and social change in many parts of the world. In 1990 the World Wildlife Fund helped organize an ecological council of faiths in Assisi, Italy, at which religious leaders, including Pope John Paul II and the Dalai Lama, affirmed the need for radical change in the direction of modern civilization if the world is to be saved from environmental catastrophe.

The ecological turn in world religions first became evident in the Christian tradition in the prophetic writings of North American theologians such as Joseph Sittler, Francis Schaeffer, Paul Santmire, and John B. Cobb in the 1960s, and in the efforts of international ecclesiastical organizations, most notably the World Council of Churches, to reexamine Christian social teachings and actions in the light of the ecological crisis. Some theologians have argued that the Christian tradition contains within it significant resources for a more sustainable way of living on the earth and have drawn on biblical motifs such as creation, covenant, reverence for life, and stewardship as crucial elements in a Christian ecological theology.

Other theologians have sponsored various ecological adaptations of Christian doctrine and ethics. Process philosophers, for example, propose that basic reality is characterized by creativity and flux rather than stasis. Theologians such as Charles Hartshorne and John Cobb argue that instead of seeing God as an unchanging absolute being who is external to the world, we should see God in a caring and dynamic relationship with the evolving processes of the biophysical world. Christian ecofeminists and liberation theologians have sponsored the idea of ecojustice, which extends ethical ideals of social justice and equality between peoples and genders to a concern for justice, and even equality, among all species on the earth. It is, however, in worship and spirituality that the most widespread influence of ecological concerns may be observed in contemporary Christianity.

New liturgies, hymns, and credal affirmations in Christian worship connect reverence for the divine creator with care for the gifts of creation and encourage Christians to exercise daily ecological responsibility for the earth through simpler lifestyles.

Efforts to green Christianity have met with considerable resistance among many conservative Christians, particularly in North America. Many Christians of a conservative disposition believe that Christians have been given dominion over the earth and that humans therefore have a divine mandate to transform the earth into useful products and to exploit its resources to the full until the return of Christ, when the earth will be destroyed in a great apocalyptic conflagration before the final redemption of all things. In this perspective, environmental regulation and taxation are seen as undue restraints on the property rights of individuals and corporations. The rollback of environmental legislation in the United States in the early and mid-twenty-first century has significant ideological roots in this conservative Christian resistance to environmentalism, as well as in the economic dogmas of neoliberalism.

What some have called the greening of religion is also evident in the religions of Asia and in Islam. Buddhist monks have fought illegal logging of the few remaining areas of tropical forest in Thailand by the practice of "ordaining" trees with a sacred thread. Criticizing the pact between statist Islam and Western capitalism fostered by Arab monarchs and political leaders, radical Muslims adopt simpler lifestyles. Hindus draw on the philosophy and practices of Gandhi, as well as on the Upanishads, in deploring the depredatory effects of industrialization and international trade on the peoples, forests, and wild animals of South Asia. Perhaps the most ecological of all Asian religions, Jainism takes the Buddhist concept of *ahimsa* (nonviolence) with such seriousness that all Jains are vegetarians, and Jain monks take enormous care never to inadvertently crush an insect. Westerners, who find in Asian traditions an emphasis on the oneness of all life forms absent from Western religion and philosophy, adopt meditative practices and philosophical ideas from Daoism and Zen Buddhism.

In the Americas the practices and religious traditions of Native Americans involved an acknowledgement of the interdependence of all life, and their deep ethical regard for the land and all its inhabitants prevented them from despoiling the land as did later colonizers. Advocates of environmental ethics argue that modern civilization needs to recover this indigenous regard for land and nature and that this recovery will involve a spiritual as well as a philosophical reorientation.

Environmentalism in its more radical ecocentric forms may be said to represent a new and growing ecological religion, even the archetypal religion of post-Christian societies, and to have sponsored the recovery of pagan and primal religious styles. Ecological religion takes a variety of forms, and some of these are increasingly influential in Western societies. Thus growing numbers of vegetarians reject the killing of animals for sport and food and ascribe equivalent moral value to all sentient life forms. Other forms of ecological religion—which may be variously described as New Age, pagan, ecofeminist, or Wiccan—reflect an explicit desire not just to prevent harm to the natural world but also to reconnect the rituals and rhythms of human life with reverence for the sacred spirit or spirits said to reside in natural elements, cycles, processes, beings, and events.

See also *Dalai Lama; Enlightenment; Feminism; Hinduism; Paganism; Science and Technology; Social Justice; Traditionalism.*

Michael S. Northcott

BIBLIOGRAPHY

Attfield, Robin. *The Ethics of Environmental Concern.* 2d ed. Athens: University of Georgia Press, 1991.

Nasr, Seyyed Hossein. *Religion and the Order of Nature.* New York: Oxford University Press, 1996.

Northcott, Michael. *The Environment and Christian Ethics.* Cambridge, U.K.: Cambridge University Press, 1996.

Oelschlaeger, Max. *Caring for Creation: An Ecumenical Approach to the Environmental Crisis.* New Haven, Conn.: Yale University Press, 1994.

Ruether, Rosemary Radford. *Gaia and God: An Ecofeminist Theology of Earth Healing.* San Francisco: HarperSanFrancisco, 1992.

World Commission on Environment and Development. *Our Common Future.* Oxford and New York: Oxford University Press, 1987.

Episcopalianism

See *Anglicanism.*

Ethnic Cleansing

See *Genocide and "Ethnic Cleansing."*

Ethnicity

Ethnic identity is predicated on the assumption that one shares a heritage with others that can be traced to a common forebear. Ethnicity differs from kinship, however, in that the links are not traced through genealogy. Instead, certain cultural attributes are taken as signifying that one shares descent with those who also share these attributes. For those who affirm an ethnic identity, certainty is found in the heritage that is believed to link them to others with whom they share descent. This belief is embedded in cultural practices such as the stories heard in childhood, ceremonies and commemorations, the expression of ethnic stereotypes encountered in relations with others, the implementation of bureaucratic rules based on ethnic distinctions, and political acts, sometimes violent, that entail the assertion of ethnic boundaries. In all cases, an ethnic identity is validated by the authority of the past, a past to which one is linked through a nongenealogical line of descent.

Religion, like ethnicity, offers certainty with reference to the authority of the past, providing truths first enunciated by elders, prophets, and messiahs who lived in former times and were followed by many successive generations. Such truths enable those who accept them to confront problems of suffering and death, chaos, and injustice that do not lend themselves to rational solutions. In a religion, such as Judaism, that is followed by those who consider themselves a chosen "people," such truths may be traced to founders who are also thought to have been forebears. Most religions, however, are open to any who choose to act in accord with their tenets and to participate in the prescribed rituals. Some religions specifically require the follower to forgo the expectations associated with kinship or membership in an ethnic group if these conflict with the practice of the faith. This has been especially true of many proselytizing religions such as Islam and certain branches of Christianity.

Ethnic Movements and Modernity

The rise of ethnic movements in the twentieth century, especially in the latter half of the century, can be traced to some of the same causes as the resurgence of religious movements in that same period. Both are manifestations of a quest for certainty about one's self and the world in which one lives in the wake of the destabilizing forces associated with modernity. Bureaucratic and economic rationalization have undermined social cohesion based on kinship, locality, and patronage. Alienation has been intensified in many cases when modern governments have intruded deeply into everyday life. In the same period scientific successes in finding cures for or ways to prevent many of the afflictions that humans have long suffered from have also served to accentuate for many the lack of scientific means for confronting those physical afflictions that still lack cures.

The intensified uncertainty that has been the by-product of modernity has led many to turn to beliefs and practices that posit unchanging and unchangeable truths about their relation to the world. Both religious and ethnic movements offer such truths, but these are based on different premises. While ethnic identity may reinforce religious identity, it is also often the case that ethnicity and religion are in tension or even in conflict with one another.

Ethnicity, Religion, and the Politics of Cultural Diversity

Both ethnicity and religion are important factors in what can be termed the *politics of cultural diversity* in modern societies. Every ethnic group and every religion is associated with distinctive cultural patterns. Some cultural patterns have generated political interest because they are seen as being in conflict with the patterns of others. Major differences in cultural attitudes toward reproduction or property rights, for example, or even something seemingly unimportant, such as the clothes a student wears to school, have proved to be divisive in some societies. The politics of culture can, and all too often do, turn violent when state power is used to curb or forbid some cultural practices considered to be central to a religious or ethnic identity.

If a modern state has made religion the basis for national identity, then ethnic divisions within the society may become associated also with religious divisions. This is evident in Sri Lanka, for example, where since the 1950s the state has promoted policies that accord a privileged position to the Sinhalese-speaking Buddhist majority. Although these policies have marginalized many groups, Tamil-speaking peoples in northern Sri Lanka, who are also predominantly Hindu, have felt especially discriminated against. Religious as well as ethnic differences have been used to justify violence by Sinhalese against Tamils in the mid-1980s and since then violence by Tamils against Sinhalese in support of a movement whose goal is the creation of an independent or autonomous Tamil polity in northern Sri Lanka. By the late 1990s, after tens of thousands of deaths, the conflict in Sri

Lanka had assumed an endemic character that appeared to be beyond resolution. A comparable situation has also existed in Lebanon, with violent conflicts in that country resulting in an ethno-religious partition of the country.

Links between religious, ethnic, and national identity have shaped the politics of Israel in fundamental ways. The definition of Israel as a Jewish state has generated many conflicts, not only with Palestinians living on the West Bank and in Gaza, but also among Christians and Muslims who hold Israeli citizenship and between secular Jews whose Jewishness is based primarily on their ethnic background and religious Jews who wish to see religious injunctions enforced by the state.

In some instances the political culture has prompted the reconstruing of religious identities as ethnic ones. A foremost example is in the former Yugoslavia, where despite markedly similar languages and cultures Serbs, Croats, and Bosnians are considered fundamentally different because of their religious heritage. Identities as Orthodox Christian, Catholic, or Muslim are taken as signifying the existence of deep historical differences that legitimate ethnonationalist divisions. The equation of religious with ethnonationalist differences also has occurred in Northern Ireland, where "Protestant" and "Catholic" have come to be seen as labels for distinct peoples.

Many indigenous peoples who have converted to Christianity or Islam have found in these religions and associated institutions sources of support for asserting their ethnic distinctiveness within the societies in which they live. A good example is that of the Karen people, found mainly in Burma but also in Thailand, who have built an ethnonationalist movement on Christian institutions and on a writing system that was developed in association with their conversion to Christianity. The Hui of China, who live among the Han Chinese and share the same language and much of the same culture but who trace their origins to Muslim converts, provide another example. In contemporary China many Hui have rediscovered their links to Islam and increasingly express their identity through religious actions.

For a religious affiliation to be construed as marking a distinctive ethnic or ethnonationalist identity, it must be understood as an essential element of one's heritage. Many religions explicitly reject such an assumption and, instead, insist that a person's faith can be demonstrated only through an act of commitment that could well entail a rejection of one's heritage. In many parts of Africa, for example, conver-sion to Christianity or Islam has made it possible for people to transcend local and tribal backgrounds and to find a new cultural identity, which they now share with others of diverse ethnic origins.

In any society in which a politics of cultural difference is significant, it can be anticipated that the relationship between ethnic and religious identity will for at least some people become a matter of political concern. At the same time, these relationships will always be shaped by the particular politics of the societies in which they are manifest.

See also *Genocide; Ireland; Israel; Prejudice; Yugoslavia.*

Charles F. Keyes

BIBLIOGRAPHY

Anderson, Benedict R. O. G. *Imagined Communities: Reflections on the Origin and Spread of Nationalism.* Rev. and expanded ed. London: Verso, 1991.

Bruce, Steve. "Fundamentalism, Ethnicity, and Enclave." In *Fundamentalisms and the State: Remaking Polities, Economies, and Militance,* edited by Martin E. Marty and R. Scott Appleby. Chicago: University of Chicago Press, 1993.

Geertz, Clifford. "The Integrative Revolution: Primordial Sentiments and Civil Politics in the New States." In *Old Societies and New States,* edited by Clifford Geertz. Glencoe, Ill.: Free Press, 1963. Reprinted in *The Interpretation of Cultures: Selected Essays,* by Clifford Geertz. New York: Basic Books, 1973.

Keyes, Charles F., Laurel Kendall, and Helen Hardacre, eds. *Asian Visions of Authority: Religion and the Modern States of East and Southeast Asia.* Honolulu: University of Hawaii Press, 1994.

Kotkin, Joel. *Tribes: How Race, Religion, and Identity Determine Success in the New Global Economy.* New York: Random House, 1993.

Europe, Eastern

In the post–World War II era, the term *Eastern Europe* often was used to refer to the Soviet bloc countries of Europe: Bulgaria, Czechoslovakia, the German Democratic Republic, Hungary, Poland, and Romania. Only after Soviet-imposed communism collapsed in 1989 in Eastern Europe did a real relationship between politics and religion begin to develop. The collapse of communism also marked the return of these countries' separate identities.

Eastern Europe is a mosaic of languages, cultures, denominations, and traditions; the imposition of the Soviet model had made the countries of the region only seem homogeneous. Indeed, "Eastern Europe" was a concept that could be understood only by reference to Soviet practices. The

went on, the largely incidental character of communist systems. Religion was capable politically of playing three liberating roles, regardless of the particular denomination in which it was practiced. At the level of individuals, confession of a faith could drive the faithful to abandon the schizophrenic attitude demanded by the communist system, which forced people to keep their actions and thoughts separate. At the level of societies, religion could help to repair the fabric of communities that the political authorities had tried hard to destroy. And, at the level of nations, religion could be liberating by revealing the historical continuity of nation-states and thereby calling into question the legitimacy of the "revolutionary" break on which the Soviet system had been based.

When the Polish church celebrated one thousand years of Christianity in the country in 1966, it revealed publicly Poles' commitment to Catholicism. The church then lost no time in identifying a strategy that would call into question the solidity of communist power in terms of both social geography and time. This strategy was to be continued by Pope John Paul II, who, as a former archbishop of Krakow, knew it well. Thus the whole interpretation of reality on which communist power relied was swept away by the emphasis on the long haul of civilization and on the historic and cultural unity of Europe rather than on the short life of political systems.

From this point of view, the pope's first visit to his native country in 1979 after becoming head of the Catholic Church had a considerable impact. John Paul II attracted huge crowds and proved that the legitimacy of political power had eroded. This proof, coupled with the pontiff's encouragement to Poles to have no fear, was largely responsible for the birth of the Solidarity movement in 1980, led by the Gdansk shipyard worker Lech Walesa and supported by the workers' union Solidarity.

Although religion had the potential to play three liberating roles, it was up to the actors on the scene to grasp this potential and turn it into an effective weapon in the fight against state power. In Eastern Europe the actors used this opportunity in a variety of ways. The end in 1956 of the dark (and relatively uniform) days of repression fomented by the Soviet Communist Party leader Joseph Stalin left the way clear for a variety of scenarios. In Poland the Catholic Church operated as the main sociopolitical force by coordinating the forces of resistance. But the Catholic and Protestant churches in Hungary followed the model of submission

Soviet model presented the struggle against religion as dictate of ideology, and, as a result, it applied a strategy to the region aimed at eventually eliminating religion. It would be too simple, however, to reduce the history of relations between religion and politics to a matter of religious persecution alone. In fact, differences among countries of Soviet-led Eastern Europe on the place of religion in society and politics very quickly became apparent—for example, the constitutional prohibition of all religion imposed by the regime in Albania and the "church within socialism" mandated in the German Democratic Republic.

The Church in Communist Eastern Europe

The main function of religion in pre-1989 Eastern Europe was to provide proof of the permanence of historic nations, the existence of pluralistic societies, and, as time to the state that had been initiated by the Habsburg emperors. And while the Orthodox churches in Bulgaria, Romania, and Russia threw themselves into legitimizing state power with theological justifications (which objectively placed them in a compromising position), in Czechoslovakia all the churches, beginning in the 1980s, came down on the side of opposition.

Entering the Post-Communist Era

Pope John Paul II's visit to newly democratic Czechoslovakia in 1990 at the invitation of President Václav Havel was of symbolic value to the church and, indeed, the whole country. Sanctioning by his journey the role played by the Catholic Church in opposing the regime, the pope also endorsed religion as a provider of the ethical values required for the moral regeneration of those societies damaged on the moral level. To some extent, history gained its revenge by ensuring that liberation from communism was celebrated in the Cathedral of St. Vitus in Prague. (The capital is located in Bohemia, a region that previously had turned Catholicism into the very enemy of the nation's historical destiny.) But this event, which blessed the crucial role played by the faithful in resisting the regime, could not conceal the profound secularization of Czech society.

Some churches, such as the Polish and Czech Catholic churches and the Protestant churches in the former East Germany and Transylvania, emerged with prestige from their long confrontation with Soviet projects and practices. This was not the case, however, for the majority of Orthodox churches, such as those in Romania and Bulgaria, whose position vis-à-vis political authorities had been so compromised that they had to seek their own people's forgiveness. For this reason, the Romanian patriarch Theoctist had to resign just after the revolution. Likewise, the Hungarian churches appeared to have generally lost their credibility. Finally, churches that had survived in secret, such as the Uniate Church in Romania and Ukraine, began to revive and inevitably to see signs of hope and revenge in the fall of the regimes that had made martyrs of them.

Regardless of how the churches entered the post-communist era, they were immediately confronted with many challenges from a sociopolitical modernity for which they were ill-prepared. The example of the West aroused fears of rationally disenchanted politics in which the social influence of churches would be lost. In fact, most religious leaders had, and continue to have, difficulty understanding what may turn out to be a provisional choice between, on the one hand, a policy of making churches the center of political life (the choice of several, mainly Protestant, churches) and, on the other hand, direct intervention in the political arena by using the prestige and institutional influence that flow from such intervention.

Analyzing Politics and Religion in Eastern Europe

Analysis of the relationship between politics and religion in Eastern Europe during the communist era relied for a long time on the use of numerous stereotypes that often said much more about the fantasies of those who used them than about the reality they were supposed to describe. The same could be said about the unrealistic image of a uniform and homogeneous "Eastern Europe" and the existence of the "Church of Silence" that was closely associated with it and tended to lend credence to it. Yet, without denying that churches and believers were really persecuted in certain countries, those who made such a categorization, because of its very inclusiveness, could not account for the wide range of different situations among the countries of Eastern Europe. Moreover, a research project carried out in January 1990 by Median in Hungary, Demoskop in Poland, and the Institute of Public Opinion Polls in the Soviet Union, and coordinated by the French CSA Institute, discovered that 90 percent of the Hungarians, 91 percent of the Poles, and 89 percent of the Soviets questioned denied they had ever been victimized because of their religious beliefs.

"Religious revival" eventually joined the original list of stereotypes and was applied to the years just before and after the collapse of communism. This stereotype tried, on the one hand, to explain both the erosion and then the fall of the Soviet system in terms of the force of religion, and, on the other hand, to give some meaning to the process triggered by this fall. It is clear how this stereotype gained credibility: everywhere and at different levels religion seemed likely to provide a privileged means of escape from communism. It did not matter whether this stemmed from, among other things, the religious symbols used by Solidarity and the presence of the church in the developments in Poland, or Augustin Navratil's petition for religious freedom in Czechoslovakia, or the position of Catholic and Protestant believers at the heart of the Charter 77 movement in the same country (a 1977 manifesto, Charter 77 denounced the lack of civil rights in Czechoslovakia), or the role played by Protestant churches in opposing the regime in East Germany or that played by Pastor Tökes in Romania in sparking the revolution.

Yet if religion really had potential as a liberating movement, it was not necessarily based on a renewal of faith; rather, it reflected the specific status granted to religion by the Soviet-type system. By making God the only category that it banned from its own ideology, this system raised God to the status of the only independent category capable of calling the system's own legitimacy into question.

Poland, which is of special importance in this context both because Pope John Paul II was born there and because of his efforts to give it "model" status, countered the false belief that the legitimacy of the country's political system rested on consensus with an equally false belief, like an echo, that the whole of Polish society was united behind its church. When the first false belief disappeared, the second was bound to follow. The return to reality in the form of a pluralized political landscape brought to light an ambiguity that shaped the way in which the system of social resistance operated. By placing its own idea of totality in opposition to that which the state claimed to impose, the church, whether or not it was aware of the fact, was defending relative values. The church represented "real pluralism" as opposed to "real socialism." Various elements of society made symbolic use of the church, its pronouncements, and its values merely as ways of questioning the legitimacy of the regime. But the people who chose to refer to a totality did not necessarily have to belong to it.

In any case, this observation was supported by the participants themselves and particularly by members of the church hierarchy. In fact, the gap between reported membership in the Polish church and respect for its moral standards often has been noted, as much by bishops as by sociologists. Indeed, since the end of the 1970s there have been many instances in Poland in which the church's authority has declined when its views have moved too far away from representing the interests of society in favor of working out its own objectives and priorities, especially on the political front. Thus Poland created the original sociological type of the "practicing nonbeliever" who used religion for purposes that were clearly nonreligious. Today in Poland in the areas of human rights and relations with modernity, the differences between the church, on the one hand, and society, on the other, are becoming sharper. As early as 1991 a survey in Poland revealed that 74 percent of respondents thought the church played too large a role in public life, and this figure

went up to 82 percent in November 1992. Fifty-seven percent thought the church should not participate in politics at all. More than 50 percent reported that priests gave political sermons, and 71 percent were in favor of separating church and state.

In general, then, the social influence of the church in Poland has continued to decline since 1989: 90 percent of Poles expressed satisfaction with its role in 1989, but only 45 percent in 1992. Since then the rate has stabilized at around 50 percent. In the same vein, the success of the former communists in the legislative elections of the fall of 1993 and the historic failure of all the parties claiming to represent Catholicism are viewed as running counter to the Polish church's attempts to perpetuate in a pluralist arena the kind of central control that it had acquired only because of particular circumstances bound up in the very nature of the Soviet-type system. The victory of Aleksander Kwasniewski, a young communist turned social democrat, over Lech Walesa in the presidential elections of the fall of 1995 is in line with this thinking.

Although the use of stereotypical ideas like "Eastern Europe," "Church of Silence," or "religious revival" in writing about Eastern Europe led to a somewhat simplistic interpretation of reality, the introduction of a new stereotype, "the transition toward democracy and the free market," created even more confusion. Promoters of the idea of transition suggested that, with the dissolution of an "abnormal" situation (communism) and the gradual progression toward "normality" measured by Western standards, the conditions for a real "religious explosion" were fulfilled. The participants themselves were expecting it: in 1990, 76 percent of Hungarians believed that democratization would boost religious activity.

By contrast, 57 percent of Poles believed at the same time that recent developments would make no difference or would bring about a decline in religious practice. The case of Poland may appear unusual, and indeed it is, precisely because of the special significance of religion and the church in the long exodus from communism. Moreover, Poles had a vague idea, which became clearer over time, that by abolishing communism as their central point of reference they also were getting rid of the central importance of struggle that they had entrusted to the church.

Above all, the situation in Poland took to an extreme conclusion certain tendencies that were found all over Eastern Europe, at least wherever religion had been used effectively as a means of escape from communism. In the mid-1970s, when reformers had to draw up a platform for attacking the legitimacy of the system without giving the appearance of entering directly into politics proper (access to this field was forbidden by the very nature of Soviet practices), the church was able to join a comprehensive resistance movement based on the fiction that all its protagonists agreed on the content of the movement for human rights. But as soon as the movement was no longer needed, the consensus disappeared with it, together with the ambiguity on which the church's potential for social influence rested.

The result was the ultra-rapid privatization of religion: as early as 1991, 81 percent of Poles thought that it was wrong for the church to get involved in the issue of contraception; 71 percent were against the church's involvement in problems relating to abortion (although the church itself, at the highest level, considers the fight against abortion to be one of its main priorities); and 63 percent rejected its stance on divorce. Moreover, the pluralization now affecting the whole sociopolitical scene in Eastern Europe is finding expression at the very center of the religious scene—and it is, to say the least, a spectacular development. In Poland, where perhaps more than anywhere else Catholicism had sought the image of a "citadel under siege," the splintering of the Catholic camp into different fragments has been brutal, leading, for example, to violent attacks by the church's hierarchy against the weekly Catholic newspaper *Tygodnik Powszechny* and a section of the Catholic intelligentsia.

Poland does not have a monopoly over privatization. Religious practice already was very weak in prewar Czechoslovakia. Even if at the end of the "Velvet Revolution" the churches, and in particular the Catholic Church, enjoyed real prestige, religion once more became a "private matter" in Bohemia. (In April 1990 half a million Czechs had traveled to see the pope during his visit to the country, whereas only fifty thousand turned up to meet the pontiff during his visit in May 1995.) In Hungary fewer than 10 percent of the population attended church.

Debates and Uncertainty

The developments just described—the church's loss of social influence and the privatization of religion—are being aggravated by the debates about the return to the churches of assets confiscated by the communists. In Hungary, where a July 10, 1991, law provided for the return of these assets (with the exception of land), the call for charity and generosity comes from the political sphere, and the declaration of the rights of property ownership comes from the church. In the Czech Republic, the trust accumulated by the church is being lost, just as it is in Hungary, precisely because of this issue of returning the church's assets.

One must not, however, be misled by a certain amount of turmoil. The growing number of new religious movements, the increase in popularity of certain groups (especially the Pentecostalists), and even upsets in the major long-established churches only show that it is difficult to find landmarks and to redefine individual and collective identities in the context of a violent transformation of scenarios from which all references to communism have been expunged.

Indeed, the withdrawal from communism has led to uncertainty and to the reconstruction of identities in all countries. In a very fluid situation, where most of the landmarks have disappeared, the temptation is strong to use religion to establish the membership of an organization and to fix a firm identity, as is the temptation to use this approach in legitimizing or managing a political clientele. Clearly, in Hungary, Poland, and Slovakia—and in Russia and in a particularly dramatic way in the former Yugoslavia—the potential to mobilize religion in the cause of nationalism has been used for political ends.

Religion as a privileged means of seeking identity also can be used as an instrument for legitimizing the nation-state with all the risks that such a function entails. Concern about Catholicism's potential for nationalist mobilization in Poland is relevant to the situations found elsewhere in Eastern Europe and the Balkans, such as in Slovakia and Croatia. As for the Orthodox churches, whether through fear, passivity, or submissiveness, they have retreated into a conservatism and a ritualism that make it difficult to predict their attitude at a time of political change tending toward democratization. Even if the Orthodox hierarchy has avoided sliding toward anti-Semitism, there still is a risk in Romania and Bulgaria that religion will be exploited by political forces that adopt a program of excluding minorities and that the churches themselves will go one better than the nationalists in order to efface the memory of their compromises with the old order. In fact, in this part of Europe, where identification with a single state was the exception rather than the rule, religion can function as a means of marking out the nation, as happened during the interwar period, with the state deriving the legitimizing stereotypes it needs from religion.

The religious processions held in Slovakia to celebrate the end of the communist era undoubtedly showed some signs of taking over an evolution that the vast majority of people had undergone. Thus the aim of such processions was to confirm a personal and collective victory over an enemy against whom the people had not really fought for most of the time. Rather, participants in the processions were trying to take their revenge on historical events, to tame a past they had rewritten, and to overcome the frustration that had built up. Participation in the processions also allowed people to express an identity—an identity that their previous experience had supposedly sought to weaken—by using religion, the privileged guardian of the foundational myths of identity, to forge links with past traditions that the communist regime had allegedly destroyed. These processions also helped to reappropriate "national space" by making the geography of everyday life sacred. A final effect of these processions was the opportunity they presented Slovaks to affirm explicitly a Slovakian identity and to open up the possibility, which was rich in potential ways to achieve political goals, of formulating a view about the Czechs and, therefore, about the union of the two peoples within the same political entity—or about their separation.

The reevaluation of the importance of Cardinal József Mindszenty, the cardinal primate of Hungary who had staunchly opposed the communist regime there, shares this logic. The solemn transfer of his remains to Esztergom in May 1991 allowed the church to take on the appearance of a victim of the old order. Thus the history of the relationship between church and state in Hungary has been rewritten—in the 1970s and 1980s historians and commentators had deliberately omitted all reference to Mindszenty. Now it is Cardinal Lekai, Mindszenty's successor as head of the church in Hungary and the person who masterminded "one-step-at-time" politics, who is going through the trap door. The idea is to endow the church with a "resistance identity," of which political parties with an interest in maintaining a link to religion will be able to avail themselves.

In Poland the stereotypical idea that "Polish equals Catholic" has been reworked in ways that have turned this very effective tool for delegitimizing the communist system into an instrument for disqualifying political opponents.

Religion can act as an indicator of a crisis of identity and as a means of handling the restructuring of identities brought about by the crisis, because it is, first and foremost, an indicator of the state of advancement of a process aimed at defining a link with the change under way. (It often does this by referring to a tradition that is peculiar in the sense of having to be continually invented at the same time as it is supposed to be undergoing protection.)

Here the position of religion is neutral. This means that any religious contents can be used equally well as a way of encouraging change (be it social, political, or other), taming it, or denying it. Such an approach entails many ambiguities: in Poland the church was punished soundly in the 1993 legislative elections, in the 1995 presidential elections, and during the 1997 referendum on the new constitution because of its desperate attempts in a pluralist situation to perpetuate a form of central control that it had acquired in the first place as a result of communism. From this point of view, it is not surprising that from 1989 to 1993 public debate in Poland centered on questions such as the legal status of the church, the constitutional nature of the state, abortion, the teaching of the catechism in schools, and divorce.

All these issues allowed Polish society to formalize its relations with pluralism, to establish the divisions necessary for forming (or beginning to form) a public space that the disappearance of communism—as a system and above all as an apparatus of legitimization in the last instance—had stripped of all its landmarks. The links with religion remain as they were before: a privileged indicator of the fact that a relation with pluralism has been established. But whereas the withdrawal from communism took place *with* the church (and, to a certain extent, thanks to it), the context has now changed, and democracy is advancing *against* the church.

Thus, in 2002, in the large Polish cities, fewer than 30 percent of young people had a religious practice. Sixty percent claim to be believers as compared with 90 percent at the end of the 1980s. Seventy percent of girls and 66 percent of boys accept the use of contraception (as compared with 35 percent and 46 percent in 1988). More than 60 percent consider it normal to have sexual relations before marriage. But this trend is part of a larger trend in which society is distancing itself from the public sphere, an estrangement in which the church is a victim as are all other authorities. The church experiences this with bitterness, stigmatizing what it perceives as a lack of gratitude.

The death of John Paul II, the "greatest of all Poles," in the spring of 2005 did indeed leave the nation feeling as an orphan. But most of all, it made it necessary, once again, to think of the Polish nation as "normal," to mourn the supposed Polish "exception," already considerably unsettled by

Polish integration into the European Union. The coming into power that same year of the traditional right, in the context of a very low electoral participation, does indeed portray the influential power of organizations such as Radio Marya and their impact on populist discourse. But it also testifies to the considerable increase of the society's disarray and the persistent difficulty of Polish Catholicism to play a role in the politics of modernity.

The political instrumentation of religion, in the context of the individualization and Europeanization of behavior, is not specific to Poland. The whole region has been marked by an extreme diversification of the forms of social investment in what pertains to religion. In its Romanian version, for instance, appropriation of what is religious may lead as much to an updating of the national orthodoxy paradigm as to the attempt to redefine believing, liberated from its national enclosure and projected onto a European horizon. In fact, wherever the social and political order emerging from communism is being called into question, elements pertaining to the religious sphere can be used to bring together the individual and collective logics constantly circulating among different spaces—local, national, European, worldwide, and global.

See also *Catholicism, Roman; Havel, Václav; Hungary; Poland; Russia; Yugoslavia.*

Patrick Michel

BIBLIOGRAPHY

Michel, Patrick. *Politics and Religion in Eastern Europe.* Cambridge: Polity Press, 1991.
———. *Les religions à l'Est.* Paris: Cerf, 1992.
———. *Politique et religion: La grande mutation.* Paris: Albin-Michel, 1994.
———. "Religion and Democracy in Central Eastern Europe." In *Religion in Contemporary Europe,* edited by John Fulton and Peter Gee. New York: Gellen Press, 1994.
———, ed. *Europe centrale, la mélancolie du réel.* Paris: Autrement, 2004.
Ramet, Pedro, ed. *Catholicism and Politics in Communist Societies.* Durham, N.C.: Duke University Press, 1990.
Swatos, William. *Politics and Religion in Central and Eastern Europe: Traditions and Transitions.* Westport, Conn.: Praeger, 1994.

Europe, Western

Western Europe encompasses the countries of the European Union post-May 2004, together with Croatia, Norway, and Switzerland. Many of the countries that joined the European Union had been under Soviet domination from 1945 to 1989 (that is, the Baltic States, Poland, Hungary, the Czech Republic, Slovakia, and Slovenia). "Western," therefore, is used in the following sense: it includes those parts of Europe that found themselves within Western, not Eastern or Orthodox, Christianity at the time of the schism between Rome and Byzantium, a division that dates from the middle of the eleventh century. The particular arrangements of church and state that emerged in the West as a result of this schism facilitated a whole succession of reforming movements—notably, the Renaissance, the Reformation, the scientific revolution, and the Enlightenment. These are shared experiences that have colored the whole evolution of religious life in the West. None of these movements made a similar impact on the Orthodox world.

In contrast, the relatively recent division between communist and noncommunist Europe becomes almost an aside to the central account, a matter of generations, not a millennium. The terms *eastern* and *central* Europe have significance in this respect, for the countries of eastern Europe (Bulgaria, Romania, and most of European Russia) belong to the Orthodox tradition, whereas the central European countries (Poland, the Czech Republic, Slovakia, Hungary, and what was East Germany) developed within Western Catholicism. The position of the Baltic states is equally revealing. Roman Catholic Lithuania and Poland are closely linked historically. In contrast, Estonia and Latvia belong essentially to northern (Lutheran) Europe.

Such distinctions have significance with regard to the future of Europe and the European Union. The former communist countries that belonged—and continue to belong—to Western instead of Orthodox Christianity have found it easier to realize their political and economic aspirations. Despite their real economic difficulties, their aim is to reestablish Western traditions. They are not learning something totally new. The vicissitudes in the Balkans in the early 1990s exemplify the same point. The postwar entity known as Yugoslavia combined within one country not only contrasting Christian traditions but a sizable Muslim presence as well. For a relatively short space of time the country held together under the personal authority of Marshal Josip Broz Tito. As that authority—and the creed that underpinned it—collapsed, Yugoslavia's pseudo-unity, not surprisingly, began to fall apart. Ethnic nationalisms, bolstered by religious differences, interacted with a multiplicity of factors (linguistic,

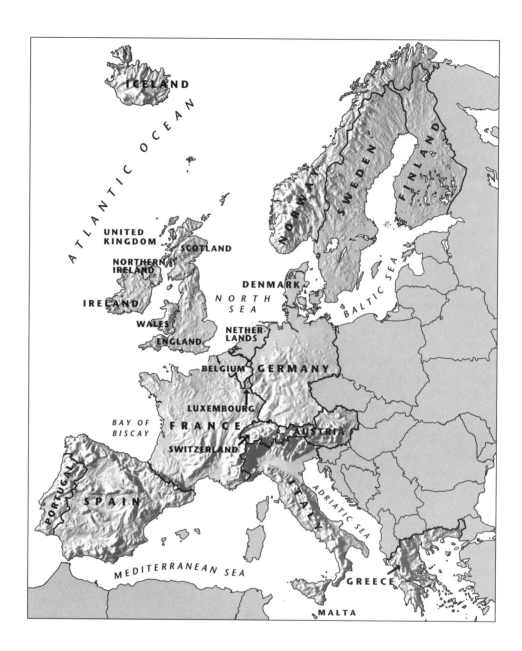

historical, and economic) to create an explosive situation. At the same time, the presence of sizable ethnic minorities within the borders of each state rendered the dissolution of the country as problematic as its retention. Long-term stability remains elusive.

Facts and Figures: Europe's Religious Profile

Europe's religious profile can be considered from several points of view. There is, first, a historical perspective that stresses the formative factors or themes that come together in the creation and re-creation of the unity that is called Europe: Judeo-Christian monotheism, Greek rationalism, and Roman organization. These factors shift and evolve over time, but their combinations can be seen forming and reforming a way of life that have come to be recognized as European. The significance of the religious strand within such combinations is self-evident. It is equally important, however, to grasp the historical complexity of European identity. One way of doing this lies in identifying the seven interlocking and overlapping blocs that exist within the European whole: the western islands, western (Atlantic) Europe, the Rhinelands, the Nordic/Baltic countries, the Mediterranean group, the former Ottoman territories, and the Slavic countries. Not all of these are covered here, but the notion of building blocs underlines a crucial aspect of modern as well as historical Europe—its diversity. The religious factor is one dimension of this diversity.

One point in particular, however, requires firm underlining: the shared religious heritage of western Europe as one of the crucial factors in the continent's development—and, possibly, in its future—and the influence of this heritage on a whole range of cultural values. Other, different sources reinforce this conclusion. One of these, the European Values System Study Group (EVSSG), provides a principal source of information for this article. Using careful sampling techniques, the EVSSG aims at an accurate mapping of social and moral values across Europe. It has generated considerable data and will continue to do so.

Two underlying themes run through the EVSSG study. The first concerns the substance of contemporary European values and asks, in particular, to what degree they are homogeneous; the second takes a more dynamic approach, asking to what extent such values are changing. Both themes involve, inevitably, a religious element. The first, for example, leads quickly to questions about the origin of shared value systems. If values in western Europe are shared (and it seems that many of them are), how had any such joint cultural experience been created? As the European values study indicates, the answer lies in deep-rooted cultural experiences that derive from pervasive social influences that have been part of western European culture for generations, if not centuries. A shared religious heritage is one such influence.

Many of these findings are unproblematic and confirm the historical perspective already outlined. As soon as the idea of value change is introduced, however, the situation becomes more contentious. A series of unavoidable questions immediately present themselves. Is the primacy given to the role of religion in the creation of values still appropriate? Has this role not been undermined by the process known as secularization? Can it be maintained that religion remains a central element of the western European value system? The influence of religion is becoming increasingly peripheral within contemporary European society. Or is it? These are the central questions facing the analyst of religious life in western Europe. The principal findings of the 1981, 1990, and 1999–2000 EVSSG surveys provide a starting point for social scientific understanding in this field.

There are, broadly speaking, five religious indicators within the EVSSG data: denominational allegiance, reported church attendance, attitudes toward the church, indicators of religious belief, and some measurement of subjective religious disposition. Two types of variables, however, emerge with respect to these multiple indicators: on the one hand, those concerned with feelings, experience, and the more numinous religious beliefs; and on the other, those that measure religious orthodoxy, ritual participation, and institutional attachment. The latter display an undeniable degree of secularization throughout western Europe, while the former demonstrate considerable persistence in some aspects of Europe's religious life. In particular, some form of religious disposition and an awareness of the moral concepts of Christianity continue to be widespread among large numbers of Europeans, even among those for whom the institution of the church has ceased to resonate.

It may, therefore, be more accurate to suggest that western Europeans remain, by and large, unchurched populations instead of simply secular. A marked falling-off in religious attendance (especially in the Protestant North) has not resulted, yet, in a parallel abdication of religion as such. (Over 70 percent of Europeans, for example, still consider themselves religious, though not always in orthodox terms.) In short, many Europeans have ceased to belong to their religious institutions in any meaningful sense, but they have not abandoned, so far, many of their deep-seated religious aspirations.

This relatively widespread—although fluctuating—characteristic of believing without belonging within European religion in the twenty-first century should not merely be assumed; it must be examined, probed, and questioned. A second point illustrates this need for questioning. It introduces two contrasting situations in which believing without belonging is not always the norm. In parts of eastern and central Europe prior to 1989, the two variables were reversed, for the nonbeliever consciously used church attendance as one way of expressing disapproval of an unpopular regime. The second, very different, contrast comes from the United States. Here religious attendance appears to maintain itself at levels far higher than those that prevail in most of Europe. About 40 percent of the American population report that they both believe and belong (in the sense that they claim to practice on a regular basis). Once again the situation should not be taken for granted. It must be examined, sociologically as well as theologically.

Returning to western Europe, there is further evidence of consistency in the shapes or profiles of religiosity that are relevant across a wide variety of European countries. One clear illustration of such profiling can be found in patterns of religious belief. Levels of belief vary from country to country, but irrespective of level of belief, the rank order among different indicators of belief is almost identical across Europe. The one exception to a consistent pattern, paradoxically, is the higher ranking given by English-speaking countries to heaven than to life after death. This kind of consistency is persuasive, the more so in that it is not easily predictable.

Correlations between different aspects of religion and socioeconomic variables confirm the existence of socioreligious patterning across national boundaries. Throughout western Europe, religious factors correlate—to varying degrees—with occupation, gender, and age (social class is more problematic). The correlation with age is particularly striking, raising the question of the future shape of European religion. The EVSSG findings (particularly the 1990 study) seem to indicate that western Europeans may be experiencing a permanent generational shift with respect to religious behavior. Markedly lower church attendance, institutional attachment, and adherence to traditional beliefs are found in younger compared with older respondents, a finding reinforced by other data. Such changes are difficult to explain simply by life-cycle differences. If this is the case, the future shape of European religion may be very different. A countertrend emerged, however, in the 1999–2000 study: the predilection of younger people for innovative forms of religious belief, notably the notion of a "God in me" and some sort of conviction about life after death. Neither change represents a return to orthodox Christianity or denotes unmitigated secularization.

The EVSSG data—like all survey data—reveal some things and fail to reveal others. There is no way of grasping, for example, why a particular country should be similar to or different from its neighbors. Apparently similar statistical profiles can mask profound cultural differences. A second difficulty concerns the presence of religious minorities. The EVSSG sample sizes for each country are too small to give any meaningful data about such communities. It would be grossly misleading, however, to present an image of Europe at the beginning of the twentieth-first century without any reference to these increasingly important sections of the European population.

Religious Minorities

The first of these, the Jews, has been present in Europe for centuries. It was a presence, moreover, that has been inextricably bound up with the tragedies of recent European history. Nor can it be said that anti-Semitism is a thing of the past. It continues to surface from time to time right across Europe, itself an accurate indicator of wider insecurities. Estimations of numbers are always difficult, but there are, currently, about one million Jews in western Europe, the largest communities being the French (500,000 to 600,000) and the British (300,000). French Judaism has been transformed in the postwar period by the immigration of considerable numbers of Sephardim from North Africa. The causes of this immigration are multiple but include the Suez crisis of 1956 (when Britain and France supported Israel's attack on Egypt), the withdrawal of France from its former colonies in the Maghrib, and the repercussions of the Arab-Israeli conflict, especially in Muslim countries. Europe's religious life is in no way self-contained.

Former colonial connections also account for other non-Christian immigrations into Europe. The Islamic communities are the most significant in this respect, although a considerable number of Sikhs and Hindus have found a home in Britain. Followers of Islam are, however, by far the largest non-Judeo-Christian population in Europe. Conservative estimates suggest a figure of twelve million; other commentators put this as higher still. Such figures, however, depend largely on accurate information about immigration, information that is not easy to come by. Bearing this in mind, Muslims likely make up approximately 5 percent of the West European population. More specifically, the colonial links between France and North Africa account for the sizable French Muslim community (4.5 million). Britain's equivalent comes from the Indian subcontinent (1.6 million). Germany has absorbed large numbers of migrant workers from the fringes of southeastern Europe and from Turkey in particular. The fate of these migrants in the face of growing numbers of ethnic Germans from the former Soviet bloc looking for work within the new Germany continues to cause tension.

Whatever the outcome of this particular situation, however, one fact remains clear: the Islamic presence in Europe is here to stay. It follows that Europeans can no longer distance themselves from the debates of the Muslim world. Whether they like it or not, the issues are present on their own doorstep. Admitting that this is the case is not easy for many Europeans, for the Islamic factor undoubtedly challenges the assumptions of European life, both past and present. Peaceful coexistence between Islam and Judeo-

Christian Europe cannot—and never could be—taken for granted. Nor can Muslims accept unequivocally the live-and-let-live religious attitudes assumed by the majority of contemporary Europeans. This remains the problem at the heart of the controversies surrounding the publication of Salman Rushdie's book *The Satanic Verses* in 1988 and the disputes about wearing the Muslim veil in French schools that took place from 1989 onward. The even more violent murders of Pim Fortuyn (2002) and Theo van Gogh (2004) in the Netherlands, together with the widespread unrest following the publication of what have become known as the "Danish cartoons" in 2005, indicate the continuing intractability of the underlying issues.

One further source of diversity should also be pointed out: the controversial presence of new religious movements in many European societies, most notably in France. New religious movements attract considerable media attention, which is often negative in tone. The numbers involved are, however, tiny. Be that as it may, such movements have inadvertently become barometers of the changes taking place in contemporary society, revealing—among other things—the limits of western European understanding concerning unconventional forms of religious life. This perspective can, moreover, be used to examine one of the most urgent questions facing Europe at the present time: the need to create and to sustain a truly tolerant and pluralist society, both in Europe as a whole and in its constituent nations. This society needs to go well beyond an individualized live-and-let-live philosophy and accommodate the person (of whatever faith) who takes religion seriously. If a country fails in its tolerance of new religious movements, it is unlikely, or at least much less likely, to succeed with respect to other, more significant (numerically speaking) religious minorities.

Church and State

A broad-brush profile of religion in western Europe provides the background for a more detailed discussion of church and state relationships. It is helpful to set these within the following framework, taken from David Martin's seminal work on the process of secularization in the Western world, *A General Theory of Secularization*. Following Martin, Europe is a unity by virtue of having possessed one Caesar and one God (hence the commonalities of faith and culture). It is a diversity by the existence of nations. The patterns of European religion derive from the tensions and partnerships between religion and the search for national integrity and identity. These tensions and partnerships are ongoing processes that have dominated four centuries of European history and have resulted in a bewildering variety of church-state relationships within the continent as a whole.

The first split within Christendom concerned the divergence of Catholic and Orthodox Europe in the eleventh century. The subsequent divisions of the West into areas or nations that are primarily Catholic or Protestant (or combinations of the two) are inseparable historically from the emergence of the nation-state as the dominant form of Europe's political life. The processes by which such division occurred are highly complex, involving economic, social, and political issues as well as religious ones. Which of these led to the others and how the whole thing was set in motion in the first place is the subject of an ongoing debate among historians, themselves of different persuasions. What remains indisputable, however, is an unprecedented upheaval in the ordering of Christian society in the sixteenth century, an upheaval that included the emergence of separate political entities, or nation-states, some of which expressed their independence from papal interference in the form of a state church. These state churches were increasingly underpinned not only by Protestant understandings of theology but also by corresponding changes in the ecclesiastical order.

Part of the ambiguity regarding the whole historical process lies in the understanding of the term *Reformation*. Does this imply innovation and the breaking of new ground? Or does it imply a return to and rediscovery of primitive excellence? Were those who endorsed the theological changes taking place at this time looking primarily for radical change or for conservative independence? Motives were bound to be mixed. The more conservative interpretation, however, appealed to those political rulers who were anxious to establish independence from external authority but who kept a careful eye on stability within. Both were possible within the Lutheran concept of a "godly prince." Sometimes the prince had jurisdiction over a whole kingdom or kingdoms. Such was the case in Scandinavia, where Lutheranism became embodied in the state churches of northern Europe. Elsewhere the process was far more local and concerned relatively small patches of land. Germany exemplifies the latter process, which led to patterns that are not only extant but also highly influential some four hundred years later.

The Reformation took different forms in different places. In addition to Lutheranism, some Europeans—notably the

Swiss, the Dutch, the Scots, some Germans, some Hungarians and Czechs, and a small but significant minority of French people—were attracted first by the Swiss reformer Ulrich Zwingli (1484–1531), and then by John Calvin (1509–1564), toward a more rigorous version of Protestantism. Calvinism was both more radical and more restrained—radical in the sense of a new kind of theology based on the doctrines of predestination and redemption but restrained with regard to its stringent moral codes. The effect of this particular combination on the subsequent economic development of Europe has provided inexhaustible material for an ongoing debate among historians and sociologists alike.

Broadly speaking, western Europe divided itself into a Catholic south (France, Italy, Portugal, and Spain, and also including Belgium and Ireland) and a Protestant north (Scandinavia and Scotland), with a range of mixed countries in between (England, Germany, the Netherlands, Northern Ireland, and Wales). Central Europe exemplifies similar categories, although the geography is more complicated. Croatia, Lithuania, Poland, Slovakia, and Slovenia are firmly Catholic; Estonia and Latvia are Lutheran and relate closely to their Scandinavian neighbors (a commonality strongly reemphasized as the Baltic republics regained their political independence); the Czech Republic and Hungary are more mixed (primarily Catholic but with significant Protestant minorities). In other words, boundaries gradually emerged all over Europe dividing one nation from another, one region from another, and one kind of Christianity from another. Boundaries, moreover, imply dominance as well as difference. Majorities and minorities were, and still are, created as a result of the location of a political boundary line. One of the most arbitrary in recent years has been the line that divides Northern Ireland from the Irish Republic. The consequences of this division compound instead of resolve the Irish question.

The confessional map of western Europe emerged in the early modern period and has remained relatively stable ever since. It would be a mistake, however, to assume that church-state arrangements necessarily follow suit. What evolves in the latter respect is a bewildering variety of arrangements that are dictated for the most part by particular historical circumstances and that change over time as political necessity requires or as economic or social shifts suggest. The following summary moves from north to south and covers the countries of the European Union prior to 2004, together with

Norway and Switzerland. The countries of central Europe are harder to analyze, given that their church-state relationships are part of newly established relationships in nations where independence remains a relative novelty. The point to recognize in all of them, however, is the significance of church-state relationships in an emergent democratic order. Freedom of belief and conscience is a universal aspiration, but how this works in practice, particularly for smaller, less recognized denominations, is much more problematic. The solutions are not self-evident, and neither are the attitudes of these various churches toward the European Union itself.

The Nordic countries (Denmark, Finland, Iceland, Norway, and Sweden) are some of the easiest to deal with from a church-state perspective. Here are the Lutheran state churches of northern Europe, which have high rates of membership although practice is universally low. Low also is the acceptance of orthodox Christian beliefs. However, in Sweden, a form of disestablishment has already been effected. In 2000 the Swedish church became a "free folk church." A state church was no longer thought appropriate in an increasingly pluralist society. Belgium and the Netherlands exemplify a pillarized society, that is, a society in which the vertical divisions between Catholic, Protestant, and secular provided until relatively recently the parameters for daily living (traditionally from the cradle to the grave). The particular nature of the pillars varies in the two countries, themselves different from a confessional point of view. In both, however, church and state are technically separate, although in neither case is the separation rigorous. It should be seen as a mutual independence, implying at the same time a considerable degree of mutual respect.

The United Kingdom is a complex case, embodying as it does four distinct nations, each with its own religious history and constitutional arrangements. England has an established church (which is Anglican) and Scotland a national church (which is Calvinist). Wales has neither, and its important Nonconformist congregations are crosscut by linguistic differences. Northern Ireland exemplifies the most problematic entity in the European Union, given its divisive religious history, with a definitive resolution still awaited. The Irish Republic, in contrast, is technically a secular state, although the preamble to its constitution is heavily Catholic and the practice of Catholicism remains unusually high compared with the European norm.

The German case is complicated by the reunification of the country after 1989. The Catholic-Protestant bi-confessionality of the country remains nonetheless the most significant feature of Germany's religious life, despite the growing presence of those with no religious allegiance (partly but not wholly explained by the population from the former East Germany) and of a sizable Muslim community. With regard to categories, Germany holds a middle position between state church and the separation of church and state. The Weimar Constitution (1919) ensured a constitutionally secured form of cooperation between church and state, structured around three principles: neutrality, tolerance, and parity. Germany continues to operate a church tax system. Despite the leakage of membership in the postwar period, especially among Protestants, the numbers who contribute through this system to the churches' budgets remain large—so, too, are the budgets themselves. Austria maintains an intermediate position between separation and state church. It is different from Germany, however, in that the population is overwhelmingly Catholic, at least in nominal allegiance.

France is a hybrid case in a different way. It is culturally part of Catholic Europe but far more like the Protestant north with regard to religious practice or patterns of belief. It is, moreover, the country of western Europe that embodies the strictest form of separation between church and state. The French state is conceived as a neutral space, privileging no religion in particular and effecting this policy by excluding the discussion of religion from all state institutions, including the school system. The incapacity of the French to accommodate the demands of young Muslim girls who wish to wear their *foulard* (or veil) in school exemplifies the limitations of this system in a rapidly changing Europe. Switzerland is entirely different. Not only is it made up of twenty-six independent cantons, but each of these also has its separate arrangements regarding church and state. Confessional (and linguistic) boundaries crosscut cantonal ones, resulting in a highly complex but ultimately stable set of checks and balances.

Italy, Spain, and Portugal remain solidly Catholic, at least in culture. The presence of the papacy within Italy influences the evolution of Catholicism within the peninsula, even though the Italian state came into being in 1870 at the expense of the temporal power of the pope. Relationships have eased since then, giving the Catholic Church a privileged position in Italian society, followed by a large number of denominations recognized by the state (including the Waldensians, an early Protestant community). A third group, which includes Muslims and Jehovah's Witnesses—more numerous than almost all the groups in the second category—are excluded from significant privileges. Spain exemplifies a different history, in which the re-creation of democracy is relatively recent. Technically speaking, there is no state church in Spain. In effect, however, the Catholic Church is privileged simply by its dominance in terms of numbers. Regional autonomy remains a life issue in Spain—it is not without relevance for the status of the churches. Portugal is in many ways similar to Spain, exemplifying once again a halfway stage between theoretical equality before the law and a certain degree of privilege for the dominant religion. The concordat, or legally privileged, status of the Catholic Church, for example, still exists in Portugal, despite the constitutional changes of the 1970s.

Greece is the only Orthodox country of western Europe. (Greece became part of the European Union for political reasons.) In modern Greece, Orthodoxy is almost identical with Greek identity; it is the official religion of the Greek state. Observance of the major festivals and the rites of passage is almost universal. The controversies surrounding the mention of religion on identity cards at the turn of the millennium provided, however, a lens through which the changing nature of Greek society and its relationship both to Orthodoxy and to the European Union could be seen.

Beneath the surface lie layers of legal complexity concerning the financial arrangements of different churches; differential access to both education systems and the mass media; questions about divorce, abortion, and family life; and the legal protection of both religious communities and religious minorities. From a legal point of view, an interesting aspect to arise in recent years has been the recourse to European, as opposed to national, law on the part of some religious minorities. Crosscutting sociological themes are different. Among them can be found the patterns of secularization in different parts of Europe (including the degree of conflict that might be embedded therein) and the likelihood or not that religion will be caught up in the destructive—instead of constructive—aspects of national identity.

Confessional Parties

Church-state relationships provide the stage set within which particular histories unfold. Like all stage sets, such relationships affect what is going on and how it is presented. Particular forms of church-state relationships permit certain actions and prevent others. Only when the strain becomes intolerable do the relationships themselves alter, for example, in the dramatic break between church and state in France in 1905 or in the reestablishment of the democratic process in Spain after the death of the dictator Francisco Franco.

The actors in such histories are many and varied. They are both collective (such as churches, religious organizations, political parties, and pressure groups) and individual (political and religious leaders and, in some cases, their followers as well). One collectivity with particular resonance in Europe is the confessional (usually Catholic) political party. Christian democracy can be understood within this context. It belongs to a particular, and probably passing, period in the history of western Europe.

The antecedents of Christian democracy go back to the nineteenth century as individual Catholics looked for ways in which to reconcile their faith to a changing world. Such initiatives were, however, heavily outweighed by the institutional—and especially Roman—dislike of democracy, whether in politics or in theology. The natural home for Catholicism remained the authoritarian political party until the collapse of fascism and National Socialism destroyed that possibility forever. It was, therefore, in the period immediately following World War II that Christian democracy proved the effective alternative for Catholics in large parts of western Europe. Despite a mixture of ideas at the outset, these Christian Democratic parties soon became parties of the moderate right. This was particularly true in Germany and Italy. In France the picture was more confused with the presence of a right-wing Gaullist Party, to which many Catholics were attracted.

Christian democracy varies from country to country. Nonetheless, common features appear in its political philosophy, many elements of which derive from a central emphasis on personalism, an approach that sees society as composed of persons, not individuals. The person is a fundamentally social being with a significant place in different types of community, for example, neighborhood, church, family, or nation. Individualism, in contrast, is the primary emphasis within liberalism—a juxtaposition that leads Christian Democrats to be critical of the excesses of capitalism. Or to put the same point more positively, Christian democracy incorporates an emphasis on welfare. However, an inherent tension exists in the politicization of welfare as a Christian Democratic philosophy in that it collides with the traditional Catholic emphasis on charity—an essentially apolitical theme. Be that as it may, the Catholic origins of Christian democracy underline its principal contrast with social democracy. The latter also emphasizes welfare within its political programs but without the formative influences of Christian teaching. Social Democrats (parties of the left) are, more often than not, rigorously secular in their outlook.

Christian democracy became for a time a significant political actor in many European countries (Austria, Belgium, France, Germany, Italy, and the Netherlands). It is important, however, to recognize its international dimensions. Christian democracy was an essentially European phenomenon, giving considerable impetus to the idea of a European Community. It is not entirely a coincidence that the treaty that brought the community into being was the Treaty of Rome, for its architects were profoundly influenced by their religious as well as political backgrounds. The implications of the treaty's title provide, moreover, one explanation for why at least some of the non-Catholic countries of Europe remain ambivalent toward the idea of a European Union and not least to the notion of an external power that may threaten the sovereignty of individual nations.

Christian democracy is certainly less influential than it was. Why this should be so is not easy to discern, although one possibility must lie in the growing indifference of Europeans to their churches and to the centrality of Christian teaching, if not to softer versions of the spiritual. Such an evolution was bound to affect parties claiming a confessional instead of a class constituency. It is not the whole story, however, for one of the most dramatic collapses of all Christian Democratic parties occurred in Italy, where the conventional indicators of religion remain relatively high. Here Christian democracy seems to have imploded partly through exhaustion (and the inevitable corruption that corrodes a party too long in power), as well as through the even more spectacular collapse of its alter ego, the Italian Communist Party. Without the potential opposition of the latter, the checks and balances within the Italian Christian Democratic Party gave way, leading to a splintering of interests among many different groups.

It is important not to jump to conclusions about the future. The partial eclipse of the confessional party does not mean the eradication of religion as a significant influence in the political life of western Europe (or elsewhere). Hence the significance of José Casanova's analyses of public religion in the modern world, even in a relatively secular continent such as Europe. European churches of all kinds, despite the history of some of them as state churches, are increasingly operating as voluntary organizations—organizations that attract appreciable numbers of people and that become significant actors in the political sphere, the more so as the comprehensive nature of the European welfare state increasingly comes under strain. At the level of civil society (as opposed to the nation-state), such churches are, and will remain, important contributors to the political life of Europe. As Casanova suggests, a healthy political democracy would be infinitely poorer without them, for they are effective—some would say the most effective—builders of social capital in societies that at times show signs of fragmentation.

Europe and Ecumenism

If the emergence of the nation-state, and the role of the religious factor within this process, has dominated European history since the early modern period, the possibility that the events of more recent decades might indicate the beginnings of a reversal in that process requires serious consideration. In 1945 Europe had come close to self-destruction for the second time in a century. The idea of European unity was barely conceivable as individual nations struggled to come to terms with what had happened and to rebuild their devastated societies. Surprisingly quickly, however, the seeds of a European Community began to generate in the form of the Coal and Steel Agreements of the 1950s. These European treaties embodied the principle that the weapons of war should themselves be subject to supranational if not international control. Since then Europe has moved inexorably, if not very steadily, toward a greater common identity.

Meanwhile, the Christian churches have made significant progress toward greater unity, for example, in the agreements between the Anglicans and the Lutherans in Germany (the Meissen Agreement of 1991), in the Nordic countries (the Porvoo Agreement of 1996), and in the ongoing conversations between Anglicans and Roman Catholics. The building of a greater European identity and the growth of ecumenical endeavor arguably are part and parcel of the same process. There is, once again, a greater (if by no means unanimous) emphasis on what Europe has in common instead of its differences. That some nations and churches find this process easier than others is part of the complexity of European religiosity. Britain, Denmark, and Greece are particularly interesting in this respect. Each of these countries is ambivalent toward the European Union. In all their hesitations, the religious factor as an exemplar of particularity plays a significant role.

Europe remains, however, a rapidly changing place. From a religious point of view, one of the most significant evolutions of the late twentieth century was the increasing representation of faiths other than Christianity. Analytical concepts will have to evolve accordingly. Europe's religion—essentially the legacy of Christendom—is giving way to the "religions of Europe." Europe has become a continent that houses a significant representation of Muslims, Sikhs, Hindus, and Buddhists in addition to the Jewish communities that have played such a crucial role in Europe's recent history. It is paradoxical that, at the moment when Europe and, to some extent, the Christian churches of the continent are attempting to draw themselves back together again, new forms of demographic and religious diversity are appearing. The tension between unity and diversity re-presents itself once again, although in forms that are peculiar to late modern, not early modern, society.

At the start of the twenty-first century, the tensions embedded in this process have become apparent in two interrelated questions. The first concerns the heated debates surrounding the mention of religion (and more specifically Christianity) in the preamble to the ill-fated European Constitution (signed in 2004). The fact that the debates took place at all reveals the continuing significance of religion in the minds of many European individuals and in at least some European nations. The fact that the solution that emerged was more favorable to a secular interpretation of Europe than a Christian one is indicative of the predominance of secular thinking in the political sphere. The fact, finally, that no one thought to clarify the nature of a preamble and the significance of a reference to religion within it is indicative of continuing confusion about religion in twenty-first century Europe. Paradoxically, one motive for clarification in this respect can be found in the second issue: the debates surrounding the possible accession of Turkey to the European Union. The religious factor is unavoidable in this discussion. If Turkey is rejected on the grounds of its Muslim identity, what does that say about Europe? An awareness that Turkey is a strictly secular state (modeled on France) has not resolved the issue. Initially tacit references to the religious culture of Turkey have become increasingly explicit. The question disturbs both Christian and secular currents in Europe. The outcome is far from clear.

See also *Christian democracy; Islam in Europe; Secularization; State Churches.* See also individual countries, religions and groups, and denominations.

Grace Davie

BIBLIOGRAPHY

Barker, David, Loek Halman, and Astrid Vloet. *The European Values Study, 1981–1990: Summary Report.* London: Gordon Cook Foundation, 1992.

Beckford, James. *Cult Controversies.* London: Tavistock Publications, 1985.

Casanova, José. *Public Religions in the Modern World.* Chicago: University of Chicago Press, 1994.

Cesari, Jocelyne, and Sean McLoughlin, eds. *European Muslims and the Secular State.* London: Ashgate, 2005.

Davie, Grace. *Religion in Modern Europe: A Memory Mutates.* Oxford: Oxford University Press, 2000.

Davie, Grace, and Danièle Hervieu-Léger, eds. *Identités religieuses en Europe.* Paris: La Découverte, 1996.

Halman, Loek, ed. *Atlas of European Values.* Boston: Brill, 2005.

Hanley, David, ed. *Christian Democracy in Europe: A Comparative Perspective.* London: Pinter Publishers, 1994.

Kalyvas, Stathis. *The Rise of Christian Democracy in Europe.* Ithaca, N.Y.: Cornell University Press, 1996.

Klausen, Jytte. *The Islamic Challenge: Politics and Religion in Western Europe.* Oxford: Oxford University Press, 2005.

Martin, David. *A General Theory of Secularization.* Oxford: Blackwell, 1978.

Nielsen, Jørgen. *Muslims in Western Europe.* Edinburgh: Edinburgh University Press, 2004.

O'Connell, James. *The Past and Future Making of Europe.* Peace Research Report 26. Bradford, England: University of Bradford, Department of Peace Studies, 1991.

Robbers, Gerhard. *State and Church in the European Union.* Baden-Baden, Germany: Nomos Verlagsgesellschaft, 2005.

Van Kersbergen, Kees. *Social Capitalism: A Study of Christian Democracy and the Welfare State.* London: Routledge, 1995.

Vincent, Gilbert, and Jean-Paul Willaime, eds. *Religions et transformations de l'Europe.* Strasbourg, France: Presses Universitaires de Strasbourg, 1993.

Webber, Jonathan, ed. *Jewish Identities in the New Europe.* Washington, D.C.: Littman Library of Jewish Civilization, 1994.

Evangelicalism

Evangelicalism describes a large extended family of Protestant denominations and religious movements bound together by common beliefs. Like many religious terms, however, *Evangelicalism* has a number of meanings, especially among those who adopt the label.

Evangelical, or *evangelical Protestant,* is a term commonly used to describe the largest Protestant tradition in the United States. Most simply put, evangelicals are Protestants who adhere to highly traditional Christian beliefs and practices and who focus on individual salvation. For this reason, evangelicals have been called the "private party" of Protestantism, as opposed to the "public party" of mainline Protestants. They are also historically white churches and thus distinguished from the historically black Protestant churches, with which they share some beliefs and practices. However, in recent times, evangelicals have become more engaged in public affairs and more diverse socially.

Origins and Development

In the New Testament the Greek word *evangelion,* often translated as *evangel*—and the Greek root of evangelize, evangelist, and evangelical—is used to describe the "good news" of salvation through Jesus Christ. In this sense, all Christians might be described as "evangelical" in that they accept the evangel in one form or another.

But in the sixteenth century *evangelical* took on a more specific meaning with the Protestant Reformation, when German theologian Martin Luther (1483–1546) used the word to describe his Protestant alternative to the Roman Catholic Church. Luther emphasized the evangel itself over church tradition, stressing the authority of scripture (the source of the evangel) and salvation by grace through faith (the message of the evangel). The term was eventually extended to other reformers, such as John Calvin (1509–1564). Many Europeans and Americans in Reformation-era churches—for example, the Evangelical Lutheran Church in America, the major mainline Lutheran denomination in the United States—still use the word in this sense today.

Ironically, the Protestant Reformation set in motion a process of periodic redefinition of the term *evangelical*. The original reformers had rejected the institutionalized Catholic Church of their time, claiming that it had diluted the evangel by accommodating itself to secular culture. But over time the Lutheran and Calvinist movements became established churches in their own rights and, in doing so, invited new efforts to recover and proclaim the evangel. This church-sect cycle has recurred many times among Protestants. Perhaps the best American example is the Methodists, who began as a sectarian movement within the Church of England but who gradually institutionalized to become the largest mainline Protestant denomination, spawning a series of sectarian revolts along the way.

The meaning of Evangelicalism at the dawn of the twenty-first century reflects several iterations of the church-sect cycle. It encompasses both the first-century meaning of the "good news" of salvation through Jesus Christ and the

Reformation meaning of the authority of scripture and salvation by grace through faith. In addition, its meaning includes the necessity of personal conversion (the mechanics of the evangel) and the centrality of witnessing and missions (sharing the message of the evangel). These experiential aspects of Evangelicalism are manifestations of the spiritual revivals (systematic efforts to bring outsiders into the ranks of the faithful) that swept through the United States at the end of the nineteenth century and that continue in a more limited fashion today.

Given this complex history, it is hardly surprising that Evangelicalism has had many meanings and that these could be applied with some validity to church institutions, sectarian movements, and beliefs. Scholars frequently employ all three to define Evangelicalism.

Denominations

The denominations generally assigned to the evangelical tradition had three sources. First, many evangelicals (or their religious ancestors) came to the United States to practice their religion freely. Examples include the Amish, members of the Dutch Reformed churches, some ethnic Lutherans, and Pietist groups. This kind of immigration continues today, notably among Latino Pentecostals. Second, many evangelical denominations were the product of revivals, especially the nineteenth-century Presbyterians, Methodists, and Baptists. And, third, many evangelical denominations arose from reactions within existing denominations and local churches, which attempted to recapture more fully spiritual excitement and which often were linked to sectarian movements. The Holiness churches (such as the Nazarenes and Salvation Army) and many conservative Baptists are good examples.

In the early twenty-first century, scholars generally recognize four large evangelical subtraditions. The largest is the Baptist, including the Southern Baptist Convention, the largest Protestant denomination in the country, and a host of other denominations. As a group, Baptists are known for their intense individualism, stressing the "soul competency" of each believer in matters of doctrine. Typical of the Baptist subtradition are the numerous independent Baptist churches. Scholars frequently include other smaller groups in the Baptist subtradition because of similarities in belief and origin. These include the Adventists, of whom the Seventh-day Adventists are best known, and the Restorationists, such as the Churches of Christ.

Another subtradition is the Reformed-Confessional composed of other churches originating in the Protestant Reformation. The Reformed elements stress traditional Calvinist beliefs, such as the sovereignty of God and predestination. The Presbyterian Church in America, the Orthodox Presbyterian Church, and the Christian Reformed Church are the best-known bodies in this category. The confessional elements, which largely originated in the Lutheran churches, stress traditional Lutheran beliefs. More examples are the Lutheran Church-Missouri Synod, the Evangelical Lutheran Synod, and the Wisconsin Evangelical Lutheran Synod. Scholars often include in this subtradition other split-offs from Reformation-era families, such as the Reformed Episcopal Church and the Congregational Christian churches.

Pentecostal-Holiness, the third evangelical subtradition, is made up of churches stressing special kinds of religious experiences. Churches in the Holiness family emphasize personal sanctification and individual purity. The Church of the Nazarene, Salvation Army, and Church of God (Anderson, Indiana) are the best-known Holiness groups. Scholars frequently include in this subtradition other churches that split off from the Methodist family, such as the Wesleyan Methodists, and from the Pietist churches, such as the Evangelical Free Church. The Pentecostal movement had roots in many Holiness churches but emphasizes the "gifts of the Holy Spirit," such as speaking in tongues and faith healing. The largest white Pentecostal denominations are the Assemblies of God, the Four-Square Gospel churches, and the Church of God (Cleveland, Tennessee).

The fourth and smallest subtradition is the Anabaptist. Many of these denominations also date from the Reformation era and include the Amish, Mennonites, Brethren groups, and some Friends (Quakers). They combine traditional doctrine and lifestyle with opposition to serving in the military or swearing public oaths—beliefs that have earned them the label "peace churches."

Sectarian Movements

All of the evangelical subtraditions put some emphasis on separating themselves from modern society. Sectarian religious movements are the fullest embodiment of this impulse and crucial to contemporary Evangelicalism. Four such movements are important today. By far the best known is Fundamentalism, an early twentieth century-revolt against accommodation in the major Protestant denominations, especially the northern Baptists and Presbyterians. Named after *The Fundamentals,* a series of pamphlets published between 1910 and 1915 that defended basic Christian beliefs, Fundamentalism is characterized by strict doctrinal orthodoxy and strident ecclesiastical separatism. This movement influenced many evangelical denominations, created new denominations, and produced a myriad of nondenominational or independent churches and institutions. The Rev. Jerry Falwell is perhaps the best-known fundamentalist leader, and Bob Jones University in South Carolina is a leading fundamentalist institution.

Another important movement is Neo-Evangelicalism, which emerged in the 1940s as a conscious rejection by some fundamentalist leaders of the strictness and extreme separatism of Fundamentalism. Instead, these leaders emphasized outreach and evangelism along with a critique of contemporary culture. The "neo" prefix was eventually dropped as the leaders and institutions generated by the movement, such as the Rev. Billy Graham and the National Association of Evangelicals, became central to the broader religious tradition. This movement's adherents are found in all four of the evangelical subtraditions and in mainline Protestant denominations. This movement has also produced nondenominational ministries and churches. Dr. James Dobson of Focus on the Family is a good example on the first count; Rev. Rick Warren and the suburban "megachurches," on the second.

The "spirit-filled" movements (Pentecostals and charismatics) are sectarian movements that stress the direct work of the Holy Spirit. Pentecostalism originated in a series of revivals at the beginning of the twentieth century that eventually produced denominations such as the Assemblies of God. (Pentecostalism gets its name from the Pentecost in the New Testament, when the Holy Spirit transformed the original followers of Jesus into the Christian Church.) Despite the founding of denominations, Pentecostalism still shows strong sectarian tendencies, and these helped to generate the charismatic movement in the 1960s (the term *charismatic* derives from the Greek word for gifts). Charismatics originated in denominations that did not emphasize spiritual gifts, although tensions with noncharismatics led many to form nondenominational churches. There is continuing foment in the spirit-filled movements today. Rev. Ted Haggard, president of the National Association of Evangelicals, is a Pentecostal, and television evangelist Pat Robertson is a charismatic.

Core Beliefs

Despite all this diversity, evangelical denominations, subtraditions, and movements share core beliefs that tie the extended family together. Scholars agree on four doctrinal distinctives, each closely linked to the historical development of Evangelicalism: (1) a belief that salvation comes only through faith in Jesus Christ; (2) a high view of scriptural authority; (3) an emphasis on witnessing and missions; and (4) the need for personal acceptance of salvation, or personal conversion. The emphasis on (4) has made a common term for personal conversion—"born again"—a frequent synonym for Evangelicalism.

Although each of these four distinctive beliefs is found among other types of Christians, they are combined with rare force among adherents to evangelical denominations and movements. As one might imagine, considerable dispute exists over the exact nature of each "doctrinal essential." For example, some evangelicals insist on a literal interpretation of scripture and a sudden born-again experience, while others allow wider latitude in biblical interpretation and a gradual process of conversion. Similarly, some evangelicals understand witness and mission exclusively as a quest for converts, while others include social reform and charity. Such disagreements help to define the various subtraditions and movements.

Politics

A religious tradition as diverse as Evangelicalism is bound to display some political diversity. The core beliefs and sectarianism of evangelicals have produced strong political tendencies at some times and abstention from politics at others. For example, in the nineteenth century, evangelicals were vigorous proponents of both religious freedom and social reform, with many of the former preferring the Democrats and many of the latter joining the Whigs and, later, the Republicans. By the early twentieth century many evangelicals, especially in the South, were strong backers of the Democratic Party for regional, cultural, and economic reasons. In the North they tended to be Republican, but many withdrew from public affairs to concentrate on saving souls.

In the 1970s, evangelicals began reentering national politics, propelled by social issue conservatism and encouraged by Christian right leaders such as Jerry Falwell (the Moral Majority), Pat Robertson (the Christian Coalition), and James Dobson (Focus on the Family). As a consequence, evangelicals increasingly identified with the Republican

Party, and by 2004 they had become one of President George W. Bush's strongest constituencies. At this time, however, evangelicals' issue agenda began to broaden beyond the social issues to foreign, economic, and environmental policy. This broader agenda may produce additional political shifts in the future.

See also *Communication; Christian Right; Fundamentalism; Pentecostalism; Revivalism.*

John C. Green

BIBLIOGRAPHY

Bebbington, D. W. *Evangelicalism in Modern Britain: A History from the 1930s to the 1980s.* Boston: Unwin Hyman, 1989.

Cromatie, Michael, ed. *A Public Faith: Evangelicals and Civic Engagement.* Lanham, Md.: Rowman and Littlefield, 2003.

Dayton, Donald W., and R. K. Johnson, eds. *The Variety of American Evangelicalism.* Knoxville: University of Tennessee Press, 1991.

Finke, Roger, and Rodney Stark. *The Churching of America, 1776–1990: Winners and Losers in Our Religious Economy.* New Brunswick, N.J.: Rutgers University Press, 1993.

Green, John C. "Seeking a Place: Evangelical Protestants and Public Engagement in the Twentieth Century." In *Toward an Evangelical Public Policy,* edited by Ronald Sider and Diane Knipper. Grand Rapids, Mich.: Baker Press, 2005.

Kellstedt, Lyman A., John C. Green, Corwin E. Smidt, and James L. Guth. "The Puzzle of Evangelical Protestantism: Core, Periphery, and Political Behavior." In *Religion and the Culture Wars,* edited by John C. Green, James L. Guth, Corwin E. Smidt, and Lyman A. Kellstedt. Lanham, Md.: Rowman and Littlefield, 1996.

Marsden, George, ed. *Evangelicalism and Modern America.* Grand Rapids, Mich.: W.B. Eerdmans, 1984.

Marty, Martin E. *The Righteous Empire: The Protestant Experience in America.* New York: Dial Press, 1970.

Noll, Mark A. *American Evangelical Christianity: An Introduction.* Oxford, U.K.: Blackwell Publishers, 2001.

Smith, Christian. *American Evangelicals: Embattled and Thriving.* Chicago: University of Chicago Press, 1998.

Evolution

See *Creationism and Evolution.*

F

Fascism

Fascism, a political movement that seeks to induce the rebirth of the nation in a "new order" based on the coordination of all political, social, and cultural energies in a homogeneous national community, first arose as a radical alternative to liberalism and communism in some nation-states of the Christian world in the aftermath of World War I (1914–1918). Its application in the ideology of Benito Mussolini's Italy and Adolf Hitler's Germany wreaked immense destruction on human life and humanistic institutions, especially during World War II (1939–1945).

The appeal of fascism, in the conditions of extreme economic hardship, social anxieties, and political crisis that prevailed in some liberal democracies during the 1920s and 1930s, could be considerable. It derives from the core myth of the nation's imminent phoenix-like resurrection from the ashes of the decadent old order—a secular vision fundamentally antagonistic to any metaphysical religion. Fascism's antagonism for religion, however, was generally obscured in the interwar period by its success in presenting itself as an ersatz or civic religion based on the cult of the leader, the nation, and the state, and further obfuscated by the hostility to Marxism that it shared with Christianity (which in the past had been used to rationalize other European manifestations of authoritarianism and imperialism). These elements enabled fascist movements in several countries not only to appropriate the energies of Christianity as a moral authority but to convince many thousands (and, where they seized power, millions) of ostensibly devout Christians, including some high-ranking clergy, to become enthusiastic recruits to their cause and hence prepared to connive with, or even participate personally in, acts of repression, violence, racial persecution, and war in blatant defiance of basic Christian values.

In the contemporary world some fascists still abuse Christian precepts and biblical references as part of the often phantasmagorical mix of ideas that they invoke to rationalize hatred, legitimize violence, and demonize the "other." Meanwhile, some radically fundamentalist forms of Christianity, Judaism, Islam, and Hinduism display several features reminiscent of interwar fascism, even if their underlying myth is distinctive, being based on a highly selective and politicized interpretation of revealed truth. But though the distinction between fascism and metaphysical religion can become blurred, a fundamental distinction remains: the belief of the fascist centers on the need for national or ethnic regeneration and not on obedience to a divine law.

Fascism as a Civic Religion

Although the precise definition of fascism has been the subject of considerable academic controversy, there are signs of a growing consensus outside the Marxist camp that it is best treated as a revolutionary form of nationalist ideology, with a specific dynamic of its own imparted by its profoundly antirational, self-consciously mythic character. The version of this approach that informs the present article identifies the ideological matrix underlying fascism's policies, propaganda, and actions as the fusion of the vision of imminent rebirth, or "palingenesis" (an archetypal human myth), with a virulently illiberal form of populist nationalism (a secular creed originating in modern Europe). This gives rise to a palingenetic variety of "ultranationalism" obsessed with the need for cleansing and renewal in every sphere of national life—political, social, economic, cultural, moral, and, in some cases, even biological (as in the case of the Nazi eugenics program). Accordingly, fascist activists believe that their political campaigning and paramilitary actions can arouse the latent patriotic fervor and sense of cultural belonging in the spiritually disoriented, disaffected, and "slumbering" masses to the point where the nation is rescued from the encroaching forces of decadence and given a new lease of life as the protagonist of an epic historical destiny.

In the aftermath of World War I, in which mass mobilization in a climate of extreme patriotism and militarism had conditioned the lives of millions, it was all the more natural that fascism's pursuit of the utopia of national unity and greatness should lead it to adopt a militarized, overtly charismatic style of politics in which rhetoric, faith, and action prevailed over debate, understanding, and coherent party programs. Legitimacy of the state was no longer to be derived from constitutional procedures but from the intensity of the displays of mass enthusiasm that could be orchestrated in support of the movement. Fascism systematically replaced the "rational" processes of liberal democratic politics with a constant stream of carefully staged and deliberately ritualized events in which the general population could take part only as more or less fervent spectators.

The typical manifestation of this "spectacular" politics was the rally or "oceanic assembly" in which the scores of thousands who participated in person, and the millions more who listened to it on the radio or watched it in newsreels, celebrated both the symbolic deification of the leader as Providence's response to the plight of the nation and their own transformation into a national community united in mind and body within a single fate. When fascism held power in Italy (1925–1943) and Germany (1933–1945), the state itself became extensively "sacralized" through such techniques as the invention of national holidays and festivals to commemorate aspects of the fascist revolution; the mounting of propagandistic exhibitions sometimes attended by hundreds of thousands of people; the emphasis placed on sport, collective calisthenics, and choreographed parades; the pervasive use of symbols (the *fasces,* the swastika); the linking of all achievements in the technological, social, or political sphere with the nation's regeneration under fascism; the erection of civic buildings and creation of public spaces on a monumental and "timeless" scale; and the pervasive use of quasi-religious discourse in references to the new order, its institutions, leadership, and total claims on the life of the individual.

In anthropological terms, the goal of this concerted attempt to revolutionize the nation's culture within a generation was to induce all members of the national community to experience a sense of supra-individual, ritual, or "sacred" time in which the limitations and problems of individual existence were transcended. In this sense fascism not only sets out to overcome the atomization and skepticism fostered by liberalism, and to ward off the class division and internationalism fomented by socialism, but eventually to replace organized religion by becoming the sole source of social and ethical values in the modern age. Although it is legitimate to apply the term "civic religion" to fascism, it is misleading to treat it as a modern form of millennialism, since the fascist transformation of society is conceived as taking place imminently within secular historical time and solely through human—not divine—agency, however religious the discourse used to articulate it.

Fascists and the Church

Fascists can adopt three basic strategies in reacting to the presence of organized religion in the nation that they intend to "regenerate": persecution, compromise, and appropriation. The dominant fascist tactic in Italy was compromise, while the policy of the National Socialist Party, or Nazis, in Germany, though ultimately geared toward persecution, oscillated between all three for reasons of expedience. A number of abortive fascist movements, however, arose in countries still dominated by Christianity to a greater extent than either Italy or Germany. Because they could not hope to gain a mass following by overtly repudiating Christian values, they set about appropriating them.

Thus the Spanish Falange and the Hungarian Arrow Cross embraced Catholicism, the South African Ossewabrandwag incorporated Dutch Reformed Christianity, the Finnish Isämaallinen Kansanliike (IKL) upheld the values of Lutheranism, while the Romanian Iron Guard stressed the role of the Orthodox Church to the point that its leader, Corneliu Codreanu, looked forward to the collective resurrection of all "true" Romanians on Judgment Day. In Belgium a radical form of reformist politics arose that started as a form of right-wing political Catholicism, taking its name from the religious journal *Christus Rex*. It was modeled on the style and ethos of fascism. When Belgium was occupied by the German Third Reich, Rexism's leader, Léon Degrelle, turned it into a fully Nazified movement and organized a volunteer legion of French-speaking Walloons in southern Belgium to fight alongside the Wehrmacht in the Third Reich's "European crusade" on the eastern front.

Even in France, where most fascist initiatives were secular in orientation, a leading ideologue of ultranationalist rebirth, Drieu la Rochelle, depicted the Third Reich as the harbinger of a new renaissance in line with that of the medieval age of the Christian faith. La Rochelle played upon the promise of renaissance, using methods perfectly adapted to the needs of the modern age, one which combined the spirituality of the First Reich (the Holy Roman Empire) with the industrial and military might of the Second Reich (1871–1918).

The attempted appropriation of Christianity by fascists to their own political ends should be seen in the context of three major currents in interwar Europe: first, the extensive conflation of "God" with "country" that had characterized the propaganda of all European states in the era of World War I; second, the widespread rejection of laissez-faire capitalism, urban living, and individualism in favor of corporatist economics combined with a nostalgia for the apparent stability of rural life and traditional family values; finally, the crisis of belief in parliamentary democracy and party politics as the best basis of stable government and the search for a "third way" between liberalism and communism.

Mainstream Christianity was until 1945 closely associated with all three ideological currents—for example, a papal encyclical of 1931, *Quadragesimo Anno,* officially endorsed the idea that the best economic basis for a Christian society was corporativism, a system in which sectors of economic activity were organized into corporations that harmonized the interests of workers, management, and the state. It thus became natural for every conservative regime (or, when it mimicked fascism and Nazism, "parafascist" regime) to broaden its support by presenting itself as the upholder of Christian values and hence antimaterialist, anticommunist, and, not infrequently, anti-Semitic. As a result it was able frequently to win the all too often uncritical support of the church and much of the laity. Antonio Salazar's Portugal, Francisco Franco's Spain, Engelbert Dollfuss's Austria, Nicolas Horthy's Hungary, Joseph Pilsudski's Poland, Ion Antonescu's Romania, Ionnis Metaxas's Greece, Henri Pétain's Vichy regime in France, and most authoritarian regimes of the Balkan and Baltic states fit this pattern. Histo-

rians sometimes use the term "clerical fascism" to refer to regimes that fuse Catholicism with paternalistic authoritarianism, such as the corporate state established in Austria between 1933 and 1938. The fact that its leader, Engelbert Dollfuss, was assassinated by Austrian Nazis underlines the necessity to distinguish modern forms of conservative dictatorship from fascism proper, which as a revolutionary movement is anticonservative and anticlerical at heart, despite its pragmatic need to forge alliances with conservative forces once in power.

Since World War II nonreligious forms of fascism have prevailed, whether neopagan (for example, based on Nazi Aryanism) or secular (for example, "scientifically" racist). There are exceptions, however, such as the *Oeuvre Française,* a small fascist movement active in the 1990s, that defines the authentic Frenchness it wants to resurrect from the "chaos" of liberal democracy as a fusion of Christian faith with French language and culture. (Achieving this goal would result in the branding of Muslim fellow citizens as "aliens.") Meanwhile, building on a tradition established by the Ku Klux Klan, the United States has witnessed a proliferation of virulently racist forms of fascism partially rationalized through a highly selective and distorted interpretation of scripture. Foremost among these are the Christian Identity movement, which fuses components of Christianity with Nazi Aryanism, and some currents of the highly disparate survivalist and militia movements (not all of which are fascist).

The Catholic Church and Fascism

The response of Christians to fascism can take one of three basic forms. The most theologically consistent one, *opposition,* stems from the urge to act on the realization that fascism, however it seeks to disguise the fact and whatever enemies it has in common with organized religion, is the antithesis of everything Christianity stands for. The theologically and morally more questionable tactic of *collusion* is rooted in the pragmatic hope that in the prevailing historical circumstances the interests of the church may be better served by cooperating with a fascist regime than by adopting a hostile position, despite the radical divergence of the ultimate ends they serve. Finally, true to a long tradition in which divine precepts become conflated with an all-too-human creed of aggression and destruction, Christians may experience a deep-seated *confusion* of their faith with the fascist world view. An example is when the Slovak Republic—

officially a "Christian national community" headed by a Catholic prelate—collaborated with the deportation of its Jewish population to the death camps during World War II. A parallel episode took place in another Nazi puppet regime, the Independent State of Croatia, where Roman Catholic priests played a conspicuous role in the mass murder of Orthodox Christian Serbs, Jews, and gypsies by the Ustasha, a paramilitary organization dedicated to the cause of Croatian independence. This violent ultranationalist movement was underpinned by a mindset and world view closely akin to those of fascists, but its goal was the creation of a nation-state through secession rather than the regeneration of an existing one.

All three permutations of the relationship are to be found under Italian fascism. Although Mussolini's movement was originally anticlerical, he quickly recognized that to establish the power base for the "new Italy" he had to compromise, which meant allying his vulnerable, numerically weak movement with the country's major conservative forces, foremost among which was the Catholic Church. As for his followers, only a few leading ideologues, notably Giovanni Gentile, the idealist philosopher of the "ethical state," were prepared publicly to attack Christianity as an obstacle to Italy's rebirth. The bulk of the fascist leadership, though agnostic, instinctively embraced Catholicism both as an integral part of "Italianness" and as another manifestation of the "universal" civilizing mission of the Italian genius first displayed in the ancient Roman Empire. (Falangists cultivated an analogous myth about Spanish Catholicism.) Meanwhile, even the less secularized rank-and-file members of the Fascist Party and its affiliated mass organizations operated a sufficiently flexible, watered-down version of Christianity to experience no fundamental contradiction between their political and religious commitments or behavior as long as the church was prepared to endorse the fascist revolution.

This the church was predisposed to do. A pact with Italy's fascist leadership offered the Vatican the unexpected opportunity to reoccupy the central place in the spiritual life of the nation, a role that had been denied it by the liberal *risorgimento,* or resurgence, which had finally unified Italy in 1870 in the teeth of papal opposition. The path to such a reconciliation was smoothed by the fact that it converged with fascism on several core issues: antiliberalism, antisocialism, and a belief in family values, patriarchy, hierarchy, and imperialism. The result of Mussolini's eagerness to turn a potential antagonist into a major source of legitimacy at home and abroad

(even if it flouted the "totalitarian" claims of his regime) was the concordat and the Lateran Pacts agreed in February 1929 between the Italian state and the Vatican. In exchange for recognizing the Kingdom of Italy, and hence enabling Mussolini to take the credit for resolving the long-standing "Roman question," the papacy, among other things, exacted recognition of the sovereignty of the Vatican state, the prerogative to assert its moral authority on issues such as divorce and abortion, and the right to teach Catholic doctrine in elementary and secondary schools. Perhaps most important for the future of Italy, the church was allowed to continue to run Catholic Action as a nationwide organization that, though strictly "nonpolitical," nevertheless had considerable potential for ensuring that a section of Italian youth grew up with non-fascist values.

Whatever its fundamental misgivings about fascism, the Vatican officially pursued a policy of active cooperation with it, at least until the alliance between Mussolini and Hitler caused Italy to adopt racial and foreign policies that made further quiescence impossible. The attitude of individual Catholics to fascism, however, could vary considerably. In the 1920s an important constituency of anti-fascism was formed by the radical faction of the Christian Democrat Italian Popular Party, established in 1919. Seen as subversively socialist by both the Vatican and Mussolini, adherents of the Popular Party were first marginalized and then suppressed, and no significant anti-fascist movement developed within the church to replace them. In July 1943 Mussolini was removed from power by the Fascist Grand Council and the king; he was imprisoned in a former hotel in a mountainous region of the Abruzzi in central Italy. Rescued in a daring SS operation four days after the armistice between Italy and the Allied forces was signed on September 8, he was installed on Hitler's orders as nominal head of the Italian Social Republic, which was effectively run by the Nazis as a puppet state. It was only then that anti-fascist political Catholicism reemerged as a significant force by inspiring one of the most important partisan factions. The church thus helped to lay the ground for the domination of the new postwar Italian Republic by the Christian Democratic Party from 1946 to 1994.

At the other end of the spectrum, ardent ecclesiastical support for the regime in its formative years was provided by the Clerico-Fascists, a loose faction of Catholic clergy, intellectuals, and politicians who advocated collaboration with Mussolini's new Italy and helped prepare the ground for the Lateran Pacts. Their cause was taken up by high-ranking church dignitaries, such as Cardinal Schuster of Milan, who enthusiastically and unashamedly used his authority to contribute to the cult of Mussolini—the Duce—and the sacralization of the fascist state. In the 1930s, however, except for an open rupture with Mussolini when he tried to curb the activities of Catholic Action, the Vatican itself came close to adopting a Clerico-Fascist position. Its representatives played a prominent part in the elaborate civic liturgy evolved by fascism, and it gave its blessing to Italy's imperialist conquest of Abyssinia (now Ethiopia), in the name of Christian civilization, and to its participation in the Spanish civil war (ostensibly to defend Catholicism from Bolshevik atheism and anticlericalism).

Pope Pius XI, despite misgivings about the fascist regime, was reluctant to compromise the concordat, from which he expected so much, by using the creation of Italy's pact (Axis) with the overtly pagan Third Reich in the autumn of 1936 or the introduction in November 1938 of Italian anti-Semitic legislation as pretexts to condemn the regime outright. Something of the pope's true feelings can be inferred from his issue in 1937 of the encyclical *Mit Brennender Sorge* ("With burning sorrow") declaring the incompatibility of Nazi paganism and racism with Christianity, an implicit condemnation of Italy's Axis partner. The Vatican also vehemently protested against the Law for Defense of the Italian Race, but these protests centered on the way the veto on marriages between Italians and Jews constituted a violation of the concordat, which recognized the primacy of the church on issues of marriage. Whether the pope's refusal to wage an all-out diplomatic and propaganda war on Nazism, the Axis, and fascist racism is to be attributed to the legacy of Christian anti-Semitism and cowardice or prudence and pragmatism is still a matter of considerable scholarly controversy. The fact remains that by the death of Pius XI, in February 1939, the collusion between the Vatican and the Italian state had given way to open hostility.

The new pope, Pius XII, a germanophile, hinted at intentions to call a truce on the racial issue, raising hopes among fascist leaders of *détente*. But though Mussolini's catastrophic decision to enter World War II as Hitler's ally prompted the same public displays of ecclesiastical approval and loyalty as had accompanied all of the regime's bellicose acts, behind the scenes the new pope had been using his authority to campaign against Italy's abandoning of its neutrality. His denunciation of racism—as in his first encyclical to the bish-

Although the Vatican was criticzed for failing to speak out against Nazi chancellor Adolf Hitler, many individual Catholics actively opposed Hitler's Third Reich, often at great personal risk.

ops of the world of October 1939—and sanctioning of thinly veiled polemics against the "pact of steel" in the Vatican organ *Osservatore Romano* led to a steady deterioration in the relations with the fascist regime. In May 1940 Mussolini denounced the papacy as a "cancer which gnaws at our national life."

Pius XII, however, never took a public stand against the policies of the Third Reich, and although the Curia was kept meticulously informed about the mounting scale of atrocities being committed by the Third Reich, he never resorted to the weapon of excommunication against the many thousands of his flock (whose ranks technically included Hitler) directly or indirectly involved in genocide and state terror. The most explicit attack on the regime's expanding system of terror and mass murder was the papal message of Christmas 1942 that managed to condemn persecution on racial or political grounds without specifically mentioning the plight of the Jews.

The precise reason for the pope's reluctance to speak out unequivocally against the Third Reich's foreign and racial policies and fascist Italy's participation in their implementation is still a matter of controversy. Certainly there is evidence that behind the scenes the pope had tried to dissuade Mussolini from entering the war and that in 1942 the Vatican initiated contacts with the British and U.S. governments as well as with anti-fascist elements within Italy bent on overthrowing the regime and negotiating a peace treaty with the Allies. There were also moves by high-ranking church dignitaries to stop the deportations of Jews to the death camps from France, Croatia, and Italy. But direct appeals for the Vatican to use the full weight of its authority to condemn the extermination of the Jews, such as those made by the British ambassador to the Holy See, D'Arcy Osborne, fell on deaf ears.

The Christian Churches and the Third Reich

The failure of the Holy See to become a source of active resistance to the Rome-Berlin Axis did not help Germany's twenty-two million Catholics adopt an attitude of unequivocal opposition to Hitler, who was deeply conscious of the power of organized religion and took care in the formative stage of the regime to emphasize its commitment to "positive Christianity." In July 1933 a concordat was signed, mediated by one-time chairman of the by then dissolved (Catholic) Center Party and former chancellor Franz von Papen and the future Pius XII. Like the Italian concordat, a degree of strictly apolitical autonomy was secured in return for recognition of the regime, thus making it all that much easier for patriotically inclined Catholics to experience no fundamental tension between their religious and their nationalist loyalties. Indeed, parts of the Catholic press called for active participation in the "national revolution," while the church gave official backing to the return of the occupied Saarland by France in 1935 and to the incorporation of Austria into Germany (the *Anschluss*) three years later. At no time did it avail itself of its still theoretically intact moral authority to mount a sustained campaign denouncing the regime's creation of a vast European empire based on organized, bureaucratized, and eventually industrialized inhumanity.

If the Catholic Church never became a major source of resistance to the Third Reich as a whole, however, it was prepared to show its opposition on specific issues. Such acts as the placing on the Catholic Index of Forbidden Books of Arthur Rosenberg's *The Myth of the Twentieth Century* (a major exposition of the Nazis' pagan, fiercely anti-Christian vision of the history of culture, published in 1930) and the protracted struggle to defend the autonomy of the Catholic Action and the Catholic Youth League from state interference were sufficiently provocative to the regime for hundreds of clergy to be sentenced to terms in concentration camps during the thirteen-year reign of state terror.

A high point of coordinated Catholic opposition to Nazism was the nationwide reading from the pulpits of the encyclical *Mit Brennender Sorge* of March 1937. A minority of Catholics also took stands on their own initiative, often at great personal risk. The most famous examples are the three sermons preached in 1941 by the bishop of Münster, Clemens von Galen. (In fact, though the bishop's prominence protected him from retribution, several Catholics were executed for distributing his sermons.) In them he used theological arguments to attack the legitimacy of the police state, accusing of murder authorities which claimed the right to carry out the "mercy killing" of those deemed to have "a life unworthy of being lived." As a direct result of von Galen's intervention, the text of which was circulated throughout Germany, the euthanasia program was officially halted, and even in practice lost much of its momentum. The courage of the "lion of Münster" inspired many acts of heroism on the part of individual Catholics, a famous example of which was the abortive attempt by Hans and Sophie Scholl, a brother and sister who were leaders of the Munich University resistance circle, the White Rose, to stir their fellow students into revolt. They were arrested, tortured, and executed in February 1943. Meanwhile, some former members of the Catholic workers' movement had joined forces with socialists to set up underground resistance to Hitler. In general, however, overt antisocialism and illiberalism combined with the covert nationalism and anti-Semitism of established Catholicism precluded the possibility that German Catholics would turn against Hitler en masse.

Germany's Protestant churches were even less well placed to put up united resistance to Nazism. In the nineteenth century, German Protestantism had closely identified itself with Prussian imperialism and the Second Reich. After 1918, with the exception of the weak liberal faction, its main groupings instinctively rejected the legitimacy of the "social democratic" Weimar Republic. Instead most aligned themselves with the ultraconservative, and fiercely antisocialist, German National People's Party (DNVP) and with the presidency of Paul von Hindenburg, a World War I hero and incarnation of the nexus between army, aristocracy, monarchy, and Protestantism, which was the foundation of the Second Reich. They also hosted currents of ultranationalism and anti-Semitism, which associated the pluralism, individualism, materialism, and skepticism of modern urban existence with moral decay. As the republic started collapsing in the wake of the Great Depression in the 1930s, these tendencies predisposed political Protestantism to be drawn into the orbit of the National Socialist Party, not just as a shield against communism but as a party that campaigned for the rebirth of Germany as an imperial power based on a healthy, organic, and spiritually reawakened national community. The path to collusion was smoothed by the influence of prominent Protestant academic theologians such as Gerhard Kittel, Paul Althaus, and Emanuel Hirsch. Their scholarship extensively rationalized the compatibility between belief in the reborn Christ and in the reborn German people, or *Volk*. As a result, the Executive Committee of the Protestant Churches, the *Kirchenausschuss,* saw no reason to use its authority to attack the National Socialists in the run-up to the crucial elections of 1933, in which the Nazis became the largest single party, hence securing Hitler the chancellorship. Its response to Hitler's victory was the promise of cooperation with the new government, which some members saw as a "gift of God."

Although Hitler feigned respect for the spiritual independence of the Protestant churches, in reality he intended to neutralize them as a rival claim on German "belief." At first he applied a covert strategy of "appropriation" *(Gleichschaltung),* encouraging the "German Christians," a faction of Nazi activists who worked within the church and promoted an Aryanized perversion of Christianity, to infiltrate the Protestant hierarchy and help engineer the election of their candidate, Ludwig Müller, as the first "Reich bishop." The rigged victory of the German Christians in the church elections of July 1933, however, provoked a backlash led by two pastors, Martin Niemöller and Dietrich Bonhoeffer, who rallied the support of a third of the Protestant clergy in Germany to create the "Confessional Church," a name chosen to indicate that it intended to stay true to its "confession," or religious principles, and hence preserve its religious autonomy from the inroads of the state. Hitler's response was to turn to persecution. Between 1935 and 1938 several thousand pastors, priests, and nuns were arrested for criticizing Nazi neopaganism, for disloyalty to the regime, or on

trumped-up charges of immorality. Indeed, the offensive launched against Christianity during the war in the new province of Germany, the "Warthegau," which had been carved out of occupied Poland, was probably a harbinger of the fate that eventually awaited the churches in Germany too had the Third Reich been victorious.

For the time being, however, the main weapon deployed against Protestantism was suppression: under the Reich Church Ministry set up in 1935, all church activities and publications were scrutinized for anything that could be construed as political interference with or veiled criticism of the regime. This muzzling tactic was generally successful. While infighting over theological issues between the increasingly factionalized German Christians and the Confessional Church continued until 1945, on only a few occasions did Protestantism take a principled stand against the inhumanity of the Third Reich. An important instance of this was the Confessional Church's detailed memorandum of June 1936 (not originally intended for publication) attacking the regime's racial ideology and anti-Semitism, the cult of the leader, and the unaccountability of the concentration camp system and the Gestapo to the rule of law. About a million copies were circulated, and three-quarters of Confessional pastors read it from the pulpit. Even more courageous was the memorandum of the Prussian synod of the Confessional Church of October 1943; it condemned the regime's policies to exterminate people on whatever grounds as "wielding a sword which is not given to the state by God" and declared the lives of the people of Israel to be "sacred to Him." Such rare moments when genuine Protestant faith triumphed over ideological and moral disorientation did little or nothing to slow down the Nazi juggernaut of mass destruction.

The Corruption of Religion by Fascism

A year into World War II, 95 percent of Germans still claimed to be members of a Christian denomination. Given the weakness of organized Christian resistance to the regime, this number suggests that compromise, denial, and double-think had become behavioral norms for the mass of the population. Only a minute proportion of theologians, clergy, and lay Christians, Catholic or Protestant, were prepared to draw the logical consequences of their faith by taking personal stands against the regime or joining the resistance movement. An outstanding exception was the Lutheran theologian Karl Barth, who scrupulously spelled out the logical consequence of the Christian faith, namely unequivocal rejection of Nazism, in his journal *Theologische Existenz Heute* ("Theological Existence Today") until he was forced to resign his professorship at the University of Bonn and return to his native Switzerland for refusing to declare an oath of allegiance to Hitler. It must be said that the cost of defying the regime was enormously high: although Clemens August von Galen, the bishop of Münster, was too famous to be touched, three priests who circulated the text of his sermons were executed and draconian punishments were imposed on some civilians suspected of tacitly supporting him. Even being in the public eye did not spare Niemöller seven years internment in concentration camps (1938–1945). Nor did it save Bonhoeffer, who, convinced that the defeat of his nation was to be preferred to the destruction of Christian civilization, joined the resistance, only to be arrested and condemned to death by the infamous "People's Court," a sentence carried out in the very last days of the war.

Bonhoeffer's personal courage and his efforts to formulate a doctrinal rationale for the resistance to the Nazi terror state were to help inspire the anti-authoritarian stands taken by some clergy in Latin America and the Soviet Empire in the years after the war. The overriding impression created by the responses of Christian communities in the face of fascist or parafascist regimes is less one of cowardice, however, than of a general failure of both the laity and the clergy at every level to adopt an appropriate moral position on them. This failure was openly acknowledged in the Stuttgart Confession of Guilt published by the Protestant churches at the end of the war, and although the Vatican has never formally conceded the inadequacy of its attempts to curb the inhumanities committed by the Axis powers, mainstream Catholicism has since 1945 flowed along democratic rather than authoritarian channels.

Symptomatic of the radical shift of postwar Vatican thinking toward a liberal humanist position was the publication of the papal encyclical *Nostra Aetate* ("In this age of ours") in October 1965. It declared a sense of solidarity with non-Christian religions, stressed the common heritage of Christians and Jews, and condemned "every form of persecution against whomsoever it may be directed." Nevertheless, the history of the Christian churches' relationship with fascism between 1922 and 1945 provides a disturbing case study in how insidiously easy it is for religious convictions to become corrupted into an ideological force that compounds rather than combats the organized inhumanity of the modern state.

See also *Anti-Semitism; Barth, Karl; Bonhoeffer, Dietrich; Christian Democracy; Civil Religion; Colonialism; Ethnicity; Fundamentalism; Genocide and "Ethnic Cleansing"; Germany; Holocaust; Italy; Millennialism; Nationalism; Papacy; Spain; Survivalism; Vatican Council, Second; Yugoslavia.*

Roger Griffin

BIBLIOGRAPHY

Buchanan, Tom, and Martin Conway, eds. *Political Catholicism in Europe, 1918–1965.* Oxford: Clarendon Press, 1996.

Chadwick, W. O. *Britain and the Vatican during the Second World War.* Cambridge: Cambridge University Press, 1986.

Eriksen, Robert P. *Theologians under Hitler.* New Haven: Yale University Press, 1985.

Gentile, Emilio. *The Sacralization of Politics in Fascist Italy.* Cambridge: Harvard University Press, 1996.

Griffin, Roger D. *The Nature of Fascism.* London: Routledge, 1993.

———. *International Fascism: Theories, Causes, and the New Consensus.* London: Arnold, 1998.

Housden, Martyn. *Resistance and Conformity in the Third Reich.* London and New York: Routledge, 1997.

Kent, Peter C. *The Pope and the Duce: The International Impact of the Lateran Agreements.* New York: St. Martin's, 1981.

Pollard, John. "Fascism." In *New Dictionary of Catholic Social Thought,* edited by Judith Dwyer. Collegeville, Minn.: Liturgical Press, 1994.

———. *The Vatican and Italian Fascism, 1929–1932.* Cambridge: Cambridge University Press, 1985.

Scholder, Klaus, *The Churches and the Third Reich.* 2 vols. Translated by John Bowden. Philadelphia: Fortress Press, 1988.

Wolff, Richard J., and Jørg K. Hoensch, eds. *Catholics, the State, and the European Radical Right.* Boulder, Colo.: Social Science Monographs, 1987.

Feminism

Feminism can be most simply defined as the belief that women have been thought to be (or have been treated as if they were) secondary or inferior to men and that this situation must change. This leaves room for many kinds of feminism, and indeed, feminist movements have been extremely varied in their diagnoses of the present situation and the prescriptions they offer for its improvement. Whatever the precise content they give to their agenda for social change, however, feminists have insisted that the full range of social institutions be confronted. Thus, although feminism is often thought of in reference to legal and policy issues (such as the Equal Rights Amendment, abortion rights, or educational opportunities for girls), feminists find work to be done elsewhere as well. As the feminist slogan goes, "the personal is political": social institutions make their impact felt in personal life, and vice versa. No sector of society, then, is off-limits for feminist reform.

Certainly, feminists have always targeted religion as one bastion of male power. Feminists have consistently demanded that male-dominated religions transform themselves such that women are given opportunities for religious leadership, theologies include the female or feminine, and scriptures be interpreted to emphasize women's equality within the religious tradition and before God. This effort to make organized religions more favorable to women is probably the most common way in which feminists have interacted with religion, but there are other ways as well. Some feminists have given up on traditional, patriarchal religions altogether, saying that they are nothing more than an elaborate cosmic justification for male dominance. Such feminists have sometimes worked to create new religions that they believe to be feminist at their core; at other times they have sought to eradicate the hold of religion on people's consciousness altogether. Finally, many feminists have used religion—traditional or otherwise—as a power base from which to demand social reforms in women's interest, stressing themes within a specific religious tradition that lend divine support to their struggle. These initiatives are not mutually exclusive; individual feminists often use one or more of these strategies simultaneously.

Early Feminism

These are approaches that have an extensive history. As long as there have been women seeking spiritual growth within religious communities or institutions, there has been some form of feminist agitation for women's rights. Early Buddhist women, for example, sought to establish spiritual orders for women and to ensure that women, like men, were given opportunities to pursue enlightenment. French poet Christine de Pisan (1364–c. 1430), writing in the late fourteenth century, argued for women's rights from a Christian standpoint. And in the United States, women such as the Puritan Anne Hutchinson (c. 1591–1643) exercised religious leadership, sometimes in vocal and controversial ways, even before this was generally considered proper.

In spite of these precedents, feminist criticism of religion as such did not gain significant momentum until the nineteenth century, and at that time it was monopolized by Christians. The rising tide of Christian evangelicalism gave women new opportunities to become involved in missionary societies and in social movements such as abolitionism and temperance. The demand for charismatic speakers meant that many women, both black and white, were preaching (although they were rarely formally ordained). This situation, coupled with the emergence of the women's movement in the mid-nineteenth century, left the field ripe for feminist religious activism.

The Declaration of Sentiments and Resolutions, written by the suffragist Elizabeth Cady Stanton (1815–1902) and adopted by the women's convention held in Seneca Falls, New York, in 1848, is often said to have launched the women's movement in the United States. Modeled on the Declaration of Independence, the connection of the Declaration of Sentiments to political activism in the United States has always been clear. What has been perhaps less noticed, but equally significant, however, is that like the Declaration of Independence, the Declaration of Sentiments relies on religious language to justify its advocacy of women's rights. "Woman is man's equal," the declaration claimed, and "was intended to be so by the Creator." And yet the Declaration of Sentiments does not spare the Christian Church from criticism; among the grievances it articulates against male dominance is the subordination of women within the church and the "perverted application of the Scriptures" in support of this subordination.

This combination of reliance on religious authority and critique of it was also present in *The Woman's Bible,* a scriptural commentary compiled by Stanton and others in the late nineteenth century (and which presaged later interest in feminist biblical criticism). Concentrating on those passages of the Christian Bible that had been most damaging to women's status, the authors offered commentary, wherever possible turning these texts to serve feminist interests. For example, Stanton interpreted the first creation story in Genesis—where God creates human beings in "his" own image, male and female—as an indication that God was "himself" both male and female.

In the suffragist politics of the late nineteenth and early twentieth centuries, feminists drew on religious resources to strengthen their cause. Some, favoring the approach pioneered by Stanton and her fellow activist Matilda Joslyn Gage (1826–1898), relied on a vision of women's religious equality in their demand for political equality, while others, like Frances Willard (1839–1898), longtime head of the Women's Christian Temperance Union, used more traditional stereotypes of femininity to argue that society needed the input—via the vote—of women's "special" perspectives. Suffrage, like the union's campaign for temperance, expanded to include other social reforms that we in more modern times would recognize as feminist, such as day care for young children, homes for unwed or impoverished mothers, medical clinics for urban women, and the "rescuing" of prostitutes. The battle for suffrage was hard won, however, and once accomplished, feminist religious activism lay more or less dormant for several decades, only to break free again with new vigor in the late 1960s and early 1970s.

Twentieth-century Feminism

This wave of feminist activism, still flourishing in the early twenty-first century, has stressed the same points raised by nineteenth-century feminists, and added new ones as well. It has broadened to include women from religions other than Christianity—most prominently, Jewish women—and has increasingly been both strengthened and challenged by the feminist (or womanist, or *mujerista*) religious activism of African American, Hispanic, and Asian American women, who are dominantly Christian.

Attempts to secure equality for women within American churches and synagogues led in the 1970s to demands for women's ordination in Jewish and Christian movements and denominations. Some denominations, such as the Baptists, Congregationalists, and Unitarians, had begun to ordain women even before 1900, but most excluded women from the clergy well into the 1970s. By the late 1980s, however, most denominations—with the exception of Roman Catholicism, Orthodox Judaism, Eastern Orthodox Christianity, and some of the more conservative Protestant denominations (including Southern Baptists, Mormons, and Seventh-day Adventists)—began to ordain women. Once women were admitted to the clergy, they rushed in with perhaps more enthusiasm than had been expected, quickly forming significant minorities—and even majorities—in more liberal denominations.

This era also saw significant activism around the issue of inclusive language. Many prayer books, liturgies, and hymn books were rewritten in an effort to include women as equal spiritual seekers. Words like *mankind* were changed to *humanity,* and the ritual invocation of female religious figures (saints, matriarchs, and heroines of the faith) alongside that of male figures was encouraged. Particularly in the 1980s, these publications made their way into American congregations, where sometimes bitterly unhappy congregants were forced to learn new words to their favorite prayers and hymns. Feminist successes were abundant in this arena, but far from complete: many prayer books, hymnals, and the like have retained the male generic to this day.

Feminists also drew attention to scripture, calling on the one hand for new translations, where these seemed warranted, and, on the other hand, for biblical interpretations that, like Stanton's *Woman's Bible,* removed the sting of divine commands that subordinated women to men. Within Christianity this enterprise embraced an entire spectrum, from biblical literalists—who could soften but not eliminate blows against women—to textual critics who dispensed with any notion of direct divine authorship of scripture, freely separating the wheat of those passages that supported women's freedom from the chaff of those that denied it. Jewish feminists, with a tradition of midrash (commentaries on scripture) behind them, have had a relatively freer hand in reinterpreting and retelling key biblical stories but a perhaps more difficult task in working around Jewish biblical law, which is still held to be authoritative by Conservative and Orthodox Jews.

Perhaps the greatest challenge for both Jewish and Christian feminists has been confronting the maleness of God. Although both traditions have, at times, emphasized that God is neither male nor female, they have also persistently referred to God with male pronouns, and even justified, with theological argument, the practice of doing so. For example, God has been said to be male in relation to humanity's femaleness, or to be uniquely paternal in his relationship to humans. Feminists have dealt with this situation in several ways. At times they have struggled to avoid the use of gendered pronouns altogether (repeating the word *God,* or using terms like *Godself*), making God as gender-neutral as possible. At other times, they have retained male pronouns for God but offered female ones for another member of the Christian Trinity, usually the Holy Spirit. They have also described God with female metaphors—some of them drawn from scripture—saying that God is like a woman in childbirth or that God nurtures humanity as a woman suckles a child. Finally, there have been efforts to reconstruct female deities or divine powers, such as the Sophia of Hebrew and Christian scriptures or the cabalistic Shechinah, and to worship God with these names.

In addition to working with preexisting materials, religious feminists have also improvised, creating new stories, rituals, and religious communities that they believe work to enhance women's spirituality. Noncanonical stories have been retold: for example, that Eve, the dutiful wife, was preceded in the Garden of Eden by Lilith, who was more of an upstart. Where male-only rituals have existed, religious feminists have created complementary ones for females. For example, in the Jewish tradition, where formerly only boys were honored with religious ritual at birth (circumcision) and puberty (*bar mitzvah*), girls are now frequently given ceremonies at birth (in which they are given their Hebrew names) and coming-of-age rituals (*bat mitzvot*) at puberty. Additional rituals with no male counterparts have been created by religious feminists, sometimes to celebrate women's life-cycle events such as childbirth, menstruation, and menopause. New, all-female religious communities, such as Women-Church (an egalitarian feminist group composed mainly of Roman Catholics) or Rosh Chodesh groups (which mark the Jewish new moon with a women's ritual), have been created broadly within the bounds of established religion.

Religious feminists have networked across denominations to share existing resources and develop new ones, sometimes finding common cause across differing religions as well. Increasingly, American women have attempted to extend their feminist religious insights to other religions besides Judaism and Christianity. They have sought to build a more global network of religious feminists. Efforts in this direction are still preliminary, but there are growing international coalitions of feminists from a variety of religious backgrounds. In addition, some American women, raised as Jews or Christians, have taken up Eastern religions such as Buddhism and sought to reform these as well in a more feminist vein.

All these manifestations of feminist religious activism occur within the religions that feminists deem patriarchal. Some, however, can find no compelling reason to stay within patriarchal religions, preferring a more secular (or less obviously religious) approach to feminism. For example, Sonia Johnson, who was branded a heretic by the Mormon Church, used her notoriety to launch an assault on patriarchal religions. Mary Daly, who in 1968 wrote *The Church and the Second Sex,* which attempted to make a home for women within Roman Catholicism, in 1971 led an "exodus" from Christianity when she preached a sermon at Harvard Memorial Church encouraging women to leave patriarchal religions behind them. Although both of these women were

steeped in religious concepts and language as young women, and continue to draw on this background and interact with other religious feminists, neither has rushed to invent a new, more feminist religion.

Others, however, have done just that. Respecting the power of religion, they believe that it cannot be abandoned but must instead be recreated in new, nonpatriarchal forms. Such feminists work to create new religions or spiritualities that do not share what they believe to be the debilities of patriarchal religions. The most prominent example of this religious creativity in the United States is the feminist spirituality movement.

The feminist spirituality movement began in the early 1970s concurrently with feminist reforms within established religions. Drawing on neopagan and New Age religions, feminist spirituality's key innovations were to worship a goddess (or goddesses) and nature and to exclude men (at least initially). Insisting that feminist principles must be the cornerstone of religion, and not an elaborate patch on a fundamentally patriarchal structure, spiritual feminists designed their new religion with women's needs and interests as their first criterion. Although the feminist spirituality movement has set itself up in opposition to established religions, it actually works to a large degree in concert with Jewish and Christian feminism (and, to a lesser extent, with Buddhist and other religious feminisms). Women sometimes participate in both a church or synagogue and in a ritual circle of goddess-worshiping women. Although some individual women do not claim a joint allegiance to patriarchal religions and feminist spirituality, religious feminists as a group have worked across this divide. Jewish and Christian feminists have adapted theologies and rituals pioneered by spiritual feminists; in turn, spiritual feminists have often supported the work of Jewish and Christian feminists, though not claiming it as their own.

Most religious feminism since 1970 has characterized itself as reforming patriarchal religions, but it has also seen religion itself as a power base upon which feminism can stand. Claiming that these religions are—or can be, or should be—fundamentally committed to human equality, feminists have sometimes used religious ethics and rhetoric in their organizing, hoping to mobilize religious congregations in the service of feminist political goals. In this area feminists have been inspired by the earlier example of black theology and the civil rights movement, which found in the very religions that were oppressing African-American communities the resources to call for an end to this oppression. As a consequence of this connection, no doubt, those feminists who have been most adept at seeing patriarchal religions themselves as agents of social change have been women of color. No less concerned about sexism than their white counterparts, African American, Hispanic, and Asian American feminists have constructed theologies that situate race more squarely in the middle as a concern every bit as pressing as sex discrimination (or more so).

Politics and religion can, of course, never be truly separated. Little can prove this better than feminist activism within and against certain practices of organized religion, religious feminism outside its boundaries, and the grounding of political feminism—at least at times—on religious principles.

See also *Gender; Paganism.*

Cynthia Eller

BIBLIOGRAPHY

Daly, Mary. *Beyond God the Father: Toward a Philosophy of Women's Liberation.* Boston: Beacon Press, 1973.

Eller, Cynthia. *Living in the Lap of the Goddess: The Feminist Spirituality Movement in America.* Boston: Beacon Press, 1995.

Gross, Rita M. *Feminism and Religion: An Introduction.* Boston: Beacon Press, 1996.

Isasi-Díaz, Ana María, and Yolanda Tarango. *Hispanic Women, Prophetic Voice in the Church: Toward a Hispanic Women's Liberation Theology.* San Francisco: Harper and Row, 1988.

King, Ursula, ed. *Feminist Theology from the Third World: A Reader.* Maryknoll, N.Y.: Orbis Books, 1994.

Plaskow, Judith. *Standing Again at Sinai: Judaism from a Feminist Perspective.* New York: Harper and Row 1990.

Ruether, Rosemary Radford. *Women-Church: Theology and Practice of Feminist Liturgical Communities.* New York: Harper and Row, 1985.

Schüssler-Fiorenza, Elisabeth, ed. *Searching the Scriptures: A Feminist Introduction.* New York: Crossroad, 1993.

Stanton, Elizabeth Cady, et al. *The Woman's Bible.* New York: Arno Press, 1972 [1895, 1898].

Williams, Delores S. *Sisters in the Wilderness: The Challenge of Womanist God-Talk.* Maryknoll, N.Y.: Orbis Books, 1993.

Foreign Mission Society

See *Maryknoll.*

France

France is a traditionally Roman Catholic country in western Europe adjusting to the growth of other religions and the loss of interest toward religion in general among its population. The first phrase of the French constitution—"France is a secular and indivisible Republic"—confirms with exceptional solemnity that the secularism of the state is a fundamental part of the republican tradition. This notion may appear curious and sometimes contradictory to the ideal of tolerance of a democratic and pluralist society. To understand its true significance, one must remember that the secular ideal originated in the long struggle of French kings to escape the yoke of the Catholic Church. Secularism is not opposed to religion as such but to all the forms of clerical control that a particular religion wishes to exercise over a political power.

Catholicism and French Society

On the eve of the Revolution of 1789, Catholicism pervaded French society. It legitimated political institutions, governed collective life, and controlled the registry office and the teaching, medical, and social service institutions. In a matter of months (May–September 1789) the Old Regime collapsed and the constitutional monarchy that followed immediately made the political system secular. The legitimacy of the monarchy lost its religious foundation. From then on it was based on a contract struck between the king and the people.

Citizens defined themselves as belonging to the nation as a community, and their religious affiliation could not be used to prevent them from participating in politics. The proclamation of the principle of religious freedom in Article 10 of the Declaration of the Rights of Man and of the Citizen (1789), the preamble to the revolutionary constitution, was a decisive step in this political transformation. Religious minorities were gradually granted all the rights associated with citizenship. The rights of Protestants to vote and to be elected to public office—as well as their admission to all employment—were rapidly established. Jewish emancipation was effected in September 1791.

The constitution adopted in September 1791 guaranteed freedom of religion, but the very question of religious freedom raised the issue of the status of Catholicism in society. The national assembly repeatedly voted down church demands that Catholicism be recognized as the state religion.

The long symbiosis between the Catholic institution and the absolute monarchy lent to political modernization a dimension of religious conflict that divided the church itself. Radicalization of the opposing positions came to mean for each the exclusion of its adversary—the republic could triumph only in bringing down the church, but this constituted a victory of one-half of France over the other.

But the revolutionaries did not question the importance of religion in society. Their objective was to join the ecclesiastical institution with civil society. The 1789 Civil Constitution of the Clergy obliged priests to swear an oath of loyalty to the new regime, splitting them between those who rallied around the new regime and those who increasingly fought it. French Catholicism divided into two factions. The hardening of resistance to the new regime, the increasing repression of those opponent clergy, and the authoritarian radicalization of the revolutionary regime drew France into a religious conflict of astounding violence. Many clergy were among those who lost their heads to the guillotine during the Reign of Terror (1793–1794).

Until the end of the nineteenth century, the struggle against the political and social power of the Catholic Church was at the center of the republican effort to build a nation. The 1905 Separation of the Church and the State law, approved in a climate of ideological war, constituted at the time the final struggle in this confrontation and the beginning of a reconciliation made possible when the Catholic masses sided in force with the republic. The celebration of the hundredth anniversary of the law also focused on its liberal aspect. Until World War II, however, French political life carried traces of this religious struggle. On one side was Catholic France, traditional and politically conservative; on the other was a republican and progressive France, where the Protestant French minority and the French Jews freed by the revolution found their place.

Paradoxically the republican culture born of opposition to the power of the Catholic Church was itself constructed along the lines of the Catholic culture that had typified the nation for centuries. The educational and moral work of the Third Republic (1870–1940) and the ceremonies, symbols, temples, and republican processions of the nineteenth century are a form of what British sociologist David Martin has called Catholicism without Christianity. The political victory of the republic did not signify the end of a religious France but the emergence of a specific identity: that of a secular country with a Catholic culture, which is today becoming less and less vigorous.

Modern France

What remains of this long and turbulent history? The passionate episodes that regularly shake up French political life (the dramatic political conflict over the wearing of the Islamic head covering by Muslim pupils in the public schools prohibited by the law passed in March 2004, secular mobilization against the official celebrations in the memory of Pope John Paul II, and so on) should not be misunderstood—the war of two Frances is over. There are many reasons for this pacification. The first, along historical lines, was the stabilization of the republican regime and the definitive adherence of Catholics to the republic, which was pledged in the trenches of World War I. In this respect the Catholic hierarchy had clearly renounced all of its direct political role (no bishops have intervened in elections since 1965).

Even if the vote of regular, practicing Catholics normally goes to the conservative right and the center right, the distinguishing trait of the last thirty years has been the pluralistic politics of French Catholicism as a whole. Regions strongly associated with the Catholic tradition that moved politically to the left (Brittany, Alsace) were the deciding factor in the election of socialist president François Mitterand in 1981. Today the political role of the Catholic Church is identified with affirming moral values that Catholics believe should preside over public life. For example, French bishops have been driven to vigorously denounce the beliefs of xenophobes, protectionists, and the anti-Semites of the extreme right headed by National Front Party founder Jean-Marie Le Pen.

This moral judiciary not only advocated by the Catholic Church but also embraced by Protestant and Jewish minorities is important to the redefinition of relations between secularism and religion under way today. The principal question is no longer the independence of the state from the Catholic Church. It is how the state can function to integrate the republic in a multicultural France in which Islam, with about five to six million followers, has become the second largest religion in the nation. In this new age, new alliances are established that form new connections between religion and politics.

See also *Anticlericalism; Catholicism, Roman; Europe, Western; Islam.*

Celine Beraud

BIBLIOGRAPHY

Bauberot, Jean. *Vers un nouveau pacte laïque?* Paris: Seuil, 1990.

Donegani, Jean Marie. *La Liberté de choisir : pluralisme religieux et pluralisme politique dans le catholicisme français contemporain.* Paris: Presse de la Fondation Nationale des Sciences Politiques, 1993.

Giry, Stéphanie. "France and its Muslims." *Foreign Affairs.* (September/October 2006).

Hervieu-Léger, Danièle. "The Past in the Present: Redefining Laïcité in Multicultural France." In *The Limits of Social Cohesion: Conflict and Mediation in Pluralist Societies,* edited by Peter L. Berger. Boulder, Colo.: Westview Press, 1998.

Hervieu-Léger, Danièle. *Catholicisme, la fin d'un monde.* Paris: Bayard, 2003.

Poulat, Emile. *Liberté, laïcité : la guerre des deux France et le principe de modernité.* Paris: Cerf-Cujas, 1987.

Freedom of Religion

Religious freedom is a two-pronged idea, granting people the right to practice their faith as they choose and to be free from supporting an established religion. More than two hundred years ago Thomas Jefferson penned a classic description of religious freedom: "No man shall be compelled to frequent or support any religious worship, place, or ministry whatsoever, nor shall be enforced, restrained, molested, or burthened in his body or goods, nor shall otherwise suffer on account of his religious opinions or beliefs; but that all men shall be free to profess, and by argument to maintain, their opinions in matters of religion, and that the same shall in no wise diminish, enlarge, or affect their civil capacities." Jefferson's definition expresses an ideal yet to be realized.

From time immemorial religions—with their rites, rituals, moral codes, and creeds—have been an integral if not central component of every culture and thus a major concern of every government. Until the past three centuries of Western civilization, there was no such thing as a secular realm in which people had choices.

Religion and culture were so intimately intertwined through most of human history that it was inconceivable for any member of a society not to share its religion. Religion was the fabric of tribal life. Nonbelievers who spoke up were probably killed or driven out, but they were so few in number that we have no records. Conflicts between religious groups usually occurred when one people or tribe conquered another, as when Rome conquered Palestine in the first century B.C.E. or Muslims invaded Hindu India in the eleventh century C.E. Conflict occasionally arose when a new indigenous religion developed and gained adherents, as when Christianity arose within Palestine in the first century C.E. or Islam arose in Arabia in the seventh century. Normally, conquered people were required to accept the religion of the conqueror or, if they maintained their own religious beliefs and practices, to pay tribute. After a few decades uniformity was reestablished and conflict disappeared.

Christian Beginnings

When Christianity originated in Judaea and Galilee, it was a heretical sect that took root within a despised minority, the Jewish people, who had only recently been conquered by the Roman Empire. Early Christians had reason to respect, or at least accommodate, the empire, if only to gain protection from Jewish leaders. Early Christians introduced a number of radical ideas, many attributed directly to Jesus. Among these was the admonition, "Give unto Caesar the things that are Caesar's and unto God the things that are God's" (Mark 12:17). It was Roman custom to have its emperors identified with the gods, so a split between the deity and the earthly ruler was a radical idea. This caused ambiguous relationships in the late Roman Empire. On the one hand, Christians could be loyal Roman citizens, for "their kingdom was not of this world" and therefore not in competition with Rome. On the other hand, it was a limited loyalty, a distinction between spiritual and temporal domains described and defended in Saint Augustine's *City of God,* written in the early fifth century. Here were the seeds of a separation of church and state idea that took centuries to germinate.

When Christians gained hegemony in the fourth century, after the emperor Constantine's conversion, they reverted to traditional patterns by establishing Christianity as the official faith of the empire, albeit with a two-swords doctrine: the Holy Roman Empire theoretically consisted of spiritual and temporal realms that were separate but coordinate. Much of

medieval history is the story of a struggle for supremacy between secular rulers and popes and between contending "Christian" nations, primarily France, England, Spain, and the Habsburg empire, with the Italian city-states, Portugal, and the small Germanic states playing lesser roles.

Heretics and schismatics were widely persecuted or protected, depending on the political circumstances of individual rulers and the power of various popes, cardinals, and bishops. Freedom of religion for individuals was not given serious consideration.

Reformation and Enlightenment

The Protestant Reformation in the sixteenth century, led by Martin Luther, John Calvin, Henry VIII, and others, initiated profound shifts in Western political thinking—particularly in the area of religious ideas. Luther's original protest was strictly against the established church, both its corruption and its doctrine. He preached the priesthood of all believers and each person's ability to interpret the Bible. He rejected the two-swords theory, substantially strengthening the hand of secular rulers. These new ideas reinvigorated an older notion of the divine right of kings, the belief that kings rule by direct authority from God, not from the will of the people. Early Calvinist thought followed in the same vein, although keeping the concept of separation of church and state, with each institution having distinct rights and duties.

Protestantism quickly spread and split into denominations—Lutheran, Calvinist, Presbyterian, Anglican, Puritan, Dutch Reformed, and the more radical Anabaptists. Ironically, the Reformation also triggered the Counter Reformation, a moral cleansing and rejuvenation of the Roman Catholic Church. The intellectual and spiritual turmoil of the period brought social upheaval and persecutions as people began to think and argue about their faiths. Lutherans and Catholics reached an accommodation in the Peace of Augsburg (1555), agreeing to the principle that each ruler could choose the religion of the people within his region (*cuius regio, eius religio*). This strengthened belief in the divine right of kings and worked against any idea of individual freedom of religion. It also backfired.

The idea of toleration, a critical step on the way to freedom of religion, was all but inconceivable to rulers except as an expedient to be espoused in times of political weakness. It was in such a time that the Edict of Nantes, proclaiming toleration for Calvinists in France, was decreed in 1598, only to be revoked by Louis XIV in 1685. The French phrase *une roi, une loi, une foi*—"one king, one law, one faith"—captured the conventional wisdom of the time. All three elements were seen as essential to maintain national unity and identity.

Attempts to enforce uniformity of belief within political realms were simply not compatible with a core Protestant principle—freedom of each person to read and interpret the Bible for him- or herself. Reformers naively believed all persons of good will would interpret the Bible the same. That was not the case. The principle that rulers could choose their citizens' religion led not to peace but to civil war, suppression of minorities, assassinations, forced conversions, emigrations, expulsions, and searing hatreds that poisoned Western civilization for generations. These disasters still influence our politics.

Religious wars and the ideas that caused them began to change in the seventeenth century as a flurry of writers, primarily but not exclusively English, began to rethink the relationships between kings and subjects. Political philosophers began thinking in terms of social contracts as a more legitimate basis for governing than divine right. Contracts imply mutual responsibilities and limits between ruled and ruler. Thomas Hobbes (1588–1679) and Jean-Jacques Rousseau (1712–1778) used the idea as a starting point for very different philosophies, but they helped the idea gain legitimacy. John Milton penned a plea for freedom of the press (except for Catholics and atheists) in his classic *Areopagitica* (1644). In a lesser-known but influential work, *Treatise of Civil Power in Ecclesiastical Causes* (1659), he argued against a professional clergy and in favor of private interpretation of scripture according to each person's conscience. His work was followed in short order by that of John Locke. In *Two Treatises on Government* (1689), published a year after the Glorious Revolution of 1688, in which the English Parliament replaced James II with William and Mary, Locke attacked the very idea of a divine right of kings. Substituting instead the idea of a social contract between ruled and rulers, he argued that religious freedom was a natural right that it was government's duty to protect.

Although these ideas did not immediately take hold in England or on the Continent, they were profoundly influential with another group of emerging leaders, the founders of the American Republic.

The American Colonial Experience

During their almost 170 years before independence, the American colonies participated in many of England's religious persecutions on a smaller scale. The first Puritans had come to the New World seeking religious freedom for themselves. They had no intention of extending that freedom to others with different religious views. The smaller scale was due partially to the ease with which dissenters could move to other colonies or to the frontier. But religious tensions and hostility were never far below the surface, especially as religious enthusiasts such as Baptists and Methodists engaged in proselytizing among adherents of the more established Anglican and Congregational churches.

Two of America's classic religious documents grew out of this tension. Thomas Jefferson first wrote a bill for establishing religious freedom in 1779, but it was not passed by the Virginia legislature until 1786. It still reads so well as a general statement of religious freedom that it was used to begin this article.

The second document, James Madison's "Memorial and Remonstrance against Religious Assessments" (1785), was written as a circular to be signed by citizens in response to an effort by Virginia's governor, Patrick Henry, to raise tax money to support teachers of the Christian religion. It is a passionate treatise on why "the religion of every man must be left to the conviction and conscience of every man" and why a tax to support any religion violates that liberty. The two documents were forever linked after the "Memorial and Remonstrance" so successfully turned public opinion that Governor Henry's tax measure was defeated and Madison successfully substituted Jefferson's bill for religious freedom. Jefferson considered this one of his greatest accomplishments.

Widely circulated and studied, the two documents set the standard when the U.S. Constitution was written in the summer of 1787. Madison had helped organize the Constitutional Convention and was so influential during its proceedings that he is rightly called the father of the Constitution. During the convention he resisted all calls to add a bill of rights. The only mention of religion in the constitution is a prohibition against using a religious test as a qualification to hold office. Madison feared listing even major rights, lest future generations would infer that rights not listed were not protected. He also believed that the very structure and design of the national government spelled out in the Constitution, with three equal branches and limited to the exercise of delegated powers, was the best protection of rights. When it became clear during debates in the state ratifying conventions that a bill of rights was the price of ratification, he agreed to propose amendments during the first term of Congress. He kept his word, and the first ten amendments are now known as the Bill of Rights.

Madison made yet another contribution to our understanding of religious liberty. During the battle for ratification he, along with Alexander Hamilton and John Jay, penned the *Federalist Papers* to explain and defend the new Constitution. In *Federalist* No. 10, Madison argued that the best way to control the violence of factions (among which he included religious groups) is to have a multiplicity of parties and sects spread over a large republic. In that way no one party or sect can gain enough power to oppress the rest. Pluralism, as we now call it, has become a stable feature of American religions. It is accepted by the churches and has become a basis for cooperating in defense of religious liberty claims—even of competing sects.

The First Amendment to the Constitution reads in relevant part: "Congress shall make no law respecting an establishment of religion or prohibiting the free exercise thereof." The two clauses are respectively known as the establishment and free exercise clauses, and they form the basis for nearly all subsequent development of religious freedom in the United States. Although it is Congress that is prohibited from legislating in this arena, two developments have altered the thrust of this amendment. The first is that the Supreme Court has emerged as the ultimate interpreter of the Constitution, so Court cases have become the primary authority for defining what freedom of religion means. The second is that, beginning in the 1920s, the Supreme Court has gradually applied the Bill of Rights to the states, that is, mandating that states and not just Congress must abide by the standards set in the Bill of Rights. Because most religious liberty claims arise in local situations, the Court's rulings have had a huge effect on the development and spread of religious freedom in the United States. The application of the Bill of Rights to the actions of subnational governments is termed *incorporation* and has occasioned a great deal of litigation in the church-state area.

The Role of the Court

The establishment and free exercise clauses sometimes appear to be in tension. The establishment clause is generally interpreted to mean that there can be no officially recognized or sponsored church (such as the Anglican Church is in England or the Roman Catholic Church once was in Spain) and that no government can support any religion either through monetary aid or display of religious symbols. The establishment clause minimally ensures that government cannot endorse a particular religion, although some analysts (generally termed *separationists*) argue that government cannot provide support or endorsement of religion in general. The free exercise clause is generally interpreted to mean that no government can prohibit religious expression or activity, discriminate against persons or organizations because of their religious beliefs, or coerce people to do things their religion prohibits.

Some analysts regard the religion clauses as internally contradictory, in that there may be instances in which policies that seem prohibited by the establishment clause seem permitted or even required by the free exercise clause. For example, opponents of organized prayer in public schools argue that such prayers amount to an unconstitutional "establishment" of religion, and supporters of school prayer insist that prohibiting such religious expressions represents a violation of the free exercise clause.

However, many contemporary scholars argue that both clauses are designed to protect religious liberty in its largest sense, one that includes equal treatment of all religions and of religious institutions with similar nonreligious (usually nonprofit) organizations. However, not every action can be allowed just because someone claims freedom of religion. Hundreds of court cases define the contours of constitutionally protected free exercise of religion. The following are discussed in chronological order to give an idea of the range of issues covered.

In the first major religious liberty case, *Reynolds v. United States* (1879), George Reynolds, a Mormon official, believed polygamy was required by his religion. He was convicted of practicing polygamy and appealed, arguing that his free exercise rights had been violated. The Supreme Court rejected his claim. The Court reasoned that a person is free to believe whatever he or she wishes, but that actions can be regulated by government and that polygamy violates social duties and is subversive of good order.

West Virginia v. Barnette (1943) considered whether Jehovah's Witness children could be required to salute the American flag, even though this act violated their religious beliefs. The Court noted that the children's refusal was peaceful and orderly and did not interfere with the rights of others. The justices were also troubled that the flag salute statute coerced children into professing a belief they did not hold. This case is particularly interesting because it reversed a decision the justices had made just three years earlier upholding a similar statute.

Twenty years later the Court heard *Sherbert v. Verner* (1963). Adell Sherbert, a Seventh-day Adventist, worked in a textile mill in South Carolina. When she refused to work on Saturday, because Saturday was her Sabbath, she was terminated. She sought unemployment benefits but was denied them, again because she refused to be available for work on Saturdays. In this case the Supreme Court began to work out a free exercise doctrine. After affirming that Sherbert's beliefs were sincere and a central component of her religious faith, the Court looked to see whether South Carolina had a compelling state interest in denying her unemployment benefits. Finding that it did not, the Court ordered the state to accommodate the needs of religious people in its unemployment benefit regulations.

The U.S. Congress has since its inception provided conscientious objector status for citizens who oppose war in all circumstances because of their religious beliefs. Men granted conscientious objector status are not required to serve in the military, but they may be required to perform alternative service in noncombatant roles. *Gillette v. United States* (1971) presented a new issue. Gillette objected to the Vietnam War—although not to all wars—because he considered it unjust. He based his objection on a humanist approach to religion—his deeply held beliefs about the purpose and obligations of human existence. The Supreme Court ruled that Gillette did not qualify for conscientious objector status. Although Congress had indeed distinguished between citizens who oppose all wars and those who oppose only "unjust" wars, the Court ruled that there were pragmatic reasons for doing so (maintaining an adequate pool of candidates, showing fairness to all, and providing administrative clarity). The statute that grants conscientious objector status is neutral and secular; it does not discriminate between religions, because it affects only individual believers. In brief, relief from the duty to serve in the military is limited to those who conscientiously oppose all wars. Individuals are not allowed to pick and choose which wars they will fight.

Unusual or minority religions have always had a difficult time in America. The Amish, descendants in the Anabaptist tradition, attempt to live simple, peaceful lives in rural areas, having as little contact with the outside world as possible.

They do not use motor vehicles, electric motors, telephones, or other modern inventions. They send their children to school until they can read, write, and do arithmetic, usually through the eighth grade. The Amish lived for many decades peaceably among their neighbors in Wisconsin until the state changed its law to require all students to attend school through their sixteenth birthday, generally the ninth or tenth grade. Amish parents refused, arguing that their children not only did not need the extra years of schooling but that they might be tempted to abandon their faith if exposed to modern ideas not compatible with their way of life. Further, these were critical years in which children would learn the farming and housekeeping skills they needed as adults in the Amish community. In *Wisconsin v. Yoder* (1972), the Supreme Court sided with the Amish, arguing that the state did not have a compelling state interest in the extra years of school and that there were alternative means to achieve its legitimate ends—the informal education given by Amish parents during their children's adolescent years. In this case the free exercise claim was upheld. Justice William Douglas raised the issue of whether this right of the parents was contrary to the right of children to be equipped to make other career choices when they became adults, but the Court was not willing to pursue this line of argument.

Goldman v. Weinberger (1986) dealt with a Jewish military officer who was told he could not wear his yarmulke indoors. Capt. Simcha Goldman argued that his religion required him to wear the head covering and that he had previously worn it without infringing on anyone's rights or disrupting military discipline. The Supreme Court reasoned that military life has unique needs for uniformity and discipline and that what might be considered an infringement on religious liberty in civilian life could be subordinated to military discipline in the armed forces.

Employment Division, Department of Human Resources of Oregon v. Smith (1990) is the most important case decided since *Sherbert v. Verner*. Two Native Americans who were counselors with a private drug rehabilitation agency were fired when their employer discovered that they had ingested peyote, an outlawed drug, at a religious ceremony in the Native American Church, of which both were members. Their applications for unemployment benefits were denied because they had been fired "for cause"—that is, for committing an illegal act—and were thus ineligible. The Supreme Court upheld the state of Oregon's right to refuse benefits, overriding the free exercise claim of the defendants.

What is most important about this case is not the outcome but the reasoning. Writing for the majority, Justice Antonin Scalia argued that so long as a state's criminal statutes were general in nature and neutral toward religion they did not have to accommodate religious beliefs. Although *Sherbert* required a government to show a compelling state interest as to why its laws should outweigh a religious liberty claim, the majority's opinion held that in the case of criminal statutes only a rational basis for the statute is required. The result is that religious liberty claims will always lose if the government can show that its laws are a reasonable way to achieve otherwise legitimate goals.

Religious interest groups and denominations from across the political and religious spectrums found this decision an alarming threat to religious liberty and combined in an extraordinary coalition to petition Congress for a law rejecting the *Employment Division v. Smith* reasoning and reinstating the *Sherbert v. Verner* rule. After intensive lobbying by these groups, Congress passed the Religious Freedom Restoration Act of 1993 (RFRA). But in a 1997 case, *City of Boerne (Texas) v. Flores, Archbishop of San Antonio,* the Supreme Court ruled, 6–3, that Congress exceeded its power to regulate state activity when it dictated that states and courts had to use a compelling interest and least restrictive means test in religious liberty cases. The current constitutional rule governing religious liberty cases is that statutes that are general in nature and not specifically written to burden religion do not have to accommodate religious beliefs, although in a case decided in 2006 (*Gonzales, Attorney General, et al., v. O Centro Espirita Beneficente Uniao do Vegetal, et al.*), the Court made a distinction between state and federal regulation in upholding RFRA against federal encroachment of religious freedom. This ruling suggests that the Court may take a more expansive view of the free exercise clause in the future. Nevertheless, many scholars see the precedents in *Smith* and *Boerne* as serious erosions of religious liberty protection. Whether that will be the case in practice remains to be seen.

If we look to the future, it seems clear that the United States, as a relatively open, changing society that accepts immigrants from around the world and emphasizes individual liberties, will continue to see a stream of ever-changing freedom of religion claims come before its courts. There will be numerous efforts to curtail religious liberty, particularly for unfamiliar minority groups with unfamiliar practices. Religious liberty enjoys a broader range of protection in the United States than anywhere else in the world, but it is never quite secure. Religious groups must be vigilant to maintain their freedom in its present form.

Global Dimensions

It is tempting to consider religious freedom in strictly American and European terms. That is a mistake, even though the roots of religious freedom are deeply embedded in these cultures. The ideals of peace, justice, and universal love are preached in all major religious traditions. The idea of toleration of others' religious beliefs can be found in Islam's sacred book, the Qur'an, which dates from the seventh century. Unfortunately, concern for freedom of religion did not become a matter of global concern until the mid-twentieth century.

Stimulated in part by a desire to protect their missionaries in colonial territories, an ecumenical group of mainline Protestants held a conference at Oxford, England, in 1937, during which they developed a common position on religious liberty as a global problem. The statement noted a close link between religious liberty and a just, stable international order. After World War II, in early 1948, the first assembly of the World Council of Churches was held in Amsterdam. This assembly issued a statement linking religious freedom to peace and urged that religious liberty become part of a new international bill of rights. Driven in part by widespread revulsion at the fate of Jews in Nazi-occupied territories, and input from the World Council of Churches, the United Nations General Assembly passed the Universal Declaration of Human Rights in late 1948. Article 18 may be considered the Magna Carta of religious freedom: "Everyone has the right to freedom of thought, conscience and religion; this right includes freedom to change his religion or belief and freedom, either alone or in community with others and in public or private, to manifest his religion or belief in teaching, practice, worship and observance."

Little was done to clarify or implement this declaration in the following years. The major world powers turned their attention to cold war issues, and colonized nations were caught up in winning their independence. The concept of religious liberty received a major boost in 1965, when the Second Vatican Council passed a Declaration on Religious Freedom that supported freedom of conscience for all people. Although the Catholic Church was the last major Christian church to embrace religious liberty for all, it was also the largest, and its statement added legitimacy to the idea.

Freedom of religion is now seen as an important universal human right, but attempts to define exactly what it requires in practice have run into a number of difficulties. Five very different but sometimes overlapping cultures have such different ideas that this area has become a complex one to negotiate.

- A Western secular tradition sees religious freedom as rooted in separation of church and state and disestablishment along the American model. Secularists are concerned that nonbelievers be treated equally and that no tax monies or government influence be used to support religion.
- A Zionist Jewish tradition believes that Israel is a special case calling for government support of Judaism because of the close identification of the Jewish faith with the land of Israel, especially Jerusalem, throughout history. Further, the unique record of persecution of Jews in other lands supports the idea of Israel as a separate Jewish state.
- A Christian tradition holds that government support for religious ideas and institutions helps preserve important cultural values and identities and is not incompatible with religious freedom as long as other religions are protected and no individuals are coerced or disadvantaged because of their faith. Long prevalent in England and Latin America, this idea is emerging in eastern Europe as newly freed nations try to return or compensate for religious properties confiscated during the communist years and to reestablish their national cultures.
- A Marxist tradition, still powerful in China and several smaller nations, sees religion as a competitor to the state, a social institution to be controlled and limited, and at best a necessary evil to be tolerated only until it withers away. This tradition is willing to accept the freedom of conscience as an "inner freedom" but rejects any social role or rights for religious institutions.
- An Islamic tradition rejects the very idea of separation of church and state and in some cases even the legitimacy of a secular state. Allah is Lord of all, and where possible Islamic law, *shariʿa,* is to be the primary source of justice. Of particular concern to Muslims is any acknowledgment of freedom for non-Muslims to proselytize or convert Muslims. The memory of the Christian Crusades and Western colonialism make this issue particularly sensitive and radically at variance with the Christian view

that religious freedom entails the right of churches to evangelize and individuals to change faiths. A growing Hindu nationalism takes a negative view of evangelism parallel to that in Islamic tradition.

Freedom of religion remains an area filled with controversy and complexity. The very idea that there is any universal set of human rights has come under attack from nations whose religious and cultural traditions do not include such emerging rights as equality for women and protection of children. Another challenge comes from religion-based nationalism, essentially the idea that a particular religion, invariably that of those in power, is the "soul of the nation" and that religious minorities are disloyal or at best second-class citizens. A further tension comes from certain churches themselves, as their self-understanding increasingly requires them to criticize social injustice and political oppression wherever it is found.

Although great progress has been made in understanding and spreading the ideal of religious freedom as a universal human right, limits on religious expression and activities and even outright persecutions continue across the globe. The fight for freedom of religion is a story without end.

See also *Constitution, U.S.; Human Rights; Nationalism; Secularization; Separation of Church and State.*

Ted G. Jelen

BIBLIOGRAPHY

Davis, Derek. "Resolving Not to Resolve the Tension between the Establishment and Free Exercise Clauses." *Journal of Church and State* 38 (1996): 245–259.

Freedom of Conscience. Proceedings. Seminar organized by the Secretariat General of the Council of Europe. Strasbourg: Council of Europe Press, 1993.

Jelen, Ted G., and Clyde Wilcox. *Public Attitudes toward Church and State.* Armonk, N.Y.: M. E. Sharpe, 1995.

Koshy, Ninan. "The Ecumenical Understanding of Religious Liberty: The Contribution of the World Council of Churches." *Journal of Church and State* 38 (Winter 1996): 137–154.

Laycock, Douglas. "Continuity and Change in the Threat to Religious Liberty: The Reformation Era and the Late Twentieth Century." *Minnesota Law Review* 80 (1996): 1047–1102.

Miller, Robert T., and Ronald B. Flowers. *Toward Benevolent Neutrality: Church, State, and the Supreme Court.* 5th ed. Waco, Texas: Baylor University Press, 1997.

"Religious Human Rights in the World Today: A Report on the 1994 Atlanta Conference." *Emory International Law Review* 10 (Spring 1996).

Reynolds, Noel B., and W. Cole Durham Jr. *Religious Liberty in Western Thought.* Atlanta, Ga.: Scholars Press, 1996.

Weber, Paul J. *Equal Separation: Understanding the Religion Clauses of the First Amendment*. Westport, Conn.: Greenwood Press, 1990.

Witte, John, Jr., and Johan D. van der Vyver, eds. *Human Rights in Global Perspectives*. 2 vols. Amsterdam: Martinus Nijhoff, 1996.

Freemasonry

A fraternal order, known to outsiders primarily for its secrecy and ritual, Freemasonry has its greatest strength in Britain and the United States. Masonry played a central role in the transformation of American society from the colonial era to the rise of Jacksonian democracy in the late 1820s. Under President Andrew Jackson, American society became increasingly egalitarian and this period became known as the era of the "common man."

The Freemasons, the largest and most influential fraternal order to come to America, trace their roots to England at the time of the Norman Conquest (1066), when building in stone was carried on with remarkable activity by stonemasons at the behest of kings, nobles, and churchmen. As early as the seventeenth century the membership of Masonic lodges began to shift from tradesmen skilled in the craft of masonry to noblemen and gentry who took an interest in planning and design. By 1717, at the time of the formation of the first Grand Lodge in London, "free," or independent, masonry had taken on the character of a nobleman's club, while continuing to employ remnants of a tradition-laden medieval institution, including a secret brotherhood; consistent identity from lodge to lodge; centrality of ritual, initiation, and myths of origin; and explicit connection to an artisan culture.

In its migration to the Continent and to North America the newly formulated Masonic order continued to alter its beliefs and practices as larger social and political contexts framed the terms in which it was understood. In Europe, reaction against Masonry's trade origins was articulated most forcefully in the development of Templarism, or Scottish Masonry. Templaric Freemasonry offered a reinterpretation of Masonic origins that traced its birth from the orders of Crusader knights such as the Knights Templars. Templarism involved the creation of more exclusive and hierarchical subgroups within Masonry. In contrast, American Masonry underwent a limited democratization.

The Enlightenment and American Revolution

The first American Masonic lodges reflected the ideals of benevolence and sociability at the heart of eighteenth-century Enlightenment social theory. Established in eastern coastal towns during the 1730s and 1740s, and dominated by many of the colonies' most prominent men, American Freemasonry erected no formal barriers of religion or nationality to membership, yet it reinforced social divisions between gentlemen and others. In its rejection of religious and political disputes, and its support for "that Religion in which all Men agree," the order embodied a liberal view of religion as an institution that brings order and harmony to society. Similarly, fraternal men believed that the proper awareness of nature's harmony would act as a corrective to the individualism and greed that threatened the social and political order. Masonic references to God as the Supreme Architect reflect this Newtonian understanding of a harmonious and ordered universe. At the same time, the first American lodges believed in the Enlightenment's ideal of a cultivated, orderly community, where a benevolent elite would be recognized and honored for selfless devotion to the public good.

In the mid-eighteenth century, new directions in Masonry placed it at the center of revolutionary changes in definitions of power and hierarchy. Beginning in the 1750s large numbers of mechanics, small merchants, and military men, some of whom had been rejected by existing lodges, proposed a variant of Freemasonry, which they termed "Ancient Masonry." Preoccupied by issues of status in a rapidly changing society, these ambitious and politically active men reshaped the social and intellectual boundaries of the fraternity. Revolutionary concepts of disinterested virtue and equality lay at the heart of this transformation, helping to buttress Ancient Masonry's claims to social distinction and to identify the order as an archetype of the republican society based on virtue and talent that they were attempting to build. In the 1790s, with the American Revolution fought and won, the order spread rapidly. Masons began to describe the fraternity as embodying the republican values of education, morality, and Christianity.

Ambiguous Relationship with Religion

The first quarter of the nineteenth century was marked by a growing convergence of Christianity and Freemasonry around ideals of the Enlightenment. Standing between Christian sectarianism and nonbiblical rationalism, Freemasonry attracted ministers and members from various proto-liberal denominations with a high incidence of Congregationalists, Episcopalians, and Unitarians among its leaders. At the same time, its members began to invest Freemasonry with explicitly Christian values and beliefs. Lodge meetings were opened with Christian prayers and Bible readings, new rituals emphasized biblical narratives and settings, Christian ministers were admitted without charge, and, by 1815, lodges were appointing their own Christian chaplains. After the shift to republican ideals and symbols—in contrast to the colonial period, when civic ritual had centered on the British monarchy and the church, with Christian ministers called upon to bless public institutions—Masons were increasingly called upon to solemnize public enterprises, even going so far as to lay the cornerstone at the foundations of churches.

Despite a positive public presence, an Anti-Masonic Party arose in the early nineteenth century. The Anti-Masons attacked the fraternity's secrecy and medieval trappings as exemplifying the evils identified by the new democratic and evangelical critique of society. The fraternity's secret brotherhood now appeared to undermine government: its exclusiveness was a sign of aristocracy, while its promotion of preference illustrated the wealthy's subversion of the open market. Masonic ideas were prominent among Joseph Smith's radically new Mormon sect, whose stories of revelation threatened the "truth" of Christian beginnings.

Finally, Masonry's affinity for a religion that arises naturally from human reason, together with its liberal view of Christian doctrine, furnished grounds for believing it was incompatible with revealed religion. By the late 1820s and 1830s Freemasonry was effectively shut down, its membership dispersed and lodges closed. By the 1840s, however, the order was reborn as a private male world quite separate from an increasingly feminized Christianity.

See also *Enlightenment*.

David G. Hackett

BIBLIOGRAPHY

Brooke, John L. *Refiner's Fire: The Making of Mormon Cosmology, 1644–1844.* Cambridge: Cambridge University Press, 1994.
Bullock, Steven C. *Revolutionary Brotherhood: Freemasonry and the Transformation of the American Social Order, 1730–1840.* Chapel Hill: University of North Carolina Press, 1996.
Carnes, Mark C. *Secret Ritual and Manhood in Victorian America.* New Haven: Yale University Press, 1989.
Clawson, Mary Ann. *Constructing Brotherhood: Class, Gender, and Fraternalism.* Princeton: Princeton University Press, 1989.
Dumenil, Lynn. *Freemasonry and American Culture, 1880–1930.* Princeton: Princeton University Press, 1984.
Goodman, Paul. *Towards a Christian Republic: Antimasonry and the Great Transition in New England, 1826–1836.* New York: Oxford University Press, 1988.
Jacob, Margaret C. *Living the Enlightenment: Freemasonry and Politics in Eighteenth-century Europe.* New York: Oxford University Press, 1991.
Lipson, Dorothy Ann. *Freemasonry in Federalist Connecticut, 1789–1835.* Princeton: Princeton University Press, 1977.

Friends, Society of (Quakers)

The Society of Friends (Quakers) is a religious movement that arose out of radical Puritanism in the seventeenth century in northwestern England. In the early twenty-first century the movement included about 135,000 English-speaking members worldwide, with larger numbers in East Africa and Latin America.

Though considered a Protestant denomination, the Friends require no creeds, outward sacraments, or ordained clergy for worship (meeting). Their worship centers on silent waiting together for the personal, direct experience of God—that is, divine guidance from an "Inner Light."

Friends have sought ethical perfection throughout their history. "Speaking truth to power," the watchword of a twentieth-century Friends committee, reflects early Friends' vision of a world ruled by evil yet conquered by the Spirit. Their experience of restoring primitive Christianity led them to pacifism, a refusal to take oaths, and simplicity in dress and speech. It also led them into the "Lamb's War" to transform the social order, as well as personal lives, and to struggles throughout their history to balance sectarian purity and political responsibility.

Early Friends (see John 15:15) became known as Quakers because they quaked upon "convincement" and because the founder of the movement, George Fox (1624–1691), urged English magistrates to tremble (or quake) before the word of God rather than before that of the law.

The Early Years

The Society of Friends was born in England in the 1650s, when civil war followed the overthrow of King Charles I, Anglican bishops, and the House of Lords by the parliamentary leaders, rising merchants, and Puritans among the parish clergy. Although Puritans saw God's hand in these events, their apocalyptic hopes were disappointed as their alliance fractured. Artisans' "separatist" congregations renounced the inclusive parishes of the Church of England.

Many became Friends, adhering to the teachings of George Fox, an English shepherd and shoemaker who felt divinely led to preach that a formal church structure with its rites and educated ministers was not necessary because God illuminated the inner soul of every person. The Quaker "Awakening" mushroomed as lay itinerants called on unchurched crowds in moorlands and cities to heed the searching "Light" or Spirit that shows all evil within: "Jesus Christ has come to teach his people himself."

Defensive gentry and some Puritans rejected Quaker claims of human perfectability. As the Puritan Commonwealth and Protectorate established in 1649 fell apart in 1659, however, radical Puritans invited Quakers to hold public office.

The restoration of King Charles II, the House of Lords, and bishops in 1660 led to two bitter decades of persecution of all dissenters from the Anglican Church. Nevertheless, Friend Margaret Fell and Fox, who had organized the "First Publishers of Truth" across Europe and America, set up a network of meetings to support Quaker community life.

Meanwhile, mutual discipline patterns turned "testimonies" of speech and dress, which began as prophetic confrontations of non-Quakers, into badges of sectarian loyalty. Quaker theologians such as Robert Barclay (1648–1690) defended silent worship and the universality of the "Light." Cautions that each person must follow "the measure of Light" within provided Friends such as William Penn (1644–1718), an aristocratic convert to the movement, with a basis on which to appeal to the consciences of even non-Quaker persecutors. Indeed, the Friends' reliance on "spiritual weapons" and "friendly persuasion" became evidence that the Spirit would never lead them to violence. Finally, by openly but peacefully refusing to restrict their worship and ethics, Friends helped to secure passage of the Toleration Act of 1689, which freed worship (though not all civil rights) in England.

Quaker Settlements in the New World

Between 1656 and 1672 Fox and other traveling Quaker preachers had gathered to meetings settlers in Barbados, Jamaica, Rhode Island, New York, Maryland, Virginia, and Carolina. The persecution continued, however; in Massachusetts four Friends were hung. Even before the 1689 Toleration Act, William Penn, who had secured a royal land grant in the American colonies in payment of debts owed his fam-

George Fox.

ily, had established the colonies of West New Jersey and Pennsylvania, which were based on his faith in the universality of the Light and conscience. Penn shared ideas with other Friends and, despite his landlord rights, placed power from the beginning in the hands of an elected assembly. Its leaders, however, were able to maintain power and outward peace among the varied settlers and native American Indians until 1755 only by frequent compromises of "Truth" with successive British monarchs and ministers, who continued to demand military defenses. Finally, in 1756, the Quakers relinquished control of the assembly.

In England and its American colonies Quakers had always been penalized for refusing militia service and tax support for clergy, but from 1790 to 1860 they escaped sectarian isolation by immersing themselves in commerce and pioneering programs for hospital and prison reform, public education, and efforts to abolish slavery. Indeed, to recover

Quaker purity, John Woolman (1720–1772), a tailor from West New Jersey, and others persuaded Friends to "disown" slave owning. Quakers Benjamin Lundy (1789–1839) and John Greenleaf Whittier (1807–1892) published newssheets. Lucretia Mott (1793–1880), Sojourner Truth (1797–1883), and the Grimke sisters lectured, defending women's rights. Black sea captain Paul Cuffee repatriated freedmen to Africa. Levi Coffin (1798–1877) coordinated the Underground Railroad and Freedmen's Aid. And Elizabeth Fry (1780–1845) reorganized women's prisons.

Nineteenth-century American Friends migrated in great numbers from the South, where laws enforced slavery, to the farmland of the Midwest. There and in cities, increasingly influenced by non-Quaker neighbors and social pressures, the Friends became permanently divided in theology and worship between the Bible-centered evangelicals and quietists, who later became liberals. Moreover, they increasingly found their patterns of congregational discipline unable to handle intermarriages and those members who had enlisted in the Union Army during the Civil War (1861–1865) to oppose slavery. In England, where since 1832 Quakers had been entitled to enter Parliament, Quaker reform politician John Bright (1811–1889) helped to maintain English neutrality in the U.S. Civil War, but lost his seat for opposing the Crimean War (1853–1856).

Relief and Reform

After the American Revolution, Friends embarked on what became long-term alternatives to sectarian purity and political compromise: alternative services in times of war, relief programs in times of natural disasters, and reform efforts at the national and international levels. For example, Friends undertook aid efforts during the Crimean War and the Franco-Prussian War (1870–1871). The outbreak of World War I (1914–1918) in 1914 saw British and American Friends, who faced hostility for opposing the war and its conscription, form the frontline Friends Ambulance Unit and American Friends Service Committee, which served in battle-ravaged northern France. In 1919 relief and reconstruction programs were extended to Germany, where until 1924 one million children were fed daily in cooperation with German teachers and social workers. Similar programs in central Europe and Russia (1917–1927) followed. In all of these programs, Quakers worked with or under Red Cross and government officials such as Friend Herbert Hoover (U.S. president, 1929–1933).

The first Friends World Conference in 1920 called for disarmament and racial justice, and in 1922 and 1929 the American Friends Service Committee and the British Friends Service Council tackled economic and social issues by aiding the families of striking textile workers and coal miners. Volunteer work camps, "peace caravans," and education programs enlisted students. Quaker senator Paul Douglas, a Democrat from Illinois, worked within Congress.

In World War II American Friends were barred by Congress from most of the ambulance, air raid, children's resettlement, and mining services open to British conscientious objectors. The historic peace churches (Mennonites, Brethren, and Friends) vainly opposed conscription and agreed to administer civilian public service camps, mostly for forestry and conservation. Frustrated with army oversight and the isolation of the work, however, the churches declined to administer similar pacifist service options during the Korean and Vietnam wars.

The Friends' four-decade battle against conscription and for disarmament and the rights of Native Americans led to the establishment of the Friends Committee for National Legislation in 1943. Under Raymond Wilson and Edward Snyder it became the pioneer among Protestant lobbies. The American Friends Service Committee oversees the Quaker United Nations office. Elsewhere over the years, individual Friends have joined in vigils against nuclear weapons and power plants, chemical and biological weapons, and the Vietnam and Persian Gulf wars, among other issues, and Friends continue to lead the worldwide network of Alternatives to Violence Programs in dozens of prisons. Except among East African and Latin American Friends, at most Quaker monthly and regional yearly meetings of varied theologies, committees present programs and resolutions for or against abortion, homosexuality, and capital punishment—issues on which Friends have no consensus nationally. Overall, the emphasis of most Quakers and their committees since the tumultuous 1960s has shifted from social service to social change.

See also *Pacifism; Protestantism*.

Hugh Barbour

BIBLIOGRAPHY

Barbour, Hugh, and J. William Frost. *The Quakers.* Richmond, Ind.: Friends United Press, 1994.

Brock, Peter. *The Quaker Peace Testimony, 1660 to 1914.* York, England: Sessions, 1990.

Fox, George. *The Works of George Fox.* 8 vols., edited by T. H. S. Wallace. State College, Pa.: New Foundation Publication, George Fox Fund, 1990.

Jones, Rufus M. *The Later Periods of Quakerism.* London: Macmillan, 1921.

Marietta, Jack D. *The Reformation of American Quakerism, 1748–1783.* Philadelphia: University of Pennsylvania Press, 1984.

Mullen, Tom, ed., and Edward Snyder. *Witness in Washington: Fifty Years of Friendly Persuasion.* Richmond, Ind.: Friends United Press, 1995.

Fundamentalism

Fundamentalism is a modern form of politicized religion by which self-styled "true believers" resist the marginalization of religion in their respective societies. Fundamentalists identify and oppose the agents of marginalization (secularists) and seek to restructure political, social, cultural, and economic relations and institutions according to traditional religious precepts and norms.

"True believers" adopt different approaches and methods in pursuing their common goals. Some battle secularists gradually on the cultural and social fronts by establishing schools, religious academies, journals, newspapers, hospitals, and orphanages to serve, educate—and convert—people in need of such services. Other fundamentalists enter the political arena by forming political parties and contesting elections. Seeking power through established, conventional means, they hope to transform society in dramatic ways. Still other fundamentalists, abandoning rule by law and conventional politics, become militants who wage a religious war to overthrow the established political order or commit violent acts of terrorism designed to intimidate the enemy into making concessions.

In recent years fundamentalist movements have combined these various roles into a single, and singular, public profile. In the twenty-first century, this became evident on September 11, 2001, with the elaborate and large-scale attacks by the Islamic fundamentalist group al-Qaida on the World Trade Center and the Pentagon. Fundamentalist groups became players in a global conflict over resources, political self-determination, and global governance. Several fundamentalist movements, particularly those rooted in Islam, adopted a three-fold approach, combining cultural and social activism, political advocacy and party politics, and military operations in a full-bore assault upon "the decadent West" and its surrogates around the world.

Defining Fundamentalists

Use of the term *fundamentalist* for everyone who pursues one of these strategies can be misleading if other considerations are not taken into account. For example, some modern religious leaders eschew political power and concentrate on fostering a return to religious practices and lifestyles by fallen-away Muslims, Christians, or Jews. It is more accurate to call such apolitical leaders revivalists and to see their movements as expressions of religious revivalism. In other words, not every person who takes her religion seriously, practices it fervently, and organizes her life and career around it is a fundamentalist. Fundamentalists, by contrast, want to change the behavior of nonbelievers as well as believers; therefore, they strive to change the laws and structures of society that impede their mission of opposing the godless and converting the nonbeliever. At the other extreme, many terrorists and so-called religious warriors are not motivated by religious sensibilities at all; rather, they are mercenaries or secular ideologues exploiting religious fervor for their own irreligious ends. The genuine fundamentalist is both religious and political; indeed, he believes that circumstances require him to act politically (and perhaps violently) in order to fulfill his religious obligations. In the late 1990s Usama bin Ladin, leader of the Sunni fundamentalist network known as al-Qaida, issued *fatwas,* or religious rulings on Islamic law, enjoining all Muslims to fight against and kill all U.S. citizens, for example. Bin Laden argued that the "soul" of Islam was at risk. The subsequent al-Qaida attacks on targets in the United States, Europe, Africa, and South Asia were designed to demonstrate to fellow Muslims that a cosmic battle against the infidels was underway—and winnable.

If fundamentalism is defined as a cross-cultural, religio-political pattern of thought and behavior rather than equated with a specific set of beliefs, rituals, or religious practices, it becomes clear that fundamentalists may be found within any historic religion that has sacred scriptures and basic teachings. They are defenders of a religious tradition that goes back centuries rather than promoters of a new religion or cult centered on one charismatic leader, such as David Koresh of the Branch Davidians, a cult centered in Waco, Texas, in the early 1990s. Although fundamentalists defend traditional beliefs and draw on the symbolic and organizational resources of their ancient religion, they are not merely conservative or orthodox believers. Being a conservative Christian, a devout Muslim, or an Orthodox Jew, in other words, does not necessarily make one a fundamentalist. Rather, fundamentalists are militant conservatives who see the world as a battleground between absolute good and absolute evil. Thus they are spiritual (and sometimes physical) warriors who oppose nonbelievers as well as the doubters or compromisers within their own religious community.

Most fundamentalists are neither uneducated, backward-looking people nor the credulous dupes of silver-tongued preachers. To the contrary, they are medical doctors, nurses, engineers, teachers, businessmen, and college-educated mothers and fathers who readily use (or even invent) the tools of technology, mass communications, and modern science. Yet they feel strongly that Western societies erred grievously when they replaced God, religion, and divine law with human reason and secular political principles as the basis for the legal and social order. For such people, religiously derived morality is the only acceptable framework for discerning the common good, evaluating human behavior, and governing society. Moreover, for most Muslims, Western ideas and institutions were imposed by European outsiders who colonized and dominated their societies, converting many of their brothers, sisters, and children to their foreign, "godless" ways.

Accordingly, fundamentalists oppose ideas and social movements that carry secular values. Whether Jewish, Christian, or Muslim, fundamentalists are, for example, antipluralist because they believe in the superiority of the one true religion (their own) and therefore reject the idea that the state should offer equal protection under law to all religions or philosophical positions. Fundamentalists also tend to be antifeminist because they believe that the movement for women's liberation from patriarchy (a society ruled by men) violates the will of God (Allah, Yahveh) who created males and females for different roles, with women destined to be subordinated to men in society and in the home.

Jewish, Christian, and Muslim fundamentalists may not share the same specific beliefs, but they do share a way of thinking about their beliefs. First, fundamentalists are selective. They are selectively traditional, choosing certain scriptures or theological teachings from the past and insisting that all true believers "fight to the death" (literally or figuratively) to protect these "fundamentals." They are also selectively modern, choosing certain twentieth-century tech-

nologies (such as modern passenger jets, Stinger missiles, television, computer, and fax machine) and processes (such as modern political parties and elections) as weapons against their enemies.

Second, the fundamentalist pattern of thought is absolutist (the truth we proclaim is perfect, complete, and irreformable); inerrantist (the truth we proclaim is free from any kind of error); and dualist (we who proclaim the truth are children of light; all others are children of darkness). Fundamentalists also believe that they are living in a special time in history, perhaps the last days, in which God is working in a new way among the true believers. This idea, known as millennialism in Christianity, helps fundamentalists to explain why they sometimes resort to violence even though their religion normally forbids it. In the final days, when the true believers find themselves in direct combat with the enemy, God wants them to retrieve teachings that justify violent action in defense of the faith.

Members of fundamentalist movements often live by strict rules of discipline; they dress, eat, drink, and perhaps marry according to rules prescribed by an authoritarian leader who always is male and also may be charismatic (gifted with special powers, including the ability to inspire heroic action in others). Members devote a great deal of energy toward maintaining the borders between themselves and outsiders, whom they may portray as witting or unwitting agents of Satan.

Fundamentalists are found within the three great monotheistic faiths—Judaism, Christianity, and Islam. Many of the characteristics of fundamentalism also appear in twentieth- and twenty-first-century South Asian religious movements, including Hindu nationalists in India, Sikh radicals in Punjab, and Buddhist militants in Sri Lanka. In the South Asian cases, the innovative and (ironically) antitraditional character of fundamentalism is especially clear: the political leaders of these movements, seeking to use religion as the basis for an ethnically and culturally exclusive nationalism, have found it necessary to "Westernize" the host religious tradition.

Hinduism and Buddhism do not readily lend themselves to the political dynamics of fundamentalism; they lack the necessary theological "raw materials"—a comprehensive religio-legal code, a concept of time as linear and progressive, and a salvation history prefigured in sacred scriptures and directed by an interventionist personal God. Thus Hindu nationalists created in the 1980s a synthetic fundamentalism by borrowing politically charged Western religious concepts and grafting them onto the diverse, local, folk-oriented traditions and practices known as "Hinduism." Members of the World Hindu Party (VHP, Vishva Hindu Parishad), the cultural wing of Hindu nationalism, staged a campaign in the 1980s and 1990s to promote the mythical deity Lord Rama to the status of a national patron of Hindustan, the imagined sacred nation whose citizens, whether they be Hindus, Muslims, Christians, Jains, Buddhists, or Sikhs, must conform to the cultural and political requirements of *Hindutva* (Hinduness). Seeking to project Rama as a historical figure with a clearly defined birthplace and political legacy, the VHP helped to popularize (and modernize) the *Ramayana,* the epic poem celebrating the deeds of the god-hero, by broadcasting it, in serial form, on national television.

The renewal of Rama's myth and cult served explicit political purposes: the secular government of India, led by the Congress Party, was at the time implementing the "affirmative action" recommendations of a national commission, and Hindu activists vigorously opposed affirmative action for "minorities" in India, especially Muslims. The most flagrant expression of the new Hindu chauvinism was the 1992 destruction of Babari Masjid, a mosque established in 1528 in the north-central town of Ayodhya by Muslim leaders of the Mughal dynasty. Hindu nationalists, claiming the site as the birthplace of Lord Rama, razed the mosque in hopes of rebuilding the ancient temple as a twentieth-century Hindu national shrine. In doing so, they unleashed a spiral of violence across India that resulted in the death of thousands of Muslims and Hindus.

In whatever religious tradition they inhabit, fundamentalists are always outnumbered by conservatives, moderates, and liberals who practice the religion without developing a principled hostility toward outsiders. Despite their relatively small numbers, however, fundamentalists usually capture media headlines and cause controversy by acting in a way that other religious believers as well as the secular public find dramatic and intentionally provocative. Fundamentalists would say that they are only fulfilling sacred obligations; such fidelity to orthodoxy (correct religious belief) or orthopraxis (correct religious practice) may seem defiant and even scandalous, they acknowledge, to people who have compromised their religious identities by cooperating with nonbelievers for political or economic gain.

Christian Fundamentalism

In 1920 Curtis Lee Laws, editor of the Baptist *Watchman-Examiner,* coined the term *fundamentalist* to describe the evangelical Christians of North America willing to do "battle royal" in defense of the fundamentals of the faith. Evangelical Christians, to paraphrase historian Grant Wacker, are Protestants who believe that the sole authority in religion is the Bible and the sole means of salvation is a life-transforming experience wrought by the Holy Spirit through faith in Jesus Christ. Fundamentalist Christians, according to the liberal Protestant preacher Harry Emerson Fosdick, are "mad evangelicals."

At the turn of the twentieth century, when they first emerged from the Protestant churches, the fundamentalists were angry because new secular ideas and methods were threatening to discredit traditional Christian beliefs. Englishman Charles Darwin's theory of evolution by means of random mutation and natural selection seemed to deny God's providence in creating and sustaining the world. When middle ground–seeking Protestants like Lyman Abbot proclaimed that evolution was simply "God's way of doing things," his bruising-for-a-fight coreligionists rankled. They saw an insidious link between evolutionism and the so-called higher criticism, a method of examining the historical and literary character of the Bible as if it were just another book. To make matters worse, liberal Protestants were importing the new methods and ideas from Germany into American Protestant seminaries and colleges.

In what would become fine fundamentalist fashion, the angry evangelical Christians reacted by selecting certain traditional beliefs—Christ's birth to a virgin, blood atonement for human sins by death on the cross, bodily resurrection, and anticipated second coming in glory—and fortifying them with a new way of describing the authority of the Bible. This fifth "fundamental," the strict inerrancy of the Bible, guaranteed that everything taught in scripture, including science and history as well as religion, was absolutely true without qualification. Adherence to the doctrine of strict inerrancy served to separate the true believer from the moderate or merely conservative evangelical, whose judgment presumably was clouded by the seductive appeal of the prestigious new sciences. (Fundamentalists earned the name "come-outers" when they fled the mainline denominations and established their own independent churches in order to worship apart from their corrupted brethren.)

The fundamentalists also were innovative in their interpretations of the Bible's teaching about the end days. The Scofield Reference Bible (1909) presented their own unique form of apocalypticism. Called dispensational premillennialism, the widely adopted theory held that Christ would soon return to punish the nonbelievers, beginning with the liberal Protestants who accepted evolution and the higher criticism, and lift the true believers directly into heaven (rapture). After vanquishing the Antichrist in a terrible battle called Armageddon, the triumphant Christ would establish a thousand-year reign.

Christian fundamentalism found its form through a series of Bible conferences held during the last quarter of the nineteenth century. From 1910 to 1915 Lyman and Milton Stewart, wealthy oil businessmen from California, financed the publication and distribution of a twelve-volume paperback series entitled *The Fundamentals,* authored by prominent evangelical thinkers who described their opponents within the churches as modernists. In 1919 these combative thinkers formed the World's Christian Fundamentals Association to oppose modernism. Charismatic preachers such as the colorful Billy Sunday popularized their antimodernist message through well-publicized revival meetings.

After World War I (1914–1918) the United States experienced "a revolution in morals," celebrated by the eastern media, including the new tabloid newspapers. Women smoked and even danced in public; popular literature discussed Sigmund Freud (1856–1939), the Austrian founder of psychoanalysis, and aberrant sexual behavior; and communal enforcement of Victorian standards of personal behavior virtually collapsed. In response, Christian fundamentalists launched a moral crusade and aligned themselves temporarily with Catholics and other Protestants to campaign for laws banning the manufacture or sale of alcoholic beverages. This effort culminated in passage of the Eighteenth Amendment, implementing Prohibition in 1919.

Despite this temporary victory in the battle against alcohol, the war for the enforcement of Victorian/Methodist behavioral standards was ultimately lost. The death knell sounded in 1925, when fundamentalists in Dayton, Tennessee—led by the legendary William Jennings Bryan and opposed by the celebrated criminal lawyer Clarence Darrow—charged schoolteacher John T. Scopes with teaching biological evolution and thereby violating Tennessee's antievolution laws. Although Bryan won the "Scopes Monkey Trial," the fundamentalists, depicted as superstitious rubes and hicks, were discredited nationally. After campaigning against Catholic presidential candidate Al Smith in 1928, they withdrew from the American cultural and political mainstream.

During their period of cultural separatism, Christian fundamentalists were not inactive. In the 1930s and 1940s they built a subculture of fundamentalist radio stations, periodicals, publishing houses, Bible colleges, missionary bands, creationist science institutes, and Christian day schools and academies. Their operative world view, a premillennialist expectation of Christ's imminent return, encouraged missionary outreach and soul winning, however, rather than political activism.

A change in attitude occurred in the 1960s, when dismayed Christian fundamentalists observed what they described as a conspiracy of secular humanists invading the nation's schools, Congress, and the Supreme Court (which banned prayer in the public schools in 1962 and 1963 and permitted abortion in 1973). In 1979 the Reverend Jerry Falwell, a gifted preacher and pastor of an independent Baptist church in Lynchburg, Virginia, explained that Christians could no longer wait for Christ to do the dirty work of rolling back the tide of atheistic humanists serving Satan; Bible-believing Christians, whom Falwell called the "Moral Majority," must reinvest the public square with the "Judeo-Christian values" on which the nation had been founded (according to the fundamentalists).

Falwell's Moral Majority was only the most prominent of dozens of Christian political action groups that sprang up in the late 1970s and had their heyday during Ronald Reagan's presidency, lobbying against abortion, pornography, and feminism, among other social forces erosive of a Christian America and "traditional family values." Politicians on the secular right helped fundamentalists perfect their mass marketing and voter mobilization techniques in exchange for support of Republican Party candidates who did not necessarily pursue the rather narrow, and controversial, Christian agenda. In 1990 Falwell disbanded the Moral Majority, claiming it had accomplished its goals. But, in fact, Congress and the Supreme Court, in their lawmaking and jurisprudence, were arguably no closer to Judeo-Christian values than they had been in the 1970s.

Nonetheless, the demise of the Moral Majority signaled only the end of the first phase of renewed Christian activism. The second phase began almost immediately with the formation of the Christian Coalition, a political action

Jerry Falwell.

board, state assembly, and Republican Party leadership.

The Christian Coalition quickly demonstrated its new political muscle by injecting strong antiabortion language into the 1992 Republican Party platform and then claiming credit for the 1994 congressional election results, in which 56 House seats, 10 Senate seats, 472 state legislature seats, and 11 governorships shifted from Democratic to Republican hands. Independent pollsters confirmed that the Christian right was indeed crucial to the electoral results. During the campaign the Christian Coalition, with 1.5 million members organized in 48 state units and 1,400 local chapters, had mobilized a network of 17,000 precinct coordinators, 30,000 local volunteers, and 23,000 "church liaisons," who distributed 33 million "nonpartisan" voter guides. Other organizations on the Christian right, including Concerned Women for America, Focus on the Family, and the Traditional Values Coalition, also helped to ensure that, for the first time, a majority of the nation's 50 million evangelical Protestants identified themselves as Republicans.

Meanwhile, the pro-life movement Operation Rescue, led by Randall Terry, recruited fundamentalists and conservative Roman Catholics, whom they trained to participate in marches on abortion clinics. Acts of civil disobedience led to prison terms for some activists, who saw their jailing as a sign of God's unfolding plan of redemption for the United States.

Christian fundamentalists and their evangelical allies seethed during the two-term presidency of Bill Clinton, and contributed financially and morally to the building of a politically conservative media network designed to attack liberalism and defend "traditional family values" in U.S. society. Heartened in 2000 by the election of George W. Bush, a born-again Methodist with a socially conservative agenda, they tended to support the U.S. invasion of Iraq and promoted a constitutional amendment to ban gay marriage.

Islamic Fundamentalism

In the twentieth century religious reformers within both major branches of Islam advocated adoption of a new practice by Islamists, or fundamentalist Muslims: identify and persecute the "infidel," or nonbeliever, including the person who pretends to be Muslim but has actually betrayed the faith by adopting Western attitudes and values. Muslim fundamentalists believe that the only remedy for the growing threat of apostasy (the renunciation of Islam) is to establish states governed exclusively by the *shari'a,* the law of Allah, inscribed in the Holy Qur'an and in the *hadith,* or traditions,

group led by Pat Robertson, a Pentecostal preacher, the son of a former U.S. senator, and a successful television entrepreneur (*The 700 Club*) in his own right. Robertson, like Falwell, established his own university as a base of operations. Unlike the fundamentalist preacher, however, the Pentecostal media mogul turned over political management of the movement to his savvy young protégé Ralph Reed, who had a Ph.D. in American history and a knack for grass-roots politics. Reed shifted the focus of Christian politics from Washington, D.C., to thousands of communities across the United States, where his operatives organized local chapters of the Christian Coalition and trained candidates to run for the school of the prophet Muhammad (570–632 C.E.), the founder of Islam.

Muslim fundamentalists focus their rage first on lax members of the faith community itself and see the world as divided sharply between true believers and corrupt sinners. Muslims, however, are unique among the major monotheist traditions because they have never formally accepted and institutionalized a distinction between religion and the state, or between the "public" and "private" realms of society. Thus many radical Muslims believe that the real enemy is "Westoxification," the slow poisoning of Muslim purity by the insinuation of foreign ideas and practices imported from Western "imperialist" nations, especially the United States, Great Britain, and France.

In Sunni Islam, followed by nine-tenths of the world's one billion Muslims, the fundamentalist tendency first emerged in the work of Hasan al-Banna (1906–1949), an Egyptian schoolteacher who founded the Muslim Brotherhood in 1928 after concluding that the shaykhs, or religious scholars, of the Islamic religious establishment in Cairo had sold out to British interests, allowing night clubs, advertising, the consumption of alcohol, and other un-Islamic activities. After the Muslim Brotherhood combined religious education with social services (child care centers, medical clinics, orphanages, and schools), the movement spread quickly throughout the Arab world.

In the 1950s the Egyptian branch of the Muslim Brotherhood began to oppose the presidency of Gamal Abdel Nasser (1918–1970), who had jailed and tortured hundreds of young Muslim activists. One of them, a literary critic named Sayyid Qutb, developed a radical fundamentalist ideology before he was executed in 1965. Published in a little book called *Milestones,* it inspired a generation of violent radicals who accepted Qutb's notion that *jahiliyya* (pre-Islamic ignorance) had descended over Muslim societies, making it necessary for true Muslims to flee society, name the infidel, and attack the nonbeliever. One group inspired by this ideology, Islamic Jihad, assassinated Egyptian president Anwar Sadat (1918–1981) as retribution for the peace treaty he signed with Israel—the group saw the treaty as a flagrant betrayal of Islamic interests to the religion's greatest enemy. Shaykh Umar Abd al-Rahman, the blind religious scholar convicted in 1996 of conspiring to blow up New York City's World Trade Center and other U.S. landmarks, was one of Qutb's intellectual disciples. So, too, is Usama bin Ladin, who is a direct spiritual and intellectual descendant of Sayyid Qutb; the organization he founded, al-Qaida, sees itself as a direct successor to the radical Muslim Brotherhood.

In the early twenty-first century the Muslim Brotherhood itself and its radical splinter groups were active in Egypt, Palestine, Sudan, Nigeria, Algeria, and several other Muslim nations. Some experts argue that the Muslim Brotherhood is a separate and distinct organization, no longer dedicated to the violent overthrow of corrupt regimes; it prefers instead to compete with secularists within the existing political system. In Jordan, for example, Islamists won election to parliament in significant numbers; in Egypt, while the Brotherhood itself was officially banned, its members were allowed to participate in the Labor Party and to operate their own press. Other analysts, however, claim that the Sunni Islamic movement simply diversified in the 1980s and 1990s, with different levels adopting different tactics—the radical *jamaat* groups going underground and fomenting violent revolution, for example—in order to reach the same ultimate goal of replacing the existing states with Islamic governments and judicial systems based on *shari'a*.

In any event, Sunni Islam produced a variety of fundamentalist parties, movements, and activists in the final decades of the twentieth century. The aforementioned al-Qaida was the brainchild of the Saudi expatriate and former engineer and businessman Usama bin Ladin. The organization grew when jihadis were recruited from across the Sunni Muslim world to contribute to the campaign to oust the Soviet Union from Afghanistan. Eventually, al-Qaida included operatives from more than a dozen countries in the Middle East and South Asia. In 1992 the strongest fundamentalist Algerian party, the Islamic Salvation Front (FIS), was poised to assume a commanding majority in the Algerian parliament. But President Chadeli Benjedid of the ruling National Liberation Front (FLN) resigned, thereby delivering the government into the hands of the military and effectively ending Algeria's three-year experiment in democracy. By winning 180 of the 231 seats contested in the December 1991 election—the first free national election since Algeria gained its independence from France in 1962—the FIS Islamists surprised their secular opponents. Exploiting widespread disgust with the FLN—the Marxist party that has controlled Algeria for thirty years despite a record of inefficiency and corruption—the Islamists mobilized the disgruntled and the zealous alike, including thousands of veiled Algerian women clad in traditional Islamic garb.

After Benjedid's resignation, a High Security Council composed of military and civilian leaders canceled the second round of elections and announced the creation of a five-man body, the High State Council, to rule the country. Described as a junta by FIS spokesmen, this ruling body was headed by a founding member of the FLN and dominated by army officials. A thorough crackdown on the FIS followed, with the arrest of hundreds of Islamists and the party's most prominent leaders. Since the government crackdown, civil war has raged between the government and tenacious radical factions such as the Armed Islamic Group, which adopted terrorist tactics (including the murder of unveiled Algerian women) in the wake of the failure of Islamic fundamentalists to gain power by legitimate means at the ballot box.

The one Sunni fundamentalist movement to have tasted significant political power, the Sudanese faction of the Muslim Brotherhood (called the National Islamic Front), hardly provided a model of Islam as a force for democratization. Its charismatic leader, the Sorbonne-educated lawyer Hassan Turabi, spoke in grandiose terms of the inevitable Islamization of Africa, the Middle East, and South Asia, but his considerable influence in the Sudanese government did not prevent, and may have abetted, the country's decline into a debilitating civil war waged by the government against Christian and animist rebels in the south. Marred by the excessive human rights violations committed by the regime he helped to govern, Turabi's carefully cultivated image as the enlightened spokesman for the "Islamic Awakening" failed to persuade Islamists in other countries, much less Westerners.

The reach of Sunni Islamic fundamentalism extends to South Asia, where al-Qaida and its Afghan counterpart, the primitivist Taliban movement, are based. The Taliban came to power in Afghanistan in the 1990s and sought to establish a patriarchal, clan-based theocracy modeled, or so they contended, after the example of the Prophet Muhammad. Secular education was abolished, women were subjected to severe human rights violations, and the Taliban became the pariah of modern society. The U.S.-led bombing of Taliban strongholds after the terrorist attacks on the United States in 2001 reduced but did not eliminate the presence or the influence of the Taliban, which emerged again in 2006 as a force in the region. In Pakistan, established in 1947, Usama bin Ladin himself sought refuge for a time; his global jihad was designed, in its first phase, to topple the regime of Pakistan's president, General Pervez Musharraf. Pakistan is also the home to the Jama'at-i Islami (Islamic Group) a fundamentalist movement that characterizes Islam as a comprehensive way of life that covers the entire spectrum of human activity, be it individual, social, economic, or political. By contrast, conservative religious scholars confine Islam to the observance of its five pillars (the profession of faith, prayer, fasting, alms giving, and pilgrimage).

Jama'at-i Islami seeks to acquire political power and establish an Islamic state on the prophetic model. Sayyid Abu al-Ala Mawdudi (1903–1979), the movement's founder, taught that Islam cannot be implemented without the power of the state. His commentary on the Qur'an reads like an Islamic legal-political text, providing guidance in the fields of constitutional, social, civil, criminal, commercial, and international law. By providing Islamic discourse with a political vocabulary, Mawdudi achieved a pervasive influence on contemporary Islamic fundamentalist groups. By defining the Islamic system of life, ideology, constitution, economic system, and political system, Mawdudi elaborated the total subordination of the institutions of civil society and the state to the authority of divine law.

Although Sunni Islamists are more numerous than their Shi'i counterparts and are organized in many more countries worldwide, the most prominent and politically consequential example of Islamic fundamentalism emerged from within Shi'i Islam, practiced by about 100 million Muslims concentrated in Iran, Iraq, and Lebanon, and scattered throughout several Persian Gulf states. Shi'i Muslims have endured a long history of persecution by the majority Sunnis and by non-Muslim rulers; part of their unique belief system holds that the Great Imam, or spiritual leader, will return from self-imposed hiding to lead the Shi'is to victory over their many enemies. When the Ayatollah Ruhollah Musavi Khomeini (1900–1989) successfully led a Shi'i revolution against the modernizing shah of Iran in 1979 and later established the Islamic Republic of Iran, many of his followers came to believe that Khomeini was the Hidden Imam returned, or at least his powerful precursor—an impression Khomeini did little to correct. Instead, he revived a little-known Shi'i teaching and developed it into a politically useful doctrine: the Rule of the Jurist. This innovative interpretation of Shi'i theology justified the establishment of an Iranian government run by Muslim religious scholars and presided over by the grand ayatollah, Khomeini himself.

While striving to consolidate the Islamic regime in Iran during the 1980s, the charismatic Khomeini and his authoritarian successor, Hashemi Rafsanjani, attempted to spread the Islamic revolution elsewhere, most successfully in Lebanon. In that fragmented nation, suffering the ravages of civil war, the Shiʿi guerrillas of Hizbullah (Party of God) carved out a homeland and launched suicide missions in 1983 against French and U.S. troops stationed in southern Lebanon. Hizbullah eventually exercised political and military control over the region and continued to hold sway there into the twenty-first century. In 2005 Iran once again emerged as a major regional player under the influence of Shiʿite radicalism and new leadership in the person of its newly elected president, Mahmoud Ahmadinejad.

The future of Islamic fundamentalism—and its influence on the development of political systems in Muslim-majority nations—remains a pressing question. Many of the Algerian supporters of the FIS, motivated more by a passion for Islam than for democracy, were obviously not preoccupied with working out a long-term alliance between the two. The Qurʾan and the shariʿa provide a sociomoral framework rather than a detailed blueprint for the political order, and allow a measure of adaptation and flexibility in state building, as the history of Islam demonstrates. The Islamic Republic of Iran, while maintaining a virulent anti-Western discourse, has nonetheless entered into economic partnership with European and American corporations and with some European governments. In Palestine, Jordan, Nigeria, Algeria, and Saudi Arabia, Sunni Islamic fundamentalists have made great demands on their governments without yet developing coherent and sophisticated alternative economic and social policies; the emphasis has been on cultural and political authenticity and self-reliance. This pattern, however, began to change in the first decade of the twenty-first century as Islamist movements evolved into viable political parties (even while retaining their own militias). Hamas (Islamic Zeal), the Islamic resistance movement of Palestine, surprised the world (and itself) not only by fielding candidates for elections but actually winning control of the Palestinian government in elections held in 2005. Hizbullah, the Lebanese Shiʿi counterpart to Hamas, won seats in the Lebanese parliament and was part of the ruling coalition in 2006, when open warfare erupted between Israel and Hizbullah outposts in southern Lebanon.

The quest for political power, sovereignty, and self-reliance does not rule out a gradual process of incorporation and Islamization of Western structures and mechanisms, including mass participation in democratic procedures. Indeed, this has been the pattern followed in the Islamists' appropriation of Western science and technology, a borrowing they describe as an act of "repossession" of a mode of discourse and production that originated, they claim, in the golden age of Islamic civilization.

Jewish Fundamentalism

Two messianic movements within modern Judaism approximate fundamentalist patterns of thought and political behavior. The religious Zionists known as Gush Emunim (Bloc of the Faithful) are found primarily in Israel, while the ultra-Orthodox, mostly Hasidic, Jews known as the *haredim* (those who tremble before God) live in communities in Israel, Europe, Canada, and the United States. Together these movements constitute a minority within a minority—that is, they are Jews (numbering only fifteen million worldwide) who practice their religion (80 percent of Israelis are nonobservant Jews). More than most other Orthodox Jews, the fundamentalists narrowly focus their energies on the eagerly awaited coming of the Messiah, the divinely sent king who will bring justice to earth and vanquish the enemies of the Jewish people (including a considerable number of lukewarm Jews).

These two groups take different attitudes toward the modern world in general and the Zionist state of Israel in particular. The six thousand hard-core members of Gush Emunim are religious Zionists; they believe that God inspired secular Jews like Theodor Herzl (1860–1904) to create a political movement of Jewish return to Zion, the name for the ancient Jewish homeland in Palestine. Even though the Zionist movement was not explicitly religious, the Jews of Gush Emunim believe that the Zionist political leaders were and are unwitting agents of the Messiah. For evidence of this divine plan, they point to the founding of the state of Israel in 1948 against all odds, and to the astounding victory of Israel against its hostile Arab neighbors in the Six-Day War of 1967, when Israel took control of the Gaza Strip and territories on the West Bank of the Jordan River, which members of Gush Emunim refer to by their biblical names, Judea and Samaria.

To advance God's plan, Gush Emunim members have pressured the Israeli government to annex the territories, which they consider to be part of "the Whole Land of Israel" promised by Yahveh to the Jewish people in the Book of

Genesis. The Palestinian Arabs who were displaced by the creation of the modern state of Israel, however, claim the same lands as their home. These competing claims to the West Bank and Gaza have led to several violent confrontations and terrorist episodes between the Jewish settlers and Arab and Muslim militants. For their part, Gush Emunim, like all fundamentalists, reject the idea of religious pluralism, divide the world into realms of evil and good (they believe that all Jews embody a "sacred spark"), and selectively retrieve the most politically useful Orthodox Jewish teachings from the past. Indeed, they selected one of the 613 Jewish ethical obligations–"settle the land"—and made it paramount.

The *haredim* are the second candidate for inclusion in a category called Jewish fundamentalism. Many returned to Israel, but not to participate in the Zionist enterprise. Indeed, *haredi* Jews denounce Zionism as an ill-advised effort by nonobservant Jews who seek to take God's work into their own hands. To them, it was not God but human pride that inspired Herzl and the other Zionist pioneers. Unlike the Jews of Gush Emunim, who wear jeans, work shirts, and other modern clothes, the *haredim* wear the long black coats and dress of the Jewish villages of early modern eastern Europe, their traditional home before the onset of the so-called Jewish Enlightenment and disasters such as the Nazi persecution and murder of six million Jews in the Holocaust.

Ultra-Orthodox Jews, known for their strict and unyielding adherence to the imperatives of Jewish law, include Hasidic, Polish, and Galician followers of a charismatic folk Judaism based on feeling, piety, and human attachments. This group also includes the Misnagdim, Lithuanian Jews who opposed the excesses of Hasidism and maintained a rigorous attachment to the letter of Jewish rabbinic law.

The *haredim* live uneasily, as exiles, wherever they are found—including in Zion (Israel), their religious and spiritual homeland. The various eastern European sects live crowded together in enclaves such as Jerusalem's Mea Shearim neighborhood, where the men spend years in yeshivas (religious schools) studying the Torah (the law, contained in the first five books of the Hebrew Bible) and shun the outside world, refusing to join the Israeli army or to interact socially with other Israelis. (By contrast, members of Gush Emunim, some of whom studied in the same yeshivas as the *haredim,* have served in the Israeli army.) *Haredi* Jews are selectively modern, however; in New York City, for example, they own a photo shop where one can purchase the latest computer and communications technology.

The *haredi* political parties, such as Agudat Israel (Party of Israel) and Neturei Karta (Guardians of the Gate), were formed primarily to settle disputes within the *haredi* community itself. In the 1980s and 1990s, however, they were drawn into the larger world of Israeli politics, where they exercised influence disproportionate to their tiny numbers, often providing the votes needed to bring a larger political coalition to power. They sought to retain their privileges in the Israeli system and to promote the passage of laws to enforce the keeping of the Sabbath and other Orthodox Jewish norms.

Pluralism and Antipluralism

Fundamentalism in the early twenty-first century is one of several political forces vying for supremacy in the post–cold war world. In most cases fundamentalists represent the noncompromising, antipluralist elements in a conflict. In Israel, for example, both the radical Jewish settlers of Gush Emunim and the Sunni activists of Hamas violently opposed the peace process pursued by the Israeli government and the Palestine Liberation Organization. Similarly, Hezbollah exercised a radicalizing influence over Lebanese politics, leading that country into war with Israel in 2006. Throughout the Islamic world, radical fundamentalists are a destabilizing minority dedicated to the overthrow, by any means, of Western-supported governments. But in the United States, with its strong traditions of pluralism and democracy, Christian fundamentalists "play by the rules" and generally eschew violence. Their hope is to transform American society gradually into a Bible-believing republic, as they believe it once was. Fundamentalism, in other words, may exist in democratic as well as undemocratic societies, but it stands a much greater chance of dominating its enemies in states where pluralism and human rights do not enjoy strong protection under the law.

See also *Banna, Hasan al-; Conservatism; Evangelicalism; Gush Emunim; Herzl, Theodor; Hinduism; Islam; Judiasm; Khomeini, Ruholla Musavi; Mawdudi, Sayyid Abu al-Ala; Millennialism; Qutb, Sayyid; Zionism.*

R. Scott Appleby

BIBLIOGRAPHY

Appleby, R. Scott. "Religious Fundamentalisms and Global Conflict." Foreign Policy Association Headline Series booklet, 1994.

Heilman, Samuel. *Defenders of the Faith: Inside Ultra-Orthodox Jewry.* New York: Schocken Books, 1992.

Kepel, Gilles. *The Revenge of God: The Resurgence of Islam, Christianity, and Judaism in the Modern World,* translated by Alan Braley. University Park: Pennsylvania State University Press, 1994.

Marsden, George M. *Understanding Fundamentalism and Evangelicalism.* Grand Rapids, Mich.: Eerdmans, 1991.

Marty, Martin E., and R. Scott Appleby, eds. *Fundamentalisms Observed.* Chicago: University of Chicago Press, 1991.

———. *Fundamentalisms Comprehended.* Chicago: University of Chicago Press, 1995.

G

Gandhi, Mohandas Karamchand

A leading practitioner of civil disobedience and acclaimed as the father of India as a nation. Gandhi (1869–1948) was born into an upper-caste Hindu family and grew up in the religiously plural environment of western India. At nineteen he went to England to train as a lawyer. There he read two religious texts that had a deep and abiding influence upon him, the great Hindu epic poem *Bhagavad Gita* and the Bible. He also read an account of the life and teachings of the Buddha. The Jain ideas of nonviolence (*ahimsa*) and non-possessiveness (*aparigraha*), the Buddhist ethic of renunciation, the Hindu attitude of detachment (*anasakti*), and the Christian values of selfless love and passive (nonaggressive) resistance to evil embodied in Jesus' Sermon on the Mount became the moral foundation of Gandhi's life and work.

On his return to India, Gandhi accepted a short assignment as a legal consultant to an Indian merchant in South Africa. He arrived in Durban in 1893 to discover that Indian settlers in the British colonies of Natal and Transvaal were the victims of extreme racial discrimination. When his contract expired, he decided to stay in South Africa to organize the Indians to fight for their personal dignity and political rights.

Gandhi developed a philosophy of action anchored in an unflinching insistence on truth, *satyagraha,* in thought and in deed. He ruled out any compromise with evil but considered it morally obligatory to try to reform the evildoer through love. It was imperative that political actors should be moral individuals, ready to acknowledge their infirmities and atone for them. At the level of collective political action

Mohandas Karamchand Gandhi.

Gandhi developed the techniques of nonviolent civil disobedience and passive resistance. He maintained that politics was a legitimate instrument, provided that it was subsumed under ultimate values. His religious vision was holistic: "For me, every, the tiniest, activity is governed by what I consider my religion" (1932).

Gandhi, who was a theist but not a ritualist or traditionalist, placed moral reason above scripture. In 1909 he wrote a confession of faith, which was followed by a political pamphlet on Indian self-governance. In these he argued that modern industrial civilization is evil.

His efforts on behalf of Indians in South Africa were attended by both successes and failures. Between 1893 and 1915, when he finally returned home, Gandhi paid several visits to India and kept in touch with developments there. He became known as a leader in the heroic mold. Rabindranath Tagore (Nobel laureate in literature) acclaimed him as a *mahatma* (great or noble soul), and the title won ready and wide acceptance. It was only in 1917, however, that Gandhi plunged into political activity, championing, first, the cause of an exploited peasant community in northern India and, then, challenging the might of the British raj in Punjab.

During the 1920s and 1930s Gandhi emerged as the unquestioned leader of the Indian National Congress Party. He perceived quite early that two major obstacles impeded the struggle for freedom: the political differences between Hindus and Muslims and the moral and social degeneration of Hindu society, represented most critically by the practice of segregating the group known as untouchables.

In a bold move in 1920 Gandhi, in his first major noncooperation movement against the British, gave support to the Turkish sultan. The sultan, recognized by Muslims worldwide as their caliph, or religious leader, had most of his territories taken away from him by the victorious powers at the end of World War I (1914–1918). Gandhi hoped that his support of the sultan's cause would bring Muslims into the Indian national movement. His success in mobilizing Muslims was exceptional, but it was short lived. His concessions to Muslim sentiments resulted in a right-wing Hindu backlash. Furthermore, conservative Muslims, who were the backbone of the caliphate movement, withdrew their support of Gandhi after the caliphate was abolished by Turkish nationalists. Thus the long-term consequence of Gandhi's strategy was the strengthening of divisive religious nationalisms. He met with greater success in his crusade against caste discrimination in Hindu society.

Muslim separatism peaked in 1940, when the demand for partition of the subcontinent on a religious basis was formally made. Gandhi opposed the idea, calling it political folly and moral evil. In 1942 he launched the "Quit India" movement against British rule. All of the senior leaders of the Congress Party were jailed. Their absence created an opportunity for Muslim separatists to mobilize support. When the imprisoned leaders were released, they found that the political situation had changed significantly. India and Pakistan emerged as free nations in 1947, in the midst of unprecedented intercommunity violence and the movement of millions of refugees.

Old, frail, and deeply disappointed, Gandhi refused to give up his vision of religious concord in the subcontinent. He called for the establishment of a secular state in India. His efforts on behalf of the Muslims who stayed in India angered Hindu fanatics. One of them, Nathuram Godse, shot Gandhi dead on January 30, 1948, when he was on his way to an evening prayer meeting.

Gandhi's emphases on the moral foundations of society and on nonviolence in politics have won universal recognition. His influence has been acknowledged in major political struggles, notably that of African Americans under the leadership of Martin Luther King Jr. In a world that has woken up to the destructive dimensions of technology, consumerism, and religious fundamentalism, Gandhi's ideas of religious pluralism, limitation of desires, and living in harmony with nature have acquired a keen relevance.

See also *Hinduism; India.*

T. N. Madan

BIBLIOGRAPHY

Chatterji, Margaret. *Gandhi's Religious Thought.* Notre Dame, Ind.: University of Notre Dame Press, 1983.

Nanda, Bal Ram. *Mahatma Gandhi: A Biography.* Delhi: Oxford University Press, 1989.

Parekh, Bhikhu C. *Gandhi's Political Philosophy: A Critical Examination.* Notre Dame, Ind.: University of Notre Dame Press, 1989.

Gender

Gender, which derives from the Latin *gener* (genus, birth, race, kind, gender), has traditionally referred to a grammatical feature of Indo-European languages that classifies nouns, pronouns, and modifiers in arbitrary groupings (masculine, feminine, and neuter). A secondary meaning of the word equates it with biological sex. Because of feminist studies gender has been recognized as a key analytical category.

Gender is understood as a system of classification and structure of domination that connotes binary power differences.

In Western societies two genders are thought to exist. They are understood as mutually exclusive and, at best, complementary: one is either a woman or a man, but not both. Generally, *male* and *female* classify beings primarily on the basis of anatomical sex differences; *men* and *women* connote social agents; and *masculine* and *feminine* or *man* and *woman* express cultural-religious ideals, values, and standards appropriate to one's gender. The cultural construct of male and female/masculine and feminine constitutes the Western sex/gender system that determines sex in terms of gender and constructs symbolic "worlds" in terms of gendered social hierarchies and values.

Gender then is not a biological or divinely "given" but a socio-political construct, a principle of classification that generates psychological, social, cultural, religious, and political meanings, and structures biological sexual identity. In the 1970s women's studies distinguished social gender roles from biological sex; by the mid-1980s gender studies emerged as a distinct field of inquiry that questions seemingly universal beliefs about women and men and attempts to unmask the cultural, societal, and political roots of gender. Gender theories understand sex as constructed by gender and gender as constructed by other relations of power, such as race, class, heterosexuality, colonialism, and religion.

Gender as an Ideological Structure

If one does not distinguish between sex as a biological given and gender as a cultural construct but sees both sex and gender as sociopolitical constructions, one can analyze the sex/gender system as a cultural symbolic structure of representation that has become "common sense." As an ideological structure, gender actively naturalizes the sex/gender system through grammar, language, biology, and culture and makes its construction of sexual difference appear to be "natural" or "god-given."

Gendered language in turn expresses power relations and reinscribes cultural-religious gender assumptions. In Western linguistic systems, masculine terms function as "generic" language. *Man, male, masculine,* and *he* stand for human and male, whereas *woman, female, feminine,* and *she* connote only femaleness. In other words, Western languages are androcentric, that is, male-centered. Grammatically androcentric Western languages explicitly mention women only as the exception to the rule or as particular individuals. Unless women are specifically mentioned, one has to decide in light of contextual linguistic markers whether women are meant to be included or not.

Western androcentric languages and discourses do not just marginalize women or eliminate them from historical records. As kyriocentric (from the Greek *kyrios,* which means emperor, lord, slave master, husband and the Greek *archein,* which means rule or domination) languages, they also construct the meaning of being a woman or a man differently. The meaning of *woman* is unstable and shifting: it depends not so much on its sex/gender relation but on the socio-political context of the time and place in which it is used.

For example, the expression *woman* today is used interchangeably with *female* and thus has become a generic sex-based term, although until very recently it was applied to lower-class females only. One can perceive the historical ambiguity of the term *woman* much more easily if one compares it with the term *lady,* an appellation that readily reveals its race, class, and colonial bias. Not only has *lady* been restricted to women of higher status or educational refinement, it also symbolized "true womanhood" and femininity. A statement such as "slaves were not women" offends our common-sense understanding, whereas a statement such as "slaves were not ladies" makes perfect sense.

In most Western languages the lady, slave mistress, and mother is the "other" of the lord, slave master, and father. All other women are marked as inferior by race, class, religion, or culture, and as the "others" of the other are not mentioned at all. One can illustrate how such supposedly generic language works, for example, with reference to position advertisements that often read: "University X is an affirmative action institution and invites applications from African, Asian, Hispanic or Native Americans and women," as though these different types of Americans are all men and women are only gendered but do not belong to racial and ethnic minority groups. African, Asian, Hispanic, or Native American women are doubly invisible in gendered language systems.

The socio-political classification of gender, like the grammatical, does not always correspond to the biological classification of sex. Anthropologists have pointed out that not all cultures and languages know of only two sexes/genders, and historians of gender have argued that even in Western culture the dual sex/gender system is of modern origins. Thomas Laqueur, for instance, has argued that a decisive shift took place in modernity: a shift from the ancient one-sex model to the present dichotomous, two-sex model. Women were once believed to have the same sex and genitals as men except that women's were inside the body whereas men's were outside. In this one-sex model the vagina was understood to be an interior penis; the labia, the foreskin; the uterus, the scrotum; and the ovaries, testicles. Not biological sex but gender was the primary category determining the order of things.

What it meant to be a man or a woman in the ancient one-sex model was determined by social rank and by one's place in the household, not by sexual organs. As a free man or a slave woman, one performed a cultural role according to one's social status and was not thought to be organically one of two incommensurable sexes. Not sex but the social status of the free, elite, propertied male head of household determined superior gender status. Hence the ancients did not need to resort to sexual difference for supporting the claim that freeborn women were inferior to freeborn men. Rather because freeborn women were subordinates, their "nature" was believed to be inferior.

Beginning with the Enlightenment in the eighteenth century the two-sex model—the notion that there are two stable, opposite sexes—emerged. It was commonly believed that the economic, political, and cultural lives of women and men, their gender roles, were based on two sexes that are biologically given. Just as in antiquity the body was seen as reflecting the cosmological order, so in modernity the body and sexuality are seen as representing and legitimating the social-political order. The social and political changes wrought by modernity produced the change from the one-sex to the assymmetrical two-sex model just as it engendered theories of racial inferiority. Because the Enlightenment's claims for democracy and equality excluded freeborn women and subordinate men, new arguments had to be fashioned if elite freeborn men were to justify women's exclusion from the public domain.

The promise of democracy, that women and disenfranchised men were full citizens, generated new antifeminist arguments based on nature, physiology, and science. Those who opposed, for instance, the democratic participation of freeborn women sought evidence for women's mental and physical unsuitability for the public sphere by arguing that women's bodies and biology made them unfit to participate. Similar arguments were made with respect to subordinate men and colonialized peoples.

The theory of separate spheres for men and women thus arose together with the dual-sex/gender model. In Enlight-

enment discourses women are no longer construed as lesser men but as totally different from and complementary to men, as beings of a "purer race," as an "angelic species" less affected than men by sexual drives and desires. With women excluded from the new civil society, the physical and moral differences between men and women were conceived to ensure that women and subordinate men were excluded from political decision making. Two incommensurable sexes/genders are the result of these ideological practices.

Gender as a Socio-political Structure

Gender is a socio-political institution as well as an ideological representation. The assumption of natural sex/gender differences serves as a preconstructed frame of meaning for individuals and cultural institutions. By presenting the sex/gender system of male and female or masculine and feminine as universal, this preconstructed frame of meaning obscures the reality that the very notion of two sexes is a socio-political construct for maintaining domination rather than a biological essence. Not all cultures know only two sexes or have gendered languages. Sexual differences depend on socio-cultural communicative practices and therefore can be developed differently or changed.

Contemporary feminist work on gender has attempted to unravel the politics of this modern sex/gender model. Teresa de Lauretis, for instance, argued that gender is the product of various social technologies, institutional discourses, and practices of daily life. Gender as a socio-cultural construct does not connote a biological, anthropological, or psychological given but a semiotic difference that assigns meaning to individuals within a society.

Individuals recognize gender and appropriate ascriptions because they are real for them. Gender is thus a product and process not only of representation but also of self-representation. The recognition of women's own participation in the construction of gender makes it possible to see that gender can also be deconstructed or differently constructed. Understanding gender as a product and process makes it possible for feminist theory to analyze cultural masculinity and femininity with the idea of changing them.

Generally accepted gender expectations define the socially recognized genders in a given society. The gendered division of labor assigns work according to gender, whereas kinship spells out family rights and responsibilities for each gender. Gender scripts prescribe behavior and grant prerogatives. Social controls, which reward conforming behavior and stigmatize aberrant conduct, produce personalities that perform culural gender dictates. Finally, gender ideology and imagery, the cultural representations of gender in symbolic language and artistic production, its reenforcement through law, custom, and religion legitimate and support dominant gender statuses.

For instance, the modern ethos of femininity, which prescribes that "good" women perform unpaid services inside and outside the family, inculcates selfless love, nurturing care, and loving kindness as feminine virtues. The ethos of "true womanhood" defines woman's nature as "being for others" in actual or spiritual motherhood. Whereas men are measured by the masculine standards of self-assertion, independence, power, and control, women are called to fulfill their true nature and destiny in self-sacrificing, loving care and motherhood. The cultural socialization of women to selfless femininity and altruistic self-negation is reinforced and perpetuated by the Christian preaching of self-sacrificing love and humble service.

Although maleness and femaleness are supposedly biological givens, they are actually cultural norms that are backed by social sanctions and enforced by medical procedures. In antiquity, for instance, menial service was seen as appropriate to the nature of slaves and serfs; in modernity it is construed as a feminine ideal appropriate to the nature of women. Public political service in turn is conceptualized as masculine, appropriate to the nature of men. This separation between the public male sphere and the private female domain is at the root of an economic system that frequently leaves female-headed households destitute, a development that has devastating effects, especially on women and children not only of developing but also of industrialized countries.

Gender as an individual identity structure rests on the ascription of a certain sex from birth on or even before birth. Gender identity constitutes a sense of self; it determines marital and procreative status as well as sexual orientation that patterns sexual desires, feelings, and identifications. The outcome is the heterosexually gendered personality fashioned by socially normative patterns and emotions inculcated through family structure, parenting, and education.

Finally, gendered practices internalize learned social gender behavior, sexual cues, and gender socialization and interaction, while gender display presents the self as a masculine or feminine person through dress, cosmetics, weight control and other body regimes. Thus the "second-class" status of women is achieved not by force but in and through individual socialization and cultural practices of femininity. Reli-

gion has played a major role in the construction and symbolic legitimization of such naturalized gender, race, class, and colonial relations.

Gender as a sociopolitical and psychological practice of superiority and inferiority is only one of several social ascriptions that promote the exploitation of women. If one realizes that gender intersects with race, class, age, religion, sexual preference, and ethnicity, one is able to demystify binary gender oppositions. Conceptualizing gender as a practice that produces sex differences that are inflected by those of race, class, sexual preference, culture, religion, age, and nationality allows one to see that individual women are not simply gendered. Rather the intersection of race, class, heterosexuality, nationality, and religion constructs what it means to be a woman differently in different socio-political, cultural contexts.

Kyriarchal societies need a "servant class" of people—be they slaves, serfs, house servants, kulaks, or mammies. The existence of a gendered "servant class" is maintained through law, education, socialization, and brute violence. It is sustained by the belief that members of a "servant class" are by nature or by divine decree inferior to those whom they are destined to serve.

Such relations of domination and subordination were first articulated in Western political philosophy in the context of Greek patriarchal democracy. By the fourth century B.C.E., the Greek philosopher Aristotle had already argued that the freeborn, propertied, educated Greek man was the highest of moral beings and that all other members of the human race were defined by their functions in his service. Political philosophy continued to assume that propertied, educated, elite Western man was defined by reason, self-determination, and full citizenship, whereas women and other subordinated peoples were defined by emotion, service, and dependence. They were seen not as rational and responsible adults but as emotional and helpless children or "beasts of burden" and sex objects. These prejudices have been mediated by Christian theological traditions and have determined modern kyriarchal forms and ideologies of democracy. Genevieve Lloyd, among others, has argued that modern (and postmodern) understandings of rationality and of the world have been articulated by white, European-American, elite, educated men. These men have not only defined white women as "others" but have also regarded all the "others" as "second-class citizens" who lack human, that is, masculine, qualities.

Nineteenth-century scientists constructed women, the "lower races," the sexually deviant, the criminal, the urban

Gender

poor, and the insane as biological "races apart." Their differences from the white male, and their likeness to each other, explained their lower position in the social hierarchy. In this scheme the lower races represented the feminine aspect of the human species, and women represented the lower race of gender. Hence it is important to see gender as one among several structures of domination constructed to serve the division of power and wealth by sex, economics, race, culture, nationality, and religion.

Religion and Gender

Feminist theologies and gender studies in religion have sought to bring about a paradigm shift in the way religion and religious texts, traditions, and communities have been seen and studied. They have sought to change and transform the discipline by engaging in a wide-ranging critique of disciplinary presuppositions, methods, and epistemology, as well as through creative reimagination and transformation of religious discourses and institutions. They have thereby sought to rediscover and elaborate women's subjectivity and agency within religious histories and contemporary communities. Insofar as feminist theory has revealed the gender encoding of all knowledge, feminist studies in religion have been able to show the gendering of religious knowledge and religious institutions. Feminist scholars in religion have used the theories of gender to understand the second-class status of women in religion.

In many religions men and masculinity are associated with the Divine and the transcendent, whereas women and femininity are seen as immanent, impure, profane, evil, and sinful. Many religious traditions such as Judaism, Christianity, Islam, Hinduism, Taoism, or Buddhism use binary gender oppositions to construct their symbolic universe. The deity (Jahwe, Allah, or Christ) is not only understood as masculine but also as allpowerful ruler and judge, whereas women are associated with sin, death, and sex (Eve, Lillith, or Kali). Men have been representatives of the divine and religious leaders in the major religions of the world. Women in turn have been excluded from religious leadership, official teaching, and sacred ritual.

Because religious symbol and systems are heavily gendered in masculine terms, they reinforce cultural gender roles and concepts and legitimize them as ordained by God or as the "order of creation." As Judith Plaskow has argued, Christian male theologians have formulated theological concepts in terms of their own cultural experience, insisting

on male language relating to God and on a symbolic universe in which women do not appear. Similar observations can be made about other world religions.

Since the industrial revolution in Europe and the United States at the beginning of the nineteenth century, religion has been pushed out of the public realm and relegated to the private sphere of individualistic piety, charitable work, and the cultivation of home and family. Religion has become culturally feminized while its leadership has remained predominantly male. Nevertheless, both religion and women were crucial in shaping Westen identity. For instance, as a "missionary religion," Christianity had the same function as the "white lady." It was to "civilize the savages," who were understood as "untamed nature."

Hence, feminist scholars and religious leaders insist that religious texts and traditions must be so reinterpreted that women and other "nonpersons" can achieve full citizenship in religion and society as well as full access to decision-making powers, and learn how to live in radical equality in religious communities. They argue that differences of sex/gender, race, class, and ethnicity are socioculturally constructed and not willed by God and must be changed. God, who created people in the divine image, has called every individual differently and is to be found in and among people who are created equal.

Replacing the religious dual-sex model with that of the divine image that is neither male nor female, white nor black, rich nor poor but multicolored and multigendered would open up the possibility of moving beyond the masculine monism of the one-sex model and the asymmetric dualism of the sex/gender system. Such a process will offer the prospect of deconstructing gender and of fashioning identity and community in the variegated image of the Divine in our midst.

See also *Feminism; Homosexuality; Sexuality.*

Elisabeth Schüssler Fiorenza

BIBLIOGRAPHY

Agosín, Marjorie, ed. *Women, Gender, and Human Rights: A Global Perspective.* New Brunswick, N.J.: Rutgers University Press, 2001.

Ahmed, Durre S., ed. *Gendering the Spirit: Women, Religion, and the Postcolonial Response.* New York: Palgrave, 2002.

Baron, Dennis. *Grammar and Gender.* New Haven, Conn.: Yale University Press, 1986.

Bussmann, Hadumond and Renate Hof, eds. *Genus. Geschlechterforschung / Gender Studies in den Kultur- und Sozialwissenschaften. Ein Handbuch.* Stuttgart, Germany: A. Kröner Verlag, 2005

Butler, Judith. *Undoing Gender.* New York: Routledge, 2004.

—————. *Gender Trouble: Feminism and the Subversion of Identity.* New York: Routledge, 1990.

Castelli, Elizabeth A., ed. *Women, Gender and Religion: A Reader.* New York: Palgrave, 2001.

Cameron, Deborah. *Feminism and Linguistic Theory.* New York: St. Martin's, 1992.

Caraway, Nancie. *Segregated Sisterhood: Racism and the Politics of American Feminism.* Knoxville: University of Tennessee Press, 1991.

Chopp, Rebecca S. *The Power to Speak: Feminism, Language, God.* New York: Crossroad, 1989.

De Lauretis, Teresa. *Technologies of Gender: Essays on Theory, Film, and Fiction.* Bloomington: Indiana University Press, 1987.

Hooks, Bell. *Yearning: Race, Gender, and Cultural Politics.* Boston: South End Press, 1990.

Juschka, Darlene M., ed. *Feminism in the Study of Religion: A Reader.* New York: Continuum, 2001.

Laqueur, Thomas. *Making Sex: Body and Gender from the Greeks to Freud.* Cambridge: Harvard University Press, 1990.

Lorber, Judith. *Paradoxes of Gender.* New Haven, Conn.: Yale University Press, 1994.

Moore, Stephen D. and Janice Capel Anderson, eds. *New Testament Masculinities.* Atlanta, Ga.: Society of Biblical Literature, 2003.

Plaskow, Judith. *Sex, Sin, and Grace: Women's Experience and the Theologies of Reinhold Niebuhr and Paul Tillich.* Washington: University Press of America, 1980.

Schüssler Fiorenza, Elisabeth. *But She Said: Feminist Practices of Biblical Interpretation.* Boston: Beacon Press, 1992.

—————. *Jesus—Miriam's Child, Sophia's Prophet: Critical Issues in Feminist Christology.* New York: Continuum, 1994.

—————. "Religion, Gender and Society: Shaping the Discipline of Religious/Theological Studies." In *The Relevance of Theology,* Nathan Söderblom and the Development of an Academic Discipline: Proceedings from a Conference held in Uppsala, April 14–16, 2002, edited by Carl Reinhold Bråckenhielm and Gunhild Winqvist Hollman. Uppsala, Sweden: Uppsala Universitet, 2002, pp. 85–99.

Genocide and "Ethnic Cleansing"

The terms *genocide* and *ethnic cleansing* were both coined in twentieth-century Europe to describe the attempted extermination of a specific group of people or their violent expulsion by their own government. *Genocide* was first used in 1944 in regard to the Holocaust, and *ethnic cleansing* was first used in the early 1990s to describe the policies of Bosnian Serb militias against Muslim civilians after the breakup of Yugoslavia. The concepts and the practices have been in use for much longer, across the globe, but the twentieth century earned the title Century of Genocide.

The 1948 United Nations Convention on the Prevention and Punishment of the Crime of Genocide defines that crime as "acts committed with intent to destroy, in whole or in part, a national, ethnical, racial, or religious group, as such." From the point of view of international criminal law, genocide is a crime against humanity that requires proof not only of acts such as "killing members of the group" but also of specific intent to destroy it. But the convention has been criticized by scholars from two major, different points of view. Some argue that the genocide convention is too sweeping, allowing the serious charge of genocide to be leveled if just a part of a group is targeted for destruction. Others argue that it is too narrow, failing to outlaw attempts to exterminate political or social groups. Conceivably, both could be correct. Yet, since the first international conviction for genocide, that of a Rwandan perpetrator in 1998, the legal definition has gained greater standing.

Social scientists and historians have proposed, first, new typologies of genocide. For example, separate categories have been established for religious, racial, and ethnic genocides, those of colonial conquest, and those prescribed by a political ideology. One typology includes "retributive" genocide, in which mass murder is perpetrated for revenge; "institutional" genocide, which accompanied military conquest in premodern history; "utilitarian" genocide, associated with colonial expansion or economic exploitation; "monopolistic" genocide, used to transform plural societies; and "ideological" genocide. Another uses the first and last of these categories, but substitutes "developmental" or "despotic" genocide for the others. And another typology distinguishes between genocides according to the motive of the perpetrator, whether it is to eliminate what is perceived to be a threat, to terrorize enemies, to increase wealth, or to impose an ideology.

Meanwhile courts and legal scholars determined that the UN convention's definition of genocide includes some nonlethal acts, such as the removal of children of a group, for instance, to "breed out the colour," as Australian officials described their policy toward some Aborigines. The definition demands no specifically genocidal motive, such as racial hatred, but excludes nonviolent or even forcible cultural assimilation, sometimes called *ethnocide*. The convention's restricted range of victim groups led to the coining of *democide* for killings of any large populations, and of *genocidal massacres* and *related atrocities* for mass killings of groups beyond the scope of the definition, either because the perpetrators targeted social or political groups, because of their lack of intent to destroy a group "as such," or because killings of members of protected groups occur sporadically or are limited to a few towns or rural locations. Thus, even as scholars slowly converged on a new academic definition, the first international implementations of the convention—the Ad Hoc International Tribunals on the Former Yugoslavia and Rwanda—refocused attention on enforcing the 1948 legal definition.

Early and Modern Cases of Genocide

Genocide was fairly common even in antiquity, less so in the medieval era. The best-known but sometimes still contentious cases since earliest times include the Athenian destruction of Melos (416 B.C.E.) during the Peloponnesian War, the Roman obliteration of Carthage in 146 B.C.E., the ravages of the Mongols under Genghis Khan in the thirteenth century, the Albigensian Crusade in thirteenth-century Europe, the persecution of Christians in early modern Japan, the mass killings of Ndwandwe people by Shaka's Zulu armies in the 1820s, and the destruction of certain Native American peoples in the New World, including the nineteenth-century United States, and of some Aboriginal groups in colonial Australia. Critics of the British imperial regime also used the term *extermination* to characterize the Irish famine of the 1840s, during which at least a million people perished. However, that term more frequently applied to direct killing.

The twentieth century opened on a continuing theme, with the near extermination of the colonized Herero people of Southwest Africa by their German conquerors in 1904–1905. Ten years later, during World War I, the Young Turk rulers of the Ottoman Empire deported the Armenian people from their homelands, causing the death of more than a million in forced marches and massacres. During World War II, in an escalating series of persecutions, deportations, mass shootings, and extermination in gas chambers, the Nazis (National Socialists) murdered nearly 6 million European Jews and 500,000 Gypsies, along with 3 million Soviet prisoners of war. This—the Holocaust—became the archetypal genocide, the most extreme case in history, if not a unique one. More recently, the Khmer Rouge genocide from 1975 to 1979 in Cambodia, then called Democratic Kampuchea; the genocide of Mayan Indians in Guatemala in 1981–1983; the mass murder of Muslims in "ethnic cleansing" operations in parts of Bosnia, especially at Srebrenica, in 1995; and in Rwanda, the ethnic Hutu regime's 1994 slaughter of perhaps a million Tutsi and their Hutu defenders in four months, have all evoked similar memories of those first modern genocides.

Two other major series of mass killings marked the last century. Not always described as genocide, these often fall into the category of ideological or political mass murder of opponents or suspected opponents, sometimes called *politicide*. First, communist regimes, most particularly Joseph Stalin's Soviet Union and the later Soviet client state Ethiopia, as well as Mao Zedong's China and its sometime client states North Korea and Cambodia, targeted entire social and political groups for physical extermination.

In the Soviet Union the kulak class of rich peasants, almost the entire Soviet political class, religious and other dissidents, and various ethnic minorities—all were targets of Stalin's murderous purges, which took many millions of lives, especially in the 1930s. Mao Zedong's extermination of China's landlord class after 1949 killed several million people. Another twenty million to thirty million Chinese perished in the greatest human tragedy of the postwar world, the famine during the "Great Leap Forward" of 1958–1961. The evidence suggests that this famine, though man-made, was not deliberately instigated but was a disastrous result of rampant ideological arrogance and extraordinary economic mismanagement. The enforced starvation of Cambodians from 1975 to 1979 by the pro-Chinese Pol Pot regime, ostensibly pursuing a "Super Great Leap Forward," also involved ideological retribution and mass political killings (as well as ethnic exterminations), accompanied by the export of food amid nationwide hunger.

Second, political mass murder by anti-communist regimes, with links to the United States and an ideological obsession with guarding "national security" and preventing social reform, plagued Latin America and Asia especially after 1945. Such regimes instigated the "Matanza" massacres in El Salvador in the 1930s and the army-organized "death squads" that killed 70,000 people there in the 1980s, the state-sponsored slaughter of 200,000 indigenous and Ladino peasants and dissidents in Guatemala from 1954 to 1996, the murderous 1973 coup in Chile, and the "dirty wars" and mass disappearances of civilians in Argentina, Brazil, Colombia, Peru, and Uruguay from the 1960s to the 1980s.

This continental phenomenon may be compared to the killings of 500,000–800,000 communists and other civilians by the Suharto military regime in Indonesia in 1965–1966

As Allied troops advanced on Nazi concentration camps at the end of World War II, prisoners of the camps—not only Jews but also homosexuals, communists, liberals, and anyone opposing the Nazis—were forced to undertake extended, deadly marches. The "death marches," including this one from the Dachau concentration camp, constituted the final initiative in the Nazi's campaign of genocide.

and of similar numbers of Vietnamese, Cambodian, and Lao civilians by U.S. and allied forces in Indochina during the wars of intervention from 1954 to 1975. To these may be added about 150,000 East Timorese victims of the U.S.-backed Indonesian army's bloody campaign to annex and incorporate their territory, from Jakarta's invasion in 1975 to its withdrawal in 1999. In that quarter-century occupation, Indonesia's commanders perpetrated "extermination as a crime against humanity," according to the report of a UN-sponsored Truth Commission completed in 2005. Meanwhile, in South and West Asia, U.S.-backed regimes in Pakistan and Iraq committed genocide against Hindus and secessionists in Bangladesh in 1971 and against Iraqi Kurds in 1987–1988. After the Baath Party regime of Iraqi dictator Saddam Hussein invaded Kuwait and met defeat at U.S. hands in 1991, it then turned its guns on Iraq's rebellious Shiite majority.

By the end of the twentieth century, a third wave of genocide had spread. The impunity enjoyed by the Pakistani military perpetrators of the Bangladesh genocide enabled Pakistan to host flourishing Sunni fundamentalist Islamist forces, some of which waged jihad, or holy war, by massacring civilians and prisoners of war during the 1979–1989 war against the Soviet occupation of Afghanistan. From that conflict emerged new genocidal groups like al-Qaida, which targeted Jews and Americans, Shiite Muslims in Iraq, and Russians in Chechnya. In 2003 Sudan's Arab Islamist regime transferred its genocidal counterinsurgency and "ethnic cleansing" campaigns against African Christians and animists of the country's south to fellow Muslims of the western region of Darfur.

Religion and Race

These three waves of postwar mass killing—communist, anti-communist, and Islamist—exemplify both the political variety of genocide and its underlying ideological features. Perpetrators of genocide and "ethnic cleansing" are usually preoccupied with ethnic or racial visions—and divisions. But their concepts can be dissimilar, internally inconsistent, or combined with a range of other political features. They may be based on notions of religious heritage, racial purity, ethnic hierarchy, biological theory, geographical origin, national citizenship, or combinations of these and other ideological preoccupations, such as class. Nevertheless, some commonalities bridge political divides.

In colonial genocides, racial divisions are usually clearcut. In other cases, religion has played an equally important role. The Armenian genocide, quickly followed by massacres of Greeks, was in part an attempt to eliminate Christian non-Turks from a newly defined Turkish Muslim nation. But it also involved attempted forcible assimilation (or ethnocide) of Muslim non-Turks. Kurdish Muslims were first mobilized to kill Armenians, then reclassified as "Mountain Turks" and forbidden to practice their separate culture—or even to speak the Kurdish language. In Cambodia, the majority religion, Buddhism, along with Islam and Christianity, was repressed by the antireligious Khmer Rouge regime. Minority and foreign languages were also banned, and Khmer became the only permitted language. The regime directed its fiercest extermination campaign at the ethnic Cham Muslim minority, who suffered a combination of genocide and ethnocide, and at the Vietnamese, all of whom were expelled or murdered. The Vietnamese Catholic cathedral in Phnom Penh was dismantled by a Khmer Rouge decision with explicit racialist overtones. In the case of Germany, anti-Semitism was central to Nazism. Adolf Hitler's pathological hatred for the Jews was perhaps best illustrated in the Nazi film *Der Ewige Jude* ("The Eternal Jew"), which depicted Jews as rats.

Genocidal regimes, radical and often unstable, make decisions on pragmatic as well as ideological grounds, in order to maintain or secure their grip on power. For similar reasons, genocidal racialism often proves deadly to many members of the supposedly privileged or protected race. This was least true in the case of the Armenian genocide, where the number of Turkish victims was low. By contrast, in absolute numbers, most victims of the Khmer Rouge regime were from the country's ethnic Khmer majority. Under Nazism, Jews were the largest single group to be exterminated; no other large group was exterminated more systematically than Jews were. But the numerous other victims were not even limited to "non-Aryans," such as Gypsies and Slavs. Hitler targeted German homosexuals, communists, liberals, trade unionists, and others who opposed him. In the Nazi purge of German culture, books and paintings were burned, literary and film criticism abolished, and modern music banned. The day after

the *Kristallnacht* (or Night of Broken Glass) pogrom on November 9, 1938, Hitler speculated that if someday the intellectual classes in Germany became unuseful, he might exterminate them.

During the Nazi invasion of Poland, more than 750,000 ethnic Germans were put into camps. The SS investigated and interrogated them. The "racially unfit," those who opposed Nazism, and those whom the SS disliked for some other reason were killed. Thousands more were mistreated before the SS decided to send them either to Germany or the east. Thus many German settlements were demolished or turned over to the Poles. This illustrates how the individual was rejected in favor of the race. Nazism did not privilege individuals by virtue of their membership in a particular race but, rather, suppressed their individual rights and gave primacy to the idealized group.

Nazi "eugenics" eliminated 70,000 Germans with hereditary illnesses. This euthanasia forms a close link with the destruction of Jews: the Nazis considered both sets of victims to be unproductive and to have an unpleasing outward physical appearance and thus to be biologically inferior and unworthy of life. By the same token, Gypsies, although defined in 1935 as "alien to the German species," were in the early years of the war persecuted not on the basis of race but on the basis of an "asocial and criminal past" and their posing a threat to security. Some more assimilated Gypsies, known as Sinti, even became members of the armed forces, where they served until 1942, when the Nazi regime ordered all Gypsies to be sent to the concentration camp at Auschwitz.

The Nuremberg Laws, designed by Hitler and approved by the Nazis in 1935, defined a "mixed-blood" Jew (*Mischling*) as anyone who had one or two "fully Jewish" grandparents. "Fully Jewish" was defined as belonging to the Jewish religious community. It has been contended that an individual was considered Jewish only if he or she had three or four Jewish grandparents or if the individual had two Jewish grandparents and belonged to the Jewish religion or was married to a Jewish person. Even in this Nazi version of biological racism, the most important issue always was the religion of the grandparents.

In Cambodia, Khmer Rouge racism was yet more inconsistent, with no attempt at "scientific" precision. Formal Nazi and communist differences aside, the Khmer Rouge considered their captive urban populations "subhuman" (*anoupracheachun*), the same term (*Untermenschen*) the Nazis had used for conquered Slavs. Democratic Kampuchea referred to its enemies as "microbes"; the Germans had talked of "vermin" and "lice." Pol Pot considered his revolution the only "clean" one in history, just as the Nazis "cleaned" occupied areas of Jews. Both regimes were obsessed with the concept of racial "purity." As a student, Pol Pot had called himself the "Original Khmer," but his preoccupations had precedents.

People and Land

Genocidal regimes often proclaim a need to "purify" not only a race but a territory. The Young Turks dreamed of a Pan-Turanian empire of Turkish-speaking peoples across Central Asia. As Christian provinces in the Balkans seceded from the Ottoman Empire in the years before World War I, there was an increasing call to make the remaining parts Turkish. The Young Turks initially chose to name their country Turkestan, with expansionist Central Asian connotations. Purification and expansion went hand in hand.

The Nazis' attempts to expand their territory and to exterminate the Jews were similarly connected. Hitler initially envisaged individual German, Polish, and Jewish areas of population from west to east. Pragmatic considerations gave priority to exchanging populations of Poles and German settlers, then expelling and eventually exterminating Jews.

Race and land were connected in two ways. First, idealization of the land itself played an important role. The Young Turk commander Enver Pasha claimed that it was the rural class that had given his army its strength. National Socialism, for its part, descended from the *völkisch* (folk) tradition, a product of the romanticism of the late eighteenth century. It is believed that Nazi nationalism sprang directly from the doctrine of "blood and soil" (*Blut und Boden*), which sought strength for the *Herrenvolk* (master race) in German soil and in peasant virtues. Hitler declared the farmer "the most important participant" in the Nazi revolution. In *Mein Kampf* ("My Struggle"), he linked German peasant farmland with German racial characteristics. Then the Nazi peasant leader Walther Darré took up the concept of *Blut und Boden* and became the main theoretician of expansion and agricultural settlement to the east.

Faith in agriculture also accentuated suspicions of city dwellers. Prefiguring Pol Pot, Hitler proclaimed that a nation could exist without cities but not without farmers. He described modern industrial cities as "abscesses on the body of the folk [*Volkskörper*], in which all vices, bad habits, and sicknesses seem to unite. They are above all hotbeds of miscegenation and bastardization." In 1975 the Khmer Rouge took this much further, evacuating the cities of Cambodia and seeing only the peasants as allies in their revolution.

The Nazis believed in the superiority and virtue of rural life. It has been asserted that *Blut und Boden* was one of National Socialism's very few consistent concepts. A film of that name made for use in Nazi Party meetings was subtitled *Foundation of the New Reich*. Hitler's minister of agriculture saw the issue in a way that Pol Pot could have put it: "Neither princes, nor the church, nor the cities have created the German man. Rather, the German man emerged from the German peasantry." Joseph Goebbels, Hitler's propagandist, commissioned at least seven feature films on the topic of "blood and soil." Another antiurban, anti-intellectual semi-documentary, *The Eternal Forest*, idealized the woods. The film depicts a master race represented by the German peasant, whose blood has fertilized the sacred soil for centuries. This view of "blood and soil" has been connected with Nazi anti-Semitism, with Jews seen as archetypal city dwellers.

Second, the land question is geographic as well as ideological. For instance, the decline of the Ottoman Empire from the sixteenth century made fear of further territorial diminution a political preoccupation for the Turks. Ottoman rulers were warned that Europeans would rule over Islamic lands unless defensive action were taken. For the Young Turks the survival of the Ottoman state was the most important issue.

Even expansion could only fuel such a relentless sense of conflict. In August 1939 Hitler recited his list of territorial gains—Austria, Czechoslovakia, the Rhineland, Sudetenland—while still proclaiming the threat of Germany's "certain annihilation." German territorial stability was unachievable. Failure to keep expanding meant annihilation. This special perception of the conditions of Germany's survival had a counterpart common among Cambodian nationalists too. The reasons were similar: a historically recent national territorial formation and the twin peaks, both heightened by extensive yet precarious gains, of national ambition and related insecurity.

Modern Germany was not the immediate heir to the medieval Holy Roman Empire. Only late-nineteenth century unification resulted in the establishment of the German Reich in 1871. Anti-Semitism increased and German colonial expansion soon began. Territorial setbacks and defeat in World War I fueled German nationalism and chauvinism.

Medieval Cambodia dominated mainland Southeast Asia, much as medieval Germany had dominated Europe. But after similar prolonged division, modern Cambodia's territory was consolidated just shortly before World War I, like Germany's a little earlier. The year 1907 saw the "return" to Cambodia (then under French colonial rule) of its entire northwest quadrant, under Thai rule since 1794. In 1914 France restored more territory to Cambodia, in an exchange with another French colony, Vietnam, to the east. A third territorial dispute (with Thailand) was resolved in Cambodia's favor in 1961.

The return of the northwest territories, which included the famous medieval temples of Angkor, had a major impact on Cambodian elite nationalism. When large territories are first regained, especially by a weak colonized state, they raise the stakes in the border conflict, but they also heighten consciousness of further ancestral losses. Cambodian nationalist attention became focused on other, longer lost, Khmer-speaking areas: several provinces of modern Thailand, whose ethnic Khmer majority still call themselves Upper Cambodians, and also Vietnam's Mekong Delta, whose ethnic Khmer minority are known as Lower Cambodians. The territorial gains made between 1907 and 1914 encouraged Cambodia to petition France for the additional transfer of the Mekong Delta from Vietnamese to Cambodian rule for the first time since the nineteenth century.

In World War II, with Japanese support, the Thais again seized the northwest of Cambodia (just as Germany had lost territories in World War I). The tide was turned again in 1946, when Thailand had to return the territories. But Khmer vulnerability had been reemphasized in both military defeat and territorial diminution. This became the nationalist nightmare, even though it had been a loss only in post-1907 terms, and only a temporary one. To the Khmer Rouge, like the Nazis, geographical stability was impossible. Cambodia had to recover its long-lost territories at the expense of its neighbors.

Some German historians have emphasized Germany's dilemma as "the country in the middle," unprotected by natural boundaries and threatened by her great neighbors: Russia on one side, France and Britain on the other. Germany has been termed Europe's No-Man's Land. For its part, Cambodia, with Thailand on one side and Vietnam on the other, has been called "The Land in Between."

Just as Hitler saw Czechoslovakia as "a dagger pointed at the heart of Germany," Pol Pot saw Cambodia's decline as uninterrupted by its twentieth-century territorial gains. His millennial view of the past stressed "2,000 years of exploitation" and rule by national traitors selling off territory. In a major public speech in 1977, Pol Pot urged his people to "prevent the constant loss of Cambodia's territory." This required both "tempering" his country's population and reconquering long-lost territory. The next year, Khmer Rouge radio exhorted its listeners not only to "purify" the "masses of the people" of Cambodia but also to sacrifice "only 2 million troops to crush the 50 million Vietnamese, and we would still have 6 million people left."

See also *Anti-Semitism; Holocaust; Human Rights.*

Ben Kiernan

BIBLIOGRAPHY

Andreopoulos, George J., ed. *Genocide: Conceptual and Historical Dimensions.* Philadelphia: University of Pennsylvania Press, 1994.

Blood, Archer K. *The Cruel Birth of Bangladesh: Memoirs of an American Diplomat.* Dhaka: University Press, 2002.

Browning, Christopher R. *The Path to Genocide: Essays on Launching the Final Solution.* Cambridge: Cambridge University Press, 1992.

Chalk, Frank, and Kurt Jonassohn. *The History and Sociology of Genocide: Analyses and Case Studies.* New Haven: Yale University Press, 1990.

Chomsky, Noam, and Edward S. Herman. *The Political Economy of Human Rights.* Vol. 1, *The Washington Connection and Third World Fascism.* Boston: South End Press, 1979.

Cook, Susan E., ed. *Genocide in Cambodia and Rwanda: New Perspectives.* New Brunswick, N.J.: Transaction Books, 2006.

Des Forges, Alison. *"Leave None to Tell the Story": Genocide in Rwanda.* New York: Human Rights Watch, 1999.

Gellately, Robert, and Ben Kiernan. *The Specter of Genocide: Mass Murder in Historical Perspective.* New York: Cambridge University Press, 2003.

Kiernan, Ben. *Blood and Soil: Genocidal Violence in World History from Carthage to Darfur.* New Haven: Yale University Press, forthcoming 2007.

———. *The Pol Pot Regime: Race, Power, and Genocide in Cambodia under the Khmer Rouge, 1975–1979.* 2d ed. New Haven: Yale University Press, 2002.

Lower, Wendy. *Nazi Empire-Building and the Holocaust in Ukraine.* Chapel Hill: University of North Carolina Press, 2005.

Melson, Robert. *Revolution and Genocide: On the Origins of the Armenian Genocide and the Holocaust.* Chicago: University of Chicago Press, 1992.

Melvern, Linda. *Conspiracy to Murder: The Rwandan Genocide.* London: Verso, 2004.

Moses, A. Dirk, ed. *Genocide and Settler Society: Frontier Violence and Stolen Indigenous Children in Australian History.* New York: Berghahn, 2004.

Totten, Samuel, William S. Parsons, and Israel W. Charny, eds. *Century of Genocide: Critical Essays and Eyewitness Accounts.* New York: Routledge, 2004.

Germany

One of the most powerful countries in modern Europe, Germany has been religiously divided between Roman Catholicism and Protestantism since the Reformation and Counter Reformation of the sixteenth century. Hence "religion" and "denomination" have been used as synonyms for centuries. This bitterly fought struggle between the faiths ended in the twentieth century. Since the 1960s, general processes of detraditionalization underminded the stability of church membership and beliefs, but in West Germany church membership nevertheless remained high. The reunification of Germany dramatically changed the situation, because East Germans had become predominantly nonmembers and nonbelievers. New developments are indicated by the growing presence and institutional representation of Islam.

From Religious Schism to the Nazi Period

Unsuccessful attempts by both the Catholics and the Protestants (Lutherans) to achieve ascendancy led to the insight early on that the respective adversary could not be defeated. This acceptance, enshrined in the Peace of Augsburg in 1555, gave the various princes the right to prescribe their subjects' religion. Recognition of religious equality created denominational equilibrium throughout the Holy Roman Empire of the German Nation, which henceforth was made up of a patchwork of denominationally homogeneous territories. A century later, after exhausting themselves in the Thirty Years' War, the two conflicting denominations reaffirmed this compromise in the Peace of Westphalia in 1648. The treaty put an end to open hostilities between the denominations until the nineteenth century.

Relations between the denominations worsened after the abolition, in 1806, of the Holy Roman Empire in the course of the Napoleonic Wars—including the disestablishment of its official (Catholic) church. A new European order was created in 1815 at the Congress of Vienna, which ratified the secularization of church territories. The creation of the Second (German) Empire in 1871 upset the equilibrium between the denominations. The exclusion of predominantly Catholic Austria reduced the Catholic population of the new empire to a one-third minority. The Catholics thus perceived in the Protestant majority under Prussian leadership a threat to their religious freedom.

The imperial chancellor, Otto von Bismarck, tried to integrate Catholics into the new empire by force. Ultimately, his *Kulturkampf,* the "struggle for culture" (1871–1878), alienated Catholics, encouraging the formation of Catholic political and social forces that remained aloof from the state. A clearly defined subculture of Catholic organizations emerged, represented politically by the Center Party, which, after its founding in 1870, astutely exploited the new opportunities presented by parliamentary representation and mass mobilization. When the National Socialists came to power in 1933, Catholic society did not initially warm to their ideology, despite the concordat in which the Catholic Church, strongly influenced by the Vatican, made peace with the dictatorship.

German Protestantism never developed institutions comparable to "political Catholicism." As the dominant Christian denomination in Prussian-oriented Germany, and its preeminent cultural marker in the nineteenth century, Lutheranism had no need for a denominational political party to represent its ideas and goals. The identification between the Lutheran Church and the authoritarian monarchy culminated in the First World War. After the state church was disestablished in 1919, German Protestants lacked a political home in the constitutionally secular, democratic Weimar Republic, with whose institutions few of them readily identified. Their disregard for democracy is reflected in widespread acceptance of National Socialism.

Only the question of church independence forced prominent Protestants to reconsider their theological position. In response to the blatant politicization of the church by the pro-Nazi "German Christians," they formed a group in 1934 that claimed to be the only legitimate German Evangelical Church. It became known as the *Bekennende Kirche* (Confessing Church). From this came many of those who opposed Adolf Hitler and became active in the resistance (such as the theologian Dietrich Bonhoeffer).

In addition to its bi-confessional structure, Germany has a strong tradition of scientism, religious critique, materialism, and atheism. It found a political expression in parts of the socialist movements in the nineteenth and twentieth centuries. Different from other countries, where scientism and religious critique predominantly remained elite projects, in Germany their support by socialist and social democratic movements contributed to the estrangement of the working classes from the churches.

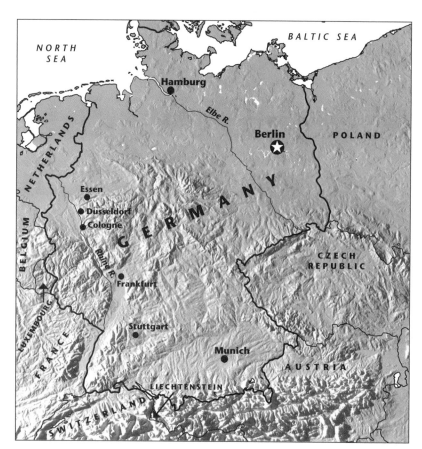

Deconfessionalization of Politics in Postwar Germany

The traumatic experience of the two Christian communities under the Third Reich profoundly affected their political attitudes. In 1945, only months after the end of the Second World War, a Christian political party that claimed to embrace both denominations was founded, the Christian Democratic Union. De facto this party was anchored much more in the Catholic population, whereas Social Democrats were anchored more in the Protestant part. The migration of enormous numbers of Germans—predominantly Catholics —toward the end of the war and in its aftermath broke up the self-contained denominational regions. This, as well as the breaking away of overwhelmingly Protestant East Germany to form the German Democratic Republic, left a new equilibrium between the denominations in the Federal Republic of Germany. Years of government under Chancellor Konrad Adenauer, a Catholic, and the mostly Catholic Christian Democratic Union erased Catholics' inferiority complex about politics.

Religion in Germany is still a relevant determinant of voting behavior and political orientation. Protestants and Catholics tend to vote differently in favor of Social Democrats on one side or Christian Democrats on the other. An additional dividing line, however, runs between people with and without close church ties. Practicing Christians of both denominations are more likely to hold traditional values and vote for conservative parties.

The churches have developed new ways of influencing public opinion. They regularly express their points of view in declarations on social and political questions. On occasion these statements have had historical significance, such as the correspondence between the Polish and German Catholic bishops (1965) that fostered reconciliation with Poland and the memorandum on Eastern Europe issued in 1966 by the Protestant Church in Germany in support of the center-left coalition's policy toward Eastern Europe. In 1991–1992 a profound conflict, which pitted Catholics, in particular, against nonreligious groups, was triggered by proposed changes to the law on abortion. In 1997 the churches' joint declaration on the consequences of flight and migration revived the controversy over the legality of the right of sanctuary that allows the churches to obstruct enforcement of the law in individual cases.

The German churches have a strong institutional position. They are bodies incorporated in public law with constitutionally guaranteed autonomy and special rights. Although the constitution charges the state to observe neutrality in religious matters, Germany does not practice radical separation of church and state. Instead, the constitution facilitates cooperation between both of them. To cover their financial needs, the churches have powers of taxation. The church tax is collected by state tax offices and employers. State-church cooperation also includes religious instruction in state schools and theological faculties at state universities. Apart from the civil service, the churches are the largest employers in the country and are especially active in health care and social work. They also have substantial economic resources.

Since the mid-1980s the decline in religious conviction and church membership as well as the demographic development have weakened the churches as institutional and financial forces, and the spread of informal forms of religious expression (the "esoteric" wave) and neoreligious movements (sects) is challenging their representational position. The general attitude toward cults is critical, however. In 1997 a dispute over Scientology came to a head when the self-proclaimed church alleged that the German government had violated the constitutional guarantee of religious freedom by discriminating against its members. German courts and authorities have defined Scientology as a new form of political extremism on account of its claim to totality and its infiltration of the corporate world and democratic institutions. Accordingly, the constitution protection agencies of most German states are obliged to keep Scientologists' activities under observation.

Throughout the time of its existence, the German Democratic Republic caused a rapid decline in religiosity and church affiliation among its citizens. With political methods ranging from open hostility over partial agreements to attempts to exploit the churches for the state's interests, the churches and religion in general were marginalized. In 1990, 69 percent of the East German population did not belong to any denomination, 24 percent were members of the Protestant Church, 5 percent belonged to the Catholic Church, and 2 percent were members of other denominations. Forty years earlier, about 80 percent of the population was Protestant, 11 percent Catholic, and only 8 percent lacked any denomination. Therefore, at the end of the German Democratic Republic, the huge majority of the population consisted of nonmembers, especially among the youth.

When the political system in East Germany collapsed in 1989, the widespread involvement of Protestant clergy in the East German opposition encouraged talk of a "Protestant revolution" in the heartland of the Reformation. The initial impression of a more Protestant Germany, however, fades on closer analysis. After 1990, the conditions for the churches changed radically because the West German model of church-state relationship was extended to East Germany. This improved the working conditions for the churches enormously, but it also suddenly made membership an issue of awareness and of a certain financial relevance. Many responded by quitting their church membership. From 1990 onward, the numbers of those leaving the churches increased rapidly, reaching its peak in 1992. Even if this tendency has declined since then, the churches up to today lose significantly more members than they gain new ones, mostly because of general demographic trends.

With unification of the two German states on October 3, 1990, the Protestant Church again became the larger denomination. The approximately 28 million Protestants outnumbered the Catholics by about 1.5 million. As a result of German unification, those who have dissociated themselves from both churches and even from Christian values and traditions represent a significant segment of the German population. The situation has consequences for Germany's political culture, as has already become visible in the debates about abortion. Also, religious instruction in state schools—as opposed to religiously neutral subjects such as ethics or religious studies—is under debate.

Islam is the third largest religious community in Germany, a result of labor migration. Of the 3.2 million Muslims in Germany (mostly belonging to the Sunni sect), most are of Turkish descent. As a rule, the Muslim congregations are organized as associations. Because of their organizational fragmentation and diverse political roots, until now they have not had the status of public bodies enjoyed by the two established Christian churches. But Muslims in Germany have started to create a structure of representation similar to the Jewish community. Successful attempts also have been made to establish Islamic instruction in school and to teach Islamic theology in public universities.

Between 1990 and 2003 Germany had its own headscarf affair. A Muslim teacher was denied the right to teach because she wore a headscarf and was considered unsuitable as a teacher because of her insistence on wearing it. But the Federal Constitutional Court of Germany in 2003 declared decisions about this case not in accordance with the constitution because they lacked legal foundation in the law of the federal states. The judges pointed out different possible solutions that could do justice to a growingly multicultural society.

Before the National Socialists came to power, 530,000 Jews lived in Germany; afterward, just 30,000. Since 1991, immigration from the former Soviet Union has more than tripled the total membership of Jewish congregations, which is about 100,000 in 2006. This shift has caused tension: the congregations' perception of themselves as communities of survivors has been called into question. Many of the immigrants have no religious traditions and have severe problems integrating socially into the Jewish community as well as into German society. Because of their precarious social situation, many used their Jewishness as a means of being accepted as refugees in Germany. In the meantime, immigration from the countries formerly in the Soviet Union is controlled more strictly. It may be considered a sign for the consolidation of the Jewish community that in 2006, for the first time after the end of the Holocaust, three rabbis were ordained in Germany.

The fundamental cleavage in Germany between the two branches of Christianity is a thing of the past. Both the Protestant and the Catholic churches have learned the lesson of the Third Reich and have used their authority in support of the democratic institutions of the Federal Republic of Germany. Nevertheless, the two churches retain some political influence through established rights and agreements as well as through their representations as public actors. Although membership is declining, 70 percent of Germans still are church members. The growing public debates about Islam not only partly give rise to ideas of a Christian guiding culture (Leitkultur), but also to secularist ideas that aim at keeping public life free from religion.

See also *Bonhoeffer, Dietrich; Catholicism, Roman; Christian Democracy; Cults; Lutheranism; Sanctuary; Taxation.*

Monika Wohlrab-Sahr

BIBLIOGRAPHY

Conway, John S. *The Nazi Persecution of the Churches, 1933–1945.* London: Weidenfeld and Nicolson, 1968.

Francis, John G. "The Evolving Regulatory Structure of European Church-State Relationships." *Journal of Church and State* 34 (Autumn 1992): 775–804.

Nowak, Kurt. *Geschichte des Christentums in Deutschland: Religion, Politik, und Gesellschaft vom Ende der Aufklärung bis zur Mitte des 20. Jahrhunderts.* Munich, Germany: C. H. Beck, 1995.

Pollack, Detlef. "Secularisation in Germany after 1945." In *The Divided Past: Rewriting Post-War German History,* edited by Christoph Klessmann. New York: Berg, 2001, pp. 105–125.

Rapaport, Lynn. *Jews in Germany after the Holocaust: Memory, Identity, and Jewish-German Relations.* Cambridge: Cambridge University Press, 1997.

Schmidt, Thomas, and Monika Wohlrab-Sahr. "Still the Most Areligious Part of the World: Developments in the Religious Field in Eastern Germany since 1990." *International Journal of Practical Theology* 7 (2003): 86–100.

Spotts, Frederic. *The Churches and Politics in Germany.* Middletown, Conn.: Wesleyan University Press, 1973.

Wohlrab-Sahr, Monika. "Integrating Different Pasts, Avoiding Different Futures? Recent Conflicts about Islamic Religious Practice and Their Judicial Solutions." *Time and Society* 13 (2004): 51–70.

Ghana

Ghana is a former British colony that gained independence under its first president, Dr. Kwame Nkrumah, on March 6, 1957. From 1966 the country experienced a series of military interventions until the last military leader, Flt. Lt. Jerry John Rawlings, metamorphosed into a democratically elected president in 1996. Having served the mandatory two terms, his party, the National Democratic Congress, lost the next election to the New Patriotic Party in 2000.

Formerly known as the Gold Coast, Ghana's political life in terms of religious influence has been shaped by African Traditional Religion, Islam, and Christianity. A number of postcolonial new religious movements also established themselves in the country. Various patterns of interaction between political structures and traditional religion prevailed in precolonial Ghana. In what is now Ghana's north, centralized, traditional, territorial rule (chieftaincy) seems to have developed apart from and later than a primeval Earth guardianship centered on shrines of larger or smaller jurisdiction. These guardians dealt ritually with the Earth as a numinous power thought to provide society not only with agricultural fertility but also with its moral base. All the ethnic groups inhabiting this area were ruled internally by elders in one or another clan, but interclan relationships, especially in the so-called stateless societies where there was no central ruler, were often regulated by the guardian of the Earth shrine.

With the stimulus of migration, long-distance trade, and intergroup warfare, centralized territorial rule did arise in some areas of Ghana's north after the sixteenth century. In the colonial era other groups in this territory developed such rule in order to deal with British colonial authorities. In recent years others have sought the recognition of self-rule where tension has developed between large stateless populations and their neighbors with centralized structures of governance.

In the Akan areas of southern Ghana, centralized rulership, characterized by ritual veneration of the chief and of dead lineage ancestors, developed early in many areas. Basically matrilineal in structure, most Akan societies link the male ruler ritually and politically with a queen mother (a royal matrilineal relative, not necessarily the mother of the chief). Akan rulers assume some of the functions associated with the Earth priesthood in northern Ghana, especially mediation between disputing segments of society and placation of the personified Earth when crimes have been committed. Unlike the Earth priest, however, until modern times the Akan ruler traditionally exercised considerable authority in warfare, long-distance commerce, and other areas of executive power.

In the 1690s the rulership in one Akan state, the Ashanti kingdom based in Kumasi, rose to hegemony over many of its neighbors. The Golden Stool, a sacred throne symbolizing the soul of the Ashanti kingdom and said to have been conjured from the skies by Okomfo Anokye, the chief priest, has proven religiously and politically more significant than the throne of any individual ruler in Ghana. Placed at the Ashanti ruler's side on the most solemn state occasions, this potent symbol of the Ashanti state and repository of the soul of the people remains a strong focus of religio-political sentiment and religious festivities, even in postcolonial Ghana.

In other major ethnic clusters of southern Ghana (the speakers of languages in the Ga-Adangme-Krobo family and the Ewe-speaking population), as well as in many smaller societies scattered throughout these areas (especially the Guan peoples), patrilineal social structures predominate, as does centralized, territorial rule with much of the same sort of sacral functions that are associated with Akan rulership,

although often over a smaller territory. In some cases centralized rulership in these areas may have arisen in conflict and competition with the Akan states.

Only about 8 percent of the country's total population of nearly twenty million people still claimed adherence to any form of traditional religion as of the early to mid-2000s. Traditional worldviews of mystical causality, however, have proven resilient in the daily affairs of people and society.

Earth priesthood and centralized territorial rulership continue to influence the politics of land tenure throughout Ghana. Recent examples of such conflicts include the 1994 Konkomba conflict and the 2001 Dagbon chieftaincy dispute, which continued to rage into the mid-2000s. Although every government since Ghana's independence in 1957 has tried to control the outbreak of violence over such matters, it would seem that not only rural populations but also many of their urban relatives continue to respond to the symbols of chieftaincy or the sacred Earth.

Islam

Islam first made its presence felt in what is now Ghana around the fifteenth century. By the middle of the sixteenth century Islamic influence emanating from a foreign commercial enclave in the Akan forest was felt in what is now the country's northern region and helped to create centralized territorial rule in the Gonja states. Islamic paraphernalia were taken up by Gonja state creators looking for a supra-ethnic system with which they could legitimate their rule over diverse populations. Actual Islamization of Gonja has been slight, but its leaders still bear Muslim names. Islamization of the non-Gonja stateless populations subject to the Gonja is minimal.

Other northern Ghanaian polities attached themselves gradually to the Islamic tradition over the seventeenth and eighteenth centuries, most notably the Wala and the Dagomba. For some of these centralized rulerships in northern Ghana, Islamization may have been a byproduct of developing such rule, but the association of Muslim clerics with various royal houses compromised the Islamic character of these clerics and reduced them to the status of amulet manufacturers and diviners for their royal patrons.

Muslims found it more difficult to penetrate the traditional courts of the Akan areas, except as amulet providers and magicians of various sorts, either in symbiosis or competition with traditional providers of such services. The matrilineal structure of most Akan chieftaincies, and especially the Ashanti hegemony, prevented Muslims—encumbered with a revealed patrilineal inheritance system—from acceding to high office. The Akan states have also blocked the access of Muslims to the patrilineal non-Akan states to their south and east, although Muslims played important roles in the commercial dealings of every large town in Ghana, especially when long-distance trade was concerned.

Muslims have, as a community, been much less involved in the politics of postcolonial Ghana than they have in many other West African states. Making up about 16 percent of Ghana's estimated twenty million people in 2000, Muslims have associated themselves with differing political traditions in the modern state. The formation of political parties along religious lines is not permitted under the 1992 constitution of the republic of Ghana. Muslims, however, have been granted two national holidays and have, since the restoration of constitutional democracy in 1992, gained increasing influence in Ghana's political life either as ministers of state or as members of parliament. The vice president of Ghana in 2006, Alhaji Aliu Mahama, was a practicing Muslim, and the Islamic vote has become so important that political parties now consciously include a Muslim face in their electioneering campaigns.

Ghanaian Ahmadi Muslims, adherents of an Indo-Pakistani Islamic sect deemed heterodox and (since 1974) even non-Muslim in its homeland, have operated Islamic schools and hospitals since the 1920s in certain parts of Ghana. Ahmadi Muslim controversies with Sunni Muslims (the majority of Muslims worldwide as well as in Ghana) stem from Ahmadi theological claims for their nineteenth-century Indian founder, Ghulam Ahmad. These religious differences have limited Ahmadi influence on the more general political life of Ghana.

In recent years various Islamic ideological tendencies emanating from the Middle East have been felt in Ghana's Muslim community. Saudi Arabia's control of the pilgrimage to Mecca has given that country much influence in Ghana. In certain urban areas Muslims influenced by the legalistic puritanism of Saudi Arabian Wahhabi thought have come into conflict with Tijani mystics, adherents of a form of fervent piety originating in eighteenth-century North Africa but popularized throughout West Africa in the nineteenth and twentieth centuries by charismatic Senegalese preachers. The Iranian Shi'i government since 1979, aware of Saudi influence on the Wahhabi opponents of Tijani mysticism, has

taken up the opposing role of sponsor for this mystical tradition of Sunni Islam. One of the major influences of the Iranian government in Ghanaian socio-polical life is the establishment of a Muslim university college in the country at the turn of the twenty-first century.

Christianity

Ghana presents itself as a Christian nation, with as much as 62 percent of the population at least nominally Christian. Although Christianity first made its influence felt on the Atlantic coast of Ghana from the late fifteenth century, the slave trade and the mortality rate among the Europeans on the coast meant that only a very few coastal people had become Christian by the beginning of the nineteenth century. European Protestants and Reformed or Basel Pietist missionaries founded Presbyterian churches and Methodist missions in various parts of southern Ghana after 1828.

The distance between the German-speaking Reformed Church missionaries and the British colonial authorities and the small number of British Methodist missionaries meant that neither of these groups was strongly affected by anti-colonial feeling as it developed among the educated Christian elite from the late nineteenth century. Catholic missions, also conducted by non-British missionaries, began to exercise considerable influence in southern Ghana after 1880 and, after 1906, in the north, where the Presbyterians and the Methodists never developed a strong base. The twentieth century also witnessed the introduction of other Christian churches, including classical Pentecostal churches like the Assemblies of God, American inspired neo-Pentecostal churches, as well as the efflorescence of dozens of local African independent or spiritual churches, mainly founded between 1920 and 1960. The neo-Pentecostals began forming in the country at the end of the 1970s and have since grown to become the most significant group of churches in Ghana in the early twenty-first century. These churches offer Christian solutions of a somewhat traditional religious orientation (ceremonies of exorcism, healing prayer, the use of blessed ointments and talismans) for problems stemming from such aspects of the worldview of traditional religion as the fear of witchcraft.

Among the most famous of indigenous prophets from whom the spiritual churches take their origin was the Liberian prophet William Wade Harris (d. 1929), who directed his many disciples in the southwestern Gold Coast, which he briefly evangelized in 1914, to the missionary churches. Not all of the mission churches were equally ready to receive these enthusiasts into their communions. The preaching of Harris and other early-twentieth century indigenous prophets like Samson Opon and John Swatson contributed to the formation of some of the earliest spiritual churches in the region.

Even if Reformed Church (after World War I, Presbyterian) piety did not encourage much participation in the process of seeking independence for Ghana, Catholics (albeit estranged ones, like Kwame Nkrumah, Ghana's first president, and military rulers Ignatius Acheampong and Jerry Rawlings) and Methodists (such as Prime Minister Kofi Busia) have shaped the political history of Ghana since independence. In the Nkrumah era (1957–1966) the Ghanaians who gradually assumed the leadership of the internationally affiliated ecclesiastical bodies took an independent stance on government policies, especially as Nkrumah developed more authoritarian tendencies.

In subsequent military regimes, especially under Acheampong (1972–1979) and Rawlings (1981–1993), the mainstream Protestant churches and the Catholic Church worked in concert to confront the government on issues of human rights, economic justice, and political freedom. Measures taken by the Rawlings military government (the suppression of the Catholic weekly newspaper, temporary deportation of foreign Mormon missionaries and Jehovah's Witnesses, and an abortive attempt to subject all religious bodies to government registration) led to some silencing of church-inspired opposition in the 1980s. Since the civilianization of the Rawlings regime in 1993, church-state relations have improved somewhat, although the government continues to remain cool towards the mainstream churches.

The indigenously developed spiritual churches at the height of their popularity in the 1950s and 1960s were very popular in southern Ghana. Their membership has declined considerably in the mid-2000s. The spiritual churches have been overshadowed by Pentecostals, and neo-Pentecostal/charismatic churches have enjoyed considerable popularity in Ghana since the closing decades of the twentieth century. The Pentecostals, both old and new, have generally avoided involvement in questions of politics, bestowing their blessings where requested on whoever happens to exercise political power at any particular time.

Social, political, and economic chaos afflicted Ghana in the late 1970s and early 1980s, the result of mismanagement of the state by successive military regimes. When the Rawlings regime renounced its earlier socialist rhetoric for reforms mandated by the International Monetary Fund and World Bank in the mid-1980s, many Ghanaians—looking for peace, prosperity, and self-esteem— preferred the apolitical prosperity gospel of Ghanaian neo-Pentecostal preachers, modeling themselves on American televangelists to the social gospel preached at least in some of the mainstream churches.

See also *Christianity in Africa; Islam; Traditional Religions, African.*

Kwabena Asamoah-Gyadu

BIBLIOGRAPHY

Apter, David E. *Ghana in Transition.* 2d rev. ed. Princeton, N.J.: Princeton University Press, 1972.

Asamoah-Gyadu, J. Kwabena. *African Charismatics: Current Developments within Independent Indigenous Pentecostalism in Ghana.* Leiden, the Netherlands: E.J. Brill, 2005.

Austin, Dennis. *Politics in Ghana, 1947–1960.* London: Oxford University Press, 1964.

Gifford, Paul. *Ghana's New Christianity: Pentecostalism in a Globalizing African Economy.* Bloomington: Indiana University Press, 2004.

———. *African Christianity, Its Public Role.* London: Hurst and Company, 1998.

———. "Ghana's Charismatic Churches." *Journal of Religion in Africa* 24 (1994): 241–265.

Jones, Trevor. *Ghana's First Republic, 1960–1966: The Pursuit of the Political Kingdom.* London: Methuen, 1977.

Levtzion, Nehemia. *Muslims and Chiefs in West Africa: A Study of Islam in the Middle Volta Basin in the Pre-Colonial Period.* Oxford: Clarendon Press, 1968.

Meyer, Birgit. *Translating the Devil: Religion and Modernity among the Ewe in Ghana.* Trenton, N.J.: Africa World Press, 1999.

Pobee, John S. *Kwame Nkrumah and the Church in Ghana, 1949–1966.* Accra, Ghana: Asempa Publishers, 1988.

———. *Religion and Politics in Ghana.* Accra, Ghana: Asempa Publishers, 1991.

Ryan, Patrick J. "Ariadne auf Naxos: Islam and Politics in a Religiously Pluralistic African Society." *Journal of Religion in Africa* 26 (1996): 308–329.

Samwini, Nathan. *The Muslim Resurgence in Ghana since 1950: Its Effects Upon Muslims and Muslim-Christian Relations.* London: Transaction Publishers, 2006.

Globalization

Globalization refers to the social institutions that emerge as the world increasingly becomes a single society. By the end of the twentieth century the term had come to be used with a wide variety of meanings, but the most common referred to the integration of world financial markets, the proliferation of transnational businesses with sales and production operations spread across numerous countries, the rapid intensification of global networks of physical and electronic communication, and the increasingly global nature of conflict and security issues.

Understanding globalization can begin by distinguishing between the technologies, such as aircraft or the Internet, that make the world smaller through rapid worldwide communication and exchange and the social institutions that arise amid such interaction. It is important to distinguish between the ability to travel anywhere in the world in a matter of hours or communicate in seconds and to understand why people do this, who does it, and what effect it has on people's lives. Globalization concerns primarily the way people live, the way they conduct their affairs, and their social relations with each other; it affects individuals, economies, collectivities, politics, and culture.

Immanuel Wallerstein, an economic historian, believes that the world-system, as he calls it, is primarily a world capitalist economy. Development of this economy has led to the unequal division of the world into core, peripheral, and semiperipheral regions. Core countries such as the United States and Japan are rich and dominate; peripheral countries like Zaire and Bangladesh are poor and exploited by the core; semiperipheral countries like Brazil and China are in between and act as intermediaries between the core and the periphery. In world-system analysis, states and cultures are the tools and expressions of this basic economic reality, and contemporary politics and religion are important expressions of global economic relations. Religion can take the form of political protest—as in the Iranian revolution under the Muslim fundamentalist Ayatollah Ruholla Khomeini in 1979 or in the liberation theology movement in Latin America in the late twentieth century—or, like Pentecostalism and the Roman Catholic Church, it can help reinforce the capitalist world-system by upholding the status quo.

World-system theory was one of the earliest to define the basic structures of world society. In the past, international relations focussed on subglobal states and their national societies, not the world as a whole. What was global would then be only the interaction—diplomacy or war, for example—among these principal units. Many scholars now believe that modern states themselves are expressions of a globalized model of what a state looks like and how it acts. For instance, the *world-polity* school, which is associated in particular with the Stanford University sociologist John W. Meyer, has argued that important ideas like development, human rights, citizenship, equality, and freedom have become global standards in terms of which states act and compare themselves with others. Each state also expects to have similar institutions, such as a military and school and legal systems. The world-polity with its attendant global culture is the larger context in which states and individuals act and see themselves.

Cultural approaches to globalization focus on several factors, especially social movements, such as feminism and environmentalism; mass media, like television and film; tourism; popular culture from Sailor Moon to Big Macs; and important cultural models, such as ethnicity, individuality, nationality, and tradition. The British sociologist Roland Robertson, probably the first scholar to use the term *globalization* in a technical sense, stresses the degree to which globalization is not simply about a global culture that all the world's people supposedly share but about how people increasingly structure and assert their local cultures, traditions, and identities in terms of general globalized models. The awareness of the local as particular and unique is possible only by comparison with similar "others." Thus, for instance, the Japanese do not just become more like the Americans and vice versa; they both become more aware of themselves as either Japanese or American. Globalization means self-aware pluralism. In related fashion, numerous approaches stress the transnational and global importance of a variety of phenomena not necessarily identified either with the system of sovereign states or the global economy. Sometimes understood as elements of a global civil society, these include an ever-increasing array of international nongovernmental organizations, ranging from scientific to development and aid organizations, various social movements, including even anti-globalization movements, and the networks, institutions, and global flows established by transnational migrants.

Religion, like the globalized idea of the nation-state, is both a universal category and a way of identifying differences. There now exists a system of states as the prime political structure of world society. Yet each of these states is deemed to be the instrument of a particular and different national society, whether ethnically based or not. Similarly, we now have the globally spread idea that religions can also be important identifying features of particular cultural groups, with the result that various religious nationalisms arise: Protestant and Roman Catholic in Ireland, Sikh in

Punjab, Jewish in Israel, Hindu and Buddhist in Sri Lanka, Protestant fundamentalist in the United States, Sunni Muslim in Chechnya or Malaysia, Shi'ite Muslim in Iran. These loyalties can and do contest for state power and the right to determine the identity of national societies. Often, in popular parlance, such religious movements are called *fundamentalisms,* but this category also includes various conservative, sometimes political and militant, transnational religious movements, such as exemplified in the Vishva Hindu Parishad (World Hindu Organization) or al-Qaida.

Religion also has a universalist face. Religions like Islam, Buddhism, and Christianity have always stressed that they are open to all people: individuals can convert to these religions, not just be born into them. In the context of globalization, all religions are increasingly under pressure to see themselves as universal in principle, whether historically they have been or not. They thus become ways of seeing humanity as a single community, a whole that should ultimately be harmonious and not divided in conflict. This ecumenical face of religions makes them resources for criticizing state, economy, and culture for failing to live up to global ideals. This universalist impulse also manifests itself in the growing importance of highly individualized, often equally critical but also globally aware, spiritual orientations, sometimes discussed under such headings as "new age." These trends largely escape the institutionalized religions but may be gaining increasing salience among middle-class and urban populations around the world.

See also *Capitalism.*

Peter Beyer

BIBLIOGRAPHY

Beyer, Peter. *Religion and Globalization.* Thousand Oaks, Calif.: Sage Publications, 1994.

Nederveen Pieterse, Jan. *Globalization and Culture: Global Mélange.* Lanham, Md.: Rowan and Littlefield, 2004.

Haynes, Jeffrey. *Religion in Global Politics.* London: Longman, 1998.

Robertson, Roland. *Globalization: Social Theory and Global Culture.* Thousand Oaks, Calif: Sage Publications, 1992.

Scholte, Jan Aart. *Globalization: A Critical Introduction.* New York: St. Martin's Press, 2000.

Thomas, George M., John W. Meyer, Francisco O. Ramirez, and John Boli, eds. *Institutional Structure: Constituting State, Society and the Individual.* Thousand Oaks, Calif.: Sage Publications, 1987.

Wallerstein, Immanuel. *World-Systems Analysis: An Introduction.* Durham, N.C.: Duke University Press, 2004.

Waters, Malcolm. *Globalization.* 2d ed. London: Routledge, 2001.

Graham, Billy

William Franklin "Billy" Graham Jr., born November 7, 1918, on a farm outside Charlotte, North Carolina, became the most famous and successful evangelist of the twentieth century. Graham preached the gospel of Christ in person to more than eighty million people and reached countless other millions via radio, television, films, books, magazines, and newspaper columns. Successful revivals (called "crusades") and international conferences sponsored by his ministry fostered widespread ecumenical cooperation, particularly among evangelical Christians.

Graham's preaching in the early 1950s was filled with political themes, and he eagerly sought ties with political leaders. President Harry Truman rebuffed him, but other politicians saw him as a valuable ally and warmly supported his 1952 crusade in Washington, D.C. Such attention convinced Graham that he wielded considerable political clout, moving him to estimate that he could personally swing at least sixteen million votes to the cause or candidate of his choice.

Graham professed neutrality in the 1952 presidential campaign but clearly favored Dwight Eisenhower. His transparent support of Eisenhower's campaign and administration led to frequent visits to the White House, unofficial diplomatic errands, and a close friendship with Eisenhower's vice president, Richard Nixon, who Graham clearly hoped would succeed Eisenhower to the presidency. When John Kennedy defeated Nixon in 1960, Graham's ties to presidential power were attenuated until Lyndon Johnson became president after Kennedy's assassination in 1963.

The evangelist provided valuable support and legitimization for Johnson's causes—the War on Poverty, the Civil Rights Act, the war in Vietnam—and drew sharp disapproval from those who felt he had compromised his ability to speak with a prophetic voice. This line of criticism intensified after Nixon finally gained the presidency in 1968. An openly enthusiastic supporter, Graham remained staunchly loyal to the beleaguered president until the revelations surrounding Watergate finally forced some recognition of his old friend's darker side. Deeply stung, Graham drew back from overt political involvement, rarely visiting the White House during the Ford and Carter administrations. Graham returned to Washington more frequently and more publicly during the presidencies of Ronald Reagan and George H. W. Bush, both of whom had been friends since the 1950s.

Billy Graham.

His contribution appears to have involved symbolic legitimization rather than strategic counsel, a course continued by his appearance and prayer at Bill Clinton's two inaugurations.

Although not issuing an official endorsement, Graham spoke warmly of George W. Bush on the eve of the 2000 election, and the grateful candidate spoke often of the famed evangelist's role in helping revive his religious commitment. Poor health prevented Graham from attending the younger Bush's inauguration, but his son Franklin appeared and prayed in his stead. Then, following the tragic events of September 11, 2001, the quite frail and elderly evangelist managed to fill his role as unofficial chaplain to the nation yet one more time, representing Protestant Christianity at an internationally televised interfaith service. Graham maintained his friendship with the Bush family but drew widespread attention in June 2005 by announcing that he was a registered Democrat and by inviting Bill and Hillary Clinton to share the stage with him during his New York City crusade, at which time he spoke warmly of their long friendship and noted that he had told former president Clinton that he was such a good speaker that "he should become an evangelist and let his wife run the country."

Graham's political connections and unique stature as a religious leader enabled him to break down formidable barriers, seen most dramatically in a series of increasingly successful forays behind the Iron Curtain between 1978 and 1992 that helped widen the scope of religious freedom in the Soviet Union and its satellite nations. Visits to North Korea in 1992 and 1994 included long visits with President Kim Il Sung and appear to have played some role in Kim's decision to allow limited international inspection of its nuclear weapons facilities.

Despite increasing wariness of excessive involvement in the political realm, Graham encouraged evangelical Christians to assume greater responsibility for social and economic justice, as well as other temporal problems, including, most notably, nuclear disarmament. In recognition of his achievements and influences, Graham has received, among many accolades and prizes, both the Presidential Medal of Freedom (1983) and the Congressional Gold Medal (1996), the highest honors these two branches of government can bestow upon a civilian.

William Martin

BIBLIOGRAPHY

Graham, Billy. *Just As I Am: The Autobiography of Billy Graham.* New York: HarperCollins, 1997.

Martin, William. *A Prophet with Honor: The Billy Graham Story.* New York: Morrow, 1991.

Great Britain

Great Britain, comprising England, Scotland, and Wales, is the "mainland" part of the United Kingdom, a collection of small islands on the northwest fringe of Europe. The population of Great Britain is about 58 million. Generalizations about the country's religion and politics must take account of the variations between the three regions in respect to their histories and cultures. (Northern Ireland, with a population of 1.7 million, is also part of the United Kingdom but is discussed in the article on Ireland.) Many of the variations stem from their individual responses to the Protestant Reformation of the sixteenth century, during which King Henry VIII (and later Queen Elizabeth I) defied the authority of the pope in Rome and asserted the independence of the English church; the Roman Catholic Counter Reformation that followed; and the evangelical revival of the eighteenth century.

In very general terms, two Reformed traditions—Calvinism and Presbyterianism—had the greatest impact on the Lowlands of Scotland and Wales, whereas Methodism acquired a stronghold in the southeast and southwest of England. Roman Catholicism was confined to isolated pockets of northern England and the Highlands of Scotland after Elizabeth I foiled attempts to retain a Catholic monarch (Mary Queen of Scots) in 1567, but it experienced rapid growth in many industrial towns and cities from the 1830s onward. Meanwhile, the Anglican Church—the Church of England—remained the largest and politically most powerful religious force throughout England.

The Role of Established Churches

The power of Anglicanism was bolstered by sixteenth-century legislation that severely penalized Roman Catholics and Protestants who dissented from the Church of England. In the seventeenth century further legal penalties were imposed on the growing numbers of Protestant dissenters until 1689, when the Act of Toleration granted limited religious liberty to all Protestant sects. Catholics had to wait until 1829 for the beginning of their legal emancipation, and Jews until 1845. Even today, the "established" churches in England and Scotland remain privileged in comparison with other churches and faiths.

Both the Church of England and the Church of Scotland are established in the sense of enjoying privileges and responsibilities that are specified in law. Their status gives

them unparalleled access to agencies of the state at national and local levels, although neither of them is aligned with any political parties.

The Church of Scotland, a self-governing Presbyterian body, is recognized by the British state, but it does not require Parliament's approval for changes in its doctrines or practices. The fact that many of its lay and clerical officeholders are elected to their positions means that the Church of Scotland's official pronouncements are widely regarded as the most authoritative expression of Scottish opinion. Before a wide range of powers and responsibilities were devolved to the newly created Scottish Parliament in 1999, the church often came close to functioning as an unofficial Scottish parliament when it debated matters of general public concern. The church is also widely regarded as a symbol of Scottish national identity and of

Scotland's relative independence from England and the British state.

By comparison, the Church of England's relations with the British state are closer and more complex. The Church of England has never served as a "state church," nor has it ever been a department of state. Yet its position is Erastian—that is, upholding state supremacy in church affairs—in the sense that it is subordinate to Parliament and to the Crown. The British monarch is both head of state and supreme governor of the Church of England. This is why Anglican clerics officiate at most state ceremonies, the twenty-six most senior bishops have seats in the House of Lords, the church's own legal system is recognized as valid, the prime minister is involved in the selection of new bishops and archbishops, and chaplaincy services in prisons, health care institutions, and the military are dominated by Anglican priests. Thus, although the state does not finance the church, Parliament monitors its economic activity and retains the right to debate proposed changes in doctrine, worship, and finances.

Establishment can therefore cause problems for both church and state. Problems for the Church of England include the perception that Parliament interferes in the church's internal affairs, that it is not free to select its own leaders, and that the state expects the "national church" to endorse or legitimize government policies. Problems occur for the state when leading Anglicans voice strong criticism of government policies concerning, for example, military action against Argentina in 1982, Prime Minister Margaret Thatcher's neoliberal economic programs from 1979 to 1990, or the United Kingdom's involvement in the invasion of Iraq in 2003. Problems for the state also occur when representatives of other churches and faiths complain that the Church of England receives excessively privileged treatment from the state.

Neither English nor Scottish law provides for the separation of religion and state, but the freedom of religion in both countries is guaranteed by the fact that the United Kingdom is a signatory to the European Union's Treaty of Amsterdam (1997) and to the European Convention on Human Rights and the International Covenant on Civil and Political Rights. Nevertheless, until these treaties are incorporated into acts of Parliament, those seeking remedy against perceived restrictions on their religious freedom can only cite the treaties in general support of their cases. The Human Rights Act (1998) and the Race Relations Amendment Act (2000) provide further protection for the right to practice—

or not to practice—a religion in Great Britain. And the Employment Equality (Religion or Belief) Regulations (2003) outlaw discrimination in employment on grounds of religion or belief.

The arrival of large numbers of Jews fleeing from persecution in central and eastern Europe in the late nineteenth century introduced a new dimension to the religious and political life of Great Britain. Even more far-reaching changes in the religious composition of the country began to occur in the 1950s, when migrants from the Caribbean, South Asia, and East Africa began to swell the numbers of Hindus, Muslims, Sikhs, and Christians in churches. The result was that Great Britain became the most religiously diverse country in Europe. Moreover, this diversity was inseparable from ethnic and "racial" diversity.

The communities associated with the major Christian churches and other faith traditions in Great Britain, according to the 2001 census, amounted to approximately the following proportions of the population: Christians, 70 percent; Muslims, 2.7 percent; Hindus, 0.9 percent; Sikhs, 0.6 percent; and Jews, 0.5 percent. Roughly 23 percent stated no religion or declined to answer the relevant census question. The trend is for the number of active Catholics and members of other faith communities to increase in the foreseeable future and for the mainstream Christian churches' share of the religious "market" to continue declining slowly.

The existence of two established churches and the growing strength of non-Christian religious minorities combine to create a highly distinctive nexus of politics and religion in Great Britain. Three aspects of this nexus are particularly important: the absence of strong ties between religious groups and political parties, the lack of ideological polarization based on religion, and the role of education in the country's state-funded schools.

Party Politics

No political party in Britain has been exclusively aligned with any particular church or faith, although in the latter half of the nineteenth century and in the first decades of the twentieth century there was a loose affinity between, on the one hand, the Liberal Party and the Nonconformist churches (Baptists, Congregationalists, Methodists, and Presbyterians) and, on the other, between some socialist organizations and Methodism. There is also a tendency for Christian supporters of the Conservative Party to identify themselves more closely with the Church of England than with any other church and for Christians from less advantaged backgrounds to support the Labour Party or the Liberal Democratic Party. But it is rare for religious issues to be expressed in party terms in mainland Britain, if not in Northern Ireland, where Catholics and Protestants tend to be divided along party lines. This is why members of Parliament are sometimes allowed to follow their individual consciences rather than their political parties' instructions when they vote on issues with strongly religious or moral relevance. It is also why the Roman Catholic bishops insisted that the unquestionably political opinions expressed in their booklet *The Common Good,* published in 1996, were independent of any particular party. *The Common Good* asserts the need for labor to take precedence over capital and the desirability of trade union membership if poverty is to be tackled effectively. The other side of this coin is that, unlike in France, Italy, or Spain, anticlericalism, aggressive atheism, and Christian Democracy have never taken root in Great Britain's politics.

The political sympathies of British Hindus, Muslims, and Sikhs seem to be following the same trajectory as those of Irish Catholics and European Jews who migrated to the United Kingdom much earlier. That is, first-generation settlers tended to support the Labour Party and trade unions, but many members of second and subsequent generations have gravitated toward parties in the center or on the right wing of the political spectrum, especially if they gained economic security or moved up the social ladder. In other words, social class exercises at least as much influence over political views as does religious or ethnic identity. But political friction between faith communities has been politicized in connection with several issues that appear in a multi-faith society: the application of zoning laws to the construction of religious buildings; the ritual slaughter of animals for food; the demand that the law against blasphemy be extended to religions other than Christianity; the proposal that unfair discrimination on the grounds of religion be outlawed in all areas of life; the pressure to provide even-handed support from public funds for prison, health care, and military chaplains from all faith communities; and the highly contentious proposal to introduce legislation to punish incitement to religious hatred. However, New Labour governments since 1997 have given high priority to policies and structures that harness religious diversity to the overall objective of promoting the values of diversity and equality. Support has been strong for interfaith initiatives, and many government departments have set up agencies for establishing liaisons with faith communities. These developments have, nevertheless, refueled long-standing controversies concerning the representativeness of faith groups and their leaders.

Conservative and Progressive Opinions

There is little evidence that "culture wars" have polarized conservative and progressive opinions about morally controversial issues in Great Britain. Of course, conservative support is strong for imposing harsher penalties on convicted criminals, for encouraging two-parent families, for controlling "adult" publications and video films, and for cutting the cost of social welfare programs. But ideological agreement on these issues has not seriously weakened the bonds of identity and loyalty that bind members of separate churches and other religious organizations together. For example, conservative Methodists are unlikely to leave their church simply to join fellow conservatives in a different church. Still, the swing away from liberal values of social justice and solidarity has been pronounced in many faith communities since the early 1980s, thereby mirroring British public opinion as a whole.

People who attend religious services frequently and who regard themselves as religious tend to hold more conservative political opinions than do people whose relations with religious organizations are more distant or nonexistent. Lay members of the Church of England (but not the clergy), for example, vote in significantly greater numbers for Conservative Party candidates in parliamentary elections than does the rest of the British population. By contrast, Quakers and Catholics are more likely to favor left-of-center parties, often lending support to campaigns for human rights, peace, ecology, justice, and the relief of oppression. Opposition to the radically conservative policies of Thatcher's governments in the 1980s drew in part on criticisms voiced by the clergy in mainstream churches. Since 1997, New Labour governments have attracted criticism from a range of groups for the decision to participate in the 2003 invasion of Iraq.

Education

Finally, education in schools has become an arena of intense political concern about religion. The 1944 Education Act, the 1988 Education Reform Act, and numerous other pieces of legislation, administrative directives, and governmental advice have sought to retain and bolster the requirement that every state-funded school should begin each day with an act of "collective worship" and should include "religious education" in its basic curriculum. The non-statutory national framework for religious education (2004), with its emphasis on students' spiritual, moral, social, and cultural development and its aim to combat prejudice and promote respect for others' beliefs and values, has overcome some of the difficulties associated with the 1988 Education Reform Act. In particular, the former requirement that the syllabus should "reflect the fact that the religious traditions of Great Britain are in the main Christian while taking account of the teaching and practices of the other principal religions represented in Great Britain" has been modified. Students are now required to study Christianity at each stage of their education and to study Buddhism, Hinduism, Islam, Judaism, and Sikhism before completing their religious education.

Although public opinion is not in favor of increasing the number of state-funded "faith schools," New Labour governments since 1997 have not only continued the 100-year-old practice of funding the 7,000 schools associated with Christian denominations and the 36 Jewish schools in England and Wales, but they have also extended funding to 5 Muslim and 2 Sikh schools. Scotland has many state-funded Catholic schools but only one school—Jewish—outside the Christian tradition. Furthermore, new policies since 2001 have enabled sponsors from business, faith, or voluntary groups to establish "academies" that are free from the control of local education authorities, although the state pays their running costs. Critics of New Labour's education policies complain that the stated aim of increasing parental choices of school has actually intensified the segregation of students along lines of ethnicity and religion.

Conclusion

There is no separation of religion and state in Great Britain, and many religious organizations are heavily involved in politics at local and national levels. The growth of Hindu, Muslim, and Sikh communities is generating fresh political and legal challenges for a country whose dissident religious minorities helped to forge basic political rights and freedoms at the dawn of modernity. Following the violent attacks on the United States in September 2001 and on London in July 2005, new measures to investigate and prevent religiously motivated terrorism have not divided politicians, but British public opinion has become more concerned about perceived Muslim separatism at home and abroad. The relation between politics and religion in Great Britain is

experiencing turbulence originating mainly in Afghanistan, Chechnya, Iraq, Iran, Palestine, and Pakistan.

See also *Anglicanism; Europe, Western; Ireland; Islam; Religious Organization; State Churches.*

James A. Beckford

BIBLIOGRAPHY

Beckford, James A. "Politics and Religion in England and Wales." *Daedalus* 120 (Summer 1991): 179–201.

Davie, Grace. *Religion in Britain since 1945.* Oxford: Blackwell, 1994.

Medhurst, Ken, and George Moyser. *Church and Politics in a Secular Age.* Oxford: Clarendon Press, 1988.

Modood, Tariq. *Multicultural Politics: Racism, Ethnicity and Muslims in Britain.* Edinburgh: Edinburgh University Press, 2005.

Weller, Paul. *Time for a Change: Reconfiguring Religion, State and Society.* Edinburgh: T. and T. Clark, 2005.

Gush Emunim

Established in 1974, Gush Emunim (a Hebrew term meaning "Bloc of the Faithful") is a religio-political movement in Israel with the aim is to extend Jewish sovereignty and presence throughout what it perceives as the Holy Land. Although never formally disbanded, the group gradually ceased to be active in the late 1980s.

Gush Emunim became a major political force in Israel amid the political and psychological turmoil that followed the 1967 Six-Day War and the 1973 Yom Kippur War. After the 1967 war in which Israel came to control all western Palestine, including the whole of the city of Jerusalem with its holy places as well as Sinai and the Golan Heights, a euphoric, messianic state of mind prevailed in wide segments of the religious and nationalist population. But after the Yom Kippur War, and in particular the subsequent Israeli withdrawal from Sinai, gloom prevailed.

Although a number of secular leaders have arisen in the movement and diverse circles have supported it, the core of its founders and leaders—as well as most of its supporters—have come from the religious Zionist movement, and the nucleus has been disciples or adherents of the messianic, mystical school established by Rabbi Abraham Kook Sr. and led by his son and successor, Rabbi Zvi Yehuda Kook Jr. Based on the notion that the current age signifies the beginning of redemption for the Jews and that the establishment of the state of Israel is a heavenly sign for this new stage,

Gush Emunim views itself as the revitalizing force of Zionism. The main tenet of its political theology ordains the sanctity of the entire land of Israel and prescribes its integrity, which in practical terms envisages the formal annexation of Judea and Samaria (and Gaza) to Israel. From the religious Zionist maxim that unifies the People of Israel, the Torah of Israel, and the Land of Israel, Gush Emunim has made the last of these its foremost responsibility.

Settling Jews on the West Bank and Gaza was Gush Emunim's overriding mission. In its earliest years this was accomplished primarily by extra-legal means, later legalized. After 1977 Gush Emunim worked to speed up mass settlement on the West Bank. A number of subsidiary groups were established that in time became semi-autonomous such as Amana (Covenant), Gush Emunim's official settlement organization, and Moetzet Yesha (the Council of Settlements of Judea, Samaria, and Gaza).

The early 1980s marked Gush Emunim's political apogee, in spite of its failure to stop Israel from withdrawing from Sinai and relinquishing the settlement of Yamit. Within a dozen or so years, more than 120,000 settlers took up residence on the West Bank and Gaza, the land on which the core of the Arab population lives. Only a minority of these settlers belonged to the movement, but it is seen as having activated others so that its influence was much wider.

When, in 1979, Gush Emunim decided not to become a political party, its leaders split, with some founding the Tehiya (Renaissance) Party together with secular nationalists. Initially, this party had remarkable electoral success, and it also participated in the government. In the early 1990s, however, it disintegrated and disappeared.

Individuals and groups connected with Gush Emunim have organized self-defense and other vigilante activities on the West Bank and Gaza. The leaders of the small so-called Jewish Underground, active around 1980, were connected to Gush Emunim. They planned to blow up the Dome of the Rock in Jerusalem, a Muslim holy site, to make room for the rebuilding of the (Third) Temple and also attacked the mayors of a couple of Arab West Bank towns. Dr. Baruch Gold-stein, who murdered twenty-nine Muslims praying in the Cave of the Patriarchs (Machpela) in Hebron, also had ties to the movement.

Since the beginning of the Arab-Israeli peace process in the early 1990s, the public role of Gush Emunim as pacemaker of the Greater Israel policy has changed. Its successor movements have been in the forefront of opposition to the 1993 Oslo agreement between Israel and the Palestine Liberation Organization. They have renewed expansion of Jewish settlements and staged legal and illegal protests against what is for them a treasonable policy of surrender of holy, indivisible, and inalienable ground.

A renewed culminating peak of these successor movements of Gush Emunim was the well-organized and vigorous, but ultimately unsuccessful, opposition to the unilateral Israeli withdrawal of the army and the dismantling of all settlements in the Gaza Strip in the summer of 2005. This traumatic episode, together with the continuing illegal settlement activities on the West Bank and the apparent ineptitude of the authorities to handle and bring these activities to an end, clearly generated further radicalization of some of these successor groups of Gush Emunim, while others became more moderate and less militant.

See also *Israel; Jerusalem; Judaism; Zionism.*

Emanuel Gutmann

BIBLIOGRAPHY

Aran, Gideon. "Jewish Zionist Fundamentalism: The Bloc of the Faithful in Israel." In *Fundamentalism Observed,* edited by Martin E. Marty and R. Scott Appleby. Chicago: University of Chicago Press, 1991.

Don-Yehiya, Eliezer. "The Book and the Sword: The Nationalist Yeshivot and Political Radicalism in Israel." In *Accounting for Fundamentalism,* edited by Martin E. Mary and R. Scott Appleby. Chicago: University of Chicago Press, 1994.

Lustick, Ian S. *For the Land and the Lord: Jewish Fundamentalism in Israel.* New York: Council on Foreign Relations, 1988.

Newman, David, ed. *The Impact of Gush Emunim.* London: Croom Helm, 1985.

Sprinzak, Ehud. *The Ascendance of Israel's Radical Right.* New York: Oxford University Press, 1991.

H

Havel, Václav

Václav Havel (1936–) is politician, playwright, and former dissident. A renowned Czech playwright, Havel was an anti-communist dissident before he served as president of newly democratic Czechoslovakia from 1989 to 1992 and was elected the first president of the Czech Republic in 1993. Reelected president in 1998, Havel left office in 2003 after the completion of his second term. He embodies the struggles of Eastern Europe during the post–World War II period under Soviet domination, both before and after the Velvet Revolution of 1989–1990 that brought Soviet rule to an end.

Of Roman Catholic descent, but with a Czech disdain for religious excess born of hard historical experience, Havel owes much of his religious and political inspiration to Tomáš Garrigue Masaryk, president of the first Republic of Czechoslovakia (1918–1937), and to the philosophers Jan Patočka and Emmanuel Levinas. Through Masaryk, he drew upon the examples of the pre-Reformation Czech religious reformer Jan Hus, who was martyred in 1415, and the group Unity of the Brethren.

When his family's assets were nationalized following the communist revolution of 1949, Havel left private boarding school at age fifteen. Denied a university education, he trained (unsuccessfully) as a carpenter, before becoming a university laboratory assistant in Prague. Aware of his ability as a writer, he turned to writing plays, in which he explored the irrationality of life under a totalitarian regime. In 1964 Havel married Olga Spichalova (who died in 1996); his *Letters to Olga* (English translation, 1988) afford insight into the private aspects of their shared struggle. Havel remarried in 1997.

Václav Havel.

357

He achieved international prominence with the creation of the civil rights group Charter 77, founded in 1977. This group monitored the implementation of the Helsinki Accords, in which the Soviet Union agreed to accept human rights provisions.

Havel's aims were to contribute to a "program for raising the general level of civility" and to "politics as practical morality." His primary commitment is to grounding the moral personality in an absolute existing beyond individual self-interest. His essay "The Power of the Powerless" is one of the great religio-political tracts of the twentieth century. Although Havel's contemporary reworking of the Hussite battle cry "Truth shall prevail" had an objective moral clarity, for some of those experiencing rapid economic privatization, his moralistic, indirect, and nonfactional politics were seen as an inadequate check on capitalist excess. His presidential successor and longtime political rival, Václav Klaus, however, is an even greater proponent of capitalism.

Richard H. Roberts

BIBLIOGRAPHY

Pontuso, James F. *Václav Havel: Civic Responsibility in the Postmodern Age.* Lanham, Md.: Rowman and Littlefield, 2004.
Duberstein, John. *A Velvet Revolution: Václav Havel and the Fall of Communism.* Greensboro, N.C.: Morgan Reynolds, 2006.

Health

See *Medicine*.

Heresy

Heresy is a belief or doctrine at variance with what orthodoxy, or a dominant belief system, holds to be true. It signifies more specifically adherence to a religious opinion contrary to the doctrine of a particular religious faith.

Origins and History

The term *heresy* derives from the Greek word *hairesis*, meaning "a choice." Originally heresy referred simply to any opinion one held; it had no pejorative connotation. To the extent that heresy was used to refer to a particular phenomenon, it indicated adherence to any of the schools of philosophical thought in late antiquity. This usage is reflected in the Acts of the Apostles (5:17; 15:5; 24:5; 26:5; 28:22) and in the writings of Jewish historian Josephus (37–c. 100) (*Antiquities of the Jews,* 13.5.9 and 18.1.2; *The Jewish War,* 2.8.14). It was later confirmed in the work of Spanish bishop and encyclopedist Isidore of Seville (c. 560–636) (*Etymologies,* 8.3.1).

The pejorative connotation of heresy developed in the late first and early second centuries in response to the theological challenge presented by the conversion to Christianity of large numbers of pagans with diverse heritages and beliefs. This development caused Christians to become increasingly concerned with defining an unambiguous Christian identity, leading them to press for a single, exclusive doctrinal orthodoxy.

The polemics of the early theologians Justin (c. 100–c. 165) and Irenaeus (c. 125–c. 202) laid the conceptual foundations of orthodoxy and heresy during the second-century gnostic controversy. The gnostics' claim that "gnosis," or divine knowledge, could be directly accessed without the mediation of bishops anointed with the power of apostolic succession—the power conferred on the apostles by Christ and passed along to their successors, the bishops—threatened the authority and, therefore, the organizational control of the leaders of the nascent Christian movement.

In response to the challenge of the gnostics, Justin provided a conceptual framework for the demonization of dissent that endures to this day. Drawing from apocalyptic Judaism, Justin associated Christian dissenters with the "false prophets" of Satan whose purpose was to cause the faithful to stray from the truth. In this way, orthodoxy came to be identified with divine truth, and all dissenters, referred to pejoratively as "heretics," identified as confederates of the devil.

Irenaeus extended the identity of the heretic from that of an external enemy of orthodoxy to that of an intimate enemy, that is, an insider who purposefully betrays or distorts the faith. With this formulation any dissenting doctrinal assertion could be discredited as heresy and its advocates branded as heretics and servants of the devil. This broadened meaning, which came to predominate in Christendom, is reflected in the New Testament evocation of "false prophets" and "false teachers among you who will secretly bring in destructive heresies" (2 Peter 2:1).

Heresy became an enforced category when orthodoxy intersected with political power upon the emperor Constantine's adoption of Christianity in the fourth century. Constantine and his immediate successors not only convened councils to settle questions of theological orthodoxy, they more importantly used their civil authority to influence the enforcement of creedal decisions. Christian bishops, previously victimized by the police for promulgating a *religio illicita* (a religion not sanctioned by the state), came to command them. With this development, the definition of heresy became primarily a function of power: it was determined by whoever had the power to enforce what they held to be truth, not by the correctness of a doctrine.

The demonization of dissent into heresy increasingly took on more serious and ominous overtones in Christianity, culminating in the fifteenth-century Spanish Inquisition, in which thousands accused of heresy were excommunicated, tortured, and even executed. In the United States the violent clash of extreme formulations of orthodoxy and heresy reached its apogee in the eighteenth-century Salem witch hunts, in which scores of women and men were hanged or burned alive as heretics.

Heresy in Modern Times

Although the definition of heresy has Christian origins, the demonization of dissent exists in every established religion and belief system. Indeed, heresy was a familiar charge in Iran in the aftermath of its Islamic Revolution in the 1980s. Although established religions have raised charges of religious heresy in recent years, the phenomenon of "secular" heresy has garnered the most media attention. From paranoid anticapitalism in the era of Joseph Stalin in the Soviet Union to paranoid anticommunism in the time of Sen. Joseph McCarthy in the United States to today, secular politicized evocations of orthodoxy and heresy have come to loom large on the political landscape. In the United States, the Christian religious right, as reflected by such religio-political groups as the Moral Majority and the Christian Coalition, represent a contemporary example of this trend. These groups attempted to develop a new orthodoxy consisting of religious elements—including legalizing prayer in public educational facilities, opposing abortion, and censoring television programs and motion pictures for moral content—as well as secular concerns—such as reducing governmental oversight, lowering taxes, supporting capital punishment, and opposing affirmative action. Of most sig-

nificance, these groups, generally known by the overarching rubric of "conservatives," seek to advance their agenda by means of well-financed and well-orchestrated lobbies and electoral campaigns. Dissenting opinions are labeled "liberal," which is meant as a pejorative term among conservatives and often as synonymous with heresy.

Despite the differences in their respective spheres of operation, religious and secular conceptions of heresy have one thing in common: Both are determined by those in power.

See also *Censorship; Inquisition; Witchcraft.*

Obery M. Hendricks Jr.

BIBLIOGRAPHY

Bauer, Walter. *Orthodoxy and Heresy in Earliest Christianity.* Translated by the Philadelphia Seminar on Christian Origins and edited by Robert A. Kraft and Gerhard Krodel. Mifflintown, Pa.: Sigler Press, 1996.

Burris, Virginia. *The Making of a Heretic.* Berkeley and Los Angeles: University of California Press, 1995.

Kurtz, Lester R. *The Politics of Heresy: The Modernist Crisis in Roman Catholicism.* Berkeley: University of California Press, 1986.

Pagels, Elaine. *The Gnostic Gospels.* New York: Random House, 1979.

Simon, Marcel. "From Greek Hairesis to Christian Heresy." In *Early Christian Literature and the Christian Intellectual Tradition: In Honorem: Robert C. Grant,* edited by William Schodel and Robert L. Wilken. Paris: Éditions Beauchesne, 1979.

Herzl, Theodor

Founder of modern political Zionism, the Jewish national movement, and regarded as one of the greatest influences on the creation of the state of Israel. Born in Budapest, Hungary, to well-to-do parents, Herzl (1860–1904) was educated in the spirit of German-Jewish enlightenment, which held that assimilation was the best way to overcome anti-Semitism. He studied law in Vienna, Austria, but became a playwright and journalist. From 1891 until 1895 Herzl served as the Paris correspondent of the *New Free Press,* an influential liberal Viennese daily. While in France, his interest in Jewish problems deepened.

Anti-Semitism made Herzl a conscious Jew: Its modern resurgence wounded his dignity. He was particularly stirred by German philosopher Eugen Dühring's anti-Semitic book *The Jewish Question as a Problem of Race, Morals, and Culture,* but it was the trial of Alfred Dreyfus (1894–1895) that shattered Herzl's hopes of assimilation and revealed the

Theodor Herzl.

deep roots of anti-Semitism in the French Third Republic. Dreyfus was a Jewish officer in the French army accused of espionage. Despite an almost complete lack of evidence against him, he was convicted of selling military secrets to the Germans.

Herzl came to believe that European nations would not be able to cope with their medieval legacy of anti-Semitism, but he also saw that the problem might ultimately prove useful for the Jewish people, forcing them to close ranks. From then on, he regarded the Jewish question as a national, rather than social or religious, issue that should be solved politically. He believed that only sovereignty over an area to which the Jewish masses could emigrate and form a nation would provide the right resolution. A Jewish state would also ease antagonism between Jew and Gentile.

In 1896 Herzl published his ground-breaking treatise, *The Jewish State.* A diplomat and a man of action as well as a visionary, he endeavored to win over European rulers to his plan. He turned first to Germany, convincing Kaiser Wil-

helm II that a Jewish settlement in Palestine would bring prosperity to the Holy Land and help develop and revive Asia Minor, thereby saving Turkey from bankruptcy and making it more difficult for the Allied powers to dismember the Ottoman Empire—a matter of great interest to Germany.

The kaiser was persuaded that Jewish emigration from Europe would weaken anti-Semitism and lessen the danger of revolutionary socialism. He also believed that protecting Herzl's project would earn the gratitude of Jews all over the world. During his 1898 visit to the Near East, the kaiser received Herzl in Constantinople and promised to ask Sultan Abd al-Hamid II to grant a concession to the Jewish Land Company under German protection. When the sultan rejected the suggestion, the kaiser's interest in Zionism waned.

Herzl had also been negotiating directly with the Ottoman Empire since 1896. During his final visit to Constantinople, in July 1902, he received a warm letter from Abd al-Hamid, but on matters of substance his efforts bore no fruit.

At the same time, Herzl was also petitioning the British government for permission to establish a Jewish colony under Britain's protection in the neighborhood of Palestine. British reaction was generally favorable, but a project in the El-Arish area of the northern Sinai proved impracticable. In the spring of 1903 Joseph Chamberlain, the British colonial secretary, offered instead the Guas Ngishu plateau near Nairobi, in East Africa, for Jewish settlement. Herzl thought it politically imprudent to reject this offer because the very fact that a great power was negotiating with him amounted to a de facto recognition of his movement. He considered the British offer primarily in political terms: rather than impeding his ultimate goal, it might bring a Jewish state nearer to realization. For Herzl, consideration of the British plan was merely a ploy to obtain British recognition of the Zionist movement, and of Jews as a people, and to bring Britain gradually to the conclusion that only in Palestine would the Jewish problem be solved. Herzl's strategy eventually was proved to be correct, although it provoked grave suspicions among some Zionists that he had deviated from the main course.

In August 1903 Herzl received a letter from Vyacheslav Plehve, the Russian interior minister. Writing on behalf of the tsarist government, he promised that Russia would intervene with the Ottoman sultan in favor of the Zionists and would assist them in organizing Jewish immigration and settlement in Palestine. Plehve's letter, which became the cornerstone of Herzl's diplomacy, opened doors in the Italian and Austrian capitals. Russia and Austria-Hungary had had a secret Near East agreement since 1897. When Russia endorsed Herzl's ideas, Austria followed the Russian lead. The Austrian foreign minister, Agenor von Goluchowski, told Herzl that the great powers should ask the Ottoman Empire for land and legal rights for five to six million Jews and suggested that England take the initiative.

Had Herzl lived, he would have gone to London to reveal to the Foreign Office Austria's proposal for creating a Concert of Powers in support of Zionist aspirations. But Herzl died in July 1904, robbing the Zionist movement of a leader of international caliber. Herzl had aroused both admiration and opposition, but nobody could ignore the magnetism of his personality, his intelligence, his sincerity, and his idealism. A shrewd, down-to-earth politician with no illusions about human nature, he was the foremost exponent of Jewish nationalism. Political Zionism became the most dynamic force in modern Jewish history.

Herzl, in his diary, foresaw a Jewish catastrophe in Europe. This prediction was fulfilled under Adolf Hitler as the Nazi Holocaust. Exactly fifty years and eight months after he had recorded his prediction of catastrophe, the State of Israel was proclaimed, in 1948.

See also *Anti-Semitism; Israel; Zionism.*

Isaiah Friedman

BIBLIOGRAPHY

Bein, Alex. *Theodor Herzl: A Biography.* Philadelphia: Jewish Publication Society of America, 1962.
Friedman, Isaiah. *Germany, Turkey, and Zionism, 1897–1918.* Oxford: Oxford University Press, 1977.
Herzl, Theodor. *The Jewish State.* New York: American Zionist Emergency Council, 1946.
Laqueur, Walter. *A History of Zionism.* London: Weidenfeld and Nicholson, 1972.
Vital, David. *Zionism: The Formative Years.* Oxford: Oxford University Press, 1982.

Heschel, Abraham Joshua

Jewish religious philosopher who applied the Hebrew prophets' demands for justice and compassion to social and political situations. The life and works of Abraham Joshua Heschel (1907–1972) exemplify how spiritual sensitivity can incite progressive activism.

As a Jewish thinker, Heschel wrote books and essays on prayer, religious philosophy, the Hebrew prophets, the state of Israel, education, poverty, war, and racial equality. As a teacher, scholar, and expert literary stylist, Heschel explained how ethical positions can be motivated by sensitivity to God's presence, or what he called "depth theology"—an encounter with divine reality that precedes formulations of creed. He believed that the living God of the Hebrew Bible (the "God of pathos") reacts to human actions.

Heschel's vivid writings and speeches combined emotion and incisive analysis as he sought to arouse in readers compassion for afflicted human beings, outrage at injustice, and intuitions of God's presence. His moral and political choices emulated the Hebrew prophets who rejected a politics of expediency and refused to compromise with human callousness and indifference to evil. Heschel supported his judgments with allusions to the Hebrew Bible, Talmud, Midrash (early rabbinical interpretations of the scriptures), Jewish mysticism, and Hasidic sources.

European Roots

Heschel's social and political activism, first in Europe and then in the United States, grew out of his early life. Born in Warsaw, Poland, in 1907, he was raised in a traditional Hasidic community and imbued from early childhood with daily prayer, study of sacred texts, and ideals of spiritual integrity. Without rejecting his religious faith, he began secular studies in a Yiddish-language gymnasium (school) in Vilnius, Lithuania, and earned a doctorate in philosophy from the University of Berlin.

Heschel's writings in Europe combined loyalty to God with a keen ethical conscience. His 1933 dissertation on the Hebrew prophets provided the foundation of his American theology. That same year he published in Warsaw a book of poetry (in Yiddish) that expressed his unique combination of intense compassion and feelings of closeness with God. In 1935 he published a biography of Moses Maimonides (1135–1204), the medieval rabbi, philosopher, and physician. And from 1936 to 1938 he placed inspirational essays on rabbis of the Talmudic period in German–Jewish community newspapers as Jews were being expelled from Germany.

By the time he emigrated to the United States in March 1940, Heschel had experienced political and ethnic conflicts, widespread Jewish poverty, anti-Semitism, the effects of

World War I, the ascent of German dictator Adolf Hitler, and the outbreak of World War II. After arriving in the United States, Heschel taught at Hebrew Union College, a Reform rabbinical seminary in Cincinnati, Ohio. In 1945 he joined the faculty of the Jewish Theological Seminary in New York (representing the Conservative movement), where he held the chair of Jewish ethics and mysticism until his death.

In the 1950s Heschel concentrated on scholarship, writing about the religious experience, and Jewish education. The importance of Heschel's works of religious philosophy—*Man Is Not Alone* (1951) and *God in Search of Man* (1955)—was recognized by Reinhold Niebuhr, the eminent Protestant theologian and political activist.

Heschel's wider public involvement began in 1960 at the first White House Conference on Youth and the next year at the White House Conference on Aging. From 1962 on, he consulted at the Second Vatican Council in Rome. There, Heschel worked closely with Cardinal Augustin Bea, head of the Secretariat for Non-Christian Religions, spoke privately with Pope Paul VI, and influenced the declaration on the Jews in *Nostra Aetate* (1965), a document expressing the Catholic Church's positive attitude toward Judaism.

Politics as a Religious Issue

Heschel, who considered politics to be a religious responsibility, a personal problem, was committed to civil rights for all Americans. In 1963 he met the Reverend Martin Luther King Jr. at the first National Conference on Religion and Race. A photograph of Heschel marching with King and Ralph Bunche of the United Nations at the 1965 Selma–Montgomery protest against racial segregation is widely reproduced as an emblem of the black-Jewish alliance of the period. Also in 1965 Heschel was appointed by the Protestant Union Theological Seminary as Harry Emerson Fosdick visiting professor.

That same year, Heschel, with John Bennett, president of Union Theological Seminary, Father Daniel Berrigan, an activist Jesuit priest, and Richard John Neuhaus, then a Lutheran pastor in Brooklyn, cofounded Clergy (later renamed Clergy and Laity) Concerned about Vietnam, which influenced King to join the antiwar movement. When the United States intervened militarily in Vietnam in the 1960s—an action Heschel forcefully opposed—he repeated phrases from his scholarly book *The Prophets* (1962), proclaiming, "In regard to cruelties committed in the name of a free society, some are guilty, while all are responsible." God is involved in history, but human beings have free will and responsibility to redeem the world. Following the biblical dictum that each and every person is an image of the Divine, Heschel sought to educate a radical sense of reverence for humankind. Religious observance should have practical consequences, he wrote, "prayer and prejudice cannot dwell in the same heart." His essays and speeches are collected in *The Insecurity of Freedom* (1966) and *Moral Grandeur and Spiritual Audacity* (1997).

Heschel also confronted painful conflicts between politics and religious integrity in *Israel: An Echo of Eternity* (1969), which explained the centuries-long attachment of the Jewish people to the land of Israel and evoked memories of the Holocaust, the mass destruction of Jews by the Germans under Hitler. His final book, *A Passion for Truth* (1973), denounced the mediocrity of religious institutions, using as models the dissident Protestant thinker Søren Kierkegaard (1813–1855) and the abrasive Hasidic rabbi Menahem Mendel. Heschel reaffirmed his loyalty to God by challenging philosophical absurdity, massive evil, the weak human conscience, and the frailty of society's devotion to truth. He died of a heart attack at age sixty-five on the Sabbath night of December 23, 1972.

See also *Civil Rights Movement; Judaism.*

Edward K. Kaplan

BIBLIOGRAPHY

Kaplan, Edward K. *Holiness in Words: Abraham Joshua Heschel's Poetics of Piety.* Albany, N.Y.: SUNY Press, 1996.

Kaplan, Edward K., and Samuel H. Dresner. *Abraham Joshua Heschel, Prophetic Witness.* New Haven: Yale University Press, 1998.

Kasimow, Harold, and Byron Sherwin, eds. *No Religion Is an Island.* Maryknoll, N.Y.: Orbis Books, 1991.

Merkle, John C. *The Genesis of Faith.* New York: Macmillan, 1983.

Merkle, John C., ed. *Abraham Joshua Heschel: Exploring His Life and Work.* New York: Macmillan, 1985.

Rothschild, Fritz A., ed. *Heschel, Between God and Man.* Rev. ed. New York: Free Press, 1975.

Hinduism

As the religion of about eight hundred million people, over 90 percent of whom live in South Asia, Hinduism in the early twenty-first century exists as a world religion in diverse political settings. Some of the linkages between Hinduism and politics have their roots in tradition (for example, the ideal of politics as morality), while others are new (such as the Indian innovation of the secular state).

The situation is complex. In fact, to write about religion and politics in the context of Hinduism immediately poses several definitional problems. The term *Hinduism* and its equivalents in various European languages derive from nineteenth-century Western discourses about the Orient, which was characterized as exotic, and owe their currency to Christian missionaries, colonial administrators, and Indologists (who study India and its peoples on the basis of classical texts). They have no exact equivalent in classical or modern Indian languages. This being so, is Hinduism purely a construct, or does it have sociocultural and historical substance? The word *Hindu*, originally in Greek and Persian (derived from the Sanskrit *Sindhu*, the name of the major river Indus of Pakistan), had a geographical denotation (peoples living east of the Indus) and was therefore quite unlike such terms as *Christian, Muslim*, or *Sikh*. Hinduism could be, therefore, at best the culture or way of life of the Hindus.

A second problem focuses on the definition of religion. Considering the fact that Hinduism does not have a founder, a set of fundamentals, a core text (comparable to the Bible or the Qur'an), or a church, it surely is not a religion in the sense of Judaism, Christianity, and Islam. Mutually exclusive Hindu sects, some of which have over time evolved into full-blown religions, do, however, have some of these characteristics.

Nevertheless, it is by now a well-established practice in modern scholarship and contemporary political discourse, whether Indian or other, to regard Hinduism as a religion, although one quite unlike other major world religions. When an Indian has to use an Indian language equivalent for Hinduism, the usual choice is *hindu dharma* or *sanatana dharma*, the Hindu or the universal and eternal norms of life. The normative aspect is of critical importance. Dharma is not how life is lived but how it should be lived, for its absence (*adharma*) means moral normlessness, or chaos.

Dharma as a moral code is comprehensive and encompasses every aspect of life. This brings us to the third and last problem. Dharma does not admit the distinction, fundamental in Western thought, between the sacred and the profane, or the religious and the secular. Within the Hindu religious tradition, legitimate kingship and, in modern times, politics are moral obligations or pursuits and therefore entirely religious in character. Classical Brahmanical formulations (Brahmans, the highest-ranked caste, have traditionally been the ideologues of Hindu society) as well as modern religious thought emphasize that politics outside the domain of religion or dharma is illegitimate.

The Morality of Politics: A Classical View

One of the most widely discussed classical formulations of the relationship of politics and morality is that given in the theory of *purushartha*, or value-oriented action. The highest of value orientations, and also the most comprehensive from which all other values derive, is of course that of dharma, or cosmic moral order. Dharma has a universal component equally applicable to one and all (for example, the requirement of truthfulness) as well as a context-specific component (for example, it is the dharma of the king and of the second-ranked warrior caste generally to engage in warfare, but the Brahman may never shed blood).

This context sensitivity makes room for the second value orientation, namely that of *artha*, or the rational pursuit of political and economic objectives within the framework of dharma. The king rules according to the dictates of dharma, which enjoin him to protect all dharmas, universal as well as specific. Similarly, the merchant trades and the agriculturist cultivates land, but not as purely economic pursuits: the dictates of dharma apply to them also. More significantly, dharma is incomplete unless it incorporates *artha*.

Finally, there is the third goal of value-oriented action, namely *kama*, or physical pleasure and aesthetic enjoyment generally. Just as *artha* should not violate dharma, *kama* may not violate artha and dharma. In other words, dharma embraces *artha* and *kama*, which are apparently its contraries, in a hierarchical grammar of values. In a typical Brahmanical twist of the argument, release (*moksha*) from the world of goal-oriented action is provided by a fourth optional value, that of total withdrawal from worldly though moral pursuits through renunciation (*sannyasa*).

Classical texts discuss at length each of the above value orientations. Thus there is a body of literature called *arthashastra*, or the combined science of governance and economics (political economy). One of the most famous of these texts, the *Arthashastra*, attributed to the scholar-statesman Kautilya (ca. 300 B.C.E.), declares at its start that *artha* is the supreme value, but the overall spirit of the work suggests that material well-being must be subordinated to spiritual good. Such a view was in fact already a thousand years old. It asserted that secular power was a blind force, not its own principle, but controlled by dharma. After the *arthashastra* period any ambiguity that one may detect about the relative importance of spiritual authority and temporal power in the texts on statecraft disappears, and the priority of dharma is reasserted. Taking an overall view of the Hindu tradition, Robert Lingat concludes in his *Classical Law of India* (1973) that it would be vain to look at the relation between the two powers of the Brahman and the king in terms of the Christian theory of the separation of the domains of God and Caesar. Indeed, if a comparison is made, the Brahmanical doctrine is analogous to the formulation by Pope Gelasius (at the end of the fifth century) that priestly power is much more important than royal power because the priest has to answer for the kings at the divine tribunal.

The Hindu (Brahmanical) and related Buddhist doctrines of the unity of the sacred and the secular predetermined the relationship of religion and politics, acknowledging the supremacy of dharma. In the dramatic imagery of the Buddhist tradition, the world conqueror was indeed also expected to be the world renouncer, and the duty of the king was to be a subject (follower) of dharma. This moral philosophy of power prevailed up to the dawn of the eleventh century, when Muslim rule was established in northern India, offering alternative perspectives on the nature of politics and religion. Although Hindu kingdoms collapsed or retreated one after another, Hindu ideas about the scope and character of kingship did not vanish. Indeed, they survived into modern times, not only in the Hindu princely states that the British tolerated (these states were ultimately integrated into the modern Indian state after independence in 1947), but also as one of the idioms of politics in contemporary India.

The Rise of Modern Hinduism

British rule was established in India in the second half of the eighteenth century, first under the aegis of the East India Company (1757–1857) and then (1858–1947) directly under the British government. The first half-century of expanding British governance in India was marked by the primacy of economic interests and an instrumental view of everything else. Political control was essential to the furtherance of these interests, as was knowledge of the cultural traditions of the land, but cultural and social transformation was not. Noninterference was the watchword, and missionary activity was explicitly forbidden. The ancient Brahmanical Vedic texts (the Vedas date back to at least 1200 B.C.E.) and later nonreligious Sanskrit literary works began to be translated into

English and other European languages in the late eighteenth century, and the discipline of Indology was born. Indologists admired the achievements of ancient India in the fields of grammar, belles lettres, and speculative philosophy; however, they had contempt for the religions and cultures of contemporary India, and what they called Hinduism was too complex and internally heterogeneous for their comfort. The merchants and the administrators, however, needed information about contemporary society, and thus ethnography too was born, almost a twin of Indology.

In 1813 the British Parliament lifted the ban on proselytization by Christian missionaries in India. Denigration of native cultures and religions became the order of the day. The attacks on Hinduism were generally ill-informed and intemperate. Many British writers considered India to be at the threshold of a new way of life under the combined impact of the new mercantile and administrative dispensations and evangelical Christianity. In their enthusiasm the critics overlooked the inner vitality of Hinduism, which had enabled it to meet many challenges, both internal (the birth of new religions, notably Buddhism and Jainism in the early sixth century B.C.E.) and external (the advent of Islam early in the eighth century C.E.). The emergence of religious reform and revival movements among the Hindus from the 1820s onward was more in the nature of a creative response to yet another external challenge than an unconsidered rejection of or an unqualified surrender to the many-sided impact of the West. These movements sought not only to rediscover the ancient roots of Hinduism but also to reinterpret it in the light of Christian ethics and liberal politics.

Among the religious and social reform movements of the nineteenth century, those led by Brahmo Sabha (founded in 1828 in Calcutta and renamed Brahmo Samaj, Society of God, in 1843) and Arya Samaj, Society of the Aryas, people of noble descent (founded in 1876 and active in Bombay in western India and in Punjab in northern India) are particularly noteworthy. Both organizations were nonpolitical in character, but their leaders had explicit views about Christianity and British rule, which were justifiably seen as mutually reinforcing in fact, although not as a matter of explicit policy. Rammohun Roy (1772–1833), the founder of Brahmo Sabha, was deeply appreciative of the ethical character of the New Testament and considered British rule a divine dispensation that all sensible and patriotic Indians should welcome. The founder of Arya Samaj, Dayananda Saraswati (1824–1883), wrote derisively about Christianity, denying it the status of a revealed and true religion. He was critical of the nexus between the missionaries and British officials. In the years to come, members of the Arya Samaj were to be active participants in the national movement.

The program of the Arya Samaj was explicitly revivalist and even fundamentalist in the domain of religion and progressive in regard to social life, disapproving of the inequities of the Brahman-dominated caste system and discrimination against women. In Bengal a reaction set in against the Brahmo Samaj in the last quarter of the nineteenth century and took the form of Hindu revivalism, which was not, however, pure traditionalism inasmuch as it was also innovative. The most outstanding figure in the shaping of modern Hinduism was Vivekananda (1863–1902), a disciple of a prominent religious mystic of Bengal but not excessively inward looking himself. He was sharply critical of Hindu ritualism and of social abuses (caste and gender discrimination). He attacked Christian missionaries but adopted their social activism as his own strategy. He proclaimed that the pluralism of Hinduism (the belief that all religions are true) and its spiritualism, respectively, were superior to proselytizing religions and materialism. He gave the call for making a world religion of Hinduism rooted in Vedanta (the philosophical texts that were the culmination of Vedic religion). Indeed, Vivekananda called Vedanta the mother of all religions, containing in itself the eternal truths of all religions. He took part in the World's Parliament of Religions at Chicago, an international goodwill conference of religious leaders, in 1896 and was reportedly its most impressive participant. Like Dayananda, Vivekananda was acutely aware of the mutually reinforcing relationship of British imperialism and the church in India, but he refrained from formulating a political agenda. This was done by others, who functioned in an atmosphere that was surcharged with religious revivalism and social reform.

The shaping of a new political consciousness among the Hindu intelligentsia all over India—more radically in some parts of the country (for example, Bengal in the east and the Bombay presidency in the west)—combined the stirrings of nationalist aspirations with religious sentiments and symbolism. This is perhaps best illustrated by the literary and social writings of Bankimchandra Chattopadhyay (1839–1894), one of the outstanding Indian intellectuals of the late nineteenth century.

For Chattopadhyay, political regeneration and cultural and religious reconstruction were two sides of the same coin. He even wrote of a "national religion," the roots of which lay in the Vedas. Added to this emphasis on roots, and on a holistic conception of life in which the social and religious were one and the same reality, was his judgment that the Hindus had been singularly and unfortunately indifferent to power. The subjection of the Hindus to the British for over a century, and before that to the Muslims for more than eight hundred years, was, according to Chattopadhyay, a consequence of this negligence and of apathy to history. It followed that the way to national freedom and honor lay through a positive attitude to power defined in material as well as cultural terms. The first task, then, was Hindu cultural regeneration defined by both patriotism and humanism. Drawing on Hindu mysticism and the enthusiasm centered on the worship of a supreme mother-goddess, Shakti (literally, "power" or "power embodied"), Chattopadhyay translated this religious idea into the powerful but very Hindu concept of the country as the divine mother, which was, however, anathema to the Muslims. The image of Mother India in chains was for the Hindus, who constituted nearly three-fourths of the population of India, easily the key symbol of political subjugation. It represented spiritual infirmity, material deprivation, and loss of national dignity. The time was thus ripe for the formal shaping of a national movement.

The Birth of the National Movement

By the 1880s the broad-minded and politically liberal among the British rulers of India, and like-minded sections of the public in Britain, had come to recognize that Indians should have a hand in their own governance, at least at the local level. It is not therefore at all surprising that a retired English civil servant should have been prominent among those who founded the Indian National Congress Party in 1885. Religion was still a highly significant aspect of social life everywhere in the world in the late nineteenth century, although it did come under attack in the West. It certainly was important in India, which had long been home or host to nearly all the major world religions. It was thus that, from the very beginning, nationalism in India was closely intertwined with religion. Indeed, some of the Hindu intellectuals who joined the national movement maintained that nationalism itself was a religion. It may be added that among Muslims, too, a widely shared point of view was that political activity could not be separated from religious obligation and that religious identity was the basic principle of social organization in India.

The situation was complex. Part of the complexity was a consequence of the plurality of religions of India, which opened the way for competing religious nationalisms. Part of it flowed from the self-contradictory character of colonial rule. On the one hand, the colonial rulers not only insisted on describing India as a land of disparate religious communities, castes, sects, and tribes but also contributed to the consolidation of such primordial identities through the codification of Hindu and Muslim family laws, compilation of ethnographic notes, and enumeration of "the peoples of India" through the decennial censuses from 1881 onward. These measures contributed to the emergence of religious nationalism, or, as it is called in India, communalism. On the other hand, British rule helped to shape a national secular identity on a subcontinental scale through administrative, judicial, economic, educational, and other policies. The country saw the emergence of a new middle class, which, notwithstanding critical deficiencies owing to its character as a colonial implant, engaged in secular politics based on the concept of equal citizenship rights within the nation-state. The politics of nationalism was thus afflicted by schisms from its birth.

Nobody, not even the secular politicians, denied the importance of religious and cultural differences. The secularists asserted that nationalism would focus on common interests, common benefits, and general reforms (the demand for self-governance and, later, full independence were things of the future) and would recognize the legitimacy of separate community interests within the larger framework. Their opponents, however, expressed deep misgivings about Hindu domination and questioned the applicability of democracy or majority rule in India. The secularists took a hierarchical view of national and community interests, maintaining that the latter should and could be accommodated in the former. Those who disagreed—most notably Sir Sayyid Ahmad Khan (1817–1898), the leader of Muslims in northern India, and Jotirao Phule (1827–1890), a low-caste social reformer from western India—considered the Indian National Congress Party primarily a high-caste Hindu organization and disagreed with its political plank of self-governance. They saw in the continuance of British rule the best means of protecting the interests of minority communities in India.

The Congress Party derived its membership from all of the major religious communities, but the predominance of Hindus was an undeniable fact. The minority communities, particularly the Parsis (Zoroastrians), were prominent in the leadership. The third president of the party was a Muslim, and it was he who tried to negotiate (unsuccessfully) with Sayyid Ahmad Khan and other like-minded Muslim leaders for their support.

With only limited support from Muslims, the national movement tended to use Hindu cultural symbols and drew upon Hindu perspectives on Indian history to mobilize mass support. A notable instance of this was the successful attempt by a prominent Hindu (of the highest Brahman caste), Bal Gangadhar Tilak (1856–1920), to inject politics into a traditional religious festival and to recruit the Hindu god Ganapati to serve secular goals. He also wrote an interpretation of the religious text *Bhagavad Gita* to promote a vigorous political philosophy of action. The formally adopted objectives of the Congress Party, however, emphasized a fuller development and consolidation of sentiments of national unity. It spoke on behalf of the people of India and not the Hindus alone.

Nevertheless, Muslims became more apprehensive with the passage of time, and in 1906 they established a new political organization called the Indian Muslim League. Those Muslims who had stayed out of the national movement because, they said, they feared Hindu domination (many of them may have simply been reluctant to recognize the end of Muslim control in India, for they continued to recall and insist upon their political preeminence) now had a platform of their own. One of their earliest demands (going back to 1896) was for the institution of separate electorates. Under such a system Muslims would choose their representatives from among reserved constituencies demarcated on the basis of community-wide distribution of population. The Muslim leadership considered this the only way Muslim interests could be defended. The British government conceded the demand in 1909. Many historians regard the partition of the subcontinent in 1947 on the basis of religious difference considered alongside of population distribution an inevitable consequence of the grant of separate electorates combined with weightage for Muslims in the Muslim-minority provinces. The Muslims also demanded special treatment because of their historical role as the community that provided the rulers of India over a period of eight hundred years. This demand was not conceded by the British.

Hindus generally resented the concession of separate electorates, but moderate politicians from within and outside the Congress Party advised their coreligionists to accommodate the Muslim demand. In 1916 the Muslim

A sadhu, *or Hindu holy man, prays in Ayodhya, one of Hinduism's most revered holy sites.*

League and the Congress Party entered into what is referred to as the Lucknow Pact. (Lucknow is a major city in northern India where the two organizations held their parleys.) Under it the Congress Party agreed to separate both electorates and weightage. Moreover, the Hindu leaders who negotiated and advocated it were inspired by Western liberal ideas, despite the rejection of the principle of individual liberty by separatist Muslims. Having joined hands, the two organizations demanded representative government in India but not full independence. The pact, however, was never implemented. A Hindu response to the pact, consciously based on the Hindu preference for religious pluralism combined with some measure of tolerance, had to await the entry of Mohandas Gandhi (1869–1948) into Indian politics.

Gandhi and Religious Tolerance

Few Indians of the twentieth century were more explicit than Gandhi in emphasizing, first, the imperative of morally or religiously informed politics and, second, the philosophy of religious tolerance. He considered it a particular virtue of Hinduism that it had, according to him (and many others), a millennia-old tradition of religious tolerance. In the minds of numerous thoughtful people in India and abroad, it was Gandhi who best exemplified the marriage of tradition and modernity in Hinduism. His admirers came to call him the Mahatma, "great soul." Gandhi was born a Hindu, and this

fact was for him the very foundation of his life and work. While acknowledging that he had learned some great truths from other religions (notably Christianity), he remained essentially a Hindu because he found Hinduism open to reinterpretation in the light of moral reason and respectful of all religions. Indeed, freedom from dogmatism was, in Gandhi's judgment, the strength of Hinduism.

Gandhi started his political career in South Africa, where he began his experiments with the conduct of political agitations in the light of moral or religious principles, such as insistence on truth, moral dignity, and nonviolence. He returned to India in 1915 and, after carefully studying the Indian political scene, gradually moved into a position of leadership in the Congress Party. He supported the Lucknow Pact and the policy of accommodation that it advocated. At the end of World War I the issue of the future of the Muslim institution of the caliphate, which was the central locus of political authority in the Muslim world and had long remained vested in the Ottoman emperor, was faced with a crisis, for Turkey was earmarked for dismemberment. The symbolic importance of the caliphate far outweighed its nominal political authority. Among many Muslim national communities that were greatly concerned about the developments were Indian Muslims. Some of their leaders informed the British government that unless the Turkish sultan was saved, Indian Muslims would have no choice but to engage in a religious war (*jihad*) or to migrate en masse to a Muslim country.

Long mindful of the importance of Hindu-Muslim harmony in both religion and politics, Gandhi lent his unqualified support to the movement for the preservation of the caliphate with all its functions. He asserted that since the issue was of the deepest religious and political significance to Muslims, it was the moral duty of all Indians, particularly the majority community of Hindus, to make the caliphate their own cause. Gandhi decided to overlook the fact that such support would entail close collaboration with traditional Muslim religious leaders, who tended to be socially conservative and politically reactionary. He made the caliphate a central issue of Indian politics and succeeded in drawing Muslims into the national movement in unprecedented numbers. The experiment failed, however, because the Turkish nationalists who captured power abolished the caliphate in 1924.

Gandhi's support of the caliphate and his involvement with conservative religious leaders seems, in retrospect, to have been a significant political blunder. It strengthened the separatist tendencies among Muslims because the conservatives among their leaders tended to be exclusivist in their politics. Consequently, Hindu-Muslim conflicts resurfaced in full force by the mid-1920s. Gandhi's religious tolerance was of little avail in producing harmony between the religious communities. Within the Hindu community itself, the entry of the masses into the national movement, for which Gandhi was largely responsible, resulted in the ascendance of folk forms of religion that were rather remote from the moral reason that he considered crucial for any living religious tradition. Far from being able always to obtain knowing support for the values of truth and nonviolence, he was recast by his mass following in the image of a holy man and miracle maker. More injuriously, his support of Muslim causes generated a reaction among certain sections of the vast and heterogeneous Hindu community. It was thus that the political ideology of "Hindutva," that is, making India a culturally homogeneous country, was born—a country in which Hindus would exercise the political dominance that their numbers entitled them to or, at least, made possible.

Hindutva—Making India Hindu

In the development of a politically motivated and culturally hegemonistic Hinduism in the twentieth century, the emergence of the religious and social reform movements of the late nineteenth century, which were at least partly revivalist, played a crucial role. These movements were not overtly political, although their members often had political interests; many of them were in the Congress. A Hindu political party, distinct from the Hindu-dominated secularist Indian National Congress, namely, the Hindu Mahasabha, was established in 1915 (ironically, the very same year in which Gandhi returned to India from South Africa). It began with a modest agenda of the protection of specifically Hindu interests but failed to make much of an impact on the nationalist politics of the day. Demands for its activation were made in the wake of the worsening of Hindu-Muslim relations after the collapse of the caliphate movement. Hindu associations made their appearance in many parts of the country, sounding the alarm that politically assertive Muslims posed a threat to the interests of the Hindu community.

A most significant development was the publication in 1923 of a small book, *Hindutva: Who Is a Hindu?*, written by a notable Mahasabha leader, Vinayak D. Savarkar, while in prison as a political detainee. The Arya Samaj had put forward a restrictive definition of the true followers of the original Vedic religion, since transformed into Brahmanism and then Hinduism, and named them "Aryas" (the noble people). They were contrasted to degenerate Hindus of the caste system, prisoners of Brahmanic orthodoxy ridden with rituals and social taboos. Savarkar emphatically favored the term *Hindu,* tracing it back to the geographical designation *Sindhu:* Hindus were the people who lived in the lands between the Sindhu (Indus) and the high seas; their original scriptures were the Vedas, as the Arya Samaj had stated. For them the country so defined was both their fatherland and their holy land, and they constituted one nation, the Hindu nation. The acknowledgment of a common race, a common culture, and a common nationality constituted, in Savarkar's opinion, the ideology of Hindutva, that is, being a Hindu and, further, making India Hindu.

Savarkar clarified that Hindutva was a complex whole of which Hinduism, the religion, was only a part or derivative. Further, he insisted that the term *Hinduism,* properly used, should denote the religions of all Hindus (including in this category not only all kinds of Hindus but also those of other religions such as Buddhists, Jains, Sikhs, and even the tribal communities). He excluded Christians and Muslims, even descendants of converts from Hinduism, on the ground that, commonalities of descent and culture notwithstanding, their holy places were not all in India. These peoples were in the country but not in the nation; they could be so included if they looked upon India as their premier holy land.

Savarkar's innovative thesis has in recent years acquired the undisputed status of the manifesto of neo-Hindu fundamentalism, which is totalitarian in relation to all those deemed to be Hindus and exclusivist toward those stigmatized as the spiritually alien "others." It is significant that Savarkar diluted the emphasis on true scripture, which was a characteristic of the concerns of the Brahmo Samaj and the Arya Samaj, and replaced it with an overwhelming stress on culture, particularly in its spiritual (rather than material) aspect. Inspired by Savarkar's rhetoric, a member of the Congress Party, Keshav B. Hedgewar (1889–1940), founded an organization for the protection of Hindu culture in 1925, which he named the Rashtriya Swayamsevak Sangh (RSS; National Volunteer Association) two years later. The justification that he provided for the new organization made it quite clear that Hindutva was being defined antagonistically as an identity that was under severe pressure from Muslims, who had been lately mobilized during the caliphate movement.

The RSS has from the very beginning emphasized character building (through physical culture and ideological instruction) rather than religion. Its principal concern is to save Hindu culture from external influences. To the extent to which religion is an aspect of Hindu culture, Hinduism too is to be saved, but that is not the primary aim. The RSS conceives of culture as encompassing all aspects of life, including religion and politics. Downplaying Hinduism and disavowing any interest in politics are therefore deceptive.

The inclusiveness of culture in the RSS ideology was fully articulated by Hedgewar's successor, M. S. Golwalkar (who assumed leadership of the organization in 1940 on the former's death). He called for the rejuvenation of the ancient Hindu nation, which, according to him, was united by geography, race, culture, religion, and language. In a well-known book (*We or Our Nationhood Defined*, 1938), he called upon the non-Hindu peoples of India to adopt Hindu culture and language, revere Hindu religion, and respect and love the Hindus. In short, he asked them to cease to be foreigners. If they did not do so, they could stay in India only under subordination to the Hindus, deprived of any privileges, even the common rights of citizens. The RSS ideology is, above all, about power. If we recognize the preeminence of the so-called Hindu nation and of its culture and religion, Hindu political domination is ensured ideologically without any elaborate political agenda.

The importance of Hinduism (or religion) in the RSS ideology is unclear. Judging by what the group's ideologues have written, or what the members do organizationally, rituals and theological concerns—particularly the latter—do not receive much attention. Scriptural authority is seldom invoked. The emphasis is consistently on culture (*sanskriti*), which is derived from dharma—a notion that, as noted earlier, includes morality as well as religion as commonly understood. It is therefore rather difficult to understand what the RSS ideologues mean when they acknowledge religious pluralism as an element of Hindu culture.

The RSS itself has never adopted a formal political agenda or participated in elections. Some of its leaders, however, formed a political party in 1951 called the Jana Sangh. It has since been renamed the Bharatiya Janata Party (BJP; Indian Peoples Party). Although it first derived its support mainly from northern India, the party has gradually spread its appeal countrywide and is now the largest single party in the national parliament, although it falls short of a simple majority. It attempted to form a government in the summer of 1996 but failed. It has formed governments in several states in northern and western India or shared power with other parties. In its formal pronouncements of policy, the BJP supports the concept of the secular state based on respect for all religions and universal human rights. Indeed, it accuses other political parties, particularly the Indian National Congress, of being pseudosecularist, given more to the appeasement of religious minorities (notably Muslims) than to the protection of universal human rights. These parties in turn consider the BJP a threat to the ideals of secularism and pluralism and have joined hands to keep it out of power. It is clear that in any discussion of politics in the context of Hinduism, the issue of secularism occupies a central place.

Hinduism and Secularism

The religious plurality and the numerical preponderance of Hindus, who account for more than four-fifths of the population of India (or less than two-thirds if the former polluting, or untouchable, castes are excluded), pose a challenge in regard to the cultural and political rights of the religious minorities. The largest of these minorities are the nearly 120 million Muslims, who comprise 12 percent of the population, followed by Christians (2.5 percent), Sikhs (2 percent), and others. In the closing years of the nineteenth century, when certain sections of the Muslim leadership sounded the alarm about Hindu political domination, Vivekananda emerged as a charismatic and articulate Hindu religious reformer. He claimed that among all the major world religions Hinduism was both the oldest and the most tolerant. Moreover, he traced Hindu tolerance back to the earliest Veda (c. 1500 B.C.E.), which declares that the Truth (or the Absolute) is one although the learned describe it variously. Vivekananda's declaration legitimized religious plurality. The importance of this attitude becomes clear by setting it off against the position of Dayananda that the Vedic religion was the only truly revealed and complete religion known to humanity. One of the most radical changes that Dayananda introduced was that of the reclamation—he called it purification—of Hindus who had been converted to other religions (Islam, Christianity, Sikhism) and were desirous of returning to the Hindu fold.

The pluralist perspective of Hinduism found its most eloquent exponent in the twentieth century in Gandhi. Indeed, his pluralism was more genuine than Vivekananda's, for he argued for the complementarity of religions. All religions, according to Gandhi, were equally true, but they were also imperfect because of the limitations of human understanding. Gandhi, however, credited Hinduism with being the most pluralist and tolerant of religions.

Religion, understood as a grammar of ultimate values and not as rituals and social taboos and prejudices, was for Gandhi the guiding principle of all activities, including politics. In other words, religion was constitutive of society. He was therefore opposed to the secularization of society, but he insisted that the state should be secular and confined to such activities as the maintenance of law and order. Many Indian social and political thinkers, including the philosopher Sarvepalli Radhakrishnan (India's second president, 1962–1967), who held similar views, put forward the idea that in India, a deeply religious country, secularism could only mean equal respect for all religions or, at least, equal treatment of all citizens, irrespective of their religions, at the hands of the state. Hindu political leaders, including the most liberal and the most conservative, were quick to claim that Hinduism was a secular religion in the foregoing sense of the term and that Hindus would lose their moral vision if they borrowed an atheistic or agnostic secularism from the West.

Many Hindus and other Indians, however, are advocates of science as the temper of society rather than religion and look forward to a gradual decrease in the importance of religion in public life if not to its total elimination from society.

The most distinguished exponent of this position among the leaders of the national movement was Jawaharlal Nehru (1889–1964), who was born a Hindu but came under the influence of rational liberal thinkers such as Bertrand Russell and of Marx, Lenin, and the British socialists. From the 1920s onward until 1946, the year before the partition of the subcontinent, Nehru consistently denied the importance of religious antagonisms. He regarded them as a side issue and, at most, a reflection (or mystification) of the clash of economic interests. A little over a year before he finally accepted the demand for the separate country of Pakistan in 1947, he had called it a product of a medieval mode of thinking and simply "fantastic." His emphasis on the material basis of society and on reason and science made him a secularist in the Enlightenment sense of the term.

Nehru was an avid student of history and had written two major historical works, one on world history and the other on Indian history. He was therefore aware of the positive as well as the negative aspects of the historical role of religion generally and of Hinduism in India. In his presentation of it, Hinduism was not to be valued for its mythology, theology, or ritual, but for its metaphysics and speculative thought. After independence, faced with the monumental task of governing a multicultural country of many religions (the formation of Pakistan reduced the proportion of Muslims in the residual state of India to 10 percent, but in absolute numbers this meant 40 million people), Nehru acknowledged that secularism in India would have to be religious pluralism in the foreseeable future, rather than a narrowing of the role of religion in society. In fact, electoral politics at all levels, ranging from the local to the national, created powerful arenas for the use of religion for the furtherance of secular ends. The formation of new, Hindu-dominated, but in principle not exclusively Hindu, parties, namely, the Jana Sangh and the Bharatiya Janata Party, has already been noted. A third organization, exclusively Hindu, for the promotion of Hinduism and the mobilization of Hindus as a worldwide cultural, religious, and political community, called the Vishva Hindu Parishad (VHP; World Hindu Assembly), also has been established. It represents the aggressive face of Hinduism in the early twenty-first century.

VHP and the Semitization of Hinduism

Founded in Bombay in 1964 by 150 religious leaders, and invoking a "Universal Hindu Society" of six hundred million people residing in eighty countries, the VHP went beyond the Hindutva concept of a subcontinentally located religion and society. Its half-dozen stated objectives included, first, the consolidation and strengthening of the Hindu society worldwide, second, the promotion of "the Hindu values of life," and third, the rendering of "social service to humanity at large." The behind-the-scenes influence of the RSS leadership in the establishment of the VHP has been asserted and is believable. As stated above, religious concerns are not prominent in the public profile of the RSS. It is common nowadays to speak of the Sangh family, comprising RSS as the cultural body, BJP as the political party, and VHP as the religious organization. It is the quest for power that is the common element, whether formally acknowledged or not. The VHP's religious concerns, symbolized, for instance, by the holding of ancient fire (sacrificial) rituals and of ceremonies designed to arouse religious consciousness, have different amounts of political content but rarely none. Not only does the VHP present Hinduism as the national religion of India, it also portrays it as a religion beleaguered by Christianity and Islam. To strengthen it, the VHP has devoted considerable attention to missionary work among low-caste Hindus and the non-Hindu tribal peoples. In 1984 the VHP established a youth wing called the Bajrang Dal, invoking the image of a band of warriors, inspired by the monkey hordes of the ancient Rama story contained in the Sanskrit epic *Ramayana*.

It is important to note that when the VHP pursues its objectives, Hinduism is transformed by the expansion of scales (of activities as well as the social spaces) and the inescapable concessions to the very diverse lifestyles of the peoples being mobilized (tribals in India to professionals in the United States). The very existence of an organization like the VHP is a major innovation, for Hinduism traditionally has not had a churchlike body. Other significant changes include the identification of a universally applicable set of values, the selection of the traditionally calm and benign Rama from the Hindu pantheon of gods as the favorite divinity and the recasting of him as a heroic warrior, and the promotion of particular versions of certain sacred texts (notably the northern Indian, sixteenth-century version of *Ramayana*). Some observers have seen in these transformations a perhaps subconscious wish to recast Hinduism in the Semitic mold to enable it to face more effectively the perceived challenges of Judaism, Christianity, and Islam.

Demolition of the Babri Mosque

Consolidation means strength, and strength posits the use of force to achieve certain objectives. The demolition of a Muslim mosque in the northern Indian city of Ayodhya on December 6, 1992, was attributed to the leaders, members, and followers of the Sangh family. The destruction of the mosque did irreparable damage to the image of Hinduism as a tolerant religion.

The historical background to this act of vandalism takes us back to the middle of the sixteenth century, when Babur invaded northern India and, defeating local Muslim kings, laid the foundations of the Mughal Empire. A mosque named after Babur was built in 1528 in the Hindu temple town of Ayodhya by one of his generals to mark his conquests. It became a source of dispute between Hindus and Muslims after the arrival of the British as the new rulers of the country. The Hindu contention was that the mosque had been constructed after the demolishing of an eleventh-century Hindu temple that commemorated the "birth place" of the god Rama as a human being in mythological time.

The controversy gained further strength after independence in 1947, and the government put the mosque under police protection, denying entry to it to members of both communities. The VHP launched a movement in 1984 for access to the mosque to offer worship to a stone image of Rama, which was placed there surreptitiously in 1949. A magistrate (who happened to be a Hindu) allowed access to the disputed site in 1986, and the performance of Hindu rituals inside the mosque commenced. Muslims refrained from offering prayers there but staged protests locally and elsewhere.

The next step for the VHP was to ask for the demolition of the mosque so that a "grand" Rama temple could be constructed in its place. The mosque was described as a symbol of Hindu defeat and national shame. The issue became crucial during the general elections of 1989 and saw the Sangh family act jointly in relation to it, although not exactly for the same reasons. Three years later (in 1992) the BJP won the elections in the state of Uttar Pradesh in which Ayodhya is located and formed the government. After benefiting in the elections by using the temple issue, it sought to distance itself from the VHP's aggressive posture of immediate action. The union (federal) government also advocated a negotiated settlement and tried to buy time in the hope that passions on both sides would cool down with the passage of time (the Muslims were represented by an all-India committee set up in 1987 for the protection of the mosque and its restoration to them). This turned out to be a grave miscalculation.

Workers of the VHP and the BJP gathered in Ayodhya on December 5, 1992, for the performance of rituals, some distance away from the mosque, in preparation for the eventual construction of the temple. The BJP government of the state had offered assurances that the mosque would not be harmed. It was reduced to rubble the next day in an apparent preplanned manner, with the law-and-order forces of the state looking on. Triumphant bands of Hindu vandals next engaged in looting Muslim properties in Ayodhya, in which more than a dozen people were killed. By this time, most Muslims had fled the town, which had never before experienced an interreligious riot. In response, Muslims retaliated with riots in other parts of India, as well as in Pakistan and Bangladesh. Thousands of Muslims were killed in Surat, a city in western India, while thousands of Hindus fled from Bangladesh to cross into India. A few months later, the Indian city of Bombay (now Mumbai) was bombed by Muslims before peace was finally restored.

The Babri mosque dispute remains unresolved. Muslim groups have advocated rebuilding the mosque while the VHP, which governed between 1999 and 2004, advocated the contruction of a new Rama temple. In July 2005, five militants, probably allied with the group Lashkar-e-Toiba, attempted to bomb the disputed site but were killed in a battle with Indian security forces. Based in Pakistani-controlled Kashmir, Lashkar-e-Toiba is designated a terrorist group by the U.S., U.K., Indian, and Russian governments.

Hinduism Today

Vivekananda, one of the founding fathers of modern Hinduism, warned that India should not cease to be a religious (spiritual) country. For it to embrace politics and materialism would be not only a break with its prized cultural heritage, he said, but actually suicide. What he failed to realize was that his vision of Hinduism in its Vedantic form, as a world religion that is the mother of all religions was hegemonic and political. By contrast, Gandhi emphasized the inseparability of religion and politics in the hope that the latter would be redeemed by the former. As it turns out, Hinduism and, indeed, Islam, Sikhism, and Buddhism have been used in South Asia as markers of ethnic identity and made to serve political goals. When this happens religion becomes, as the French anthropologist Louis Dumont stated in his *Religion, Politics, and History* (1970), its own shadow.

Still, Hinduism as *collective ideology* has not completely displaced Hinduism as *personal faith*. There are millions of Hindus around the world in the early twenty-first century for whom Hinduism is a means to spiritual advancement and a way of relating to the Absolute through the path of ritual, knowledge, or devotion to a personal deity—or through a combination of these paths. Given the rate of construction of new neighborhoods and larger temples, of attendance at daily rituals, of participation in pilgrimages, and of the emergence of new deities (for example, Santoshi Ma), new sects (such as the Radhasaomi Satsangh), and new cults (for instance, that around the spiritual guru Sathya Sai Baba), Hinduism as a religion does not seem to be in danger of being swallowed up by politics. For such Hindus, Hinduism is an eternal religion (morality), *sanatana dharma*.

See also *Ahmad Khan, Sir Sayyid; Gandhi, Mohandas Karamchand; India; Pakistan.*

T. N. Madan

BIBLIOGRAPHY

Anderson, Walter K., and Shridhar D. Damle. *The Brotherhood in Saffron: The Rashtriya Swayam Sevak Sangh and Hindu Revivalism.* New Delhi: Vistar, 1987.

Babb, Lawrence A. *Redemptive Encounters: Three Modern Styles in the Hindu Tradition.* Berkeley: University of California Press, 1986.

Baird, Robert D., ed. *Religion in Modern India.* New Delhi: Manohar, 1995.

Dalmia, Vasudha, and H. von Steitencron, eds. *Representing Hinduism: The Construction of Religious Traditions and National Identity.* Thousand Oaks, Calif.: Sage, 1995.

Jones, Kenneth W. *Socio-religious Reform Movements in British India.* Cambridge, England: Cambridge University Press, 1989.

Larson, Gerald J. *India's Agony over Religion.* Albany: State University of New York Press, 1995.

Ludden, David, ed. *Making India Hindu: Religion, Community, and the Politics of Democracy in India.* 2d ed. Delhi: Oxford University Press, 2005.

Madan, T. N. *Modern Myths, Locked Minds: Secularism and Fundamentalism in India.* Delhi: Oxford University Press, 1997.

Nandy, Ashis, et al. *Creating a Nationality: The Ramjanambhumi Movement and the Fear of Self.* Delhi: Oxford University Press, 1995.

Nehru, Jawaharlal. *The Discovery of India.* Bombay: Asia Publishing House, 1961.

Sontheimer, Günther D., and Hermann Kulke, eds. *Hinduism Reconsidered.* New Delhi: Manohar, 1989.

Van der Veer, Peter. *Religious Nationalism: Hindus and Muslims in India.* Berkeley: University of California Press, 1994.

Hobbes, Thomas

Prominent (and controversial) English philosopher and political theorist. Hobbes (1588–1679) was active during a period of social and cultural change. In content, his writings on politics and religion reflect the momentous civil conflicts experienced in seventeenth-century England—including the civil wars, the execution of Charles I, and the restoration of the monarchy. In method and perspective, his works manifest the influence of the European intellectual revolution of the time, a radical shift from medieval modes of thought to modern forms of science and philosophy.

Hobbes received a traditionally classical education at Oxford University, which he later subjected to withering criticism. After graduation, he entered the employ of the Cavendish family as tutor and companion, a position he held (except for two periods including eleven years of self-imposed exile in Paris) to the end of his life. While serving as tutor, Hobbes spent some years on the continent, especially in Italy and France, during which he interacted with several noted intellectuals (among them, René Descartes, a French philosopher, and Galileo Galilei, an Italian scientist). He became convinced, through his discovery of Euclid's work, that the geometric method of reasoning constituted the most reliable form of scientific and philosophical inquiry.

That conviction, combined with his reaction to civil strife in England, led Hobbes to develop a scientific model of politics (centered in a doctrine of sovereignty) and a critical understanding of Christianity (in which the only essential principle of faith is that Jesus is the Christ). In political thought, Hobbes was opposed by Royalists, who adhered to the doctrine of the divine right of kings, and Parliamentarians, who advocated a form of mixed government, in which the Crown was subordinate to Parliament.

In Hobbes's materialist philosophy, reality is nothing but matter in motion. On a human level, this means that we, in our natural state, live in a condition of constant conflict—a war of all against all—in which we are driven by a ceaseless desire for power yet intimidated by a constant fear of death. But reason (by deducing a set of "laws of nature," which constitute, at the same time, commands of God) provides an alternative: the creation, through covenantal agreement with each other, of a single governing authority—a sovereign or Leviathan—with full power to adopt and enforce a system of laws by which civil order is sustained. Subjects are obliged to obey the sovereign in all things, including religious prac-

Thomas Hobbes.

tice, with one singular exception—when their natural right to self-preservation is seriously threatened.

Religious authority (church) and political authority (state) are thus, within Hobbes's model of social order, merged in the office of the sovereign, at least in a Christian commonwealth. Given this version of Erastianism (the subordination of ecclesiastical to secular power), Hobbes leveled vigorous attacks on Roman Catholicism, Presbyterianism, and Dissenting Protestant churches—all of which, in his judgment, were causes of civil unrest. Hobbes, in turn, was charged with atheism and, in his later years, was banned from publishing his works because of his anticlericalism and materialist philosophy. Hobbes, however, well read in theology, defended his positions, developing modern critical methods in his interpretations of Scripture and Christian doctrine.

Throughout his life Hobbes remained a practicing Anglican, receiving, at his own request, the sacraments on his deathbed.

See also *Anticlericalism; Covenant.*

Douglas Sturm

BIBLIOGRAPHY

Hobbes, Thomas. *Leviathan,* edited by Richard Tuck. Cambridge: Cambridge University Press, 1991.

Martinich, A. P. *The Two Gods of Leviathan: Thomas Hobbes on Religion and Politics.* Cambridge: Cambridge University Press, 1992.

Sommerville, Johann P. *Thomas Hobbes: Political Ideas in Historical Context.* New York: St. Martin's, 1992.

Sorrell, Tom, ed. *The Cambridge Companion to Hobbes.* Cambridge: Cambridge University Press, 1996.

Holidays

Referring most broadly to periods of time free from work, the word *holidays* is derived from the word *holyday* and has come to mean special days of celebration and commemoration. These days can be based on religion, politics, and regional, ethnic, or racial affiliation, and they may or may not be officially recognized by city, state, or national governments.

For instance, in the United States some holidays are widely and popularly celebrated even though they are not recognized by the government or businesses as official holidays. Both Halloween (October 31) and Valentine's Day (February 14) fall into this category. Other American holidays receive official government sponsorship at the local, state, or national level, including Evacuation Day (March 17), in Massachusetts's Suffolk County; Juneteenth (June 19), in Texas; and Independence Day (July 4), nationwide.

The British use the word *holidays* to refer to what Americans call vacation. In the following discussion *holidays* will be defined more generally as socially recognized days celebrating an important person or event, such as saints' days or Christmas, or marking a transition of some kind, such as the beginning of the new year or the turning of the season.

Origin of Holidays

Some holidays, such as Halloween and Valentine's Day, have been celebrated in Europe and America for centuries or are related to preexisting, pre-Christian celebrations. Many holidays on the national American calendar, for example, have ancient origins and have been exploited in more recent times by commercial industries, Valentine's Day being a good example. The day is referred to in the medieval writings of Geoffrey Chaucer and, later, in the work of William Shakespeare. Moreover, many holidays, while specific to the United States, are similar to and heavily influenced by preexisting festivals. The American Thanksgiving, for instance, commemorates a feast at Plymouth Colony in 1621 that was most likely inspired by the British harvest home traditions. However, holidays are always being created as social circumstances demand. Thus we see the addition of clergyman and civil rights leader Martin Luther King Jr.'s birthday to the American calendar and the increasingly widespread observance of Kwanza by African Americans.

Controversial Holidays

Despite their celebratory nature, holidays are frequently contested. The establishment of a national day of commemoration for King, for instance, was met with resistance from President Ronald Reagan and the officials of several states, who eventually accepted the holiday only with great reluctance. The ways in which holiday celebrations may reinforce a sense of community for those who participate in them while alienating those who do not are revealed in the controversy surrounding Kwanza.

Kwanza is celebrated from December 26 through January 1. It was invented in the mid-1960s by Dr. Maulana Kerenga, a leading scholar of African and African American studies. He is well known for championing an Afrocentric perspective in the study of culture and society. Sensing that African Americans were alienated from the Eurocentrism and commercialism of Christmas, he adapted African symbols and harvest traditions to construct a festival for African Americans. *Kwanza* is derived from a Swahili word meaning first fruits. The festival is not intended to supplant Christmas so much as to complement it. Many families choose to celebrate both. Kwanza is not a religious holiday but instead speaks to ethnic and racial identity and tradition within the United States. In this sense Kwanza involves the cultural dynamics of identity politics, reflects the growing awareness of pluralism in the United States, and helps create that sense of pluralism as well. When Kerenga invented Kwanza, he provided a ritual for the expression of ethnic and racial identity. In spite of his benevolent intentions, the celebration is sometimes an occasion for racial debate and exclusion.

Similar dynamics can be seen in the increasingly national celebration of Cinco de Mayo, a Mexican celebration of military victory. In the United States it has become something of a pan-Latino holiday, shared by Latino people of many backgrounds, and therefore not without controversy.

Any such sharing of one holiday by people representing a variety of national and regional cultures (for example, Puerto Rican, Colombian, Cuban, and so on) does injustice to their real differences. Similarly, traditional occasions such as the Day of the Dead (Día de los Muertos) are growing in popularity in the United States. While these pan-Latino holidays reflect the growth of a culturally diverse population, they can also be seen as a force for standardization. The Day of the Dead traditions taught in schools and presented as authentic in museums and cultural centers are largely based on phenomena found mostly in central and southern Mexico. Like all such traditions, their manner of celebration varies widely from locale to locale; there is no one right way to celebrate them.

The adaptation of the Day of the Dead and other traditional celebrations in the United States demonstrates that celebrations serve different purposes in different circumstances and that meanings change as do personal, social, and cultural contexts. Still, in America, even major holidays such as Independence Day, Thanksgiving, and Christmas are fraught with identity politics and controversy, although this has not always been acknowledged. For instance, in the eighteenth and nineteenth centuries African Americans, both free and slave, held countercelebrations near Independence Day, as an ironic commentary on the celebration of freedom in a land of slaves. More recently Native Americans have declared Thanksgiving a national day of mourning.

Politics and Holidays

Politics and holidays, depending on one's definition of politics, become intertwined whenever a politician marches in a St. Patrick's Day Parade, the public celebrates civil holidays or debates the constitutionality of publicly sponsored nativity scenes, or special interest groups lobby to establish particular days of observance. The American Christmas shows the strain of being both a national, official holiday and a Christian holy day. It is difficult to be an American citizen and not celebrate this major festive occasion, but it is equally difficult to participate if one is not Christian. Moreover, the celebration is complicated by the doctrine of separation of church and state. These contradictions are played out in controversies over the display of crèches, or nativity scenes, on public property such as town squares. Those who object to the presence of nativity scenes, or indeed any Christmas symbolism, on public property maintain that such displays violate the principle of separation of church and state. In contrast, those who support the displays often claim that the United States is essentially a Christian country. Again, these debates reflect people's sense of their own identity as Christians, although the arguments are not usually presented in those terms. Interestingly, a common response to objections to publicly sponsored Christmas decorations is to include other traditions in the public celebration, rather than to ignore Christmas entirely. So along with the national Christmas tree in Washington, D.C., for instance, there is a national menorah representing the Jewish festival of Hanukkah, as well as an Islamic star and crescent.

Holidays have always involved politics in many ways; that association has become overt as holidays increasingly are recognized as public expressions of identity. Thus gay pride days are growing in popularity, Halloween is claimed as a high holy day by neopagans, and Latino people lobby for a day of national recognition for American labor leader Cesar Chavez. Each of these movements is met with organized resistance from other groups within the United States.

Civil Religion

Scholar Robert Bellah has used the term "civil religion" to refer to the use of religious symbols and concepts in the public political discourse of nation states, particularly the United States. The phrases "under God" in the American Pledge of Allegiance and "In God We Trust" on U.S. coins are examples of civil religion. Moreover, Bellah notes the frequency with which politicians invoke God in their speeches, particularly inauguration speeches. Indeed, it is fair to say that most national governmental ceremonial displays in the United States include a religious component such as a prayer or an oath sworn on a Bible.

This blending of the political domain with the religious domain is a means of making sacred the political system itself. If we separate the concept of the sacred from the concept of the religious, we can view politics as having its own sacred realm, beyond that of religion. For instance, the American flag is sacred though not religious. It occupies a special position in public and private spaces, is raised and lowered at certain prescribed times, must be folded in a certain way, and is burned when it has outlived its useful life. However, in spite of its sacred aspect, the flag is subject to civil authority, as the American flag burning controversy has shown. It is the U.S. Congress, after all, that determines whether burning the flag in protest is illegal.

Other examples of sacred symbols in the American political system include the narratives of the pilgrims in Plymouth, those of the War of Independence, and those of the country's founders, which are analogous to the mythic narratives of many cultures; they, too, are sacred without being specifically religious. Likewise, national texts such as the Constitution and the Declaration of Independence are sacred, almost biblical charters.

Sacred and political symbols often overlap and mimic each other. For example, the monuments to Abraham Lincoln and Thomas Jefferson in Washington, D.C., resemble classical temples. The U.S. Vietnam War Memorial is reminiscent of a gravestone: a slab of granite with the names of the deceased inscribed upon it. It is no wonder that people leave personal memorabilia at this site. Moreover, the sacred-political realm has its holidays, including the American Memorial Day, Flag Day, and especially Independence Day. Interestingly, Labor Day, a celebration of the value of labor and the rights of workers, has been incorporated into this group of sacred-political holidays in the United States, unlike its May Day analogues in Europe.

Until recently the national anthem in Great Britain was sung before theatrical presentations. National anthems are still routinely sung before sporting events throughout the world. In Belfast at the Queen's University, many students have refused for political reasons to participate in singing the British national anthem during commencement exercises.

In the United States professional sporting events are increasingly adapting the devices of festivity, such as the use of fireworks, to extend their appeal. According to its organizers the Super Bowl has become an "unofficial American holiday." It is important to note, however, that the Super Bowl (the championship game of the National Football League) was initiated during the television era and is very much a mediated event. People gather together in small, festive groups to watch it. The cost of commercials is higher than that of any other television advertising, and the commercials themselves are advertised in advance of the broadcast. The Super Bowl celebrates the consumerist, capitalist system of which it is a part. It is made sacred by formal religious invocations and the opening rituals of the game. The graphics promoting the game employ Roman numerals, equating this event with ancient gladiatorial contests, while the winning team receives a congratulatory phone call from the president of the United States. The values and symbols of government, the media, commercial industry, and religion

are fused in this one event, justifying and supporting one another.

Commemorating Rites of Passage

Many holidays, both political and religious, commemorate life cycle rites of passage. The Christian church calendar is based on the birth, circumcision, life, death, and resurrection of Jesus, for instance. Holidays also mark the births of great people (at present, exclusively male) such as American president George Washington and Martin Luther King Jr. The assassination of U.S. president John F. Kennedy, in 1963, and his subsequent funeral, was followed by a national ritual of mourning that gripped the entire country for several days.

Similarly, people experience their own rites of passage through the life cycle (and the anniversaries of those events) as personal and family holidays. Birthdays, name days, bat mitzvahs, weddings, jubilees, and even wakes and funerals are occasions for celebration and commemoration.

These personal celebrations occur within families or among groups of friends (associational groups). Large-scale holidays are usually sponsored by church or state and, more recently, by commercial industry. Some holidays are in fact created entirely by self-interested industries. Events such as Secretaries Day and Grandparents Day, which acknowledge relationships, are based on a principle of created guilt: once a day has been set aside to recognize and honor a person occupying a certain social role, such as a secretary or grandmother, it is difficult for people to ignore the day without feeling guilty. Moreover, those who ignore such days, especially those in unequal power relationships, run the risk of being punished for their refusal to participate. If, for instance, a worker overlooks Bosses Day, that worker might invite retaliation.

Imposing and Opposing Ideology

One could argue that the commercialization of holidays is itself a political act. Because the United States is a capitalist, consumerist society, commercializing public celebrations is another way of imposing ideology. In addition to serving the interests of the established political order, holidays are often used to subvert or oppose established political ideas or practices. Opposition groups invert the primary symbols associated with a holiday, as when animal rights groups prepare a vegetarian Thanksgiving dinner and have a live turkey present at the feast, or when a group in Maine holds a Memorial Day antiwar rally. Other examples include the creation of new, oppositional days such as the Native American National Day of Mourning held at Thanksgiving. Scholar David Waldstreicher has noted that slave and free African Americans often held celebrations on or near significant dates such as Independence Day. Also, many groups create days of celebration on which they can display publicly a stigmatized identity, such as Gay Pride Day.

Holidays are developed either from the top down (by the state, the church, or some other overarching institution) or from the bottom up (at the grassroots level, as in the case of a truly popular or folk celebration). Most contemporary holidays include both institutional and popular aspects, such as Halloween, which is clearly promoted by the candy industry but which also involves popular customs such as pranks, street festivals, and masquerades that are often thought to be dangerously uncontrollable by local officials. The arson of Devils Night (October 30) in Detroit is an example of the extent to which holiday celebrations can oppose the established order. Commercialism reigns in the United States, but clearly carnivalesque celebrations such as Halloween and Mardi Gras allow for more popular participation than some other holidays, and that participation is occasionally inversive.

Holidays and celebrations frequently involve conflict. To the extent that a certain group identity is being celebrated, an outgroup is necessarily created. Despite the popular rhetoric, not everybody is Irish on St. Patrick's Day, as the reaction to a group of gay and lesbian Irish Americans at the parades in Boston and New York in the 1990s demonstrated. In Northern Ireland, where religion and politics are thought to be the same, efforts at ending the guerrilla war between Protestants and Catholics often fell apart on more than one occasion over the issue of parade routes: who got to parade where on the national commemorations of the Twelfth of July, St. Patrick's Day, and at other times as well.

Reflecting Society

Holidays are always changing in accordance with society. New holidays replace old ones. Still, among many of our holiday observances there is an air of tradition, a sense of continuity with the past. While the overt and covert ramifications of holiday traditions, especially along race, class, and gender lines, cannot be overlooked or minimized, there is much of great value to be found in holiday celebrations, including the sense of coming together and sharing that we frequently associate with them. Holidays are social and cultural artifacts, and so they reflect the society in which they occur, for better and for worse.

See also *Civil Religion; Public Theology; Sacred Places; Separation of Church and State.*

Jack Santino

BIBLIOGRAPHY

Jarman, Neil. *Material Conflicts: Parades and Visual Displays in Northern Ireland.* Oxford and New York: Berg, 1997.

Kertzer, David I. *Ritual, Politics, and Power.* New Haven: Yale University Press, 1988.

Moore, Sally F., and Barbara G. Myerhoff. *Secular Ritual.* Assen, Netherlands: Van Gorcum, 1977.

Santino, Jack. *All Around the Year: Holidays and Celebrations in American Life.* Urbana: University of Illinois Press, 1994.

———. *New Old-Fashioned Ways: Holidays and Popular Culture.* Knoxville: University of Tennessee Press, 1996.

Schmidt, Leigh Eric. *Consumer Rites: The Buying and Selling of American Holidays.* Princeton: Princeton University Press, 1995.

Swanson, Wayne. *The Christ Child Goes to Court.* Philadelphia: Temple University Press, 1990.

Waldstreicher, David. *In the Midst of Perpetual Fetes: The Making of American Nationalism, 1776–1820.* Chapel Hill: University of North Carolina Press, 1997.

Holocaust

A holocaust (from the Greek *holos,* whole, and *kaustos,* burnt) was originally a sacrifice to the Greek gods in which the victim was burned whole, but the word has come to mean slaughter or destruction on a mass scale, especially by fire and nuclear warfare. When written *Holocaust,* now the most frequent use, the term refers to the period (1933–1945) of persecution and extermination of six million Jews and other minorities by Nazi Germany, also known as the Catastrophe, the Sho'ah, the Hurban.

Aftermath of World War I

Any discussion of the Holocaust must begin with World War I, the defeat of Germany, and the punitive measures of the Versailles treaty of 1919. Germany lost one-eighth of her land along the eastern and western borders, her colonies, and her overseas investments. The German army was limited to one hundred thousand men, the navy curtailed, and the German people obligated to pay enormous reparations. The war guilt clause, which blamed the war solely on Germany, infuriated all of German society. The first republican government resigned rather than sign the treaty. Matthias Erzberger, who signed because Germans were near starvation and the Allies threatened to withhold food shipments until signatures were affixed, was assassinated three years later.

The harshness of the Versailles treaty was compounded by Germany's lack of political experience with democracy and the institutional weaknesses of the newly established Weimar Republic, a coalition government. The Weimar constitution included Article 48, referred to as the suicide clause, which allowed the president to suspend the constitution during emergencies. This undemocratic clause exposed the nation to political exploitation by the left (communists, Bolsheviks, socialist radicals) as well as the right (ultra-nationalists). Indeed, Hitler would enact the clause to help facilitate his rise to power.

The German economy after World War I was a disaster. Prices soared when the German government urged workers of the French-occupied Ruhr to strike and the government supported them by printing paper money not backed by gold. The shortage of goods led to an inflation difficult to comprehend in today's world. At the end of the war, for example, $1 equaled 8.4 marks. In 1922 it bought 70,000 marks, and by December 1923 trillions of worthless marks traded for $1. The middle class saw their painstakingly amassed reserves wiped out, with lifetime savings buying only one loaf of bread. Investments were quite literally not worth the paper on which the certificates were printed. Labor unions were nearly destroyed because they could not provide their members with job security and a living wage. But some industrial giants profited mightily as debts melted away, paid off with cheap money. Workers were powerless, and real estate speculators increased their holdings.

All this hardship contributed to increasing political polarization. By 1923 the government controlled runaway inflation by putting the mark on par with the prewar German currency. The medicine was strong, and many already-weak businesses collapsed. The overall standard of living declined as unemployment and low wages demoralized wage earners. The bitter pill was, however, swallowed, leading to partial economic recovery. By the mid-1920s the German people were reviving, and had this trend continued, Germany might have achieved political stability.

Unfortunately, the Great Depression, especially the Wall Street Crash of 1929 and the failure of the Bank of Austria, caused drastic declines in production, employment, and individual and corporate purchasing power. Banks closed, busi-

nesses went bankrupt, and farmers lost farms. In the daily struggle for survival the centrally planned economies that could function without foreign interference or dependence found new supporters.

Industrialists wanted no part of communism, and this fear sent conservative industrial barons searching for alternatives. Into this mood of political hopelessness and economic disintegration entered the Nazi Party, which promised to right the wrongs of the Versailles treaty, offered a scapegoat for political aimlessness, and claimed to know how to decrease restrictions on private property while still managing the nation's business life without foreign meddling.

Hitler and the Rise of the Nazi Party

Born in 1889 in Lower Austria, Adolf Hitler failed the entrance examination for the Vienna Academy of Fine Arts and eked out a living selling picture postcards. He resented groups he saw as non-German who flocked to the heart of the Austro-Hungarian Empire. Hitler came under the influence of Karl Lueger, anti-Semitic mayor of Vienna from 1895 to 1910.

World War I provided Hitler direction, and he was devastated by the armistice. He returned to Munich, where he became the seventh member of the German Worker's Party, a small political party made up of penniless ex-soldiers. Hitler quickly reshaped this group of malcontents and discovered his powers as an orator. With an air of absolute assurance in a world he saw as black and white, he offered simple, bold solutions based on his anti-Jewish and antidemocratic convictions, admiration for the outstanding individual, and contempt for the masses, swaying followers with appeals based on emotion, not logic. The party platform of the renamed National Socialist German Workers' Party, or Nazi Party, was highly nationalistic, with membership in the German nation denied to all Jews.

In 1921 Hitler created the Storm Troops, or SA, a semi-military band of men to protect Nazi Party meetings and harass rivals. These men wore brown shirts (and hence were called Brownshirts) and were mostly unemployed military people. In 1923 Hitler's Nazis attempted a coup in Munich. Known as the Beer Hall Putsch, it collapsed when three thousand SA men ran after being confronted by only one hundred policemen. Hitler was captured and used his trial as a publicity platform. Even though he was found guilty and sentenced to five years in prison, all Germany suddenly knew him. He served less than two years in comfort and wrote his autobiography, the openly anti-Semitic *Mein Kampf* (My Struggle), during that time.

Hitler decided to take power using legitimate means and used the right-wing industrialists' fears of Bolshevism to increase Nazi support in the 1930 Reichstag elections. He challenged Paul von Hindenburg in 1932, when Hindenburg's first term as president ended. Hitler received 30 percent of the vote and forced the aging war hero into a runoff. Hindenburg won, but in the Reichstag elections of 1932, the Nazis held 230 seats and became the largest single party. According to the newly instituted republican constitutional traditions, Hitler should have been appointed chancellor, but Hindenburg resisted, turning instead to Franz von Papen, an aristocrat who thought he could control Hitler.

Hitler was offered the vice chancellorship. He refused, and von Papen called a new election. The Nazis again held the most seats in the Reichstag, despite a thirty-four seat decline. Von Papen then resigned the chancellorship and General Kurt von Schleicher became the last chancellor of Weimar. Von Schleicher tried to check the Nazis by creating a coalition between the army and the trade unions. When this pairing proved too odd, von Schleicher tried to convince Hindenburg that only a military dictatorship would save Germany. Hindenburg responded that he had sworn to uphold the constitution and would not sign such an order. Although Schleicher resigned, Hitler remembered his attempt to block the Nazi ascent, and during the 1934 Blood Purge six Nazi members murdered von Schleicher in front of his family.

Hindenburg finally was persuaded to ask Hitler to form a government, and Hitler was appointed chancellor on January 30, 1933. Von Papen served as the vice chancellor, still mistakenly believing his titles and experience would keep Hitler in check. On August 2, 1934, Hindenburg died and on August 3 Hitler declared himself president as well as chancellor; this act was ratified by a 90 percent vote in a referendum on August 18, 1934.

Anti-Semitism and Racism as Law

From the birth of the party in 1920, Nazi racial principles linked citizenship to race, characterizing Jews as subhuman parasites who had infected the German nation and caused all German misfortunes. Only people of "pure" German blood—those the Nazis referred to as Aryans—could be German citizens. Nazi policy was to make Germany and German-controlled areas free of Jews, and the Nazis insti-

tuted racial anti-Semitism as a fundamental part of governmental policy soon after they took office.

On April 1, 1933, the Nazis staged a boycott of Jewish shops and businesses. On April 11 they issued a decree defining as non-Aryan anyone with at least one Jewish grandparent or parent. On April 26 they established the Secret State Police, the Gestapo, and in June opened the Dachau concentration camp, with Buchenwald, Sachsenhausen, and Ravensbruck soon to follow. On July 14 the Nazi Party was declared the only legal party in Germany. Between September and May 1934 various measures were passed to make life unbearable for Jews, thereby forcing Jews to emigrate—for example, Jews were eliminated from citizenship, public office, the professions, and the intellectual and artistic life of the country. The infamous Nuremberg Laws of September 15, 1935, denied Jews citizenship in the Reich and forbade the "desecration of the race" to protect the purity of German blood by preventing intermarriage.

These laws were followed by a series of anti-Jewish economic measures designed to take away the Jews' economic independence: the "aryanization" of Jewish business concerns and the liquidation of Jewish-owned retail businesses and industrial enterprises; locally enforced sales of property and business; and the registration and marking of Jewish-owned businesses. Other policies were intended to enforce further personal isolation and ostracism. The first census conducted on a racial basis was on May 17, 1938. Public schools were closed to Jewish children on November 15, 1938, and compulsory identification cards were issued after January 1, 1939.

Physical violence against Jews escalated during the pre–World War II period once the Nazis took power. On May 10, 1933, Jewish books were burned. There were anti-Jewish riots by the SA in Berlin (March 9–10, 1933). Jewish judges and lawyers were chased from the Breslau court on March 13, 1933. The Munich synagogue was destroyed on June 9, 1938, and the Nuremberg synagogue, on August 10, 1938. This was followed by the infamous *Kristallnacht,* the Night of the Broken Glass, on November 9–10, 1938. A massive pogrom, it was so named because thousands of windows were smashed and the shards glistened in the streets like crystal. All 275 of Germany's synagogues were destroyed, and some seventy-five hundred Jewish businesses demolished. Firemen and police did nothing, and most non-Jewish citizens looked the other way. The arrests and the violence continued for two days, and some thirty thousand Jewish men were shipped to concentration camps. Most were later released, but eight hundred did not survive.

Throughout this period "Jews not wanted" signs were posted on businesses, sports stadiums, and roads leading to towns and resorts, and the names of Jewish dead were erased from war memorials. These policies had their anticipated effect. In 1933 there were 500,000 people in the two-thousand-year-old Jewish community in Germany, including foreign and stateless Jews; by 1939, only 220,000 remained.

These actions against the Jews took place under increasing totalitarianism within Germany, with the German Gestapo essentially above the law after February 10, 1936. The failure of the world to react to these early outrages signaled other countries, especially those in Eastern Europe, that anti-Semitism was an acceptable state policy.

The reaction of the German people during this time ranged from widespread Nazi support or apathy to individual acts of humanity. Most Protestant churches accepted the Nazi racial policies, although the dissenting Confessing Church took a strong stand against such racism on March 17, 1935, an act that resulted in the arrest of some seven hundred ministers. The Catholic Church took no public stand, although there were registered cases of Catholic protests such as that of the Canon Bernhard Lichtenberg who, after Kristallnacht, used to pray daily and openly for all those persecuted.

It was difficult for Jews themselves to grasp the enormity of what was happening to them. German Jews were highly assimilated and were shocked and bewildered by the slow escalation of so-called legal measures and acts of violence. Many continued to hope they could live in Germany; others argued that expulsion was only a matter of time, and emigration, especially to Palestine, was widely advocated. Some 280,000 Jews did emigrate, despite the legal, financial, and psychological difficulties of doing so. The hard times created by the economic depression made the arrival of poor Jewish immigrants unpopular, and Nazi propaganda made much of this anti-Jewish reaction.

Wartime Acts

After Hitler invaded Poland on September 1, 1939, Nazi policy toward Jews accelerated in its lawlessness, resulting in the mass murder of the Jewish population in any areas occupied or influenced by the Nazis. This violence culminated in the extermination of millions by shooting and gassing from 1941 to 1945 and was accompanied by the starvation, forced labor, and death marches of many other Jews. Most of these atrocities were carried out under the code name the Final Solution. The Wannsee conference of January 20, 1942, coordinated the mass murder and moved the Holocaust beyond mass shootings—such as the SS [Elite Guard] murder of 33,771 Jews at Babi Yar near Kiev, Russia, in September 1941—and killings in mobile gas vans to more technologically sophisticated, bureaucratized mass murder. The killing took place in concentration camps, such as at Auschwitz. As the war neared the end, the Nazis forced those held in the camps on death marches designed to cover their crimes by destroying all traces of victims.

Range of the Holocaust

Although Nazi treatment of many subject peoples (Slavs, homosexuals, and gypsies) was inhumane and cruel, the Jews seemed particularly singled out for mistreatment. Decisions on the ultimate fate of many of the other subject groups within the Reich, for example, were postponed until Hitler's anticipated victory, but the destruction of the Jews was carried out immediately, even taking precedence over Nazi wartime aims.

As the Nazis captured more territory, the geographic areas affected by anti-Jewish measures expanded. Nazi policies extended into Poland after September 1, 1939; to Denmark and Norway after April 9, 1940; and to the Netherlands, Belgium, Luxembourg, and France (including French Africa and the French Levant) after May 10, 1940. The Germans occupied part of Italy as of September 8, 1943, and Yugoslavia and Greece after April 16, 1941. From June 22, 1941, anti-Jewish measures were imposed on the occupied parts of the Soviet Union, and once the United States had entered the war against Japan, these policies were applied to the Jews living in Japanese-controlled parts of Asia, such as Shanghai.

Jews living in geographic areas occupied by the Italians were more fortunate because the Italians were much more humane in their treatment of them. But other German satellites were just as cruel toward the Jews as were the Nazis. The extent of this mistreatment remains the subject of controversy to this day.

Religion and the Churches

Religion played an integral part in the Holocaust. Christian churches from the time of Constantine in the fourth century had wanted to convert Jews, and medieval Christian

One of the death trains used by the Nazis to transport Jews and other Holocaust victims to concentration camps at the end of World War II. Allied forces discovered this train after liberating Dachau.

churches throughout Europe engaged in varying degrees of anti-Semitic persecution because they felt it was the Jews who had crucified Christ. This belief formed the basic foundation for anti-Semitism and was never contradicted, or even addressed directly, by any religious groups throughout this period. The Nazi assault on the Jews thus took place in a climate of opinion conditioned by centuries of anti-Semitism that existed throughout the Christian world. Indeed, various canonical laws from 306 to 1434 bear striking similarity to Nazi laws against the Jews.

The extent to which religion and cultural differences lay at the core of the Holocaust is clearly seen in the Nazi genocidal psychology, which requires the intentional identification of a particular group for destruction. For the Nazis, religion, as well as the cultural and ethnic differences that flowed from religious differences, became the foundation for discrimination and destruction. Nazis claimed—and appeared to believe in many cases—that Jews as non-Chris-

tians represented a threat to the majority German population. An individual German could not be Jewish, the Nazis argued, and still share the same desires for Germany non-Jewish Germans did. Allegiances and goals were believed to be ascriptive, flowing inevitably from birth into a particular group. This belief sets genocide apart from other conflicts in which allegiances can shift and opponents can be converted and means that victims are killed not for their individual acts or beliefs but rather because of their membership in a particular group.

The specific reaction to various aspects of the Holocaust among religious groups was mixed. In general the Roman Catholic church under Pope Pius XII was one of studied neutrality. The response of Protestant churches varied greatly by country, with protest found more often among churches in occupied countries in Western Europe, as part of patriotic resistance to the Nazis. National differences also affected churches' willingness to protest Nazi policies, with church leaders in Western Europe, especially in Belgium, France, Holland, and Italy, taking much stronger stands in support of Jews than did Christians in Eastern Europe, where anti-Semitism had far deeper roots.

Pope Pius XI, who held office when the Nazis began their persecution of the Jews, limited his public concern to Catholic non-Aryans. His encyclical of March 1937 rejected the myth of race and blood as being contrary to Christian truth but did not mention anti-Semitism itself. During a reception for Catholic pilgrims from Belgium on September 7, 1938, Pius XI supposedly condemned Christian participation in anti-Semitic movements, noting that Christians were spiritual descendants of Abraham and therefore spiritually Semites, but this statement was not published in the accounts of the Italian papers.

After Pius XII succeeded Pius XI in the spring of 1939, official papal comments became even more circumscribed. Although the Vatican had been informed about the murder of Jews in concentration camps as of 1942, Pius XII's public comments were limited to carefully crafted expressions of sympathy for victims of injustice in general and to calls for more humane conduct of wartime hostilities. (In his Christmas message of 1942, for example, Pius XII expressed concern for those innocent people who had been killed merely because of nationality or descent.)

The Vatican policy of neutrality was more difficult to maintain once the Nazis began rounding up the eight thousand Jews of Rome late in 1943. German authorities had feared Pius XII might speak out and were relieved when he was silent as, on October 18, 1943, more than one thousand Roman Jews, mostly women and children, were transported to Auschwitz. Some seven thousand Roman Jews went into hiding, with four thousand of these given refuge in the many houses of religious orders in Rome, apparently with the pope's knowledge and approval. A few dozen were hidden in the Vatican itself, and the rest were concealed by ordinary Italians, who had never liked the Fascists' anti-Jewish policy.

Pius XII's failure to speak publicly against Nazi atrocities, especially after the arrests of the Italian Jews, drew criticism from many, who pointed out that the Vatican's silence endangered its moral prestige. Wladislaw Raczkiewica, president of the Polish government in exile, called on the pope to denounce Nazi violence unequivocally, arguing that this would strengthen the willingness of Poles to help Jews. The chief rabbi of Palestine, Isaac Herzog, and Bishop Preysing of Berlin were other prominent officials who urged the pope

to speak out. They argued that the pope could have threatened the Germans with an interdict or with the excommunication of Hitler, Nazi propagandist Joseph Goebbels, and other leading Catholic Nazis. Furthermore, the critics continued, even though the pope could not have halted the machinery of destruction itself, just a public papal statement would have saved many lives, if only by encouraging Catholics living under Nazi rule to resist anti-Jewish policies. These critics pointed to the effective public protest led by the German episcopate against the euthanasia program. And finally, the critics argued, a public broadcast over the Vatican radio would have made clear to all what awaited the Jews in the East, thereby encouraging more Jews to attempt escape and more Christians to shelter them.

Would a papal decree of excommunication against Hitler have had any effect? What were the pope's private views on Nazi policies? Did his inaction reflect lack of concern or a more statesmanlike fear of pushing too far? The pope's defenders argue that a strong stand by the pope on the Jewish question would have led to mass desertion from the church, but no one knows the answers to these questions. Whatever his motive, the pope would not take such action, arguing that doing so would risk the allegiance of the German Catholics, who he felt were largely indifferent to the fate of the Jews. Beyond this, the pope saw the Nazis as aiding the fight against communism, and he considered Bolshevism more dangerous than German National Socialism.

The failure of the pope to take part in public protest contrasts sharply with activities of several papal nuncios. Nuncios in Slovakia, Romania, Turkey, and Hungary saved many thousands of Jewish lives. (The nuncio in Istanbul, Monsignor Roncalli, who saved thousands of Jews, later became Pope John XXIII.) It seems doubtful, but by no means clear, that these individuals acted on orders from Rome. In general, Rome's attitude seems to have followed the political winds, with Pius XII becoming more willing to speak out publicly only after it was evident that Germany was losing the war.

The church and state had long ties in Germany, and the official Lutheran Church did little to protest Nazi policies, even excluding Christians of Jewish origins from membership in the church. This attitude reflected centuries of Protestant anti-Semitism as embodied by Luther's ugly depiction of the Jews as vermin who craved world domination.

The Confessing Church took a more courageous stand; it defended the rights of its members who had Jewish origins but did not publicly oppose persecution of such Jews outside the church. The Confessing Church did send a memorandum to Hitler on May 1936, arguing that even when anti-Semitism was forced on the Christian by National Socialist ideology, the Christian nonetheless has a divine commandment to love his neighbor. Many ministers of the Confessing Church refused to cooperate with anti-Jewish directives and were sent to concentration camps as a result.

Protestant churches in occupied countries spoke out more aggressively against Nazi policies. The Lutheran churches in Denmark and Norway protested publicly when the Nazis began deportations from their countries, and both Protestant and Catholic churches in Holland sent similar protests. Some of these protests were read from the pulpits, as was a letter from the Reverend Marc Boegner, president of the Protestant Federation, addressed to the French chief rabbi and to important French political leaders.

Orthodox Church leaders stood up for the Jews. In Greece the archbishop of Athens sent a strong protest against Jewish deportations to the prime minister of the German puppet regime, and the bishop of Salonika intervened to help Jews. But many of the Orthodox were persecuted, and many of these protests appear to have been based mainly on national, rather than religious, considerations.

Given the extent of Nazi control and the deeply embedded anti-Semitism in eastern Europe, it is perhaps noteworthy how many church leaders did speak out publicly for Jews. The Lutheran Church in Slovakia protested in November 1939 and again in May 1942. Patriarch Nicodemus of Romania personally—and successfully—intervened with the Romanian government on behalf of Jews. In Bulgaria the metropolitan of Sofia and the metropolitan of Plovdiv intervened with King Boris, and the Holy Synod of the Bulgarian Orthodox Church repeatedly sent strong written protests to the government. This resulted in the rescue of many Bulgarian Jews. The Hungarian situation was more mixed, with the Lutheran bishops voting for the first and second anti-Jewish laws of 1938 and 1939; when the bishops did finally draft a statement against the deportations in 1944, they caved in to government pressure and never read the statement publicly.

Protestant church leaders in Britain, France, Sweden, Switzerland, and the United States had protested the first anti-Semitic measures in Germany, the promulgation of the Nuremberg Laws, and Kristallnacht in 1938. The Church of Sweden protested publicly against the deportation of Nor-

wegian Jews. And protest by the Protestant churches of Switzerland helped change the Swiss government's policy of returning illegal Jewish refugees to their countries of origin. Church leaders in both Britain and the United States protested against their governments' policies of turning away Jewish refugees but had little effect on actual policy. The churches did collect aid money for refugees and sent parcels to Jews in concentration camps.

What Caused the Holocaust?

Did Hitler's rhetoric seduce an otherwise civilized people? How much of the Holocaust resulted from fear and forceful intimidation by a small group of marginal thugs? How widespread was support for the Nazis? Why did the Holocaust happen in Germany and not elsewhere?

As early as 1946 British historian A. J. P. Taylor traced the roots of Nazism back to Luther and suggested the German tendency toward authoritarianism and brutality was a fact established long before Hitler. The view that there is a special path of German history that led to Hitler was expanded on by many scholars and became known as the Sonderweg theory, which stressed the idiosyncrasy of German history that lay at the heart of the Nazis' power and that set Germany apart from France or Britain. Original proponents emphasized the structural factors of German history, such as the Thirty Years' War (1618–1648), which gave Germans a fear of being encircled. Other historians rejected the Sonderweg theory, with Marxist scholars viewing the Holocaust as a result of Fascism, itself a part of a dying capitalism. German-born American political scientist Hannah Arendt argued that the Holocaust was an inherent part of totalitarianism, but others treated the Holocaust as part of Europe's tradition of anti-Semitism, which dated back to the Middle Ages and which was enhanced by the turn-of-the-century pseudo-science of eugenics and social Darwinism, movements that appeared in other countries, too.

Most historians conclude that Hitler's role was central but far from predetermined. One debate focuses on the extent to which the Holocaust was a calculated attempt to solve the population problem in newly conquered lands or a policy carried out in spite of its economic irrationality. The intentionalists make Hitler central, claiming that he had always intended to kill all the Jews and that the timing of the Final Solution merely reflected Hitler's waiting for the most appropriate moment. They stress Hitler's ideology, explaining the Jewish policy as determined primarily by Hitler himself, whose efforts were calculated or intended to realize the goals of an ideologically derived plan that Hitler had always advanced with fanatical consistency. Functionalists, however, emphasize the structure and institutions of the Third Reich, arguing that the Holocaust was unplanned, more the result of the chaotic decision making of an ideologically focused regime. These historians stress the extent to which the different bureaucracies within the Nazi system competed for Hitler's attention by developing solutions that became increasingly more extreme, arguing that the development of the Final Solution came only after much indecision and trying other policies (for example, expulsion).

Why Germany? Was there something unique in Germany that made the Holocaust more likely there, or was it merely chance? Most experts point to several factors that led to the Holocaust's occurring in Germany. Unstable political conditions after World War I threatened the social order. The First World War and the harsh terms of the Versailles treaty brought great geographic and psychological dislocations and gave the German people a grievance and a feeling that they had been wronged. A weak Weimar government attempted to establish a democratic government in a political culture that had little democratic roots. Unlike other countries of Western Europe, Germany had no liberal democratic tradition on which to build. The forces of moderation were essentially drowned out by extremists during the Weimar period. The economic chaos of the depression was made worse in Germany because of the harsh terms of the Versailles treaty, especially the reparations.

All of these factors prepared the Germans psychologically to look for a scapegoat, which Hitler supplied them through both the Jews and the democratically elected politicians who supposedly betrayed Germany at Versailles. Hitler exploited the ancient stereotype of Jews as cosmopolitan elites who feel no loyalty to the homeland. This view prevailed throughout much of Europe, and Nazi propaganda fanned this fear shamelessly. And the Holocaust was carried out secretly, under conditions that discouraged intervention by the outside world. The tight control of information by the totalitarian Nazi regime greatly facilitated the massacre of the Jews. In addition, there existed among Germans and non-Germans alike a widespread desire not to know too much. It was difficult to face facts too horrible to comprehend, let alone believe, a phenomenon that affected both Jews and non-Jews as they slowly learned more details of the Holocaust.

It would be comforting to attribute the Holocaust to "backward" people, crippled by lack of education and socioeconomic poverty, but even the most respected academic, political, and social circles in the nineteenth and early twentieth centuries fell under the sway of beliefs that linked biology, prejudice, and genocide. (Indeed, the British delegation to the first international eugenics conference, called to improve the race through the science of eugenics, was led by Winston Churchill.) In Germany, Nazi double-think existed at all levels of society, and support for the Holocaust extended into the well-educated classes. Even Nobel Prize winner Konrad Lorenz, prominent professor of Asian studies Paul de Lagarde, and other respected scholars were supporters.

How widespread was public support for the Holocaust? Was support greater in Germany than in other countries? How much cooperation resulted from fear and force? Most psychosociological explanations look to the identification of Jews and other minorities as outsiders, internal strife, territorial ambitions, propaganda, organized destruction, and the failure of social control. Analysts groping for explanations for the worst aspects of the Holocaust point to factors ranging from the geographic origin or social background of the perpetrators to party membership and ideology, virulent eliminationist anti-Semitism, and the suggestion that personality characteristics of certain individuals lie dormant until particular conditions awaken them. Such explanations build on the idea that most people are capable of great cruelty and simply fall into the roles society assigns them. Ironically, these explanations return to the kind of authoritarian explanation originally offered in the postwar period, suggesting that it is the rare individual who resists such assignment and follows personal ethics instead. The reasoning echoes Theodore W. Adorno's early arguments on authoritarianism and Stanley Milgram's work on obedience to authority, not obedience out of fear of immediate reprisals but rather obedience more akin to deference and arising out of long-term socialization.

General works on genocide all suggest a psychological connection to a victim affects perpetrators' willingness to participate in inhumane behavior toward members of the persecuted group. This connection was clearly evident during the Holocaust. In a process replicated in other genocides, the Nazis changed the way people looked at the Jews. Extensive ideological indoctrination, stressing the importance of keeping the Aryan blood pure, and a tightly controlled press that sanctified the German people and blood community were critical. The German people were depicted as facing a constant struggle for survival, ordained by nature, against the weaker peoples who would contaminate them with their impure blood.

Arendt explained the Holocaust's mass psychology as one of banality, in which killing becomes mechanized and impersonalized, thus removing the individual from moral responsibility. This concept of impersonal and bureaucraticized murder has been challenged in recent work focusing on the killing units in Eastern Europe. Arendt's explanation of impersonal, bureaucratic murder cannot apply to these men, who killed face to face. This does not discount the general value of her explanation, since the reserve order policemen found it vastly easier to put Jews on transports and send them to their death that way than to physically murder the Jews themselves. It does, however, suggest that segmentation and routinization, the depersonalizing aspects of bureaucratized killing, are not sufficient to explain much of the ugly brutality and sadism directed against the Jews.

Typically in genocides, both a scapegoat and a victim are needed to explain the disintegration of the old economic, political, and social order and to justify the beginning of the new. The stereotype of the wealthy, cosmopolitan Jews provided a handy scapegoat; the good German people filled the role of victims. Both elite and masses responded to threats to their economic situation, political power, and way of life. The political elite may have done so in a more cynical and calculating way, but the followers, the ones who actually performed the genocidal acts, were moved out of their own personal frustration and hostility as much as a response to orders.

The psychological effect of this deluge of racist and anti-Semitic propaganda, when combined with the reprisals for helping Jews—the Nazis killed the families of those found guilty of rescuing Jews—made it easier for people to conform to the norms of their immediate community. The years of anti-Semitism were accentuated by the polarizing effects of war. The dichotomy of racially superior Germans and racially inferior Jews, central to Nazi ideology, easily merged with the image of a beleaguered Germany surrounded by warring enemies.

Ironically, the Nazi genocide seems related to the German search for national identity and power. Because it is state sanctioned, if not state induced, genocide requires a legitimizing principle or ideology to justify its scale of human destruction. Anti-Semitism and the myth of Aryan superiority fit this purpose. The doctrine of biological determinism served to provide additional justification for the Holocaust, so the massacres of the Jews became identified with a holy crusade to free the German body politic of diseased tissue. Thus the Holocaust was defended as a scientifically necessary response to prevent contamination by agents of racial pollution who were viewed as parasites and bacteria causing sickness, deterioration, and death in the host peoples. The mass murder of the Jews was justified through a twisted logic in which it becomes necessary to prevent the members of a biologically degenerate group from destroying a biologically superior group.

See also *Anti-Semitism; Fascism; Genocide and "Ethnic Cleansing"; Germany; Prejudice; Zionism.*

Kristen Renwick Monroe

BIBLIOGRAPHY

Adorno, Theodor W., et al. *The Authoritarian Personality.* New York: Harper, 1950.

Arendt, Hannah. *The Origins of Totalitarianism.* New York: Harcourt Brace, 1958.

Bauman, Zygmunt. *Modernity and the Holocaust.* Ithaca, N.Y.: Cornell University Press, 1989.

Browning, Christopher. *Ordinary Men: Reserve Police Battalion 101 and the Final Solution in Poland.* New York: Aaron Asher, HarperCollins, 1992.

———. *The Path to Genocide: Essays on Launching the Final Solution.* New York: Cambridge University Press, 1993.

Burleigh, Michael, and Wolfgang Wippermann. *The Racial State: Germany 1933–1945.* New York: Cambridge University Press, 1991.

Goldhagen, D. J. *Hitler's Willing Executioners.* New York: Knopf, 1996.

Hilberg, Raul. *The Destruction of the European Jews.* Vol. 1–3. New York: Holmes and Meier, 1985.

Martin, Gilbert. *Atlas of the Holocaust.* New York: DaCapo Press, 1982.

Milgram, Stanley. *Obedience to Authority: An Experimental View.* New York: Harper and Row, 1974.

Monroe, Kristen R. "The Psychology of Genocide: A Review of the Literature." *Ethics and International Affairs* 9 (February 1995): 215–239.

Steiner, John M. "The SS Yesterday and Today: A Sociopsychological View." In *Survivors, Victims, and Perpetrators: Essays on the Nazi Holocaust,* edited by Joel E. Dimsdale. Washington, D.C.: Hemisphere Publications, 1980.

Taylor, A. J. P. *The Course of German History.* New York: Capricorn Books, 1946.

Holy See

See *Vatican.*

Homosexuality

German scientists coined the term "homosexual" in the nineteenth century to describe both same-sex erotic behavior and persons attracted to others of the same sex. Throughout history labels have existed for same-sex erotic behavior, some loosely synonymous with homosexual as an adjective, but "homosexual" as a noun is a recent invention. Scholars disagree on whether self-identified homosexuals lived in various times and cultures. Essentialists believe that homosexuals, keenly aware of their sexual orientation, existed in many societies including those described in the Bible. Constructionists hold that gay or lesbian self-perception is a modern creation, reasoning that in agrarian societies, where the biological families were the main economic unit, people lacked the leisure time to build a sexually based self-identity. Constructionists do not dispute that homosexual behavior can be found throughout history but argue that these individuals lived in urban settings such as the city-states of ancient Greece and Rome or of the Renaissance. City life allowed leisure time for community with others who shared the same sexuality and erotic pursuits. Industrialization undermined the family as an economic unit and brought spare time to the masses, enabling the rise of modern gay communities.

The Biblical Record

Because homosexual is a recent addition to the vocabulary, biblical inferences about it are complicated. The word "homosexual" does not appear in the Bible, and no known writings in Hebrew or ancient Greek contain a synonym for it. The belief that homosexual behavior is immoral is rooted in several biblical passages. The most well known is probably the story of the destruction of Sodom in Genesis 19. Although "sodomy" eventually became closely synonymous with homosexuality, most biblical scholars now posit that the city was destroyed because its residents were inhospitable to visitors sent by God. Chapters 18 and 20 of Leviticus contain statements condemning male same-sex behavior. The theme of these chapters is the distinctiveness or purity of the Jews contrasted with the habits of other peoples. These passages describe acts considered unclean, such as eating pork, rather than inherently evil, like theft. Therefore, one interpretation of Leviticus is that it condemns same-sex behavior but only as a practice of non-Jews. The distinction between these two types of wrongdoing may have been obscured as early as the third century B.C.E., when Leviticus was translated from Hebrew into Greek.

Three of Paul's New Testament writings are thought to deal with homosexuality: 1 Corinthians 6:9; 1 Timothy 1:10; and Romans 1:26-7. These passages denounce lust and unrestrained sexual behavior, not specifically homosexuality. Paul's letters implored believers to stay on the path they had chosen and eschew worldly pleasures. In Christian antiquity the idealized life was sexual abstinence. This view contrasted with Jewish beliefs that embodied an obligation to multiply. Historian John Boswell (1980) amassed much empirical evidence to support the controversial proposition that throughout the first millennium the Christian Church often was accepting of same-sex friendship in which eroticism played a central role. By the thirteenth century, however, the church had grown hierarchical and become hostile to sexuality in general. For example, until that time priests had been allowed to marry.

Thereafter, Christianity served as the cornerstone of Western reproach toward homosexuality. Religious opposition to homosexuality undoubtedly influenced its late-nineteenth-century medical construction as illness. (Only in 1973 did psychiatry drop the classification of homosexuality as a mental illness.) Many religions are silent on the question of same-sex relations. Christianity, however, continues to be a formidable source of opposition for gays and lesbians.

Changing Attitudes

The status of gays and lesbians in secular and religious institutions is remarkably similar. After the end of World War II, in 1945, homosexual communities emerged in most large U.S. cities. They first organized around issues touching their personal lives, notably police entrapment and harassment. Local governments, which regulate public safety, were the objects of the first protests by homosexuals. Then, with safety more assured, lesbians and gays sought protection from discrimination. They also took these demands to local governments. More than one hundred municipalities in the United States ban discrimination based on sexual orientation. In 1982 only one state, Wisconsin, and the District of Columbia had similar laws, but by 2005 seventeen states had passed anti-discrimination laws.

When lesbians and gays first enter any political arena, their claims to legitimacy tend to be debated in terms of morality. As they become familiar to policy makers, they establish themselves as an interest group to be accommodated in a pluralist society. The issues mature from morality to rights.

Acceptance of gays and lesbians in religious institutions followed a parallel track. Religious opinion on same-sex eroticism spreads across the board. To some, homosexuality is another gift from God. To others, it is a mortal sin. The gay and lesbian rights movement brought homosexuality to the attention of religious leaders. In many denominations this generated profound changes in teachings about sexuality. Quakers were the first major U.S. religious organization to reevaluate their position on homosexuality. They debated the morality question but before settling it moved on to accept homosexuals in their congregations. Unitarians also pioneered in welcoming gays and lesbians. Both composed ceremonies for the union of same-sex couples. Other liberal religious organizations, including the United Church of Christ and Reformed Jews, began to acknowledge a place for homosexuals in their denominations and to ordain them into the clergy. They viewed the biblical injunctions against homosexuality as focusing on condemning pagan religions and unbridled lust. Gay Christians in 1968 organized the Universal Fellowship of the Metropolitan Community Church. It takes as an article of faith that humans are sexual beings and has a primarily gay and lesbian membership, with about three hundred congregations across the United States. These denominations have all voiced their support for the civil rights of gays and lesbians when they have been a political issue.

Continuing Opposition

At the other end of the spectrum are fundamentalist Christians who maintain that homosexual behavior is sinful and immoral. Their congregations have few if any openly gay or lesbian members, but even within some of these denominations formal organizations have been established as support groups for gays and lesbians. These include the National Gay Pentecostal Alliance, Evangelicals Concerned, and Dignity (which was organized among Roman Catholics). Although many religious organizations are hostile to lesbians and gay men, studies of urban politics have found three distinct groups to be the most active in mobilizing opposition in secular matters. First are white evangelicals, represented by denominations such as Assemblies of God and Seventh-day Adventists. The Southern Baptist Convention, the largest of the numerous Baptist denominations in the United States, steadfastly opposes the civil rights of lesbians and gays. Most

but not all Baptist organizations share this position. In 1998 gay Christians from the evangelical tradition formed an organization, called SoulForce, to be a voice for acceptance in that wing of the faith. Second, black evangelicals are concentrated in many Baptist denominations. It is the strength and political activism of the evangelicals that likely causes efforts to ensure the civil rights of lesbian and gay citizens to be met with much fiercer opposition in the United States than in other Western democracies. Third, Catholic Church leaders have maintained a firm position against legal protection for homosexuals, whose behavior they regard as sinful. The position of the Catholic Church is more complex than that of the evangelicals. Although it labels homosexual behavior immoral, it views same-sex erotic orientation as a disorder but not inherently wrong.

Mainline white Protestant denominations have gay or lesbian organizations formed by their members and engage in dialogue with their parent churches. The Evangelical Lutheran Church in America, the United Methodist Church, and the Presbyterian Church (U.S.A.) prohibit sexually active gays and lesbians from serving as clergy. Nevertheless, all of these denominations are on record as opposing discrimination against lesbians and gays in civil society and confirm that gays and lesbians are welcome in their congregations. The numerous black Methodist denominations are also seen as generally supportive of gay and lesbian rights.

Marriage: Sacrament and Right

Religions recognize sexuality through ceremonies and the sacrament of marriage. Marriage is both a religious commitment and a civil contract. Gays and lesbians have sought marriage as a civil right to ensure same-sex couples enjoy the same legal benefits of married heterosexuals. At first, these same-sex legal ties were usually labeled "unions" or "partnerships." In the early and mid-2000s this has become a push for marriage equality as activists argue that labels matter. Governments label the objects they regulate. Just as butter and margarine have legal definitions so do marriage and partnerships. When objects are named, one can be viewed as superior to another. When partnerships become labels, they may be viewed as inferior to marriages. Although the idea of same-sex marriage appeared revolutionary in the context of the late twentieth century when it emerged as a matter for public debate, it appears that the early Christian Church of the first millennium had blessed same-sex relationships (Boswell, 1994).

The acceptance of same-sex civil unions appeared first in the more secular countries of northern Europe. Denmark was the first in 1989 to recognize "Registered Partners." Partnerships give same-gender couples most but not all of the civil rights of marriage. Partnership status also became policy in Norway, Sweden, Iceland, and Finland. Scandinavia has a Lutheran heritage and currently a large atheist population bloc. Partnership laws offering fewer rights than does marriage have been adopted in France, Germany, and the United Kingdom. Hungary became the first post-communist European country to recognize same-sex unions. Belgium was the first country to recognize same-sex marriage, and the Netherlands, Spain, the Czech Republic, and Slovenia followed. With the exception of Spain, this list of nations is comprised of countries where active religious participation is largely lacking. Although the proliferation of marriage rights is growing in patterns that are not always predictable, it is unlikely that countries with firmly entrenched Catholic populations will quickly add any sort of partnership rights. In July 2003, Pope John Paul II approved a twelve-page statement labeling "homosexual acts" as against "natural moral law" and warning Catholic politicians that support of same-sex unions is "gravely immoral."

In North America the politics of same-sex unions has been shaped by the religious diversity of Canada and the United States, the federal structures of the governments in both countries, and the intervention of the court systems. In both countries, clergy of select denominations or of particular congregations have for decades been performing same-sex commitment ceremonies that have no legal standing.

Court orders directed the provinces of British Columbia, Ontario, and Quebec to recognize same-sex marriages. Legislation by the Canadian Parliament then extended marriage rights to the rest of the country. In the United States a 1999 decision of the Vermont Supreme Court ordered the state legislature to enact a civil equivalent of marriage for same-sex couples. The legislature passed a civil unions bill. Legislatures in California, Connecticut, and New Jersey have established forms of legal partnerships short of marriage. Massachusetts became the first state to offer same-sex marriage in 2004 after its supreme court ordered it to do so. Meanwhile, states where evangelical Christianity is strong have been amending their constitutions to prohibit same-sex unions.

Conclusion

At the middle of the twentieth century no U.S. religious organization welcomed homosexual members, much less considered their ordination as clergy. Conditions changed rapidly. This process of change is far from over, especially among the mainline Protestant denominations. Within their ranks are members who accept the interpretations of the Bible that are supposed to refer to homosexuality as describing Jewish distinctiveness and condemning wanton sexual behavior. Others cling to the belief that the Bible intends a strict prohibition on same-sex erotic behavior. The fact that virtually all major religious organizations have gay and lesbian members who have formed their own associations guarantees that discussion of homosexuality will continue even among the most conservative of the evangelical Protestant denominations. The dialogue may work itself out along the lines of earlier religious conflicts over issues perceived in terms of morality, such as divorce or birth control.

See also *Gender; Sexuality.*

Steven H. Haeberle

BIBLIOGRAPHY

Boswell, John. *Christianity, Social Tolerance, and Homosexuality: Gay People in Western Europe from the Beginning of the Christian Era to the Fourteenth Century.* Chicago: University of Chicago Press, 1980.

———. *Same-Sex Unions in Premodern Europe.* New York: Villard Books, 1994.

Button, James W., Barbara A. Rienzo, and Kenneth D. Wald. *Private Lives, Public Conflicts: Battles over Gay Rights in American Communities.* Washington, D.C.: CQ Press, 1997.

Haeberle, Steven H. "The Role of Religious Organizations in the Gay and Lesbian Rights Movement." In *The Role of Religious Organizations in Social Movements,* edited by Barbara M. Yarnold. New York: Praeger, 1991.

Hartman, Keith. *Congregations in Conflict: The Battle over Homosexuality.* New Brunswick, N.J.: Rutgers University Press, 1996.

Pinello, Daniel R. *America's Struggle for Same-Sex Marriage.* New York: Cambridge University Press, 2006.

Human Rights

The notion of "human rights" is a quintessential twentieth-century phenomenon. It is a concept that has evolved from a historical, religious emphasis on collective entitlements earned as a result of having performed certain obligations, to a modern recognition of individual rights grounded in the inherent humanity of the person. In the early twenty-first century, as a result of parallel and, sometimes, intersecting political and religious endeavors, "human rights" includes civil, political, social, economic, developmental, *and* spiritual rights, that is, an aggregate of freedoms that characterize a broad contemporary commitment to both social justice and the right of conscience.

Religious Notions of Rights

Since recorded history, the theological interpretation of man's rights has been inextricably tied to his collective and personal obligations to God, to his fellow man, and to the community. Among the world's religions, group responsibilities have overshadowed the importance of individual rights and freedoms. In Judaism, for example, man's covenant with God was epitomized by the collective obligations that defined those who were his Chosen People. Faith in a divine mandate to maintain a separate and revealed path to holiness led to the development of a legalistic approach to rights within Judaism. Codified societal prohibitions and duties enumerated in the books of Leviticus and Deuteronomy in the Bible, as well as the divine precepts handed down in the Ten Commandments, became the basis of Hebraic law. Interpreted through the centuries by rabbis, these rules have reflected an *implied,* collective approach to rights, one in which individual entitlements have emerged as an unintended result.

Islam, too, has primarily stressed man's religious obligation, that is, his responsibility to submit to God's will. To ensure the maintenance of monotheism and a public order based on justice and mercy, Islam has based its concept of rights on divinely promulgated moral principles and collective legal regulations as codified in the Qur'an and the shari'a. Serving as the supreme law and legal framework of the state, these holy regulations have emphasized the public responsibilities, contractual obligations, and social rules that would make it possible for man, as a member of the community, to surrender to "the One." In fact, these rules were regarded as so sacred, that the state was expected to enforce divine law and extend it by jihad, or holy war, if necessary.

Hinduism has understood group rights in the context of obligations as well. Based on polytheism, mysticism, asceticism, and the teaching tradition of the Vedas, the Hindu belief system assumes order. The maintenance of the cosmic design in the social order, then, is determined by the distribution of responsibilities among the various strata of groups in society. One's position in this life is determined by one's actions in a prior life. The notion of reincarnation, therefore, carries with it obligations that are identified in the Upanishads, or the teachings of the high tradition. They spell out the dharma, or the meaning of righteousness, religion, and law; in short, all that is morally binding on human beings according to their birth (*jati*). Equally as important is the belief that all beings seek unity with the spiritual force that sustains the universe. Such beliefs have been used historically to maintain the social order and have served as a justification for the caste system, that is, the establishment of a system of rights based on birth and the responsibilities necessitated by one's social position.

Buddhism, a major world religion, is also a philosophy. Divided into three main traditions, Theravada, Mahayana, and Vajrayana, it is concerned with the discovery of true reality though religious practice and meditation. Based on sensitivity and appropriateness, individuals are expected to seek an understanding of the suffering of worldly life, its causes, and the path to its end. Buddhism teaches that by grasping the weaknesses of the world, persons are capable of becoming compassionate, and in turn becoming enlightened themselves. Such a state brings true knowledge, or liberation, gained by following the "middle path," or a course of moderation based on wisdom, virtuous behavior, and a meditative mind.

Shintoism has traditionally based a notion of "rights" within a three-dimensional universe, one in which man is part of the middle domain. It is believed that this position is maintained through the clan system and a series of obligations that individuals must carry out to serve their ancestors. Ritual purifications, offerings, supplications, and feasts place the major stress, again, on duty rather than on the rights of the individual in this patristic system.

Christianity, in contrast, has developed differently from other religions, by emphasizing both a legalistic and a relational approach to rights. This is the result of its seminal theological belief in *imago dei,* that is, the notion that individuals are created in the image and likeness of God, that they possess a spiritual nature embodied in the soul, and that they are destined to seek their own eschatological end. Christianity has, therefore, understood that people have certain natural, collective obligations to God and others, but that they also have certain personal obligations and *rights* because they possess souls. This affinity with the spiritual has generated the justification and pursuit of those rights within the state or temporal world in the pursuit of one's salvation. Thus, secular law and institutions have always been understood to be subservient to one's conscience, and thus were to be served in the context of God's revealed, codified law of the Old Testament as well as the new teachings of Jesus. Found in the Beatitudes and the commandment to love one's neighbor as oneself, the New Testament calls on Christians to obey the spirit, as well as the letter, of the law, and to respect the rights of others in their quest for salvation.

Thus for much of history, institutionalized religions emphasized and enforced the collective obligations of their adherents over personal freedoms. As a consequence, the traditional relationship between religion and the state revolved around the necessity of religions to maintain their autonomy in order to carry out their divine missions. In the past, and in many parts of the world still, religious groups have demanded a privileged status within various states to complete their spiritual tasks. Historically, some have gone so far as to pursue a fusion of church and state, or even to establish theocracies. Many have acted with fanaticism and zeal, a phenomenon that can be seen historically in the Crusades, the Inquisition, jihads, witch hunts, the writing of concordats, the establishment of class systems, and ancestor, as well as emperor, worship.

Political Notions of Rights

By the seventeenth century, political philosophers began to question traditional religious teachings and to argue for a new notion of rights: one that was universal that acknowledged duty, and that also merged notions of natural *law* with natural *rights*. The English had established the earliest political document institutionalizing rights with the writing of the Magna Carta in 1215, but this granted certain civil rights only to the nobility.

In 1625, however, Hugo Grotius wrote *De Jure Belli ac Pacis* and codified the jurisprudence that regulated the relations between sovereign states. Based on the natural law, Grotius's international legal system was founded on pragmatism and rationality, attributes that maintained an orderly state, protected property, and promoted general agreement about the conduct of society.

In 1651 Thomas Hobbes translated Grotius's natural law theory into individualistic terms in *The Leviathan*. Hobbes reasoned that man, consumed with the need for self-preservation, had a "right" to protect himself and to establish a corporate body, or state. Headed by a sovereign whose duty it would be to maintain societal order and stability, the government would thus ensure the individual's right to existence.

Thirty years later, John Locke advanced the theory of inalienable rights in *The Second Treatise on Government*. Moving traditional political thinking about rights from collective obligations to individual entitlements based on humanity, Locke maintained that all individuals, because they were *human*, had certain inherent claims against society. These included the rights to life, liberty, and property as well as the right to consent to a government by means of a social contract. Locke's philosophical notions were compatible with the English Bill of Rights. It guaranteed the right to petition, habeas corpus, taxation based on representation, free elections, the appointment of jurors, free speech and debate in the Parliament, and protection from excessive bail as well as cruel and unusual punishment.

The notion of inalienable rights also became the basis for the American democratic experiment and was reflected in the principles advanced by Thomas Jefferson in the Declaration of Independence. Honed and refined, these ideas took the form of civil and political rights in the United States and were enumerated in the Bill of Rights of its Constitution; for the first time in history, the right to the free exercise of religion and the prohibition of a state religion were expressed within a founding political document.

Renewed and Redefined Notions of Rights

A global insistence on the definition and protection of religious freedom and other human rights began to coalesce around the events leading up to World War II. President Franklin D. Roosevelt's commitment to the Four Freedoms in 1941 made clear the U.S. intention to support the right of all people to freedom of speech and expression, the right to worship, and to be free from fear and free from want. By the end of the war, a broad confluence of political events created an even greater concern for human rights. First, the Holocaust brought world attention to genocide based on religious as well as ethnic discrimination against Jews. Second, the spread of communism after the war was predicated on the enforcement of atheism in Eastern Europe, China, and various developing countries in Africa. Third, the rise of repression in autocratic states led to an exaggerated role of the state and the persecution of clerics, particularly in Latin America. Fourth, the establishment of the United Nations provided a forum for the discussion and implementation of human rights covenants in a global context.

The human rights movement was initially impelled forward as part of the mandate of the United Nations. In the

1950s that organization fostered international agreements to create a common standard of achievement among its member nations, particularly through the adoption of the Declaration of Human Rights and a series of covenants on genocide; fundamental freedoms; civil and political rights; economic, social, and cultural rights; and racial discrimination. Taken together, these documents reaffirmed the inherent dignity and equality of all people, stressing their inalienable rights to freedom, justice, and peace. Thus, the pursuit of human rights by the United Nations reawakened a political interest and commitment to them, particularly as emergent nations began to cast off their colonial yokes and seek their own nationalistic identities and interpretations of freedom and social justice.

The most significant religious group to move in a parallel direction with the United Nations to advance human rights was the Catholic Church. In 1962 it held a General Council, known as Vatican II, to renew its spiritual mission and to reappraise its relationship to the world. As a result, the council officially promulgated major decrees that changed the religious and political course of the Catholic Church and its nearly one billion adherents for all time.

The Declaration on Religious Freedom (*Dignitatis Humanae*) accepted the notion that theology is evolutionary, that conscience is formed in different ways, and that each individual has the right to the freedom of his or her own beliefs. The Declaration on the Constitution of the Church (*Lumen Gentium*) rejected the privileged political status of Catholicism in the world and committed itself to supporting those organizations and governments that would work toward the advancement of human rights. The Decree on the Bishops' Pastoral Office in the Church (*Christus Dominus*) supported the establishment of regional organizations to work on matters of social justice; and in the Decree on Ecumenism (*Unitatis Reintegration*) the council accepted the notion of interfaith cooperation to further a religious and political agenda for human rights and social justice.

In 1967 Pope Paul VI gave impetus to this institutional commitment by establishing the Pontifical Commission for Justice and Peace within the Vatican state infrastructure. Charged with the defense and advancement of international human rights, the work of the commission was further supplemented by the pope's landmark encyclical entitled *Populorum Progressio* in the same year, and his subsequent apostolic letter *Octagesima Adveniens*. Both papal writings called for the integral development of individuals and nations in society and the community of nations.

With the accession of Pope John Paul II to the papacy in 1978, the Vatican moved its international human rights agenda even further along the political continuum. By making over 100 visits to numerous nations during his pontificate, John Paul spoke "truth to power," evangelizing against unjust leaders, unresponsive political structures, and repressive governmental policies. He challenged autocratic and dictatorial regimes, raised consciousness about the persecution of indigenous peoples, called for the end of racial and ethic discrimination, and supported the right to life, work, and development. Many believe that by castigating tyrants and joining with democratic leaders John Paul was able to play a major role in the eventual downfall of communism in Eastern Europe and the rest of the world.

Although the pope's journeys served as a world forum to address political and religious leaders personally, John Paul also used encyclicals to engender a greater concern for social justice. His most important writings include *Sollicitudo Rei Socialis* and *Centesiumus Annus,* both of which call for a reappraisal of international economic rights, a recognition of the gulf between technologically developed and developing countries, and the implementation of an authentic democracy. Clearly, the Catholic notion of individual "rights" had changed radically within the twentieth century.

In conjunction with Vatican efforts to advance human rights and social justice, regional and international meetings of the Catholic hierarchy were also held in Mar Del Plata (1968), Rome (1971 and 1974), and Puebla (1979). The bishops also made breakthroughs, declaring that social justice is a "constitutive dimension" of the work of the church, that evangelization and liberation are inextricably intertwined with its mission, and that the church should give a preferential option to the poor in its mission to transform society. Thus, the Catholic Church began to shift away from many of its former expedient relationships, such as those in Latin America. Instead, it established Christian-based communities, spurred on and often challenged by lay and clerical activists, many of whom espoused liberation theology.

From the Vatican down to the grass roots, the Catholic Church had firmly established itself as a force for human rights and social justice. Creating a structural revolution, the church worked to bring an end to the "dirty war" in Argentina; to challenge the *mano blanco* in Guatemala; and to bring about an end to the dictatorship in Nicaragua, the tyranny of the right in El Salvador, and the successive military regimes in Brazil. It reached out to Eastern Europe and developing countries to create a moral vanguard against atheistic communism. It has been credited with ousting the Marcos regime in the Philippines and the Jaruzelski government in Poland.

Other Christian denominations played various roles around the world as well. In Germany, the Evangelische Kirche, that is, a combination of Lutheran and Reformed churches, led major protests and played a critical part in the transition of the former German Democratic Republic to democracy. In South Africa, the Council of Churches challenged the policy of apartheid, and with the Nobel Prize–winning Anglican archbishop, Desmond Tutu, is credited with the demise of institutionalized racial discrimination and the establishment of truth commissions to reconcile the crimes of both whites and blacks on each other. The Presbyterian Church took on the task of providing sanctuary for political exiles in the United States. The Quakers have served as the conscientious objectors of U.S. war policies, as conciliators in the Nigerian civil war, and as facilitators in the transition of Rhodesia to Zimbabwe.

Thus, Christian religious institutions have played a significant role in the advancement of human rights in the post–World War II and post–cold war world. Intersecting with various governments, they have worked to monitor repression, to educate governments and the media about human rights violations and social injustice, to lobby and bring pressure to bear on social and public institutions, and to use their resources to transform society. Recently, however, critics have claimed that Christians, in general, and Catholics, in particular, have become complacent and have missed opportunities to play positive roles in bringing about peace in places such as Kosovo, Rwanda, and Darfur. There, genocide and ethnic cleansing occurred with little religious opposition.

Other critics of religious groups also point out that many religions have not even moved to the point of trying to advance human rights in their interactions with political structures, whereas others, at the opposite end of the spectrum, have become politically involved in partisan ways. In short, religion and politics are increasingly at a crossroads over human rights.

For example, the rise of Islamic fundamentalism, particularly as it emerged in Iran under the Ayatollah Khomeini, reflected a reactionary religious response to modernism, equal rights for women, freedom of conscience, and other

basic civil, social, and economic rights for all. Afghanistan under the rule of the Taliban became even more repressive, creating conditions under which women could no longer work or be educated. Within some Islamic states there have emerged drives to create Islamic republics, that is, theocracies based on the Qur'an and the *shari'a,* thus denying religious freedom to non-Muslims. Other states, such as Turkey, reject a fusion of religion and politics and have illustrated the quandary of a nonsecular Islamic state attempting to interact with the modern world. Thus, traditional Islam, as a religion, currently faces a political human rights dilemma. How can it preserve its religious heritage and historical understanding of freedom within Islam, balance increasing calls for radical separatism among some of its followers, and allow more social tolerance, equality, reconciliation, and human rights for others?

Many institutionalized religions in a variety of developing countries also still reject modern notions of human rights. Hindu society, for example, is based largely on kinship and ethnicity rather than on social contracts or societal constructs. Others see Western interpretations and calls for human rights based on individuality as a form of "cultural imperialism." Thus they reject many contemporary ideas about human rights as expressions of "colonial" thought, and they often oppose movements toward the establishment of democracy and social justice within their societies as threats to their long-standing cultures. In an exception to this kind of thinking the Dalai Lama (Tenzin Gyatso) has been calling for freedom for the people of Tibet, who have been subjected to the rule of the Chinese since the country's takeover in 1959.

Other religions, such as Judaism, interpret personal rights today in terms of religious, ethnic, and national survival—with such historical and experiential claims based on anti-Semitism and the genocide of the Holocaust. Thus, Judaic religious belief in God's special covenant with the Jews plays an implicit role in its treatment of the political enemies of Israel within its own sphere of political influence.

Although some faith groups have taken the lead to advance human rights in the post–World War II and post–cold war world, many have not been able to continue to do so: as a new world order emerges, religious polarization, rather than spiritual reconciliation, has become the dominant force in a new type of global, spiritual politics. Some religious groups, indeed, have changed the political landscape, becoming problem makers rather than problem solvers.

In the Middle East, for example, the rise of Islamic fundamentalism has become synonymous with repression and jihad, with terrorism and martyrdom, particularly after the events of September 11. Used by Osama Bin Laden, Islamic teachings have become the rallying cry for the training of young men as terrorists and martyrs for al-Qaida. Its part in the destruction of the World Trade Center in New York triggered not only a war between the United States and Afghanistan but a division between Islamic religious moderates and radicals and a growing breach between Christians and Muslims around the world.

Yet, in this new century, the major world religions must put aside their dogmatic and political differences. They have crucial roles to play, roles that will challenge them to use the transcendent values of their spiritual beliefs for the advancement of human rights. They will be called on to help re-create the world: to mediate conflicts; to oppose oppression; to reconcile enemies; to open lines of communication; to reduce suspicions; to act as peacemakers; to provide sanctuary, resources, and support for the least free; to help reorder values; to serve as information gatherers; to promote moral discussion; to ensure disciplined listening; to promote solidarity and witness; and to continue objective truth telling. Thus, religion and politics will need to work together as the world becomes more complex and interdependent, in order to advance human rights and social justice for all.

See also: *Separation of Church and State as a Principle of Human Rights; Social Justice.*

Jo Renee Formicola

BIBLIOGRAPHY

Appleby, R. Scott. *The Ambivalence of the Sacred.* Lanham, Md.: Rowman and Littlefield, 2000.

De Bary, Theodore, and Tu Weiming, eds. *Confucianism and Human Rights.* New York: Columbia University Press, 1999.

Donnelly, Jack. *International Human Rights.* Boulder, Colo.: Westview Press, 2006.

Formicola, Jo Renee. *Pope John Paul II: Prophetic Politician.* Washington, D.C.: Georgetown University Press, 2002.

Keown, Damien V., Charles S. Prebish, and Wayne R. Husted, eds. *Buddhism and Human Rights.* Richmond, Surrey: Curzon Press, 1998.

McGraw, Barbara A., and Jo Renee Formicola, eds. *Taking Religious Pluralism Seriously.* Waco, Texas: Baylor University Press, 2005.

Meyer, Elizabeth Anne. *Islam and Human Rights.* Boulder, Colo.: Westview Press, 2006.

Rittner, Carol, John K. Roth, and Wendy Whitworth, eds. *Genocide in Rwanda: Complicity of the Churches?* St. Paul, Minn.: Paragon House, 2004.

Sharma, Arvind. *Hinduism and Human Rights: A Conceptual Approach.* New Delhi: Oxford University Press, 2004.

Humanitarianism

Humanitarianism refers to theologies of moral agency focusing on the transformation of spiritual life through active commitments to changing social, political, and economic conditions. The movement represents both a specific doctrinal strand in the evolution of American religion and a broad theme involving the commitment of many religious groups to charitable, philanthropic, and reformist endeavors.

As a specific body of doctrine, humanitarianism was a component of seventeenth-century liberal Anglican and Calvinist theology, which, evolving out of Arianism and Arminianism, emphasized the role of good works as a dimension of spiritual development and, in particular, stressed the integration of spiritual and worldly concerns. The theological rationale for humanitarianism, like its institutional expressions, developed as part of a transatlantic culture of religious and social reform.

In the eighteenth century the Enlightenment gave rise to contradictory—but ultimately complementary—religious impulses. On the one hand, it nurtured a spirit of rationalism that de-emphasized the emotional and mystical aspects of religion, humanized Christ, and portrayed the natural order as an expression of divine reason. For some, it led to the deism of American statesmen Benjamin Franklin and Thomas Jefferson. On the other hand, the Enlightenment influenced the revivalists. Jonathan Edwards (1703–1758), an American who was the intellectual leader of the Great Awakening (the revivalist movement that swept through the American colonies from 1740 to 1750), drew on the philosophy of Englishman John Locke both to conceptualize the psychology of religious experience and to promote a voluntaristic approach to religious institutions. However profound their differences, both strands of Protestantism came to share a common belief in the importance of institutions in shaping religious experience and in the capacity of individuals to change the world through reforming institutions.

Unitarian Humanitarianism

Although late eighteenth-century religious rationalism took many forms in the United States, among its most influential spokesmen were the Congregationalist clergy of eastern Massachusetts. In the 1780s they began to question openly the divinity of Christ, to argue for the possibility of universal salvation, and to advocate strict congregational independence. By the 1820s a clearly defined body of

Unitarian doctrine had emerged and, along with it, an infrastructure of charitable and cultural institutions (among them, the Boston Athenaeum and Massachusetts General Hospital) anchored by Harvard University and supported by new mercantile and industrial wealth.

Typifying Unitarianism and its humanitarian concerns was William Ellery Channing (1780–1842), a Boston clergyman who, in the first decades of the nineteenth century, emerged as an influential commentator on social and political issues. His 1816 sermon on war led to the organization of the Massachusetts Peace Society. In 1822, influenced by the efforts of the Rev. Thomas Chalmers among Edinburgh's poor, Channing organized the Beneficent Association whose goals reflected an ambitious agenda for social reform.

The association became a platform for launching an assortment of reform efforts, the most notable of which was a mission to Boston's growing population of impoverished citizens. One of Channing's colleagues, the Rev. Joseph Tuckerman (1778–1840), gave the effort national visibility through his essays on the condition of the poor. Although grounded in a social and theological conservatism that viewed poverty as a product of spiritual deficiency, the work of Tuckerman and his successors, in calling attention to the importance of social and economic factors, gave rise to a host of institutional efforts to relieve and prevent poverty.

By the 1830s, Channing, who also visited the West Indies, had become an outspoken opponent of slavery. Although he died before antislavery agitation reached its height, his forcefully expressed concerns led the way for a younger generation of Unitarian activists such as Theodore Parker (1810– 1860) and Thomas Wentworth Higginson (1823–1911), who became leaders of the movement on the eve of the Civil War.

Despite their role as pioneers in the use of voluntary associations, many Unitarians, such as Channing's colleague Ralph Waldo Emerson (1803–1882), rejected all forms, traditions, and institutions that stood in the way of spiritual self-discovery. Emerson's protégé, Henry David Thoreau (1817–1862), took this anti-institutionalism to an extreme by withdrawing from society and building a hermitage at Walden Pond in Massachusetts. (This physical withdrawal was not in any sense an intellectual disengagement, however. It was during his sojourn in the woods that Thoreau wrote "Civil Disobedience"—an essay that later would have a profound impact on humanitarian reformers such as India's Mahatma Gandhi and America's Martin Luther King Jr. as

well as trenchant criticisms of capitalist society.) Others in the Unitarian tradition pursued reform by organizing alternative communities such as Brook Farm in Massachusetts, where from 1841 to 1847 a group of writers and scholars experimented in cooperative living.

Trinitarian Humanitarianism

For Trinitarians (believers in the doctrine of the Trinity, unlike Unitarians), resolving the tension between their Calvinist belief in the omnipotence of God and the efficacy of human action was no easy task. The influence of Enlightenment psychology led Jonathan Edwards to explore the theological implications of the link between the emotions and the intellect. His psychology of conversion clarified the role of human agency by suggesting that believers did not have to wait passively for God to act. A variety of activities—the reform of individual behavior, family worship, "social religion," and evangelical preaching—could "awaken" and prepare them for "evidences of God's saving mercy." Thus Edwards both revitalized Calvinism and legitimated assertive lay piety.

The efforts to shift the center of spiritual gravity from the clergy to the congregation and legitimate religious voluntarism would have a dramatic political impact. Because the church was a public institution, debate over the fundamentals of spiritual sovereignty and ecclesiastical polity inevitably involved the newly awakened laity. As time went on, then, the debate moved from a theological to a political focus, encouraging a shift in the nature of public discourse. That shift, in turn, helped to fuel the struggle for American independence from Britain, which began in 1763, and the emergence of political voluntarism based on abstract principles and harnessed to tactics of popular mobilization and electoral and legislative strategizing.

Through the 1780s political, not social, reform framed the Trinitarians' agenda, and politics, not theology, ultimately moved Trinitarians into the forefront of social movement activity. Led by Timothy Dwight (1752–1817)—preacher, poet, politician, and president of Yale University from 1795 to 1817—Trinitarians began to create entirely new kinds of voluntary organizations in the hope of stemming the rising tide of religious dissent and irreligion in Connecticut and in the nation at large.

Though maintaining the central tenets of Calvinism, Dwight and his protégés—Nathaniel W. Taylor (1786–1858), Lyman Beecher (1775–1863), and Leonard Bacon (1802–

1881)—built Edwards's ideas about the importance of human agency in advancing God's purposes into a theological justification of the role of institutions in social and political reform.

Taylor, Yale's first professor of divinity, emphasized the role of man's free, moral, rational, and creative nature in the process of salvation and, in doing so, highlighted the role of churches in nurturing those capacities. This theological innovation enabled Taylor and his followers to replace conceptions of humankind as passive instruments of divine will with a more activist vision.

Beecher, a brilliantly persuasive preacher, pioneered a pragmatic and profoundly influential activist response to the new religious marketplace. Dismayed by the political and economic disorder that characterized the presidency of Andrew Jackson (1829–1837), Beecher became convinced that the churches—not as direct political actors but as forces for the political empowerment of their members—could play a central role in the redemption of society. To this end he encouraged believers to create voluntary associations to act in every domain of public life. These associations became vehicles for a broad range of social reform efforts, including antislavery, Bible, debating, library, mechanics, and temperance societies; schools and colleges; and a national network of lyceums, which provided forums for Americans to discuss public issues and hear the ideas of leading philosophers, scientists, and literary figures.

Leonard Bacon, pastor of New Haven's Center Church and professor of divinity at Yale, focused his theological energies on organizational issues, writing pioneering essays on stewardship and the governance of associations. He engineered the emergence of Congregationalism as the nation's first denominational body, as well as played a leading role in antislavery agitations.

If Beecher and Bacon mapped the forward integration of Edwardsian logic from the church to the world, Horace Bushnell (1802–1876), another avatar of the "New Haven theology," integrated backward from church to family life by redefining religious conversion as a developmental process involving child-rearing, schooling, and family life. This step necessarily extended spiritual citizenship to women and children and, in doing so, constructed a theological rationale for intensive religious investment in innovative educational and youth-serving activities.

Conservative Dissent

In the years leading up to the Civil War the rising power of the Trinitarians' voluntary enterprises alarmed some Americans. Theological conservatives such as Francis Wayland (1796–1865), the leading political economist and Baptist intellectual of the period, challenged the Trinitarians' notion that individuals could delegate moral responsibility to associations. They feared that Trinitarians would lead people to believe that benevolence consisted only of giving money, thereby excusing the giver from "personal service and self-denial in the cause of charity." Despite Wayland's qualms, Baptist and Methodist institutions were springing up all over the country by the mid-nineteenth century. Unlike the Congregationalist enterprises, which sought to serve the general public and a broad variety of humanitarian purposes, the conservatives' institutions primarily served their coreligionists and tended to be local rather than national in focus.

The Congregationalists' increasing attention on humanitarian concerns led ultimately to a basis for accommodation with rival denominations and to alliances among theological liberals in support of national reform initiatives. The most important of these was the U.S. Sanitary Commission, a private group that provided public health services for the Union Army. A national enterprise modeled on the Trinitarians' antebellum "benevolent empire," the commission eventually aroused the opposition of theological conservatives, who argued that its professionalized, bureaucratic institutionalization of relief efforts and emphasis on quantifiable efficiency and effectiveness drained these activities of the essential attributes of Christian charity, particularly the spiritual bond between giver and receiver. Such struggles, replayed with greater intensity after the Civil War, nearly wrecked the effort to reconstruct the defeated Confederacy.

Religion and Social Reform: 1870–1930

In the late 1860s religious humanitarians turned their attention to the problems of poverty, dependency, and public order resulting from industrialization and urban growth. In doing so, they took the lead in organizing state boards of charities that sought to centralize, rationalize, and professionalize relief for the poor. By the mid-1870s a more ambitious agenda had emerged. It sought not merely to ameliorate poverty but also to prevent it through scientific fact-gathering and cooperation between public and private agencies. These efforts laid the groundwork for a national organization—the National Conference of Charities and Corrections

—which helped to launch a national charities reform movement.

By the late 1880s many Christians, liberal and conservative alike, were becoming uncomfortable with approaches to poverty and dependency whose calculated punitiveness was plainly at odds with scriptural conceptions of charity. The response, like so many aspects of American humanitarianism, drew on the transatlantic culture of charity, particularly initiatives such as London's pioneering settlement house, Toynbee Hall, which opened its doors in 1884. Within two years American clergy and religiously committed laity were experimenting with workingmen's clubs, neighborhood guilds, and settlement houses. By 1910 more than four hundred settlement houses were operating in the United States.

Jane Addams (1860–1935), the movement's most articulate and influential advocate, gave voice to a uniquely American combination of pragmatism and spirituality, calling for the extension of "democracy beyond its political expression," bringing "the accumulation of civilization to those portions of the race which have little," and promoting a revival of Christianity's "early humanitarian aspects." Viewed as particularly important was the capacity of the movement to address the spiritual impoverishment of the upper classes. The settlement house offered a setting in which one could combine spirituality with the practical tasks of political education and organizing.

The settlement houses played a key role in the development of the social sciences and social work. Pursuing social, educational, health, housing, and economic initiatives, settlement workers were transformed from well-intentioned amateurs into social service professionals. Close ties to universities ensured that the work of these community-based enterprises was both guided by and served to enrich broader, more systematic forms of knowledge building and to inform the creation of social policy. Ultimately, however, the conditions for successful settlement house work—political pragmatism, the cultivation of expertise, professionalism, and nonsectarianism—undermined the movement's religious commitment.

Though certainly the most influential manifestation of Social Gospel humanitarianism, the progressively oriented settlement houses were only one of many humanitarian responses to the urban crisis. Challenging the comfortable assumptions of middle-class parishioners, Kansas Congregationalist minister Charles M. Sheldon sought in his best-selling novel *In His Steps* (1896) to promote social activism by pointing out the ways in which social ills resulted from the failure of Christians to carry their professed beliefs into their public and private lives. Baptist Walter Rauschenbusch, who spent the 1890s preaching to a working-class congregation in New York's Hell's Kitchen, articulated an encompassing rationale for the affirmative role of religion in public life in his 1907 bestseller, *Christianity and the Social Crisis.* His delineation of the stake of the church in the social movement not merely as an instrument for shaping the consciences of individuals but also as a centrally important social institution in its own right did much to define the role of religion in American public life for the rest of the twentieth century.

Although at the beginning of the century interest in the social implications of the Social Gospel was limited to a small group of social reformers and theological students, as the Progressive Movement gained momentum all the leading Protestant, Catholic, and Jewish denominations embraced the Social Gospel. By the late 1920s the churches' social mission had begun to include international affairs, social justice, racial problems, the family, education—almost every phase in the development of the individual and society. Through the 1920s denominational bodies, congregations, and interdenominational organizations made significant commitments to various forms of service provision, particularly youth-serving activities. Churches also became active promoters of secular philanthropy, particularly the Community Chest and community foundation movement.

If religious and other private charitable initiatives were eclipsed by the Great Depression of the 1930s and the Second World War, the challenges of the postwar years—particularly America's emergence as the preeminent leader of the free world—did much to rekindle activist humanitarian commitment. America's donning of the mantle of global leadership set in motion a process of national self-examination that focused on broad issues of public values as well as on the nation's failure to live up to its own ideals, particularly racial equality and religious tolerance. Often working through denominations and ecumenical bodies such as the Federal Council of Churches and the National Council of Churches, clergy and laity led efforts to right long-standing wrongs. In the fifties and sixties, churches were in the forefront of the civil rights, antipoverty, and anti–Vietnam War movements—even though the clergy and denominational executives often positioned themselves considerably in advance (and to the left) of the attitudes of the faithful.

The Rise of Conservative Humanitarianism

In the postwar years liberal elements in Protestantism, Catholicism, and Judaism had forged a humanitarian consensus that sought relevance by de-emphasizing spirituality in favor of "civil religion" and liberal reformism that promoted internationalism, religious tolerance, women's rights, and racial and economic equality. But in doing so, liberals opened the way for a resurgence of religious conservatism embraced by Catholics disenchanted with the edicts of the Second Vatican Council; ultra-Orthodox Jews rooted in mystical traditions and Zionists for whom the national interests of the state of Israel eclipsed social democratic pluralist ideals; Southern Baptists, Methodists, Presbyterians, and a variety of fundamentalist and evangelical groups resisting the civil rights movement; and groups within every faith tradition for whom "relevance" and authenticity were spiritual, not political, issues.

The theological anti-institutionalism of conservative Christians was affirmed by the increasing secularism of American culture after World War I. But political events after World War II pushed conservative groups toward activism and into unlikely partnerships over issues such as government support for religious institutions, race, women's rights (including reproductive freedom), and patriotism. Legislation and court decisions on race, reproductive rights, and religious freedom alarmed believers disenchanted with the liberal tilt of the mainstream denominations and helped to transform conservative Christians into activist Christian conservatives.

By 1990 Christian conservatives had moved from being a reactive voting bloc that reluctantly chose between the lesser of evils to a tightly organized, proactive political force that not only played a major role in the national nominating process but also began to articulate its own political program. The key actor in this process was Marvin Olasky, a young Yale-educated journalist, whose book *The Tragedy of American Compassion* (1992) offered a harsh critique of the liberal welfare state and a thorough reinterpretation of the history of American social welfare and its religious roots. Rejecting mainline religion's perfectionist humanitarianism (the evolution of which paralleled and justified the growth of the liberal state), Olasky offered a radical anti-institutionalist approach to charity that stressed the importance of one-to-one relationships between those who give and those who receive. Offering a common meeting ground for secular and religious conservatives, Olasky's religiously grounded

rationale for a fundamental reordering of social welfare policy served as the intellectual road map for the "Republican revolution" that began to unfold in 1994 with the midterm congressional elections. However, Olasky's greatest influence probably came from his relationship with George W. Bush. In 1995 he became an occasional adviser to Bush, the newly elected governor of Texas, who put some of Olasky's policy proposals into practice, especially the use of religious charities to solve social problems. Bush believed these initiatives were successful, and they influenced his policies when he entered the White House. As president, he created the White House Office of Faith-Based and Community Initiatives. Olasky is credited as the source of the term "compassionate conservative," the theme of Bush's 2000 presidential campaign.

Olasky's significance went well beyond politics. In surprising ways, his writings and role as editor of *World* magazine gave voice to ideas that had become increasingly important to countercultural elements in the liberal community, particularly those involved with disabilities rights and the provision of human services. When the states, forced by the federal courts to release the mentally disabled from institutional care, sought help in establishing community-based treatment mechanisms, the federations of Jewish, Catholic, and Protestant charities proclaimed themselves unequipped to deal with the problems of the profoundly disabled who made up the bulk of the population of state institutions. Much greater enthusiasm was found among less traditional groups: minority social services organizations spawned by President Lyndon B. Johnson's War on Poverty, new groups created by members of Catholic religious orders newly empowered by the Second Vatican Council, and radical social workers disenchanted with the traditional institutional methods of social provision. Between the mid-1970s and mid-1980s state governments placed the majority of institutionalized mentally disabled clients in nonprofit group homes, many of them operated by conservative religious individuals and groups.

Developing incrementally over two decades, deinstitutionalization and privatization became components of the devolutionary policies of the Republican revolutionaries for whom Olasky's work had supplied a coherent, if contested, rationale. While these ideas and practices present a compelling alternative to the agendas of liberal religion and the liberal state, the question remains as to whether such individualized and spiritualized approaches to helping others constitute *humanitarianism* as the term is commonly understood. Olasky's claim—summarized in *Renewing American Compassion* (1996)—suggests that, framed by government policy and phrased in reformist rhetoric, such efforts to transform society from the inside out and the bottom up might be, for all of their emphasis on individuals, no less socially and institutionally perfectionist and, as such, might appropriately be viewed as a new variant of humanitarianism.

See also *Civil Society; Enlightenment; Philanthropy; Social Gospel; Unitarianism.*

Peter Dobkin Hall

BIBLIOGRAPHY

Black, Amy E., Doughlas L. Koopman, and David K. Ryden. *Of Little Faith: The Politics of George W. Bush's Faith-Based Initiative.* Washington, D.C.: Georgetown University Press, 2004.

Davis, Allen F. *Spearheads for Reform: The Social Settlements and the Progressive Movement, 1890–1914.* New York: Oxford University Press, 1967.

Foster, Charles I. *An Errand of Mercy: The Evangelical United Front, 1790–1837.* Chapel Hill: University of North Carolina Press, 1960.

Frederickson, George M. *The Inner Civil War: Northern Intellectuals and the Crisis of the Union.* New York: Harper and Row, 1965.

Griffen, Clifford S. *Moral Stewardship in the United States, 1800–1865.* New Brunswick: Rutgers University Press, 1960.

Hall, Peter Dobkin. *The Organization of American Culture, 1700–1900: Institutions, Elites, and the Origins of American Nationality.* New York: New York University Press, 1982.

Hodgson, Godfrey. *The World Turned Right Side Up: A History of the Conservative Ascendancy in America.* Boston: Houghton Mifflin, 1996.

Katz, Michael B. *In the Shadow of the Poorhouse: A Social History of Welfare in America.* New York: Basic Books, 1986.

Olasky, Marvin. *Renewing American Compassion: how Compassion for the Needy Can Turn Ordinary Citizens into Heroes.* New York: Free Press, 1996.

———. *The Tragedy of American Compassion.* Washington, D.C.: Regnery, 1992.

Wright, Conrad Edick. *The Transformation of Charity in Postrevolutionary New England.* Boston: Northeastern University Press, 1992.

Wuthnow, Robert, ed. *Faith and Philanthropy in America.* San Francisco: Jossey-Bass, 1990.

Hungary

A partly Catholic, partly Protestant country in central Europe, Hungary between the ninth and early twentieth centuries included contemporary Croatia, Slovakia, and parts of Austria, Romania, Serbia, and Ukraine.

Hungary is a buffer between the East and the West. For centuries wars were fought against non-Christians attacking from Asia. Acting as a "fortress of Christianity" and "defender of the Christian faith" created a strong feeling among Hungarians of having been chosen for a historical mission, and this became a key notion of the national identity.

The Reformation started rather early in Hungary, and it resulted in many religious wars during the sixteenth and seventeenth centuries. These wars divided the country into two parts: western Catholic and eastern Protestant. The Hungarian national identity emerged mainly from the Protestants. The Hungarian principality of Transylvania declared very early the principle of religious tolerance, even for Unitarians (1568), and Hungary has ever since remained multidenominational. During the seventeenth century a heavy Counter-Reformation policy was launched. Mainly during the eighteenth century heavy restrictions were placed on Protestants. In the Counter Reformation the Habsburgs-dominated state cooperated with the Catholic Church. Joseph II, the anticlerical and enlightened absolutist Habsburg emperor—who was not coroneted and refused to swear to the old laws of the country—not only attacked the traditional laws and institutions but also codified religious tolerance.

In Hungary, Catholics and Protestants have ever since enjoyed equal rights. Still, until the end of the nineteenth century the Catholic Church enjoyed special rights in public life, working as a kind of established church.

Although the Hungarians were predominantly Catholic, the national revival was begun mainly by the Protestant nobility and educated middle class. Therefore, the Hungarian national identity absorbed many Protestant elements, including a new, Protestant official national anthem to replace the old one, Our Lady.

The modernization of the state has, since the end of the nineteenth century, been driven mainly by the liberal Protestant aristocracy. During this period this political elite started secular legislation to implement civil marriage and divorce as well as public education, following the idea of separation of state and church. This process made for much conflict between the Catholic Church and the political elite (Kulturkampf).

Between the two world wars a strong cooperation emerged between state and churches in reaction to the Treaty of Trianon (1920) and the communist coup (1919). During this period the Hungarian political community labeled itself Christian-nationalist. Although the legal situa-

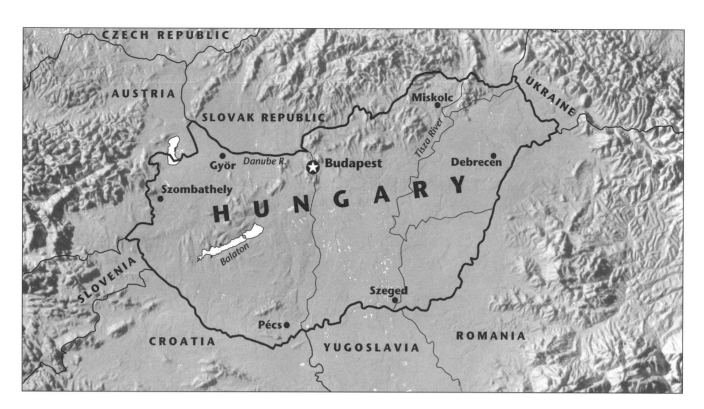

tion of the Catholic Church and the two large Protestant churches didn't change, religion had a tremendous influence on the life of the state. At the same time, the Hungarian national identity absorbed a lot of religious elements, and the Catholic Church adapted itself to Hungarian nationalism, opposed by the church before World War I. This period was characterized by the cooperation of the Protestant, now antiliberal political elite and the Catholic Church.

Totalitarianism and Religion

Communist leaders, imposed by the Soviet Union following World War II, tried to replace the indigenous society with their own ideological order. Political parties, civil organizations, even informal clubs were forbidden. After 1948–1949 the network of religious associations was prohibited, as were all other associations. The state attempted to destroy the public presence and influence of religion. Still, the churches remained the only public bodies not entirely controlled by the state. They became the refuge of the disinherited and the persecuted, all those people who were not willing to accept totalitarianism. The religious organizations were destroyed, their property was confiscated, and thousands of priests, ministers, and members of religious orders were imprisoned, deported, or exiled. Show trials against church dignitaries—such as Cardinal Mindszenty (1949) and

Cardinal Grösz (1951)—were used to weaken the social prestige of church leaders. Prelates and church activists were placed under surveillance by the police or by the agents of the Communist Party. The last imprisoned Catholic priest was released only in 1976. The churches were placed under the authority of the State Church Office. This state agency, together with the secret police, controlled religious life, even putting religious services and the content of sermons under surveillance.

Still, the destruction or paralysis of these organizations did not eliminate the faithful or their religious needs. Lay persons soon began to fulfill religious duties by themselves. The churches started to live from their social roots, in parishes and in newly emerging religious circles—"basis communities"—often unknown even to the church authorities. Totalitarian legislation labeled underground church groups, similarly to all other autonomous groups, as "organizations against the state." Activists and members in such "illegal" groups and communities became a central target of persecution. In their continuous regeneration, religious communities relied on the religious socialization in the family. It broke the monopoly of communism by organizing society and shaping its culture. Religious communities maintained cultural and social positions that contradicted the official expectations and ideology as espoused in the schools and the media. These groups consciously cultivated their faith and culture by educating their members. Their mutual support created a visible social alternative to the totalitarian system, before and independently from the political opposition movements of the 1970s and 1980s. By this role the underground churches exercised a political function even if they did not issue political declarations in explicit opposition to the communist system.

Social Discrimination of the Believers

The most basic and enduring dimension of the confrontation between religion and politics during the communist era was the attempt by the regime to form a new society without ties to the old system and culture. This goal coincided with the antireligious Marxist ideology. The denial of religion became a formal requirement for party members. Believers were discriminated against in admission to higher education. Practicing Christians could not become (or remain) teachers, journalists, police or army officers, or high-ranking administrators. They could not reach leading positions at all, because the precondition for these was party membership. Discrimination in evaluations and promotions reduced incomes and living standards, and it led to less access to information and fewer chances of sociopolitical participation. Curriculum content and propaganda furthered the same antireligious reeducation. For four decades, openly confessed belief resulted in formal social discrimination. Communism did not create a new society but, rather, a secularist upper class.

Official policy was to appoint only those who were avowed secularists and atheists as heads and chief executives in the state-owned economy and the entire public domain. Believers who were in the lower ranks of the social hierarchy had to hide their religious convictions if they wanted to keep white-collar jobs. Communism succeeded in implanting the impression that nonreligiosity was a normal requirement for an academic career, for higher appointments, and for occupations in education and the media. After some decades of communism, these formal proscriptions received tacit acceptance by the ruling strata. Educated in a totalitarian and secularist spirit, many people were prejudiced against any faith and against believers, whom they dismissed as not being able to convert to modernity. The institutionalization

of the second-rate status of religious citizens thus became independent from the state and its political structure. It also became a social fact that survived the political changes of 1989 and the disintegration of the communist system.

After the Collapse of the Communist State

During the collapse of the communist state, many groups protested against the State Church Office. Thus, in 1989, even before the free elections, the office was closed. A new constitution written by the communists and the opposition leaders stated (section 60) that in Hungary everyone has the right to freedom of thought, conscience, and religion. It also called for the separation of state and church. A new law was enacted concerning the right and method of church registration (a formal legal process done by a court in the capital; a registered church has privileges such as tax exemption). This law required only one hundred signatures (from anyone) and a copy of the main tenets of a religious community. Since that time church registration has been rather easy.

The renewal of the big churches in post-communist Hungary includes the restoration of their institutional framework. The law on restitution of church property excludes lands and commercial or industrial buildings but guarantees the restitution of former denominational institutions. More than eighty Catholic religious orders reemerged. Even the present proportion of 4 percent religious schools is an important step to plurality. Similarly, churches gained broadcasting time in the public media. Although Hungary has been a dominantly Catholic country (the denominational distribution in 1997: 54.1 percent Catholic, 14.7 percent Calvinist, 4.5 percent Lutheran, 0.4 percent Jewish, 1.0 percent other, 0.7 percent unknown, and 24.6 percent nonaffiliated), it is a rather secularized country. Its degree of secularization is about the European average.

The consensus concerning religion and churches collapsed shortly after 1990 when the first freely elected government wanted to adopt the German state-church pattern. It would mean religious education in public schools and financial subsidies for religious institutions and schools. Still, churches claimed back a large part of their school buildings confiscated by the communist state. The rightist government supported these claims, whereas the liberals and post-communist parties heavily blocked them. Thus a new conflict arose concerning the relation between politics and religion. Since 1990 Hungarian political life has been divided into two large political camps, differing from each other in regard to their relations to the communist past and religion. The main political dividing line is neither an economic nor a class conflict; it is a cultural clash. And even the presence of religion, in various degrees, in public life is itself highly debated by political actors.

The strong association between nonreligion and upward mobility under communism divided the Hungarian population both culturally and structurally. Socialists and left liberals represent a historically stabilized ideological opposition to religion and churches. Rightists and conservatives receive most of the religious votes. The religious holidays, state subsidies to churches, tax exemption, and the clash of human rights and the religious taboos of homosexuality and abortion are the main subjects of these debates in which two large camps import the main arguments from the West. It is important to note that the Hungarian Socialist Party and its allies promote the idea of a neutral state, whereas both the left and the right argue for religious freedom. Still, public life has kept some religious characteristics: the national anthem starts with a prayer to God; one of the largest state holidays is St. Stephen's Day (August 20), on which the political elite attend a Catholic mass despite their personal religious affiliations.

Religion and Political Community

In Hungary, as in the other central and eastern European countries, the meaning and history of nation and state are quite different from those in western states. Here, the loyalty to the ethnic-cultural group was and still is more important than loyalty to state, because political society is a cultural-linguistic entity that is independent of any state. The state and its institutions, symbols, laws, and constitution are important only if they serve the interest of the ethnic nation. Of course, in these countries one can also find political religions that integrate political society and support political order, political identity, and loyalty, but these religions refer only to one ethnic group. The ethnic religion is civil religion in the wider sense, because it integrates society and political order; it has many community and political functions. However, ethnic religion differs significantly from Western civil religion, because although ethnic religion can transcend socioeconomic differences, it is not intended to be an overarching worldview of every citizen of the state.

In brief, there is neither civil religion nor ethnic religion in Hungary. Because about one-third of the world's Hungarian-speaking people live outside Hungary, the Hungarian

national identity has focused more on ethnicity than citizenship both inside Hungary and among the Hungarian minorities in neighboring countries. Hungarians belong mainly to Catholic or Calvinist churches. Whereas Calvinism (and Unitarianism as well) is strongly connected to Hungarian ethnicity, the relation of Catholicism to Hungarian minorities varies. The majority of Hungarians are Catholic, and in the Orthodox countries (like Romania, Serbia, and Ukraine) Catholicism, in addition to language and culture, is the marker of the Hungarian ethnic group. Hungarian minorities in Orthodox countries can be considered to have an ethnic religion. Catholic or Calvinist churches are used for national celebrations, and in these countries more than 80 percent of the Hungarians are religious. One can see national flags even at a wholly religious feast, as national feasts are held in churches. The ethnic and religious borders do not coincide with each other in the case of the Hungarian minority in Slovakia because the overwhelming majority of Hungarians and the majority of Slovaks are Catholic. Thus, in Slovakia, because Catholicism cannot signify and strengthen ethnic divisions, it is far from being the Hungarian ethnic religion.

Hungary is a different question than the Hungarian minority abroad. The nonexistence of any civil or ethnic religion in Hungary refers to the lack of moral and symbolic consensus and to the lack of a religion legitimated by the government. Each government over the years must legitimate itself only through the fulfillment of its economical or material promises.

After World War II the Hungarian nation (the identity of the people) and state (the government) contradicted each other because of the ideological considerations of the party-state. At the end of the war Hungary was seen as a defeated country. Because of historical-political reasons, the people were dealt with as fascists. The succeeding generations have lived in a society without revered flags, national holidays, national hymns, or state symbols. Indeed, they are there, but they awaken enthusiasm only in one segment of the society, and they are highly debated.

Hungarian political society split into two parts during the modernization of the country at the end of the nineteenth century. This split, which still exists today, is not along class or ethnic lines. The main division between the two societies is their relation to cultural modernization and local society. During the years of socialism this division of Hungarian society was covert; now it is more open. The two societies not only have different parties, but they tend to build up their own institutional establishments. Thus, public religion can actually be found in Hungary, but it does not refer to the entire society. One of the two societies is integrated and symbolized by the common values contained in Christianity—without denominational differentiations.

Ethnic religion exists mainly among Hungarian minorities in Orthodox countries, but it opposes rather than supports the political order of these states. Ethnic religion can also be found in Hungary, but although it has features similar to the civil religions in the West, its role and effects are very different because it exists as an island in the society.

Attila K. Molnar

BIBLIOGRAPHY

Andras, Emeric, and Julius Morel. *Hungarian Catholicism: A Handbook.* Toronto: St. Elizabeth of Hungary Parish, 1983.

Beeson, Trevor. Discretion and Valour. *Religious Conditions in Russia and Eastern Europe.* Rev. ed. Philadelphia: Fortress Press, 1982.

———. "Church and Religion in a Communist State, 1945–1990." *New Hungarian Quarterly* (spring 1991): 59–69.

———. "Religion in Eastern and Central Europe." Social Compass 1 (1995): 17–26.

Tomka, Miklós. "Stages of Religious Change in Hungary." In *World Catholicism in Transition,* edited by Thomas M. Gannon. New York: Macmillan, 1988.

I

Ibn Khaldun

Distinguished Muslim historian, sociologist, and philosopher. Abd al-Rahman Ibn Khaldun (1332–1406) wrote *Muqaddimah,* the acclaimed first volume of his world history, *Kitab al-Ibar. Muqaddimah* described his philosophy of human culture and civilization, and, in particular, the reasons for the rise and fall of civilizations.

Life and Work

Born in Tunis to an influential family who served a succession of Muslim dynasties in Spain and then in Tunis, Ibn Khaldun pursued an education that followed the traditional Islamic model. At age twenty he entered public life as secretary to the sultan of Fez, Morocco, but the political turmoil that ensued after the collapse of the Almohad dynasty in North Africa spurred his departure in 1362 for Spain, where he entered the service of the king of Granada.

It turned out to be a brief interlude, however, for shortly Ibn Khaldun left Spain for reasons of political prudence and returned to North Africa, where he served as prime minister in the court of the sultan of Bourgie, Algeria. Over the next several years Ibn Khaldun's life was entangled in a complex web of political and diplomatic intrigue and military skirmish.

In 1375, weary of this turbulent life, he retired to a castle near Oran, Algeria, to begin work on *Muqaddimah.* In 1382, en route to Mecca, Ibn Khaldun arrived in Cairo, which appealed to his cosmopolitan political interests. Not surprisingly, when the Mameluke sultan offered him the post of chief justice, Ibn Khaldun needed little persuading, putting off his pilgrimage plans.

As chief justice, Ibn Khaldun swept away the political corruption that had clogged up the city and suffocated the courts, leading his enemies, in revenge, to instigate a commission of inquiry into his tenure. Although no charges leveled against him were upheld, the inquiry affected his usefulness for the patronage-minded rulers. When the sultan requested his resignation, Ibn Khaldun, having recently lost his family in a shipwreck between Tunis and Egypt, resumed his interrupted pilgrimage to Mecca in 1387 and then returned to Egypt, intending to lead a quiet life.

The retired life was not to be. In 1400 the sultan took him and a group of leading jurists and scholars to Damascus to undertake urgent negotiations with the Tartar conqueror Tamerlane. The Tartar reputedly was impressed enough with Ibn Khaldun's abilities to offer him a court position, which Ibn Khaldun declined. He took advantage of the offer, however, to collect valuable historical information on Mongol and Tartar history and to rehearse with Tamerlane some Maghrebi history. Later he was able to escape the Tartar sacking of Damascus, rescuing in the process many of the city's important nobles before returning to Egypt. There, as a reward for his services, he was reappointed chief justice. Shortly thereafter, in 1406, he died at age seventy-four.

On Politics and Religion

In *Muqaddimah* Ibn Khaldun was able to draw on his vast practical experience of public life and on his meticulous scholarly investigations to delineate the relationship between political affairs and religious life. He was ambivalent, however, about where to place religion in society, whether as an established value at the center or as a secondary source of influence. For him religion had two senses: it was either a social ornament or a ruling ideology, useful or necessary.

Ibn Khaldun looked at the secular roots of political institutions, convinced that the theocratic view of history was too simplistic and lacking in empirical realism. He argued that political society is founded on group cohesion, or solidarity (*asabiyah*). Aware of other traditions that have the prophet Muhammad abolishing kinship, Ibn Khaldun preempted criticism by turning to the same source to find the Prophet intending his followers to understand how kinship is useful only when blood ties lead kin to cooperate and help one another in the face of danger. Indeed, Ibn Khaldun defended kinship by asserting that the Prophet did not intend to neglect group solidarity, but merely to emphasize its relative merit as a worldly arrangement vis-à-vis the higher obedience centered in revelation. In all this, Ibn Khaldun was seeking to discern the sociological laws in collective historical institutions and hierarchies while distancing himself from dogma. According to him, rulership as such was not divine but was the outgrowth of social development because rulership evolved naturally from social solidarity. Indeed, the establishment and the effectiveness of laws, religions, and institutions depended on the underlying social solidarity.

In his writings, Ibn Khaldun gave preeminence to such solidarity, calling it identical with the spiritual community. No religious movement can succeed unless it is based on solidarity, he concluded. Solidarity is the backbone of religion as it is of the state. Such views also have implications for political legitimacy, Ibn Khaldun noted. He was at pains to point out that effective leadership is a matter not of revealed truth but of pragmatic competence. Good leaders are determined by the quality of their rule as seen by their subjects rather than by the purity of the ideals to which they subscribe. Governments, then, are the just deserts of the societies in which they are found: "If such rulership is good and beneficial, it will serve the interests of the subjects. If it is bad and unfair, it will be harmful to them and cause their destruction" (*Muqaddimah*). Ibn Khaldun, writing here as a scholar, was not primarily concerned with spelling out the practical institutional arrangements by which harm may be determined and remedied. Rather, his insights would be compatible with modern notions of democratic political liberalism, constitutional accountability, and participation.

Ibn Khaldun's views on the relation of politics and religion continued to be ambivalent. He seemed in one move to lean toward the centrality of politics only to revert to religion in the next. One must note, however, that Ibn Khaldun's theory of history received its most cogent and explicit development from the preponderance of fact and practice, thereby implying he downgraded religious speculation in favor of empirical observation. In his methodology, he was a pragmatist first and a moralist last. Thus it is still a valid question about where religion stands after the dust has settled.

See also *Islam*.

Lamin Sanneh

BIBLIOGRAPHY

Gibb, H. A. R. "The Islamic Background of Ibn Khaldun's Political Theory." In *Studies on the Civilization of Islam, Collected Essays,* edited by Stanford J. Shaw and William R. Polk. London: Routledge and Kegan Paul, 1962.

Issawi, Charles. *An Arab Philosophy of History.* London: John Murray, 1963.

Weber, Max. *The Sociology of Religion.* Translated by Ephraim Fischoff. Boston: Beacon Press, 1963.

Ibn Taimiyya

Islamic theologian and scholar. Ibn Taimiyya (1263–1328) is perhaps the most important medieval theologian inspiring the thought and actions of modern Muslim fundamentalists. Born in northeastern Syria, at age six he and his family moved to Damascus, fleeing advancing Mongol armies. The rest of his life was spent in the Mamluk realms of Syria and Egypt. His was a family of scholars, and he followed that tradition, later succeeding his father as professor of Hanbali law in Damascus. His temperament and the times, however, worked against a quiet life of scholarship. Ever inclined to act on his theological principles, Ibn Taimiyya was often jailed or placed under house arrest. His death came while he was imprisoned, yet again, in the Damascus citadel. Even so, at other times he was often favored by the Mamluk rulers and more than once was appointed to exhort the faithful to *jihad* (holy war).

Ibn Taimiyya was a strict scripturalist. He insisted on the supremacy of the Qur'an, the Islamic holy book, and the *hadith,* narratives of the sayings and actions of the prophet Muhammad, in their literal sense to such an extent that his theological rivals accused him of anthropomorphism. His stern literalist stance pitted him against the more esoteric interpretations advanced by the Sufi mystics.

He was uncompromising in his approach to both non-Muslims and to non-Sunni Muslims. He was first jailed for agitating for summary punishment against a Christian alleged to have insulted the Prophet. His strictures on the Shi'i Alawis were as harsh. They were, he maintained, more infidel than Jews or Christians, and fighting them was obedience to God. Such fulminations from past centuries resonated into the twentieth century, finding acceptance among Muslim Brethren in Syria in their resistance to the rule of Hafiz al-Asad's Alawi-dominated government. Ibn Taimiyya even questioned the more accommodationist positions of the mainstream Sunni theologians.

To Ibn Taimiyya, religion and the state were necessarily linked. Without the coercive power of the state, religion would be in danger, but without the comprehensive body of Islamic law (the shari'a) government would become tyranny. His most famous work, Al-Siyasa al-Shari'iyyah, might be loosely translated as Shari'ah Politics or, perhaps more accurately, Shari'ah Public Policy.

In modern times the ideas of Muhammad ibn Abd al-Wahhab (1703–1787) build in large measure on the doctrines of Ibn Taimiyya, whose influence continues in present-day Saudi Arabia. Certain of Ibn Taimiyya's ideas were picked up by the more meliorist and modernist stance of Egyptian theologian Muhammad Abduh (1849–1905) and his followers, especially the emphasis on individual intellectual effort to establish religious doctrine (ijtihad) and resistance to the consensus of the conservative orthodox ulama (legal scholars).

The fit between the ideas of Ibn Taimiyya and those of today's radical Islamists is striking. The strict scripturalism and the belief that any pious Muslim can understand and thus live according to Qur'anic injunctions has roots in Ibn Taimiyya's thought. The same holds for the idea that government is necessary to protect and preserve religion but that the only legitimate government is one that carries out the shari'a. Ibn Taimiyya offers a dramatic example of confronting the establishment ulama, just as do modern Islamists.

Moreover, the sharpest break with conventional Muslim political thought advanced by contemporary Islamists is the notion that Muslim rulers who do not adhere to the strict canons of the faith have become like infidels. They have lapsed into jahilivya. A jihad is, accordingly, proper against such rulers. This idea too comes from Ibn Taimiyya. The

Mongols, by Ibn Taimiyya's time, had become at least nominal Muslims, but they remained no less a threat to Mamluk rule. The Mamluks sought a legal opinion (fatwa) justifying a jihad against the Mongols, and Ibn Taimiyya obliged them. To him, their laws remained tainted with infidel sources. The Mongols, he maintained, should be combated until they complied with the laws of God.

A prolific scholar, Ibn Taimiyya wrote on many subjects. His many legal opinions, for example, fill thirty-five volumes. Virtually all of his works are available in modern Arabic editions, and many have been translated into other languages.

See also Islam; Jihad; Sufism.

L. Carl Brown

BIBLIOGRAPHY

Ibn Taimiyya. Ibn Taimiyya on Public and Private Law, or Public Policy in Islamic Jurisprudence (Translation of Al-Siyasa al-Shari'iyyah). Translated by Omar A. Farrukh. Beirut, Lebanon: Khayat's, 1966.

Laoust, Henri. Essai sur le doctrines sociales et politiques d'Ibn Taymiyya. Cairo, Egypt: Imprimerie de l'Institut Fran.ced.cais d'Archéologie Orientale, 1939.

Sivan, Emmanuel. Radical Islam: Medieval Theology and Modern Politics. New Haven, Conn.: Yale University Press, 1985.

Independent Churches, African

African independent churches (AICs), also called African-initiated or instituted churches, are a Christian phenomenon in sub-Saharan Africa. The movement comprises thousands of churches founded by black Africans for black Africans and is devoted to the well-being, salvation, and liberation of African people.

Origins and Growth

African independent churches date to the early eighteenth century, when a young woman, Kimpa Vita, resisted Portuguese rule in the Congo by proclaiming a black Christ and a utopian African kingdom. In 1706 the Portuguese rulers burned her at the stake as a heretic and forcibly subdued her followers. By the beginning of the twentieth century, when African nationalism emerged as a significant force in southern Africa, AICs had established themselves as an enduring, fast-growing movement. After the first major schism in South Africa in 1884, led by Nehemiah Tile, a

Methodist minister, and the formation of the first "Ethiopian" church by Mangena Mokone in 1892, Ethiopian-type churches began to flourish. The Zionist movement, in turn, came into being after Daniel Bryant, an "overseer" of Dowie's Christian Catholic Apostolic Church in Zion, near Chicago, baptized the first converts in South Africa, in 1904. Independent of the Western-led mission churches, African missionaries of both these movements soon operated throughout South Africa, establishing new churches. When rapid AIC expansion triggered a process of ecclesial fragmentation, many new groups emerged. Through the conversion of labor migrants from neighboring countries, the AIC movement spread from South Africa to Botswana, Namibia, Mozambique, Zimbabwe, Zambia, and Malawi. While many of the early movements in South Africa and the Congo were distinctly nativistic, millennialistic, and radically anti-white in political disposition, the West African AICs developed more peacefully, with an emphasis on placing the Christian faith within the context of African culture and religion.

African independent churches vary in size, from small, single-family churches consisting of only a few related adults and their children to the more widely known churches with millions of adherents. Some of the most prominent of the latter are the amaNazareta of Isaiah Shembe and the Zion Christian Church of Engenas Lekganyane in South Africa; Samuel Mutendi's Zion Christian Church and Johane Maranke's African Apostolic Church (the vaPostori has some two million members with congregations as far north as Zaire) in Zimbabwe; Alice Lenshina's Lumpa Church in Zambia; Simon Kimbangu's Church of Jesus Christ in Zaire (the largest AIC, with an estimated membership of between ten and fifteen million); and the Cherubim and Seraphim Church and the Church of the Lord (Aladura), both in Nigeria.

Types and Distinctive Features

AICs stem from pre-Christian as well as Christian movements. The neo-pagan pre-Christian movement represents a reversion to traditional African religion in an attempt to achieve stability in the face of intrusive religious influences from the West. The vast majority of AICs are distinctly Christian; they believe in the triune Christian God as portrayed in the Old and New Testaments, consider the Scriptures part of their lives, develop congregations for joint worship and use of the sacraments, and develop spiritualities that convincingly witness to the existential reality of Christ and the movement of the Holy Spirit in their existence. Some AICs suffer from a lack of theological training among their leadership, limited doctrinal development, fragmented Bible interpretation, and syncretistic trends of interreligious encounter. Yet, in terms of missionary activity, numerical strength, holistic Christian communities that cater to both the spiritual and physical needs of people, and Bible-oriented church life, AICs qualify as mainline Christianity rather than as peripheral or sectarian Christian movements.

Scholars tend to classify AICs originating in the Christian movement into three main types. The *Ethiopian-type churches,* or nonprophetic movements, adopt patterns of church leadership, organization, and worship that are fairly similar to those of the Anglican, Congregationalist, Methodist, Reformed, and other mission churches on which they are partly modeled. These churches originated largely as a reaction to white-led mission churches. Political development and the knowledge that a colonial power, the Italians in Abyssinia (now Ethiopia), had been successfully resisted in East Africa contributed to the development of an Ethiopian ideology, which tended to foster a sense of self-esteem and responsibility for the expansion of God's kingdom in Africa. This ideology took root mainly in East Africa and South Africa between 1890 and 1920. Despite the decline of the ideology, "Ethiopian" continues to feature in the names of some AICs.

The *Spirit-type churches,* or prophetic movements, emphasize the work of the Holy Spirit, manifested in emotional forms of worship, speaking in tongues, prophetic activity, and faith healing. This category comprises all Zionists, such as the Zion Christian churches, and a wide range of Apostolic churches. Prophetic faith healing, based on the diagnostic and therapeutic powers of the Holy Spirit and manifested in a wide range of exorcistic and individual- or group-cleansing ceremonies, is at the center of the Spirit-type churches.

The so-called Messianic churches represent a development of leadership within the prophetic movements. Messianism occurs when the eminence of a movement's founder-leader—his or her mystical powers, healing miracles, image as resistance figure against colonial rule, or closeness to God as mediating representative of his or her followers—captures the attention of members to such an extent that Christ's salvific work is obscured either wholly or in part. This classification is controversial because few AIC leaders actually claim to be black Christ figures, and members of

AICs generally consider the "gate-keeping function" at the portals of heaven as an extension of the leaders' ecclesial duties on earth, without it necessarily circumventing the salvific mediation of Christ or the final judgment of God.

Religiocultural and Socioeconomic Liberation

AICs have served as sources of religiocultural and socioeconomic liberation for their members. The spontaneous, celebratory life of the AICs—especially in song, dance, sermons, and healing—is largely the result of their emancipation from the paternalist structures and austere and dogmatically correct forms of worship that the Western mission churches maintained by means of funding and staffing. This liberative process, insofar as it includes a reevaluation of indigenous culture and religion, has led to numerous rites informed by African worldviews. Trends of confrontation and Christianizing transformation are evident in the Spirit-type churches. As a result, the Gospel message is introduced at an existential level to cater to Africans' needs in a new way, just as the High-God cult, ancestor veneration, and magical rites had done in earlier times.

Faith-healing practices in the Spirit-type churches in Zimbabwe clearly reveal that religiocultural liberation is not just a reaction against Western control and medical science accompanied by uncritical affirmation of indigenous custom. It also implies liberation from the besetting fear of spiritual powers and life-threatening sorcery inculcated by traditional religion. The Zionist and Apostolic prophets' healing rites represent pastoral, psychological liberation for people threatened by destructive forces. Prophetic diagnosis still rests on the ancient worldview in which the traditional causes of misfortune or danger are demonstrated and taken seriously. In prophetic therapy, however, the healing and protective power of Christ and the Holy Spirit emerges in symbolic purificatory or exorcist rites. Thus the Christian God is convincingly and visibly presented as a God directly involved in the joys and sorrows of the community.

The socioeconomic liberation represented by AICs is evident in rural and urban areas of Africa. In rural areas the extensive leadership structures of the AICs enable people who have little political say or social standing to enjoy greater recognition and improve their social status. At the weekly gatherings, church members, appearing in their dignified uniforms or robes bearing their leadership monograms, proudly assume a meaningful new identity as well as responsibility for the attainment of congregational goals.

This helps to enliven their village life and give them a sense of control over the problems of their peasant existence. Leadership structures have been adapted to the traditional kinship codes and codes of authority, making it possible to distribute group responsibilities in a way that makes sense to the people. All this liberates participants from the blight of social obscurity and drudgery.

In a subsistence peasant economy the AICs also represent economic progress. The good news they communicate is that of freedom from economic impotence and from fatalism in the face of poverty and inefficient farming methods. This message is conveyed through identification with the poor and concerted application of modern farming methods resulting in improved cash crop yields. In Zimbabwe, the Zionist bishops in particular have been economically progressive, qualifying as master farmers and buying up farms in the erstwhile Native Purchase Areas. In recent years, ecumenical AIC institutions, notably Fambidzano in Zimbabwe, have attempted to raise funds for member churches to engage in economic development projects.

Most rural Africans who migrate to the city encounter almost insurmountable problems. Lack of mobility often breaks up families. The stabilizing kinship codes and tribal mores no longer function in heterogeneous mass society, resulting in social isolation or degeneracy. New models and criteria are needed for a meaningful existence. In this complexity, the independent churches act as "reorientation centers"—communities offering security and a chance for reintegration, a new home providing stability in a harsh, competitive world.

Political Liberation

The political liberation offered by the AICs is found in both rural-tribal politics and national politics. The history of many African churches contains an element of struggle against colonial domination in which a politically oriented liberation theology is implicit, although the leaders of these churches did not necessarily use such terminology. In colonial southern Africa, the traditional Supreme Being sometimes appeared indifferent to Western pressures on tribal politics. The sermons and catechesis of mission churches created an impression of a God concerned about individual morals and salvation rather than one directly involved in the lives of rural headmen, in the problems of divided loyalties in tribal politics, in the dispossession of territory, in boundary disputes, and in the inheritance of tribal leadership.

In this situation the prophetic church leaders in particular transformed the image of a remote God into one of direct divine involvement in tribal and national politics. Outstanding prophetic figures—such as Shembe and Lekganyane Senior in South Africa, Mutendi and Maranke in Zimbabwe, and Kimbangu in Zaire—were all leaders who through their close contact with tribal heads were aware of the problems of local administration and addressed their Gospel messages to these issues. Like Shembe in South Africa, Bishop Samuel Mutendi of the Zimbabwean Zion Christian Church recruited a large number of chiefs and headmen for his church. Tribal leaders were attracted by his resistance to colonial rule in the educational and religious spheres, for which he was arrested by the Rhodesian administration on several occasions and spent short spells in detention. As a figure of resistance against the white regime and a representative of indigenous political and cultural values, Mutendi appeared to his followers as an emissary, a "man of God"—a title by which he always was respectfully addressed in the religious sense as well as in the political arena.

Bishop Mutendi introduced the Christian message into tribal politics by having his Zionist prophets appointed to the tribal courts of affiliated chiefs. In this way the guidance and revelations of the Holy Spirit, as experienced by Zionists, could directly influence the traditional judiciary and various facets of rural government. Thus Mutendi established a wide network of mutual allegiance between the "man of God" in Zion City and traditional leaders across large parts of the country, giving him considerable influence over tribal politics. Well aware that headmen were being torn by the opposing claims of the administration, on the one hand, and the tribesmen, on the other—two worlds that because of differing cultural and religious values were in continual friction—the "man of God" set himself the aim of offering frustrated headmen spiritual anchorage and protection that helped them to function optimally in a situation that constantly highlighted their impotence in the face of the white overlords. It was in this kind of context that a message of liberation evolved. This message did not promise easy solutions or revolutionary changes in the political constellation that would bring sudden freedom from bondage. Yet it was through the involvement and continuous availability of Zionist prophets that God drew nigh in the affairs of tribal dignitaries. The once remote deity now enabled chiefs and headmen to cope with a complex and often critical political situation and liberated them from their fears and anxiety.

In the national politics of Zimbabwe, the independent churches generally kept a low profile. Their sympathies with their people's struggle for political independence did not lead to unreserved participation in militant political activities, largely because they were reluctant to allow their organizations to be used as a platform for party politics. Their liberation theology was not confined to religiocultural freedom from the mission churches, socioeconomic advancement of their members, and overt opposition to the administration of the day such as Mutendi's. It also concerned maintaining a unique identity in the midst of political pressure. A classic example of the refusal of AICs to be manipulated politically occurred in the 1960s in Zambia, where members of Alice Lenshina's Lumpa Church were massacred because of the prophetess's refusal to order her followers to join the ruling United National Independence Party.

During the 1950s and 1960s, some of the more prominent Zimbabwean independent churches openly defied the black nationalist parties ZANU (Zimbabwe African National Union) and ZAPU (Zimbabwe African People's Union) by rejecting violent resistance. Their motives were pragmatic ones of self-preservation. The church leaders were aware of the omnipresence of members of the Rhodesian intelligence service and that they could not effectively oppose the colonial power with their own numbers. Their aloofness from organized violence did not, however, imply political apathy. Black nationalist sentiments were continually expressed in the sermons and activities of the AICs in the form of propagation of ideas of racial equality, the dignity of the black race, and blacks' competence to rule themselves. Thus the main contribution of the AICs to political liberation lay in providing religious justification for the liberation struggle, for which they could, moreover, adduce the necessary scriptural proofs. In this sense, the AICs represented the religious vanguard of black nationalism.

Among the vaPostori, resistance to white rule was manifested in sermons and in charges that whites had killed Christ and deliberately withheld his message from blacks. The prophet Johane Maranke had brought an end to the age of white privilege and had restored the despised house of Ham (that is, black Africans) to glory in order that they, guided by the Holy Spirit, might fulfill Jesus Christ's task in the world under a new dispensation.

The role of the independent churches in the liberation history of Zimbabwe, as enacted in the bush war (the second *chimurenga,* or liberation struggle, 1965–1980), still has to be written. For members of both mission and independent churches, it largely was a matter of survival between the Scylla of the Rhodesian forces and the Charybdis of the guerrilla freedom fighters. In the 1970s, virtually all independent churches appeared to have actively supported the freedom fighters, notwithstanding that some guerrilla groups—under the banner "Down with Jesus, the white man's god"—actively opposed the churches, burning their buildings and even Bibles.

The Zimbabwean independent churches clearly contributed significantly to the second *chimurenga,* and many of them are justly proud of their role in the reconquest of their "lost territory" and the attainment of political independence. Given the Zimbabwean history of AIC political involvement, it would be difficult for South African exponents of black theology to criticize the allegedly apolitical attitude of AICs on the subcontinent. If one considers the combination of pragmatic and prophetic-ideological elements of Bishop Mutendi's resistance strategy, it is conceivable that in South Africa Zionist Christian Church bishop Lekganyane's public statements, which during apartheid rule seemed to be supportive of the political status quo, did not preclude either individual involvement of Zionist Christian Church members in the liberation struggle or the provision of religious justification for and active support of black nationalist ideals. Comprehensive studies of the histories of AICs are bound to compel African theologians, who have tended to limit the merits of these churches to the indigenization of church praxis, to accord greater recognition to their sociopolitically liberative roles.

Although black theology is undeniably more militant and revolutionary than Zionist theology, this by no means implies that the former has a kind of monopoly on liberation and sociostructural change. In academic circles and in the communications media, the exponents of black theology have conducted an impressive public campaign that is recognized internationally. At the grass-roots level of church life, the independent churches—through their marked identification with the struggle and aspirations of black Africans, expressed in a holistic, enacted theology—have made an existential contribution to liberation whose impact on African society has been insufficiently assessed and appreciated in academic circles.

See also *Botswana; Christianity in Africa; Colonialism; Liberation Theology; Millennialism; Nativism; Nigeria; Pacifism; South Africa; Traditional Religions, African; Zimbabwe.*

Marthinius L. Daneel

BIBLIOGRAPHY

Anderson, Allan. *African Pentecostals in South Africa.* Pretoria: University of South Africa, 1992.

Barrett, D. B. *Schism and Renewal in Africa: An Analysis of Six Thousand Contemporary Religious Movements.* Nairobi: Oxford University Press, 1968.

Campbell, James T. *Songs of Zion: The African Methodist Episcopal Church in the United States and South Africa.* New York: Oxford University Press, 1995.

Comaroff, Jean. *Body of Power. Spirit of Resistance. The Culture and History of a South African People.* Chicago: University of Chicago Press, 1985.

Daneel, M. L. *Old and New in Southern Shona Independent Churches.* Vol. 1, *Background and Rise of the Major Movements.* The Hague: Mouton, 1971.

———. *Old and New in Southern Shona Independent Churches.* Vol. 2, *Church Growth: Causative Factors and Recruitment Techniques.* The Hague: Mouton, 1974.

———. *Quest for Belonging: Introduction to a Study of African Independent Churches.* Gweru, Zimbabwe: Mambo Press, 1987.

Hastings, Adrian. *The Church in Africa 1450–1950.* Oxford: Clarendon Press, 1994.

Maxwell, David. "Historicizing Christian Independency: The Southern African Pentecostal Movement ca 1908–1960." *Journal of African History* 39, no. 2 (1999).

Ndiokwere, Nathaniel I. *Prophecy and Revolution: The Role of Prophets in the Independent African Churches and in Biblical Tradition.* London: SPCK, 1981.

Sundkler, Bengt. *Zulu Zion and Some Swazi Zionists.* Oxford: Oxford University Press, 1976.

Sundkler, B. G. M. *Bantu Prophets of South Africa.* London: Oxford University Press, 1961.

Turner, H. W. "A Typology for African Religious Movements." *Journal of Religion in Africa* 1, no. 1 (1967).

West, M. *Bishops and Prophets in a Black City: African Independent Churches in Soweto, Johannesburg.* Cape Town: Phillip, 1975.

India

The largest and most populous of the countries of South Asia, India, with 1.1 billion people, is home to many faiths, including such world religions as Hinduism (80 percent of the population), Islam (12 percent), Christianity (3 percent), and Sikhism (2.5 percent). The notion of separate sacred and secular domains of society, which is characteristic of the Christian (Roman Catholic) tradition and of social science literature, must be abandoned when speaking of India in the context of religion and politics. Instead, the focus becomes the relationship between sacred and secular power, derived from dynastic succession or popular election.

In the oldest Indian religious traditions (Buddhism, Hinduism, and Jainism) the sacred and the secular are united; the secular is only relatively autonomous and ultimately encompassed by the sacred. The ethical principle that guides the wielders of secular power is an aspect of the overarching moral principle, *dharma,* that sustains not only human society but the entire cosmos. The Sikhs hail the sword as a symbol of the divinity but place it at a lower level than the holy scripture in the temples. In Islam the nondifferentiation of the secular from the sacred is even more emphatically stated through a repudiation of the secular. The Islamic holy book, the Qur'an, teaches that whatever is apparently secular is sacred in its very roots.

The Nineteenth Century

Classical formulations of the relationship of religion and politics provide the background, but they do not anticipate contemporary complexities. An appropriate starting point for discussion is the early nineteenth century, when the ruling British Parliament allowed evangelical efforts by Christian missionaries to begin in India. Religious differences ultimately became politicized in the late nineteenth century, following the introduction of administrative reforms, which included local self-government.

Many Indian intellectuals were deeply impressed by the moral tone of the New Testament. While some of them embraced Christianity, others endeavored to combine what they considered the best elements of Hinduism and Christianity. One notable effort, based in Bengal, was by Rammohun Roy, who founded the Brahmo Samaj (Society of God) in 1828 as a new religious way of life. Such experiments were countered within a generation, however, most significantly by Hindu revivalism. Bengal witnessed the emergence of an ecstatic form of Hinduism, centered on the worship of a supreme mother-goddess. Politically sensitive intellectuals translated this religious idea into the mystical concept of the country as divinity, Bharat Mata (Mother India). Her liberation from foreign rule thus emerged as a sacred duty, and nationalism assumed a religious mantle.

A rejuvenated Hinduism was different from the religious hybrids in that it appealed to an exclusive though reinterpreted past. The need for reinterpretation arose from the perceived corruption of the original (Vedic) religion over the millennia, accompanied by social degeneration. Many late-nineteenth-century religious reform movements, among the Hindus and among the Sikhs, had a dual agenda: the restoration of the purity of religious belief and ritual and the eradication of undesirable social practices, including gender- and caste-based discrimination.

The most successful movement among the Hindus was led by Dayananda Sarasvati, who founded the Arya Samaj (Society of Noble People) in Bombay (now Mumbai) in 1875. It was in the north, however, that the Arya Samaj achieved its most notable success, and the reason for this was political. Not only had Punjab been under Muslim domination longer than other parts of India, during which time it had acquired a considerable Muslim population through immigration and conversion, but it had also become the site of Christian missionary activity after the British annexed the province in the middle of the nineteenth century. A crusade against Islam and Christianity was, according to Dayananda, essential to Hindu rejuvenation and, indeed, to patriotism.

Regional socioreligious reform movements were active in the last quarter of the nineteenth century among Hindus, Sikhs, and Muslims alike. These movements had implicit political significance, even in the absence of explicit political agendas. A national political party, the Indian National Congress (INC), was established in 1885 by a group of urban elites drawn mostly from the Hindu community but also including Muslims and Parsis. (The Parsis were a religious community descended from refugees who had fled from Persia in the eighth century to escape persecution by Muslim conquerors.) From the very beginning, however, the representative character of the INC was undercut by the refusal of many prominent Muslim leaders, including Sayyid Ahmad Khan, to join. Muslim separatism from then on became a significant issue in Indian politics; it eventually led to the partition of the subcontinent in 1947 and the creation of Pakistan.

A thousand years of Muslim rule in India ended in 1857 with the banishment of the Mogul emperor Bahadur Shah from Delhi, the imperial capital, for his support of a soldiers' mutiny directed against British rule. The period of Muslim decline had begun a century and a half earlier, and when the so-called Sepoy Mutiny erupted, the old shah was little more than its symbolic head. The Muslim community came under suspicion, or so its leaders believed, of being disloyal to the British rulers. They reacted in two ways, both of which focused on the need for education. Sayyid Ahmad Khan chose the path of modern education and of cooperation

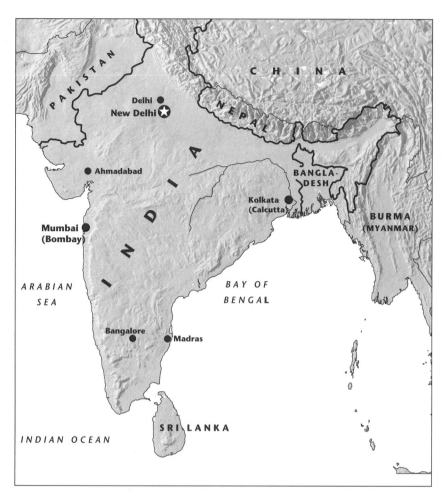

with the British, from whom he sought protection against future domination by a resurgent Hindu community. A college he established at Aligarh in northern India sought to reconcile the basic teachings of a reinterpreted Islam with the ideals of the European Enlightenment. Other, more conservative leaders, opted for religious and cultural revival through traditional forms of education and abstention from politics. They established a seminary at Deoband, not far from Aligarh, and trained teachers who would communicate the Islamic principles of everyday life to the common people through the widely understood Urdu language. Thousands of decrees and opinions issued from Deoband, providing guidance in the Muslim way of life.

The Early Twentieth Century

Gradually, the Deoband *ulama* (religious scholars) cultivated political interests and sided with the avowedly secular politics of the INC. They believed that the Muslim way of

life would be safe if politics were religiously neutral. The Aligarh modernists also joined the struggle for self-rule but on the basis of the notion that Sayyid Ahmad Khan had first put forward and which had been taken up by the Muslim League, founded in 1906—that of two nations, the Hindus and the Muslims. One of the first demands of the Muslim League was for the institution of separate electorates in local elections, which were the only elections then held in India. The Muslims would choose their own representatives (obviously Muslim), and the other religious communities would choose theirs. The ideology of religious nationalism—or communalism, as it is generally called in India—was thus introduced into Indian politics. Communalism meant that nationhood was to be defined primarily in religiously exclusive terms and only secondarily by political boundaries.

The basic premise of communalism was (and is) that the political interests of a religious community are unaffected by ethnic, linguistic, class, or any other such divisions within the community. These interests were defined antagonistically in relation to other, similarly conceived religious communities. In contrast, religiously neutral, or secular, nationalists regarded themselves as primarily engaged in a struggle to end colonial domination and therefore considered religious as well as linguistic, ethnic, and similar differences to be of secondary importance, if not illusory. Secular nationalism and communalism thus emerged as rival ideologies of political emancipation. Communalists, who were religious nationalists in their own eyes, maintained that the fight against colonialism could not be joined unless the postindependence political and economic rights of the religious minorities were first guaranteed.

In the rhetoric of religious nationalism, religion appears as a collective ideology of renewal rather than a personal faith of redemption. When faith becomes political, as it does under communalism, ultimate values recede from view, and religion becomes a sign of political differentiation. Secular nationalism generated its own problems because it acknowledged religious pluralism rather than favoring religious rationalism or agnosticism. The INC recognized the plurality of interest groups but considered subnationalisms as the enemy of secular nationalism unless their proponents accepted its priority.

At the very beginning of his political career in India Mohandas Karamchand Gandhi espoused the cause of the distant Ottoman sultan, who claimed the status of caliph, the religious leader of Muslims worldwide. Gandhi had returned in triumph to India in 1915 from South Africa, where he had organized and led people of Indian origin in their struggle for political rights. He made the sultan's cause part of the noncooperation movement against British rule in India because Indian Muslims were deeply concerned about the fate of the ancient Muslim institution of the caliphate. His mixing of religion and politics produced serious misgivings among secularists. At first Gandhi seemed to have worked a miracle as Muslim participation in the INC-led national movement reached unprecedented heights. But the abolition of the caliphate in 1924 by secular Turkish nationalists brought the Hindu-Muslim collaboration to a quick end, never to be revived again.

In fact, Hindu-Muslim hostility resurfaced with greater intensity. The political accommodation of Muslims by the INC leadership, particularly Gandhi, was deeply resented by right-wing Hindu leaders. The currently popular communal ideology of Hindutva (Hindu identity) was put forward in

1924. An apparently nonpolitical cultural organization, the Rashtriya Swayamsevak Sangh (RSS), was established soon afterward. Hindutva promulgated a restrictive definition of Indian identity by merging the notions of "native land" and "holy land." This meant, in effect, that those Indians whose most holy lands were outside India—namely, Christians, Jews, and Muslims—were likely to be treated as foreigners, and even denied citizenship rights, unless they assimilated with the Hindu cultural mainstream. A concept of "national culture" was put forward, denying the religious pluralism that the INC had advanced, as the distinctive character of Indian nationalism, rooted in Indian history and arguably in the Hindu religious tradition itself.

Although secularism as religious pluralism was the dominant mode of thinking within the INC, some leaders, including Jawaharlal Nehru, its president for many years and the first prime minister of independent India, were secularists in the Western sense of the term. Nehru had been greatly influenced by British socialist thinkers and by Marxist-Leninist thought. From the 1920s to the eve of the partition of India, he consistently denied that nationalism had any legitimate connection within religious identities. He considered national independence a prerequisite to the reordering of socioeconomic relations in society. Once such a reconstruction was achieved, Nehru was convinced, religious differences would retreat into the privacy of individual lives. As things turned out, Nehru's faith in the primacy of an economic approach to nationalism remained a minority, though strongly articulated, viewpoint within the nationalist movement. It had a severe setback when the country was partitioned in 1947.

Partition and Afterward

The partition of India on the basis of religio-cultural difference was far from a satisfactory solution to the clash of multiple identities and subnationalisms. The Muslim majority areas of the northeast and northwest were constituted into Muslim homelands (East and West Pakistan) and, potentially, an Islamic state. In the months after partition several million Muslims left their homes in India to migrate to Pakistan, just as Hindus and Sikhs moved in the other direction. About 40 percent of the 100 million Muslims of the subcontinent remained in India, scattered over most parts of the country.

These Muslims decided, out of conviction or necessity, to dissociate themselves from the ideology of religious nationalism. For the limited purpose of the preferred form of government, they supported the concept of a secular state, but many among them did not embrace the broader ideology of secularism as a worldview. In the years following partition, the ideology of communalism seemed to wane in India. Religion as the principal marker of collective identities was replaced by others, notably language and ethnicity.

The respite turned out to be temporary, however. As the shock of partition abated, the economic improvements that the secularists had hoped would end communal hostility reinforced it in some places, while in others the older forms of communal politics and competition for scarce resources resurfaced. A major irritant has been an unresolved dispute over whether Jammu and Kashmir should be part of India, of which it is a constituent state by virtue of constitutional status, or of Pakistan, in view of the region's Muslim majority. Following partition, Pakistan and India went to war over the issue. A United Nations ceasefire, introduced at the start of 1949, effectively divided the disputed region, which nevertheless remained a hot spot in subsequent decades. Moreover, in the mid-1980s an Islamic fundamentalist movement, largely pro-Pakistan, and a cultural-nationalist, or ethnic, movement, which is pro-independence (secessionist), emerged. At present, both the Indian State of Jammu and Kashmir and, on the opposite side of the so-called Line of Control, the Pakistani-administered Azad Kashmir and Northern Areas (the regions of Baltistan, Diamir, and Gilgit), have secular governments in which Muslim-affiliated political parties have typically played leading roles. Nevertheless, the confluence of interests and forces has caused much bloodshed and destruction.

A similarly volatile situation had earlier developed in Punjab. Economic grievances, combined with political skulduggery by right-wing Hindus and the federal and state governments, strengthened an earlier demand for independence put forward by a sector of the Sikh political leadership. In June 1984, in a misconceived and ill-executed military action code-named "Bluestar," the government attempted to arrest a charismatic fundamentalist preacher, Jarnail Singh Bhindranwale. He, along with heavily armed followers, had taken sanctuary inside a major Sikh temple in Amritsar called the Akal Takht (the Golden Temple). There were heavy casualties on both sides. Bhindranwale was killed, and the temple was severely damaged. Fundamentalism and terrorism swept Punjab, and on October 31 Prime Minister Indira Gandhi was assassinated by her Sikh bodyguards. It took ten years to bring militancy under control and restore normal politics in the state.

Meanwhile, Hindu fundamentalism was emerging as a major feature of state and national politics, partly in protest against the alleged partiality of the government toward Muslims. In the early 1990s an abandoned Muslim mosque at Ayodhya, Uttar Pradesh, became a symbolic focus in that it had once been the site of a sacred Hindu temple. Hindu communal organizations called for the demolition of the mosque, which, they asserted, had been erected in the mid-sixteenth century as a symbol of Muslim power. The Hindu fundamentalists proposed building a new, grand temple on the site. In addition to generating ethnic unrest, in November 1990 the conflict contributed to the fall of the country's coalition government following the withdrawal of support by the right-wing Hindu Bharatiya Janata Party (Indian People's Party, or BJP), which had close ties to the RSS. Subsequently, while the federal government dithered, the state government, run by the BJP, provided covert assistance to the agitators, and the mosque was razed in a matter of hours in December 1992. Widespread killings of Muslims followed, bringing about violent Muslim retaliation, mainly in Mumbai (formerly Bombay).

The bloody consequences of mixing religion and politics generated serious misgivings about the future of secularism. Although the BJP suffered reverses in state elections in 1993, it emerged from the 1996 parliamentary elections with a plurality of seats, but its leader, Atal Bihari Vajpayee, was unable to form a stable government. Thereafter, the party moderated its Hindu nationalist image and forged ties to state and regional parties. As a consequence, the BJP, supported by some 20 allied parties, both communal and secular, carried the February–March 1998 legislative election and formed a government with Vajpayee as prime minister. The defection of a key state party precipitated another parliamentary election in September–October 1999 that saw the BJP lead a National Democratic Alliance (NDA) of 24 parties to victory. The NDA election platform had emphasized the economy and omitted Hindu nationalist goals, but Prime Minister Vajpayee's apparent moderation did not allay suspicions that the BJP continued to be heavily influenced by the RSS and the linked Swadeshi Jagran Manch (SJM), a leading Hindu proponent of economic nationalism.

In 2000 India experienced a dispersed series of anti-Christian attacks, many of them allegedly committed by members of the Vishwa Hindu Parishad (World Council of

Hindus) and its youth wing, but the worst intercommunal violence continued to involve Hindus and Muslims. On February 27, 2002, nearly 60 people died when Muslims set fire to train cars filled with Hindu activists who had been visiting Ayodhya. Reprisals by Hindi vigilantes cost an additional one thousand Muslim and Hindu lives. Subsequent reports by the United Kingdom and the European Union asserted that the anti-Muslim riots had been organized, rather than spontaneous, and that government personnel may have acquiesced or even been directly involved. In September 2003 the supreme court criticized the Gujarat state government, headed by the BJP, for failing to convict anyone for the Muslim deaths.

The government's inadequate response to the communal violence brought into question its commitment to India's secular union, which helped an INC-led alliance register an upset win over the NDA at the April–May 2004 national election. The INC's Manmohan Singh, a Sikh senator and economist, was named prime minister after INC president Sonia Gandhi withdrew her name from consideration, in part because of Hindu objections to her Italian birth. Thus both of India's highest offices, prime minister and president, were held by members of religious minorities, A. P. J. Abdul Kalam, a Muslim, having been elected president in July 2002. (A scientist new to politics, Kalam was widely admired for his leading role in India's ballistic missile program. In that light, his religious background was incidental to his election.)

Meanwhile, following a November 2003 ceasefire along Kashmir's Line of Control, relations between India and Pakistan had improved, permitting a "composite dialogue" on bilateral issues and leading to an April 2005 joint announcement that the peace process was "irreversible." Militant Islamic fundamentalists, however, did not agree. A host of shifting Kashmir-based extremist groups, chief among them Lashkar-i-Taiba (Army of the Pure) and Hizb-ul-Mujaheddin, were increasingly employing terrorist tactics to achieve the separation of Jammu and Kashmir from India and the establishment of an Islamist regime. Many of the extremist leaders, trained in *jihad* (holy war) during the Soviet occupation of Afghanistan during the 1980s or the Afghan revolution of the 1990s, had ties to the Taliban and al-Qaida.

In their various guises the extremists have claimed responsibility for or been implicated in innumerable bombings, suicide missions, and other attacks within Kashmir and elsewhere. In October 2001 militants attacked the state assembly building in Srinagar, the summer capital of Jammu and Kashmir, causing nearly forty deaths. In December 2001 terrorists attacked India's Parliament, with fourteen fatalities. Bombings in Mumbai in August 2003 killed more than fifty people. In October 2005 bombs left another sixty dead in New Delhi. In July 2006 a series of bombs on Mumbai commuter trains killed over 180 and injured another eight hundred. Although the union government in 2006 engaged in discussions with more moderate elements within the pro-independence All Parties Hurriyat Conference—an umbrella for more than two dozen parties and other Kashmiri organizations, many of them Muslim—such negotiations were unlikely to satisfy the demands of Islamist extremists.

India thus found itself, at the end of 2006, confronting clamorous, sometimes violent pressures from communal extremes, both Hindu and Muslim, that reject the secular principles on which the Indian union has been based. In the preceding decade, however, India's spectacular rate of economic growth, despite gross inequalities of wealth, added another factor to the equation, raising the possibility that improved material well-being may mitigate some of the less volatile religio-political pressures.

See also *Gandhi, Mohandas Karamchand; Hinduism; Islam; Nationalism; Pakistan.*

William R. Overstreet

BIBLIOGRAPHY

Brass, Paul. *The Politics of India since Independence.* 2d ed. Cambridge: Cambridge University Press, 1994.

Gopal, Servepalli, ed. *Anatomy of a Confrontation: The Babri Masjid-Ramjanambhumi Issue.* New York: Viking Penguin, 1991.

Jones, Kenneth W. *Socio-religious Reform Movements in British India.* Cambridge: Cambridge University Press, 1989.

Madan, T. N. *Modern Myths, Locked Minds: Secularism and Fundamentalism in India.* New York: Oxford University Press, 1997.

Nehru, Jawaharlal. *The Discovery of India.* New York: New American Library, 1946.

Pandey, Gyanendra. *The Construction of Communalism in Colonial North India.* 2d ed. New York: Oxford University Press, 2006.

Van der Veer, Peter. *Religious Nationalism: Hindus and Muslims in India.* Berkeley: University of California Press, 1994.

Individualism

Individualism is a political, religious, and social theory and a set of associated institutions that view each individual as possessing intrinsic dignity and whose autonomous moral and religious choices, accordingly, must be given the highest level of respect and protection. Max Weber, one of the most celebrated sociologists of the twentieth century, wrote in 1905 that individualism includes the most heterogeneous things imaginable and that individuality and individualism can mean very different things. Although some disagreement remains over the meaning of individualism (and individuality), during the twentieth century scholars have moved close to a consensus on its meaning, at least in political and religious matters.

At the center of this consensus is the belief that every human being is a unique, rights-bearing moral entity and the final arbiter of the moral and religious truths that he or she believes and chooses to put into practice. Furthermore, this widely accepted understanding requires that the political system be designed to protect, at the minimum, all adults from inappropriate public or private intrusion into their protected sphere of choice, especially concerning religious or moral matters. In a more aggressive stance, one with a romantic tinge, individualism finds that the self-development of each decision-making individual is the most important social goal, with the meaning of self-development defined by each individual. Most important, individualism thus demands of associated political systems that they facilitate individuals in realizing their religious-like choices in a wide range of social spheres.

This understanding of the individual and his or her elevated relationship vis-à-vis political and religious authorities was not one traditionally embraced by either Western or non-Western cultures. Indeed, for nearly all of recorded human history, articulate elites condemned essential elements of what became individualism as a form of selfishness and godlessness. In fact, not until the nineteenth century was *individualism* even recognized as a distinct concept. But the development of individualism began much earlier, and the history of individualism provides a panoramic backdrop against which to view the development, after 1650, of modern thought and practices. This history is essentially one of changing standards in Western thought by which claims of moral and religious truth are judged. Matters of conscience that had once been viewed as reflecting an innate, divine, and wholly objective moral compass within humankind, so aptly described in the moral teachings of medieval Roman Catholic natural law, over time became increasingly subjectivized and, depending on the preferred school of thought—Enlightenment or romantic—best understood by the individual's own reason or sentiments.

The Elements of Individualism

Individualism, by its support or opposition, is central to almost every major modern intellectual, social, political, and artistic movement; thus, understanding it is essential in order to make sense of modernity. Indeed, individualism does much to divide the modern world of ideas. Capitalism, liberalism, existentialism, progressive religiosity, rationalism, libertarianism, and anarchism lie on the liberating side of this divide; conservatism, corporatism, collectivism, communitarianism, and fascism lie on the other, restrictive side; and romanticism and Marxism draw from both. Steven Lukes, an Oxford University political philosopher, has already done much of the work of cataloging the major elements and varieties of individualism.

Individualism insists that each human being enjoy an inherent dignity and intrinsic value (traditionally awarded uniquely to humans and denied to other species, although this discrimination has recently become philosophically more difficult to maintain). Individualism next emphasizes that each individual must be morally autonomous, that is, self-directing and free from coercive and intrusive societal direction in all moral and religious matters of conscience. Each adult, thus, is to be protected within a cocoon of privacy in which his or her most essential concerns are to be pursued free from intrusive public intervention. Put in popular vernacular, these essential features of individualism treat as a hallowed right individuals doing as they wish as long as the similar capacity of others is respected. When given more of a romantic coloration, individualism additionally emphasizes the fullest development of each person's inherent abilities.

Less a particular goal and more a way of understanding or viewing individuals, *abstract individualism* holds that hypothetical individuals logically and historically precede an existing social or political setting whose principal goal is to meet the needs of such individuals. Although associated with such celebrated thinkers as Thomas Hobbes and John Locke, the seventeenth-century English philosophers of the social contract, and John Rawls, the late-twentieth-century

American political philosopher, this attribute of individualism, from the moment it was articulated in the mid-seventeenth century until today, has been subject to attack from both political philosophers and incipient sociologists. They have found this thesis incapable of describing or explaining how individuals are created without being first constituted by the cultures that they are claimed to have preceded.

Individualism manifests itself in all the most significant cultural realms of modern Western life, and particular variants have developed in distinct ways. Among the most important is *political individualism,* which describes a form of politics in which the state is nothing other than the protector of the inherent rights of abstract individuals who, through their representatives, consent to the actions of the state. The legitimate goals of the state, from this perspective, must be limited to those that are consistent with the autonomous choices of individuals. This precludes the state from pursuing corporate ends that interfere with individual self-direction or matters of conscience.

In the economic domain or *economic individualism,* individualism insists on the freedom of individuals who are self-possessing of themselves and their labor to pursue their own interests in buying and selling, owning private property, and employing human labor in a lightly regulated market. The hoped-for goal of this form of individualism, first widely defended at the end of the seventeenth century, is that wealth will be created for individuals and the society at large, thus fully satisfying, through a generally self-regulating system, the essential needs of both.

Religious and *moral,* or *ethical, individualism* hold in common the equal sanctity of the individual and the inviolate nature of his or her moral conscience. In each instance, an individual's spiritual well-being is believed to depend on his or her religious and moral commitments being unmediated and uncoerced by society or government. From this perspective, the only life that is worth living is one in which individuals closely examine their religious and moral choices and follow the pathway their consciences demarcate. In both cases, the individual carries a heavy burden and, therefore, must be afforded considerable latitude in making choices.

The difference between these two forms of individualism turns on the religious form being necessarily tied to objective standards that have been handed down by a superior, ordinarily a divinity, whereas ethical individualism need not (but may) be committed to objective standards. Indeed, many forms of contemporary moral philosophy that exhibit key features of ethical individualism, such as existentialism and emotivism, deny in a godless world the existence of anything resembling objective moral principles. Yet, Immanuel Kant, a late-eighteenth-century German philosopher and one of the most famous proponents of ethical individualism, held that true moral standards must be objective and universal, even if not formally religious.

Two forms of individualism are primarily philosophical and are readily associated with Hobbes: *epistemological individualism,* which views all knowledge as necessarily possessed only by individuals, and *methodological individualism,* which argues that all social phenomena are, in truth, wholly reducible to the action of individuals following their particular ends. Each tends to dismiss as fictitious trans-individual phenomena. Although distinct from the other forms of individualism outlined above, epistemological and methodological individualism are necessitated by the collective insistence of these other varieties of individualism on the primacy and inviolability of individual experience and self-direction. These two philosophical perspectives, though, like the idea of the abstract individual, have been regularly subjected to the critiques of sociologists, anthropologists, and political theorists who question the accuracy of placing individuals before or outside of a defining formative culture.

The Individual and the Group

Individualism stands in stark contrast to collectivism and communalism, ideas that themselves are often confused with one another. Collectivism, most recently defended in the early twentieth century by the German National Socialists (Nazis) and Italian Fascists, describes a political and social vision that views individuals as incomplete elements of the whole, who flourish only through their subordination to the corporate good (of the religious group, people, nation, state, or class). The relationship is not dissimilar to that between a finger and a hand, in which it makes little sense to talk of the finger (the individual) having an end or good distinct from that of the hand (the collective whole).

Different from both collectivism and individualism is communalism. Similar to individualism, communalism holds that one of the highest moral ends is the flourishing of individuals as individuals, but it holds that this is not likely to be achieved through an individual's autonomous self-direction. Instead, communalism, the most traditional of moral teachings, stretching back to the ancient Greek philosopher Aristotle and beyond, argues that individual human advancement is best pursued through familial and communal shaping of individual character by means of the active inculcation of corporately agreed-on virtues. Moreover, this sanctioned formation of individual character by intermediate social and political institutions is guided by an underlying moral, invariably religious, definition of a well-lived human life. This template necessitates a common morality that is unacceptably intrusive when judged by the standards of individualism. In effect, the communal quest after personal virtue is not a fully private or even wholly familial project but rather a corporate and public one that involves political, social, and usually theological elements. But for communalism, as with individualism and unlike collectivism, one of the most important moral ends remains individual human development.

Individualism is distinct from but related to individuality. Each concept anchors contrasting visions of *liberalism,* a political philosophy with at least two significant varieties: in its classical form, it leaves to individuals the direction and implementation of their personal development and overlaps with individualism, but in its more intrusive and ambitious romantic form, liberalism shows greater affinity to the demands of individuality. Individuality, though, is not wholly distinct from individualism; rather, it describes an uncompromising commitment to two features of individualism, self-development and autonomy. Compared with most proponents of individualism, the mostly romantic (and often French or German) defenders of individuality settle for nothing less than a total dedication to the fullest development of the absolutely free individual.

Such a perspective, though, contains elitist overtones and often demonstrates, in contrast to individualism, little regard for human equality or the importance of individual heroic action serving societal ends. The truly individuated individual, as celebrated by the nineteenth-century American essayists Henry David Thoreau and Ralph Waldo Emerson, must be capable of standing against the tide of common perceptions and norms, and resolutely must follow his or her own way regardless of the social costs or benefits. Yet the influential nineteenth-century English philosopher John Stuart Mill defended individuality not only on these grounds but as well by arguing that geniuses were essential to a society's overall welfare. For Mill, social utility and human progress ultimately depended on the thought and actions of extraordinary men and women, truly individuated individuals, cut-

ting through customary nostrums and experimenting in novel lifestyles.

Individuality is of particular interest because it provides a lens with which to assess the fit between individualism's normative principles and its institutional arrangements. It is regularly assumed that the political and social institutions readily associated with individualism will necessarily facilitate the normative end most commonly advanced by individualism, the creation of fully flourishing individuals. Yet a political system that systematically, in the memorable language of Kant, treats each individual as a moral end rather than only as a means may prove, in fact, to be an impediment to the development of those characteristics associated with true individuality. Indeed, the creation of egalitarian political and social institutions, with no appropriate social obstacles to oppose, may create only soft and flabby individuals without any heroic features. For the romantic defenders of individuality, the true individual's development requires struggle and the overcoming of powerful opposition, quite often that of the majority. This is a dilemma without an immediate resolution, but it should raise concern over the desirability of individualist political and social institutions among those most attracted to the elevated goals of full individuality.

Although romantic liberals may be little concerned with the absence of widespread and egalitarian individual well-being, they should be troubled by the possibility that individualist political and social institutions might have debilitating effects on even those few with heroic potential. As the disturbing nineteenth-century German philosopher Friedrich Nietzsche predicted, individualism would produce what he described as a race of last men, pathetic creatures incapable of nobility of spirit or soul, rather than the heroic types defended by those most interested in individuality.

In better understanding individualism, there is one other distinction worth noting, that between individualism and familism. Because the nuclear family is small compared with other social groupings, it is easy to confuse with the self-directing individual, thus, individualism with familism. Yet the subordination in traditional families of the individual to the values and demands of the corporate unit surely makes familism distinct from individualism. Contemporary critics are, thus, right to contend that the traditional patriarchal family is an institution guilty of suppressing the individual freedoms of subordinate women and children. They hold that it is only when liberated from the bonds of the family that all individuals can achieve full independence from each other, although not equally so from the state and its professional providers of economic and personal assistance. As contemporary feminists have shown, a doctrine that subordinates a woman's individual interests to a corporate body, even a small one such as the family, cannot be equated with the tenets or goals of authentic individualism.

The persistent strength of familism, until recently, limited the appeal of individualism, be it religious or political, because of the often encountered attraction and necessity of the nuclear family. But the combined effects of feminist-guided individualism, changes in post-modern service economies, and the continuing emphasis on the quest for personal happiness, independent of all familial and communal ties and duties, seems to be taking its toll on the strength of the family. Even among socially conservative Catholics, the previously controlling language of Ephesians 5, in which orthodox Christians are commanded to observe a patriarchal familism, has become liturgically optional. Among many fundamentalists, though, an insistence on strict observance of this biblical injunction has become a defining quality. On balance, with the exception of the lingering Christian traditionalism of such families, it seems that the distinction between individualism and familism will become less salient with the continual decline in the nuclear family's social and economic importance.

Origins of Individualism in the West

The history of individualism, both as a normative aspiration and a set of institutional arrangements, is neither short nor simple. Pericles, leader of Athens during the Peloponnesian War in the fifth century B.C., had boasted that each Athenian citizen was the rightful lord and owner of his own person. Clearly, then, critical elements of individualism have been long present in Western thought. Still more striking is the degree to which the Hellenistic philosophies of Cynicism and Stoicism and, in particular, the legalism, voluntarism, atomism, and hedonism of Epicureanism anticipated the inward turn of modern individualism. But these philosophies defended an elevated spiritual realm and elite, and the everyday features and universal and egalitarian claims of modern individualism would have to find another route along which to reach maturity in modern European thought.

It would be in Christianity, and its insistence on the sanctity of the individual conscience and the necessity of right intention, that many of the central elements of individualism would find a vehicle to carry them to maturity in the early years of the nineteenth century. This is not to say that other religions, for example, Judaism, lack individualist tendencies. For in the teachings of the major prophets, Judaism gives voice to powerful personalities who opposed the people, their leaders, and their national norms. Ezekiel is especially insistent in defending individual accountability in which each will suffer for his or her own sins, clearly an early instance of the triumph of the individual conscience over that of the collective. Yet, Judaism remained a religion primarily of law, in which God's covenant was with a nation. It was not, as is Christianity, principally concerned with proper belief and the inner conscience of each individual, where God's covenant (of grace) is made with individuals rather than a people. Indeed, Christianity defined itself through its emphasis on the authentic belief and religious intentions of its adherents and through its rejection of the legalism of Judaism and its consequentialist emphasis on an individual's correct actions.

It is with Christianity and its claim of God's generous and loving sacrifice of his son for fallen human beings that the idea of each individual's infinite worth, regardless of earned merit, develops. And by focusing on the individual's right intention rather than the consequences of his or her actions, Christianity highlighted the sanctity of individual religious conscience. Still, the distance between these authentic seedlings in early Christianity and their expression in late Roman law and what would become individualism is so great that it would take well over a millennium to blossom fully. What had to be overcome before modern individualism could emerge from historic Christianity was its adherents' widespread belief in objective moral truths, their dependence on Christ's mediation, their acceptance of corporate intrusiveness, and their depressing (to modern sensibilities) belief in human original sin. Overcoming these not so negligible obstacles did much to form the substance of Western religious and political history.

Across the eighteen centuries after Christianity's introduction, major elements of what would become individualism continued to develop. But as to when individualism stepped forth fully grown on the world stage, there remains considerable disagreement. Some scholars have argued that its coming of age was during the Italian Renaissance; some hold that it was with the rise of Protestantism; others find its take-off point to be the rapid growth of market forces in seventeenth-century England; and yet others associate it with nineteenth-century romanticism. There is, accordingly, little controversy concerning individualism's close association with the rise of modernity and even less regarding the first use of the term itself.

It was in the 1820s that Joseph de Maistre, a French opponent of a then-emerging understanding of the individual as an absolute moral center, coined the term *individualism*. For him and other French reactionaries, individualism designated the disintegration of society and the spread of egoism, which they believed had resulted from the dissemination during the French Revolution of the doctrine of individual natural rights. What they most objected to was the new understanding of rights that arose at the end of the eighteenth century, which failed to distinguish between pre-social natural civil rights and civil rights awarded by governments upon the surrender of the former. Additionally, they found especially troubling the abandonment of the traditional linkage between rights and duties, such that rights, in being closely tied to duties, were as much a limitation on the freedom of the possessor as they were a form of protection. Interestingly, it was during these years that *inalienable,* meaning that the possessor was not free to surrender a right or some property, and *inviolable,* that is, that a certain right or possession could not be taken from an individual, began to be confused. But in the early nineteenth century, the reactionaries were not alone in their condemnation of these changes and the rise of the new concept, individualism. Other European thinkers and political figures, even progressive ones, initially rejected the new concept, found it to be a form of abuse, or employed it themselves as a pejorative label.

The first use of *individualism* in English would also be derogatory and would come with the translation of the work of one of two French authors who had used the new term to criticize early-nineteenth-century American social and political life. Henry Reeve, in his 1840 translation of French man-of-letters Alexis de Tocqueville's second volume of *Democracy in America,* noted that he adopted the term from the French because he knew of no English equivalent for the expression. And if not then, the word had made its first appearance in English a year earlier, in 1839, in the translation of Michel Chevalier's *Society, Manners, and Politics in the United States.* But from then on, *individualism* gradually began to assume a more favorable sense in the English-speaking world, particularly in Great Britain. Indeed, by the second half of the nineteenth century, all manner of English liberals

had begun to use the term *individualism* and to embrace it; it had in truth become almost synonymous for them with liberalism. (At about the same time, the meaning of liberalism in America and Great Britain began to diverge so that today, in America, liberalism is most readily associated with the political left, and in Britain, with the center-right.)

But in embracing individualism, Anglo-American elites had stood on its head the traditional Western condemnation of idiosyncratic inwardness. Individualism's defense of the particularity of each individual occurred as an older Christian consensus and the more recent rationalist one, specifying the objective nature of religious and moral claims, began to unravel among progressive thinkers. With a loss of confidence in the objective character of the moral cosmos, the uniqueness and particularity of the self became less objectionable; indeed, with the close of the nineteenth century, it came to be the source and standard of moral value.

Modernity and the Rise of Individualism

How did a culture like the West, recognized as Christendom for more than a millennium, become one in which God was replaced by each individual as the source and arbiter of religious and moral truth? No simple explanation, ideal or material, can be given. But any attempt at answering this question, ironically, must begin with the nature of Christianity itself and its development over two millennia. What is immediately obvious is that the history of individualism and Christianity are inextricably linked. Quite possibly, the central elements of no other concept have moved as promiscuously from the spiritual and religious realm of thought and practice to that of the temporal and political, and back again, as have those of individualism.

Over a two-thousand-year history, central elements of what would become individualism in the nineteenth century, most importantly the scientifically impossible-to-defend claims of equal human dignity and the structural beneficence of the cosmos, moved from one sphere to the other, only later to be reflected back, although slightly altered, into intellectual and lived provinces from which they had migrated. Such transference from one sphere to another has not occurred in a fully transparent manner, and not surprisingly, the foundation that made individualist tenets reasonable in one realm has proved incapable of following them and providing the needed foundation in another. Thus, Western elites now find themselves confronting a range of widely shared moral, religious, and political values, such as equal moral dignity, the inviolability of individual conscience, and universal benevolence, for which they are unable to provide adequate philosophical or theological foundations. Significantly, this reiterative process continues even today as liberal political theory, originally derived from important elements in Christian theology and moral thought, reshapes progressive Christianity in its own image.

Still left unidentified, though, are those features of Christianity that facilitated the West's transformation from a God-centered to an individual-centered culture. In partial explanation, Tocqueville noted in the early nineteenth century that elite society had distanced itself more from Christian theology than from Christian philosophy. This shift is of critical importance, because when one turns away from Christian theology to philosophy, one must also turn away from the Protestantism of the sixteenth-century Reformers. Those scholars who hold Protestantism singularly responsible for this transformation, while overlooking Catholicism's rich and long development of Christian humanism, have missed Catholicism's essential contribution to the development of individual-centered religiosity and politics. In particular, the dignity and almost sacred character awarded to the natural reason of each individual and his or her unredeemed conscience in Catholic thought, especially as envisioned by Saint Thomas Aquinas, the thirteenth-century Italian theologian, and his influential followers, are entirely absent in the thought of the most influential early Protestant Reformers. Instead, Reformers like Martin Luther and John Calvin argued that the natural reason found in fallen humanity elevated human beings only marginally above the level of God's other creatures. Calvin, one of the most influential of sixteenth-century Christian Reformers, went so far as to argue that man's likeness to God had been eviscerated with the Fall.

In a manner too often overlooked, only Catholicism is able to teach that the unredeemed individual, through his or her intact reason, is largely able to know the moral good and to will it. The most influential of the Reformers, in their insistence on the total depravity of humans, reject the idea that the individual can significantly know the full nature of the good and, more emphatically, are confident that fallen humanity is incapable of willing it. This failure leaves the individual in a dependent relationship—on Christ, on the Holy Spirit, on family, and on a gathered community of witnessing fellow-Christians. Accordingly, the elevated status, self-direction, and self-centeredness that modern thought

accords the free individual is difficult to envision flowing out of the Reformers' theology of total human depravity and God's irresistible grace. It is not so surprising, then, to find the contemporary Catholic Church championing without reservation "the primacy of human dignity and basic human rights."

The hugely disruptive effects of the Reformation on the unity of Western Christendom and European political life were also essential in facilitating the rise of modern individualism, but these effects were less direct than many have suggested and resulted from consequences wholly unintended by the Reformers. Protestantism's valuation of the unregenerate individual was anything but elevated; indeed, quite the opposite. But beyond the rupture created by the Reformation itself, what the Reformers critically added to the mix of ideas that culminated in modern individualism was their distrust of human-made hierarchies, particularly ecclesiastic; their sacralization of everyday life, of work, and of family; and their tactical but shared insistence with Catholicism on the inviolability of religious conscience and the centrality of right intention rather than right action. These aspects produced a theology in which the divisions present in Catholicism between Christian professionals, that is those who profess (priests, nuns, and monastics), and lay persons, and between heavenly demands and those of daily life, were rejected. The individual, and his or her tender conscience, was accordingly given a new, still more elevated standing.

The magisterial Protestant Reformers and their followers, though, demanded that all true Christians, regardless of occupation or wayward conscience, give themselves entirely to Christ and that ordinary life be dedicated to glorifying God. There was no other acceptable choice; there was only one right answer. When removed from their theological moorings and transformed by emboldened forms of humanism, however, such teachings supported a form of egalitarianism in which each man and woman enjoyed equal human dignity; each moral conscience—right or wrong as viewed against external objective standards—was inviolate, and each person became the final arbiter of all values. But again, the Protestantism of the Reformers is able to help create these effects only when the centrality of original sin, of God, and of a community of brothers and sisters joined in Christ that closely follows and disciplines the actions of its member sinners is denied.

In the modern period, the West moved with the seventeenth-century French philosopher René Descartes, rationalism, and Kant from holding that the individual's inner self or conscience was the principal conduit to objective truth to embracing the romantic's defense of the individual's feelings as the sole standard of truth. Finally, in the contemporary period, there has been a transition to an existentialist and postmodern denial of truth as such and the apotheosis of the radically free and self-determining individual. Yet this modern reverence for the individual is founded on a mixture of an empirically indefensible secular faith in human goodness and equality, and an irremediable epistemic uncertainty about the particular ends humans are to pursue—a seemingly unstable combination of ideas.

This unstable foundation, in spite of individualism's having triumphed across a wide array of cultural arenas, led in the early years of the twentieth century to its being attacked from various sides in an inflamed cultural war. Indeed, for much of the early twentieth century it seemed certain that individualism had passed its zenith and would be eclipsed by one or more prevalent collectivist political alternatives, of both the right and the left. This did not happen. Quite likely, though, what prevented individualism from waning was not necessarily the superiority of its ideas but the physical defeat in World War II of forces representing certain of these collectivist perspectives and the horrific and uninspiring nature of others. Defeat and horror helped produce the relative intellectual cautiousness or quietism of the post–World War II era, which is unlikely to continue indefinitely.

Among late-twentieth-century intellectuals, it once again became fashionable to attack individualism, in particular, what is described as the ideal of the abstract individual and the associated concept of methodological individualism. Yet those doing so—communitarians, animal-rights activists, feminists, and postmoderns—are caught in a curious bind. They are free to attack the putative flaws and excesses of contemporary individualism but only if they decline to challenge the sacrosanct claims of individualism: individual dignity, autonomy, equality, privacy, and self-development. To do so, they must realize, would relegate their writings to obscurity. Still, one must wonder how much longer Nietzsche's challenge to confront the disparities between the West's individualist values and its lack of a credible and coherent epistemic foundation can be delayed. How much longer can the magical table of values, without legs, continue to stand?

The answer might be, unexpectedly, for some time to come. For individualism, in the various guises described above, in spite of Nietzsche's insights, works. That is, individualism has contributed greatly to improving human life, particularly in reducing all manner of physical suffering and increasing material abundance, across a wide range of activities and environments.

Its most potent current religious, political, and military challenges come not from Western elites but from militant Islamist movements that reject much, if not all, of the religious, social, and political practices associated with contemporary individualism, and the Christian familism of American fundamentalists that continues to defend Christian communalism and biblically sanctioned patriarchy. Yet also of possible concern are the increased loss of confidence by Western elites in the legitimacy of their power and their God and the persistently declining birth rates in western and central Europe, where populations could drop by 50 percent over the next fifty years while becoming increasingly Islamic.

Still, as long as the Western economies remain robust, people from developing countries are willing to do much of their menial labor, and their military superiority remains intact, individualism should continue to be the central organizing principle of Western religiosity, politics, economics, ethics, and art and literature. The question remains, though, whether Islam in its competition with the West will embrace much of the West's individualism before the West is forced to abandon it as no longer able to meet its most essential religious and political needs. Only time will tell.

See also *Calvinism; Catholicism, Roman; Communitarianism; Conservatism; Enlightenment; Fascism; Feminism; Hobbes, Thomas; Liberalism; Natural Law; Protestantism; Reformation; Secular Humanism; Secularization; Tocqueville, Alexis de.*

Barry Alan Shain

BIBLIOGRAPHY

Arieli, Yehoshua. *Individualism and Nationalism in American Ideology.* Baltimore, Md.: Penguin, 1966.

Coleman, Janet, ed. *The Individual in Political Theory and Practice.* Oxford: Clarendon Press, 1996.

Curry, Richard O., and Lawrence B. Goodheart, eds. *American Chameleon: Individualism in Trans-National Context.* Kent, Ohio: Kent State University Press, 1991.

Dumont, Louis. *Essays on Individualism: Modern Ideology in Anthropological Perspective.* Chicago: University of Chicago Press, 1992.

Gurevich, Aaron. *The Origins of European Individualism.* Oxford: Blackwell, 1995.

Izenberg, Gerald N. *Impossible Individuality: Romanticism, Revolution, and the Origins of Modern Selfhood, 1787–1802.* Princeton, N.J.: Princeton University Press, 1992.

Lukes, Steven. *Individualism.* Oxford: Blackwell, 1973.

Macpherson, C. B. *The Political Theory of Possessive Individualism: Hobbes to Locke.* New York: Oxford University Press, 1962.

Morris, Colin. *The Discovery of the Individual, 1050–1200.* Toronto, Ont.: University of Toronto Press, 1995.

Paterson, Orlando. *Freedom: Freedom in the Making of Western Culture.* New York: Basic Books, 1991.

Shain, Barry Alan. *The Myth of American Individualism: The Protestant Origins of American Political Thought.* Princeton, N.J.: Princeton University Press, 1994.

Shanahan, Daniel. *Toward a Genealogy of Individualism.* Amherst: University of Massachusetts Press, 1992.

Taylor, Charles. *Sources of the Self: The Making of the Modern Identity.* Cambridge: Harvard University Press, 1989.

Trevor-Roper, Hugh. *The Crisis of the Seventeenth Century: Religion, The Reformation, and Social Change.* Indianapolis, Ind.: Liberty Fund, 1967.

Indonesia

A Southeast Asian country made up of 12,000 islands, Indonesia is the fourth most populous nation and the largest majority-Muslim country in the world. Some 88.7 percent of its 230 million citizens profess Islam. With more than 300 ethnic groups, Indonesia is also one of the most culturally diverse countries in the world.

Although in the fourteenth century the Hindu Javanese kingdom of Majapahit exercised nominal suzerainty over parts of the Indonesian archipelago, it was Dutch colonialism that carved out the nation's present-day expanse. The Dutch introduced Christianity into a few tribal territories. However, as a result of a great wave of Islamic conversion that swept maritime Indonesia prior to the Dutch arrival, most of the native population was already Islamic to varying degrees of orthodoxy. Unlike the Spanish in the nearby Philippines, Dutch officials remained half-hearted promoters of Christianity, prohibiting mission activity outright in Muslim strongholds. Today 9 percent of Indonesia's population is Christian, 1.5 percent is Hindu, and 1 percent is Buddhist or Confucian.

Religion and Colonialism

In the final decades of the nineteenth century, Dutch forces launched an ambitious assault on the last remaining native states. By the early 1900s, all of the archipelago was under Dutch rule. The subsequent colonial peace facilitated a significant growth in commerce and communications. It also contributed to the spread of reformist variants of Islam and new movements of anticolonial resistance.

Inspired by Arabia's Wahhabis (puritanical reformists who had arisen in Arabia at the end of the eighteenth century), Islamic reformists appeared in central Sumatra in the early 1800s. The advent of steamboat travel in the mid-nineteenth century, however, allowed for greater contacts between Indonesia and the Middle East. An upsurge in religious pilgrimage and new patterns of religious education eventually gave rise to a mass movement for Islamic reform back in the Indies. Reformists decried what they regarded as heretical "innovations" and called for a return to the Qur'an and the Sunna (canonical traditions of the prophet Muhammad). Traditionalist Muslims took exception to the reformists' rejection of classical scholarship and authority. Muslims of a mystical or nominal Islamic persuasion disliked what they regarded as the reformists' intolerance.

Despite these disagreements, Islam provided the symbols around which the first modern organization against colonialism took shape in the early twentieth century. Founded in 1912, the Islamic Association (Sarikat Islam) attempted to use Islam to unite the country's diverse populations. From its inception, however, the movement was torn by rivalries between those committed to the establishment of an Islamic government and nationalists committed to the idea of a multiconfessional state. Most of the association's nonconfessional nationalists were Javanese of a nominally Islamic, or *abangan* ("red," "of the earth," connoting "peasant") persuasion. Half of Indonesia's polyglot population is ethnic Javanese, and, until the Islamic resurgence of the late twentieth century, the majority professed an Islam of a localized and ethnic cast. "Javanist" Islam emphasized a pantheistic mysticism rather than Islamic legalism.

Rivalry between Islamic nationalists and nonconfessional nationalists remained a central feature of Indonesian politics for most of the twentieth century. In the 1910s, as the Islamic Association's base expanded, tensions grew between the organization's Islamist and secular-socialist wings. In 1921 the orthodox leadership expelled members who refused to renounce their allegiance to Marxist socialism. During preparations for independence in mid-1945, Muslims and nonconfessional nationalists again clashed, this time over the state constitution. The nationalist leaders Sukarno and Mohammad Hatta favored nonconfessional nationalism. The 1945 constitution, however, affirmed that the Indonesian nation was not strictly secular but based on its citizens' belief in God. The constitution also made clear that, rather than

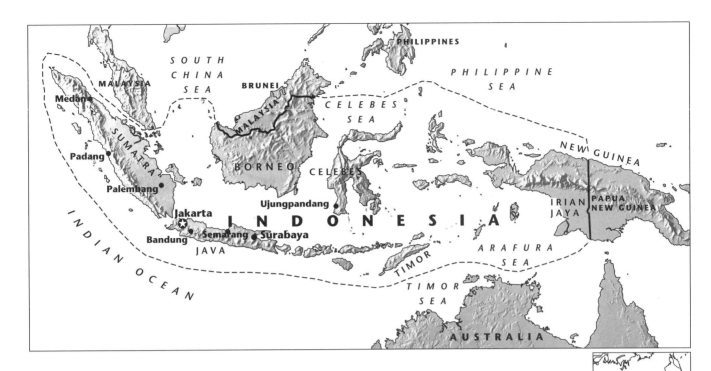

making Islam the state religion, the state recognized several separate-but-equal religions.

Independence

At the end of the war for independence in 1949, tensions between Islamists and nonconfessional nationalists exploded again, this time in the form of struggles between political parties organized along religious lines. The rivalry polarized the countryside and, aggravated by the country's economic decline, eventually degenerated into violence. In September 1965, there was a failed left-wing army officers' coup in Jakarta, in which the Communist Party leadership appeared implicated. The military command blamed the entire Communist Party for the coup and mobilized the army and Muslim parties in a systematic campaign against the communists. Over the next eight months, between 250,000 and 500,000 people were killed, and the Communist Party, heretofore the largest in the non-communist world, was destroyed. The violence also prompted two million nominal Muslims to convert from Islam to Christianity and Hinduism—the largest mass conversion from Islam in modern times.

The "New Order" government that came to power in 1966 placed strict limits on mass politics and social freedoms. Buoyed by Western and Japanese investment, however, the regime's economic programs catapulted Indonesia from the ranks of the world's poorest societies to one of Asia's emerging industrial giants. During the first two decades of his rule,

President Suharto imposed strict limits on Muslim political organizations and promoted an authoritarian variant of nonconfessional nationalism.

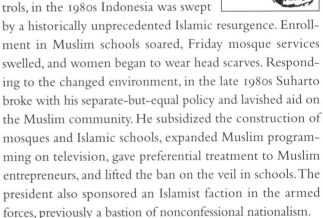

Notwithstanding government controls, in the 1980s Indonesia was swept by a historically unprecedented Islamic resurgence. Enrollment in Muslim schools soared, Friday mosque services swelled, and women began to wear head scarves. Responding to the changed environment, in the late 1980s Suharto broke with his separate-but-equal policy and lavished aid on the Muslim community. He subsidized the construction of mosques and Islamic schools, expanded Muslim programming on television, gave preferential treatment to Muslim entrepreneurs, and lifted the ban on the veil in schools. The president also sponsored an Islamist faction in the armed forces, previously a bastion of nonconfessional nationalism.

During the last ten years of his rule, the president also tried to co-opt the mainstream leadership of the country's two largest Islamic organizations, the Nahdlatul Ulama and the Muhammadiyah. Established in the early years of the twentieth century, these associations are today the largest mass-based religious organizations in the Muslim world, with some forty million and thirty million members, respectively. Both groups have long prided themselves on their commitment to Indonesian nationalism and their independence from government control.

In the 1990s, Indonesia also developed the largest Muslim-dominated prodemocracy movement in the world. President Suharto attempted to turn back the movement by appealing to the Muhammadiyah and Nahdlatul Ulama leaders for support, but Muslim leaders made clear that they supported calls for democratic reform. Rebuffed by the moderates, Suharto changed tack and reached out to hardline conservatives. The hardliners condemned the democracy movement as Christian-dominated and anti-Islamic. With the onset of the Asian economic crisis in late 1997, however, support for the Suharto regime waned, and the president was forced from power in May 1998. The months leading up to his resignation were marked by widespread violence against Chinese and Christian Indonesians. Some of these riots bore the signs of old-regime provocation, but others reflected simmering ethno-religious tensions.

The Post-Suharto Transition

The habit of using ethno-religious appeals for private political advantage did not end with Suharto's resignation. With the loss of control at the country's center, politicians and bosses in the provinces used the tactic to outflank their rivals. The practice had an especially unhappy consequence in the Moluccas, Central Kalimantan, and South Sulawesi, where rival Christians and Muslim groupings clashed. In Central Kalimantan, tribal Dayaks, nominally Christian, launched brutal campaigns of ethnic cleansing against Madurese Muslim immigrants. In the Moluccas, Christian and Muslim gangs battled each other from 1999 to 2003, leaving 9,000 dead and a million homeless.

In the months following Suharto's resignation, hundreds of radical Islamist paramilitaries also sprang up across the country. Most were tiny, but the largest had thousands of members organized in military-style battalions. Some among these latter groupings enjoyed the backing of disaffected members of the Suharto-era elite, who hoped to use the militants to block efforts to reform the military and bureaucracy. Other militant groupings, however, like the Jemaah Islamiyah (blamed for bombings on the resort island of Bali in October 2002 and 2005), were entirely independent of old-regime sponsorship. The Jemaah Islamiyah had ties to al-Qaida. After the Bali bombings in October 2002, the activities of the largest Islamist paramilitaries diminished dramatically, but the underground Jemaah Islamiyah has survived.

Notwithstanding the turbulence of the early post-Suharto period, the majority of Indonesia's Muslims remain moderate or moderately conservative in their political views. Since 1999, the national assembly has twice rebuffed efforts to implement Islamic law. The country has also made great progress toward the consolidation of a democratic electoral system. Surveys have shown that the majority of Muslims see democracy and human rights as compatible with Islam. The elections of 1999 and 2004 were a triumph of moderation, with conservative Islamists winning less than one-fifth of the vote.

Although their support in the electoral arena is limited, conservative Islamists have taken advantage of democratic freedoms to press for restrictions on the rights of non-Muslims. Working through regional governments susceptible to backroom lobbying and pressure-point demonstrations, conservatives continue to campaign for the implementation of Islamic law, as well as restrictions on the rights of secular Muslims and non-Muslim minorities. Indonesia is making impressive progress toward a democratic consolidation, but skirmishes over the proper role of Islam in politics are likely to continue for many years to come.

See also *Colonialism; Islam; Islam in Southeast Asia.*

Robert W. Hefner

BIBLIOGRAPHY

Aragon, Lorraine V. *Fields of the Lord: Animism, Christian Minorities, and State Development in Indonesia.* Honolulu: University of Hawaii Press, 2000.

Barton, Greg. *Indonesia's Struggle: Jemaah Islamiyah and the Soul of Islam.* Sydney, Australia: University of New South Wales Press, 2004.

Bertrand, Jacques. *Nationalism and Ethnic Conflict in Indonesia.* Cambridge: Cambridge University Press, 2004.

Cribb, Robert. *The Indonesian Killings, 1965–1966: Studies from Java and Bali.* Clayton, Victoria, Australia: Centre of Southeast Asian Studies, Monash University, 1990.

Hefner, Robert W. *Civil Islam: Muslims and Democratization in Indonesia.* Princeton, N.J.: Princeton University Press, 2000.

———. "Muslim Democrats and Islamist Violence in Post-Suharto Indonesia." In *Remaking Muslim Politics: Pluralism, Contestation, Democratization,* edited by Robert W. Hefner, 273–301. Princeton, N.J.: Princeton University Press, 2005.

Ramstedt, Martin, ed. *Hinduism in Modern Indonesia: A Minority Religion between Local, National, and Global Interests.* London: Routledge Curzon, 2004.

Reid, Anthony. "A Religious Revolution." In *Southeast Asia in the Age of Commerce, 1450–1680.* Vol. 2, *Expansion and Crisis.* New Haven, Conn.: Yale University Press, 1993.

Inquisition

A system of inquiry *(inquisitio)* in the Roman Catholic Church dating from the thirteenth century and associated principally with the countries of southern Europe, the inquisition was originally a normal part of the judicial process. It was taken over by the church in order to inquire into a particular offense—heresy—that began to be identified and persecuted with special vigor during the later Middle Ages. The accused came principally from sectarian movements, such as the Cathars (twelfth century), that questioned the political power of secular princes, who consequently gave their full support to persecution and backed the establishment of inquisitions.

The Inquisition as an institution did not exist in medieval times: the term was a generic description for the various commissions issued by the papacy for inquiries into heresy. These inquisitions were created by papal bull and then supported by the laws of the local prince. They came into existence from the 1230s in France and Aragon and above all in the Holy Roman Empire, where the emperor, Frederick II (1272–1337), gave them his firm support and extended them into his Italian dominions, including Sicily. As a result, the machinery of inquisitions could be found in most states from the Mediterranean to the North Sea but not in Castile, England, and Scandinavia. A papal decree for the Inquisition was first issued by Gregory IX (1143?–1241) in 1233, and administration of the commissions was put into the hands of the Dominican and Franciscan orders. The first full-scale Inquisition, directed against the Cathars, was set up in Languedoc in 1233–1234, and jurisdiction over heresy was put in the hands of the new tribunals and taken out of the hands of bishops.

Pope Innocent IV (d. 1254) in his bull *Ad Extirpanda* (1252) laid down a detailed constitution for the prosecution of heresy. In most countries the close alliance of state and papacy created an Inquisition that was subject directly to the pope and allowed to override local laws when necessary. In late-fourteenth-century Germany the papal inquisitors were influential in the persecution of Waldensians, members of a Protestant religious sect, and Beghards, religious associations of men.

The most famous of the Inquisitions was that in Spain. Social pressure against converts of Jewish origin *(conversos),* who were suspected of embracing Catholicism publicly but continuing to practice Judaism privately, led the Spanish rulers Ferdinand (1452–1516) and Isabella (1451–1504) to ask the papacy to sanction the establishment of a tribunal in Castile to inquire into their orthodoxy. The bull for an Inquisition was issued in 1478, and the new tribunal began functioning in 1480. Three years later the tribunal was also established in Aragon, where it replaced the medieval tribunal. In time local tribunals were set up all over the peninsula and also (from 1571) in the American colonies of Spain.

There were important differences between the medieval and the Spanish Inquisition. In Spain, for example, the Inquisition was in practice dependent wholly on the state and extended its functions beyond the mere pursuit of heresy. Most of its activity also involved persecution of cultural minorities not found in other countries: the *conversos* and later the Moriscos (descendants of the forcibly converted Muslim population of Spain). The tribunal was famous for the *auto de fe,* a normally public ceremony at which sentences were decreed; executions were later carried out in a different location. Though notoriously savage in its treatment of the *conversos,* the Inquisition executed fewer people than is generally believed. Deaths in its first fifty years, when most prosecutions occurred, are unlikely to have exceeded two thousand.

In the sixteenth century three important new Inquisitions were set up. In the Netherlands a papal Inquisition was founded in 1522 and acted vigorously against the new heresies of the Protestant Reformation. In Italy Pope Paul III (1468–1549) in 1542 set up a central tribunal, the Sacred Congregation of the Holy Office, which received further powers in 1588. Though busy in Naples and Milan, its main sphere of activity was the Papal States. Among its more lasting acts was the creation of an Index of Prohibited Books. The Spanish Inquisition was the model for the new Portuguese Inquisition, initially established in 1536 and then fully set up in 1547 by papal bull. The new tribunal was also exported to the colonies (in Goa in Portuguese India from 1560).

In the eighteenth century, when in most of Europe heresy had ceased to be a secular offense, the Inquisitions were restricted largely to a political role and were usually inactive. In Spain a few dissidents were prosecuted, but the activity of the tribunal was limited mainly to censorship and blocking the entry of Enlightenment ideas. In the second half of the century only four people were burnt at the stake. The Spanish Inquisition was suppressed by the French when they invaded Spain in 1808 but was afterwards restored by Ferdinand VII (1784–1833). It was not finally abolished until 1834. The Roman Inquisition survived into the twentieth century, but the Congregation of the Holy Office, which had administered the Inquisition, no longer carries out that role and was merged into the Congregation de Propaganda Fide in line with the reforms of the Second Vatican Council (1962–1965), the twenty-first ecumenical council recognized by the Roman Catholic Church, which became the symbol of the church's openness to the modern world.

See also *Enlightenment; Heresy; Protestantism; Reformation; Spain; Vatican Council, Second.*

Henry Kamen

BIBLIOGRAPHY

Bethencourt, Francisco. *L'Inquisition á l'époque moderne: Espagne, Portugal, Italie, XVe–XIX siècle.* Paris: Fayard, 1995.

Kamen, Henry. *The Spanish Inquisition: An Historical Revision.* New Haven, Conn.: Yale University Press, 1998.

Lea, Henry Charles. *A History of the Inquisition of Spain.* New York: Macmillan, 1906–1908.

van der Vekene, Emil. *Bibliotheca Bibliographica Historiae Sanctae Inquisitionis.* 2 vols. Vaduz, Liechtenstein: Topos Verlag, 1982–1983.

Iqbal, Muhammad

Indian poet and philosopher. Sir Muhammad Iqbal (1877–1938), a Muslim in British-ruled India, was influential in the movement for a separate state for India's Muslims and accordingly is regarded as the spiritual father of Pakistan. Born on the Kashmir border, between what is now India and Pakistan, Iqbal was exposed early on to the modernist ideas of Sayyid Ahmad Khan and the Aligarh movement, which advocated that Indian Muslims adapt European scientific knowledge to their own cultural situation.

After studying in Lahore, Iqbal went to London to study law and then took a Ph.D. in philosophy from the University of Munich. His poetry in Urdu and Persian addressed the issues of modernity as framed by European thinkers while retaining classical Islamic idioms and references. Iqbal was knighted by the British Crown in 1924 for his literary achievements. His English lectures on *The Reconstruction of Religious Thought in Islam* (1930) argued the need to incorporate an awareness of modern European philosophy and science into Islamic theology.

Politically, Iqbal was impressed by the Russian Revolution of 1917, though the dilemmas of colonialism and social justice also preoccupied him. His most important political legacy was his recommendation to the Muslim League (the principal political party representing the interests of Indian Muslims) in 1930 to form a Muslim state of the provinces of northwestern India. He believed a state that was separate from Hindu India was necessary for the self-determination of Indian Muslims. His formulation of the two-nation theory of India and Pakistan was adopted by Muhammad Ali Jinnah, who in 1947 with the creation of Pakistan became the new nation's first head of government.

In religious terms, Iqbal was highly critical of certain aspects of Sufism, a branch of Islam that he regarded as passive, fatalistic, and excessive in claiming union with God. The complexity of his religious and political thought is exhibited best by poems like *The Book of Eternity,* a Dante-inspired journey through the heavens (led by the thirteenth-century Persian mystic poet Rumi), which includes encounters with many Eastern and Western politicians, philosophers, and religious figures.

See also *Islam; Pakistan; Sufism.*

Carl W. Ernst

BIBLIOGRAPHY

Malik, Hafeez. "Iqbal, Muhammad," in *The Oxford Encyclopedia of the Modern Islamic World,* vol. 2. Edited by John L. Esposito. New York: Oxford University Press, 1995: 221–224.

Schimmel, Annemarie. *Gabriel's Wing: A Study into the Religious Ideas of Sir Muhammad Iqbal.* 2d ed. Lahore, Pakistan: Iqbal Academy Pakistan, 1989.

Zakaria, Rafiq. *Iqbal: The Poet and the Politician.* New Delhi, India; New York: Viking, 1993.

Iran

Iran, officially the Islamic Republic of Iran, is located in southwestern Asia between Iraq and Afghanistan and is the world's first theocratic republic. About 93 percent of its population belong to the Twelver Shi'i branch of Islam, and some 6 percent to the Sunni (mainstream) branch. Bahais and Armenian Christians constitute the larger religious minorities, and there are smaller religious communities of Jews, Nestorian Christians, and Zoroastrians.

Religion and Revolutionary Change in Iranian History

Iran is the birthplace of Zoroastrianism, the oldest millenarian world religion, whose fundamental dualism of the eternal struggle between good and evil has served as powerful imagery for numerous religio-political movements in several religious traditions. The only Muslim country where Shi'ism, which also has a strong millenarian component, has been the state religion for centuries, Iran has been a fertile land for the growth of religious hierarchies, or hierocracies, as in the Catholic Church. The Zoroastrian hierocracy, with extensive control over social life, grew during the Sassanian dynasty in the fourth and fifth centuries C.E. Since the sixteenth century, Iran has witnessed the continuous growth of a Shi'i hierocracy. This hierocracy survived the modernization of the Iranian state through the first three-quarters of the twentieth century, overthrowing the secularizing state in 1979 and declaring Iran a Shi'i theocratic republic under a supreme religious leader.

Four revolutions in which religion played a major role can be found in Iran's long history: those accompanying the rise of the Sassanian dynasty in the third century and the Safavid dynasty at the beginning of the sixteenth century, the constitutional revolution of 1906–1911, and the Islamic revolution of 1979. Furthermore, Iran was critically important in the revolution in which the Abbasid dynasty overthrew the Umayyad caliphs in the eighth century, Islam's first social revolution. In that revolution, too, religion played a major role.

The rise of the Sassanian dynasty in the third decade of the third century can be considered a revolution because it unified a large number of feudal petty kingdoms to make an empire. There was no organized Zoroastrian clergy when Ardashir (d. 240), the founder of the Sassanian dynasty, posed as the restorer of Zoroastrian religion. The gradual growth of a Zoroastrian hierocracy, which became enormously powerful by the end of the fourth century, was the long-term consequence of the central role given to the restoration of religion in the nationalist ideology of the Sassanian revolution.

The foundation of the Sassanian empire was shaken by the massive religious rebellion of Mazdak, who preached an early form of communism at the end of the fifth century. The empire was overthrown by the conquering Muslims in the second quarter of the seventh century. The conversion of Iran to Islam was slow, however, and occurred on a large scale only after the Abbasid revolution in the mid-eighth century. The proselytizing Islamic movements, which proposed equality between Arabs and the non-Arab converts, played a critical role in the Abbasid revolution, as did the long-settled Arab Muslims of Khurasan in the northeast. The Abbasid revolution thus opened the way for the full integration of Iranians into Islamic society and brought about the conversion of the majority of the Iranian population to Islam.

Until the end of the Middle Ages, the majority of the Iranians were Sunni Muslims. In the fourteenth and fifteenth centuries, however, a number of Shi'i millenarian movements appeared in Iran, usually in connection with Sufism (popular, mystical Islam). The last of these, the Safavid movement, culminated in what may be considered the first successful Shi'i revolution. The leader of the Safavid movement, Shah Isma'il I (1486–1524), was considered the mahdi (Islam's messianic restorer and rightly guided leader of the end of time) and the incarnation of God by his Turkoman followers. His millenarian movement turned the Turkoman tribesmen into a zealous fighting force for the conquest of Iran and its subsequent conversion to Shi'ism. Once in power, the Safavid rulers modified their millenarian claims, saying that their reign would continue until the mahdi appeared. The Twelver Shi'ism that was spread in Iran under the patronage of the Safavid rulers by Shi'i *ulama* (religious leaders), who often came from Lebanon and Arab Iraq, was more doctrinally systematic than the extremist faith of the conquering Turkomans. These *ulama* also founded a Shi'i hierocracy, which became increasingly powerful and began to assert itself against the Safavid monarchs in the latter part of the seventeenth century.

After the collapse of the Safavid dynasty in the eighteenth century, the Shi'i religious authorities were forced to subsist on their own without state support. They developed the doctrinal basis of their juristic authority during the civil wars of that century and emerged as a powerful hierocracy at the end of it. The hierocracy remained independent of the state and consolidated its power throughout the nineteenth century. Its highest ranking members assumed the title of Ayatollah (sign of God) by the beginning of the twentieth. State and *ulama* were drawn together in the face of the common threat from the Babi millenarian movement, which initiated the Bahai religion, in the middle of the nineteenth century. The incipient modernization of the autocratic state and the accompanying subservience to imperialist powers, however, drew them increasingly apart thereafter.

The Shi'i religious authorities appeared in the forefront of the massive popular protests that forced the shah to grant Iran a constitution in 1906, in what was Asia's first modern political revolution. As the secularizing implications of parliamentary legislation became clear and, especially as secularization of the judiciary could be seen as loss of clerical power, some religious leaders distanced themselves from the constitutionalists, while others actively opposed them. The Shi'i hierocracy generally withdrew from politics in disillusionment at the end of the revolutionary period.

The modernization of the state under Reza Shah Pahlavi (1877–1944) in the 1920s and 1930s resulted in a drastic diminution of the institutional prerogatives and social power of the hierocracy. However, it did not impair the legitimacy of the exclusive hierocratic authority of the *ulama*. Consequently, the hierocracy not only survived but also withstood the modern state's challenge to its virtually exclusive control over religious learning and over the authoritative interpretation of Shi'i Islam.

The Islamic Revolution

The establishment of an Islamic theocracy ruled by the Shi'i *ulama* can be regarded as the last stage of the evolution of clerical authority in Shi'i Islam. After the Shi'i hierocracy had freed itself from the tutelage of political authority characteristic of the Safavid era, the next logical possibility was to assert the superiority of the hierocracy over the state by extending clerical authority to the political sphere. This logical possibility was actualized when Ayatollah Ruhollah Khomeini (1900–1989) transformed a sizable section of the Shi'i hierocracy into a revolutionary political party. The projected final stage of the growth of Shi'i clerical authority then became the blueprint for the militant clerics who overthrew the shah in 1979.

Khomeini and his followers drew on the cult of martyrdom and on the millenarian elements in the Shi'i tradition to mobilize the Iranian masses for the revolution that was to realize the Shi'i clerical rule. With the emergence of an Islamic revolutionary movement in the late 1960s, for instance, the lay Islamic ideologue Ali Shari'ati interpreted the belief in the coming of the mahdi as an allegory of the imminent revolution of the oppressed masses of the developing countries.

As massive demonstrations and strikes paralyzed the government, all political groups that formed the revolutionary coalition against the shah, Mohammad Reza Pahlavi,

accepted the leadership of Khomeini, who was a Grand Ayatollah. After the overthrow of the monarchy in 1979, Khomeini appointed Mehdi Bazargan, the leading member of the liberal and nationalist elements in the revolutionary coalition, as the prime minister of a provisional government. Nevertheless, a clerically dominated Assembly of Experts, elected in place of a constituent assembly, bypassed a draft constitution submitted by the provisional government and proposed a theocratic government based on the Mandate of the Jurist, as advocated by Khomeini, with an elected parliament (Majlis) and president. This was approved by a referendum in December 1979, shortly after the occupation of the American embassy and the taking of its staff as hostages resulted in the toppling of the provisional government of Bazargan. Although another moderate, Abol-Hasan Bani-Sadr, was elected president in January 1980, the Majlis, which was controlled by the clerical party, impeached him in June 1981. The revolutionary power struggle moved into the streets and entered its most violent phase. The new president and prime minister and some seventy organizers of the clericalist Islamic Republican Party died in explosions, while many important members of the clerical elite were assassinated by suicide attackers belonging to the *mujahedin,* the Islamic radical group that had supported Bani-Sadr. The revolutionary terror did not abate until early 1983, after thousands of men and women belonging to the *mujahedin* and other rival revolutionary groups had been executed or killed in street fights.

With the ending of the revolutionary power struggle and elimination of nonclericalist partners in the revolutionary coalition of 1978, Khomeini's clericalist theory of government on the basis of the Mandate of the Jurist was implemented. Iran became the first theocratic republic in the world. The constitution of the Islamic Republic of Iran gives its *rahbar,* the head of state and supreme religious jurist, extensive religious and secular powers, including appointment of the commanders of the armed forces and the head of the judiciary and confirmation of the elected president. The position was held by Khomeini until his death in 1989. Ayatollah Sayyid Ali Khamanei succeeded him. Although the 270 representatives in the Majlis are elected, all Majlis legislation must conform with Islam as determined by six clerical jurists of the Council of Guardians. This council automatically reviews all enactments. The constitution was amended in 1989 to strengthen the presidency by eliminating the position of the prime minister. The amendment also clarified the authority of the clerical Assembly of Experts in electing and dismissing the *rahbar.* The Council for the Determination of the Interest of the Islamic Republic, which had been set up by Khomeini to arbitrate in cases of deadlock between the Majlis and the Council of Guardians, was given the additional function of acting as an advisory body to the *rahbar.*

The Reform Movement

The major cause of the victory of the Islamic revolution in Iran, or to be more precise, the independence of the Shi'ite hierocracy from the state, was structural. The development of an Islamic political ideology, or what is generally called political Islam, was not impressive, as compared with Egypt, Pakistan, and other Muslim countries, and its chief architect, Shari'ati (d. 1977), was out of favor with Khomeini and the Islamic regime. Nevertheless, the 1979 Constitution of the Islamic Revolution declared "the Islamic ideology" its basis. The post-revolution reform movement was part of a political liberalization during the pragmatic administration of President Akbar Hashemi Rafsanjani (1989–1997). Intellectually, it had its roots in the rejection of Khomeini's theocratic ideology as part of a more general call for Islamic reform.

In the early 1990s, the lay Islamic intellectual Abd al-Karim Sorush made a radical break with the Shari'ati's revo-

lutionary characterization of Islam as an ideology, arguing that Islam as a world religion is "richer than ideology." An ideological society, he said, stifles free enquiry and intellectual development, whereas Islam as a world religion allows for a variety of different interpretations that open the road to intellectual creativity. Sorush also advanced the idea of "Islamic secularism," arguing for the separation of religion from the state and implicitly rejecting the justification of theocratic government. At about the same time, the cleric Mohammad Mojtahed-Shabastari rejected the fundamental premises of "Islamic political jurisprudence" by arguing that Islamic jurisprudence was never constitutive of political order, was always pragmatic, and was designed to answer practical questions that arose within the framework of existing political regimes. Mojtahed-Shabastari proposed a hermeneutic approach to Islamic law and religion. This led to the popularization of the idea that different readings of Islam were legitimate and to an equally radical break with the twentieth-century apologetic Islamic modernism by Sorush's advocacy of religious pluralism in the latter part of the 1990s.

The advocacy of Islamic reform by Sorush and Mojtahed-Shabastari paved the way for the political reform movement led by President Mohammad Khatami (1997–2005), who endorsed Mojtahed-Shabastari's justification of different readings of Islam and Sorush's idea of religious democracy. His administration instituted freedom of the press in 1997, and his reformist supporters won a considerable majority of Majlis seats in the national election of 2000. They met, however, with the staunch and determined opposition of the clerical establishment and Ayatollah Sayyed 'Ali Khamane'i, Khomeini's successor as the supreme leader, and were in the end defeated. Although the reform movement can be said to have failed politically, it had a profound and lasting cultural impact, undermining the legitimacy of theocratic government.

In August 2005 hard-liner Mahmoud Ahmadinejad was elected president. During his first year in office Ahmadinejad refused to heed international calls to halt uranium enrichment in Iran's nuclear program and provocatively threatened to "wipe Israel off the map." He maintained popular support at home, however, speaking to Iranians about matters close to them, such as the economy and education, and promising to address their concerns.

See also *Bahai; Islam; Khomeini, Ruhollah Musavi; Mahdi; Revolutions; Sufism; Theocracy.*

Said Amir Arjomand

BIBLIOGRAPHY

Akhavi, Shahrough. *Religion and Politics in Contemporary Iran.* Albany: State University of New York Press, 1980.

Amanat, Abbas. *Resurrection and Renewal: The Making of the Babi Movement in Iran, 1844–1850.* Ithaca, N.Y.: Cornell University Press, 1989.

Arjomand, S. A. *The Shadow of God and the Hidden Imam: Religion, Political Order, and Societal Change in Shi'ite Iran from the Beginning to 1890.* Chicago: University of Chicago Press, 1984.

———. *The Turban for the Crown: The Islamic Revolution in Iran.* New York: Oxford University Press, 1988.

———. "The Rise and Fall of President Khatami and the Reform Movement in Iran." *Constellations* 12, no. 4 (2005): 502–520.

Bakhash, Shaul. *The Reign of the Ayatollahs.* New York: Basic Books, 1984.

Brown, E. G. *The Persian Revolution, 1905–1909.* Cambridge: Cambridge University Press, 1910.

Hairi, A. H. *Shi'ism and Constitutionalism in Iran.* Leiden, Netherlands: Brill, 1977.

Jahanbakhsh, Forough. *Islam, Democracy, and Religious Modernism in Iran (1953–2000).* Leiden, Netherlands: Brill, 2001.

Keddie, Nikki R. *Religion and Rebellion in Iran: The Tobacco Protests of 1891–92.* London: Frank Cass, 1966.

Iraq

Situated in southwest Asia, Iraq is a multiethnic and sectarian republic with a history of cohabitation among different religions and sects. Some 97 percent of the population is Muslim; the remaining 3 percent are Christians. Historical Iraq (Mesopotamia) is perhaps the oldest civilization in the world and is called the cradle of civilization. The first code of laws was drawn up there under Hammurabi around 1800 B.C.E. A small community of Jews still exists but their numbers can be counted in the tens.

Since the founding of the state of Iraq in 1921 until 2003 successive Iraqi governments have sought to create a secular and unified state, relegating religion mostly to the private domain. Although Iraq's Muslim population is divided between the Sunni and Shi'i sects, Sunnis have dominated government for centuries. This changed, however, after the invasion of Iraq by the United States and its allies in March 2003. This invasion led to the downfall of the Sunni-dominated regime of Saddam Hussein. Since then the basis of government in the state has changed. Two changes have been striking. First has been the sharp rise in religious feeling together with hostility between the two main Muslim communities in the country, the Shi'is and the Sunnis. The second has been the form of government, which is moving from a unitary state to a federal state. The Kurds, who compose some 20 percent of the Iraqi population of about twenty-eight million, gained autonomy in their region in northern Iraq.

Politics and Religion in Iraq, 1921–1958 (The Era of the Monarchy)

Most of the Shi'i Arabs live in southern and central Iraq and most of the Sunni Arab population (about 20 percent of the total) live in the center, in Baghdad, and in the northwest. There are heavily mixed areas where Sunnis and Shi'is live together, especially in the greater Baghdad region and in the eastern province of Diyala. Under the monarchy, Sunnis and Shi'is lived peacefully together. They often entered partnership relations in business and trade, and in urban areas there was considerable intermarriage. Some estimates put intermarriages in mixed areas close to 40 percent. The Jews of Iraq trace their origin to the Babylonian captivity of the sixth century B.C.E. They were often prosperous and influential merchants. One of them, Sassun Hasqail, became a minister of finance in the 1920s and played a role in strengthening the foundation of the newly established Iraqi state. The Jews in Iraq lived mainly in Baghdad and played an important role in enriching Iraqi culture, especially in the field of music and song. After the Arab-Israeli war of 1948 their numbers were gradually reduced. Today they number less than one hundred.

The Christians in Iraq live mainly in Baghdad and in or around the city of Mosul in the north. Christians (estimated at 750,000) are slowly migrating outside Iraq, mainly to the United States and Europe. They are primarily fleeing political instability and seeking better economic conditions.

Since the rise of the state of Iraq in 1921, however, the Sunni Arabs have had the upper hand in government and the army. When Iraq was occupied by the British during the First World War, they created the new state as a mandate under the League of Nations. The Shi'is chose to boycott this process and refused to cooperate with the British. Some Sunnis, however, came forward and worked with the British. As a result, during the era of the mandate and the monarchy, few Shi'is rose to the higher ranks in the government and the army. However, many Shi'is became rich landlords and merchants. While the upper ranks of the army were filled with Sunni officers, the lower ranks were both Sunni and Shi'i. In the famous 1920 revolt against the British, both Sunnis and Shi'is participated. The participation of the Shi'i

Arab tribes in central and southern Iraq drove the British to concede to some of the demands of the Iraqis for independence. The monarchy in Iraq was toppled by a military coup on July 14, 1958, and, for the following ten years Iraq was governed by military rulers. During that period Iraq saw several coups d'état by Arab nationalist officers.

Iraq under the Ba'th Party, 1968–2003

The Ba'th Arab Socialist Party came to power in Iraq after staging a successful military coup in July 1968. The Ba'th Party announced itself as a secular, pan-Arab, socialist party whose membership was open to Sunnis, Shi'is, and even Christians. The real power, however, remained in the top leaders of the party who were mostly Sunnis and belonged to an Arab tribal clan situated in or around the town of Tikrit, some one hundred miles north of Baghdad. During the 1970s internal feuds and struggles among Ba'th leaders enabled Saddam Hussein, a member of that clan, to become president of the Iraqi Republic. During Saddam's tenure, which lasted twenty-four years (from 1979 to 2003), he ruled with an iron fist, concentrating all power in his hands. He put his relatives and clan members, all of whom were Sunni Arabs, into leading positions. Although many Shi'is were members of the Ba'th Party or were in the army and the security forces, Shi'i religious leaders and scholars were largely hostile to the regime and were under suspicion, imprisoned, and assassinated. Many Shi'is fled the country. Shi'i rituals, such as religious processions and gatherings, were strictly forbidden.

Under the monarchy, dissatisfied Shi'i youth joined extremist underground parties, such as the Iraq Communist Party, but the influence of the Communist Party diminished under Ba'th rule. In its place, dissatisfied Shi'i clerics and other personalities started, in the late 1950s and 1960s, to form underground Islamic movements. Chief among these was al-Da'wa al-Islamiyya (The Islamic "Call"). In the 1960s and 1970s, it spread and increased its membership steadily. The Da'wa became so powerful by the end of the 1970s that it committed several acts of sabotage against public buildings and tried to assassinate some important figures in the Ba'th regime. The Ba'th regime responded harshly to the Shi'i opposition. During the 1970s and early 1980s, it ordered the deportation of several hundred thousand Iraqis of Persian origin to Iran, accusing them of not being genuine Iraqis and of disloyalty to the state of Iraq. But in general, Shi'i officers and soldiers fought along with their Sunni counterparts

against Iran in the Iran-Iraq war (1980–1988). Arab Sunnis also formed underground opposition groups such as the Muslim Brotherhood.

Saddam Hussein's occupation of Kuwait (August 1990–February 1991) ended in a disaster when the United States, under the banner of the United Nations (UN), organized an international military force that attacked the Iraqis and drove them out of Kuwait. In March 1991 the Kurds in northern Iraq and the Shi'is in southern Iraq revolted against the government in Baghdad. When Kurds fled into neighboring Turkey and Iran, U.S. and UN intervention helped protect the Kurds by imposing a No-Fly Zone on some of northern Iraq, obliging Saddam to withdraw his forces from Kurdish areas. This withdrawal gave the Kurds a free hand in ruling themselves. In southern Iraq, however, Saddam put down the Shi'i revolt with brutality.

Iraq was greatly affected by the 1979–1980 Islamic revolution in Iran. This revolt was successful in putting an end to the Iranian monarchy and in installing an Islamic republic that threatened to export its revolution throughout the Muslim world. Encouraged by the Iranian revolution and reacting to Saddam's persecution, many Iraqi Shi'i political activists and politicians took refuge in Iran. Others went to other countries such as Syria and the United Kingdom. One of the leading Iraqi Shiʻi clerics who went to Iran was Muhammad Baqir al-Hakim. In 1982, with the help of the Iranians, he established a Shiʻi opposition movement to Saddam Hussein's regime, under an umbrella group known as the Supreme Council of the Islamic Revolution in Iraq (SCIRI).

The Overthrow of Saddam Hussein

The invasion of Iraq by U.S.-led coalition forces in 2003 not only toppled Saddam Hussein's regime, but also led to a fundamental shake-up of the country and its historically accepted socio-political order. It opened the door to Sunni-Shiʻi sectarian feuding. The invasion and the new political order that followed put an end to the Sunni hegemony over the country that had lasted since the establishment of the state of Iraq in 1921. It also opened the door for Shiʻis to gain political control over Iraq. On March 19, 2003, a U.S.-led international military expedition against Saddam invaded Iraq from neighboring Kuwait. It was able to occupy the country with relative ease and entered Baghdad on April 9, 2003. The attack was justified by the United States on the grounds that Saddam was still holding weapons of mass destruction contrary to UN resolutions that had demanded that he give them up. The invasion opened the door for many former Iraqi opposition leaders to return to Iraq from exile, chief among them Ahmad Chalabi, Ayyad Allawi, and Muhammad Baqir al-Hakim, all of whom brought with them their military and political organizations. Muhammad Baqir al-Hakim, who returned with his Badr Brigade, was killed on August 29, 2003; his brother, Abd al-Aziz al-Hakim, took control of SCIRI and, with the Badr Brigade, a para-military body, became a major player in Iraqi politics.

Soon after the occupation, Sunni Arab resistance against the occupation began to operate, mainly in Sunni-dominated areas in central, northern, and western Iraq. Acts of sabotage and hit-and-run operations were undertaken against U.S. and coalition forces in these areas and the rest of the country. The Shiʻis, however, cooperated with the Americans, at least to some extent, slowly extending their political power over the country. They did so on the basis of the idea that, as Shiʻis, they represented the majority of the population. The first indication of a transfer of power to Shiʻis came on July 13, 2003, when Paul Bremer, the American administrator of Iraq, nominated a twenty-five-member Iraqi government body called the Iraqi Interim Governing Council.

Its members included a majority of Shiʻis—thirteen. There also were five Sunnis, five Kurds, one Turkman, and one Assyrian Christian. The Sunnis generally attacked that council, accusing its members of being puppets of the Americans. Since that time, Iraq has gone through two general elections in 2005 in which Shiʻi parties and personalities won either a majority or a plurality of seats in parliament. This enabled them to choose the prime minister (always a Shiʻi) and to form cabinets in which Shiʻis constitute a majority.

Sunni Arabs are fighting on several fronts to reverse their loss of position. First, Sunni insurgents are fighting Americans and many of those collaborating with Americans—whether Sunni or Shiʻi. Many of these Sunnites are composed of followers of the old regime (Baʻthists or former Saddam supporters). There are also a number of armed Sunni religious extremist groups (Salafis), as well as Arab nationalists and tribal contingents. These groups work under different names. They use extreme violence and are responsible for killing thousands of Americans and Iraqis using direct confrontation, suicide bombings, car bombs, roadside explosive devices, and mortars and rockets. Working alongside these Sunni groups are elements of the lethal terrorist al-Qaida organization in Iraq, headed by a Jordanian-born terrorist, Abu Musab al-Zarqawi, who has ties to al-Qaida. Zarqawi not only recruited Iraqis but also had volunteers from the rest of the Arab world who entered Iraq through its poorly guarded borders, mainly with Syria. In 2005 Zarqawi declared a holy war, against Americans and against the Shiʻis whom he accuses of being heretics. His followers use extreme methods on their enemies such as torture, beheading, and the slaughter of innocent civilians.

Zarqawi was killed on June 8, 2006, after an American air attack on one of his hideaways near the city of Baquba. His group, al-Qaida in Iraq, said a few days later that it had chosen a new leader whose identity as of September 2006 remained unknown. Sunni political parties have changed their attitude toward the political process in Iraq. After boycotting it for almost two years (2003–2005), they slowly started to participate. Two main Sunni groups are represented in the parliament formed after the December 2005 election. They are the Iraqi Consensus Front and the National Dialogue Front. Only one main Sunni group, the Association of Muslim Scholars, is boycotting the political process, claiming that it will continue to do so as long as the Americans are in Iraq.

Shi'i Opposition to the U.S. Presence in Iraq

SCIRI and al-Da'wa, both Shi'i, are ambivalent on the question of the American military presence in Iraq. However, one important Shi'i political group is opposed. This organization goes under the name of al-Tayyar al-Sadr (the Sadri Current). The group is headed by Muqtada al-Sadr, a Shi'i cleric with a Shi'i militia of some ten thousand, known as the Jaysh al-Mahdi (The Messiah's Army). Sadr fought the Americans on two occasions in 2004. These three main Shi'i groups (al-Da'wah, SCIRI, and the Sadrists) together with four less important groups formed a unified Shi'i front, the Unified Iraqi Coalition, and their candidates won a plurality of 48 percent in the December 15, 2005, elections.

A voice of Shi'i moderation in Iraqi politics is that of the highly respected Grand Ayatallah Ali Husain al-Sistani, an Iranian-born cleric who has lived in Najaf since the 1950s. Sistani injects himself into politics through statements, religious edits (fatwas), and meetings with personalities. In general he has acted to calm the situation.

Iraq on the Brink of Civil War

In 2006 Iraq was passing through a critical phase of its history. There were calls to divide Iraq into three ethnic and sectarian components (Sunni, Shi'i, and Kurdish), united only by a loose federation. The Shi'is would form a region in the south and parts of the center; a second region would be made up of the Sunnis in the northwest and parts east of Baghdad; and the Kurds would have a third region in the north. Equally important for the future of Iraq is the ongoing sectarian feud between the Sunni and Shi'i Arabs that is leading to bloodshed and, in some cases, sectarian cleansing. This sectarian conflict started at the end of 2003, as the Sunnis complained of the increasing power of the Shi'is in government, as well as the rising influence of Shi'i political groups and their militias. Such complaints became louder in 2004, when preachers raised these issues in Sunni mosques. Shi'is retaliated in their rhetoric. Soon thereafter, politicians on both sides began to accuse one another of sectarianism. Sunni bands of insurgents together with criminals and vigilantes began to attack Shi'i passengers in buses and cars, especially in the areas south of Baghdad. Shi'is began to retaliate in kind. Matters took a downward turn under the cabinet of Ibrahim al-Jafari (May 2005–May 2006). Sunnis accused the Shi'i minister of interior, Bayan Jabr Solagh, of recruiting security and police forces from the Badr Brigade. Sunnis accused the police and security forces of arresting, torturing,

and even executing Sunnis. After a powerful explosion destroyed a revered Shi'i shrine in Samarra north of Baghdad on February 22, 2006, Shi'i militia and bands of vigilantes attacked tens of Sunni mosques in Baghdad. These events were followed by an underground war between Sunnis and Shi'is in mixed parts of Baghdad, where Sunnis and Shi'is have lived together. Thousands of Shi'i and Sunni families left their homes and took refuge in predominantly Sunni or Shi'i areas in Baghdad and elsewhere. Sectarian violence in Iraq continued despite the appeals for calm and reconciliation from many Iraqi clergymen and political leaders. This phenomenon must be viewed in the context of the deteriorating situation in Iraq, where the institutions of state have weakened; unemployment was very high; infrastructure and public services had declined; and social illnesses, such as corruption, were rampant.

See also *Islam*.

Louay Y. Bahry

BIBLIOGRAPHY

Batatu, Hanna. *The Old Social Classes and the Revolutionary Movements in Iraq.* 2d ed. Princeton: Princeton University Press, 1982.
Farouk-Sluglett, Marion, and Peter Sluglett. *Iraq since 1958: From Revolution to Dictatorship.* Rev. ed. London: I.B.Tauris, 2001.
Hashim, Ahmed. *Insurgency and Counter-Insurgency in Iraq.* Ithaca: Cornell University Press, 2006.
Jabar, Faleh. *The Shi'ite Movement in Iraq.* London: Saqi Books, 2003.
Jabar, Faleh, ed. *Ayatallahs, Sufis, and Ideologues: State, Religion, and Social Movements in Iraq.* London: Saqi Books, 2002.
Luizard, Pierre-Jean. *La Formation de l'Irak Contemporain.* Paris: CNRS Editions, 1991.
Marr, Phebe. *The Modern History of Iraq.* 2nd ed. Boulder, Colo.: Westview Press, 2004.
Meijer, Roel. "The Association of Muslim Scholars in Iraq." *Middle East Report* 237 (Winter 2005).
Nakash, Yitzhak. *The Shi'is of Iraq.* 2d ed. Princeton: Princeton University Press, 2003.
Tripp, Charles. *A History of Iraq.* 2d ed. Cambridge: Cambridge University Press, 2002.
Wiley, Joyce. *The Islamic Movement of Iraqi Shi'as.* Boulder, Colo.: Lynne Reinner, 1992.

Ireland

An island to the west of Britain, Ireland is politically divided into the 26 counties of the Republic of Ireland—a sovereign state since 1922—and the six counties of Northern Ireland, which remains part of the United Kingdom. The

Republic of Ireland has four million people, 90 percent of whom are Catholic. Northern Ireland has one and a half million people. Roughly 60 percent are Protestant and unionist (pro–United Kingdom), and the remainder are Roman Catholic and nationalist (pro–united Ireland). The historical origins of division go back four centuries to English colonialism, when English and Scottish Protestants settled in Catholic Ireland.

Division and Partition

Over time, three religious groups developed in Ireland and can be ranked hierarchically in terms of power. The rulers were "the Ascendancy," or landowning elite, whose origin was English. They formed the leadership of the Protestant (Anglican) Church of Ireland, set up after the English Reformation of the sixteenth and seventeenth centuries, and favored those farmers and servants who were its members. Their church membership came to make up more than 10 percent of the Irish population. The Presbyterians and related smaller churches were next, also at about 10 percent. Mainly from Scotland, they settled largely in the northern province of Ulster and had few rights until the late eighteenth century. Third were the majority Catholic Irish, who preceded by centuries the Scottish and English settlers. They were pauperized by the elite until the late eighteenth century, when they began their slow struggle to attain power. The nineteenth century began with the struggle for religious freedom, which led into a struggle for control and ownership of the land and, finally, towards political independence.

As the Catholic Irish began to achieve their aims, Presbyterians and the Church of Ireland in the north combined to form a political alliance against them (1886–1912) in the form of the Unionist Party. In 1912 their pact was sealed with the mass signing of a "Solemn League and Covenant," committed to removing Ulster from any future united Ireland. Catholic Republicans in the south were undeterred and, in 1916, many of them took part in a doomed rising against the British state. This led to a War of Independence that concluded in 1922 with the partition of the island into separate states in the South and North.

The state in the South while never completely dominated by the Catholic Church was heavily influenced by its social teachings. The Catholic Church developed a monopoly over the vision of Irish society and saw itself as its moral guardian. The Church only influenced the economic and more political policies of the new state indirectly, but it had enormous power and influence in education, health and social welfare. Southern Protestants felt and became increasingly marginalized. Northern Protestants felt threatened by what they saw as a premodern Roman Catholic state on their doorstep and by the ongoing rhetoric by nationalists for the abolition of Northern Ireland and the creation of a United Ireland.

The newly constituted Northern Ireland included half a million Catholic nationalists who suffered economic and political discrimination for most of the twentieth century. The British government turned a blind eye as Northern Ireland became dominated by Protestants. Catholic nationalists found it difficult to obtain jobs or decent housing, and the Northern Irish parliament (set up in 1922) adjusted the voting system and electoral boundaries to the detriment of Catholic representation. The police were given draconian powers of arrest and detention, using them mainly against Catholics. Only with the development of the civil rights movement in the 1960s did unrest grow and threaten Protestant unionist supremacy. Public order collapsed in 1969 as riots broke out. In 1971 local minorities were forcibly cleared from their homes, and terrorist paramilitaries from both sides, including the Irish Republican Army (IRA), began campaigns of bombing and assassination. The violence continued, leaving some 3,500 people dead. By 1972 the British government felt compelled to act decisively. The British abolished the provincial parliament and introduced direct rule from London.

Until 1997 the British government in effect backed the unionist cause by maintaining the status quo. Then the new Labour government restarted talks to bring about a political solution. The negotiators recognized that the continuation of civil disturbance and demonstrations was encouraged by the lack of a form of government in the province that was acceptable to both unionists and nationalists. The result was an agreement signed April 10, 1998, known as the Good Friday (or Belfast) Agreement, which was designed to bring peace to Northern Ireland. Voters in the Republic of Ireland amended their constitution, abandoning claims to the North. By voting for a new assembly that would fairly represent Catholics and Protestants alike, a strife-weary majority in the North rejected the sectarian violence that had plagued the province for so long. Elections for the new Northern Ireland assembly were held and, later, a power-sharing Executive of Unionists and Nationalists was formed.

This was fraught with difficulties, particularly in relation to continued Unionists claims that Sinn Féin, the main nationalist party in the Executive, still had links with its military wing, the Provisional IRA (PIRA).

Protestantism and Northern Ireland

The Protestant coalition arose as a result of the need for unity to sustain the separate status of Northern Ireland. Protestantism is strong, with half its population attending church on a regular basis, with youth, young adults, and the urban working class the least likely among them to attend. The Presbyterians and the Church of Ireland remain the largest denominations, but there are also some twenty smaller ones, including the Free Presbyterians, a breakaway church founded by the Reverend Ian Paisley. Paisley, a militant unionist, is leader of the Democratic Unionist Party, which has taken over from the Ulster Unionists to become the largest political party in the North. Paisley is renowned and has become on iconic figure of resistance not just to Sinn Féin and the IRA but also to the Roman Catholic Church. He has led numerous demonstrations aimed at preventing any compromise between Protestants and Catholics. The predominant characteristic shared by Protestant churches and sects in Northern Ireland is Calvinism. This sometimes appears in the form of Sabbatarian politics, with efforts to keep alcohol, sports centers, and places of entertainment inaccessible on Sundays (the Sabbath, the biblical day of rest).

Although Protestants from various churches are frequently kept apart by differences over biblical interpretation and matters of church order, they are bound together by biblical preaching and common opposition to a united Ireland dominated by Catholic, nationalist, and republican traditions. There is even some direct element of anti-Catholicism. Rhetoric is frequently derived from the Reformation period, with the papacy and the Catholic Mass particular targets. Powerful stereotypes of Irish Catholics as drunks, with large families, who are ruled by priests, bishops, and pope, are still part of populist imagery. Large numbers of the working- and middle-class populations are involved in religious-political societies dedicated to the defense of "a Protestant state for a Protestant people." The most important of these are the Orange Order, the Apprentice Boys of Londonderry, and the Black Preceptory (a small society made up of the Protestant elite). These societies help bind political activists on a local basis from their diverse church affiliations. As well as being part of these organizations as chaplains, a

number of Protestant clergy are involved directly in formal party politics. The unionists are split between moderate, British-oriented politics and more obstinate, Ulster-oriented politics. The latter, who describe themselves as loyalists, are made up of a largely unchurched, proviolence wing and a

religious fundamentalist wing. Roy Wallis and Steve Bruce argue that the exclusivity of some forms of Calvinism, particularly the stress on being chosen, reinforces ethnic ideas of Protestant superiority over Catholics and strengthens the sense of being a people apart. This argument seems supported by the Protestant fundamentalists' affirmation that their religious freedom is under threat from the tyranny of a Catholic state, which the Republic of Ireland is purported to be. They see the British government as unfaithful to them and likely to betray their cause.

Catholicism and the Republic

Sinn Féin, the political party that originated the southern state, split internally over Britain's treaty demands. Although most of Sinn Féin's leadership was republican, the majority still voted reluctantly to accept the king as head of state. The dissenting minority, led by Eamon De Valera, split away and fought a civil war (1922–1923), which it soon lost. The bitter division set the pattern for politics in the southern state for sixty years, with continuing confrontation between protreaty and antitreaty parties; until the 1980s the antitreaty republicans usually won. A major victory was the replacement of the British-imposed constitution of 1922 with the republican constitution of 1937, which was infused with Catholic themes. The preamble identified the "fathers" of the people of Ireland as the oppressed Catholic community of the past. Articles 41–44 embodied papal social teaching grounded in natural law theory: the state was deemed to play a subsidiary role to the family, which in turn was seen as the basic unit of society. Divorce was banned; private property was protected, as was religious ownership of schools and other institutions. The Catholic Church even had a special position "as the guardian of the faith professed by the great majority of the citizens," until a referendum in 1971 removed this phrase.

The church influenced decisions on ordinary legislation. Bishops advised on various acts, including those concerning censorship of films (1923) and publications (1929), vocational education (1929), and public health (1945). They successfully and secretly opposed the introduction of health and welfare measures for mothers and their children in the 1947–1951 period, though this was to be the high point of their power.

Within the new state, the leadership of the Catholic Church controlled significant aspects of moral culture. This type of religious politics, termed "monopoly Catholicism" by David Martin, was characteristic of the church's approach to state rulers (kings, dictators, democratic governments) in the predominantly Catholic countries of Austria, Spain, Portugal, Italy, and Poland, as well as Ireland. The church encouraged loyalty and law and order in return for control over the people's beliefs and moral values. It was often successful in developing and running education, health, and social welfare systems funded by the state and in obtaining legislation to preserve family morality, such as banning birth control and censoring publications. Since then there has been a steady erosion of its influence, and a successful referendum in 1995 overturned the constitutional ban on divorce—against the bishops' wishes. Popular support for the Church remains high, with almost half of Catholics attending church at least once a week: this is a reduction from the 9 in 10 who attended in 1973. The decline of monopoly Catholicism has been partnered by a diminution in the

power of republicanism and a new mood of realism within the nationalist alliance. The growing acceptance of the rights of the Protestant unionist minority and the need for compromise over the Northern Ireland question led to the Good Friday peace agreement in 1998.

See also *Anglicanism; Calvinism; Catholicism, Roman; Great Britain; Nationalism; Natural Law; Papacy; Presbyterians; Protestantism; Reformation; State Churches.*

Tom Inglis

BIBLIOGRAPHY

Bruce, Steve. *The Edge of the Union: The Ulster Loyalist Political Vision.* Oxford: Oxford University Press, 1994.

Fulton, John. *The Tragedy of Belief: Division, Politics, and Religion in Ireland.* Oxford: Clarendon Press, 1991.

Garvin, Tom. *Preventing the Future: Why was Ireland so Poor for so Long?* Dublin: Gill and Macmillan, 2004.

Harkness, David W. *Ireland in the Twentieth Century: Divided Ireland.* New York: St. Martin's, 1996.

Inglis, Tom. *Moral Monopoly: The Rise and Fall of the Catholic Church in Modern Ireland.* 2d ed. Dublin: University College Dublin Press, 1998.

Martin, David. *A General Theory of Secularization.* Oxford: Blackwell, 1978.

O'Halloran, Clare. *Partition and the Limits of Irish Nationalism: An Ideology under Stress.* Atlantic Highlands, N.J.: Humanities Press International, 1987.

Ruane, Joseph, and Jennifer Todd, eds. *After the Good Friday Agreement: Analysing Political Change in Northen Ireland.* Dublin: University College Dublin Press, 1999.

Todd, Jennifer. "Two Traditions within Ulster Unionism." *Irish Political Studies* 2 (1987): 1–26.

Whyte, John H. *Church and State in Modern Ireland, 1923–1979.* 2d ed. Dublin: Gill and Macmillan, 1980.

Islam

Beginning as the faith of a small community of believers in Arabia in the seventh century, Islam rapidly became one of the major world religions. The core of this faith is the belief that Muhammad (c. 570–632), a respected businessman in Mecca, a commercial and religious center in western Arabia, received revelations from God that have been preserved in the Qur'an. The heart of this revealed message is the affirmation that "there is no god but Allah (The God), and Muhammad is the messenger of God." The term *islam* comes from the Arabic word-root *s-l-m,* which has a general reference to peace and submission. Specifically, Islam means submission to the will of God, and a Muslim is one who makes that submission.

This submission or act of Islam means living a life of faith and practice as defined in the Qur'an and participating in the life of the community of believers. The core of this Islamic life is usually said to be the Five Pillars of Islam: publicly bearing witness to the basic affirmation of faith; saying prescribed prayers five times a day; fasting during the month of Ramadan; giving a tithe or alms for support of the poor; and making a pilgrimage to Mecca at least once during the believer's lifetime, if this is possible.

Muslims believe that Islam is the basic monotheistic faith proclaimed by prophets throughout history. The Qur'an is not seen as presenting a new revelation but rather as providing a complete, accurate, and therefore final record of the message that had already been given to Abraham, Jesus, and other earlier prophets. As the basis for a historical community and tradition of faith, however, Islam begins in Mecca with the life and work of Muhammad in the early seventh century.

The Early Community

Muhammad's life as a preacher and leader of a community of believers has two major phases. He proclaimed his message in a city in which the majority did not accept his teachings. Mecca was a major pilgrimage center and sanctuary in the existing polytheism of Arabia, and the proclamation of monotheism threatened this whole system. The message presented in the Meccan period emphasizes the general themes of affirmation of monotheism and warnings of the Day of Judgment. Muhammad did not set out to establish a separate political organization, but the nature of the message represented a major challenge to the basic power structures of Mecca.

The second phase of Muhammad's career and the early life of the Muslim community began when Muhammad accepted an invitation from the people in Yathrib, an oasis north of Mecca, to serve as their arbiter and judge. In 622 Muhammad and his followers moved to Yathrib, and this emigration, or hijrah, is of such significance that Muslims use this date as the beginning of the Islamic calendar. The oasis became known as the City of the Prophet, or simply al-Madina (the city).

In Muslim tradition the sociopolitical community that was created in Madina provides the model for what a truly Islamic state and society should be. In contrast to tribal groups, the new community, or umma, was open to anyone who made the basic affirmation of faith, and loyalty to the umma was to supersede any other loyalty, whether to clan, family, or commercial partnership. The political structure of the new community was informal. Although Muhammad had great authority as the messenger of God, he could not assume a position as a sovereign monarch because he was only human and only a messenger. The emphasis on the sole sovereignty of God provides an important foundation for Islamic political thinking throughout the centuries, challenging both theories of monarchy and absolutism, as well as later theories of popular sovereignty.

In this early era the characteristically Islamic sense of the umma or the community of believers, rather than a concept of church or state, was firmly established as the central institutional identification for Muslims. In this way Islam is frequently described as a way of life rather than as a religion separate from politics or other dimensions of society. In Madina Muhammad provided leadership in all matters of life, but Muslims carefully distinguish the teachings that are the record of revelation and recorded in the Qur'an from the guidance Muhammad provided as a person. Because of his role as the messenger of God, Muhammad's own personal actions and words have special prestige. In addition to the Qur'an, the accounts of these, called hadith, provide the basis for a second source of guidance for believers, the sunna (customary practice) of the Prophet.

By the time of Muhammad's death in 632, the new Muslim community was successfully established. Mecca had been defeated and incorporated into the umma in important ways. The Ka'ba, a shrine in Mecca that had been the center of the polytheistic pilgrimage, was recognized as an altar built by Abraham, and Mecca became both the center of pilgrimage for the new community and the place toward which Muslims faced when they performed their prayers.

Sunni and Shi'i

When Muhammad died, Muslims faced the challenge of creating institutions to preserve the community. Muslims believe that the revelation was completed with the work of Muhammad, who is described as the seal of the prophets. The leaders after Muhammad were described only as khalifas (caliphs), or successors to the Prophet, and not as prophets themselves. The first four caliphs were companions of the Prophet and their period of rule (632–661) is described by the majority of Muslims as the age of the Rightly Guided

Muslim pilgrims pray at the Grand Mosque in Mecca, Saudi Arabia, sight of the holy Kaʻba. Muslims believe that the Kaʻba was an altar built by Abraham. Believers face the cubic, black-draped stone structure during their prayers and circumambulate it during the hajj, *the pilgrimage that Muslims try to make at least once in their lifetime.*

Caliphate. This was an era of expansion during which Muslims conquered the Sasanid (Persian) Empire and took control of the North African and Syrian territories of the Byzantine (Eastern Roman) Empire. The Muslim community was transformed from a small city-state controlling much of the Arabian Peninsula into a major world empire extending from northwest Africa to central Asia.

This era ended with the first civil war (656–661), in which specific conflicts between particular interest groups provided the foundation for the broader political and theological divisions in the community and the Islamic tradition. The first two caliphs, Abu Bakr and Umar, had been successful in maintaining a sense of communal unity. But tensions within the community surfaced during the era of the third caliph, Uthman, who was from the Umayyad clan. Uthman was murdered in 656 by troops who mutinied over matters of pay and privileges, but the murder was the beginning of a major civil war.

The mutinous troops and others in Medina declared the new caliph to be Ali, a cousin of Muhammad who was an early convert and also the husband of Muhammad's daughter Fatimah (and, therefore, the father of Muhammad's only grandsons, Hasan and Husayn). According to Shiʻi Muslim tradition, there were many people who believed that Muhammad had designated Ali as his successor. An Arabic term for faction or party is *shiʻah*, and the party or shiʻah of Ali emerged clearly during this first civil war. Ali's leadership was first challenged by a group including Aisha, the Prophet's most prominent wife and a daughter of the first caliph, Abu Bakr. Although Ali defeated this group militarily, it represented the tradition that became part of the mainstream majority, or Sunni, tradition in Islam, recognizing that all four of the first four caliphs were rightly guided and legitimate.

Ali faced a major military threat from the Umayyad clan, who demanded revenge for the murder of their kinsman, Uthman. The leader of the Umayyads was Muawiya, the governor of Syria. In a battle between the Umayyad army and the forces of Ali at Siffin in 657, Ali agreed to arbitration. As a result, a group of anti-Umayyad extremists withdrew from Ali's forces and became known as the Kharijites, or seceders, who demanded sinlessness as a quality of their leader and would recognize any pious Muslim as eligible to be the caliph. When Ali was murdered by a Kharijite in 661, most Muslims accepted Muawiya as caliph as a way of bringing an end to the intracommunal violence.

Many later divisions within the Muslim community were to be expressed in terms first articulated during this civil war. The mainstream, or Sunni, tradition reflects a combination of an emphasis on the consensus and piety of the community of the Prophet's companions, as reflected in the views of Aisha and her supporters, and the pragmatism of the Umayyad imperial administrators. The Sunni tradition always reflects the tension between the needs of state stability and the aspirations of a more egalitarian and pietistic religious vision.

Shiʻi Islam has its beginnings in the party of Ali and the argument that God always provides a special guide, or *imam,* for humans and that this guide has special characteristics, including being a descendant of the Prophet and having special divine guidance. Leadership and authority rest with this imamate and are not subject to human consensus or pragmatic reasons of state.

The Kharijites represent an extreme pietism that expects sinlessness from its leaders and asserts the right of the pious believer to declare others to be unbelievers. Over the centuries, explicitly Kharijite movements have declined in importance within the Muslim world, and by the early twenty-first century were represented by small communities in the Arabian Peninsula and North Africa. The spirit of puritanical anarchism, however, although always a minority position within the Muslim community, has continued to provide a marginal but significant critique of existing conditions. Activist, sometimes militant, movements of puritanical renewal that exist throughout Islamic history are sometimes accused of being Kharijite in method if not in theology.

Another major period of civil conflict followed the death in 680 of the first Umayyad caliph, Muawiya. The Umayyad victory by 692 affirmed the pragmatic, consensus-oriented approach of the rising Sunni mainstream. Umayyad military power and the emerging pious elite's fear of anarchy resulted in the majoritarian compromise that is fundamental to Sunni views of society, community, and state. There is a tension between the pragmatic needs of soldiers and politicians and the moral aspirations of religious teachers. The Sunni majority usually accepted the necessary compromises, legitimized by the authority of the consensus of the community.

The main opposition to the structures of the new imperial community came from developing Shiʻi traditions. Husayn, Ali's son, and a small group of his supporters were killed by an Umayyad army at Karbala in 680, and Husayn became for later Shiʻis a symbol of pious martyrdom in the path of God.

When the Umayyads were overthrown in the civil war of 744–750, the core of the revolutionary movement was Shiʻi. Piety-minded scholars, who were increasingly opposed to the worldly materialism of the Umayyads, joined the opposition. The organizers of the revolution were supporters of the Abbasids, the family of Abbas, an uncle of the Prophet, and when an Abbasid was proclaimed caliph following the defeat of the Umayyads, the supporters of the line of Ali remained in opposition. The new Abbasid caliphs reestablished the pragmatic compromise with the pious mainstream, and the Abbasid state succeeded as the new version of the Sunni caliphate.

Caliphs, Sultans, and the New Community

The world of Islam continued to expand, even during periods of civil war. By the mid-eighth century Muslim conquests extended from the Iberian Peninsula to the inner Asian frontiers of China. The new Muslim state was, in many ways, the successor to the imperial systems of Persia and Rome, but the caliphates were clearly identified with Islam.

The boundaries of the state and the Muslim community were basically the same, and the rulers, even when they were not known for piety, were still viewed by the majority as the successors to the Prophet.

It was the people of knowledge, or *ulama,* and not the caliphs who defined Islamic doctrine. Although there were state-appointed judges, Islamic jurisprudence (*fiqh*) was defined by independent ulama. The Sunni majority came to accept four schools of legal thought—the Hanafi, Maliki, Shafiʻi, and Hanbali—as legitimate. By the eleventh century the ulama had also compiled authoritative collections of hadith, providing a standard for understanding the Sunna of the Prophet. In this way, the Sunni tradition developed within the caliphal state but was not identical to it.

By the middle of the tenth century the effective political and military power of the Abbasid caliphs had been greatly reduced. Power shifted to the military commanders who frequently took the title of sultan, meaning authority or power. The Abbasid caliphs continued to reside in Baghdad and provided formal recognition to sultans. Increasingly, military leadership was Turkish. Turks had come to the Middle East from Central Asia as slaves and mercenaries, but by the eleventh century there was a significant migration of Turkish peoples into the region. In 1055 Turks, under the leadership of the Seljuqs, took control of Baghdad and established a major sultanate in cooperation with the Abbasid caliphs. The new Seljuq sultanate represented a reorganization of Muslim institutions with great patronage for the ulama and establishment of the sultanate as the legitimate political system. This caliph-based sultanate system came to an end when the Mongols invaded the Middle East and conquered Baghdad in 1258.

In the era of the decline of the Sunni caliphate, Shiʻi influence increased. During the eighth century Jaʼfar al-Sadiq, the sixth imam in the line of succession from Ali, provided the first fully comprehensive statement of Shiʻi beliefs that became the basis for subsequent Shiʻi mainstream groups. He provided opposition ideology to the Sunni definition of the community but did not advocate revolution or virulent opposition to the Abbasids. The role of the imam was emphasized, and by the middle of the tenth century the moderate Shiʻi mainstream accepted the imamate as spiritual and eschatological guide. This view defined a succession of twelve imams, the last of whom would enter a state of occultation and return as a messiah, or *mahdi,* in the future. The willingness to postpone expectations of a truly Islamic society until that return is an important part of Twelve-Imam (*ithna ashari*) Shi'ism. A minority maintained a more radical opposition, calling for messianic revolt, and identified with Ismail, a son of Sadiq who was not recognized by the Shi'i majority as being in the succession of imams. Ismaili Shi'ism provided the basis for the Fatimid movement in North Africa, which conquered Egypt in the tenth century and established a powerful Shi'i caliphate that lasted for more than two hundred years.

The fall of Baghdad to the Mongols did not mean the end of the sultanates. The military commanders continued to rule as sultans, even in the absence of caliphs, working with ulama and popular societal associations. This system of rule by military commanders without caliphs but identified as defenders and supporters of Islam became common in many parts of the Muslim world. The Mongol advance had been stopped by the Mamluk commanders of Egypt. Mamluks were legally slaves, and in the crisis of the thirteenth century, the commanders simply took control of the state and created a distinctive, self-perpetuating slave elite that ruled Egypt and much of Syria until the early sixteenth century.

In northern India, Turkish slave-soldiers established the Delhi Sultanate, and in Anatolia remnants of the Seljuq state provided a basis for a number of Turkish military states, including the Ottomans, who gradually came to dominate the region. Even the Mongol commanders in the Middle East and Central Asia, often with the title of khan rather than sultan, converted to Islam and ruled sultanate-style states. In North Africa caliphal authority had been supplanted in the eleventh and twelfth centuries by first the Almoravids (Murabitun) and then the Almohads (Muwahhidun). Successor states in Morocco, Algeria, and Tunisia were more in the sultanate model.

Although the Muslim world was no longer politically unified, the era of the sultanates was a time of creativity and dynamism when the classical formulations of many aspects of Islamic faith and community were fully articulated. The schools of Islamic law were consolidated and supported by the rulers, and standard texts came to be used throughout the Muslim world.

The traditions of mystic piety, called Sufism in the Islamic world, were formulated in works of people such as Abu Hamid al-Ghazali (1058–1111), who promoted acceptance of inner spirituality as an important part of Islamic life, and Muhyi al-Din Ibn al-Arabi (1165–1240), who extended Sufism with a more pantheistic outlook that became the

heart of subsequent presentations of Muslim mysticism. More puritanical renewalism received a classic articulation in the works of Ahmad Ibn Taimiyya (1263–1328), who argued that rulers who did not strictly rule in accord with Islamic law should be considered infidels and opposed by jihad if necessary. He defined this position in opposition to the newly converted Mongol rulers of the early fourteenth century, but his works have been an inspiration to many later activist movements.

Spread of Islam

From the end of the effective power of the caliphs in the tenth century to the beginning of the sixteenth, the size of the Muslim world almost doubled. The vehicles for expansion were not conquering armies so much as traveling merchants and itinerant teachers. In Saharan and sub-Saharan Africa, in Central Asia, and in the many different societies in the Indian Ocean basin, a growing number of people came to be included within the world community of Islam.

Islamization usually involved an increasing familiarity with the basic texts and teachings of Islam and an awareness of being part of a larger community of believers. In contrast to early expansion in the Middle East, where monotheistic faiths like Christianity, Judaism, and Zoroastrianism were well established, much of this later growth was in areas where faith traditions were polytheistic or naturalistic. As Muslim teachers and merchants interacted with local rulers, they helped to transform political systems that had been based on divine rule or rulers with special naturalistic powers and obligations. In the courts of Java and West Africa, as well as among the shamans of Central Asia, the coming of Islam changed both political structures and popular faith. Often this involved incorporating local beliefs and customs that created distinctive local Muslim communities within the intercontinental community of believers.

Devotional teachers were also important in the world of the sultanates. The spiritual life associated with Sufism came to be institutionalized in organizations identified by the devotional paths, or *tariqas,* of famous Sufis. One of the earliest of these was the Qadiriyya Tariqa, tracing itself back to Abd al-Qadir al-Jilani in twelfth-century Baghdad. Because they were tied to popular piety, *tariqas* often served to meld local practices with Islamic ideas, and the brotherhoods were a major force in the gradual Islamization of many societies.

By the end of the fifteenth century the Muslim world was very different from what it had been at the height of Abbasid power. No single state could be identified, even in theory, with the whole community of believers. Although the society and culture of the early caliphates were primarily Middle Eastern, the Islamic world of the fifteenth century brought together peoples from different civilizations and nonurban societies. Islam was no longer a faith identified with a particular world region; it had become more universal and cosmopolitan in its articulation and in the nature of the community of believers.

Early Modern Expansion and Transformation

The Muslim world continued to expand in the early modern era. A broad belt of societies undergoing Islamization stretched across the Eastern Hemisphere. More than seven centuries of Muslim rule in the Iberian Peninsula came to an end in 1492 with the completion of the Spanish Christian reconquest. Elsewhere, however, new states and social institutions consolidated the gains of previous centuries and initiated a new wave of growth. Eventually, interaction with the rising states of Europe brought conflict on a global scale, with European military victory but continued conversion of peoples and societies to Islam.

A number of major Islamic states emerged during the sixteenth century. The largest was the Ottoman Empire, which had been expanding from its original base as a Turkish warrior state in western Anatolia. Ottoman forces conquered Constantinople in 1453 and Syria and Egypt in 1516–1517. Under the rule of Sultan Sulayman the Magnificent, virtually all of the Balkan Peninsula became part of the empire in the sixteenth century. In South Asia, Babur, a Central Asian military adventurer, used gunpowder to defeat the Delhi Sultanate and establish the foundations for the Mughal empire. By the end of the reign of Babur's grandson, Akbar, in 1605, the Mughals ruled virtually all of India.

Small military states in Iran were conquered by a new movement, the Safavids. Under Ismail al-Safavi, who proclaimed himself Shah in 1501, the movement was transformed from a Sufi-style organization to a dynastic state. Twelver Shi'ism was proclaimed the official religion and, although most Iranians had been Sunni, Shi'ism soon became the religion of the general population as well.

The empires of Mali and Songhay in West Africa, the merchant city-states of East Africa, the expansion of the Uzbek state under Shaybanid leadership, and the sultanates of the peninsulas and islands of Southeast Asia all reflect the political and social influence of Islamization by the sixteenth century.

By the seventeenth century this picture started to change as empires began to weaken in the face of war and internal strife. Ottoman expansion ceased in the seventeenth century, and the empire lost wars and territories to expanding European states. The Safavid Empire came to an end when Nadir, a military commander, assumed the title of shah. Nadir Shah was militarily successful, but his state collapsed after his death in 1747. The Mughals faced similar internal conflicts, revolts by non-Muslims, and ultimately, conquest by the British. Elsewhere, smaller Muslim states also suffered from civil wars and conquests by outside forces.

During the next two centuries, most of the Muslim world came under direct or indirect European control, and cultural life was increasingly shaped by European influences. There were, however, important movements of Islamic renewal that also had long-term significance.

European expansion in Muslim areas was relatively limited during the eighteenth century. The Ottoman Empire lost territories, but the continued existence of the empire itself was never in question. In the Indian Ocean basin Islamization continued alongside European expansion. The rise of the Muslim states in Southeast Asia had stopped Portuguese expansion. The Dutch and British often worked with local rulers, and the network of Malay sultanates was preserved by imperial rule. Mughal sultans still ruled even as they lost much effective power to local princes and the British East India Company. Muslim societies in Central Asia were gradually being conquered by the neighboring Russian and Chinese empires in a sequence completed by the end of the nineteenth century. Large Muslim states in West Africa collapsed primarily as a result of internal developments.

Movements of self-conscious reform developed during this transition. Within the Ottoman Empire, leaders like the grand viziers from the Kuprulu family tried to restore administrative and military effectiveness through reform. Some local Ottoman governors also worked to create more efficient and relatively autonomous administrations. In these efforts Islam provided only the background for the political system as a whole. But throughout the Muslim world, there were also movements of reform with explicitly Islamic programs of renewal.

Movements of renewal have been a long-standing part of Islamic history. By the eighteenth century there was a broad repertoire of traditions that Islamically based reform efforts could draw on. In some areas, as Islamization continued, syncretist adaptations would be rejected as non-Islamic by scholars more familiar with the more universal forms of Islam. Scholars who had been on pilgrimage often would oppose local customs on their return. Sometimes this would lead to open conflict with authorities whose position reflected the syncretism of earlier stages of Islamization.

In West Africa a tradition of renewalist jihad developed during the eighteenth century, reaching a climax with the efforts of Uthman Dan Fodio (1754–1817), whose holy war of reform resulted in the establishment of the caliphate of Sokoto in northern Nigeria and a network of related renewalist principalities. One of the last of these jihads was proclaimed by al-Hajj Umar in 1852. Although it began as a more traditional renewalist movement, it soon became a part of the new, nineteenth-century pattern of conflict with European imperialism. Similar movements of reformist jihad, often associated with tariqas, were established in western China and Southeast Asia.

Scholars interpreted the message of Islamic reform in ways significant even through the twentieth century. In the Arabian Peninsula Muhammad Ibn Abd al-Wahhab (1703–1792) presented an absolutist vision of reform based on a strict interpretation of the Qur'an in the tradition of Ibn Taimiyya. He was supported by a local prince, Muhammad Ibn Saud, laying the foundations for the Saudi state in Arabia and the Wahhabi style of reformism. In south Asia Shah Wali Allah of Delhi attempted a broad synthesis of traditional Muslim legal thought and hadith scholarship. His vision of socio-moral reconstruction inspired generations of south Asia scholars, and his influence is still visible in twentieth-century Muslim intellectual movements. Ahmad Ibn Idris (d.1837), a North African scholar in Mecca, emphasized the importance of Sufi spiritual piety and organization. His students established a number of *tariqas,* like the Sanusiyya and the Khatmiyya, that gave birth to organizations of social cohesion, resistance to European imperial expansion, and twentieth-century political parties.

Imperialism and Reform

During the nineteenth century European expansion became an increasingly important force in Muslim societies. Many observers identify the ease with which Napoleon conquered Egypt in 1798 as a symbol of the new era. The major states that remained independent undertook a wide range of reforms, although these were not generally defined in explicitly Islamic terms. Ottoman state reforms began

with attempts by Selim III to institute a *Nizam-i cedid,* or "New System," of military and bureaucratic organization. Although he was overthrown in 1807, his successor, Mahmud II, significantly changed both military and administrative institutions. At his death in 1839 Mahmud's successor, Abdal-Majid, issued an imperial proclamation that enhanced the secular and more liberal aspects of reform as a part of the Tanzimat (reorganization), which led to promulgation of the Ottoman Constitution of 1876. Although advocates of these reforms at times tried to show that they were not contrary to Islam, the programs were not presented as Islamic reform.

In Egypt, Muhammad Ali, the Ottoman governor after French withdrawal, initiated similar reforms, and by the second half of the century, Egypt was virtually independent and undergoing major sociopolitical transformations. Iran was reunified by the conquests of the Qajar dynasty in the 1790s. Qajar Iran remained independent, but the leadership initiated only piecemeal reforms. Reform did not prevent continued military losses to European powers. Britain occupied Egypt in 1882, the Ottomans lost other territories in the Balkans and North Africa, and Iran was politically and economically dominated by European powers by the end of the century.

The most effective direct resistance to European expansion came from Islamic organizations, although they were also unsuccessful. In West Africa the jihad tradition became an important part of resistance to European expansion, as can be seen in the wars of al-Hajj Umar and his Tijaniyya forces. In Algeria it was the Amir Abd al-Qadir, with his Qadiriyya organization, that led the strongest opposition to the French invasion in 1830.

In the Caucasus opposition to Russian expansion was strongest from the Naqshbandiyya, led by the imam Shamil, and at the end of the century, the most visible war against imperialists was the jihad of Muhammad ibn Abdallah in Somalia. The Mahdi in Sudan led a holy war that successfully drove out the modernized Egyptian army, defeated British-led forces, and established a state that lasted from 1884 to 1898, when it was reconquered by Anglo-Egyptian forces. This tradition of resistance continued into the twentieth century, when the Sanusiyya provided the only effective resistance to the Italian invasion of Libya.

The old-style resistance of the brotherhoods did not create an effective alternative to European expansion in either military or intellectual terms. Intellectual and ideological responses developed during the second half of the nineteenth century. Some of these were Western in style and represented the beginnings of nationalism, but others were more explicitly Islamic. The ideal of pan-Islamic unity was expressed by a number of people, most importantly in the work of Jamal al-Din al-Afghani (1838 or 1839–1897) and, in official terms, by the policies of the Ottoman sultan at the end of the century, Abd al-Hamid II.

The major new development was the emergence of Islamic modernism, in which people in a number of areas worked to create an effective synthesis of Islam and modernity. Muhammad Abduh in Egypt argued that faith and reason were compatible and that Islam was a reason-based faith. He and his student, Rashid Rida, published *al-Manar,* a journal that helped to inspire modernist groups from Morocco to Indonesia. In India Sayyid Ahmad Khan led another major modernist trend, which emphasized the compatibility of scientific understandings of nature with Islam and established a college in Aligarh that combined Islamic and modern Western studies.

The Jadid movement developed in the Russian Empire under the inspiration of Ismail Gasprinskii, whose periodical *Tarjuman* was widely read. The Jadid curriculum for schools combined Russian and Muslim traditions. Islamic modernists tended to accept the realities of European military domination, working to reform Muslim societies from within and create a synthesis that could be both effectively modern and authentically Islamic.

Muslims in the Twentieth Century

World War I was the beginning of a new era in the history of Islam. The last of the older Muslim political systems came to an end in the aftermath of the war. The Ottoman Empire, which had been allied with Germany, was defeated and occupied, and the sultanate was formally abolished as a part of the reforms of the new Turkish nationalism led by Mustafa Kemal Atatürk. The Qajar dynasty in Iran was overthrown and, although the monarchy was retained, Reza Shah, the new leader, worked to create a new state system.

Both Kemal Atatürk and Reza Shah were secularists who worked to limit the influence of Islamic institutions. In most of the rest of the Muslim world, similar Westernizing reform and the development of more secularist nationalism dominated. In this, Islam was not rejected but it did not define the central concerns of emerging Arab nationalism in the Fertile Crescent or of Egyptian nationalism under Sa'd Zaghloul.

In the period between the two world wars, some explicitly Islamic movements emerged, but they usually developed in the context of more secular radicalism or nationalism. Islamic perspectives ranged from those of the communist intellectual, Mir Said Sultangaliev, whose efforts to create a national communism for Muslims within the revolutionary movement ended when he was purged by Soviet leader Joseph Stalin, to the *Manar*-influenced Association of Algerian Ulama, which protested the growth of a French-inspired intellectual elite in North Africa and sought to affirm the Islamic base of Algerian culture.

Indian Muslims began to define their communal identity in terms of Indian nationalism. Some, such as Abu al-Kalam Azad, worked closely with the Indian National Congress Party and advocated Hindu–Muslim nationalist cooperation. At the end of World War I Azad and others mobilized Muslim opinion through the Khalifat movement, supporting the preservation of the Ottoman caliphate and working with the National Congress in opposition to British imperial policy. Other Indian Muslims began to define themselves as a separate community, which ultimately led to the partition of India when it achieved independence in 1947 and the creation of the Muslim state of Pakistan. A leader in this movement was Muhammad Iqbal, who was also important in the continuing development of Islamic modernist thought, further synthesizing Western philosophy and Islamic thought.

In a few isolated areas states maintained older Islamic traditions of rule in the 1920s–1930s. In southern Arabia Zaydi Shi'i imams ruled with the support of conservative mountain peoples in Yemen, and the Kharijite state of the sultans of Oman continued. In central Arabia the Wahhabi religious and political tradition was revived under the leadership of Abd al-Aziz Ibn Saud (c. 1888–1953), whose conquests in the first three decades of the century created the basis for the Kingdom of Saudi Arabia. Neither nationalist nor modernist, the new Saudi state was a distinctive attempt to carry out a strict interpretation of traditional Islamic law.

New movements advocating a more direct adoption of Islam in modern society also developed. Their followers came from the modern educated elements in society, and their leadership was not explicitly ulama in background. Among the most important of these movements were the Muslim Brotherhood, established in Egypt in 1928 by Hasan al-Banna (1906–1949), and the Jama'at-i Islami (Islamic Society), founded in India in 1941 under the leadership of Mawlana Abu al-Ala Mawdudi (1903–1979). These groups, and others like them, opposed the more traditional, popular Islamic practices and conservative ulama, as well as criticized the secularism of the Westernizers. They argued that Islam defined a whole way of life and should be applied in economics and politics as well as in individual religious life.

In the second half of the twentieth century Muslim societies became politically independent as the era of European imperialism came to an end. A final step in this process was the end of the Soviet Union and the emergence of new states in Muslim-majority areas of the old Russian Empire in the 1990s. Nationalism and the rise of Western-style radicalism were the most visible political dynamics in the first three decades after World War II as states in the Middle East and South and Southeast Asia gained their independence. In the already independent states of Turkey, Iran, and Saudi Arabia, political patterns established in the interwar era continued, with Turkey committed to upholding a democratic Kemalism, Iran to continuing Reza Shah's Westernizing reforms under the leadership of his son, Muhammad Reza Shah, and Saudi Arabia to maintaining its strict Islamist approach in the new context of great wealth from the sale of oil.

In some of the newly independent states, socially conservative interpretations of Islam legitimized monarchies. In Morocco, Jordan, Oman, and Malaysia, these monarchies continued through the end of the century, although monarchies were overthrown by more secular and radical movements in Egypt (1952), Tunisia (1957), Iraq (1958), Yemen (1962), and Afghanistan (1973). In Iran the monarchy was overthrown in 1979 by an Islamic revolution, a major indication of the resurgence of political Islam in the late twentieth century. In other areas older elites were also overthrown or displaced by newer and frequently more ideologically radical groups. By the 1960s Western-style radicalism was the most dynamic element in the politics of the newly independent Muslim world. The most visible leaders were people like Sekou Toure in Guinea, Gamal Abdel Nasser in Egypt, and Sukarno in Indonesia and parties such as the National Liberation Front, which spearheaded the war for Algerian independence, and the Ba'th (Arab Socialist) Party in Syria and Iraq.

This new radicalism did not directly reject Islam. It often attempted to include Islamic images in its platforms, sometimes talking about Islamic socialism, but the creation of Islamic societies or implementation of Qur'anic rules was not a prominent feature of ideologies or programs.

Rise of Islamist Movements

Movements with primarily Islamic identification existed, but with less political influence. Pakistan, as an explicitly Islamic state, was unable to develop a clear constitutional self-definition. Internal divisions led to a civil war in 1971 and the secession of Bengal as independent Bangladesh. The Jama'at-i Islami continued to advocate its Islamist program and was respected but had limited political influence.

The Muslim Brotherhood in Egypt cooperated briefly with the new military revolutionaries led by Nasser, but they were suppressed in 1954. In the 1960s the Brotherhood message was reshaped into more radical terms by Sayyid Qutb, who condemned Westernized societies as being ruled by sinful ignorance (*jahiliyya*) and called for jihad against existing states in Muslim societies. Qutb was executed in 1966, but his writings laid the foundation for a new generation of underground Muslim revolutionaries. During the 1970s movements like Islamic Jihad and Takfir wal-Hijrah in Egypt may have differed in doctrinal specifics from Qutb, but they followed his mode of analysis. In many areas of the Muslim world, Qutb helped to define Islamic revolution.

There were other Muslim movements of revolutionary opposition to the establishment of the nationalist and sometimes socialist states. The Darul Islam movement in Indonesia fought a jihad against the new state from 1948 until its founder's execution in 1962. In Iran the Fida'iyan-i Islam was created in 1945, advocating a strict application of Islamic law and engaging in a series of terrorist assassinations. The organization ended with the execution of its founder in 1956, but former members were a part of later militant antigovernment groups.

Other Islamic organizations opposed to the increasing secularism and Westernization of Muslim societies adopted methods of education and mission to transform and Islamize societies. One of the largest Muslim associations in the world is the Tablighi Jama'at (in Urdu, "Party which Propagates"), which began as a devotional and educational organization in northern India in the 1920s. After World War II the movement spread rapidly throughout the world among Muslims in Western Europe and North America, as well as in Muslim societies. Many of the established Sufi orders have also adapted themselves to the conditions of modern society and quietly grew to be large devotional associations in virtually every Muslim community. In the United States a major movement developed among African Americans that was self-identified as Muslim, though the Nation of Islam association created by Elijah Muhammad (1897–1975) was not recognized as Islamic by most Muslims because of its distinctive doctrines of black separatism. But Malcolm X, a major figure in the movement, broke with its leaders in the mid-1960s and espoused a more mainstream Islamic perspective. When Elijah Muhammad died in 1975, he was succeeded by his son, Imam Warith Deen Muhammad, who transformed the movement into a clearly Sunni Muslim one. A smaller organization led by Louis Farrakhan continued to advocate the older black nationalist and separatist beliefs.

The Islamic Resurgence

A new Islamic spirit of renewal gained increasing visibility in the final quarter of the twentieth century. The most dramatic manifestation of this was the Islamic revolution in Iran. Secular and Islamic opposition to the autocratic rule of the shah increased in intensity during the 1970s. Leftist definitions of resistance had little appeal, and opponents increasingly mobilized around Islamic aspirations. Ali Shariati, who died in exile in 1977, presented a call for a rejection of state Shiʿism, advocating an egalitarian program of social justice that some saw as an Islamic form of Marxism.

The central figure of the revolution and the republic it created was Ayatollah Ruhollah Khomeini. He declared the possibility of an authentically Islamic state, even in the absence of the imam, if it represented the rule of the Islamic legal scholars (*wilayat al-faqih*). The constitution of the new republic created a system that survived a series of major political crises, including a long and costly war with Iraq in the 1980s and the death of Khomeini in 1989. Political life was strictly controlled, and minorities and opposition groups were suppressed. Within the limitations of the constitution, however, there was a remarkable degree of debate and disagreement over policy, which was confirmed in the presidential elections of 1997, when Muhammad Khatami, an advocate of a more open and reformist but still Islamically committed line of policy, decisively defeated a more hardline candidate supported by the more conservative clergy.

As leftist ideologies and nationalist state policies proved ineffective in coping with the social, economic, and political transformations of the late twentieth century, there was a significant shift to more Islamically oriented approaches throughout the Muslim world. This frequently was centered in movements of modern-educated professionals and students that neither advocated Qutb-style jihad nor accepted conservative ulama leadership. They viewed Islam as providing a comprehensive program for society but generally worked for the gradual Islamization of state and society rather than a revolutionary overthrow of existing institutions. The rise of movements of this type represents the emergence of what came to be called "Political Islam."

A variety of Islamic groups developed in Egypt, separate from the Muslim Brotherhood although similar in aspirations. Former student militants became leaders of professional syndicates in the mid-1980s and helped to direct official policy and general public opinion in a more openly Islamic direction. Others formed political parties that were severely restricted but gained some support in Egyptian elections during the 1990s. In Malaysia the Islamic student movement ABIM was an important force on campuses, and in the 1980s its leader, Anwar Ibrahim, became a major political figure in the leading political coalition. The Islamic Tendency Movement in Tunisia gained political influence during the 1980s under the leadership of Rashid al-Ghanoushi. Although it was suppressed and its leadership jailed or exiled, in its reorganized form as the Nahda Party in the late 1980s and 1990s, al-Ghanoushi and most of the movement continued to advocate democratic participation rather than violent revolution.

In Algeria the emergence of political Islam as a major force took place quite rapidly when the National Liberation Front, facing demands for greater political participation, agreed to hold competitive elections. The Islamic Salvation Front won municipal elections in 1990 and was on the verge of gaining control of the national parliament when a military coup suspended the election in 1992. Throughout the 1990s open conflict between government and Islamist forces caused more than sixty thousand deaths.

In Lebanon, Shiʿi political activism was expressed initially through the teachings of a popular preacher and scholar, Musa al-Sadr. In the late 1970s, before his disappearance and presumed death in 1978, he developed Amal, a social welfare organization and militia to protect Shiites in the context of the growing Lebanese civil war. By the 1980s Amal became a major political party in Lebanon and, following the end of the war, its leader served as speaker of parliament. In addition, as a consequence of the Israeli invasion of Lebanon in 1982, militant Shiites organized Hizbullah as a special guerrilla force to oppose Israel's occupation in south Lebanon, where the majority of the population is Shiʿi. With the end of the civil war, Hizbullah also became active in Lebanese electoral politics. The unilateral Israeli withdrawal from south Lebanon in 2000 was viewed as a victory for Hizbullah, increasing its political influence as well as its military reputation.

Among Palestinian activists an Islamist movement, Hamas, developed alongside the long-established Palestine Liberation Organization led by Yasir Arafat (1929–2004) and won significant support among those who mistrusted Arafat for his willingness to negotiate with Israel. Even in Turkey, where religion-based political parties are illegal, the Welfare Party and its successors, which advocated a greater formal Islamization of Turkish life, won the prime ministership with more than 20 percent of the parliamentary vote in 1996, and one third of the vote in 2002.

The only country outside of Iran in which an Islamist movement came to power was Sudan. The Sudanese Muslim Brotherhood had been organized in the early 1950s and had participated actively in the politics of the parliamentary periods in 1956–1958 and 1964–1969 but had never had much electoral success. As an active political party in the third era of multiparty politics (1985–1989), the Brotherhood, reorganized as the National Islamic Front, was an important but minority force, winning about 20 percent of the votes. The military coup in 1989 was led by Islamically oriented officers who soon became closely identified with the front and its leader, Hasan al-Turabi. Turabi had an international reputation as an imaginative advocate of renewal and rethinking the foundations of Islamic law. He helped the regime establish a system of elective consultative councils and application of Islamic law, but the suppression of minorities and opposition in a brutal civil war raised doubts about the long-term Islamic significance of the Sudanese experience.

The New Islamists

At the beginning of the twenty-first century Islamic activist movements and advocates of greater Islamization of public and private life entered a new era. In the heyday of radical socialism in the 1960s, such groups were marginal. In the 1970s they came to be viewed in many areas as a dangerous militant minority that could disrupt society through terrorism. By the 1980s political Islam became an important part of the mainstream of politics in the Muslim world. The threat of groups such as Nahda in Tunisia and the Islamic Salvation Front in Algeria was that they might be able, through democratic processes, to win the support of a majority and gain control of governments. Political Islam frequently advocated democracy.

By the mid-1990s a new generation of Islamically oriented intellectuals, activists, and militants transformed Islamism. The new Islamists represent a wide spectrum of programs and perspectives, ranging from militant advocates of global jihad to new intellectuals articulating pluralist perspectives to emerging multicultural movements and communities within a broadly defined *umma*.

The terrorist attacks on the World Trade Center and the Pentagon in the United States on September 11, 2001 ("9/11") are a major symbol of the transformation in the development of militant, extremist movements. This tendency has important roots in the jihad in Afghanistan during the 1980s. Foundations for global networks of militants were created by volunteers, who came from many countries to fight the Soviet Union and then dispersed following the Soviet withdrawal in 1989. A loose core organization, al-Qaida, was developed by Usama bin Ladin, a wealthy young Saudi who gradually emerged during the 1990s as the center of militant and terrorist activities. Al-Qaida provided the framework and resources for the 9/11 attacks and was considered the primary terrorist organization of extremist Muslims during the first years of the twenty-first century.

In the first decade of the twenty-first century radical militant Islam was not monolithic, despite the high visibility of al-Qaida. Throughout the Muslim world, a number of extremist groups developed, some in loose association with al-Qaida and others more independent. Following the American invasion of Iraq in 2003, an organization loosely affiliated with al-Qaida and led by Abu Musaab al-Zarqawi (d. 2006) emerged as a major part of the Sunni resistance to American and coalition forces. In Southeast Asia, bombings of tourist sites in Bali and Western hotels in Jakarta reflect the existence of militant groups like Jemaah Islamiyah, sometimes associated with Abu Bakar Ba'asyir, an extremist, theologically conservative scholar.

The radical ideology as articulated by Ayman al-Zawahiri, an Egyptian from the Islamic Jihad group who was associated with bin Ladin and a number of others, has a core concept that jihad must be global. Local and particular jihads must be seen as part of a global Muslim effort. The ultimate goal is the establishment of an *umma*-wide caliphate that could revive the faithful purity of the early Community. In this perspective, the enemies are not just non-Muslims but also leaders in Muslim countries who are seen as "unbelievers" because they do not impose a literalist interpretation of Islam on their societies.

At the other end of the wide spectrum of Islamic experience at the beginning of the twenty-first century are many intellectuals and activists who continue the tradition of the early modernists in rearticulating Islamic fundamentals in contemporary terms. Some scholars concentrate on reconceptualizing the basic disciplines. Jamal al-Banna in Egypt is one among many intellectuals who are redefining *fiqh,* the legal studies discipline. These efforts are changing the meaning of having state and society based on *shari'a* from an application of specific legal regulations elaborated in medieval sources to a recognition of the importance of a more general normative framework based on revelation. Other activist scholars, such as Mohsen Kadivar in Iran, give emphasis to defining the relationship between Islam and human rights. Still others are articulating what some call "Islamic feminism," working to eliminate "patriarchal" restrictions on women in Muslim societies. Some leaders in this are the American scholar Amina Wadud and the Pakistani political scientist, Asma Barlas.

Developments among Muslims in non-Muslim majority societies exert growing influence on Muslims throughout the world. Highly visible public intellectuals like Tariq Ramadan present many of the new approaches in the contexts of Western Europe and North America. Ramadan speaks of the emergence of "European Islam." Farid Esack, a South African Muslim who was active in the African National Congress's struggle against apartheid, articulates an openly pluralist vision of Islam.

In the first half decade of the twenty-first century a number of critical events occurred which show the changing nature of the *umma* in the era of globalization. Elections emphasized the importance of organized Islamic groups in many places. In the Turkish parliamentary elections of 2002, the Justice and Development Party, a successor to the Welfare Party, won an outright majority in the parliament and established a government without interference from the secular military. In Egypt, despite strict governmental controls, opposition candidates associated with the still-illegal Muslim Brotherhood won significant numbers of seats in elections to the People's Assembly in 2000 and almost a quarter of the seats in 2005. The presidential elections in Iran in 2005 brought to power Mahmoud Ahmadinejad, a populist who emphasized issues of poverty and economic justice. (He was not the first non-cleric president in the Islamic Republic of Iran—Bani-Sadr and Rejai in the early 1980s were the first.) Ahmadinejad had support from some of the more conservative clergy against the political clerical establishment. Although the president has limited powers, he initiated popular domestic economic programs and he soon clashed with the United States as a result of his expansion of Iranian nuclear power capacity.

Conflicts in 2006 involving militant groups tended to obscure other developments in the Muslim world. Terrorism related to the Kashmir dispute in south Asia, a resurgence of the Afghan militant group, the Taliban, and the role of Muslim militants in Iraqi resistance to U.S. forces in the country all gained public attention. Early in the year, in the elections for the Palestinian Legislative Council, Hamas gained a resounding victory, defeating the old Palestine Liberation Organization political establishment. The rejection of the Hamas government by Israel and the United States set the stage for the renewal of hostilities between Israel and Palestinian militants during the spring and summer of 2006. Parallel hostilities developed between Hizbullah and Israel during the summer when Hizbullah militants shelled settlements in northern Israel and captured two Israeli soldiers, and Israel responded with massive military force. The impact of all these disputes on broader developments in the global Muslim community was not clear.

The Islamic experience over the centuries provides a rich repertoire out of which social institutions and political systems can be created, and Muslim societies in the modern era vary in their interpretations of that repertoire. Even specific movements like Islamist renewals are not monolithic or identical. Despite these differences, however, all Muslims continued to affirm the basic core of the faith in monotheism as defined by the revelation to Muhammad and preserved in the Qur'an.

See also *Afghani, Jamal al-Din al-; Ahmad Khan, Sir Sayyid; Algeria; Atatürk, Kemal; Banna, Hasan al-; Crusades; Egypt; Ibn Taimiyya; India; Indonesia; Iqbal, Muhammad; Iran; Islam in Africa; Islam in Europe; Islam in Southeast Asia; Islam in the United States; Islam's Encounters with the West; Islam, Radical; Jihad; Khomeini, Ruhollah Musavi; Mahdi; Malaysia; Mawdudi; Mecca; Morocco; Muhammad; Nasser, Gamal Abdel; Nation of Islam; Pakistan; Qutb, Sayyid; Sudan; Sufism; Sukarno, Achmad; Syria; Turkey.*

John O. Voll

BIBLIOGRAPHY

Abu-Rabi, Ibrahim M. *Intellectual Origins of Islamic Resurgence in the Modern Arab World.* Albany: State University of New York Press, 1995.

Ahmed, Akbar S. *Discovering Islam: Making Sense of Muslim History and Society.* 2d ed. London: Routledge, 2002.

Esposito, John L. *Islam, The Straight Path.* 3d rev. ed. New York: Oxford University Press, 2004.

———, ed. *The Oxford History of Islam.* New York: Oxford University Press, 1999.

Hodgson, Marshall G. S. *The Venture of Islam: Conscience and History in a World Civilization.* Chicago: University of Chicago Press, 1974.

Hourani, Albert. *Arabic Thought in the Liberal Age, 1798–1939.* New York: Cambridge University Press, 1983.

Keddie, Nikki R. *Modern Iran: Roots and Results of Revolution.* New Haven, Conn.: Yale University Press, 2003.

Lapidus, Ira. *A History of Islamic Societies.* 2d ed. New York: Cambridge University Press, 2002.

Lewis, Bernard. *What Went Wrong? Western Impact and Middle Eastern Response.* New York: Oxford University Press, 2002.

Rahnema, Ali, ed. *Pioneers of Islamic Revival.* 2d ed. London: Zed, 2006.

Roy, Olivier. *Globalized Islam: The Search for a New Ummah.* New York: Columbia University Press, 2004.

Schulze, Reinhard. *A Modern History of the Islamic World.* Gardners Books, 2002.

Islam in Africa

African Islam is strong particularly in North Africa and West Africa but has a significant presence in other parts of the continent, too. The total number of Muslims is about the same as that of Christians. North African states such as Algeria and Tunisia, as well as Somalia in the east, may be called Islamic in that they have Islam as the established religion and almost 100 percent Muslim populations. In the north, Egypt is an exception because of its sizable minority of Coptic Christians (about 5–10 percent). Countries with predominantly Muslim populations include, for example, the Sudan and Senegal. Muslims in West Africa tend to be concentrated primarily in the northern areas. In Nigeria, as well as Ethiopia in the east, somewhat less than half of the inhabitants are Muslim. States in central, East, and southern Africa have significant Muslim minorities, especially Tanzania, where the Muslims, who live primarily along the coast and on islands such as Zanzibar, make up at least one-third of the population. In various ways Islamic organizations and people have exerted an influence on politics and, inversely, have been influenced by political institutions and forces.

Early History

In North Africa, the Muslim expansion started in the seventh century, not long after the death of the prophet Muhammad. Islam is deeply rooted there. During the Middle Ages, Arab and Berber traders and religious leaders from the north to some degree spread Islam to West Africa. Principally, people who took part in commerce converted to Islam. Local rulers were among the first who became influenced by Islam, although only some converted, and states such as Mali and Ghana often played an important role in the process of Islamization. Traders, kings, and others who adopted Islam fused elements of the new religion to their pre-Muslim beliefs and practices, thus creating new forms of Islam.

Further east, Muslims advanced south along the Nile valley, despite resistance from Christian Nubians and others. On the coast of the Red Sea, several early Muslim settlements sprung up. By the ninth century, the town Harar in present-day Somalia had developed into an important center for trade and Islamic learning. In the highlands of Ethiopia, however, Islam's advance was arrested by the Orthodox Christian state. By the eighteenth century Oromo chiefs south of this state embraced Islam, and a century later it took root among Oromo commoners.

On the islands and along the coast of East Africa, Muslims appeared shortly after the time of the Prophet. They were mainly merchants enticed by opportunities to find, for instance, ivory and slaves. Arab immigrants frequently intermarried with African women, and some self-governing and generally independent states gradually emerged. During the nineteenth century, the sultan of Oman established himself as the leading ruler. Even though several towns remained self-governing, they paid some part of their customs dues to this sultanate.

Paradoxically, it was not until the nineteenth and twentieth centuries, under European colonial rule, that a wide expansion of Islam occurred in black Africa. For example, in West Africa, new roads facilitated the Muslim spread into the tropical forest regions and down to the coast. In Nigeria, the British colonizers used the Muslim emirs in the north, who had emerged as a result of the *jihad* (holy war) initiated by Uthman dan Fodio in the early nineteenth century, in the local administrative system of indirect rule. Similarly, in German East Africa, literate Muslims from the coastal areas were used for colonial administration in the interior, which contributed to a remarkable wave of conversions. The British welcomed substantial numbers of traders and others from South Asia, many of whom were Muslims, to settle particularly along the coast of the Indian Ocean in eastern and southern Africa. Before the British, Dutch settlers in South Africa had brought Muslim slaves from Southeast Asia.

While Christian missions were, more or less, associated with the European colonizers, Islam could more easily become a religion of resistance and independence. Its adaptation to local beliefs and practices, as well as a predominantly indigenous African leadership, enhanced its anticolonial and nationalist role. Normally, however, *jihad* had to be rejected as a doomed enterprise. Compromises and concessions were made on both sides. Regarding the spread of Islam, as well as of the competing Christianity, the overall effects of colonization were generally conducive. Thus, both of these world religions expanded rapidly at the expense of African indigenous religions, although many traditional ideas and practices could survive within the framework of the new religions.

In Islam, Sufism in particular has been able to integrate many pre-Islamic elements. Especially since the eighteenth century, Sufi shayhks and orders (*turuq,* sing. *tariqa*) have played prominent roles in the spread of Islam. Virtually all over Africa, and particularly south of the Sahara, Sufism is strong. *Tariqa* means "way" but refers also to the organization of Sufis in various orders led by shayhks on different levels. Largely because of their organizational strength, Sufi leaders and disciples have often played important political roles. Shaykhs, or *marabouts*(a common designation in North Africa and West Africa) have special knowledge and power, gained through an initiation process, which may give them strong religious as well as political and socioeconomic authority. This authority, or "blessing" (*baraka*), is also based on their *silsila,* spiritual chain of transmission, which connects them to earlier shaykhs in various saintly ancestries, sometimes back to the Prophet himself.

As in most parts of the Muslim world, the Sunni forms of Islam have been and still are predominant in Africa. Perhaps the most important historical exception was the Shi'i empire of the Fatimid rulers in the north, who founded Cairo and made it their capital. The Fatimid empire lasted from the tenth century until 1171, when Salah al-Din (Saladin) conquered Egypt and restored Sunni rule. Of the four Sunni law

Muslim faithful attend prayers at the Nasfat Mosque in Lagos, Nigeria.

schools (*madhahib,* sing. *madhhab*), Maliki—with the main exception of the Fatimid period—became predominant in North Africa and West Africa, while the Shafii tradition prevailed in East Africa, along the Red Sea coast and in parts of Egypt. In black Africa, however, local traditions of royal or chiefly authority could thrive in many areas, although more strict observance of Islamic law (*shari'a*) could be practiced in enclaves of Muslim traders and others. In the nineteenth century, first the caliphate of Uthman dan Fodio in West Africa and later the Madhist state in the Sudan, whose founder Muhammad Ahmad proclaimed himself *mahdi* ("divinely guided," Messiah), called for a strict observation of Islamic law and "purification" from pre-Islamic elements. During the colonial period, both British and French administrations, among others, sought to centralize Muslim judicial systems in Africa, which reduced the degree of local political influence in legal affairs. South of the Sahara, attempts also were made to promote customary law as a barrier to the expansion of Islam. Besides, Islamic law was often administered locally on an informal basis.

Early Post-Colonial Times

When African countries became independent, in most cases around 1960, Islam as a rule was politically marginal. In multireligious states, Christian politicians and administrators who had attended mission schools had an educational advantage and tended to dominate in new leadership positions. In Islamic and predominantly Muslim countries, Islam was seldom an ideological priority. During the early colonial period of the 1960s and 1970s, the predominant ideological currents were liberal or socialist, albeit with a more or less Islamic orientation, instead of more strictly Islamic.

Of special importance at that time was the Arab or Islamic socialism of which the Egyptian president Gamal Abdel Nasser was a pioneering proponent. While Morocco and Mauritania chose more liberal policies, other Islamic countries in the north followed the Egyptian example of opting for various nationalistically and idealistically inspired forms of socialism. Nasser presented Arab or Islamic socialism as a third way, different from Western capitalism and Eastern communism. Islam, not Marxism, was depicted as the basis and source of inspiration. During Nasser's time as president, from the 1950s until 1970, when he died of a heart attack, a great deal of political propaganda was distributed from Egypt and strongly influenced several other political leaders in Africa. Before most other African countries became independent, he prepared in Egypt a middle way for African Muslims, which until the rise of Islamism became the strongest alternative to the Christian capitalism of the Western colonizers and the communism of the Eastern atheists.

In Egypt, as well as in Algeria, Islamic socialism included many economic reforms, such as partial nationalization, which created mixed economies with strong state influence. Tunisia was economically less but socially more radical than Algeria and Egypt. The longtime Tunisian president Habib Bourguiba spearheaded several changes that caused much criticism from Islamic leaders. As early as 1956, for instance, Islamic law was replaced by a personal status code, which forbade polygamy and made marriage and divorce civil matters. Unilateral repudiation on the part of the husband was outlawed and, following recommendations of the United Nations, a minimum age for marriage was stipulated (fifteen for girls and eighteen for boys). In public schools, segregation of sexes was abandoned. Although the Tunisian type of socialism was not antireligious as such, the Bourgouiba regime clearly intended to reduce the influence of religious leaders and Islamic law.

In Libya as well as in Somalia, socialism was introduced in 1969. The new Libyan leader Muammar Qaddafi was strongly influenced by Nasser but had a stronger religious orientation. Like Nasser, Qaddafi became active trying to spread his message internationally, particularly in Africa. Siad Barre in Somalia talked about scientific instead of Islamic socialism, but it was not to be equated with Marxism. In his view, the socialism of Somalia, with its mixed economy, was fully compatible with Islam. However, the decisions to outlaw polygamy and give equal rights of inheritance to men and women (1975) were strongly criticized by some Islamic leaders for being against the *shari'a*.

The Sudan and Senegal are examples of predominantly Muslim countries that also became socialist. Like Qaddafi and Barre, Jafar Nimeiri seized power, in 1969, championing a radical form of Sudanese socialism, which was opposed by many Islamic leaders. Senegal is to a considerable degree exceptional in that there the interests of some religious leaders, especially the *marabouts* of the Muridiyya Sufi order, converged with the less radical socialist interests of Catholic president Léopold Senghor. This *tariqa* was founded in the nineteenth century by Senegalese Ahmadu Bamba, who previously belonged to the large and established Qadiriyya order, and controlled most of the peanut production, a particularly important cash crop of this country. Tanzania in East Africa was similar to Senegal in that a Catholic president, Julius Nyerere, championed an ideology of African socialism that was supported primarily by the Muslim part of the population, while particularly Christian leaders such as bishops voiced criticism. In both countries, it was above all Sufi Muslims who supported the idealistic socialist policies—in Tanzania, especially the Qadiriyya.

Arab, Islamic, or African socialism in Islamic and predominantly Muslim nations in Africa was anticolonialist and nationalist, championing selected features of the traditional past. Religion was subordinated to politics, but religious leaders were asked to assist in the struggle for socioeconomic change. While religion, interpreted in a socialist way, was said to be a source of political inspiration, there was a process of institutional secularization in that, for instance, secular schools were prioritized and the *shari'a* lost much of its grip of legislation. While the state had a leading economic role, small-scale private ownership and capitalist ventures were accepted. In general, the socialist political parties aimed at being mass parties instead of vanguard parties and the idea of class struggle was rejected.

Contemporary History

Throughout the history of Islam, reformist movements have championed a more pure Islam. In recent decades, Islamist movements, organizations, and individuals have argued that Islam is a comprehensive way of life, a universal, all-inclusive societal order based on the *shariʿa*. Hence, in their view, Islam provides answers to all questions. However, old answers may not be relevant today, and Islamists stress the importance of the principle of *ijtihad* (new interpretations of Islamic law), asserting the idea of Islamic modernization. Among others, Sufi and socialist conceptions of Islam are criticized for mixing with non-Islamic ideas and practices. Consequently, a call has been made for purification of Islam and a complete application of Islamic law.

In Africa, modern Islamism started developing mainly in the 1970s and 1980s, influenced by pioneering ideologists such as Hasan al-Banna, the Egyptian who in 1928 founded the Muslim Brotherhood; Sayyid Qutb, another leading Egyptian representative of this Brotherhood, who was sentenced to death and killed by Nasser's regime (1966); and Mawlana Mawdudi in South Asia, who in 1941 established the Islamic Society (Jamaat-i-Islami). Despite being Shiʿi-oriented, Ayatollah Khomeini and the creation of the Islamic republic in Iran (1979) was another important source of inspiration and support. Whereas Islamist conceptions of Islam grew stronger in the late twentieth and early twenty-first centuries, socialist as well as various forms of liberal interpretations of Islam instead weakened.

As of the 1970s the Egyptian presidents Anwar Sadat and Hosni Mubarak made certain concessions to the Islamist opposition, while continuing to oppose it. For instance, after a constitutional reform in 1980, the role of the *shariʿa* was at least formally reinforced in that it became the principal source of legislation. After an initial honeymoon, the Muslim Brothers and other Islamists became increasingly critical of the new regimes, which countered with strong repressive actions. In Algeria, socialism was abandoned in the 1980s and multiparty politics was rendered possible. In the early 1990s, the Islamist party Front islamique du salut (FIS, Islamic Salvation Front) won the parliamentary elections. However, the second round of elections that promised to bring the Islamists to power was halted by the military. Instead, FIS was

banned and a devastating civil war started, resulting in the deaths of tens of thousands of people.

In the Sudan, the Islamist movement gradually grew strong. Nimeiri soon left the socialist path and started cooperating with the Muslim Brotherhood and its well-known Sudanese leader Hasan al-Turabi, an internationally prominent ideologist. In 1983 Nimeiri announced the full adoption of the *shariʿa*. Among other things, this led to tensions with Sufi Muslims. After the military takeover in 1989, led by Umar Hasan al-Bashir, Islamist policies were further strengthened. The Islamization process has aggravated the conflicts between the north and the mainly non-Muslim and non-Arab south of the country.

In neighbouring Ethiopia, much discontent arose among Muslims because of the discriminatory policies of the old Christian state. Under the Marxist military regime in the 1970s and 1980s, which strongly opposed the previously established Orthodox Church and its old privileges, Muslims first believed in improvements, but the new government's antireligious policies soon affected them negatively, too. After 1991, when the military regime was overthrown, Muslims witnessed a revival, even though the growth of Islamist groups led to tensions with Christians as well as Sufis.

In West Africa, the most far-reaching results of the Islamist wave are found in Nigeria, Africa's most populous country. The Islamic legacy in the form of the *shariʿa*-based Sokoto caliphate, founded by dan Fodio, has been glorified by Islamists as a local historical example that should be followed. After the presidential victory in 1999 of a born-again Christian, Olusegun Obasanjo, who unlike most previous Nigerian presidents hails from the southeast, not the Muslim-dominated north, several northern constituent states of the federation, starting with Zamfara in 2000, decided to implement the full gamut of *shariʿa,* including criminal law. As in the Sudan, this development has worsened the tensions between Muslims and Christians.

In other parts of West Africa, as in East Africa and southern Africa, the stronger position of Sufism, among other things, has counteracted the growth of Islamist influence. However, a growing attachment to the *shariʿa* and the idea of Islamic states can be found also among some Sufi Muslims, for instance, in Sufi-dominated Senegal, which sometimes tends to blur the distinction between Islamists and Sufis. On the Tanzanian islands of the Indian Ocean, another part of Africa with a historical legacy of an Islamic state, some Muslims fight for independence from the mainland and a new state with a strong commitment to the *shariʿa*. Further south, for instance, in South Africa, Islamist groups are too small to have any major political impact, but within the Muslim communities their increased presence is clearly felt there as well.

In the early twenty-first century, Islamism seems to be the most significant ideological current within Islam in Africa. Islamists see it as the solution to failures of other ideologies and poorly fulfilled promises of secular modernization. Like before, however, most African Muslims are Sufis; and there is a multitude of political interpretations of Islam, such as the feminist views of, among others, the Moroccan Fatima Mernissi and the socialist ideas of the Egyptian Hasan Hanafi. Also, in markedly multireligious countries (the majority of Africa's states), it is difficult for Islamists—or other religiously exclusive groups—to influence state policies in any far-reaching way.

See also *Islam; Shariʿa;* specific countries.

David B. Westerlund

BIBLIOGRAPHY

Brenner, Louis, ed. *Muslim Identity and Social Change in Sub-Saharan Africa.* London: Hurst, 1993.

Evers, Rosander, Eva Westerlund, and David Westerlund, eds. *African Islam and Islam in Africa: Encounters between Sufis and Islamists.* Athens: Ohio University Press, 1997.

Hiskett, Mervin. *The Course of Islam in Africa.* Edinburgh: Edinburgh University Press, 1994.

Levtzion, Nehemia, and Randall L. Pouwels. *The History of Islam in Africa.* Athens: Ohio University Press, 2000.

O'Brien, Donal B. Cruise. *Symbolic Confrontations: Muslims Imagining the State in Africa.* New York: Palgrave Macmillan, 2003.

O'Brien, Donal B. Cruise, and Christian Coulon, eds. *Charisma and Brotherhood in African Islam.* New York: Oxford University Press, 1988.

Trimingham, J. S. *The Influence of Islam upon Africa.* 2nd ed. London: Longman, 1980.

Islam in Europe

Muslims were in the early years of the twenty-first century, the largest religious minority in Western Europe. The presence of Islam in this part of the world is a direct consequence of the immigration into Europe that began in the early 1960s from former colonies in Asia, Africa, and the Caribbean. The official end of work-based immigration in 1974, along with subsequent policies on family reunification, have caused these immigrant populations to take root and expand, contributing to the noticeable increase in family size within Europe. In such a context, belief in Islam becomes a powerful identity marker around which many groups cohere. The resulting visibility of Islam in Western European countries has prompted questions, doubts, and even open violence against Muslim communities.

A combination of factors characterizes the specific condition of Islam in Europe: European Muslims are mostly immigrants; they have vastly different ethnicities and cultures; they are socioeconomically marginalized; they are obliged to integrate into politically and culturally varied nations; and finally, their integration is occurring against a background of international constraints such as the war on terror.

European Muslims Are Mostly Immigrants

According to the best estimates, Muslims in the early twenty-first century constitute approximately 5 percent of the European Union's 425 million inhabitants. There are about 4.5 million Muslims in France, 3 million in Germany, 1.6 million in the United Kingdom, and more than half a million in both Italy and the Netherlands. In other countries such as Austria, Sweden, and Belgium, Muslim populations number less than 500,000, but still represent significant minorities. Approximately half of European Muslims are foreign born. In general, the Muslim population is younger and produces more children than the corresponding domestic populations.

In France and the United Kingdom, Muslim populations began arriving in the mid-twentieth century, primarily from former colonies. This led to a predominately North African Muslim ethnicity in France, and a predominantly South Asian one in the United Kingdom. In Germany the community began with an influx of "guest workers" during the post-war economic boom, mostly from Turkey. Immigration of guest workers in the Netherlands led to a largely Moroccan and Turkish population. Along with the other nations in the European Union, all of these populations have been substantially augmented by continuing immigration flows over the last twenty years. Although immigrants have come from all over the world, the countries with existing populations tend to attract more of the same ethnic background.

The majority of Muslims in Europe place their origins in three areas of the world. The largest ethnic group is Arab (45 percent), followed by Turkish and South Asian. Although there are sizable populations of Turks in several countries, the majority is in Germany, while most of the South Asians reside in the United Kingdom. Most European countries closed their doors to simple economic migration in the 1970s, but asylum and family reunification policies continue to encourage substantial numbers of new arrivals. Muslims have also entered Europe in large numbers as refugees from violence. Bosnian and Kosovar Muslims fleeing the wars during the breakup of Yugoslavia generated large flows across Europe, with more than 300,000 fleeing to Germany. Violence in Somalia also drove many to emigrate.

The growing number of Muslims in the European Union (EU) and the proposed admission of Turkey as an EU member state have sparked a debate about the demographics of Islam in Europe. Some commentators believe that current trends will lead to the development of a Muslim majority in Europe by the end of the twenty-first century. In a 2004 interview the social critic and noted author Bernard Lewis predicted that Europe would eventually become part of the Arab West. With Muslims currently constituting only 5 percent of the European Union, this would require an unprecedented surge in immigration. Even the addition of Turkey to the European Union would not come near to generating an overall Muslim majority. In certain locations within Europe, however, including the Netherlands' three largest cities, Muslim majorities may emerge within the next few decades.

Muslims Are Part of the European Underclass

The socioeconomic condition of European Muslims is one of great fragility. The unemployment rate for immigrant Muslims in the early 2000s was, as a general rule, higher than the national average: 31 percent and 24 percent for Moroccans and Turks, respectively, in the Netherlands. In Britain, persons originating from Bangladesh and Pakistan, most of whom are Muslim, had a level of unemployment three times higher than that of society at large. In inner cities, almost half of all Bangladeshi men and women were unemployed. This marginality is passed on to the generation born and educated in Great Britain: in 2002, the unemployment rate for young people of Bangladeshi origin aged 16 to 24 was almost 40 percent, whereas the unemployment rate for white men of the same age was 12 percent (www.statistics.gov.uk 2002). This disadvantage is not limited to jobs requiring only basic qualifications, but also concerns high-profile domains such as medicine and education.

This socioeconomic marginality is in most cases accompanied by residential segregation. Data from the British census shows that Pakistani immigrants tend to live in the most dilapidated and unhealthy kinds of housing. Disparities in ethnic concentration per residential area or per residence are also notable in the inner cities of Germany and in France's poorer suburbs.

Such marginalization has important consequences for Islam in Europe. On the one hand can be found the political temptation to associate Islam with poverty and to assume a causal link between the two. On the other, there is a tendency for Muslims to use Islam in a defensive or reactive way. A collusion occurs between ethnicity, religion, and poverty. Frustrated by poverty and a lack of equal opportunity, some groups withdraw from society, preserving their Muslim identity as a defense against cultural isolation. In Great Britain this has led to segregation along racial and religious lines at every level of society, from education and employment to housing and social services.

The ethnic character of social disparity is also noticeable within the urban spaces of France, Germany, and the Netherlands, where the poorest segment of the population (a majority of which are Muslim) becomes concentrated in the poorer suburbs. The riots in France in the winter of 2005 involved such a group. The correlation between social problems and Islam has been invoked as one of the reasons for the resurgence of extreme-right political movements, not only in France, but also in Belgium, Austria, and the Netherlands. Links between Islam and poverty are used to justify the idea that Islam is incompatible with, and threatening to, Western culture.

One of the consequences of the attacks of September 11, 2001, has been the accentuation of stigma through the association of Islam, the poor suburbs, and terrorism. The Madrid bombing in March 2004 and the London bombings in July 2005 have intensified this correlation.

Islam and European Secularism

The ethnic diversity of European Muslims is often underlined. It is also important, however, to take into account the diversity of national contexts: the status of religion within different societies; the modes of acquiring nationality; the presence of multiculturalism, or lack thereof; as well as the specific characteristics of each European country that have a direct influence on the dynamics of the formation of Muslim minorities and on the construction of identities.

Muslims pray in the main square in Graz, Austria, during a protest demonstration in February 2006. Muslims across Europe protested the publication of cartoons depicting the prophet Muhammad in a Danish newspaper.

The dominant argument advanced to explain difficulties of Muslim integration is the supposed incompatibility of Islam with secular principles. Being secular implies that political power is defined by its neutral interactions with religious institutions, bearing in mind that the principle of neutrality is not necessarily synonymous with the separation of church and state. Regarding the latter, European countries can be divided into three broad categories: those that endorse cooperation between the state and the churches, those with a state religion, and those that have effected a separation between the state and religion. Throughout Europe, however, it is clear that Islam's arrival has reopened a debate, previously considered closed, about the relationship between the state and religion.

The institutional agreements between Islamic organizations and the secular state are only one aspect of the status of religions within Europe. Underpinning differentiation between the political and religious spheres and the notion of neutrality can be found an ideological component that originated with the philosophy of the Enlightenment. The idea that religion cannot play a legitimate role in the general well-being of societies—a mark of the secularized mind—is common throughout Europe, despite differences in national contracts between states and organized religion. One conse-

quence of this invalidation of the religious is that the various manifestations of Islam in Europe become troublesome, or even unacceptable. The first major manifestation of this tension occurred in 1989 over Salman Rushdie's book *The Satanic Verses*. The novel, which Muslims all over the world denounced as an insulting portrayal of the Prophet Muhammad, prompted Iran's Ayatollah Khomeini to issue a fatwa against Rushdie, calling for his execution.

Simultaneously, an intense debate began in France about the permissibility of the *hijab* (Islamic headscarf) in public spaces. According to the dominant secularist attitude, the headscarf was an expression of private religious devotion, and therefore a violation of the neutrality of French public space. Interpreted as a symbolic rejection of progress and of individual female emancipation, the hijab provokes the wrath of groups who spearhead the defense of secular ideology: teachers, intellectuals, feminists, and civil servants, among others. The culmination of this controversy, the 2004 French law prohibiting religious signs in public schools, is an example of this secular ideology at its peak, although there have been similar incidents involving the wearing of *hijab* or *niquab* (veils that cover the face) all over Europe.

The protests of Muslims both in Denmark and worldwide against the caricatures of the Prophet Muhammad published on September 30, 2005, in the Jyllands-Posten newspapers reopened the debate about the compatibility of Islamic principles with secularism and especially with freedom of expression. The demands and requests of Muslims, often perceived as suspect, and sometimes as backward, provoked highly emotional reactions. Equally significant was the response of the Norwegian atheist association, which sought the right to proclaim for several minutes everyday the non-existence of God in order to offer competition to Oslo's muezzin.

All over Europe, the establishment of Islam has, simply by its presence, questioned the dominant culture as this culture reflects on its own arbitrariness and limitations. In France this happened with the controversy surrounding the headscarf and the resurgence of a debate on the definition of secular society. In Great Britain the Rushdie affair created the conditions for a critique of public culture. Until that point, the debate about multiculturalism had mainly been led by members of the majority population; the role of minorities was largely passive. Before the Rushdie affair, integration had been seen as the adjustment of minorities to dominant society; after the Rushdie affair, it was understood to be a mutual process that would also transform the majority population. Muslim leaders stressed their desire that the existing legislation on blasphemy, which until then had only been applicable to the Anglican Church, be extended to incorporate the Muslim minority, as well as all other minorities. The consequences of such a request are very clear: political adhesion is seen as a bilateral relationship in which the host society must enter into negotiations in order to reach a consensus that will respect the fundamental aspects of the minority's way of life. For British Muslims, in other words, equating political adhesion with adhesion to British culture constitutes an attack on their moral and cultural integrity.

Although conflicts with incoming non-European migrants may have been inevitable, cultural differences between immigrants from Muslim countries and secularized European populations are likely to make them more dramatic. In contradiction to Samuel Huntington's thesis about the inherent divergence of Islam from Western political values, the conflicts do not center around the nature of the state in Europe, the claim for Islamic governance, or the accommodation of *shariʿa* (Islamic law) in the common law. Instead the clash concerns life styles, gender equality, and the question of homosexuality.

The most explicit case of cultural conflict has taken place in the Netherlands over homosexuality. Prior to his assassination in 2002, the openly gay politician Pim Fortuyn ran a highly successful political movement against Muslim immigration prompted by what he described as their un-Dutch intolerance. In the mid-2000s the Netherlands introduced a video for the socialization of immigrants into Dutch society. The video is clearly intended to challenge these cultural differences with its many references to homosexuality and portrayals of nude sunbathing. Although the Dutch case has been the most prominent, the differences are broad in scope. Attitudes in Muslim countries are notably more conservative with regards to abortion, homosexuality, gender equality, and divorce. For European societies attempting to integrate Muslim minorities, this difference can be difficult to accommodate, leading to an increase in cultural conflicts with an anti-Muslim sentiment.

This divergence between the European secular mind and Muslim religious values highlights a broader challenge. Islam makes it necessary both to rethink and to contextualize the principle of equality between cultures, thus bestowing on the principles of tolerance and pluralism an entirely new resonance. The multicultural policies that predominate in European societies do not really allow for equality and pluralism to be rethought along the lines of an incorporation of the minority culture's values.

Conclusion: Religious Integration under International Constraints

The attacks of September 11, 2001, were rapidly followed by new anti-terrorism and immigration policies in most European countries and at the European Union level. The attacks in Madrid (2004) and London (2005) have also led to legal and political initiatives to prevent terrorism. Legislation passed since September 11 shows a trend towards conflating immigration and nationalization policies with internal and external security in a way that will have negative long-term effects on the Muslim populations of Europe.

Some estimate that 1 to 2 percent of all European Muslims (between 250,000 to 500,000 people) may be involved in radical activities. Since 9/11, the nations of the EU have arrested more than twenty times the number of terrorist suspects as the United States. More recently, there have been strong suspicions that groups from Iraq have been recruiting in Europe. States are naturally concerned that individuals recruited and trained for overseas battles may eventually turn towards terrorism against Western nations. This is undoubtedly the case for the generation of fighters trained ideologically and militarily in the battle to cast off Soviet domination of Afghanistan (1979–1989). Many of these individuals would eventually gravitate towards radical Islamic groups. Because of this threat, states may take a view of domestic Muslims as "foreign enemies," a classification that implies a much lower level of legal and social rights and privileges.

The conflation of internal and external security has led to a particular emphasis on controlling the speech of Muslim religious leaders. That emphasis can be seen in the rising numbers of imams expelled from European countries and in increasingly frequent attempts to control and infiltrate mosques. Across Europe, dozens of imams have been expelled for preaching beliefs that the state considers threatening. Probably the most famous have been the British imams, Abu Hamza al-Masri and Sheik Omar Bakri Muhammad, who were accused of speaking in favor of Osama bin Laden, and even of helping to recruit terrorists. Lower-profile cases have been a frequent occurrence in France, Germany, and Italy. The laws allowing police to spy on religious groups, passed in various countries, including Germany, the Netherlands, and Britain, are part of an effort to control the speech of religious leaders.

As Muslims are already in difficult social and economic situations, these types of activities are likely to increase sentiments of alienation and disaffection. If Muslims begin to feel that they are not legitimate members of the nation in which they live, this may well lead to negative reactions against that nation, creating a vicious cycle.

See also *Islam;* specific countries.

Jocelyne Cesari

BIBLIOGRAPHY

Cesari, Jocelyne. *When Islam and Democracy Meet: Muslims in Europe and in the United States.* New York: Palgrave Macmillan, 2004.

Cesari, Jocelyne, and Sean Mcloughin, eds. *European Muslims and the Secular State.* Burlington, Vt.: Ashgate, 2005.

Cesari, Jocelyne, Alexandre Caeiro, and Dilwar Hussein. *Islam and Fundamental Rights in Europe.* Report for the European Commission, Directorate-General Justice and Home Affairs, October 2004.

Dassetto, Felice, Birgitte Maréchal, and Jorgen Nielsen, eds. *Convergences musulmanes, aspects contemporains de la présence musulmane dans l'Europe élargie.* Louvain-la-Neuve, France: Academia-Bruylant, 2001.

Fekete, L. "Anti-Muslim Racism and the European Security State, Race and Class." *Race and Class* 46, no. 1 (2004): 3–29.

Giry, Stéphanie. "France and Its Muslims." *Foreign Affairs* (September/October 2006).

Huntington, Samuel P. *The Clash of Civilizations and the Remaking of World Order.* New York: Simon and Schuster, 1996.

Norris, Pippa, and Ronald Inglehart. *Sacred and Secular: Religion and Politics Worldwide.* Cambridge, U.K..: Cambridge University Press, 2004.

Parekh, Bhikhu. "Integrating Minorities," in *Race Relations in Britain, A Developing Agenda.* Tessa Blackstone, Bhikhu Parekh, and Peter Sanders, eds. London: Routledge, 1998: 19–21.

Postiglione, Gerard A. *Ethnicity and American Social Theory: Toward Critical Pluralism.* Lanham, Md.: University Press of America, 1983.

Savage, T. M. "Europe and Islam: Crescent Waxing, Cultures Clashing." *Washington Quarterly* 27 (2004): 25–50.

Islam in Southeast Asia

Far from the Middle Eastern lands in which Islam originated, Southeast Asia is home to the largest majority-Muslim country in the world (Indonesia) and contains an aggregate Muslim population greater than that of the Arab Middle East. Spread across Indonesia, Malaysia, Brunei, Singapore, Cambodia, southern Thailand, and the Philippines, the Muslim population in Southeast Asia is comprised of hundreds of ethnic groups, most of whom live alongside representatives of other world religions.

Southeast Asia's pluralist legacy has left a deep imprint on the local practice of Islam. This is a region where Islam has always varied in its regional and ethnic expressions. Southeast Asian Islam is also known for the relatively elevated status it accords women and its eclectic attitude towards Islamic law. Since the 1980s Muslim communities in the region have experienced an Islamic resurgence of unprecedented proportions. The revival has generated a struggle over the proper forms and meanings of Muslim politics, the outcome of which will have serious implications for Southeast Asia and the broader Muslim world.

Premodern Precedents

For many years Western scholars believed that the most distinctive quality of Islam in Southeast Asia was the strength of pre-Islamic cultural survivals. By comparison with Persia and the Arab heartland, it is true that Islam became a civilizational force in Southeast Asia late in the region's history, long after most of its kingdoms had assimilated an assortment of Hindu–Buddhist traditions. Some non-Islamic influences are still apparent in the classical arts of this region, as well as in aspects of folk ritual and popular belief.

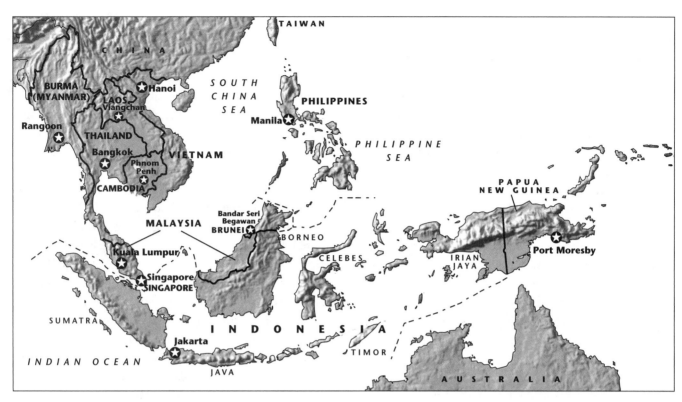

The more distinctive feature of Southeast Asian Islam is not its pre-Islamic survivals, however, but its social pluralism. Islam did not come to this region on the heels of armies of horse-mounted warriors. Islamization was also not accompanied by Arabization or a comparable process of ethnic homogenization. Islam was instead introduced through trade and a network of city-states dispersed across the region. The first Islamic settlement was established in the late thirteenth century in a north Sumatran port involved in the trade with Arabia and Muslim India. In the fifteenth and sixteenth centuries the new religion spread east, first to ports along Java's north coast, and then to the Malay Peninsula and southern Thailand. By the late seventeenth century Islam had completed its eastward journey, becoming the dominant religion in coastal principalities across eastern Indonesia and the southern Philippines. Interior portions of island Southeast Asia and agrarian states on the mainland were less intensely involved in this pan-Asian trade and, as a result, they either remained non-Islamic or, as in interior Java, adopted an Islam of a markedly syncretic cast.

The diffusion of Islam to Southeast Asia occurred at a time when Sufism played a central role in Middle Eastern and South Asian Islam. Sufism is a general term for a variety of Islamic mystical traditions, the unifying characteristic of which is believers' concern for achieving personal closeness with God. Some, but not all, Sufis also place less emphasis on implementation of Islamic law (*shari'a*). Sufi literature and ritual were among the first items borrowed into popular Islam in Southeast Asia. The ease with 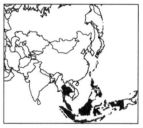 which this transfer took place reflected the fact that Sufism shared ritual and doctrinal traits with the region's pre-existing religious traditions. This included the belief that, rather than standing apart from the world, divinity infuses it. In recent decades Muslim reformists have succeeded at suppressing heterodox (especially pantheist) Sufi traditions, but orthodox mysticism remains popular to this day.

Local kings involved in the Asian trade also played a central role in conversion to Islam. Court-based variants of Islam emphasized that the ruler, rather than jurists (*ulama*), was the final arbiter in religious matters. Across the region, sultans and *rajas* were represented as the defender of the faithful and the "shadow of Allah on earth." Although on a few rare occasions it was systematically applied, most rulers were selective in their application of Islamic law. They gave primary responsibility for legal matters, not to Islamic courts, but to village- and kin-based organizations, which typically applied a variety of customary (*adapt*) laws.

Unlike many Middle Eastern countries this pluralistic pattern was reinforced rather than diminished in the colonial era. In the Dutch East Indies, in particular (the territory that today comprises Indonesia), the colonial government enforced a strict separation of religion and state, and in so doing pushed Muslim institutions away from the state and out into society. In the nineteenth century a network of Qur'anic schools, similar to Middle Eastern and north Indian *madrasas,* spread across Java, introducing ordinary Muslims to orthodox learning for the first time. This vast educational network developed independently of the colonial state. Muslim institutions in Cambodia, southern Thailand, and the Philippines showed a similar degree of institutional autonomy. The pattern of Muslim independence was less pronounced in colonial Malaya. Drawing on their experience in India, the British in Malaya sought to depoliticize Islam but also encouraged rulers to play a central role in the management of religious affairs.

Reform and Resurgence

In the first decades of the twentieth century Southeast Asia witnessed new movements of Islamic reform demanding far-reaching changes in religion and public life. Influenced by reformist trends emanating from Egypt and Arabia, the reformists emphasized the self-sufficiency of scripture and decried what they regarded as heretical "innovations" in matters of worship. They were also critical of folk and courtly traditions, which they regarded as rife with heretical polytheism. Welcoming such Western innovations as modern science and mass education, the reformists aimed to create a Muslim community at once modern and pious.

National independence after the Second World War allowed the reformists to intensify their efforts to reshape local Islam. The post-war period also witnessed a great increase in Southeast Asians' contacts with Muslim reformists in the Middle East. Middle Eastern influence gave an especially important boost to reformist fortunes in Cambodia, southern Thailand, and the southern Philippines, where the Muslim community's minority status left it vulnerable to cultural influences from the non-Muslim majority. By the early 1970s reformists across the region were making steady progress toward their goal of abolishing indigenous traditions they viewed as contrary to Islam. In the 1980s the reformists helped to bring about an Islamic revival of historically unprecedented proportions. Mosques were erected in towns and villages across insular Southeast Asia; religious schools and devotional programs expanded;

and a vast market in Islamic books, magazines, and newspapers developed.

The resurgence has complicated but not done away with the Muslim community's legacy of internal pluralism. The resurgence ushered in a new religious activism that challenged the authority of traditionalist scholars, the *ulama,* and sought to make religion relevant for a broad array of social and political concerns. In place of esoteric doctrine, new Muslim intellectuals and activists demanded that Islam serve as a practical guide for affairs of the world. Inspired by the Middle East's Islamic brotherhoods and Iran's Islamic revolution (1978–1979), some among the new Muslim activists insisted that their religion demands the establishment of an Islamic state. For these activists, Islam is a total way of life and allows no separation of religion from government. Western political concepts like civil society and democracy, these Muslims argued, amount to an abnegation of the idea that religion should serve as the foundation for politics and society. Taking exception to this view, however, other Southeast Asian leaders have insisted Islam and democracy are compatible. In the 1990s Southeast Asian Muslims were at the forefront of the global Muslim community's efforts to develop democratic politics.

Nation and Islam in Indonesia

For most of the twentieth century Indonesian politics has revolved around an often bitter rivalry between activists demanding the establishment of an Islamic state and Muslim and non-Muslim nationalists opposed to any such religious establishment. One index of the intensity of the rivalry was the fact that, notwithstanding the country's solid Muslim majority (about 88.7 percent of the total in 2006), in the late 1950s Indonesia had the largest Communist Party in the non-communist world. In 1965, in the aftermath of a failed left-wing officers coup, conservative army generals mobilized the army and Muslim organizations in a campaign to destroy the Communist Party. The military-dominated government that emerged in the aftermath of the violence set out to reduce the influence, not just of communism, but of Muslim political parties.

Notwithstanding the state's efforts, Indonesia experienced a far-reaching Islamic resurgence during the 1980s and 1990s. The pietistic wave, however, did not translate into greater support for radical Islamism. Earlier, in the 1970s and 1980s, a new class of influential Muslim intellectuals had devised sophisticated religious arguments in support of democracy and civil society. In the 1990s Indonesia developed the largest Muslim-led prodemocracy movement in the world. The movement played a central role in the overthrow of the authoritarian Suharto government in May 1998. In the elections of 1999 and 2004 a small proportion of the electorate cast their vote for Islamist parties advocating the establishment of an Islamic state, but some 80 percent voted for parties committed to a multiconfessional and nationalist state.

There has always been, however, a politically radical stream in Indonesian Islam. At the height of the war for independence in 1948, a movement known as the Darul Islam ("abode of Islam") took shape in West Java, demanding that the republican government be replaced with an Islamic state. The Darul Islam rebellion dragged on for fourteen years. Even after the capture of the movement's leader in 1962, his supporters maintained a loose network of Islamic schools and secret cells through which they spread the message that secular government is sinful, only God's law is legitimate, and the best way to achieve the latter is through the creation of small communities (*jemaah*) of believers dedicated to the implementation of Islamic law. It was from the ranks of these activists that, in the 1990s, a shadowy and violent organization known as the Jemaah Islamiyah emerged. Between 2002 and 2005 the Jemaah Islamiyah carried out a series of bomb attacks on Western and civilian targets in parts of Indonesia. The violence alienated even the militant fringe of the Muslim community, however, and the Jemaah Islamiyah does not appear capable of destabilizing Indonesia's broader political system.

Ethnicity and Politics in Malaysia

The basic social divide in Malaysian politics is that separating Malays, who are Muslim, from non-Muslim Chinese and Indians. The pervasiveness of ethnoreligious divisions reflects two historical facts. The first is that, under British rule, the Malay peninsula experienced Chinese and non-Muslim Indian immigration on such a scale that, on the eve of the Second World War, the Malays were on the verge of becoming a minority in their own country. Equally important, in those years Malays were predominantly agrarian, while non-Malays dominated the cities and the booming national economy. In the run-up to independence in 1956, however, the British gave control of the state to Malays. Although excluded from the commanding heights of the economy (which was largely in British and Western hands) the Malay leadership used the state and national media to instill a sense of ethnic pride in the Malay population. The

Malay-dominated state also provided preferential contracts to Malay businesses, improved Malay education, lifted the economic fortunes of rural Malays, and, by the 1990s, brought a new Malay middle class into existence. Malaysia's forty-year experiment with affirmative action remains one of the modern world's most successful.

For the last thirty years of these social programs, Malay society also experienced a powerful Islamic resurgence. Two features distinguished the Malaysian resurgence from its Indonesian counterpart. First, notwithstanding the efforts of a few scholars, the tone of the Malaysian resurgence is more theologically conservative than that in Indonesia. The conservatism is especially apparent in the statements of the leading Islamist party, the All-Malaysia Islamic Party (PAS). Although it originated in the 1950s as an alliance of religious scholars and populist politicians, since the 1970s PAS has taken a theologically conservative tack, aimed at implementing the letter of Islamic law, including its controversial provisions on adultery, theft, and apostasy.

The second characteristic of the Malaysian resurgence is equally distinctive. Notwithstanding their theological conservatism, Malaysian Islamists have shown a willingness to work within the bounds of constitutional government. Conversely, they have been reluctant to dabble in the paramilitarist adventurism that has marked the Islamist fringe in Indonesia, Thailand, and the Philippines. In the 1980s and 1990s Malaysia witnessed only a few minor incidents of Islamist violence. In contrast to the pattern seen in neighboring Muslim lands, no armed Islamist grouping has ever enjoyed significant mass support in Malaysia.

The success of Malaysia's development programs and, especially, the forging of a new Malay middle class, have done much to curb adventurist tendencies in the Malay Muslim community. As the ranks of the Muslim middle class have grown, ethnic tensions have diminished, although they have not disappeared. The Malay leadership has shown a new confidence in the viability of Malaysia's multireligious federation and in a moderately conservative but pluralist understanding of Islam.

Muslims as Minorities: Southern Thailand and the Philippines

In the Philippines and southern Thailand, Muslim culture and politics have been intertwined with ethnic and regionalist struggles. In southern Thailand since the 1930s and the southern Philippines since the 1950s, the non-Muslim governments' programs for nation building were accompanied by heavy-handed efforts to assimilate the Muslim minority to the non-Muslim majority's ways. In Thailand's three southern provinces, Muslims in 2006 remained a solid majority (about 80 percent of the local population) despite the influx of non-Muslims. In the heartland of Muslim settlement in the Philippines, the province of Mindanao, however, Muslims had been reduced to just 40 percent of the local population by 1975.

The political and demographic transformation of the Muslim homeland in these two countries occurred at a time when Muslims in both areas were forging new contacts with Islamic agencies in the Middle East. From the 1950s on, private and state-sponsored organizations in Libya, Saudi Arabia, and the Gulf states provided scholarships for study in the Middle East. Middle Eastern patrons also subsidized programs of mosque and *madrasa* construction, and dispatched religious proselytizers (*da'i*) to the region. In both countries, these programs undercut traditionalist and more apolitical forms of Islamic piety and accelerated the development of an overarching sense of Muslim identity.

By the late 1970s the trend in both southern Thailand and the southern Philippines was for the secular–nationalist organizations that had once led Muslim resistance to cede their leadership role to new Islamist groupings. Conflicts once described in ethnic and territorial terms slowly acquired a religious cast as well. As armed conflict with the central government escalated in the 1970s, militants in both southern Thailand and the southern Philippines turned to conventional guerrilla warfare. Both rebel movements, however, also attracted criminals and freelance adventurers less interested in Islam than in economic gain. The presence of these freelancers has added an incendiary and terrorist element to both conflicts.

Since the late 1990s southern Thailand and the Philippines have seen renewed outbreaks of secessionist violence. In Thailand the violence's primary catalyst remains Muslim anger with what is seen as the repressive hand of the central government. Although in the late-1990s Thai authorities seemed to be making headway in their negotiations with Muslim rebels, violence escalated again in 2003–2004. It is unclear whether any among the Muslim militants in Thailand are receiving assistance from al-Qaida or the Jemaah Islamiyah, as Thai authorities have claimed. Angered by an upsurge in attacks on civilians (including Buddhist monks), school teachers, and government officials, Thai authorities launched a crackdown on militants in early 2004. The cam-

paign culminated in the killing of one hundred lightly armed militants in a historic mosque on April 28, 2004, and the suffocation death of another seventy-eight protestors in police custody on October 26, 2004. Although moderates on both sides of the conflict have attempted to dampen tensions, incidents like these have greatly complicated efforts to bring about a peaceful resolution of the dispute.

The armed conflict between the government and Muslim insurgents in the southern Philippines is the most serious in all of Southeast Asia. The Muslim insurgency has operated with various levels of intensity since the 1980s. In 2006 there were ten to fifteen thousand fighters associated with the Moro Islamic Liberation Front (MILF), and another one thousand or so associated with the more extremist Abu Sayyaf Group. More than one hundred thousand youth have also received some form of military training and stand ready to assist the full-time fighters. In July 2000 the Philippine army captured the most important of the MILF military bases, after an offensive that displaced almost a million people. The army's offensive severely damaged the MILF infrastructure, but it also dispersed MILF fighters, weakening the leadership's command over its units in the field. Some of the latter have turned to random acts of hit-and-run violence. The resulting pattern of low-level but recurring conflict is likely to continue until a peace deal can be negotiated.

The Jemaah Islamiyah (JI)

The stated ambition of the most well known of Southeast Asia's *jihadi* groupings is to establish a pan-Southeast Asian polity based on the Qur'an and Sunna. The JI's roots lie not in al-Qaida but in Indonesia's own home-grown rebels, the Darul Islam. The Jemaah Islamiyah was founded in 1993 by a splinter group of militants earlier involved in the Darul Islam underground. Many of the second-tier leadership of the JI also underwent military training in Afghanistan in the late 1980s and early 1990s. There the future leaders of the organization made contact with militants from the Philippines' MILF. These international contacts became the basis for limited cooperation between the Jemaah Islamiyah and the MILF in the mid-1990s. From that point on, the Jemaah Islamiyah and the MILF—or, at the very least, factions within each of these groups—cooperated to carry out several terrorist attacks on civilian targets.

The long-term prospects for these two groups remain unclear. With significant arrests in Singapore, Malaysia,

Indonesia, Thailand, and the Philippines, Southeast Asian governments have dealt the JI leadership a serious blow. The Philippine army's attacks on MILF camps have also damaged the MILF infrastructure. Although both achievements have weakened these organizations, they have also decentralized and dispersed armed militants. The type of hit-and-run attacks seen in the southern Philippines and southern Thailand may well continue for some time to come.

The diversity seen within Southeast Asian Islam shows that there is no single civilizational determinant of Muslim politics. Southeast Asian Muslims are varied in their political views and include in their ranks ardent democrats as well as hardline militants. The central role of democratic Muslims in overthrowing Indonesia's Suharto in May 1998 stands as one of the most important achievements of democratic Islam in modern times. The low-level conflicts that have raged for decades in several Southeast Asian countries, however, also demonstrate that the future of Muslim politics in this region will depend on local patterns of power and justice as much as on enduring religious aspirations.

See also *Civil Society; Islam; Pluralism;* specific countries.

Robert W. Hefner

BIBLIOGRAPHY

Abdillah, Masykuri. *Responses of Indonesian Muslim Intellectuals to the Concept of Democracy (1966–1993).* Hamburg: Abera Verlaag Meyer and Co., 1997.

Ackerman, Susan E., and Raymond L.M. Lee. *Heaven in Transition: Non-Muslim Religious Innovation and Ethnic Identity in Malaysia.* Honolulu: University of Hawaii Press, 1988.

Chalk, Peter. "Militant Islamic Separatism in Southern Thailand." In *Islam in Asia: Changing Political Realities,* edited by Jason F. Isaacson and Colin Rubenstein, 165–186. New Brunswick, N.J.: Transaction Publishers, 2002.

Che Man, W. K. *Muslim Separatism: The Moros of Southern Philippines and the Malays of Southern Thailand.* New York: Oxford University Press, 1990.

Van Dijk, Cees. *Rebellion under the Banner of Islam: The Darul Islam in Indonesia.* The Hague, the Netherlands: Martinus Nijhoff, 1981.

Hefner, Robert W. *Civil Islam: Muslims and Democratization in Indonesia.* Princeton, N.J.: Princeton University Press, 2000.

Hefner, Robert W., and Patricia Horvatich, eds. *Islam in an Era of Nation-States: Politics and Religious Renewal in Muslim Southeast Asia.* Honolulu: University of Hawaii Press, 1997.

Hooker, M. B., ed. *Islam in South-East Asia.* Leiden, the Netherlands: E. J. Brill, 1983.

International Crisis Group. "Al-Qaeda in Southeast Asia: The Case of the 'Ngruki Network' in Indonesia." Brussels: ICG Asia Briefing, 8 August 2002.

Laffan, Michael Francis. *Islamic Nationhood and Colonial Indonesia: The Umma below the Winds.* London: RoutledgeCurzon, 2003.

McKenna, Thomas M. *Muslim Rulers and Rebels: Everyday Politics and Armed Separatism in the Southern Philippines.* Berkeley: University of California Press, 1998.

Reid, Anthony. *Southeast Asia in the Age of Commerce, 1450–1680.* Vol. 2, *Expansion and Crisis.* New Haven, Conn.: Yale University Press, 1993.

Riddell, Peter G. *Islam and the Malay-Indonesian World: Transmission and Responses.* London: Hurst and Company, 2001.

Islam in the United States

Islam is one of the fastest-growing religions in the United States today. It comprises several racial and ethnic groups, including South Asians, Arabs, and African Americans.

Islam is an Arabic term that means surrender or submission to God, and one who submits to God is called a Muslim. Today, Islam is the largest faith tradition in the world—one out of five people belong to the Islamic religion. South Asia is home to the largest Muslim nations, with 215 million Muslims in Indonesia (88 percent of the country's population) and another 160 million in Pakistan (97 percent of the country's population). Predominantly Muslim populations are also located in North Africa (Egypt, Algeria, Morocco, and Tunisia) and western Asia (Syria, Iraq, Iran, and Jordan). Although many of these countries are Arab, the majority of Muslims globally are of non-Arab ethnicity, including Pakistanis, Indians, and Persians.

This diversity is reflected in the Muslim population of the United States, which is the most ethnically diverse Muslim population in the world, originating from over eighty countries. Size estimates of the U.S. Muslim population are contentious, ranging anywhere from 2 to 8 million. Because of the constitutional separation of church and state, the U.S. Census Bureau does not collect information on religion and so official counts of Muslim Americans are nonexistent. Scholarly studies conducted by Muslim sociologists in the late 1990s projected that the population would number around 7 million by 2000, an estimate that was later revised to 5.7 million in 2003. Similarly, the 2001 Mosque Study Project placed the Muslim American population at 6–7 million. By contrast, a 2001 study sponsored by the American Jewish Committee put the number much lower, at 1.9–2.8 million. A plausible estimate is that found in the *CIA World Factbook,* which places the Muslim population at 1 percent of the U.S. population, or roughly 3 million persons.

Although there is considerable debate over the size of the population, scholars tend to agree more on the social and demographic composition of the U.S. Muslim community. About two-thirds of these Muslims are indigenous to the Middle East, South Asia, and Africa; one-third of the population is African American; and a small but growing number are U.S.-born Anglo and Hispanic converts to the religion. The vast majority of the indigenous population is immigrant, and most have resided in the United States for ten or more years (that is, they are not new arrivals). Muslim immigration to the United States, which reached its peak in the 1970s and 1980s, has been relatively slow over the past ten years because of the restrictive Illegal Immigration and Reform Act, passed in 1996. Although most of the indigenous population is foreign-born, an increasing number are the second- and third-generation offspring of earlier immigrant arrivals. The indigenous population is also diverse by ethnicity; South Asians (30–35 percent) and Arabs (20–25 percent) make up the two largest ethnic groups.

A sizable and growing percentage of the population consists of U.S.-born African Americans. African American Muslims differ from the indigenous population in several ways—most notably they are typically converts to the religion. Most African American converts to Islam adhere to mainstream Islam (Sunni or Shi'a), like the indigenous population. Mainstream, or orthodox, Islam refers to those branches of Islam that are rooted in the fundamental philosophies of the Islamic religion as laid out in the Qur'an and hadiths, which are second-hand reports of the prophet Muhammad's personal traditions and lifestyle that detail how he dealt with daily issues and problems. A large number of African American Muslims also belong to the Nation of Islam, which was established in 1930 by Wallace Fard Muhammad and is considered a more politically oriented branch of Islam. Under Muhammad's successor, Elijah Muhammad, conversion to Islam became popular among African Americans during the civil rights era, not only as a sign of religious expression but also as a distinct marker of cultural identity that separated black Americans from mainstream American Christianity. Because the Nation of Islam focuses primarily on black-white racial issues in American society, indigenous Muslims often distance themselves from this group in order to establish organizations that focus more on cultural and religious (rather than racial) oppression. Furthermore, some adherents of mainstream Islam see the Nation of Islam as blasphemous because its members teach

Two Muslim girls look out the window of their school bus after leaving the Islamic Al Noor school in Brooklyn. Many American Muslim children attend Islamic private schools or Muslim weekend schools, which teach them the basics of their faith.

that God will manifest himself in a human form, which is diametrically opposed to the most central article of faith in mainstream Islam, "There is no God but Allah, and Muhammad is His Prophet."

The Religion–Politics Connection

In addition to being ethnically diverse, the Muslim American community is characterized by considerable diversity with respect to the socioeconomic and demographic factors that are known to affect the democratic participation of other racial/ethnic and immigrant groups, such as Hispanics and Asians. Similar to many U.S. immigrant populations, Muslim immigrants have characteristics that distinguish them markedly from Muslims in their countries of origin. For example, on average they tend to be more highly educated and more politically conscious than those in their homelands, and they have extremely high levels of English language fluency, all of which suggests a positive profile for political engagement. Yet at the same time, the community is composed primarily of immigrants, many of whom may feel they have less at stake in political outcomes than their U.S.-born counterparts.

One of the most important characteristics to consider when examining Muslim American political attitudes and behaviors is degree of religiosity, or strength of Muslim religious identity. Religion is an important characteristic to consider, because religious institutions can foster and promote a sense of collective identity, or common fate, that helps to mobilize congregants to participate in the political process in order to remedy group grievances such as discrimination. The black church has historically played such a role in the African American community, but to date there has been limited evidence on how Muslim identity affects U.S. political participation. The general sentiment among the American public is that Islam cannot coexist with democracy—recent nationwide polls conducted by the Pew Forum on Religion and Public life found that a majority of Americans feel that Islam is a violent religion, that Muslims are anti-American, and that Islam is incompatible with democracy.

However, Muslim Americans are quite diverse in their religious identities, ranging from the religiously devout to those who are nonpracticing and secular (that is, basically Muslim in name only), similar to a good proportion of U.S. Christians and Jews. Among the more religiously devout, there is still a sharp distinction between being a good Muslim and being an Islamic fundamentalist. Indeed, in part to practice their religion and politics more freely in the United States, many Muslim Americans emigrated from countries in the Middle East that are now considered an enemy of the state. But whether and how religious identity influences Muslims' participation in the American political system are less clear, and the limited evidence that does exist suggests mixed outcomes for the political integration of this minority group. On the one hand, some Islamic scholars contend that Muslims should not participate in non-Muslim political systems, such as the United States, because it compromises their religious principles that promote living is a society guided entirely by Islamic teachings. Other scholars argue not only that can Muslims participate in American politics, but also that it is their duty to do in order to resolve social injustices against all persons, not just Muslims.

For the most part, social scientists have found support for the second argument. And mosque involvement increases the political consciousness and activity of Muslim Americans, which corresponds with the evidence in the larger literature on the influence of religion on American political participation. However, the influence of religious participation on political involvement appears to vary by gender—it has a stronger effect on men than on women. This difference may reflect the fact that men and women do not intermingle at the mosque, and thus what they get out of mosque attendance might be quite different. Unlike Judeo-Christian services in which men and women congregate together, about two-thirds of mosques have separate prayer rooms for women, and this practice is increasing, up from 50 percent of mosques in 1994.

The one thing that is clear is that Muslim religious institutions are flourishing in the United States, and, as such, have the potential to play an important role in the political mobilization of a sizable number of Muslim Americans. According to the Mosque Study Project conducted in 2000, over 1,200 mosques are spread throughout the United States, which represents a 60 percent increase since the 1980s; the average attendance at Friday prayers increased 94 percent between 1994 and 2000, from 150 to 292 persons; and over 2 million Muslims are associated with the religious life of mosques, for an average of 1,625 persons per mosque nationwide. The Mosque Study Project was part of a larger study of American congregations, *Faith Communities Today,* conducted by Hartford Seminary's Hartford Institute for Religious Research.

Muslim Organizations and Political Involvement Post–September 11

The terrorist attacks on the United States of September 11, 2001, propelled Muslims into the spotlight of American public discourse and debate. Muslim American organizations such as the Council on American-Islamic Relations (CAIR) and the Islamic Society of North America (ISNA) responded to the backlash of September 11 by unequivocally denouncing the terrorist acts and proclaiming their loyalty to the United States. At the national level, CAIR worked and continues to work with state and local law enforcement authorities to improve community relations by coordinating forums with Islamic leaders, conducting sensitivity training for law enforcement officials, and providing diversity training workshops. At the state and local levels, Muslim American organizations have participated in outreach programs aimed at educating the American public on Islam and differentiating mainstream Islam from the radical Islam of terrorist groups.

The events of September 11 also served to heighten Muslim American political consciousness, which has facilitated mobilization efforts by Muslim American organizations to increase their participation in the political process. The ongoing wars in Iraq and against terrorism, interpreted by some Muslim Americans as a war against Islam (both radical and mainstream Islam), have ensured that Muslim advocacy groups have an active and vocal base. In the 2004 national elections, CAIR worked diligently to get out the Muslim vote, especially in key battleground states such as Ohio, Florida, and California. Their efforts included opening "Get Out the Muslim Vote" election centers throughout Ohio, calling thousands of Ohio and Florida Muslim voters to ask for a commitment to vote, busing Florida Muslim voters to early polls after Friday prayers, and publishing a voter guide for Muslim voters in California. These efforts resulted in the unprecedented successful mobilization of Muslim American voters. In 2004 a record high number of Muslim Americans were elected to public office—nearly 50 percent of the one hundred Muslim American candidates nationwide—in positions ranging from city council to mayor to state senates. And there was a dramatic shift away from President George W. Bush—only 7 percent of Muslim American voters supported his reelection, down from over 40 percent in 2000. Only time will tell whether Muslim Americans will have a voice in American politics and whether and how they choose to exercise that voice.

See also *Islam; Islam's Encounters with the West.*

Jen'nan Ghazal Read

BIBLIOGRAPHY

Bagby, Ihsan, Paul M. Perl, and Bryan T. Froehle. "The Mosque in America: A National Portrait." Washington, D.C.: Council on American-Islamic Relations. http://www.cair-net.org/mosquereport, 2001.

Haddad, Yvonne Y., Jane I. Smith, and John L. Esposito, eds. *Religion and Immigration: Christian, Jewish, and Muslim Experiences in the United States.* New York: Altamira Press, 2003.

Jamal, Amaney. "The Political Participation and Engagement of Muslim Americans: Mosque Involvement and Group Consciousness." *American Politics Research* 33 (2005): 521–544.

Pew Research Center. "Plurality Sees Islam as More Likely to Encourage Violence." Pew Forum on Religion and Public Life. Press release from telephone survey, http://pewforum.org/publications/surveys/islam.pdf, 2004.

Strum, Philippa, and Danielle Tarantolo, eds. *Muslims in the United States: Demography, Beliefs, Institutions.* Washington, D.C.: Woodrow Wilson International Center for Scholars, 2003.

U.S. Central Intelligence Agency. *The World Factbook.* Annual. http://www.cia.gov/cia/publications/factbook.

Islam, Nation of

See *Nation of Islam.*

Islam, Radical

Since the 1970s the world has witnessed rebellions and acts of terrorism in the name of Islam. From Afghanistan and India to Iraq and Algeria, Islamic activists have risen up to challenge the ruling authorities, dislodge occupying powers, or overturn the existing social order. The 1979 Iranian revolution led by Ayatollah Khomeini ushered in the first Islamic republic in the modern age and inspired many movements to mobilize for social change. The defeat of the Soviet Union in Afghanistan at the hands of Islamic insurgents during the 1980s was another milestone that motivated radical Muslims like Usama bin Ladin to take up arms against their own governments and to declare holy war (*jihad*) against Western powers. The goal of these radicals is to establish a new government based on Islamic law (*shariʿa*) and unify the Islamic nation (*umma*) under a single Muslim ruler (*khalifa* or caliph). Radical Islam arose in the context of failed economic modernization by secular nationalist elites, political exclusion by authoritarian regimes, and a cultural shift toward religious revivalism or fundamentalism. Militant Islamic activists rely on informal organizations and networks to build social ties with Muslim communities and to foster legitimacy for the broader Islamic movement. Above all, radical Muslims put forward an extreme interpretation of Islam to justify rebellion against the existing order.

Definition of Radical Islam

Radical Islam refers to Muslim individuals, groups, organizations, and parties that see in Islam a guiding political doctrine that justifies and motivates mobilization on behalf of that doctrine. They are radical because they reject accommodation with the existing social order, refuse to participate in its institutions, and insist on the necessity of violent revolution or terrorism to achieve their objectives.

There are secular Muslims who engage in violence, including nationalists and socialists. They are not part of radical Islam because they do not aspire to create an Islamic state. They might opportunistically draw on Islamic symbols, but their underlying motivations are based on non-Islamic worldviews. There are devout Muslims who call for establishing an Islamic state, but who do not engage in violence or do not advocate the violent overthrow of the existing social order. They, too, are not part of radical Islam because they seek to work gradually and peacefully to reform their polities. Radical Islam, therefore, entails an ideological commitment to establish an Islamic state and a strategic commitment to engage in violent mobilization.

Historical Context of Contemporary Islamic Radicalism

The widespread phenomenon of Islamic violence in the Muslim world has its origins in the social transformations that shaped the lives of millions of Muslims in the post-colonial era (1920s–1960s). Following independence from their former colonial rulers, many revolutionary governments in the Muslim world promoted rapid structural, demographic, and social transformations in order to modernize their societies and compete with their former colonial "masters." These reforms entailed the expansion of secondary and university education; development of public-sector employment; implementation of land reforms and Western-style legal systems; imposition of state control over religious institutions; modification of family, marriage, and divorce laws; and promotion of state-led industrialization. Secular leaders and technocratic elites with an affinity toward Western models of development usually carried out these reforms with the intent of consolidating their rule, expanding their legitimacy, and promoting genuine economic progress in their societies. They equated successful development with secularization and Westernization of society and saw institutions rooted in rural economies and religious traditions as impediments to modernization. Kamal Atatürk in Turkey, Reza Shah in Iran, Habib Bourguiba in Tunisia, Houari Boumedienne in Algeria, and Gamal Abdel Nasser in Egypt are primary examples of post-colonial modernizing reformers who embraced secular and Western models of development and relegated religion to the private sphere.

These post-colonial transformations, despite improving the lot of many people, manifested serious contradictions. Industrialization, initially a source of national pride, quickly turned into a heavy societal burden that could only be sustained through national debt. The expansion of education significantly increased literacy rates and produced many engineers, doctors, and lawyers. Prospects for meaningful employment for this "new middle class," however, diminished over time; many of the new professionals could not find employment or simply withered away in state-sector jobs where their talents were underutilized. Land reforms did not improve the lot of peasants, but instead forced many of them to migrate to already overcrowded cities, where they ended up in shantytowns. Legal reforms did not ensure rule of law or put an end to corruption; instead, they became the principal means by which to deprive civil society of an independent voice in politics. The rhetoric of progress that accompanied efforts at modernization produced high expectations among people. Many state regimes sought legitimacy by promoting grandiose national projects that promised to raise the living standards of ordinary people and combat poverty, inequality, and exploitation associated with pre-independence years. Thus, many people came to believe that hard work and education could result in a better life for themselves and their children. This talk of progress resulted in a rapid increase in urbanization as many peasants flocked to cities expecting to benefit from modern education and employment. As time passed, however, it became apparent that the attempt at state-led development in Muslim societies disproportionately benefited a well-positioned few while leaving many with unfulfilled expectations and broken promises.

Cultural Underpinnings of Radical Islam

The failure of secular regimes to meet the rising expectations of ordinary people and their unquestioning emulation of Western lifestyles resulted in feelings of generalized discontent and alienation. This context created an opportunity for Islamic movements to step forward as untainted critics of secularism and excessive Westernization. Underlying this Islamic challenge was a genuine cultural shift toward greater religiosity in everyday living. The Muslim world experienced an Islamic revival characterized by the spread of public displays of piety, growing mosque attendance, and the spread of Islamic networks, social movements, and political parties. Just as Christian fundamentalism emerged in the United States, Jewish fundamentalism in Israel, and Hindu fundamentalism in India, the Muslim world developed its own fundamentalist movements. Women donned their headscarves and men grew their beards. Muslims began to purchase books about Islam, Islamic history, and contemporary figures of Islamic revivalism. Young men and women in the universities gravitated toward Islamic social clubs and unions, and Islamic activists reaped the benefits by expanding their representation in local student elections.

Heightened Islamic consciousness created a cultural opportunity for politicizing religion and demanding a "return to Islam." Islamic groups began to organize around political issues and, when possible, formed parties in order to challenge the hold of secular nationalists on government. Their ultimate aim was to establish governments bound by Islamic law (shari'a). Those that were excluded from the political process sometimes organized violent insurgencies or engaged in terrorism.

Islamic fundamentalism contested the hold of secular left-ists and nationalists in almost every arena of competition—student unions, professional associations, local and national elections, and in the cultural sphere. Even the state-controlled media of secular regimes had to placate the growing religious sentiment of their publics by adopting more religious programming as well as censoring content deemed inappropriate or sinful. Islamists did not just offer a critique of existing social arrangements; they also advanced social and charitable projects to present a tangible alternative to secular governments. In Egypt, for instance, Islamic groups at impoverished neighborhoods organized food distribution to families during the holidays. In Algeria, Islamists organized "free" mosques to circumvent sermons approved by secular state officials. In almost every Muslim country, Islamic activists sought to compete with leftists and nationalists over the vision and direction of their societies. Networks of charity and non-governmental mosques were created by entrepreneurial Islamic activists who saw an opportunity to present viable public spaces free from the "corrupting" influence of the secular state, as well as to foster legitimacy for the Islamic movement through tangible provisions to the public.

Intellectual and Organizational Roots of Radical Islam

Radical Islam has its origins in intellectuals and organizations that were not always radical or violent. The three most prominent ideologues of Islamic resurgence are Hassan al-Banna, the founder of the Egyptian Muslim Brotherhood movement in 1928; Abul Ala Mawdudi, the founder of the South Asian Jama'ati Islami movement in 1941; and Sayyid Qutb, a leading intellectual in the Muslim Brotherhood movement executed by the Egyptian government in 1966.

Hassan al-Banna was a school teacher who was disappointed with the secular turn Egypt was taking during the first two decades of the twentieth century and at British domination of his country. In 1928 he founded an activist organization, the Society of Muslim Brothers, which eventually spread to every part of the Muslim world. The Muslim Brotherhood was a revivalist movement, not a violent jihadist group. It concentrated on moral and social issues; its goal was to win the hearts and minds of ordinary people and turn them toward religious observance and piety. Al-Banna wanted to create a cadre of preachers and educators that would go and spread the word to others. Education, not violent jihad, was the key to revival.

Abul Ala Mawdudi was a journalist influenced by the anti-colonial struggle in India. Accordingly, his rhetoric took on an anti-Western tone. He was also influenced by the India–Pakistan split in 1947 and actively called for the formation of an Islamic state. Like al-Banna, Mawdudi formed a formidable and influential movement known as the Jama'ati Islami. This vanguard organization aimed to Islamize society through winning over the professional middle classes and students.

Both al-Banna and Mawdudi had a shared worldview that laid the foundations for the fundamentalist revival and Islamic militancy in the latter half of the twentieth century. They both saw Islam as a political religion that does not recognize the separation between religion and the state. They both saw the return to Islam as a solution to the persistent weakness of Muslims in the modern world. They interpreted the Western threat not merely in terms of military hegemony or economic domination, but also in terms of a cultural invasion that supplanted Islam with secular values. They did not, however, see a contradiction between Islamic revival and modernization. Both al-Banna and Mawdudi wanted to take advantage of modern developments to advance Islam. Their goal was to recruit the modern educated class and impart to them an Islamic orientation. Their movements not only attracted traditional Muslim scholars, they also recruited workers, teachers, engineers, doctors, journalists, and students mainly in urban areas.

Al-Banna and Mawdudi established an important precedent for radical Islam through their disdain for the official scholars of Islam. They believed that religious elites were tied to traditional hierarchies and old ways of doing things. These elites legitimated or at least did not challenge the existing order or the prevailing ideological currents in society and government. Above all, the official scholars did not seek to mobilize people for the revivalist project. They waited in

A Palestinian gunman looks over the balcony of the dormitory housing the Israeli Olympic team in Munich, Germany, September 5, 1972. Nine Israeli athletes were kidnapped and two were killed by terrorists bargaining for the release of 200 Palestinian prisoners in Israel. The hostages were later killed along with five of their captors and a West German policeman in a failed rescue attempt.

mosques or Islamic seminaries for the people to come to them.

Another innovation of al-Banna and Mawdudi that became a model for radical Islam is their mosque-centered activism. The mosque for them was not just a place to pray and worship God, it was also a social center for education, charitable giving, sports, and mediation of communal disputes. They turned mosques into integral institutions of their communities and derived legitimacy from their social and practical outreach activities.

A third important precedent set by the Muslim Brotherhood and Jama'ati Islami is their concentration on recruitment within the middle and lower middle classes. The social base of the contemporary radical Islamist movement is that of students and professionals in their twenties and thirties. These students tend to be educated in the technical fields such as engineering, physics, computer science, and medicine. They exhibit high motivations and aspirations. Militant Islamists also attract members of the lower-middle class and recent migrants to cities, many of whom feel alienated by the rapid shift from rural to urban settings.

The extremist turn in contemporary Islamic revivalism came with the Egyptian Sayyid Qutb. Qutb lived during the height of Pan-Arab nationalism that advocated unity among all Arabs, not a broader unification based on Islam. Qutb recognized that not all Muslims are Arabs. As a matter of fact,

the majority of Muslims are not Arabs. Pan-Arab nationalism, therefore, was a narrow identity that deprived Muslims of a more powerful and inclusive basis for solidarity.

For Qutb, the Muslim world completely shunned religion and turned toward secularism, nationalism, and socialism. More importantly, Qutb and his Muslim Brotherhood cadres encountered tremendous repression in society and torture in jail. His tormentors not only ridiculed him and his movement, they also ridiculed religion in general and took pleasure at being physically and mentally cruel. In 1965, while in jail, Qutb wrote a controversial book entitled *Signposts on the Road*. In it, he declared the Egyptian government to be an infidel regime. A year later, he was executed by that same regime. The ideas in that book set the major themes of radical Islam.

Ideology of Radical Islam

Radical Islamists promote seven major themes to mobilize for rebellion and justify violence and terrorism. The first theme is the widespread ignorance (*jahiliyyah*) of the contemporary Muslim world. Ignorance does not refer to the lack of scientific, artistic, or common knowledge. Instead, it refers to the historical era that preceded the rise of Islam in the Arabian Peninsula (modern-day Saudi Arabia) in 610 CE. In that period, people lived in a rich oral culture and enjoyed the fruits of commerce. Their ignorance, therefore, did not stem from a lack of civilization or wealth. Rather, their ignorance stemmed from their polytheism; they worshiped multiple idols instead of the one God worshiped originally by Abraham and his Jewish and Christian descendents. The Prophet Muhammad introduced monotheism to the Arabs and turned them away from their ignorance.

Contemporary radical Islamists believe that *jahiliyyah* has returned. Muslims today think that by adopting the values of Western civilization, they are adopting the most advanced knowledge of the world. Just as the people of pre-Islamic Arabia thought that they had the best culture, today nominal Muslims think they are imitating the best civilization. In reality they are polytheists because they embrace nationalism, socialism, communism, liberalism, humanism, and other isms rather than embracing the one God and his religious commands.

The second theme of radical Islam is closely linked to the first: God's sovereignty (*hakimiyyat allah*). According to radicals, God is the only lawgiver and He alone can define right and wrong, good and evil, permissible and forbidden. All other sovereignties—monarchies, republics, or the democratic will of the majority—are subordinate to God's sovereignty; there can be no higher authority than God. All systems that displace God's sovereignty or supplement it with another are polytheistic systems (worshiping multiple Gods). They must be rejected and overthrown. Radical Islamists do not believe that humans can arrive at the truth or distinguish between right and wrong through human reasoning. There are limits to human rationality and humans can never comprehend God's plan beyond what He has revealed to them. The best that humans can do is to follow the word of God as revealed in the Qur'an and exemplified by the sayings and deeds of His Prophet and the pious ancestors (*al-salaf al-salih*). Discovering and applying the intended meaning of the Qur'anic verses, therefore, is the ultimate form of devotion to God. Conversely, altering, ignoring, or nullifying God's revelation is violating God's sovereignty and subverting His will.

The third theme of radical Islam is rejection of democracy because it violates God's sovereignty. Democracy is a secular innovation that gives the right to legislate to someone other than God, which is equivalent to deifying the people. The majority in a democratic system can make permissible something that God has forbidden, which means their authority is higher than God's will. The only way to reaffirm God's sovereignty is by making His laws the sole source of legislation.

The fourth theme in radical Islamic discourse is the comprehensiveness and universalism of religion. Radical Islamists believe the Qur'an to be a comprehensive guide by God, covering matters of worship (*'ibadat* or how to exhibit faith in God) and social relations (*mu'amalat,* such as economics, warfare, marriage, taxes, and so on). Therefore, there is no need for ancillary worldviews or ideologies such as Marxism, liberalism, or humanism. God has said it all. Radicals believe in the universalism of the Qur'an; it is applicable in all places on earth and at all times. Therefore, one cannot say that "times have changed" and "new rules are necessary." Saying so violates God's sovereignty on earth. The comprehensiveness and universalism of Islam is the source of its superiority vis-à-vis secularism, socialism, nationalism, and all the other religions on earth. All other ideologies promote human-centered systems based on fallible reasoning and selfish interests that perpetuate the subjugation of people to foreign and domestic rulers. Making God the only master frees humans from all other masters.

The fifth theme of radical Islam concerns the permissibility and necessity of *takfir* (declaring a Muslim to be outside of the creed, somewhat equivalent to excommunication in Catholicism, though there is no single pope or church hierarchy in Islam with universal authority to engage in excommunication; there have always been multiple Islamic authorities, and Islamic radicals now appoint themselves as authorities without significant seminary training). Muslims can be judged to have committed major transgressions that put them outside of the Islamic faith. Radicals disagree among themselves as to when *takfir* must take place. An extreme strand maintains that if a Muslim exhibits great unbelief (*kufr kabir*) and persists in his or her unbelief despite being warned and given a chance to repent, that person is considered an infidel or apostate. A second strand rejects this extreme disposition. It maintains that if a person commits a great sin, but does not publicly justify the sin, then he or she is not an infidel. In other words, the most extreme position judges people on their actions, not just their words; the less extreme position judges people on their words alone, not their actions. The issue of *takfir* is the stepping stone to violence. Many radicals today argue that existing Muslim regimes rule according to secular laws, thus violating God's sovereignty and can no longer be considered Muslims. Consequently, it is permissible to reject them and rebel against them until they repent and apply Islamic law or until they are removed from power.

The sixth theme of radical Islam is the presumed conspiracy against the Muslim world. Radical Islamists portray their struggle as a fight against an international conspiracy led by the combined forces of Jewish Zionists, atheistic communists, and Christian crusaders who are out to subvert Islam, divide the Muslim world, and pilfer its resources. The triad of Zionists, communists, and crusaders fear the truth of Islam and unity of Muslims and, consequently, conspire to distort Islam and weaken the faith of Muslims. Secularism and nationalism are instruments of this nefarious international plot because they deny the totality of Islam and split Muslims into many small states. Existing rulers in the Muslim world are instruments of the broader conspiracy against Islam. They are either imposed by colonial powers or supported by them against their own people. These rulers collude with their "masters" to maintain their positions of power and enrich themselves at the expense of ordinary Muslims.

The seventh theme of radical Islam is *jihad* in the path of God. Radical Islamists believe that *jihad* is an Islamic obligation against infidel regimes who do not rule according to God's laws. Jihad is an indispensable component of comprehensive Islamic activism, which begins with preaching (d'awah), progresses to forbidding vice on a local level, and culminates with holy war. This three-pronged strategy is the only appropriate one because it comes from the Qur'an and it is how the Prophet Muhammad spread Islam in the Arabian Peninsula in the seventh century CE. Jihad is also an imperative to counter foreign aggression and ward off the international conspiracy against Islam. Finally, jihad is continuous until Judgment Day. Jihad for the radicals is an aggressive doctrine, not a defensive concept.

Diversity in Radical Islam

Despite continuity in radical Islamic thought, militant Islamists often disagree over strategy, tactics, targets, organization, and leadership. In this respect, radical Islam is not different from other radical fundamentalist movements or secular nationalists and leftist groups. There are at least three forms of radical Islamic activism. The first is *revolutionary Islamism,* which seeks to transform the existing political order in any given state or national government. Revolutionary Islamists target their own governments and societies in order to overthrow the system and establish an Islamic order in its place. The current generation of Revolutionary Islamism appeared in the Iranian revolution of 1979, when Ayatollah Khomeini inspired masses to rise up and overthrow the secular shah of Iran; he ultimately established an Islamic theocracy. Revolutionary Islamism also appeared in Egypt and Algeria during the 1990s. In both countries, armed Islamic groups rebelled against the state and sought to undermine its economic infrastructure. They targeted the state's security forces, police, government officials, intellectuals, artists, tourists, and ordinary civilians in the hope of collapsing the ruling order and mobilizing a social revolution.

The second form of radical activism is *Islamic nationalism,* which seeks to harness the power of Islam to fight foreign occupiers, make irredentist claims, or demand regional autonomy. Islamic groups such as Hamas in the Israeli-occupied Palestinian territories and Hezbollah in southern Lebanon appeal to Islam in order to fight Israeli occupation of lands they consider theirs. Similarly, Moro rebels in the southern Philippines and Chechen insurgents in Russia advocate Islamic unity in order to distinguish themselves from the non-Muslim majorities in each country, laying the groundwork for regional separation or greater communal autonomy.

The third form of radical activism is *transnational Islamic terrorism,* which seeks to mobilize disparate Islamic groups to attack Western "enemies." The first two forms of radicalism focus their violence on the "near enemy" while transnational Islamic terrorism puts emphasis on attacking the "far enemy." Usama bin Ladin, the supreme leader of al-Qaida, is the pioneer of global *jihad.*

Al-Qaida grew into a movement out of four developments. The first was the defeat of the Soviet Union in Afghanistan in 1989 as a result of the resistance of the Afghan *mujahidin* (holy fighters), who were aided in small part by Arab volunteers from various parts of the Muslim world. This victory confirmed to some Muslims around the world that resistance and rebellion is the way forward. This victory gave jihadists the symbolic capital necessary for recruiting and motivating future cadres for jihad.

The second development that contributed to the rise of al-Qaida during the 1990s was the presence of U.S. forces in Saudi Arabia following the Iraqi invasion of Kuwait in 1990. The United States led a multinational coalition that contained both Western and Muslim forces against Iraq. Following the liberation of Kuwait in 1991, the United States maintained forces in the Arabian Peninsula to deter Iraqi leader Saddam Hussein from embarking on another attack on his neighbors. The presence of U.S. forces near the holiest sites of Islam (Mecca and Medina) angered many Saudis and gave rise to internal critiques of the Saudi monarchy and its close alliance with the United States. The Saudi ruling family dealt with this criticism by repressing the opposition. Usama bin Ladin was deprived of his Saudi citizenship after refusing to cease his "advice" to the ruling monarchs. Failure to alter policies in Saudi Arabia through peaceful means gave bin Ladin the legitimacy to wage war on the Saudi regime and its ally the United States.

The third major development that contributed to the rise of al-Qaida during the 1990s was the failure of Islamist insurgencies around the Muslim world. Had some of these insurgencies succeeded, the strategy of rebellion against the "near enemy" (as opposed to attacking the United States and other Western powers) would have been viewed as effective by Islamic movements. Usama bin Ladin benefited from these failures by taking in the experienced leaders and cadres of these insurgencies.

The fourth development that contributed to the consolidation of al-Qaida during the 1990s was the rise of the Taliban regime in Afghanistan in the mid 1990s. After years of factional infighting in Afghanistan, the Taliban movement swept to power and subdued many of the groups that wreaked havoc in the impoverished Central Asian state. The ultra-traditional Taliban acquiesced to having al-Qaida terrorist training camps on its territory.

These four developments laid the foundations for al-Qaida's September 11, 2001 attacks on the United States. Bin Ladin believes that Muslim activists around the world could be more effective if they concentrated all their time, effort, and resources on attacking Western powers that presumably prop up un-Islamic governments in the Muslim world. Fighting the "near enemy" alone is not sufficient to produce success because Western states invariably come to the aid of those regimes and help them stay in power. Attacking the "head of the snake" is the best way to undermine regimes in the Muslim world.

Political Context of Radical Islam

Violence by Islamic radicals since the 1980s is not a product of an inherent tendency in Islam toward militancy. On the contrary, Islamic opposition movements adopt a variety of strategies to effect social and political change. Some opt for militancy, violence, and revolution as the recent histories of Algeria, Egypt, and Iraq demonstrate, but many more eschew violence and seek accommodation with their secular states. Islamists in Turkey, Jordan, Morocco, Malaysia, and Indonesia, to name a few, are generally committed to legality, gradualism, and constitutionalism. Therefore, the rise of Islamic radicalism must be seen as one form of Islamic activism, but not the only or most prevalent form.

The resurgence of Islamic movements as serious competitors in the political process has put many secular regimes in the Muslim world on the defensive. Some states pursued a strategy of unmitigated repression (Tunisia since 1990, Algeria since 1992, and Syria in 1982). Others opted for formal inclusion (Jordan, Indonesia, Malaysia, and Pakistan). Still others have chosen a mixed strategy of toleration and repression (Turkey since the 1970s, Egypt during the 1980s, and Morocco since the 1990s). Although the reactions of governments to Islamic politics have varied between accommodation and exclusion, or co-optation and repression, nearly all sought to maneuver in order to avoid ceding real power to Islamic opposition movements in the system. Governments that were increasingly viewed by large segments of the public as corrupt, illegitimate, and ineffectual in running state affairs engaged in legal and institutional manipulation to provide Islamic opposition forces with procedural access to state ministries, but simultaneously sought to deny them substantive influence in the political process.

Circumscribed inclusion of the Islamic opposition resulted in two dynamics that ultimately contributed to mass rebellions in some of these societies. The first dynamic was the expansion of Islamic networks and legitimacy in society. The policy of partial inclusion allowed Islamists to grow in strength and popularize their message, which meant that they had societal and organizational resources with which to fight state repression and political exclusion. The second dynamic was the delegitimization of moderate Islamic strategies. Moderates who wanted to work within the system were constantly frustrated by their inability to exert power. Their radical critics pointed out their futility in implementing reforms through conventional political processes. As a result, radical strategies became more appealing to the broader Islamic movement.

See also *Fundamentalism; Islam.*

Mohammed M. Hafez

BIBLIOGRAPHY

Bergen, Peter. *The Osama bin Laden I Know: An Oral History of al-Qaeda's Leader.* New York: Free Press, 2006.

Dekmejian, R. Hrair. *Islam in Revolution: Fundamentalism in the Arab World.* 2d ed. New York: Syracuse University Press, 1995.

Esposito, John L. *The Islamic Threat: Myth or Reality?* 3d ed. New York: Oxford University Press, 1999.

Gerges, Fawaz A. *The Far Enemy: Why Jihad Went Global.* New York: Cambridge University Press, 2005.

Hafez, Mohammed M. *Why Muslims Rebel: Repression and Resistance in the Islamic World.* Boulder, Colo.: Lynne Rienner, 2003.

Kepel, Gilles. *Muslim Extremism in Egypt: The Prophet and Pharaoh.* Berkeley: University of California Press, 2003.

Kurzman, Charles. *The Unthinkable Revolution in Iran.* Cambridge: Harvard University Press, 2004.

Milton-Edwards, Beverly. *Islamic Fundamentalism since 1945.* New York: Routledge, 2004.

Nasr, Seyed Vali Reza. *The Vanguard of the Islamic Revolution: The Jama'at-i Islami of Pakistan.* Berkeley: University of California Press, 1994.

Wickham, Carrie R. *Mobilizing Islam: Religion, Activism, and Political Change in Egypt.* New York: Columbia University Press, 2002.

Wright, Lawrence. *The Looming Tower: Al-Qaeda and the Road to 9/11.* New York: Knopf, 2006.

Islamic Law

See *Shari'a.*

Islam's Encounters with the West

Both the Muslim world and the West have been seminally shaped by their encounters with one another through the centuries, both benign and hostile, polemical and dialogic. Islam is a universal religion and from its inception in the seventh century saw itself as the natural heir to the cognate faith traditions of Judaism and Christianity. Christianity, born in the East, became a state religion and a civilization in Europe after the conversion of Constantine in 312 C.E., and also envisioned a universal role for itself. The two religio-political entities mostly contended with one other for political control over the same realms and sometimes for the souls of the same people, but they also exchanged emissaries and traders, scholars and learning. Islamic civilization flourished in the High Middle Ages and had much to teach Christian Europe. Islamic sciences and philosophical learning in particular were transmitted to Europe, eventually leading to a revival of classical learning there. By the Late Middle Ages the tide would begin to turn and a large slice of an increasingly fragmented and fractious Islamic world would be occupied by European colonizers, a traumatic experience from which most Muslim-majority countries till today have not recovered. In the post-colonial and post-September 11 state of affairs, much soul-searching continues among Muslims, and issues of identity, religious revival, governance, and extremism take center stage. The emergence of political Islam is probably the most striking feature of post-colonial twentieth century Islamic trends and movements, a response in considerable part to the rise of secular modernity and globalization spearheaded by a perceived hegemonic West.

The Formative Period of Islam

The Qur'an (verses 30:1–4) took sides in the rivalry between Persia and Byzantium in the seventh century and predicted the victory of the latter over the former on account of its monotheistic faith and praxis. In the Qur'anic *weltanschauung,* belief in a common God and subscription to shared standards of piety dissolved geographical distinctions. "It is not righteousness that you turn your faces towards the East and the West" (Qur'an 2:177). European Christians were assumed to form a continuity with Arab and other Christians in western Asia on the basis of their shared faith, although Muslims emerging out of the Arabian peninsula in the seventh century would encounter a different reality on the ground.

Before his death in 632 C.E., the Prophet Muhammad is reported to have sent invitations to the rulers of Byzantium and Persia to accept Islam. Later Muslim scholars have understood this act to underscore the universalist nature of Islam and the duty to propagate the faith among non-Muslims, ideally without coercion (cf. Qur'an 2:256). According to the Prophet's biographer, Ibn Hisham (d. 834), the Persian emperor, Khosrow II, was enraged by this missive while Heraclius, the Byzantine ruler, received it thoughtfully, recognizing within it a message of possible religious kinship worthy of at least respect. Heraclius's attitude, as depicted in the Islamic sources, testified to a shared genealogy and worldview between Christianity and Islam and pointed to an optimistic belief that Christianity would prove to be an ally, not a rival, in a common religious mission to supplant polytheism with a belief in the one God.

Under the Rightly-Guided Caliphs, the four men who ruled the Muslim community between 632 and 661, the great Islamic conquests began, which dramatically expanded the geographical realms of Islam and brought Muslims into increasing contact with the older established communities of

Eastern Christians. Most of these Christians—Nestorians, Jacobites, Copts, Assyrians—were Monophysite Christians who subscribed to the belief that the human and divine natures of Christ had become fused into one. This had been declared heretical by the Council of Chalcedon in 325, which adopted the Diophysite doctrine asserting two distinct and separate natures of Christ, a position adopted by the Byzantine church. Byzantine rulers of Eastern Christian realms consequently treated their subjects harshly, taxing them severely and persecuting them for their heretical beliefs. When Muslim armies arrived in Syria and Egypt, both Arabic and Syriac sources report that the local populations welcomed them as liberators and actively colluded with them in ousting their Byzantine rulers.

Muslim encounters with the West in the first century of Islam continued through more ambitious military expeditions to the continent of Europe. Most of Spain fell to Muslim control by the early eighth century, and Muslim armies reached the south of France, where they were decisively defeated at the Battle of Poitiers in 732 C.E. Regarding this event, the historian Edward Gibbon (d. 1794) famously remarked that had it not been for this defeat, "perhaps the interpretation of the Koran would now be taught in the schools of Oxford." Such a fear has not totally receded from the Western consciousness and in fact has been revived in certain quarters today in the post-September 11 environment, especially under the guise of the "Clash of Civilizations" thesis, discussed below.

The Classical and Medieval Periods

The middle of the eighth till roughly the twelfth century represents the acme of pre-modern Islamic civilization. The cultural and intellectual efflorescence associated with this period may be regarded in many ways as a coming together of different civilizational strands in the Islamic crucible. Knowledge of classical antiquity—from Greece, Persia, and India—became accessible through translation to an increasingly sophisticated elite, eager for learning and entertainment in cosmopolitan Baghdad, the capital of the 'Abbasid caliphate. The Abbasid caliph al-Ma'mun (d. 833) is said to have sent emissaries to the Byzantine emperor, Leo the Armenian, seeking Greek manuscripts and receiving in return a number of works, including those of Euclid. Under al-Ma'mun's patronage, a number of the medical works of Galen and the philosophical treatises of Aristotle and of neo-Platonic commentators were translated in the Bayt al-

Hikma, an academy–library set up by him to house his coterie of Syriac and Arabic speaking Christian translators. The fusion of Eastern and Western learning in Islamic realms represented a cross-cultural encounter that was to have far-reaching consequences for the subsequent intellectual history of humankind. Through al-Andalus (Muslim Spain) and Sicily under the Muslim Kalbid dynasty (948–1052), much of this learning would be transmitted to Europe. Two of the most enduring legacies of this transfer of knowledge are: 1) the rise of the college in twelfth century Europe, whose structure and curriculum appear to have been strongly influenced by the *madrasa,* the institution of higher learning that became widespread in the Islamic world from after the tenth century; and 2) the start of the European Renaissance in the fourteenth century.

It was during the 'Abbasid period that distinctive notions of governance took shape and the duties of the caliphs and his subjects became fully articulated. It has become a truism to state that there is no separation between religion and politics in Islam and that Islam mandates a specific political office, namely the caliphate. As rigorous scholarship has shown, however, there developed fairly early a de facto separation between religion and the state, with the caliph and his retinue exercising political power while the *ulama,* the religious scholars, interpreted the *shari'a* (religious law). During the early caliphate in Medina, the Righly-Guided Caliphs are reported to have eschewed self-aggrandizing titles, such as *Khalifat Allah* ("deputy of God"), adopting instead more modest titles such as *Khalifat Rasul Allah* ("successor to the messenger of God") and *Amir al-Mu'minin* ("Commander of the Faithful"). Such titles reflected more accurately the caliph's rather pedestrian political role of primarily maintaining law and order and applying the religious law, in the interpretation of which they did not exercise exclusive or any control.

Under the influence of Persian and Hellenic ideas of divine kingship in particular, the 'Abbasid caliphate grew in stature and royal mystique, reflected in the adoption of titles such as "the Deputy of God" (a title already adopted by the Umayyads) and "the Shadow of God on Earth." Al-Mawardi (d. 1058), perhaps the best known political theorist of the pre-modern period, writing during a period when Islamic realms had become splintered and controlled by a multitude of rulers, attempted to shore up the caliphate by imputing to the caliph a certain religio-political authority. Such authority was based on his required descent from the Quraysh (the

Prophet's natal tribe), his superior intelligence, and his role as upholder of the religious law and defender of Islamic realms. To read al-Mawardi's manual as reflective of an unchanging political reality is, however, to grievously misread the history of the evolution of the office of the caliph and its function.

In the tenth century the renowned Sunni theologian al-Ash'ari (d. 935) asserted the doctrine that the caliphate (or the imamate as it was often called) was a requirement of the religious law. Yet Mu'tazili theologians before him, like Abu Bakr al-Asamm (d. 816) and Abu Ishaq al-Nazzam (d. ca. 835) had maintained that Muslims did not require a ruler as long as they remained faithful to the religious law. Al-Ash'ari's position became axiomatic among Sunni Muslims, since by his time a consensus had developed among scholars that the caliphate was necessary to ensure the moral and material welfare of the polity. Ironically, it was this consensus, which had evolved through deliberative historical processes, that ultimately conferred on the caliphate the imprimatur of a divinely ordained institution. Some scholars later than al-Ash'ari, however, continued to subscribe to the notion that the caliphate was an office that Muslims could adopt, or not, if either alternative was held to conduce to the collective welfare of the polity.

The eleventh century Mu'tazili theologian 'Abd al-Jabbar (d. 1095) indicates in his writings that there were three schools of thought in his time on the subject of the caliphate. The first, a minority, held that the caliphate was not necessary; the second believed that it was necessary for rational reasons; and the third believed that it was required by the religious law. A fourteenth century scholar, 'Adud al-Din al-Iji (d. 1355), was of the opinion that popular consensus from the time of Abu Bakr onwards and social utility, rather than religious doctrine, had established the necessity of the caliphate. Historical evidence shows in fact that political practices and traditions in Sunni Islam developed over time through recourse to an amalgam of interpreted Qur'anic injunctions, prophetic precedent, ad-hoc pragmatic measures, and adapted institutions and policies of ancient Arab, Persian, and Byzantine provenance. In contrast to the Sunni position, Shi'i Islam by the ninth century had developed the notion of the charismatic religio-political office of the imam, inherited only by the Prophet's direct descendants through divine election.

Another important development in the ninth century was the articulation of the four sources of jurisprudence (usul al-fiqh) by the jurist Muhammad b. Idris al-Shafi'i (d. 820). Al-Shafi'i was also instrumental in promoting a rather dichotomous view of the world encoded in the notions of the "Abode of Islam" (Dar al-Islam) and the "Abode of War" (Dar al-Harb), to which he added a third "Abode of Treaty or Reconciliation" (Dar al-Sulh). These abodes were a piece of legal fiction, sanctioned neither by the Qur'an nor by the sunna, but which reflected a certain historical and political reality at the time. The Qur'anic term jihad fi sabil allah, which broadly means "struggling/striving in the path of God" through a variety of means, including charity and armed combat, became semantically and functionally circumscribed by many jurists, who were influential in official circles, to primarily signify "armed combat." Jihad in this sense became a duty of the caliph, according to these jurists, and the means through which the abode of war could progressively be added to the abode of Islam.

According to al-Shafi'i, non-Muslim polities who chose to sign a treaty and pay a tribute to the Muslim ruler, however, could become part of the abode of treaty and safe from military aggression. This was in contrast to the view of an earlier jurist, Abu Hanifa (d. 767), who said that non-Muslim polities who entered into treaties with Muslims became part of the abode of Islam. Al-Shafi'i's embrace of the possibility of expansionist jihad was also in contrast to the position of an earlier jurist, Sufyan al-Thawri (d. 778), who would recognize the permissibility of armed combat only in self-defense. It is significant that Sufyan lived in the Arabian peninsula, away from the center of caliphal power, and disinclined to justify the military adventurism of the worldly Umayyad rulers of his time.

The High and Late Middle Ages

One of the critical defining points of Muslim–Western Christian encounters whose repercussions are still with us in the twenty-first century are the Crusades, the military expeditions launched by medieval Europe starting at the end of the eleventh century to wrest Jerusalem and Palestine away from what was perceived to be wrongful Muslim occupation. The period of the Crusades deeply affected European Christian perceptions of Muslims, leading to the image of the latter as an inveterate enemy whose religion and prophet, conceived of as fundamentally antithetical to Christianity and Christians, were deserving of virulent denigration, as expressed in Dante's Divine Comedy, for example. The Christian–Muslim toleration that had characterized the

Seeking to recover the Holy Land from the Muslims, European Christians waged a series of wars known as the Crusades between the eleventh and fourteenth centuries. This painting, "La Prise de Jerusalem," records the Christian conquest of the Holy City in 1099.

court of Roger II in Norman Sicily, attracting Muslim notables such as the geographer al-Idrisi to his court, would become a dim memory during the Crusades.

Among Muslims of the time, the Crusades, however, did not have such a devastating impact. In the chronicles that deal with these wars, the Muslim counter-offensive was not cast in terms of a cosmic battle against all of Christianity; Christian Arabs after all could be enlisted on the Muslim side. The Crusaders were typically termed Faranj (Franks) by Arabs, a term that above all forefronted their northern European background. One of the best known accounts of the Crusades is a biography written by the Syrian Muslim physician and warrior Usama ibn Munqidh (d. 1188), who registers both horror and amusement at some of the barbaric and outlandish practices of the Franks he personally witnessed. Importantly, Usama provides accounts of benign interactions with the Frankish invaders as well. He records

the details of his visit to the house of a Crusader settled in Palestine and conversations with individual Franks. Crusaders who settled in Arab lands often married Arab women and became Arabized over the years. Those who returned to Europe brought back with them valuable knowledge regarding science, culture, and the arts. In the contemporary period, Muslim polemicists and extremists have resurrected the Crusades to recast them as events that embody within them the unflagging hatred of the Christian West towards Islam, manifested today, they maintain, in Western political and cultural imperialism.

The Crusaders were finally decisively defeated by 1293 by the Mamluks, a Turkic dynasty that set up its capital in Cairo and ruled in the name of the 'Abbasid caliph, now reduced to a figurehead. In 1453 the Ottoman Turks entered the world stage by defeating the Byzantines and capturing the latter's capital of Constantinople, which they renamed

Istanbul. The Ottoman Empire lasted for almost six hundred years. During its heyday in the sixteenth and seventeenth centuries its territories included Anatolia, Greater Syria, parts of North Africa, and a broad swath of southeastern Europe up to the Caucasus. The Ottoman rulers on the whole were efficient administrators and great patrons of learning, and known for their tolerance towards religious and ethnic minorities, who lived in autonomous communities known as *millets* within their empire. When Spain finally fell to European Christians in 1492, many of the Jews fleeing the Spanish Inquisition were welcomed by the Ottoman sultan Beyazit II into his realms.

A very different story, however, begins to unfold by the end of the seventeenth century. In 1699 the Ottomans signed the Treaty of Karlowitz, which required them to cede control over extensive territories in Europe for the first time. European powers also began to increasingly interfere in Ottoman internal affairs and obtained "capitulations," or contracts from the government, that conferred specific rights and privileges in favor of the subjects of various European nations residing or trading in Ottoman lands. By the end of World War I, the Ottoman Empire (now dubbed by Europeans "the Sick Man of Europe") had collapsed and much of its European territories were conquered and divided among the Allied Powers. The winds of change had definitely begun to blow in the "wrong" direction, as far as Muslims were concerned.

Colonization, Resistance, and Revival

Progressive European encroachment eastward culminated in the colonization of much of the Islamic world between 1798 and 1922. In the Middle East the period of European domination began with Napoleon's expedition to Egypt in 1798, followed shortly thereafter by British occupation. European colonization reached its greatest geographical extent when the League of Nations gave France and Britain mandates to rule the newly-created Arab states in 1920. The League of Nations thus upheld the terms of the notorious Sykes–Picot Agreement signed between England and France in 1916, which had carved up the Middle East into British and French controlled domains after Arabs had been promised independence for their help against the Ottomans.

In 1924 the Young Turks abolished the caliphate that had existed since the first century of Islam and set up the Republic of Turkey, an event that caused much consternation in the Islamic world. Another catastrophic event for Muslims that occurred in this period was the creation of the Jewish state of Israel on Palestinian soil in 1948, and the subsequent homelessness of hundreds of thousands of Muslim and Christian Palestinians, further embittering the attitudes of Arabs and Muslims toward the West.

It appeared that things had started to go awry in the house of Islam, now much in need of self-cleansing and revival. Why had Muslim societies declined so much that they had become easily colonizable by others? How could Muslims renew themselves and be in control of their destinies once again? Muslim thinkers and scholars pondered these questions and tried to formulate effective responses to them, sometimes setting in motion religio-social revivalist movements.

The first such movement of significance occurred in the eighteenth century, launched by Muhammad ibn ʿAbd al-Wahhab (1703–1792), after whom it is called Wahhabism. Ibn ʿAbd al-Wahhab was by training a jurist or a lawyer and a theologian who had also studied Sufism in the two principal cities of Mecca and Medina. He maintained that the moral decline of the Muslim community was a result of deviation from the original practices of the *umma* or the Muslim community. For the community to regain its vitality and moral vigor, these practices had to be uprooted and replaced with a society that resembled the early Muslim community set up by Muhammad.

Ibn ʿAbd al-Wahhab's movement acquired a political dimension when he joined forces with a local tribal chief by the name of Muhammad ibn Saud (d. 1765). ʿAbd al-Wahhab has been compared by some to Martin Luther, a Christian who ushered in the period of Reformation. This comparison is quite apt. Like Luther, ʿAbd al-Wahhab was a puritan and a literal scripturalist. Both had contempt for scholarly learning and wished to rid their religious traditions of the elaborate theological and intellectual interpretations that had grown up over the years. "Sola scriptura!" The clarion call of both movements to return to an unadulterated reading of scripture alone divorced from contextualizing exegeses has led to literalism and anti-intellectualism among Christian and Muslim "fundamentalists." And just as Luther's Reformation led to some of the bloodiest and most savage religious wars in Europe, the legacy of a militant strand within Wahhabism, as reflected in the ideology of the Taliban in Afghanistan and al-Qaida today, has been barbaric violence.

The nineteenth century gave rise to two individuals indelibly associated with Islamic reform and modernism. They are Jamal al-Din al-Afghani (d. 1897), a brilliant thinker and intellectual at large, and his disciple, Muhammad Abduh (d. 1905), rector of al-Azhar University. Both men stressed the importance of *ijtihad* ("independent reasoning") as their main tool of effecting reform, and they advocated using this tool to arrive at new interpretations of Islam, rather than slavishly following the interpretations of the medieval scholars.

Both al-Afghani and Abduh emphasized that Muslims had lost their way because they had ceased tapping into the dynamic, progressive spirit of Islam that had made it a world civilization in an earlier period. Abduh in particular stressed that religion was completely compatible with reason, and that independent reasoning should lead to sweeping social and legal reforms. Although Western political domination should be resisted and Muslim countries liberated from colonial occupation, Western civilization itself was not to be regarded as a threat to Islam. Muhammad Abduh's thought has been influential to a certain extent among reform-minded Muslims, although during his lifetime he could not implement many of his reforms and had his share of detractors.

In the aftermath of the abolition of the caliphate in Istanbul in 1924, a distinctively new and thoroughly modern phenomenon arose that is usually termed by scholars "political Islam" or "Islamism." Like the revivalists of the eighteenth and nineteenth centuries, the Islamists also believe that contemporary Muslim society should be reformed from within by modeling themselves closely on the early Muslim community at Medina. Only by regenerating itself can it successfully establish a righteous, genuinely "Islamic" government that would rule its subjects wisely and justly while successfully resisting Western imperialism. Emphasis on a highly politicized Islam is a defining characteristic of these Islamists, who claim to derive a broad political ideology from Islamic principles.

The earliest such groups are the Muslim Brotherhood, established by Hasan al-Banna (1906–1949) in Egypt, and the Jamaat-i (Islamic Society), established by Mawlana Abu al-Ala Mawdudi (1903–1979) of India, later of Pakistan. Both men were personally pious and educated in the traditional Islamic and modern Western disciplines. Both came to react strongly against British imperialism, in whose shadow they lived the greater part of their lives. Importantly, they were also reacting against a local elite which, under European colonial influence, had become Westernized to the extent that members of this elite spoke the language of the colonizers, imitated their dress and customs, and considered themselves secular. Thus, as al-Banna and Mawdudi saw it, they were fighting the influence of both external and internal forces against Islam, which they conceived of as a reified body of doctrine capable of yielding a blueprint for a utopian "Islamic State." Many Islamists believe in what Mawdudi called "theo-democracy"; in other words, a democracy that called for power-sharing through consultation, according to the Qur'anic concept of *shura*. Mawdudi and al-Banna believed it needed to be an "Islamic democracy" subject to the tenets of the religious law, the *shari'a,* as interpreted by them, and which recognized only God as political sovereign (in Arabic, *al-hakimiyya*).

During the 1960s the movement's leading ideologue was Sayyid Qutb, a schoolteacher who turned fervently anti-Western after his sojourn in the United States between 1948 and 1950. Appalled by the racism he witnessed in the United States at that time and by what he regarded as the superficiality and immorality of American society, he joined the Muslim Brotherhood and became its chief publicist. In 1954 Gamal Abdel Nasser, the president of Egypt, accused the Muslim Brotherhood of attempting to assassinate him and imprisoned Qutb and others after banning the Brotherhood that year. In prison for ten years, Qutb wrote some of his most fiery tracts, in which he explained his radical opposition to any form of government that was not Islamic, as he defined it. Accused of treason, he was hanged by Nasser in 1966, but his fiery legacy lived on among the more radical elements, leading to the formation of militant groups such as the Jihad Organization in Egypt, and Hamas and the Islamic Jihad in the Palestinian Occupied Territories. More recently, terrorist groups such as al-Qaida have derived their inspiration from Qutbian-style rejectionism.

Clash of Civilizations? And Counter-Responses

In the post-September 11 environment, the controversial "Clash of Civilizations" thesis first propounded by Samuel Huntington in 1993 is being discussed again with renewed vigor. Huntington had provocatively argued in a 1993 journal article that the fault lines of conflict in the future would be along civilizational and religious lines. In a book-length monograph three years later, he effectively characterized

Islam as a whole as unregenerate and ill-suited for adaptation to modern times. As might be expected, his thesis has provoked much criticism from a number of historians and specialists in Islam who have underscored *inter alia* his poor knowledge of an assumed monolithic Islamic world, past and present, particularly its history and religious sociology, and his failure to take into consideration intra-cultural dynamics and differences. As a conscious rejoinder to Huntington's scheme, Richard Bulliet, a professor of Islamic history at Columbia University, coined the term "Islamo-Christian civilization" in the early 2000s to underscore in particular the intellectual and epistemic commonalities that have historically existed between the two world civilizations. Interestingly, in Muslim-majority societies, Huntington's dichotomous worldview resonates among hard-line Islamists, who similarly imagine a fundamental civilizational divide predicated on irreconcilable values and worldviews.

Historical evidence can be cited more in support of Bulliet's position than Huntington's. The historical record shows in fact that fundamentally dichotomous and adversarial Western attitudes towards the Islamic world, as articulated by Huntington, mainly came into being in the nineteenth century with the onset of Western colonization. Between the sixteenth and the eighteenth centuries European scholarly studies of the Muslim East leaned more towards objectivity and even sympathy. This was due to the rationalist trend that prevailed in academic circles and to the absence of European overt political involvement in western Asia during this period. Those who were seeking to reform Christianity in light of this new spirit of rationalism found in Islam, regarded as combining a balanced regard for the demands of both spiritual and social life, a kindred system more to their liking. In this spirit, some European scholars of this period, such as Richard Simon, Simon Ockley, and Edward Gibbon, could provide fairly impartial accounts of Islam and its civilization. This attitude persisted more or less through the eighteenth century. In this age of Enlightenment, cultivated Europeans in this period continued to cling to a universalist view in which East and West played complementary roles.

This state of affairs began to change drastically in the nineteenth century, when the period of European conquests and imperialism in the East began. A utilitarian sense of Western cultural superiority and a romantic exoticism with its delight in an imagined magical East produced, in synergy with one another, an academic discipline termed "Orientalism." Such an enterprise focused on the study of languages of the East, leading to the translations of a number of texts produced in these languages. Because of its provenance, Orientalism came to be regarded as a highly politicized and tendentious discipline, famously and devastatingly criticized by Edward Said, a professor of comparative literature at Columbia University. In his seminal book appropriately titled *Orientalism,* Said lambasted this phenomenon for having engendered what he described as the process of organizing knowledge about the East, embedded in a discourse of power, which subjected knowledge to the political concerns of the three great empires (as he calls them) of the nineteenth and twentieth centuries, British, French, and American. Whether one fully agrees with Said or not, the impact of his work has wrought a sea change in the way scholarship about the Middle East and Islam is conducted in the Western academy, particularly in the United States, allowing for more rigorously analytical and considerably more objective methodologies to emerge that acknowledge the complexities of Muslim societies and the multiple inflections of the Islamic tradition.

In contrast to hard-line Islamists, many contemporary Muslim modernist and reformist thinkers have strenuously refuted the Clash of Civilizations thesis, deeming its reification of Islam and its traditions reprehensible. They rather point to the inherent resiliency of the *shariʿa* and its ability to respond to changing historical circumstances. Unlike most Islamists and traditionalists, modernists and reformists regard the *shariʿa* not as a fixed legal code but as a set of moral guidelines from which specific legal rulings may be derived through human reasoning, in accordance with the objectives of the religious law (in Arabic, *maqasid*). Such rulings are thus historically contingent and susceptible to change. Adherence, however, to the basic objectives of the *shariʿa,* which seek to safeguard justice and mercy and promote the welfare of society (in Arabic, *maslaha*), is a binding requirement. Thus, modern standards of justice and the concept of collective welfare allow for the hermeneutic annexation of pre-modern concepts such as *shura* and *ijmaʿ* ("consensus") to support of democracy and democratization in Muslim-majority societies. Equal rights for women may be adduced from women's visible and robust participation in particularly early Islamic society. This contemporary group of modernist Muslim thinkers include Saʿid Ashmawy of Egypt, Muhammad Shahrour of Syria, and western Muslims such as Tariq Ramadan, Khaled Abou el Fadl, Azizah al-Hibri, and Muqtedar Khan. Theirs is the task of negotiating modernity (or competing views of modernity) and articulating legitimate responses to it based on a thoughtful (re)consideration of the Islamic religio-intellectual tradition. Theirs is a project full of pitfalls but also of exhilarating challenges, a project, one may add, that is long overdue.

See also *Clash of Civlizations; Islam.*

Asma Afsaruddin

BIBLIOGRAPHY

Afsaruddin, Asma. "The 'Islamic State': Genealogy, Facts, and Myths." *Journal of Church and State* 48 (2006): 153–173.

Bulliet, Richard. *The Case for Islamo-Christian Civilization.* New York: Columbia University Press, 2004.

Euben, Roxanne. *The Enemy in the Mirror: Islamic Fundamentalism and the Limits of Modern Rationalism.* Princeton, N.J.: Princeton University Press, 1999.

Gibbon, Edward. *Decline and Fall of the Roman Empire.* New York: Modern Library, 1932.

Hourani, Albert Habib. *Arabic Thought in the Liberal Age, 1798–1939.* Cambridge, England: Cambridge University Press, 2003.

Huntington, Samuel P. "The Clash of Civilizations?" *Foreign Affairs* 72 (1993): 22–49.

Ibn Munqidh, Usama. *An Arab-Syrian Gentleman and Warrior in the Period of the Crusades.* Translated by Philip K. Hitti. Princeton, N.J.: Princeton University Press, 1987.

Khan, M. A. Muqtedar, ed. *Islamic Democratic Discourse: Theory, Debates, and Philosophical Perspectives.* Lanham, Md.: Lexington Books, 2006.

Kurzman, Charles, ed. *Modernist Islam, 1840–1940: A Sourcebook.* New York: Oxford University Press, 2002.

Lapidus, Ira. "State and Religion in Islamic Societies." *Past and Present* 151 (1996): 3–28.

Mawardi, ʿAli ibn Muhammad. *The Laws of Islamic Governance.* Translated by Asadullah Yate. London: Ta-Ha, 2005.

Mottahedeh, Roy and Ridwan al-Sayyid. "The Idea of the Jihad in Islam before the Crusades." In *The Crusades from the Perspective of Byzantium and the Muslim World.* Edited by Angeliki E. Laiou and Roy Parviz Mottahedeh. Washington, D.C.: Dumbarton Oaks Research Library and Collections, 2001.

Said, Edward W. *Orientalism.* New York: Vintage Books, 1979.

Israel

Established as a state in 1948, Israel is bounded on the north by Lebanon, northeast by Syria, east by Jordan, southwest by Egypt, and west by the Mediterranean Sea. Some 5.2 million (74 percent) of the approximately 7 million Israelis are Jews. Israel is also home to more than 1 million Muslims, more than 100,000 Arab Christians, more than 100,000 Druze, approximately 28,000 non-Arab Christians, and a quarter million residents whose religion is unknown. Many of the non-Arab Christians and individuals whose religion is not indicated are family members of recent Jewish immigrants from the former Soviet Union.

Israel is a small country of 7,800 square miles, about the size of Massachusetts. After the June 1967 war with Egypt, Jordan, and Syria (aided by Iraq, Kuwait, Saudi Arabia, Sudan, and Algeria), Israel occupied sizable additional territories in the Sinai Peninsula, Gaza, and West Bank. It returned the largest of these, the Sinai Peninsula, to Egypt in 1982, after the signing of a peace treaty, and withdrew from Gaza in 2005. The ongoing occupation of areas in the West Bank has been a source of conflict between Israel and its neighbors, and among Israelis who have wanted to return the areas or hold on to them as religious patrimony or as essential to national defense.

Founding of the State of Israel

The pre-state Jewish community of Palestine had two major religious parties, which differed in their orientation toward Zionism, the Jewish national movement. Mizrahi, founded in 1902 in eastern Europe, supported the Zionist enterprise in Palestine, because its adherents saw in the resettlement of the land—even if by secularists acting unawares—the hand of the divine. Agudat Israel, founded in Germany in 1912, interpreted the Zionist enterprise as a usurpation of God's own messianic (and unknowable) timetable.

After World War I, the League of Nations formally approved, in 1922, the terms of a British mandate over Palestine. These terms recognized "the historical connection of the Jewish people with Palestine" and called on mandate authorities to help "secure the establishment of a Jewish National Home." To this end, the Jewish Agency instituted by the World Zionist Organization undertook formal representation of the Palestinian Jewish community to the mandatory power. It also coordinated efforts within the Jewish community itself, and it established an extensive infrastructure of public services in the Jewish sector of Palestine.

By the end of the mandate in 1948, many of the institutions of a sovereign state were already in place. An elected assembly presaged the Knesset (parliament); the Jewish Agency had executive functions; and various militia formed the basis of the Israeli army. There were also numerous political parties, from religious to secular and leftist socialist to rightist capitalist.

As the extent of the European Holocaust became known after World War II, the anti-Zionist party Agudat

Israel softened its stand against Zionism in return for concessions from the new state. These concessions, gained in 1947 from the Jewish Agency, became known as the "status quo agreement." They formed the basis for the institutionalization of Judaism in postindependence Israel. According to this agreement, the Jewish Shabbat would be the official day of rest for Jews, and the observation of dietary laws (kashruth) would be maintained in the army and other governmental institutions. The existing Mizrahi religious school system would remain separate from secular schools, but, as part of the national education system, would receive funding from the state. Ultra-Orthodox (including Agudat Israel) schools would also remain separate and outside the national system, retaining their autonomy entirely. Ultra-Orthodox youth would be exempt from army service, and rabbinical courts would decide on matters of personal status (such as marriage, divorce, or inheritance) concerning Jews.

Although between two-thirds and three-quarters of Jewish Israelis are not religiously observant and do not vote for the religious parties, the Orthodox minority has been able to maintain considerable power, because members of the Knesset are chosen under the proportional list electoral system. Because no party has ever received an absolute majority in national elections, the "winning" party has always had to form a coalition government with other parties. In negotiating coalition agreements, smaller parties extract promises and resources in return for their support. One or another religious party has usually been within the governing coalition.

Religion and Politics

The nature of Judaism, and how it differs from Christianity and Islam, is important in understanding the interplay between religion and politics in Israel. Judaism is not simple. It differs from Christianity and Islam in that ethnicity figures prominently. Membership in the ethnic community, rather than belief, determines one's status as a Jew. Humanists, agnostics, and atheists who are Jews can be no less at home in Israel than the ultra-Orthodox. Argument about the meaning of religious law is well established in Jewish tradition. And there is no central authority to resolve disputes.

Also contributing to the religious disputes in Israel is the multiplicity of backgrounds represented by Israelis. Major waves of immigrants originated from Eastern Europe, the Balkans, Germany, North Africa, Yemen, Iraq, Iran, Ethiopia, and a dozen or so subregions of the former Soviet Union. These immigrants brought with them—and their children preserve—differences in ritual and tradition, as well as conflicting sentiments about the proper role of religion in a modern state.

During Israel's first half-century, points of chronic contention among Jewish citizens revolved around the following questions:

- Which aspects of religious law should be enforced by state authorities, and which bodies should have the final say in determining the nature of religious law or its application to individual cases? This cluster of disputes includes prohibitions of work, public entertainment, and transportation on the Sabbath and religious holidays; the availability of nonkosher food; abortions, autopsies, burials, marriage, and divorce; the definition of "modesty," which concerns mostly the attire of women who live in or visit religious neighborhoods and the women who are pictured in advertisements; who should be considered a Jew; and who should be given the designation and authority of "rabbi" to perform marriages, divorces, and conversions to Judaism?
- What is the basic law of the nation? Claims about religious law have stood in the way of creating a constitution for Israel. One religious position is that a central legal

document with high status would challenge the importance of the Torah in Jewish law. Israel has stumbled through an ongoing procedure of adopting basic laws, or a constitution in stages, that deal with some of these issues while avoiding others.

- What should be the rights and privileges of various categories of Jews? Religious and secular Jews, ultra-Orthodox and non-Orthodox communities, as well as the communities of Jews from North Africa, Asia, and Ethiopia, each feel that they have been treated unfairly by some other group of Jews.
- As for the significance of the biblical Land of Israel, how much of that imprecise landscape should be insisted on in negotiations, bargained away for the sake of peace, or incorporated into Israel unilaterally without agreement by Arab claimants?

The diversities within Judaism, its mixture of ethnicity, doctrines, and traditions, and the dominance of Israel's polity by Jews give every public issue in Israel something of a religious element. Political activists add claims about *Jewish values* to their arguments about social policy and public finance; assert the safety of the *Jewish people* and the *Jewish state* when talking about the budgets for the police and the military; and emphasize the sanctity of the *Land of Israel* when demanding more attention for environmental protection.

Surveys find that about 10 percent of the population falls within each of the "ultra-Orthodox" and "Orthodox" categories, 30 percent into the "traditional" category, and 50 percent into the secular category. Israelis who consider themselves "traditional" are typically from North African or Asian backgrounds. Many of them observe dietary laws and the Sabbath and the men wear skullcaps, but they are not as rigorous about observances as those who consider themselves Orthodox. It is estimated that fewer than 50,000 Reform and Conservative Jews live in Israel, many of them with roots in North America. They suffer in the distribution of public benefits by virtue of their small size and their lack of a political party to represent them in the Knesset. However, they carry considerable weight in international Jewish organizations that have some influence on the Israeli government. Individual disputes between Orthodox and non-Orthodox religious Jews can be grouped into clusters concerned with conversion to Judaism; marriage, divorce, and burial; the rights of women, the practice of Reform or Conservative rituals at the Western Wall; and the representation of non-Orthodox Jews on local religious councils.

Religious parties elected to the Knesset in 2006 include a new joint venture between the National Religious Party and the right-wing party National Union, aimed primarily at maintaining Jewish control of the Land of Israel; Torah Judaism, an ultra-Orthodox party that includes what had been Agudat Israel along with congregations of anti-Hasidic or Lithuanian ultra-Orthodox Jews; and SHAS, an ultra-Orthodox party composed mostly of Jews from North Africa and Asia. Shinui had been a prominent antireligious party from the 1990s to the 2006 election, but it split as a result of personality conflicts, and neither of its factions won any seats in the new Knesset. Meretz is a left-of-center party whose agenda has an anticlerical element.

Despite the chronic and intense nature of disputes in Israel, the outcomes of political quarrels about religion among Israel's Jews often amount to sound and fury with little significance, and so they are allowed to play themselves out. They have not provoked mass violence or threatened the security of the state in the same way as recent conflicts between Israelis and Palestinians or other groups, such as Hezbollah in Lebanon. Activists who work for some issues claim a quarrel among Jews typically begins with a charge by religious or antireligious activists that there has been a violation of the status quo. When a dispute catches hold, the rhetoric begins to escalate, with speakers for both religious and secular interests proclaiming that the other side is anti-Semitic and that it provoked the confrontation by threatening the status quo. The next step may be street demonstrations with overturned trash dumpsters, fights between religious and antireligious participants, and the presence of mounted police trying to minimize the damage and jailing the most extreme demonstrators for a few hours.

Characteristically, policy makers do not try to settle general problems once and for all. They limit their efforts to finding a way out of a particular situation. Thus they may deal with the issue of a particular instance of Sabbath controversy (for example, a particular shopping center that insists on remaining open for business on the Sabbath, thereby provoking religious protests) rather than ruling conclusively what activities will be permitted and what will be forbidden on the Sabbath. Although limited treatment is possible but often difficult, the larger goal of full treatment would be more threatening to a religious or a secular posture and would be likely to escalate religious-secular animosity.

Several problems stand in the way of a systematic, quantitative reckoning of who wins individual confrontations, or determining whether religious or antireligious interests have been dominant in recent Israeli history. For one thing, the ambiguities in Judaism hinder that their postures are derived from "Jewish norms" or would benefit the Jewish state, but they are not making claims that are clearly religious. Additional problems arise from judging the outcomes of individual confrontations. For example, how can success be claimed if one side has won the enactment of a law, but the measure is seldom enforced, or it is implemented in ways that are criticized by those who supported its enactment? And how can a general conclusion be reached when the same general problem (for example, public modesty, Sabbath observance, the availability of nonkosher food) returns over and over with variations in the character of the demands and subtle nuances in the ways in which the issue is resolved. The weight of the argument is that neither side has won. Religious activists have scored some victories, but so have secular Israelis. It is difficult to weigh the closure of a road against the opening of discotheques, cinemas, and restaurants on the Sabbath. The score is tied, more or less.

The Arab uprising that began in September 2000 has left its mark on the issue of religion and politics in Israel. Until Prime Minister Ariel Sharon revealed the outlines of his disengagement plan in December 2003, tensions between religious and secular Jews had declined. Arguments about Shabbat, kashruth, modesty, or the rights of non-Orthodox rabbis paled in significance when violent Arabs seemed intent on killing Jews of all religious persuasions. As disengagement, or the withdrawal of Jewish settlements from Gaza and from the northern area of the West Bank, moved toward reality in August 2005, tensions between secular and religious Jews increased. The predominant issue became the Land of Israel and the right of Jews to remain wherever they had settled on the land. The overwhelming majority of Israelis who protested by distributing leaflets, blocking traffic, and ultimately resisting removal with force were religious Zionists of the kind that traditionally voted for the National Religious Party. For the most part, the ultra-Orthodox abstained from activity in keeping with their lesser concern for Israeli control over the Land of Israel.

In 2006 it appeared that the new government headed by Ehud Olmert was committed to extensive further withdrawals from the West Bank under the labels of relocation or consolidation. Olmert proclaimed that he wished to com-plete the separation from the Palestine National Authority within clear boundaries of Israel. Religious Zionists expressed strong opposition to the plan, and the conflicts with Hamas and Hizbullah in summer 2006 may have removed such proposals from the Israeli political agenda as attention shifted to security concerns along Isreal's borders and as public opinion hardened.

See also: *Nationalism; Palestine; Violence; Zionism.*

Ira Sharkansky

BIBLIOGRAPHY

El-Or, Tamar. *Educated and Ignorant: Ultraorthodox Jewish Women and Their World.* Boulder, Colo.: Lynne Rienner, 1994.

Etzioni-Halevy, Eva. *The Divided People: Can Israel's Breakup Be Stopped?* Lanham, Md.: Lexington Books, 2002.

Heilman, Samuel. *Defenders of the Faith: Inside Ultra-Orthodox Jewry.* New York: Schocken Books, 1992.

Liebman, Charles, and Eliezer Don-Yehiya. *Religion and Politics in Israel.* Bloomington: Indiana University Press, 1984.

Medding, Peter. *The Founding of Israeli Democracy, 1948–1967.* New York: Oxford University Press, 1990.

Sharkansky, Ira. *The Politics of Religion and the Religion of Politics: Looking at Israel.* Lanham, Md.: Lexington Books, 2000.

Sprinzak, Ehud, and Larry Diamond, eds. *Israeli Democracy under Stress.* Boulder, Colo.: Lynne Rienner, 1993.

Italy

A country in southern Europe, bordered by the Mediterranean Sea on three sides and by the Alps to the north, Italy achieved political union only between 1860 and 1870. Before then the Italian peninsula was divided among a number of small states, some self-governing, some dominated by other European powers, and one ruled directly by the pope as a sovereign prince. The story of politics and religion in Italy during the nineteenth and twentieth centuries is in large part the story of the pope's gradual reconciliation to his loss of temporal power and his equally gradual acceptance of the reality and legitimacy of the Italian state. The attitude of the Holy See to a unified Italy progressed from bitter opposition, through denial and passive hostility, to acceptance, recognition, and finally cooperation. It was only late in this process, in 1913, that the pope even permitted obedient Catholics to take part in the political life of their country.

The attitude of the Roman Catholic Church toward the new Italian state was supremely important because its citizens were almost exclusively of Catholic background. Many Italians, although nominally Catholic, had no use for the clergy. But a significant number felt some duty to obey a pope who believed he had a right to lay down the law on political as well as religious matters. Immediately before Italy's final unification serious thought had been given to turning the peninsula into a federal, democratic union of states, presided over by the pope. But Pius IX (reigned 1846–1878) would not compromise what he felt was his divine right to rule over state as well as church, and the idea came to nothing.

The Roman Question

The Kingdom of Italy, which was basically established by 1860, comprised all of the peninsula except a small area, including Rome, which the pope ruled directly. It was not until September 1870 that the new Italian government decided to take over Rome and establish it as the kingdom's capital. A final—almost symbolic—assault deprived the pope of his personal residence at the Quirinal and made him a "prisoner in the Vatican," as he termed himself. After a thousand years of temporal power, the papacy had to deal with a completely new situation.

The decision of the First Vatican Council, in July 1870, to recognize the primacy of the pope and his infallibility when he spoke on faith and moral matters "from the throne"

(Latin *ex cathedra*) was made for religious reasons, but it had some political side effects. Among other things it tended to increase hostility between the Vatican and some national governments. The Prussian chancellor, Otto von Bismarck, for example, declared that his state would refuse to talk with the Prussian bishops because only the pope could make decisions. Bismarck's declaration led to an official explanation of the council's position by Pius IX, making clear the unchanged responsibility of local bishops. In Italy nothing of this kind ever happened.

The intractable problem of the pope's status, known as the Roman Question, caused a global rejection of any relationship between the Vatican, supported by bishops naturally beholden to the pope, and the new Italian state. By an act of an anticlerical Parliament the Italian government protected some of the church's properties and its right to operate, but this act received no thanks from the pope. The sincere Catholic was discouraged (in the papal statement known by its opening Latin words *Non Expedit*—"It is not appropriate") from taking any active part in political life. But the strictest prohibitions often had little force in the country as a whole. Catholic movements such as cooperative associations, savings banks, and trade unions were alive and well, even if the pope formally prohibited more than this level of political activity.

It is hard to overestimate the importance of the Roman Question in shaping Catholic participation in and exclusion from political life in the late nineteenth century. On the side of the state, the political establishment was vigorously anticlerical, and those voices urging a more open attitude toward the church were silenced as dangerous, naive, or both. On the church's side, a battle was raging by the end of Leo XIII's pontificate (1878–1903) between those opposed to modern society (and specifically opposed to any political compromise with the state) and those who looked for a point of contact between liberal positions and Catholic doctrine. However, any attempt to organize a political party free and committed to developing "Christian democracy" was not only stopped but condemned as political modernism. Pius X (1903–1914) used the term *modernism* as an accusation with which to persecute the spirit of free inquiry on religious matters. Even some of the leading branches of the Catholic social movement were singled out and destroyed. Prominent leaders, priests as well as layman, were denounced and deprived of chairs in seminaries and schools, denied responsibility, and even made to lose basic acceptance by other Catholics.

Socialism and World War I

By the turn of the century a new scare had arisen to distort the relations between religion and politics in Italy—namely, the spirit of socialism. The efforts of a generation of Italian Catholics to fight socialism on its own ground, by the side of the workers, were wasted. After a general strike in 1904 the pope permitted Catholic politicians in local government to take an active role as conservative support to the liberal order. But bishops who expressed their personal views about social problems were immediately suspected of not being loyal to the pope.

Italian Catholics became officially and directly involved in electoral politics in 1913, when for the first time the vote was extended to almost all male citizens. Catholic voters were urged to help nonsocialist candidates at the polls, even those not affiliated with the church. The electoral strength of Catholic voters was thus directed toward helping conservative candidates.

World War I (1914–1918) showed that Italian Catholics felt themselves to be Italians not only by geography but also by citizenship. Movements of troops (often accompanied by priests in uniform) to the northeast front from all over the country made the war and ultimate victory the first event in which all Italians could feel a sense of unity and participation—even if papal consent was lacking.

In 1919 the pope nullified the prohibition on participation in national elections. At about the same time a Sicilian priest, Luigi Sturzo, founded the Italian Popular Party, which aimed to bring Catholics, "free and strong," into the political arena, not as representatives of the church but as autonomous citizens. Suspected of excessive independence by the church hierarchy, the Popular Party was nonetheless a success in elections, and the first hundred Catholic representatives entered Parliament, in Rome. The Popular Party, however, was unable to foresee that the immediate danger to the liberal state was not so much from socialist and communist strikes but from a silent alliance that linked northern agrarian interests, industrialists, and middle-class people—often deriving from a Catholic culture of authority and order—with a new political force, the Fascist Party of Benito Mussolini.

Mussolini's Regime and World War II

Mussolini came to power in stages. At the beginning his regime appeared only authoritarian, but even the revelation of his tyrannical goals did not arouse serious opposition in the Vatican. Many church leaders were pleased that Mussolini supported them in matters in which they were interested (for instance, the rescue of the Bank of Rome, where Vatican money was heavily invested), and they accepted the exile of Sturzo from Italy as a favor to the Vatican: had not Mussolini stopped the communist danger?

Mussolini achieved his greatest success in solidifying Catholic support for his regime in February 1929, when he signed, with the papal secretary of state, a set of agreements between Italy and the Vatican. The Lateran Treaty, by which pope and state recognized each other's existence, "gave back the pope to Italy, and Italy to the pope." The papal enclave at the Vatican was recognized as a tiny independent state, and Roman Catholicism became the official religion of Italy, with a special status recognized for priests and seminarians. The act was greeted as something more than the overdue resolution of a problem that belonged to the past; indeed, it was hailed as the fruit of a divine plan, accomplished by "the man of Divine Providence," as the pope called Mussolini.

Some small opposition to fascism did exist among Catholics, but it took a long time to become visible. Between 1931 and 1933 there were confrontations in several towns between Catholic Action, a church organization, and corresponding Fascist organizations. These confrontations showed how unrealistic was the idea of "Christianizing" fascism. At Easter 1937 three papal documents were issued, condemning Nazism, communism, and the Mexican revolution (with some difference of severity). Although nothing was said about Mussolini, it was a symptom of a growing papal willingness to be critical. When, in October 1938, Mussolini applied racist and anti-Jewish laws to Italy, Catholics were split in their attitude. Many were indifferent, and a few actively supported Mussolini's action, but some priests and lay people offered their help to persecuted Jews. When he died in 1939, Pius XI had not finished working out a policy of appropriate reaction, and war was on its way. The new pope, Eugenio Pacelli, elected as Pius XII, had been the papal secretary of state.

The beginning of World War II gave the Catholic hierarchy problems of interpretation. The old justification for war—that it comes as a punishment for sin—was advanced again, but it was no longer convincing. The Vatican diplomat (and future pope) Giovanni Battista Montini; some lay members of Catholic Action, such as the future prime minister Aldo Moro; and some young professors of the Catholic University saw beyond the war the need to reconstruct a non-Fascist Italy, where Catholics could find their place.

The tragedy of the war and the destruction caused by fascism climaxed when Mussolini's regime collapsed in July 1943. There followed rapidly an armistice with the Allies, the occupation of much of Italy by the Germans, and finally the installation of Mussolini as dictator of northern Italy in a short-lived, Nazi-supported Italian Social Republic. These events were paralleled by a growing resistance from young people, from such diverse backgrounds as the Communist Party, liberal circles, and even Catholic parishes. A new generation of Catholics discovered democracy as a way to rebuild the nation. The radio broadcasts of Pius XII, especially his Christmas broadcasts between 1942 and 1944, gave greater impulse to this new commitment.

Early Postwar Politics

A new generation of Catholics entered politics after the war, but the Italian religious situation had not really changed. There was no national church organization—not even a national conference of Catholic bishops, which would have been considered an offense to the privilege of having the pope "among us." But although there was no national identity for the church, there was a national Catholic party. The Christian Democrats took over from the old Popular Party the role of representing Catholic interests in Italian democracy. During the working out of the new constitution, where Catholic and Communist leaders reached significant agreements, the Christian Democratic members represented both the hopes of a new generation and the interests of the Holy See: preservation of the concordat, freedom for Catholic schools, and a constitutional prohibition of divorce. There was, on the ecclesiastical side, no further interest in the nature or form of Italian democracy. The only aim was to repel the communist threat and to ensure Catholic control over society, even if this meant an undeclared attitude of tolerance for illegal organizations like the Sicilian Mafia.

The final version of the constitution was decided upon in 1947, after the Marxist parties had been ejected from the cabinet, in accordance with an agreement between the prime minister, Alcide De Gasperi, and the United States. The first democratic elections, in April 1948, saw a large victory by the Christian Democrats over the Socialist and Communist alliance and confirmed the exclusion of leftist parties from the government. Although the Christian Democrats won, it was the end of the dream of a young generation of Catholic politicians, who hoped to direct Catholic politics toward a more equal society, with all classes participating in the democratic process. The leadership of De Gasperi and his young aides gave to the Catholic political presence a moderate, even conservative stamp. This conservatism was strengthened in 1949, when the church excommunicated Communists and their supporters.

Vatican II

The election, in 1958, of a new pope, John XXIII, marked a watershed in politics and in religion. The elderly cardinal Roncalli had been elected as a transitional pope, his papacy to be a moment of rest after the turbulent theological controversies in the last years of Pius XII. However, his summoning of the Second Vatican Council (1962–1965), which was intended to reconsider the position of the church in the modern world, had profound repercussions. With the new attitude of reform and diversity that came from Vatican II, Christian Democratic leaders in Italy were enabled to involve the Socialist Party in the country's government and proceed with far-reaching economic reforms, through the nationalization of energy and heavy industry.

The effects of this mutual accommodation between a Catholic and Vatican orientation, on the one hand, and the political choices of the ordinary citizen, on the other, were impressive. Within the church the responsibility for political affairs was shifted from the office of the "substitute" (a sort of vice secretary of state) to the newly created national conference of Catholic bishops. The person to order this change was Pope Paul VI, himself a former substitute, who succeeded John XXIII in 1963 and continued the reforms of Vatican II. For the first time Italian bishops did not regard themselves simply as the "life jacket" of the Roman papacy. They began to feel a sense of responsibility toward their country.

Most Italian bishops, even after Vatican II, shared the opinion that "Catholic political unity" was necessary. The acceptance of a Socialist presence in the government did not prevent the bishops from urging all Catholics to vote for Christian Democratic candidates. Thoughtful Catholic voters often had to make political choices in conflict with their bishops. Political pluralism (which meant votes for the Communist Party) had long been a general practice, but it became a controversial issue at the end of the 1960s. Instead of being the voice of order, priests were urging the young to refuse military service in the army in the name of Christian pacifism.

Terrorist Campaigns

Three events jolted the relations between church and state during the 1970s. Two national laws, permitting divorce and abortion, were approved by Parliament. In both cases the reaction of the church was one of discomfort, even shock. Instead of accepting that the times were demanding radical changes, the bishops and some Christian Democratic leaders tried to abolish the laws through the constitutional procedure of referendum. Only a minority of voters were for abolition, and many Catholics even supported the laws. The defeat of the bishops' challenge was seen in many circles as a symptom of a crisis, but fears were even greater when hundreds of young people, coming both from the ranks of the Communist Party and from Catholic families, started a terrorist campaign.

Increasingly, after 1973, these terrorists described democratic institutions as a masquerade for capitalist power. Brutal murders and attacks were used as a means to force the government to abandon what the terrorists believed was a sham democracy and by revealing its true face to bring the masses to revolution. Both Christian Democrats and Communists—now coming together in a common government of "national solidarity"—were favorite targets. Among hundreds of other crimes, the Red Brigades in 1978 kidnapped Aldo Moro, the former prime minister and president of the Christian Democrats, who was a personal friend of Paul VI. Political leaders refused to consider negotiations to save Moro, and even the Vatican accepted this strategic choice. Moro was killed by the Red Brigades in August 1978, a few months before the end of Paul VI's pontificate. The first pope with leanings to the Christian Democrats ended his life in the realization that the support offered by the church to one political party was having an effect on the church and its choices.

Change and Rebuilding

The election of a Polish cardinal to the papacy in 1978 increased the independence of Catholics in political life, but Italian politics was still dominated by an international situation that was beyond Italy's power to alter. There had been no fundamental changes since World War II—during the cold war no change was possible—and the effects on the morality of the political establishment had been disastrous. It was with the end of European communism and the disintegration of the Soviet Union in 1991 that this crisis came to the surface. Many political parties simply disappeared after their leaders were put on trial for corruption.

Between 1992 and 1995 the Christian Democratic Party splintered into several minor political groups and signed alliances with parties that were proving more stable in the new political atmosphere. Some Catholic voters went to a conservative alliance, strengthened by the support of the extreme right movement (formerly neofascist, now converted to democratic methods). Others, resurrecting the name of the Popular Party, went to the left and allied with the parties that inherited the electoral weight of the old Communist Party, now renamed the Democratic Party of the Left.

The first election after these big changes, in 1994, was won by the conservative groups led by a media businessman, Silvio Berlusconi, who was discharged by the groups' own allies in some eighteen months. Berlusconi was forced to resign soon after going to court to answer charges of corrupt payments made by parts of his business empire. On the eve of the 1996 general election (won by Romano Prodi and the center-left alliance) the Conference of Catholic Bishops released a statement recognizing the complete freedom of each Catholic voter. This statement marked the end of an era: even if it is known that the Catholic voter decided on his or her own and voted Christian Democratic for political reasons, even if the immense audience of parish faithful and the small groups known as "movement" had opposite needs of political visibility, the assertion marked the lack of ability of the Bishops' Conference and its president, Cardinal Ruini, to rescue a very peculiar past.

During the center-left governments and the five years of the government of Silvio Berlusconi (who won the 2001 election), the Bishops' Conference, primarily its president, shaped a direct political role for the church. The Bishops' Conference entered into the technicalities of the political fight. This meant that the "foreign" pope was represented by the bishops' president that he had appointed, and the president was called to represent to the pope byzantine politics. Such a state of being disabled some tools of "the Vatican," such as the secretary of state and the international position of John Paul II (for instance against the American wars on Iraq), and the cardinal expressed different views.

In the Ruini era the debate centered on legal-moral topics, such as abortion, stem cell research, and medically assisted procreation techniques. In some cases (abortion, for example) the bishops simply requested Catholics to express concerns about existing laws; in other cases (such as the debate on the MAP Act, or Law N. 40), the Bishops' Conference appealed to the Catholic and other sympathetic members of parliament to legally implement at least some of the Catholic moral principles. The majority boycotted a referendum called by anticlerical movements against this law, as they had other referendums in the past decade. The boycott, however, was read by the cardinal as a victory opening a new era, when Catholics and atheistic Italian conservatives supporting Catholic culture could be rallied in a common ideological framework against, for example, uncontrolled scientific research or against the threat of a "Western and Christian" identity represented by the presence of an Islamic minority.

This program has suffered difficulties since the beginning of 2006. The bishops and the new pope (the German Cardinal Ratzinger, reigning as Benedict XVI since April 19, 2005) looked for a church committed more to pastoral issues than to political variability. The general election of 2006 marked a defeat for the center-right (which supported church views and passed laws adding a minor tax exemption to the grant of 1.2 billion dollars to the church per year,) and a victory for the center-left alliance led again by Romano Prodi. In this new situation the Catholic Church had three options: to put an end to the Italian polarity concerning moral issues (such as euthanasia or the nonmarriage agreement, called Pacs, as in France) in order to rebuild a center party inspired by the church; to act as political subject within a framework of democratic competition, using its economic power for campaigning; or to commit Catholics to both Italian and European nation building, where religious and cultural identities could be formed in a peaceful society. The future will tell which option the church will choose and what the destiny of the church as a community will be.

See also *Anticlericalism; Christian Democracy; Papacy; Vatican; Vatican Council, Second.*

Alberto Melloni

BIBLIOGRAPHY

Alberig, Giuseppe, ed. *History of Vatican II,* edited by Joseph A. Komonchak (English ed.). Maryknoll, N.Y.: Orbis Books, 1995.

Gentile, Emilio. *The Sacralization of Politics in Fascist Italy.* Translated by Keith Botsford. Cambridge, Mass.: Harvard University Press, 1996.

Giammanco, Rosanna Mulazzi. *The Catholic-Communist Dialogue in Italy: 1944 to the Present.* New York: Praeger, 1989.

Ginsborg, Paul. *A History of Contemporary Italy: Society and Politics, 1943–1988.* New York: Penguin, 1990.

Kertzer, David I. *Comrades and Christians: Religion and Political Struggle in Communist Italy.* New York: Cambridge University Press, 1980.

Leonardi, Robert, and Douglas A. Wertman. *Italian Christian Democracy: The Politics of Dominance.* New York: St. Martin's, 1989.

Mack Smith, Denis. *Modern Italy: A Political History.* New Haven: Yale University Press, 1997.

McCarthy, Patrick. *The Crisis of the Italian State: From the Origins of the Cold War to the Fall of Berlusconi.* New York: St. Martin's, 1995.

Miller, James Edward. *From Elite to Mass Politics: Italian Socialism in the Giolittian Era, 1900–1914.* Kent, Ohio: Kent State University Press, 1990.

Tarrow, Sidney G. *Democracy and Disorder: Protest and Politics in Italy, 1965–1975.* Oxford: Clarendon Press, 1989.

Ivory Coast

Ivory Coast, also known as Côte d'Ivoire, a former French colony situated along the Atlantic Coast of West Africa, is a country of great cultural, linguistic, and religious diversity with a population of approximately 12.5 million inhabitants. Its 122,000 square miles are bisected into different climactic zones: tropical rain forest covers most of the southern half of the country, whereas the north is all grasslands.

The Precolonial Period

The frontier between the forest and the grasslands was the locus for exchange of commodities as well as ideas. Kola nuts from the forest were traded for rock salt mined in the Sahara. However, these exchange networks tended to orient the peoples of the forest and the grasslands in opposite directions. Northbound trade was controlled by Muslims, many of whom settled along trade routes throughout the grasslands. For the most part, these Muslim traders lived as minorities and subjects of non-Muslim rulers. The larger trading towns, such as Kong and Bondoukou, were also major centers of Muslim learning. It was generally in the interest of both chiefs and their Muslim subjects to maintain close relationships. About 1700, a Muslim leader, Sekou Wattara, seized power in the kingdom of Kong; however, the coup d'état was not in any sense a jihad, an attempt to construct an explicitly Muslim state. All in all, Islam as practiced in northern Ivory Coast was not of a militant variety.

The forest region, in contrast, was more oriented toward the coast and to overseas trade with Europe. In 1637 five Capuchin missionaries landed at Assinie, along the coast. However, the mission was a total failure. Fifty years later, the French established a fort there, but this, too, was soon abandoned. Subsequently, European powers took little interest in Ivory Coast until the nineteenth century, when it began producing palm oil for export to Europe. Despite this European presence, Christianity made no significant inroads in Ivory Coast, unlike Islam in the north.

The Colonial Period

In 1893 France declared Ivory Coast as its colony. At that time, the territory was relatively peripheral, both economically and strategically. The French had already established a series of outposts along the coast, which were linked by the creation of the colony to French territories along the Niger River. The major obstacle to these French projects of expansion was Samory Toure, a Muslim warlord who controlled much of northern Ivory Coast in the 1890s. Nonetheless, the French were not entirely hostile toward Islam during the early years of rule, when the colony was under military leadership. Most of the French colonial troops were Africans from the colonies of Senegal and Sudan (now Mali), many of whom were Muslims themselves. Louis Gustave Binger, the first governor of the colony, had earlier been among the first to explore its interior. He and other military officers, convinced that Muslims were more "evolved" than African "fetishists," were not at all averse to the spread of Islam. At the same time, Binger also called for the establishment of Catholic missions in the new colony. Initially, these missions were restricted to the coastal regions, the most accessible to Europeans.

The outcome of the Dreyfus affair in France had profound repercussions for colonial policy concerning religion. By 1906 the official policy of the French government was the strict separation of church and state. The army, which until then had enjoyed relatively free rein in France's African colonies, was particularly suspect, along with the Catholic Church and organized religion in general. Any official collaboration between Catholic missionaries and the colonial government of Ivory Coast was categorically ruled out. Unlike many British colonies, where education was largely left in the hands of missionaries, the colonial government of Ivory Coast was committed in principle to the establishment of a secular school system. Catholic missions were permitted to establish their own schools, and they attempted to proselytize in the southern half of the country. However, the separation of church and state dictated that the colony be open to Protestant as well as Catholic missionaries.

This openness had its limits. In 1913 William Wade Harris, a native of Liberia, crossed the border into Ivory Coast,

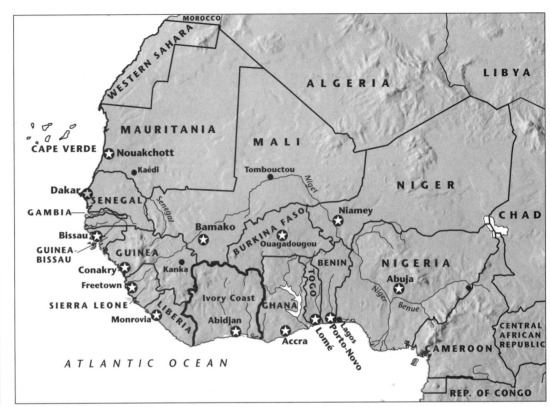

baptizing people and announcing his prophetic mission. He urged the local populations to burn their masks and statues, to renounce their gods, and to practice Christianity. Harris was apprehended and jailed but quickly released. He continued to proselytize, making his way along the coast and ultimately into the Gold Coast (modern Ghana). The British authorities sent him back to Ivory Coast, where he continued to preach. The outbreak of World War I fueled French suspicions of outsiders, especially anyone like Harris who could mobilize masses of people, and Harris was expelled back to Liberia. Nevertheless, the Harrist Church, among the oldest independent African churches in West Africa, continued to flourish in Ivory Coast.

The colonial government was equally suspicious of Muslims, fearing that pan-Islamism would constitute a threat to colonial domination. At the outbreak of World War I, France was at war with Turkey, the world's leading independent Muslim power. During the war, the French actively solicited declarations of support from notable *ulama,* or Muslim clerics. Throughout the colonial period, the French kept very close watch on all *ulama,* even though they never posed any serious threat. More generally, French authorities were con-

cerned to "contain" Islam, hoping both to discourage followers of traditional religions from converting to Islam and to foster varieties of Islam which they identified as more "African" and less orthodox. It is one of the paradoxes of colonial rule that the same authorities who welcomed "African" Islam were highly suspicious of "African" Christian movements such as Harrism. French efforts to insulate Muslims in Ivory Coast from global currents in Islam were doomed to failure. After World War II, young Africans returning from the pilgrimage to Mecca or from study in the Middle East (notably Cairo) began to challenge local Islamic practices. Bouaké, in central Ivory Coast, was one of the leading centers of these Wahhabis, as the French called them. Many local African Muslims were even more resolutely hostile to the Wahhabis than were the French, but although tempers ran high, no violence erupted in Ivory Coast—as it did in nearby Mali—between supporters and opponents of the new movement.

After Independence

Since Ivory Coast's independence in 1960, no religious community could claim a majority. A substantial proportion of the population continues to adhere to traditional religions. Catholics and Protestants of various denominations, including Harrists, are concentrated in the southern half of the country. This is by far the most prosperous half, where coffee and cocoa (Ivory Coast's major export commodities) are planted and consequently where most cities and towns are located. Muslims predominate in the north, but there are also very large communities of Muslims in the south, where peoples from the north have migrated in search of better opportunities. Ivory Coast's prosperity relative to most of its neighbors has attracted large numbers of immigrants from neighboring countries, many of whom are Muslim. As a result, Islam has expanded rapidly and is now the country's largest religious community.

Until his death in 1993, Félix Houphouët-Boigny, the country's first president, remained in relatively firm control. In a country as diverse as Ivory Coast, this control could be maintained only through a pattern of strategic alliances with representatives of all sectors of the population. In religious terms, this entailed the distribution of money and services to different religious communities and organizations for the construction of churches and mosques; the organization of national religious youth conferences; and the attribution of air space on public radio and television. As Houphouët-Boigny's reign drew to a close, there was increasing concern that he was favoring his own religion, Catholicism. Such concerns peaked with the construction of a sumptuous basilica in Yamoussoukro, the president's home town, which he had also made the capital city.

The situation deteriorated seriously in the struggle for Houphouët-Boigny's succession in 1993. Henri Konan Bédié was designated heir apparent but was under international pressure to hold prompt elections. His principal opponents were Laurent Gbagbo, who led the perennial opposition against Houphouët-Boigny, and Alassane Ouattara, Houphouët-Boigny's last prime minister. In an attempt to narrow the field and corner the elections, Konan Bédié amended the constitution to stipulate that any candidate had to be of pure Ivorian descent. Ouattara's mother allegedly hailed from nearby Burkina Faso, and he was barred from running for office. Ouattara is a Muslim from the north, and his exclusion was understood by northerners, especially Muslims, as proof that they were disenfranchised and assimilated to the status of foreign immigrants. To justify his move, Konan Bédié promulgated an official ideology of Ivoirité (Ivorianness), which confirmed Muslim suspicions that they were considered second-class citizens at best.

In 1999 Konan Bédié was overthrown in a military coup led by Robert Guei, who promised to hold elections and return the country to civilian rule. The coup initially met with general approval in the Muslim community. However, in the course of the 2002 elections, Guei presented himself as a candidate, maintaining the exclusion of Alassane Ouattara. When Guei proclaimed himself the winner, riots broke out in Abidjan, the country's largest city. The riots turned violently xenophobic, specifically targeting Muslims and burning mosques to the ground, even though the Muslim candidate had been excluded. In the wake of the riots, Guei stepped down and his opponent, Laurent Gbagbo, acceded to the presidency.

Gbagbo continued to rely on the xenophobic and implicitly anti-Muslim ideology of Ivoirité to maintain himself in power, and in 2002, segments of the military attempted to stage a second coup. The attempt failed, but as a result the country was partitioned de facto into a rebel zone in the north and part of the west and a government-controlled area in the remainder of the country. French and United Nations forces positioned themselves in between the two zones, avoiding a bloodbath but also maintaining the partition of the country. As a reaction to the attempted coup and to the role of the French forces, government sympathizers formed a militia, the Young Patriots, which has been accused of violent acts of vigilantism.

Notably, the country is not split strictly along religious lines, and the current conflict does not pit Muslims against Christians. The population of the rebel zone is not all Muslim by any means. The political leader of the rebels, Guillaume Soro, is a former seminarian. Moreover, many Muslims continue to live in territory under government control. However, the official ideology of Ivoirité implicitly sanctions the xenophobic assimilation of Muslims to "foreign" status. Certain Christian religious leaders, in particular the senior evangelist Ediémou Blin Jacob of the Celestial Christian Church, head of the national Forum of Religious Faiths, have actively asserted their solidarity with the Muslim community and promoted ecumenism and tolerance. There have been no expressions of anti-Christian sentiments on the part of Muslims. The current situation, while exacerbating religious antagonisms, especially anti-Muslim sentiments, is primarily a regional rather than religious conflict.

See also *Africa, Christian; Colonialism; France; Independent Churches, African; Islam; Traditional Religions, African; Ulama*

Robert G. Launay

BIBLIOGRAPHY

Dufka, Corinne. *Côte d'Ivoire: The New Racism.* New York: Human Rights Watch, 2001.

Haliburton, Gordon Mackay. *The Prophet Harris.* New York: Oxford University Press, 1973.

Harrison, Christopher. *France and Islam in West Africa, 1860–1960.* Cambridge: Cambridge University Press, 1988.

Kaba, Lansine. *The Wahhabiyya: Islamic Reform and Politics in French West Africa.* Evanston, Ill.: Northwestern University Press, 1974.

Launay, Robert. *Beyond the Stream: Islam and Society in a West African Town.* Berkeley: University of California Press, 1992.

Le Pape, Marc, and Claudine Vidal, eds. *Côte d'Ivoire: l'année terrible, 1999–2000.* Paris: Karthala, 2002.

Walker, Sheila. *The Religious Revolution in Ivory Coast: The Prophet Harris and the Harrist Church.* Chapel Hill: University of North Carolina Press, 1983.

Index

Laws of Ecclesiastical Polity, 30
Lazar, Prince, 150
LDP. *See* Liberal Democratic Party (LDP)
Lebanon
  civil war, 550–551
  the Druze, 252–254
  origins, 549
  political parties in, 254
  post-civil war, 551–552
  post-independence, 549–550
Lee, Edwin, 867
Lee v. Weisman, 212
Lekai, Cardinal, 280
Lemon v. Kurtzman, 211, 212, 225
Lenin, Vladimir, 191–192, 771
Lenski, Gerhard, 187
Leopold II, King, 202
Leo XIII, Pope, 102, 103, 106, 131, 149, 152, 917, 920
Le Pen, Jean-Marie, 24, 308
Lessing, G. E., 269
Letters to Olga, 357
Levellers, 268
Levinas, Emmanuel, 357
Levine, Harry G., 868
Lewis, Bernard, 182
Liberal democracy
  and voluntarism, 930
Liberal Democratic Party (LDP), 496, 497
Liberalism
  betterment of humankind, 557–558
  characteristics of, 553
  conception of good, 556
  democracy and, 554–555
  liberty and, 553–554
  multiculturalism and neutrality, 558–559
  political ideologies overview, 552
  rights, natural and equal, 555–556
  secularization of, 557
Liberation theology
  changes to, 561–562
  origins, 559–560
  as political theology, 560–561
  problems and prospects, 562–563
Liberation Tigers of Tamil Eelam (LTTE), 82
Liberation War (Zimbabwe), 963
Libya
  domestic and economic policies, 567
  foreign policy, 565
  historical background, 563–564, 739–740
  Qaddafi's regime, 564–565, 739–740
  terrorist activities and, 740
  U.S. relations, 565–567
Life and Times of Frederick Douglass, 252
Li Hongzhi, 130
Lilburne, John, 268
Lilly, Eli, 747
Lilly, J. K., Jr., 747
Lilly, J. K., Sr., 747
Lilly Endowment, 747–748, 750
Lincoln, Abraham, 204–205, 219, 881
  antislavery position, 5
  draft laws of, 27
  Emancipation Proclamation, 6
  on religion and politics, 907
Lingat, Robert, 364
Lippman, Walter, 880
Lipset, Seymour Martin, 97
Liturgy
  defined, 568
  purification or scapegoating, 569–570
  restoration liturgies, 570
  rituals of aversion, 569

transormation rituals, 568–569
Lloyd, Genevieve, 333
Lobbying, religious
  influence in the United States, 570–572
  outside the United States, 573–574
  tactics, 572–573
Locke, John, 94, 163, 167, 218, 269, 310, 393
  inalienable rights, 390
Locke v. Davey, 210
London Missionary Society, 72
Looking Backward, 909, 910
Lord's Resistance Army (LRA; Uganda), 897, 899
Lorenz, Konrad, 384
Losing Ground, 207
L'Ouverture, Toussaint, 6
Lovelock, James, 272
Low Countries, 574–576
Löwith, Karl, 911
LTTE. See Liberation Tigers of Tamil Eelam
Lubac, Henri de, 45, 104
Lucknow Pact, 367
Luegar, Karl, 378
Luker, Kristin, 10
Lumumba, Patrice, 202
Lundy, Benjamin, 318
Luther, Martin, 759
  as evangelical, 290
  on "holy war," 927
  Reformation and, 309, 743
Lutheranism
  history of, 576–577
  and Nazi policies, 382–383
  and politics, 578
  restistance to authority of man, 577–578
  in Scandinavia, 285
  in the United States, 577
  view of God's authority, 577
Luwum, Janani, 33
Lynch v. Donnelly, 212

M
Macdonald, John A., 97
Macedonia, 56
Mackenzie, Alexander, 97
Madani, Abbasi, 23
Madison, James, 499, 579–580
  Federalist Papers, 311
  and religious freedom, 310
Magic. *See* Witchcraft
Magna Carta, 43, 390
Mahama, Alhaji Aliu, 346
Mahdi, 580–581
Mahfouz, Naguib, 266
Mahidol, Ananda, 874
Mahmud II, Sultan, 894
Maimonides, Moses, 517
Maistre, Joseph de, 887–888
Makarios III (Mihail Mouskos), 675
Malaysia, 581–583
Malbim, Meyer Leibush, 518
Malcom X, 445
Mali, 16
Malthus, Thomas Robert, 257
Malula, Joseph Albert (Cardinal), 203
Mandela, Nelson, 942
Mandeville, Bernard, 178
Mande world. *See* Africa, West
al-Ma'ni, Fakhr al-Din, 254
Manning, Preston, 97
Mansfield, Harvey, 207
Manual of the Mother Church, 143
Maori, 671

Mao Zedong, 48, 128, 194, 200, 235, 928
  genocide by, 336
  and Tibet, 86–87
Maranke, Johane, 963
Maritain, Jacques, 131, 148, 152, 583–584
Markward of Anweiler, 232
Marshall, John, 865
Marshall, T. H., 163–164
Marsh v. Chambers, 212
Marsilius of Padua, 146
Martin, David, 285, 308
Marty, Martin E., 879
Martyrdom
  conciousness of martyrs, 587
  control of martyrs, 587–588
  defined, 584–585
  social and cultural supports of, 585–587
  social functions of, 585
Marx, Karl, 47, 48, 100, 178, 191, 223, 910, 911
  on religion, 757
Marxism, 757
  and atheism, 48
  defined, 588
  history of theory, 589–590
  liberation theology, 590–592
  and religious freedom, 314
  treatment of religion, 588–589
  and utopianism, 912
Marxist Partiya Karkeren Kurdistan. *See* Kurdish
    Workers Party (PKK)
Mary, Queen, 759
Mary, the Virgin, 755
Maryknoll, 105, 592–593
Masaryk, Tomás Garrigue, 357
Masire, Ketumile, 72–73
Masjid, Babari, 321
al-Masjid al-Aqsa, 503
Matabeland, 964
Mathews, Basil J., 184
Mau Mau. *See* Kenya
Maurin, Peter, 242
Mawdudi, Sayyid Abu al-Ala, 325, 593–594
Maxim, Patriarch, 194
May, Samuel J., 903
Maylasia
  colonial rule, 581–582
  federation government, 582–583
  overview, 581
McCarthy, Joseph, 359
McCollum v. Board of Education, 211, 212
McCreary Co. v. Kentucky, 212
McDonald, Forrest, 207
Mclean v. Arkansas Board of Education, 225
McPherson, Aimee Semple, 187, 756
Mecca, 594–596
Mechanical solidarity, 255
Medellín, Colombia
  Latin American Bishops Conference, 765
Media and religion, 596–600
Medicine
  in colonial America, 600–601
  pre-Civil War, 601–602
  and religion and law, 602–603
  and religion in North America, 600
  religious origins of private hospitals, 602
Meeks, Douglas, 99
Mein Kampf, 339, 379
Meir, R. of Rothenberg, 517
Melanesia, 669–670
Melville, Andrew, 93
"Memorial and Remonstrance against Religious
    Assessments," 310

ENCYCLOPEDIA OF POLITICS AND RELIGION

Cover designed by Matthew Simmons

Typeset by MacPS, Indianapolis, Indiana

Printed and bound by Data Reproductions, Auburn Hills, Michigan

Composed in Bembo, a typeface designed by Stanley Morrison in 1929,

based on a design by Francesco Griffo in 1495